ALSO BY RICHARD LYMAN BUSHMAN

From Puritan to Yankee:
Character and the Social Order in Connecticut, 1690–1765

Joseph Smith and the Beginnings of Mormonism

King and People in Provincial Massachusetts

The Refinement of America: Persons, Houses, and Cities

Believing History: Latter-day Saint Essays

JOSEPH SMITH

ROUGH STONE ROLLING

Pen and ink sketch of Joseph Smith
by Sutcliffe Maudsley, 1844.

JOSEPH SMITH

—◆—

ROUGH STONE ROLLING

RICHARD LYMAN BUSHMAN

with the assistance of

JED WOODWORTH

ALFRED A. KNOPF · NEW YORK 2005

THIS IS A BORZOI BOOK
PUBLISHED BY ALFRED A. KNOPF

Copyright © 2005 by Richard Lyman Bushman

All rights reserved. Published in the United States by Alfred A. Knopf,
a division of Random House, Inc., New York,
and in Canada by Random House of Canada Limited, Toronto.

www.aaknopf.com

Knopf, Borzoi Books, and the colophon are registered trademarks
of Random House, Inc.

Grateful acknowledgment is made to the University of Illinois Press for
permission to reprint material from *Joseph Smith and the Beginnings of
Mormonism* by Richard Lyman Bushman. Copyright © 1984 by the Board of
Trustees of the University of Illinois. Reprinted by permission of the
University of Illinois Press.

Library of Congress Cataloging-in-Publication Data

Bushman, Richard Lyman.
Joseph Smith : rough stone rolling / Richard Lyman Bushman, with the
assistance of Jed Woodworth.—1st ed.
p.   cm.
Includes bibliographical references and index.
ISBN 1-4000-4270-4
1. Smith, Joseph, 1805–1844.   2. Mormons—United States—Biography.
I. Woodworth, Jed.   II. Title.

BX8695.S6B875 2005   289.3'092—dc22   [B]   2004061613

Manufactured in the United States of America

First Edition

FOR
DEAN JESSEE AND RONALD ESPLIN
MASTERS OF LATTER-DAY SAINT HISTORY

[I am like a] rough stone roling down hill.

JOSEPH SMITH, May 21, 1843

I [am] a rough stone. The sound of the hammer and chisel
was never heard on me nor never will be.
I desire the learning and wisdom of heaven alone.

JOSEPH SMITH, June 11, 1843

This is the Case with Joseph Smith. He never professed to be a
dressed smooth polished stone but was rough out of the mountain & has been rolling among the rocks & trees & has not hurt
him at all. But he will be as smooth & polished in the end as any
other stone, while many that were so vary poliched & smooth in
the beginning get badly defaced and spoiled while theiy are
rolling about.

BRIGHAM YOUNG, September 9, 1843

CONTENTS

MAPS

JOSEPH SMITH CHRONOLOGY

1805	Dec. 23	Born at Sharon, Vermont
1811		Smith family moves to Lebanon, New Hampshire
1816		Smith family moves to Palmyra, New York
1820	Spring	First Vision
1823	Sept.	First visit of Moroni
1827	Jan. 18	Marries Emma Hale
	Sept. 22	Obtains *Book of Mormon* plates
	Dec.	Moves to Harmony, Pennsylvania
1828		Translates *Book of Mormon* with Martin Harris
	June	116 pages of *Book of Mormon* manuscript lost
	July	First records a revelation
1829	Apr.–June	Translates *Book of Mormon* with Oliver Cowdery
	May 15	Visit of John the Baptist
	June	Translation of *Book of Mormon* completed
1830	Mar.	*Book of Mormon* published
	Apr. 6	Church of Christ organized
	June	Receives vision of Moses
	Oct.	Missionaries leave on mission to Western Indians
1831	Jan.	Moves to Kirtland, Ohio
	Feb. 9	The "Law" of the Church revealed
	June 3	Ordination to high priesthood
	July 20	Jackson County, Missouri, designated as Zion
	Sept.	Moves to Hiram, Ohio
	Nov.	Elders approve *Book of Commandments*
1832		Exaltation revelations
	Apr.–June	Visits Jackson County
	Oct.–Nov.	Trip to Albany, New York City, and Boston
1833	July 23	Cornerstones for Kirtland temple laid
	July	Missouri Saints told they must leave Jackson County
	Oct.–Nov.	Missionary tour in Canada
	Nov.	Missouri Saints expelled from Jackson County
1834	Feb. 17	Organizes Kirtland High Council
	May–Aug.	Zion's Camp to Missouri

	Nov.	School of the Prophets begins in Kirtland
1835	Feb. 14	Organizes quorum of Twelve Apostles
	Mar. 28	Revelation on priesthood
	July	Purchases Egyptian mummies
	Aug. 17	Church approves *Doctrine and Covenants*
1836	Jan.–Feb.	First washings and anointings in Kirtland temple
	Mar. 27	Kirtland temple dedicated
	Apr. 3	Vision of Christ in Kirtland temple
	July–Sept.	Trip to New York City and Salem, Mass.
	Nov. 2	Kirtland Safety Society articles drafted
1837		Failure of Kirtland bank
		Dissension in Church
	June	First missionaries to Great Britain
	Sept.–Dec.	Visits Missouri
	Dec.	Dissenters expelled from Church
1838	Jan. 12	Flees Kirtland for Far West, Missouri
	Mar. 14	Arrives at Far West
	Aug. 6	Fight at Gallatin election
	Oct.–Nov.	Mormon war in Missouri
	Nov. 12	Court of inquiry at Richmond
1838–39	Dec.–Apr.	Imprisoned at Liberty, Missouri
1839	Apr. 16	Escapes Missouri captors
	Apr. 22	Reaches Quincy, Illinois
	May 10	Moves to Commerce, Illinois
	Sept.	Twelve Apostles depart for Great Britain
1839–40	Nov.–Feb.	In Washington, D.C., and Philadelphia area
	Dec.–Feb.	Petitions for redress in Washington, D.C.
1840	March	Returns to Nauvoo, Illinois
	Dec. 16	Nauvoo Charter granted
1841	Apr. 5	Marries Louisa Beaman, first of many Nauvoo plural marriages
	Apr. 6	Lays cornerstones for Nauvoo temple
	June 5	Arrested on old Missouri charges
	Nov. 8	Temple font dedicated for baptisms for the dead
1842	Mar. 1	First installment of Book of Abraham published
	Mar. 15	Freemasonry lodge organized in Nauvoo
	Mar. 17	Female Relief Society organized
	Apr.	Joseph applies for bankruptcy
	May 4	Temple endowment introduced
	June	Excommunication and departure of John C. Bennett
	Aug. 8	Arrest for alleged complicity in Boggs shooting
	Aug.–Nov.	Joseph in hiding much of the time

1843	Jan. 5	Joseph discharged from arrest in Boggs case
	May 28	Sealed to Emma Smith for eternity
	June 23	Joseph arrested on old Missouri charges
	July 12	Revelation on priesthood marriage recorded
	Sept.	Endowment of women beginning with Emma
1844	Jan. 29	Twelve Apostles nominate Joseph for U.S. presidency
	Mar. 11	Council of Fifty organized
	Apr. 7	King Follett discourse
	June 7	*Nauvoo Expositor* published
	June 10	*Expositor* press destroyed
	June 25	Surrender at Carthage, Illinois
	June 27	Joseph shot to death in Carthage jail

FOUR GENERATIONS OF JOSEPH SMITH'S FAMILY

GRANDPARENTS	PARENTS, AUNTS, UNCLES	BROTHERS AND SISTERS (SPOUSES LISTED IN ITALICS)	CHILDREN
	Jesse Smith (1768–1853)	Unnamed son (about 1797)	Alvin Smith (1828–1828)
	Priscilla Smith (1769–1867)	Alvin Smith (1798–1823)	Louisa Smith (1831–1831)
	Joseph Smith Sr. (1771–1840)	Hyrum Smith (1800–1844) *Jerusha Barden* *Mary Fielding*	Thaddeus Smith (1831–1831)
	Asahel Smith (1773–1848)		Julia Murdock Smith (adopted twin) (1831–1880)
	Mary Smith (1775–1844)	Sophronia Smith (1803–1876) *Calvin Stoddard* *William McCleary*	Joseph Murdock Smith (adopted twin) (1831–1832)
Asael Smith (1744–1830) Mary Duty (1743–1836)	Samuel Smith (1777–1830)		
	Silas Smith (1779–1839)	Joseph Smith Jr. (1805–1844) *Emma Hale*	Joseph Smith III (1832–1914)
	John Smith (1781–1854)	Samuel Harrison Smith (1805–1844) *Mary Bailey* *Levira Clark*	Frederick Granger Williams Smith (1836–1862)
	Susan Smith (1783–1849)		Alexander Hale Smith (1838–1909)
	Stephen Smith (1785–1802)	Ephraim Smith (1810–1810)	Don Carlos Smith (1840–1841)
	Sarah Smith (1789–1824)	William Smith (1811–1893) *Caroline Amanda Grant* *Roxy Ann Grant* *Eliza Elsie Sanborn* *Rosa Surprise*	(Unnamed son) (1842–1842)
			David Hyrum Smith (1844–1904)
	Jason Mack (1760?–?)		
	Lovisa Mack (1761?–1794)	Katharine Smith (1813–1900) *Jenkins Salisbury* *Joseph Younger*	
	Lovina Mack (1762?–1794)		
	Lydia Mack (1764–1826)	Don Carlos Smith (1816–1841) *Agnes Coolbrith*	
Solomon Mack (1732–1820) Lydia Gates (1732?–1818)	Stephen Mack (1766–1826)	Lucy Smith (1821–1882) *Arthur Millikin*	
	Daniel Mack (1770?–?)		
	Solomon Mack (1773–1851)		
	Lucy Mack (1775–1856)		

PREFACE

Two hundred years should be long enough to gain perspective on Joseph Smith. Over the years, hundreds of books and articles have been written on every detail of his life. There have been at least eighteen biographies, and more will appear in 2005 during the bicentennial of his birth. A six-volume collection of original documents has long been available, and many more sources are accessible on DVD and in archives. We are dealing with mountains of information.[1]

Yet, it is unlikely there will ever be consensus on Joseph Smith's character or his achievements. The multiplication of scholarly studies and the discovery of new sources have only heightened the controversies surrounding his life. The central difficulty is that Joseph Smith lives on in the faith of the Mormons, like Abraham in Judaism or Muhammad in Islam. Everything about Smith matters to people who have built their lives on his teachings. To protect their own deepest commitments, believers want to shield their prophet's reputation. On the other hand, people who have broken away from Mormonism—and they produce a large amount of the scholarship—have to justify their decision to leave. They cannot countenance evidence of divine inspiration in his teachings without catching themselves in a disastrous error. Added to these combatants are those suspicious of all religious authority who find in Joseph Smith a perfect target for their fears. Given the emotional crosscurrents, agreement will never be reached about his character, his inspiration, or his accomplishments.

A believing historian like myself cannot hope to rise above these battles or pretend nothing personal is at stake. For a character as controversial as Smith, pure objectivity is impossible. What I can do is to look frankly at all sides of Joseph Smith, facing up to his mistakes and flaws. Covering up errors makes no sense in any case. Most readers do not believe in, nor are they interested in, perfection. Flawless characters are neither attractive nor useful. We want to meet a real person. My model for this book has been W. Jackson Bate's biography of the eighteenth-century man of letters, Samuel Johnson. Bate saw all of Johnson's weaknesses, including his crippling doubts and fears, and yet found nobility and genius in his mammoth personage.

Joseph Smith had none of Johnson's learning or finesse, but he was mammoth too and a genius in what the literary scholar Harold Bloom has called "religion making."[2]

Joseph Smith is one of those large Americans who like Abraham Lincoln came from nowhere. Reared in a poor Yankee farm family, he had less than two years of formal schooling and began life without social standing or institutional backing. His family rarely attended church. Yet in the fourteen years he headed the Church of Jesus Christ of Latter-day Saints, Smith created a religious culture that survived his death, flourished in the most desolate regions of the United States, and continues to grow worldwide after more than a century and a half.[3] In 1830 at the age of twenty-four, he published the *Book of Mormon*, the only person in American history to produce a second Bible—an entirely new revealed work to stand beside the traditional scriptures. He built cities and temples and gathered thousands of followers before he was killed at age thirty-eight.

Smith is interesting for what he was as well as for what he did. He was the closest America has come to producing a biblical-style prophet—one who spoke for God with the authority of Moses or Isaiah. He was not an eloquent preacher; he is not known to have preached a single sermon before organizing the church in 1830.[4] But he spoke in God's voice in revelations he compiled and published. A revelation typically began with words like "Hearken O ye people which profess my name, saith the Lord your God."[5] Many thought him presumptuous if not blasphemous, and he made no effort to prove them wrong. He did not defend his revelations or give reasons for belief. He dictated the words and let people decide. Everything he taught and most of what he did originated in these revelations. The question of this book is how such a man came to be in the age of railroads and the penny press. What was the logic of his visionary life?

Joseph Smith did not offer himself as an exemplar of virtue. He told his followers not to expect perfection. Smith called himself a rough stone, thinking of his own impetuosity and lack of polish.[6] He was sensitive to insults and could not stand to be crossed. Twice he was brought to trial before one of his own church councils for scolding offenders too severely. He so dominated the rooms he entered that some thought him arrogant. But it was his iron will that brought the church, the cities, and the temples into existence.

He was warm and affectionate too. He loved to sit in council with his brethren. When imprisoned with a group of them he wrote his wife Emma about being chained together in the bonds of love. Letter after letter to Emma expressed affection for her and the children. That his doctrine of plural marriage drove a wedge between the two of them was the great sorrow of his life. He said once to his people, "You never knew my heart."[7] Perhaps he cannot be entirely known, but my aim has been to imagine him as fully as the records allow.

I have also undertaken to explore a side of Joseph Smith not adequately examined in other biographies: his religious thought. There are good reasons for this neglect. His thought is not easily encapsulated or analyzed. His teachings came primarily through his revelations, which, like other forms of scripture, are epigrammatic and oracular. He never presented his ideas systematically in clear, logical order; they came in flashes and bursts. Nor did he engage in formal debate. His most powerful thoughts were assertions delivered as if from heaven. Assembling a coherent picture out of many bits and pieces leaves room for misinterpretations and forced logic. Even his loyal followers disagree about the implications of his teaching.

Despite the difficulty in extracting its essence, the thought cannot be neglected. Doctrine attracted the early converts, most of whom had not met Joseph Smith before joining the Church, and remained a significant reason for the survival of Mormonism after his death. His followers derived their energy and purpose from the religious world he brought into being. Imperfect as a summary must be, that world has to be re-created to understand Joseph Smith's life and influence.

A rhetorical problem vexes anyone who writes about the thought of Joseph Smith. Are his ideas to be attributed to him or to God? Some readers will consider it obvious that the revelations came from Joseph Smith's mind and nowhere else. His revelation of the afterlife, for example, can be summed up by saying "Joseph Smith imagined a heaven divided into three degrees of glory." Only a Mormon reader would say bluntly, "God revealed a heaven with three degrees of glory," without any disclaimer. Out of respect for the varied opinions of readers, it would seem judicious to compromise with "Joseph Smith *purportedly* received a revelation about a heaven with three degrees of glory."

But there are reasons for not inserting a disclaimer every time a revelation is mentioned, no matter how the reader or writer feels about the ultimate source. The most important is that Joseph Smith did not think that way. The signal feature of his life was his sense of being guided by revelation. He experienced revelation like George Fox, the early Quaker, who heard the Spirit as "impersonal prophecy," not from his own mind but as "a word from the Lord as the prophets and the apostles had." Joseph's "marvilous experience," as he called his revelations, came to him as experiential facts. Toward the end of his life, he told a Pittsburgh reporter that he could not always get a revelation when he needed one, but "he never gave anything to his people as revelation, unless it was a revelation."[8] To blur the distinction—to insist that Smith devised every revelation himself—obscures the very quality that made the Prophet powerful. To get inside the movement, we have to think of Smith as the early Mormons thought of him and as he thought of himself—as a revelator.

Karen Armstrong makes a similar point in her biography of Muhammad.

Though subscribing to no particular religion herself, Armstrong believes "the great religions, seers and prophets have conceived strikingly similar visions of a transcendent and ultimate reality." Muhammad had "such an experience and made a distinctive and valuable contribution to the spiritual experience of humanity."[9] That irenic viewpoint permits Armstrong to write about Muhammad's visions as if they actually occurred, giving readers unimpeded access to his mind. My aim, like Armstrong's, is to recover the world of a prophet. The skeptics in that world must be allowed to speak, to be sure, and the contradictions and incongruities in the Prophet's record have to be dealt with. But the book attempts to think as Smith thought and to reconstruct the beliefs of his followers as they understood them.

Mormon children grow up knowing Joseph Smith as well as they know George Washington. He is referred to familiarly as "Joseph," or, a bit more formally, as "the Prophet," never as the distancing "Smith." Even Fawn Brodie, who was on her way out of Mormonism when she wrote her landmark biography *No Man Knows My History*, reflected her Mormon upbringing by calling him "Joseph." In this book, "Joseph" occasionally becomes merely "Smith," but out of respect for Mormon custom, I usually refer to him by his more familiar name. Perhaps this attempt to draw close to Joseph Smith will reveal a little more of the heart that he said no one knew.

This study has been helped immensely by the project to collect and publish Joseph Smith's papers in a scholarly edition. Many of the papers have long been available but sometimes in doctored form and not carefully annotated. A comprehensive sweep of the nation's archives has produced many more, all of them now being published at Brigham Young University through the Joseph Fielding Smith Institute for Latter-day Saint History. Although I have not had the benefit of all the annotation and cannot cite the new edition now going to press, I have been given access to the materials as they have been assembled. For this I am grateful.

That collected-papers project began a quarter of a century ago, when Dean Jessee was asked by LDS Church historian Leonard Arrington to produce an edition of the papers of Joseph Smith. Jessee published two volumes and had largely completed a third when he envisioned a larger project involving many more editors. He joined forces with Ronald Esplin at the Smith Institute to organize an editorial team that would produce volumes at a much faster pace.

This book is dedicated to these two scholars out of respect for their work over many decades. They now stand out as preeminent figures in Latter-day Saint history. Ronald Esplin came to me more than a decade ago to ask if I would write a biography of Joseph Smith. Although I had vaguely considered such a study, it was not until Esplin made this proposal that I decided to begin the work. The book would not be without him.

Esplin also responded to my suggestion that the Smith Institute sponsor a summer seminar on Joseph Smith for graduate students and advanced undergraduates. Beginning in 1997, a half dozen students from all over the country met in Provo, Utah, for two months of research into the cultural context of Joseph Smith's life and thought. My association with these young scholars has been the most pleasurable experience of my academic life. Papers on subjects ranging from Ann Lee's visionary religion to ordination practices in Protestant churches have been published by the Smith Institute with another volume to come. References to their studies are found throughout this volume. Their work was funded by a group of generous donors mobilized by Karen and David Davidson, who have backed this work in countless ways. The Davidsons are patrons of the highest order.

Through the summer seminar, I became acquainted with Jed Woodworth, my collaborator on this book. Jed began as an editor and research assistant running down secondary work, checking facts and quotes, and improving style. As time passed, it became evident he was doing much more. He proved to be an excellent copy editor whose judgments I came to accept as invariably sound. He checked my text against the sources, tested my claims, elaborated ideas, and enriched the scholarship. Probably only scholars will appreciate the depth of the research reflected in the notes. All of this he accomplished while pursuing his own graduate studies in history at the University of Wisconsin and beginning married life. At one point his wife, Shawna, complained that she felt like a plural wife. Her husband was wed to Joseph Smith as well as to her. Jed earned his place on the title page many times over.

My wife, Claudia, on the other hand, has been as much married to Joseph Smith as I have been. When she saw the magnitude of the project, she volunteered to integrate and coordinate the notes and bibliography. She has also labored over the prose, unknotting the obscure constructions, and pruning my flowery phrases. Thanks to her, some of my best writing expired on the cutting room floor. Her compulsion to complete projects drove the work from the start. She persuaded me to write from the outset rather than accumulate research notes for years. As always, she was right.

I have called on friends to read chapters along the way. James Lucas in New York City has willingly taken on every batch of manuscript I thrust upon him and told me what I was thinking before I knew it myself. Richard Brown at the University of Connecticut, one of the wise men of the historical profession, can always be counted on for astute judgments. He warned me when my defensiveness was getting in the way of the exposition. Beyond these two, George Marsden, whose biography of Jonathan Edwards has been a model, gave some gentle advice on Joseph Smith's thought. David Hall, whose own work in American intellectual and religious history has been so influential, gave a characteristically subtle reading of my chapter on the Book of Mormon. Larry Porter and Ronald Esplin at BYU, both legendary for their encyclopedic knowledge of Latter-day Saint history, made an heroic effort to read the manuscript from beginning to end, coming up with errors and misinterpretations. Others have commented on chapters, papers, or essays: Jon Butler, Stephen Stein, Richard Anderson, Alex Smith, Mark Ashurst-McGee, David Paulsen, Bruce Nichols, Shawna Cluff Woodworth, and Rick Turley. Much of the work was presented in primitive form to the Smith Institute summer faculty seminar, where the participants were both merciless and generous, especially Jack Welch, Ronald Walker, Alexander Baugh, and Ralph Hancock. Greg Prince, who has written with much insight on priesthood authority in early Mormonism, gave me his extensive e-mail research files, a resource that should be in a library.

I began the study in the Edenic climes of the Huntington Library presided over by Robert (Roy) Ritchie, and enjoyed a fruitful year at Princeton University's Shelby Cullom Davis Center, which in my year was headed by Anthony Grafton. Both scholars were helpful and hospitable beyond measure. The Smith Institute staff, headed by Jill Derr, director, and Marilyn Parks, executive secretary, have hosted Claudia and me for eight summers now. They are generous and kindly but also efficient, the perfect combination. The Smith Institute provided funds at a key point to support the source checking.

This book began as a study published by the University of Illinois Press in 1984 under the title *Joseph Smith and the Beginnings of Mormonism*. Elizabeth Dulany and Richard Wentworth shepherded that book through the press, as they have so many studies of Mormonism. The press must be recognized as a key factor in the fluorescence of Mormon studies over the past three decades. The press gave permission to use large portions of chapters 1, 2, 3, and 5 in this book. At Knopf, Jane Garrett, the best of editors and bearer of the noble Knopf tradition in American history publication, befriended the project from the beginning.

Generous help with the illustrations came from William Slaughter at the Latter-day Saint Church Archives, who believes his trove of Church history images is a scholarly resource rather than a source of income, Richard Oman at the Church Museum of History and Art, David Whittaker and Russell Taylor in BYU Special Collections, and the Daughters of the Utah Pioneers. Whitney Fae Taylor of the Brigham Young University Geography Department drew the maps.

Thanks above all to Claudia. We will celebrate our fiftieth anniversary the year this book is published.

RICHARD LYMAN BUSHMAN
New York City

JOSEPH SMITH

◆

ROUGH STONE ROLLING

PROLOGUE

JUST BEFORE MIDNIGHT ON MAY 14, 1844, the small upper Mississippi steamer *Amaranth* landed at Nauvoo. Two passengers, Josiah Quincy Jr. and Charles Francis Adams, decided to come ashore. A fellow passenger, Dr. W. G. Goforth, had persuaded the pair of tourists to stay over at Nauvoo and meet the Mormon prophet Joseph Smith. Goforth was coming to seek Mormon votes for Henry Clay in the 1844 presidential election, an election in which Joseph Smith himself was a candidate. Two days later, supporters would carry Joseph Smith about on their shoulders at a Nauvoo political convention, their progress lighted by a barrel of burning tar.[1]

Both of the visitors knew politics. Quincy, a successful railroad executive and son of the president of Harvard College, would be elected Boston's mayor the next year. Adams, son of former president John Quincy Adams and a member of the Massachusetts legislature, had a distinguished career as statesman and diplomat ahead of him.

No carriage was available to carry Quincy and Adams to the inn on this dark rainy night, but Goforth shouted from the shore that he had found a bed nearby. The two followed him to an old mill shanty. Sweeping cockroaches from the coverlet, they lay down in their dressing gowns. During the night, the rain turned Nauvoo's roads to bogs of mud, but word of their arrival preceded them, and the next morning Smith sent a wagon to the landing for them.[2]

They alighted before a two-story frame house with a white picket fence and found a group of "rough-looking Mormons" awaiting them. Wrote Quincy:

> Pre-eminent among the stragglers by the door stood a man of commanding appearance, clad in the costume of a journeyman carpenter when about his work. He was a hearty, athletic fellow, with blue eyes standing prominently out upon his light complexion, a long nose, and a retreating forehead. He wore striped pantaloons, a linen jacket, which had not lately seen the wash-tub, and a beard of some three days' growth.

Not thrown off by the rough clothes, Quincy remarked that "*a fine-looking man* is what the passer-by would instinctively have murmured." "This was the founder of the religion which had been preached in every quarter of the earth."[3]

Looking for a place to talk, Smith opened a door to a first-floor room and found someone asleep. Heading upstairs, he interrupted the rest of three sleepers in one room and two more in another. Finally finding a room with only a single sleeper, "our host immediately proceeded to the bed, and drew the clothes well over the head of its occupant. He then called a man to make a fire, and begged us to sit down."[4]

Quincy and Adams had breakfast with Joseph and thirty other people in the long mansion house kitchen. Had he been able, Joseph would have entertained Adams in the large hotel under construction across the street, but he had given up work on the Nauvoo House when the strain of building a temple and houses for the rapidly expanding population proved too great. He had constructed a wing on his own house, called the Nauvoo Mansion, and opened it as an inn. Unable to run it profitably, he had leased it to an innkeeper and moved his family of six, along with two serving people, into three of the rooms.[5]

Quincy's account of his Nauvoo visit, published the winter before his death in 1882, was filled with puzzled skepticism. He balked at the stories Joseph told him, and he knew his readers would find Mormon beliefs "puerile and shocking," yet Smith struck him: "One could not resist the impression that capacity and resource were natural to his stalwart person." Quincy was impressed that Smith had come so far in his short life. "Born in the lowest ranks of poverty, without book-learning and with the homeliest of all human names, he had made himself at the age of thirty-nine a power upon earth." (Smith was actually thirty-eight.) He reminded Quincy of Rhode Island Congressman Elisha R. Potter, a giant of a man whose wit and intelligence had impressed Quincy in Washington. Potter, Quincy said, "was one of the men who carry about them a surplus of vital energy, to relieve the wants of others." When Quincy met Joseph Smith, he immediately thought of Potter. "These two seemed best endowed with that kingly faculty which directs, as by intrinsic right, the feeble or confused souls who are looking for guidance."[6]

A plank in Smith's political platform caught Quincy's attention: "Smith recognized the curse and iniquity of slavery, though he opposed the methods of the Abolitionists." He proposed to pay for the slaves with proceeds from the sale of public lands, thus respecting the rights of property while freeing all bondsmen. Quincy noted that eleven years later Ralph Waldo Emerson, "who has mixed so much practical shrewdness with his lofty philosophy," had made the same proposal. Considering "the terrible cost of the fratricidal war," Smith and Emerson's proposal, in Quincy's judgment, was "worthy of a Christian statesman."

> But if [Emerson] the retired scholar was in advance of his time when he advocated this disposition of the public property in 1855, what shall I say of the political and religious leader [Smith] who had committed himself, in print, as well as in conversation, to the same course in 1844?[7]

What puzzled Quincy most about Smith were the converts to the movement. Quincy happened by chance on a letter from an English Mormon writing from Manchester on gilt-edged paper and including a gift of a hat, black satin stock, and brooch. Until he accepted Mormonism, the man had been a Sunday singer in the Church of England; the rest of the week, he worked in a hat shop. Quincy quoted long passages from the letter to show "what really good material Smith managed to draw into his net." Such a person, Quincy thought, "would seem to be intellectually superior to so miserable a delusion."[8] Yet the Englishman found the light he was looking for in Mormonism.

To add to the puzzle, when Quincy wrote his essay four decades later, Smith's religion had not sunk into the earth. The Prophet's death had not slowed Mormonism's progress. Considering its expansion in the face of so much opposition, Quincy speculated that Smith's influence would reach further still:

> It is by no means improbable that some future text-book, for the use of generations yet unborn, will contain a question something like this: What historical American of the nineteenth century has exerted the most powerful influence upon the destinies of his countrymen? And it is by no means impossible that the answer to the interrogatory may be thus written: *Joseph Smith the Mormon prophet.*[9]

The prospect appalled Quincy, but the success of Joseph Smith's Mormonism was not to be denied.

Quincy's Boston education had ill fitted him to understand Joseph Smith's place in nineteenth-century religion. Reared a Unitarian, Quincy could not understand the desire for revelation in his time. He didn't pick up on a clue in the English convert's letter. The man wrote Joseph that he was "assured that you are a man of God and a prophet of the Most High, not only from testimony given by the brethren, but the Spirit itself beareth witness."[10] The phrase about the Spirit bearing witness was not one Quincy noted. He did not understand people who lived for spiritual manifestations.

That need was voiced in more sophisticated language by Ralph Waldo

Emerson, Quincy's classmate in the Harvard College class of 1821. In 1838, Emerson warned the graduates of the Harvard Divinity School—most of them Unitarians—that they were in danger of losing sight of true religion. Emerson worried that "men have come to speak of the revelation as somewhat long ago given and done, as if God were dead." Now was no time to deny inspiration. "It is my duty to say to you, that the need was never greater of new revelation than now." He urged each graduate to become a "newborn bard of the Holy Ghost." Friends of Joseph Smith would have considered Emerson prophetic when he told the graduates, "I look for the hour when that supreme Beauty which ravished the souls of those Eastern men, and chiefly of those Hebrews, and through their lips spoke oracles to all time, shall speak in the West also."[11]

Had Emerson looked, he would have found thousands of kindred spirits among unsophisticated Christians, who longed for visions, visitations, inspired dreams, revelations, and every other outpouring of the Spirit. These seekers were Joseph's natural constituency. Quincy was too caught up in Smith's personality to see him as his followers did, as another Moses who brought news from heaven. One recent convert, writing from Independence, Missouri, in 1832, told her sister, "Did you know of the things of God and could you receive the blessings that I have from the hand of the Lord you would not think it a hardship to come here for the Lord is revealing the misteries of the heavenly Kingdom unto his Children."[12]

William Clayton, an educated Englishman like Quincy's letter writer, was forced into farming after migrating to Nauvoo. Living in miserable circumstances, he wrote home that everything about Joseph Smith confirmed his faith. "We have abundance of proofs," he wrote, "that Joseph Smith Jun[ior] is what he pretends to be viz a P[rophet] of the most high God and this is the work of God . . . and will roll forth to the ends of the earth and the Lord will gather his people." Clayton was to know Joseph Smith better when he later became his clerk, but he loved him from the start. "Last night a meeting of us was in company with brother Joseph. Our hearts rejoiced to hear him speak of the things of the Kingdom. He is an affectionate man and as familiar as any of us. We feel to love him much and so will you."[13]

In his single day in Nauvoo, Quincy missed the Mormons' affection for Joseph Smith. If he had glimpsed it, it would have only compounded his confusion. Loyalty and love for the Prophet were what Quincy least understood. After forty years of reflection, he was still perplexed. "If the reader does not know just what to make of Joseph Smith," he wrote in the concluding sentence of his essay, "I cannot help him out of the difficulty. I myself stand helpless before the puzzle."[14]

At the end of the day, on their way to the landing, Joseph flashed a side of his personality that Quincy had not previously seen. Quincy remarked to

Smith, "You have too much power to be safely trusted to one man." Joseph replied that in Quincy's hands or another person's "so much power would, no doubt, be dangerous. I am the only man in the world whom it would be safe to trust with it. Remember, I am a prophet!" The manner of Joseph's answer intrigued Quincy. "The last five words were spoken in a rich, comical aside, as if in hearty recognition of the ridiculous sound they might have in the ears of a Gentile."[15] Joseph knew his visitor was amused and skeptical, yet remained unfazed, sure of himself no matter what the Bostonian thought.

Smith's diary entry for May 15, 1844, noted that "a son of John Quincy Adams, Mr. Quincy and Dr. Goforth visited at the Mansion." "Much rain this A.M."[16]

ONE

THE JOSEPH SMITH FAMILY

TO 1816

My Last request & charge is, that you will Live together in an undivided bond of Love; you are maney of you, and if you Join together as one man, you need not want aney thing; what counsil, what comfort, what money, what friends may you not help your Selves unto, if you will, all as one contribute your aids.

ASAEL SMITH, "A few words of advice," 1799

LUCY MACK SMITH BADE FAREWELL to her sons Joseph and Hyrum a few days after their deaths in June 1844. Joseph's secretary, Willard Richards, and their brother Samuel had brought the bodies back from Carthage to Nauvoo, and after the corpses were washed and dressed in burial clothes, the Smith family was admitted to the room. "I had for a long time braced every nerve," their mother wrote,

> roused every energy of my soul, and called upon God to strengthen me; but when I entered the room, and saw my murdered sons extended both at once before my eyes, and heard the sobs and groans of my family, and the cries of "Father! Husband! Brothers!" from the lips of their wives, children, brother, and sisters, it was too much, I sank back, crying to the Lord, in the agony of my soul, "My God, my God, why hast thou forsaken this family!"[1]

Six months later, Lucy began a narrative of the early life of Joseph Smith. She was sixty-nine, afflicted with disease and saddened by "the cruelty of an ungodly and hard hearted world."[2] Within a month she had lost three sons: Joseph and Hyrum to vigilante bullets and Samuel to a fever contracted while escaping the mob. Of her seven sons, only the unstable William survived. Her husband, Joseph Sr., had died four years earlier, and she lived with her daughter, another Lucy, and later with Joseph's widow, Emma, who was carrying her husband's unborn son.

In this troubled and uncertain moment, the question of the Prophet's successor remained unsettled. Lucy's son William was soon to be among the contenders. The "Gentile" countryside expected the Mormon kingdom to crumble and the Saints to disperse. When they proved inconveniently adamant, the citizens forced the Mormons to leave. But trouble did not slow Lucy's dictation to Martha and Howard Coray through the winter of 1844–45. One crisply told story after another covered the pages, making her narrative the central source for the early life of Joseph Smith.[3]

Lucy Smith reacted to the sorrows and distresses of her life with indignation, not regret. Recollecting the murder of her sons, she wrote that "my blood curdles in my veins." At the close of the book, she consigned the malicious and indifferent government officials who had darkened her family's lives—the governors Lilburn W. Boggs, Thomas Carlin, and Thomas Ford, and President Martin Van Buren—to the judgment of God. She was a proud, high-strung woman, belligerent, capable of anger, grief, and sublime confidence in the final triumph of the innocent. She concluded her account with a lofty judgment: "And I shall leave the world to judge, as seemeth them good, concerning what I have written. But this much I will say, that the testimony which I have given is true, and will stand for ever."[4]

Lucy did not mention the name of Joseph Smith Jr. until page 56 of her record. As she told the story, no signs or portents accompanied the birth of her most famous son. She said quite simply that "in the meantime we had a son, whom we called Joseph, after the name of his father; he was born December 23, 1805. I shall speak of him more particularly by and by."[5] Joseph's revelations and writings, his part in constructing the city of Nauvoo, the tens of thousands of followers, and his national notoriety—none of this overwhelmed Lucy Smith's story.

The Smith family stood at the center. Lucy's pride was the pride of family. When she saw the bodies of Hyrum and Joseph, she spontaneously asked why had God "forsaken this family." Her narrative began with her father, Solomon, and devoted six chapters to her brothers and sisters before telling about herself. Lucy calculated that six Smith martyrs had fallen because of persecution: Joseph Sr.; sons Don Carlos, Hyrum, and Samuel; William's wife Caroline; and Joseph the Prophet.[6]

She had little worldly to boast of. Lucy knew of the "attention and respect which are ever shown to those who live in fine circumstances," but of her sister Lydia, who "sought riches and obtained them," Lucy wrote but two paragraphs: not that Lydia was less loved, "but she seemed to float more with the stream of common events."[7] Lucy's pride arose from the way her family met adversity. Joseph and Hyrum lay in triumph in their coffins because justice and charity gave them power over their enemies. She honored those who overcame. Her narrative turned the misfortunes of the Smith family into exemplifications of family character.

SOLOMON AND LYDIA MACK

Lucy Mack Smith was the youngest of eight children born to Solomon Mack and Lydia Gates. Lucy briefly mentioned her father's adventures in the French and Indian War and the American Revolution, and then said little more about him. He was absent for years at a time while Lucy was growing up, and until he experienced a drastic change of heart late in life, he was preoccupied solely with the pursuit of wealth. Solomon was born September 15, 1732, in Lyme, Connecticut, the grandson of John Mack, one of Lyme's prospering traders. When Solomon was four, his father, Ebenezer Mack, lost the land he had inherited in Lyme, and Solomon was bound out to a hard-hearted and miserly farmer, about whom he wrote in his memoir:

> I was treated by my Master as his property and not as his fellow mortal; he taught me to work, and was very careful that I should have little or no rest. . . . His whole attention was taken up on the pursuits of the good things of this world; wealth was his supreme object. I am afraid gold was his God.

Solomon grew up "like the wild ass's colt," feeling "no obligation with regard to society."[8]

Free at age twenty-one, Solomon Mack tried "to make myself great and happy, in the way I was educated," by accumulating property. Defeated in one venture after another, wounded by falling trees and spills from horses, afflicted with fits and permanently lame, shipwrecked, betrayed by business associates, he always recovered his health and courage and set forth on new undertakings. He enlisted for service in the French and Indian War and with his discharge pay purchased a farm in Lyme. In 1759, at twenty-six, he married Lydia Gates, daughter of Deacon Daniel Gates in nearby East Haddam. But then, carried away by ambition, he purchased rights to 1,600 acres in New York, freighted a vessel for New York City, and sold his Lyme property to purchase a proprietary right in New Hampshire. By July 8, 1775, when Lucy Mack was born in Gilsum, New Hampshire, Solomon had eight children, had cleared scores of acres and owned hundreds more, risked his capital in a variety of ventures, and yet despite all his efforts, "the Lord would not suffer me to prosper."[9]

The battle of Bunker Hill took place in Boston three weeks before Lucy's birth. George Washington's greatest need was for supplies. Sensing a renewal of the opportunities of the French and Indian War, Solomon learned from his brother-in-law in Connecticut how to make saltpeter for gunpowder and earned a dollar a day teaching the art from town to town. During the Revolution, Solomon was one of seven Gilsum men to enlist in the army. He alternated between enlistments and profit-making enterprises like carting the army's baggage. In 1778, he signed on with the crew of a privateer.[10]

For fourteen years, Solomon lived at home less than half the time. Instead of satisfying himself with a small farmstead, the traditional base for a household economy, he reached for one handhold after another in the larger economy. After the war he freighted a vessel bound for Liverpool, Nova Scotia, sailed with a fishing schooner, and ended up purchasing it after it was damaged in a hurricane and abandoned. He and a son carried passengers to New London, Connecticut, and conducted a coasting trade between Halifax, Nova Scotia, and St. John, New Brunswick. For four years Solomon heard nothing from his family. Finally around 1788, he returned home with little to show for his exertions. He was fifty-six, and after all his "hard labor and perplexity of mind, I had won nothing." "The best of my days were past and gone and had to begin entirely anew." He discovered on his return that Lydia and the children had been turned out of their house in Montague, Massachusetts. A misunderstanding on an old debt from Lyme and the underhanded dealings of one John McCurdy, who fell heir to Solomon's promissory note, led to the ejection. This news took the heart out of him. "I now thought all was gone, and I did not care whether I lived or died."[11]

Solomon's doleful account of his life should not be read as a narrative of failure. He wrote his story after his religious conversion in 1811 to show that God had repeatedly humbled him and taught him the vanity of the world, and yet he had remained deaf to the Lord's call. Solomon's purpose required him to emphasize defeat and despair. Although they suffered reverses, the Mack family did not dwell in mean poverty. At various times, they owned farms and houses. Solomon had the capital to purchase land, freight vessels, buy a schooner, and to owe and be owed hundreds of dollars. In 1786, his daughter Lydia married Samuel Bill from one of Gilsum's prominent families. Solomon's disappointments never broke his spirit. After lamenting that he cared not whether he lived or died, he reported that "I went to work and shifted from plan to plan till at length I moved to Tunbridge." Neither failure, old age, nor broken bones defeated him. The significance of Solomon's account lies less in his actual success or failure in acquiring wealth than in his sense of life as made up of toil, hurt, defeat, and death. Outside of the war episodes, there is no happiness or triumph until the end, when "God did appear for me and took me out of the horrible pit and mirey clay, and set my feet on the rock of Christ Jesus."[12]

Much of Solomon's grim endurance passed to his daughter. Lucy measured the early years not by happy friendships or childish adventures but by deaths and illnesses. Her memories, she said, were "engraved upon my heart

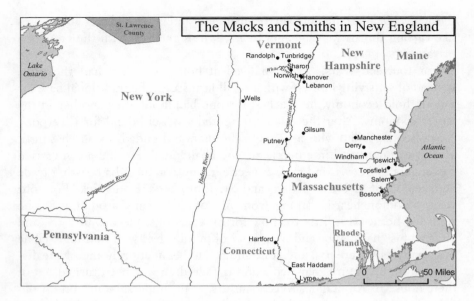

The Macks and Smiths in New England

with a pen of Iron." When a chance meeting reminded her of her youth, the thought would come to her, " 'The friends of my youth! where are they?' The tomb replies, 'here are they!' "[13] Lucy's life could be recounted as a series of losses. When she was three, Solomon was carried home half-dead from a falling tree. Later she watched while he suffered from a waterwheel fall and then from bodily fits caused by a blow on the head from a tree limb. Solomon left for Nova Scotia when Lucy was about eight. Soon after, her mother suffered a "severe fit of sickness" and came so near death that, in the absence of Solomon, she assigned eight-year-old Lucy to her brother Stephen for safekeeping.[14] When Lucy was about fourteen, her married sister Lovisa fell ill with consumption, and for five years, either Lovisa or Lovina, a year younger and stricken with the same disease, hovered on the edge of death.

At age sixteen or seventeen Lucy was able to carry Lovina, then twenty-nine, from chair to bed. As Lovina died, she told Lucy of the cold creeping into her fingers and face. A few months later, in 1794, Lovisa's consumption flared up after a three-year remission. Solomon went at once to South Hadley, Massachusetts, where she lived with her husband, and tried to bring her back to Gilsum, but she died in an inn on the way home. Lucy's "mournful recital" evoked feelings that "must last while life endures." In summing up her early life, Lucy spoke only of these illnesses and deaths.[15]

Probably in 1794, when Lucy was nineteen, grief began to prey upon her. "I was pensive and melancholy, and often in my reflections I thought that life was not worth possessing." Depressed and restless, Lucy sought comfort in religion: "I determined to obtain that which I had h[...] of so much from the pulpit—a change of heart." She gave hersen[...] reading and prayer but stumbled over one obstacle. "If I remain a n[...]ber of no church, all religious people will say I am of the world; and it [...] join some one of the different denominations, all the rest will say I am in error. No church will admit that I am right, except the one with which I am associated."[16]

Her father had no answers. At sixty-two, he still sought happiness in an elusive prosperity, the false hope of his faithless upbringing. Lucy's mother, Lydia, reared in a deacon's house, joined the Congregational church at age thirty after she married Solomon. He gave her full credit for instructing the children in habits of "piety, gentleness, and reflection," and for calling them together morning and evening to pray. Lucy said that all of her religious instruction came from her "pious and affectionate" mother.[17]

The Mack children bore Lydia's imprint. As Lovina and Lovisa approached death, they warned their hearers to prepare for eternity. The oldest son, Jason, became a lay preacher at twenty, and by the end of his life was practicing faith healings and "holding meetings, day and night, from place to place." He became a religious seeker before he was sixteen, pursuing the spiritual gifts of early Christianity outside of established churches. Religious currents ran deep in Lucy. She believed that God had healed her sister, Lydia, and her mother, and she solemnly recorded the account of Lovisa's vision of "the Saviour, as through a veil." Her sisters' deaths led her thoughts to eternity, judgment, and the worthlessness of life. But the only mention of a church in Lucy's childhood reminiscences occurs in the reference to Lovisa after her marriage to Joseph Tuttle.[18] Lucy groped through her depression looking for a church and a change of heart and found nothing. Mack religion was family religion, and nothing outside the family satisfied her.

Lydia had charged Stephen Mack, Lucy's brother, with looking after her. After their sisters' deaths, he invited the depressed Lucy to visit him in Tunbridge, eighty miles north and across the Connecticut River in Vermont. In 1793, Stephen had moved from Gilsum to Tunbridge, where he thrived as a merchant. Tunbridge was a new town, like Gilsum or Marlow thirty years earlier when Solomon had moved there from Lyme. Among the new settlers was Asael Smith, who first acquired land in 1791 and was clearing and settling his sons on it when Lucy visited Stephen. Asael became Stephen's "intimate acquaintance," though twenty-two years separated the two. Lucy spoke of the Smiths as "a worthy, respectable, amiable, and intelligent family." Asael was a selectman of Tunbridge, one of the three active men chosen to look after the town's affairs. During her visit Lucy met Joseph Smith, Asael's second son, a strong, tall young man of twenty-three. After a year she returned to Gilsum by way of Marlow, where Mack rela-

tives still lived. She was hardly home when Stephen came again and
"insisted so hard upon my returning with him" that she agreed. On January 24, 1796, justice of the peace Seth Austin married Lucy Mack and
Joseph Smith.[19]

ASAEL AND MARY SMITH

Until Asael's generation scattered to the north and west, the Smith ancestors of Joseph Smith were rooted in Topsfield, Massachusetts. Twelve-year-
old Robert Smith had sailed from England in 1638 at the height of the
Puritan migration, and his descendants settled in Topsfield, a farm village
ten miles north of Salem. Robert's son, the first Samuel Smith, was among
the accusers of a witch at the famous trials.[20] Asael was the fourth generation of Smiths in the town. His father, the second Samuel, received nearly
all the honors the town could bestow. He was repeatedly chosen assessor,
selectman, town clerk, representative to the General Court (the Massachusetts legislature), and delegate to the Provincial Congress. Most important,
Samuel was frequently chosen moderator of the town meeting, a position
commanding universal respect. When he died in 1785, his obituary in the
Salem Gazette noted that he "was esteemed a man of integrity and uprightness . . . a sincere friend to the liberties of his country, and a strenuous
advocate for the doctrines of Christianity."[21]

Samuel's distinction in Topsfield gave Asael no economic advantage as he
started in life. Selectmen, though respected, were not necessarily wealthy.
Asael was the youngest of five children, each of whom had to be provided
for: land for the two boys and marriage portions for the three daughters.
After helping the older children and reserving enough to keep him through
old age, Samuel lacked the resources to set Asael up in Topsfield. Cast loose
from the old village moorings, Asael scrambled for a toehold in the spare
New England economy, much like Solomon Mack, who began life with
nothing.

In 1767, at twenty-two, Asael married Mary Duty of Windham, New
Hampshire. For five years they probably lived with father Samuel and his
second wife, Priscilla. Their first three children were born in Samuel's
house, including Joseph, the second son, on July 12, 1771. The next year,
Asael and Mary began twenty years of shuffling from farm to farm in eastern Massachusetts and southern New Hampshire, trying to get their feet
under them. They lived in three different New Hampshire towns, interrupted only briefly by Asael's enlistment in the army in 1776. Then in 1785,
Samuel Smith died in Topsfield and Asael inherited half the property.
Samuel Jr., who was listed as a gentleman in the land records, ran the farm
probably in hopes of succeeding to his father's place, but he soon realized
the estate was insolvent. The depression of the mid-1780s made it nearly

impossible to collect the debts owed the estate and pay off creditors. Hoping for a fresh start, Samuel Jr. offered to exchange the Topsfield property for Asael's farm in Derryfield. Asael rashly agreed to the exchange, he later said, because "I am not willing that my father, who has done so much business, should have it said of him that he died insolvent." He worked the farm for five years before admitting defeat. In 1791 the farm was sold. Asael and Mary, with their eleven children, were once again looking for a home.[22]

Asael's son John said the family was destitute when they left Topsfield, but they were not without recourse. With proceeds from the Topsfield property and a loan, Asael purchased eighty-three acres of uncleared land in Tunbridge, Vermont. He planned to send the two oldest sons, Jesse and Joseph, ages twenty-three and twenty, to clear the Tunbridge land before the family's arrival the next spring; he and Mary and the others would lease dairy land in Ipswich, a few miles from Topsfield. The plan worked through the summer until Asael "changed his mind," John wrote later, "as He could not bare to have his boys so far from him as he always loved to have his children close by." In October 1791, Asael sold his Ipswich crops on the ground, hired three yoke of oxen and a wagon, and set out with the family on the 140-mile journey to Tunbridge. En route they met Joseph on his way back to Ipswich with a "partly fractured" leg bone. In November, the Smiths crowded into the fourteen-by-ten-foot hut built by Jesse and Joseph and prepared for the Vermont winter.[23]

Asael's seven sons, his greatest asset and his greatest responsibility, were valuable workers, but all needed farms as they came of age. Jesse married a year after their arrival and set up on fifty acres received from Asael. The rest of the boys labored alongside Asael until they married. By 1796, he reported to an old friend in Topsfield that one farm was ready and a new house built on a second. Joseph, the second son, received a farm when he married Lucy Mack in 1796 and worked it on halves. Asael used his half to support his family while he brought in new farms for the others. In 1794 and 1795, he purchased two additional lots, 83 and 100 acres, close to the first farm, and another purchase soon followed. By the time the third son, Asael Jr., married in 1802, the Smiths had a compound of adjoining farms totaling between 300 and 400 acres. The plan brought Asael modest eminence in Tunbridge. Beginning in 1793 he was frequently elected one of three selectmen to manage town affairs; he occasionally served as moderator and highway surveyor. His son Jesse was chosen trustee of the school district when it opened in the southern portion of the town near the Smith farms and later was elected selectman and town clerk. After a rocky start, Asael came close to replicating his father's Salem life.[24]

When Asael was fifty-five in 1799, each of his four married children bore him a grandchild, prompting him to write "A few words of advice" to his family, "whom I expect ear Long to Leave." Asael was a quiet and a sad man. "I Never found any thing too hard for me in my calling," he said, "but Discouragement and unbileaf." "Above evry thing," he advised his children, "avoid a Malaancholly Disposition, that is a humer that admits of aney temptation and is capable of aney impresson and Distemper. shun as Death this humour, which will work you to all unthankfulness against god, unlovingness to men, and unnaturalness to your Selves and one another."[25]

Asael's mother had died when he was six months old. His mother's cousin, who married his father a year later, "did not treat him [Asael] so kindly as some Mothers treat their Children." His experience determined him to bind his large family together:

> Wherefore my Dear children, I pray, Beseach, and adjure you by all the relations and Dearness that hath Ever been betwixt us, and by the heart rending pangs of a Dying father, whos Soul hath been ever bound in the bundle of Life with yours, that you know one anothr visit (as you may) each other comfort, counsel, relieve, Succour, help and admonish one another. and while your mother Lives, meet hear (if posably once Evry year)[.] when She is Dead, pitch on Some other place; if it may be, your older Brothers house; or if you cannot Meet, Send to and hear from each other yearly, and oftener if you can. and when you have Neither father nor mother Left, be so maney fathers and mothers to each other, So you Shall understand the blessing mentioned in the 133 psalm.[26]

His appeal for family unity took a concrete form during one last migration. Between 1811 and 1820, Asael and Mary and at least seven of the eleven children moved from Tunbridge. Six of the seven settled around their parents in Stockholm and Potsdam in St. Lawrence County, New York, where, presumably with the aid of grandchildren, they opened new farms.[27]

They were living close together in 1828 when Joseph Smith Sr. wrote about the visions of his son. In 1830, he visited personally, bringing copies of the Book of Mormon. Eventually, four of the five surviving sons became Mormons, and Asael and Mary were well disposed. In 1836 the clan moved again, this time without Asael, who died in 1830. Asael Jr., Silas, John, and Mary Duty Smith took the five-hundred-mile journey to Kirtland to join the Mormons. When Joseph Jr. and Hyrum met their ninety-two-year-old grandmother in her Fairport hotel room, "Joseph blessed her and said she was the most honored woman on earth." Mary told Lucy, "I am going to have your Joseph [Jr.] baptize me, and my Joseph [the patriarch] bless me." She did not live long enough for that to happen, but there was time for a reunion with four sons, several grandsons, and a score of great-grandchildren, fulfilling Asael's admonition that the children meet yearly and "live together in an undivided bond of Love."[28]

The switch to Mormonism was not difficult for Asael. He had been dislodged from the crumbling orthodoxies of New England Congregationalism. His father had seen to the baptism of all four of his children in Topsfield's Congregational church, but after the Revolution, Asael drifted away from orthodoxy. He was drawn to the teachings of John Murray, a Universalist preacher, who emigrated from England in 1770 and began preaching in Gloucester, Massachusetts, about fifteen miles from Topsfield, in 1774. Murray was neither Boston-born nor Harvard-bred; his teachings appealed mostly to common people. He answered to a growing desire to make God more reasonable and benevolent than Calvinism allowed. Murray taught that Christ assumed the sins of all men. Christ's atoning grace was powerful enough to redeem everyone without exception—thus "universal" salvation. Murray carried the Calvinist idea of irresistible grace to its logical conclusion and included every soul within the circle of divine love.[29]

In "A few words of advice," Asael tried to bring his children to the same conclusion. In Asael's opinion, Christ "came to Save Sinners mearly because they [were] such," not because of repentance. Grace saved people and saved them all. Asael saw no reason why God should favor Vermont Christians over "the worst heathen in the Darkest corner of the desarts of arabia." "And if you can believe that Christ [came] to save Sinners, and not the righteous, pharisees or Self rightious. that Sinners must be saved by the rightiousness of Christ alone, without mixing any of their own rightiousness with his; then you will See that he can as well Save all, as aney."[30]

Murray's followers organized an association in Massachusetts in 1785, and in 1793 a New England convention of Universalists met. From all reports, Vermont was one of their strongholds. In 1790, five Congregational clergymen on the upper Connecticut converted to Universalism. In 1797 the town clerk recorded a request from seventeen members of the Tunbridge Universalist Society to be exempted from ecclesiastical taxes. Asael was moderator of the group, and Joseph and Jesse were among the seventeen. That was the high point of the family's Universalism. Thereafter, Asael's children gravitated back toward orthodoxy before turning to Mormonism; Universalism became an overlay on family religion. But Asael's own convictions did not waver; his grandson George A. Smith remembers him writing "quires of paper on the doctrine of universal restoration" before his death.[31]

JOSEPH AND LUCY SMITH

Both sides of the family helped Joseph Smith and Lucy Mack begin married life. Asael provided his son with part ownership of a "handsome" four-year-old farm, and Lucy's brother Stephen Mack and his partner John Mudget presented Lucy with $1,000 for a wedding present. Lucy bought her household furnishings with other resources and laid away the $1,000 as a cash reserve. After visiting Solomon and Lydia Mack in Gilsum, she and Joseph set to work in a promising year. Wheat prices in 1796 were up a third from the previous decade. The New England farm economy had left the doldrums of the 1780s behind. A first son died in childbirth, and then two years after their marriage Lucy bore a second son, Alvin, followed two years later by a third boy, Hyrum.[32]

The Smiths remained in Tunbridge for six years before leaving the farm and turning to storekeeping. Perhaps in hopes of advancing their fortunes, perhaps prodded by the ambitious Stephen Mack, Joseph and Lucy rented out their Tunbridge house and land and moved to Randolph, a village seven miles to the west. By 1810, Randolph had 1,841 inhabitants to Tunbridge's 1,324, making it the largest town in Orange County and the fourteenth largest in the state. By 1820 Randolph had grown to 2,255 inhabitants and was the eighth largest town in Vermont. Instead of Vermont's usual hills, largely unusable for tillage, Randolph lay on a broad plateau stretching between two rivers. Nearly 20,000 acres of arable land attracted settlers. After 1802, growth was further stimulated by a canal at Bellows Falls, which gave Vermont water access to the lower Connecticut. A weekly Vermont-Boston stage line began service in 1801.[33]

Joseph Smith opened his Randolph store with a line of goods purchased on credit from Boston. His inventory sold quickly, not for cash but for promise of payment in commodities at harvest. Joseph meanwhile turned his thoughts to ginseng, a wild root prized in China for its supposed capacity to prolong life and restore virility. The *Empress of China*, the first American ship to reach Canton after the Revolution, carried forty tons of ginseng. The next year the Americans shipped over twice that amount without lowering the price. Joseph collected the root, probably from local farmers, and crystalized it. A merchant named Stevens from Royalton, a few miles south of Randolph, offered him $3,000 for the lot, but Joseph refused, preferring to handle it himself for the full price.[34]

It was a fateful turning point in the Smith family fortunes. Joseph took the ginseng to New York and contracted for shipment on consignment. He stood to make as much as $4,500 by circumventing the middlemen, but he also assumed the whole burden of risk. And he lost. Stevens's son sailed for China on the same ship as Joseph's cargo. On his return, he reported the sad news that the venture had failed, and presented Joseph with a chest of tea as the only compensation. The venture was, in fact, a failure, but not because of a poor market. According to Lucy Smith, Stephen Mack suspected foul play when the young Stevens opened works for crystalizing ginseng and hired eight or ten men. Catching Stevens in his cups, Mack deftly extracted the information that the ginseng had brought a chestful of money. Joseph had been cheated of his just returns. Stevens fled for Canada, and though Joseph set out after him, the pursuit was in vain. Joseph returned from the chase disheartened, perhaps wiser, and financially ruined.[35]

Meanwhile the debt for the original inventory of store goods was due. With his shelves empty, Joseph found he had $2,000 in bad debts from his customers and nothing to pay the $1,800 owed in Boston. Forced to the wall, he took the step that blighted the Smith family fortunes for thirty years: he sold the farm. Lucy contributed her $1,000 wedding gift, and the farm went for $800. Lucy said they made the sacrifice to avoid the "embarrassment of debt," but they soon knew the "embarrassment of poverty." They crossed the boundary dividing independent ownership from tenancy and day labor.[36]

One of the misfortunes of the propertyless was the necessity for frequent moves. Tenants sometimes rented farms in the process of being sold and available only for a few years. If the farm was not sold out from under them, a better opportunity elsewhere might impel a move. Over the next fourteen years, the Smiths moved seven times. Between 1803 and 1811 all the moves were in a tiny circle around Tunbridge, Royalton, and Sharon, immediately adjoining towns, and probably never involved a distance of more than five or six miles. Then in 1811 they moved twenty miles across the Connecticut River to Lebanon, New Hampshire, and finally, after a few years back in Vermont, in Norwich, the Smiths broke entirely free of the network of family and friends and in 1816 migrated to New York.[37]

Until that final break, family members smoothed the way. In spring 1803, the Smiths were back on their Tunbridge farm, close to Asael's children, for the birth of Sophronia. After the sale of the farm, they spent a few months in Royalton and then rented a farm from Solomon Mack, who on August 27, 1804, purchased a hundred acres straddling the Sharon-Royalton line. Stephen Mack remained in Tunbridge for a few years; Daniel Mack, Lucy's brother, married in Tunbridge in 1799; and Solomon and Lydia Mack were close at hand. Though poor, Joseph and Lucy would not starve or be shorthanded when they needed help.[38]

Joseph taught school in Sharon in the winter and farmed in the summer, and with him working two jobs, the Smith family circumstances, as Lucy reported, "gradually improved." She was feeling optimistic when another son, Joseph Smith Jr., arrived on December 23, 1805.[39] The little boy probably had no memories of the sloping hill farm that now bears a monument to his name: his family moved when he was barely two. They were back in Tunbridge on March 13, 1808, for the birth of Samuel Harrison. Two years later to the day, Ephraim was born and exactly one year later William followed, both in Royalton. Little Ephraim died eleven days after birth, the second of Lucy's children lost in childhood.[40]

Despite the moves and occasional sorrows, there is no evidence of excessive stress in the Smith family during Joseph Jr.'s early years.[41] Lucy remembered them as happy, progressive times. Joseph Jr. probably had enough schooling from Deacon Jonathan Finney in Royalton to learn his letters. If not, his father could teach him. When they crossed the Connecticut River to Lebanon, New Hampshire, in 1811, the Smiths congratulated themselves on their prosperity. "We looked around us and said what do we now lack," Lucy recalled. "There is nothing which we have not a sufficiency of to make us and our children perfectly comfortable both for food and raiment as well as that which is necessary to a respectable appearance in society both at home and abroad." Still not content, they purchased 100 pounds of candles to permit them to work into the winter nights, and with them 200 yards of cloth for a stock of family clothing. Hyrum, age eleven, was sent a few miles north to Moor's Charity School, associated with Dartmouth College. Alvin, thirteen, and Sophronia, eight, went to common school. Joseph Jr., five, and his two younger brothers, Samuel and William, three and six months, remained at home. In the summer of 1812 a baby girl, Katharine, joined the family.[42]

For all of its modest comfort, the life of the Smith family was far from secure. Lucy and Joseph Sr. knew they were unprepared for the two great economic challenges of every nineteenth-century farm family: provision for children as they came of age, and provision for their own old age. Adult life was a race to accumulate sufficient goods to give the children a start, and still have enough to be independent and comfortable in old age. "We doubled our diligence, in order to obtain more of this world's goods, with the view of assisting our children, when they should need it; and, as is quite natural, we looked forward to the decline of life, and were providing for its wants." They had to own property to clear both hurdles. Without land, the margin between comfort and mean poverty was too thin. A single calamity could consume their resources and leave them penniless.[43]

In 1812 and 1813, calamity struck. Typhoid fever swept through the upper Connecticut Valley and left 6,400 dead in five months. One after another, the Smith family fell ill, until all but the parents lay prostrate. Sophronia went through a ninety-day sickness that left her limp and motionless. Joseph Sr. and Lucy clasped hands, knelt, and uttered a grief-stricken prayer. Lucy caught the apparently dead girl up in a blanket, pressed her close, and paced the floor until the child sobbed and began to breathe. The fever had broken. None of the children died.[44]

The fever left six-year-old Joseph after two weeks, but a sore formed in his armpit and was wrongly diagnosed as a sprain. After two weeks of intense pain, the doctor identified the true cause and lanced the sore, which discharged a quart of purulent matter. Though that infection healed, Joseph complained of a pain in his left shin and ankle. Hyrum sat beside him "holding the affected part of his leg in his hands, and pressing it between them, so that his afflicted brother might be enabled to endure the pain."[45] After three weeks, a Dr. Stone was called in and this time an eight-inch incision was made between ankle and knee. Opening the leg helped temporarily, but infection had now entered the bone. As the wound healed over, the infection flamed up again. The doctor made another, larger incision, going down to the bone.

When the healing wound began to swell once more, Dr. Stone consulted a "council of surgeons," headed by Nathan Smith and Cyrus Perkins of Dartmouth Medical College. They proposed amputation, the sensible treatment of osteomyelitis in the age before antibiotics. Lucy remembered seven physicians riding up to the house in Lebanon; Joseph remembered eleven. Probably some were medical students who came to witness the surgery. Lucy refused to permit the amputation, and young Joseph protested too. As she remembered the event, Lucy appealed to the doctors to cut out the diseased portion of bone instead. Lucy also remembered young Joseph refusing wine or brandy and assuring the doctors that cords were unnecessary. Fortunately, Joseph had come under the care of a renowned surgeon. In his extensive practice with typhoid patients suffering from bone infection, Nathan Smith had developed a surgical procedure in advance of his time. He may have suggested amputation to prepare the family for accepting an unconventional alternative.[46]

As the operation began, Lucy went out into the fields and left Joseph in his father's arms, the infected leg resting on folded sheets. The surgeons bored holes on each side of the leg bone and chipped off three large pieces. Joseph Jr. screamed when they broke off the first piece, and Lucy rushed back into the room. Sent away, she came back again as the third piece came off. Blood gushed from the open wound, and Joseph lay on the bed drenched in blood. He was "pale as a corpse, and large drops of sweat were rolling down his face, whilst upon every feature was depicted the utmost agony!"[47]

After three months of constant pain, Joseph Jr. passed the crisis, and the leg began to mend. The ordeal, however, continued. The wound healed cleanly, but fourteen additional pieces of bone worked their way to the surface. The disease and pain so wasted his body that his mother easily carried him about in her arms. Convalescence dragged on for three years. To speed his recovery, the family sent him to Salem, on the Massachusetts coast, with his uncle Jesse to enjoy the sea breezes. Until the family moved to New York, Joseph hobbled around on crutches. From age seven to ten, he was either in bed or on crutches. To the end of his life he was slightly lame, possibly because of the trauma.[48]

The typhoid fever episode revealed relationships in the Smith household that were less visible in placid times. We see Lucy bold and determined. When the medical men walked into her house in Lebanon intending to cut off Joseph's leg, she blocked the way. As she told the story, she posed the crucial question: "Gentlemen, what can you do to save my boy's leg?" When they answered, "We can do nothing," she proposed another procedure.[49] On the long journeys from Norwich to Palmyra, and later from New York to Kirtland, she took the same role. She was the one who knew the right thing to do, to set matters in order, to stand up to error, and eventually to save the day. She was a spirited woman, outspoken and candid, forceful under pressure. Confronting the doctors, she declared, "You will not, you must not, take off his leg until you try once more. I will not consent to let you enter his room until you make me this promise."[50]

A different picture of Joseph Sr. emerges in Lucy's account. Lucy said he "was constantly with the child." She reported that after learning of the decision to operate again, Joseph Sr. "seemed for a moment to contemplate my countenance . . . then turning his eyes upon his boy, at once all his sufferings, together with my intense anxiety rushed upon his mind, & he burst into a flood of tears, and sobbed like a child." She saw her husband's softness in contrast to her resolution. She contended with the doctors while he sat by the boy.[51]

Lucy thought of herself as a comforter too. She was the one to pace the floor with Sophronia clasped to her bosom until the child began breathing again. When Joseph Jr.'s leg began to swell, Lucy carried him much of the time. She had convenanted with God during an earlier religious crisis to comfort her family to the best of her ability, but her comfort was more high-strung. After Sophronia caught her breath, Lucy sank to the bed, "completely overpowered by the intensity of my feelings." She carried Joseph Jr. so much, she said, that she was taken ill herself. "The anxiety of mind that I experienced, together with physical overexertion, was too much for my constitution, and my nature sunk under it."[52]

Joseph Sr.'s strength was of another kind. He cried at the thought of an operation, but he also held his son while the doctors cut into his leg. When the pain first struck, Joseph Jr. cried out to his father, not to Lucy, and in refusing to be tied with cords, said, "I will have my father sit on the bed and hold me in his arms." He sent his mother from the room, telling her, "I know you cannot bear to see me suffer so; father can stand it, but you have carried me so much, and watched over me so long, you are almost worn out." The steadier father stood by when Lucy's nerves could not bear the strain.[53]

Though Lucy saw herself as the family fighter, she needed her husband's steady strength. In retelling the story, she gave him full credit for his part in the operation. In the flinty fashion of nineteenth-century Yankees, she was circumspect about her feelings for him, but her affection and admiration comes through. A few years earlier, when she was trying to interest her husband in religion, she dreamed of Joseph Sr. and his brother Jesse. She saw herself standing in a meadow "of peculiar pleasantness" where stood two large trees that she later understood represented Joseph and Jesse:

> These trees were very beautiful, they were well proportioned, and towered with majestic beauty to a great height. Their branches, which added to their symmetry and glory, commenced near the top, and spread themselves in luxurious grandeur around. I gazed upon them with wonder and admiration.

One of the trees was fixed and rigid in the wind, the other flexible and joyous. The dream comforted Lucy, because her husband was the flexible tree, which later she took to mean he would embrace the gospel her son Joseph would teach, while the unbending Jesse stubbornly refused. The unconscious point of the dream was the beauty of her husband and her admiration for him.

> I saw one of them was surrounded with a bright belt, that shone like burnished gold, but far more brilliantly. Presently, a gentle breeze passed by, and the tree encircled with this golden zone, bent gracefully before the wind, and waved its beautiful branches in the light air. As the wind increased, this tree assumed the most lively and animated appearance, and seemed to express in its motions the utmost joy and happiness. . . . Even the stream that rolled beneath it, shared, apparently, every sensation felt by the tree, for, as the branches danced over the stream, it would swell gently, then recede again with a motion as soft as the breathing of an infant, but as lively as the dancing of a sunbeam. The belt also partook of the same influence, and as it moved in unison with the motion of the stream and of the tree, it increased continually in refulgence and magnitude, until it became exceedingly glorious.

This happy tribute to the radiance of Joseph Sr. must have magnified Lucy's pleasure after each separation "in once more having the society of my husband."[54]

Lucy's only explicit reservation about her husband was his diffidence about religion. After his brief flirtation with Universalism in 1797, Joseph Sr. hovered on the margins of the churches. Her own quest for peace of mind and a church had not slackened since girlhood, and her husband's refusal to become involved troubled her. Lucy's concern culminated in Randolph in 1803 while they were operating the store. She came down with a cold and then a fever that the doctor diagnosed as consumption. The sickness so wore on her that she could not bear the sound of a footfall or voices above a whisper. The knock of a well-meaning Methodist exhorter agitated her nerves unbearably.[55]

Lucy dreaded to hear the man speak; she feared he would ask if she was prepared to die. "I did not consider myself ready for such an awful event, inasmuch as I knew not the ways of Christ; besides, there appeared to be a dark and lonesome chasm, between myself and the Saviour, which I dared not attempt to pass."[56] In that frame of mind, she was a ready mark for the Methodist exhorter, although Lucy's mother forbade him to speak for fear of jangling Lucy's nerves. The main purpose of evangelical preaching was to set people on a quest for salvation. The conventional method was to convict people of their sins, to persuade them that they were utterly unable to please God through sheer obedience. Lucy's sense of "a dark and lonesome chasm, between myself and the Saviour" was a classic expression of the feeling the preachers wished to evoke. Having been brought so low, she should have been prepared to throw herself entirely on the mercy of God and plead for grace. In the ideal case, a new hope arises in the heart, and the person begins to rejoice in the glory and goodness of God. That realization opens a flood of happiness and love and an overwhelming sense of the beauty of the world. The scriptural phrase "born again" describes exactly the renewal that has occurred.

In 1803 a season of revivals that would soon surpass the Great Awakening of the 1740s began in Connecticut and Vermont. In the west and south, vast camp meetings were being organized at which hundreds and thousands of persons came under evangelical preaching. Lucy's personal concern in 1803 connected her with a vast movement, one that would course in great waves through the entire nineteenth century; to this day it has not spent itself completely.[57]

Lucy listened to no evangelical preaching during her illness, but doubtless she had heard the doctrine of new birth many times. At the height of her illness, when her husband despaired of her life, she pleaded with the Lord to spare her that she might bring up her children and comfort her husband.

My mind was much agitated during the whole night. Sometimes I contemplated heaven and heavenly things; then my thoughts would turn upon those of earth—my babes and my companion.

During this night I made a solemn covenant with God, that, if he would let me live, I would endeavour to serve him according to the best of my abilities. Shortly after this, I heard a voice say to me, "Seek, and ye shall find; knock, and it shall be opened unto you. Let your heart be comforted; ye believe in God, believe also in me."

In a few moments her mother entered the room and said, "Lucy you are better."[58]

Lucy recovered her health, but her mind still was "considerably disquieted" and "wholly occupied upon the subject of religion." When she was able, she looked for someone to give her direction "in the way of life and salvation." Her attempts to connect with a church, however, were scarcely more successful than after the deaths of her sisters. She visited Deacon Davies, a local man noted for piety, but he was wholly concerned for her physical comfort and said nothing "in relation to Christ or godliness." Lucy returned to her house disgusted and sorrowful. Anxious to keep her covenant with God, she looked on every side for a congenial spirit. A notable itinerant Presbyterian preacher only convinced her that he "neither understood nor appreciated the subject upon which he spoke." His discourse was all "emptiness vanity vexation of spirit," and palled her heart "like the chill night air." The cold words could "not fill the aching void." She concluded "that there was not then upon the earth the religion" she sought. She resigned herself to Bible reading and self-instruction. Eventually she found a minister to baptize her without requiring that she join a church. Like her brother Jason in his early life, Lucy was a seeker.[59]

While still searching for direction, Lucy attended Methodist meetings in Tunbridge, and Joseph Sr. obligingly accompanied her. The news of this angered Asael and Jesse, who pressed Joseph to stop. Lucy reported that one day Asael came to the door "and threw Tom Pain's age of reason into the house and angrily bade him read that until he believed it."[60] While the details are somewhat out of character for Asael (Lucy told the story only in her draft manuscript), it is not surprising that Asael should oppose Joseph Sr.'s association with an evangelical church. Universalists thought evangelical belief slandered a loving heavenly father. If grace could save one, it could save all. There was no need for the anxiety, humiliation, and depression of rebirth. Asael was understandably disgusted with Joseph for listening to Methodists, who preached little else but conversion. Asael may have thrown Paine at his son to startle him into reconsideration.

Joseph Sr. was not lacking in religion. He spontaneously knelt with his wife to pray for Sophronia in her illness and insisted on morning and evening family prayers.[61] Revival seasons aroused his desire for religion. When Solomon Mack was converted during the revival of 1810 and 1811, Joseph Sr. "became much excited upon the subject of religion." What he could not embrace was the institutional religion of his time. The reason became clear in one of his prophetic dreams. In the first dream, around 1811, Joseph Sr. found himself traveling in a barren field covered with dead fallen timber: "Not a vestige of life, either animal or vegetable, could be seen; besides, to render the scene still more dreary, the most death-like silence prevailed, no sound of anything animate could be heard in all the field." The attendant spirit, according to Lucy, told Joseph Sr. that "this field is the world which now lieth inanimate and dumb, in regard to the true religion or plan of salvation." Then appeared "all manner of beasts, horned cattle, and roaring animals . . . tearing the earth, tossing their horns, and bellowing most terrifically." That was the religious world as Joseph Sr. saw it: empty and silent, or fiercely hostile to true wisdom and understanding. He concluded from his dream that the "class of religionists" knew no more of the Kingdom of God than "such as made no profession of religion whatever." Partly because of her husband's attitude, Lucy hovered on the edge of respectable religion, attracted and repelled at the same time. Without the help of minister or church, her son William later remembered, Lucy made "use of every means which her parental love could suggest, to get us engaged in seeking for our souls' salvation."[62]

In following his father to Vermont, Joseph Sr. had been detached from the comfortable village religion of Topsfield. Grandfather Samuel had been a Congregationalist, a leading townsman, a man of property. Asael broke those religious moorings as surely as he left the family's farm. He was drawn to Universalism, read Tom Paine, and repudiated evangelical religion. Joseph Sr. was even more adrift. In the first generation, Asael experimented; in the second, Joseph Sr. was lost.

It would be hard to place the Smiths in any one religious tradition. The family's religious culture was too eclectic. Smith and Mack relatives comprised an inventory of late-eighteenth-century alternatives. Joseph Sr.'s dreams linked him to radical Protestantism with its taste for spiritual manifestations. Solomon Mack underwent a classic evangelical conversion at the end of his life. Lucy's crisis in 1803 took the same form. Her brother Jason was a seeker. Asael's Universalism was a form of vernacular rationalism, an offspring of the Enlightenment. Asael used Thomas Paine's *Age of Reason* to quash Joseph Sr.'s flirtation with Methodism. Possibly in Vermont and certainly later in New York, Joseph Sr. was involved in magical practices, an unorthodox but not unusual way of connecting with the supernatural.[63] The Smiths were exposed to a conglomeration of doctrines and attitudes, some imported from Europe, others springing up in New England, none sorted or ranked by recognized authority, all available for adoption as personal whim or circumstances dictated. The result was a religious melee.

Buffeted by these currents, the family was marginalized religiously, but in a peculiar way. The historian David Hall has called indifferent seventeenth-century churchgoers "horse-shed" Christians because they talked animals and crops between Sunday meetings rather than religion.[64] Solomon Mack and his master could be numbered among these worldlings, unconcerned for the condition of their souls. The Smiths were not "horse-shed" Christians. Orthodoxy seemed inaccessible, inanimate, and hostile, but the distance between the Smiths and the churches did not harden their hearts. They were anguished souls, starved for religion. If there was a personal motive for Joseph Smith Jr.'s revelations, it was to satisfy his family's religious want and, above all, to meet the need of his oft-defeated, unmoored father.

MIGRATION

At the end of the Smiths' year-long stay in Lebanon, medical bills had broken them financially. Around 1814, they moved back across the Connecticut River to Norwich, Vermont, where they rented a farm from "Squire Moredock" and went into "business." Their low condition and residence in a new village may have left them without credit to tide them over until their first crop, and compelled them, like other poor people, to truck for a living. Sometime before the move to New York, Lucy learned to paint oilcloths, which were popular for floor coverings and tablecloths. Joseph Sr. might have peddled small items and hired out as a farmhand. When their crops failed the first year, they lived on the sale of fruit from their orchard and took work in town.[65]

Unfortunately, the Mack and Smith backup was ebbing away. Solomon Mack was over eighty and unable to help. The Smith clan in Tunbridge were uprooting themselves and moving west. By 1815, all of Joseph's brothers, except Jesse, had migrated to New York, and he and Asael soon followed. Joseph and Lucy were increasingly on their own.[66]

In the next two years nature conspired to drive them from Vermont. The second year on the Norwich farm, crops failed again. Joseph planted the third spring, in 1816, with a resolve to try just once more. The result was conclusive. This was known as the year without a summer. Lucy spoke of an "untimely frost." Actually on June 8 several inches of snow fell all across the highlands of northern New York and New England, and ice formed on the ponds. The entire summer was cold and dry. Famine compelled farmers to pay $3 a bushel for imported corn. As Lucy remembered it, "This was enough: my husband was now altogether decided upon going to New York." Thousands of Vermonters left the state. Migration in 1816 and 1817 dealt a blow to the state's prospects from which it did not recover for a century. The population in Orange County, which contained Tunbridge, had more than doubled between 1790 and 1800 and had grown by almost 40 percent more by 1810. After the cold summer the 1820 census showed 600 fewer people than in 1810, and thereafter growth was spasmodic at best. In 1880, the population of Orange County was 3,000 less than it had been in 1810.[67]

The many reasons for leaving Norwich did not make the decision easy for Joseph Sr. Lucy had borne a son, Don Carlos, in March 1816, and would be traveling with a baby at her breast. While Joseph Sr. was locating a new place, she would have to handle the family's business affairs and prepare for the trip. There was also the question of where to resettle. Joseph's brothers and father had all moved to St. Lawrence County on the northern rim of New York. If he were to follow, Joseph Sr. and Lucy could turn to their kinsmen in emergencies, but was it the best place? It might also be difficult to extricate themselves from Norwich. By 1816 the Smiths had woven themselves into the web of debts and credits that substituted for money in that period. All of the debts had to be paid, a point of honor with the Smiths. They would not run out on their creditors as others did.[68]

For over a decade, weather, crop failures, creditors, illness, and business failures had battered the Smith household economy. They were in desperate shape by the time they left Norwich, but not without resources. Stories of New York land available on long credit gave them hope. They were never forced to bind out their children, the ultimate admission of failure. The four boys and two girls were all potential workers. Family, as always, held their world together.

Lucy assured Joseph Sr. of her ability to make the preparations and suggested that "he might get both his creditors and debtors together, and arrange matters between them in such a way as to give satisfaction to all parties concerned." That satisfactorily accomplished, Joseph Sr. felt free to go. A local man, Mr. Howard, was going to Palmyra, and the offer of a traveling companion convinced Joseph Sr. to look in New York. The Vermont papers advertised new land in the Genesee country for $2 to $3 an acre. Palmyra looked promising. In the summer of 1816, Joseph Sr. set out. Alvin and Hyrum walked out along the road with their father to say goodbye.[69]

Lucy had the help of her mother and the older boys to collect provisions and clothing and pack the wagon. She had sewn woolen clothing for the children and "had on hand a great deal of diaper and pulled cloth in the web." When the word came, they were ready to go. Joseph Sr. arranged for Caleb Howard, the cousin of his traveling companion, to come with a team. Then, just as the family was about to depart, the old debts rose to plague them. Some of the creditors had not brought their books to the first settlement and waited until the last to make their claim. A departing family was particularly vulnerable at the moment of leave-taking. Under ordinary circumstances creditors knew that the scarcity of money made collection impractical and waited patiently for credits to balance the account. Departure was, of course, the last opportunity to collect; it was a time when the family, having sold all of its possessions to obtain cash for the trip, was most liquid. Apparently some of Joseph's creditors unscrupulously held back their accounts until this moment when they could hope for a better settlement. Two well-wishers offered to take Lucy's case to court, but to avoid delay she chose to settle. The creditors took $150 of the funds Lucy had assembled to pay expenses, leaving her only $60 or $80. By the end of the trip she was paying innkeepers with clothing and bits of cloth.[70]

Snow covered the ground when Lucy and the eight children left Norwich. They went by sleigh to Royalton, where they left Lucy's mother with Daniel Mack after she was severely injured in a sleighing accident. Lydia Mack wept over her daughter and admonished her to "continue faithful in the service of God to the end of your days, that I may have the pleasure of embracing you in another and fairer world above." Transferring their goods to a wagon, the little party turned their backs on family and familiar places and headed for Palmyra, three hundred miles distant.[71]

The driver, Caleb Howard, proved troublesome from the start. The Smiths fell in with a Gates family traveling west in sleighs, and Howard wanted the Gates daughters to ride beside him. To make room, he drove Joseph Jr. from his place. For days at a time young Joseph, who had just discarded his crutches and was still lame, limped along in the snow. When Alvin and Hyrum protested, Howard knocked them down with the butt of the whip. A few miles west of Utica, still nearly a hundred miles from Palmyra, the Smiths ran out of money. Seeing no hope for more from Lucy, Howard threw their goods into the street and was about to set off with the Smiths' wagon and team. Lucy confronted him in the barroom before a company of travelers and demanded the reason for his outrageous action. When he attempted to drive off, Lucy grabbed the reins and shouted to the bystanders that she was being robbed and left destitute with eight children. "As for you sir," she announced to Howard, "I have no use for you and you can ride or walk the rest of the way as you please but I shall take charge of my own affairs."[72]

Howard left them, but Joseph Jr.'s hardships were not at an end. He was assigned to the Gates sleigh, and one of the sons in the Gates family knocked him down as he attempted to find a place. Joseph said he was "left to wallow in my blood until a stranger came along, picked me up, and carried me to the Town of Palmyra."[73]

Lucy arrived at Palmyra, after a journey of three to four weeks, with a few possessions and nine cents. Her last payment to the innkeepers was made with Sophronia's eardrops. At last the strain of caring for the family passed partly back to Joseph Sr.

> The joy I felt in throwing myself and My children upon the care and affection of a tender Husband and Father doubly paid me for all I had suffered The children surrounded their Father clinging to his neck, covering his face with tears and kisses that were heartily reciprocated by him.

Refreshed by that reunion, energy returned and all eyes looked forward. "We all now sat down, and counselled together relative to the course which was best for us to adopt in our destitute circumstances."[74]

TWO

THE FIRST VISIONS

1816–27

*While I was thus in the act of calling upon God, I discovered a light appearing
in the room which continued to increase untill the room was lighter than at
noonday when immediately a personage appeared at my bedside standing in the
air for his feet did not touch the floor.*

JOSEPH SMITH, Manuscript History, 1838

JOSEPH AND LUCY SMITH WERE second-generation members of families
that left the coastal villages of Massachusetts and Connecticut at the end of
the eighteenth century for towns at the edge of settlement. Both Solomon
Mack and Asael Smith moved from old towns—Lyme and Topsfield—to
new towns in Vermont and New Hampshire. Still not rooted, the Smiths
and Macks kept moving from town to town and farm to farm. Asael formed
the most lasting connection in Tunbridge but migrated again in old age to
St. Lawrence County, New York. Following their parents' pattern, Joseph
and Lucy circulated among villages in the upper Connecticut Valley before
migrating to Palmyra and Manchester, New York, where they lived for
fifteen years before moving to Ohio.

The Smiths arrived in western New York in the winter of 1816–17. The
area had opened for settlement just twenty-five years earlier when the first
permanent white settlers moved north of Lake Canandaigua to the area of
Palmyra.[1] The major western New York settlements formed at the northern tips of the Finger Lakes, where goods carted from the east could be
boated southward to the lakeside villages. Geneva, in Seneca township at
the head of Seneca Lake, and Canandaigua, twelve miles directly south of
Palmyra on Canandaigua Lake, came into existence at about the same time
as Palmyra. By 1824 Canandaigua was characterized as a "populous and
opulent" town, and the author of that year's gazetteer feared that "extravagance and fashion" would corrupt its farmers. The main street south from
Palmyra was called Canandaigua Road. By 1824 a stage ran daily between
the two towns.[2]

Between Palmyra and Canandaigua lay Farmington, a large rectangular township with various village centers. One of the most prosperous, Manchester village, was to become the nucleus of a new township in 1822, and there the Smiths purchased land. As suggested by the name, the founders hoped for a manufacturing center, until the Erie Canal dashed their hopes.[3] The canal was a boon to farmers who shipped their harvests to New York City, but death to small manufacturers who had to compete with goods from Albany and New York.

The canal affected Palmyra differently. The canal route paralleled Red Creek, on which Palmyra had been settled, and passed just a few hundred yards north of the village center at the corner of Main and Canandaigua. Construction began in 1817, and the Palmyra section was completed in 1822. When finished in 1825, the canal spanned the entire 363 miles from Albany to Buffalo on Lake Erie. Palmyra's fortuitous location positioned it to become a trading center for the immediate region.[4]

The canal not only stimulated internal growth but reoriented the village geographically. Before 1820, Palmyra looked southward to Canandaigua and Geneva. The canal turned towns on the north ends of the lakes eastward toward Albany and New York City and westward toward Rochester. Less than twenty-five miles away along the canal, Rochester's commercial and cultural influence soon enfolded Palmyra. The southern towns did not lose their influence while the Smiths lived in Palmyra; stages carried traffic daily to Canandaigua and twice weekly to Geneva. Palmyra operated on two axes, east-west to Rochester and Albany and north-south toward Canandaigua and Geneva.[5]

As it turned out, Smith family affairs moved mainly along the southerly route. Joseph Jr. went southward along the area's earliest roads to the Susquehanna for work, for a wife, and eventually for religious converts. Joseph's first backer, Martin Harris, applied for a loan in Geneva to finance the Book of Mormon. The Rochester route figured much less prominently until events compelled the Mormons to pack their belongings on a canal boat and move west via the canal and Lake Erie to Kirtland, Ohio.[6]

SETTLEMENT

For a year and a half after their arrival, the Smiths lived in Palmyra without a farm. Since selling their property in 1803, they had rented land and supplemented farming by hiring out their labor and engaging in small enterprises. In Palmyra they lived by their labor alone. Lucy painted oilcloth table coverings, and the family sold refreshments from a small shop. On public occasions, they peddled the goods from a cart. Joseph Sr. and the older sons hired out for haying and harvesting in the peak seasons when every farmer needed extra hands, and took on odd jobs like gardening and

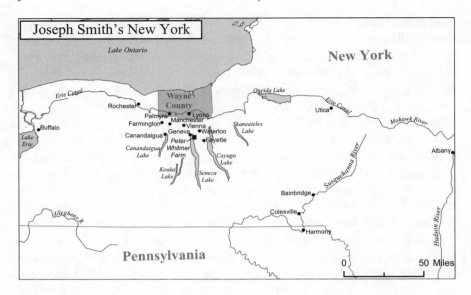

digging wells. High wheat prices from 1812 to 1819 enabled farmers to pay
for extra labor. The contributions of Alvin and Hyrum made a big addition
to the family income. When the census taker came to the Smiths in 1820,
Joseph Jr. was not listed, probably because he was living elsewhere earning
during the growing season.[7]

The combination of Palmyra's flourishing economy, the wages of Alvin
and Hyrum, and the family's industry allowed the Smiths to contract for a
farm for the first time in fifteen years. The growing population had not yet
occupied all of Palmyra's and Farmington's virgin land, and the Smiths
located a wooded tract less than two miles south of Palmyra village on
Stafford Road. The property, part of a purchase made in 1788 by Massachusetts speculators, had passed through the hands of various owners until
Nicholas Evertson of New York City purchased a large tract before his
death in 1807. In July 1820, Joseph Smith Sr. contracted with Zechariah
Seymour, land agent of the Evertson heirs, to pay $600 to $700 for 100
acres.[8]

The Smiths moved onto their land in stages. Before obtaining title to the
land, the Smiths raised a log house adjacent to their prospective purchase
on the land of a local merchant, Samuel Jennings, possibly to begin clearing
land they intended to buy.[9] Purchase was delayed until the Evertson estate
appointed an agent in June 1820, but the Smiths were living on the Jennings property by 1819 and perhaps a year earlier.[10] An early visitor described the house as having two rooms on the ground floor—one doubtless
a kitchen–dining room—and a low garret divided in two. When they built
the house in 1818 or 1819, the Smiths had to find sleeping spaces for ten

people: six boys ages nineteen to two; two girls, fifteen and six; and the parents.[11] They soon added a bedroom wing of sawed slabs to the dwelling. Crowded though it was, the "snug log house, neatly furnished," with "the means of living comfortably," satisfied Lucy for the time being.[12]

The acquisition of land changed the tempo of family life. Instead of odd jobs and shopkeeping, interspersed with stretches of arduous work in harvest and hay seasons, father and sons now cleared the land and cultivated a crop. A man working alone might clear ten acres the first year, though at the risk of neglecting fences, a garden, and the construction of a barn and outbuildings. Lucy remembered that "something like thirty acres of land were got ready for cultivation the first year," a herculean achievement even with the aid of Alvin, Hyrum, and Joseph Jr. William Smith said the clearing was "mostly done in the form of fire."[13]

The farm began to produce a little income at once. The asheries in Palmyra purchased the remains of brush and log fires for working into potash. The Smiths sold cordwood in the village and made maple sugar. William said his father engaged in coopering. Most farmers planted corn for family and animals on the first cleared land. Wheat followed in the second year, with the possibility of a small surplus beyond the family needs.[14] The Smiths harvested their first wheat crop in 1821, but the panic of 1819 and the subsequent depression had lowered the price of wheat by more than a third in two years.[15]

The Smiths needed a cash crop to meet the worrisome payment for their land. Failure to make the payment gave the land agent the right to reclaim the farm, improvements and all, with no compensation for the family's labor. Lucy reported that after the first year the Smiths made "nearly all" of the first payment without being ejected. But repeated shortfalls stretched an agent's patience and endangered all the family had worked for. The Smiths manufactured small items for sale—black ash baskets and birch brooms—and kept up their refreshment business with cakes, sugar, and molasses. Joseph Jr. said that all of the children who "were able to render any assistance . . . were obliged to labor hard" to support the family. He took an occasional odd job at a village store when he was there on an errand, and probably worked for established farmers nearby. Lucy credited Alvin, the eldest, with helping with the payments. "Alvin went from home to get work," and in later years, the other boys dispersed across the countryside in search of employment.[16]

Lucy took pride in the Smiths' accomplishments since they arrived in Palmyra "destitute of friends, house, or employment." She spoke happily of their "snug comfortable though humble habitation built and neatly furnished by our own industry." She claimed the townspeople accepted the family. "Never have I seen more kindness or attention shown to any person

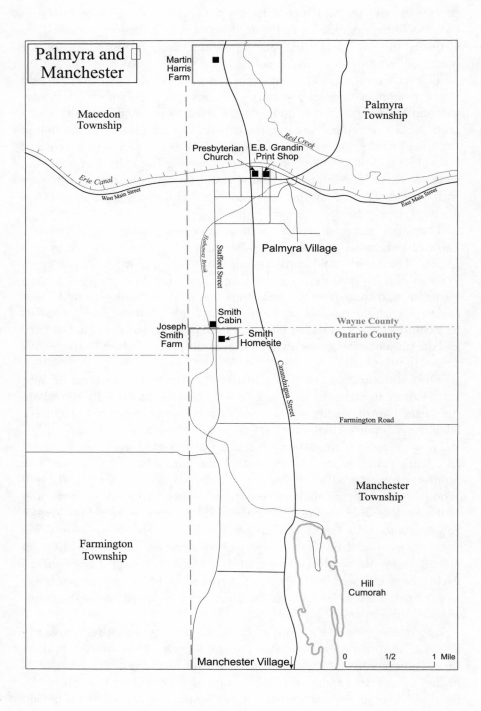

Palmyra and Manchester

Martin Harris Farm

Macedon Township

Palmyra Township

Red Creek

Presbyterian Church

E.B. Grandin Print Shop

Erie Canal

West Main Street

East Main Street

Hathaway Brook

Stafford Street

Palmyra Village

Smith Cabin

Joseph Smith Farm

Smith Homesite

Wayne County

Ontario County

Canandaigua Street

Farmington Road

Manchester Township

Farmington Township

Hill Cumorah

0   1/2   1 Mile

Manchester Village

or family than we received from those around us." But the first draft of
her *Biographical Sketches* told about a humiliation she left out of the final
version.

> A friend of mine having invited several of her associates to take tea with her
> one afternoon sent an urgeant request for me also to call on her with the rest
> the lady's invited were some wealthy merchants wives and the minister's lady
> we spent the time quite pleasantly each seeming to enjoy those reciprocal
> feelings which renders the society of our friends delightful to us—when tea
> was served up we were passing some good-natured remarks upon each other
> when one lady observed Well I declare Mrs [Smith] ought not to live in that
> log house of her's any longer she deserves a better fate and I say she must have
> a new house. so she should says another for she is so kind to every one She
> ought to have the best of every thing.

Perhaps oversensitive, Lucy took the ladies' solicitude badly. She was
insulted by the suggestion that the Smiths' cabin was a cause for shame. "I
have tis true suffered many disagreable disapointments in life with regard to
property," she admitted, "but I now find myself very comfortably situated
to what any of you are." Her riches were her family's virtues. "We owe no
man we never distressed any man which circumstance almost invariably
attends the Mercantile life." The minister's family had problems with sons
"in habitual attendance on the Grog Shop & gambling house." Lucy pretended to be indifferent to the comments about her house, but they stung.
The next entry in her account described plans to build a new frame house.[17]

REVELATIONS

During the fourteen years following the Smiths' move to Palmyra in 1816,
Joseph Jr. had the experiences that led him to believe he was a prophet. In
1818, when he was twelve, he began to be troubled about his sins, though
apparently no one in the family knew about it. Around 1820, the visions
began, first of the Father and the Son and then, three years later, of the
angel who gave instructions about the gold plates. In 1830, at twenty-four,
he published the *Book of Mormon*, organized a church, and was identified as
"a seer, a translator, an apostle of Jesus Christ."[18]

Lucy had no premonitions of such a future for her son. She remembered
him as a "remarkably quiet, well disposed child," "much less inclined to the
perusal of books than any of the rest of our children, but far more given to
meditation and deep study."[19] Judging from later accounts by the Smiths'
neighbors, Joseph's religious struggles were unknown in the village. The
publication of the *Book of Mormon* surprised everyone. The villagers had no

idea that the nondescript farm boy who occasionally appeared in town to buy a paper for his father had any ambition or religious character. He seemed slow and "destitute of genius" or lazy and superstitious.[20] The townspeople who later recorded their memories thought of the family as treasure-seekers, not eager Christians. Nothing the townspeople knew about Joseph or the Smiths prepared them for his claims to revelation.[21]

The best barometer of the household's religious climate are seven dreams Joseph Sr. had in the years before and after his son's first vision. Lucy wrote down five of them, calling them visions. Since no other member of the family gave an account of the dreams or even referred to them, and Lucy recorded them thirty years later, there is no way of testing the accuracy of her memory. One of Lucy's accounts echoes passages in the *Book of Mormon*, suggesting a tendency to make her husband the predecessor of her son. But if the details are questionable, the visions' recurring themes do reveal a religious mood.[22]

In many of the dreams, Joseph Sr. found himself alone, decrepit, or ill, or on a vaguely defined quest. In one, he traveled alone in "the desolate world," on a road "so broad and barren, that I wondered why I should travel in it." In another he was in a "gloomy desert" amidst "the most death-like silence." Usually the desolation was followed by redemption, a flower-filled garden or the fruit of an "exceedingly handsome" tree representing the love of God. In every dream, a yearning for relief or redemption or beauty moved the dreamer. The visions held the promise that beyond a gate, through a door, under a tree could be found healing and salvation. In some, Joseph Sr. reached his goal; in others it hovered just beyond reach, promised but not attained.[23]

The Palmyra churches which tried to offer villagers like Joseph Sr. hope of salvation and peace sometimes figured in the dreams. Four churches met within a few miles of the Smiths' house. Presbyterians had the largest congregation in Palmyra village and in 1820 the only meetinghouse in the center. The Methodists, the next largest group, constructed a building of their own in 1822, followed by the Society of Friends in 1823. Two miles west of the village, a large congregation of Baptists had met in a meetinghouse since 1808, and in the eastern part of the township stood a second Presbyterian church.[24]

The churches were augmented by the revivals that touched one town after another in the early decades of the nineteenth century.[25] A hundred people joined the Baptist church in Palmyra during a revival in 1808, making it necessary to construct a meetinghouse. The great revival of 1816 and 1817, which nearly doubled the number of Palmyra Presbyterians, was in progress when the Smiths arrived. Joseph Sr. felt the appeal of the Palmyra revivals, as he had in 1810–11 in Vermont. He dreamed of going to meeting with hundreds of others. "When I came in sight of the meeting-house, I saw multitudes of people coming from every direction, and pressing with great anxiety towards the door of this great building; but I thought I should get there in time, hence there was no need of being in a hurry." When he knocked, the porter told him he had come too late, and Joseph Sr. was told what he would have heard at a revival meeting: "it was necessary to plead the merits of Jesus, for he was the advocate with the Father, and a mediator between God and man." With that, the door opened and Joseph Sr. entered, just as he would had he made the same confession in a waking moment at a revival.[26]

Joseph Smith Jr. began to be concerned about religion "at about the age of twelve years," in late 1817 or early 1818, when the aftereffects of the revival of 1816 and 1817 were still being felt.[27] Between the ages of twelve and fifteen, he read the scriptures, "believing as I was taught, that they contained the word of God." He was confused by the failings of the Christians in the town. Like his mother earlier, he was aware of more hypocrisy and contradiction than harmony or devotion. "My intimate acquaintance with those of differant denominations led me to marvel excedingly for I discovered that they did not . . . adorn their profession by a holy walk and Godly conversation agreeable to what I found contained in that sacred depository this was a grief to my Soul." The revivals created a "stir and division amongst the people" where there was supposed to be love. "All their good feelings one for another (if they ever had any) were entirely lost in a strife of words and a contest about opinions."[28]

His confusion did not prevent him from trying to find a religious home. Two printer's apprentices at the *Palmyra Register* who knew Joseph Jr. remembered Methodist leanings. One said he caught "a spark of Methodism in the camp meeting, away down in the woods, on the Vienna road." The other remembered Joseph joining the probationary class of the Palmyra Methodist Church. Joseph himself said he was "somewhat partial to the Methodist sect," and had "some desire to be united with them." He wanted, he later said, "to get Religion too wanted to feel & shout like the Rest but could feel nothing."[29]

Sometime in the half dozen years after 1818, the religious rift in the family broke open again. Lucy joined the Western Presbyterian Church in Palmyra, probably the best established church in the village. Hyrum, Sophronia, and Samuel went to church with their mother, but Joseph Sr., Alvin, William, and Joseph Jr. stayed home.[30] Forced to choose between his father's and his mother's religion, Joseph stood by his father.

Joseph's acquaintances in the newspaper office may have complicated his predicament. Orsamus Turner, one of the apprentices, said Joseph came to the meetings of a "juvenile debating club," which gathered in the red schoolhouse on Durfee Street, to "solve some portenous questions of moral or political ethics." Very likely the young debaters raised the question of how to know of God's existence, a question posed by Deists. The Deists did not doubt the reality of God but wished to base their belief on reason. Oliver Cowdery later said that Joseph wondered for a time whether "a Supreme being did exist." In recounting his thoughts in the time of confusion, Joseph partly rested his faith on the beauty of the created universe:

> the sun the glorious luminary of the earth and also the moon rolling in their magesty through the heavens and also the stars shining in their courses and the earth also upon which I stood and the beast of the field and the fowls of heaven and the fish of the waters.

"All these," he said, using the usual rationalist language, bespoke "an omnipotant and omnipresant power a being who makith Laws and decreeeth and bindeth all things in their bounds."[31]

Caught in these crosscurrents, Joseph said his "mind at times was greatly excited, the cry and tumult were so great and incessant." He had two questions on his mind: which church was right, and how to be saved. The two questions were actually one. His anguish for himself mingled with his anguish for religion generally. The corruption and confusion in the churches seemed to stand in the way of his own salvation.

> From the age of twelve years to fifteen I pondered many things in my heart concerning the sittuation of the world of mankind the contentions and divi[s]ions the wicke[d]ness and abominations and the darkness which pervaded the minds of mankind my mind become excedingly distressed for I became convicted of my sins and by searching the scriptures I found that mankind did not come unto the Lord but that they had apostatised from the true and liveing faith and there was no society or denomination that built upon the gospel of Jesus Christ as recorded in the new testament and I felt to mourn for my own sins and for the sins of the world.[32]

In this state of mind, he came across the Bible verses that promise that "if any of you lack wisdom, let him ask of God, that giveth to all men liberally . . . and it shall be given him." The words spoke to him: "Never did any passage of scripture come with more power to the heart of man than this did at this time to mine. It seemed to enter with great force into every feeling of my heart. I reflected on it again and again, knowing that if any person needed wisdom from God, I did." In his desperation, he saw no other way. The contradictory views of the clergy had destroyed his confidence "in settling the question by an appeal to the Bible." "At length I came to the conclusion that I must either remain in darkness and confusion or else I must do as James directs, that is, ask of God."[33]

Probably in early 1820, Joseph determined to pray—the first time, he said later, he had prayed aloud.[34] With no hope of privacy in the little cabin filled with children and household activity, he went to a place in the woods where he had left his ax in a stump in a clearing. In the minds of Mormons today, the events of that morning marked the beginning of the restoration of the Gospel and the commencement of a new dispensation. The vision is called the First Vision because it began a series of revelations. But at the time, Joseph did not know this was the First Vision. Like anyone, he understood the experience in terms of the familiar.[35]

By 1832, when he first recorded the vision, Joseph knew that his experience was one step in "the rise of the church of Christ in the eve of time," along with Moroni's visits, the restoration of the Aaronic Priesthood, and the reception of the "high Priesthood." But twelve years after the event, the First Vision's personal significance for him still overshadowed its place in the divine plan for restoring a church. He explained the vision as he must have first understood it, as a personal conversion. In 1832, he remembered that "a pillar of light above the brightness of the sun at noon day come down from above and rested upon me and I was filled with the spirit of god and the Lord opened the heavens upon me and I saw the Lord and he spake unto me saying Joseph my Son thy sins are forgiven thee. go thy way walk in my statutes and keep my commandments." It was the message of forgiveness and redemption he had wanted to hear. A glancing reference to the vision in an 1830 revelation called it the time when Joseph "received a remission of his sins." Like countless other revival subjects who felt forgiven, Joseph said his "soul was filled with love and for many days I could rejoice with great Joy and the Lord was with me."[36]

He had also mourned the sins of the world and pondered the confusion in the churches. In the vision he was told that "the world lieth in sin at this time and none doeth good no not one they have turned asside from the Gospel and keep not my commandments they draw near to me with their lips while their hearts are far from me and mine anger is kindling against the inhabitants of the earth." The vision included a brief apocalyptic note: "behold and lo I come quickly as it [is] written of me in the cloud clothed in the glory of my Father."[37]

At first, Joseph was reluctant to talk about his vision. Most early converts probably never heard about the 1820 vision. "The angel of the Lord says that we must be careful not to proclaim these things or to mention them abroad," he told his parents after one early vision. A subsequent vision of the angel who led him to the gold plates was not mentioned in the first edition of the Book of Mormon. Accounts of John the Baptist and Peter,

James, and John, other early visions, did not appear in the early editions of the revelations. When he described the First Vision in 1832, he abbreviated the experience.[38]

As Joseph became more confident, more details came out. In later accounts, he explained that a dark power had prevented him from praying. As he tried to speak, he recalled in 1835, "my tongu[e] seemed to be swolen in my mouth, so that I could not utter." Just then he heard a noise behind him like someone walking toward him. "I strove again to pray, but could not, the noise of walking seemed to draw nearer, I sprung up on my feet, and looked around, but saw no person." It seemed then "as if I were doomed to sudden destruction . . . not to an imaginary ruin but to the power of some actual being from the unseen world." Deliverance came when the pillar of light or pillar of fire descended from heaven and fell on him. In his first narrative, Joseph said only that he saw the Lord in the light and heard His words of forgiveness. In 1835, he said that first one personage appeared and then another. In 1838, he reported that the first pointed to the other and said, "This is my beloved Son, Hear him."[39]

In the 1835 account and again in 1838, the balance of the two parts of the story—personal forgiveness as contrasted to the apostasy of the churches—shifted. Joseph's own salvation gave way to the opening of a new era of history.[40] The promise of forgiveness through faith in Christ was dropped from the narrative, and the apostasy of Christian churches stood as the central message of the vision. The 1832 report emphasized general moral degeneration: "the world lieth in sin at this time and none doeth good." In 1838, by contrast, Joseph reported that he was told to join none of the sects. "All their Creeds were an abomination in his sight. . . . 'They teach for doctrines the commandments of men.' " The decay was doctrinal and institutional, as well as moral.[41] The later accounts of the vision supplied the church with a founding story.

When Joseph came to, he found himself lying on his back. Returning to the house, he spoke to his mother but said almost nothing about the vision. When she asked about his apparent weakness, Joseph said, "Never mind all is well.—I am well enough off." All he would report was that he had learned for himself that Presbyterianism was not true. His refusal to say more may have been the natural reticence of a teenage boy keeping his own counsel, or he may have held back for fear of ridicule. Two or three years later when the angel appeared to him, he again said nothing until explicitly commanded to speak to his father. As late as 1831, he was slow to say much about Moroni. He was not interested in notoriety.[42]

Joseph did tell a Methodist preacher about the First Vision. Newly reborn people customarily talked over their experiences with a clergyman to test the validity of the conversion. The preacher's contempt shocked Joseph. Standing on the margins of the evangelical churches, Joseph may not have recognized the ill repute of visionaries. The preacher reacted quickly and negatively, not because of the strangeness of Joseph's story but because of its familiarity. Subjects of revivals all too often claimed to have seen visions. In 1826 a preacher at the Palmyra Academy said he saw Christ descend "in a glare of brightness, exceeding ten fold the brilliancy of the meridian Sun." The *Wayne Sentinel* in 1823 reported Asa Wild's vision of Christ in Amsterdam, New York, telling him that all denominations were corrupt. At various other times and places, beginning early in the Protestant era, religious eccentrics had claimed visits from divinity. Norris Stearns published an account in 1815 of two beings who appeared to him: "One was God, my Maker, almost in bodily shape like a man. His face was, as it were a flame of Fire, and his body, as it had been a Pillar and a Cloud. . . . Below him stood Jesus Christ my Redeemer, in perfect shape like a man."[43]

The clergy of the mainline churches automatically suspected any visionary report, whatever its content. "No person is warranted from the word of God," a writer in the *Connecticut Evangelical Magazine* said in 1805, "to publish to the world the discoveries of heaven or hell which he supposes he has had in a dream, or trance, or vision. Were any thing of this kind to be made known to men, we may be assured it would have been done by the apostles, when they were penning the gospel history." The only acceptable message from heaven was assurance of forgiveness and a promise of grace. Joseph's report of God's rejection of all creeds and churches would have sounded all too familiar to the Methodist evangelical, who repeated the conventional point that "all such things had ceased with the apostles and that there never would be any more of them."[44]

The dismissal widened the gulf between Joseph and the evangelical ministry. He felt that the clergy had picked him out for persecution. The reviling angered him all the more because he spoke from direct experience. "I had actualy seen a light and in the midst of that light I saw two personages, and they did in reality speak unto me, or one of them did, And though I was hated and persecuted for saying that I had seen a vision, yet it was true." His vision, instead of bringing him into the mainstream, as conversions ordinarily did, set him on a course of his own.[45]

MORONI

The 1820 vision did not interrupt the Smith family's round of work. "I continued to pursue my common avocations in life," Joseph later wrote. William Smith remembered sixty acres being cleared and fenced, and an orchard planted. Regular schooling was impossible while loss of the farm was a possibility. "As it required the exertions of all that were able to render any assistance for the support of the Family," Joseph recalled in 1832, "we were deprived of the bennifit of an education. Suffice it to say I was mearly instructed in reading writing and the ground rules of Arithmatic which constuted my whole literary acquirements." Joseph may have attended school briefly in Palmyra, and a neighbor remembered the Smiths holding school in their house and studying the Bible.[46]

Financial pressures increased in 1822 after Joseph's elder brother, Alvin, began to build a frame house for the family. They managed this extravagant undertaking by making a fatal mistake. Lucy reported that as the time for the next land payment approached, Alvin left home "in order to raise the money, and after much hardship and fatigue, returned with the required amount." But the payment was apparently not applied to the mortgage. The Evertson agent had died in 1822, and no one had been appointed to collect. Rather than putting the money aside for the inevitable time when payment would be required, the Smiths chose to build a new house. Lucy felt the social pressure to move up from their log house, and the birth of a new baby, Lucy, in 1821 added to the crowded conditions. In a few years they would reap the consequences of their decision.

Alvin, his mother's favorite son, took responsibility for the "management and control" of construction, which began in November after the fall harvest. Lucy credited him with wanting to provide for her comfort in her old age. Joseph Jr. said of him that "from the time of his birth, he never knew mirth. He was candid and sober and never would play; and minded his father, and mother, in toiling all day. He was one of the soberest of men."[47]

Alvin may have taken the lead because his discouraged father could not. Alvin had cosigned the articles for the land purchase in 1821, suggesting he was serving as auxilary family head.[48] Joseph Sr., worn down by setbacks, may have partially abdicated family leadership. "I have not always set that example before my family that I ought," he confessed in 1834. Speaking of himself in the third person, he gratefully told Hyrum that "though he has been out of the way through wine, thou has never forsaken him nor laughed him to scorn." Joseph Sr.'s drinking was not excessive for that time and place; only two of the hostile affidavits collected in 1833 mentioned it.[49] But he feared his sons' scornful laughter. Joseph Sr. had lost his Vermont farm, and a few years later at age fifty-four would lose the land they were buying in Manchester. There would be no inheritances for his sons. By the standard measures of success in a rural society, he had failed. Even his dreamy yearning for religion had led to nothing; he felt that he had let his children down. "I have not been diligent in teaching them the commandments of the Lord," he admitted, "but have rather manifested a light and trifling mind." All the boys loved and honored their father, Joseph Jr. particularly, but their affection may have included sympathy for a life blighted by shame.[50]

In the years after his First Vision, Joseph Jr. said little about his spiritual development. He had no sense of mission, no emerging prophetic identity unless a mysterious reference to "many other things did he say unto me which I cannot write at this time" is interpreted to mean religious instructions. What Joseph said explicitly was that the vision led to trouble, though his youthful sensitivity probably exaggerated the reaction. The talk with the minister, he remembered, brought on ridicule by "all classes of men, both religious and irreligious because I continued to affirm that I had seen a vision." Local people seemed to have discussed his case, even though he had said nothing to his parents. Eighteen years later when he wrote his history, the memories of the injustices still rankled.[51] For whatever reason, his father's family suffered "many persicutions and afflicitions," he recalled, deepening a previous sense of alienation. William Smith remembered people throwing dirt, stones, and sticks against the Smith house. Later, after Alvin died, it was rumored someone had disturbed his body, and Joseph Sr. published a notice in the paper that the body had been exhumed and found to be untouched. Once someone fired a shot at young Joseph for no apparent reason.[52]

Joseph's conscience bothered him too. In the brief summary of his experiences written for the Church's creed in 1830, he said of this time "he was entangled again in the vanities of the world." His sins were not "great or malignant," he later said, but "I was guilty of Levity and sometimes associated with Jovial company &c. not consistent with that character which ought to be maintained by one who was called of God as I had been." From time to time he drank too much. As one Palmyran later said: "every body drank them times."[53] Joseph regretted his "gratification of many appetites offensive in the sight of God," without specifying which ones. These transgressions, he wrote in 1832, "brought a wound upon my soul." There is no reason to think he spent all his time in lonely brooding; he "fell into many foolish errors" because he was "mingling with society." But privately he was concerned about his "state and standing" before God.[54]

A turning point came in the fall of 1823. The Smiths had spent the evening of September 21, as Lucy recalled, "conversing upon the subject of the diversity of churches . . . and the many thousand opinions in existence as to the truths contained in scripture."[55] That night after the others in the crowded little house had gone to sleep, Joseph remained awake to pray "to Almighty God for forgiveness of all my sins and follies."[56] While praying he noticed the room growing lighter until it was brighter than broad daylight. Suddenly, as he later reported, a person appeared in the light standing above the floor.

He had on a loose robe of most exquisite whiteness. It was a whiteness beyond anything earthly I had ever seen, nor do I believe that any earthly thing could be made to appear so exceedin[g]ly white and brilliant, His hands were naked and his arms also a little above the wrist. So also were his feet naked as were his legs a little above the ankles. His head and neck were also bare. I could discover that he had no other clothing on but this robe, as it was open so that I could see into his bosom. Not only was his robe exceedingly white but his whole person was glorious beyond description, and his countenance truly like lightning.

This time all the accounts agree on the burden of the message. If Joseph initially understood the First Vision as his conversion, similar to thousands of other evangelical conversions, this vision wrenched Joseph out of any ordinary track.

The being, who identified himself as Moroni, assured Joseph that his sins were forgiven, but then said God was giving Joseph a work unlike any envisioned in his time. He was told about a book "written upon gold plates, giving an account of the former inhabitants of this continent and the source from whence they sprang. He also said that the fulness of the everlasting Gospel was contained in it as delivered by the Saviour to the ancient inhabitants." Besides that, "there were two stones in silver bows and these stones fastened to a breast plate constituted what is called the Urim & Thummim deposited with the plates, and the possession and use of these stones was what constituted seers in ancient or former times and that God had prepared them for the purpose of translating the book."[57] All this was buried in a nearby hill that Joseph saw in his vision.

The rest of the vision was more familiar and comprehensible. Moroni quoted Old and New Testament prophecies relating to the final days of the earth: the third and fourth chapters of Malachi, Acts 3:22–23, Joel 2:28–32, and Isaiah 11. These were the texts the clergy used to teach about the millennium. Joseph knew them well enough to note small departures from the words in the Bible. Hearing the familiar texts from the angel confirmed the common belief that the last days were near and Joseph was to prepare.[58]

Moroni warned him not to show the plates and the Urim and Thummim to anyone, and then the light began to gather around him until the room was dark except near his person. "Instantly I saw as it were a conduit open right up into heaven, and he ascended till he entirely disappeared." Joseph lay back in astonishment, trying to understand what had happened, when the room brightened again, and the angel reappeared. Moroni repeated every word he had said before and then added comments about "great judgements which were coming upon the earth with great desolations by famine, sword, and pestilence." Moroni again ascended but soon after appeared a third time to repeat everything again. This time he added the warning that "Satan would try to tempt me (in consequence of the indigent circumstances of my father's family) to get the plates for the purpose of get-ting rich." Joseph was to have no other object "but to glorify God."

Not long after the third appearance, day broke and the family began to stir. Joseph said nothing and went to the fields. Reaping wheat alongside Alvin, Joseph stopped and seemed to be in a deep study. As Lucy Smith later told the story, Alvin chided him, saying, "We must not slacken our hands or we will not be able to complete our task." Joseph went back to work but stopped again. Noticing his son's drained face, Joseph Sr. sent the boy back to the house. Climbing over a fence, Joseph Jr. fainted. The first thing he recognized was a voice calling his name. Looking up, he saw the angel standing above him in a bright light. Moroni repeated the entire mes-sage of the previous night and commanded Joseph to tell his father.[59] Dis-belief from his father could have tipped Joseph's confidence against his own experiences. But probably because he was a visionary himself, Joseph Sr. accepted the story. Do exactly as the angel said, he counseled his son.[60]

The hill where the plates were supposed to be buried stood about three miles south and east of the Smith farm and just a few hundred feet to the east of the main road between Palmyra and Canandaigua. Later it was called "Cumorah," from a name in the *Book of Mormon*. As he told the story, Joseph had seen the hill in vision the night before in enough detail to know exactly where the plates were. The steep northern side was an open pasture; to the south trees grew. The stone covering the plates lay among the scat-tered trees on the western slope, near the top. Joseph dug away the earth and pried up the stone with a lever. Under the top stone was a box made of five stones set in cement with their flat sides turned in. Inside lay the plates, the Urim and Thummim, and the breastplate.[61]

Thoughts of the money value of the plates troubled Joseph. The angel had cautioned him about the temptation to get rich. He was told he must have "no other object in view in getting the plates but to glorify God, and must not be influenced by any other motive than that of building his king-dom." Despite the warning, the sight of the gold was too much, and Joseph gave way to the very temptation he had been cautioned about. Oliver Cow-dery and Lucy Smith said that Joseph felt a severe physical shock when he touched the plates, and that the angel appeared and severely rebuked him. Joseph reported three failed attempts at lifting out the plates, causing him to cry "unto the Lord in the agony of my soul why can I not obtain them." The angel told him that he was "tempted of the advisary [adversary] and saught the Plates to obtain riches and kept not the commandment that I should have an eye single to the glory of God therefore I was chastened and saught diligently to obtain the plates and obtained them not untill I was twenty-one years of age."[62]

The evening after the visit to the hill, Joseph told the rest of the family about the angel and the plates. William said they were "melted to tears, and believed all he said." He had made his first converts. Typically, Lucy understood the finding of the plates as a family event. She remembered them "all seated in a circle, father, mother, sons and daughters." It struck her that her "family presented the most peculiar aspect of any family that ever lived upon the Earth," all "giving the most profound attention to a boy, eighteen years of age; who had never read the Bible through in his life." "The sweetest union and happiness pervaded our house, and tranquility reigned in our midst." Joseph Jr. warned of troubles ahead for the Smiths. "The world was so wicked that when they came to a knowledge of these things they would try to take our lives." For that reason they had to keep what he told them to themselves, but they still rejoiced to know that God was about to give them "a more perfect knowledge of the plan of salvation and the redemption of the human family." At last, as Lucy said, the Smiths had "something upon which we could stay our minds."[63]

MONEY

The tranquility of those first evenings after Moroni's visit soon ended. The misfortunes that followed the Smiths in Vermont and that had receded after the move to New York descended upon them again. Less than two months after Joseph went to the hill, Alvin fell sick with bilious colic. The doctor prescribed a large dose of calomel, a compound of mercury and chlorine thought to promote the discharge of bile. Lucy thought the calomel lodged in Alvin's stomach, and, according to her, the combined exertions of four physicians could not remove it.[64]

Feeling death was near, Alvin called the family to the bedside. He urged Joseph Jr. "to be a good boy, and do everything that lies in your power to obtain the Record." On November 19, 1823, Alvin died. His death brought an end to the family gatherings. Alvin had taken a greater interest in the gold plates than any of the other family members, Lucy said, and consequently they "could not bear to hear anything said upon the subject." With Alvin gone, Joseph assumed larger responsibilities in the family on the basis of his visions. Where his father had failed in achieving religious unity, he succeeded. He later said, "I brought salvation to my fathers house, as an instrument in the hand of God, when they were in a miserable situation."[65]

The year after Alvin's death, a revival struck Palmyra and nearby towns. Even Joseph Sr. attended two or three meetings before refusing to go again, but Joseph Jr. held back. He told his mother he could learn more in the woods from the Bible than from any meeting. He saw too much greed among purported Christians to be comfortable in church. You are "mistaken in them," he told his mother, "and do not know the wickedness of their hearts."[66]

For the moment, religious questions gave way to temporal concerns. Alvin's death sharply reduced the family's earning power. Work on the new frame house was completed in late 1824 and had to be paid for on top of the burdensome annual contract payment. While the Evertsons' land agent was not on the scene, the Smiths had diverted money for the land purchase into construction of the house.[67] Now they had at least two land payments to make and no Alvin to help out. To raise money, Joseph Jr. and Hyrum scouted the countryside for work. In October 1825, Joseph and his father took jobs in Pennsylvania digging for Josiah Stowell Sr., who believed that a Spanish silver mine was buried near Harmony, Pennsylvania, just south of the New York–Pennsylvania state line. About the same time, the family determined to borrow on next year's wheat crop. Sometime after November 17, when Joseph came back from the digging expedition, Stowell, who lived three miles south of the village of South Bainbridge, New York, and Joseph Knight Sr. of Colesville visited Palmyra looking for wheat or flour, as they may have been doing for a number of years. Stowell and Knight agreed to lend the Smiths money with next year's wheat crop as collateral.[68]

They needed every penny they could scrape together. Russell Stoddard, the carpenter who had completed the house, had sued the Smiths for payment in February 1825, a matter not settled until April 1826. Meanwhile the new agent for the Evertsons, John Greenwood, was foreclosing on occupants who were too far behind in their payments. The Smiths probably had made no payments save the first in 1821. As Lucy tells the story, Stoddard had designs on the property, offering them $1,500 for it at one point.[69] He persuaded the land agent that Joseph Sr. and Joseph Jr. were running away and Hyrum was cutting the sugar orchards and tearing down the fences. Lucy says the agent gave them a deadline of December 25, 1825, to make their payment, leaving them too little time to raise the money. As a second-best alternative, the Smiths persuaded a third party, Lemuel Durfee, a local Quaker landholder, to purchase the farm and permit them to rent and benefit from their improvements.[70]

The loss of the farm in 1825 hurt Lucy more than the sale of their Tunbridge property in 1803. Then "we were young," she said, "and by making some exertions we might improve our circumstances." In 1825, Lucy was fifty and Joseph Sr. fifty-four, both weary from lives of toil. They no longer had the help of Alvin, and Hyrum and Joseph were nearing marriage age. The moment when the unified effort of father and sons could raise the money to buy a farm had passed. They were doomed to revert to tenancy, and when old age overtook them, instead of the dignity of a house and land of their own, they would live as guests in the house of one of the children. Durfee permitted Joseph Sr. and Lucy to work the farm until 1829, when with five of the younger children they moved back into their log house, now occupied by Hyrum with the wife he had married in 1826.[71]

The loss of the farm did not end Joseph Jr.'s work excursions. The family had to pay rent in place of the contract payment, and Joseph, at twenty, was looking ahead to marriage and a house and farm of his own. He had to make provisions for himself as well as for his parents. Samuel and William, ages eighteen and fifteen, could handle the work on the Smith farm while Joseph took employment elsewhere.[72] He was drawn back to the area about 140 miles southeast of Palmyra where he had been working before the loss of the farm. Josiah Stowell Sr. employed him to do farm chores and perhaps work in his mills. Stowell, who was fifty-six in 1826, owned hundreds of acres of woodlots and ran a number of sawmills in the southern part of the state. Joseph's experience in clearing the Smith farm made him a useful hand in the Stowell enterprises. When he was not employed by Stowell in 1826, Joseph worked for Joseph Knight Sr. who ran carding machinery and a gristmill in addition to his farms. Stowell's property lay on the Susquehanna River in Bainbridge (now Afton), Chenango County, and Joseph Knight lived in Colesville, Broome County, on the south (or east) side of the river, just a few miles north of the Pennsylvania line.[73]

TREASURE

Joseph Knight Jr. said his father thought Joseph Smith Jr. was "the best hand he ever hired," but that was not the reason Stowell brought young Joseph all the way from Palmyra to work in 1825. Stowell believed that he had located the site of an ancient Spanish mine where coins had been minted and buried. Through the summer of 1825 he put his hired hands to work on the site, which lay some twenty-six miles downriver from his farm in Harmony township, Pennsylvania. When his men failed to locate the cache, Stowell enlisted the Smiths' help, and Joseph Smith Sr. and Joseph Jr. agreed to join the diggers in Harmony. A set of "Articles of Agreement," dated November 1, 1825, indicated that Joseph and his father were to receive two-elevenths of the ore in the mine or "the coined money and bars or ingots of Gold or Silver" reputed to lie hidden underground. The articles created a company to share the profits and bear the labor and expenses of mining. Lucy said that after less than a month Joseph Jr. prevailed upon Stowell to stop digging, and in mid-November the group dispersed. Joseph and his father returned to Manchester during the crisis over the farm.[74]

Stowell went to the trouble of bringing Joseph Jr. from Manchester, Lucy Smith explained, "on account of having heard that he possessed certain keys by which he could discern things invisible to the natural eye." Joseph had discovered two stones, one in 1822 while digging a well with Willard Chase a half mile from the Smith farm.[75] The source of the other stone is uncertain. These stones were the keys that enabled Joseph to see things, as Lucy said, "invisible to the natural eye."[76] Emma Smith described one of them as "a small stone, not exactly black, but was rather a dark color." In 1841 Joseph showed his other, whitish stone to the Council of the Twelve in Nauvoo and told them, Brigham Young reported, "that every man who lived on the earth was entitled to a seer stone and should have one, but they are kept from them in consequence of their wickedness." In 1888, when Wilford Woodruff consecrated a seerstone upon a temple altar in Manti, Utah, he wrote that it was the stone "that Joseph Smith found by revelation some thirty feet under the earth (ground), and carried by him through life."[77] For a time Joseph used a stone to help people find lost property and other hidden things, and his reputation reached Stowell. Later, after Joseph was arrested for his activities, Stowell testified in court that while still in Palmyra, the "prisoner looked through stone and described Josiah Stowell's house and out houses" correctly. Having failed on his own to find the Spanish bullion, he thought Joseph could help.[78]

All of this was later used against Joseph Smith. In 1833, an excommunicated Mormon named Doctor Philastus Hurlbut collected affidavits in Palmyra and Manchester from people who remembered the Smith family. One of the repeated charges in the affidavits was that Joseph Sr. and his sons hunted for treasure and looked in stones. The aim of the affidavits was to discredit the Smiths, but the reports revealed more than the witnesses intended. The firsthand accounts of treasure-seeking necessarily came from people who had gone on expeditions themselves and were participant observers. In exposing the Smiths, the neighbors inadvertently described a culture of magic in which they and many others in nineteenth-century New York were involved.[79]

Willard Chase, one of the Smiths' neighbors and a friend of Joseph's, found one of the stones. Chase let Joseph take the stone home, but as soon as it became known "what wonders he could discover by looking in it," Chase wanted it back. As late as 1830, Chase was still trying to get his hands on the stone. His younger brother Abel later told an interviewer that their sister Sally had a stone too. A nearby physician, John Stafford, reported that "the neighbors used to claim Sally Chase could look at a stone she had, and see money. Willard Chase used to dig when she found where the money was." After Joseph obtained the plates, Willard Chase led the group that searched the Smiths' house, guided by Sally Chase and a "green glass, through which she could see many very wonderful things."[80]

A clan of Staffords who lived about a mile and a half from the Smiths had their own money-digging operations. William Stafford told Hurlbut about twice hunting for treasure with Joseph Sr., but after a time the "people of this vicinity" lost faith in the Smiths, and presumably fell back on their own resources. Joshua Stafford, Dr. John Stafford's father, was said to have a stone "which looked like white marble and had a hole through the center." Cornelius Stafford said, "There was much digging for money on our farm and about the neighborhood. I saw Uncle John and Cousin Joshua Stafford dig a hole twenty feet long, eight broad and seven deep."[81]

Money-digging was epidemic in upstate New York. Stories of spirits guarding buried treasure were deeply enmeshed in the region's rural culture. In Vermont, too, buried treasures and lost mines were detected through dreams, divining rods, or stones. From 1800 to 1802, the Nathaniel Woods family in the Wells-Putney area of Vermont set out with one Winchell, who used a "St. John's" rod to find treasure guarded by a hostile spirit. The father of one of Joseph's later associates, Oliver Cowdery, lived in the Woods's neighborhood and may have picked up some of this lore.[82]

Buried treasure was tied into a great stock of magical practices extending back many centuries.[83] Eighteenth-century rationalism had failed to stamp out belief in preternatural powers aiding and opposing human enterprise. Enlightened newspaper editors and ministers scoffed at the superstitions of common people but were unable to erase them. Ordinary people apparently had no difficulty blending Christianity with magic. Willard Chase, the most vigorous of the Manchester treasure-seekers, was a Methodist class leader at the time he knew the Smiths, and in his obituary was described as a minister. At the time he employed Joseph to use his stone to find Spanish bullion, Josiah Stowell was an upright Presbyterian and an honored man in his community. The so-called credulity of the money-diggers can be read as evidence of their general faith in invisible forces. Christian belief in angels and devils blended with belief in guardian spirits and magical powers.[84]

The Smiths were as susceptible as their neighbors to treasure-seeking folklore. In addition to rod and stone divining, the Smiths probably believed in the rudimentary astrology found in the ubiquitous almanacs. Magical parchments handed down in the Hyrum Smith family may have originally belonged to Joseph Sr. The visit of the angel and the discovery of the gold plates would have confirmed the belief in supernatural powers. For people in a magical frame of mind, Moroni sounded like one of the spirits who stood guard over treasure in the tales of treasure-seeking.[85] The similarities may even have made the extraordinary story more credible in the Smith family. Lucy recognized the crossover in prefacing her narrative of the plates with a caution against thinking

> that we stopt our labor and went at trying to win the faculty of Abrac drawing Magic circles or sooth saying to the neglect of all kinds of buisness we never during our lives suffered one important interest to swallow up every other obligation but whilst we worked with our hands we endeavored to remember the service of & the welfare of our souls.

Lucy's point was that the Smiths were not lazy—they had not stopped their labor to practice magic—but she showed her knowledge of formulas and rituals and associated them with "the welfare of our souls." Magic and religion melded in Smith family culture.[86]

According to Oliver Cowdery's 1835 report, Joseph could not suppress his baser motives on the first walk to the Hill Cumorah. When he saw the "sacred treasure," he began to calculate how to "add to his store of wealth . . . without once thinking of the solemn instruction of the heavenly messenger, that all must be done with an express view of glorifying God." When he was stopped from lifting out the plates, Cowdery said, Joseph's mind flashed back to the tales of the treasure-hunters: "He had heard of the power of enchantment, and a thousand like stories, which held the hidden treasures of the earth, and suposed that physical exertion and personal strength was only necessary to enable him to yet obtain the object of his wish." Lucy told of Moroni describing "the operation of a good Spirit and an evil one" and urging Joseph to "keep your mind always staid upon God that no evil may come into your heart." The angel's instructions connected the greed of the money-digger with the powers of Satan. Joseph was to follow a different course. Cowdery reported Moroni as saying that "the commandment was strict, and . . . if ever these sacred things are obtained they must be by prayer and faithfulness in obeying the Lord."[87] It may have taken four years for Joseph to purge himself of his treasure-seeking greed.

Joseph Jr. never repudiated the stones or denied their power to find treasure. Remnants of the magical culture stayed with him to the end. But after 1823, he began to orient himself away from treasure and toward translation. Martin Harris, another early supporter, remembered Joseph saying that "the angel told him he must quit the company of the money-diggers. That there were wicked men among them. He must have no more to do with them. He must not lie, nor swear, nor steal." After 1823, he continued to be involved in treasure expeditions but not as the instigator or leader; perhaps he resisted by dragging his feet. William Stafford depicts Joseph Sr. hunting for gold and going back to the house to seek further instructions from Joseph Jr., as if the son was trying to stay out of the picture while the father pushed on.[88] In 1825, when the family needed money, Joseph Jr. agreed to help Stowell find the Spanish gold, but with misgivings. Lucy said of Stowell's operation that "Joseph endeavored to divert him from his vain pursuit." Alva Hale, a son in the household where the Smiths stayed in Harmony while digging for Stowell, said Joseph Jr. told him that the "gift in seeing with a stone" was "a gift from God" but that " 'peeping' was all d—d nonsense"; he had been deceived in his treasure-seeking, but he did not intend to deceive anyone else.[89] By this time, Joseph apparently felt that "seeing" with a stone was the work of a "seer," a religious term, while "peeping" or "glass-looking" was fraudulent.

Notes of a March 1826 court appearance in South Bainbridge shed light on the Smith family's attitudes toward treasure-seeking on the eve of receiving the plates.[90] Peter Bridgeman, nephew of Josiah Stowell, entered a complaint against Joseph Smith Jr. as a disorderly person in South Bainbridge, Chenango County, New York. New York law specified that anyone pretending to have skill in discovering lost goods should be judged a disorderly person. Joseph had continued working for Stowell after the abortive mining operation in November 1825, and during that time, besides working on the farm and going to school, Joseph may have helped look for lost mines again. Presumably, Bridgeman believed that Joseph was trying to cheat the old man by claiming magical powers. In the court record, Stowell said that he "had the most implicit faith in the Prisoners skill," implying that was the reason for hiring Joseph.[91]

Under examination, the twenty-year-old Joseph said that he had looked for "hidden treasures in the bowels of the earth" and had helped Stowell several times. For the past three years at Palmyra (going back to the time he found the seerstone in 1822), "he had frequently ascertained in that way where lost property was." But he was not happy with this work. "Of late he had pretty much given it up on account of injuring his Health, especially his eyes, made them sore." Treasure-seeking, he said, was not his idea. "He did not solicit business of this kind, and had always rather declined having anything to do with this business." He had been under pressure from neighbors, from the enthusiastic and well-off Stowell, and from his own father. They kept after him even though the hunts invariably failed.[92]

By the time of the court appearance, Joseph Sr. may have been backing off too. W. D. Purple, a skeptical observer at the hearing, said one statement particularly impressed him. Joseph Sr. testified that "both he and his son were mortified that this wonderful power which God had so miraculously given him should be used only in search of filthy lucre, or its equivalent in earthly treasures. . . . His constant prayer to his Heavenly Father was to manifest His will concerning this marvelous power. He trusted that the Son of Righteousness would some day illumine the heart of the boy, and enable him to see His will concerning him." A neighbor who knew Joseph Sr. around 1827 reported that the old man "stated their digging was not for money but it was for the obtaining of a Gold Bible. Thus contradicting what he had told me before."[93]

MARRIAGE

Joseph spent most of 1826 in southern New York. He went to school and worked for Stowell in Bainbridge, and possibly labored in Joseph Knight Sr.'s carding mills, three and a half miles down the Susquehanna River in Colesville.[94] He made a good impression while there. John Reid, a local farmer versed in the law who later defended Joseph in court, said Joseph was truthful and intelligent. Josiah Stowell Jr. said Joseph was "a fine likely young man & at that time did not Profess religion he was not a Profain man although I did onc[e] in a while hear him swair he never gambled to my knowledge . . . I never new him to git drunk." The Knight boys, Joseph Jr. and Newel, had the same impression. Joseph Smith Jr. formed lifelong friendships with both families. In 1843, through his son, Stowell wrote of Joseph that "he never knew anything of him but that was right als[o] know him to be a Seeer & a Phrophet & Believe the Book of mormon to be true." In November 1826, Joseph told the Knights about Moroni and a "gold book of ancient date." At first the two older boys had no faith in the story, but Joseph Knight Jr. and his father believed at once. The Knights later became the nucleus of a small branch of the Mormon Church in Colesville and migrated to Ohio with other Mormons.[95]

Joseph returned to Manchester in the fall of 1826 to comply with Moroni's instructions to report at Cumorah every year on September 22. He did not stay for long, possibly not even for Hyrum's marriage to Jerusha Barden on November 2, since Joseph Knight Jr. remembered Joseph being at their house in Colesville in November.[96]

Work on the Stowell and Knight farms was not the only magnet drawing Joseph Smith back. While at home, he told his mother about Miss Emma Hale, who "would be my choice in preference to any other woman I have ever seen." Joseph had kept company with two of Stowell's daughters, but he had been attracted to the tall, dark-haired Emma while he and his father boarded at the Hale home in Harmony during the treasure-hunting expedition. Isaac Hale, Connecticut-born and sixty-two years old, had moved into the area around 1790, acquired land, and won notoriety as a hunter. Hale was close enough to the Stowell mining venture to witness the signatures on the agreement that Stowell, the Smiths, and others signed. Later, however, he turned against the treasure-seekers. When Joseph came to court Emma and eventually ask for her hand, Hale objected that Joseph was "a stranger, and followed a business that I could not approve."[97]

In January 1827, Emma visited Josiah Stowell in Bainbridge and saw Joseph. He was a handsome young man, over six feet tall with broad chest and shoulders, light brown hair, blue eyes, and long thick lashes, bushy brows, and a little beard. She later told her son, "I had no intention of marrying when I left home; but during my visit at Mr. Stowell's, your father visited me there. My folks were bitterly opposed to him; and being importuned by your father, aided by Mr. Stowell, who urged me to marry him, and preferring to marry him to any other man I knew, I consented." Joseph was twenty-one and Emma twenty-two when they "eloped to marry" at the house of Zechariah Tarble in South Bainbridge, January 18, 1827.[98]

Apparently without returning to Harmony, the young couple moved to

Manchester, where Joseph farmed with his father. The next summer Emma timidly wrote home to ask if she might obtain her clothing and some furniture and cows that belonged to her. When Isaac Hale assured her of the availability of her belongings, Joseph hired his neighbor Peter Ingersoll to haul the goods back to Manchester. In Harmony, Joseph and Emma met Isaac Hale for the first time since the marriage. The old man tearfully rebuked Joseph for stealing his daughter and said he would rather follow her to her grave than have her married to Joseph, who assured his father-in-law that treasure-seeking was behind him, and "he expected to work hard for a living, and was willing to do so." Apparently convinced, Isaac offered to let the couple live on the Hale property and to help Joseph get started in business.[99]

Joseph had long been trying to free himself from the treasure-seekers. He told Peter Ingersoll on the way back to Manchester that he intended to keep the promise he had made to his father-in-law, but "it will be hard for me, for they will all oppose, as they want me to look in the stone for them to dig money." Ingersoll confirmed Joseph's predictions: "They urged him, day after day, to resume his old practice of looking in the stone."[100] Later, when they heard he had the plates, Sally Chase would come with her stone to try to find the hiding place.

FAMILY RELIGION

When he married Emma Hale in 1827, Joseph was on the eve of realizing himself as a prophet. He may still have been involved in magic, but he was sincere when he told Emma's father that his treasure-seeking days were over. Magic had served its purpose in his life. In a sense, it was a preparatory gospel. Treasure-seeking lore may have made it easier for his father to believe his son's fabulous story about an angel and gold plates. Joseph Sr. might have dismissed the report had not tales of spirits guarding treasure prepared his mind.

Traces of a treasure-seeking mentality still appeared in the family's reactions to the angel. His parents admonished Joseph to be rigorously obedient to the messenger's instructions, just as exact compliance with prescribed rituals was required for successful money-digging. Stories circulated of a requirement to bring Alvin to the hill to get the plates; and when he died, someone else. Emma, it was said, was designated as a key.[101] The stories have a magical flavor, but other stories have the angel warning Joseph about greed and the evildoings of the money-diggers, as if the messenger was moving him away from his treasure-hunting ways. The danger of treating the plates as treasure was underscored time after time. By 1826, even Joseph Sr. had come around to a more biblical conception of Joseph's mission. The plates were seen less and less as a treasure and more and more as a religious history, preparing Joseph to conceive of himself as a translator and prophet.

Was there anything uniquely powerful in Smith family dynamics to produce a prophet son? Family culture must have played some part. The Smiths' confusion about religion made Joseph an independent seeker. Both parents had broken out of the standard church orthodoxies while at the same time remaining pious and searching. Joseph Sr. was filled with yearnings for peace and salvation combined with deep distrust of churches and ministers. He bestowed on his son a concern for the failures of the churches. Lucy, who wanted the comfort of religion and the respectability of church membership, also had trouble finding a church to join. The two imparted faith to their children but no clear direction or institutional support. Joseph Jr. was left on his own to find answers. Although the revivals brushed his life and probably awakened concerns about his sins, he found salvation in a private vision, not in a camp meeting. He was bred to independence. The message of apostasy in the First Vision coupled with the rebuff received when he reported his vision widened the gulf between Joseph and the churches. After 1820, it was fairly certain he would cut a path for himself.

But independence did not imply prophethood. Did anything else in family dynamics empower him to make large claims? His parents were loyal to him. They believed in his visions and followed him wherever he led his new church. But Lucy, a high-strung, proud woman, intensely devoted to her family's standing in the world, did not select her fourth son as the chosen vessel of family accomplishment; the oldest, Alvin, was favored at first.[102] Only after Alvin's death when Joseph was seventeen did responsibility for family leadership fall on Joseph, under the tacit family agreement that Joseph Sr. was not fully adequate. He was a gentle, disappointed man with an inclination to compensate for his failures with magic and drink. He loved his sons as Asael had loved him and was grateful for their support despite his weakness. Joseph Jr. eventually restored his father's dignity by giving him an honored place in the church. If there was any childhood dynamic at work in Joseph Jr.'s life, it was the desire to redeem his flawed, loving father, but was this enough to make him a prophet?

The Smiths have been diagnosed as a dysfunctional family that produced a psychologically crippled son.[103] They did suffer traumas both personal and social: typhoid fever infections, poverty, humiliation about their log cabin, alienation from the respectable village population, religious confusion. But these were complaints of the age. Poor families everywhere suffered poverty, humiliation, and sickness. Perhaps the Smiths' afflictions prepared Joseph for leadership. He had endured the agonies of thousands in his generation and could speak to their sorrows. His religion may have touched people all the more because it came out of experiences common to them all.

After Joseph and Emma's return to Manchester in 1827, Joseph Sr. sent his son into the village on business. When it grew dark and Joseph was still not back, the parents started to fret. At last an exhausted Joseph came through the door and dropped into a chair. For a long time he sat silent while his father plied him with questions. Lucy held back. "The fact was," she said, "I had learned to be a little cautious about matters with regard to Joseph, for I was accustomed to see him look as he did on that occasion, and I could not easily mistake the cause thereof." Finally Joseph said quietly, "I have taken the severest chastisement that I have ever had in my life." The angel had met Joseph on the road near Cumorah and warned him that he "had not been engaged enough in the work of the Lord; that the time had come for the Record to be brought forth; and that I must be up and doing, and set myself about the things which God had commanded me to do." Joseph appeared calm. "I now know the course that I am to pursue, so all will be well."[104]

THREE

TRANSLATION

1827–30

In writing for J[oseph]. S[mith]. I frequently wrote day after day, often sitting at the table close by him, he sitting with his face buried in his hat, with the stone in it and dictating hour after hour, with nothing between us. He had neither mss nor book to read from. If he had had anything of the Kind he could not have concealed it from me. The plates often lay on the table without any attempt at concealment, wrapped in a small linen table cloth, which I had given him to fold them in. I felt of the plates, as they lay on the table, tracing their outline and shape. They seemed to be pliable like thick paper, and would rustle with a metallic sound when the edges were moved by the thumb, as one does sometimes thumb the edges of a book. O[liver] Cowdery and JS wrote in the room where I was at work. JS could neither write nor dictate a coherent and well worded letter, let alone dictating a book like the Book of M[ormon].
EMMA SMITH BIDAMON, Notes of Interview with Joseph Smith III, 1879

BY THE FALL OF 1827, Joseph Smith stood on the line dividing visionary supernaturalism from rational Christianity—one of the many boundaries between the traditional and modern world in early-nineteenth-century America. He was difficult to place in relation to that line because he faced in both directions. Joseph looked backward toward folk beliefs in divine power communicated through stones, visions, dreams, and angels. At the same time, he turned away from the money-diggers' passion for treasure and reached for higher, spiritual ends. The gold plates and angels scandalized rational Christians, while the religious impulse confused the money-diggers.

Inevitably, Smith was misunderstood. Newspaper editors and clergymen vilified him for reviving old superstitions, and the Palmyra magicians harassed him for not playing their game. Neither group could believe that Joseph's powers advanced the purposes of God. Even those who helped with the translation, Oliver Cowdery and Martin Harris, questioned at times. They heard the story with a mixture of amazement, joy, and cautious disbelief. In their first encounters with Joseph, they wavered between fasci-

nation and incredulity, devising one test after another to safeguard themselves against deception. Though neither sophisticated nor truly skeptical,
they asked for proof of Joseph's gifts in the same spirit of doubt that moved
his Enlightenment critics.

THE PLATES

The events surrounding the translation of the *Book of Mormon* can be pieced
together from the recollections of a dozen or so contemporaries. A few
non-Mormons wrote brief accounts: Orsamus Turner, Pomeroy Tucker,
Isaac Hale, Charles Anthon, Willard Chase, Peter Ingersoll, and others.
The detailed, close-up reports come from Mormons: Lucy Smith, Joseph
Knight Sr., Joseph Knight Jr., David Whitmer, Oliver Cowdery, Emma
Smith, William Smith, Katharine Smith Salisbury, Martin Harris, and
Joseph himself. The story that emerges from their accounts is perplexing.
The Mormon sources constantly refer to the single most troublesome item
in Joseph Smith's history, the gold plates on which the *Book of Mormon* was
said to be written. For most modern readers, the plates are beyond belief, a
phantasm, yet the Mormon sources accept them as fact. Interspersed with
descriptions of journeys, illnesses, business deals, and lost horses are trips
to the Hill Cumorah, boxes holding the plates, and times when the plates
are hidden, touched, lifted, and translated. Mundane details mix with an
incredible artifact whose very existence is debated.

To account for the plates' presence in the records, skeptics look for signs
of trickery. Fawn Brodie, the most eminent of Joseph Smith's unbelieving
biographers, referred to a neighbor's account of Joseph filling his frock with
white sand and telling his family it was gold plates. Dan Vogel, a recent
biographer, hypothesizes that Joseph fabricated plates from tin while he
was at Cumorah.[1] Contemporaries speculated that he wrapped a tile brick
in a cloth. One deception led to another until Joseph had fabricated a fabulous tale. These explanations keep the story within the realm of the ordinary but require considerable fabrication themselves. Joseph "may" have
done this and "probably" did that. Since the people who knew Joseph best
treat the plates as fact, a skeptical analysis lacks evidence. A series of sur-
mises replaces a documented narrative.[2]

Incredible as the plates were, hunting for deception can be a distraction.
It throws us off the track of Joseph Smith the Prophet. In devising a story
of a charlatan, we lose sight of the unprepossessing rural visionary who
became a religious leader admired by thousands. What is most interesting
about Joseph Smith is that people believed him. To understand the emergence of Joseph the Prophet, we must follow the stories told by family and
friends who believed they were witnessing a miracle. From their accounts
issues the Joseph Smith who has a place in history.

In September 1827, Joseph Knight Sr., Joseph Smith's Colesville friend, and Josiah Stowell, Joseph's Bainbridge employer, visited the Smiths in Manchester. Knight had arranged a business trip to Rochester to coincide with the date of Joseph's next visit to Cumorah. Knight remembered Joseph saying that the angel told him "if he would Do right according to the will of God he mite obtain [the plates] the 22n Day of Septemer Next and if not he never would have them." According to Knight, he was at the Smith house on the evening of September 21 and observed Joseph making preparations. Joseph foresaw the possibility that Samuel Lawrence, a neighbor who searched for treasure with the Smiths, would try to interfere. Joseph asked his father to scout the Lawrence house in the late afternoon and, if he saw signs of movement, to warn Lawrence off. Joseph Sr. returned at nightfall with nothing to report.[3]

The angel had commanded Joseph to come to the hill on September 22. To be precise in his compliance and still to throw off meddlers who knew of the date, Joseph chose to go to Cumorah in the dead of night, almost the minute September 22 arrived.[4] Lucy stayed up past midnight on September 21. Around twelve o'clock Joseph came into the room to ask if his mother had a chest with lock and key. Knowing at once why he wanted it, Lucy was upset when she was unable to provide one. "Never mind," Joseph assured her. "I can do very well for the present without it—be calm—all is right." Minutes later Emma passed through the room in her bonnet and riding dress, and Lucy heard the two of them drive off in Joseph Knight's wagon.[5]

Joseph and Emma did not return until after breakfast. When the men were seated at the table, Joseph Sr. asked after his son. Lucy tried to put him off, but her husband insisted: "I must have Joseph sit down here and eat with me." "Well, now, Mr. Smith," Lucy came back, "*do* let him eat with his wife *this* morning; he almost always takes breakfast with you." A few minutes later Joseph Knight came in with the disturbing news that his horse was missing. "Never mind the horse," Lucy parried. "Mr. Knight does not know all the nooks and corners in the pastures; I will call William, he will bring the horse immediately." Satisfied for a moment, Knight soon discovered his wagon gone and was convinced that some rogue had taken both. Lucy put him off again until finally Joseph Jr. returned.[6]

Lucy was trembling as Joseph came into the house, fearful that through some failure of obedience all was lost. When she left the room to conceal her feelings, Joseph stepped aside with her. "Do not be uneasy mother, all is right—see here, I have got a key," he said, and handed her an object covered with a silk handkerchief. Lucy said she felt "two smooth three-cornered diamonds set in glass" and fixed in bows that were connected, as she said, like old-fashioned spectacles. After breakfast Joseph called Joseph Knight into another room and, with the happy enthusiasm of a young man, told him that everything was "ten times Better then I expected." He described the plates but was more excited about the Urim and Thummim: "I can see any thing; they are Marvelus." As for the plates, they were "writen in Caracters," Joseph said, "and I want them translated."[7]

From then on, Joseph's life revolved around the plates: how to store the plates, how to protect them, how to translate them. Probably to forestall interference, Joseph did not bring the plates home on September 22. Lucy said he concealed them in an old birch log by cutting out a segment of bark, carving out the interior, depositing the plates, and replacing the bark. This interim hiding place also gave him time to have a box made. Lucy directed him to a cabinetmaker who had made furniture for Sophronia. Always short of cash, the Smiths worried a little about how to make payment. Lucy told Joseph to promise half cash, half produce, the same arrangement as for the furniture. The next day, Joseph learned of a well-digging job in Macedon, just east of Palmyra, and left immediately.[8]

The Smiths' efforts to keep the plates secret were of no avail. The day after Joseph left for Macedon, his father learned that ten or twelve men working with Willard Chase were conspiring to find the plates, and had sent for a conjuror sixty miles away whom they believed could discover the hiding place. Brigham Young said the conjuror traveled the sixty miles three times that season. "The man I refer to was a fortune-teller," Young said, "a necromance, an astrologer, a soothsayer, and possessed as much talent as any man that walked on the American soil, and was one of the wickedest men I ever saw." The next morning Joseph Sr. walked over the hill east of the Smith farm to the Lawrence place and found Willard Chase, Samuel Lawrence, the conjuror, and a group of others laying plans. Joseph Sr. heard enough to learn that the gang aimed at getting the "gold bible," as they called it. When he got back, Emma went off at once to fetch Joseph from Macedon. Joseph left the well, borrowed a horse, and hastily rode through Palmyra to the Smith farm. He reassured the family that the plates were safe but decided that now was the time to bring them home.[9]

Joseph set out alone, still dressed in the linen frock he had been wearing to dig the well. Lucy Smith said he wrapped the plates in the frock and put them under his arm. Martin Harris later estimated that the plates weighed forty or fifty pounds, and Joseph carried them three miles. Wary of interference, Joseph thought it better to leave the road and travel in the woods. His caution proved useless. While he was scrambling over a tree that had fallen across the path, a man struck him with a gun. Joseph knocked the man down and ran off at full speed, still with the heavy plates under his arm. A half mile further he was assaulted again and again made his escape. Yet a third time someone tried to stop him before he finally reached home, speechless with fright and fatigue and suffering from a dislocated thumb.[10]

Joseph's brother Carlos ran off at once to get Hyrum, who came with a chest made of cherrywood. Once the plates were safely locked inside,

Joseph told his father, Knight, and Stowell what had happened. A number of neighbors gathered to listen, for word of the plates had spread and curiosity ran high. All wanted to know "something in regard to the strange circumstance which had taken place." Offers of cash and property were made to be given a glimpse of the plates.[11]

Lucy Smith said the angel warned Joseph as the record was turned over to him that "wicked men" would "lay every plan and scheme that is possible to get it away from you, and if you do not take heed continually, they will succeed." Willard Chase's gang, for one, was still plotting to get possession. According to Lucy, Joseph kept the seerstone on his person to keep track of the plates. Alerted to an approaching danger, Joseph took up hearthstones in the west room and buried the box of plates there. They had scarcely replaced the stones when a collection of armed men rushed up to the house. Thinking quickly, Joseph threw open the doors, yelled loudly, and all the men in the house, including eleven-year-old Carlos, ran out in a fury. Surprised and disorganized, the mob fell back, ran for the woods, and disappeared.[12]

As Joseph's former partners, the treasure-seekers thought the plates were partly theirs. "The money-diggers," Martin Harris explained, "claimed that they had as much right to the plates as Joseph had, as they were in company together." Over a year later, David Whitmer met a group of incensed young men in Palmyra who claimed that before Joseph got the plates, "he had promised to share with them." One of them, Samuel Lawrence, allied with Alva Beaman, a "rodsman" from Livonia, came to the Smith house to try to persuade Joseph to give them a share.[13] Joseph Knight, who was still at the Smiths', said that "they Proposed to go shares with him and tried every way to Bargain with him. But Could not." Whereupon Beaman held up his rods (sticks like dousing rods) until they pointed to the hearth where the plates were hidden.[14]

To elude Chase and Lawrence, Joseph moved the plates from the hearth to the cooper's shop in the yard where Joseph Sr. carried on his trade. He buried the box under a floorboard and hid the plates themselves in a pile of flax in the shop loft. That night Willard Chase and his sister Sally Chase with her green glass came with their friends to search. They rummaged around outside but did not come in. Lucy learned later that Sally Chase told the men the plates were in the coopering shop. The next morning, the Smiths found the floor torn up and the box smashed. To their relief, the plates were safely buried in the flax.[15]

MARTIN HARRIS

After these intrusions, Joseph, realizing he must move, asked his mother to invite Martin Harris, a possible source of aid, to come to the Smith farm.

The Harrises, a prosperous, second-generation Palmyra family, had frequently given Joseph work on their farm a mile and a half north of the village. Martin was considered the most respectable of Joseph's converts, though he was given, the townspeople thought, to superstition and visionary beliefs. Harris knew of Joseph's gifts as a seer, and talk of the plates was all over the village. Harris was laying a hearth when Lucy arrived. While waiting for him to finish up, she talked to Mrs. Harris about the plates. Lucy Harris was enthralled. She immediately pressed money on Lucy Smith to assist in the translation. Lucy put her off and asked that Martin Harris pay them a visit.[16]

Lucy and Martin Harris combined credulity and suspicion. People like the Harrises were looking for wonders like their Puritan ancestors but as children of the Enlightenment were wary of being deceived. They wanted to believe but would retaliate if they detected fraud. When the curious Lucy Harris visited the Smiths, she pled for a glimpse of the plates and even offered payment. Joseph told her, as he had told all the villagers, that he was forbidden to show them. That night Mrs. Harris dreamed of an angel and the plates and awoke more eager than ever. To satisfy her, Joseph accepted her offer of a $28 loan. Martin Harris, more cautious than his wife, arrived a few days later while Joseph was off earning money for flour. When he first heard of the plates, he had stood up for Joseph. "He that answereth a matter before he heareth it," he had cautioned the detractors in the village, "it is foolishness unto him. I do not wish to make myself a fool." But now he wanted proof that he was not being deceived. When Harris visited the Smiths, he ran a little test on Emma and the other Smiths. "I talked with them separately," he later reported, "that I might get the truth of the matter." Then he compared their accounts with Joseph's report to check for contradictions.[17]

To Harris's surprise, Joseph told him the angel had revealed that Harris was to assist in the translation. "If it is the devil's work," Harris answered, "I will have nothing to do with it; but if it is the Lord's, you can have all the money necessary to bring it before the world." "You must not blame me for not taking your word," he added. Harris hefted the box containing the plates and went home. He later said that he went to his bedroom, prayed, and was shown by God that "it was his work, and that it was designed to bring in the fullness of his gospel to the gentiles. . . . He showed this to me by the still small voice spoken in the soul."[18]

Others in the village were more suspicious. Martin Harris heard that a mob planned to tar and feather Joseph unless he showed them the plates. Seeing that he would have no peace in Palmyra, Joseph wrote to Alva Hale, Emma's brother, asking him to come up from Harmony with a wagon to take them back, and Harris gave him $50 to pay off his debts before leaving.

Before Joseph departed, a few townsmen were determined to see the plates. Lucy Smith said a mob of fifty men asked Dr. Alexander McIntyre to lead them in an effort to get the "gold bible," but he dismissed them as a "pack of devilish fools." To avoid trouble, Harris advised Joseph to leave two days in advance of the announced departure day. They put the plates in a barrel one-third full of beans and topped it off. On a Saturday night in late fall, they loaded their belongings into the wagon, helped in the pregnant Emma, and set out for Harmony armed with cudgels.[19]

For the next year and a half, Joseph had to provide for Emma while attempting to translate in a house that her parents reluctantly provided as a place to work. The previous August, Isaac Hale had agreed to help Joseph after exacting a pledge that he would settle down to serious business. The "wonderful book of Plates," as Isaac Hale called them, was not what he had in mind. "I was allowed to feel the weight of the box," he said, "and they gave me to understand, that the book of plates was then in the box—into which, however, I was not allowed to look." Hefting the box was not enough. Hale told Joseph, "If there was any thing in my house . . . which I could not be allowed to see, he must take it away." The neighbors also pestered Joseph for a glimpse of the plates. To placate his father-in-law and escape the curious, Joseph hid the plates in the woods. That winter he and Emma moved into a two-room house with a loft owned by Emma's brother Jesse and standing on her father's land about 150 yards from the main house. The two of them lived there for two and a half years while the translation went on. Joseph purchased the house and thirteen acres for $200, making the last payment in August 1830.[20]

Though finally settled, Joseph had to learn how to "translate" the curious characters. He had told his friend Joseph Knight Sr. he wanted the plates translated, but now they were there before his eyes, how was he to begin? Developing a method took time. His mother said, "Joseph was very solicitous about the work but as yet no means had come into his hands of accomplishing it." With Emma's help, he began by copying off "a considerable number" of the intricate figures and translating "some of them."[21]

Martin Harris arrived in Harmony in February 1828, two months after the Smiths. In his 1832 account Joseph said that because of Harris's righteousness "the Lord appeared unto him in a vision and shewed unto him his marvilous work which he was about to do and he imediately came to Su[s]quehanna and said the Lord had shown him that he must go to new York City with some of the caracters." The vision may have confirmed a plan already agreed on, for Lucy Smith said Joseph had previously arranged with Harris to come to Harmony and take the characters east to a linguist.[22]

Why Harris went is unclear. Joseph Knight Sr., who from his home in nearby Colesville aided Joseph while the translation went on, said that

Joseph and "his wife Drew of[f] the Caricters exactley like the ancient and sent Martin Harris to see if he Could git them Translated." Lucy Smith gave the same reason. She said Joseph was instructed "to take off a facsimile of the characters composing the alphabet which were called reformed egyptian Alphabetically and send them to all the learned men that he could find and ask them for the translation of the same." Lucy implied that once Joseph had a translation of all the basic characters, he could carry on by himself—thus the need to copy a great number of characters. Harris went to the "professed linguists," Lucy said, to give them "an opportunity to display their talents in giving a translation of the characters." Joseph himself did not say why Harris went to the linguists, except that he was commanded to go. But when Harris spoke with the scholars, he asked if the translation was correct. The answer would interest Harris and the citizens of Palmyra. Perhaps Joseph wanted a check on his work too.[23]

Where Martin Harris went, whom he saw, and what happened are clouded in contradictory reports. He stopped at Albany, probably to see Luther Bradish, a New York state assemblyman with a reputation for knowledge of the Middle East. Someone referred Harris to the illustrious philomath Samuel Latham Mitchill, then vice president of Rutgers Medical College in New York City and famed as a "living encyclopedia," a "chaos of knowledge." Accounts vary as to whether he saw Mitchill or Charles Anthon, another scholar, first, or if he saw Mitchill before and after Anthon, but the Mitchill episode was of slight importance. According to Harris, Mitchill encouraged him and referred him to Anthon, where a more important exchange took place.[24]

Charles Anthon was professor of classical studies at Columbia College from 1820 until his death in 1867. In February 1828, when Harris arrived, the scholarly work that was to establish Anthon as "the principal classical bookmaker of his time" lay ahead of him, but he was already noted for his 1825 edition of *A Classical Dictionary*, really an encyclopedia, first published by John Lempriere in 1788. Anthon added four thousand entries to the dictionary, and among the most notable were many on Egypt. In the preface he professed familiarity with the most eminent authorities on Egypt and cited Jean-François Champollion's "elaborate treatise on Hieroglyphics of Egypt." Anthon was probably as well equipped as anyone in America to answer Harris's questions.[25]

Anthon and Harris differed substantially in their accounts of their encounter. Anthon wrote letters in 1834 and 1841 to critics of the Mormons, denying that he had verified Joseph's translation or the authenticity of the characters. Anthon claimed he saw through the hoax at once, feared that Harris was about to be cheated of his money, and warned the "simplehearted farmer" to beware of rogues. Anthon, however, contradicts himself on an important detail. In the first letter Anthon said he refused to give Harris a written opinion; according to the second, the opinion was written "without any hesitation," in an attempt to expose the fraud.[26]

There is also confusion about what he actually saw. Anthon said that on the paper Harris showed him was a "singular medley" of Greek and Hebrew letters with other strange marks, with "sundry delineations of half moons, stars, and other natural objects, and the whole ended in a rude representation of the Mexican zodiac." Inexplicably, no moons, stars, or natural objects appear on the surviving copy of the "Anthon Transcript," as it was published in 1844. The characters are identifiably Egyptian, though not formed into Egyptian sentences.[27] One scholar has argued there were two separate transcripts, one with a translation and one without.[28] Harris said he showed Anthon both Joseph's translation and the untranslated characters and received confirmation of both. According to Harris, Anthon then said that the characters were Egyptian, Chaldaic, Assyriac, and Arabic, and gave Harris "a certificate certifying to the people of Palmyra that they were true characters, and that the translation of such of them as had been translated was also correct."[29] Satisfied with the professor's observations, Harris was leaving when Anthon inquired about the origins of the plates. When he was told that an angel had revealed their location, he asked for the certificate and tore it up. Anthon wanted to see the plates themselves, but Harris said they could not be shown because part was sealed. "I cannot read a sealed book," Harris reported Anthon saying. With that they parted.[30] Whatever happened, Martin Harris came back more convinced than before. He went right to translating and later funded publication of the *Book of Mormon*.[31]

For Joseph, Anthon's certification meant less than a discovery made sometime after Harris's return. Someone realized that Harris and Anthon had inadvertently fulfilled a prophecy in Isaiah that speaks of the "words of a book that is sealed, which men deliver to one that is learned, saying, Read this I pray thee: and he saith, I cannot; for it is sealed: And the book is delivered to him that is not learned, saying, Read this, I pray thee: and he saith, I am not learned." That realization thrilled Joseph. When he began writing his history in 1832, he took the pen in his own hands to describe the Anthon incident in terms that made it an exact fulfillment of Isaiah 29:11–12. He wrote that Martin Harris

took his Journy to the Eastern Cittys and to the Learned saying read this I pray thee and the learned said I cannot but if he would bring the plates they would read it but the Lord had forbid it and he returned to me and gave them to me to translate and I said cannot for I am not learned but the Lord had prepared spectacles for to read the Book therefore I commenced translating the characters and thus the Prophicy of Isaiaah was fulfilled which is writen in the 29 chapter concerning the book.[32]

At a time when Joseph's prophetic identity was jelling, a reference in the Bible was far more important than a verification of the translation. The Anthon incident brought Joseph into the biblical narrative, connecting him to the primary source of his creative energy. The Bible had prophesied his life.

When Martin Harris told his wife he planned to help translate the plates, she insisted on going with him. This time Lucy Harris was determined to see the plates and settle the question of their existence. She searched every possible hiding place in the Smiths' house and then the ground outside. Frustrated and angry at her failure, Lucy Harris took lodging nearby and told people that Joseph intended to cheat her husband of his farm. When the Harrises returned to Palmyra after two weeks, Lucy vainly attempted to persuade Martin to give up the translation. After he left for Harmony again, she hid the movable articles in the house to put them out of reach of Joseph's supposed design.[33]

Martin Harris was back in Harmony by mid-April 1828, and the translation began in earnest. For two months, from about April 12 to June 14, 1828, Joseph and Harris were hard at work. Joseph translated using the interpreters (also called the Urim and Thummim, crystals mounted on a breast plate), and Harris wrote down the text as it was dictated. A curtain divided the men to prevent Harris from seeing the plates.[34] By mid-June 1828, they had covered 116 pages of foolscap with text. Yet uncertainty still beset Harris. The ever-lengthening manuscript and the tests to which he put Joseph did not quiet his doubts. He could not forget his wife's skepticism or the hostile queries of Palmyra's tavern crowd. Was Joseph making a fool of him? Was he the classic dupe, to be cheated of his money and farm when the fraud was complete? Lucy Smith said that Harris asked Joseph for a look at the plates, for "a further witness of their actual existance and that he might be better able to give a reason for the hope that was within him." When that request was denied, he asked about the manuscript. Could he at least take it home to reassure his wife? Joseph asked through the interpreters and was told no. Harris pressed again and received the same answer. Still he was not satisfied. Finally, Joseph later reported, "After much solicitation, I again enquired of the Lord, and permission was granted him to have the writings" on the condition that Harris show the pages only to five people: his wife, his brother Preserved, and his father, mother, and wife's sister. Uneasy about the whole proceeding, Joseph required Harris before he set off to bind himself in a solemn covenant to comply.[35]

That decision began a sorrowful season. Soon after Harris left, Emma gave birth to a son after an exhausting labor. Whatever happiness the child brought was short-lived. The baby, named Alvin after Joseph's older brother, died that very day, June 15, and was buried near Emma's grandparents in sight of the house. Emma came close to death herself, and Joseph attended her night and day. After two weeks, as she began to mend, Joseph's mind turned back to the manuscript. Sensing his anxiety, Emma suggested that he go to Manchester to check up on Martin Harris. Mrs. Hale agreed to care for Emma, and Joseph caught the first stagecoach north.[36]

As soon as he got home, the Smith family sent for Harris, expecting him at eight for breakfast. The morning hours dragged by, and he did not come. At half past twelve, Lucy reported, "we saw him walking with a slow and measured tread towards the house, his eyes fixed thoughtfully upon the ground. On coming to the gate, he stopped instead of passing through and got upon the fence, and sat there some time with his hat drawn over his eyes." When he finally came in and sat down for the long-delayed breakfast, Harris "took up his knife and fork as if he were going to use them, but immediately dropped them." He "pressed his hands upon his temples, and cried out, in a tone of deep anguish, 'Oh, I have lost my soul! I have lost my soul!' " Joseph sprang up and demanded to know about the manuscript. "Have you broken your oath, and brought down condemnation upon my head, as well as your own?" "Yes, it is gone," replied Martin, "and I know not where."[37]

Lucy Smith said that seeing the manuscript had placated Mrs. Harris, as Martin had hoped. She was so pleased that she let him lock the papers in her bureau, from which the manuscript was retrieved from time to time to show the relatives named in the covenant. Martin Harris's first mistake came when he wished to show the pages to a close friend. His wife was away and, having no key, he picked the lock, marring the bureau. Having broken his promise once, he showed the manuscript to any friend who came along. Lucy Harris castigated him when she returned and found her bureau damaged, but that was not the worst. By the time the Smiths sent for Martin, the manuscript had disappeared. He had spent the morning searching without success. Joseph demanded that he go back and look again, but Harris said further search was useless: "I have ripped open beds and pillows; and I know it is not there." Lucy Smith surmised that Mrs. Harris stole the manuscript with the intention of altering it. The discrepancies between the second translation and the first would make the whole appear a fraud. Whatever the reason, the manuscript was gone, never to be recovered.[38]

"O, my God!" moaned Joseph, clenching his hands. "All is lost! all is lost! What shall I do?" He blamed himself for the calamity. "It is I who tempted the wrath of God. I should have been satisfied with the first answer." What would Emma think? "Then must I . . . return to my wife with such a tale as this? I dare not do it, lest I should kill her at once." No one could comfort him, his mother said; everyone felt his despair: "Sobs and groans, and the most bitter lamentations filled the house." "I well remember that day of darkness," Lucy Smith recalled, "both within and without. To us, at least, the heavens seemed clothed with blackness, and the earth shrouded with gloom." Joseph paced the floor, weeping and grieving, until sunset when he finally consented to eat.[39]

Joseph went back to Harmony in July 1828, suffering, as he later wrote, much "affliction of soul." As he later told the story, the angel appeared and returned the interpreters, which had been taken from him when Harris went off with the manuscript. Through them Joseph received his chastisement:

> For God doth not walk in crooked paths; neither doth he turn to the right hand nor to the left; neither doth he vary from that which he hath said: Therefore his paths are strait, and his course is one eternal round. Remember, remember, that it is not the work of God that is frustrated, but the work of men.

The revelation was inexorable. Joseph was at fault for yielding to Harris, but the revelation made it sound like a larger problem: "behold, how oft you have transgressed the commandments and the laws of God, and have gone on in the persuasions of men." He had listened to Harris, whose friendship and aid he needed, rather than to God. "For, behold, you should not have feared man more than God, although men set at nought the counsels of God, and despise his words, yet you should have been faithful." The voice was adamant. "Behold thou art Joseph, and thou wast chosen to do the work of the Lord, but because of transgression, if thou art not aware thou wilt fall."[40]

The words were hard for a young man who had just lost his firstborn son and nearly lost his wife, and whose chief error was to trust a friend, but there was comfort in the revelation: "Remember God is merciful: Therefore, repent of that which thou hast done, and he will only cause thee to be afflicted for a season, and thou art still chosen, and wilt again be called to the work." Lucy said Joseph was put on probation. If he showed proper penitence, the interpreters would be returned on September 22, the day of his annual interview with Moroni for the past four years.[41]

The revelation printed as section 3 of the current *Doctrine and Covenants* holds a significant place in Mormon history. So far as can be told, it is the first revelation written by the Prophet. He and others remembered earlier revelations, but they were written later. The current section 3 appeared as section 2 in the first printed edition of revelations, immediately following the introduction revealed in 1831. The revelation gave the first inkling of how Joseph would speak in his prophetic voice. The speaker stands above and outside Joseph, sharply separated emotionally and intellectually. The rebuke of Joseph is as forthright as the denunciation of Martin Harris. There is no effort to conceal or rationalize, no sign of Joseph justifying himself to prospective followers. The words flow directly from the messenger to Joseph and have the single purpose of setting Joseph straight. "For although a man may have many revelations, and have power to do many mighty works, yet, if he boasts in his own strength, and sets at nought the counsels of God, and follows after the dictates of his own will, and carnal desires, he must fall and incur the vengeance of a just God upon him." At twenty-two, Joseph was speaking prophetically.[42]

Eighteen twenty-eight was a turning point in Joseph Smith's development. It was the year when he found his prophetic voice. Not two years earlier, he was entangled with the money-diggers and struggling to scrape together rent money for his family. In 1828, he dictated 116 pages of the *Book of Mormon* and received a revelation spoken in God's voice. By this time, the treasure-seeking language has disappeared. Neither the lore nor the greed of the money-diggers enters the picture. The plates are being translated, the revelation said, that God's people might "rely upon the merits of Jesus Christ, and be glorified through faith in his name." The language was biblical rather than occult.[43]

With Joseph's realization of himself as a prophet, the rearrangement of memory began. When Joseph tells his history from 1828 on, his search for treasure as a boy became an irrelevant diversion of his youth. Treasure-seeking did not lead to the person he had become. His true history began with his search for a church and his plea for forgiveness. These led to the revelation of the Father and the Son and the visit of Moroni, the cardinal events of his boyhood. After 1828, Joseph could no longer see that magic might have prepared him to believe in a revelation of gold plates and translation with a stone. It did not occur to him that without magic his family might have scoffed at his story of Moroni, as did the minister who rejected the First Vision. Magic had played its part and now could be cast aside.[44]

OLIVER COWDERY

Sometime in this dark period, Joseph attended Methodist meetings with Emma, probably to placate her family. One of Emma's uncles preached as a Methodist lay minister, and a brother-in-law was class leader in Harmony. Joseph was later said to have asked to be enrolled in the class. Joseph Lewis, a cousin of Emma's, rose in wrath when he found Joseph's name. Lewis objected to the inclusion of a "practicing necromancer" on the Methodist roll. He confronted Joseph and demanded repentance or removal. For some reason Joseph's name remained on the roll for another six months, although there is no evidence of attendance.[45]

Lucy Smith said that Joseph received the interpreters again on September 22, 1828, and he and Emma did a little translating, but the need to prepare for winter intervened.[46] Emma's family, still suspicious, gave no aid. That fall Joseph worked the land purchased from Isaac Hale and tried to collect supplies. In early winter, he and Emma visited their old friend Joseph Knight Sr. in Colesville and told him that they were in need. Knight could do little between his own straitened circumstances and his wife's lack of sympathy. He gave Joseph some food, a pair of shoes out of the store, and three dollars.[47]

The period between the loss of the manuscript in the summer of 1828 and the burst of rapid-fire translation beginning in April 1829 appears like a fallow moment in Joseph's history. He seems to have been quiescent, waiting for help or direction. But in these months his conception of his mission was expanding. Until this time, his energies had been bent on recovering the plates and starting the translation. In the winter of 1829, a new revelation gave a glimpse of something more. A revelation for his father referred to a larger undertaking: "A marvelous work is about to come forth among the children of men," Joseph Sr. was told. The revelation implied a grander project, involving Joseph's family and friends: "If ye have desires to serve God ye are called to the work," though what the work was went unsaid.[48]

For the moment the work was translation. Joseph began dictating again while Emma wrote, aided occasionally by Joseph's brother Samuel. Emma, unlike Martin Harris, had no problem believing. When the plates were not in her red morocco trunk, they lay on the table wrapped in a linen tablecloth. "I felt of the plates, as they lay on the table," she later told Joseph Smith III, "tracing their outline and shape. They seemed to be pliable like thick paper, and would rustle with a metallic sound when the edges were moved by the thumb, as one does sometimes thumb the edges of a book." She occasionally moved them around on the table as her work required it. When Joseph III asked if his father might have written the manuscript beforehand or memorized what he dictated, Emma said no. Joseph at that time "could neither write nor dictate a coherent and well worded letter; let alone dictating a book like the *Book of Mormon*." Furthermore, "he had neither mss nor book to read from." "If he had had anything of the Kind he could not have concealed it from me." The whole thing was marvelous to her.[49]

Emma joined the small group of converts consisting of Joseph's immediate family, the vacillating but useful Martin Harris, and the interested bystanders Josiah Stowell and Joseph Knight Sr. The next spring brought a significant addition. Near sunset on Sunday, April 5, Joseph's brother Samuel arrived at the Smith cabin in Harmony accompanied by a stranger named Oliver Cowdery. Samuel was coming to spend the spring with Joseph, probably to help with the planting. Cowdery came seeking information about the plates. Twenty-two years old, a year younger than Joseph, and unmarried, Cowdery had learned of Joseph's work while teaching the district school in Manchester and boarding with the Smiths. Lucy Smith said Cowdery became so obsessed with the story of the plates he could think of nothing else. When he learned that Samuel was going to Harmony, Cowdery asked to go along.[50]

Oliver Cowdery was born in Wells, Rutland County, Vermont, not fifty miles from Joseph's birthplace, and moved to western New York with his family about the same time as the Smiths. The district school committee on which Hyrum Smith served hired his brother Lyman Cowdery but accepted Oliver in his place when Lyman was unable to honor the contract. Oliver had blacksmithed, clerked in a store, and worked in New York City, trying to help his family and to accumulate enough for a start in life.[51]

Joseph Sr. had been reluctant to say much when Cowdery first inquired. Experience had taught caution. But Cowdery won the family's trust and was told enough to whet his curiosity. In early April, he and Samuel set out in the rain to walk to Harmony on the muddy spring roads. On the way south, they stopped in Fayette to see David Whitmer, a friend of Oliver's, and promised to send back information about the plates.[52]

Joseph and Cowdery talked late into the evening the Sunday of his arrival. Cowdery learned more of the story and decided to stay. On April 6, he witnessed the purchase agreement for the Isaac Hale property, and the next day the translation began again, moving forward with only a few pauses until the book was completed by late June. "Day after day," Cowdery reported in 1834, "I continued, uninterrupted, to write from his mouth, as he translated with the *Urim* and *Thummim*." When Martin Harris had taken dictation from Joseph, they at first hung a blanket between them to prevent Harris from inadvertently catching a glimpse of the plates, which were open on a table in the room. By the time Cowdery arrived, translator and scribe were no longer separated. Emma said she sat at the same table with Joseph, writing as he dictated, with nothing between them, and the plates wrapped in a linen cloth on the table.[53] When Cowdery took up the job of scribe, he and Joseph translated in the same room where Emma was working. Joseph looked in the seerstone, and the plates lay covered on the table.[54]

Neither Joseph nor Oliver explained how translation worked, but Joseph did not pretend to look at the "reformed Egyptian" words, the language on the plates, according to the book's own description. The plates lay covered on the table, while Joseph's head was in a hat looking at the seerstone, which by this time had replaced the interpreters. The varying explanations of the perplexing process fall roughly into two categories: composition and transcription. The first holds that Joseph was the author of the book. He composed it out of knowledge and imaginings collected in his own mind, perhaps aided by inspiration. He had stuffed his head with ideas for sermons, Christian doctrine, biblical language, multiple characters, stories of adventure, social criticism, theories of Indian origins, ideas about Mesoamerican civilization, and many other matters. During translation, he composed it all into a narrative dictated over the space of three months in Harmony and Fayette.[55]

Composition is the naturalistic explanation for the *Book of Mormon*—the way books are always written—but it is at odds with the Joseph Smith of the historical record. The accounts of the neighbors picture an unambitious, uneducated, treasure-seeking Joseph, who had never written anything and is not known to have read anything but the Bible and perhaps the newspaper. None of the neighbors noted signs of learning or intellectual interests beyond the religious discussions in a juvenile debating club. To account for the disjuncture between the *Book of Mormon*'s complexity and Joseph's history as an uneducated rural visionary, the composition theory calls for a precocious genius of extraordinary powers who was voraciously consuming information without anyone knowing it.[56]

The transcription theory has Joseph Smith "seeing" the *Book of Mormon* text in the seerstone or the Urim and Thummim. He saw the words in the stone as he had seen lost objects or treasure and dictated them to his secretary. The eyewitnesses who described translation, Joseph Knight, Martin Harris, Oliver Cowdery, and David Whitmer, who was in the house during the last weeks of translation, understood translation as transcription. Referring to the seerstone as a Urim and Thummim, Knight said: "Now the way he translated was he put the urim and thummim into his hat and Darkned his Eyes then he would take a sentance and it would apper in Brite Roman Letters. Then he would tell the writer and he would write it. Then that would go away the next sentance would Come and so on."

Joseph himself said almost nothing about his method but implied transcription when he said that "the Lord had prepared spectacles for to read the Book." Close scrutiny of the original manuscript (by a believing scholar) seems to support transcription. Judging from the way Cowdery wrote down the words, Joseph saw twenty to thirty words at a time, dictated them, and then waited for the next twenty to appear. Difficult names (Zenoch, Amalickiah) were spelled out.[57] By any measure, transcription was a miraculous process, calling for a huge leap of faith to believe, yet, paradoxically, it is more in harmony with the young Joseph of the historical record than is composition. Transcription theory gives us a Joseph with a miraculous gift that evolved naturally out of his earlier treasure-seeking. The boy who gazed into stones and saw treasure grew up to become a translator who looked in a stone and saw words.

Whatever the process, the experience thrilled Oliver Cowdery. "These days were never to be forgotten," Cowdery reflected in 1834. "To sit under the sound of a voice dictated by the *inspiration* of heaven, awakened the utmost gratitude of this bosom!" The young prophet more than fulfilled Cowdery's expectations. On the other hand, the shock of the sudden immersion in a supernatural work now and then gave Cowdery pause, and like Harris he needed further reassurance.[58] A revelation helped put Cowdery's doubts to rest by telling of two spiritual experiences he had never mentioned to Joseph and that only a prophet, as Cowdery saw it, could have known about.[59]

Cowdery was open to belief in Joseph's powers because he had come to Harmony the possessor of a supernatural gift alluded to in a revelation as the "gift of Aaron," or "gift of working with the rod." Most likely, Cowdery used a rod to discover water and minerals. The revelation spoke of divine power causing "this rod of nature, to work in your hands." His family may have engaged in treasure-seeking and other magical practices in Vermont, and, like others in this culture, melded magic with Christianity. For a person with his cultural blend, an angel and gold plates had excitement and appeal. The revelation said nothing to discourage Cowdery's use of his special powers. "Behold thou has a gift, and blessed art thou because of thy gift. Remember it is sacred and cometh from above." Rather than repudiate his claims, the revelation redirected Cowdery's use of his gifts. "Thou shalt exercise thy gift, that thou mayest find out mysteries, that thou mayest bring many to the knowledge of the truth."[60]

Soon after Cowdery began work on the *Book of Mormon*, he wanted to exercise the greater gift of translation. Characteristically, Joseph made no effort to monopolize the work. In a peculiar form of democratic generosity, he held out the expectation throughout his life that his followers could receive revelations or see the face of God as he did. The first revelation to Cowdery promised "a gift if you desire of me, to translate even as my servant Joseph." Hearing this, Joseph remembered, Cowdery "became exceedingly anxious to have the power to translate bestowed upon him."[61]

Cowdery tried the experiment but failed. He began and then stopped, apparently mistakenly believing that he needed only to ask God and look in the stone. A revelation explained his mistake. "Behold I say unto you," the revelation chided, "that you must study it out in your mind; then you must ask me if it be right, and if it is right, I will cause that your bosom shall burn within you. . . . You feared, and the time is past, and it is not expedient now." Cowdery was to return to writing, "and then behold, other records have I, that I will give unto you power that you may assist to translate."[62]

By May 1829, Joseph and Cowdery had not yet translated what are now the opening books of the *Book of Mormon*. After the loss of the 116 pages, Joseph did not begin again at the beginning. Joseph and Emma took up the translation where Joseph and Harris had broken off the previous June, that is, around the first part of the Book of Mosiah in the reign of King Benjamin. Joseph and Cowdery kept on in sequence. Sooner or later, Joseph had to decide what to do about the loss of the previous manuscript, containing the first four hundred years of *Book of Mormon* narrative. In May he received a revelation telling him not to retranslate. Were he to bring out a new translation contradicting the first version, the people who had stolen the manuscript would say that "he has lied in his words, and that he has no gift," and claim "that you have pretended to translate, but that you have contradicted your words." Another component of the record, the plates of Nephi, the revelation said, covered the same period. Joseph was to translate them instead and publish them as the record of Nephi. In late May or June, probably after the rest of the book was done, he and Cowdery began work on 1 Nephi.[63]

While the translating went on, the Smiths had to keep food on the table. Looking for help, Joseph and Cowdery walked the twenty-six miles to Joseph Knight Sr.'s place in Colesville only to find him away. Back in Harmony, they searched for work, a frustrating dissipation of time when so much translation remained. One day, after looking unsuccessfully, they arrived home to find that the good-hearted Knight had brought nine or ten bushels of grain, five or six bushels of potatoes, a pound of tea, a barrel of mackerel, and, of course, lined paper.[64]

Despite the hard work and the spartan diet, the two young men enjoyed the two months they spent translating in Harmony. They paused occasionally to talk over the unfolding story of the Nephites. In April, they differed over the question of whether John the ancient apostle died or continued to live, a question suggested by *Book of Mormon* passages on prophets who had never died. They agreed to settle the matter through the interpreters, and learned that the Lord permitted John to tarry until the Second Coming.[65]

They also wondered about the authority to baptize. "After writing the account given of the Savior's ministry to the remnant of the seed of Jacob, upon this continent," Cowdery remembered, "it was as easily to be seen, that amid the great strife and noise concerning religion, none had authority from God to administer the ordinances of the gospel." Joseph said the question of authority disturbed them enough that they broke off the translation and went to the Susquehanna River to pray. In the middle of the prayer, in the brightness of day, a "messenger from heaven, descended in a cloud of light." As Joseph told the story in 1838, the person said he was John the Baptist and that he had been sent by Peter, James, and John. Then he laid his hands upon their heads to ordain them:

Upon you my fellow servant in the name of Messiah I confer the priesthood of Aaron, which holds the keys of the ministring of angels and of the gospel of repentance, and of baptism by immersion for the remission of sins; and this shall never be taken again from the earth, untill the sons of Levi do offer again an offering unto the Lord in righteousness.

The angel told them they would later receive a higher priesthood, the Melchizedek Priesthood, and the power to lay on hands for the gift of the Holy Ghost. Now they were to baptize one another and ordain each other again to the Priesthood of Aaron. Foreshadowing future events, Joseph was told that his title was to be First Elder of the Church, and Cowdery's Second Elder. Joseph took Cowdery into the Susquehanna and baptized him and Cowdery did the same for Joseph. Then they ordained one another.[66]

That was the story in its ripe form, but Joseph did not tell anyone about John the Baptist at first. Summarizing the key events in his religious life in an 1830 statement, he mentioned translation but said nothing about the restoration of priesthood or the visit of an angel. The first compilation of revelations in 1833 also omitted an account of John the Baptist.[67] David Whitmer later told an interviewer he had heard nothing of John the Baptist until four years after the Church's organization. Not until writing his 1832 history did Joseph include "reception of the holy Priesthood by the ministring of angels to administer the letter of the Gospel" among the cardinal events of his history, a glancing reference at best. Joseph had not told his mother about his First Vision, and spoke to his father about Moroni only when commanded. His reticence may have shown a fear of disbelief. Although obscure, Joseph was proud. He did not like to appear the fool. Or he may have felt the visions were too sacred to be discussed openly. They were better kept to himself. The late appearance of these accounts raises the possibility of later fabrication. Did Joseph add the stories of angels to embellish his early history and make himself more of a visionary? If so, he made little of the occurrence. Cowdery was the first to recount the story of John's appearance, not Joseph himself. In an 1834 Church newspaper, Cowdery exulted in his still fresh memory of the experience. "On a sudden, as from the midst of eternity, the voice of the Redeemer spake peace unto us, while the vail was parted and the angel of God came down clothed with glory, and delivered the anxiously looked for message, and the keys of the gospel of repentance!"[68] When Joseph described John's visit, he was much more plainspoken. Moreover, he inserted the story into a history composed in 1838 but not published until 1842. It circulated without fanfare, more like a refurbished memory than a triumphant announcement.

In his 1838 history, when the story was finally told in full, Joseph spoke of their happiness afterwards: "Immediately upon our coming up out of the water after we had been baptized we experienced great and glorious blessings from our Heavenly Father." Their study of the scriptures yielded more knowledge than ever before, Joseph observed. "Our minds being now enlightened, we began to have the Scriptures laid open to our understandings, and the true meaning and intention of their more mysterious passages revealed unto us, in a manner which we never could attain to previously, nor ever before had thought of."[69]

WITNESSES

Joseph's activities had not gone unnoticed in the neighborhood. He and Cowdery said nothing publicly about the vision of John the Baptist, but people knew about the translating. "We had been threatened with being mobbed, from time to time," Joseph said, "and this too by professors of religion." He had won over the Hale family far enough to receive their protection, but he needed uninterrupted time to complete the translation.[70]

Sometime in the latter part of May 1829, Cowdery wrote David Whitmer to ask if they could work in his father's house in Fayette. The Whitmer farm lay about twenty-seven miles east of Palmyra, between Seneca Lake and Lake Cayuga. Joseph knew the Whitmers too. He had met David's father, Peter Whitmer Sr., soon after the translation began, and the Smith parents traveled by way of the Whitmer farm on their way to visit Joseph in February 1829. The Whitmers were Pennsylvania Germans who had moved to Fayette around 1809, purchased a farm, and joined the German Reformed Church. The town elected Peter Whitmer Sr. overseer of highways and a school trustee. The whole family took an interest in the translation. The four older boys, including the two married sons, later became witnesses of the plates. Another witness, Hiram Page, was the Whitmers' son-in-law, the husband of their daughter Catherine. Her younger sister, Elizabeth Ann, would later marry Oliver Cowdery.[71]

Joseph and Cowdery began to translate the day after they arrived at the Whitmer farm. David Whitmer thought they worked hard. "It was a laborious work for the weather was very warm, and the days were long and they worked from morning till night." Various persons relieved Cowdery as clerk. Whitmer remembered his brother Christian and Joseph's Emma each taking a turn. One of the hands in the manuscript of 1 Nephi looks like John Whitmer's, and Joseph said, "John Whitmer, in particular, assisted us very much in writing during the remainder of the work." But Cowdery did most of the transcribing.

Occasionally circumstances interrupted the flow of translation. David Whitmer said sometimes Joseph "found he was spiritually blind and could not translate. He told us that his mind dwelt too much on earthly things, and various causes would make him incapable of proceeding with the translation." Whitmer told the story of one interruption:

One morning when he was getting ready to continue the translation, something went wrong about the house and he was put out about it. Something that Emma, his wife, had done. Oliver and I went up stairs and Joseph came up soon after to continue the translation, but he could not do anything. He could not translate a single syllable. He went down stairs, out into the orchard and made supplication to the Lord; was gone about an hour—came back to the house, asked Emma's forgiveness and then came up stairs where we were and then the translation went on all right. He could do nothing save he was humble and faithful.[72]

Spotted around the countryside were people fascinated by the story of the plates. Joseph later said he found "the people of Seneca County in general friendly and disposed to enquire into the truth of these strange matters which now began to be noised abroad." What did he say to them when he talked? His primary concern was daily translation of the plates, but in his account written in 1838 he said Seneca County people were "wishful to find out the truth as it is in Christ Jesus, and apparently willing to obey the Gospel when once fairly convinced." When people believed, they did not just subscribe to the book; they were baptized. Joseph named Hyrum Smith, David Whitmer, and Peter Whitmer Jr., but then said "many became believers, and were baptized."[73] The translation project was transmuting into a gospel program of conversion. Joseph was becoming a minister as well as a seer and translator.

As he began to seek converts, the question of credibility had to be addressed again. Joseph knew his story was unbelievable. Outside of his immediate family and close associates, he faced a wall of skepticism. Martin Harris, Joseph's most willing assistant in the beginning, had doubts about the plates from the start. When he asked for proof again in March 1829, a revelation came back saying, "Behold if they will not believe my words, they would not believe you, my servant Joseph, if it were possible that he could show them all things."[74]

The March revelation, while stalling Harris, hinted at the possibility that others might see the plates. Harris was to be patient and "if he will go out and bow down before me, and humble himself in mighty prayer and faith, in the sincerity of his heart, then will I grant unto him a view of the things which he desireth to know." The translation coming along in these months also referred prophetically to future witnesses of the plates. Harris, Cowdery, and David Whitmer wondered if they might be the ones. Joseph was slow to respond to their inquiries. Previous requests had brought admonitions of patience. Finally the three solicited Joseph so ardently that he asked for a revelation, which promised them a view not only of the plates but of the breastplate, the Urim and Thummim, and two sacred objects accompanying the plates—the sword of Laban and the Liahona, the miraculous ball with a compass given to Lehi by the Red Sea to set his course.[75]

Joseph Sr. and Lucy Smith came over to the Whitmers' after the translation was completed around July 1 and spent their first evening reading the manuscript. The next morning after the usual daily religious services, reading, singing, and praying, Joseph stood, as Lucy recalled, and turned to Martin Harris. "You have got to humble yourself before your God this day, that you may obtain a forgiveness of your sins. If you do, it is the will of God that you should look upon the plates, in company with Oliver Cowdery and David Whitmer."[76]

Whitmer was plowing the field when Joseph and Cowdery came to say they were to seek a witness that day. Whitmer tied his team to the fence, and when Harris joined them, the four men entered the nearby woods. They had agreed to take turns praying, first Joseph, then the other three. The first attempt brought nothing, and they tried again. Again nothing. Before they made a third attempt, Harris offered to leave, saying he was the obstacle. The remaining three knelt again and before many minutes, according to their account, saw a light in the air over their heads. An angel appeared with the plates in his hands. David Whitmer said the breastplate, Lehi's Liahona, and the sword of Laban lay on a table. He heard the angel say, "Blessed is he that keepeth His commandments." That was all Whitmer could remember him saying. Then a voice out of the light said, "These plates have been revealed by the power of God, and they have been translated by the power of God; the translation of them which you have seen is correct, and I command you to bear record of what you now see and hear."[77] Cowdery later said: "I beheld with my eyes. And handled with my hands the gold plates from which it was translated. I also beheld the Interpreters."[78]

After the appearance to Cowdery and Whitmer, Joseph went searching for Harris, who had gone further into the woods. Harris asked Joseph to pray with him, and at length, they later reported, their desires were fulfilled. Joseph said he saw the same vision as before, and Harris cried out "in an ecstasy of Joy": "'Tis enough; 'tis enough; mine eyes have beheld." At the close of the vision he jumped up, shouted "Hosanna," and blessed God. Harris later signed a statement with Cowdery and Whitmer saying that they had seen an angel and heard a voice commanding that "we should bear record."[79]

Lucy Smith said Joseph seemed immensely relieved when they returned to the Whitmer house. He threw himself down beside her and exclaimed that "the Lord has now caused the plates to be shown to more besides myself." "They will have to bear witness to the truth of what I have said, for now they know for themselves, that I do not go about to deceive the people. . . . I feel as if I was relieved of a burden which was almost too heavy for me to bear, and it rejoices my soul, that I am not any longer to be entirely alone in the world."[80]

A few days later, Joseph, Cowdery, and four Whitmer sons went over to Palmyra to make printing arrangements. By that time the elder Smiths had left their frame house and moved into their old log house with Hyrum, whose eighty-acre farm immediately adjoined their former property.[81] A company of Whitmer and Smith men, including four Whitmer boys, Christian, Jacob, Peter Jr., and John, and their brother-in-law Hiram Page, plus Hyrum, Samuel, and Joseph Smith Sr., eight men in all, walked out to the place where the family went to pray. There Joseph showed them the plates, this time without an angel present. They turned over the leaves, examined the characters and the workmanship, and held the plates in their own hands. They later signed a statement saying what they had seen and testifying that they knew "of a surety, that the said Smith has got the plates of which we have spoken."[82]

The testimonies of the three and eight witnesses appearing at the back of the first edition of the *Book of Mormon* were not a final answer to the unbelievers. The claims of the witnesses were nearly as incredible as the existence of the plates. Critics pointed out how many of the witnesses were members of the Smith and Whitmer families, implying that they signed out of loyalty or from a self-serving motive. Others have suggested the imagined scene was viewed only through "spiritual eyes," or that Joseph pressured the witnesses into thinking they saw the angel and the plates.[83] The witnesses were no substitute for making the plates accessible to anyone for examination, but the testimonies showed Joseph—and God— answering doubters with concrete evidence, a concession to the needs of post-Enlightenment Christians.

While finishing up the translation at the Whitmers', Joseph continued to think about John the Baptist's promise of a higher priesthood.[84] He and Cowdery, he wrote years later, "had for some time made this matter a subject of humble prayer, and at length we got together in the Chamber of Mr Whitmer's house in order more particularly to seek of the Lord what we now so earnestly desired." Here, to their "unspeakable satisfaction," their prayers were answered, "for we had not long been engaged in solemn and fervent prayer, when the word of the Lord, came unto us in the Chamber, commanding us; that I should ordain Oliver Cowdery to be an Elder in the Church of Jesus Christ, And that he also should ordain me to the same office, and then to ordain others as it should be made known unto us, from time to time." They were not to ordain each other immediately but to await a time when all who had been baptized could be assembled to accept Joseph and Cowdery as "spiritual teachers." At that time they were to bless bread and wine, call out others to be ordained, and, by laying on hands, give the gift of the Holy Ghost to those who had been baptized.[85]

On June 11, 1829, Joseph deposited the title page of the *Book of Mormon* in the Utica office of R. R. Lansing, clerk of the U.S. district court for the Northern District of New York, and obtained a copyright. At the same time, he was negotiating with Egbert B. Grandin, a Palmyra bookseller, printer, and publisher of the *Wayne Sentinel*, one of Palmyra's papers, to print the book. Grandin doubted the book's commercial feasibility, considering that many Palmyrans felt the book should be suppressed. Meeting rejection in the village, Joseph and Harris went to Rochester looking for a printer. They twice applied to Thurlow Weed, publisher of the *Anti-Masonic Enquirer*, without success. Finally, Elihu F. Marshall, another Rochester publisher, agreed to print the book. Pomeroy Tucker, who worked in the Palmyra printing office, said that before signing with Marshall, Joseph and Harris made a last appeal to Grandin, pointing out that the book was to appear anyway. Some of Grandin's friends urged him to go ahead, and an agreement was reached.[86]

Martin Harris mortgaged his farm for $3,000 as security in case the books did not sell. Mrs. Harris refused to be a party to the mortgage, and their marriage soon ended. In a sense she was right about the consequences of Martin's involvement with Joseph. Martin did sell his farm on April 7, 1831, even though Tucker judged that Harris could have paid the bill from other resources.[87]

With financial arrangements complete, printing began. Joseph, Cowdery, and Harris stood together in the printing office when the printer drew the first proof sheet of the title page and celebrated the "dawning of a new gospel dispensation." Joseph foresaw trouble during the printing. Hostility was growing in Palmyra. As a security measure, Joseph told Cowdery to recopy the entire manuscript and never take both copies to the printing office at once. Someone was to accompany him while he carried the pages back and forth, and a watch was to be kept at the house. Cowdery set to work, and about the middle of August delivered the first twenty-four pages to Grandin's print shop on the third floor of the Exchange Building on Palmyra's Main Street. One of Grandin's typesetters said the copy came "on foolscap paper closely written and legible, but not a punctuation mark from beginning to end." Cowdery spent time in the office, now and again picking up a stick and setting type. In December, Cowdery wrote to Joseph, "It may look rather Strange to you to find that I have so soon become a printer." Grandin's typesetter said that Cowdery set ten or twelve pages in all of the first edition.[88]

On October 4, Joseph returned to Harmony, where Emma awaited him, but was forced to come back within a few months.[89] Abner Cole, a one-time justice of the peace, began publishing a Palmyra weekly entitled *The Reflector* in September, under the pseudonym O. Dogberry. Through the fall, Cole inserted brief observations on the "Gold Bible," but then, on December 29, he filled the front page with a long excerpt from the opening pages of the *Book of Mormon*.[90] Cowdery and Hyrum, who had been forewarned about Cole's pirating of the manuscript, discovered the editor hard at his labors in Grandin's shop one Sunday afternoon, with a prospectus promising subscribers more from the *Book of Mormon*. Hyrum warned Cole about the copyright but to no avail. "I don't care a d—n for you," Lucy Smith reported him saying. "That d—d gold bible is going into my paper, in spite of all you can do." Sensing a crisis, Joseph Sr. set off for Harmony and returned the next Sunday with Joseph Jr.[91]

Finding Cole at work in Grandin's shop, Joseph apprised him again of the copyright and told him to stop meddling. As Lucy reported the incident, the feisty Cole rose to the occasion. He threw down his coat, rolled up his sleeves, and came at Joseph smacking his fists together: "Do you want to fight, sir? do you want to fight?" Smiling, Joseph told Cole to put his coat back on. "It is cold, and I am not going to fight you." "Sir," bawled out the wrathful gentleman, "if you think you are the best man, just pull off your coat and try it." "There is law," Joseph returned, "and you will find that out, if you do not understand it." At length Cole cooled off and agreed to arbitration. The next two issues of *The Reflector*, dated January 13 and 22, contained excerpts from the *Book of Mormon* text, but Cole printed nothing more.[92]

The imminent publication of the *Book of Mormon* added to the ire of Palmyrans. Judging from newspaper comments even before it came off the press, the book was seen as a blasphemous rival to orthodox Christianity. The Western Presbyterian congregation in Palmyra thought the matter serious enough to send Deacon George Beckwith and two others to visit the Smiths. When Lucy would not back down on her belief, a church court suspended her, Hyrum, and Samuel from communion and censured them for their contumacy.[93]

The alarmed inhabitants of "the surrounding country" resolved never to purchase the *Book of Mormon* and tried to persuade Grandin to stop publication. They argued that since the Smiths had lost their farm they could not pay him unless the book sold, and they were not buying. Having entered the contract reluctantly in the first place, Grandin stopped work until he could be assured of payment. In an attempt to start the presses again, Harris consented to sell part of his farm to raise some cash, although only after getting a signed agreement from Joseph Sr. giving Harris the right to sell books on his own account. Impatient with Harris's reluctance, Hyrum urged Joseph to leave him out entirely and raise the money by other means. Hyrum had heard that the copyright could be sold in Canada and asked Joseph to inquire of the Lord. David Whitmer later reported that Joseph told Cowdery and Hiram Page to go to Toronto and promised them success, but the two returned empty-handed. They had to depend on Harris after all. Lucy said that Joseph and Harris together allayed Grandin's fears, and the work went on.[94]

In the March 26, 1830, edition of the *Wayne Sentinel*, Grandin published the title page of the *Book of Mormon* and announced: "The above work, containing about 600 pages, large Duodecimo, is now for sale, whole sale and retail, at the Palmyra Bookstore, by HOWARD & GRANDIN."[95]

Harris soon discovered that the citizens' boycott was effective. The book did not sell well. Traveling up from Harmony in the spring, Joseph Knight Sr. and Joseph met Harris crossing the road with a pile of books in his arms. "The Books will not sell for no Body wants them," Harris reported dejectedly. "I think they will sell well," Joseph replied encouragingly. "I want a Commandment," Harris said, meaning a revelation. "Why . . . fullfill what you have got," Joseph said, implying Harris had received ample instructions about his role already. "I must have a Commandment," Harris insisted three or four times. The next morning, after a night at the Smiths', Harris repeated his demand. According to Joseph Knight, Joseph received a revelation on Harris's behalf in which he was told he must not covet his own property but to "impart it freely to the printing of the book of Mormon, which contains the truth and the word of God." "Pay the printer's debt. Release thyself from bondage."[96]

The publication of the *Book of Mormon* made Joseph Smith a minor national figure. He first received newspaper attention on June 26, 1829, two weeks after he registered the title page with the clerk of the Northern District. The *Wayne Sentinel* published the title page and a brief notice. In late August and early September, two Rochester papers picked up the news from another article in the *Palmyra Freeman*, and other papers took notice. In the spring of 1830, after publication of the book, the *Rochester Republican*, the *Rochester Daily Advertiser*, and the *Rochester Gem* all published substantial comments. A local minister called it "the greatest fraud of our time in the field of religion," a dubious but notable distinction.[97]

The papers elevated Joseph from an obscure money-digger of local fame to full-blown religious impostor. The *Rochester Daily Advertiser* and the *Horn of the Green Mountains* headed their reports "Blasphemy" and "Fanaticism." A Rochester editor called the *Book of Mormon* "the greatest piece of superstition that has come within our knowledge."[98] The editors classed Joseph Smith and his followers with other fraudulent claimants to supernatural power: "It partakes largely of Salem Witchcraft-ism and Jemima Wilkinson-ism."[99] The editors drew on two vocabularies to discredit Smith; words like "enthusiasm" or "fanaticism" were used for false religions, but predominantly they called him a charlatan, a word for conspirators in treasure-seeking schemes.

The Smiths paid no attention to the reviews. Neither Lucy nor Joseph Jr. mentioned any of the articles in their histories. Joseph seemed most sensitive to the possible appearance of a doctored version of the lost 116 pages. He was still fretting over the fallout should it turn up. The preface to the *Book of Mormon* informed readers that some persons had stolen the account translated from the Book of Lehi, and despite Joseph's "utmost exertions" the pages had not been recovered. He feared that if he "should translate the same over again, they would publish that which they had stolen, and Satan would stir up the hearts of this generation, that they might not receive this work."[100] A translation from the plates of Nephi, he explained, replaced the missing part.

For all the effort and trouble he put into the translation, Joseph made little of the book's appearance. Neither he nor his mother named the day when bound copies were available. The first edition said virtually nothing about Joseph himself, the angel, or the process of translation. The preface contained one sentence—in the passive voice—about his part in the work: "I would also inform you that the plates of which hath been spoken, were found in the township of Manchester, Ontario county, New-York." His own name appeared only on the title page and in the testimony of the eight witnesses at the back. It was an unusually spare production, wholly lacking in signs of self-promotion. Joseph presented his handiwork to the public and moved on. The book thenceforth had a life of its own.[101]

FOUR

A NEW BIBLE

1830

Our lives passed away, like as were unto us a dream, we being a lonesome and a solemn people, wanderers cast out from Jerusalem.

JACOB, *Book of Mormon*, 142 (Jacob 7:26)

And it came to pass that when we had gathered in all our people in one to the land of Camorah, behold I, Mormon, began to be old; and knowing it to be the last struggle of my people, and having been commanded of the Lord that I should not suffer the records which had been handed down by our fathers, which were sacred, to fall into the hands of the Lamanites, (for the Lamanites would destroy them,) therefore I made this record out of the plates of Nephi, and hid up in the hill Camorah, all the records which had been entrusted to me by the hand of the Lord, save it were these few plates which I gave unto my son Moroni.

MORMON, *Book of Mormon*, 529 (Mormon 6:6)

THE *BOOK OF MORMON* IS A thousand-year history of the rise and fall of a religious civilization in the Western Hemisphere beginning about 600 BCE. A briefer history of a second civilization, beginning at the time of the Tower of Babel and extending till a few hundred years before Christ, is summarized in thirty-five pages near the end. The founders of the main group were Israelites who migrated from Jerusalem and practiced their religion in the New World until internal wars brought them to the verge of extinction in 421 CE, when the record ends. During the thousand years, wars are fought, governments crumble, prophets arise, people are converted and fall away, and Jesus Christ appears after His resurrection.

The book has been difficult for historians and literary critics from outside Mormondom to comprehend. A text that inspires and engages Mormons baffles outside readers. Mark Twain dismissed it as "chloroform in print." Bernard DeVoto called it "a yeasty fermentation, formless, aimless and inconceivably absurd . . . a disintegration." Histories of American literature usually ignore the *Book of Mormon*. It seems subliterary, either simple or unintelligible. Harold Bloom, sympathetic to Mormonism in other respects, could not "recommend that the book be read either fully or closely, because it scarcely sustains such reading." Perhaps because she had been reared a Mormon, Fawn Brodie saw the *Book of Mormon* differently: "Its structure shows elaborate design, its narrative is spun coherently, and it demonstrates throughout a unity of purpose." Mormon scholars find depth in the book and offer readings that uncover layer after layer of meaning. "I'm drawn to its narrative sweep, complexity of plots, array of characters who inhabit this world, and the premise that the book is about ultimate matters," says the literary critic Robert Rees.[1] And so opinion divides. The book has been controversial from the moment of its publication until now.

Contemporaries thought of the book as a "bible," and that may be the best one-word description. Martin Harris referred to the manuscript as the "Mormon Bible" when he was negotiating with the printer. Newspapers derisively called it the "Gold Bible."[2] Eber D. Howe, the Painesville, Ohio, editor who took an interest in Mormonism, described the recovery of the *Book of Mormon* as "a pretended discovery of a new Bible, in the bowels of the earth." The literary historian Lawrence Buell, after describing the desire of New England authors to write books with the authority of the Bible, notes that "the new Bible did not get written, unless one counts the *Book of Mormon*."[3]

The table of contents has a biblical feel. It lists fifteen books with titles like "The Book of Jacob," "The Book of Mosiah," "The Book of Helaman," and so on through Nephi, Enos, Jarom, Alma, Mormon, Ether, and Moroni, just as the Bible names its divisions after Jeremiah, Ezekiel, Amos, and Micah. But unlike the Bible, these books are not divided into histories and prophetic books. History and prophecy are interwoven, sermons and visions mingling with narrative.

The *Book of Mormon* tells the story of a family founding a civilization. The main story opens in Jerusalem on the eve of the Babylonian captivity.[4] Lehi, one of many prophets foretelling the city's doom, is told to flee the city with his wife and children and one other family. Drawn by the lure of a promised land, they are led into the wilderness of the Arabian peninsula. Like Abraham leaving Ur and Moses departing Egypt, Lehi is told God has a place for them. Lehi's band wanders in the wilderness for eight years (not forty like the children of Israel), until somewhere along the seacoast (seemingly the Arabian Sea) they are told to construct a ship. After a protracted voyage, they reach their promised land. The name America is never used, but readers universally thought Lehi's company had arrived in the Western Hemisphere.[5]

In the New World, the migrants build a temple and follow the law of Moses much like the society they left in Palestine, but their religion is explicitly Christian. They live under the constant threat of war, not from outside invaders, but between factions of their own society. The sons of Lehi quarrel, and brothers Laman and Lemuel attack the families of brothers Nephi, Sam, Jacob, and Joseph. Out of a family dispute grows a lasting division between Lamanites and Nephites who battle year after year until, after a thousand years, the Lamanites destroy the Nephites. Moroni, the last of the Nephite prophets to record the history, writes his closing words on the gold plates that had been accumulating since the beginning. He buries them, and fourteen hundred years later, returning as an angel, he directs Joseph Smith to the plates.[6]

Nephite prophets teach the coming of Christ and are told of the star that will rise at the time of Christ's birth. At the Crucifixion, three days of darkness settle on the New World, and after the resurrection, Christ descends in glory. As He is about to appear, the Father speaks from heaven, echoing events at Jesus's baptism and at the Mount of Transfiguration: "Behold my Beloved Son, in whom I am well pleased." During His stay among the Nephites, Christ repeats the Sermon on the Mount. He blesses children, prophesies the future of the descendants of Lehi, appoints twelve disciples, and tells them to baptize and administer bread and wine in remembrance of His death.[7] Altogether, the *Book of Mormon* can be thought of as an extension of the Old and New Testaments to the Western Hemisphere.

The book explains itself as largely the work of Mormon, a military figure who leads the Nephites, from about 327 to 385 CE, in the twilight of their existence as a nation. Mormon is one of more than a score of powerful personalities to emerge in history. Precociously eminent, he is appointed at fifteen to lead the Nephite armies. (He gives no reason for his elevation except that "notwithstanding I being young was large in stature.") In the same year, "being somewhat of a sober mind," he is "visited of the Lord," making him both prophet and general. From then until the Lamanites cut him down, still fighting in his seventies, Mormon and his people are swept this way and that by the tides of battle.[8]

Mormon writes at a time when Nephite civilization has fallen into decay. Much of the time, Mormon despairs of victory because of his people's iniquity. Even the bitterness of war does not soften their hearts. Theirs is "the sorrowing of the damned, because the Lord would not always suffer them to take happiness in sin." Rather than come to Jesus in humility as Mormon desires, "they did curse God, and wish to die." Mormon stands by his people despite their wickedness and "loved them, according to the love of God . . . with all my heart." He prays for them, but "without faith, because of the hardness of their hearts," leading them into battle year after year until an especially great victory convinces the Nephites that final vengeance is possible through an offensive war. At this point, Mormon refuses to lead the people any longer. The Lord tells him that "vengeance is mine, and I will repay," and adds that because of their wickedness this people "shall be cut off from the face of the earth."[9]

While out of the Nephite wars, Mormon goes to the hill Shim where the records of the nation are buried. The prophets have kept accounts of their prophesying, governing, and wars, and Mormon undertakes to compile a history from the plates they have produced. The title page calls the book "an abridgment of the Record of the People of Nephi." As editor, Mormon is unusually forthcoming about his sources. One segment comes from Nephi, another portion from Alma. A little headnote by Mormon, for example, indicates *"the words of Alma which he delivered to the people in Gideon, according to his own record."* Or *"*THE RECORD OF ZENIFF*, An account of his people, from the time they left the land of Zarahemla, until the time that they were delivered out of the hands of the Lamanites."* At one point, Mormon interrupts the narrative to say that when he was halfway through the record, he stumbled across another set of plates, which he is now adding: "After that I had made an abridgment from the plates of Nephi, down to the reign of this king Benjamin, of whom Amaleki spake, I searched among the records which had been delivered into my hands, and I found these plates, which contained this small account of the Prophets, from Jacob, down to the reign of this king Benjamin."[10]

One gets a picture of Mormon surrounded by piles of plates, extracting a narrative from the collection, and not completely aware of all there is. At various points while hurrying through the records, he interjects a comment about how much he is leaving out, as if overwhelmed by his abundant sources. Mormon makes no effort to hide his part in constructing the book. The entire *Book of Mormon* is an elaborate framed tale of Mormon telling about a succession of prophets telling about their encounters with God. Read in the twenty-first century, the book seems almost postmodern in its self-conscious attention to the production of the text.[11]

Mormon introduces a large number of characters and places into his saga. Nearly 350 names are listed in the pronunciation guide at the back of modern editions—Paanchi, Pachus, Pacumeni, Pagag, Pahoran, Palestina, Pathros.[12] Quite out of nowhere, Mormon describes a system of weights and measures in senines, seons, shums, and limnahs, following a numerical system based on eight rather than the conventional ten. He moves the armies, the prophets, and the people about on a landscape, taking time to sketch in the geography of the Nephite nation. Naturally, Mormon the general gives special attention to armaments, military tactics, and battles.[13] Architecture, animals, and trade are dealt with. Although the book is above all a religious history of prophesying, preaching, faithfulness, and apostasy, Mormon evokes an entire world.

Among the leading characters are Nephi, the unbendingly good younger brother; Sariah, the dutiful, outspoken mother; Benjamin, the righteous king who speaks to his people from a tower; Ammon, the warrior missionary who wins hearts by faithfully serving a Lamanite king; Alma, the prodigal son who is converted like Paul and becomes a champion of the gospel; the hot-blooded General Moroni; Samuel, the brave Lamanite prophet who stands on a wall to warn the Nephites until they drive him away. Then there are the heretics, Sherem, Nehor, and Korihor, who challenge the Nephites with wayward dogmas ranging from universalism to atheism. Korihor, the atheist, claimed that belief was the "effect of a phrensied mind," and that "every man prospered according to his genius, and that every man conquered according to his strength."[14] Along with the heretics are the villains Kishkumen, the assassin of judges, and Gadianton, the organizer of secret bands for robbery and murder. Such characters and their stories are incorporated into the broader account of peoples prospering and failing and civilizations rising and falling.

A writer in 1841 commented that "it is difficult to imagine a more difficult literary task than to write what may be termed a continuation of the Scriptures." Yet Joseph Smith dictated the bulk of the *Book of Mormon* from early April to late June 1829. When forays for food, travel from Harmony to Fayette, and applications to printers are deducted, the amount of time available for translating most of the book's 584 pages was less than three months.[15]

CRITICISM

Even before the *Book of Mormon* was published in March 1830, the press had an explanation for its creation. In its first announcement in June 1829, the *Wayne Sentinel* commented that "most people entertain an idea that the whole matter is the result of a gross imposition, and a grosser superstition." The book was part of a scheme to swindle gullible victims. In this case, Martin Harris, "an honest and industrious farmer," was thought to be Joseph Smith's mark. Everyone else in town, the *Palmyra Freeman* reported, treated the gold plates story "as it should have been—with *contempt*."[16] They discouraged publication to stop Joseph Smith from ensnaring more victims like Harris.

In a slightly more philosophical spirit, the editors offered an additional explanation. They placed Joseph Smith in a long line of false prophets beginning with Muhammad. Abner Cole, the obstreperous editor of the *Palmyra Reflector*, listed a set of examples as he began his account of Joseph Smith: "By way of introduction, and illustration, we shall introduce brief notices and sketches of the superstitions of the ancients—the pretended science of alchymy . . . of Mahomet (properly Mahommed) and other ancient impostures . . . the Morristown Ghost, Rogers, Walters, Joanna Southcote, Jemima Wilkinson, &c."

Joseph was categorized as a false prophet with the usual following of ignorant dupes. Hapless uneducated souls always stood ready to believe the most extravagant tales. As Cole put it: "The page of history informs us, that from time immemorial, MAN has more or less been the dupe of superstitious error and imposition; so much so, that some writers in derision have called him 'a religious animal,' and it often happens that the more absurd the *dogma*, the more greedily will it be swallowed."

The categories were well entrenched and beyond contradiction; the only question was why Joseph Smith's appearance in an enlightened age. "It was hardly to be expected, that a *mummery* like the one in question, should have been gotten up at so late a period, and among a people, *professing* to be enlightened."[17] In mock despair, Cole lamented the failure of humanity to progress.

The categories of false prophet, superstition, and dupe so commanded the thinking of most editors that credit has to be given to the best informed of the early critics, Alexander Campbell, for reading enough of the *Book of Mormon* to offer a reasoned critique. Founder of the Disciples of Christ and one of the country's most notable theologians and preachers, Campbell turned his attention to the *Book of Mormon* when Mormon missionaries made converts in one of his strongholds in northeastern Ohio in 1830 and 1831 and won over Sidney Rigdon, a luminary in Campbell's reformed Baptist movement. Campbell's critique appeared in his own *Millennial Harbinger* on February 7, 1831, and was reprinted in Boston in 1832 under the title *Delusions: An Analysis of the Book of Mormon; with an Examination of Its Internal and External Evidences, and Refutation of Its Pretences to Divine Authority.* The words "internal and external evidences" in the title referred to the usual methods for proving the Bible in Campbell's time, indicating he took the *Book of Mormon* seriously.

Campbell thought Joseph Smith was "as ignorant and as impudent a knave as ever wrote a book." He had cobbled together fragments of American Protestant culture, mixed theological opinions with politics, and presented the whole in Yankee vernacular. The book had touches of anti-Masonry and republican government, interspersed with opinions on all the contemporary theological questions: "infant baptism, ordination, the trinity, regeneration, repentance, justification, the fall of man, the atonement, transubstantiation, fasting, penance, church government, religious experience, the call to the ministry, the general resurrection, eternal punishment."

For Campbell, the *Book of Mormon* was anything but another Bible. "I would as soon compare a bat to the American eagle, a mouse to a mammoth . . . as to contrast it with a single chapter in all the writings of the Jewish or Christian prophets." Here was an awkward effort to treat "every error and almost every truth discussed in N. York for the last ten years."[18]

Campbell dismissed the intricate plot and the huge array of characters as "romance." Subsequent critics were less dismissive. They felt they had to explain the origins of the *Book of Mormon*'s complex story. The problem, as one newspaper editor wrote in 1839, was to account for a work "being evidently the production of a cultivated mind, yet found in the hands of an exceedingly ignorant illiterate person."[19] Two years after Campbell's pamphlet, an explanation was forthcoming from Eber D. Howe, the editor of the *Painesville Telegraph*, a few miles from Mormon headquarters in Kirtland. In 1834, Howe published the findings of Doctor Philastus Hurlbut, an excommunicated Mormon and a violent enemy of Joseph Smith who had been employed by followers of Campbell to collect derogatory reports on Smith. Hurlbut found a half dozen old-timers in Conneaut, Ohio, who thought the *Book of Mormon* resembled a novel written twenty years earlier by Solomon Spaulding, a Dartmouth graduate and former town resident. The Conneaut people swore that the Spaulding story described lost tribes of Israel moving from Jerusalem to America led by characters named Nephi and Lehi. One deponent remembered the names Moroni and Zarahemla.[20]

Hurlbut tracked down Spaulding's widow, who was living in Massachusetts, and eventually located a manuscript called "Manuscript Found." Spaulding's story told of a party of Romans blown off course en route to Britain during the heyday of the Roman Empire. Landing in America, the Romans lived among the Indian tribes and wrote an account of their experiences addressed to future generations. Spaulding purportedly discovered the parchments and translated them from the Latin. To Hurlbut's disappointment, none of the telltale names cited by his informants appeared in the novel, and the story bore little resemblance to the *Book of Mormon* apart from the migration to the New World. Hurlbut concluded his deponents must have had another manuscript in mind and laid the "Manuscript Found" aside. Piecing together one surmise after another, he and Howe decided that Sidney Rigdon, the only Mormon with the wit to write the *Book of Mormon*, had obtained Spaulding's non-extant second manuscript in Pittsburgh, where Spaulding had submitted his work for publication and where Rigdon had lived for a time. According to the theory, Rigdon transformed the novel into the *Book of Mormon* by adding the religious parts. He conveyed the manuscript to Smith without being detected, and then pretended to be converted when the missionaries brought the *Book of Mormon* to Kirtland in 1830. Given the complexity of the book, there had to have been "from the beginning of the imposture, a more talented knave behind the curtain."[21]

The Spaulding theory remained the standard explanation of the *Book of*

Mormon for more than a century. As long as thirty and forty years after the book's publication, new witnesses were discovered, linking Rigdon to the manuscript and verifying the resemblances between the two works. In the 1860s, accounts of Joseph Smith's early life began to make references to shadowy strangers in the neighborhood, presumably Rigdon smuggling in the manuscript, even though Rigdon, still alive at the time, vigorously denied it.[22] The theory was elaborated year after year as witnesses remembered incriminating facts they had forgotten earlier.

The downfall of the Spaulding theory began in 1884 when "Manuscript Found"—still never published and subsequently lost—turned up in Hawaii and came into the hands of James Fairchild, president of Oberlin College. In an article on the Spaulding theory, Fairchild concluded that the manuscript Hurlbut found was the novel that the witnesses remembered and that the alleged second manuscript never existed. He said evidence for any Spaulding manuscript coming into the hands of Rigdon and thence to Smith was tenuous. Although conservative in his judgment, Fairchild concluded that the theory did not hold water.[23]

Around the turn of the nineteenth century, a few students of Mormonism—I. Woodbridge Riley, Theodore Schroeder, and Walter Prince—offered a new explanation of the *Book of Mormon*'s composition. They did not so much refute Spaulding as supply an alternate theory in the spirit of Alexander Campbell. The book, these authors hypothesized, showed signs of Joseph Smith's psychology and culture, and so must be his work. In 1945, Fawn Brodie, whose biography was acknowledged by non-Mormon scholars as the premier study of Joseph Smith, explicitly rebutted the Spaulding theory, noting chronological inconsistencies, dubious testimonies, and the absence of evidence for a link to Rigdon. Brodie turned instead to the analysis of Riley and, before him, Campbell. The *Book of Mormon* was best explained, Brodie argued, by Joseph Smith's "responsiveness to the provincial opinions of his time."[24] Interest in the Spaulding theory revived in 1977 when handwriting experts speculated that Spaulding's writing appeared in the original manuscript of the *Book of Mormon*, but on further consideration the experts backed off, and the theory assumed the status of an historiographical artifact without credibility among serious scholars.

The fall of the Spaulding theory turned critical scholarship in a new direction. In the half century since Brodie, all the critics have assumed that Joseph Smith wrote the *Book of Mormon*. They have pointed to the signs of its nineteenth-century production, on the one hand, and the lack of supporting archeological evidence in the supposed *Book of Mormon* lands, on the other. In one sense, the modern critics have perpetuated the older project of proving the fraudulence of the *Book of Mormon* by showing it is not the historical text it claims to be; in another sense, latter-day critics have broken with their predecessors. Much of the current critical scholarship comes from disaffected former Mormons who are still fascinated by Mormon texts. Some have sought less to destroy Mormonism than to reshape it. Much of their work is supported by Smith Research Associates or the Smith-Pettit Foundation and is published by Signature Books, all headed by George D. Smith, a San Francisco businessman with a Mormon pedigree. Much of this scholarship aims to convince readers that the *Book of Mormon* can be inspiring even if it is not historically authentic, much as critical readings of the Bible do not foreclose its use as a devotional text.[25] They do not deny the book's "interesting and impressive literary, theological, psychological, and spiritual qualities"; they claim that "such writing can be as powerful in providing people with spiritual guidance as non-fiction." These critics want to make Joseph Smith a compelling religious writer rather than a visionary revelator, adopting the posture of enlightened friends trying to persuade Mormons to adjust to the modern world.[26]

The modern critics write with the same confidence as the nineteenth-century skeptics. They are certain that any reasonable person who takes an objective, scientific approach to the *Book of Mormon* will recognize "the obvious fictional quality" of the book. They point to evidence in the book of the anti-Masonic agitation stirring New York in the years when it was being translated. In the doctrinal portions, they see anti-Universalist language and imitations of camp-meeting preaching. The critics complain that the Isaiah passages quoted by Nephi draw upon portions of the book now thought to be pseudepigrapha, composed long after the Nephites left Jerusalem. Turning to archeology, they point out that archeological digs have produced no evidence of Nephite civilization, yielding no horse bones, for example, an animal named in the *Book of Mormon*. Most recently, an anthropological researcher has claimed that Native American DNA samples correspond to Asian patterns, precluding Semitic origins. In view of all the evidence, the critics believe defense of the book's authenticity is hopeless.[27]

Proponents of the *Book of Mormon* face an uphill battle in resisting this onslaught. They not only have to reply to the criticism, they must work against the prevailing belief that the story of the plates and the angel must be fantasy. As Harold Bloom has observed, in modern times "angels violate the law of nature."[28] According to contemporary reasoning, Joseph Smith's story of translating gold plates simply cannot be true. The proponents have to overcome this ingrained disbelief along with the specific criticisms. Yet they refuse to concede that the *Book of Mormon* is no more than inspiring sacred fiction. For them, the value of the book goes beyond the inspiration offered readers. Its historicity is the foundation for believing that Joseph Smith was commissioned by God. To put him in the category of devotional writer, reducing his work to the level of purely human achievement, rips the heart out of Mormon belief.[29]

With so much at stake, the proponents are as energetic and ingenious as the critics in mustering support for the historicity of the *Book of Mormon*. On the whole better trained, with more technical language skills than their opponents, they are located mainly at Brigham Young University and associated with the Foundation for Ancient Research and Mormon Studies (FARMS).[30] As a loosely coordinated group, they are as assiduous in demonstrating the historical authenticity of the book as the critics are in situating it in the nineteenth century. The two scholarships almost mirror one another, one drawing parallels with nineteenth-century culture and the other with antiquity.[31]

The proponents are not searching for a single conclusive proof that the *Book of Mormon* is ancient; instead they draw attention to scores of details that resemble the local color and cultural forms of ancient Hebrew culture, many of them unknown even to scholars when Joseph Smith was writing. They find passages written in the Hebrew poetic form of chiasmus, where a series of statements reverses at a midpoint and repeats itself in reverse order.[32] The proponents note how chapters about a Nephite king bestowing his crown on his son conform to the coronation rituals of antiquity. The "reformed Egyptian" in the *Book of Mormon*, the proponents say, compares to ancient Meroitic, which used Egyptian characters to write Meroitic words. The extended parable of the olive orchard in Jacob 5 reveals an accurate understanding of olive tree culture. In response to the absence of horse bones in Latin American archeology, the proponents point out that no archeological evidence of horses has been found in regions occupied by the Huns, a society dependent on horses. Proponents are quick to note that a *Book of Mormon* archeological site in the Middle East has been tentatively located. The *Book of Mormon* describes Lehi's journey down the Arabian peninsula and directly east to the Gulf of Arabia. Here Lehi's people came upon a pocket of fertile land and bounteous food in an otherwise desert area. A site in Oman fulfills many of the *Book of Mormon* requirements. Along this route, a site has been located that bears the name "Nhm," corresponding to the name Nahom given in the *Book of Mormon* as one stop on Lehi's journey.[33] On point after point, the proponents answer the critics and assemble their own evidence.[34] Unlike the critics, they do not claim their case is conclusive; they accumulate evidence, but admit belief in the *Book of Mormon* requires faith.[35]

One of the most interesting turns in recent Mormon argumentation is a revised conception of the extent of *Book of Mormon* lands. Early readers assumed the *Book of Mormon* people ranged up and down North and South America from upstate New York to Chile. A close reading of the text reveals it cannot sustain such an expansive geography. Measured by journeys on foot, events occurred much closer to one another than previously thought. The entire area, these scholars now estimate, was perhaps 500 miles long and 200 miles wide, a patch of land comparable in size to ancient Palestine.

Under this thesis, other people may have simultaneously inhabited the land. In fact, tiny hints of their presence turn up in the text, leaving room for the conventional Bering Strait migrations that dominate the standard explanations of Western Hemisphere populations.[36]

Mormon's proponents have received a little help from outside scholars in the *Book of Mormon* wars.[37] One early reader, perhaps the only non-Mormon of her time to find any merit in the *Book of Mormon*, sensed some of the book's genius. Writing in a New York newspaper in 1841, "Josephine" judged the *Book of Mormon* "remarkably free from any allusions that might betray a knowledge of the present political or social state of the world. The writer lives in the whole strength of his imagination in the age he portrays."[38] In more recent times, Cyrus Gordon, the maverick Semiticist, has argued for multiple transatlantic contacts in the pre-Columbian period, including ones from the Middle East. He finds traces of many Eastern Hemisphere cultures at American sites.[39] Here and there a few others pick out authentic Middle Eastern qualities in the text.[40] Recently a pair of Protestant evangelical critics gave the work of the proponents a serious review. Trying to warn their slumbering colleagues of the mounting body of work, the pair concluded that "the increased sophistication of LDS scholarly apologetic is clearly seen in their approach to the *Book of Mormon*." "LDS academicians are producing serious research which desperately needs to be critically examined."[41]

INDIANS

The efforts to situate the *Book of Mormon* in history, whether ancient or modern, run up against baffling complexities. The Book of Mormon resists conventional analysis, whether sympathetic or critical. Early Mormons themselves had trouble grasping the book's nature. When required to offer a brief summary, they often called it a history of the Indians. Samuel Smith, Joseph's brother, on a tour to win followers in 1830, tried to sell the book as "history of the origins of the Indians." Joseph himself wrote a newspaper editor in 1833 that "the Book of Mormon is a record of the forefathers of our western Tribes of Indians." Outsiders saw it the same way. Abner Cole described the end of the Nephites as the time when "God sent the *small pox* among them, which killed two thirds of them, and turned the rest into Indians." Almost as frequently as the book was called a "gold bible" it was called a history of the Indians.[42]

While the Indian label intrigued potential readers, it obscured as much as it revealed. The label does not help, for one thing, with the puzzle of motivation. Why would an uneducated farmer write a lengthy volume on the origins of the Indians? Nothing in Joseph Smith's immediate environment propelled him to investigate Indians. The question of origins was not a pressing issue for New York's rural population in 1830. By the 1790s, the great Iroquois tribes had been driven away by warfare or decimated by disease. According to the *Wayne Sentinel*, only 4,820 Indians remained in the state in 1829. Most lived on a half dozen small reservations in the woods on the edges of the towns.[43] Indian relics turned up in newly plowed furrows, and remnants of old forts and burial mounds were accessible to the curious, but none was known in Palmyra or Manchester. In this post-Indian environment, the Smiths exhibited no particular interest in the original occupants of the land until Joseph got involved with the gold plates.[44] Andrew Jackson's presidential campaign of 1828 revived talk about the old Indian fighter's earlier campaigns. A second edition of Daniel Clarke Sanders's *A History of the Indian Wars with the First Settlers of the United States*, published in Rochester in 1828, discoursed about Indian culture and speculated about probable origins. It mentioned theories about a wayward Carthaginian vessel, about "Malayans," Laplanders, the Kamschatkans, Scythians, Israelites, the Tungusi in northern Asia, and Egyptians. Sanders inclined toward some form of migration from Asia as the best explanation of Indian origins, possibly via the Bering Strait, possibly when the continents were joined, or perhaps by boat. An essay in the *Palmyra Herald* in 1823 propounded roughly the same idea: "The first settlers of North America were probably the Asiatics, the descendants of Shem." "The Asiatics at an early period, might easily have crossed the Pacific Ocean and made settlements in North America."[45] Although pundits were propounding theories, there is no reason to think the Smiths brooded over these possibilities.

Among the welter of speculations in the 1820s, the lost tribes theory with which the *Book of Mormon* is associated stood out. According to this view, Indians descended from the lost ten tribes of Israel carried away by the Assyrians in the eighth century BCE. Though popular because of the biblical connection, the ten tribes theory did not command universal assent. *A History of the Indian Wars* devoted only a few sentences to the possible Israelite origins of the Indians. In the Palmyra newspapers, the lost ten tribes went unmentioned in the scattering of articles about Indian origins, save for one report on the theories of Mordecai Noah, a Jewish eccentric who designated an island in the St. Lawrence River as a gathering place for Jews.[46] At Dartmouth, where Hyrum Smith briefly attended Moor's Charity School in the 1810s, many hypotheses about Indian origins were propounded by Professor John Smith, a distant relative of Joseph's, but he came down against the Israelite theory. Smith told his students, "It is almost certain the aboriginal inhabitants of America are not the descendants of Jews, Christians, or Mahometans because no trace of their religions have ever been found among them."[47]

Though not predominant, the lost tribes theory did appeal to religious thinkers eager to link Indians to the Bible. From the seventeenth century onward, both Christians and Jews had collected evidence that the Indians had Jewish origins. Jonathan Edwards Jr. noted the similarities between the Hebrew and Mohican languages. Such Indian practices as "anointing their heads, paying a price for their wives, observing the feast of harvest" were cited as Jewish parallels.[48] Besides Edwards, John Eliot, Samuel Sewall, Roger Williams, William Penn, James Adair, and Elias Boudinot expressed opinions or wrote treatises on the Israelite connection.

Did any of this speculation filter down to Joseph Smith? The evidence compiled by the Israelite school was summarized in an 1823 volume, *View of the Hebrews*, by Ethan Smith, a Congregational minister in Poultney, Vermont. Since Oliver Cowdery's family lived in Poultney, and Cowdery did not leave until after the book's publication, critics have speculated that *View of the Hebrews* might have fallen into Joseph Smith's hands and inspired the *Book of Mormon*.[49] Both books speak of migrations from Palestine to America and of a great civilization now lost; both describe a division that pitted a civilized against a savage branch with the higher civilization falling to the lower; both books elicit sympathy for a chosen people fallen into decay. Even though Joseph Smith is not known to have seen *View of the Hebrews* until later in his life, the parallels seem strong enough for critics to argue that Ethan Smith provided the seeds for Joseph Smith's later composition.

But for readers of Ethan Smith, the *Book of Mormon* was a disappointment. It was not a treatise about the origins of the Indians, regardless of what early Mormons said. The *Book of Mormon* never used the word "Indian." The book had a different form and purpose than the earlier works on Indian origins. The assembling of anthropological evidence was the central endeavor of *View of the Hebrews* and the books that preceded it. Ethan Smith and his predecessors looked for signs of a deteriorating Jewish culture in Indian society, ticking off instances such as similarities in sacrifices and feasts. The *Book of Mormon* gave almost no attention to Old Testament parallels; its prophets taught pure Christianity. *View of the Hebrews* was an anthropological treatise, combining scripture and empirical evidence to propound a theory. The *Book of Mormon* was a narrative, not a treatise. Anyone looking for a scientific investigation of Indian origins in its pages would have found ancient American Christianity instead.

Early Mormons disregarded the differences in their book and the writings on Indian culture. They eagerly cited all of the scholarship about the original inhabitants of North and South America as proof of the book's accuracy. The editor of the Mormon newspaper *Times and Seasons* was thrilled by John L. Stephens's immensely popular *Incidents of Travel in Central America, Chiapas, and Yucatan in 1841*. In the Saints' eyes, all reports on the glories of ancient American civilization vindicated the *Book of Mormon*. Among the rest, they casually cited Ethan Smith's work to prove the validity of the Hebrew connection.[50] But their *Book of Mormon* was another kind of book.

When other authors delved into Indian origins, they were explicit about recognizable Indian practices and the location of particular tribes. Solomon Spaulding's romance had characters traveling through a recognizable landscape from the east coast to the "Owaho" river formed by the confluence of two great rivers. There they met a people called "Kentucks" and another called "Delewans."[51] A reader going through Spaulding's pages could readily locate Indian places on a modern map. Burial mounds in his manuscript reminded readers of modern remains. Readers easily oriented themselves in time and place on an Indian landscape.

The *Book of Mormon* deposited its people on some unknown shore—not even definitely identified as America—and had them live out their history in a remote place in a distant time, using names that had no connections to modern Indians. All modern readers had to go on was the reference to a "narrow neck of land."[52] Lacking specific orientation points, Mormon scholars still debate the location of the Nephite nation.[53] Once here, the *Book of Mormon* people are not given an Indian character. None of the trademark Indian items appear in the *Book of Mormon*'s pages. In his parody of the *Book of Mormon*, Cole dressed his characters in blankets and moccasins. They traveled in bark canoes and suffered from smallpox. Spaulding's Indians lived in wigwams and raised corn, beans, and squash.[54] The *Book of Mormon* contains none of the identifying words like squaw, papoose, wampum, peace pipes, tepees, braves, feathers, and no canoes, moccasins, or corn. Burial mounds, supposedly a stimulus for investigation of the Indians, receive only the slightest mention.[55] Nephites and Lamanites fought with bows and arrows, but also with swords, cimeters, slings, and shields, more like classical warriors than Native Americans. The closest the book comes to an Indian identification is the description of Lamanites as bloodthirsty and bare-chested. Neglecting to scatter obvious clues through its pages, the *Book of Mormon* seems more focused on its own Christian message than on Indian anthropology. The book refuses to argue its own theory.[56]

LAMANITES

Despite the absences in the text, the *Book of Mormon* has been universally thought of as an attempted history of the American Indians. One of the evidences, in the critics' view, is its blatant racism. Not far into the story, the Lamanites, the presumed ancestors of the Indians, are marked with a dark skin: "The Lord God did cause a skin of blackness to come upon them."

This act resembles the curse of God on Cain in Genesis, the beginning, according to later Christian readings, of the black race. In the Book of Mormon, the curse comes because of the Lamanites' stubborn adherence to a false tradition about Nephi's usurpation of authority. These troublesome ideas about skin color are followed with stereotypical descriptions of Lamanite savagery. The Lamanites are "an idle people, full of mischief and subtlety, and did seek in the wilderness for beasts of prey." Ferocious and bloodthirsty, half-naked and garbed in skins, they launch unprovoked attacks on civilized Nephite cities.[57] These passages sound like the Jacksonian view of Indians common to most Americans in 1830.

But the fact that these wild people are Israel, the chosen of God, adds a level of complexity to the *Book of Mormon* that simple racism does not explain. Incongruously, the book champions the Indians' place in world history, assigning them a more glorious future than modern American whites. All the derogatory descriptions of Lamanites notwithstanding, the Indians emerge as God's chosen people. They are not viewed as a pathetic civilization moving inevitably toward their doom, as sympathetic observers in Joseph's time depicted them.[58] According to the *Book of Mormon*, the Lamanites are destined to be restored to favor with God and given this land, just as Jews are to be restored to the Holy Land. A similar ambivalence about Indians runs through all Christian missionary efforts in these years, but the *Book of Mormon* carries it to an extreme. While the Lamanites are cursed and degraded, they are also at times the most righteous of all the *Book of Mormon* peoples. In one episode, as the Lamanites bury their weapons and refuse to fight, a narrator asks, "Has there been so great love in all the land? Behold, I say unto you, Nay, there has not even among the Nephites." At one point the Nephites become so wicked, a Lamanite prophet calls them to repentance. Lamanite degradation is not ingrained in their natures, ineluctably bonded to their dark skins. Their wickedness is wholly cultural and frequently reversed. During one period, "they began to be a very industrious people; yea, and they were friendly with the Nephites; therefore, they did open a correspondence with them, and the curse of God did no more follow them." In the end, the Lamanites triumph. The white Nephites perish, and the dark Lamanites remain.[59]

In its very nature, the *Book of Mormon* overturns conventional American racism. The book makes Indians the founders of civilization in the New World. The master history of America's origins is not about Columbus or the Puritans but about native peoples. History is imagined from the ancient inhabitants' point of view. European migrants are called "Gentiles" in the *Book of Mormon* and come onstage as interlopers. They appear late in the narrative and remain secondary to the end. The land belongs to the Indians.[60]

The primary role of the Gentiles is to serve the natives, to build them up by bringing them the Bible and the *Book of Mormon*. If the Gentiles fail to help Israel, they are doomed. After nourishing the remnant of Jacob, they must join Israel or perish.[61] If they don't choose Israel, the native peoples will terrorize the Gentiles. Christ tells the *Book of Mormon* people that "ye shall be among them, as a lion among the beasts of the forest, and as a young lion among the flocks of sheep, who, if he goeth through, both treadeth down and teareth in pieces." One might expect predictions of violent retribution against whites in the writings of a black abolitionist like David Walker, who predicted the vengeance of God on slaveholders for their abuse of African slaves, but it is extraordinary coming from a white northern farmer speaking about Indians. As one scholar puts it, the *Book of Mormon* is a "ruthlessly tragic narrative that chronicles the destruction of the white race and foresees the fruition of the dark race."[62] The *Book of Mormon* is not just sympathetic to Indians; it grants them dominance—in history, in God's esteem, and in future ownership of the American continent.

THE BIBLE

All the efforts to situate the *Book of Mormon* in the nineteenth century are frustrated by contradictions like these. The book elusively slides off the point on one crucial issue after another. Mormons talked up the *Book of Mormon* as an explanation of Indian origins, but the book does little to identify its peoples with Indian culture. The Lamanites are both a cursed and a chosen people. The Indians, targets of prejudice, are also the true possessors of the lands whom the Gentiles must join or perish. The text repeatedly trespasses standard categories.

The *Book of Mormon* is equally perplexing in its comments on the Bible, the book from which Joseph's translation primarily drew its strength. The *Book of Mormon* can be seen as an extension of the Bible, as a mammoth apocryphal work; the modern Church calls it "Another Testament of Jesus Christ." On opening the book, a reader hears the intonations of King James Version diction. Thousands of phrases are common to the Bible and the *Book of Mormon*.[63] Whole chapters of Isaiah are inserted into the text. "My soul delighteth in the words of Isaiah," said the prophet Nephi, who in one stretch copies thirteen consecutive chapters (Isaiah 2–14) onto the plates. In all, twenty-one chapters of Isaiah are reproduced in part or in full, including Isaiah 54, inserted by Christ during his time with the Nephites. The *Book of Mormon* presents itself as offspring of the Bible. If you believe one, the *Book of Mormon* says, you will believe the other. "These last records . . . shall establish the truth of the first."[64]

And yet for all the similarities and mutual confirmations, the *Book of Mormon* challenges the authority of the Bible by breaking the monopoly of the Bible on scriptural truth. Certain passages in the *Book of Mormon* even throw doubt on the Bible's accuracy. Over time, the *Book of Mormon* says, biblical revelation has been depleted. In a vision of the future, Nephi sees the Bible going "forth from the Jews in purity, unto the Gentiles, according to the truth which is in God." But the Gentile church takes away "from the Gospel of the Lamb, many parts which are plain and most precious." The *Book of Mormon*, in other words, declares the Bible to be deficient. "There are many plain and precious things taken away from the Book, which is the Book of the Lamb of God." Later a Mormon article of faith was to say "we believe the Bible to be the word of God as far as it is translated correctly; we also believe the Book of Mormon to be the word of God."[65]

The *Book of Mormon* actually recasts the meaning of the original scriptures by offering what has been called a strong reading of the Bible.[66] Instead of seeing the Bible as a book of holy words, inscribed by the hand of God in stone, the *Book of Mormon* has a rather modern sense of scripture coming out of a people's encounter with God. In places, the prophets grow impatient with those who separate sacred texts from the people who produced them. Speaking to modern Christians, Nephi says: "O fools, they shall have a Bible; and it shall proceed forth from the Jews, mine ancient covenant people. And what thank they the Jews for the Bible which they receive from them? Yea, what do the Gentiles mean? Do they remember the travels, and the labors, and the pains of the Jews, and their diligence unto me, in bringing forth salvation unto the Gentiles?"[67] In the vein of modern scholarship, the passage seems to say that scripture is the product of a people whose labors and pains must be honored along with their records.

Expanding on this idea, the *Book of Mormon* multiplies the peoples keeping sacred records. The Jews have their revelations in Palestine, the Nephites have theirs in the Western Hemisphere. Beyond these two, all the tribes of Israel produce bibles, each containing its own revelation: "For behold, I shall speak unto the Jews, and they shall write it; and I shall also speak unto the Nephites, and they shall write it; and I shall also speak unto the other tribes of the house of Israel, which I have led away, and they shall write it; and I shall also speak unto all nations of the earth, and they shall write it."

Wherever Israel is scattered on "the isles of the sea," prophetic voices are heard and histories recorded. Every nation will receive its measure of revelation: "For behold, the Lord doth grant unto all nations, of their own nation and tongue, to teach his word; yea, in wisdom, all that he seeth fit that they should have."[68] The tiny land of Palestine does not begin to encompass the revelation flooding the earth. Biblical revelation is generalized to the whole world. All peoples have their epic stories and their sacred books.

Though the Bible and the *Book of Mormon* come from the same God, Nephi foresees a contest between the two books. The misguided will cling to the Bible when they should accept new revelation: "And because my words shall hiss forth, many of the Gentiles shall say, A Bible, A Bible, we have got a Bible, and there cannot be any more Bible."

> Wherefore, because that ye have a Bible, ye need not suppose that it contains all my words; neither need ye suppose that I have not caused more to be written: for I command all men, both in the east, and in the west, and in the north, and in the south, and in the islands of the sea, that they shall write the words which I speak unto them.

The world is a hive of bible-making, and in the end all these records will come together, and people will know one another through their bibles. "And it shall come to pass that the Jews shall have the words of the Nephites, and the Nephites shall have the words of the Jews; and the Nephites and the Jews shall have the words of the lost tribes of Israel; and the lost tribes of Israel shall have the words of the Nephites of the Jews."[69] The *Book of Mormon* is but one record in a huge world archive.

In the *Book of Mormon* reading, the Bible becomes not the book of books but the mother scripture for a brood of bibles. Divine revelation cannot be confined; it is delivered wherever people will listen. The *Book of Mormon* not only prepares the way for itself by ridiculing those who think the Bible sufficient; it warns readers against restricting God in the present. Revelation may break forth anywhere and anytime. The hard-hearted pay no heed and despise the words of God. The receptive are instructed line upon line:

> Wo be unto him that shall say, We have received the word of God, and we need no more of the word of God, for we have enough. For behold, thus saith the Lord God: I will give unto the children of men line upon line, precept upon precept, here a little and there a little; and blessed are they that hearken unto my precepts, and lend an ear unto my counsel, for they shall learn wisdom: for unto him that receiveth, I will give more; and from them that shall say, We have enough, from them shall be taken away even that which they have.

Rather than being the sum total of revelation, the Bible is but one example of what should happen even here and now. If *Book of Mormon* reasoning holds true, America should produce its own sacred text. Thus the way is paved for Joseph Smith.[70]

AMERICA AND ISRAEL

The *Book of Mormon* can be read as a nationalist text. The book gives the United States a deep past, reaching back centuries beyond any known his-

tory of the continent to 600 BCE and through the Jaredites even further
back to the Tower of Babel, millennia before Christ. Embedding America
in the Bible necessarily hallowed the nation, but the *Book of Mormon* also
created a subversive competitor to the standard national history.[71] In the
classic version of America's past, the first settlers flee the oppressions of
Europe to establish themselves as a free people in the new land. When
oppressed by their mother country, Americans rise in revolt and establish
an independent empire of liberty. This story makes a cameo appearance in
the *Book of Mormon* in one of Nephi's visions. Nephi sees the Spirit of God
work upon a man (presumably but not indisputably Columbus) who "went
forth upon the many waters, even unto the seed of my brethren, who were
in the promised land." The Spirit then works upon "other Gentiles; and
they went forth out of captivity, upon the many waters." In time "their
mother Gentiles were gathered together upon the waters, and upon the
land also, to battle against them." In the ensuing struggle, presumably the
American Revolution, the power of God delivers these Gentile migrants,
and they go on to "prosper in the land."[72] That was the story that Americans would recognize as their own.

But the American story does not control the narrative. The *Book of Mormon* allots just nine verses to the deliverance of the Gentiles, and the rest of
the book concentrates on the deliverance of Israel. The impending American republic is barely visible. Even at points where it should have been
foreshadowed, such as in the passages on government, republican principles are not sketched in. American constitutionalism is faintly invoked and
then dismissed. *Book of Mormon* governments are monarchies and judgeships, Old Testament governments, not democratic legislatures and elected
presidents. Monarchy is terminated at one point in the *Book of Mormon*,
surely a republican moment, but not by revolution. The king gives up his
throne and persuades his people to change the form of government. He
abdicates rather than the people rising as they should in a proper revolution. The king's recommendations for a new government, moreover, are
not democratic. He recommends a return to judgeships, the primitive form
of Old Testament government before the kingship of Saul, not the establishment of constitutional government. Mosiah is "exceedingly anxious
that every man should have an equal chance," but by equal chance he
means personal responsibility for one's own sins, not an equal opportunity
to get ahead.[73]

There is one apparently democratic gesture at this turning point. The
first judge is selected by the voice of the people. But this step toward
democracy is immediately retraced. Successors to the chief judge inherit
their offices—the aristocratic turn toward the hereditary officeholding
that Americans most feared. Thereafter, judges are appointed. The voice

of the people is consulted only when the former judge's sons fight over the judgment seat or no natural successor is available. These hereditary judges follow traditional law and make additions to the law of the land without the consent of the people. The most valued features of republican government—regular elections, a representative legislature, and checks and balances—are absent. Moreover, throughout the text, church and state are liberally intermixed. The first chief judge is also the high priest, and the prophets and the judges collaborate in ruling the people.[74] Righteous rule is the prophets' object rather than limitations on power.

The *Book of Mormon* does not plant seeds of democracy in the primeval history of the nation. Instead of tracking the history of liberty, as a nationalist work might be expected to do, the *Book of Mormon* endlessly expounds the master biblical narrative—the history of Israel. Israel's covenant with God, Israel's rebellion and apostasy, and Israel's eventual restoration—Isaiah's basic themes—recur nearly a dozen times. Israel, of course, was a metaphor Americans had always applied to themselves, beginning with the Puritans. The term had expanded over the centuries to include the church, the people of God, even the United States as a favored nation. The *Book of Mormon* returned to the Hebrew Bible's more restricted meaning of Israel as a specific nation and a particular people, the actual twelve tribes. The restoration of one tribe, the Jews, was a fixture of the millennial calendar in virtually every account of the last days, but they were usually but one part of the larger triumph of the Christian church, the new Israel. The *Book of Mormon* reversed the emphasis. The restoration of literal Israel was the centerpiece. The rehabilitation of the world was to begin with literal Israel and expand from there.

In the *Book of Mormon*, Gentile Christianity has apostatized. The book repeatedly condemns Gentile religion—for disbelief in revelation and miracles, for preaching for pay, for disregard of the poor, for erasure of key parts of the Bible. Although long favored by God to become a mighty people, the Gentiles have built up false churches as monuments to their own pride. Now they have a choice. They must either join Israel or be cast off. "If the Gentiles shall hearken unto the Lamb of God . . . that they harden not their hearts against the Lamb of God, they shall be numbered among the seed of thy father; yea, they shall be numbered among the House of Israel." But unless they turn to God and ally with Israel, the Gentiles are to be pruned from the natural root and cast aside. All are invited to join—ideally Israel would encompass all nations—but Israel is the central player. God calls upn modern Christians to assist in this work of restoration—and to become Israel themselves.[75]

The implications of restoring Israel remain vague in the *Book of Mormon*. Who are the favored people? In Joseph's time, the only peoples known to be Israel were Jews and (after the *Book of Mormon*) Indians, both outcast groups. Literal Israel consisted of once-chosen ones who had been lost and forgotten and now must be restored. The general import of the Israel story was that the world had come to a turning point when the favor of God was shifting from one people to another. The mighty Gentiles were falling, and forgotten Israel was being restored. The Gentiles must serve these lost ones, the outcasts, and then join them or lose their place in history.

The *Book of Mormon* stood at the center of this pivotal moment. Its appearance was the sign of God's renewed activity. When the voice of an ancient people spoke from the dust, the time of restoration had come. God's great work, moreover, was to be accomplished through the book. It was not only the herald of restoration; the *Book of Mormon* was the instrument for accomplishing it. The book works on the premise that a history— a book—can reconstitute a nation. It assumes that by giving a nation an alternative history, alternative values can be made to grow. As inscribed on the title page by the ancient historian, the book's purpose was "to shew unto the remnant of the House of Israel how great things the LORD hath done for their fathers; and that they may know the covenants of the LORD, that they are not cast off forever." The book was to inform Israel of its true history.

All this turned American history upside down. The story of Israel over- shadowed the history of American liberty. Literal Israel stood at the center of history, not the United States. The book sacralized the land but con- demned the people. The Indians were the chosen ones, not the European interlopers. The *Book of Mormon* was the seminal text, not the Constitution or the Declaration of Independence. The gathering of lost Israel, not the establishment of liberty, was the great work. In the *Book of Mormon*, the bib- lical overwhelms the national.[76]

Taken as a whole, the *Book of Mormon* can be read as a "document of pro- found social protest" against the dominant culture of Joseph Smith's time. That may not have been most readers' first impression. Many converts said it confirmed their old beliefs. The book read like the Bible to them; its gospel was standard Christianity. The book patriotically honored America by giving it a biblical history. And yet on closer reading, the *Book of Mormon* contests the amalgam of Enlightenment, republican, Protestant, capitalist, and nationalist values that constituted American culture. The combination is not working, the book says. America is too Gentile, too worldly, too hard-hearted. The Gentiles "put down the power and miracles of God, and preach up unto themselves, their own wisdom, and their own learning, that they may get gain, and grind upon the faces of the poor." The nation must remember God and restore Israel—or be blasted.[77]

The *Book of Mormon* proposes a new purpose for America: becoming a realm of righteousness rather than an empire of liberty. Against increasing wealth and inequality, the *Book of Mormon* advocates the cause of the poor.[78] Against the subjection of the Indians, it promises the continent to the native people. Against republican government, it proposes righteous rule by judges and kings under God's law. Against a closed-canon Bible and nonmiraculous religion, the *Book of Mormon* stands for ongoing revelation, miracles, and revelation to all nations.[79] Against skepticism, it promotes belief; against nationalism, a universal Israel. It foresees disaster for the nation if the love of riches, resistance to revelation, and Gentile civilization prevail over righteousness, revelation, and Israel. Herman Melville said of Nathaniel Hawthorne, "He says NO! in thunder." A NO can be heard in the *Book of Mormon*'s condemnation of an America without righteousness.[80]

A REVELATION OF JOSEPH SMITH

The *Book of Mormon*, the longest and most complex of Joseph Smith's revelations, by rights should have been written in his maturity, not when he was twenty-three. Emerson, Joseph's nearly exact contemporary, was still finding his voice when he was that age, with only his journals to show for his extensive study. Joseph dictated the *Book of Mormon* without any practice runs or previous writing experience. It came in a rush, as if the thoughts had been building for decades.[81] Talking to her son late in her life, Emma remembered how fluidly Joseph dictated:

> When acting as his scribe he would dictate to me hour after hour, and when returning after meals or after interruptions, he could at once begin where he had left off, without either seeing the mss or having any portion of it read to him. This was a usual thing for him to do. It would have been improbable that a learned man could do this, and for so ignorant and unlearned as he was it was simply impossible.

During the three months of rapid translation, Joseph seemed to be in the grip of creative forces outside himself, the pages pouring from his mind like *Messiah* from the pen of Handel.[82]

Dictating so rapidly, he must have spoken from his heart. In some respects, the *Book of Mormon* can be seen as a revelation of Joseph Smith as well as a translation of the gold plates. Indeed some scholars have reduced the book to almost pure autobiography. They account for virtually every character and every incident by locating precedents in Joseph's personal history. Though illuminating at times, when carried to extremes these attempts break down; the parallels are too tenuous, too inconclusive. Are we really to believe that wicked King Noah is a version of Joseph Smith Sr. because both drank wine? Biographical analysis runs the risk of making creative works little more than a mirror of the author's life. As one critic puts it, "the book is far grander, much broader, and its internal logic and power go well beyond the life of Joseph Smith."[83]

Still, in places, one can imagine Joseph seeing himself in the text, as a year later he was to discover himself in his revelations about Moses and Enoch. Did the prophet Jacob capture one of Joseph's moods in saying the *Book of Mormon* migrants from Jerusalem felt like "a lonesome and a solemn people, wanderers cast out from Jerusalem"? A later revelation said Enoch's people "confessed they were strangers and pilgrims on the earth."[84] If Joseph felt lonesome and estranged like the people in his writings, his campaign for Zion could be interpreted as making a home for outcasts and wanderers—like his own struggling family.

At the very least, the *Book of Mormon* may outline possibilities for a young man still forming his own identity. Nephi, the leading character in its opening books, was, like Joseph, a strong younger brother, the one to have visions and teach the others. Joseph had no rival brothers like Nephi's Laman and Lemuel, but Nephi did set a pattern for taking charge of a family in place of one's father and older brother. Nephi was a model in his weakness too. He led his people through the wilderness, defended them against enemies, and eventually allowed them to make him a king, and yet lamented his inability to overcome his own sins. In one passage, sometimes labeled "the Psalm of Nephi," Nephi laments:

> O wretched man that I am; yea, my heart sorroweth, because of my flesh. My soul grieveth, because of mine iniquities. I am encompassed about, because of the temptations and the sins which do so easily beset me. And when I desire to rejoice, my heart groaneth because of my sins.

One can imagine the young Joseph hearing echoes of his own humiliation at having backslid after the First Vision. Throughout his life, he was overcome with anguish for his personal weakness. A few years later, he wrote to Emma, "I have Called to mind all the past moments of my life and am left to morn and Shed tears of sorrow for my folly in Sufering the adversary of my Soul to have so much power over me." Nephi's words convey some of that same desperation. Borne down by his sorrow, Nephi cried out, "O Lord, wilt thou encircle me around in the robe of thy righteousness? O Lord, wilt thou make a way for mine escape before mine enemies? Wilt thou make my path straight before me? . . . O Lord, I have trusted in thee, and I will trust in thee forever."[85] Religion here is called on to heal the wounds inflicted by sin.

We can only conjecture about how the *Book of Mormon* interacted with Joseph's inner life, but the book does shed light on the struggle between Joseph the treasure-seeking magician of the neighbors' reports and Joseph the earnest young Christian of his own autobiography. If the book is evidence of Joseph's religious character in 1830, the Christian had won out. God hovers over everything in the *Book of Mormon*, rebuking, promising, warning. With unrelenting diligence, the prophets teach Christ. Magic figures in its pages no more than in the Bible. Sin and redemption define the great issues, not arcane formulas for eluding guardian spirits. The book thinks like the Bible.[86]

The *Book of Mormon* also makes religion a public concern. Its religion has a broader scope than the salvation of individuals. Sermons are directed to kings and cities with the intent of converting whole societies. Mormon charts the spiritual health of the whole Nephite people, knowing their fate hangs on their corporate faith. The rise and fall of a civilization over a thousand-year period depends on national righteousness.[87] Individuals suffer in the concluding debacles—Mormon, Moroni, Coriantumr, Ether—but the epic tragedy is the obliteration of two nations. The Nephites and the Jaredites are ultimately the book's protagonists. They illustrate the book's main point that submission to God is necessary for society to survive. The *Book of Mormon* shows an Old Testament—or Puritan—concern for national sin and the fate of entire peoples. The book prepares us for the Joseph who would construct a world religious capital and run for president of the United States.

It is hard to tell what aspects of the *Book of Mormon* appealed to the early converts. Did they find themselves in the book as Joseph did? They never explained why they believed; they simply found it convincing. When the book fell into the hands of Parley Pratt, he "read all day; eating was a burden, I had no desire for food; sleep was a burden when the night came, for I preferred reading to sleep." Pratt said nothing about what gripped him except that "as I read, the spirit of the Lord was upon me, and I knew and comprehended that the book was true, as plainly and manifestly as a man comprehends and knows that he exists." For others, the very idea of the book was an attraction. Hyrum Smith handed Ezra Thayer a copy during a meeting in the Smiths' yard. "I said, let me see it. I then opened the book, and I received a shock with such exquisite joy that no pen can write and no tongue can express." All this without reading a word. When Thayer opened the book again, he felt "a double portion of the Spirit." "I did not know whether I was in the world or not. I felt as though I was truly in heaven."[88]

Considering the book's contents, it is not likely that converts believed because the *Book of Mormon* explained the Indians or because it stirred their resentments against the established social order, both of which could be overlooked in a rapid reading. The manifest message of the *Book of Mormon* is Christ's atonement for the world's sins. The Christian gospel overwhelms everything else—Indian origins, race, the Bible, America. No reader could miss the Christian themes. As the subtitle now says, it was another testament of Jesus Christ. The closing words of Moroni summed up the message:

> Yea, come unto Christ, and be perfected in him, and deny yourselves of all ungodliness; and if ye shall deny yourselves of all ungodliness, and love God with all your might, mind and strength, then is his grace sufficient for you, that by his grace ye may be perfect in Christ; and if by the grace of God ye are perfect in Christ, ye can in no wise deny the power of God. And again, if ye, by the grace of God are perfect in Christ, and deny not his power, then are ye sanctified in Christ by the grace of God, through the shedding of the blood of Christ, which is in the covenant of the Father, unto the remission of your sins, that ye become holy without spot.[89]

Passages like this anchored Mormonism in orthodox Christianity. In later years, Joseph's revelations redefined the nature of God and man so radically that Mormonism has been seen as a departure from traditional Christianity as serious as Christianity's from Judaism.[90] The critics have questioned if the temple, priesthood, baptism for the dead, and plural marriage were Christian at all. But however extensive the innovations, the Saints never left basic Christianity behind; the *Book of Mormon*, their third testament, held them to the fundamentals. Joseph Smith called it the "key stone of our religion." A few decades later, higher criticism would undermine faith in the orthodox gospel. Many Christians came to doubt the scriptures, the divinity of Christ, and the efficacy of the atonement. In that turbulent time, the *Book of Mormon* bound Mormons to traditional belief. The higher criticism could not unsettle people who had overcome much greater difficulties in accepting the *Book of Mormon*.[91]

FIVE

THE CHURCH OF CHRIST

1830

Joseph stood on the shore when his father came out of the water and as he took him by the hand he cried out Oh! My God I have lived to see my father baptized into the true church of Jesus christ and he covered his face . . . in his fathers bosom and wept aloud for joy as did Joseph of old when he beheld his father coming up into the land of Egypt.

LUCY SMITH, Preliminary Manuscript, 1844–45

SOMETIME IN EARLY 1830, Joseph Knight Sr. picked up Joseph Smith at his house in Harmony and drove him to Palmyra, where the elder Smiths were living with Hyrum in the old Smith cabin. On the way, Joseph told Knight "there must be a Church formed." Knight said he was not told the day, but Joseph had a precise date in mind. He had made the long journey to Palmyra twice the previous winter, to stop Abner Cole's plagiarism and to keep Grandin at work on the *Book of Mormon*, but both times had returned to Harmony without forming a church. Organization of the "Church of Christ" had to wait until April 6, the date given by revelation, probably as far back as the summer of 1829.[1]

The location of the Church's organization has become a matter of historical debate. In his 1838 history, Joseph said the organization took place at the Whitmer house in Fayette; in an 1842 letter to John Wentworth, a Chicago newspaperman, Joseph said Manchester. Although Fayette has been accepted traditionally as the place, the evidence for Manchester is not insubstantial. Historians have speculated that a Fayette meeting shortly after April 6 was confused with the Manchester organizational meeting. The official organizers for legal purposes were Joseph Smith Jr., Oliver Cowdery, Hyrum Smith, Peter Whitmer Jr., Samuel H. Smith, and David Whitmer. Whitmer spoke of forty or fifty others in attendance.[2]

In Joseph's account, after the meeting was opened with "solemn prayer," he asked if the brethren accepted him and Cowdery as teachers and whether they wanted to organize. After receiving unanimous approval, Joseph ordained Cowdery an elder, and Cowdery ordained Joseph. They

blessed bread and broke it with the brethren, and blessed wine and drank it.
Then Cowdery and Joseph laid hands on many of those present to give
them the Holy Ghost and confirm them. Some prophesied while others
praised the Lord and rejoiced. Joseph Knight reported that "Joseph gave
them instructions how to Bild up the Church and exorted them to Be faithful in all things for this is the work of God." Joseph and Cowdery ordained
some of the brethren to priesthood offices "as the Spirit manifested unto
us," and "after a happy time spent in witnessing and feeling for ourselves
the powers & the blessings of the Holy Ghost," they departed.[3] The
records say nothing about a sermon. No one present had much experience
with preaching.[4]

The organization of a church was a momentous event in the Smiths'
family history. Lucy had looked for a church since her 1802 illness in Randolph. In Palmyra, perhaps under revival influence, she had joined the
Presbyterians, bringing three children with her. Joseph Sr. attended for
short stretches, but soon gave up. In his dreams, he saw the religious world
as a desolate barren field covered with dead fallen timber and devoid of animal or vegetable life. The intimation of Lucy's minister, the Reverend Benjamin Stockton, that Alvin had gone to hell because of his refusal to attend
church confirmed Joseph Sr.'s convictions about clerical hypocrisy. Lucy
said her husband thought "no order or class of religionists" understood the
Kingdom of God. And yet he longed for a church. He dreamed of people
going to judgment on their way to the meetinghouse. When he arrived too
late, he "was almost in a state of total despair." After satisfying the porter of
his faith in Christ, he was permitted to enter but only in a dream.[5]

Following the organization of the Church of Christ, Joseph Smith Sr.
was baptized in a small stream on Hyrum's farm. Lucy said that Joseph Jr.
grasped his father's hand as he came from the water and cried out, "Oh! My
God I have lived to see my father baptized into the true church of Jesus
christ"! According to Joseph Knight, Joseph Jr. "bast out with greaf and Joy
and seamed as tho the world Could not hold him." He "went out into the
Lot and appeard to want to git out of site of every Body and would sob and
Crie and seamed to Be so full that he could not live." Knight and Oliver
Cowdery went after Joseph and finally brought him back to the house. "He
was the most wrot upon that I ever saw any man," Knight said. "His joy
seemed to Be full."[6] Some great tension had been relieved.

For over a year before the Church's organization, the revelations to individuals had repeated the sentence "a great and marvelous work is about
to come forth among the children of men."[7] Well before the translation
was completed, the people around Joseph had a sense of an impending
campaign. Through the spring of 1829, while Joseph dictated the *Book of
Mormon*, the revelations shifted focus away from the book toward the conversion of souls. In May, a revelation announced directly that "if this gener-

ation harden not their hearts, I will establish my church among them." The *Book of Mormon* became less an end and more a means of bringing people to repentance. In March 1829, before Oliver Cowdery arrived to write for Joseph, a revelation said, "I will establish my church, like unto the church which was taught by my disciples in the days of old."[8]

The beginning of the "marvelous work" in 1830 was nearly as much of a leap for Smith as the passage from rural visionary to prophet and translator two years earlier. At age twenty-four, Joseph seemed unprepared. He had attended church meetings haphazardly and had no experience with complex organizations. His natural bent was charismatic, not bureaucratic. His influence had come through his visionary gifts, not by appointing officers and assigning duties. Yet he formed institutions almost intuitively, showing a surprising aptitude for one with limited experience.

Initially, the Church organization followed conventional lines. Joseph appointed elders, priests, and teachers, offices found in the *Book of Mormon* and familiar from the churches around him.[9] Elders were to meet in quarterly conferences "to do church business whatsoever is necessary," reminiscent of the Methodist annual conference of elders. Perhaps the most radical departure was the lack of provision for a professional clergy. Although never enunciated as a policy, the practice of ordaining every worthy male member quickly took effect. David Whitmer said six men had been ordained elders by August 1829, and ordinations flowed readily from Joseph's hands thereafter. The *Book of Mormon* foreshadowed the practice. "All their priests and teachers should labor with their own hands for their support," Alma and Mosiah had taught. The purpose was explicitly democratic: "the priest, not esteeming himself above his hearers, for the preacher was no better than the hearer, neither was the teacher any better than the learner; and thus they were all equal."[10] Joseph and Cowdery were the First and Second Elders, and soon after were designated apostles, lifting them up a level, but there were many elders, and a revelation of the previous June had foreshadowed twelve apostles to be appointed later. Smith and Cowdery were literally first among equals.[11]

The most important office was the one designated for Joseph in a revelation on the day of the Church's organization: "Behold there shall be a record kept among you, and in it thou shalt be called a seer, a translator, a prophet, an apostle of Jesus Christ, an elder of the church through the will of God the Father, and the grace of our Lord Jesus Christ." From the time of the first seerstone through the completion of the translation, Joseph's influence had been based on his supernatural gifts. The revelation told the Church that "thou shalt give heed unto all his words, and commandments, which he shall give unto you, as he receiveth them, walking in all holiness before me."[12] He governed through his power to speak for God.

But the consequences of Joseph's charismatic authority can easily be misconstrued. He was not the luminous central figure he is sometimes made out to be. Attention focused on his gift, not his personality. Although he served the vital function of revealing God's word, he was thought of as an instrument. The early missionaries told audiences that revelation had been restored; they rarely named the revelator. When Joseph summarized Church principles for the public in 1833, he obscured his own part in the movement. "The Lord has declared to his servants," he said, referring to a revelation.[13] The point was not that a great prophet had arisen among them, but that revelation had come again. His own person was effaced.

His revelatory gifts received a modest accounting in a summary of Church principles recorded around the time of the organization in 1830. The revelation on organization, now section 20 in the *Doctrine and Covenants* and originally called "the Articles and Covenants of the church of Christ," seemed more intent on presenting the Church as a standard denomination than in announcing the arrival of a prophet. The First Vision and the visit of Moroni were mentioned so briefly they were barely recognizable. For the most part, the articles made no effort to distinguish the new church from other denominations. The purpose seems to have been just the opposite: to identify the new organization as a respectable Christian church, holding to the established principles of the Gospel. Joseph's visions were simply acknowledged as one part of the Church's history.[14]

The Articles and Covenants resembled the confessions of faith of Christian denominations, both in the form of the language and the topics covered: the Fall, the nature of man, the atonement, resurrection, redemption, justification, and sanctification. The Articles defined the Mormon position on a few controversial issues. The question of infant baptism was resolved with the provision that "not any one can be received into this church of Christ who has not arrived to the years of accountability before God, and is not capable of repentance." The Calvinist principle of perseverance of the saints was struck down in favor of the idea that "there is a possibility that men may fall from grace and depart from the living God," in harmony with the emphasis in the *Book of Mormon* on human freedom and responsibility.[15] Both principles were announced without fanfare. The articles presented the Church of Christ as a church among churches, stable, disciplined, and orthodox.

CONVERSIONS

On the first Sunday after the organization, Oliver Cowdery preached and a half dozen people were baptized. Cowdery baptized another eight in Seneca Lake the next Sunday. In April about twenty-three people in all joined the Church. The first to be baptized were Joseph's family and close friends:

Oliver Cowdery, Martin Harris, the Whitmers. These early converts had in common a sympathy for visionary religion, a side of Mormonism not evident in the sober Articles and Covenants. Even before the organization, a few strangers with visionary inclinations gravitated toward Joseph. Thomas Marsh, who had heard of the "gold bible" while visiting Lyons, New York, was at age twenty-eight a disillusioned Methodist and a seeker. Solomon Chamberlin, a Lyons resident, heard of the *Book of Mormon* in 1829 when a journey to upper Canada brought him within a mile of the Smith house. He had long believed that "there was no people on the earth that was right, and that faith was gone from the earth, excepting a few and that all Churches were corrupt." In a vision he had seen a church raised up "after the Apostolic Order," with "the same powers, and gifts that were in the days of Christ." When Chamberlin called on the Smiths, his first question was "Is there any one here that believes in visions or revelations?" Hyrum replied, "Yes, we are a visionary house," and gave Chamberlin sixty-four pages of *Book of Mormon* proofs to take into Canada. Soon after the organization of the Church, Joseph baptized him in Seneca Lake.[16]

The word "visionary," a term commonly applied to the Mormons, referred to an amorphous religious culture flourishing along the margins of the standard Christian denominations. Visionaries were a variant of a restless seeker population that wanted more religion than conventional Protestantism offered. Some seekers looked for a return to the exact forms of the New Testament church; others sought a bestowal of divine authority. The greatest hunger was for spiritual gifts like dreams, visions, tongues, miracles, and spiritual raptures, making the visionaries the natural audience for the Mormon missionaries and the new revelation.[17]

Even among visionaries and seekers, conversions came slowly at first. In June 1830, Joseph's brother Samuel tried to sell copies of the *Book of Mormon* in Livonia, a day's journey away. On his first day, Samuel was turned out at five different places, including the inn where he had planned to stay the night. At Bloomington, a Methodist preacher, John P. Greene, somewhat gingerly agreed to take around a subscription paper on his next circuit for a book he believed to be a "nonsensical fable." When Samuel returned two weeks later, no copies had been sold. But in the fall Greene's wife, Rhoda, read the book and took an interest. When Samuel presented her with a copy "she burst into tears," he reported, "and requested me to pray with her." He instructed her to pray for a testimony of the truth as she read. Both Greenes soon were baptized. Rhoda Greene's brothers— Phinehas, Lorenzo, Brigham, and Joseph Young—read the book and joined the Church two years later.[18]

Belief in the *Book of Mormon* spread along family lines. Not just brothers and sisters but cousins, in-laws, and uncles listened and believed. Five

Whitmer children and three of their spouses were baptized in the first few months. Eleven Smiths, six Jollys, and five Rockwells joined in the same period. The most remarkable collection of kin was the offspring and relatives of Joseph Knight Sr. and his wife, Polly Peck Knight, the Colesville family that befriended Joseph after he dug for Josiah Stowell. Two of Polly Knight's brothers and a sister, their spouses, and a sister-in-law accepted the *Book of Mormon* and were baptized. Seven of the Knight children joined, four of them with spouses, plus Joseph Knight's sister Mary Knight Slade and five of her children. Twenty-one people came into the Church through the Knight-Peck connection in the first few months, forming the core of the Colesville branch. The Knights and the other four families accounted for sixty baptisms in the first nine months.[19]

To spread the word to his own family, Joseph Smith Sr. and young Don Carlos Smith, still a boy of fourteen, set out in August 1830 for Stockholm, St. Lawrence County, New York, a Smith stronghold. The Manchester Smiths had written to the family in the fall of 1828 about Joseph Jr.'s revelations. Jesse Smith, the eldest son, scoffed at such pretensions, but the other St. Lawrence Smiths were interested. Father Asael, eighty-six and about to die, read the *Book of Mormon* nearly through without the aid of glasses. He said "he always knew that God was going to raise up some branch of his family to be a great benefit to mankind."[20] Jesse's efforts to seal Joseph Sr. off from the rest of the family were to no avail. Jesse became so obnoxious that Silas, another brother, threatened to throw him out of the house if he continued to insult Joseph Sr. Still another brother, John, kept the visitors overnight at his house by a trick and heard the story. By the time Joseph left Stockholm, the family had copies of the *Book of Mormon* and knew about the Church. John was baptized in 1832, and Silas and Asael Jr. soon followed. Their mother, Mary Duty Smith, traveled to Kirtland to see Joseph Jr. Jesse was the only one of the living brothers not to join, and even he felt the tug of the powerful clan ties. When Joseph Sr. left Stockholm, he gave Jesse his hand and bade him farewell. "Farewell, Jo, for ever," Jesse said stiffly. Joseph replied, "I am afraid, it will be for ever, unless you repent." As the two parted, Jesse broke into tears.[21]

While the missionary work went forward, Joseph Jr. shuttled among the clusters of believers. He and Emma still lived in the house in Harmony near Isaac Hale, while the elder Smiths lived with Hyrum in Manchester. One group of sympathizers clustered around the Whitmers in Fayette, and another around the Joseph Knight family in Colesville. Joseph characterized Knight as a Universalist; Knight spoke of himself as a "Restorationar," one who believed all would be saved after a period of punishment. When Joseph visited in April, neighbors and family members met to hear Joseph and pray for "wisdom to understand the truth."[22]

At their meetings, the little group "got into the habit of praying much," and Joseph once asked Newel Knight, Joseph Knight's son, to pray. Knight begged off, saying he would rather pray alone in the woods. When he tried it the next morning, however, he was no more able to pray privately than publicly. On his return home, his appearance worried his wife and she sent for the Prophet. Joseph found him "suffering very much in his mind, and his body acted upon in a very strange manner. His visage and limbs distorted and twisted in every shape and appearance possible to imagine; and finally he was caught up off the floor of the apartment and tossed about most fearfully."[23]

Joseph looked on aghast, along with eight or nine others who had collected in the house. Newel begged Joseph to cast out the devil, and Joseph said, "If you know that I can, it shall be done." Joseph rebuked the devil, and Newel cried out that he saw the devil leave. Newel's body relaxed and he could be laid on his bed. He later reported that "the visions of heaven were opened to my view." Those who witnessed the scene were impressed, and most finally joined the church. Newel Knight visited the Whitmers in Fayette in late May, and David Whitmer baptized him.[24] Writing eight years later, Joseph could not hide his pleasure in the miracle. He was not inclined to enlarge on the sensational, but manifestations of extraordinary powers gave him confidence that God was with them.

Joseph returned to Fayette in May to hold a conference on June 9, 1830, in keeping with the requirement for quarterly conferences in the Articles and Covenants. Thirty members, among them seven elders, met along with others who were "anxious to learn." The Articles and Covenants were read and "received by unanimous voice of the whole congregation, consisting of most of the male members of the Church." The official business included confirmation of newly baptized members, ordination of priests, and the issuance of licenses. The license to Joseph Smith Sr. read, "Liberty Power & Authority Given to Joseph Smith sen. signifying and proveing that he is a Priest of this Church of Christ established and regularly Organized in these last days A D 1830 on the 6th day of April." Joseph Smith Jr. and Oliver Cowdery signed as First and Second Elders.[25]

The official minutes kept by Oliver Cowdery briefly noted the formalities. Still lacking a preacher, Joseph read Ezekiel 14, prayed, and exhorted the members. In closing, prayer was offered "by all the Brethren present and dismissed by Br. Oliver Cowdery." The staid depiction in the minutes was the churchly part of the story. The visionary side of the meeting did not go into the official minutes, but Joseph remembered for his history that "the Holy Ghost was poured out upon us in a miraculous manner many of our number prophecied, whilst others had the Heavens opened to their view." Some were so overcome they had to be laid on beds, among them

Newel Knight, who "saw Heaven opened, and beheld the Lord Jesus Christ, seated at the right hand of the Majesty on high." Joseph said that in a vision of the future, Knight "saw there represented, the great work which through my instrumentality was yet to be accomplished." Nine years later, Joseph still remembered the excitement:

> To find ourselves engaged in the very same order of things, as observed by the holy Apostles of old; To realize the importance and solemnity of such proceedings, and to witness and feel with our natural senses, the like glorious manifestations of the powers of the Priesthood; the gifts and blessings of the Holy Ghost; and the goodness and condescension of a merciful God, unto such as obey the everlasting gospel of our Lord Jesus Christ, combined to create within us, sensations of rapturous gratitude, and inspire us with fresh zeal and energy, in the cause of truth.[26]

TRIALS

By the summer of 1830, Joseph could no longer be merely derided and dismissed. He held enough power, at least over the credulous, to be feared. Opposition mounted after the June 1830 conference. Joseph returned to Harmony, and then set out again with Emma, Cowdery, and David and John Whitmer to visit Joseph Knight Sr. in Colesville. On Saturday afternoon, June 26, they dammed a small stream to make a pond for baptisms and appointed a meeting for the Sabbath. That night the dam was torn out.[27] The Mormons replaced the dam early Monday morning and held their baptism later that day. Oliver Cowdery baptized Joseph and Polly Knight along with eleven others connected to the Knights, plus Levi Hall and Emma Smith. On their way back, a collection of the Knights' neighbors scoffed at the new Mormons as they passed by. Later about fifty men surrounded Joseph Knight's house, Joseph Smith said, "raging with anger, and apparently determined to commit violence upon us." When Joseph left for Newel's, the mob followed along, threatening physical attack.[28]

Joseph was to become accustomed to ridicule and rough treatment. He lived in a time when citizen vigilantes considered it their duty to discipline disruptive elements in the community. When village toughs failed to stop the baptisms, the law stepped in. Before the newly baptized members could be confirmed, a constable from South Bainbridge delivered a warrant for Joseph's arrest. Doctor A. W. Benton of Chenango County, whom Joseph Knight called a "catspaw" of a group of vagabonds, brought charges against Joseph as a disorderly person. On June 28, he was carried off to court in South Bainbridge by constable Ebenezer Hatch, trailed by a mob that Hatch thought planned to waylay them en route. When a wheel came off the constable's wagon, the mob nearly caught up, but, working fast, the two men replaced it in time and drove on. Hatch lodged Joseph in a tavern in South Bainbridge and slept all night with his feet against the door and a musket by his side.[29]

The nature of the charges brought against Joseph in the court of Justice Joseph Chamberlain of Chenango County is not entirely clear. Joseph Smith said it was for "setting the country in an uproar by preaching the Book of Mormon," which was his most recent offense, but Joseph Knight Sr. said Benton swore out the warrant for Joseph's "pretending to see under ground," going back to the old money-digging charges of the 1826 trial. The fact that Josiah Stowell, Joseph's employer in the silver mine venture, was called to testify suggests that the accusers wished to reopen the case. Benton himself said Joseph Smith was brought to trial "in order to check the progress of delusion, and open the eyes and understandings of those who blindly followed." From that perspective, money-digging and the *Book of Mormon* were both fraudulent schemes. Benton said in a report to the *Evangelical Magazine and Gospel Advocate* the next year that "the Book of Mormon was brought to light by the same magic power by which he pretended to . . . discover hidden treasure."[30]

Joseph Knight hired James Davidson to defend the Prophet, but Davidson, sensing the hostility of the crowd and the intensity of the prosecutions, said that "it looked like a sqaley Day" and advised engaging John Reed as well, a local farmer noted for his speaking ability. Reed later said that Joseph "was well known for truth and uprightness; that he moved in the first circles of community, and he was often spoken of as a young man of intelligence, and good morals." Reed thought bigots among the sectarian churches were responsible for bringing the charges. The hearing dragged on until night, when Justice Chamberlain, whom Reed considered a man of "discernment," acquitted Joseph.[31]

Joseph had no sooner heard the verdict than a constable from neighboring Broome County served a warrant for the same crimes. The constable hurried Joseph off on a fifteen-mile journey without a pause for a meal. When they stopped for the night, the constable offered no protection from the tavern-haunters' ridicule. After a dinner of crusts and water, Joseph was put next to the wall, and the constable lay close against him to prevent escape.[32]

At ten the next morning, Joseph was in court again, this time before three justices who formed a court of special sessions with the power to expel him from the county. Newel Knight was interrogated about his healing, and the prosecution rehearsed the old money-digging charges. Reed said witnesses were examined until 2 a.m., and the case argued for another two hours. The three justices again acquitted Joseph. Most of the onlookers were won over, including the constable, who apologized for his bad treatment and warned Joseph that his enemies planned to tar and feather him. The constable took Joseph out a back door, and he made his way to Emma's sister's house, where his wife was waiting. The next day Joseph and Emma were safely home in Harmony.[33]

Joseph and Cowdery tried to steal back to Colesville a few days later to complete the confirmations that the trials had interrupted, but their enemies were too alert. They had no sooner arrived at the Knights' than the mob began to gather. The Knights had suffered along with Joseph. On the night of the South Bainbridge trial, their wagons had been turned over and sunk in the water. Mobbers piled rails against the doors and sank chains in the stream. On Joseph's and Cowdery's return to Colesville, there was no time for a meeting or even a meal before they had to flee.[34]

Joseph said they traveled all night, "except a short time, during which we were forced to rest ourselve[s] under a large tree by the way side, sleeping and watching alternately." It may have been on this occasion that Peter, James, and John appeared to Joseph and Cowdery and, as a later revelation said, "ordained you and confirmed you to be apostles, and especial witnesses of my name, and bear the keys of your ministry: and of the same things which I revealed unto them." Erastus Snow later said that Peter, James, and John appeared to Joseph and Cowdery "at a period when they were being pursued by their enemies and they had to travel all night, and in the dawn of the coming day when they were weary and worn who should appear to them but Peter, James and John, for the purpose of conferring upon them the Apostleship, the keys of which they themselves had held while upon the earth, which had been bestowed, upon them by the Savior." In a conversation between Hyrum and Joseph overheard by Addison Everett, Joseph spoke of a trial involving Mr. Reed. In trying to escape the mob,

> Joseph & Oliver went to the woods in a few rods, it being night, and they traveled until Oliver was exhausted & Joseph almost Carried him through mud and water. They traveled all night and just at the break of day Olive[r] gave out entirely and exclaimed O! Lord! How long Brother Joseph have we got to endure this thing; Brother Joseph said that at that very time Peter James & John came to them and Ordained them to the Apostleship.[35]

DISSENSION

Three and a half years of marriage had afforded Emma few moments of uninterrupted peace. She had nearly perished when her firstborn son died shortly after his birth in June 1828. Joseph had been gone from home more than half of the time since the spring of 1830, seeing to the publication of the *Book of Mormon*, organizing the Church, exhorting, and baptizing. She accompanied him sometimes, but on her most recent trip to Colesville she had seen her husband arrested, tried twice, and pursued by a mob. In July 1830, when Joseph and Oliver fled home to Harmony from Colesville, she may have already been pregnant with the twins who were born the next April.[36]

In July, a revelation admonished Emma to "murmur not because of the things which thou has not seen," but Emma was a believer. Oliver Cowdery had baptized her at Colesville in late June, and she was soon to be confirmed. Long after Joseph's death and her own remarriage, Emma held on to her belief in the *Book of Mormon*. She was convinced that Joseph could not have written the book himself. The July revelation envisioned a substantial role for her in the Church. Besides being wife to Joseph, she was to be "ordained under his hand to expound scriptures, and to exhort the church." Emma may have had literary inclinations, for the revelation also said that "thy time shall be given to writing, and to learning much." Her first assignment was "to make a selection of sacred Hymns," a task completed in 1835 when the first Mormon hymnal was published.[37]

Like her father, Isaac, Emma worried about Joseph as a provider. The July revelation told her to "lay aside the things of this world, and seek for the things of a better." But injunctions did not feed the household or provide for the future. An earlier revelation had said that Joseph's support was to come from the Church. "In temporal labors thou shalt not have strength, for this is not thy calling." He was to "continue in calling upon God in my name, and writing the things which shall be given thee by the Comforter; And expounding all scriptures unto the church." Joseph was to derive his support like the itinerant Methodist preachers. "Thou shalt take no purse nor scrip, neither staves, neither two coats, for the church shall give unto thee in the very hour what thou needest for food and for raiment, and for shoes and for money, and for scrip." Yet he was not to abandon farming altogether; the revelations commanded him to sow his fields, and in late August 1830, Joseph borrowed money to finish paying for the thirteen acres he had purchased from Isaac Hale.[38]

For a time Hale protected Joseph against growing resentment among the neighbors, but Hale's brother-in-law, Nathaniel Lewis, a leader among the Methodists, was determined to discredit the Prophet. He may have been the one to turn Hale against his son-in-law. Without Isaac's protection, Joseph and Emma were defenseless. They completed the purchase of the farm on August 25 but were already planning to leave. Peter Whitmer Sr. once again offered his house as a refuge, and in the last week of August, Newel Knight moved Joseph and Emma to Fayette.[39]

Joseph was needed in Fayette for other reasons. Through the summer,

Oliver Cowdery and the Whitmer family began to conceive of themselves as independent authorities with the right to correct Joseph and receive revelation. Cowdery had witnessed at least three major revelations with Joseph and been granted the title of Second Elder in the Articles and Covenants. Perhaps he thought his duty was to detect errors. While Joseph worked on a compilation of the revelations, Cowdery wrote him about a mistake in the Articles and Covenants. The objectionable passage, relating to the qualifications for baptism, stated that candidates shall "truly manifest by their works that they have received of the Spirit of Christ unto a remission of their sins." Though apparently innocuous, Cowdery may have felt that the requirement of the Spirit verged dangerously close to the traditional Puritan practice of insisting on evidence of grace. Evaluating a candidate's experiences before admission to the Church gave ministers great power. Cowdery saw in those words the seeds of priestcraft.[40]

Joseph wrote Cowdery at once, asking "by what authority he took upon him to command me to alter or erase, to add to or diminish from, a revelation or commandment from Almighty God." To straighten out the matter, Joseph made a special trip to Fayette, perhaps realizing the Church was in peril. Acknowledging every rival claim to revelation would quickly lead to anarchy. Cowdery had the whole Whitmer family on his side, and Joseph was hard-pressed to convince them they were wrong. It was, he said, "with great difficulty, and much labour that I prevailed with any of them to reason calmly on the subject." Christian Whitmer came over to Joseph's side first and gradually the others followed. Joseph believed the error had "its rise in presumption and rash judgement," and from the experience they were all to learn "the necessity of humility, and meekness before the Lord, that he might teach us of his ways."[41]

Cowdery's criticism was not the last of the challenges. When Joseph arrived in Fayette in September, the Whitmers and Cowdery were studying the revelations of Hiram Page, the husband of David Whitmer's sister Catherine. He had a "roll of papers," as Newel Knight reported it, full of revelations through a stone. Joseph had put aside his seerstone after completing the *Book of Mormon*, and David Whitmer thought this a big mistake. Only the seerstone revelations received through June 1829 were trustworthy in Whitmer's view. He may have believed Page because he used a stone when Joseph had stopped.[42]

Joseph had suppressed the previous criticism of his revelation by force of argument. This time he "thought it wisdom not to do much more than to converse with the brethren on the subject," and wait for the conference scheduled for September 26. Joseph recognized the danger of the competing revelations. Acknowledging every visionary outburst could splinter the church. Newel Knight, who came up for the conference, found Joseph "in great distress of mind." The two of them occupied the same room before the conference, and Newel said that "the greater part of the night was spent in prayer and supplication." Rather than face the brethren individually and risk another outburst later, Joseph turned to the Church to settle the matter for good. Joseph brought a new revelation dealing with Hiram Page to the conference, but it was not by revelatory power that Joseph prevailed. He insisted rather that Page's revelations "were entirely at variance with the order of Gods house, as laid down in the New Testament, as well as in our late revelations." He turned the question into a constitutional issue: did Hiram Page have the authority to promulgate revelation? The new revelation emphasized that the reception of revelation for the Church had "not been appointed unto him, neither shall anything be appointed unto any of this church contrary to the church covenants." The Articles and Covenants now proved their usefulness. They laid out procedures and leadership structure that inhibited erratic claims, the downfall of other charismatic religious groups. "For all things must be done in order," the revelation insisted, "and by common consent in the church, by the prayer of faith." Joseph had Cowdery read the Articles and Covenants to the conference, and then Joseph explained their meaning. After the investigation "Brother Joseph Smith Jr. was appointed by the voice of the Conference to receive and write Revelations & Commandments for this Church."[43] Charisma was to be focused, not left free to run wild.

The conference established Joseph's authority by clarifying his office as "seer, a translator, a prophet, an apostle of Jesus Christ," particularly in relation to Cowdery, the Second Elder. Joseph was Moses, to "receive commandments and revelations in this church." Cowdery was Aaron, "to declare faithfully the commandments and the revelations . . . unto the church." Cowdery might speak authoritatively but was not to "write by way of commandment, but by wisdom." The Prophet alone was to inscribe scripture. To leave no question, Cowdery was told not to "command him who is at thy head, and at the head of the church," for only Joseph had the "keys of the mysteries, and the revelations."[44]

Joseph was proving to be a tough administrator. Speaking of the confrontation, Newel Knight said that "it was wonderful to witness the wisdom that Joseph displayed on this occasion, for truly God gave unto him great wisdom and power, and it seems to me, even now, that none who saw him administer righteousness under such trying circumstances, could doubt that the Lord was with him, as he acted." The revelations instructed Cowdery to tell Hiram Page that he had been deceived, and by the end of the investigation "Brother Page, as well as the whole church who were present, renounced the said stone, and all things connected therewith, much to our mutual satisfaction and happiness."[45] In that moment, the fledgling movement was put on a course to becoming a church rather than remaining a visionary sect.

GATHERING

Shortly after the organization of the Church in April, Joseph thought for a time that the innovations were over. He told David Whitmer "he was through the work that God had given him the gift to perform, except to preach the gospel."[46] At other points in his life, he was to think he had finished, and then a new revelation would drive him on.[47] He perpetually initiated new campaigns and taught new doctrines. His administrative style was almost excessively dynamic. In the fall of 1830, while his identity as prophet was still damp in the mold, Joseph unfolded the first of the Church's missions, a massive program combining the biblical ideas of New Jerusalem, millennium, and gathering.

The September revelations began at a logical starting point for believers in the *Book of Mormon:* missionary work to the Indians. The same revelation that directed Cowdery to subordinate himself to Joseph also commissioned Cowdery to go to the Lamanites. Peter Whitmer Jr. and two recent converts, Parley Pratt and Ziba Peterson, were called to join him. The *Book of Mormon* gave the missionaries ample reason for going: the book's purpose was to recover the lost remnant of ancient Israel. Joseph translated the plates so that "through the knowledge of their fathers," the doctrine of Christ would reach the "Lamanites, and the Lemuelites and the Ishmaelites, which dwindled in unbelief."[48]

The mission to the Lamanites soon came to be seen as a part of a larger plan. In a covenant signed on October 17, Oliver Cowdery promised, in addition to teaching the Indians, "to rear up a pillar as a witness where the Temple of God shall be built, in the glorious New-Jerusalem." Cowdery was to locate a site for the holy city prophesied in both St. John's Revelation and the *Book of Mormon*. The New Jerusalem, the revelation said, was to be situated "on the borders by the Lamanites," which they all knew was the western edge of Missouri, to which the federal government was forcibly removing the eastern states' Indians.[49] The foursome were to convert Indians, if possible, and to locate the place of the New Jerusalem along this frontier.

The references to the New Jerusalem assumed more importance because of another revelation given to Joseph Smith just before the September conference. The revelation described in gruesome detail the calamities to come upon the earth before Christ's Second Coming: a plague of flies, maggots, signs in the heavens, destructive hailstorms, and devouring fire. In the meantime, the revelation said, the Church was to find the righteous and bring them to safety.

And ye are called to bring to pass the gathering of mine elect, for mine elect hear my voice and harden not their hearts:

Wherefore the decree hath gone forth from the Father that they shall be gathered in unto one place, upon the face of this land, to prepare their hearts and be prepared in all things, against the day when tribulation and desolation are sent forth upon the wicked.

The New Jerusalem was to be a refuge against the coming calamities. The conversion of the Indians, the building of the New Jerusalem, and the gathering of the elect came together in a single plan to prepare the world for the Savior's Second Coming.[50]

The revelation on the millennial gathering brought all the routine activities of everyday life into question. Were the Mormons to stay in New York or were they to be gathered elsewhere? What would be required in preparation for the Second Coming? Through the fall of 1830, the future was unclear. Joseph and Emma labored under a double uncertainty. Besides awaiting light on a gathering place, they were without a house or a farm in New York, and hostility in Harmony made return there uninviting.[51]

News from the west put everything in a new light. En route to Indian territory, the Cowdery group stopped in northeast Ohio to meet with Sidney Rigdon, a leader in the Campbellite movement and a friend of Parley Pratt's. Rigdon and over a hundred followers in Mentor, Painesville, and Kirtland had accepted Mormonism. On December 10, 1830, Rigdon and Edward Partridge, a prosperous hatter and one of Rigdon's followers, arrived in Waterloo in the middle of a meeting at the house where Joseph Smith Sr. had recently moved. Partridge, who had withheld judgment until he met the Prophet, was baptized the next day.[52]

Sidney Rigdon was Mormonism's most auspicious convert to date. Reared on a farm in central Pennsylvania, he had qualified as a Baptist minister in 1819 at age twenty-six by dint of self-education. He preached in Trumbull County, Ohio, and in Pittsburgh until 1824, when he broke with the Baptists over the doctrine of infant damnation. While he worked as a tanner for two years with his brother-in-law, Rigdon discussed religion with Alexander Campbell and Walter Scott, two independent and vigorous young preachers who wished to restore the Christian church to its original purity. In 1826, Rigdon moved to Bainbridge, Ohio, where he preached the doctrines he had developed in discussions with Scott and Campbell. Scott meanwhile was preaching what he called the "restored gospel" in nearby New Lisbon, Ohio. In the course of a thirty-year ministry, he was said to have converted a thousand souls a year. Attracted by similar doctrines, people in Mentor, Ohio, asked Rigdon to preach, and although he refused a salary, they began building a house for him. He was preaching in a number of nearby towns when Parley Pratt fell under his influence and set out on a preaching tour in the summer of 1830. Along the way, Pratt encountered the *Book of Mormon* and was converted.[53]

In October, Pratt presented his old teacher with a copy of the *Book of Mormon*. Rigdon was impressed. He did not believe that a twenty-four-year-old could have written the book. After two weeks of close study, he accepted baptism at Pratt's hands. His Mentor congregation was furious, refusing him the house, but Rigdon moved to Hiram and formed a little church of Mormon converts. In the late fall, he and Edward Partridge determined to meet Joseph Smith in person.[54]

David Whitmer said Rigdon was "a thorough Bible scholar, a man of fine education, and a powerful orator." He had qualities none of them could match. Resentment and jealousy tinged Whitmer's comments. He later observed that Rigdon "soon worked himself deep into Brother Joseph's affections, and had more influence over him than any other man living." "Brother Joseph rejoiced believing that the Lord had sent to him this great and mighty man Sydney Rigdon, to help him in the work." Joseph was impressed, but he did not defer to Rigdon, though Rigdon was thirteen years his senior and far his superior in education. A revelation explained the relationship of the two. Joseph had "the keys of the mystery of those things which have been sealed." Rigdon, with all his learning, was to watch over Joseph and "write for him: and the scriptures shall be given even as they are in mine own bosom, to the salvation of mine own elect." Joseph was the revelator and Rigdon the scribe, who was to "preach my gospel, and call on the holy prophets to prove his words, as they shall be given him."[55] With Cowdery on a mission, Rigdon became Joseph's primary assistant.

In the early winter, Joseph and Rigdon toured the Church centers in New York. Wherever he spoke—Fayette, Canandaigua, Palmyra, or Colesville—Rigdon made an impression. Emily Coburn, one of the converts, said that when Rigdon came to Colesville "we did not class him as a Mormon, as we were informed that he was a Baptist minister, from Paynesville, Ohio." He seemed like a different order of being from the ragged group Joseph had collected in the Church. At Palmyra "the people stood trembling and amazed, so powerful were his words, and some obeyed."

Despite the respect temporarily afforded Rigdon, "it was all in vain," John Whitmer said. No amount of learning or eloquence could stop the growing opposition. The enemies of the Prophet threatened to kill both Joseph and Rigdon. He was "too smart for them therefore they wanted to trouble him."[56] As the opposition mounted, a revelation commanded them both to "go to the Ohio." In fact, the entire Church was to move and await word from Oliver Cowdery about the Lamanites and the city of Zion. John

Whitmer was sent ahead with a letter of introduction to the Ohio Mormons, while Joseph made preparations to leave.[57]

The quarterly conference met as scheduled at Peter Whitmer Sr.'s in Fayette on January 2, 1831. The usual business was conducted, but a further revelation about the move to Ohio preempted everyone's attention. One reason for going, the revelation said, was "that the enemy in the secret chambers, seeketh your lives." The other reason was to begin the gathering. "And that ye might escape the power of the enemy, and be gathered unto me a righteous people, without spot and blameless: Wherefore, for this cause I gave unto you the commandment that ye should go to the Ohio." The members interpreted this to mean that they were now "to begin the gathering of Israel." The revelation contained hints of a new society to be founded: "There I will give unto you my law, and there you shall be endowed with power from on high." "Hear my voice and follow me," they were promised, "and you shall be a free people, and ye shall have no laws, but my laws when I come, for I am your Lawgiver, and what can stay my hand?" From their base in Ohio, missionaries would "go forth among all nations," and "Israel shall be saved, and I will lead them whithersoever I will."[58]

Quick sale of property to effect a sudden move inevitably meant poor prices and substantial losses. The revelation foresaw the difficulty. "And they that have farms, that cannot be sold, let them be left or rented as seemeth them good." The members were reminded that "the riches of the earth is mine to give," and said that the Lord would give them "greater riches, even a land of promise; a land flowing with milk and honey, upon which there shall be no curse when the Lord cometh." Meanwhile they were not to forget the poor. Men should be appointed to "look to the poor and the needy, and administer to their relief, that they shall not suffer; and send them forth to the place which I have commanded them."[59]

By the last week of January the advance party was ready for departure. Sidney Rigdon delivered a parting sermon from the courthouse steps in Waterloo, warning the populace to flee from the wrath to come. Joseph traveled with Emma and Joseph Knight in a sleigh provided by Joseph Knight Jr. By the first week in February the Prophet was in Kirtland.[60] Through the winter and early spring the other members made their way west to Kirtland in small parties. Thomas Marsh left with a party of about thirty Waterloo Saints May 3 or 4, reaching Buffalo by May 8. The Colesville members traveled together. At Buffalo, heavy ice on Lake Erie blocked further passage of both parties. While others marked time, Lucy Smith loaded her group of fifty onto a steamboat and told them all to pray for clear water. A crack appeared in the ice, the captain cast loose, and the boat scraped through as the ice closed behind them. Lucy reached Fairport, just eleven miles from Kirtland, about May 11. The others arrived three days later, after the ice had cleared.[61] Martin Harris with a group of about fifty set out for Kirtland in mid-May, the last of the large migrations. By June 1831, the bulk of the first year's converts had left New York.

Missionaries crisscrossed through the state in subsequent years, teaching and baptizing such kinsmen as Brigham Young and Heber Kimball, but New York would never again be Mormon headquarters. The Hill Cumorah, the place of the First Vision, the Smith farmhouse, the Peter Whitmer farm, all memorialized with monuments in the next century, were left behind.[62] The money-diggers and the critical neighbors were left too. In Ohio, Joseph was free to start fresh in a new place. He was unable to put aside his treasure-seeker and glass-looker past completely; affidavits advertising those episodes would soon be published. But the religious identity he had forged in New York would flourish in Ohio. He arrived as a prophet, the head of a church, and the leader of Zion. All the rest was now irrelevant.

SIX

JOSEPH, MOSES, AND ENOCH

1830

& they came forth to hear him, upon the high places, saying unto the Tent keepers, Tarry thou ye here & keep the Tents, while we go yonder to Behold the Seer, for he prophesieth; & there is a strange thing in the land; a wild man hath come among us.

Book of Moses, 1830

ELIZABETH ANN WHITNEY, an early Mormon convert in Ohio, remembered when Joseph Smith strode into her husband's store in Kirtland in February 1831. "I am Joseph the Prophet," he said on meeting the Whitneys for the first time. The declaration seemed natural when Whitney wrote almost fifty years later in Utah.[1] By then, the Mormons had built a thriving society on the premise of Smith's revelations. But in 1831, it was a startling claim for an unprepossessing young man of twenty-five.

The title appalled the Palmyrans who thought of Joseph as a poor, rural visionary with pretensions to "see" with a stone. After making inquiries in Palmyra in 1831, the New York reporter James Gordon Bennett concluded that Joseph was "a careless, idle, indolent fellow."[2] When questioned, neighbors described the Smiths as "lazy, intemperate and worthless," given to money-digging and lying.[3] One onlooker later recalled Joseph's occasional attendance at revival meetings, but most denied that he had any religious character. He appeared to be an easygoing boy with little ambition. No one imagined him as a prophet.

He assumed that title with little support from anyone outside his family. Only a handful of people valued his revelations at first: Martin Harris, Joseph Knight, Josiah Stowell, Oliver Cowdery. The Whitmers appeared only after Joseph's first translation was nearly complete. Otherwise, Joseph met only scorn at the beginning. His father-in-law, Isaac Hale, refused to allow him to stay in the house with the gold plates. Most Palmyra villagers thought the *Book of Mormon* a fraud and boycotted the book to prevent Joseph from profiting by it. In recounting his experience years later, Joseph remembered only skepticism and ridicule.[4] Joseph was more popular as a money-digger.

Few clues about Joseph's reading, other than the Bible, remain to explain how he came to think of himself as a prophet. Books of all kinds were in circulation in his immediate environment, but he was not bookish; Joseph was no Abraham Lincoln borrowing books and reading when he finished plowing a furrow. No minister reported conversations about religious writings. He may have known of New England prophets who saw visions or heard God's voice, but none lived nearby or are known to have influenced him. Commerce with the supernatural among his acquaintances was of the magical and treasure-seeking variety. All outside sources of Joseph's prophetic identity must be hypothesized—save for the Bible and his own "marvilous experience."[5]

Joseph stepped into the prophetic role with surprising confidence. It was a remarkable achievement, except that, as he said, he did not invent his prophethood. He understood his calling as a gift, not an achievement, beginning with his teenage visions and then rapidly accelerating in 1828 when he began translating the *Book of Mormon*. Where his gifts came from will probably never be explained to everyone's satisfaction. What is known is that in his early twenties, Joseph began acting like a prophet. He spoke in the voice of God, and defined a prophetic role for himself. Relying on biblical examples, Joseph worked out—or found out—how he should conduct a prophetic life. He tried to explain himself in his later histories, but his revelations themselves reveal the most about what he meant when he said, "I am Joseph the Prophet."

REVELATION

In the fall of 1830, Joseph began to compile the two dozen revelations that made up his prophetic record.[6] From 1828 on, he had prized the words that came to him from heaven enough to write them down. To the believers, the revelations sounded like scripture. They were immediately treated like the Bible, a status that no other contemporary visionary writings achieved. A few Shaker "instruments" initially made high claims for their revelations, but they did not retain that status for long.[7] Ann Lee, founder of the Shakers, is not known to have written her visions, and the Adventist Ellen White, who filled several large volumes with revelations, never equated them with scripture.[8] In 1833, Joseph's revelations were published as the *Book of Commandments*, later the *Doctrine and Covenants*, and put alongside the Bible in the Mormon canon.

How they achieved their status so quickly is not easily explained, but the revelations' language made an impression. One rhetorical feature may partly account for their authority: the voice in them is purely God's. Joseph as a speaker is absent from the revelations, just as he is from the *Book of Mor-*

mon. In the opening lines of the 1833 *Book of Commandments*, he does not utter a sound:

> HEARKEN, O ye people of my church, saith the voice of Him who dwells on high, and whose eyes are upon all men; yea, verily I say, hearken ye people from afar, and ye that are upon the islands of the sea, listen together.[9]

God speaks, with no human intermediary present. When Joseph figures in the revelations, he stands among the listeners, receiving instructions. When reprimands are handed out, he is likely to receive one. The first written revelation chastised him for losing 116 pages of the *Book of Mormon* translation. Since there was no church and few followers, the revelation was addressed to him alone. He stands before the Lord to receive a rebuke in words coming from his own mouth.

> Remember, remember, that it is not the work of God that is frustrated, but the work of men: for although a man may have many revelations, and have power to do many mighty works, yet, if he boasts in his own strength, and sets at nought the counsels of God, and follows after the dictates of his own will, and carnal desires, he must fall and incur the vengeance of a just God before him.[10]

In this case, as in virtually all the revelations, the voice is imperious but never argumentative. The words make no appeal to reason or scripture or experience. God pronounces what is and what will be without giving evidence. Hearers must decide to believe or not without reference to outside authority—common sense, science, the Bible, tradition, anything. The hearer faces the personage who speaks, free to hearken or turn away.[11]

Joseph's followers reacted quite differently to the words spoken as revelation and the words he spoke as a man. When Joseph asked John Whitmer to be Church historian, Whitmer agreed only if the Lord would "manifest it through Joseph the Seer."[12] Whitmer complied only when he was told in the voice of the Lord, "Behold it is expedient in me that my servant John should write and keep a regular history."[13] When a new edition of the revelations was being prepared, the editor of the Mormon newspaper, William W. Phelps, wrote his wife: "The Saints must learn their duty from the Revelations. We must live by every word that proceeds from the mouth of God, and not by what is written by man or is spoken by man."[14] Joseph showed the revelations the same respect. Writing in 1831, he advised his brother Hyrum to come to Ohio, "for the Lord has Commanded us that we should Call the Elders of this Chur[c]h to gether."[15] He spoke as if the revelations commanded him along with everyone else.

The revelations carried authority even though Joseph did not fall into trances like Ellen White or withdraw into the desert like Muhammad. Most of Joseph's revelations came while he sat in council with his followers. Parley Pratt, one of Joseph's early converts, described how the revelation on discerning spirits was received. John Murdock and several other elders asked Joseph to inquire of the Lord. They joined in prayer in the translating room, Pratt said, and Joseph dictated a revelation.

> Each sentence was uttered slowly and very distinctly, and with a pause between each, sufficiently long for it to be recorded, by an ordinary writer, in long hand.
>
> This was the manner in which all his written revelations were dictated and written. There was never any hesitation, reviewing, or reading back, in order to keep the run of the subject; neither did any of these communications undergo revisions, interlinings, or corrections. As he dictated them so they stood, so far as I have witnessed.[16]

Once recorded, the revelations were recopied and carried around by Church members.[17] Joseph once said his revelations "have been snatched from under my hand as soon as given."[18] Most converts believed on the basis of these writings alone without ever meeting Joseph Smith.[19]

TRANSLATION

Besides the revelations in the *Book of Commandments*, with their biblical ring, Joseph's prophethood was based on a gift peculiarly his own. In an 1830 revelation, Joseph was called "a seer, a translator, a prophet, an apostle of Jesus Christ, an elder of the church." The series of titles implied that prophethood was connected to translation. Though unusual for one of his education and social status, "translator" became his permanent role. Had Joseph followed the course of other Yankee dreamers and visionaries, he would have become a preacher.[20] Charles Finney, the rural New York lawyer who had a vision of Christ a few years after Joseph, immediately began preaching and in time became the leading evangelist in America. The self-taught radical Baptist reformer Elias Smith, a restorationist and visionary like Joseph, interpreted success in preaching as evidence of his call.[21] Joseph did not pretend to mastery of the pulpit. He began by translating a book, and, though entirely unqualified by any conventional standard, continued translating to the end of his life.

News about scholarly translations could only have touched Joseph lightly. In 1822, the French scholar Jean-François Champollion first deciphered Egyptian hieroglyphics through close study of parallel documents inscribed on the Rosetta stone. Discussion of the hieroglyphs appeared in an elite American periodical, the *North American Review*, in 1823, and a follow-up article in 1828 discussed Champollion's translation the very year Joseph Smith was translating the "reformed Egyptian" on the plates. Conceivably, news of Champollion's triumph could have reached Palmyra, but the translation of the Rosetta stone was a work of the most advanced scholarship, a tour de force of ingenuity and learning. Champollion, a prodigy, delivered a paper on Coptic at age sixteen and was appointed a professor of history at the Grenoble lyceum at eighteen. A chair was created at the College de France especially for him.[22] Smith could not aspire to enter this learned world.

Neither his education nor his Christian upbringing prepared Joseph to translate a book, but the magic culture may have. Treasure-seeking taught Joseph to look for the unseen in a stone. His first reaction when he brought home the Urim and Thummim was delight with its divining powers. "I can see any thing," he told his friend Joseph Knight. He knew from working with his own seerstone what to expect from the Urim and Thummim: he would "see."[23] Practice with his scrying stones carried over to translation of the gold plates. In fact, as work on the *Book of Mormon* proceeded, a seerstone took the place of the Urim and Thummim as an aid in the work, blending magic with inspired translation.[24]

The *Book of Mormon* contained an example of an inspired translator, King Mosiah, who deciphered the twenty-four gold plates of the Jaredites. Limhi, the king of a Nephite colony, who had discovered the plates, asked Ammon, a Nephite explorer, about translation. Ammon said he knew "a man that can translate the records: for he hath wherewith that he can look, and translate all records that are of ancient date." Mosiah had "interpreters" like Joseph Smith's. Ammon explained that a title went with the command to look in the interpreters. He who looked "the same is called seer. . . . A seer is a revelator and a prophet also; and a gift which is greater, can no man have." In a curious refraction, the text Joseph was translating mirrored his act of translating.[25] He doubtless saw himself in those words, just as he had found himself in Isaiah's unlearned man.[26] The *Book of Mormon* helped Joseph to piece together a prophetic identity that included a peculiar form of translation as part of his divine call.

Over his lifetime, Joseph produced three inspired "translations": the *Book of Mormon*, the Book of Moses, and the Book of Abraham, plus the "revision" of the Bible, a form of translation. Each book purported to be the record of another people of another time. In all these works, Joseph Smith does not introduce himself as the narrator of the story. The *Book of Mormon* opens with the phrase "I, Nephi, having been born of goodly parents"; the Book of Moses begins, "The words of God which he spake unto

Moses, at a time when Moses was caught up into an exceeding high mountain"; Abraham starts "In the land of the Chaldeans, at the residence of my
father, I, Abraham, saw that it was needful for me to obtain another place of
residence."[27] The reader is immediately immersed in another time and
place and absorbed into the narrative without the help of an intermediary,
like reading Beowulf or Thucydides.

The Book of Moses differed technically from Abraham and the *Book of
Mormon* in not being based on purported ancient writings. The Book of
Mormon came from gold plates and the Book of Abraham from Egyptian
scrolls purchased from a dealer in 1835. For the Book of Moses and the
inspired revision, Joseph worked from the King James Version of Genesis
without promptings from another manuscript. But in the method of their
creation, the three translations were alike. Joseph did not translate in the
sense of learning the language and consulting dictionaries. He received the
words by "revelation," whether or not a text lay before him.

The three historical translations all grew out of the Bible. They centered
on Moses, Enoch, and Abraham, and took place in Bible lands: Jerusalem,
Canaan, and Egypt. All had the character of expansions, enlarging a few
verses in the old scriptures into lengthy accounts unknown to Bible readers.
The *Book of Mormon* took off from the Jerusalem prophets in the time of
Jeremiah. Abraham added four chapters to the Bible story of the patriarch.
Much of the Book of Moses conformed to Genesis 1 through 5:25, describ-
ing the Creation, Adam and Eve, and the first generations after the Fall.
But instead of beginning with the Creation, Joseph's Book of Moses inserted
a preceding chapter describing Moses's call to write Genesis.

Joseph received the first chapter of Moses in June 1830 as an independent revelation, but over the next six months, he came to conceive it as the
beginning of a grand, new project: to revise the Bible. He would work his
way through the text, straightening out contradictions, correcting errors,
and adding lost portions. New translations of the Bible were common in
these years, but Joseph's revision was not based on a review of ancient
sources. He sat with a large King James Version, marking passages and dictating changes to Sidney Rigdon and other scribes. Until 1833, his day-to-
day activity was to work over the text, making changes large and small.[28]

It is hard to imagine now how this twenty-four-year-old came to believe
that he could revise the Bible. It was a striking demonstration of his outrageous confidence. To take on this hallowed book, he had to think of himself
as a prophet among prophets. Nearly all Protestants thought the Bible contained the final word on Christian doctrine and practice. The watchword
for radical reformers was the "all-sufficiency and the alone-sufficiency of
the Holy Scriptures."[29] By presuming to alter the Western world's most
revered literary work, Joseph appeared to rise above holy writ, risking the

wrath of every Christian. Yet revising the Bible was only a logical extension of translating the *Book of Mormon*. Both were expansions of the scriptures. Joseph's role as revelator authorized him to add to the Bible and correct the translation where it had gone astray. He did not question the authenticity of the Bible as did the German scholars who were identifying signs of human authorship about this time.[30] Rather than doubting the Bible's inspiration, Joseph believed the original text had been marred in its descent through the ages and proposed to strengthen biblical authority by recovering the original.

Other translations of the Bible in Joseph's time simplified the language to make the scriptures more accessible. In 1826, the Baptist reformer Alexander Campbell published a new version of the New Testament, combining portions of three new translations selected by Campbell for their intelligibility and their recognition of baptism by immersion. In 1836, Noah Webster, author of the dictionary, published a translation designed for American audiences.[31] Joseph's revision was more like Thomas Jefferson's treatment of the New Testament. Without referring to the ancient manuscripts, Jefferson altered the text to suit his own preferences, except that Jefferson pared back the text to the bare bones of Jesus's moral teachings, while Joseph added long passages and rewrote sentences according to his inspiration.[32] As a son of the Enlightenment, Jefferson cut out the mysterious doctrines; as a prophet and seer, Joseph expanded and elaborated them. Unlike the scholarly translators, he went back beyond the existing texts to the minds of the prophets, and through them to the mind of God. As he said later in life, "I believe the Bible, as it ought to be, as it came from the pen of the original writers."[33]

MOSES

The revelation that initiated revision of the Bible came at a difficult time. After Joseph had organized the Church in April 1830, he returned to Harmony, Pennsylvania, to farm his scrap of land. During a visit to followers in Colesville, twenty-six miles away, he was harassed by a "raging" mob and twice hauled into court, charged as a disorderly person.[34] Then in June 1830 came the revelation of Moses, now found in the first chapter of the Book of Moses. In his history, Joseph said that "amid all trials and tribulations we had to wade through, the Lord, who well knew our infantile and delicate situation, vouchsafed for us a supply, and granted us 'line upon line, here a little and there a little,' of which the following was a precious morsel."[35] The revelation had no apparent relation to his court battles, or to his precarious finances, the new Church, or the lives of his followers. It said nothing about the familiar stories of the Exodus, or the reception of the Ten Commandments, or the forty years in the wilderness. It dealt instead with the story of Creation that Moses was believed to have described in Genesis. It is worth close attention because it laid down themes Joseph would return to for the rest of his life and reveals a little more of what being a prophet meant to him.

The June 1830 revelation of Moses consists of a grand vision, more far-reaching than Joseph's own First Vision. "Moses was caught up into an exceeding high mountain, & he saw God face to face, & he talked with him, & the glory of God was upon him; therefore he could endure his presence."[36] Incongruously for a supposedly Old Testament text, Christ enters the discourse almost at once and remains present throughout the book. "Behold, thou art my Son," the Lord says to Moses, a son like "mine only begotten; and mine only begotten is & shall be the Savior." Joseph Smith's Moses is a Christian, as are the prophets in all his translations. The *Book of Mormon* had also Christianized prophetic discourse, even in pre-Christian times. In the Book of Moses, God uses Christian language as naturally as Paul. Worlds without number has God created, Moses learns, "and by the same I created them, which is mine only Begotten." When Moses prays, he is "filled with the Holy Ghost which beareth record of the Father & the son."[37] A Christian godhead with Father, Son, and Holy Ghost presides over the world from the beginning.

Joseph's translation of Moses went a step beyond Protestant readings of the Old Testament. Protestants saw only foreshadowings of Christ in the Hebrew scriptures. Humankind was cut off from the full knowledge of the Gospel at the Fall. From then on, Christ was only hinted at in symbols or clues called types. Jonathan Edwards, New England's leading eighteenth-century theologian, said the first hint of the Christian gospel came in the warning in the Garden that the serpent would have power to bruise man's heel, but God would have power to crush the serpent's head. This statement was "an obscure revelation of the gospel." Edwards likened the gradual increase of gospel light to the building of a house. "First, the workmen are sent forth, then the materials are gathered, then the ground fitted, then the foundation is laid, then the superstructure is erected, one part after another, till at length the top stone is laid, and all is finished." For two hundred pages in *A History of the Work of Redemption*, Edwards catalogued the prefigurements of Christ in the Old Testament, building toward the final revelation during His life on earth.[38]

Joseph Smith's Book of Moses fully Christianized the Old Testament. Rather than hinting of the coming Christian truth, the Book of Moses presents the whole Gospel. God teaches Adam to believe, repent, "and be baptized even by water, in the name of mine only begotten Son, which is full of grace and truth, which is Jesus Christ."[39] Together the *Book of Mormon* and the Book of Moses give history a different shape from the Old Testament. There is no sharp drop after the Fall, followed by gradual spiritual enlightenment. Theologically, the ancient patriarchs were the equals of later Christians. The problem of history was to hold on to the Gospel, not to prepare for its coming.

The Moses narrative opens with a dramatic scene. Moses receives a vision of "the world and the ends thereof, and all the children of men," at which he "greatly marveled & wondered." He is shown everything about the earth, but then God abruptly withdraws. Moses falls to the ground, left weak and helpless without "his natural strength." Astonished, Moses says "for this once I know that man is nothing which thing I never had supposed."[40] In this weakened condition, Moses faces a test that echoed Joseph's struggle with darkness before his First Vision. Satan appears and tempts Moses: "Son of man worship me." A battle of words and wills ensues that must be read in full text to recapture the spirit.

Moses lifted up his eyes and looked upon Satan & said who are thou for behold I am a son of God in the similitude of his only begotten & where is thy glory that I should worship thee for behold I could not look upon God except his glory should come upon me & I was transfigered before him but I can look upon thee in the natural man! shurely blessed is the name of my God For his spirit hath not altogether withdrawn from me. I say where is thy glory for it is darkness unto me & I can Judge between thee & God for God said unto me, Worship God for him only shalt thou serve

Get thee hence, Satan, deceive me not, for God said unto me Thou art after the similitude of mine only begotten. & he also gave unto me commandment, when he called unto me out of the burning bush, Saying, call upon God, in the name of mine only begotten, & worship me.

And again, Moses said, I will not cease to call upon God, I have other things to enquire of him for his glory has been upon me & it is a glory unto me wherefore I can Judge between him and thee. Depart hence, Satan.

And now when Moses had said these words Satan cried with a Loud voice & wrent upon the Earth, & commanded, saying, I am the only begotten, worship me.

And it came to pass that Moses began to fear exceedingly, & and as he began to fear he saw the bitterness of Hell, Nevertheless, calling upon God he received strength & he commanded Saying, Depart hence, Satan, for this one God only will I worship, which is the God of glory.

And now Satan began to tremble, & the Earth shook, & Moses received strength & called upon God in the name of his Son saying to Satan depart hence.

And it came to pass that Satan cried with a loud voice with weeping &

wailing & gnashing of teeth, & departed hence yea from the presence of
Moses that he beheld him not.[41]

Satan's terrible rage shakes the earth, causing Moses to fear, and yet he finds
strength to command Satan's departure. Satan weeps and wails as he
retreats, vanquished by Moses' courage and faith. The Book of Moses,
more than any of Joseph's works, conveys the sense of prophethood as an
ordeal. Visions of light and truth alternate with evil and darkness.

Having survived the trial, Moses is restored to God's presence. "Blessed
art thou Moses," God says, "for I, the almighty have chosen thee, And thou
shalt be made stronger than the many Waters." Moses receives a call to lead
God's people, "even Israel my chosen," from bondage. Then in a confirmation of the call, God opens another vision of literally everything in and on
the earth:

> And it came to pass, as the voice was still speaking, he cast his eyes & beheld
> the Earth yea even all the face of it & there was not a particle of it which he
> did not behold, decerning it by the spirit of God.
>
> & he beheld also the Inhabitants thereof & there was not a soul which he
> beheld not, & he dicerned them by the spirit of god, & their numbers were
> great, even numberless as the sand upon the Sea shore.
>
> & he beheld many lands & each land was called Earth, & there were
> inhabitants on the face thereof.[42]

Strengthened and amazed, Moses turns to God with a question: Why
creation?

> And it came to pass that Moses called upon God saying shew me I pray thee
> why these things are so & by whom thou madest them
>
> & Behold, the glory of God was upon Moses so that moses stood in the
> presence of God & he talked with him face to face. & the Lord God said unto
> Moses, For mine own purpose have I made these things, here is wisdom, & it
> remaineth in me.[43]

God, still distant and terrible, refuses to say why he created the worlds,
other than to declare that "worlds without number have I created, & I also
created them for mine own purpose, & by the same I created them, which is
mine only begotten." That is all you need to know, God says. But Moses has
grown bold, and his curiosity about these creations cannot be contained.
"Be mercifull unto thy servant, O God," he pleads, "& tell me concerning
this Earth & the inhabitants thereof & also the Heavens & then thy Servent
will be content. Please, Lord." Finally, God answers:

The Heavens . . . these are many, & they cannot be numbered unto man but they are numbered unto me for they are mine & as one Earth shall pass away & the Heavens thereof even so shall another come And there is no end to my works neither to my words.

for Behold this is my work and my glory to bring to pass the immortality and eternal life of man.[44]

There is the answer: God made multiple earths and heavens to bring humans to eternal life.

Did Moses' vision give meaning to Joseph's life as the Church got started? A prophecy in the *Book of Mormon* had linked a modern prophet named Joseph with Moses and Israel, making Moses a model for Joseph Smith.[45] The two 1830 court trials must have been interpreted in part as battles in an eternal war between God and Satan. Even more, Joseph identified with Moses' cosmic curiosity. His third historical translation, the Book of Abraham, presented another account of creation, paralleling but differing from the Genesis of the Book of Moses. The heavens and the earth, the history of God, the making of worlds, the nature of matter, and cosmic purpose all returned in subsequent revelations. Joseph's kind of prophet was one who inquired about God's creations and received answers.

The literary critic Harold Bloom claims that Joseph Smith went back beyond Puritan and Augustinian Christianity to find the God of the Bible's Moses. In Bloom's opinion, Joseph Smith restated "the archaic or original Jewish religion" from the earliest tales of the Pentateuch. The "Yahweh who closes Noah's ark with his own hands, descends to make on-the-ground inspections of Babel and Sodom, and who picnics with two angels under Abram's terebinth trees" is very close "in personality and dynamic passion" to the God of Joseph Smith.[46] The relationship is reminiscent of 4 Ezra (sometimes called 2 Esdras) in the Apocrypha, a book available in Protestant Bibles in Joseph's time. Ezra aggressively interrogates an angel whom he calls "my Lord," pressing him relentlessly for answers to imponderable questions. Ezra asks, Why did God leave an evil nature in men? Ezra wants to know why Israel, God's people, suffers at the hands of other nations. Why does He not let the Israel possess the world?[47] Although Joseph's question is not "Why evil?" but "Why creation?" his Book of Moses is written in the spirit of Ezra's dialogue, and can be said to continue the apocryphal tradition of cosmic inquiry.[48]

ENOCH

After recording Moses' vision in June, Joseph began work on the succeeding chapters of Genesis. In the fall of 1830, while the New York missionar-

ies preached in Ohio, and on through December when the newly converted
Sidney Rigdon and Edward Partridge came to visit, Joseph translated while
Emma, Oliver Cowdery, John Whitmer, or Rigdon took down the dictation. This work inaugurated the much larger project of revising the whole
Bible.[49] By the end of the year, Joseph had completed the first five chapters
of Genesis, enlarging eight pages of the Bible into twenty-one of what
became the Book of Moses.[50]

In redoing the early chapters of Genesis, the stories of Creation, of
Adam and Eve, and the Fall were modified, but with less extensive interpolations than in the revelation to Moses. Joseph wove Christian doctrine into
the text without altering the basic story. But with the appearance of Enoch
in the seventh generation from Adam, the text expanded far beyond the
biblical version. In Genesis, Enoch is summed up in 5 verses; in Joseph
Smith's revision, Enoch's story extends to 110 verses.

Bible readers had always been curious about Enoch and the city transported into heaven. Joseph's expansion appeared when a vast apocryphal literature on Enoch was first being rediscovered. In 1821, Richard Laurence,
the Archbishop of Cashel and professor of Hebrew at Oxford, published an
English translation of an early Ethiopic text discovered in Abyssinia by
James Bruce and deposited in Oxford's Bodleian Library. Called the Book of
Enoch or, later, 1 Enoch, the text purported to be the teachings and visions
of the ancient patriarch, though its true authorship was unknown. Up until
that time, modern biblical commentators on Enoch had been restricted to
the five verses in Genesis and the three in the New Testament that speak of
Enoch's genealogy, prophecy of judgment, and ascent into heaven without
dying. Later in the nineteenth century, more texts were uncovered, and
Enoch's importance among Jewish Kabbalists, the Qumran community, and
second-century Christians has come to be generally understood.[51] It is
scarcely conceivable that Joseph Smith knew of Laurence's Enoch translation, but the coincidence of their appearance within a few years of each
other is a curiosity.[52]

Laurence's 105 translated chapters do not resemble Joseph Smith's
Enoch in any obvious way. The Ethiopic Book of Enoch, for example, tells
the story of two hundred angels called the Watchers who conspired to wed
the daughters of men. They brought forth a race of giants and introduced
sorcery, warfare, and luxury into the world. Nothing like that appears in the
Book of Moses. The chief resemblance between the Ethiopic Enoch and
the Enoch and Moses narratives of Joseph Smith is their common messianism. References to the Son of Man and other New Testament titles for
Christ are sprinkled throughout the Ethiopic text.[53] But differences pre-
dominate, so that a casual reader might not notice a relationship.[54] The
ancient and the modern Enoch appear to be independent productions.

Enoch's story merits close attention because, like the vision of Moses, it bears on Joseph's prophetic identity. Later, when Joseph disguised his identity to elude his enemies, he took the name of Enoch as pseudonym.[55] As he was a modern Moses, so was he a modern Enoch. Enoch's call comes not on a high mountain like Moses', but in a voice from heaven, saying, "Enoch my Son, prophesy unto this people, & say unto them, repent." In a response that echoes Smith's unease about his own prophethood, Enoch protests, "Why is it that I have found favour in thy Sight, and Am but a lad, & all the people hate me, for I am slow of speech: Wherefore am I thy Servent?"[56] Joseph had been a boy, with no desire to preach, when he received his call. He later remembered "the bitterest persecution and reviling."[57] In the Enoch story, the prophet overcomes his adversaries by following God's instructions to anoint his eyes with clay. Afterward, Enoch beholds "things which were not visable to the natural eye," becoming a seer like Joseph. "From thenceforth came the saying abroad in the land, a seer hath the Lord raised up unto his people." When Enoch finally did preach, he frightened his hearers so that no one dared touch him. "No man laid hands on him, for fear came on all them that heard him, for he walked with God."[58] By becoming a seer, the unfavored boy was revenged on his antagonists. The voice issuing the call to Enoch announces the dominant theme in the Enoch passage: the evil in the hearts of men:

> I am angery with this people, and my firce anger is kindeled against them; For their hearts have waxed hard, & their ears are dull of hearing, & their eyes cannot see afar off, & for these many generations, even since the day that I created them, have they gone astray, & have denied me, & have sought their own councils in the dark, And in their own abominations have they devised murder, & have not kept the commandments which I gave unto their father, Adam.[59]

Enoch, poised between his progenitor Adam and his grandson Noah, speaks with a God who contemplates the destruction of the earth by a flood. Enoch is told to cry repentance to a doomed world.

After the call, the narrative adopts an apocalyptic architecture. A voice from heaven tells Enoch to go up upon Mount Simeon. There, like Moses, "I saw the Lord; he stood before my face, and he talked with me, even as a man talketh one with an other face to face; and he saith unto me, Look, and I will shew unto thee the world for the space of many generations." When that vision closes, Enoch goes forth to preach, but then another vision opens, and Enoch is given a view of all the earth's inhabitants:

> Enoch was high and lifted up, even in the bosom of the Father, and the Son of man; and behold the power of Satan was upon all the face of the earth! And he saw angels descending out of heaven; and he heard a loud voice, saying, Wo,

wo, be unto the inhabitants of the earth! And he beheld Satan, and he had a great chain in his hand, and it veiled the whole face of the earth with darkness, and he looked up and laughed, and his angels rejoiced.[60]

Beginning with this awful scene, the last half of Enoch's narrative is a vision of the future from Noah and the flood, to the crucifixion and resurrection of Christ, down to the last day when the wicked are judged and Christ returns.

The most compelling theme in this complicated narrative is the suffering of God for the sins of His people. On the eve of the flood, Enoch knows God's anger is kindling against His wicked children. Yet Enoch sees God's tears. "And it came to pass that the God of heaven looked upon the residue of the people, and he wept," causing Enoch to marvel and boldly ask: "How is it that thou canst weep, seeing thou are holy and from all eternity to all eternity? . . . Were it possible that man could number the particles of the earth, yea, and millions of earths like this, it would not be a beginning to the number of thy creations." Nothing but "peace, justice and truth is the habitation of thy throne; and mercy shall go before thy face and have no end; how is it that thou canst weep?"[61]

In answer, God tells Enoch his brethren were commanded "that they should love one another; and that they should choose me their father." But they refused. "Behold they are without affection." Humanity has become hardened and vicious; hence God's lament. For "among all the workmanship of mine hand, there has not been so great wickedness." And so "misery shall be their doom; and the whole heavens shall weep over them," and "wherefore, should not the heavens weep, seeing these shall suffer?"[62] Wrath and sorrow alternate in God's heart. Enoch now understands God's anguish at knowing his own children must suffer. They have turned against him and one another; they "hate their own blood." Seeing the horrible wickedness that has blighted the earth, Enoch too "wept, and stretched forth his arms, and his heart swelled wide as eternity; and his bowels yearned, and all eternity shook."[63]

The words echo Mormon in the *Book of Mormon* bemoaning the fall of his people with the cry "O ye fair ones, how could ye have departed from the ways of the Lord! . . . O ye fair sons and daughters, ye fathers and mothers, ye husbands and wives, ye fair ones, how is it that ye could have fallen!"[64] The Book of Mormon tells of the prophets' failure to prevent the descent into wickedness and chaos. After a thousand years of labor, the Nephite prophets go down in defeat. Their civilization disappears in the bloody battles of opposing armies.

In Enoch, the earth itself joins the lament. As Enoch looks upon the earth, he hears a voice intoning, "Wo, wo is me the mother of men? I am pained: I am weary because of the wickedness of my children? When shall I rest, and be cleansed from the filthiness which is gone forth out of me?" The earth's cry moves Enoch to plead for the Lord's compassion, echoing the question "When shall the earth rest?"[65]

Against this tale of sorrow and wickedness, God reveals to Enoch the time of Christ's return and the spread of truth around the earth. Then the earth will find peace. This is not a restoration, as has sometimes been argued. The coming of the last day is not a triumphant ascent toward utopian perfection, nor a return to a golden age of innocence and purity.[66] The last day is a long-delayed release from an ancient sorrow. God and the earth have too long mourned for a people who turn against their Father and hate their own blood.

This cosmic lament returns us to the sorrow in the *Book of Mormon*'s "Psalm of Nephi." Joseph Smith, of a self-confessed "native cheery Temperament," knew of sin—in himself and in the world. A March 1830 revelation had spoken of Christ's suffering causing Him, "even God, the greatest of all, to tremble because of pain, and to bleed at every pore." Under Joseph's confident exterior lay a despair for human sinfulness so intense that God Himself weeps. The "holy men" in Enoch who wandered the earth as "strangers and pilgrims" in search of peace "found it not because of wickedness and abominations."[67] In these early writings, Joseph was a prophet of sorrow.[68]

The Enoch narrative created a deep history for the young church.[69] The revelation came while Oliver Cowdery and the missionaries to the Lamanites headed west to find a site for the City of Zion. The writings gave the little flock a pattern for their own city-building. Enoch's people dwelt in a city called Zion "because they were of one heart and of one mind, and dwelt in righteousness; and there was no poor among them," a city so righteous it "was taken up into heaven." Though modeled after Enoch's Zion, Joseph's New Jerusalem was not to follow Enoch's "City of Holiness" into heaven. Quite the reverse. In Enoch's vision, latter-day people gather from all over the earth into a holy city, "called ZION, a New Jerusalem." Rather than rising, this city stays put, and Enoch's city descends from heaven to meet the people of the New Jerusalem on earth. "Then shalt thou and all thy city meet them there, and we will receive them into our bosom, and they shall see us, and we will fall upon their necks, and they shall fall upon our necks, and we will kiss each other." Joseph's people and the city of Enoch were to converge at the end with the promise that Enoch would come down from heaven one day to kiss the Latter-day Saints. "And it shall be Zion which shall come forth out of all the creations which I have made; and for the space of a thousand years the earth shall rest."[70] The millennium begins in a happy union of two holy peoples on a cleansed earth.

Bloom uses the word "transumption" for this blend of a distant past with the present, when the people of one age think they are continuing the history of another. In Joseph's revelations, figures from the Bible return to bestow their powers on the Church, joining past and present. The past in Enoch's narrative breaks into the present in order to complete the scriptural story. More than restoring the New Testament church, the early Mormons believed they were resuming the biblical narrative in their own time.[71] Linking the "latter-day" church to an ancient sacred history was to become a hallmark of Joseph's prophesying.

REVISION

After moving to Ohio, Joseph intermittently carried on translation of the Bible until 1833 when he declared the work finished, although the Church lacked the funds to publish the revision during his lifetime.[72] For nearly three years, his everyday work, between dealing with crises and managing the Church, was this "New Translation." In March 1831, instructed by a revelation, he switched from the Old Testament to the New.[73] As he worked his way through the text, aided by Sidney Rigdon, his methods changed. After the Enoch revelations, he made no more heroic additions. Here and there the text was dramatically expanded, but mostly he appears to have been reading and rereading in search of flawed passages. The changes did not always come in a flash of insight or a burst of revelation. The manuscript shows signs of him searching his mind for the right words, as a regular translator might do.[74]

These smaller revisions read more like improvements than fresh revelations. Unlike the many additional pages about Moses and Enoch, the later alterations added only a few verses at a time, clarifying meaning in small ways.[75] Not working from an ancient text, Joseph still obviously relied on inspiration to make the changes, but he gave up the Urim and Thummim, as Orson Pratt later explained, because he had become acquainted with "the Spirit of Prophecy and Revelation" and no longer needed it. Later, he moved still closer to conventional translation. In 1835 the Church hired Joshua Seixas to teach Hebrew to the elders. Joseph joined the classes along with everyone else. The inspired translator of the Bible and *Book of Mormon* received instruction from a professor, as if he wanted to blend conventional learning with his own special gifts.[76]

Blending was an issue for Joseph. His whole life divided between the ordinary and the strange. At times he appeared to be two persons. We can hardly recognize Joe Smith, the ignoramus and schemer of the Palmyra neighbors, in the writings of Joseph Smith, the Prophet and Seer. The writings and the person seem to have lived in separate worlds. In the neighbors' reports, he was a plain rural visionary with little talent save a gift for seeing in a stone. No flashes of intelligence, ambition, or faith distinguish him. Even his family members, who thought he was virtuous, had no premonition of his powers. They could not envision him writing about Moses' epic encounter with God or telling of God's sorrow over humanity's iniquity in Enoch. In his inspired writings, Joseph entered into other worlds and looked across time and space. Strange and marvelous narratives come from his mouth. No one, friend or foe, expected any of that.

In the decade leading up to his introduction in the Whitney store, Joseph had become a prophet of puzzling complexity. Even he could not reconcile what he had become with what he had been. Near the end of his life, he said he could not fault the skeptics for their disbelief: "If I had not experienced what I have, I should not have believed it myself."[77]

SEVEN

THE KIRTLAND VISIONARIES

JANUARY–JUNE 1831

*And then received ye spirits which ye could not understand, and received them to
be of God, and in this are ye justified? . . . That which is of God is light, and he
that receiveth light and continueth in God, receiveth more light, and that light
groweth brighter and brighter, until the perfect day.*
Book of Commandments, 53:14, 21

KIRTLAND, OHIO, HAD BEEN SETTLED for about twenty years when Joseph
and Emma arrived in February 1831. Surveyed in 1798, the town first
formed a government in 1818. In 1820, 481 residents lived on twenty-five
square miles, fewer than twenty per square mile. By 1830, the population
had doubled to 1,018 people in 162 households, well under the 2,500
required to meet the census definition of a town. Church members could
easily become a major presence in such a small population. Nine Kirtland
families joined the Mormons in the first wave of conversions, and over the
next six years, many others were baptized or migrated in. By 1835 when the
town's population stood about 2,000, some 900 Mormons lived in Kirtland
with another 200 nearby. Two years later, the Mormons probably were a
majority.[1]

In those early years, Newel K. Whitney and Algernon Sidney Gilbert,
two converts baptized in 1830, did business in Kirtland Flats, a village in
the far northwest corner of the township on the East Branch of the Chagrin River. Near their country store was a small hotel, and scattered along
the stream were saw, grist, and carding mills. The main road led up a hill
south of the village to Geauga County's rolling tablelands. A visitor called
it "rough, broken, country." On this broad expanse, intermittent fields
appeared amid the largely wooded landscape with gorges as deep as 100 feet
cut by streams flowing into Lake Erie.[2]

Once more Joseph and Emma moved into an area stimulated by canal
traffic. The construction of the Ohio & Erie Canal between 1825 and 1832
greatly improved the commercial prospects of Geauga County, just as New
York's Erie Canal had boosted Palmyra's. Starting north from the Ohio

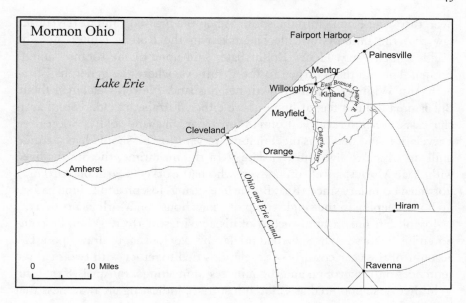

River, the Ohio & Erie terminated at Cleveland on Lake Erie, just twenty miles west of Kirtland in Cuyahoga County. The canal provided an alternate means of transportation for Mormon excursions to Independence, Missouri, soon to become the Church's secondary headquarters. For five dollars, a canal boat would carry a passenger the 308 miles from Cleveland to Portsmouth, Ohio, in eighty hours. From there steamboats went west.[3]

By 1840, the canal had turned Cleveland into an energetic city numbering 6,000 people, but a decade earlier only 1,075 inhabitants lived in a village about two-thirds of a square mile.[4] Kirtland was more influenced by Painesville, twelve miles to the east. Painesville had no canal terminus (and thus no future), but it was situated near Fairport, the Lake Erie entry point for migrants moving into Geauga County from New York. With its bank, school, and newspaper, Painesville figured prominently in Mormon affairs. Eber D. Howe, the editor of the *Painesville Telegraph*, took an immediate interest in the Mormons, writing about the first missionaries who arrived in the fall of 1830.[5] In 1834, he published the exposé *Mormonism Unvailed*, a book, that despite its negative tone, was filled with much good reporting.[6]

Joseph entered a new world when he arrived in Kirtland. In Palmyra he was derided and persecuted; in Kirtland admirers and believers surrounded him. Within five years, he would build a temple and gather thousands of followers. Even so, when Joseph and Emma arrived on February 1, 1831, they had no place to go. They were welcomed at the Gilbert and Whitney store, but no house awaited the pregnant Emma. Gilbert's invitation to stay with his family was ill-fated from the start. On the way, the wagon turned over, throwing Emma into the snow. When the bruised Emma arrived, she saw that the Gilberts already had taken in the Rollins family, and she decided not to stay. Henry Rollins later said none of the rooms "suited" Emma. The Smiths returned to the Whitneys, where the generous Elizabeth Ann Whitney, a convert with her husband, Newel, welcomed them. But Emma did not feel at home there either. Elizabeth's elderly and anticlerical aunt Sarah received Emma's "preacher" husband coldly.[7] Soon after, a revelation said that "it is meet that my servant Joseph should have a house built, in which to live and translate."[8] In the meantime, the Smiths lived with Isaac Morley, a well-off convert who had worked a farm on Kirtland's northern boundary since 1812. By the late spring, Joseph and Emma had set up housekeeping in the single room of a new house on Morley's property.[9]

Joseph left only a brief record of his activities in 1831. When he composed his history in 1838, he had no day-by-day journal to draw upon. His account of the year consists of revelations tied together with two or three sentences of background and the minutes of meetings. In April 1831, John Whitmer was appointed as Church historian, indicating an awareness that history should be recorded, but no contemporaneous history is known to exist. The history Whitmer later wrote consisted of a few observations about Church events filled out with transcriptions of the revelations.[10]

In his history, Joseph wrote that in Kirtland he "continued to translate the scriptures as time would allow." The translation, though it proceeded in fits and starts, was his ongoing work. Between April 4 and April 7, he and Rigdon completed chapters 1 through 8 of Matthew, but by September 26 they were only up to Matthew 26. A few more 1831 events are recorded in the "Far West Record," a spare account of Church conferences copied into a ledger purchased to hold minutes of the Far West, Missouri, high council a half dozen years later.[11] Little was said about Joseph's personal life.

VISIONARIES

In many ways, northeast Ohio was an extension of the New York region Joseph and Emma had just left. Kirtland was located in a block of land awarded by the federal government to Connecticut in return for the state's giving up its much more extensive claims to western lands. Ohio governed this "Western Reserve," but Connecticut dispensed the land. Yankees and "Yorkers" flowed into the area in the first decades of settlement, bringing to the Western Reserve a form of New England culture much like Palmyra's. The migrants had the same excitable religious temperament that earned upstate New York the description "burned-over district." In both places, religious intensity and spiritual independence gave birth to a host of innovations in worship and belief.

The fertility of the religious landscape in the northeastern United States was evident as early as the 1740s. Scores of independent religious groups sprang up in the first Great Awakening as zealous believers splintered from established congregations in search of more exciting preaching. After the American Revolution, the number of independent congregations multiplied. Most of these groups came and went, but a few persisted beyond the lives of their founders. By 1815, the Freewill Baptists, the Shakers, and the Universalists each had a hundred or more congregations. According to the most complete account, these radical sects had their "ultimate source" in "the charismatic, visionary experience of prophetic leaders." Benjamin Randal, founder of the Freewill Baptists, received a revelation in a New Hampshire cornfield instructing him to forsake other religious traditions and teach only the Bible. Caleb Rich, an early Universalist in New England, ascended Mount Zion accompanied by a "celestial friend." In vision he saw "the house of God and the gate of heaven." An angel said that no existing church "stood in the Apostolic rectitude or that contended for the Faith once delivered to the saints." Ann Lee, founder of the Shakers, had "astonishing visions and divine manifestations." These visionaries differed in the details of their revelations, but each of them received "direct personal confirmation of their unique and world-saving mission through visionary and providential experiences."[12]

The outbursts of religious enthusiasm point to the existence of a widespread visionary population hungering for more of God than standard church worship provided. John Wigger, an historian of early Methodism, defines their "supernaturalism" as "a cluster of beliefs and practices that place great stock in dreams, visions, supernatural impressions, miraculous healings, speaking in tongues." Enthusiasts wanted "a more interactive faith in which the believer and God actively work together to meet life's daily challenges and in which God communicates directly with the believer or community of believers." Methodism, the fastest-growing branch of American Protestantism from the Revolution to the Civil War, began as a visionary religion. Wigger has uncovered numerous stories of visions and dreams in the lives of early Methodist preachers, leading him to conclude that "this quest for the supernatural in everyday life was the most distinctive characteristic of early American Methodism."[13]

Many early converts to Mormonism came out of this culture. In one affidavit, the Palmyra neighbors observed that "all with whom we were acquainted, that have embraced Mormonism from this neighborhood, we are compeled to say, were very visionary, and most of them destitute of moral character." Elizabeth Ann Whitney, who took the Smiths into her house on their arrival in Kirtland, remarked to her husband, Newel, that Mormonism "was the fulfillment of the vision we had seen of a cloud as of glory resting upon our house." Before his conversion, Jonathan Crosby "dreamed that some new preachers came with a book containing new doctrine, and which threw new light on the bible, and their preaching was different from that of all others, and that I rejoiced in it."[14] Looking back in 1877, Edward Tullidge, an English convert, remembered that "at about the same time Joseph Smith was receiving the administration of angels, thousands both in America and Great Britain were favored with corresponding visions and intuitions."[15]

By the 1820s, the Methodists were retreating from their visionary beginnings, taming extravagant impulses as the church grew in size and respectability.[16] Visionary religion was still a current within denominational religions but less of a generative force. Mormons (and Shakers) preserved a type of religion that was gradually dimming. Conventional churches already prevailed in Kirtland when the Smiths arrived. The Congregationalists had organized in 1819 and a few years later constructed a frame meetinghouse. From about 1820 on, Methodists had a small church across the street from the future Mormon temple site. A Calvinist Baptist church (as distinguished from the Freewill Baptists) was meeting by 1830.[17]

Not everyone found a spiritual home in these congregations. Elizabeth and Newel Whitney chose to go outside the established churches looking for religion. "We united ourselves with the Campbellites," she later explained, "who were then making many converts, and whose principles seemed most in accordance with the Scriptures."[18] Campbell condemned visionary religion, but shared the desire for a more pure and powerful religion based on the New Testament. Visionaries sought spiritual gifts; Campbell sought exact conformity to New Testament organization and doctrine.

Alexander Campbell's followers, calling themselves Reformed Baptists, sought to strip away everything added since the age of the apostles. Campbell's fellow reformer, Walter Scott, reduced the Gospel to five simple points: faith, repentance, baptism by immersion, remission of sins, and the gift of the Holy Spirit. Claiming to establish the "scriptural order of the gospel," the Reformed Baptists made hundreds of converts. Sidney Rigdon, who taught doctrines close to Campbell's, built up a congregation of fifty members in Mentor, the township directly north of Kirtland, and another fifty in Kirtland itself.[19] The Reformed Baptists provided a home for people like the Whitneys who wanted stronger religion.

Though committed to the New Testament, Campbell was averse to "gifts"—prophecy, visions, tongues, and healings. He wanted to restore only the ancient doctrine and church practices. Miracles in the time of Christ, Campbell believed, supported the original apostles' claim to divine revelation. They were not to be enjoyed by modern Christians—except as evidence. The Campbellite response to Joseph Smith was to demand miracles, but only as proof of his purported visions.[20] Campbell was unsympathetic to the visionaries' desire for stronger spiritual food as a regular diet. He could not understand Sidney Rigdon's search for something more. In late October 1830, on the eve of the Mormons' arrival, Rigdon "had often been unable to sleep, walking and praying for more light and comfort in his religion." The next month, he led a parade of believers into Joseph Smith's fold. Campbellites were appalled that people would blindly accept revelations on so little evidence.[21]

Campbell was equally opposed to the New Testament practice of common property, a principle a few families in the Kirtland area with Rigdon's encouragement tried to follow.[22] Isaac Morley, a member of Rigdon's congregation, organized a communitarian system of property under which Morley shared property with eleven families called "the Family," and spawned a smaller branch of five families under Lyman Wight in nearby Mayfield. Uncertainty about who owned what led to "confusion and disappointments," but the group persisted from February 1830 until Joseph and Emma arrived the next year.[23] Virtually all members of the Family were baptized in the first wave of Mormon conversions.

Independent spirits like these made up the congregations that greeted Joseph Smith when he arrived in Kirtland in 1831. Many were ready to believe before they saw the Prophet. Philo Dibble was immediately interested when he learned "that four men had come to Kirtland with a golden Bible, and one of them had seen an angel." Dibble refused to "make light of such a subject," though others scoffed. He "thought that if angels had administered to the children of men again, I was glad of it." When he heard Oliver Cowdery's preaching, Dibble asked for baptism—against the warnings of his wife.

> When I came out of the water I knew that I had been born of water and of the spirit, for my mind was illuminated with the Holy Ghost. I spent that evening at Dr. F. G. Williams. While in bed that night I felt what appeared to be a hand upon my left shoulder, and a sensation like fibers of fire immediately enveloped my body. . . . I was enveloped in a heavenly influence and could not sleep for joy.[24]

Rigdon was baptized within ten days after the four New York missionaries arrived in Mentor on October 28, 1830, and though the majority of his congregation withdrew its support, a few families in Kirtland followed his lead. Before the four missionaries left near the end of November, Rigdon, Isaac Morley, Lyman Wight, and John Murdock were ordained elders and put in charge of more than a hundred converts.

As the news spread, curiosity attracted investigators from the surrounding towns. Rigdon's conversion dumbfounded John Corrill, who had expected Rigdon to demolish the Mormons' outrageous claims. Corrill attended the Mormon meetings to dissuade the converts, but he found them "enjoying as they supposed, the gift and power of the Holy Ghost" and was converted himself. Writing as a cool-headed rationalist nine years later, after he had left Mormonism, Corrill admitted that the Mormons' spiritual gifts had impressed him.

> The meeting lasted all night, and such a meeting I never attended before. They administered the sacrament, and laid on hands, after which I heard them prophecy and speak in tongues unknown to me. Persons in the room, who took no part with them, declared, from the knowledge they had of the Indian languages, that the tongues spoken were regular Indian dialects, which I was also informed, on inquiry, the persons who spoke had never learned. I watched closely and examined carefully, every movement of the meeting, and after exhausting all my powers to find the deception, I was obliged to acknowledge, in my own mind, that the meeting had been inspired by some supernatural agency.[25]

Impressed by the visionary phenomenon, Corrill consulted his Bible.

> I found, on searching the Scriptures, that from the commencement of time, through every age, God continued to send prophets to the people, and always when God had a message for the people, he chose a special messenger to send it by, and it was always headed with a "thus said the Lord". . . . If he supplied every other age and people with prophets and special messengers, why not this?

On January 10, 1831, Corrill was baptized a Mormon.[26]

Sometime in the early winter, after the New York missionaries had gone on to Missouri, the visionary impulse got out of hand. Eber D. Howe, the Painesville editor with Campbellite inclinations, reported "fits" of "the most wild, frantic and horrible fanaticism." In the nightly prayer meetings, some made "the most ridiculous grimaces, creeping upon their hands and feet, rolling upon the frozen ground," aping "all the Indian modes of warfare, such as knocking down, scalping, ripping open and tearing out the bowels." Levi Hancock, a hardheaded carpenter who had come to Mormonism through Parley Pratt's preaching, thought some of his fellow Mormons like Burr Riggs had gone too far. "I have seen him jump up from the floor, strike his head against the joist in the Baldwin's new house and swing some minutes, then fall like he was dead. After an hour or two he would come to. He would prophesy and tell what he had seen." Hancock saw Heman Bassett "behave like a baboon."[27] The cautious Corrill was unnerved too. "Many improprieties and visionary notions crept into the church, which tried the feelings of the more sound minded," but the wild conduct did not derail him. There were, he thought, "but a very few of the Church who were exercised in that way."[28]

The Kirtland Saints' antics were unlike anything Joseph had known in New York. Howe said he "appeared astonished at the wild enthusiasm and scalping performances, of his proselytes there." Joseph later wrote that "some strange notions and false spirits had crept in among them" which had to be "overcome." But, of course, he could not discredit visionary experience. When Levi Hancock told about his vision of Christ after baptism, Joseph said it showed the Lord's favor. He could scarcely say otherwise when the promise of visions and gifts was one of Mormonism's great appeals. Corrill said Mormons "believe rather more firmly . . . than others do" in biblical promises "that these signs shall follow them that believed; in his name they shall cast out devils, heal the sick, &c."[29] Joseph had to restrain the excesses without discouraging spiritual gifts altogether.

Soon after arriving in Kirtland, he received a revelation in response to a woman named Hubble "who professed to be a prophetess of the Lord" and wanted to set up as "a teacher in the Church." Joseph was sensitive about rival prophets after the Hiram Page episode the preceding fall. He did not want anyone else "revealing commandments, laws, and other curious matters." The new revelation firmly announced that only one was "appointed unto you, to receive commandments and revelations from my hand," and "there is none other appointed unto you to receive commandments and revelations until he be taken, if he abide in me."[30] The revelation sought to block the natural tendency of visionary religion to descend into confusion.[31]

Containing excesses was not easy when Joseph's own revelatory powers excited the desire for spiritual gifts. Corrill reported that "those visionary spirits spoken of before continued in the church, and rose to such a height that the elders became so dissatisfied with them that they determined to have something done about it." Visiting branches outside of Kirtland, Parley Pratt came across "strange spiritual operations" that were "disgusting, rather than edifying." People would swoon, make unseemly gestures, fall into ecstasies and cramps. Pratt felt that "a false and lying spirit seemed to be creeping into the Church." In March Joseph wrote his brother Hyrum about the devil's attempts to overthrow the disciples. Joseph was called from bed late one night to heal a frenzied woman. "Had an awful strugle with satan but being armed with the power of God he was cast out."[32] The visionary spirit had become a bane.

To discipline the ardor, a second revelation condemned the excesses and gave rules for judging the spirits. Members were told to follow the Spirit of truth, not the mindless ecstasies of the visionaries. "He that is sent forth to preach the word of truth by the Comforter, in the Spirit of truth, doth he preach it by the Spirit of truth or some other way?" The phrase "Spirit of truth," borrowed from the Gospel of John, was repeated five times in three verses. Truth must pass between a preacher and his listeners, not just spiritual exhilaration. "He that preacheth and he that receiveth, understandeth one another, and both are edified and rejoice together." To the word "edify" was added the metaphor of light. "That which is of God is light, and he that receiveth light and continueth in God, receiveth more light; and that light groweth brighter and brighter, until the perfect day." The words "truth," "light," and "edify" resonated with terms like "learning," "pure knowledge," and "intelligence" in later revelations. Spiritual gifts were meant to instruct, not merely to excite. "If thou shalt ask, thou shalt receive revelation upon revelation, knowledge upon knowledge."[33] Never an enthusiast himself, Joseph Smith turned visions away from sensation toward doctrine.

Gradually the excesses of the visionaries were checked. Hancock, who did not know what to make of Burr Riggs swinging from a house joist, was given a way to decide. If he met an unintelligible spirit and failed to receive it himself after asking for it, "then you may know it is not of God." The Saints were to proclaim against the evil spirit and overcome it. Joseph's revelation did not bring visionary outbursts to a halt, but he had laid down a line between Mormonism and the visionary culture of its first converts.[34]

THE LAW

The Kirtland converts' excesses briefly diverted Joseph from his main concern since the September 1830 conference: finding the site for the City of Zion. The revelations required the Saints to gather as soon as possible "to prepare their hearts, and be prepared in all things, against the day when tribulation and desolation are sent forth upon the wicked." Zion was their refuge against the coming calamities. Among the Mormons, the phrase "to bring forth Zion" soon came to mean building a city and gathering the people. For the next year, the revelations said little about doctrine, focusing almost completely on organizing the Church and gathering to the city. In early 1831, the revelations instructed Joseph to organize a new social order in preparation for the millennium. "Ye shall have no laws but my laws, when I come," one said. He was told that the "law" for the new society would be given after they got to Ohio, and ten days after Joseph's arrival in Kirtland, the revelation came.[35]

The "law" began with directions for missionary work, making it a responsibility of the entire adult male population. "Ye shall go forth in my name, every one of you," was the command. John Corrill was ordained an elder just three or four days after joining the Church, and within a few weeks he was on his way west on a proselytizing mission.[36] The missionaries went without training or indoctrination. The revelation simply said to "teach the scriptures which are in the bible, and the book of Mormon, in the which is the fulness of the gospel." No education was required. Eber D. Howe considered it an effrontery to ordain uneducated plain people so freely. "Nearly all of their male converts, however ignorant and worthless, were forthwith transformed into 'Elders,' and sent forth to proclaim, with all their wild enthusiasm, the wonders and mysteries of Mormonism."[37]

The Methodist precedent probably helped Mormon converts understand what was expected. In Methodism "a vast cadre of short-term and local preachers, exhorters, and class leaders" filled in between their celebrated itinerants' visits or added enthusiasm to the spirit of a meeting.[38] Even more populist than Methodism, Mormonism relied entirely on regular members for preaching; it had no clerical class at all. No salaried itinerants or settled ministers stood above the plain men sent out to teach the Gospel. The *Book of Mormon* spoke of teachers and priests set off from the Nephite lay members, but this class of leaders and preachers never developed in the modern Church. The line between laity and clergy, the most significant social division in Christian ecclesiastical society, was erased. Joseph, a plain man himself, inexperienced in preaching, trusted ordinary men to carry the message.

In a democratic time, the Mormons emerged as the most democratic of churches, rivaled only by the Quakers.[39] Yet at the same time, the seeds of hierarchy were sown early. The "law" revelation spoke of elders, priests, and teachers, implying grades and divisions of authority. The revelation forbade unauthorized preaching. No one was to go out without being "ordained by some one who has authority, and it is known to the church that he has authority, and has been regularly ordained by the hands of the church."[40] The authority to teach did not descend on every adult head, as did Luther's priesthood of all believers. Church leaders controlled ordinations, and Joseph as revelator was first among the leaders. The Church's ministry was both democratic and authoritarian.

To help these plain men carry out their mission, the revelations provided a simple gospel formula: "And this is my gospel: Repentance and baptism by water, and then cometh the baptism of fire and the Holy Ghost, even the Comforter, which showeth all things, and teacheth the peaceable things of the kingdom."[41] The missionaries taught a gospel almost exactly like Walter Scott's Campbellite doctrine that had converted hundreds in northeast Ohio. Although Mormonism appeared to be a bizarre offshoot of mainline Christianity, the revelations and the *Book of Mormon* actually stressed a basic Christian message of faith in Christ, repentance, and baptism with promises of spiritual blessings.

The straightforward message did not prevent opposition from forming. At the Masonic Hall in Cleveland John Murdock "warned the inhabitants of that place to flee the wrath to come," and angered listeners blew out candles and threw inkstands and books. In other places, as John Whitmer reported, people shouted, "False prophets, false christ," and their "priests" cried, "Delusion! delusion!!" After a few weeks in the field, some of the elders had to come back for "rest and instructions."[42] Occasionally, the missionaries' lack of tact led to trouble. In March, Sidney Rigdon and Parley Pratt visited a Shaker community at North Union near Cleveland, hoping for a warm reception from a people who believed in continuing revelation. Leman Copley, a former Shaker turned Mormon, went along to introduce the missionaries to Ashbel Kitchel, the local Shaker leader. After the Shakers' sabbath meeting, the missionaries read a revelation declaring that marriage was ordained of God—contrary to the Shaker belief in celibacy. When the irked Kitchel dismissed the Mormon delegation, the irrepressible Pratt shook his coattails, saying, in good New Testament fashion, that he shook the dust from his garments as a testimony against them. At this Kitchel blew up, called Pratt a "filthy Beast," and told him never to return, while Pratt sat in his seat with his hands covering his face. Pratt simply reported that "this strange people . . . utterly refused to hear or obey the gospel."[43]

Despite the opposition, the missionaries soldiered on. John Whitmer wrote the Church's history as if he were composing another Book of Acts, reporting that "the disciples increased daily, and miricles were wrought such as healing the sick casting out devils, and the church grew and multiplied in numbers, grace, and knowledge." Membership grew to about six hundred within three months of Joseph's arrival in Kirtland.[44]

After the section on missionaries, the remainder of the revelation on the "law of the Church" laid down rules for organizing society in Zion, reiterating a modern version of the Ten Commandments forbidding murder, theft, lying, and adultery. Then the revelation added a seemingly simple injunction to "administer to the poor & needy." As the plan was elaborated, however, caring for the poor entailed a radical new economic order. Members were to "consecrate" their properties for support of the poor by deeding all their land and goods to the Church's bishop with an irrevocable deed. In return, they were to receive back "stewardships" proportionate to the needs of their families, thus equalizing property. Year by year, the equalization was to continue. Stewards were to work their properties— presumably farms or shops or stores—and then give back their annual surplus for distribution to the poor. The desired end was that "every man may receive according as he stands in need." The officer appointed to administer the system, a bishop, would redistribute the consecrated properties according to people's needs and capacities. Surplus properties would be kept in a storehouse to provide for the poor and for "purchasing lands & the building up of the New Jerusalem."[45] The storehouse was to supply capital for city-building, as well as land and tools for the needy.

The economic reforms put Joseph Smith's Zion in company with scores of utopians who were bent on moderating economic injustices in these years. One startling revelation declared that "it is not given that one man should possess that which is above another: Wherefore the world lieth in sin."[46] Such a call for equality of property could be read as a criticism of the capitalist order more far-reaching than Robert Owen's plans for New Harmony, Indiana, which self-consciously aimed at creating a new moral order within industrial society, or the Transcendentalists' attempt at Brook Farm to stop the degradation of labor.[47]

But condemnation of the market economy was not the prevailing spirit in the Zion social order. The revelations did not generate resentment against social injustice or try to motivate reform through outrage.[48] The leading motif was concern for the poor rather than resentment of their exploiters. A later version of the law began "remember the poor" and ended with the reminder that "inasmuch as ye do it unto the least of these ye do it unto me." Growing up poor, Joseph knew deprivation firsthand. A January 1831 revelation could have been referring to his own parents when it called for the appointment of certain men to "look to the poor and the needy, and administer to their relief, that they shall not suffer."[49]

In the view of Joseph's revelations, inequality poisoned society. "Wo unto you rich men, that will not give your substance to the poor, for your riches will canker your souls," declared one, and then immediately continued "wo unto you poor men . . . whose bellies are not satisfied, and whose hands are not stayed from laying hold upon other men's goods, whose eyes are full of greediness, and who will not labor with their own hands!" Wealth itself was not the evil; in the *Book of Mormon*, righteousness brought prosperity. The evil was the social distance separating rich and poor. The rich "despise the poor, and they persecute the meek." In their pride, men adorn themselves "with that which hath no life, and yet suffer the hungry, and the needy, and the naked, and the sick, and the afflicted to pass by . . . and notice them not."[50] Unequal property prevented people from being "of one heart and one mind," the ideal of Enoch's city.

AN ENDOWMENT OF POWER

While plans for Zion were maturing, Joseph and Emma spent the winter and spring on the Morley farm, located near Kirtland's northern boundary. Three months after their arrival, Emma gave birth to twins named Thaddeus and Louisa. Both died at birth. After four years of marriage, Emma had borne three children and lost them all. The day after Emma lost the twins, Julia Clapp Murdock, wife of John Murdock, died six hours after giving birth to twins in nearby Orange. Burdened with five children and no wife, Murdock offered the twins to the Smiths. Within ten days, Emma had Julia and Joseph Murdock to care for.[51] The Smiths treated the two children like their own, giving them the Smith name. Their household was complicated further by the May arrival of Lucy Smith with a company of New York Saints, joining Joseph Sr., who was already living in the Smiths' one-room house.[52]

While Joseph was coping with children and helping to settle the New York Saints, the visionary enthusiasm of the first months in Kirtland subsided.[53] The calmer atmosphere allowed Joseph to pursue his own version of spiritual power. The revelation about the Ohio move had said, "I will give unto you my law, and there you shall be endowed with power from on high." The law came in February 1831; that left endowment of power yet to come. Through the spring, the revelations continued to portend an outpouring. "Sanctify yourselves and ye shall be endowed with power." The promise became more specific in the command to convene the elders, and "I will pour out my Spirit upon them in the day that they assemble themselves together." The words seemed to promise a day of Pentecost, when some gift from heaven, a spiritual endowment, would descend on the Saints.[54]

In early June, forty-four elders, four priests, and fifteen teachers met in a log schoolhouse near Isaac Morley's farm, hoping for a spiritual endowment. Levi Hancock, who had earlier been startled by visionaries, was baffled by what happened that day. In an expansive spirit, Joseph said that Christ's kingdom, like a grain of mustard seed, "was now before him and some should see it put forth its branches and the angels of heaven would some day come like birds to its branches." According to Hancock, Joseph promised Lyman Wight he would see Christ that day. Wight soon turned stiff and white, exclaiming that he had indeed viewed the Savior. According to Hancock, Joseph himself said, "I now see God, and Jesus Christ at his right hand."[55]

Then the meeting unraveled. Joseph ordained Harvey Whitlock to the high priesthood, the most important business of the meeting, and Whitlock reacted badly. "He turned as black as Lyman was white," Hancock reported. "His fingers were set like claws. He went around the room and showed his hands and tried to speak, his eyes were in the shape of oval O's." Astonished at the turn of events, Hyrum exclaimed, "Joseph, that is not of God." Joseph, unwilling to cut the phenomenon short, told Hyrum to wait, but Hyrum insisted: "I will not believe . . . unless you inquire of God and he ownes it." Hancock said, "Joseph bowed his head, and in a short time got up and commanded satan to leave Harvey, laying his hands upon his head at the same time." Then, Hancock said, Leman Copley, who weighed over two hundred pounds, somersaulted in the air and fell on his back over a bench. Wight cast Satan out of Copley, and Copley was calmed. The evil spirit, according to Hancock, was in and out of people all day and the greater part of the night. Joseph, who was ordaining men to the high priesthood, came eventually to Hancock and assured him he had a calling "as high as any man in the house." The words brought Hancock relief: "I was glad for that for I was so scared I would not stir without his liberty for all the world."[56]

This was not the spiritual endowment the elders had expected, and the outburst may have contributed to "trouble and unbelief" among the disciples. John Whitmer noted that about this time "some apostatized, and became enemies to the cause of God, and persecuted the saints."[57] But others understood it as Joseph did—as a manifestation of "the man of Sin." Walking back from the meeting, Hancock heard Harvey Green, one of the possessed, say that "he could not describe the awful feeling he experienced while in the hands of Satan." As John Whitmer reported in the minutes, "the Lord showed to Joseph the Seer the design of this thing, he commanded the devil in the name of Christ and he departed to our joy and comfort."[58]

During the turbulent meeting, Joseph ordained five men to the high priesthood, and Lyman Wight ordained eighteen others, including Joseph.[59] The ordinations to the high priesthood marked a milestone in Mormon ecclesiology. Until that time, the word "priesthood," although it appeared in the *Book of Mormon*, had not been used in Mormon sermonizing or modern revelations. Later accounts applied the term retroactively, but the June 1831 conference marked its first appearance in contemporary records.[60] The term "authority" frequently appeared, but not "priesthood." The absence of the word to this point may have been because of its generally negative associations for radical Protestants in Joseph's time. Priesthood was associated with Roman Catholicism and the old regimes of Europe. The radical religious tradition from which many Mormon converts came denounced priesthood as popish, emphasizing preaching rather than sacraments administered by priests. Universalists like Joseph Smith's grandfather linked priesthood with priestcraft and preaching the gospel for hire.[61] In most New England churches, ministers were ordained as pastors of specific congregations and were not admitted to a priesthood at all. The idea of priesthood descending in a line of authority was Roman, not Puritan.

Because priesthood was an alien concept to Yankee Christians, Joseph may have considered it prudent to say nothing about priesthood in the early years, or possibly he did not understand it himself.[62] So far as can be told now, before 1831 men were called to church offices—elders, priests, and teachers—given authority, and licensed without reference to a bestowal of priesthood.[63] At the June conference, the word "priesthood" was used and priesthood was bestowed as if it was an addition to previous authority. Both the minutes of the meeting and John Whitmer's history noted ordinations to "the High Priesthood," also known as the Melchizedek Priesthood, named for a mysterious biblical figure from the time of Abraham.[64] Writing about the meeting years later, Joseph said that "the authority of the Melchisedek priesthood was manifested and conferred for the first time upon several of the Elders."[65] That statement startles modern Mormons because they believe that elders receive the higher or Melchizedek Priesthood when they are ordained, making an additional ordination unnecessary. Because Mormons emphasize the transmission of priesthood, from person to person by laying on of hands, the moment when it was actually received from heaven for the first time makes a difference. The Melchizedek Priesthood, Mormons now believe, had been bestowed a year or two earlier with the visit of Peter, James, and John. If so, why did contemporaries say the high priesthood was given for the first time in June 1831? Joseph Smith himself was ordained to this "high priesthood" by Lyman Wight.[66] If Joseph was already an elder and apostle, what was the necessity of being ordained again?

The usual explanation is that Joseph meant to say "high priest," one of the offices in the Melchizedek Priesthood, not "high priesthood."[67] By this interpretation, high priests, officers in the priesthood, were ordained for the first time at the conference, though the Melchizedek Priesthood was received earlier. But that is not what Joseph said. He said the Melchizedek Priesthood was conferred for the first time. Men close to him put it the same way.[68] Parley Pratt, who was present, later recalled that "several were then selected by revelation, through president Smith, and ordained to the High Priesthood after the order of the Son of God; which is after the order of Melchisedec. This was the first occasion in which this priesthood had been revealed and conferred upon the Elders in this dispensation."[69]

The confusion may indicate that the division into two priesthoods, with elders in the higher and priests and teachers in the lower, was not clear before 1831. Joseph may not have realized that elders were part of the Melchizedek Priesthood already and were being ordained to the office of high priest rather than receiving the powers of the high priesthood. Although he understood the distinction by the 1840s, he seems to have fallen back into the confusion of those early years when he wrote about the ordinations.[70] In this case, experience may have outrun comprehension. Because he knew so little about priesthood at the beginning, Joseph could no more grasp its meaning than he comprehended the full significance of the First Vision as a teenager.[71] Although he understood such Church offices as teacher and elder, it took time to comprehend that the powers of priesthood were included in the authority that went with those offices.

Priesthood would grow into one of the defining principles of Mormonism. Despite Protestant aversion to the term, Joseph continued to expand priesthood down to his final days in Nauvoo. The June 1831 conference ordinations hinted at the direction his theology would take. Joseph had hoped for an endowment of power at the conference. He had tolerated exorbitant behavior in hopes of receiving a pentecostal manifestation. Though disappointed, his reaction indicated a line of thinking: that the endowment of power would come to the Saints by way of priesthood. A year later, a revelation would say that in the ordinances of the priesthood, "the power of godliness is manifest; and without the ordinances thereof, and the authority of the priesthood, the power of godliness is not manifest unto men in the flesh."[72] Eventually the quest for the endowment of power would be transferred to the temples, the site of the highest priesthood rituals. In the world of Joseph's revelations, the ancient authority of priests would become preeminent. One of his gifts was to sense the power in biblical passages that others had long overlooked. His inspiration told him to restore priesthood to the central position it had occupied in ancient Hebrew religion, and the idea appealed to the searching nineteenth-century Christians who came to Mormonism. In priesthood, they found a key to the godly powers they longed for.

The source of this incongruous development in Joseph Smith's theology has puzzled historians. Unwilling to believe Joseph learned about priesthood from his revelations, Fawn Brodie suggested that Joseph Smith borrowed his ideas from a contemporary book on Melchizedek. Indeed the subject was much debated in rarified theological circles in the half century before the Church's organization. In the Bible, the name comes up in Genesis, where Melchizedek was a king of Salem who collected tithes from Abraham, and in the Book of Hebrews, where Christ is a priest forever after the order of Melchizedek. Not knowing exactly what to make of these clues, Bible commentators generally concluded that only two men held the Melchizedek Priesthood: Melchizedek and Christ. It was a messianic priesthood.[73]

If Joseph Smith tapped into this recondite debate, he took the subject of Melchizedek Priesthood in a new direction. He was more influenced by the *Book of Mormon* and the Bible than by the learned writings of his contemporaries. The prophet Alma in the *Book of Mormon* spoke of men "ordained unto the High Priesthood of the holy order of God," and referred to Melchizedek having received "the office of the High Priesthood, according to the holy order of God." The name came to Joseph's attention again while he was translating the Bible during the winter of 1831. The three brief verses on Melchizedek in Genesis 14 were among those he embellished most elaborately. In the expansion, Enoch received the Melchizedek Priesthood along with Melchizedek and Christ. Moreover, the revision said, the high priesthood was to be bestowed on "as many as believed on his name."[74] Far from being a messianic priesthood, all believers were to be ordained high priests, a presumptuous act from the viewpoint of Protestant scholarship.

Joseph's expansion of Genesis went on to describe the Melchizedek Priesthood's tremendous powers:

> Every one being ordained after this order & calling, should have power, by faith, to break Mountains, to divide the Seas, to dry up waters, to turn them out of their course, to put at defiance the armies of Nations, to divide the Earth, to break evry band, to stand in the presence of God; to do all things according to his will, according to his command; subdue principalities & powers, & this by the will of the Son of God, which was from before the foundation of the world.[75]

Although the men in the log schoolhouse had not seen the passage when they received ordination that turbulent day in June 1831, these visions were on Joseph's mind as he conferred the Melchizedek Priesthood. They were all to become Enochs and Melchizedeks—reason enough for Satan to seize them. Joseph was trying to install them in the order of the Son of God, "to stand in the presence of God; to do all things according to his will." If he had silenced the visionaries in Kirtland, he never intended to hinder the flow of power. He wanted to invest all the men among his followers with the powers of heaven descending through the priesthood.

The scene at the June 1831 conference typified Joseph's relationship with his people in the early years. In a log schoolhouse on a hill in a forested countryside, plain people of little education and much zeal sit before him on slab benches. He is one of them, an ordinary man among ordinary men. He speaks of his visions and their possibilities, trying to invest them with power and intelligence beyond his capacity to describe. They listen transfixed, puzzled, and sometimes fearful. They know a power beyond the ordinary plays around them. They want to grasp it and make it their own. Can they break mountains and divide the seas? Can they put the armies of nations at defiance? Sometimes they are uncertain. Sometimes they burn with perfect certainty. They feel their lives are being elevated, their persons empowered. The concerns of farms, shops, and families drop away, and they dedicate their lives to the work.

EIGHT

ZION

JULY–DECEMBER 1831

Wherefore this is the land of promise, and the place for the city of Zion. And thus saith the Lord your God, if you will receive wisdom here is wisdom.— Behold the place which is now called Independence, is the center place, and a spot for the temple is lying westward upon a lot which is not far from the court house.
Doctrine and Covenants [1835], 27:1

THE DAY AFTER THE JUNE 1831 CONFERENCE, a revelation commanded fourteen pairs of elders to leave for Missouri, where Oliver Cowdery had been teaching the Indians for several months. Through the spring, Cowdery was enthusiastic about the Delawares' reactions to the *Book of Mormon.* "The principle chief says he believes evry word of the Book & there are many more in the Nation who believes." His enthusiasm was dampened when Richard W. Cummins, the U.S. agent to the Shawnee and the Delaware, stopped the Mormons from proselytizing (they had not received official permission), but Cowdery still believed the time had come when God would "redeem his ancient covenant people."[1]

After access to Indian territory closed, the other half of the missionaries' charge became paramount. When they left New York in October, they had been told to find the site for "the city" on "the borders by the Lamanites."[2] Both the *Book of Mormon* and the Book of Moses spoke of a holy city in the last days, and every Christian was familiar with biblical passages about the "New Jerusalem" coming down from heaven. Church members were thrilled to think that Cowdery's band of missionaries was to locate the exact spot. Joseph said that the expedition to find the site "was the most important subject which then engrossed the attention of the saints." In the spring and summer of 1831, every activity anticipated the building of the city. The missionaries were told to raise up churches in Ohio until "the time shall come when it shall be revealed unto you, from on high, when the city of the New Jerusalem shall be prepared that ye may be gathered in one." The consecration of properties was for the "building up of the New Jerusalem, which is hereafter to be revealed." When the call to the Missouri mission came, the revelation assured the twenty-eight elders that "I the Lord will hasten the city in its time."[3]

With the founding of a city in mind, Joseph left for Missouri on June 19 with a party of eight, taking wagon, canal boat, and stage to Cincinnati, where Sidney Rigdon introduced him to Walter Scott, Rigdon's old Campbellite colleague. The interview was fruitless. The Campbellites had made up their minds that Mormon claims to spiritual gifts were an insidious delusion. The party went on to St. Louis by steamboat, traveling down the Ohio River and up the Mississippi. Finding no waiting vessel in St. Louis, Joseph and four others walked the 250 miles to Independence in the summer heat, preaching as they went. The *Book of Mormon* got a bad reception in the scattered Missouri settlements, but the men comforted themselves by praying and reading the Bible.[4]

When they arrived at the Independence frontier in mid-July 1831, Joseph recoiled at the village's ragged collection of settlers. Jackson County had been organized only six years earlier, and Independence was not laid out and made the county seat until 1827. The town had no more than twenty dwellings. The chief attraction was its location at the edge of settlement with access to the Santa Fe trade and the fur traffic coming down the Missouri River. Along with a population of southern farmers, the county had attracted a tough crowd of traders and trappers. An agent of the American Home Missionary Society said that even the Christian ministers were "a sad lot of churchmen, untrained, uncouth, given to imbibing spirituous liquors." They were not the worst, as "many suspicious characters . . . headquarter here. . . . When intelligence arrives that a federal marshall is approaching this county, there is a hurried scurrying of many of this element into Indian country."[5]

Writing after the Missouri persecutions, Joseph remembered feeling that he came from "a highly cultivated state" compared to "the degradation, leanness of intellect, ferocity and jealousy of a people that were nearly a century behind the times." Like other travelers to the West, Joseph felt he had retreated in time as he traveled through space, coming upon the primitive people of another age. In 1839, he remembered asking himself, "When will Zion be built up in her glory, and where will thy temple stand, unto which all nations shall come in the last days?"[6]

Joseph may have been disappointed by the thin harvest of souls in Independence. He had expected to find a thriving branch, but only a handful had been converted. Edward Partridge, the man appointed to take charge in Missouri, who had understood Joseph's expectations as prophecy, was disillusioned. A few weeks after Joseph's arrival, a revelation rebuked Partridge for his "unbelief and blindness of heart." Partridge wrote his wife in Ohio "as I am occasionally chastened I sometimes fear my station is above what I can perform to the acceptance of my Heavenly Father."[7] The whole operation ran on faith. Joseph suppressed his own anxieties and required the same of everyone else.

A few days after the party arrived, a revelation confirmed that "this is the land of promise, and the place for the city of Zion." Independence, Jackson County, Missouri, was declared the "center place." Four years earlier, the town had been laid out in 143 lots. One of them, an unpurchased, thickly wooded lot near the courthouse, was declared to be the spot for the temple. They were to buy land—all the land—from there to the state's western boundary twelve miles to the west. Then the consecration of properties would begin. Bishop Edward Partridge was to grant inheritances to each family. Another migrant, Sidney Gilbert, Newel Whitney's partner, was to open a store. William W. Phelps, a newspaper editor from Canandaigua, New York, was to start a press.[8]

Meanwhile, the Saints from Colesville, New York, arrived in Independence. On August 2, they laid a log for the first house, on land purchased in Kaw township twelve miles west of Independence. "The log was carried and placed by twelve men, in honor of the twelve tribes of Israel." Sidney Rigdon dedicated the land for the gathering of the Saints by asking the thirty-one present if they would receive the land as an inheritance from God. "Do you pledge yourselves to keep the laws of god on this land, which you have never . . . kept in your own land," he inquired of them, using the language of Israel. "We do," they replied, whereupon Rigdon pronounced the land consecrated to the Lord for the possession of the Saints "to the rimotest ages of time." The next day, Rigdon "dedicated unto the Lord forever" the ground for the City of Zion, and Joseph laid a stone at the northeast corner of the temple site.[9]

Enveloped in these promises, the land became beautiful in Joseph's eyes. In his history, using poetic language provided him by Phelps, he remembered gazing out on the "sea of meadows . . . decorated with a growth of flowers." The trees, the watercourses, the shrubbery, everything struck his eyes happily. He resorted to language used by real estate promoters since the founding of America. He could foresee the rich soil, "from three to ten feet deep, and generally composed of a rich black mould," yielding wheat, corn, sweet potatoes, and cotton. Like a farmer in paradise, he observed that horses, cattle, and hogs "seem nearly to raise themselves" by grazing on the prairie. Turkeys, geese, swans, and ducks grace "the delightful regions of this goodly land of the heritage of the children of God." A revelation continued in the same lyrical spirit. "The fulness of the earth is yours," yea, all things are "made for the benefit and the use of man, both to please the eye, and to gladden the heart." He sounded like Moses looking upon Canaan.[10]

Somewhat incongruously, a somber revelation tempered this enthusiasm. Warning that only "after much tribulation cometh the blessings," the revelation implied that the enjoyment of Zion lay in the future. The missionaries had been sent "that you might be honored of laying the foundation, and of bearing record of the land upon which the Zion of God shall stand," and no more.[11] They were not to enjoy a triumphant entrance into the promised land. The elders themselves were told not to move to Zion. Their assignment for now was to funnel people from the ends of the earth—and to do it cautiously. The gathering was to proceed "not in haste, nor by flight."[12] The Saints were to collect funds to buy land and enroll workmen, but to leave only a small group to start the settlement. The revelation set up a tension between the urgency of the oncoming calamities and a measured gathering. Joseph may have sensed that the excitement of constructing a holy city would stir up more zeal than was practical, and the warning was well taken. More converts flocked to Jackson County than their combined wealth could adequately support. By November 1833, 1,200 Saints were in the area.

Joseph and the missionaries headed home on August 9. They began the trip down the turbulent Missouri in frail little canoes. On the third day, after passing through a bad stretch of water, one of their number received a shock. William Phelps saw a vision of "the Destroyer, in his most horrible power" riding on the river.[13] Praying for guidance, Joseph was told that some missionaries should leave the river for the land, preaching as they went. The Lord would preserve the faithful on the waters, they were assured, but Rigdon and Joseph were to avoid river travel until they got to the canal. The two of them, along with Oliver Cowdery, went overland to St. Louis, passing a group of missionaries preaching their way to Missouri. Traveling by coach until they reached the canal, Joseph arrived in Kirtland on August 27.[14]

NEW JERUSALEM

During his month in Missouri, Joseph transformed a bedraggled frontier village surrounded by vast stretches of empty prairie into a sacred place. The sacralization of space usually results from a succession of holy events like repeated miracles, or from accumulated layers of worship and veneration over centuries, in the way of Lourdes and Jerusalem.[15] Rather than growing from repeated sacred happenings, Joseph's Zion was created in a stroke. A few words from heaven declaring Independence to be the site of the New Jerusalem inscribed indelible marks on the land—forever. Though eventually evicted never to return, Mormons have never forgotten Jackson County. The defeat of all their efforts has not erased the site from Mormon memory.[16] A remote location in the middle of North America became the place where Mormons from around the globe believed they were to gather, build a temple, live by consecration, have no poor, and be of one heart and one mind.

The name—New Jerusalem—helped to imprint Zion on the Mormon imagination. John the Revelator saw "the holy city, new Jerusalem, coming down from God out of heaven, prepared as a bride adorned for her husband," and Ether, the *Book of Mormon* prophet, looking beyond the days of Christ's mortal life on earth, "spake concerning a New Jerusalem upon this land." Mentioned only twice in the Bible, the New Jerusalem had gathered meaning and force through centuries of interpretation, always stirring anticipation and hope among Christians. Beginning with the Puritans, religious idealists in America had formed communities large and small called New Jerusalem.[17] Joseph sanctified Independence just by naming it.

In establishing his Zion, Joseph joined a large company of utopian community builders. Between 1787 and 1860, 137 communitarian experiments were undertaken in the United States.[18] All sought to improve the world by forming miniature societies on ideal principles. Naming the city New Jerusalem, however, gave Joseph's city a particular cast. More than a social experiment, Joseph's New Jerusalem was a place for hungry souls. A revelation in March 1831 had spoken of "a city reserved until a day of righteousness shall come a day which was sought for by all holy men." Saint Augustine struck that same plaintive note in *The City of God*, in writing of "an ancient city, this City of God: always enduring its existence on earth, always sighing for heaven—whose name is also Jerusalem and Sion." The New Jerusalem was home for people, one of Joseph's revelations said, who "confessed that they were strangers and pilgrims on the earth," who could find no peace until "wickedness and abominations" ended.[19] Missionaries were to collect the Saints into the one safe place on earth during the calamities of the last days.

> And it shall be called the New Jerusalem, a land of peace, a city of refuge, a place of safety for the saints of the most high God . . . and there shall be gathered unto it out of every nation under heaven: And it shall be the only people that shall not be at war one with another.[20]

Zion went forward under the looming shadow of the Second Coming.

The dedication of the Missouri site occurred during an upswing in millennial thinking in the transatlantic world. In the late eighteenth century, the American and French revolutions had spurred speculation about the imminent coming of Christ. Millenarians saw the two revolutions as signs of the coming Kingdom. Expectations had not dimmed a generation later.

Eighteen thirty-one was a signal year for millenarian activity. Besides Joseph's dedication of Zion, William Miller, later famed for predicting an exact date in 1843 for the Second Coming, began preaching his chronology of millennial events, matching historical occurrences with scriptural predictions. In Southampton County, Virginia, Nat Turner, the slave visionary, was awaiting a moment for his people to rise against their masters. In February 1831, he interpreted a solar eclipse as the signal. Five months later, moved by further signs, Turner acted. In August, while Joseph returned from Missouri, fifty slaves armed with knives and clubs slew fifty-seven whites before the outbreak was stopped. Over a hundred slaves were executed in retribution.[21]

Although they coincided in time, Joseph Smith's Zion was of another order from Turner's and Miller's millenarianism. Unlike Turner, Mormon converts had no oppressive masters to overthrow and no program of violence. The revelations specifically forbade the Saints to use force to obtain the land. If they sought it violently, they were told, "as you are forbidden to shed blood, lo, your enemies are upon you, and ye shall be scourged from city to city." Nor did the Mormons indulge in the historical speculations of Miller. None of Joseph's revelations linked prophecy to history in the fashion of the chronological millenarians. Mormons watched for signs of the times in the skies and noted news reports of earthquakes and fires, but never named the moment when the world was to end.[22]

Mormon millenarianism was more akin to that of the Shakers. Ann Lee, a working-class English Quaker visionary, came to the United States in 1774 and founded the United Society of Believers in Christ's Second Coming. Its members, called Shakers, eventually collected into communities where they exercised spiritual gifts and established a code of behavior called "Millennial Laws." Rather than pointing to a date for Christ's return, Shaker millenarianism served more to inject urgency into the sect's reform efforts. Both Shakers and Mormons felt the pressure of time. The errors of the present pressed against the calamities of Christ's Coming, making radical change a necessity.[23]

In the early years, the Saints thought a half dozen years would bring the end. Awakened one morning at 4 a.m. to see the signs in the heavens, Joseph reported, "I arrose and beheld to my great Joy the stars fall from heaven . . . a sure sign that the coming of Christ is clost at hand." An imminent transformation called for radical behavior. The Shakers practiced celibacy, as an imminent Second Coming did not require perpetuation of the community. The Mormons warned the world to flee to Zion.[24]

Taking their lead from the violent passages in Revelation and Christ's predictions of the temple's destruction in Matthew, the millenarians expected catastrophes. Joseph's early revelations dwelt on the calamities in the end times: "The proud, and they that do wickedly, shall be as stubble, and I will burn them up, saith the Lord of Hosts, that wickedness shall not be upon the earth." The forces of nature would be hurled against the unbelieving. "The heavens shall shake and the earth shall tremble. . . . thunders shall utter their voices from the ends of the earth. . . . the lightnings shall streak forth from the east unto the west, and shall utter forth their voices unto all that live, . . . saying these words: Repent ye, for the great day of the Lord is come." At times the language became gory: "their tongues shall be stayed that they shall not utter against me, and their flesh shall fall from off their bones, and their eyes from their sockets."[25] The words reflected a feeling that the world had gone horribly awry. Something fundamental and essential was wrong for the world to deserve these calamities.

Millenarians clashed with the legendary optimism of Jacksonian America, but radical reformers, especially abolitionists, were equally pessimistic about a society rotting at the core, ready to be hewn down and cast into the fire. The abolitionist Angelina Grimké Weld looked forward to "the downfall of every Earthly throne," the "overthrow of every political government," the annihilation of "every Ecclesiastical Establishment & the dissolution of every sect and party under the sun." William Lloyd Garrison's warning to slave owners in the opening issue of *The Liberator* in 1831 was full of woe:

> *Woe if it come with storm, and blood, and fire,*
> *When midnight darkness veils the earth and sky!*
> *Woe to the innocent babe—the guilty sire—*
> *Mother and daughter—friends of kindred tie!*
> Stranger and citizen alike shall die!

Though hardy and upbeat by nature, Joseph Smith shared the reformers' bleak outlook. The *Book of Mormon* mercilessly indicted America for its pride and selfishness. Enoch in the Book of Moses saw that the earth would not rest until the end: "The heavens shall be darkened, and a veil of darkness shall cover the earth . . . and great tribulations shall be among the children of men."[26] A sense of pervasive evil underlay Joseph's optimism, an evil that only divine intervention could end.

Filled with such forebodings, Joseph passed through a fundamental transition during his summer in Missouri. A resolve to build Zion clamped itself on his soul. The words "city," "New Jerusalem," and "Zion" had been in the air at least since September 1830, when the four missionaries to the West had been told to locate the city, but until he was on the ground, Joseph could not have understood all that was involved. The "leanness of intellect" and "ferocity" of the Jackson County people must have suggested the immensity of his task. He was attempting to create a godly civilization in a barbaric wilderness. Carrying that one log to lay the foundation of a single house must have driven home what it would take to construct a temple and a city.[27] Yet nothing would discourage him. To the end of his life, he gathered his followers into cities no matter the cost.

When Joseph returned to Kirtland, Church members in Ohio showed "great anxiety" over Zion, "the most important temporal object in view." By now, the theological framework was in place: the judgments of the last day were near, and the faithful must flee to Zion for safety. "The day of wrath shall come upon them as a whirlwind, and all flesh shall know that I am God," one revelation said, necessitating a gathering. "Wherefore seeing that I the Lord have decreed all these things upon the face of the earth, I willeth that my saints should be assembled upon the land of Zion." The Saints were to bring all who would come. Everyone must "lift a warning voice unto the inhabitants of the earth; And declare both by word and by flight, that desolation shall come upon the wicked."[28]

In Joseph's mind, the Zion drama overshadowed everything, including politics. Concerns about the American republic scarcely figured in the early revelations, an indifference found among early Methodists too. For Mormons, the United States was but one country among the "nations of the earth," and like the others must hearken or face extinction. The righteous, the revelations said, would be gathered from all nations. The United States had no special part in the early millennial revelations. In the first few years, America was not even named. The only quasi-national division that mattered was the divide between Israel and the Gentiles, with America on the Gentile side.[29] The United States government in all of its democratic glory was not the model for Zion; the value of the Constitution as the "law of man" was acknowledged only later, after the Missouri persecutions. In the millennium, the revelations said, the Church would have no laws but God's laws.[30]

A later promotional tract located Zion in the "center of the continent." Considering the distribution of the American population in the East and the location of the nation's commercial cities and political capitals, to emphasize the city's centrality seems anomalous, since it lay on the margins of the civilized world, not at the center. But New York, Washington, and London combined did not outweigh Zion in the geography of Joseph Smith's revelations. The New Jerusalem oriented the world to a new capital, forming its own space at the edge of American settlement and at the vortex of its own history.[31]

OBJECTIONS

Not everyone was happy with the Zion mission. Ezra Booth, a convert of the preceding May, came back from Missouri disillusioned. Booth complained to Smith, Rigdon, and Cowdery about Joseph's behavior on the trip. Booth pushed so hard that at a September conference his right to preach was withdrawn, and soon after, he renounced his membership. In nine impassioned letters to the *Ohio Star* published from October through December 1831, Booth explained his reasons for considering Joseph unworthy.[32] Booth was the first of a half dozen outspoken apostates who broke with Joseph and mounted campaigns to bring him down.

Booth and his wife had witnessed a miraculous healing in the spring of 1831. During a conversation concerning spiritual gifts, a perennial interest among people striving for New Testament Christianity, someone asked about the rheumatic arm of Elsa Johnson, another visitor. The person wanted to know if God had "given any power to men now on the earth to cure her." The conversation had turned in another direction when Joseph rose, walked across the room, took Elsa Johnson by the hand, and solemnly said, *"Woman, in the name of the Lord Jesus Christ, I command thee to be whole."* Johnson raised her arm, and the next day did her washing without pain.[33]

The incident had persuaded Booth, a Methodist minister of more than ordinary gifts. Convinced by his own eyes, he accepted Mormonism. But from then on, every attempt at healing became a test, and, as his faith waned, he noted only failures, overlooking or not witnessing the successful healings recounted by the believers such as John Whitmer. In Booth's eyes, the June 1831 conference was a fiasco. He expected an outpouring of miraculous events but saw instead Harvey Whitlock in contortions. Booth's dwindling faith was strong enough to get him to Missouri and back, but by the time he wrote his letters in the fall, he could remember nothing good about the journey.[34]

Booth admitted that Mormon belief carried "the face of plausibility." When he first encountered Mormonism, he saw it as "the restoration of the apostolic church, with all the gifts and graces" enjoyed in New Testament times, including promise of "signs and wonders." Mormonism offered an "everlasting inheritance" in the land of Zion, where the Savior was to appear; and a temple of God in the City of Zion, which would be "a city of Refuge, and a safe asylum when the storms of vengeance shall pour upon the earth." On a more material note, "the riches of the Gentiles [were to] be consecrated to the Mormonites; they shall have lands and cattle in abundance, and shall possess the gold and silver, and all the treasures of their enemies."[35]

Because of the doctrines, honest men remained with the Mormons even after they saw Joseph Smith's failings. "Adherents are generally inclined to consider the system too perfect, as to admit of no suspicion; and the confusion and disappointment, are attributed to some other cause." But in Booth's opinion, Mormonism's signal weakness was Joseph Smith. He held too much power. As Booth pointed out, "the relation in which Smith stands to the church, is that of a Prophet, Seer, Revealer, and Translator; and when he speaks by the Spirit, or says he knows a thing by the communication of the Spirit, it is received as coming directly from the mouth of the Lord." This held true for small, everyday matters, as well as for grand doctrines. "When he says he knows a thing to be so, *thus* it must stand without controversy."[36]

In Booth's eyes, Joseph Smith's demeanor fell short of a prophet's proper character. Joseph lacked "sobriety, prudence and stability," frequently showing "a spirit of lightness and levity, a temper easily irritated, and an habitual proneness to jesting and joking." Joseph himself repeatedly told his followers not to expect perfection of him, but whatever his disclaimers, Joseph's prophethood left him exposed. Symonds Ryder, a Campbellite converted by Booth, left in disgust when his name was misspelled in a revelation.[37] At any sign of weakness, converts tumbled off the wagon.

Booth was one of many to drop away. Eleven of sixty-three attendees at the June 1831 conference "denied the faith" or were "cut off" within a few years, and another dozen attendees left later. More than one-fifth of priesthood-holding converts in Joseph Smith's lifetime were cut off from the Church or turned against it. Many others drifted away.[38] For apostates like Booth, Mormonism was too good to be true. They wanted to live in the biblical world that Joseph brought into existence, but after a period within millennial time-space, something shook their faith—an unfulfilled prophecy, a harsh word, a failed miracle—and the imagined world collapsed. The revelations rang false, and the plan to build a New Jerusalem looked absurd.[39]

Joseph took these defections in stride; he dismissed individual apostates as blind gnats. But he was not indifferent. The loss of members troubled him, especially experienced preachers like Booth. Every soldier was needed to build Zion. Whom could he rely on to gather the willing to the holy city? At any given moment, he could not be sure. As the years went by, and one stalwart after another deserted him, Joseph came to value loyalty above every other virtue.

While he was dealing with Ezra Booth in September, Joseph, Emma, and the twins moved thirty-six miles south to the John Johnson farm in Hiram, Ohio.[40] For six months, the Smiths lived with Johnson and his wife, Elsa, who had joined the Mormons after the healing that had converted Booth. One of the few convert families with substantial property, the Johnsons offered the Smiths free rooms, a benefaction the Smiths welcomed. The small house purchased from Isaac Hale was the only place they had ever owned; most of the time since their marriage they had lived with friends or their parents. The Johnsons were the latest to take them in. Collected money went for Missouri land purchases instead. Joseph lived more like a poor Methodist itinerant than a prophet and seer leading a church.

Sidney Rigdon, Joseph's companion and ally, joined the Smiths in Hiram. The Johnsons provided a log cabin for Sidney and Phebe Rigdon and their six children. Since Rigdon's visit to Palmyra the previous December, he and Joseph had worked together on the translation project to which they now planned to return. Although Sidney was thirteen years Joseph's senior, their relationship was summed up in the titles John Whitmer assigned them in his history: "Sidney the Scribe" and "Joseph the Seer." Sidney's learning far exceeded Joseph's. Sidney had been the bookish child that Joseph never was, reading by the light of burning hickory bark when his father denied him candles, and remembering everything he read. He had been a success-ful Reformed Baptist preacher for nearly a dozen years before the two met. Out of respect, Joseph often deferred to him on public occasions.[41] In Mis-souri, Sidney had dedicated the land and the temple site. Sidney was the superior preacher of the two, but the unlearned Joseph's revelations, rather than Sidney's eloquent speeches, formed the foundation of Mormon belief. Joseph by his nature took the lead—the seer over the scribe.

Sidney's temperament ran to excess. He was prone to overstatement and frothy fury. Joseph was capable of anger but remained more composed in debate. The difference was evident during the visit of Nancy Towle to Kirt-land in the fall of 1831. Towle, a thirty-five-year-old itinerant, was one of a corps of female evangelists who helped to satisfy the nation's hunger for preaching in the 1830s. Given to visions herself, Towle said in her memoirs that "God has not infrequently spoken to me, in dreams, and in visions of the night." Preaching in Methodist and Baptist meetinghouses through New England and New York, Towle learned of the Mormons. "I had heard much of the people," she wrote, "and in many places, the excitement I found considerably in their favor." Deciding to investigate, she spent a day in Kirtland and attended a Mormon meeting. She saw nothing "indeco-rous" in Mormon worship, and yet concluded "that it was one of the most deep-concerted-plots of Hell, to deceive the hearts of the simple that had ever come, within the limits of my acquaintance."[42]

Once Rigdon sensed hostility, he attacked, saying that Towle was in the "*gall of bitterness, and the bond of iniquity.*" Furthermore "all, that you have ever done in the world, was mischief." According to Towle's account, Joseph said nothing until she turned to him and demanded that he swear he had seen an angel. He replied that he never swore at all. "Are you not ashamed, of such pretensions?" she insisted. "You, who are no more, than an ignorant, plough-boy of our land!" Joseph calmly noted that "the gift, has returned back again, as in former times, to illiterate fishermen."[43]

BOOK OF COMMANDMENTS

In November 1831, a conference of elders and high priests decided to col-lect and publish Joseph's revelations. Ever since 1828, he had recorded the words he believed came to him from God, and the stack of manuscripts with the revealed words on them was growing. On November 1, a conference at Hiram voted to print 10,000 copies of the *Book of Commandments*, a number later reduced to 3,000, but a sign of the book's importance to the Church.[44] The title page as it appeared in the 1833 publication calls the volume *A Book of Commandments, for the Government of the Church of Christ, Organized According to Law, on the 6th of April, 1830*. Joseph apparently felt a need to regularize Church procedures and perhaps lay down the primary elements of belief. At the organization of the Church, "The Articles and Covenants of the church of Christ" outlined basic beliefs and a few ecclesiastical rules; after a year and a half, a more complete statement was needed.[45]

Church doctrine and practices could have been presented in another way. When Alexander Campbell summed up his theology after thirty years of study, he reduced his ideas to doctrinal principles organized in a treatise called *The Christian System*. Other churches distilled their beliefs into brief creeds. The New England Congregationalists wrote "Platforms" to serve as church constitutions. But Joseph had an aversion to creeds. Later he criticized the very idea of them.[46] They circumscribed truth when he wanted expansion. Revelation overturned old ideas and was forever evolving.

Within a few years, various Church elders, beginning with Oliver Cowdery, attempted to summarize Church doctrines; later Joseph borrowed from a formulation by Orson Pratt to prepare thirteen "Articles of Faith." But these were never meant to encompass all Church doctrine or even to distill its essence. Instead, the Church published the revelations in all their diversity and complexity, making no attempt to distinguish the significant from the trivial. Brief revelations about personal callings intermingled with visions of the future and broad statements of belief and policy. Save for the revealed preface that was put first in the book, the revelations were arranged in chronological order. The result was a melange much like the Bible: unsystematic, concrete, sometimes sweeping, other times pedestrian, both effulgent and spare.

The *Book of Commandments* contained 160 printed pages of revelations received through September 1831. In a sense, these sixty-five revelations bound in a small pocket-size book about two and a half by four inches constituted the Church. The revelations exercised authority comparable to the hold of the Bible on Christians or the Constitution on the United States government. The revelations directed the Church's program as a will directs the disposition of an estate. Besides establishing a framework, the revelations regulated day-to-day operations. To get the elders to Missouri and back, Joseph received eleven revelations between June 7 and August 13, 1831. No other visionary sect of the nineteenth century was so dependent on immediate revelation to carry on business.[47]

Other visionaries prized revealed words: seventeenth-century Quakers published their ecstatic experiences in such volume that their pamphlets at one time constituted thirteen percent of all the titles printed in England.[48] But no one else valued revelations more than Joseph Smith. In arranging for publication, Joseph could not find strong enough words to underscore their worth. He knew the entire Zion enterprise and every other aspect of the Church depended on these messages from God. For two weeks, he kept bringing new ideas to the conference to emphasize the revelations' significance. To parallel the *Book of Mormon*'s testimony of witnesses, Joseph asked the nine elders in the meeting to testify to the revelations. They arose one by one and bore witness "to the truth of the Book of Commandments." Afterward, Joseph expressed his "feelings & gratitude concerning the Commandment & Preface received yesterday." Then he wrote a "testimony of the witnesses to the book of the Lord's commandments," for the elders to sign. Ten days later at a follow-up conference in Hiram, Joseph asked that the "sacred writings" and the elders bearing them to the printer be "dedicated to the Lord by the prayer of faith." He wanted everything possible done to guard and honor the precious words. He called for a vote in consideration of the "Revelation now to be printed being the foundation of the Church & the salvation of the world & the Keys of the mysteries of the Kingdom & the riches of Eternity to the Church." The conference affirmed that the writings "be prized by this Conference to be worth to the Church the riches of the whole Earth speaking temporally."[49]

Judging by his actions, Joseph believed in the revelations more than anyone. From the beginning, he was his own best follower. Having the word of God at his back gave him enormous confidence. He unselfconsciously exercised authority not only among people of his own social class, but with men of learning and broader experience. He recognized Sidney Rigdon's talent, but Rigdon never assumed the Prophet's authority. The imaginative newspaper editor William W. Phelps, a potential rival for intellectual leadership, published the Church newspaper under Joseph's direction. Forceful men like Brigham Young were put to work in the Church. They all deferred to the Prophet and the revealed commandments despite his lack of education and social position. Faith in the revelations, added to his innate personal strength, made him indifferent to rank. He believed in himself and the cause to the point of arrogance, as more than one critic pointed out. Indeed, the Church was built on his confidence. Members came and went, leaders rose and fell, but Joseph persisted. He believed, as the revelations assured him, that "no weapon that is formed against you shall prosper," and the work of God will roll forth.[50]

Because they were so important, the revelations were bound to be criticized. During the November conference a question arose about their language. Was the simple language of Joseph Smith worthy of the voice of

God? "Some conversation was had concerning Revelations and language," Joseph noted in his history. The inquiry could have come from Phelps, who wrote with considerable elevation, or the eloquent Rigdon, or William E. McLellin, a schoolteacher. A revelation brought the matter into the open: "Your eyes have been upon my servant Joseph Smith, jun.: and his language you have known; and his imperfections you have known." While all were believers in the Prophet, a few wondered about the capacity of an uneducated young man to do justice to his own revelations. "You have sought in your hearts knowledge," they were told, "that you might express beyond his language."[51]

The question was not trivial. The revelations' style could have brought Joseph's revelatory powers into question. The beauty of the Qur'an's language convinced many believers of its divinity; ragged language from Joseph Smith might have led to doubts. The November revelation sidestepped the issue by challenging the conference to appoint "the most wise among you" to manufacture an imitation. Take the least of the revelations, it offered, and try to "make one like unto it." William McLellin took up the challenge, "having more learning than sense," as Joseph put it.[52] McLellin's failure to produce a revelation settled the question, and the elders bore testimony of the book.[53]

Not long after this attempt, the issue arose again. A conference on November 8 instructed Joseph Smith to review the commandments and "correct those errors or mistakes which he may discover by the holy Spirit."[54] Correcting "errors" in language supposedly spoken by God again raised the question of authenticity. If from God, how could the language be corrected? Correction implied Joseph's human mind had introduced errors; if so, were the revelations really his productions?

The editing process uncovered Joseph's anomalous assumptions about the nature of revealed words. He never considered the wording infallible. God's language stood in an indefinite relationship to the human language coming through the Prophet. The revealed preface to the *Book of Commandments* specified that the language of the revelations was Joseph Smith's: "These commandments are of me, and were given unto my servants in their weakness, after the manner of their language, that they might come to understanding." The revelations were not God's diction, dialect, or native language. They were couched in language suitable to Joseph's time. The idioms, the grammar, even the tone had to be comprehensible to 1830s Americans. Recognizing the pliability of the revealed words, Joseph freely edited the revelations "by the holy Spirit," making emendations with each new edition.[55] He thought of his revelations as imprinted on his mind, not graven in stone. With each edition, he patched pieces together and altered the wording to clarify meaning. The words were both his and God's.

Edited or not, the revelations carried great weight. They were valued as scripture equal to the Bible, raising Joseph above everyone else. The revelations that condemned Hiram Page's rival revelations a year before had set the pattern. No one was to receive revelations for the Church "excepting my servant Joseph, for he receiveth them even as Moses."[56] In Kirtland, he had silenced the visionaries when they competed with his authority. And yet in a perplexing reversal, the revelations also said everyone was to receive inspiration and speak for God. Despite Joseph's monopoly on Church-wide revelation, the Lord promised these untutored elders revelation of their own. The preface to the *Book of Commandments* declared that "every man might speak in the name of God." A revelation at the November 1831 conference told the elders that "whatsoever they shall speak when moved upon by the Holy Ghost, shall be scripture; shall be the will of the Lord; shall be the mind of the Lord; shall be the word of the Lord; shall be the voice of the Lord, and the power of God unto salvation."[57]

Even though he was the seer and God's spokesman to the Church, Joseph wanted his followers to experience God as he did. As he was collecting the revelations, Joseph seems to have believed a vision of God might be given to everyone at the November conference. He told the Church that if "we could come together with one heart and one mind in perfect faith the vail [*sic*] might as well be rent to day as next week or any other time." He had entered the June 1831 conference with the same anticipation; he failed both times. In November, a follow-up revelation explained that they had not received "the blessing which was offered unto you" because "there were fears in your hearts." But they were not to give up. "As you strip yourselves from jealousies and fears, and humble yourselves before me, for ye are not sufficiently humble, the vail shall be rent and you shall see me and know that I am.[58]

In an inexplicable contradiction, Joseph was designated as the Lord's prophet, and yet every man was to voice scripture, everyone to see God. That conundrum lies at the heart of Joseph Smith's Mormonism. The amplification of authority at the center was meant to increase the authority of everyone, as if the injection of power at the core energized the whole system. Although the Prophet's ability to speak for God put his supreme authority beyond dispute, power was simultaneously distributed to every holder of the priesthood and ultimately to every member. From the outside, Mormonism looked like despotism, if not chaos. On the inside, subservience to the Prophet's authority was believed to empower every member. Though he was Moses and they were Israel, all the Lord's people were prophets.[59]

A revelation in the spring of 1832 demonstrated the power of Joseph's revelation to make major changes in an instant. A few phrases on Zion gave the New Jerusalem project a new meaning. In April 1832, a revelation added an expansive codicil to the instructions on Zion: "Zion must increase in beauty, and in holiness: her borders must be enlarged; her stakes must be strengthened: yea, verily I say unto you, Zion must arise and put on her beautiful garments." The revelation introduced a new word into the Saints' vocabulary, "stake," which was taken from a passage in Isaiah about the expansion of Zion in the last days: "enlarge the place of thy tent, and let them stretch forth the curtains of thine habitations; spare not, lengthen thy cords, and strengthen thy stakes." The revelation announced that Zion in Missouri was not the only gathering place for the Saints. Zion was to expand like a great tent, extending ever more curtains secured by stakes. Kirtland was to be a stake of Zion, making it an outpost of the holy city and an authorized place of gathering. The April 26 revelation said the Lord had "consecrated the land of Shinehah [Kirtland] in mine own due time for the benefit of the saints of the Most High, and for a stake to Zion."[60] That meant, of course, that both people and funds could be collected in Ohio as well as Missouri, though the preeminence of Missouri went unchallenged.

Theologically, the revelation implied that Zion was not a single small spot in the center of the continent, but an elastic concept that encompassed any place where the Saints lived under divine law. One cannot help but sense an American expansiveness in this announcement. Instead of being a singular site, a uniquely powerful focal point like the great religious capitals of antiquity, the New Jerusalem was to be multiple. By combining New Jerusalem imagery with Isaiah's tent, curtains, and stakes, Joseph's revelation allowed satellite cities to increase without number, anticipating the multitudes that would throng to the modern Zion. The City of Zion remained in Missouri, but Kirtland was to be a "city of the stake of *Zion*."[61] Zion's glory could be lent to additional city-stakes. Just as Joseph had established Zion with a few words of revelation, he altered its meaning with a few more, making the idea of a holy city suitable for a growing nineteenth-century America and a rapidly enlarging Church.

NINE

THE BURDEN OF ZION

1832

*I have much care and tribulation calculated to weigh down and distroy
the mind.*

JOSEPH SMITH to WILLIAM W. PHELPS, July 31, 1832

BEARING THE SHEAF OF REVELATIONS, on November 20, 1831, Oliver
Cowdery and John Whitmer left Kirtland for Independence, where
William Phelps was setting up a press for printing the *Book of Commandments.* Joseph and Sidney returned to the translation of the Bible, until a
revelation on December 1 sent them on a preaching tour to counteract
Ezra Booth's letters in the *Ohio Star.* Some readers considered Booth's letters devastating.[1] Sidney Rigdon replied to Booth in the *Star* and invited
him to meet in public debate. Not until early 1832 did Joseph and Sidney
feel they had allayed the "excited feelings."[2] Booth then dropped from
sight. Only his letters, republished in Eber D. Howe's 1834 exposé of Mormonism, remained to mark his trail across Joseph's life.

Booth thought Joseph was "highly imperious and quite dictatorial."
When criticized, he gave way to "violent passions, bordering on madness,
rather than the meek and gentle spirit which the Gospel inculcates."[3] Booth
thought God would never honor a man like Joseph with revelations. Unruf-
fled, Joseph dismissed Booth's fumings as the outpourings of an evil heart.
The letters, Joseph thought, "exposed his weakness, wickedness and folly
and left him a monument of his own shame." The criticisms were dismissed
as baseless.

Booth's observation, however, was not entirely unjustified. Bitter and
disillusioned though he was, Booth was right about Joseph's strong reactions. He lashed back at critics and could be a bulldog when contradicted.
As his response to Booth showed, he brushed off the jibes of his enemies.
"Their shame shall be made manifest," he would say of opponents, sure he
was in the right. Incongruous as it seemed to Booth, that kind of strength
may have been a requirement of Joseph's position. He had to be tough. A
weaker, gentler soul could scarcely have survived the incessant hammering

he endured as head of the Church. By 1832, Joseph led an organization of a thousand members, with multiple problems, and huge projects under way, and he was just a twenty-six-year-old, learning on the job. Only by shrugging off criticism and maintaining rock-hard resolve could he keep going. Even then, strong as he was, the burdens of office were sometimes too much.[4]

TAR AND FEATHERS

In early 1832, opposition took a violent turn. On Saturday, March 24, Joseph was dragged from his bedroom in the dead of night. His attackers strangled him until he blacked out, tore off his shirt and drawers, beat and scratched him, and jammed a vial of poison against his teeth until it broke. After tarring and feathering his body, they left him for dead. Joseph limped back to the Johnsons' house and cried out for a blanket. Through the night, his friends scraped off the tar until his flesh was raw.[5]

Accounts differ on how many men were involved. Joseph said about a dozen hauled him from the room where he was sleeping in a trundle bed with one of the twins. Someone tapped gently on the window, perhaps to see if anyone was awake, and then the men burst through the door. Outside there may have been fifty others.[6] About 150 yards from the house, Joseph saw Sidney Rigdon lying on the ground apparently dead, dragged there by his heels. Joseph said "one McClintic" clutched his hair and Felatiah Allen, Esq., gave the mob "whiskey to lift their spirits." Joseph heard calls of "Simonds, Simonds," presumably meaning Symonds Ryder, the former Mormon and custodian of a Campbellite congregation in Hiram.[7]

The attack came as the culmination of a number of petty harassments over the preceding weeks. Booth's letters in the *Ohio Star* brought the opposition to the boiling point. Booth claimed that Joseph Smith was an insidious fraud. Behind Joseph's plans for Zion, Booth saw a plot to trap the unsuspecting "in an unguarded hour [as] they listen to its fatal insinuations. The plan is so ingeniously contrived, having for its aim one principal point, viz: the establishment of a society in Missouri, over which the contrivers of this delusive system, are to possess unlimited and despotic sway." Booth thought Joseph's doctrines were "designed to allure the credulous and the unsuspecting, into a state of unqualified vassalage."[8]

Booth's friend Symonds Ryder shared the fears. Like Booth, Ryder had been a Mormon for only a few months before becoming disillusioned. Writing thirty years later, Ryder could remember only evil of the Mormons. Naive converts soon learned "the horrid fact that a plot was laid to take their property from them and place it under the disposal of Joseph Smith the prophet." Ryder wrote without embarrassment that some who had been the dupes of this deception, determined not to let it pass with impunity; and, accordingly, a company was formed of citizens from Shalersville, Garrettsville, and Hiram, in March, 1832, and proceeded to headquarters in the darkness of night, and took Smith and Rigdon from their beds, and tarred and feathered them both, and let them go. This had the desired effect, which was to get rid of them.[9]

Ryder felt the mob "cleansed" the community of a dangerous element.

In a later memoir, Luke Johnson, one of John Johnson's sons, said that during the attack Joseph was

> stretched on a board, and tantalized in the most insulting and brutal manner; they tore off the few night clothes that he had on, for the purpose of emasculating him, and had Dr. Dennison there to perform the operation; but when the Dr. saw the Prophet stripped and stretched on the plank, his heart failed him, and he refused to operate.[10]

The mob apparently meant to castrate Joseph. The historian Fawn Brodie speculated that one of John Johnson's sons, Eli, meant to punish Joseph for an intimacy with his sister Nancy Marinda, but that hypothesis fell for lack of evidence.[11] Whatever the reason for the punishment, a kind of primitive terror took control. The mob did not take him to court or attack him in pamphlets or sermons; they inscribed their anger on his body. In a strange conflation of cultural impulses, one of the mobbers fell on the naked Joseph, and "scratched my body with his nails like a mad cat," muttering, *"God dam ye, that's the way the Holy Ghost falls on folks."*[12]

Luke Johnson saw a battle of manhoods in the encounter that night. He said, "Waste, who was the strongest man on the Western Reserve, had boasted that he could take Joseph out alone." Waste had hold of one foot as Joseph was hauled from the house when "Joseph drew up his leg and gave him a kick, which sent him sprawling in the street. He afterwards said that the Prophet was the most powerful man he ever had hold of in his life." Johnson liked to think that Joseph had bested his opponent. Joseph was not so assertive. When he thought they had killed Rigdon and would execute him next, he pled, "You will have mercy and spare my life, I hope." He did acknowledge that before making his plea, "I made a desperate struggle, as I was forced out, to extricate myself, but only cleared one leg, with which I made a pass at one man, and he fell on the door steps." He was proud the next day when members of the mob found him at his pulpit. "With my flesh all scarfied and defaced, I preached to the congregation as usual, and on the afternoon of the same day baptized three individuals."[13]

The morning after, Joseph found Sidney suffering from the thumping his head had taken as he was dragged along the frozen ground. Delirious, Sidney asked his wife, Phebe, to bring him a razor to kill Joseph; when she refused, he asked Joseph for a razor to kill her. The trauma of the mobbing may have deepened Sidney's tendency to manic-depression.[14] Closer to home, little Joseph Murdock Smith, weakened by the measles, caught cold from the exposure and died after five days, the fourth child the Smiths had lost.

The fallout from the attack lasted for months. The mobbers continued to menace the Johnson farm until they drove Sidney and Joseph away. In early April, they left for Missouri. Joseph advised Emma to leave the Johnson farm for the Whitneys' house in Kirtland, where the Smiths had stayed the previous year. Unfortunately, Elizabeth Ann Whitney's hostile aunt Sarah turned Emma away at the door, a crushing humiliation for that proud woman. Emma moved from house to house that summer, no more settled than when she had married Joseph Smith five years before.[15]

TROUBLE IN ZION

For a time, no place around Kirtland was safe. Sidney Rigdon tried moving to town, but a second mob forced him out. The tar-and-feather episode required Joseph to accelerate a Missouri trip he had been planning for a month in order to administer the Zion he had so exuberantly created in the summer of 1831. Managing two centers—Independence and Kirtland separated by hundreds of miles—added inordinately to the burden of his leadership. Rigdon and Joseph met a few miles away in Warren, and along with Newel Whitney, Peter Whitmer, and Jesse Gause, left for the West. To be sure Joseph was gone, the mob followed him to Cincinnati.[16]

Gause, a new face among the Church leaders, had impressed Joseph after converting from the Shakers. At forty-seven, Gause was eight years older than Rigdon and an experienced Quaker schoolteacher. He later held responsible positions in Shaker communities in Pennsylvania and Ohio. Not long after Gause was baptized, Joseph ordained him a high priest and called him and Rigdon as counselors in the newly organized Presidency of the High Priesthood.[17] In Missouri, Gause was one of the handful of men appointed to oversee Mormon economic affairs. He remained in Independence until he left on a mission later in the summer. Then he disappeared. In December 1832, Gause was dropped from the Church and faded from sight. His was not an exceptional case. In his need for talent and experience, Joseph frequently placed unjustified confidence in untried converts.[18]

With Gause in the company, the five men left their wagon at Steubenville on the Ohio River and went upstream by boat to Wheeling, Virginia, where they purchased paper for William Phelps's press. Backtracking, they took passage to Louisville and transferred to a steamer bound for St. Louis. From there, they took the stage for the final three hundred miles across Missouri to Independence, arriving on April 24, completing the nine-hundred-mile journey in about three weeks.[19]

Joseph's first business was to settle a quarrel between Sidney Rigdon and Edward Partridge, the Missouri bishop. Rigdon had not forgiven Partridge for questioning Joseph's prediction of a large branch in Jackson County in 1831. The same age as Rigdon and a successful hatter in Painesville, Partridge had been a member of Rigdon's Campbellite congregation in Mentor. When the missionaries arrived in Ohio in November 1830, Partridge's wife, Lydia, was attracted to Mormonism; Edward thought the Mormons were impostors. He and Rigdon visited Joseph Smith in New York in December, and satisfied with what he found, Partridge was baptized. Joseph recognized his ability and called him to be the first bishop.[20]

Although questioning Joseph's prediction that there would be many Jackson County converts, Partridge did not defect when rebuked for "unbelief and blindness of heart." Ezra Booth appealed directly to Partridge in his *Ohio Star* letters, but the bishop did not follow Booth out of the Church. Partridge's basic faithfulness was never in doubt. He had joined the Mormons even though his relatives in Massachusetts considered him deranged and sent a brother to look after him. In Missouri, he took his censure about the "prophecy" of converts to heart and worried about failing in his position.[21]

Joseph seems to have forgiven Partridge for his "unbelief," but Rigdon complained of Partridge "having insulted the Lord's prophet." Rigdon was assured that "br. Edward" was "willing to make every confession" that Rigdon could require. Why not "bury the matter"? At a conference in Independence two days after Joseph's arrival, the "difficulty or hardness" between Partridge and Rigdon was "amicably settled," and "all hearts seemed to rejoice."[22]

Joseph wanted good feelings to abound in meetings. Unlike many preachers of the time, he did not measure success by his own "liberty" in speaking, but was more concerned about harmony and uplift. At the morning meeting of the Independence conference, Joseph was acknowledged as president of the High Priesthood, the position the Kirtland church had endorsed in January. Afterwards, he was given "the right hand of fellowship" by Bishop Partridge on behalf of the Church. Preparing his history seven years later, Joseph remembered "the scene was solemn, impressive, and delightful."[23]

The most important business of the conference dealt with the problem of consecrated properties. The Zion Saints were trying to provide an "inheritance" for each migrant family according to the law of consecrated properties, but most had almost nothing on arrival. Resources went out of the storehouse, while little came in. A revelation in Hiram had commanded

Joseph to coordinate the Missouri storehouse with the one in Kirtland. According to the instructions, Joseph, Rigdon, and Newel Whitney, the newly appointed bishop for Kirtland, were to "sit in council" with the Saints in Zion to resolve the difficulty.[24]

At an afternoon session in Jackson County, Joseph received a follow-up revelation on organizing a firm comprising nine men who were "to manage the affairs of the poor, and all things pertaining to the bishopric both in the land of Zion, and in the land of Shinehah [Kirtland]." Everyday management of the storehouse remained with the two bishops, Partridge in Missouri and Whitney in Ohio, but overall direction was to come from this higher council. Called the United Firm or the United Order, it functioned like a company, managing a tannery, steam sawmill, a printing press, and real estate in hopes of serving the Saints and turning a profit for the storehouse.[25]

The two revelations on the firm, like the others on consecrated properties, were long on principles and short on detail. They presented a theological message, not a business plan. Almost nothing was said about division of responsibilities, organizational structure, or procedures. One revelation dwelt instead on the connection of earthly and heavenly societies. The revelation put forward the arresting doctrine that the economies of earth and heaven must correspond: "If ye are not equal in earthly things, ye cannot be equal in obtaining heavenly things." The leveling of property introduced the Saints to the heavenly order. "For if you will that I give unto you a place in the celestial world, you must prepare yourselves by doing the things which I have commanded you."[26]

One cannot tell if Joseph Smith understood how much he was asking of his followers in requiring the consecration of property. Questions about self-interest and obstinacy were not ones he entertained. The revelation said everyone was entitled to draw on the storehouse of common property, that "every man may improve upon his talent, that every man may gain other talents, yea, even an hundred fold." Afterwards, whatever surplus was acquired was to "be cast into the Lord's storehouse, to become the common property of the whole church." The Saints were to work hard for each other. That asked a lot of individualistic farmers and artisans in the expanding market economy of nineteenth-century America. Nothing was more sacrosanct in American ideology than the individual's right to the fruits of his labor. Equalizing wealth required each person to be "seeking the interest of his neighbor, and doing all things with an eye single to the glory of God." Could they? The little band of Saints had no prior experience with equality of property. Equality had always meant equality of rank in political society and equality before the law. Not even the most radical voices in the Revolution had called for a leveling of wealth. Only a few utopians like the Shakers had experimented with the redistribution of property.[27] Joseph expected people to sacrifice personal advantage for the good of the whole in a society long devoted to private gain.

The system never worked properly. The lack of property to distribute among the poverty-stricken early members hampered the system's effectiveness from the start. Joseph struggled on, aided by Partridge and the loyal Colesville Saints, who made up a large part of the Mormon population in Zion. In 1833, the Mormons' expulsion from Jackson County would close down everything. The system's two-year existence was about average for the various communal experiments being undertaken in the period.[28]

After its brief life in Jackson County, Joseph never put consecration of property into full effect again. He attempted a modified form in a second Mormon settlement at Far West, Missouri, but nothing in Nauvoo. It had a second life as an ideal invoked whenever a cooperative effort was required. The short-term Zion experiment came to stand for individual sacrifice for the good of the whole. Brigham Young later called upon the consecration tradition to motivate the organization of cooperatives in Utah, and to this day the principle of consecration inspires Mormon volunteerism and the payment of tithes to the Church.[29]

EVENING AND MORNING STAR

While in Missouri, Joseph saw to the founding of the first Mormon newspaper. Although not a bookish person, he knew that the mission to spread the Gospel required publications. He envisioned Independence as a publishing center whence the word would go forth into the world. The only experienced Mormon editor, William W. Phelps, was assigned to live there, and a press and paper were ordered. To house the press, Partridge purchased (or perhaps built) a two-story brick office. Dedicating the building on May 29, he remarked on "the important duties devolving upon those whom the Lord has designated to spread his truths & revelations in these last days to the inhabitants of the earth."[30]

During the Missouri conference, the Literary Firm, which had been organized in November in Kirtland to handle publications, arranged for the printing of the revelations under the title *A Book of Commandments*. A committee for reviewing the manuscripts—its members were William Phelps, Oliver Cowdery, and John Whitmer—was to "make all necessary verbal corrections," and even to select the revelations deemed "proper" for printing. The Literary Firm also instructed Phelps to work on publishing the hymns chosen by Emma. Doubtless the conference discussed publication of the *Evening and Morning Star*, the newspaper whose prospectus had appeared in February 1832.[31]

In putting their message in print, the Mormons were in step with every

other Christian denomination of the day. An estimated 605 religious journals had been founded in America by 1830, all but 14 of them since 1790.
The Mormons claimed their Independence press was the westernmost in
the state, but it was not unusual for small towns to have a newspaper. Printing had moved out from the cultural centers in Boston, Philadelphia, and
New York to 195 cities and towns in every state but Mississippi. The "truth"
sects—the Mormons, the Millerites, the Disciples of Christ, and the Universalists, each emphasizing doctrinal principles and a particular view of
history—produced huge numbers of printed works, far out of proportion to
their sizes. The Millerites printed four million pieces of literature in four
years after 1839.[32] Methodists and Baptists were just as eager to distribute
devotional literature pointing souls toward religious conversion.

William W. Phelps managed the press and lived above the printing office
with his wife, Sally, and their large family. Phelps, thirty-nine, had joined
the Mormons in June 1831 and been immediately called to "do the work of
printing, and of selecting, and writing books for schools, in this church."
Before his conversion, he had edited newspapers in upstate New York for
ten years, most recently the anti-Masonic *Ontario Phoenix*, and sought his
party's nomination as state lieutenant governor on the anti-Masonic ticket.
He was a Bible-believing seeker and millenarian when he heard of the *Book
of Mormon*'s publication in Palmyra just twelve miles north of his home
in Canandaigua. The book struck him as true on first reading, and a visit
to Joseph Smith in December 1830 confirmed the initial impression. He
delayed baptism until a decline in his fortunes the following spring, including a brief stay in debtors' prison, persuaded him to move to Kirtland and
throw in his lot with the Mormons.[33]

Phelps's writing delighted Joseph. The first issue of the *Star*, published in
June 1832, "was a joyous treat to the Saints," Joseph later wrote. Phelps's
editorials had the grand sweep of Joseph's revelations. The first article,
titled "To Man," announced that the *Star* "comes to bring good tidings of
great joy to all people, but more especially the house of Israel scattered
abroad, that the day of their redemption is near, for the Lord hath set his
hand again the second time to restore them to the lands of their inheritance." The *Star* would "show that the ensign is now set up, unto which all
nations shall come, and worship the Lord, the God of Jacob, acceptably."
That was Joseph's kind of language. The first three issues so pleased him
that he later inserted long extracts into his history. Phelps's writing combined generous inclusion along with the warnings of coming disaster. "The
Star comes in these last days as the friend of man, to persuade him to turn
to God and live, before the great and terrible day of the Lord sweeps the
earth of its wickedness." Joseph was sure the *Star*'s contents would "gratify,
and enlighten the humble enquirer after truth." For a time that summer
and fall, Joseph felt as akin to Phelps as to anyone in the Church.[34]

SADNESS

On the way back to Kirtland, Newel Whitney was injured in a runaway stage accident. While the frightened horses were galloping at full speed, Whitney jumped from the coach and caught his foot in a wheel, breaking his foot and leg in several places. Joseph, who had leapt out unhurt, sent Rigdon on to Kirtland and remained behind to nurse Whitney back to health. They put up at a tavern in Greenville, Indiana, where Dr. Porter, the tavern keeper's brother, tended Whitney. During the month-long convalescence, Joseph was afflicted with food poisoning. He got up from the table one day, rushed to the door, and vomited blood so violently he dislocated his jaw. He set the jaw in place himself and hurried to the bedside, where Whitney laid on hands. Joseph said he was healed instantly, though the poison caused "much of the hair to become loosened from my head."[35]

Forced into uncharacteristic quietude for a month, Joseph morosely walked the woods. On June 6, after news came from Kirtland, Joseph wrote Emma that his situation was a "very unpleasent one." Nearly every day he visited the woods to pray. With nothing to do but meditate, old sorrows came flooding back. In giving "vent to all the feelings of my heart," he wrote,

> I have Called to mind all the past moments of my life and am left to morn and Shed tears of sorrow for my folly in Sufering the adversary of my Soul to have so much power over me as he has had in times past but God is merciful and has f[o]rgiven my Sins and I r[e]joice that he Sendeth forth the Comforter unto as many as believe and humbleeth themselves before him.

The passage gives us once again a Joseph weighed down with regret and yearning, the Joseph reflected in Enoch's lament in the Book of Moses and Nephi in the *Book of Mormon*, grieving because of his sins: "O wretched man that I am." Around this time (the date is not known exactly), Joseph recorded the account of the First Vision in which he speaks of mourning "for my own sins" and hearing the welcome words "Joseph my son thy sins are forgiven thee."[36]

This sorrowful submissiveness would surface again in his writings, especially near the end of his life. After telling Emma of his misery, he wrote: "I will try to be contented with my lot knowing that God is my friend in him I shall find comfort I have given my life into his hands I am prepared to go at his Call I desire to be with Christ I Count not my life dear to me only to do his will." The long period of isolation coming after the tar-and-feathering in Hiram had stripped Joseph down to a vulnerable inner self: should God will it, he was ready to die; perhaps he would welcome death. He later said of this moment, "I often times wandered alone in the lonely places seeking consolation of him who is alone able to console me."[37] The words "lonely" and "consolation" would appear again in Joseph's writings at times when separation from friends brought thoughts of death.

Joseph concluded the letter with observations about friends in Kirtland. He was disappointed that the mercurial William McLellin had left his mission to marry. Joseph remembered his parents and his brother Hyrum and sister Sophronia. He missed his family. "I Should Like [to] See little Julia and once more take her on my knee." And he wanted time with Emma, to "converse with you on all the subjects which concerns us things . . . [it] is not prudent for me to write." The letter suggests a marriage where everything was talked over—the family, the gossip, Church problems, and Joseph's inward battles. The letter ended: "I subscribe myself your Husband the Lord bless you peace be with [you] so Farewell untill I return."[38]

Four weeks after his accident, Newel Whitney was still bedridden. Joseph walked into Whitney's room one day and told him that if they started for home the next morning, the way would be opened. Joseph predicted they would take a wagon to the Oho River, ferry across, take a hackney to the landing, find a boat, and be on their way. Taking courage, Whitney agreed, and events came about as predicted. Sometime in June, Joseph was back in Kirtland.[39]

IRRITATIONS

When he later wrote his history, Joseph passed rapidly over the summer of 1832. He said he spent most of the time translating the Bible, his regular occupation, and filled the space in the history with articles from the *Evening and Morning Star*. The unmentioned events may have been too painful to reiterate. While Joseph was in the West for two months, Emma moved from house to house. Still unsettled after his return, they moved back to the Johnsons' in Hiram for a while and finally took three rooms in the storage area over Newel Whitney's Kirtland store. In these cramped quarters, the Smiths found space for boarders, a hired girl, and Joseph's "translation" room. Through the moves and summer heat, Emma was pregnant with a baby due the next November.[40]

Nothing was said in the history of a small tempest in the Church a few weeks after Joseph's return. On July 5, Sidney Rigdon burst into a Kirtland prayer meeting crying that the "keys of the kingdom are rent from the church." He forbade the group to pray and proclaimed the keys gone "untill you build me a new house."[41] Rigdon had long been deprived of a home for his large family and perhaps was suffering mentally, but Hyrum

Smith took the disturbance seriously enough to ride horseback to Hiram, awaken Joseph in the middle of the night, and get him to Kirtland immediately. The Saints were assured that the keys had not been removed, and a council was called to deal with Rigdon. Sensing his counselor's instability after the mobbing, Joseph suspended his license and dressed him down. Not cast aside, as perhaps he should have been, Rigdon was restored to fellowship in three weeks. Joseph stuck by his friend for ten more years.[42]

While dealing with Kirtland troubles, Joseph worried about the spirit of the Saints in faraway Missouri. His anxieties were set off by a letter from Phelps written in a "cold and indifferent manner." Worse, John Whitmer said a few Missouri Saints were "raking up evry fault." Joseph had admitted to an error while he was there and chafed when it was dredged up again. He was further annoyed by William McLellin's disregard of a mission assignment to the South, and a party of Mormon migrants refusing to get recommendations from their congregations before departing from Kirtland.[43] A lot of little things added up to a sense of something being wrong.

Joseph was frustrated when he wrote a long reply to Phelps in late July. The burden of Zion was wearing him down. He thought he was in good standing with God—"my heart is naked before his eyes continually"—but his devotion went unrecognized among the Saints. "I am a lover of the cause of Christ and of virtue chastity and an upright steady course of conduct & a holy walk." And yet he was criticized. If only he could convey his true feelings, but "neither can toungue, or language paint them to you." He seemed to long for some elusive communion of hearts. He wished that his "feelings . . . might for once be laid open before [you], as plain as your own natural face is to you by looking in a mirror," as if perfect transparency would bring them together. He thought of himself as "your unworthy yet affectionate brother in the Lord travling through affliction and great tribulation." If only the Missouri Saints would return "that fellowship and brotherly love." They had to know he loved them. He had labored "with tender and prayerful hearts continually for there salvation." "I have ever been filled with the greatest anxiety for them, & have taken the greatest intrest for there welfare." He wanted their love in return.

When harmony eluded him, he lashed out. In the Phelps letter, he reproved "evil surmisings" and promised the "buffitings of the adversary" for "eniquitous person and rebelious." The response may reflect the pressure on an overburdened young man. As he said, "I have much care and tribulation calculated to weigh down and distroy the mind." Instead of being blessed with experienced people to assist in the work, he had to make do with the "weak things of the world," people of limited means and little learning. Sometimes they were "u[n]stable unbeleiving, unmerciful & unkind."[44] How could he help but worry when he saw them faltering? He needed their loyalty, and when they turned against him, he was disheartened and angry. The burden of Zion was too much.

"With much grief" he had "veewed the frowns of the heavenly hosts upon Zion." Its flaws were troubling because the Saints needed a haven more than ever. Joseph reported on the cholera epidemic afflicting American cities—one of the worst in United States history—striking down people in New York, Boston, Rochester, Albany, and Buffalo. A letter from Detroit, he told Phelps, informed him "the cholera is raging in that city to an alarming degree, hundreds of families are a fleeing to the country and the country people have become alarmed and torn up the bridges and stopped all communication and even shot peoples horses down under them." The news was a sign of the times, one calamity among many more on the way. The hearts of Saints and sinners were failing them, causing them to cry "to whom shall we go or whethe[r] shall we flee." Joseph's answer: "O my God spare Zion that it may be a place of Reffuge and of safety."[45]

NEW YORK

About two months later, a revelation underscored the perils of the time: "I the Almighty, have laid my hands upon the nations to scourge them for their wickedness." The revelation instructed Bishop Whitney to warn the eastern cities of "the desolation and utter abolishment which awaits them if they do reject these things." With his usual alacrity, Joseph set off with Whitney in early October, leaving Emma, eight months pregnant, at home. Though the bishop's leg was still tender from the stagecoach accident, they traveled to Albany and New York City, where they talked to the Episcopal Bishop Benjamin T. Onderdonk, a conversation regrettably not recorded, and then through New England, visiting Providence and Boston.[46]

Joseph wrote an illuminating letter to Emma about his New York City experiences. He recorded his reactions just six months before he produced a plan for the City of Zion in Missouri. The following spring he would send off instructions for laying out a city of 15,000 to 20,000 people. Until this trip, his experiences with cities had been limited to Salem, Massachusetts, as a boy of seven or eight and brief stops in Cincinnati and St. Louis on the first trip to Missouri in 1831. Now in a single month, he visited two of the nation's oldest and most distinguished cities, Boston and New York, giving him a startling view of modern urbanism. New York, with a population of over 200,000, was the nation's largest city and its commercial and cultural center. Pearl Street, where Joseph and Whitney stayed, lay in the section of crooked streets below Wall Street, but the new rectangular city with its straight streets was rapidly extending to the north, and shops and great houses in open spaces like Union Square were beginning to rival the famous squares of London.[47]

Joseph wrote Emma while his pulse was still racing. "This day I have been walking through the most splended part of the City of New Y— the build-ings are truly great and wonderful to the astonishing of eve[r]y beholder." Translating his thoughts into the religious language he knew best, he asked if this urban magnificence pleased God. "The language of my heart is like this[:] can the great God of all the Earth maker of all thing[s] magnificent and splendid be displeased with man for all these great inventions." For a man of Joseph's apocalyptic temperament and rural background, the answer could have been yes, the city did anger God; but, he said, "my answer is no it can not be seeing these works are calculated to mak men comfortable wise and happy."[48]

But God's anger was kindled against the city's wicked inhabitants, because they failed to give Him the glory. Joseph described the people as walking sepulchers, supported by appearance alone. "Nothing but the dress of the people makes them look fair and butiful." Inside he detected "defor-mity." "Their is something in every countinance that is disagreable with few exceptions." Seeing them was almost more than he could bear. He asked, "How long Oh Lord Shall this order of things exist and darkness cover the Earth?" He looked as long as he could and then returned to his room, "to meditate and calm my mind." New York was another Nineveh with confused and deluded residents. "My bowels is filled with compasion towards them and I am determined to lift up my voice in this City." He felt like a Jonah or an Amos, a wilderness prophet, warning the proud inhabi-tants of a decadent city.[49]

After that one walk, Joseph spent most of the time in his room, reading and "holding comuneion with the holy spirit." He had one satisfying con-versation with a "butiful young gentleman" from "Jersey" who listened while Joseph talked deep into the night. Otherwise, he took his meals with the hundred other boarders in the house and got a laugh from watching the waiters run about the table. Writing to Emma, he wanted to "say something to you to comfort you in your beculier triel and presant affliction." He assured her that he was her "one true and living friend on Earth." In late October, Joseph and Whitney left and were home by November 6, 1832, when at two in the morning Emma delivered her fourth child. The first to live for more than a few days, he was called Joseph, or "young Joseph," and would preside over a branch of Mormonism after his father's death.[50]

BRIGHAM YOUNG

A few days after young Joseph's birth, the man who years later would lead a larger body of Mormons to the West appeared in Nauvoo. While Emma was still in bed with the baby, her husband brought three strangers into the house. The tall, lanky Heber Kimball had arrived in Kirtland with Joseph

Young and his younger brother Brigham, a sturdy carpenter four years older than Joseph.[51] They had come by wagon from Mendon, New York, where a small Mormon outpost had formed around the John and Hannah Young family and their ten children and spouses. Brigham's brother Phinehas, a Methodist circuit rider, had believed the *Book of Mormon* when he first read it, and so did father John and sister Fanny. Brigham Young held back, wanting to test its ideas and meet some Mormons. He was slow to commit to any religion, scarred by a severe Methodist upbringing, where dancing was forbidden and violin music was thought to set one's feet on the road to hell. Young delayed joining the Methodists until he was twenty-three. Even then, he felt "cast down, gloomy, and despondent," weighed down by a vague guilt.[52]

Mormonism came like a liberation. Young afterwards said he loved its broad scope. "Were you to ask me how it was that I embraced 'Mormonism,' I should answer, for the simple reason that it embraces all truth in heaven and on earth." Mormonism was "light, intelligence, power, and truth."[53] In January 1832, Young visited a Mormon meeting in Bradford County, Pennsylvania, where he heard members speak in tongues and prophesy. That April, Young followed his father and brothers into baptism, and other Youngs soon joined them. Like so many converts in the early years, a group of family members came to Mormonism together.

After baptism, Young gave himself over entirely to his new religion. That summer, he left his tubercular wife and two daughters, abandoned his carpentry shop and tools, and went on the road to preach. He and Heber Kimball went from town to town "without purse or scrip" in the approved New Testament fashion. When he returned, he nursed his ailing wife until her death in September, and then was gone again. Leaving his daughters with the Kimballs, he circled through nearby towns with the Mormon message.[54]

For Brigham Young, as for most converts, Joseph Smith was not the issue in accepting the Mormon gospel. The Youngs studied the *Book of Mormon*, met other Mormons, and felt the spirit, but did not think it was necessary to know Joseph. When converts came to Kirtland, they were curious to see the Prophet, but rarely were they overwhelmed by his charisma. In later reports of these first meetings, they usually passed over the event without registering an impression.[55] Upon encountering Joseph for the first time and being served cider and pepper, one young man found him to be "a friendly, cheerful agreeable man," but "a queer man for a prophet of God." When Brigham Young met him for the first time in Kirtland, Joseph was chopping wood. Young's autobiographical sketch said nothing about Joseph's magnetic qualities.[56]

The highlight of the visit came during evening prayers. While the group knelt, Young spoke in tongues. Others in the room looked immediately for Joseph's reaction, knowing his aversion to extravagant gifts, and were reassured the gift was from God. Later that night, Joseph himself spoke in tongues for the first time. In his later accounts, Young said nothing of Joseph's gift.[57] He seemed more concerned about his own spiritual experiences than with evidence of Joseph's prophetic authority.

On this first meeting, no magnetism drew the two men together. Brigham Young was not swept into Joseph's inner circle as Sidney Rigdon and William Phelps had been. Joseph was most impressed with well-spoken, educated men. Brigham Young was a solid, plain person, not especially voluble at this stage of his life.[58] Young was not invited to stay for the school Joseph planned to hold that winter. Instead, he returned to Mendon and preached through the winter in New York and Canada.

SOUTH CAROLINA

The trip to New York City had the millennial purpose of warning the cities of imminent danger. Wherever he was, Joseph observed the world through a millennial lens. Mindful of the apocalyptic future, he watched for calamities signaling the end. While cholera was "cutting down its hundreds in the city of New York," he wrote Phelps, "the Indians are spreading death and devestation wherever they go." In December, news of a political disaster as dire as the cholera caught his attention. An excessively high tariff favoring northern manufactures had set off a "rebellion": a South Carolina convention had unilaterally nullified the tariff and forbade its collection. President Andrew Jackson, refusing to acknowledge this assertion of state power, called out troops. By Christmas 1832, a military confrontation appeared imminent.[59]

On Christmas Day, when the Kirtland brethren were discussing possible repercussions of the confrontation, South Carolina was mentioned in a revelation. The naming of a state was a departure for Joseph; political institutions had rarely been named in the revelations. The site for the temple in Missouri, the Lord had said, was in "the place which is now called Independence," as if the name was temporary and of no lasting significance. In revelations on missionary work, men were sent to compass points, not to named states. The United States figured only as one of the unnamed nations that were to suffer in the last days. Mormons, like other millenarians, tended to dismiss human political institutions as ephemera doomed to disappear. But the Christmas Day revelation linked the "appearances of troubles among the nations" to prophecies of the last days.[60] The revelation foresaw war in South Carolina that would spread through the world. First the North and the South would fight, and later Great Britain as a southern ally.

"After many days," the slaves would rise up against their masters, and eventually the Indians, "the remnants who are left of the land," would join in. Reference to the "remnants" would have reminded the Saints of *Book of Mormon* prophecies about the remnants of Jacob in America, the Lamanites, vexing the Gentiles if they refused to join Israel.

The Christmas Day revelation was the first Mormon revelation to correlate political events with the millenarian calendar, the central project of most millenarian thinkers, who had linked the career of Napoleon, for example, to prophecies in the Bible. Joseph's revelation foresaw a series of wars unfolding out of one another—North versus South, Great Britain and the nations, slaves rising up, then Indians "will marshall themselves, and shall become exceeding angry"—until "the consumption decreed, hath made a full end of all nations." The "rebellion" of South Carolina would "terminate in the death and misery of many souls."[61]

Little was made of the Civil War revelation in Joseph's time. He did not publish it during his lifetime, and not until 1876 did it stay in the *Doctrine and Covenants* for good.[62] The revelation responded to events of the hour, in the spirit of the cholera reports, and then was put aside. Interest revived in the 1850s when the conflict between North and South flared up again. In 1861, in the middle of the secession crisis, a Philadelphia newspaper reprinted the revelation as a curiosity, ending the article with the query, "Have we not had a prophet among us?"[63]

REPRISE

As 1832 ended, Joseph wrote Phelps again. He apologized for sending a second letter so soon but the affairs of Zion, he said, were "laying great with weight upon my mind." He was worried about all the faithful families coming to Zion "and yet rec[e]ive not there inheritance by consecration by order or deed from the bishop." Although Partridge was struggling to eke out inheritances for migrants, the resources were not there. Joseph was angry with the settlers who refused to enter into the consecration of properties. They were not to have "there names enrolled with the people of God, neithe[r] is the geneology to be kept." Their names and their fathers' names would not be written in the book of the Law of God. Implicitly criticizing Partridge, Joseph felt that a stronger hand could compel these unwilling souls to consecrate the property and make the system work. At this point in the letter, he ascended into the revelatory spirit to deliver a blast against the Missouri church:

> Thus saith the still small voice which whispereth through and pierceth all things and often times it maketh my bones to quake while it maketh manifest

saying and it shall come to pass that I the Lord God will send one mighty and strong holding the scepter of power in his hand clothed with light for a covering whose mouth shall utter words Eternal words while his bowels shall be a fountain of truth to set in order the house of God and to arrange by lot the inheritance of the saints whose names are found and the names of their fathers and of their children enroled in the Book of the Law of God while that man who was called of God and appointed that puteth forth his hand to steady the ark of God shall fall by the shaft of death like as a tree that is smitten by the vivid shaft of lightning.[64]

The mighty and strong one was never identified, though the man who put forth his hand to steady the ark was likely the faithful Partridge, who could never shake off the onus of having criticized a prophecy in 1831.[65] The question of who was the mighty one became moot the following year when the Mormons were expelled and property consecration ended. The letter shows Joseph attempting to use revelatory language to solve an insoluble administrative problem. His compulsion to make Zion work and his frustration when it proved intractable generated immense rhetorical force.

In the midst of this outburst, he abruptly stopped threatening and spoke almost plaintively:

> Oh Lord when will the time come when Brother William [Phelps] thy Servent and myself behold the day that we may stand together and gase upon Eternal wisdom engraven upon the hevens while the magesty of our God holdeth up the dark curtain until we may read the round of Eternity to the fullness and satisfaction of our immortal souls.

The switch from rebuke to vision suggests the relief Joseph found in the contemplation of eternity. When the strains of managing Zion became too great, visions restored his strength. It rested him to "gase upon Eternal wisdom engraven upon the hevens." In vision, he and Phelps stood together peacefully. Words were unnecessary. Indeed, they were a hindrance:

> Oh Lord God deliver us in thy due time from the little narrow prison almost as it were totel darkness of paper pen and ink and a crooked broken scattered and imperfect language.[66]

He yearned for communion without words, possible perhaps only while viewing "the round of eternity."

Joseph had good cause to seek respite from the vexations of his work. The year began with tar and feathers and ended with a prediction of civil war. The world was in turmoil, and worse was coming. His own life was a struggle. The recalcitrance of the Saints in Zion, added to persecution and criticism from outside, bore him down. From these discouragements, he turned to his visions for relief. While slogging through the mire in 1832 and early 1833, he received four seminal revelations, matching in importance any he had received previously. Welcomed as gifts from heaven, they marked a new stage in his development. They went beyond Zion, the gathering, and the millennium, the governing ideas of the early years, to priesthood, endowment, and exaltation, the distinguishing doctrines of the later years.

TEN

EXALTATION

1832–33

The glory of God is intelligence, or, in other words, light and truth.
Doctrine and Covenants [1835], 82:6

IN THE MIDDLE OF FEBRUARY 1832, Joseph received a revelation that introduced a new understanding of what he called "the economy of God."[1] During the previous years, the revelations had dealt primarily with establishing the Church and building the City of Zion. They established policy, made assignments, or dealt with current Church problems. The emphasis was on this world. Gathering to Zion received more attention than preparing for the afterlife. The revelations promised an inheritance on earth with little mention of a reward in heaven.

A long February revelation, called "The Vision," returned to the questions of human destiny initially addressed in the 1830 revelation of the Book of Moses. "The Vision" dealt with life after death for the first time since the *Book of Mormon*. It was the first of four revelations over the next fifteen months introducing the theme of exaltation.[2] To the fundamentals of sin and atonement, the exaltation revelations added visions of life after salvation. After redemption by Christ, after death, after entry into heaven, what then? With "The Vision," exaltation took its place alongside the Zion project as a second pillar of Mormon belief.

Until 1832, an apocalyptic message of sin and ruin had run through the revealed texts. In the *Book of Mormon*, two civilizations collapse. In the Book of Moses, the earth weeps for the world's sins. The Zion revelations described devastating catastrophes in the world's immediate future. All had a somber cast. The four exaltation revelations looked beyond the sorrows of this world to the serene expanse of "eternal wisdom." They were more promising than threatening, more light than dark.

Out of the exaltation revelations came a new idea of salvation. Protestant evangelicals were preoccupied with the Fall, sin, grace, faith, and redemption; they said little about heaven. Salvation consisted of bridging the abyss between humans and the divine. To be accepted by God was heaven enough. Mormonism too bridged the abyss. Salvation through Christ appeared on page after page of the *Book of Mormon* and again in the summary of beliefs prepared at the organization of the Church.[3] "The Vision" went on from there, dwelling less on reconciliation with God than on achieving the highest realms of God's glory. Heaven contained degrees of glory. The aim was to be exalted to the highest degree, to receive what the revelations called "the fulness," meaning the fulness of God's glory.[4]

By the standards of systematic theology, all of Joseph's exaltation revelations are undisciplined and oracular, like the Bible itself. He did not address a set of outstanding issues, as Jonathan Edwards did in combating eighteenth-century Deism and Arminianism. The exaltation revelations never reply to other texts, give reasons, or make arguments. They are tangled and spontaneous, connecting here and there with other writings like the Swedish theologian Emanuel Swedenborg's discourses on heaven or the Universalists' doctrine of universal salvation, but without engaging in debate. They stand alone, energetic and illuminating, disorderly. Interpretation involves piecing together the parts into a coherent whole and must be undertaken provisionally with no assurance that even believing Mormons will concur.

"THE VISION"

The degrees of glory revelation came in answer to a question about a New Testament passage. As he and Rigdon revised the Bible, Joseph puzzled out the plain meaning of the text. When stumped, he would ask for a revelation.[5] In January 1832, Joseph inquired about 1 Corinthians 7:14, concerning the marriage of believers and unbelievers. In reply to his inquiry, a brief revelation about the effects of mixed marriages on children was received. A month later, John 5:29 posed another problem: where was the justice of God in dealing out rewards and punishments? The passage said the dead "shall come forth; they that have done good, unto the resurrection of life; and they that have done evil, unto the resurrection of damnation." The scripture raised the question of how God could divide people into stark categories of saved and damned when individuals were so obviously a mix in ordinary life. "It appeared self-evident," Joseph wrote, "that if God rewarded every one according to the deeds done in the body, the term 'heaven,' as intended for the Saints eternal home, must include more kingdoms than one."[6]

The question Joseph posed was a classic post-Calvinist puzzle. For over a century Anglo-American culture had struggled to explain the arbitrary judgments of the Calvinist God who saved and damned according to his own good pleasure with little regard for human effort. In severe Calvinism, striving made no difference until God bestowed grace on an aspiring soul. Moral behavior was the product of God's redeeming grace, not the reason for His forgiveness and acceptance. Human effort alone counted for nothing.

During the preceding century, the Calvinist notion of arbitrary sovereignty had come to seem incongruous and offensive. In politics, the requirement of reasonable authority, respectful of human rights, underlay the revolutionary movements of the eighteenth century. In religion, theologians and preachers worked to make God appear just, loving, and reasonable, while preserving the semblance of traditional Calvinist doctrines. Calvinism still flourished in sophisticated forms in theological circles, but people were asking questions much like Smith's.[7] Is God's judgment of humanity consistent with His benevolent character?

The resulting revelation was received in the usual way: in plain sight, with others looking on. More surprising, Sidney Rigdon and Joseph, according to the text, viewed the vision together. Sitting on chairs with perhaps a dozen men watching, they spoke in a plural voice:

> We, Joseph Smith, jr. and Sidney Rigdon, being in the Spirit on the sixteenth of February, in the year of our Lord, one thousand eight hundred and thirty two, by the power of the Spirit our eyes were opened, and our understandings were enlightened, so as to see and understand the things of God.

Together they saw the "glory of the Son, on the right hand of the Father," and jointly bore witness.

> And now, after the many testimonies which have been given of him, this is the testimony, last of all, which we give of him, that he lives; for we saw him, even on the right hand of God; and we heard the voice bearing record that he is the only begotten of the Father; that by him, and through him, and of him, the worlds are and were created; and the inhabitants thereof are begotten sons and daughters unto God.[8]

Rigdon never commented on the experience, though an eyewitness writing in 1892 said Rigdon was drooping by the end while Joseph was still fresh. "Brother Sidney is not as used to it as I am," Joseph is reputed to have said.[9]

The words "economy of God in his vast creation through out all eternity," written in a note on the manuscript, referred to the state of human spirits after the resurrection. "The Vision" divided the spirits into four broad categories: three "kingdoms" of glory and one of no glory. The realm of no glory was the destination of the "sons of perdition," those who had once partaken of the glory of the Lord and rebelled against it. These rebels were worse than bad. They were souls who knew God's power, like Satan, who once "was in the bosom of the Father" and rebelled against Him. The sons of perdition suffered the devil to overcome them and "to deny the truth, and defy my power." Sinning against the light, these were "doomed to suffer the wrath of God, with the devil and his angels in eternity."[10]

These lost ones stand in contrast to the conventionally wicked "liars, and sorcerers, and adulterers, and whoremongers, and whosoever loves and makes a lie." These souls, the revelation said, will suffer on earth, and undergo the "vengeance of eternal fire" in hell after death, but in the last resurrection, after Christ has perfected his work on earth, they too are resurrected into a kingdom of glory, the "telestial."[11] Theirs is to be a lesser glory, no more than the brightness of stars compared to the sun, but still a glory "which surpasses all understanding."[12]

The grade above the telestial, the "terrestrial kingdom," receives the "honorable men of the earth, who were blinded by the craftiness of men: these are they who receive of his glory, but not of his fulness." They are the believing Christians who are not valiant in the faith. At the top is the "celestial kingdom," the "church of the first-born," for believers in Jesus who accept all the ordinances, keep the commandments, and overcome by faith. "Wherefore, as it is written, they are gods, even the sons of God: wherefore all things are theirs, whether life or death, or things present, or things to come, all are theirs, and they are Christ's and Christ is God's."[13]

"The Vision" showed God to be just by granting rewards and punishments in three divisions, roughly corresponding to human experience. The telestial kingdom contained visible sinners who flouted God's commandments; the terrestrial kingdom housed good people who observed Christian conventions but failed to receive the truth in its fulness; and the celestial kingdom was for those who accepted the fulness of the Gospel. Each group had its place, with room for even finer gradations in the telestial kingdom, where glories differed as stars differ in brightness.

The three heavens scheme came from Paul's teaching on the resurrection:

> There are also celestial bodies, and bodies terrestrial: but the glory of the celestial is one, and the glory of the terrestrial is another.
> There is one glory of the sun, and another glory of the moon, and another glory of the stars: for one star differeth from another star in glory.
> So also is the resurrection of the dead.[14]

Building on Paul, "The Vision" made the three resurrected glories of sun, moon, and stars into three heavenly realms. The same scripture inspired eighteenth-century Swedish scientist and visionary Emanuel Swedenborg to divide the heavens into three parts, "celestial," "spiritual," and "natural," equivalent to sun, moon, and stars. Like Joseph and Rigdon, Swedenborg thought the sharp division of the afterlife into heaven and hell underestimated God's desire to bless his children.[15] Since Swedenborg attracted the attention of New England intellectuals (his *Treatise Concerning Heaven and Hell* had its first American edition in 1812), his ideas may conceivably have drifted into Joseph Smith's environment, but it was more likely the passage from Paul sparked the revelations of both men.[16] Joseph later taught that there were three "heavens or degrees" within the celestial kingdom, further dividing the economy of God.

The most radical departure of "The Vision" was not the tripartite heaven but the contraction of hell. In Joseph and Rigdon's economy of God, the sinners ordinarily sent to hell forever remained there only until "Christ shall have subdued all enemies under his feet." Then they are redeemed from the devil in the last resurrection to find a place in the telestial kingdom. Only those rare souls who know God's power and reject it suffer everlasting punishment. God redeems all save these sons of perdition, "the only ones on whom the second death shall have any power."[17]

The doctrine recast life after death. The traditional division of heaven and hell made religious life arbitrary. One received grace or one went to hell. In Joseph's afterlife, the issue was degrees of glory. A permanent hell threatened very few. The question was not escape from hell but closeness to God. God scaled the rewards to each person's capacity. Even the telestial glory, the lowest of the three, "surpasses all understanding."[18]

A later revelation further softened divine judgment. In December 1832 the elders were told that glory was granted according to the law each person could "abide," whether celestial, terrestrial, or telestial. One's glory, it was implied, was tailored to one's capacity. "He who is not able to abide the law of a celestial kingdom, cannot abide a celestial glory." The glory one received was the glory one found tolerable. "For what doth it profit a man," the section concluded, "if a gift is bestowed upon him, and he receive not the gift? Behold he rejoices not in that which is given unto him." One's place in heaven reflected more one's preference than a judgment. "Intelligence cleaveth unto intelligence; wisdom receiveth wisdom; truth embraceth truth." The last judgment matched affinities.[19]

The three degrees doctrine resembled the Universalists' belief that Christ's atonement was sufficient to redeem everyone, or, alternately, that a benevolent God would not eternally punish his own children. No sinners were beyond salvation. The Universalists derived their name from the doctrine that salvation was as universal as Christ's atoning sacrifice was powerful. Though sinners might be punished for a time as a form of discipline, Christ would ultimately save everyone. Joseph's grandfather Asael Smith was among many small farmers and workers attracted to Universalist doctrine.[20] In a sense, "The Vision" perpetuated Smith family doctrine.

Strange to say, the *Book of Mormon* argued against universal salvation. A teacher of universalist doctrine, Nehor, was labeled a heretic in the *Book of Mormon*, and his followers, a band of rebellious priests called the Order of Nehor, disrupted Nephite society. Alma, a preeminent prophet, refuted universal salvation in a discourse to his son Corianton, and another prophet, Lehi, delivered an elaborate philosophical discourse to show that the law must impose punishment on transgressors or good and evil had no meaning.[21] In opposition to universal salvation, the *Book of Mormon* envisioned the afterlife as heaven or hell.

In a perplexing reversal, a revelation received in the very month the *Book of Mormon* was published contradicted the book's firm stand. The revelation said that the phrase "endless torment" did not mean no end to torment, but that "Endless" was a name of God, and "endless punishment" meant God's punishment.[22] Torment for sins would be temporary, just as the Universalists taught. In this tug-of-war between the *Book of Mormon* and the revelations, "The Vision" reinforced the Universalist tendency against the *Book of Mormon's* anti-universalism.

Where was Joseph Smith coming down on the question of universal salvation? Contradictory as they sound, the universalist tendencies of the revelations and the anti-universalism of the *Book of Mormon* defined a middle ground where there were graded rewards in the afterlife, but few were damned. "The Vision" did not actually endorse universal salvation any more than the *Book of Mormon* did. It imposed permanent penalties for sinning, rewarded righteousness with higher degrees of glory, and assigned the sons of perdition to permanent outer darkness. But "The Vision" also eliminated the injustices of heaven-and-hell theology. The three degrees of glory doctrine lay somewhere between the two extremes.

Whatever these oscillations meant for Joseph, "The Vision" confused Mormons who saw only its universalist bent. For most Christians, universal salvation exceeded the limits of acceptable orthodoxy. One Mormon reflected later that "my traditions were such, that when the Vision came first to me, it was so directly contrary and opposed to my former education, I said, wait a little; I did not reject it, but I could not understand it."[23] Others who were "stumbling at it" did object. At a conference in Geneseo, New York, held to deal with the controversy, one brother declared "the vision was of the Devil & he believed it no more than he believed the devil was crucified." Ezra Landon was cut off from the Church for insisting "the vision was of the Devil came from hel[l]." Eventually, Joseph counseled missionaries against publicizing "The Vision" prematurely. The first missionaries to England were told to stick to the first principles of the Gospel. Other members found it thrilling. William Phelps immediately published "The Vision" in the Church newspaper in Missouri.[24]

The three degrees doctrine aside, "The Vision" incorporated common Protestant beliefs about heaven. There was nothing in it like the idiosyncratic details the angels revealed to Swedenborg. In Swedenborg's heaven, people were said to have a clergy and worship in churches. Maidens embroidered flowers on white linens. People lived like innocent children without clothing. They underwent growth, struggle, and change.[25] Avoiding all such description, "The Vision" used language common to Protestants. The words of a Salem pastor in 1819 might have appeared in Joseph's revelation. Because of faith in Christ, Brown Emerson wrote, "believers will share in his honor and blessedness." Christians are "exalted, as joint heirs with the Son of God, to all the glory and felicity of the heavenly kingdom!" The saved would be raised to "celestial thrones, with crowns of glory on their heads, and unwithering palms in their hands, reigning kings and priests unto God!"[26] "Fulness," "glory," and "kings and priests," all well-known New Testament words, were the language of "The Vision." Joseph's statement that the inhabitants of the celestial kingdom were those "into whose hands the Father has given all things" would not have shocked other Christians. Many could have accepted the declaration of "The Vision" that residents of heaven would be, in the words of John's Revelation, "priests and kings, who have received of his fulness, and of his glory."[27]

The difference lay in the emphasis. Protestant sermons on heaven spoke mostly of surcease from sorrows and the joy of knowing Christ. "Pietists, Puritans, Methodists, and others," two historians of heaven have written, "created a powerful model of paradise as an ethereal world filled with psalm-singing or silent contemplation."[28] The emphasis was on serenity and joyful peace. Ideas highlighted in "The Vision," like the possibility of becoming "joint heirs with Christ" and partaking of his glory, were minor Protestant themes. Joseph's revelation, by contrast, paraphrases one biblical scripture after another on the exalted condition of humans in the celestial heavens. They enjoy godly power, dominion, and rank. "They who dwell in his presence . . . know as they are known, having received of his fulness and of his grace; and he makes them equal in power, and in might, and in dominion." In context, "equal" implied equal with God, even though all were to bow "in humble reverence and give him glory forever and ever." And most startling, "as it is written, they are gods, even the sons of God: wherefore all things are theirs, whether life or death, or things present, or things to come, all are theirs, and they are Christ's, and Christ is God's."[29] "Fulness" was the critical word in Joseph's exaltation revelations. The word implied that no blessing, power, or glory of God would be withheld from worthy humans.

Joseph loved "The Vision." "Nothing could be more pleasing to the Saint[s], upon the order of the kingdom of the Lord," he wrote later, remembering only the favorable reception,

than the light which burst upon the world, through the foregoing vision. . . .
The sublimity of the ideas; the purity of the language; the scope for action; the continued duration for completion, in order that the heirs of salvation, may confess the Lord and bow the knee; The rewards for faithfulness. & the

punishments of sins, are so much beyond the narrow mindedness of men, that, every honest man is constrained to exclaim; *It came from God.*[30]

His enthusiasm may have come from the altered relationship with God implied by the revelation. The perfection of the stern and mysterious Calvinist God distanced Him from His children. The law erected an impassable barrier, requiring perfect compliance. In "The Vision" the workings of heaven were made intelligible, and the law became less a set of forbidding commandments than of instructions on how to reach heaven. The laws were helpful and informative rather than distancing. Knowledge made heaven accessible.

PRIESTHOOD

One of the verses in "The Vision" struck a note that would eventually sound through all of Joseph's theology. Inhabitants of the celestial kingdom, the revelation said, were "priests of the Most High, after the order of Melchizedek, which was after the order of Enoch, which was after the order of the only begotten Son." Others in Joseph's time associated priesthood and salvation; a Protestant description of heaven quoted Saint John saying to the seven churches God "hath made us kings and priests unto God." But no one said that the saved priests were members of the order of Melchizedek.[31] Most Protestants, and certainly the radical visionary sects most akin to Mormonism, put little stock in priesthood; it was papist, hierarchical, and insidious. Their impulse was to reduce and dilute priesthood, spreading it thinly among all Christians.

Priesthood figured in Joseph's theology from the time of the June 1831 conference when elders were ordained to the Melchizedek Priesthood, but a year passed before he grasped the central role priesthood was to play in the Church. In November 1831, he was told to appoint a "President of the high Priesthood." In time this office was recognized as the highest in the Church—the Mormon equivalent of pope—but its importance eluded him for six months. Joseph was sustained as President of the High Priesthood at the Amherst Conference in January 1832, but his later history failed to mention the fact. He only noted that "considerable business was done to advance the kingdom."[32] In a similar lapse, Joseph failed to record the date of the visit by Peter, James, and John to restore the apostleship, nor did he include the event in the first edition of his revelations. For years, priesthood appeared only dimly in his thinking.

Near the end of September 1832, Joseph received the revelation "On Priesthood," the first to explain priesthood doctrine. As with all of his major doctrinal revelations, it was linked to the Bible. The seventh chapter of Hebrews mentioned two priesthoods, one the Levitical priesthood "after the order of Aaron," and the other the priesthood "after the order of Melchizedek." In the teaching of Hebrews, one priesthood was for administration of the law, the other for the new dispensation of Christ. Following Hebrews, Joseph's revelation described "greater" and "lesser" priesthoods, one associated with Aaron and the other with Melchizedek.[33]

The introduction to priesthood began with a lengthy genealogy:

> And the sons of Moses, according to the holy priesthood, which he received under the hand of his father-in-law, Jethro,
>> and Jethro received it under the hand of Caleb,
>> and Caleb received it under the hand of Elihu.

And so on, name by name, back through Jeremy, Gad, Esaias, Abraham, Melchizedek, Noah, Enoch, and through "the lineage of the fathers" to Abel and Adam. It seemed like an oblique approach to the subject.[34] Why start with the lineage of the priesthood rather than with divine ordination? The descent of the priesthood through the patriarchs is given more attention than its origins with God.

The point seems to be that priesthood is an ancient divine order, "the holiest order of God," going back through a chain of patriarchs. Not just God, but ancient priests hallowed this authority. An original ordination by God, though implied, is not even mentioned. The priesthood goes back to "Adam, who was the first man." A later revelation explained that "this order was instituted in the days of Adam, and came down by lineage in the following manner," from Adam to Seth to Enos to Cainan, and so on. By emphasizing the historical carriers of priesthood, the revelations linked modern priests to Moses, the patriarchs, and Adam as much as to God. Priesthood made the Saints "sons of Moses and of Aaron and the seed of Abraham," part of an ancient family of priests. "Which priesthood continueth in the church of God in all generations, and is without beginning of days or end of years."[35] Though organized less than three years before, Joseph's new religion felt old. The Saints had an instant history. They did not stand alone as individuals in looking for God; they were embedded in an order of priests going back through time, part of an ancient brotherhood.

The priesthood had one purpose in every age: exaltation. Rather than being a governmental hierarchy or a corporate organization, the priesthood held the sacral power to bring people into the presence of God. The revelation said that "in the ordinances thereof the power of godliness is manifest." Without priesthood, "no man can see the face of God, even the Father, and live," as if priesthood allowed humans to face God in person.[36] Moses, who saw God's face, tried to bring his people into God's presence through the priesthood. According to the revelation, Moses "sought diligently to sanctify his people that they might behold the face of God; but they hardened their hearts and could not endure his presence."[37] The verse referred to the instructions at Sinai, recorded in the Bible, to "go unto the people, and sanctify them to day and to morrow, and let them wash their clothes, and be ready against the third day: for the third day the LORD will come down in the sight of all the people upon mount Sinai." But Joseph's revelations informed him that they were not ready and pled for God not to speak to them, for they would die. Had they not hardened their hearts, the Children of Israel would have seen God while still mortals. Joseph was told that as punishment Moses and the Melchizedek Priesthood were removed from Israel: "he took Moses out of their midst and the holy priesthood also." Only the lesser priesthood remained, which permitted no more than the ministering of angels, not the vision of God.[38] Moses' failure defined Joseph's mission. Could he succeed where Moses had failed? Would Joseph's people sanctify themselves and see God or harden their hearts like ancient Israel?

For almost two years, Joseph had been looking for an "endowment of power," expecting it when the Melchizedek Priesthood was bestowed in June 1831. His revision of the Melchizedek passages in Genesis connected priesthood with the power to "stand in the presence of God."[39] In the fall of 1831, he was told that "inasmuch as you strip yourselves from jealousies and fears, and humble yourselves before me . . . the vail [sic] shall be rent and you shall see me and know that I am." The endowment of power, it now seemed, meant coming into the presence of God. Going one step further, the 1832 priesthood revelation associated the endowment of power with the temple. "And the sons of Moses and of Aaron shall be filled with the glory of the Lord upon mount Zion in the Lord's house."[40] A few years later, as the dedication of the Kirtland temple drew closer, a view of God's face was promised again.

What was the origin of this extraordinary aspiration? Joseph had unknowingly tapped into the centuries-old Catholic theology of the "beatific vision," the ultimate reward of the faithful and the height of human desire. In Catholic thought, the face-to-face vision required the aid of the "light of glory," and was reserved almost exclusively for the redeemed in their final state.[41] For unknown reasons, Joseph took it upon himself to bring his people into the presence of God here and now, taking his cue from Moses and Exodus.

Some readers may have missed the implications of the priesthood revelation. John Whitmer was most excited by the verse warning Boston, New York, and Albany of coming desolation. Those verses reflected the millenarian thinking of the gathering to Zion and constructing the New Jerusalem, which had occupied the Saints for the last two years. The part about "exaltation"—the preparation to stand in God's presence and commune with Him—did not register with Whitmer. Eager as the Saints were for spiritual gifts, not all were ready for the mysticism of the priesthood revelation. How could plain people obtain in this life a privilege usually reserved for the sanctified after death?[42]

If unappreciated at the time, the priesthood revelation laid the foundation for the later development of Joseph's temple practices. Once he had reinvigorated a sacral priesthood, he could adopt rituals manifesting that power. Passages from the Bible began to speak to him. After being inspired by the tenth chapter of Hebrews, he consulted New Testament passages on washing feet and examined Exodus on the consecration of priests.[43] From these texts, the temple rituals would emerge over the next four years. As early as the winter of 1833, he began foot washing, expanded in the winter of 1836 to washings, anointings, and sealings patterned after the consecration of priests. The priesthood doctrines opened a ritual world that Protestantism, with its emphasis on preaching, had closed off. Joseph's temple ordinances had the spirit of Roman Catholic practices but resembled even more the rituals of ancient Israel.

Priesthood countered the atomistic tendencies in American religion. Writing as a religious critic, Harold Bloom sees solitude as the characteristic position of the worshiping American. "The American finds God in herself or himself" only through "a total inward solitude."[44] Evangelical conversion brought people individually before God to receive grace, and Ralph Waldo Emerson said he enjoyed sitting quietly in church before the service more than listening to the sermon with other worshipers. Mormonism had individualist tendencies, but priesthood involved Latter-day Saints in communal religion. Priesthood embedded individuals in a hierarchy of priesthood offices and a line of priesthood holders. Mormons needed the ordinances of the priesthood to come to God, and as priests they ministered to others. Bloom says that "the American spirit learns again its absolute isolation as a spark of God floating in a sea of space"; Joseph's Mormons never floated alone. Priesthood was an order reaching back into antiquity. A later revelation called it "the holy priesthood, after the order of the Son of God."[45] The priesthood web prevented Mormons from ever spinning free into isolation with God. Their lives were interwoven with priesthood from the foundations of the earth.

LIGHT AND TRUTH

In December 1832, three months after the priesthood revelation, Joseph received a lengthy, conglomerate revelation that took two days to complete. Begun during a meeting in the "translation room" above the Whitney store in one of the three rooms where the Smiths were living, it broke off about nine o'clock. The minutes report that "the revelation not being finished the conference adjourned till tomorrow morning 9 oclock AM." The next day, Joseph "proceded to receive the residue of the above revelation." When he mailed it to William Phelps in Missouri, Joseph called it "the Olieve leaf which we have plucked from the tree of Paradise."[46]

Like other revelations, the "Olive Leaf" moves from subject to subject. Nothing in nineteenth-century literature resembles it. The writings of Swedenborg come closest, but they were much less concerned with millenarian events.[47] The "Olive Leaf" runs from the cosmological to the practical, from a description of angels blowing their trumpets to instructions for starting a school. Yet the pieces blend together into a cohesive compound of cosmology and eschatology united by the attempt to link the quotidian world of the now to the world beyond. The revelation offers sketches of the order of heaven, reprises the three degrees of glory, delivers a discourse on divine law, offers a summary of the metahistory of the end times, and then brings it all to bear on what the Saints should do now.

Among the provocative passages in the "Olive Leaf" is a brief metaphysical discussion of light and matter. Joseph's earlier revelations had employed the light metaphor in the usual sense of Christ lighting the way to salvation. The passage in the "Olive Leaf" extended the metaphor into a physical description of the universe. Christ, the revelation explains using a phrase from the Gospel of John, is "in all, and through all things; the light of truth."

> This is the light of Christ. As also he is in the sun, and the light of the sun, and the power thereof by which it was made.
>
> As also he is in the moon, and is the light of the moon, and the power thereof by which it was made.
>
> As also the light of the stars, and the power thereof by which they were made.
>
> And the earth also, and the power thereof; even the earth upon which you stand.
>
> And the light which shineth, which giveth you light, is through him who enlighteneth your eyes, which is the same light that quickeneth your understandings;
>
> which light proceedeth forth from the presence of God, to fill the immensity of space.
>
> The light which is in all things; which giveth life to all things; which is the law by which all things are governed: even the power of God, who sitteth upon his throne, who is in the bosom of eternity, who is in the midst of all things.[48]

The radiant energy proceeding from the presence of God enters every particle of the universe, giving life and intelligence to all existence. The elders sitting in the Whitneys' storage room were told that "if your eye be single to my glory, your whole bodies shall be filled with light, and there shall be no darkness in you; and that body which is filled with light comprehendeth all things."[49] Everything was charged with divine intelligence, putting God into every leaf, every stone. The elders themselves were to be illuminated by the blazing light sustaining all existence.

This conception of a divine light permeating every particle of matter could have turned Mormon theology toward nature. If the light of Christ activates both the human intellect and the natural world, a medium existed for finding God in the planets or in plants and animals. For centuries, alchemists, Hermeticists, and finally Emanuel Swedenborg had pursued illumination through knowledge of nature. Hermeticists sought power over nature through divine knowledge, encapsulating their hopes for divinization in the figure of the magus who tried to reunite with God by knowing and manipulating nature.[50] Swedenborg believed he could find higher levels of meaning in nature by grasping the "correspondence" of natural objects with spiritual truths. Through nature humans could rise to the spiritual or intellectual and finally to the celestial and God. Four years after Joseph's revelation, Emerson would write in his seminal essay "Nature" that "the noblest ministry of nature is to stand as the apparition of God. It is the organ through which the universal spirit speaks to the individual, and strives to lead back the individual to it."[51]

Though Joseph's light of truth doctrine pointed that way, he did not follow the Transcendentalists' path to spiritual enlightenment. A revelation in May 1833 put Christ, rather than nature, at the center of salvation. The incarnate Christ, the revelation said, received "not of the fulness at the first, but received grace for grace." Eventually "he received all power, both in heaven and on earth; and the glory of the Father was with him, for he dwelt in him."[52] The Saints were to follow the same course. "If you keep my commandments you shall receive of his fulness and be glorified in me as I am in the Father: therefore, I say unto you, you shall receive grace for grace." The fulness promised to humans, in other words, was the same as the fulness bestowed on Christ: "all power, both in heaven and on earth." The Saints were told to follow the path of Christ toward this fulness, not to search nature for signs of divinity.[53]

The fulness theology bore some resemblance to the "perfectionist" theology of the revivalist Charles Finney and other contemporaries. Through the 1830s, various zealous souls asked if moral perfection was possible through the grace of Christ. By the 1840s many perfectionists concluded that "the blood of Jesus Christ cleanses from all sin." The next step after conversion was complete sanctification. As Finney said, "entire sanctification, in the sense that it was the privilege of Christians to live without known sin, was a doctrine taught in the Bible." Phoebe Palmer, a powerful

Methodist preacher, thought that once faith was on the altar, unbelief was sinful. Failure to "go on to perfection" nullified previous regeneration.[54]

Though similar in intent, Joseph's May revelation differed from standard perfectionism in defining "fulness" as truth rather than holiness, returning to his earlier doctrine of light. Protestant perfectionists strained toward moral sanctification, Joseph toward a perfection of knowledge. Christ "received a fulness of truth, yea, even of all truth," the revelation said. The Saints were enjoined to obey and sanctify themselves, but to the end of being enlightened. "He that keepeth his commandments, receiveth truth and light, until he is glorified in truth, and knoweth all things." The choice of words to describe perfection gave a distinctive cast to Joseph's revelations. The perfectionists' words were "holiness" and "sanctification"; the governing words in the May revelation were "truth," "light," and "intelligence." Joseph's revelation declared that "the glory of God is intelligence, or, in other words, light and truth."[55] To become like God, as the word "fulness" implied, was to grow in light and truth—to be filled with intelligence. Holiness was not an end in itself but the avenue to intelligence. One kept the commandments in order to receive truth and light.

This was not the truth of science or the knowledge found in libraries, although Joseph would include these in the larger category of truth: "truth is knowledge of things as they are, and as they were, and as they are to come."[56] Intelligence was a capacity for comprehension and insight, accounting for past, present, and future, grasping the moral and spiritual meaning of things, and radiating power. The uneducated Joseph Smith used the word "intelligence" to describe the glory of God. That capacity for seeing and comprehending supernaturally—with the spiritual mind, as he called it— was to him the zenith of human experience.

Joseph combined words—truth, light, intelligence—to encompass his vision, but words still fell short. He was caught in the narrow prison of a crooked and broken language, as he had complained to Phelps. In the May 1833 revelation, he recorded pointed aphorisms without elaboration, as if to point at the truth without fully explaining it.

Man was also in the beginning with God.

Intelligence, or the light of truth was not created or made, neither indeed can be.

All truth is independent in that sphere in which God has placed it, to act for itself, as all intelligence also, otherwise there is no existence.

Behold here is the agency of man, and here is the condemnation of man because that which was from the beginning is plainly manifest unto them, and they receive not the light.

And every man whose spirit receiveth not the light, is under condemnation, for man is spirit.

The elements are eternal, and spirit and element, inseparably connected,
receiveth a fulness of joy;
    And when separated, man cannot receive a fulness of joy.[57]

The exact meaning of the passage is elusive, and interpretations differ. What does it mean that "intelligence, or the light of truth was not created or made"? Is intelligence an independent principle like a law of nature, or does intelligence refer to individual human intelligences? The implication seems to be that man himself is eternal. The revelation states that Christ was in the beginning with the Father, and so were the Saints: "Ye were also in the beginning with the Father." This seems to be saying that Christ's spirit, and the spirit of each human, went back to the same beginning. A few Protestant theologians had speculated that the human spirit was created at the same time as the rest of the universe, but these passages of Joseph's implied that spirits existed before the earth, in the beginning when God and Christ conceived the universe.[58] The revelation states that "the elements are eternal"; was individual intelligence eternal too? The revelation suggests more than it precisely defines.

In later years, Joseph would elaborate these hints into a doctrine of the free intelligence. Human beings in their essence were uncreated intelligences as eternal as God, and so radically free. In choosing the word "intelligence" to characterize this primal individual, Joseph invited comparison to the Enlightenment conception of the autonomous, reasoning individual. The individual, as conceived by Enlightenment thinkers, was autonomous because he or she possessed reason and therefore could choose. The individual had the right to consent to government, as the Declaration of Independence insisted, and to worship as he or she chose. In Enlightenment religion, even God respected reason. For people to believe, they had to have reasons. In one variety of Enlightenment religion, miracles like the parting of the Red Sea provided a reason for belief; in another, creation itself was the greatest miracle and the evidence that God existed. Given one or another form of proof, the reasoning individual could believe and worship.

Like the autonomous, reasoning individual, Joseph's free intelligence had powers of mind. As the word "intelligence" implied, its great capacity was to grasp truth. But by using the word "intelligence" rather than "reason" to characterize this being, Joseph's revelations bound the free intelligence to God rather than setting it free to reason for itself. For God was the source of light and truth, and His light and truth were to be gained only by obedience. The idea of free intelligence combined the moral being of the Bible with the reasoning individual of the Enlightenment. In Joseph's revelations, truth could not be discovered in rebellion and wickedness. "That wicked one cometh and taketh away light and truth, through disobedience."[59] The test of one's humanity was not whether one would abide by the independent dictates of one's own reason, in accord with the Enlightenment ideal, but whether one would accept the light coming from God.

By the time of the May 1833 revelation, a variety of meanings clustered around the idea of exaltation. "The Vision" had introduced the term "fulness" into the conception of celestial life. The revelation said the Saints would inherit a fulness of God's glory. All that the Father had would be theirs. The texts put no limits on the extent of this fulness. The revelation on priesthood said that "all that my Father hath shall be given unto him."[60] These passages altered the idea of salvation from making peace with God to becoming like God. The words "salvation" and "exaltation" contained a world of difference. One implied escape—from sin or hell or Satan—and the other elevation to glory and godhood.

Exaltation also meant intelligence, equated by the revelations with light and truth. In a sense, the central purpose of life was to absorb light and truth, the basis of judgment. Rejecting light was the great error. Living in darkness meant living on the side of evil. "Light and truth forsaketh that evil one." Since the glory of God was intelligence, growing in intelligence was progress in godliness. Later in Nauvoo, Joseph would use the word "intelligence" as a name for the primal essence of the human spirit, and would elaborate the history of God and the free intelligences.[61]

In a characteristic transition, the concluding verses of the May revelation descend from the heavens into the everyday concerns of Joseph and his friends. The Lord scolds them for not keeping order in their families. Joseph is told, "You have not kept the commandments, and must needs stand rebuked before the Lord."[62] Sidney Rigdon and Newel Whitney are admonished for not keeping better track of their children. Ordinary daily concerns mingle with the grand structure of the universe. While taking care of their children, it was implied, the Saints could be growing in glory and intelligence.

THE SCHOOL OF THE PROPHETS

The practical point of the "Olive Leaf" revelation of December 1832 was the organization of a school for training the elders for the next spring's missionary work. They were to study doctrine, history, politics, and more, in classes with instructors and books. Besides suggesting a curriculum and school regulations, the revelation set the school in a broad framework of history and metaphysics that focused the powers of heaven on the elders at their studies.

The school has been represented as an early adult education effort, but the name "the School of the Prophets" indicated a higher purpose. By alluding to the bands of prophets who received instruction under Samuel, Elijah, and Elisha, it implied preparation for a holy work. Missionaries had been going into the field without instruction; in the school, they were to teach one another the "doctrine of the kingdom," and virtually everything else—"things both in heaven, and in earth, and under the earth; things which have been; things which are; things which must shortly come to pass." They were to study "languages, tongues and people" and "wars and the perplexities of the nations." There seems to have been no limit on the knowledge needed to take the Gospel to the ends of the earth.[63]

The "Olive Leaf" placed as much emphasis on spiritual preparation as on subject matter. "Sanctify yourselves; yea, purify your hearts, and cleanse your hands and your feet before me, that I may make you clean." They were told to be careful about idle thoughts and excessive laughter. They were to cease to be idle and stop sleeping longer than was needful. Lustful desires, pride and light-mindedness, and all "wicked doings" had to be abandoned. The school required spiritual and moral discipline along with study out of the "best books."[64] Learning and sanctification went together.

Little was said about engaging a teacher. The pupils were to instruct one another, pooling their knowledge, taking care that only "one speak at a time" while all listened "that all may be edified of all, and that every man may have an equal privilege." The revelation envisioned egalitarian rather than authoritarian instruction.[65] To that end, the revelations concluded with instructions on how to mold the elders into a brotherhood. "Above all things, clothe yourselves with the bond of charity," they were told, and, to give that injunction form, a ritual was established for welding the students together. The president was to enter the schoolroom first and pray. As the students came in, he was to greet them with uplifted hand and the words

> Art thou a brother or brethren? I salute you in the name of the Lord Jesus Christ, in token, or remembrance of the everlasting covenant, in which covenant I receive you to fellowship in a determination that is fixed, immovable and unchangeable, to be your friend and brother through the grace of God, in the bonds of love.

The brethren in turn were to lift up their hands and repeat the covenant or say amen.[66]

The School of the Prophets tells more about the desired texture of Joseph's holy society than anything he had done thus far—and more of what he was up against. The directions to quell excessive laughter and all light-mindedness implicitly reflect the rough-hewn characters who had joined him in the great cause. Few were polished—and he would never teach them gentility—but he wanted order, peace, and virtue. One verse said to organize "a house of prayer, a house of fasting, a house of faith, a house of learning, a house of glory, a house of order, a house of God." That succession of words captured his hopes for the whole society he was attempting to create. Zion was to be orderly, godly, and brotherly. At the center was learning—about God, creation, and the world. One verse in the "Olive Leaf" was repeated later in other of Joseph's scriptures: "Seek ye diligently and teach one another words of wisdom; yea, seek ye out of the best books words of wisdom: seek learning even by study, and also by faith."[67] The School of the Prophets was the prototype for the good society, a fraternity united by study and faith. It met again in 1834–35 and 1835–36, then the school fell into abeyance for decades until revived periodically by Brigham Young and John Taylor. Perhaps not surprisingly for the 1830s, women were conspicuously absent; it was a decade before they were formally included in the holy sodality.

The perfection Joseph sought was physical as much as spiritual. The September priesthood revelation had said priesthood holders would be "sanctifyed by the Spirit unto the renewing of their bodies." A few months later, a revelation promised that their bodies would be filled with light.[68] To refine their bodies, a revelation received a month after the School of the Prophets began advised the men to give up tobacco and alcohol. During the conferences, they had smoked and chewed tobacco. Emma may have objected to the stains on the floor and the smell in the room and asked Joseph to do something about it. If so, she was not the only one disgusted by tobacco chewers. Frances Trollope, the British traveler, castigated American men for soiling the carpet and dirtying the ladies' long skirts with their spitting.[69]

The revelation counseled a diet of "wholesome herbs," fruits and grains, and spare use of meat. "Hot drinks," later interpreted to mean tea and coffee, were eschewed. All who conformed were promised "health in their navel, and marrow to their bones." Their bodies would be vigorous and their minds active.[70] The "Word of Wisdom," as the revelation was later called, came at a time when temperance and food reforms were flourishing in the United States. In 1835, Sylvester Graham lectured in New York and Philadelphia against tobacco, tea, coffee, and alcohol, advocating a diet based on whole grains. Graham presented his teachings as science; Joseph linked his version of reform to the doctrines of exaltation, giving dietary counsel a scriptural basis.[71] Quoting Isaiah, the revelation promised the observant they will "run and not be weary, and shall walk and not faint," but also, they would "find wisdom and great treasure of knowledge." As in ancient Israel, treatment of the body was combined with ministration to the spirit.[72]

The Saints differed over how rigorously to apply the "Word of Wisdom." Some were inclined to make exact compliance a requirement of membership. Others were more relaxed. Joseph drank tea and a glass of wine from time to time. It was left to a later generation of Saints to turn the "principle with a promise" into a measuring rod of obedience.[73]

The underlying idea of the "Word of Wisdom" was not to escape the physical, as hermetic and mystical philosophies taught, but to preserve and purify the flesh.[74] Joseph's religion made the body essential to human fulfillment and godliness. The exaltation revelations had told the Saints that "the spirit and the body is the soul of man," and only when joined eternally could a person receive "a fulness of joy." "When separated, man c[a]nnot receive a fulness of joy." Joseph exalted the body rather than seeking to free the spirit from the flesh. Dead souls considered "the long absence" of their spirits from their bodies "to be a bondage." The highest reward for a worthy spirit, the "Olive Leaf" had said, was to receive a "natural body." Even God and angels, Joseph would later teach, had bodies of flesh and bone.[75] The School of the Prophets added bodily discipline to the students' spiritual purification.

Minutes were not kept after the initial meetings, but the students later recalled the routine.[76] They met at the Whitney store early in the morning and continued until late in the afternoon, often fasting through the day. New members were added to the original class of fourteen until the number rose as high as twenty-five. In the school's first term in the winter of 1833, English grammar, taught by Orson Hyde, was the chief subject under discussion, a reflection on the educations of the pupils. Joseph was told to "become acquainted with all good books, and with languages, tongues and people," and the curriculum of the school doubtless was to follow along the same lines. It was to provide all the training needed for the immense task of conveying the Gospel to the world.[77]

A spiritual outburst on January 22, 1833, foreshadowed what lay ahead for the School of the Prophets. A conference was suddenly visited with the gift of tongues. Joseph spoke in another tongue, followed by Zebedee Coltrin and William Smith, and finally all the elders, along with "several of the members of the Church both male & female." "Much speaking & praying all in tongues" occupied the conference before adjournment "at a late hour." The next day, the men came together again and started "speaking praying and singing, all done in Tongues." Lucy Smith remembered hearing of the spiritual outpouring while she was baking bread. She dropped her work and rushed to join the meeting.[78]

Joseph loved these times when the Spirit enveloped the Saints in "long absent blessings," proof that New Testament religion had returned. In another return to primitive Christianity, the brethren began the washing of feet. The elders washed their own feet, and then Joseph knelt before each one and washed. When he came to his father, Joseph Jr. asked for a blessing and was promised he should continue in the priest's office until Christ should come. After he had passed around the circle, Joseph's feet were washed by his friend and counselor Frederick G. Williams as a token of the latter's determination to stand by Joseph "in life or in death."[79]

Joseph told the brethren the washing had made them clean from the "blood of this generation." Having been cleansed and sealed up to eternal life, they were to sin no more or Satan would buffet them. Joseph wanted these rough men packed into a tiny room over the Whitney store to understand they could be pure and holy. He was convinced that their tawdry appearance and ragged manners did not disqualify them for godliness. In January, two of the students wrote to the Missouri church that "the Lord has commanded us to purify ourselves to wash our hands and our feet that he may testify to his father and our Father to his God & our God that we are clean from the blood of this generation." "The smallest and weakest among us," Joseph told his people, "shall be powerful and mighty."[80]

In April 1833, the school disbanded, and the elders went out again to proclaim the Gospel.

ELEVEN

CITIES OF ZION

1833

Let them importune at the feet of the Judge; and if he heed them not, let them
importune at the feet of the governor; and if the governor heed them not, let
them importune at the feet of the President; and if the President heed them not,
then will the Lord arise and come forth out of his hiding place, and in his fury
vex the nation.

Doctrine and Covenants [1835], 97:12

THE SCHOOL OF THE PROPHETS was a huge success, in spite of the occasional arguments during the meetings. When the members finally dispersed in April 1833 to attend to spring work, the two dozen students had received their first training in preaching the Gospel. Earlier missionaries had taught from their own experience, "full of notions & whims," as David Whitmer put it.[1] No one had summarized the message or defined the key doctrines. After listening to Joseph and comparing notes for three months, the missionaries must have come closer to a unified message.

The school's meetings through the winter of 1832–33 were held in the crowded translating room above the Whitney store. No other meeting space was available in Kirtland. On Sundays the 150 or so Church members crowded into private houses or small rented spaces.[2] Characteristically nonchalant about weekly congregational worship, Joseph failed to mention regular Sunday worship in his history, much less inadequate meeting space, until late 1833.[3] Perhaps his own meeting-free childhood kept him from feeling the need. Converts from more conventional Christian backgrounds, however, looked for a solution. In March, Jared Carter raised $30 to build a meeting place, prompting discussion about frame versus log construction, but by then, more ambitious plans were maturing in Joseph's mind. He was thinking of a structure that would solve the space difficulties in a grand manner.[4]

TEMPLE

The first hints of a great building had been given months before in December 1832 in the revelation on the School of the Prophets, when the Saints were told to establish a "house of God."[5] The name could have referred to a meetinghouse with the chapel serving as a classroom, but that was not Joseph's intention. He envisioned a larger, more ambitious building, a curious edifice that he called a "temple."

The word "temple" had no single meaning for Americans. Its application to buildings and churches of every kind emptied the word of any distinctive architectural significance.[6] James Fenimore Cooper spoke of the Hudson River mansions as temples sitting on their mountaintops. Greek temples, epitomizing high architectural beauty for this generation, were widely imitated in American banks and churches, and Greek Revival influences can be seen in the pilasters, window trim, and columns in the Kirtland temple too. But Joseph's idea of a temple did not come from classical civilization; he omitted Greece and Rome entirely from his many recapitulations of world history. He was familiar with Masons who met in buildings called temples, but Freemasonry was not an attractive model in the aftermath of anti-Masonic political campaigns, and Masonic temples were non-existent in areas where Joseph lived. Country Masons conducted their rituals in the upper rooms of taverns that weren't built to be temples.[7] It is not likely that Joseph ever saw a Masonic temple before he began building in Kirtland. Not only did he lack models, temples were foreign to the low church Protestants he was familiar with from childhood. Temples were associated with the animal sacrifice of the obsolete Mosaic law. Presbyterians and Methodists might casually refer to their meetinghouses as temples but only to add a little dignity to ordinary chapels.

Joseph turned quite naturally to the Bible for inspiration. In the *Book of Mormon*, Nephi built a temple "after the manner of the temple of Solomon." Geauga County's *Chardon Spectator* reported that the Mormons "contemplated erecting a building of stone on a magnificent plan, to be called, after the one erected by King Solomon, '*The Temple*.'" The Kirtland temple did not resemble the temple of Solomon; it had the outward appearance of a large, vaguely neoclassical meetinghouse. But the pair of auditoriums, one on top of the other, were called inner courts, suggesting biblical antecedents.[8]

By seizing upon the temple rather than the church for a center of worship, Joseph put aside Christian tradition in favor of ancient Israel. During the course of his life, he never built a standard meetinghouse, even in Nauvoo, where the Mormon population exceeded 10,000. Although Sunday services were held regularly, the Nauvoo Saints met in houses, public buildings, and an outdoor "bowery." Wherever Joseph lived—in Kirtland, Independence, Far West, or Nauvoo—his architectural imagination focused on temples. Where he did not build a temple, he planned one. Having Christianized the Hebrew prophets in the Book of Moses and the *Book of Mor-*

mon, he turned to the Old Testament for inspiration.[9] Gathering Israel to temples was in keeping with the Old Testament character of the entire Zion project.

Joseph had only vague ideas about the purpose of the temple when the revelations first mentioned the idea. In the *Book of Mormon* the idea of worshiping in temples appears only dimly. After the Church's organization, "temple" first came up in a revelation about Christ appearing: "I will suddenly come to my temple," Joseph was told in late 1830. Otherwise, temples had no purpose when a site was designated for one at the "center" of the City of Zion in 1831.[10] Temples at first were an empty form, awaiting content.

By spring 1833, however, when plans were laid for the Kirtland temple, its value as an all-purpose Church building had become evident. The main floor was for worship services, the second floor would house the School of the Prophets, and the attic would contain offices for the presidency of the Church.[11] Along with the practical purposes, the idea of the temple as a holy place and dwelling for God was not forgotten. In the temple, the long-awaited endowment of power was to take place. Joseph hoped his Saints would face God as Moses' people never could. At the completion of Solomon's temple, God came in a cloud of glory. A fall 1832 revelation said that when the Kirtland temple was finished, "a cloud shall rest upon it, which cloud shall be even the glory of the Lord." In May they were promised "my glory shall be there, and my presence shall be there."[12]

Plans moved ahead speedily. Frederick G. Williams was appointed to supervise the brick-making, until September 1833, when a switch to stone facing led to quarrying just south of Kirtland. A committee to purchase land agreed to pay $5,000 for the Peter French farm and sited the temple on the bluffs overlooking Kirtland Flats and the Chagrin Valley.[13] In May, a revelation showed the dimensions of the temple's inner court: fifty-five by sixty-five feet, a cavernous space. (The same revelation called for a second temple, never built, of exactly the same dimensions, to serve as a printing office.) On June 1, a building committee of Hyrum Smith, Reynolds Cahoon, and Jared Carter began a subscription list among the branches. To raise funds, the temple was presented as a place for preparing the elders to go out among the Gentiles for the last time.[14] Everyone was to contribute.

Economically, the temple was a disaster. The temple diverted funds needed for the City of Zion to a huge, costly building project. Construction artificially boosted the Kirtland economy for a time and then knocked out the props when the temple was completed. The project was far out of proportion to the Church's pitiful resources. Joseph Smith went deeply into debt and was hounded by his creditors ever after. But the economic realities gave Joseph no pause. In his determination to follow his inspiration, he extended himself and the Church far beyond their capacity. Beginning in Kirtland, temples became an obsession. For the rest of his life, no matter the cost of the temple to himself and his people, he made plans, raised money, mobilized workers, and required sacrifice.

A revelation told Joseph in June 1833, "Let it be built after the manner which I shall show unto three of you." Years later, Truman Angell, who supervised construction in Kirtland, said that plans for the Kirtland temple came to Joseph, Sidney Rigdon, and Frederick G. Williams in a joint revelation. These three, constituting the First Presidency, saw the exterior from a distance and then looked inside the building. From then on, they judged the actual construction by its conformity to this image. Joseph gave no account of receiving the plans in vision, but a revelation said the temple was to be built after the manner of God, not the world. While the exterior gave the impression of a large New England neoclassical church with Gothic windows, the interior was Joseph's own.[15] The inside stacked two meeting spaces, the lower and upper courts, on top of one another. These assembly rooms had the uncommon feature of two front walls. A set of pulpits stood on both the west and the east walls. Movable chairs in pews allowed hearers to rotate when addressed by speakers from opposite pulpits. In addition to that peculiarity, the pulpits at each end ascended in four levels, each assigned to particular priesthood offices, exhibiting the hierarchical structure of the priesthood. On the west wall was the Melchizedek, or higher, Priesthood. A top bank of pulpits was for the First Presidency; below them was another for the three members of the bishopric, the next down for the high priests, with the elders at the bottom. On the opposite wall, the Aaronic, or lesser, Priesthood was similarly divided into four levels with the presidency of the Aaronic Priesthood on top, and the priests, teachers, and deacons in order below. The main court on the first floor could be divided into temporary rooms by lowering curtains with a system of pulleys and ropes, just as veils divided the temple of Solomon.[16] Joseph was apparently fascinated by separate compartments. He believed that the body of the Church functioned best in "quorums," the subdivisions of the two priesthoods, suggesting a segmented conception of ecclesiastical society, more Catholic than Protestant.

Groundbreaking began June 5, 1833. Members dug a trench in a wheat field on the Peter French farm, and hauled stone from the quarry for the foundation. By July 23, the cornerstones were in place. From then on, every member was asked to contribute funds or labor; one day in seven was the rule for labor. On June 25, Joseph sent plans for a similar temple to Missouri, along with a letter of instructions and answers to questions. The Missouri temple was to have a simple shedlike exterior, but the interior had the same plan as Kirtland's.[17] The fledgling Church with only a few thousand members planned for two large temples for studying good books and receiving revelations from God.

CITY PLANS

Construction of a temple in Independence as well as in Kirtland added to the complexity of overseeing two Mormon centers. During the early 1830s, Joseph had managed affairs in Zion from a distance, even though the numbers in Missouri in June 1833 approached eight hundred, while many fewer lived in Kirtland.[18] The long-distance government rarely worked well. The letters are a record of turbulent feelings. Joseph usually wrote Phelps, the newspaper editor, rather than Bishop Partridge, the man in charge of dividing properties in Zion.[19] Joseph blamed the leadership in Zion for not making the consecrated properties system work. He also resented the criticism and innuendos in letters coming from Zion. Hyrum Smith and Orson Hyde referred to charges against Joseph for "seeking after monarchal power and authority." Joseph, who disliked criticism of any kind, told Phelps "we have the satisfaction of knowing that the Lord approves of us."[20]

Tensions with Zion relaxed, however, after Hyrum and Hyde wrote a conciliatory letter to Missouri in January 1833. One can imagine Hyrum, the wise elder brother, protecting Joseph from his own impulsive nature. Hyrum was reason and sympathy where Joseph was will and energy. In February, the Missouri leaders wrote a conciliatory reply that the Kirtland Council found satisfactory. Joseph toned down his writing and expressed his understanding of the strain of "much business." A revelation noted that the brethren in Zion "begin to repent and the angels rejoice over them."[21] By late June, Joseph could reveal his plan for Zion, confident the Saints there could be trusted to carry it forward.

With the design for the temple, Joseph included a plat for the City of Zion, a layout for an entire city with temples at the center. In the plat's margins, the draftsman, Frederick G. Williams, described Zion's major features. The city was to occupy one square mile, the size of the sections being laid out in the West by the United States government. An amended plan expanded the size to a mile and a half square. Ten-acre blocks, divided into half-acre house lots, surrounded public squares at the center.

City planning, while unusual for a minister, was common for utopian and religious visionaries. In many respects, the Zion format, with its square blocks and central squares, resembled plans devised by other town founders in these years.[22] But the Zion plan had singular features. Joseph's house lots were set at right angles on alternate blocks. On one block the long, narrow lots fronted the east and west sides of the block. On the next block, the lots faced north and south. Consequently, houses did not look across the street at other house fronts, but into the long back gardens of the lots across the street. Walking down a street, residents would see house fronts on one side and back gardens on the other.[23]

The most unusual aspect was the three public squares at the center with twenty-four temples, twelve to a block, standing on two of these squares. According to the description, the temples would serve as "houses of worship, schools, etc."[24] One can imagine a town hall, a courthouse, and perhaps stores among the "temples," much like the public buildings around the green in a New England town. But the names assigned to the temples do not support this simple reading. The temples were grouped into threes and assigned to priesthood "quorums," the organizations of the various levels of priesthood. One group was to be called "House of the Lord for the presidency of the High and most holy priesthood after the order of Melchizadek, which was after the order of the Son of God." Another was "the Sacred Apostollic Repository for the use of the Bishops," and still another group "the house of the Lord for the Elders of Zion, an ensign to the nations." And so on down to "House of the Lord for the Deacons in Zion, helps in governments." Those elaborate titles do not relate to any standard functions of public buildings. Stores lined the main streets of most American towns, surrounding a courthouse or jail at the center. But neither commerce nor civil government is given architectural form in the City of Zion. Everything is subsumed under priesthood quorums, which presumably absorbed all other institutions. The plan specified that "Underneath must be written on each House—Holiness To The Lord."[25]

The unusual temple names transformed a standard plat into a plan for a holy city. The presence of temples and the absence of ordinary civic buildings suggest a higher purpose. Speaking of the United States as a whole, Garry Wills has noted "there is no more defining note to our history than the total absence of a sacred city in our myths." The only exception, he noted, "is the Mormons' temple, fetched (like Jerusalem's) from heaven."[26] The American landscape dispersed religious energy widely through the society into thousands of churches; Joseph's city plat concentrated holiness in one place, in a sacred city and its temple, where religion absorbed everything.

However culturally anomalous, the City of Zion occupied a central place in Joseph Smith's design for world renewal. He conceived the world as a vast funnel with the city at the vortex and the temple at the center of the city. Converts across the globe would be attracted to this central point to acquire knowledge and power for preaching the Gospel. Trained and empowered in the temple, the missionary force would go back into the world and collect Israel from every corner of the earth. The city, the temple, and the world, existed in dynamic relationship. Missionaries flowed out of the city and converts poured back in. The exchange would redeem the world in the last days.[27]

Joseph's plat has been explained as a remodeled New England town carried over from his childhood, and the city as an effort to recover order and peace in a world being shattered by industrialization.[28] But that gloss fails to note that the plans called for a population of 15,000 to 20,000 people—a city, not a town. Only seven cities in the United States in 1830 had more than 25,000 inhabitants and only sixteen had populations between 10,000 and 25,000. St. Louis had around 10,000. Zion would have dwarfed every city west of the Mississippi. Moreover, the straight streets, square blocks, and public squares followed an urban aesthetic rather than the casual layouts of New England villages.[29] Joseph wanted everyone, including farmers with lands outside the plotted area, to live in a city. Contrary to his own upbringing, he would urbanize society. As the explanation said, "When this square is thus laid off and supplied lay off another in the same way and so fill up the world in these last days and let every man live in the City for this is the City of Zion."[30]

Zion was to be the capital, but Kirtland was to be a city too, implying an expandable network of urban places, with Zion first among many. People could gather to any of these cities, not to Zion alone. Joseph thought of the Church as an assemblage of cities, rather than a scattering of parishes and congregations. New converts met in branches, but only temporarily until they could gather to a city. When Joseph formed parishes in Nauvoo, he called them "wards," the term used for urban political divisions.[31]

Joseph called this entire process "the work," meaning the work of the Lord. Building cities was like building temples: wherever Joseph lived, he prepared a plat. Hounded out of Kirtland, he planned Far West, Missouri. After Far West, Nauvoo was next, the only city he came near to completing. After Joseph's death, Mormons in the mountain West based the scores of towns they founded on the original plan for Zion.[32]

Only in the New World could such a scheme have been conceived, much less carried out. In the more tightly packed societies of the Old World, only kings and nobles dreamed of founding new towns, while in the United States, speculators laid out hundreds of towns on the millions of acres stretching westward from the edges of settlement. The open landscape unleashed Joseph's imagination.[33] He became a developer, promoting the Church's land in Missouri and, later, Illinois. American conditions allowed him to move beyond the organization of a church toward the creation of a society. Rather than establishing beachheads in the form of church buildings all over the country, he took over a complete city, occupying all its space, consecrating every activity to God.

The conception of a church of cities rather than a church of congregations had wide-reaching—and disastrous—implications for the Mormons. Even in America, the scheme was doomed. No American community was ready for that degree of religious rejuvenation. What would happen to citizens who refused to put "Holiness to the Lord" on their storefronts? Zion could not be forced on a settled area without meeting resistance. Church leaders could not take over city planning, require holiness, equalize property, and control politics without making enemies. Wherever the Saints settled, conflict followed. In the thrall of his visions, Joseph overlooked the practical obstacles.

In mid-1833, he was unprepared for the storm about to burst upon him. Having made peace with the leaders and dispatched plans for city and temple, he had high hopes for Zion. A revelation on August 2 painted a bright picture. Parley Pratt was commended for opening a school to study the scriptures. The people were told to build the temple speedily "that they may be perfected in the understanding of their ministry." If they kept the temple holy, "the pure in heart that shall come into it, shall see God." If the Saints followed instructions, Zion "shall prosper and spread herself and become very glorious." Even the nations of the earth would say "surely Zion is the city of our God."[34]

PERSECUTION

On August 9, 1833, Oliver Cowdery arrived in Kirtland with bad news. Jackson County citizens were demanding that the Mormons leave, and, under pressure, the Church leaders had agreed to go. Within six months, the Saints were expelled from Jackson County with no realistic prospect of returning. Zion was suddenly abolished.

Conflict had been brewing for over a year as alarmed locals watched the growing Mormon numbers.[35] Non-Mormon citizens threw rocks and bricks at Mormon houses or burned haystacks. Mormon children began to wake up with nightmares about "the mob" coming. As Parley Pratt noted, the Jackson County inhabitants "became jealous of our growing influence and numbers. Political demagogues were afraid we should rule the county." An unanticipated consequence of gathering was the build-up of Mormon political power. By summer 1833, the Mormons, numbering nearly a thousand, were a third of the county's population. Soon every office in the county would be at the disposal of the Mormons. John Corrill, a Mormon leader on the scene, agreed with Pratt's analysis. The settlers saw "that if let alone they would in a short time become a majority, and, of course, rule the county."[36]

The revelation calling for gathering to Missouri used the word "enemies" to describe the current residents, and indeed they were becoming so.

The Mormons spoke of the land being redeemed by its rightful inheritors. The *Evening and Morning Star* wrote matter-of-factly about "tak[ing] possession of this country." Josiah Gregg, a merchant living in Independence, said the Mormons grew bolder in their predictions as their numbers increased. "At last they became so emboldened by impunity, as openly to boast of their determination to be the sole proprietors of the 'Land of Zion.' " By summer 1833, the Saints held over 2,400 acres of land in and around Independence and threatened a complete takeover.[37]

Opposition burst into the open in July 1833. William Phelps published an article in the *Evening and Morning Star* about the legal requirements for bringing free Negroes into the state, and locals interpreted the description as an invitation. Phelps quickly disavowed any such intention, insisting he was actually warning future immigrants against importing free blacks, but the damage had been done.[38] On July 15, the local citizens posted a manifesto, with a copy presented to the Saints. Signed by about three hundred residents, it called for a mass meeting on July 20.[39]

"An important crisis is at hand, as regards our civil society," the manifesto declared, which "the arm of the civil law" cannot redress. Although the Mormons had broken no law for which they could be prosecuted, they presented a dire threat. Locals felt they must resort to the time-honored American tradition of vigilante action, which went back to attacks on Stamp Tax distributors in 1765 and the closing of courts to prevent debt collection during Shays' Rebellion in 1786–87.[40] Following this long line of precedents, the Jackson County citizens believed they could act legally against the Mormons. They were not a mob but the people in action. The men who signed the manifesto listed themselves as jailor, county clerk, Indian agent, postmaster, judge, attorney-at-law, justice of the peace—the most respectable characters in the county. They met on the courthouse steps to make plans. In their manifesto, they pledged "our lives, fortunes, and sacred honors," borrowing the famous last line of the Declaration of Independence.[41]

According to the report of the July 20 meeting, a committee of twelve was commissioned "to wait on the Mormon leaders" and inform them that the press must close and every Mormon leave the county. When Phelps and Partridge asked for ten days to consider, the meeting "unanimously resolved" to raze the printing office and Phelps's house.[42] "Which resolution was, with the utmost order, and the least noise or disturbance possible, forthwith carried into execution, as also some other steps of a similar tendency."[43] The "steps of a similar tendency" were to tar and feather Bishop Partridge and Church member Charles Allen, and dump the goods from Sidney Gilbert's store in the street.[44] The report was signed Richard Simpson, "Chairman," and S. D. Lucas and J. H. Flournoy, "Secretaries."[45]

The group charged the Mormons with religious fanaticism. Mormons pretended to speak in tongues, claimed communications direct from heaven, attempted to heal the sick, and tried "all the wonderworking miracles wrought by the inspired apostles & prophets." Nearly as bad, Mormons were "the very dregs" of society without property or education, elevated but little "above the condition of our blacks." So close to the slaves were the Mormons that the non-Mormons suspected them of tampering with the labor force and of bringing free blacks into the county.[46] The manifesto authors envisioned an amalgam of slaves, free blacks, and impoverished religious fanatics taking over their society.

Where would it all end? "The day is not far distant, when the civil government of the county will be in their hands. When the Sheriff, the Justices, and the County Judges will be Mormons, or persons wishing to court their favor from motives of interest or ambition." Another religious group might be permitted this degree of control, but not Mormons: "What would be the fate of our lives and property, in the hands of jurors & witnesses, who do not blush to declare and would not upon occasion hesitate to swear, that they have wrought miracles, and have been the subjects of miracles and supernatural cures; have converse with God and his Angels, and possess and exercise gifts of Divination and of unknown tongues." In their minds, the horrors of domination by pretenders to the powers of apostles and prophets staggered the imagination. The non-Mormon settlers claimed that decisive action was necessary to protect the "good society, public morals, and the fair prospects" of the county.

The committee demanded that half the Mormons, including most of the leaders, leave the county within six months and the rest by the following April. The citizens reported that on July 23 their committee had "entered into an amicable agreement with them," as if the two parties had politely agreed on a mutually acceptable arrangement. The secretary did not mention the destruction of the Phelps family's house or Partridge's burns from a corrosive agent in the tar, but fastidiously noted that "no blood was spilled, nor any blows inflicted."[47] Had the Mormons not yielded, they faced whippings and wrecked houses.

The Mormon presence in Jackson County, as in every other county they occupied during the next fifteen years, tested democracy. The Mormon case illustrated an underlying democratic dilemma: can a majority, in defense of the public good as they see it, strip a minority of its rights? The Jackson County citizens believed their procedures were democracy in action. The citizens came together to prevent a social and political disaster of alarming proportions; in their view, they acted purely in self-defense. But for Mormons, Jackson County democracy meant repression and expulsion. Under the terms of the agreement, Mormons could not vote, could not own property, could not print a newspaper, and could not work in the county.

The July 23 agreement gave Mormon leaders time to consult with Joseph in the six months they were given before they had to leave the county. Joseph may have already anticipated the mounting hostility. Letters sent from Missouri in early July, now lost, probably carried news of growing opposition. Perhaps in response to these rumors, a revelation on August 6 counseled moderation: "Be not afraid of your enemies." Instead of fighting back, they were to "renounce war and proclaim peace."[48] Avoid retaliation, they were told, and rely on God.

Whether they were forewarned or not, Cowdery's arrival in Ohio with news of the citizens' ultimatum threw Kirtland into an uproar. An emergency council first advised the Missouri Saints to look for another home, assuring them that "an other place of beginning will be no injury to Zion in the end." The council agreed with the decision to leave. "There was no other way to save the lives of all the church in Zion." Joseph, devastated by the news, tried to comfort the brethren with a plaintive postscript wishing he was there to share the suffering. "My spirit would not let me forsake you unto death." Be of good cheer, he urged. "Oh God save my Brethren in Zion Oh brethren give up all to God forsake all for Christ sake."[49]

As the days passed, Joseph became more and more troubled. On August 18, he wrote the most anguished letter of his life, all of it in his own hand, addressed to "Brother William, John, Edward, Isaac, John and Sidney"— the Missouri leaders.[50] He was driven nearly to "madness and desperation," he said, not understanding why the grand plan for Zion, the heart of the whole restoration movement, had been set back. God "will spedily deliver Zion for I have his immutible covenant," but He "keep[s] it hid from mine eyes the means how exactly the thing will be done."[51] Joseph scarcely knew what to say or do.

The letter commiserated with the brethren in one line, promised them deliverance in the next, and condemned their enemies a few lines later. The letter opens with a prayer to "thou disposer of all Events" asking for "some kind word to these my Brotheren in Zion." They had sacrificed for Zion; why must they suffer? "O Lord what more dost thou require at their hands before thou wilt come and save them?" Joseph prayed that God's anger might consume their enemies and render quick punishment. "They will go down to the pit and give pl[a]ce for thy Saints." He promised that "the cloud shall pass over and the sun shall shine as clear and as fair as heaven itself." They had his support. "There is not one doubt in my heart not one place in me but what is filld with perfect confidince and love for you."[52]

A few practical suggestions emerged from the letter. They should start a newspaper in support of the current administration in Washington and then appeal for protection. Meanwhile, he advised a more unyielding stand than Cowdery had proposed a week earlier. Cowdery had told them "to look out another place to locate on." On August 18, Joseph told the Missouri Saints they must not sell one foot of land in Jackson County, for they would never get it back. They must act secretly, for the residents would immediately suspect them of reneging on the agreement, but the Saints must stand firm. He was less certain about using force to counter attacks. On this delicate question "we wait the Command of God to do whatever he plese and if he shall say go up to Zion and defend thy Brotheren by the sword we fly and we count not our live dear to us."[53] The question of an armed defense plagued Joseph for the next six months—and for the rest of his life.

The conflict in Missouri changed Joseph's politics dramatically. For the first time, government figured in his thought as an active agent. The revelations had never before acknowledged a nation or government, not even the Constitution. Zion had been considered a society unto itself. "There is and can be no ruler nor lawgiver in the Kingdom of God save it be God our Saviour," Sidney Rigdon wrote in 1831.[54] But the Jackson County attacks made government an essential ally in recovering the Saints' lost lands. The moderate revelation on August 6 advised the Saints to befriend constitutional law. The rights and privileges in the Constitution, the revelation said, belonged to all mankind and were justifiable before God, elevating those principles from the national to the universal. "As you know," he told his Missouri brethren in his August letter, "we are all friends to the Constitution yea true friends to that Country for which our fathers bled."[55] From then on, Joseph was never far removed from politics. For a decade, he sought protection from the government, usually without success, until finally, frustrated by his inability to rally government to the Saints' side, he ran for president.

In the long run, the appeals to government had an unexpected effect on the Church's self-image. The need to gather support for their petitions led the Saints to tell their story not as a narrative of revelations, but as one of persecutions. By the 1840s, when Joseph wrote about the Jackson County expulsion in great detail, he had perfected the form. The story of the Church had become an account of "wicked, outrageous and unlawful proceedings." The history of Missouri featured beatings of "women, and children . . . driven or frightened from their homes, by yells and threats." As the persecution and sufferings mounted through the years, the Mormon story became more heart-wrenching. When Joseph received visitors, he was as likely to describe the mobbings as he was to explain his revelations. "In this boasted land of liberty," the Saints "were brought into Jeopardy, and threatened with expulsion or death because they wished to worship God according to the revelations of heaven, the constitutions of their country, and the dictates of their own consciences. Oh Liberty, how art thou fallen!"[56] This persecution story, even without rhetorical embellishment, was persuasive. People who had no respect for the Saints' theology, including much of the Missouri press in 1833, recognized the injustice of their treatment.[57] The persecution was all the more poignant because it happened in a land presumably free.

The success of the appeal changed the Saints' relation to the world. The customary language of conversion and gathering implicitly conceived of non-Mormons as potential converts who accepted or rejected the missionaries' message. When a town rejected them, missionaries washed the dust off their feet and left that people to their fate.[58] The persecution story, by contrast, recognized an unbaptized, sympathetic middle group, not joiners or enemies, but somewhere in between. Accounts of persecution, paradoxically, bridged the gulf between the Saints and the unbelieving world by envisioning a body of sympathizers with whom friendly relations could be established without converting them.[59]

The Church came to conceive of itself differently too. A general "Appeal" from the Missouri Mormon leadership in July 1834 claimed the Mormons were fulfilling biblical prophecy in gathering to Zion, as if they alone were carrying out God's mission; but when the appeal switched to the Mormons' right to "worship God according to the dictates of our own consciences," Mormonism became one religion among many. The Mormon paper pointed out that if "a majority may crush any religious sect with impunity," any religion could suffer; "the fate of our church now might become the fate of the Methodists" and then the Catholics.[60] By asking for toleration and the right to worship, Mormonism had to present itself not as the one true church but as one church among a society of churches, all on an equal plane.

REDRESS

Within a few months of the July agreement, Church leaders had adjusted to the setback in Missouri. Even though the Missouri Saints remained in Jackson County, by the fall of 1833, the Kirtland brethren were already shifting emphasis to Ohio. The *Evening and Morning Star*, now under Oliver Cowdery's editorship, was moved to Kirtland and converts were advised to remain in Kirtland rather than move to Independence.[61] The migrant stream was diverted from Zion in Missouri to the "stake of Zion" in Kirtland.[62] After his first agonized letter, Joseph spoke more philosophically about the disaster. In September, he told a suffering Missouri Saint that he was "not at all astonished at what has happened to you neither to what has happened to Zion."[63]

The shift did not mean the Church was giving up on Jackson County.

Although the Mormons had been warned that any attempt to obtain redress would put their lives in jeopardy, they submitted an unsuccessful petition to Missouri governor Daniel Dunklin in September 1833, asking for protection. The governor assured the Saints that the justice system would enforce the law without the backing of troops. Dunklin thought that a complaint brought before the circuit judge or justice of the peace would produce a warrant against the attackers, ignoring the fact that the court officers themselves were deeply involved. To pursue every possible redress, the Saints hired four non-Mormon lawyers from Clay County, just north of Jackson, for the exorbitant fee of a thousand dollars.[64]

When this news leaked out, the old settlers were outraged. For seven days and nights, from October 31 to November 6, they lay siege to the Saints. Believing the Mormons had gone back on the July 23 agreement, the non-Mormon citizens were determined to evict them immediately.[65] In keeping with the unwritten rules of vigilante action, the Missourians at first tried to avoid bloodshed, mainly attacking property. They threw stones at houses, stuck long poles through windows, and tore off roofs. Several Mormons were whipped or beaten, and one had his head creased by a ball from a pistol. The mob tore down part of Sidney Gilbert's store, broke windows, and scattered inventory. Throughout the Mormon settlement, houses and furniture were ruined.[66]

The attacks escalated after an exchange of fire in which a Mormon and two Missourians were killed. Bloodshed removed the restraints on mob tactics. Some old settlers believed the Mormons planned on "butchering us all," and began attacking persons as well as property.[67] A clergyman on the Jackson County side learned of mobbers who "were determined to kill." Mormon leaders had to be held in prison for their safety. Under dire threat, the Saints agreed to give up their arms. From then on, the Mormons were helpless. No massacre occurred, but Missourians went from house to house forcing out women and children and demanding to know where the men were hiding. Fearing their husbands would be murdered, the women fled. By November 7, most of the Saints were camped on the southern bank of the Missouri River, awaiting ferries to Clay County, where the citizens had granted them temporary refuge.[68]

In recounting the story in the 1840s, Joseph emphasized the feeble efforts of the government to aid the Saints. One justice of the peace refused to book a Missourian caught in the act of throwing bricks at Gilbert's store, and a few days later charges were brought against Gilbert for false imprisonment of the culprit. Fearing the mob, another justice refused to issue a peace warrant while depredations were occurring all around. Militia colonels Lucas and Pitcher disarmed the Saints and then stood by while they were evicted. At first, the Saints placed their confidence in Lieutenant Governor

Lilburn Boggs, a large landholder in Jackson County, thinking him their protector. Five years later, as governor of Missouri, he issued the notorious order requiring Mormons to leave the state. In light of this later history, Joseph's account of the 1833 expulsion castigated Boggs: "All earth and hell can not deny that a baser knave, a greater traitor, and a more wholesale butcher, or murderer of mankind, never went untried, unpunished, and unhung."[69]

News of the violence reached Kirtland on November 25. This time Joseph had little to say. Nothing had come from heaven. An October revelation, the only one that fall, dealt mainly with a mission to Canada and only incidentally promised that "Zion shall be redeemed, although she is chastened for a little season." Frederick G. Williams wrote in early October that "we have received no revelations for a long time." A December 5 letter from Joseph could only say "the destinies of all people are in the hands of a just God." He repeated the previous counsel to hold on to the lands and seek redress from the government. Zion was not to be moved. Five days later another letter said, "I cannot learn from any communication of the spirit to me that Zion has forfeited her claim to a celestial crown." Joseph had to deduce God's will from what was *not* revealed. Meanwhile he searched the old revelations for light and seized upon a passage in the dedicatory revelation about glory coming to Zion "after much tribulation."[70]

Distraught and confused, Joseph began to murmur against the Lord. He asked how long Zion's tribulation would last, and was told, "Be still, and know that I am God!" Considering all that he had been blessed with, Joseph knew he should not complain. "I am sensible that I aught not to murmur and do not murmur only in this, that those who are innocent are compelled to suffer for the iniquities of the guilty; and I cannot account for this." He agonized that the bad news from Zion "weighs us down; we cannot refrain from tears." When government fails you, he wrote, "and the humanity of the people fails you, and all things else fails you but God alone," rely on Him to execute judgment.[71] Joseph ended the December letter with a long prayer asking God to restore the Saints to their Zion.

Finally, after months of silence, the Lord spoke. Oliver Cowdery is reported to have dramatically announced, "Good morning Brethren, we have just received news from heaven."[72] Like biblical accounts of Israel's defeats, the revelation blamed the losses in Missouri on Zion's own sins. God suffered affliction to come upon the Saints "in consequence of their transgressions." But, again like Israel, the Saints were not cast off. "Yet, I will own them, and they shall be mine in that day when I shall come to make up my jewels." They were not to give up Zion but to purchase even more land in Jackson County.[73]

Joseph gradually regained his footing after December, but the events of

1833 cast a long shadow over Mormon history. For the first time, the Saints felt their helplessness before popular enmity. While the government looked on and did nothing, they were driven from their homes. The Saints learned that the mobs were the people and the people were the government. No law officer or court would come to their defense. In a destructive irony, the people of Jackson County, in the name of democracy, deprived the Mormon people of their democratic right to live, work, and vote in the county.

The only recourse in 1833 was to flee. But what about the next time? Was flight their only option? Forming a private militia had no part in the revelations, but self-defense required one. How else could they react to depredations? The seeds of Mormon militarism were sown in this moment. The Mormons were later accused of threatening the peace with violence born of religious fanaticism. But their resort to militias was the result of being treated violently themselves. Violence originated in the democracy, not in religion. From 1834 onwards, Mormons uneasily experimented with various forms of self-protection. Most Mormons were pacific by nature, but a fierce minority longed for battle. They pressed Joseph to declare war on their enemies. Events of the year initiated a spiral of suspicion, resistance, and persecution that resulted a decade later in Joseph's death.

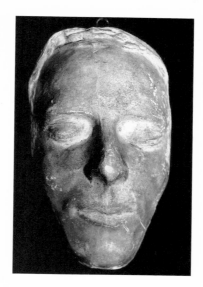

Death mask of Joseph Smith.

Lucy Mack Smith by Sutcliffe Maudsley, 1843.

Emma Smith with David Hyrum Smith,
born November 17, 1844,
four months after his father's death.

Hyrum Smith by
Sutcliffe Maudsley, 1843, a companion
piece to the profile of Joseph Smith
on the cover. Hyrum holds a Doctrine
and Covenants in his hands, while
Joseph holds a Bible.

Three witnesses
to the Book of Mormon:
(from left to right)
Oliver Cowdery, David Whitmer,
and Martin Harris.

Sidney Rigdon.

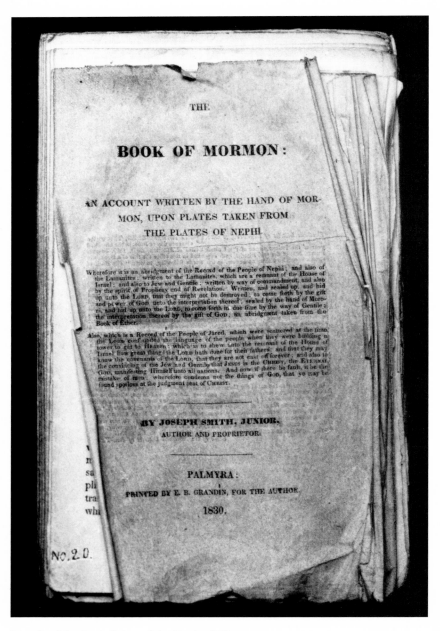

Proofs of the first edition of the Book of Mormon.

CHAPTER VII.

AND now I, Moroni, write a few of the words of my father Mormon, which he spake concerning faith, hope and charity: for after this manner did he speak unto the people, as he taught them in the synagogue which they had built for the place of worship. And now I, Mormon, speak unto you, my beloved brethren; and it is by the grace of God, the Father, and our Lord Jesus Christ, and his holy will, because of the gift of his calling unto me, that I am permitted to speak unto you at this time; wherefore I would speak unto you that are of the church, that are the peaceable followers of Christ, and that have obtained a sufficient hope, by which ye can enter into the rest of the Lord, from this time hence forth, until ye shall rest with him in Heaven. And now my brethren, I judge these things of you because of your peaceable walk with the children of men: for I remember the word of God, which saith, By their works ye shall know them: for if their works be good, then they are good also. For behold, God hath said, A man being evil, cannot do that which is good: for if he offereth a gift, or prayeth unto God, except he shall do it with real intent, it profiteth him nothing. For behold, it is not counted unto him for righteousness. For behold, if a man being evil, giveth a gift, he doeth it grudgingly; wherefore it is counted unto him the same as if he had retained the gift; wherefore he is counted evil before God. And likewise also is it counted evil unto a man, if he shall pray, and not with real intent of heart; yea, and it profiteth him nothing: for God receiveth none such; wherefore, a man being evil, cannot do that which is good; neither will he give a good gift. For behold, a bitter fountain cannot bring forth good water; neither can a good fountain bring forth bitter water; wherefore a man being the servant of the Devil, cannot follow Christ; and if he follow Christ, he cannot be a servant of the Devil. Wherefore, all things which are good, cometh of God; and that which is evil, cometh of the Devil: for the Devil is an enemy unto God, and fighteth against him continually, and inviteth and enticeth to sin, and to do that which is evil continually. But behold, that which is of God, inviteth and enticeth to do good continually; wherefore, every thing which inviteth and enticeth to do good, and to love God, and to serve him, is inspired of God. Wherefore take heed, my beloved brethren, that ye do not judge that which is evil to be of God, or that which is

37

Smith family house in Manchester, New York, as restored to historical accuracy.

Hill Cumorah as photographed by George Edward Anderson, 1907.

Page from Joseph Smith's journal.

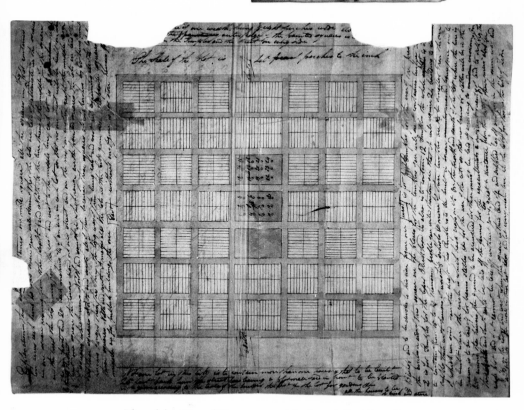

Plat of the City of Zion prepared by Joseph Smith and Frederick G. Williams in 1833. Similar plats were prepared for Kirtland, Ohio, and Far West, Missouri.

Kirtland temple as photographed by George Edward Anderson.

Altars on facing walls in Kirtland temple,
photographed by George Edward Anderson.

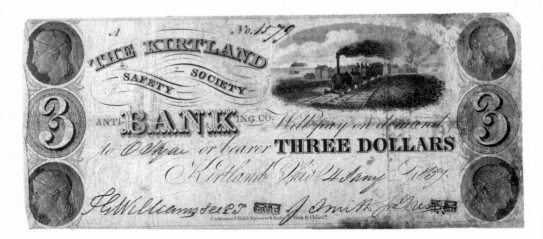

Kirtland Safety Society note issued January 4, 1837.

Jail in Liberty, Missouri,
where Joseph was incarcerated in the winter of 1839.

John C. Bennett,
from his *History of the Saints* (1842).

Willard Richards, Joseph Smith's clerk
and journal keeper from 1842 through 1844.

Mansion House in Nauvoo, where Joseph and his family lived in the last two years of his life. George Edward Anderson, 1907.

Downspout on Joseph's Nauvoo Mansion House with sun and star symbols echoing those on the temple.

The Nauvoo temple was only half finished when
Joseph Smith died in 1844.

Eliza Partridge Smith Lyman, one of two sisters married to
Joseph on March 8, 1843, and later married to Amasa Lyman.
Sutcliffe Maudsley, 1843.

Robert Campbell, *General Joseph Smith Addressing the Nauvoo Legion*,
painted in 1845 of an event that occurred in June 1844.

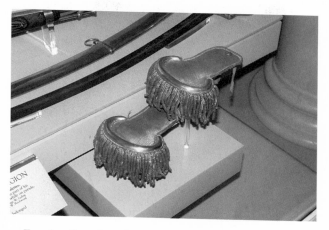

Epaulets from Joseph Smith's Nauvoo Legion uniform.

Benjamin West, *Death on the Pale Horse*.
A smaller version of this immense painting,
larger than 14 by 25 feet, was on display in Nauvoo in June 1844.

Brigham Young,
1851.

This sampler (1846–49) of the Nauvoo temple surrounded
by the names of the Twelve Apostles illustrates one person's
sense of Joseph Smith's legacy to the Saints.

THE CHARACTER OF A PROPHET

1834

*Behold I say unto you, the redemption of Zion must needs come by power; there-
fore, I will raise up unto my people a man, who shall lead them like as Moses led
the children of Israel, for ye are the children of Israel, and of the seed of Abraham; and ye must needs be led out of bondage by power, and with a stretched
out arm.*

Doctrine and Covenants [1844], 101:3

FROM THE MOMENT JOSEPH began receiving revelations, people were curious to know more about him. Believers and unbelievers came to inspect
him and report their impressions. His own followers were sometimes disappointed. He was a "lubberly fellow," one said.[1] "He looked green and not
very intelligent," wrote another. Others were struck by his charisma. Mary
Hales said that "on shaking hands with Joseph Smith, I received the Holy
Spirit in such great abundance that I felt it thrill my whole system, from the
crown of my head to the soles of my feet. I thought I had never beheld so
lovely a countenance. Nobility and goodness were in every feature." Some
doubted his capacities: one genteel visitor to Nauvoo found "his language
and manner were the coarsest possible." A few skeptics found his personal
power surprising.[2]

In 1834, Joseph's character became the subject of public debate. Doctor
Philastus Hurlbut, the man who discovered the Spaulding manuscript,
tracked down neighbors in Palmyra who remembered Joseph Smith and his
family. Hurlbut collected a batch of disparaging affidavits, which Eber D.
Howe, the Painesville editor, published. Joseph's character has been a matter of dispute ever since.

Given the name "Doctor" because he was a seventh son with presumed
healing powers, Hurlbut, a former Methodist preacher, had joined the
Mormons in March 1833, at age twenty-four. Three months later he was
tried by a bishop's council for "unchristian like conduct with the female
sex." On appeal to a council of high priests presided over by Joseph Smith,
Hurlbut was forgiven after "liberal confession," but two days later, after

new testimony was received, he was excommunicated.[3] Furious, he returned to Pennsylvania, where he had once preached for the Mormons, and began lecturing against them. Hurlbut collected the affidavits while returning from his search for Spaulding's supposed manuscript source of the *Book of Mormon*. His search had been funded by a group of Campbellites who were still smarting from Sidney Rigdon's defection and hoping to discredit Joseph.[4]

While lecturing in Palmyra, Hurlbut met people who described the Smiths as lazy, money-digging liars. During November and December 1833, Hurlbut collected fifteen statements that he exhibited when he lectured in Kirtland and surrounding towns in January 1834.[5] One Ohio Mormon reported that the "rediculous stories" gathered in New York had "fired the minds of the people with much indignation against Bro Joseph and the Church." Joseph said Hurlbut was "lieing in a wonderful manner and the peopl are running after him and giveing him mony to brake down mormanism which much endangers our lives at prasent."[6]

In the ensuing battle of words, the impassioned Hurlbut threatened to wash his hands in Joseph's blood. The reason for Joseph's four-week preaching mission to New York and upper Canada in October and November 1833 may have been to escape Hurlbut. Upon his return, Joseph appointed bodyguards and filed a complaint in court, perhaps remembering the tarring and feathering in Hiram two years before. In his journal, Joseph wrote out a prayer, offered with five of his friends, asking that "the law of the land may be magnified" in bringing Hurlbut to justice. After his experience with the impotent Missouri courts, Joseph could not take justice for granted. He prayed the Lord would "destroy him who has lifted his heel against me even that wicked man Doctor P. H[u]rlbut." To Joseph's relief, the court placed Hurlbut under a $200 bond to keep peace for six months.[7] Discredited, Hurlbut gave up his campaign and sold the depositions to Eber D. Howe, who included them in his history of the Mormons published in November 1834. *Mormonism Unvailed* presented Hurlbut's speculation about Solomon Spaulding's authorship of the Book of Mormon and printed the fifteen negative depositions along with other derogatory reports.[8]

Joseph was less troubled by the Palmyra neighbors' critical comments than by Hurlbut's threats on his life. After the court restrained Hurlbut, the Mormons felt that his "influence was pritty much distroyed." He disappeared from the scene, and Joseph turned his attention back to rescuing Zion. But Hurlbut's depositions left an indelible mark on Joseph's reputation. The former neighbors' sworn statements allowed Howe to claim that these witnesses counterbalanced the eleven witnesses to the gold plates. Colorful and detailed, the neighbors' statements paint a less-than-ideal Joseph. Joshua Stafford remembered the Smiths as "laboring people, in low circumstances" who in the early 1820s "commenced digging for hidden treasures, and soon after they became indolent, and told marvellous stories about ghosts, hob-goblins, caverns, and various other mysterious matters." Eleven citizens of Manchester said the Smiths were "a lazy, indolent set of men," and "their word was not to be depended on." The statement closed with happy relief: "we are truly glad to dispense with their society."⁹ Howe and Hurlbut brought the money-digging Joseph back from the past to trouble the Joseph who was now a prophet.

In 1832, a year before Hurlbut came on the scene, Joseph had written a history of his life covering the same period described by the affidavits. Though not written as a defense, the history does serve as an implicit rejoinder. Joseph had tried to keep histories before 1832 but with poor results. Neither Oliver Cowdery nor John Whitmer, who were appointed to keep accounts of Church events, did an adequate job. After looking over Whitmer's record in 1832, Joseph decided to tell his own story and launched "A History of the life of Joseph Smith Jr." The six-page narrative began with his birth and stopped as he was about to translate the *Book of Mormon.* To improve records in the future, he began a diary in November 1832, which ran for a few months, faltered, and then picked up a year later and lasted for a longer time. By 1835 clerks were recording his day-by-day activities, and these raw materials helped him compile a history, beginning in 1838 and published serially during his lifetime.¹⁰

The two accounts—the neighbors' affidavits and the 1832 brief history— show how differently a man's life could be represented. The Palmyrans never knew the Joseph of his own history. They saw him as a careless, indolent treasure-seeker; Joseph remembered growing up anguished and searching, anything but slack and careless. All of the familiar visionary events of his early life are seen as struggles. He comes across as a restless, yearning soul. Not even his own family knew this Joseph. His mother remembered a boy who brooded a lot, but she had no idea of his adolescent anguish. The failure of religious people to follow a "holy walk" was "a grief to my Soul." He became concerned with "the wicke[d]ness and abominations and the darkness which pervaded the minds of mankind." "Exceedingly distressed," he feared the world was lost. Everyone had "apostatised from the true and liveing faith," leaving him to "mourn for my own sins and for the sins of the world."¹¹

After his bout with skepticism as a teenager, the affirmation of his belief in the God of Creation did not calm him. He "cried unto the Lord for mercy for there was none else to whom I could go and obtain mercy." The vision of God in a "piller of light" was pacifying, but soon after, his transgressions and sins again "brought a wound upon my soul," and the "persicutions and afflictions" suffered by his family left him in need once more.

Another prayer brought the vision of Moroni and instructions about the *Book of Mormon*, but his sharpest memory was his inability to get the plates from the hill on the first try. "I cried unto the Lord in the agony of my soul why can I not obtain them."[12] Rather than rejoicing in the marvel of seeing gold plates, he remembered primarily the angel's chastisement.

By his own account, Joseph frequently felt cast down, lacking, or falling short, never enjoying all that he needed, whether wealth or spiritual assurance. He spent more time recounting Martin Harris's loss of the first translated pages than he did describing the translation itself. He remembered the chastisement and how he regained the plates only "after much humility and affliction of soul." Joseph was capable of gratitude; he opened the "History" with a phrase saying he would give an account of "his marvilous experience and of all the mighty acts which he doeth in the name of Jesus Ch[r]ist." But his voice was not triumphant. He broke off the narrative with a sentence about the poverty he and Emma suffered when her father threatened to turn them out of their house: "I had not where to go and I cried unto the Lord that he would provide for me to accomplish the work whereunto he had commanded me."[13] Joseph's "History" contains more pleading with God than excitement about revelation.

The entries in the journal that Joseph started in November 1832 were written in the same spirit. At the top of the first page, he noted the book was "to keep a minute acount of all things that come under my obse[r]vation," and then lapsed into the yearnings of his earlier writing. "Oh may God grant that I may be directed in all my thaughts Oh bless thy Servant Amen." The next entry, November 28, 1832, noted that he had spent the evening reading and writing and then observed "my mind is calm and serene for which I thank the Lord." On December 4, he happily reported, "feel better in my mind then I have for a few days back," but not knowing how long the peace would last, he added, "Oh Lord deliver thy servent out of temtations and fill his heart with wisdom and understanding."[14]

The journal entries, usually five or six lines jotted down casually when he had a spare moment, reveal a striving young man uncertain of his standing with God, yearning to be worthy, grateful when he finds peace. He often included small prayers. "Oh may God bless us with the gift of utterance to accomplish the Journy and the Errand on which we are sent," reads one. His appeals were sometimes specific and material: "it is my prayer to the Lord that three thousand subscriber[s] may be added to the Star in the term of three yea[rs]." Often he prayed for family: "O Lord bless my little children with health and long life to do good in thi[s] generation for Christs sake Amen."[15] Without God's help, his own powers fell short.

The forced exodus from Missouri in 1833 set Joseph to praying once more. "Oh my God have mercy on my Bretheren in Zion for Christ Sake," he wrote in January 1834. Perhaps to strengthen his prayers, he joined five friends in a petition that sounded like a formal appeal to the government. In the first clause, they asked the Lord to "watch over our persons and give his angels charge concerning us and our families." Then they prayed for their economic organization, the United Firm; asked for success in the suit against Hurlbut; sought means to discharge the Church's debts; and requested protection of the printing press "from the hands of evil men" and for the deliverance of Zion.[16] The items were listed and entered in the journal as a record of their desires.

ZION'S CAMP

Joseph's confidence gradually returned in the winter of 1834. When two emissaries from the Saints in Clay County, Missouri, arrived in Kirtland in February, he took action. After hearing the report, Joseph declared that he was going to Zion to redeem the land and called for the council's assent. The members agreed unanimously, nominating Joseph as "Commander in Chief of the Armies of Israel."[17] Provoked by the outrages in Missouri, another side of Joseph's character surfaced. In place of the struggling Christian stood the militant leader of Israel's armies.

The revelations did not explain how the Saints were to respond to violence. The *Book of Mormon* contained examples of extreme pacifism and equally vigorous militarism.[18] Joseph's early revelations had a pacifist side. The Saints were told to obtain Zion by purchase, not violence, for "if by blood, as you are forbidden to shed blood, lo, your enemies are upon you." The first rumor of anti-Mormon action in Missouri in the summer of 1833 had brought a revelation telling them to "renounce war and proclaim peace." But the same revelation explained that the Saints were expected to forbear only so long. If smitten once, twice, or thrice by their enemies, they were to "bear it patiently and revile not against them, neither seek revenge." After that, resistance was justified. If their enemies repeatedly injured them, armed defense was justifiable.[19]

One historian sees in the revelation on submitting to three attacks the basis for an independent, militant kingdom under the umbrella of the United States government, with power to make war on its own authority.[20] Joseph's designation by the Kirtland High Council as "Commander in Chief of the Armies of Israel" strengthens the impression of a military operation. But this peculiar elaboration of Church organization only reflected the position in which the Jackson County expulsion had placed the Mormons. The mob had treated them like an enemy nation. The citizens did not prosecute the Saints in court; they attacked them like Indians and drove them out as if they were wartime foes. What could the Mormons do but defend themselves like a nation, organizing an army and preparing for war? The only alternative seemed to be slaughter or expulsion.[21]

A revelation at the time of the February 1834 council meeting told the Saints that "the redemption of Zion must needs come by power," and the Lord would "raise up unto my people a man, who shall lead them like as Moses led the children of Israel." That sounded like a call to action, but the comparison was to Moses leading Israel out of bondage and not Joshua invading Canaan. The comparison left some question about the nature of the "power" by which Zion was to be redeemed. Was it the power of arms conquering an enemy, or the power of God opening the sea? The Saints were promised they would possess "the goodly land," a clear reference to Canaan, and told to assemble as many as five hundred men. But how these men were to engage the enemy is not explained. If attacked in Zion, were they to fight? The revelation said to "avenge me of mine enemies," but nothing about fighting. The Saints were to "curse them," not shoot them. When the little band finally reached Missouri, it was disbanded before a shot was fired.[22] Joseph's military flourishes usually stopped short of battle.

The Mormons had no intention of invading Jackson County. The Saints believed that Governor Daniel Dunklin had promised to escort them back under armed guard when he brought the state's witnesses to the trial of the Jackson County perpetrators. The Mormons became vulnerable only at the trial's conclusion. Dunklin said he lacked authority to maintain a permanent militia attachment to prevent further depredations. To protect themselves, the Mormons were encouraged to organize a militia and acquire public arms, a possible invitation to war, but the only course Dunklin could suggest. He could call out the militia only in a time of public danger, he said, and the Mormons' distress did not qualify. The U.S. Congress, however, did have the authority to call out the militia to execute the laws or suppress insurrection. Taking the hint, the Mormons appealed to President Andrew Jackson, but were turned down because no federal laws had been broken. With neither federal or state government able to maintain the peace, the Mormons organized themselves as Dunklin recommended. They wrote him in April that "a number of our brethren, perhaps 2 or 3 hundred, would remove to Jackson Co," with the object "purely to defend ourselves and possessions against another unparalleled attack from that mob." Since the governor lacked the authority to protect them, they said, "we want therefore the privilege of defending ourselves."[23]

Through the spring of 1834, Joseph raised men for Jackson County. Two days after the council meeting resolved to go to Zion, he set out with Parley Pratt on a month-long recruiting tour of Pennsylvania and New York while three other pairs of elders recruited elsewhere. The February revelation called for the enlistment of five hundred men if possible and one hundred

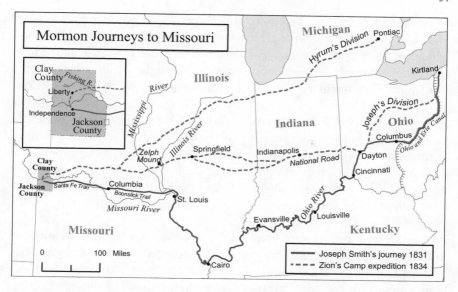

minimum. Back in Kirtland in March, Joseph continued the campaign, circling out to the branches near Kirtland and writing letters to the Saints
about the importance of "obtaining a place of reffuge" and an "inheritance
upon the Land of Zion." The camp would depart in May.[24]

On the way to a conference at New Portage, Ohio, a few weeks before
the camp's departure, Joseph stopped in Norton with Cowdery, Rigdon,
and Zebedee Coltrin. After getting settled, the four went into the woods to
pray. Their written prayers constituted the longest entry in Joseph's journal
that month. They asked God to give Joseph "strength, and wisdom, and
understanding sufficient to lead the people of the Lord." He needed assistance to "gather back and establish the Saints upon the land of their inheritances." Somehow he had to "organize them according to the will of heaven,
that they be no more cast down forever." All the tasks were more than he
could handle alone. After the prayers, Joseph asked the others to lay their
hands on his head and confirm "all the blessings necessary to qualify him to
stand before the Lord in his high calling." Then each of the men in turn
received a blessing for his particular responsibility. Having been fortified,
their "hearts rejoiced, and we were comforted with the Holy Spirit."[25]

The initial company of what became known as "Zion's Camp" or the
"Old Camp" set out from Kirtland on May 1. Joined by Joseph in New
Portage on May 6, the company totaled about a hundred men, the number
eventually doubling as other parties of Mormons trickled in from midwest
branches. Hyrum Smith and Lyman Wight recruited a company that ren-
dezvoused with Joseph's group north of St. Louis.[26] The departure of so
many Kirtland males attracted the attention of the vigilant Eber D. Howe,

who wrote a humorous report in the *Painesville Telegraph's* May 9 issue. His story was an early warning of the fears the Mormons would arouse whenever they appeared militant. Even before the march began, Howe characterized the expedition as a "fanatical," if slightly ridiculous, military campaign. The Mormons had done nothing warlike save to set out for Missouri, and yet Howe discerned at once a "holy zeal" for combat. He named all the weapons they had been accumulating: "Dirks, knives, swords, pistols, guns, powder-horns, &c. &c. have been in good demand in this vicinity. Some have equipped themselves with four or five pistols. The prophet, it is said, has a sword over *four feet long*." Though writing sarcastically, Howe portrayed the Mormons as a band of zealots, armed to the teeth, ready to draw blood. He likened Joseph to "Peter the Hermit, in the days of the crusades."[27]

Zion's Camp did attempt a mild military order, but Joseph was short on military discipline. The company, which included women and children, averaged about twenty-five miles per day.[28] The men were organized into companies of twelve with a captain over each, but their duties were to cook, make fires, prepare tents, fetch water, and attend to horses, more like trail companies than a military troop. The officers were quartermaster and historian, commissaries of subsistence, adjutant, and captain of the guard.[29] This regimen was accompanied by morning and evening prayers and weekly Sunday services. Zion's Camp set a guard each night, worried about being spied on by "the enemy." They feared that the Jackson County citizens would use force to stop the Mormons en route. After it became known that a Mormon company was coming, the Jackson citizens had burned over a hundred abandoned Mormon dwellings.[30]

Once the camp conducted a sham battle as a "diversion" while they waited for one of the men to buy a horse, and after crossing into Missouri, the camp attempted a more military style. Joseph was acknowledged as commander in chief; Lyman Wight, one of the more militant converts, was general of the camp. According to Wight, Joseph called him to the position while recruiting in New York state. At "Father Bosley's" farm, "Joseph ordained me to the office of Benamey [*sic*] in the presence of an angel." Joseph was given the name Baurak Ale, "the officer of the highest rank in the army of the strength of the Lord's hosts and Banemy is an appendage there unto." Joseph chose twenty men for his bodyguard, fearing that he was a particular target for the Missourians. To give some small measure of discipline to this odd lot of men, Joseph held an inspection of firearms and had them discharged to be sure they worked, and then Wight marched the men about in platoons for half a day. Joseph went no further toward turning the camp members into soldiers. He seemed more intrigued with military flourishes like appointing to himself an "Armour Bearer" who carried a brace of silver-mounted brass-barreled horse pistols that Joseph discharged from time to time.[31]

It is hard to know what the camp experience meant to Joseph as he traveled the nearly thousand miles from Ohio to Missouri during May and June of 1834. His journal for those months, kept by camp historian Frederick G. Williams, was lost. A brief account prepared during Joseph's lifetime was not printed until after his death. The expanded account in the official *History of the Church* was the work of clerks who borrowed from the notes of participants such as Heber C. Kimball, George A. Smith, and the conscientious diarist Wilford Woodruff. In the expanded version, clerks combined all the available sources of information into entries that sounded as if Joseph himself wrote them. Where he was in this welter of sources is hard to know.[32]

Much of the Zion's Camp story in the later accounts came from George A. Smith, Joseph's admiring younger cousin who went on to become a leader in the Church hierarchy.[33] "George A." was nearly seventeen when the camp left Kirtland in May 1834, a plain country boy with weak eyes, wearing a crushed straw hat and striped ticking pantaloons, too short for his long body. Joseph sent him out when the camp passed through towns to answer questions the townspeople might direct to a simple boy rather than a more forbidding adult. Joseph invited George A. to sleep in his tent and assigned him to carry water for their irascible cook, Zebedee Coltrin.[34]

George A. made note of food and sore feet. Forced on one hot day to drink slough water, he learned to "strain Wiglers" with his teeth. He was grateful to Joseph for lending him a pair of his own boots to ease his painful feet. He watched the Prophet bear up under hardships along with everyone else. When Joseph was given sweet bread rather than sour like the others, he asked for the sour. He walked all day rather than riding because the wagons were overloaded with supplies. Joseph "had a full proportion of blistered, bloody and sore feet, which was the natural result of walking from 25 to 40 miles a day in a hot season of the year."[35]

George A. picked up the camp lore and especially the feeling of divine protection. Though apparently on their own as they trudged along the famed National Road to the West, the camp members believed heaven watched over them. A revelation had said an angel would go before them like Israel in the wilderness, and one camp member, Heber C. Kimball, said angels were seen. When a man turned over a spadeful of earth and found water, some exclaimed that "it was as much of a miracle as when Moses smote the rock and water came out." Happenings like this led Levi Hancock to say, "Truly we had seen the hand of God in our favor all the way."[36]

George A. remembered an occasion when onlookers were unable to gauge the camp's numbers: "In passing through the Village of Middlebury an attempt was made to count us and we were declared to be 450, those who counted said they did not think they included all: there were not in reality 100 of us." Joseph made the same observation to Emma: "In counting us the[y] make of our 170 men from five to seven hundred," he wrote in early June.[37] The exaggeration benefited the Saints, Joseph thought, by intimidating the Jackson County spies.

In George A. Smith's retelling, supernatural power focused on Joseph. George A. noted the times when Joseph's greater wisdom prevailed over the foolishness of camp members. When some feared they would take ill from milk, Joseph calmed them. "If they would follow his counsel and use all that they could get from friend or enemy it should do them good and none be sick in consequence of it." George A. happily reported that "although we passed thro neighbourhoods where many of the people and cattle were dying with the sickness, yet his words were fulfilled."[38]

Mormons inherited the Puritan habit of seeing Providential interventions in everyday events. When an argument broke out involving Sylvester Smith, a perpetual troublemaker, Joseph warned that "they would meet with misfortunes, difficulties and hindrances; as the certain result of giving way to such a spirit and said, you will know it before you leave this place." George A. reported that the next morning "almost every horse in the Camp [was] so badly foundered, that we could scarcely lead them a few rods to water." When he learned of the problem, Joseph told the men to humble themselves and the horses would be restored. By noon, George A. happily reported, they were "as nimble as ever, with the exception of one of Sylvester Smith's which soon afterwards died."[39]

Like everyone else, Joseph wanted evidence of God's backing. The expulsion from Zion had shaken his confidence. Although he never doubted his revelations, he was less certain about everyday events. The periodic instructions from heaven were beacons for the Church, but Joseph was on his own in carrying out the commandments. When reporting the magnified camp numbers to Emma, he saw God's hand in it. "The Lord shows us to good advantage in the eyes of their spies."[40]

A rather prosaic idea of prophecy lay behind the camp's attention to Joseph's sayings. Everyone thought a prophet should foretell the future, and Joseph's accuracy in even small matters confirmed their belief. Joseph's gifts, however, were of a different nature. In early June when several camp members stopped near the Illinois River to investigate a mound, they came across three piles of stones that looked like possible altars, with bones scattered on the ground nearby. Digging down about a foot, they found a skeleton with an arrow point stuck in its ribs. According to the account prepared under his direction, Joseph said: "The visions of the past being opend to my understanding by the Spirit of the Almighty. I discovered that the person whose Skeleton was before us was a white Lamanite, a large thick set man, and a man of God." Named Zelph, the man fought for "the great prophet Onandagus, who was known from the hill Cumorah, or eastern sea, to the Rocky Mountains." According to Joseph, Zelph had his hip broken by a rock flung from a sling during the last great battle between Lamanites and Nephites.[41] Stories like this perplexed Levi Hancock, who later noted, "I could not comprehend it but supposed it was alright."[42]

George A. Smith understood that Joseph saw himself as the camp's instructor. The camp members were "prayerless, thoughtless, careless, heedless, foolish or devilish and yet we did not know it." "Joseph had to bear with us and tutor us, like children." Joseph told the men around him "to cultivate thro' life a modest and graceful demeanour, avoiding vulgarity," a hard lesson for these rough-cut men. He told them to be careful about their posture while praying. "When we Kneel to pray we should be in a graceful manner such as would not cause a disgusting impression to arise in the mind of any spectator."[43]

On another occasion, Joseph taught a little millennial ecology. He stopped some men from killing three rattlesnakes by telling them: "When will the Lion lie down with the Lamb and the venom of the Serpent cease, while man seeks to destroy and waste the flesh of beasts, waging a continual war against reptiles, let man first get rid of his destructive propensities and then we may look for a change in the serpents' disposition." They avoided killing snakes from them on, said George A., and shot wild animals only for food.[44]

A month into the trip, Joseph wrote to Emma that "a tolerable degree of union has prevailed among the brethren." Were it not for the absence of their families, he told her, "wandering over the plains" with these "social honest and sincere men" would be "as a dream, and this would be the happiest period of all our lives." He saw the camp as a rehearsal for a future journey to Zion when all would come peacefully "in the enjoyment and embrace of that society we so much love."[45]

The harmony did not last. On June 5, the day after Joseph wrote home, Sylvester Smith, captain of one of the companies, began an argument that lasted three months. It started when Sylvester marched his company smartly into camp to the sound of a flute, and a dog given to Joseph by a camp member snapped at the men. Sylvester berated Joseph and threatened to kill the dog. The next morning, Joseph mimicked Sylvester's wrath, saying, "If a dog bites me I will kill him—if any man insults me, I will kill him—if any man injures me I will injure him . . . This spirit keeps up division and bloodshed through the world." That a soft answer turneth away wrath was a worthy principle, but then Joseph contradicted his own lesson by snapping at Sylvester, "If you kill that dog I will whip you." He predicted that if

Sylvester "did not get rid of that spirit the day would come when a dog should bite him, and gnaw his flesh and he would not be able to resist it." Furious, Sylvester spat back, "You are prophecying lies in the name of the Lord."[46]

In mid-June, a disagreement over a campsite sparked another outburst between the two men. On a night when they feared an attack by Missourians, Joseph thought they should camp on the prairie where approaching forces could be seen. Sylvester, backed by General Lyman Wight and others, preferred to remain hidden in the trees. As the company pulled out onto the prairie, Sylvester placed himself in its path and shouted, "Are you following your general or some other man?" All but about twenty men followed Joseph, and when the smaller group caught up the next morning, Joseph "called them together and reproved them for tarrying behind and not obeying his counsel." That was George A.'s polite account. Actually a shouting match ensued in which Joseph was said to have thrown the camp bugle at Sylvester.[47] Lyman Wight backed down immediately, but Sylvester, in George A.'s tactful phrase, "manifested refractory feelings."

Disputes within the camp were matched by troubles with Missourians. The approach of the camp threw Jackson County into a frenzy. Sentries were placed along the south bank of the Missouri to warn the county of the approaching invaders. On June 6, Governor Dunklin appealed to state militia colonel John Thornton of Clay County, where most of the displaced Saints resided, to effect a compromise between the warring parties. Dunklin acknowledged the right of the Mormons to their lands and their constitutional right to arm themselves in self-defense, but thought they were better advised to settle elsewhere because of "the eccentricity of the[ir] religious opinions." He urged the Jackson County leaders to buy out Mormon property.[48]

On June 16, with the camp getting closer, more than eight hundred people gathered at the courthouse in Liberty to settle the differences with resident Mormons. Probably as a result of the governor's initiative, Judge John Ryland in neighboring Ray County called together representatives of both parties. Sidney Gilbert, the Mormon storekeeper who handled the negotiations along with the Mormons' attorneys, Alexander Doniphan and David Rice Atchison, warned the judge that the Mormons would never sell, but that was precisely what the Jackson County committee proposed. Doniphan thought the Mormons had the right to oppose "mob violence." "If they don't fight they are cowards," one account of the June 16 meeting had him saying. On the other side, a Clay County minister said that the Mormons "must either clear out or be cleared out." Calmed by the Church's attorneys, the Jackson County committee finally proposed to purchase all Mormon lands at double the market value with payment due in thirty days. As an alternative, the Saints could buy all Jackson County lands on the same terms: double the fair price.[49]

For the Saints, the terms were impossible. As Gilbert wrote to the attorneys, to sell their inheritances in Zion "would be like selling our children into slavery." As for the alternative, how could so much money be raised so quickly to buy out far wealthier settlers? The offer could only have been made in full realization of its impossibility. The Mormon counterproposal a few days later was to buy out the Jackson County citizens at full value—not double value—within a year and not to return until full payment was made. The cost of damages to Mormon property would be deducted from the price.[50]

In the meantime, a catastrophe killed all hope for compromise. Returning to Jackson County on the evening of the June 16 meeting, seven citizens, most of them members of the committee, crossed the Missouri River on William Everett's ferry. Although the ferry was believed to be in solid condition, it sank about two hundred yards from shore. Five men drowned, including Everett and two ferrymen. An investigation found nothing suspicious, but rumors quickly circulated that the Mormons had bribed one of the drowned men to bore large holes in the gunwales of the boat.[51]

Joseph was grimly satisfied with the ferry disaster. James Campbell, one of the victims, was reported to have sworn at Liberty that "the eagles and Turkey buzzards shall eat my flesh if I do not fix Joe. Smith and his army so that their skins will not hold shucks, before two days are passed." In his history, Joseph happily repeated the story that Campbell "floated down the river some four or five miles, and lodged upon a pile of drift wood, where the Eagles, Buzzards, ravens, crows and wild animals eat his flesh from his bones, to fulfil his own words, and left him a horrible looking skeleton of God's vengeance."[52] To the end of his life, Joseph took dismal pleasure in stories of Jackson County suffering.

A furious storm a few nights later, on June 19, showed God exacting vengeance once again. Camped between two branches of the Fishing River, the Mormons learned from five men who rode into camp that they would "see hell before morning." Two hundred Jackson County men, to be joined by sixty from Ray County and seventy from Clay, were crossing over to attack. Not long after the advance party rode off, the Mormons "discovered a small black cloud rising in the west; and not more than twenty minutes passed away before it began to rain and hail." Drenched and pelted by hailstones, the Mormons barely got through the night. Exposed to the fury of the storm, the Jackson men were unable to cross the river. Joseph said that the "wind and rain, hail and thunder met them in great wrath, and soon softened their direful courage, and frustrated all their design to 'kill Jo Smith and his Army.'" Joseph was sure the battered attackers had learned "that when Jehovah fights, they would rather be absent. The gratification is too terrible."[53]

If the storm slowed the mob, it also slowed Zion's Camp. With the direct route to Jackson County temporarily flooded, the men marched north around the headwater, stopping on a plain in Ray County for a few days while Joseph considered his next move. The camp had learned on June 15 that the governor would not escort them back to their lands; they would have to fight their way into the county. That was a setback; they had never envisioned a bloody battle. Joseph told mediators from Ray County that the camp had assembled only to assist their abused brothers and sisters. "It is not our intention to commit hostilities against any man, or set of men; it is not our intention to injure any man's person or property." He admitted they were well armed, but added that "we have every reason to put ourselves in an attitude of self defense, considering the abuse we have suffered." Although Joseph felt he had won over the Ray delegation, there was no chance for a settlement.[54] After the sinking of the ferry, the Jackson citizens refused to deal.

On Sunday, June 22, the Mormons' attorneys made their counterproposal for purchasing the Jackson County lands to Clay County sheriff Cornelius Gillium, who published the plan in the (Liberty) *Missouri Inquirer.* By then, however, the negotiations were dead. That same day, Joseph, still well outside of Jackson County, received a revelation telling the camp to disband for the time being. On Monday, their lawyers advised them to give up any ideas of military action and depend on the courts for redress. With no practical alternatives, Joseph agreed.[55]

The more bellicose camp members were unhappy. George A. Smith said that "several of the brethren apostatized because they were not going to have the privilege of fighting." John Whitmer felt hopes "were blasted at least for a season" when the decision was made to disband. These militants had marched to Missouri expecting to redeem Zion by force. Now they were told to abandon the campaign. The June 22 revelation forbade aggressive action. Before the army of Israel could "become fair as the sun, and clear as the moon" and her banners terrible unto the nations, she must be sanctified, and the Saints were far from that state. The failure to redeem Zion, the revelation made clear, was ultimately the Saints' responsibility, not that of the Jackson citizens. The Missouri Saints had refused to impart their substance to the poor, and the Church at large did not volunteer enough men for the camp. Before they could succeed in Zion, the Saints must learn to consecrate. For now, the elders were to gather up their money, purchase land, and only then might they be found "throwing down the towers of their enemies" and taking possession. "But firstly, let my army become very great, and let it be sanctified before me."[56]

The revelation was not a signal to retreat, foreshadowing an abandonment of the gathering: "next year in Zion" remained Joseph's motto. But the revelation did reroute the Zion impulse. By making sanctification the answer for Zion, the revelation united the Church's two programs: the gathering to Zion in Jackson County, and the exaltation of the Saints. Zion could not go forward until the Saints were sanctified. The elders must "know more perfectly, concerning their duty, and the things which I require at their hands," the revelation said. And how were they to learn all they must do? "This cannot be brought to pass until mine elders are endowed with power from on high." The endowment of power, central to the exaltation of the Saints for the past three years, became the first step in the redemption of Zion. Both depended on construction of the Kirtland temple, where the endowment was to be given. The day after the revelation was received, a council appointed "the first Elders," as they were called, "to receive [their] endowment in Kirtland with the power from on high and to assist in gathering up the strength of the Lord's house, and proclaim the everlasting gospel." Fifteen leading men from Zion were named. In the meantime, the Saints in Clay County, the June 22 revelation said, were to lie low, not talk of the judgments on the land, and to make friends. "Sue for peace, not only [to] the people that have smitten you, but also to all people. . . . Lift up an ensign of peace, and make a proclamation for peace unto the ends of the earth."[57]

That was the hope, but for the moment, the Saints knew no peace. Seeing a man with cramps earlier in the week, George A. Smith suspected Asiatic cholera, a plague that had ravaged the country in recent years. During the week beginning June 23, one member after another of the now demilitarized camp was struck with terrible stomach pains. On June 25, the first death occurred, followed a half hour later by the second. Sixty-eight members of the camp contracted the disease during a four-day siege, and fourteen died.[58] George A. and others rolled the dead in blankets and buried them without coffins in the bank of a stream. Among the fatalities was Sidney Gilbert, the storekeeper who had managed the negotiations for the Mormons over the past few weeks. When struck blind while praying, Heber C. Kimball "saw no way whereby I could free myself from the disease, only to exert myself by jumping and thrashing myself about, until my sight returned to me, and my blood began to circulate in my veins." Jesse Johnson Smith, another of Joseph's cousins, died on July 1. The last entry in Jesse's diary read: "the journey was long and tedious temporally speaking, but [we] believ[ed] it to be according to the mind and will of the Lord."[59]

Long afterward, Joseph remembered the suffering that week. "While some were digging the grave others stood sentry with their fire arms, watching their enemies." The camp was trapped between the hatred of the

Missourians and the onslaught of cholera. Responding to the shrieks of pain that filled the camp, Joseph gave the victims flour and whiskey and ministered by laying on hands. Nothing worked. Each time Joseph laid hands on a victim, the disease passed into his own body. "I quickly learned by painful experience," he later wrote, "that when the Great Jehovah decrees destruction upon any people, makes known his determination, man must not attempt to stay his hand." Why else would God punish camp members for seeking relief? Joseph remembered the unsettling contradictions. "Elder John S. Carter was the first man who stepped forward to rebuke it, and upon this, was instantly seized, and became the first victim in the camp." The men who buried Carter "united, covenanted and prayed, hoping the disease would be staid; but in vain, for while thus covenanting, Eber Wilcox died."[60] Pleading with God attracted a bolt of lightning.

Joseph had warned the brethren of punishment for their contentious spirit, and now their bickering brought misery and destruction.[61] No revelation told Joseph that God had sent the cholera. He read his own ideas about Deity into the event. In the retelling, Joseph called Him Jehovah, whose Old Testament character punished recalcitrants with suffering and death. In the camp's extremity, Joseph seems to have called up a God out of his Puritan past, a God who would destroy His own people if they neglected His commands. This was the God, we must assume, to whom Joseph felt responsible for establishing Zion and preparing his people for exaltation, a God harsh and implacable, inflicting punishment on those who failed.

Ravaged by disease, Zion's Camp broke up. On June 25, Joseph wrote his attorneys that the camp was separating into bands and dispersing about the countryside. The campaign was over. George A. Smith received his honorable discharge and $1.16, his share of the common fund into which all had deposited their money at the outset. Joseph reorganized the Clay County Saints with David Whitmer as president of the council and spent a week giving instructions. On July 9, Joseph started home with fifteen brethren, including George A.[62]

The company trudged east through the oppressive summer heat. Crossing one stretch of prairie, they took turns driving off green-headed flies reputedly able to kill a tethered horse in thirty minutes. During the arduous three-week journey, the company's problems were more physical than moral or spiritual. Only once did Joseph detect disunity among the group. Rather than contention, George A. remembered maggott-ridden cheese and watered milk. On July 27 in Indiana, the party divided. Joseph and three others climbed on a coach, leaving the rest of the party to trail along on foot and horse. He arrived in Kirtland around August 1; George A. got home three days later. At the door of his house, George A. overheard his father praying for his safe arrival.[63]

The expedition to Missouri in 1834 has been called Joseph Smith's first major failure. Nothing that Joseph aimed to accomplish came about. Several hundred men spent three months walking two thousand miles; fourteen of them never came home. Nothing the camp did improved the situation in Jackson County. The Saints were still refugees, living in Clay County as barely tolerated aliens. Hoping to pacify the Clay people, the Mormons agreed among themselves to abstain from voting and not to hold public meetings, all to no effect.[64] Four years later, Missourians combined to drive the Mormons across the Mississippi into Illinois.

Was Zion's Camp a catastrophe? Perhaps, but it was not the unmitigated disaster that it appears to be. Most camp members felt more loyal to Joseph than ever, bonded by their hardships. The future leadership of the Church came from this group. Nine of the Church's original Twelve Apostles, all seven presidents of the Seventy, and sixty-three other members of the Seventy marched in Zion's Camp.[65] Joseph's own devotion to Zion and the gathering grew more intense. When the Jackson County committee gave the Saints an opportunity to sell out, cut their losses, and start again elsewhere, he refused. A revelation had designated Independence as the place for a temple, and no other would do. After experiencing Jackson County anger and backing off, Joseph still predicted a return within two years.[66]

CHARGES

Not everyone was happy when Zion's Camp returned. Within two weeks after getting back from Missouri in early August 1834, Joseph was brought before a high council by the quarrelsome Sylvester Smith. Smith brought charges of "criminal conduct" against the Prophet for mismanagement of monies and properties, and was even more angry about the rebukes he had received. The property issue was soon cleared up, but the council spent days investigating Joseph's correction of Sylvester. A settlement reached on August 11 broke down when Sylvester disavowed the decision, and a second council meeting called on August 28 to review the case did not end until almost three in the morning on August 30. Meanwhile, reports circulated that Joseph had maligned Sylvester with "insulting and abusive language" in a manner out of harmony with Joseph's "profession as a man of God." Jacob Bump admitted that "his mind had been agitated" by what he had heard. To clear Joseph's name, the *Evening and Morning Star* printed the council's findings for the benefit of the Church. Everyone wanted to know how their prophet behaved and if he lived in accord with "the true principles of his profession as a man of God."[67]

On one of the occasions when Joseph was supposedly out of control, he was said to have rebuked Sylvester for refusing bread to Parley Pratt, not one of Sylvester's company. Probably wanting to husband the meager supply for his own men, Sylvester told Pratt to look elsewhere for food. Joseph, who could not abide stinginess, was irate. A year before he had criticized Sidney Gilbert for not extending loans to poor migrants in Independence, whether or not they were credit risks. A continuing theme in the revelations was the requirement to look after the poor. Incensed by Sylvester's refusal, Joseph gave him a tongue-lashing. Luke Johnson "thought at the time the reproofs were rather severe."[68]

Sylvester came in for chastisement again over the incident with Joseph's dog. Joseph threatened to whip Sylvester after Sylvester threatened to kill the dog. According to Brigham Young, Joseph backed off quickly from this heated exchange and asked the men standing nearby if they were not ashamed of such a spirit, confessing that he was. He must have recognized that he had lost control. Young said Joseph's explanation satisfied the men, implying that at first they were shocked by the exchange. David Elliot admitted the occurrence gave him "some disagreeable feelings."[69]

In a third incident, the one involving disagreement over a campsite when an enemy attack was expected, the witnesses testified about the degree of Joseph's anger. When Joseph chastised Sylvester and Lyman Wight for disobeying orders, Sylvester claimed Joseph had thrown the camp bugle at him. Luke Johnson, who saw it all happen, doubted the charge because the two were so close that Joseph could easily have hit Sylvester had he tried. Johnson thought Joseph had thrown the horn to the ground. Johnson noted somewhat ambiguously that Joseph's reproofs were "no more severe than he had often heard him give previously," and "that he did not consider him mad as he has been represented." Reproof was to be expected; rage was off-limits.[70]

Sylvester had hardly brought the charges against Joseph when the hearing turned into a trial of Sylvester himself for bringing false charges. The men hearing Sylvester's complaints composed themselves into a council with Bishop Newel Whitney presiding. The question became what was to be done "to arrest the evil," meaning the circulation of false reports about Joseph. Isaac Story, believing "the plaster ought to be as large as the wound," urged that an apology from Sylvester be published in the *Evening and Morning Star*. That opinion prevailed, and an article was prepared announcing that after thorough investigation the council had determined that during the journey to Missouri, Joseph acted "in a proper manner and in every respect has conducted himself to the satisfaction of the church."[71] Fifteen men, not council members but present at the proceedings, signed a statement attesting to the justice of the results.

But the case was not over. A few days later, Sylvester reneged on his agreement to publish a confession in the *Star*, and his retraction required a second and more laborious investigation, which again concluded with a requirement that he confess his wrongs against the Prophet. Sylvester signed a single-sentence confession and then wrote below "signed for fear of punishment," a grudging concurrence at best. His departure from the Mormon fold seemed imminent, but surprisingly he stayed on. On October 28, he published the irksome confession and attested that Joseph had conducted himself worthily. He told the Saints everywhere that he sought to "put a final end to all evil reports."[72]

The camp incident triggered strong feelings. While Sylvester was raging and the members gossiping about reports from the camp, Joseph wrote the Missouri Saints that he was "met in the face and eyes as soon as I had got home with a catalogue [of charges] that was as black as the author of lies himself . . . the cry was Tyrant,! Pope!! King!!! Usurper!!!! Abuser of men!!!!! Ange[l]!!!!!! False Prophet!!!!! Prophesying Lies in the name of the Lord." The list showed Joseph understood how he looked to his enemies, but the charges infuriated him. He told the Missouri Saints he had been unable "to regulate my mind" sufficiently to give them counsel, but was sure his accusers were "meet for the devourer the shaft of the . . . distroying Angel."[73]

If the Sylvester Smith case brought Joseph's leadership into question, it also vindicated the procedures he had put in place for dealing with controversy. The long debates in council settled the "great difficulty," as Joseph called it. Sylvester stayed on to become a president of the soon-to-be-appointed Seventy and act for a time as Joseph Smith's clerk. Looking back, Joseph concluded that such experiences may be "necissary to perfect the Church." A council with many Church members present had heard both sides, deliberated, and decided. The fifteen outside members attested to the results and assured the Church "that every appearance of evil is, in this place, searched out," by implication meaning purported evil in the Prophet himself.[74]

The high council hearings, along with events during Zion's Camp, revealed Joseph's weaknesses along with his strengths. He was a man of strong feeling and will, as was apparent in his commitment to this risky and difficult venture in the first place. He would not be defeated by the mobbers in Jackson County or the resistance of the Missouri government. Supported by militants like Lyman Wight, Joseph even showed a willingness to make the military gesture. He spoke of the armies of Israel and gave himself a military title. Some have argued he later made a war department a permanent feature of Church organization.[75] But when it came to military action, he backed down. The revelations authorized the Saints to defend themselves but made peace the better course. When an actual battle with the Missourians loomed, Joseph negotiated, as he was to do later in Missouri and again in Illinois. His own nature and the military culture of his time prompted militant rhetoric, but he stopped short of bloodshed.

As Sylvester Smith learned, Joseph did not like to be crossed. His own followers were sometimes shocked by his flashes of anger. But in the end they backed him. The high council found Sylvester Smith at fault, not Joseph. They sensed that their prophet had the right to rebuke his followers, fiercely if necessary. Their dismay at his anger was balanced by their love of his good nature. Joseph enjoyed the comradeship of the march and bore the discomforts of the trek without complaint. They knew he did not elevate himself above the ordinary when hardships were involved. He joked and laughed and enjoyed their company. His warm-hearted friendship more than compensated for the occasional tirades.

Probably no one in the camp sensed the anxiety under his confident exterior. It was the anguished Joseph of the 1832 history who walked with Zion's Camp. Probably referring to the threatened loss of Zion, Joseph wrote to Emma on the way to Missouri, "You know that my situation is a very critacal one." He might fail. He realized that "our numbers and means are altogether too small for the accomplishment of such a great enterprise." He hoped at best to "deter the enemy, and terrify them for a little season." Emma's affection sustained him through the difficult time. "I hope you will continue to communicate to me by your own hand for this is a consolation to me to convirse with you in this way in my lonely moments which is not easily discribed." The bonhomie and business of the camp could not salve his sorrows. He ended one letter: "from your's in the bonds of affliction." He told Emma to comfort the family "and look forward to the day when the trials and the tribulations of this life will be at an end."[76]

THIRTEEN

PRIESTHOOD AND
CHURCH GOVERNMENT

1834–35

The decisions of these quorums . . . are to be made in all righteousness; in holiness and lowliness of heart; meekness and long suffering; and in faith and virtue and knowledge; temperance, patience, godliness brotherly kindness and charity.
                                   Doctrine and Covenants [1835], 3:11

MORMONISM SUCCEEDED WHEN other charismatic movements foundered on disputes and irreconcilable ill feelings partly because of the governing mechanisms Joseph put in place early in the Church's history. The Sylvester Smith case, involving the Prophet himself, showed the strength of the councils and conferences that governed the Church. When the charges brought before the August 11 meeting proved serious, the men knew how to form a council. They had been gathering for years into councils of seven or eight men to decide on mission calls and handle transgressors. During the course of Sylvester Smith's hearings, twenty-eight men spoke their minds, some as members of the council, others as observers in the meeting. By the end of the hearings, all sides having spoken, Joseph could say, "I now swim in good *clean* water, with my *head* out."[1]

The characterization of Joseph Smith as the prophet with no gift for administration, whose inchoate movement was saved by the genius of Brigham Young, misses the mark. Joseph did not attend to details the way Young did, but he could certainly organize. Almost all of his major theological innovations involved the creation of institutions—the Church, the City of Zion, the School of the Prophets, the priesthood, the temple. Joseph thought institutionally more than any other visionary of his time, and the survival of his movement can largely be attributed to this gift.

Soon after the Church was organized Joseph adopted the practice of bringing councils together. Rather than restricting himself to the Methodist pattern of quarterly conferences of elders, Joseph convened conferences or councils (the words were used interchangeably at first) whenever there was business to conduct. Attended on average by eight elders, the meetings were run by a moderator with a clerk taking minutes. In one particularly intense period between the end of August and the middle of November 1831, twelve conferences were convened in addition to the general Church conference on October 25 and 26.[2]

The conferences considered priesthood ordinations, the settlement of Church disputes, decisions about who was to go to Zion, the construction of the temple. Ezra Booth was "silenced from preaching" on September 6, as he slid into apostasy. On October 10, arrangements were made to manage Frederick G. Williams's farm. A conference on October 21 took up an accusation against two brethren for "offering abuse to Newel K. Whitney's little child," resulting in a charge to Joseph and Sidney Rigdon to ask the two men to acknowledge their sin or be dealt with according to the law of the Church. One conference sent out six elders to "visit the several branches of this church setting them in order," suggesting how congregational organization was handled.[3]

Joseph was not always in charge of the councils he attended. The group itself chose the moderator, shifting the responsibility from one to another of the more experienced men like Sidney Rigdon or Oliver Cowdery, but sometimes turning to new converts like William E. McLellin. Since Joseph received revelations right in the conferences, reports of how revelations came were common. In some respects, revelation became part of the routine.[4]

Joseph could absent himself from these meetings without crippling business. He left Kirtland for months at a time, and the councils carried on in his absence. The men in Missouri managed their affairs without him for years. In 1831, when Oliver Cowdery and John Whitmer stopped in Indiana on their way west with the revelations, they held two long conferences in Randolph County, Indiana, to settle a controversy over common property.[5] Councils made the Church self-governing.

The process seems incongruous in an organization led by a man who was believed to receive revelation from the mouth of God. How could any opinion but the Prophet's count? The incongruity brings us back to the conundrum of Joseph Smith's Mormonism: how could an authoritarian religion distribute so much power to individual members? Just as every member was expected to speak scripture by the Holy Ghost, so individual priesthood holders were allowed a voice in church governance, giving them ownership of the kingdom to which they had subjected themselves.

The array of governing bodies and relationships formalized in 1834 and 1835 was among Joseph Smith's greatest achievements. In July, after the Clay County high council was organized, he told it that he had now completed the organization of the Church and made it independent enough to function without him. He was premature in proclaiming an end to organizational development, but the statement underscored his belief that organization was crucial to his mission.[6] A revelation told him that "this shall be your business and mission in all your lives to preside in counsel."[7]

In many ways, the organization of Church government revealed Joseph's thought as much as the doctrine. He believed the structure he created followed the "order of heaven in ancient councils." In a time when Protestant churches had lost interest in organizational forms, save to democratize them as far as possible, Joseph built an ever more elaborate structure in emulation of the ancient church as he understood it. While other churches were simplifying and flattening their structures, he erected complicated hierarchies.[8]

LAYERS

In March 1835, the newly called Twelve Apostles asked Joseph for a "great revelation" to "enlarge our hearts, comfort us in adversity and brighten our hopes amidst the powers of Darkness."[9] In response, Joseph received the "great revelation" on priesthood now recorded in section 107 of the LDS *Doctrine and Covenants*. A hundred verses long in the modern edition, the revelation summarized and regularized all the governmental forms that had developed over the past five years, the high councils in Zion and Kirtland, the traveling Twelve Apostles, the presidency of the Church, the division into Melchizedek and Aaronic priesthoods, the quorums of elders, priests, teachers, and deacons, the appointment of evangelical ministers or patriarchs.

This culminating statement of Joseph's church-building project looks like a blueprint of Church structure, but any effort to extract an organizational chart ends in confusion. The overlapping parts and peculiar extensions cannot be sorted out on the basis of the revelation alone. It is best understood as an archeological site, containing layers of organizational forms, each layer created for a purpose at one time and then overlaid by other forms established for other purposes later. The totality has the appearance of an ancient city occupied by a number of civilizations yet composed into a unity by the harmonizing effects of time. In practice, the pieces came together into a complicated but coordinated whole.[10]

Picking through the revelation, the limits of Joseph's vision when he organized the Church in 1830 quickly become evident. At the outset, he envisioned a simple structure. The statement of beliefs and organization prepared by Cowdery and Joseph in 1829 and 1830 listed a set of officers much like the officers in other churches—elders, priests, teachers, and deacons—and closely following the church described in the *Book of Mormon*. Joseph and Cowdery were the First and Second Elders like the elders in Congregational or Presbyterian churches. The officers had familiar duties like baptizing, blessing the sacrament, and preaching. Very little distinguished them from parallel figures in other denominations. General supervision was exercised by quarterly conferences made up of elders representing their home churches.[11]

Nothing in this initial organization would have surprised a Methodist, save for the absence of a bishop to superintend the whole. In 1830, the Church was organized as a church like other churches. Priesthood was not mentioned, even though priesthood authority had been given by John the Baptist a year before. In the beginning Joseph and Cowdery did not seem to grasp the importance of the ordination they had received.[12] It took a year or more before the priesthood principle had much effect.

This simple plan was soon expanded. Within six months, the initial organization was inadequate for the complicated program Joseph had launched. The society of Zion in his millenarian world involved operations unknown in ordinary churches, including the Zion economic system that called on immigrants to deed their property to the Church and receive back a "stewardship" proportionate to their needs and talents. A bishop, the missing Methodist officer, was named to accept the consecrations and reassign them according to individual wants and needs.[13]

Step by step, the hierarchy unfolded as doctrine and program required new officers. The designation of gathering cities in Independence and Kirtland created a need for governing bodies for each municipality, and high councils were formed to serve the purpose. The high council to regulate Kirtland was organized on February 17, 1834, with twelve high priests called as standing members, contrasted to the earlier ad hoc councils that were composed of whoever was available.[14] Twelve men were named to constitute the council, and "the high priests, Elders, priests, teachers and deacons that were present who had not been nominated as counsellors" were then asked "to pass their vote whether they were satisfied with the appointment or nomination of the twelve to compose the Church Council." They agreed unanimously, and the first high council came into existence. Rules were laid down for trying transgressors and handling other church business.[15]

Although stationed in Kirtland, this council served as a council for the whole Church. Kirtland was the seat of government, Joseph explained, as Jerusalem was for the New Testament church. Five months later, Joseph organized an equivalent council in Clay County for the Saints expelled from Jackson, appointing David Whitmer as president.[16] By the end of 1834, the two councils in Kirtland and Clay had become city councils for the two gathering cities. By implication, the number of councils could then be expanded as more cities were founded. Each new "city of a stake of Zion" would have its high council of twelve high priests and a presidency of three members.

The two councils were a response to a geographical concept emerging from the Church's missionary program. Implicit in revelations received in late 1830 and 1831 was a world divided in two, into the mission field and the Zion cities.[17] Missionaries went out into the mission field and brought Israel back to Zion. There was an outside and an inside. In 1834, the portion of the globe considered to be Zion and its stakes came under the jurisdiction of the high councils, providing the stakes with a regular form of government. But the remainder of the world, where there were only scattered branches of the Church, remained unorganized.

At first Joseph seems to have felt that worship in the mission field would occur spontaneously under the supervision of whatever priesthood was on the scene. Branches by their nature were ephemeral; they were temporary holding tanks where members prepared to gather to Zion. An elder or high priest could call on local members to preach and administer the sacrament—and they did.[18] No more organization was necessary.

Joseph became more aware of the branches in 1833 and 1834, during his journeys to recruit men and money for Zion's Camp. He realized then that these scattered little groups were essential to the Church. He needed their men for Zion's Camp and their funds to purchase land and pay for temple construction. The branches were not interim places of worship for the scattered Saints, but resources to be organized and mobilized in support of the Church centers.

The responsibility for regulating them fell to the council of Twelve Apostles whose calling had been foreseen in a revelation in 1829, before the Church was organized. The formation of this council met the need for worldwide direction of the Church. In February 1835, the apostles were chosen from the Zion's Camp men, a group for whom Joseph had particular affection.[19] He prefaced the selection of the apostles with an account of the trials and sufferings of the camp "and said God had not designed all this for nothing." The three witnesses to the *Book of Mormon* called out the twelve men and gave each one a blessing, emphasizing the role of the twelve to "go forth and gather the Elect," implying they were to be the core missionary force.[20] In a sermon after the blessings were completed, Oliver Cowdery told them to "bid a long farewell to Kirtland . . . even till the great day come." They would be about their missionary business "till your heads are silvered over with age." A few days later, Joseph selected another body of men, largely out of the Zion's Camp contingent, to be the Seventy, a title borrowed from several obscure biblical references. Seventies were traveling quorums, as the priesthood units were called, "also called to preach the gospel, and to be especial witnesses unto the Gentiles and in all the world."[21]

Although charged to "preach the gospel of the son of God to the nations of the earth," the Twelve, in Joseph's conception, fulfilled a second important function of regulating the mission field branches as the high councils regulated Zion and the stakes. Joseph told them they were "to preside over all the churches of the Saints among the Gentiles." At a meeting in May just before the Twelve left Kirtland, he drew the line more sharply: "The Twelve will have no right to go into Zion or any of its stakes and there undertake to regulate the affairs thereof where there is a standing High Council. But it is their duty to go abroad and regulate all matters relative to the different branches of the church." By the same token, "no standing high council has authority to go into the Churches abroad and regulate the matters thereof, for this belongs to the Twelve."[22] The world was divided between the two types of councils, traveling and standing, rounding out the plan for Church government.[23] A purely expedient method for conducting business had been transformed into a system for governing a world divided between the cities of Zion and the mission field.[24] For the time it met the need, though later Joseph gave the Twelve supervising authority over both stakes and mission field.

So far as the records tell, the idea of councils did not originate in a standard revelation. The councils in Kirtland evolved over a three-year period. The founding document for both high councils appointed in 1834 (and for all future high councils) was a set of minutes composed by clerk Orson Hyde for the February 17, 1834, meeting of one of the ad hoc councils. The minutes regularized and extended procedures that had been developing for years. Ad hoc councils had been meeting since the fall of 1831, and one such meeting, on February 17, created the high council system. The minutes of the meeting were revised by Joseph Smith and then discussed, amended, and approved by the council itself.[25]

The council served as a kind of constitutional convention for Church government. Speaking of the occasion, Joseph's history said "the minutes were read three times, and unanimously adopted and received for a form and constitution of the High Council of the Church of Christ hereafter." The priesthood holders plus "fourteen private members" ratified the decision.[26] The procedure set a startling precedent for the Church. The establishment of a basic governing body by the members of the council themselves gave their work the status of revelation. The minutes of the council were included in the *Doctrine and Covenants* alongside revelations coming directly to Joseph Smith. By putting the work of the councils on the same plane as his own revelations, Joseph set a precedent for inspiration other than his own: revelation through a council. The more formal March 1835 revelation, ratifying the past year's developments in Church government, came at the end of the process rather than at the beginning.[27]

Joseph acknowledged the inspiration of the council in the provision that the president of the council was to receive revelation. In case of doubt about true policy, the minutes said, the president "may inquire and obtain the mind of the Lord by revelation." That was nothing new so long as Joseph Smith presided at the council—he had frequently received revelations in council meetings—but the policy applied to Frederick G. Williams or Sidney Rigdon when they held the chair in Joseph's absence, and to David Whitmer running the high council in Clay County. These presidents could learn the mind of the Lord, as could any president of any high council in any stake of Zion. Joseph told the high council in Clay that through them "the will of the Lord might be known on all important occasions in the building up of Zion, and establishing truth in the earth." Rather than monopolizing inspiration, Joseph spread it widely, always with the proviso that revelation at one level did not regulate the authority above.[28]

In his concluding charge to the Twelve Apostles, Joseph admonished them to record their decisions. If a more complete record had been kept of previous council meetings, he said, the minutes "would decide almost every point of doctrine, which might be agitated." The apostles' minutes, he said, will be one of the most important records ever seen. "Such decision[s] will forever remain upon the record, and appear an item of covenant or doctrine."[29] Those words were weighted with meaning because "Doctrine and Covenants" was the title for the compilation of revelations Joseph was preparing for publication. His charge implied that the Twelve Apostles as well as the Prophet would be a conduit for revelation.

Joseph seemed surprisingly eager to reduce his own part in receiving revelations. He seemed uneasy about constantly appealing to heaven for direction. He told one inquirer that the Lord should not be petitioned for every little thing, especially if revelations on the same subject had already been given. "It is a gre[a]t thing to enquire at the hand of God or to come into his presence and we feel fearful to approach him upon subject[s] that are of little or no consequence . . . especially about things the knowledge of which men ought to obtain in all cencerity before God for themselves." They should search out their instructions and rely more on their own judgment. Years before, Edward Partridge had been told in a revelation that "it is not meet that I command in all things."[30]

That reluctance, contradictory as it might seem in a man who gained great authority from his revelations, became more pronounced in 1835. After the organization of the Twelve Apostles, the frequency of canonical revelations dropped precipitously. The commandments to particular people, included among the revelations in the early years, were omitted from later compilations. Instead, Joseph's history was filled with the minutes of the Twelve Apostles' meetings, as if they had become the source of inspiration. The Acts of the Apostles from the New Testament—a history of their activities—became the pattern for revelation rather than the visions of Moses on Sinai. At a moment when Joseph's own revelatory powers were at their peak, he divested himself of sole responsibility for revealing the will of God and invested that gift in the councils of the Church, making it a charismatic bureaucracy.

PRIESTHOOD

The "great revelation" of March 1835 actually combined two revelations. The latter half, comprising verses 59–100 in the current LDS *Doctrine and Covenants*, was received in November 1831, and the first half, verses 1–58, three and a half years later, in connection with organizing the Twelve in February 1835.[31] The earlier revelation, as would be expected, emphasized the offices known up until 1831—elders, priests, teachers, and deacons, from the original simple organization—plus a bishop for the City of Zion, and high priests as revealed to Joseph in June 1831. The 1835 portion contains the passages on councils, a later development. One verse mentions the "standing high councils, at the stakes of Zion"; another "the high council in Zion"; and a third "the twelve traveling counsellors . . . called to be the twelve apostles, or special witnesses of the name of Christ, in all the world."[32] These were the councils formed to govern the gathering cities on the one hand and the mission field on the other.

Besides these two organizational layers, a priesthood strata runs through the 1835 revelation. In its schema, priesthood infuses the two preceding layers, the simple church of April 1830 and the councils for managing the cities of Zion and the branches. The importance of priesthood was not primarily organizational, but grew out of its part in exaltation. Priesthood administered the critical ordinances of baptism and laying on of hands for the gift of the Holy Ghost. The higher priesthood, the priesthood of Melchizedek, held "the key of the mysteries of the kingdom, even the key of the knowledge of God." One revelation said its power was to "have the privilege of receiving the mysteries of the kingdom of heaven—to have the heavens opened unto them—to commune with the general assembly and church of the first born, and to enjoy the communion and presence of God the Father, and Jesus the Mediator of the new covenant."[33] But priesthood with its mysterious exalting power was also integrated into the organizational structure. The mystical powers of priesthood blended with the everyday business of running the church. The president of the High Priesthood was the president of the Church. The bishop, whose office was basically for managing property in Zion and caring for the poor, was made president of the Aaronic Priesthood. High councils were composed of high priests.[34]

It took nearly two years for priesthood to emerge as the ruling principle of Church government. The ordination of high priests in June 1831 had a huge impact on Joseph's conception of priesthood. The extraordinary experience of having the powers of God and of the adversary manifest on the same occasion was not soon forgotten. But the governing scheme laid out in 1830, of first and second elders aided by quarterly conferences of elders, left no room for high priests in the management of Church business, even though after June 1831 they were the ranking priesthood officers. High priests administered spiritual blessings, but what was their role in Church government?

The first revelation of their leadership function came in November 1831 with a commandment calling for "one to be appointed of the High Priesthood to preside over the priesthood, and he shall be called president of the High Priesthood of the Church."[35] At the time, the revelation had surprisingly little effect. The office of president remained in the background for more than a year. Joseph was running the Church through his informal councils, each chaired by a moderator chosen for the occasion. He did not preside in these councils in any formal sense, although his influence was paramount. The 1831 revelation calling for a president of the High Priesthood was not even included in the first batch of revelations prepared for publication that fall. As much as Joseph valued his revelations, he did not ascribe much importance to this one, so far as can be told.[36] The 1831 revelation received little public attention until he attached it to the great revelation on priesthood given to the Twelve Apostles in March 1835.[37] He showed no eagerness to grasp the power that the presidency of the High Priesthood seemingly granted him. Not until the spring of 1833 did the presidency of the High Priesthood register as a notable office in Church government.

The grand priesthood revelation of 1835, however, indicated that the very nature of the Melchizedek priesthood was administrative and presidential. "The Melchizedek priesthood holds the right of presidency, and has power and authority over all the offices in the church," said the priesthood revelation, and by 1835, priesthood controlled the entire structure of Church government.[38] This blending of priesthood and administrative authority extended down through the ranks to the extremities of the Church. Every priesthood holder, virtually every male member, held membership in a "quorum," a word meaning a "select company." Deacons, teachers, priests, and elders were formed into separate quorums made up of between twelve and ninety-six members, each with its own presidency. In their quorums, the men received instructions from their presidencies on the duties of their offices.[39]

The combination of sacral priesthood power and Church government was unusual in the visionary tradition. The Shakers, like the Mormons in many ways, also had authoritarian leadership and structured organization to go with their ecstatic visions; elders and eldresses governed "families" of a hundred or so, and deacons and deaconesses managed temporal affairs. The mature men, a kind of council, played a leading role. Strict obedience was required of all members. But no sacral priesthood exercised leadership or held office.[40] In emphasizing priesthood, Mormonism moved to the other end of the religious spectrum, toward Roman Catholicism with its sacraments and the mysterious power of the priests to transform bread and wine into Christ's flesh and blood. The sacral and the ecclesiastical combined in Mormonism as in Catholicism, adding to the strength of Church government.

This vision of priesthood governance was crystalizing in the spring of 1833 when Joseph and Frederick G. Williams were planning the temples for Zion and Kirtland. The potency of the priesthood was manifest in the "altars"—really banks of seats and pulpits—constructed in the assembly rooms of the temples. At one end of the room, altars were provided for the president of the High Priesthood and his counselors, for the bishop, for high priests, and elders—all offices of the higher priesthood. At the other end, the presidency of the lower priesthood, the priests, the teachers, and the deacons each had an altar. The priesthood structure stood preeminent among the governing agencies of the Church. The councils that managed the day-to-day business had no place on these stands. No seats were set aside for the high councils or the Twelve Apostles. The Presidency, the bishop, and the priesthood quorums were the primary structures of Church government. Judging from the temple altars, the names of the temples in the City of Zion, and the constitutions given by revelation, the Church as a whole was conceived as an organization of priesthood. "All other authorities, or offices in the church," the 1835 priesthood revelation said, "are appendages to this priesthood."[41]

Absent from these leadership positions was a place for women. They were unrepresented on the stands and in Church government, except to the extent that their husbands and fathers stood in for them. Women had no equivalent to the quorums for men. The organizational plan would continue to evolve but at this point women were subsumed under the men, the same assumption prevailing in the American political system in 1835. Mormon women received instruction from their fathers and husbands, spoke their minds in the family, and exercised spiritual gifts in public meetings.[42]

FAMILY

Winding through the great priesthood revelation of 1835 was a fourth theme that would in time bring women into priesthood government. In addition to the simple Church, the councils for the city stakes of Zion, and priesthood, the final layer was lineage and family. A passage in the 1835 revelation on bishops provided that "no man has a legal right to this office, to hold the keys of this priesthood, except he be a literal descendant of Aaron."[43] Claiming an office by virtue of descent struck a dissonant note in a Protestant and republican world where calls to the ministry came from God and public office went to the meritorious. The idea went back to monarchical society with its hereditary titles and to ancient Judaism with its tribe of hereditary priests, the Levites, and the requirement that priests should be sons of Aaron.

The return to ancient lineage priesthood appears to be another manifestation of Joseph's penchant for Hebrew religion and no more than a gesture, considering that the next verse provides that high priests may fill the office of bishop as they may officiate in any office. The assignment of the bishopric by lineage had no practical effect if high priests could occupy the office regardless. Yet the idea was not allowed to drop. Later in the 1835 revelation, the principle of descent in the office of bishop was restated with greater emphasis: "For unless he is a literal descendant of Aaron he cannot hold the keys of that priesthood," immediately qualified again by the provision of high priests qualifying to be bishop.[44] With little chance of actually installing descendants of Aaron as bishops, since none were known in the Church, Joseph seemed to be highlighting the general principle of descent through bloodlines, as if that had some importance in itself.

Appointment by lineage governed appointment to another office first announced in the 1835 revelation. The Twelve Apostles were authorized to appoint "evangelical ministers" in large branches of the Church and told that "the order of this priesthood was confirmed to be handed down from father to son, and rightly belongs to the literal descendants of the chosen seed." The title "evangelical minister" quickly went out of usage in the Church, replaced by the term "patriarch." Why "evangelical minister" was ever used, considering the title suggested a gospel preacher, was never explained, though it probably was based on the use of the word "evangelist" in the New Testament, the model for Church organization.[45] "Patriarch" much more accurately conveyed the duties of the office, which were to bless people as Abraham, Isaac, and Jacob blessed their offspring and prophecied their futures. As was true for the ancient patriarchs, the priesthood office of patriarch descended from father to son.

The office emerged out of the practice of public blessings administered by Joseph and by various fathers, most notably Joseph's own father, Joseph Smith Sr. Gradually these spontaneous blessings evolved into more systematic blessings of comfort and direction and were regularized in the office of patriarch. At the School of the Prophets in January 1833, as Joseph was about to wash his father's feet, he asked for a father's "blessing." Joseph Sr.

laid his hands on his son's head and promised that he would "continue in his Priests office untill Christ come."[46] The following fall, Joseph began blessing the men closest to him, Sidney Rigdon and Frederick G. Williams and others. Joseph wrote down meditations on their characters that melded into blessings. Williams, Joseph felt, "is not a man of many words but is ever winning because of his constant mind." "God grant that he may overcome all evil." The next month he entered similar blessings for his father, mother, and sisters; his brothers Hyrum, Samuel, and William; and Oliver Cowdery. Of his father, Joseph wrote that "when his head is fully ripe he shall behold himself as an olive tree whose branches are bowed down with much fruit." In these early meditations, he wove blessings, family, and the Old Testament patriarchs into a fabric of clan, spirituality, and priesthood.[47]

In late 1833 or 1834, Joseph ordained his father as patriarch (there is a dispute over whether it was December 1833 or December 1834).[48] Although couched in formal language, Joseph's blessing on Joseph Sr. expressed the feelings of a son for a father who had suffered repeated defeats. This was a man who had lost one farm when his storekeeping business failed, who had been reduced to tenancy for fourteen years while his children were young, and then lost a second farm when he missed the mortgage payments. Fifty-eight years old when the Church was organized, Joseph Sr. was back in tenancy, with no house or land to call his own. Defeated by the rigors of the economic order, he was told by his son he would be a prince over his posterity. "Blessed of the Lord is my father," Joseph said, "for he shall stand in the midst of his posterity and shall be comforted by their blessings when he is old and bowed down with years, and he shall be called a prince over them." Like Adam, he would assemble his children—his one undoubted accomplishment—and "sit in the general assembly of patriarchs, even in council with the Ancient of Days when he shall sit and all the patriarchs with him—and shall enjoy his right and authority under the direction of the Ancient of Days." Whatever else Joseph Sr. lacked, "his seed shall rise up and call him blessed. . . . his name shall be had in remembrance to the end."[49]

Joseph Sr. seemed to understand that his sons had redeemed his life. When he blessed Joseph and Hyrum in December 1834, he thanked them for enduring the hardships of their early lives. Hyrum, Joseph Sr. said, had "borne the burthen and heat of the day" and "labored much for the good of thy father's family." The father was grateful for Hyrum's kindness in tolerating Joseph Sr.'s weakness. "Thou hast always stood by thy father, and reached forth the helping hand to lift him up, when he was in affliction, and though he has been out of the way through wine, thou has never forsaken him, nor laughed him to scorn." Joseph Sr.'s candid words speak the sorrows of a failing father in a cruel time. Besides his business failures, his weakness for wine brought him down and opened him to the scorn of his own children. Joseph Sr. was grateful that his sons did not laugh: "For all these kindnesses the Lord my God will bless thee." In return, he could bless Hyrum with "the same blessings with which Jacob blessed his son Joseph, for thou art his true descendant." He could not give his son wealth, but he could say "thy posterity shall be numbered with the house of Ephraim, and with them thou shalt stand up to crown the tribes of Israel."[50]

Joseph Sr. could make these promises because Joseph Jr. had given him priesthood, while the father had given his son only hardship. Joseph Sr.'s blessing on Joseph Jr. acknowledged that "thou has suffered much in thy youth, and the poverty and afflictions of thy father's family have been a grief to thy soul." Joseph Jr. had mourned his family's humiliations and assumed responsibility for lifting them from their low state. "Thou has stood by thy father, and like Shem, would have covered his nakedness, rather than see him exposed to shame." There must have been times when Joseph supported his father through public humiliation. "When the daughters of the Gentiles laughed," Joseph Sr. said to his son, "thy heart has been moved with a just anger to avenge thy kindred." The words may explain why Joseph joined his father in money-digging ventures despite his reluctance, why he stayed home from church when his mother took the other children to Presbyterian meetings, why Joseph wept when his long unchurched father was baptized into the Church of Christ on the day of its organization. He had made his father's pain his own. Now, at last, the father could bless his son "with the blessings of thy fathers Abraham, Isaac and Jacob." Joseph Sr. had given his son nothing for a worldly inheritance, and Joseph Jr. had met this lack by giving his father the power to bless his sons. In the seating in the Kirtland temple, Joseph Sr. sat in the highest pulpit above his son.[51]

Joseph Sr.'s blessings suggest the personal meaning of priesthood to early members. Whether weak or strong, rich or poor, priesthood holders could pass priesthood to their sons. The 1835 priesthood revelation named the patriarchs who received the priesthood from father Adam: Seth, Enos, Cainan, Mahalaleel, Jared, Enoch, and Methuselah; after Adam died, Lamech received the priesthood from Seth and Noah from Methuselah. As a later revelation was to say, the priesthood "came down from the fathers." Priesthood was a father's legacy to his son, counting for more than lands and herds. In the overall plan, material possessions had a part too. Zion promised an "inheritance" to all who migrated there. Fathers who lacked the wealth to provide for their children, as many did in this fast-moving age, were promised land in the holy city. The word "inheritance" for describing properties in Zion expressed a father's wish to bestow a legacy on his children.[52] In restoring priesthood, Joseph restored fatherhood.[53]

All of these themes were layered into the revelation on priesthood in March 1835. The remnants of the first Church organization of April 1830 can be glimpsed in the offices of elders, priests, teachers, and deacons, the most familiar Protestant offices in 1830. By early 1831, the Zion layer of bishops was added and then, in 1834, high councils to regulate the Church in Zion's city and its stakes; a year later, the traveling council of apostles was formed to carry the gospel to the world (assisted by the Seventies) and regulate branches in the mission field. Running through all the offices is the authority of priesthood with its power to perform ordinances and bestow spiritual blessings, the exalting authority that brought people to God. Instead of remaining an ethereal force, set above practical affairs, priesthood ran the Church. High priests served as bishops, they occupied the seats in the high council, and the three presidents of the High Priesthood, the First Presidency, presided over the whole Church. The final office, evangelical minister, or patriarch, linked the Church to the antiquity of Adam and his descendants down to Noah, harking back to a time when priesthood came through lineage, and priesthood and fatherhood were equated. The revelation restored those familial elements of priesthood, perhaps to heal the wounds inflicted on fatherhood by the modern economy.

LAYERS OF CHURCH ORGANIZATION, 1831–35

YEAR	LAYER	OFFICES
1830	Simple organization	Elders, priests, teachers, deacons
1831	City of Zion	Bishops
1834–35	Zion geography	High councils over stakes
		Twelve Apostles over branches
1831–35	Ordinances and endowments	Aaronic and Melchizedek priesthoods
1833–35	Lineage priesthood	Bishops, patriarchs

CHURCH ORGANIZATION CHART, 1835

ADMINISTRATIVE:

First Presidency
    President of the High Priesthood
        First Counselor
        Second Counselor
Twelve Apostles
    Preside over branches in the mission field
High Councils of Twelve High Priests
    Preside over stakes of Zion

PRIESTHOOD:

    Melchizedek Priesthood
        High Priests
        Seventies
        Elders
    Aaronic Priesthood
        Bishop (President)
        Priests
        Teachers
        Deacons
    Patriarch

POLITICAL THEORY

What did this vision of priesthood and Church government mean to Joseph? What was accomplished by raising up a priesthood hierarchy in a democratic age? The implications of this labyrinthine organization are complex and contradictory. The democratic elements are easily identified in the overall structure: the distribution of offices to all male members and the elimination of a professional clergy. No clerical class ever formed in Mormon congregations, and no special education was required of its preachers. Ordinary converts took charge of the little branches that grew up in the missionaries' wake. Priesthood was a right of citizenship in the Kingdom of God. The democratic elements were underscored by calling the chief Church officer and the leaders of quorums "president." In the same spirit, a later addition to an early revelation provided that "no person is to be ordained to any office in this church, where there is a regularly organized branch of the same, without the vote of that church."[54] Even the three members of the Church Presidency were brought before conferences of members for approval.

But the confirmation of officers was not an election. Approval by the people indicated that officers were "upheld by the confidence, faith, and prayer of the church," not that the officers represented the people's interests.[55] "The people" had no political standing in Mormon thought. The word "people" never appears in the revelations except in phrases like "all nations, kindreds, tongues, and people." The Church system was quite different from popular government. The latter was based in a fundament of popular sovereignty. Church officers served the people but were not beholden to them. In the Church, God was sovereign.

The revelation on priesthood does not locate the origins of authority exactly in divine ordination either. One would expect Joseph Smith to buttress his authority by highlighting his call from God, but one looks in vain in the revelation on priesthood for a passage about transmitting power from heaven to earth, from God to Joseph Smith. The priesthood revelation is not even given in the voice of God. It opens with an oblique sentence obscuring the identity of the speaker: "There are, in the church, two priesthoods, namely: the Melchizedek and the Aaronic, including the Levitical priesthood." The speaker remains unidentified until halfway through the text, where the older portion of the revelation begins. Until then, a knowing guide describes priesthood as if to neophytes. The classic "thus saith the Lord" is never sounded. An experienced priest leads us through a temple he knows well. "Why the first is called the Melchizedek Priesthood," we are told in the opening lines, "is because Melchizedek was such a great high priest." Our guide knows priesthood ways. "Before his day it was called *the holy priesthood, after the order of the Son of God.*" The title has been shortened "out of respect or reverence to the name of the Supreme Being."[56]

The origins of priesthood are never revealed and, according to the revelation, it had no beginning. The priesthood goes back before the foundation of the world. This ancient order has always existed, descending from one ancient priest to the next. Only an occasional disruption in the orderly sequence required reordination under the hands of God, and Joseph Smith is not such an exception. He received his priesthood from John the Baptist, Peter, James, John, and, later, Elijah. The revelation locates the source of authority in an ancient order coming down through time. The Melchizedek priesthood, we are told, has presided over "all the offices in the church, in all ages of the world."[57] Now priesthood order is being reconstituted in the latter days.

These peculiar conceptions make it difficult to understand how priesthood could find its place among the governments of Joseph's day. Would not priesthood look like an alien system from another age? The revelations have little to say about democracy, the form of government to which priesthood had to be compared, but the contradictions, it would seem, would make it impossible for converts to live under the priesthood in the Church and function as democratic citizens in the general society.

In theory, the great advantage of democratic government was the effective containment of power, the traditional enemy of liberty. The change from monarchical to republican government had been motivated by a desire to contain the abuses suffered under British rule.[58] By placing ultimate political authority in the hands of the people, democracy kept rulers in check. Subjecting them to regular elections meant they could not stray too far from the public interest.

Like a democracy, Church government had provisions for removing bad officials, including fallen prophets. The president of the Church could be tried before the Church's "common council," consisting of the bishop and twelve counselors.[59] John Corrill, the coolheaded member who left when he would not yield to Joseph's authority, claimed he was assured of democratic procedures for checking power:

> Smith and Rigdon taught the church that these authorities, in ruling or watching over the church, were nothing more than servants to the church, and that the church, as a body, had the power in themselves to do any thing that either or all of these authorities could do, and that if either or all of these constituted authorities became deranged or broken down, or did not perform their duty to the satisfaction of the church, the church had a right to rise up in a body and put them out of office, make another selection and re-organize them, and thus keep in order, for the power was in the people and not in the servants.[60]

But Corrill exaggerated the importance of restraints on power under priesthood government. Limitations on the higher authorities functioned only at the margins of Church activity. The provision for trying the Church president resembled impeachment in a democratic government, a drastic resort in an emergency.[61] Ordinary, day-by-day checks on power had almost no place in priesthood government.

The democratic concern about political power seemed beside the point when the power of the priesthood was the power of God. In the revelations, the word "power" referred to the Lord's power, not to the power of government. "The power and authority of the higher, or Melchizedek priesthood, is to hold the keys of all the spiritual blessings of the church." The connection with God transformed power from a necessary evil to a power to be magnified, embraced, pursued. Rather than restricting God's power, people wanted it to fill their lives. Instead of being a danger, power fulfilled their deepest desire. Priesthood government was desirable because "in the ordinances thereof the power of godliness is manifest."[62] Instead of suspicion, there was trust and yearning. Power was not to be checked but released and expanded.

The problem of priesthood power was not containment, but worthiness. To acquire the power of God and exercise it suitably, the holders of power had to make themselves acceptable. "What manner of men ought ye to be?" was the question. Priesthood councils aimed for righteous administration, for decisions made "in all righteousness, in holiness and lowliness of heart; meekness and long suffering; and in faith and virtue and knowledge; temperance, patience, godliness brotherly kindness and charity."[63] Men qualified themselves for office by their virtue. High council trials for unworthy behavior served the purpose of elections in democratic government by removing the unworthy from office.

Joseph learned by hard experience about the temptations of power. A

few years later, he reflected on the universal tendency of men to abuse
authority: "We have learned by sad experience that it is the nature and disposition of almost all men as soon as they get a little authority as they suppose they will imediatly begin to exercise unritious dominion."[64] But he
would not resort to institutional restraints like the United States Constitution's checks and balances. Repentance was the solution to bad government. "No power or influance can or ought to be maintained by virtue of
the priesthood, only by persuasion by long suffering, by gentleness and
meakness and by love unfaigned." He assumed that the priesthood instilled
"kindness," and "pure knowledge." The identity of priesthood holders as
servants of God was expected to overcome the human tendency to dominate. As he said, "the rights of the priesthood are inseperably connected
with the powers of heaven and . . . the powers of heaven cannot be con-
troled nor handled only upon the principals of rightiousness." Priesthood
had to be heavenly and godly. It created the moral environment that established the terms of power.

As an ideal, righteousness served priesthood government as equality
serves democracy. Never perfectly realized in practice, righteousness and
equality constitute the inner spirit of their respective governmental systems. Ultimately, God checked unrighteous exercise of priesthood power.
Unrighteous Church government would collapse. "The heavens with draw
themselves the spirit of the Lord is grieved and when it has withdrawn
amen to the priesthood or the authority of that man."[65]

The priesthood model of righteous government was akin to political
theories of the eighteenth century. In its emphasis on virtue in rulers and
people, Church government resembled the classical republicanism of the
revolutionary generation and government by a patriot king who sought
only the good of the nation. In either republican or monarchical forms,
good government in these theories required virtue at the center. In the dark
times of the Confederation, John Jay wrote to George Washington that
"the mass of men are neither wise nor good, and the virtue like the other
resources of a country, can only be drawn to a point and exerted by strong
circumstances ably managed, or a strong government ably administered."[66]
The problem was how to bring virtuous men to power, whether as patriot
kings or as a corps of dedicated citizens ruling for the public good.

Though kindred in spirit, priesthood government went far beyond classical republicanism or idealized monarchy in bringing people to God. Priesthood government sought to redeem people, not just serve their interests.
Priests were godly teachers rather than protectors of the people's rights.
Priesthood government was redemptive. High priests held "the keys of
all the spiritual blessings of the church." Aaronic priests held "the keys of the
minstring of angels" and administered ordinances like baptism. People did

not "submit" to the priesthood in the sense of yielding their wills to higher authority. They "received" it, as an 1832 revelation said:

> All they who receive this priesthood receiveth me, saith the Lord, for he that receiveth my servants receiveth me, and he that receiveth me receiveth my Father, and he that receiveth my Father receiveth my Father's kingdom. Therefore, all that my Father hath shall be given unto him.[67]

Under priesthood authority, as outlined in the revelations, the exercise of power was to be wholly benevolent, receiving and giving, not ordering and submitting. Government was to bless people. Properly exercised, authority eliminated coercion. Priests in this kingdom would rule like God Himself—without force. "Thy dominion shall be an everlasting dominion, and without compulsory means it shall flow unto thee for eve[r] and ever."[68] Joseph Smith is famous for saying that he governed his people by a thread. "I teach them correct principles, and they govern themselves."[69]

Joseph Smith knew, of course, that Church power, especially his own, would not appear benevolent. In a democratic society, so much authority in a single person set off alarms. As he told the Missouri Saints, people looked on him as a "Tyrant,! Pope!! King!!! Usurper!!!!"[70] Besides the repeated charges of his enemies, close associates criticized him for abusing authority. Considering the traditional dread of unchecked power, the charges seem inevitable. Joseph's confidence in the righteousness of rulers seems naive. The accepted wisdom of the founding era in United States history was that, as David Hume put it, "in contriving any system of government . . . every man out to be supposed a knave."[71] Joseph's plan of church government assumed the opposite; priesthood holders could be trusted with power. They would constitute a government that blessed and redeemed people and was received with gladness rather than fear and suspicion.

FOURTEEN

VISITORS

1835

Curiosity to see a man that was reputed to be a Jew, caused many to call during the day and more particularly at evening Suspicions were entertained that the said Joshua was the noted Mathias of New York, spoke so much of in the public prints on account of the trials he underwent in that place before a court of justice . . . after supper I proposed that he should deliver a lecture to us, he did so sitting in his chair.

JOSEPH SMITH, Journal, November 9, 1835

BY THE MID-1830S, Joseph was spending hours each week with visitors. While engaged in copying blessings one day, Cowdery noted that "we were thronged a part of the time with company, so that our labor, in this thing, was hindered; but we obtained many precious things." The next day Joseph wrote that while he "was at home writing blessings for my most beloved Brotheren[.] I have been hindered by a multitude of visitors."[1]

Joseph enjoyed the company. One entry recorded a visit from a party leaving for Missouri. "Joy filled our hearts and we blessed them and bid them God speed and promised them a safe Journy and took them by the hand and bid them farewell for a season Oh! May God grant them long life and good days."[2] Joseph wrote those sentences in his own hand, expressing, as always, more emotion than entries made by his scribes.

Some of the visitors were strangers, curious about Mormonism. By 1835, news of the Mormons was becoming public knowledge. As early as the summer of 1831, James Gordon Bennett, touring the state with Martin Van Buren, filed a story with the *Morning Enquirer and Courier* in New York City that began: "You have heard of MORMONISM—who has not? Paragraph has followed paragraph in the newspapers, recounting the movements, detailing their opinions and surprising distant readers with the traits of a singularly new religious sect which had its origin in this state."[3] Looking for the sensational, newspaper editors seized upon reports and passed the word along.

A Mormon-owned newspaper led to the visit of the Rev. John Hewitt in

June 1835. Hewitt came to investigate the Mormons on behalf of a congregation of Christians in Barnsley, England. A letter from the group referred to "one of your papers brought here by a merchant from New York." On the basis of this report, the English believers recognized the Mormons as kindred spirits. "The Lord hath seen our joy and gladness to hear," the letter said, "that He was raising up a people for Himself in that part of the New World, as well as here." Hewitt's visit, though it led nowhere, raised the question of affiliations and alliances with other religious movements in the 1830s.

Hewitt was introduced as a one-time mathematics teacher in the Rotherham Independent Seminary and pastor of a church in Barnsley. Excommunicated from the Church of England for teaching new doctrines, he had been preaching to a flock who followed him out of the church. After two years, he had come to America to explore the possibility of migration, perhaps to join forces with the Mormons. "Many will follow," the letter assured the Saints, "should he approve of the country, etc., who will help the cause, because the Lord hath favored them with this world's goods." Joseph's eyes must have lingered on that sentence, considering the impoverished state of the Church treasury. The Barnsley Christians assured the Saints of their resolve to come whatever the opposition. They had heard of the attacks on the Mormons and were not discouraged. "We understand that persecution had been great among you, or would be, but we were commanded not to fear, for He would be with us."[4]

Although Joseph knew nothing of Hewitt's church, the group's beliefs resembled those of the Mormons. Following the New Testament practice, they too called themselves "saints." One sentence in the letter prayed, "O, may our faith increase that He may have Evangelists, Apostles, and Prophets, filled with the power of the Spirit, and performing His will in destroying the works of darkness." The Catholic Apostolic Church, as the Barnsley group's larger affiliation was later called, sought to restore the apostleship and other offices of the New Testament church. Between 1832 and 1835, church leaders in London had appointed twelve apostles by revelation, and the congregation in Barnsley, hearing of the Mormon prophet and possibly of the appointment of the Twelve, had been intrigued. The English apostles were set apart on July 14, 1835, just six months after the Mormon apostles in Kirtland.[5]

The Catholic Apostolic Church (or "congregations gathered under apostles," the name they preferred) originated in the preaching of Edward Irving, a Scottish Presbyterian who had moved to London in 1822 and quickly attracted a fashionable following. So large and stylish were his congregations that listeners' coaches lined up for four miles outside the Caledonian Chapel in Hatton Garden. His followers included members of

Parliament, rich lawyers and bankers, and clergymen from the Church of England and the Scottish Kirk. Thomas Carlyle, the famed essayist, came to hear him, and George Canning, the British foreign minister, mentioned Irving's name favorably in Parliament.[6]

Irving's views resembled those of the millenarians who had convened in Albury, England, in 1826 to study the timing of the Second Coming. The clergymen and laymen, though differing on details, agreed that "our blessed Lord will shortly appear," accompanied by heavy judgments on the church and its final destruction. During this time, the Jews would be restored to their own land, and at the end of the judgments, the "universal blessedness" of the millennium would commence. Preaching on millennial themes, Irving shared the excitement spreading through England and Ireland between 1826 and 1830 about the coming end.[7]

In preparation for these final events, Irving believed, spiritual gifts, like tongues, prophecy, and healing, would be bestowed on the church along with the apostolic authority to give the Holy Ghost. When he heard stories of people speaking prophetic utterances in the west of Scotland, he went to investigate. His followers prayed fervently for a return of spiritual powers, relying on the same promise in Joel 2 that Moroni quoted to Joseph Smith about "your sons and your daughters shall prophesy." In 1831, prophesying and tongues broke out in Irving's London congregation. Many were impressed, but public opinion, offended by doctrinal excesses, turned against him. The trustees of his London church, backed by the London Presbytery, removed him from office. In 1833 Irving was cut off from the Church of Scotland.[8]

His followers regrouped and formed independent congregations as a movement to warn and prepare Christianity. Seven congregations met in London, and others collected throughout England and Scotland. Unfortunately for Irving, he was discredited after his excommunication. In 1834, broken in spirit, he died, and the movement came under the control of a strong-willed lawyer, J. B. Cardale, allied with the millenarian Henry Drummond. They set about to institutionalize prophecy and speaking in tongues. During worship services, prophets sat alongside the preachers and interrupted sermons with spontaneous "utterances." Apostles were called by the utterances of these prophets. Cardale, the first apostle, went about the church with Edward Taplin, one of the prophets, selecting others. The "Council of Zion," made up of representatives of the seven London churches, set apart the apostles in imitation of the missionary calls of Paul and Barnabas.[9]

The Kirtland Mormons knew nothing of this history when Hewitt arrived in 1835. He came in the spirit of investigation that had taken Irving's friends to the west of Scotland to investigate spiritual gifts. The Barnsley congregation, a satellite of the London churches, wanted to know if there was in fact a prophet with the Holy Ghost in America. They may also have been contemplating the advantages of migration as the letter suggested. In any event, Hewitt's involvement with the Mormons was brief. He left at once for Fairport, ten miles north of Kirtland on Lake Erie. The Kirtland brethren expected a prompt return but never heard from him again. A letter to Fairport followed by a visit from Cowdery evoked no response. The last the Mormons heard, Hewitt had opened a school in Painesville.[10]

Were the Mormons ready to join forces with kindred spirits like the Catholic Apostolic Church? Irving emerged from a vortex of English millenarianism that bore many resemblances to Mormonism. The Irvingites shared the Mormon sense of an imminent Second Coming for which the world must prepare. Both thought the Christian churches were irreparably dysfunctional. The millenarians believed the Jews would return to their own land and be converted. They doubtless knew of Joseph S. C. F. Frey, a converted Jew and head of the London Society for Promoting Christianity amongst the Jews, who believed the ten lost tribes dwelt among the American Indians. If Joseph had learned of these groups, would he have considered a combined effort to preach the Second Coming of Christ? The millenarian fervor burned brightly in Britain in the late 1820s.[11] Were there grounds for an alliance?

Other religious movements were amalgamating to form stronger denominations. The most notable was the merger of the followers of Alexander Campbell and Barton Stone. Both had broken from the Presbyterians earlier in the century over the restoration of New Testament Christianity. Campbell had gathered followers in western Virginia and Ohio, Stone in Kentucky and Ohio. In 1832, representatives of these "restorationist" groups merged under the name Disciples of Christ. Restorationist Christian congregations in New England allied themselves under the working title of the Christian Connection, which later evolved into the Christian Church. Where actual denominations were not formed, people with similar doctrinal interests met in conferences, like the millenarians at Albury, to work on biblical prophecies. The Mormons were left out of all these conversations. They were not even considered—save for Hewitt's congregation in Barnsley—as candidates for an alliance. Mormonism resisted ecumenism.[12]

An 1842 editorial in the Nauvoo *Times and Seasons* about the Catholic Apostolic Church, possibly by Joseph Smith, indicated why a merger was impossible. The editorial acknowledged that the Irvingites had come close to the "truth perhaps the nearest of any of our modern sectarians." They had apostles, prophets, and the gifts of tongues and healing. But Irving mistakenly believed "all supernatural manifestations" were of God and honored the prophetesses who spoke "strange utterances." This recognition put Irving in a subordinate position. When his followers prophesied, "Mr. Irving, or any of his ministers had to keep silence," a position Joseph Smith would never accept.[13] Joseph kept the ultimate authority to himself. While encouraging all the brethren to speak by the Holy Ghost and bestowing on every council the authority to receive revelation for its domain, Joseph remained the prophet for the Church, the only one to write in the name of God. He had seen the error in acknowledging Hiram Page's seerstone in the very first year of the Church's organization. Six months later, he quelled the visionaries in Kirtland, shutting down the kind of spontaneous outbursts that paralyzed Irving and his colleagues. So eager were Irvingites for divine manifestations that they embraced the slightest trace of spiritual gifts as words of prophecy, and as a result prophecy brought chaos to the church. Joseph, blessed with an abundance of revelation, felt no need to embrace every outburst as precious intelligence from heaven. His own revelations came so frequently and authoritatively that he dismissed lesser manifestations, reserving the role of chief revelator for himself. Any effort at ecumenical collaboration had to come to terms with Joseph's authority.

Differing views of the canon also stood in the way. Others could see that the Bible did not restrict Joseph's revelations. He expanded as well as explicated scripture. While saturated with Bible language, the *Book of Mormon* was an entirely new history of a people whose existence was scarcely glimpsed in the Bible.[14] In the Book of Moses, Joseph added pages to the biblical accounts of Enoch, Moses, and Adam. His new histories and doctrines were tied to the Bible, and the Mormon elders claimed they taught an authentic Bible gospel, but for Joseph, the Bible was a gate, not a fence. Joseph's daring—his blasphemous audacity, his enemies would say—erected a barrier to collaboration. "Monstrous claims," Josiah Quincy called them in 1844.[15] What point was there in looking for common ground, when Joseph had departed for other realms entirely? He created a transbiblical world unlike anything known in the Christian churches and had no interest in forming alliances with less venturous souls.

MATTHIAS

Later that fall, Joseph received a visit from another potential ally. On a Monday morning in November, a man fated to influence the modern understanding of Joseph Smith far out of proportion to the length of his stay arrived in Kirtland. Some historians define Joseph's place in American history by his seeming similarities to this tall, slender, gray-bearded visitor who called himself Joshua the Jewish Minister. The stranger wore a "sea green frock coat, & pantaloons of the same, black fur hat with narrow brim," and while he spoke, he shut his eyes and scowled.[16] Not one to be put off by appearances, Joseph may have taken Joshua seriously at first. They talked for most of the day. Joseph gave a lengthy account of his early visions, a story he did not often tell, and, at Joseph's invitation, Joshua discoursed on Daniel's vision of the figure with feet of iron and clay, which Joshua said symbolized the confusion and disunion in modern society. He recommended withdrawal from this blighted nation to avoid being trapped in its ruins, sentiments with which Joseph would have agreed.

Curious to see a reputed Jew, a number of Kirtland Saints called to meet the visitor. Some speculated that he was the notorious Robert Matthias, who had recently stood trial for murder in New York and served time for whipping his daughter. Undeterred, Joseph invited Joshua to lecture that evening, and during his discourse, the guest admitted to being Matthias. The next morning, Joshua claimed descent from the apostle Matthias, chosen to replace Judas in the original twelve apostles. Matthias's spirit was resurrected in him, and eternal life consisted of this transmigration of souls from father to son. At this point, Joseph moved to end the discussion. He told Matthias that "his doctrine was of the Devil that he was in reality in possession of [a] wicked and depraved spirit." Matthias remained another night with the Smiths, and the next day after breakfast Joseph "told him, that my God told me that his God is the Devil, and I could not keep him any longer." "And so I for once," Joseph reflected in his journal, "cast out the Devil in bodily shape."[17]

Joseph quickly dismissed Matthias, but he has since been plagued by Matthias's ghost. Their two names are still linked as "seers of the new republic" who "went beyond evangelical orthodoxy into direct and often heretical experience of the supernatural." The opening chapter of the best modern study of Matthias is entitled "Two Prophets at Kirtland." Joseph and Matthias are classed as leading examples of an extraordinary American tradition. "Extremist prophets have a long and remarkably continuous history in the United States," coming down to modern cult leaders.[18] Joseph and Matthias met in Kirtland, and many believe they have remained together ever since.

Born of strict Calvinist parents in Washington County, New York, in 1788, and named Robert Matthews, Matthias had mixed success as a carpenter and storekeeper. Exhibiting strong animosity toward women, he beat his wife and failed to provide for his six children. In 1830, he had a vision of a flood about to descend on Albany and fled the city. Leaving his wife, Matthias wandered alone through western New York. In 1831, he decided his family name meant he was a reincarnation of the biblical Matthias and began to tell all who would listen. Returning to New York City, he convinced a Christian perfectionist named Elijah Pierson that Pierson was a reincarnation of Elijah the Tishbite. Pierson and Benjamin and Ann Folger, a pair of devout Christians, joined Matthias and offered him support. In 1832 they and a few other believers began living communally in the Folger country house in Sing Sing, New York.

In lectures given at the supper table, Matthias taught the household that he was the governing spirit, or God, sent to establish male government over women. People were not to pray or read the scriptures but to listen to him, the Father. He outfitted himself in his trademark green frock coat with varicolored pantaloons and a crimson sash with twelve tassels. When people got sick or things went wrong, he blamed the trouble on the sufferer's disobedience. He assigned couples to marry by designating them as match spirits. For himself he chose Benjamin Folger's wife, proclaiming her Mother in the Kingdom. When Elijah Pierson died, increasingly suspicious locals brought charges against Matthias. Murder could not be proven, but Matthias was convicted of beating his grown daughter and sentenced to four months in prison. He arrived in Kirtland not long after his release in the summer of 1835.[19]

Joseph sensed the gulf between himself and Matthias when he said Matthias's God was the devil, but considering the two together actually clarifies the nature of early Mormonism. Was it a radical cult, as the comparison to Matthias implies, led by a charismatic figure whose credulous followers blindly obeyed his commands? One difference was that, unlike Matthias's little household, Mormonism had an existence apart from Joseph Smith. Missionaries preached the gospel without mentioning his name; most converts accepted Mormonism without meeting the Prophet. The opposite was true of Matthias. His followers were under the spell of his personality. He was the God of the kingdom. After his downfall, his religion perished with him. After Joseph Smith died, Mormonism went on growing. Matthias's religion was driven by his personality, Joseph's by doctrine, program, and organization. Matthias created a perishable cult, Joseph a viable church.

Paradoxically, it was the revelations, the main reason for linking Joseph to Matthias, that differentiated the two. Unlike other American prophets, Joseph wrote his revelations down, turning them into scripture. The *Book of Mormon* and the published books of revelations made Mormonism conservative in a churchly sense. Recorded, available for study in printed compilations, and canonized, the texts formed a body of doctrine inviting interpretation and the formation of orthodoxy. The texts anchored Mormonism in the same way that the Bible and the creeds anchor Christian orthodoxy or the Constitution limits lawmaking. Mary Baker Eddy's *Science and Health with Key to the Scriptures* helped Christian Science evolve from a potentially radical sect into a respectable, staid church. In the same fashion, the Doctrine and Covenants stabilized the doctrines of Mormonism.[20]

Early Mormonism was further regularized by its organization. Joseph Smith's interest in ecclesiastical structure, unlike cult leaders and extremist prophets, led to the creation of offices, councils, and diffused authority. The success of Mormonism, compared to Matthias's short-lived Kingdom, was due to Joseph's instinct for institution-building. In Utah, Mormonism easily moved from sect to established religion, because all the elements of a church were present already.

In one respect, Matthias and Joseph were similar: both men believed in immediate revelation. They both discerned what orthodoxy had forgotten: that biblical authority rested on communication from God. Believers embraced the Bible because its words originated in heaven. Protestantism had smothered this self-evident fact by relegating revelation to a bygone age, making the Bible an archive rather than a living reality. The extremist prophets brought revelation into the present, renewing contact with the Bible's God. In that, Joseph and Matthias stood together. Even the evangelist Charles Finney, before his conversion, marveled that prayers for the spirit of God were never answered: "Did I misunderstand the promises and teachings of the Bible on this subject, or was I to conclude that the Bible was not true?"[21] Joseph Smith—along with Ann Lee, founder of the Shakers; the Irvingites in England; and thousands of early Methodists and Quakers—wanted more revelation than conventional Protestantism offered.[22]

Reliance on revelation made Joseph and the other visionaries appear marginal, but like marginal people before them, the prophets aimed a question at the heart of their culture: if believers in the Bible dismissed revelation in the present, could they defend revelation in the past? For centuries Christian apologists had been debating the veracity of miracles and the inspiration of the prophets with Deists, skeptics, and infidels. In the intellectual wars of the later nineteenth century, believers steadily lost ground. The loss, later characterized as the disenchantment of the world, was only dimly perceived by everyday Christians in Joseph Smith's time, but in the century to come, the issue divided divinity schools and troubled ordinary people.[23] Was the Bible inspired writing or purely a historical work? Did biblical miracles actually occur, or were they fabulous tales made up long afterwards? Was God, in other words, active in human affairs?

Joseph Smith resisted that ebbing current. Revelation was the essence of his religion. "Take away the book of Mormon, and the revelations, and where is our religion? We have none." He received revelation exactly as Christians thought biblical prophets did. In effect, he reenacted the writing of the Bible. Most put him aside as an obvious charlatan, but if revelation in the present was so unimaginable, why believe revelation in the past? One incredulous visitor marveled that Joseph—"nothing but a man"—claimed revelation, to which Joseph replied that "they look upon it as incredible that a man should have any intercourse with his Maker." Joseph's life posed the question: does God speak?[24]

In this sense, Joseph was indeed an "extremist prophet." He forced the question of revelation on a culture struggling with its own faith. Joseph's historical role, as he understood it, was to give God a voice in a world that had stopped listening. "The Gentiles shall say, A Bible, a Bible, we have got a Bible, and there cannot be any more Bible": so said the *Book of Mormon*. "O fools," the Lord rejoins, "know ye not that I am the same yesterday, to-day, and forever; and that I speak forth my words according to mine own pleasure." One reason for restoring the *Book of Mormon*, an early revelation said, was to prove "that the holy scriptures are true." In reply to a minister's inquiry about the distinguishing doctrine of Mormonism, Joseph told him that "we believe the bible, and they do not."[25] It was the power of the Bible that Joseph and the visionaries sought to recover. Not getting it from the ministry, they looked for it themselves.

FIFTEEN

TEXTS

1835

They knew that the church was evil spoken of in many places—its faith and belief misrepresented, and the way of truth thus subverted. By some it was represented as disbelieving the bible, by others as being an enemy to all good order and uprightness, and by others as being injurious to the peace of all governments civil and political.

We have, therefore, endeavored to present, though in few words, our belief, and when we say this, humbly trust, the faith and principles of this society as a body.

Doctrine and Covenants [1835], iii–iv

WILLIAM E. MCLELLIN, the former schoolteacher chosen an apostle in February 1835, left the church a year and a half later, disillusioned by his failure to receive a manifestation at the Kirtland temple dedication and critical of the Church leaders' worldly conduct. His devotion had wavered ever since his conversion in 1831, but his energy and speaking ability had qualified him for the apostleship. The journal he kept of a missionary journey with the Twelve from May through September 1835 is the best account we have of Mormon missionary work in the early years. The journal shows how completely missionaries lived off the land. Stopping in one little town after another as they traveled northeast through New York and New England, the missionary pairs found a place to preach, gathered an audience, and hoped for a favorable reception. For their accommodations, they relied on kindly souls. Coming to the house of Stephen Jones, McLellin wrote, "we called and told them that we were preachers of the ——— church of the 'Latter Day Saints' and we would be glad to be entertained for the night and also to get to preach in the neighbourhood."[1]

The missionaries' effectiveness depended on the population's taste for preaching. Like itinerants of all kinds, the missionaries made an appointment to preach, often in a schoolhouse or a barn, and relied on the word to get around. McLellin was interrupted while preaching in a schoolhouse one Sunday on a 4 p.m. appointment. A Methodist preacher rose to say he had an appointment at five and needed the space. McLellin called for a vote, and the majority favored him continuing. On another occasion, he was disappointed to find the schoolhouse door locked and "only One person who was an old lady attended." That evening some wild boys laughed and talked so much his companion stopped preaching. Usually the audiences were more receptive. The missionaries could fill a schoolhouse, and once seven hundred people crowded into a large barn.[2]

The people who came would hear a sermon of an hour or more followed by an exhortation or a second sermon. McLellin noted the sermon's topic in his journal. "After reading a portion of the Saviour's teaching in the book of Mormon," Elder "B. Young . . . spoke about 1½ hours contrasting the religions of the day with the *truth*." Others spoke about the nature of the priesthoods, judgments, the power of the resurrection, the Kingdom of Christ, or "faith &c." Even if the sermons ranged widely under these headings, it is doubtful any one preachment covered the whole story of the Church. Joseph Smith was never a topic, and no explicit mention was made, so far as can be told, of the gathering to Zion. The missionaries apparently aimed not to convey the broad idea of the restoration, but rather to make an impression. McLellin himself had been converted by first hearing Samuel Smith and Reynolds Cahoon preaching in Paris, Illinois, on their way to Missouri in the summer of 1831. "When I heard it," McLellin later wrote, "I made up my mind that there was more in it than any religions I had ever before heard advocated." A few days later, David Whitmer and Harvey Whitlock came through on their way to Missouri. Of Whitlock's sermon, McLellin said, "I never heard such preaching in all my life. The glory of God seemed to encircle the man and the wisdom of God to be displayed in his discourse." McLellin closed his school and followed the missionaries to Missouri. After a long talk with Hyrum Smith, McLellin accepted the Book of Mormon and was baptized in Jackson County on August 20, 1831.[3]

The missionaries had no plan, no pamphlets or books for the investigators to study, no standard message. The *Book of Mormon* was the only printed literature. The School of the Prophets had deepened their knowledge, but the missionaries did not learn key points or a set of principles. Joseph made no effort to homogenize the message or dictate topics. He exercised little oversight over Church communications save for publication of the revelations themselves. William W. Phelps published the *Evening and Morning Star* in faraway Missouri with little oversight. During the paper's brief life in Independence from June 1832 to July 1833, Joseph read as a subscriber, not as publisher or monitor. He never told Phelps what to print, and complained only once—about flagging interest. "If you do not render it more interesting than at present," Joseph told Phelps, "it will fall, and the church [will] suffer a great Loss thereby."[4] Joseph would not tolerate criticism of himself or of the Church, but he granted the editors wide latitude otherwise.

Mormons needed an answer to the question "What do Mormons believe?" In the October 1834 issue of the *Messenger and Advocate*, the Church's newspaper in Kirtland, Oliver Cowdery attempted a summary.

That our principles may be fully known we here state them briefly:

We believe in God, and his Son Jesus Christ. We believe that God, from the beginning, revealed himself to man; and that whenever he has had a people on earth, he always has revealed himself to them by the Holy Ghost, the ministering of angels, or his own voice. We do not believe that he ever had a church on earth without revealing himself to that church: consequently, there were apostles, prophets, evangelists, pastors, and teachers, in the same.—We believe that God is the same in all ages; and that it requires the same holiness, purity, and religion, to save a man *now*, as it did anciently; and that as HE is no respecter of persons, always has, and always will reveal himself to men when they call upon him.

We believe that God has revealed himself to men in this age, and commenced to raise up a church preparatory to his second advent, when he will come in the clouds of heaven with power and great glory.

We believe that the popular religious theories of the day are incorrect; that they are without parallel in the revelations of God, as sanctioned by him; and that however faithfully they may be adhered to, or however zealously and warmly they may be defended, they will never stand the strict scrutiny of the word of life.

We believe that all men are born free and equal; that no man, combination of men, or government of men, have power or authority to compel or force others to embrace any system of religion, or religious creed, or to use force or violence to prevent others from enjoying their own opinions, or practicing the same, so long as they do not molest or disturb others in theirs, in a manner to deprive them of their privileges as free citizens—or of worshiping God as they choose, and that any attempt to the contrary is an assumption unwarrantable in the revelations of heaven, and strikes at the root of civil liberty, and is a subvertion of all equitable principles between man and man.

We believe that God has set his hand the second time to recover the remnant of his people, Israel; and that the time is near when he will bring them from the four winds, with songs of everlasting joy, and reinstate them upon their own lands which he gave their fathers by covenant.

And further: We believe in embracing good wherever it may be found; of proving all things, and holding fast that which is righteous.

This, in short, is our belief, and we stand ready to defend it upon its own foundation when ever it is assailed by men of character and respectability.[5]

The summary was helpful, but incomplete. Nothing was said of priest-hood and authority, the promise of exaltation, or the three degrees of glory. Cowdery never mentioned the Book of Mormon or the revision of the Bible. He said little about Zion. Instead he emphasized revelation in all ages of the world, the shortcomings of modern religion, and the gathering of Israel, plus religious freedom—a lesson from the Missouri persecutions. Despite the omissions, this description was probably acceptable to most Mormons in 1835. Amid the diversity, a loose consensus was forming.

DOCTRINE AND COVENANTS

A major step toward correlating the message was taken in August 1835, when Joseph's revelations were published in a revised and expanded edition called the *Doctrine and Covenants*, a change in title from the 1833 *Book of Commandments*. The leaders had labored on the book for nearly two years, ever since the Mormon press in Independence was destroyed and the proofs of the *Book of Commandments* scattered. To assist Oliver Cowdery, Sidney Rigdon, the press manager, was charged in April 1834 with arrang-ing the "church covenants," and the project moved slowly and steadily along. In June, Joseph issued an appeal for funds to help publish all the rev-elations, including the revised version of the Bible.[6] On September 24, the Kirtland High Council assigned the task of correcting the revelations to a committee composed of Cowdery and the First Presidency.

Progress may have been slowed by disagreement about the contents. The directions to the committee in September gave signs that the book's conception was in flux. A compilation of Joseph Smith's revelations—the idea behind the *Book of Commandments*—was giving way to a systematic presentation of Church doctrine, using scripture from all sources with Joseph's revelations as a part. The high council instructed the committee to "arrange the items of the doctrine of Jesus Christ for the government of the church of the Latter Day Saints," taken from "the bible, book of mor-mon and the revelations."[7] The book was to be a summary drawing on all scriptures, rather than a record of Joseph's work. Ultimately, Bible and *Book of Mormon* scriptures were omitted, but the idea of gathering "items of . . . doctrine" for the "government of the church" prevailed. The 1835 *Doctrine and Covenants* was meant to summarize the Church's major beliefs and provide a handbook of its policies. Joseph Smith's role in receiving revelations was played down. They were referred to as "the revelations which have been given since its organization" without mentioning his name, and characterized as "items or principles for the regulation of the church."

In the first sentence of the introduction, the First Presidency states that the book contains "the leading items of the religion which we have professed to believe," and later speaks of presenting "a system." The body of the text then opens with seven theological lectures "on the doctrine of the Church of the Latter Day Saints," given at the School of the Prophets. In the second part, containing the revelations themselves, seven revelations, each one called a "section," are pulled out of chronological order and moved to the front to highlight their significance. Following the section designated the "Lord's Preface," the second section is the current section 20 of the modern *Doctrine and Covenants*, the so-called "constitution" of the Church given in the spring of 1830. The third section, the current section 107, is the grand revelation "on priesthood." The fourth is the current section 84, also on priesthood, and so on. The compilers featured the sections that offered systematic descriptions of Church organization and belief. The revelation on the organization of high councils comes fifth. Then the book reverts to roughly chronological order. The compilation concludes with statements by Phelps and Cowdery on marriage and on government. In the back, an index guides readers to topics like "Aaronic Priesthood" or "Baptism" or "Children."[8] The word "section" as a heading for the individual revelations, replacing "chapter" in the *Book of Commandments*, suggests the committee was thinking of a code of laws or a constitution.

The book came at a time when the prophetic impulses of the movement were being regularized and systematized. The standing and traveling high councils had given form to Church administration. The Twelve were touring the country organizing branches into conferences and putting their affairs in order. The First Presidency had emerged as the leading quorum in Church government. The time had come to channel energy and bring order to the movement. In January 1835, seven months before the *Doctrine and Covenants* was presented to the Church, Alexander Campbell put the finishing touches on *The Christian System*. In the same years, the Methodists were restraining the supernaturalist impulses among believers. The mainline churches, in the words of the historian Gordon Wood, "wanted to offset the personal and emotional character of revivalism by restoring the corporate rituals and doctrines of the historic churches." John Higham has characterized the overall change going on in American society as a transition from "boundlessness to consolidation."[9]

The "Lectures on Faith" were a perfect example of orderly presentation. Given in the fall of 1834 by Sidney Rigdon and others, with input from Joseph Smith, the lectures were included in every edition of the *Doctrine and Covenants* from 1835 through 1921. They are a surprising departure from Joseph's unsystematic and often sprawling revelations. Tightly organized, self-consciously logical, and overtly rational, the lectures have the air of sermons meant to persuade a skeptical audience. They accept the definition of theology in Buck's *Theological Dictionary* as a "revealed science," claiming that "any rational and intelligent being" may exercise faith in God. In the review questions following each lecture, students are asked for rational proof. "How do you prove that faith is the principle of action in all intelligent beings?" "How do you prove that God has faith in himself independently?"[10] The Saints were given a tightly wound package of logic and evidence to help them make the case. If the spirit of the lectures had governed the Church after 1835, a systematic theology like Alexander Campbell's might have soon followed.

On August 17, 1835, while Joseph was away in Michigan, Sidney Rigdon and Oliver Cowdery presented the *Doctrine and Covenants* to a general assembly to "become a law unto the church, a rule of faith and practice." They were accepted by way of an elaborate ritual that came to be observed on later occasions when important business was transacted. The various priesthood quorums and councils sat together and each group voted in turn: the two high councils (Kirtland and Missouri), the bishoprics, the Seventies, elders, priests, teachers, and deacons. When the book was brought before the assembly, the head of each group rose and attested the book's truth. The absent Twelve Apostles, away on mission, were represented by a written testimony affirming that "these Commandments were given by inspiration of God, and are profitable for all men, and are verily true." At the end, the whole assembly "gave a decided voice in favor" of the book.[11]

The ceremonial endorsement of the book did not persuade everyone to embrace it. The maverick Lyman Wight thought that "the Book of Covenants and Doctrine was a telestial law and the Book of Commandments . . . were a Celestial law." Others were apprehensive about adopting a creed. Some of the Saints liked the improvisational character of early missionary preaching. Soon after the acceptance, Elder Almon Babbitt was charged with saying that "we have no articles of faith except the Bible." The introduction anticipated these objections to regularization. "There may be an aversion in the minds of some," the First Presidency acknowledged, "against receiving any thing purporting to be articles of religious faith, in consequence of there being so many now extant." But "if men believe a system, and profess that it was given by inspiration, certainly the more intelligibly they can present it, the better. It does not make a principle untrue to *print* it." This was not good enough for David Whitmer, who later complained that the *Doctrine and Covenants* established "a creed of religious faith."[12]

Although listed on the title page as one of the four compilers of the *Doctrine and Covenants* and obviously in favor of its publication, Joseph Smith was also uneasy about creeds. Later Joseph formulated his own "Articles of Faith" when a curious newspaper editor requested a statement, but he never intended this or any single statement to represent the totality of belief. The flow of revelations prevented him from ever saying the work was finished. Even near the end of his career, he resisted any attempt to stanch the springs of inspiration. "The most prominent point of difference in sentiment between the Latter Day Saints & sectarians," a clerk later recorded him saying, "was, that the latter were all circu[m]scribed by some peculiar creed, which deprived its members the privilege of believing any thing not contained therein; whereas the L. D. Saints had no creed, but are ready to believe *all true principles* that exist, as they are made manifest from time to time."[13] Creeds fixed limits. They seemed to say "thus far and no further," while for Joseph the way was always open to additional truth: "The creeds set up stakes, & say hitherto shalt thou come, & no further.— which I cannot subscribe to." He wanted the door left ajar for truth from every source. He revised his own revelations, adding new material and splicing one to another, altering the wording as he saw fit. He felt author-ized to expand the revelations as his understanding expanded. In later edi-tions of the *Doctrine and Covenants* this freewheeling style prevailed. Instead of putting the key revelations first, as if they had preeminence, the later edi-tions became once more a chronological compilation of Joseph's revelations in all their tangled, unsystematic glory.[14]

Joseph once said that Methodists "have creeds which a man must believe or be kicked out of their church. I want the liberty to believe as I please, it feels so good not to be trameled." Revelation meant freedom to Joseph, freedom to expand his mind through time and space, seeking truth wher-ever it might be. But as the form of the 1835 edition suggested, a desire for order balanced the freeing impulse. By licensing his followers to speak with the Holy Ghost, he risked having the whole movement spin out of control. Against the centrifugal force of individual revelation, Joseph continually organized and regulated.[15] Though he was the chief visionary of the age, he showed little sympathy for the extravagant behavior of people possessed by spirits. He preferred edification and orderly worship to the uncontrolled emotion of the camp meeting or the idiosyncratic excursions of the Irving-ite prophets. The balance between freedom and control makes it difficult to keep Mormonism in focus. Was it authoritarian or anarchic, disciplined or unbounded? The printed word of God constituted a doctrinal authority that at the same time was open-ended, allowing visionary freedom to Joseph's successors after his death.

ABRAHAM

In the summer of 1835, Joseph returned to translating, the peculiar form of revelation he had set aside in 1833 when revision of the Bible was com-pleted. Reawakening his interest was the visit of one Michael H. Chandler, who arrived in Kirtland on July 3, 1835, with four mummies and some rolls of papyrus. Something of an opportunist and promoter, Chandler had exhibited the artifacts in Cleveland in March and come to Kirtland, he said, because of Joseph Smith's translating powers.[16] Chandler's account of the mummies is full of contradictions. He claimed he inherited the artifacts from his uncle, Antonio Lebolo. Lebolo had indeed obtained Egyptian artifacts around 1820 and distributed the finds to various European museums before he died in 1830, but no mention of Chandler or mummies was made in Lebolo's probate papers. He had earlier arranged for a Trieste merchant to sell eleven mummies that were forwarded to New York, and probably Chandler purchased the artifacts in New York, thinking to exhibit and then sell them.[17] On inspecting the papyri, Joseph announced that one roll contained the writings of Abraham of Ur and another the writings of Joseph of Egypt. Excited by this discovery, he encouraged some of the Kirtland Saints to purchase four mummies and the papyri for $2,400, a huge sum when money was desperately needed for other projects.[18]

In late July and off and on through the fall and winter, Joseph worked on the translation, until events interrupted the work. William W. Phelps, who helped with the project, wrote as early as September that there was little chance of getting back to it. The first chapter and part of the second of the Book of Abraham were completed by 1837, and probably earlier; the remainder may not have been produced until early 1842, shortly before the publication in the Church newspaper, the *Times and Seasons*. The translation of the writings of Joseph of Egypt never appeared.[19]

The prospect of another translation excited the Kirtland Saints. John Whitmer commented that the completed translation "will be a pleasing history and of great value to the saints."[20] Oliver Cowdery felt the translations would be "an inestimable acquisition to our present scriptures." The writings moved the world toward the time when "the earth shall be full of the knowledge of the Lord as the waters cover the sea." All through the winter of 1835–36, curious people stopped by to view the papyri and to hear Joseph's explanations. He would continue showing the relics until his death.[21]

Joseph Smith's Book of Abraham is best thought of as an apocryphal addition to the Genesis story of Abraham, in the same vein as the Enoch passages in the Book of Moses. Characteristically, Joseph's translated account did not repeat the familiar biblical stories, instead expanding on a few verses about Abraham's origins in Ur of the Chaldees, adding material not mentioned in the Bible.[22] The published version contained two chapters giving an account of Abraham's ordeal in Ur and his departure for Canaan and Egypt. In keeping with Abraham's curiosity about the heavens, the third chapter is an excursion into astronomy and cosmology, and the fourth and fifth chapters are another account of creation, paralleling the one in the Book of Moses.

Like all of Joseph's historical narratives, the Abraham story begins without a translator's introduction. The reader is suddenly dropped into Abraham's mind and world, and Joseph the translator is entirely invisible. Geographical locations like Potiphar's Hill, Bethel, Sechem, Haran, and Hai dot the text. "In the land of the Chaldeans, at the residence of my fathers, I, Abraham, saw that it was needful for me to obtain another place of residence." At once we have a character, a place, and a plot. Abraham is a restless, striving person.

> And finding there was greater happiness and peace and rest for me, I sought for the blessings of the fathers and the right whereunto I should be ordained to administer the same; having been myself a follower of righteousness, desiring also to be one who possessed great knowledge, and to be a greater follower of righteousness, and to possess a greater knowledge, and to be a father of many nations, a prince of peace; and desiring to receive instructions, and to keep the commandments of God, I became a rightful heir, a high priest, holding the right belonging to the fathers.[23]

To the familiar idea of Abraham as a prince and the father of many nations, Joseph's account adds priesthood, a theme running through the entire story. The Book of Abraham can be considered an extension of the priesthood revelations that had influenced the Church in the past few years—in contrast to the earlier Book of Moses, which rarely used the word. In Abraham's case, the priesthood is not given by ordination alone but is received as an inheritance. Priesthood is a "right belonging to the fathers." It descends to Abraham "from the fathers, from the beginning of time, yea, even from the beginning, or before the foundations of the earth, to the present time, even the right of the first born, o[r] the first man, who is Adam, or first father."[24]

Before obtaining priesthood, Abraham passes through an ordeal that takes the narrative toward Egypt and a rival priesthood. Abraham's father Terah has apostatized to the false gods of Egypt. Their worship involves human sacrifices conducted in Ur by the priest of Pharaoh. After offering a child and three virgins, the priest then seized Abraham. They take him "that they might slay me, also, as they did those virgins, upon this altar." Bound on the altar, Abraham cries to the Lord, and an angel comes to his rescue. The voice of Jehovah commands Abraham to depart for a strange land that the Lord will reveal to him. Then in a confrontation like Elijah's duel with the priests of Baal, the altar is broken down and the priest smitten, causing "great mourning in Chaldea, and also in the court of Pharaoh."[25]

At this point, the narrative detours into Egyptian history. Pharaoh, we are told, is descended from Ham, the son of Noah. Ham's daughter Egyptus discovered the land of Egypt, and her oldest son was the first Pharaoh, who ruled "after the manner of the government of Ham, which was Patriarchal." The lineage of Ham, we learn, comes through the Canaanites, who are cursed. Pharaoh is "of that lineage, by which he could not have the right of Priesthood, notwithstanding the Pharaoh's would fain claim it from Noah, through Ham."[26] Like Abraham, Pharaoh yearns for the priesthood, but is denied it because of his lineage.

These verses have had a troubled history. Later they were used as a justification for refusing black people the priesthood. The Abraham verses say nothing of skin color, but the 1830 revelation of Moses had spoken of a blackness coming upon "all the children of Canaan, that they were despised among all people," and Abraham said Pharaoh "was a partaker of the blood of the Canaanites, by birth." Joining the verses in Abraham and Moses, some concluded that black people had descended from the Canaanites, the lineage cursed "as pertaining to the Priesthood."[27]

In coming to this conclusion, later Mormons borrowed from the common nineteenth-century belief that Africans descended from Ham and bore a curse. In the Bible, Noah's son Ham mocked his father's drunkenness and nakedness, and in revenge Noah cursed Ham's son Canaan. "Cursed be Canaan; a servant of servants shall he be unto his brethren." Over the centuries, biblical interpreters, including Jews and Arabs, identified "Canaan" with people they wished to enslave, and the cursed people, whoever they happened to be at the time, were then thought of as innately inferior—dishonest, lazy, irresponsible, intemperate. Around 1000 CE, the curse was assigned to black Africans.[28]

Joseph's Book of Abraham, while partially paralleling this tradition, deviated significantly from the pattern of Hamitic interpretation. The Abraham verses spoke of Noah, Ham, and a curse, but said nothing of servitude. Slavery was left out of the picture altogether. The Pharaoh who bore the curse was anything but an impoverished servant or lazy and dishonest. He "established his kingdom and judged his people wisely and justly all his days." He sought "to imitate that order established by the fathers in the first generations." Blessed with kingship and "the blessings of the earth," Pharaoh founded the mighty Egyptian civilization famed for its magnificence and power. In Joseph Smith's time, Egypt was believed to have been the starting point for western civilization. Advocates of black equality stressed their connection with Egypt to prove African achievements. Their favorite biblical passage was Psalm 68:31: "Princes shall come out of Egypt; Ethiopia shall soon stretch forth her hands unto God."[29] By associating the cursed descendants of Ham with Egypt, the Book of Abraham ran at cross-purposes with the usual arguments for black cultural inferiority and black slavery. The book exhibited an idiosyncratic type of racial thinking. Neither inferiority nor servitude was at issue, only priesthood.

Was Joseph racist in other contexts? The exclusion of black men from the priesthood was publicly stated only after his death.[30] Except for a brief lapse in early 1836, Joseph advocated taking the gospel to "both bond and free," ignoring race. An essay against abolitionism published over his name in 1836 (a year when fear of abolitionism was at its peak) exhibited the conventional prejudices of his day in asserting that blacks were cursed with servitude by a "decree of Jehovah," but there was no follow-up. That spring, the house rules for the Kirtland Temple, the Saints' most sacred building, allowed for the presence of "male or female bond or free black or white." The same policy was followed in Nauvoo, where "persons of all languages, and of every tongue, and of every color . . . shall with us worship the Lord of Hosts in his holy temple." Nothing was done during Joseph's lifetime to withhold priesthood from black members. Joseph knew Elijah Abel, a black man who was ordained at seventy, and is said to have entertained him.[31] As Joseph began to take positions on national issues, he came out strongly against slavery. Blacks "come into the world slaves, mentally and physically," he once said in private conversation. "Change their situation with the white and they would be like them." He favored a policy of "national Equalization," though he retained the common prejudice against intermarriage and blending of the races.[32] When he ran for U.S. president in 1844, he made compensated emancipation a plank in his platform. He urged the nation to "ameliorate the condition of all: black or white, bond or free; for the best of books says, 'God hath made of one blood all nations of men, for to dwell on all the face of the earth.' "[33] Joseph never commented on the Abraham text or implied it denied priesthood to blacks.

Joseph's concern in the first chapter of Abraham was with civilizations and lineage more than race. Pharaoh, Ham, and Egypt figure in one lineage and Abraham in another. The implications for modern race relations interested Joseph less than the configuration of family lines and the descent of authority. Abraham says he will "delineate the chronology, running back from myself to the beginning of the creation," though the text never returned to that subject. In two other places in his revelations, Joseph traced the lineage of priesthood back to Adam.[34]

Abraham is the third of Joseph's foundational biographies, stories of individuals who founded nations. One great character dominates each story. The *Book of Mormon* opens with "I, Nephi," matching the opening of Abraham: "In the land of the Chaldeans, at the residence of my fathers, I, Abraham." A person immediately flashes on the screen. The first chapter of Moses begins in the third person but immediately switches into Moses' first-person account of seeing God face-to-face. From these individuals come peoples and civilizations. Nations spring up in these narratives and, in Moses and Abraham, humankind itself. The writings tell why earth was created, or how a people came into existence, through the account of a single figure. Nephi blends the dispersal of Israelite civilization to the New World with the story of his family. The Book of Abraham shows the founding of the Abrahamic nation, the people with priesthood who will bless the earth. In a sidebar to Abraham's story, Egyptus and Pharaoh found Egypt. These stories are preoccupied with beginnings.

Joseph wrote in a time of epics, when American literary figures were creating foundational stories for the new nation. Joel Barlow, the late-eighteenth-century Connecticut poet, attempted an epic in *The Columbiad*, his long vision of Columbus, as did Timothy Dwight in his recounting of the biblical Joshua as a barely disguised George Washington in *The Conquest of Canaan*. Both were narratives of nation founding told as the story of great individuals. Joseph Smith's Moses, Abraham, and Nephi compare to the leading figures in Barlow's and Dwight's epic poems, but in daring and originality, Joseph exceeds them. The American poets overlaid familiar biblical events with blunt references to the United States; Joseph's expansion of the biblical stories transcended the national.[35] He stepped out of his own time into antiquity in search of the origins of civilization. Moses and Abraham even have cosmological dimensions. All three betray a fascination with how the world began.

TRANSLATING

The Abraham texts gave Joseph another chance to let his followers try translating. While working on the Book of Mormon in 1829, Joseph invited Oliver Cowdery to translate: he tried and failed. Now with the Egyptian papyri before them, Joseph again let the men with the greatest interest in such undertakings—Cowdery, William W. Phelps, Warren Parrish, and Frederick G. Williams—attempt translations. Parrish was told he "shall see much of my ancient records, and shall know of hiden things, and shall be endowed with a knowledge of hiden languages."[36]

Through the fall of 1835, the little group made various attempts.[37] "This after noon labored on the Egyptian alphabet, in company with [brothers] O. Cowdery and W. W. Phelps," Joseph's journal notes. They seem to have copied lines of Egyptian from the papyrus and worked out stories to go with the text. Or they wrote down an Egyptian character and attempted various renditions. Joseph apparently had translated the first two chapters of Abraham—through chapter 2, verse 18, in the current edition—and the would-be translators matched up hieroglyphs with some of his English sentences.

Their general method can be deduced from a revelation given to Oliver Cowdery after he failed to translate the gold plates: "You must study it out in your mind; then you must ask me if it be right, and if it is right, I will cause that your bosom shall burn within you." One can imagine these men staring at the characters, jotting down ideas that occurred to them, hoping for a burning confirmation.[38] They tried one approach after another. Joseph probably threw in ideas of his own. Eventually they pulled their work together into a collection they called "Grammar & A[l]phabet of the Egyptian Language," written in the hands of Phelps and Parrish.[39]

Of all the men working on the papyri, only Joseph produced a coherent text. What was going on as he translated? For many years, Mormons assumed that he sat down with the scrolls, looked at each Egyptian word, and by inspiration understood its meaning in English. He must have been reading from a text, so Mormons thought, much as a conventional translator would do, except the words came by revelation rather than out of his own learning. In 1967, that view of translation suffered a blow when eleven scraps of the Abraham papyri, long since lost and believed to have been burned, were discovered in the Metropolitan Museum of Art in New York City and given to Latter-day Saint leaders in Salt Lake City. Color pictures were soon printed and scholars went to work.[40] The texts were thought to be the Abraham papyri because Joseph had published facsimiles from the papyri with his translation, and the same pictures appeared on the museum fragments. Moreover, some of the characters from the Egyptian grammar appeared on the fragments. The translation of these texts by expert Egyptologists would finally prove or disprove Joseph's claims to miraculous translating powers. Would any of the language correspond to the text in his Book of Abraham? Some Mormons were crushed when the fragments turned out to be rather conventional funerary texts placed with mummified bodies, in this case Hôr', to assure continuing life as an immortal god. According to the Egyptologists, nothing on the fragments resembled Joseph's account of Abraham.[41]

Some Mormon scholars, notably Hugh Nibley, doubt that the actual texts for Abraham and Joseph have been found. The scraps from the Metropolitan Museum do not fit the description Joseph Smith gave of long, beautiful scrolls. At best the remnants are a small fraction of the originals, with no indication of what appears on the lost portions.[42] Nonetheless, the discovery prompted a reassessment of the Book of Abraham. What was going on while Joseph "translated" the papyri and dictated text to a scribe? Obviously, he was not interpreting the hieroglyphics like an ordinary scholar. As Joseph saw it, he was working by inspiration—that had been clear from the beginning. When he "translated" the *Book of Mormon*, he did not read from the gold plates; he looked into the crystals of the Urim and Thummim or gazed at the seerstone. The words came by inspiration, not by reading the characters on the plates. By analogy, it seemed likely that the papyri had been an occasion for receiving a revelation rather than a word-for-word interpretation of the hieroglyphs as in ordinary translations. Joseph translated Abraham as he had the characters on the gold plates, by knowing the meaning without actually knowing the plates' language. Warren Parish, his clerk, said, "I have set by his side and penned down the translation of the Egyptian Heiroglyphicks as he claimed to receive it by direct inspiration of heaven." When Chandler arrived with the scrolls, Joseph saw the papyri and inspiration struck. Not one to deny God's promptings, the Prophet said what he felt: the papyri were the writings of Abraham and Joseph. The whole thing was miraculous, and to reduce Joseph's translation to some quasi-natural process, some concluded, was folly.[43]

The peculiar fact is that the results were not entirely out of line with the huge apocryphal literature on Abraham. His book of Abraham picked up themes found in texts like the *Book of Jasher* and Flavius Josephus's *Antiquities of the Jews*. In these extrabiblical stories, Abraham's father worshiped idols, people tried to murder Abraham because of his resistance, and Abraham was learned in astronomy—all features of Joseph Smith's narrative. Josephus says, for example, that Abraham delivered "the science of astronomy" to the Egyptians, as does Joseph's Abraham. The parallels are not exact; the Book of Abraham was not a copy of any of the apocryphal texts. In the *Book of Jasher*, Abraham destroys the idols of King Nimrod with a hatchet and is thrown into a furnace; Joseph's Abraham offers no violence to the idols and is bound on a bedstead.[44] The similarities are far from complete, but the theme of resisting the king's idolatry and an attempted execution followed by redemption by God are the same. The parallels extend to numerous small details.

Joseph may have heard apocryphal stories of Abraham, although the *Book of Jasher* was not published in English until 1829 and not in the United States until 1840. A Bible dictionary published by the American Sunday School Union summed up many of the apocryphal elements. Whether Joseph knew of alternate accounts of Abraham or not, he created an original narrative that echoed apocryphal stories without imitating them. Either by revelation, as his followers believed, or by some instinctive affinity for antiquity, Joseph made his own late—and unlikely—entry in the long tradition of extrabiblical narratives about the great patriarch.[45]

Despite his gift for "translating," Joseph wanted to learn language in the ordinary way and translate rationally as well as miraculously. When he returned to the translation of Abraham in 1842, he again proposed an Egyptian grammar.[46] He apparently hoped to transform his inspired interpretation of the text into a mastery of the Egyptian language. In the fall of

1835, when he first began work on the Abraham text, he was also planning to study languages conventionally. Dr. Daniel L. M. Peixotto, a professor of medicine at Willoughby University four miles from Kirtland, was hired to teach Hebrew in the School of the Prophets. When Peixotto could not come, the brethren hired Joshua Seixas, a Jewish convert to Christianity then teaching at the Western Reserve College.[47] In the interim, Joseph studied Hebrew on his own and, after Seixas arrived in January 1836, attended class conscientiously—a prophet learning from a scholar. He proudly recorded Seixas's comment that "we are the most forward of any class he ever taught." Joseph was one of ten to meet for extra sessions with the professor. Seixas called Joseph an "indefatigable" student. Excited by his learning, Joseph resolved "to persue the study of languages untill I shall become master of them, if I am permitted to live long enough." The Hebrew classes continued until the dedication of the temple in March, when Seixas dropped from sight.[48]

In light of Joseph's language study, the Egyptian grammar appears as an awkward attempt to blend a scholarly approach to language with inspired translation. Like Abraham, Joseph wanted to be one who "possessed great knowledge." He began his career as a prophet by translating gold plates inscribed in "reformed Egyptian." As late as 1842, he worked on the translation of papyri from an Egyptian tomb. The allure of the ancient comes through in the revelation to Oliver Cowdery about "those ancient records which have been hid up, that are sacred." Beyond the *Book of Mormon* people, other Israelites had kept records that would flow together in the last days. The sealed portion of the gold plates was yet to be revealed, and revelations to sundry others had generated caches of records, all part of the Lord's work, all to be recovered in time.[49] Translation gave him access to the peoples of antiquity.

Full of wonders as it was, the Book of Abraham complicated the problem of regularizing Mormon doctrine. The *Doctrine and Covenants* was meant to stabilize Mormon beliefs, but in the very year of its publication, the papyri rode into Kirtland in Michael Chandler's wagon, bringing news of Abraham from the tombs of Egypt. Every attempt to regularize belief was diffused by new revelations. Who could tell what would be revealed next— what new insight into the patriarchal past, what stories of Abraham, Moses, or Enoch, what glimpses into heaven? Joseph himself could not predict the course of Mormon doctrine. All he could say he summed up in a later article of faith: "We believe all that God has revealed, all that he does now reveal, and we believe that he will yet reveal many great and important things pertaining to the kingdom of God."[50]

SIXTEEN

STRIFE

Be assured brethren I am willing to stem the torrent of all opposition, in storms in tempests in thunders and lightning by sea and by land in the wilderness or among fals[e] brethren or mobs or wherever God in his providence may call us and I am determined that neither hights nor depths principalities nor powers things present or to come nor any other creature shall separate me from you.
JOSEPH SMITH TO THE TWELVE APOSTLES, January 1836

JOSEPH'S JOURNAL FOR SEPTEMBER 22, 1835, through April 3, 1836, was the most extensive, comprehensive, and revealing he ever kept. Earlier journals ran a few months and petered out; his letters give only a brief glimpse of one moment in time. The 1835–36 journal contains almost daily entries for six months. Only a few passages were written in his own hand, but the bulk of the entries appear to have been dictated rather than composed by his clerks.[1] After this, Joseph's journals lose the personal touch. Clerks wrote them for his approval, introducing an intervening mind between readers and the Prophet.

The personal nature of the 1835–36 journal clarifies, at least a little, the meaning of Mormonism to Joseph Smith himself. How did his religion relate to his temperament and feelings? If Joseph thought the historical significance of his work was to renew biblical revelation and to prepare for the Second Coming, what personal satisfactions did Mormonism bring? The 1835–36 journal says enough about Joseph's needs and tensions to permit speculation on a difficult question.

His personal hopes for Zion were interwoven with an inherited burden from his New England ancestors. Incidents through the fall of 1835 reveal how fully Joseph was immersed in a system called by historians the "culture of honor," illustrated at the highest level of American society by the duel between Alexander Hamilton and Aaron Burr in 1804.[2] Joseph Smith had no part in the code duello, but versions of the honor culture did affect him. By the time of his young manhood, the northern middle and upper classes were beginning to adopt genteel and commercial mores that weakened the hold of the honor culture, but it still prevailed in the South, in the northern rural backcountry, and among urban immigrant groups.

The culture of honor bred deep loyalties to friends and family, while instilling a fierce urge to avenge insults. Andrew Jackson killed a man in a duel over a perceived slight to his wife's honor. The greatest fear in life, a fear stronger than death or damnation, was public humiliation. A man must fight for honor, whether in a duel like Jackson's or Hamilton's at the upper levels of society, or in a brawl among ordinary people. Like everyone raised in this culture, the Smiths had a clannish loyalty to one another and a fiery resentment against the slightest derogation of their worth. In the culture of honor, one would battle to the death in defense of reputation. An honorable man who suffered an insult would spare nothing to get even.[3]

In a sense, these qualities were aspects of one's personal character, a matter of individual moral responsibility. In another sense, they were social and cultural. The honor culture was a legacy from one's family and society, a burden imposed on children by their world. Joseph's reaction to insults was learned behavior, shared with his society. His anger was both his own and an expression of a cultural practice—what honorable men were taught to do.[4]

Unfortunately for his peace of mind, Joseph's angry responses conflicted with the harmony and brotherhood he prized. Through the fall of 1835, he engaged in a series of small quarrels, domestic disturbances, and squabbles. He did not rise above the fray in the serene majesty of his calling. The culture of honor moved him to contend with the offending parties to protect his easily bruised pride, even though all the while he wanted peace. He hated contention and tried to make peace by mutual confessions and brotherly arbitration. But his own sensitivity entangled him in further rows, repeatedly recycling resentment and reconciliation. By January 1836, when he made peace with his antagonists, the meaning of Zion to a man of his temperament was clear. To live in harmony with his brothers and sisters, as the revelations required, was reason to rejoice.

Harmony was valued in all the Church's councils. The Kirtland High Council's hearings examined the attitudes of offending parties as well as their actions. The minutes refer to "the spirit of meekness," or "feelings of the heart," or the "spirit of justification and pride." On September 19, Jared Carter answered charges about his presentation on the temple building committee. No one objected to the topic, but Carter had threatened that "if any man spoke against the Committee, God would curse him." In asking others to pray for his committee, he "demanded it in the name of the Lord with an authoritative voice & gesticulation which are not according to the meekness of the spirit of Jesus." Joseph ruled that "Elder Carter has not designed to do wickedly, but he erred in judgement and deserves reproof."

He was to stand before the congregation and say he had "erred in spirit" and "now ask your forgiveness." Carter accepted the ruling and promised to comply.[5]

While Joseph was sensitive to the spirit of others, he may have been tone-deaf to the spirit of his own words. Unable to bear criticism, he rebuked anyone who challenged him. Benjamin Johnson, a great admirer, said, "Criticism, even by associates, was rarely acceptable, and contradiction would rouse in him the lion at once, for by no one of his fellows would he be superseded or disputed."[6] When one Brother Aldridge accused Joseph of paying too much for the patriarchal blessings book and Joseph lashed back, an observer, Brother Henry Green, accused Joseph of "rebuking Brother Aldridge wrongfully & [being] under the influence of an evil spirit." Aldridge was justified, in Green's estimation, and "Presidents Joseph & Hiram Smith were wrong in abusing the old man." Green said anyone who talked like Joseph was a "scoundrel" and "must have the Devil in him." The high council, where the dispute was aired on September 16, 1835, ruled Green was at fault for criticizing the president. When an "indignity" is "offered to the high council, then it is the privilege of the Presidency of the High council to stamp it with indignation under foot."[7] The people around Joseph divided on the degree of suitable indignation, suggesting that cultural norms were in flux.

Green's objection echoed Sylvester Smith's complaint against Joseph after the Zion's Camp expedition in 1834. Sylvester had charged that Joseph's angry chastisement was unworthy of a man of God, but after a month he agreed to publish a retraction. A year later, Sylvester was the clerk at Green's trial, standing with Joseph against Green and Aldridge on basically the same charge. During the intervening year, Sylvester had accepted the principle that the leaders of the Church, and especially the president, were not to be criticized. They were to be honored and regarded, even when a charge was brought against them. The disaffected were not required to stifle their complaints; Sidney Rigdon ruled that Green should have gone to Joseph privately. Public humiliation was the issue. There was no justification "in opposing the servant of the Lord while in the actual discharge of his duty."[8]

Theologically, the office of Prophet was essential to the well-being of the entire society. The high council seemed to have concluded the Presidency held by Joseph could not be undermined. Aldridge's error was to question "the integrity of the heads of the Church." Joseph's office required him to detect evil spirits, and reproofs were necessary. As he said a few years later, "he rebuked and admonished his brethren frequently, and that because he loved them; not because he wished to incur their displeasure or mar their happiness." In that spirit, Samuel Smith argued that "President Smith was in the line of his duty when he reproved bro. Aldridge for his evil." Oliver Cowdery warned that to call Joseph a scoundrel threatened to "destroy the character of the heads of this church."[9]

Joseph was concerned about the reputation of the entire general leadership, not just his own standing. He was furious when apostles Orson Hyde and William E. McLellin scoffed at the Kirtland school run by Sidney Rigdon. While away from Kirtland in the summer of 1835, McLellin had learned that it was not possible for his wife to attend Rigdon's school. "I am glad that it is not," McLellin wrote home, "since Elder Hyde has returned and given, me a description of the manner in which [the school] is conducted, though we do not wish to cast any reflections." Joseph and the Kirtland High Council considered the comment "the highest insult" to the Church and the Presidency.[10] McLellin and Hyde summarily had their membership suspended until they explained themselves. They were warned that any who spoke evil "of the dignities which God has set in his Church" would suffer.[11] When the Twelve returned to Kirtland in late September, the Presidency reviewed the dispute and other differences that had arisen while the Twelve were away. McLellin and Hyde admitted their error, and Joseph, feeling the matter was settled, closed the case.[12]

Through the fall, other disagreements roiled Joseph's relations with the Twelve. When a branch leader criticized the Twelve for soliciting funds for Missouri and neglecting the Kirtland temple, the high council told the Twelve that you "set yourselves up as an independent counsel, subject to no authority of the church—a kind of out laws." Casting further doubt on the Twelve's judgment, a council member questioned their decision in the trial of Gladden Bishop who had been charged with heresy. Joseph was also disturbed by stories of how the Twelve managed their funds during their summer mission. A revelation on November 3 announced that the Twelve "are under condemnation, because they have not been sufficiently humble in my sight, and in consequence of their covetous desires, in that they have not dealt equally with each other in the division of the moneys which came into their hands." Three of the Twelve were mentioned by name for their "grevious" sins, and the revelation said "the residue are not sufficiently humble before me."[13]

When word of the revelation got around, McLellin and Hyde, the offenders in the school matter, came to hear it read; later Brigham Young, one of the Apostles, asked to hear it too. Objections were raised, but Joseph thought the offenders acknowledged their wrongs eventually. "After examining their own hearts," Joseph said of McLellin and Hyde, "they acknowledged it to be the word of the Lord and said they were satisfied." Joseph met a week later with the Twelve and assured them they had "my utmost confidence."[14]

Typically, Joseph's anger evaporated after admission of error on both sides. He wanted to put difficult matters behind him. But those who were affected could not always forget so easily. In January 1836, Thomas Marsh, president of the Twelve, asked for a meeting with the Presidency to air a number of hurts. He complained that the Twelve had "been in this work from the beginning almost and had born[e] the burden in the heat of the day and passed through many trials"—and still the Presidency doubted them. Each of the quorum members rose to echo Marsh's protestations. Joseph acknowledged that the letter rebuking them "might have been expressed in too harsh language," which "was not intentional and I ask your forgiveness in as much as I have hurt your feelings," but he insisted that McLellin's criticism of the school justified the tone. He admitted sometimes being too "harsh from the impulse of the moment."[15]

Then his affection returned. "In as much as I have wounded your feelings," he implored the Twelve, "I ask your forgiveness, for I love you and will hold you up with all my heart in all righteousness before the Lord." A flood of pledges followed:

> Be assured brethren I am willing to stem the torrent of all opposition, in storms in tempests in thunders and lightning by sea and by land in the wilderness or among fals[e] brethren or mobs or wherever God in his providence may call us and I am determined that neither hights nor depths principalities nor powers things present or to come nor any other creature shall separate me from you.

He promised to "place unlimited confidence in your word" and asked the same of them, for "I will not tell you I know anything which I do not know." Sidney Rigdon and Frederick Williams asked forgiveness too, admitting they had spoken harshly. Satisfied, Marsh called upon the Twelve to accept the explanation and enter into a covenant of mutual trust. They "rais[ed] their hands to heaven, in testimony of their willingness and desire to enter into this covenant and their entire satisfaction with our explanation," and then grasped hands. Joseph reported "a perfect unison of feeling" as "our hearts over flowed with blessings, which were pronounced upon each others heads as the Spirit gave us utterance." Joseph ended with prayer: "May God enable us all, to perform our vows and covenants with each other in all fidelity and rightiousness before Him."[16]

While bickering with the Twelve through the fall of 1835, Joseph seemed to be in a mood for finding fault, as if some frustration or worry eroded his patience. On one vexing Sunday in November, he fell upon one person after another. He objected to the way his uncle John Smith and Sidney Rigdon dealt with a transgressor during a Church meeting. He noted in his journal that William Phelps and John Whitmer were "under condemnation before the Lord, for their errors." Later in the day, he admonished John Corrill for not partaking of the sacrament and upbraided Emma for leaving the meeting early. He noted "she made no reply, but manifested contrition by weeping."[17]

Contention broke out over small matters. Joseph argued with Orson Pratt in the elders' school over the pronunciation of a Hebrew letter. As teacher, Joseph thought his opinion should prevail, but Pratt "manifested a stubborn spirit." Joseph spent the next morning "setling, the unplesant feelings that existed in the breast of Elder O[rson] Pratt." Pratt eventually backed down and "confessed his fault." As usual, he asked "forgiveness of the whol[e] school and was cheerfully forgiven by all."[18] Once people gave way, Joseph forgave and forgot the matter. He could not understand how others felt when shamed. Emma wept and said nothing.

When he could not have his way, Joseph sometimes rained down curses on his opponents. He was outraged when the Chardon County court fined his brother Samuel twenty dollars for avoiding militia duty. Apparently, Samuel's claim to be a clergyman was denied for lack of a verifying document, and Joseph assumed the large sum was prejudiced, "a base insult practised upon us on the account of our faith, that the ungodly might have unlawful power over us and trample us under their unhallowed feet." When Samuel had to sell his cow to pay the fine, Joseph condemned the court: "I say in the name of Jesus Christ that the money that they have thus unjustly taken shall be a testimony against them and canker & eat their flesh as fire." The words conveyed the outrage of poor rural people defeated by official procedures they did not wholly understand and could not master.[19]

The most violent outburst came during a dispute with Joseph's younger brother William, the most volatile of the Smiths.[20] Near the end of October, William brought charges against a Brother David Elliot for whipping his teenage daughter. Called to testify, Joseph backed Elliot against William. Although softhearted toward children and opposed to whippings, Joseph had spoken with the family and concluded the girl was at fault and the neighbors were meddling.[21] The council concluded that "the charge had not been fully sustained, but [Elliot] has acted injudiciously and brought a disgrace upon himself, upon his daughter & upon this Church, because he ought to have trained his child in a way, that she should not have required the rod at the age of 15 years."

Later that day, Joseph presided in the case of Mary Elliot, David's wife, who was brought before the council on the same charges. During the hearing, when Lucy Smith, William and Joseph's mother, testified, Joseph objected that she was hauling up old charges. William lost his temper, accusing Joseph of "invalidating or doubting my mothers testimony," an unforgivable betrayal of family. Joseph told William he was out of place and ordered him to sit down. "He refused," Joseph reported; "I repeated my request [and] he become enraged." Ordered again to sit, William "said he would not unless I knocked him down." Only the appeal of Father Smith stopped Joseph from walking out. Finally order was restored and the council delivered its ruling. The Elliots confessed their wrongs and were restored to full fellowship.[22]

The next day, William wrote Joseph that the council was censuring him for misbehavior, and he wanted to settle the matter. Joseph said he thought they had "parted with the best of feelings," his usual reaction when agreement had been reached. The next morning, William came anyway to resolve their differences. Joseph proposed that they tell their stories, confess their wrongs, and ask forgiveness, letting Joseph's clerk Warren Parrish and Hyrum judge between them. The proposal gave William a chance to vent his basic grievance. But he said, Joseph reported, "that I was always determined to carry my points whether right or wrong and there fore he would not stand an equal chance with me." William thought Joseph had to have the upper hand. Joseph took this as an insult but restrained himself. Unfortunately, telling their stories got them nowhere. All efforts to "calm his stormy feelings" failed. William declared he wanted nothing more to do with the Church and rushed out.[23]

William, an apostle, did not leave as threatened. A revelation three days after William stormed off said God would "yet make him a polished shaft in my quiver." Perhaps to pacify his brother, Joseph gave William more credit at the Church store than the other apostles, leading Orson Hyde to complain that he could not buy cloth on credit when William had run up $700 in bills. Joseph feared the bickering was tearing up the Church.[24] The adversary was destroying the work by causing division among the Twelve. Joseph prayed that William would be delivered from the "power of the destroyer" and that he and all the elders would receive their endowment in the temple.

Prayers notwithstanding, the situation grew worse. While quieting Hyde's complaint against William, Joseph got involved in another row with his brother. On a frigid December night, Joseph attended a debating school at William's house. The school had been open for over a month, treating such questions as "Was or was it not the design of Christ to Establish his gospel by miracles?" (decided in the negative), and "Was it necessary for God to reveal himself to man, in order for their happiness?" (decided in the affirmative). On December 16, a question was raised about the propriety of continuing the debates—or at least William thought the question was being raised. Hyrum asked to speak, and before he said a word, William forbade him to abuse the school in his house. Joseph thought it unfair to prejudge what Hyrum would say, and also to claim that the house was William's: Joseph had helped finish the house, and Joseph Sr. had part possession. Joseph fruitlessly tried to reason with William. Meeting "an inconciderate and stubourn spirit," Joseph told him "you was ugly as the Devil."[25]

Joseph Sr. commanded his boys to stop, but William insisted he would say what he pleased in his own house. Joseph Jr. again protested William's claim of ownership and the right to speak. Despite his father's command of silence, Joseph felt justified in giving reproof in a house he had built. (He later admitted this was an exaggeration; he had only helped.) At this, William rushed Joseph, who had pulled off his coat to defend himself. Joseph had to be rescued from William's blows. When he got home, he could not sit or stand without help. Ashamed of being beaten, Joseph explained why his younger brother had won the fight. Joseph had been "marred" by mobbers who had debilitated his body, he reminded William, "and it may be that I cannot boast of being stronger, than you." Joseph was further humiliated when Almon Babbitt reported that Joseph "got mad because he was overpowered in argument." Insulted by the comment, Joseph brought Babbitt before the high council for "misrepresenting me to certain of the brethren."[26]

Joseph hated to feud. He was depressed by the "abuse, anger, malice, hatred, and rage" of that evening. "To mangle the flesh or seek revenge upon one who never done you any wrong," Joseph wrote William, "can not be a source of sweet reflection, to you, nor to me, neither to an honorable father & mother, brothers, and sisters." He begged William to curb his passion and not leave the Church. "May God take away enmity, from betwe[e]n me and thee, and may all blessings be restored, and the past be forgotten." In private, he prayed earnestly for William that "the Lord will not cast him off but he may return to the God of Jacob and magnify his apostleship."[27]

Weeks later, Joseph was still depressed. On January 1, he brooded in his journal about the low state of the Church. "My heart is pained within me because of the difficulty that exists in my father's family." To make matters worse, William had won a brother-in-law and another family member to his side. The "powers of darkness," Joseph reflected, "cast a gloomy shade over the minds of my brothers and sisters, which prevents them from seeing things as they realy are." Once again, the devil was determined to overthrow the Church by causing division, all to "prevent the Saints from being endowed."[28]

Joseph met with William, Hyrum, Joseph Sr., uncle John Smith, and Martin Harris on New Year's Day to make peace. Joseph Sr.'s opening prayer melted their hearts, according to the journal, and then "Br. William made an humble confession and asked my forgiveness for the abuse he had offered me and wherein I had been out of the way I asked his forgiveness."

He promised mutual trust to the family in the same spirit as the promises made to the Twelve. "The spirit of confession and forgiveness, was mutual among us all, and we covenanted with each other in the sight of God and the holy angels and the brethren, to strive from hence forward to build each other up in righteousness." Lucy and Emma, doubtless apprehensive about the outcome, were called in to hear the promises of mutual aid. "Gratitude swelled our bosoms, tears flowed from our eyes," Joseph recounted; "I was then requested to close our interview which I did with prayer, and it was truly a jubilee and time of rejoiceing."[29]

Joseph and William regretted the outbursts—William's petition for forgiveness was pitiful in its abjection—but their sensitivities repeatedly involved them in quarrels and fighting. Joseph rebuked critics and berated the defiant William. Outsiders who demeaned the Prophet or his family were cursed. On the other hand, he warmly welcomed them back when they were contrite. When Harvey Whitlock, a backsliding Saint, wrote a repentant letter, pleading for acceptance, Joseph wrote that "the floodgates of my heart were broken up: I could not refrain from weeping." "The angels rejoice over you." To modern eyes, Joseph's impulsiveness looks raw, but he was also vivid and strong. The expression of feelings bound people to him. Joseph summed up his own personality in a letter of instruction from the Liberty jail three years later: "Reproving betimes with sharpness when moved upon by the holy ghost and then showing forth afterwords an increas of love to ward him whom thou has reproved lest he esteem the[e] to be his enemy that he may know that thy faithfulness is stronger than the cords of death."[30]

Zion promised to end all this. In Zion, there would be no lacerating offenses, no insults, no vengeance, no infringements on honor. The inhabitants of Enoch's city "were of one heart and one mind." The Saints would live together amicably, escaping the ceaseless round of insults and reprisals, of rebuke and reconciliation. For Joseph, burdened with the contentious culture of New England's rural poor, social peace was heaven. After a particularly happy Sunday meeting in January, he wrote, "I verily realized that it was good for brethren to dwell together in unity, like dew upon the mountains of Israel."[31]

He caught a glimpse of Zion when a group of friends cut his winter's wood in December. Joseph was "sincerely grateful to each and every, one of them, for this expression of their goodness towards me." In a remarkable passage in his journal, he moved from simple gratitude to exaltation of the woodcutters.

In the name of Jesus Christ I envoke the rich benediction of heav[e]n to rest upon them and their families, and I ask my heavenly Father to preserve their health's, and those of their wives and children, that they may have strength of body to perform, their labours, in their several occupations in life, and the use and activity of their limbs, also powers of intellect and understanding hearts, that they may treasure up wisdom, understanding, and inteligence, above measure, and be preserved from plagues pestilence, and famine, and from the power of the adversary, and the hands of evil designing, men and have power over all their enemys; and the way be prepared before them, that they may journey to the land of Zion and be established, on their inheritances, to enjoy undisturbe[d] peace and happiness for ever, and ultimately to be crowned with everlasting life in the celestial Kingdom of God, which blessings I ask in the name of Jesus of Nazareth.[32]

If Joseph's theology had any foundation in his character, the footings are revealed in those words. Starting with appreciation for the winter's wood, he went on to strength of body, powers of intellect, and understanding hearts. Finally, he crowned the woodcutters with everlasting life.

NEXT YEAR IN ZION

Through all the bickering in the fall of 1835, Zion was never far from Joseph's mind. The expulsion from Jackson County and the failure of Zion's Camp to recover Mormon lands had not dulled his zeal. In May 1835, on the eve of the Twelve's departure for their summer mission, Joseph proposed to the Church in Kirtland that "we never give up the struggle for Zion, even until Death, or until Zion is Redeemed." "The vote, was unanimous and with apparent deep feeling."[33] The "salvation of Israel in the last days," an article in the *Messenger and Advocate* proclaimed, consists "in the work of the gathering."

> Men and angels are to be co-workers in bringing to pass this great work: and a Zion is to be prepared; even a new Jerusalem, for the elect that are to be gathered from the four quarters of the earth, and to be established an holy city: for the tabernacle of the Lord shall be with them.[34]

The return, they were assured, would be soon. Joseph told the Twelve in October 1835 that "they should take their families to Missouri next season." With eight other leaders, he prayed the Lord "will open the way and deliver Zion in the appointed time and that without the shedding of blood." He asked for means to "purchase inheritances, and all this easily and without perplexity, and trouble." At supper with Joseph and Emma one evening, Newel Whitney observed to Edward Partridge that next year at this time "they might be seated together around a table on the land of Zion." Emma added her hope that "the company present might be seated around her table in the land of promise." Joseph noted that "the same sentiment was reciprocated from the company round the table and my heart responded amen God grant it."[35]

How could they recover their lands? The Jackson citizenry would not permit a court trial for redress of grievances. Any Saint who set foot in the county put his life in jeopardy. Since the Missourians were certain to wage war, the Saints had to defend themselves. Joseph prayed for eight hundred to a thousand well-armed men to accomplish the work. David Whitmer was appointed "Capt of the lords host." In September Joseph challenged the Kirtland High Council that "we go next season to live or dy in Jackson County." The prospect of a battle with his comrades beside him cheered Joseph's heart. "We truly had a good time and Covena[n]ted to strugle for this thing u[n]till death shall desolve this union and if one falls that the rest be not discouraged but pe[r]sue this object untill it is accomplished which may God grant u[n]to us in the name of Christ our Lord."[36]

Meanwhile, the Saints in Missouri were to keep quiet. Joseph told them to "make little or no stir . . . and cause as little excitement as posible and endure their afflictions patiently until the time appointed." Like captive Israel in Babylon, "their harps must be hung upon the willows: and they cannot sing the songs of Zion." They were to talk not of judgments but only the first principles of the gospel. "Preach Christ and him crucified, love to God, and love to man." Whenever they could, they were to "make mention of our republican principles, thereby if posible, we may allay the prejudice of the people." Although little could be done at the moment to speed the day, the Saints collected petitions from branches all over the country and mailed them to Missouri in December.[37]

But arms and petitions figured less in their minds than spiritual strength. Ever since the dissolution of Zion's Camp, Joseph had believed the Saints would not prevail in Missouri without the endowment of spiritual power they had been anticipating for five years—their own Pentecost. The high council minutes for August 4, 1835, noted that "God has commanded us to build a house in which to receive an endowment, previous to the redemption of Zion, and . . . Zion could not be redeemed until this takes place."[38] To prepare for that time, Joseph assembled his leadership corps in Kirtland. The high council and the bishopric came from Missouri, and the Twelve Apostles and the Seventy from the mission field. "We look for the grate indowment to take place soon now theare will be a grate gathering of the saints to Zion next season," George Hinkle wrote a friend in October.[39] William Phelps told his wife, Sally, in Missouri to remain patient. He did not know "when Zion *will* be redeemed." "Little is said or known." But the endowment had to come first. "Don't reckon too much on my coming home in the spring," he warned. "Keep up your faith and pray for the endowment; as soon as that takes place the elders will anxiously speed for their families."[40]

SEVENTEEN

THE ORDER OF HEAVEN

JANUARY–APRIL 1836

Now to let you know a few of the thousand great things of God that is passing in this place. . . . some have seen the heavens opend & seen the savior others have seen angels on the four corners of the house of the Lord with drawn swords & also stood thick on the ridge Elisha with his chariot of Fire, Peter John & James, & the highway cast up the ten tribes returning in chariots as far as the eye could extend some saw the Redemtion of Zion.

BENJAMIN BROWN, KIRTLAND, TO SARAH BROWN, March 1836

THE WINTER AND SPRING MONTHS OF 1836 were among Joseph's happiest. For a time, everything went right. The strife of the previous fall ended; temple construction was progressing; the brethren studied Hebrew by day and gathered for spiritual meetings at night; weekly councils dispatched business and planned for the temple's dedication. After a long day in council, he wrote that "this has been one of the best days that I ever spent, there has been an entire unison of feeling expressed in all our p[r]oceedings this day." Paraphrasing Peter on the Mount of Transfiguration, Joseph exulted that "it has been good for us to be here."[1]

In early January, he attended a "sumptuous feast" at Bishop Whitney's. The guests sang, prayed, and Father Smith gave blessings. "Our hearts were made glad," the Prophet reported, in anticipation of "joys that will be poured upon the head of the Saints w[h]en they are gathered together on Mount Zion to enjoy each others society forever more even all the blessings of heaven and earth where there will be none to molest nor make us afraid." Here was a plain man's dream: a feast and genial companionship, safe from enemies. Bishop Whitney invited everyone back a few days later.[2]

Joseph said the feast "was after the order of the Son of God," a curious description of a party where people ate and laughed. A revelation a year earlier had attached the phrase "after the order of the Son of God" to the Priesthood; here it was applied to a dinner party. Joseph said that "the lame the halt and blind wer[e] invited according to the in[s]tructions of the Saviour," and the presence of the downtrodden probably made the feast seem Christlike.[3] But he applied the word "order" to other occasions that winter as if he felt that the "order of heaven"—the template of a good society—was beginning to regulate every aspect of his people's lives.

LIFE IN KIRTLAND

Joseph's own domestic life had become more orderly by the winter of 1836. In the fall, the Smith house had been full of people. Boarding temple workers crowded the rooms some nights, forcing Joseph and Emma to sleep on the floor. The strain on Emma may account for the premature departure from services that brought on Joseph's scolding. Earlier he had asked the boarders to leave, helping to ease Emma's burden, but the next month, Joseph's parents moved in, having left William Smith's after the November argument at the debating society. Their arrival was less of a burden for Emma.[4] Though prickly, Lucy got along well with her daughter-in-law.

Sometime in the fall, Emma became pregnant with her fifth child. Three of her four children had died at birth or soon after. Only Joseph Smith III, born in 1832, had survived. The Smiths had also lost one of the twins adopted when their own twins died in 1831. The other adopted twin, Julia Murdock Smith, was five in July 1836 when Frederick was born to Emma and Joseph.

How the Smiths paid the bills in these years is a mystery. Joseph's journal shows no evidence of working for money. In 1834, he had been granted the stewardship of a farm near the temple site, but he recorded no income or benefit. He never mentioned doing farm work or supervising anyone's labors. Later he opened a store in Kirtland, but the store was not profitable.[5] Joseph's followers helped by bringing food—half a fattened hog from John Tanner, a quarter beef from Shadrach Roundy. Others gave Joseph money or forgave borrowed sums. The Smiths never lived well, but in their small house on the hill neither did they starve.[6]

For others, temple construction provided an undependable income. Contributions from around the Church paid wages and provided building materials. A line of little houses on half-acre plots, a kind of temple village, was built near the temple for the workers. Jacob Bump plastered the inside of the temple, placing stoves in the cellar to warm the house and hurry drying. Artemus Millett, who supervised the framing, employed a crew of young men to stucco the exterior with broken glassware in the finish coat. Brigham Young glazed the windows and oversaw the painting.[7]

The workers were poor. Young once came to the printing house looking for assistance, saying "he had nothing in his house to eat, and he knew not how to get any thing." To feed his family, he borrowed twenty-five dollars from a newcomer in town. The temple committee was so far in debt, it appealed constantly for contributions in order to pay the workers. Women

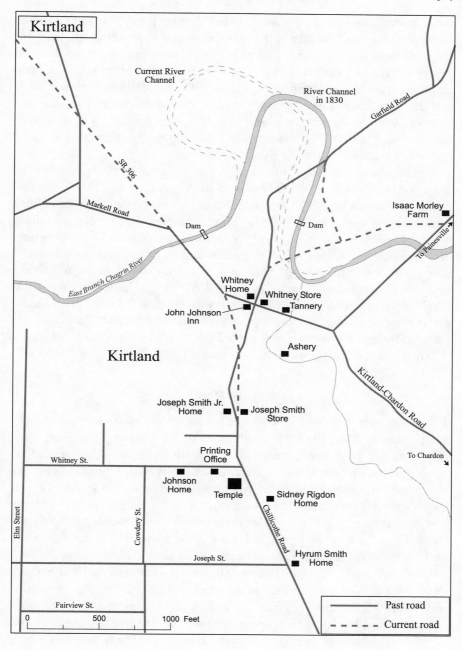

Kirtland

Current River Channel

River Channel in 1830

Garfield Road

SR 306

Markell Road

Dam

Dam

Isaac Morley Farm

To Painesville

East Branch Chagrin River

Whitney Home

Whitney Store

Tannery

John Johnson Inn

Kirtland

Ashery

Kirtland-Chardon Road

Joseph Smith Jr. Home

Joseph Smith Store

Printing Office

To Chardon

Whitney St.

Johnson Home

Temple

Sidney Rigdon Home

Elm Street

Cowdery St.

Chillicothe Road

Joseph St.

Hyrum Smith Home

Fairview St.

0   500   1000 Feet

Past road

Current road

spun, knitted, and sewed clothes for the laboring poor. Joseph negotiated loan after loan until the size of the debt drove him to pleading and bargaining with the Lord. He and Cowdery promised that if means were obtained to pay their debts, they would give one-tenth of their income to the poor and the same for their children and their children's children.[8] Heber Kimball later estimated final construction costs at between $40,000 and $50,000, a huge sum when a laborer was lucky to earn $400 a year. A large part was paid by one wealthy convert, John Tanner, who donated $13,000 and may have loaned another $30,000.[9]

By the summer of 1835, the Saints were assembling for worship in the shade of the temple walls. In January, the School of the Prophets, also called the School for the Elders, which had met in the printing office since November, moved into the temple. The December 1832 revelation calling for the temple's construction had spoken of it as a house of learning and described how to conduct a school according to divine order. During the school's five-month term, the students studied Greek, Hebrew, and theology. The instruction did not go much further, though English grammar was taught as a remedial course, along with geography.[10] In the four rooms under the eaves, the priesthood quorums assembled for instruction. While the workmen's tools were still scattered about, a singing school met in the "Chapel," as the temple was sometimes called.[11]

ENDOWMENT

The elders were meeting in the temple primarily to prepare for the "endowment of power." Joseph had awaited five years for this long-promised heavenly gift. An 1830 revelation had promised the Saints they would be "endowed with power from on high" when they got to Ohio, and an 1832 revelation said priesthood ordinances would help them to see the face of God. Spiritual blessings, much like an endowment, were received at the first session of the School of the Prophets in 1833. But later the Saints learned that the endowment would come in the temple, a house where God could "endow those whom I have chosen with power from on high."[12]

Oliver Cowdery told the Twelve, when they were ordained in February 1835, that they were "not to go to other nations till you receive your endowments." Because they had not known Jesus in mortality, these modern apostles had to know Him by revelation. "Never cease striving until you have seen God face to face," Cowdery told them. That time seemed close in October 1835. Joseph told the Twelve they were to attend the School of the Prophets that fall and "prepare the[i]r hearts in all humility for an endowment with power from on high." Indeed all priesthood holders were to ready themselves by "reigning up our minds to a sense of the great object that lies before us, viz, that glorious endowment that God has in store for the faithful." The Saints expected to relive the Pentecost in the Book of Acts when the powers of heaven rained down on the first Christians. The gift from heaven would energize all other projects—missionary work, the gathering, and the recovery of Zion.[13]

On a cold night in November 1835, when an inch of slush covered the ground, Joseph told the Twelve that new ordinances were coming to "be done in Gods own way." He had thought the Church was on a "permanent foundation" a year earlier when he had organized the high council in Missouri. He was ready to die, he said, thinking his work was complete. But now God "requires more at my hands." A solemn assembly was to be called and organized "according to the order of the house of God." Joseph was beginning to glimpse an unchanging and timeless temple order. "The order of the house of God has and ever will be the same," he told the Twelve, "even after Christ comes, and after the termination of the thousand years it will be the same, and we shall finally roll into the celestial Kingdom of God and enjoy it forever."[14]

As preparations were made, Joseph was preoccupied with the right order for everything. Church councils had to follow the pattern of the ancients. His history said the cornerstones of the Kirtland temple were laid "after the order of the priesthood," which was to divide twenty-four priesthood holders into four groups of six and assign each to a corner, beginning at the southeast.[15] In 1835 and 1836, ceremony began to infuse ordinary church business. Joseph instituted an elaborate voting method involving the Presidency of the Church, the Twelve Apostles, the Seventy, and the high councils of Missouri and Kirtland. Before this time, a single council—usually the high council in Kirtland—had made administrative decisions for the Church as a whole, but once the priesthood revelation of March 1835 explained that the governing quorums constituted the "spiritual authorities" of the Church, the possibility of them all working together had to be considered.[16]

A variant of this assemblage of authorities, called "the Grand Council," had sustained the *Doctrine and Covenants* in August 1835. A representative of each priesthood quorum, seated in order of seniority, arose in turn to approve the book, making in all ten different quorums voting one by one, plus the congregation as a whole. Through the winter of 1836, Joseph managed Church affairs this same way. At a large assembly on January 13, 1836, proposals to appoint men to bishoprics and high councils were presented for confirmation. The sustaining and ordaining of officers went on from 10 a.m. until evening, the quorums once again voting individually on each proposal. Since the voting was unanimous, the procedure was largely ceremonial, an act of confirmation rather than contest. Joseph loved it. He relished "the Spirit of the God of Israel" resting on them "in mighty power." William W. Phelps wrote his wife that the "Grand Council" was "one of the most interesting meetings I ever saw."[17]

Women remained invisible in the organization and were absent from most ritual events. Some resented it. During the 1836 pentecostal sessions, George A. Smith remembered, a few women thought "that some mischief was going on, some were right huffy about it." They were most sensitive about exclusion from spiritual occasions, gifts being their vital connection with the Church.[18] Joseph would not define a place for women in the order of heaven for another half-dozen years.

But in this spiritual season, weddings and dinners involving women were turned into holy celebrations. At the marriage of John Boynton and Susan Lowell, Joseph pronounced the "blessings of Abraham Isaac and Jacob" upon the pair, before Sidney Rigdon delivered a "forcible address." After prayer, Joseph blessed "three servers filled with glasses of wine," which were passed around, followed by cake. "Joy filled every bosom, and the countenances of old, and young, alike, seemed to bloom with the cheerfulness and smiles of youth and an entire unison of feeling seemed to pervade the congregation." Joseph enjoyed these social occasions as much as the meetings of authorities in the Grand Council. "I doubt whether the pages of history can boast," he noted in his journal, "of a more splendid and inocent wedding and feast than this for it was conducted after the order of heaven."[19]

During the winter, a small committee under Joseph's direction worked out nine rules for temple conduct. They prohibited going up the stairs during worship, marring the house with knife or pencil, and children playing in the rooms. Speakers were not to be interrupted by laughing, whispering, or "menacing Jestures," and the presiding officers were not to be insulted. Joseph solemnly told the assembled authorities that they were under "great responsibility" to enforce the rules "in righteousness before God, inasmuch as our decisions will have a bearing upon all mankind and upon all generations to come."[20] Decorum apparently had to be perfect for the Saints to receive the outpouring of heaven. Even the walls and the furniture were to be honored, if people were to change from "natural" to heavenly conduct. Later the Saints removed their shoes and dressed in white on entering the temple.[21]

PENTECOST

In mid-winter, the elaborate attention to heavenly order bore fruit. At Sunday meeting on January 17, Joseph organized the attendees into the several quorums, and instead of the usual preaching, the First Presidency and the Twelve confessed their faults to one another.[22] "The congregation were soon overwhelmed in tears," Joseph said, "and some of our hearts were too big for utterance, the gift of toungs, come upon us also like rushing of a mighty wind, and my soul was filled with the glory of God." William W. Phelps could scarcely talk. "When I was speaking," he wrote Sally, "which was but few words, the Spirit of the Lord came upon me so that I could not *speak*, and I cried as little children cry in earnest and the tears from my eyes ran in streams; the audience, which was the largest ever convened in the said room, sobbed and wept aloud."[23]

The temple rituals began with washings. Earlier, in January 1833, Joseph had washed the feet of thirteen brethren, following the example of Jesus in the Gospel of John.[24] In 1836, a new kind of washing, one for the whole body, was instituted, following Old Testament practices. On Thursday afternoon, January 21, "we attended to the ordinance of washing our bodies in pure water," Joseph wrote in his journal. "We also perfumed our bodies and our heads, in the name of the Lord."[25] Oliver Cowdery gave a fuller description of washings performed the previous Saturday.

Met in the evening with bro. Joseph Smith, jr. at his house, in company with bro. John Corrill, and after pure water was prepared, called upon the Lord and proceeded to wash each other's bodies, and bathe the same with whiskey, perfumed with cinnamon. This we did that we might be clearn before the Lord for the Sabbath, confessing our sins and covenanting to be faithful to God. While performing this washing unto the Lord with solemnity, our minds were filled with many reflections upon the propriety of the same, and how the priests anciently used to wash always before ministering before the Lord. As we had nearly finished this purification, bro. Martin Harris came in and was also washed.

When the brethren met the following Thursday, they added an anointing with oil. Dark having fallen, the west room of the temple was lit by candles. While the high councils from Kirtland and Missouri waited in two adjoining rooms, Joseph and six other men attended to "the ordinance of annointing our heads with holy oil." Recording exactly how he proceeded, Joseph wrote that "I took the oil in my left hand, father Smith being seated before me and the rest of the presidency encircled him round about.—we then stretched our right hands to heaven and blessed the oil and consecrated it in the name of Jesus Christ." The circle laid their hands on Father Smith and blessed him, after which Joseph anointed his father with the oil, and the others "laid their hands upon his head, beginning at the eldest, untill they had all laid their hands on him, and pronounced such blessings, upon his head as the Lord put into their hearts," as they did so rubbing their hands over his anointed face and head. Having been anointed and blessed himself, Joseph Sr. rose and anointed the others in order of age. When he came to his son, he "sealed upon me the blessings, of Moses, to lead Israel in the latter days, even as moses led him in days of old,—also the blessings of Abraham Isaac and Jacob." All of the Presidency followed Father Smith with blessings and prophecies on Joseph.[26]

One searches in vain for such rituals among Joseph's Protestant contemporaries. The Shakers' mountaintop feasts of the Passover were in another vein entirely, and the Baptists' feet-washing in imitation of the New Testament practice never came to full washings or anointings with oil.[27] Oliver Cowdery reveals Joseph's source in commenting that "those named in the first room were annointed with the same kind of oil and in the man[ner] that were Moses and Aaron, and those who stood before the Lord in ancient days." In Exodus, the Lord commanded Moses to "bring Aaron and his sons unto the door of the tabernacle of the congregation, and wash them with water." Then "thou shalt put upon Aaron the holy garments, and anoint him, and sanctify him; that he may minister unto me in the priest's office." The washing and anointing of ancient Hebrew priests became the pattern for the modern temple. Even the cinnamon perfume was in the biblical recipe for anointing oil. Exodus called for myrrh and calamus to be mixed with "sweet cinnamon," but cinnamon was all these poor Latter-day priests could manage. In an era when many Christians were sloughing off the Hebrew Bible and taking their Gospel solely from the New Testament, Joseph drew upon ceremonies in Exodus.[28] Later the Saints clothed themselves in holy garments like Aaron.

After Joseph's anointing, he wrote, "the heavens were opened upon us and I beheld the celestial kingdom of God, and the glory thereof, whether in the body or out I cannot tell." He saw the throne of God "whereon was seated the Father and the Son" and the streets of heaven looking like gold. He saw Adam, Abraham, and Michael and his older brother Alvin, who had died when Joseph was seventeen. How could Alvin be in heaven without being baptized? Joseph wondered. A voice told him that "all who have died with[out] a knowledge of this gospel, who would have received it, if they had been permited to tarry, shall be heirs of the celestial kingdom of God." He saw the Twelve Apostles in a foreign land "standing together in a circle much fatiegued, with their clothes tattered and feet swolen, with their eyes cast downard, and Jesus standing in their midst, and they did not behold him, the Saviour looked upon them and wept." All through the night, Joseph saw visions: Elder McLellin in the South healing a lame man, and Brigham Young in a southwest desert preaching from a rock to "a dozen men of colour, who, appeared hostile." Young was protected by an "angel of God standing above his head with a drawn sword." Joseph said that many of the brethren "saw glorious visions also."[29]

After the Presidency, Joseph anointed the bishops of Kirtland and Clay County with their counselors, the high councils of the two cities, and then the presidents of each quorum. The Bishop of Missouri, Edward Partridge, wrote that "a number saw visions & others were blessed with the outpouring of the Holy Ghost. The vision of heaven was opened to these also, some of them saw the face of the Saviour, and others were ministered unto by holy angels." Finally, after 1 a.m., the brethren sang, invoked the blessing of heaven with uplifted hands, and went home.[30]

The next day no one could concentrate on school. They wanted to talk over "the glorious scenes that transpired on the preceding evening."[31] Joseph had now established a procedure for the priesthood to follow in the temple: washing the body, anointing with oil, and sealing the anointing with prayer.[32] That evening the Twelve Apostles and the Seventy underwent the same procedure. Joseph anointed Thomas Marsh, head of the Twelve, and he in turn anointed his brethren, from oldest to youngest, sealing a blessing on each. The Twelve anointed and blessed the presidency of the Seventy, who did the same to each of their fellow seventies. Following the ordinances, "toungs, fell upon us in mighty pow[e]r, angels mingled their voices with ours, while their presence was in our midst, and unseasing prasis swelled our bosoms for the space of half an hour." At two in the morning they went home, and, Joseph said, "the spirit & visions of God attended me through the night."[33]

Six days later, in the west room of the temple attic, the presidency of the high priests were anointed and then their quorum. At the other end of the room, the elders' presidency were anointed and they anointed their brethren. In another room, Joseph found the Twelve Apostles meeting with the Seventy, and instructed them in an additional step: "to call upon God with uplifted hands to seal the blessings which had been promised to them by the holy anointing." And so the ordinances were elaborated, each one bringing more spiritual manifestations. Joseph retired filled with the Spirit and "my soul cried hossannah to God & the Lamb through the silent watches of the night & while my eyes were closed in sleep the visions of the Lord were sweet unto me & his glory was round about me."[34]

Through January and February, the brethren read Hebrew by day, and washed, anointed, prayed, and beheld visions by night.[35] The occasional sermons were not recorded in Joseph's journal. Ordinances and spiritual gifts filled the entries, showing more concern with ritual order than doctrine. One Saturday evening, he "went to the upper rooms of the Lord's house & set the different quorems in order," telling them how to anoint. In the evening, "I returned to my house being weary with continual anxiety & labour in puting all the Authorities in [order] & in striving to purify them for the solemn assembly according to the commandment of the Lord."[36]

Oliver Cowdery prayed in his diary, "O may we be prepared for the endowment,—being sanctified and cleansed from all sin." William Phelps captured the mood in a verse of "The Spirit of God," sung at the temple dedication in March.

We'll wash, and be washed, and with oil be anointed
    Withal not omitting the washing of feet:
For he that receiveth his PENNY appointed,
    Must surely be clean at the harvest of wheat.[37]

Joseph's method for bringing his people to holiness differed from the approach of evangelical preachers. Rather than convicting people of their sins, thus humbling them before God, Joseph relied upon the power of ritual to arouse their spirits. The Saints did not have to admit their helplessness as a first step toward reaching Christ. They were washed, anointed, and blessed—ministered to, rather than upbraided—a more liturgical than evangelical method. Phelps wrote his wife, "We are preparing to make ourselves clean, by first cleansing our hearts, forsaking our sins, forgiving everybody, all we ever had against them; anointing washing the body; putting on clean decent clothes, by anointing our heads and by keeping all the commandments. As we come nearer to God we see our imperfections and nothingness plainer and plainer."[38]

Ritual form was crucial. One Saturday night in early February, Joseph "called the anointed together to receive the seal of all their blessings." They were organized by quorums: the high priests and the elders in one room, the Seventy and the Twelve in the next, the bishoprics adjoining. He told each quorum to proceed with silent prayer, concluding with a sealing prayer by President Rigdon when all the quorums were to shout a "solemn hosannah to God & the Lamb." Then all were to be seated and lift up their hearts in silent prayer, and if one had a vision or prophecy he was to rise and speak. For some reason, all the quorums did not comply. "I went from room to room repeatedly," he said impatiently, "and charged each separately—assuring them it was according to the mind of God." And yet while talking to the bishops he felt something was wrong with the elders and sent Hyrum and Cowdery to investigate. Requested to "observe order," the elders replied that "they had a teacher of their own & did not wish to be troubled by others." Joseph reported as a result "this quorem lost th[e]ir blessing in a great measure." A "cloud of darkness" filled the elders' room, their minutes reported, while the more careful quorums "enjoyed a great flow of the holy spirit" that was "like fire in their bones."[39]

Joseph said nothing about a revelation on washings and anointings. The only scriptural authorization came from Exodus. Yet Joseph assured the brethren that the order was "according to the mind of God." He introduced the washings, anointings, and sealings as rigorously as any commandment.[40] Ritual now assumed as much importance as the gathering or Zion or the organization of councils in the overall program of the Church. The Kirtland rituals amounted to another form of revelation, comparable in importance to the visitations of angels, the voice of the Spirit speaking for God, the translations of historical texts, and the organization of Church councils by precedent and experience.

DEDICATION

In March, the temple washings and anointings ended, and the month was devoted to Hebrew study in the school. "Attended School as usual" was Joseph's typical diary entry. The temple neared completion and dedication loomed. The "quorum of singers" was practicing in the chapel, Joseph reported on March 16, likely perfecting songs that Emma and William Phelps had compiled for a book of hymns. Five of the six hymns sung at the dedication were written by Phelps and Parley Pratt, the leading Latter-day Saint poets.[41]

The First Presidency spent the Saturday before the dedication working on seating arrangements and ordering events. At this climactic moment, the priesthood organization would be displayed and the accumulated organizational layers ordered spatially. In his notes on the planning meeting, Joseph specified the seating chart for the meeting.

At the west end of the temple:

1. In the altars, the Patriarch, First Presidency, Presidency of Zion, and Presidency of the High Priests.

2. The Twelve Apostles on the right in the three highest seats with the Presidency of the Elders just below them.

3. The twelve High Councilors of Kirtland on the left in the three first seats with Joseph's scribes below them.

At the east end of the temple:

1. The Bishoprics of Kirtland and Zion in the first two altars with the Presidencies of the Priests and Teachers below them.

2. The twelve High Councilors of Zion to the right with the Presidency of the Deacons below them.

3. The Presidents of the Seventy to the left.[42]

Every quorum was given a place roughly in order of precedence. The Twelve Apostles, on the right of the First Presidency, were coming to be seen as the quorum next in authority. The Kirtland High Council sat next to the Presidency at the west end, indicating a rank slightly above the high council in Missouri, seated by the bishops at the east.

The dedication on March 27 was open to the general public. "A great many strangers came from the country to see it," reported Ira Ames, who collected donations at the door. People arrived at 7 a.m., and 500 or 600 were waiting outside when the doors opened at 8:00. Joseph, Cowdery, and Rigdon seated 900 to 1,000 in the lower court of the temple. The overflow went to the schoolhouse for a meeting, and the dedication was repeated the following Thursday for their benefit. Recognizing a general interest, the dedicatory prayer was published in a *Messenger and Advocate* broadside.[43]

As often happened on grand occasions, Sidney Rigdon, the most polished of the Church's preachers, took the leading role. Opening the meeting, he read two psalms, prayed, and then spoke two and a half hours on a text from Matthew 8: "the Son of man hath no where to lay his head." Joseph called Rigdon's address "forcible and sublime, and well adapted to the occasion," but said nothing about the content. Joseph was more interested in the business of the meeting. Rigdon asked the quorums to acknowledge Joseph as "a prophet and seer" and to uphold him by their prayers of faith. The voting followed the procedures worked out in the Grand Council meetings of the previous winter: "all the quorums in their turn" gave "their assent by rising on their feet." After an intermission, Joseph gave a short address—on what subject he did not say—and then asked the quorums to acknowledge the entire First Presidency as "Prophets and Seers." "I then called upon the quorums and congregation of saints to acknowledge the 12 Apostles who were present as Prophets and Seers." By now they were into the third round of polling. Quorum by quorum, they voted for the Kirtland High Council, the bishoprics of Kirtland and Missouri, the High Council of Missouri, the presidents of the Seventy, the Presidency of the Elders, and finally "the quorums and congregation of saints were . . . called upon to acknowledge and uphold by their prayers the Presidents of the Priests, Teachers, and Deacons and their counsellors, which they did by rising." Depending on possible combined votes, there could have been twelve different sustainings by ten or twelve different quorums, plus the congregation—all rising to show each other support.[44]

This tedious ritual testified to the importance of organization in Joseph's mind. The daylong meeting dedicated Church government as well as the temple. Joseph described the organizational business in detail while skipping over the sermons and the accounts of spiritual gifts. Constructing a kingdom of priests meant as much to him as propounding a set of doctrines. The dedication gave him the opportunity to display the Church's organization, one of his masterpieces, before the Saints and the world.[45]

Only after this extended presentation of officers did Joseph come to the dedicatory prayer. He wrote the prayer by revelation, he later reported, with help from counselors and clerks.[46] The prayer sums up the Church's concerns in 1836, bringing before God each major project.

1. The temple was presented to God for acceptance. Joseph asked "that thy holy presence may be continually in this house."

2. He prayed for the promised endowment to come to the Saints. "Let the annointing of thy ministers be sealed upon them with power from on high: let it be fulfilled upon them, as upon those on the day of Pentecost."

3. Feeling increasing opposition, Joseph asked that "no weapon formed against them shall prosper." He desired that "no combination of wickedness shall have power to rise up and prevail over thy people."

4. Joseph prayed that the righteous could gather to Zion and that the Lord would remember "those who have been driven by the inhabitants of Jackson county, Missouri, from the lands of their inheritance."

5. Then he prayed for the missionaries and for success in gathering Israel from among the nations.

6. Finally, Joseph asked for the exaltation of the Saints, that at the last day "our garments may be pure, that we may be clothed upon with robes of righteousness, with palms in our hands, and crowns of glory upon our heads, and reap eternal joy for all our sufferings."[47]

The meeting closed with a ceremonial gesture—a shout in the Methodist tradition. "We then sealed the proceedings of the day," Joseph reported, "by shouting hosanah to God and the Lamb 3 times sealing it each time with Amen, Amen, and Amen."

The dedication was over, but was this the Pentecostal endowment of power Joseph had so long anticipated? Joseph mentioned the appearance of angels. Frederick G. Williams testified "that while Presdt Rigdon was making his first prayer an angel entered the window and took his seat . . . between father Smith, and himself." Others saw angels, and two apostles sang and spoke in tongues. Although Joseph made no record of the events, others reported "great manifestations of power, such as speaking in tongues, seeing visions, administration of angels." Oliver Cowdery "saw the glory of God, like a great cloud, come down and rest upon the house, and fill the same like a mighty rushing wind. I also saw cloven tongues, like as of fire rest upon many . . . while they spake with other tongues and prophesied."[48]

But the congregation did not see the face of God, and the level of spiritual manifestations did not equal the outpourings of January and February. Had the long-sought endowment finally been granted? Apparently satisfied with what had happened, Joseph returned to practical matters. The campaign to redeem Zion had been on hold for months, and he was eager to get busy. Two days after the dedication, Joseph and four counselors met "in

the most holy place in the Lords house" (probably the west room in the
attic) and sought "a revelation from Him to teach us concerning our going
to Zion."[49] But then the Spirit whispered to come into the holy place three
times with the other presidents and the bishoprics, fasting through the
day and night, and, if they were humble, a revelation on Zion would be
given.

No record of such a revelation survives, but once the brethren were
gathered in the temple, the meeting took another direction. Joseph decided
to remain in the house until morning. Followers were to cleanse their feet
and take the sacrament "that we might be made holy before Him, and
thereby be qualified to officiate in our calling upon the morrow in washing
the feet of the Elders." The brethren washed feet and partook of the sacrament. "The Holy S[p]irit rested down upon us," Joseph reported, "and
we continued in the Lords house all night prophesying and giving glory
to God."[50]

The next day, March 30, more priesthood joined them "and all the official
members in this stake of Zion amounting to about 300." To provide for the
multitude, Joseph called for towels and tubs of water and took up a collection to purchase bread and wine. The First Presidency washed the feet of
the Twelve and then the brethren began prophesying on each other's heads,
often sealing the prophecies with "Hosanna and Amen." After lowering the
veils, "they prophesied, spoke and sang in tongues in each room." Exhausted
after the all-night session, the Presidency retired, but the rest of the
brethren remained, "exhorting, prophesying and speaking in tongues" until
5 a.m. A few skeptics wondered if the brethren had become drunk on sacrament wine, but according to Joseph's journal, the nonstop Tuesday and
Wednesday meetings were, finally, the endowment.[51]

> The Saviour made his appearance to some, while angels minestered unto oth-
> ers, and it was a penticost and enduement indeed, long to be remembered for
> the sound shall go forth from this place into all the world, and the occur-
> rences of this day shall be hande[d] down upon the pages of sacred history to
> all generations, as the day of Pentecost.[52]

Not many saw the face of God or the Savior, but enough had been given
to say that the endowment was now theirs.[53] As one brother wrote later,
"Some brethren expressed themselves as being disappointed at not receiving more and greater manifestations of the power of God, but for our
part, we had found the pearl of great price, and our soul was happy and
contented, and we rejoiced greatly in the Lord." Joseph told the quorums
"that I had now completed the organization of the church and we had
passed through all the necessary ceremonies, that I had given them all the

instruction they needed." Now they needed to "build up the kingdom of God."[54]

These exhausting and exhilarating three months, the zenith of the Saints' ecstatic experience, came in the 1830s, at a high point of visionary religion in American history.[55] In 1837, Emerson would tell Harvard Divinity School graduates "that the gleams which flash across my mind, are not mine, but God's."[56] In the next year, the "Era of Manifestations" began in Shaker communities at New Lebanon and Watervliet, New York, where visions, tongues, and spiritual "operations" took over entire congregations. In 1844, Ellen G. White, the Adventist prophetess, would receive the first in a series of visions that eventually filled many volumes. In the late 1830s a cluster of evangelical theologians around Charles G. Finney at Oberlin contemplated the doctrine of sinless perfection. Under the influence of grace, a person could live a perfectly sinless life.[57] For a number of groups, the cap on human experience seemed to be lifting.

AFTERMATH

Joyous as the endowment was, Joseph's attention went back to Zion immediately. After the seven-month suspension, the missionaries were to return to the field to gather Israel, empowered now by their spiritual experiences. If ever the Saints were slain or driven from their lands in Missouri again, Joseph vowed, we would "give ourselves no rest until we are avenged of our enimies." They would preach or fight, whichever was required, confident that God was with them. The Saturday following the last endowment experience, Joseph's clerk noted him talking on "his favorite theme," which was "the redemption of Zion." The clerk observed that "the positive manner in which he [Joseph Smith] expressed himself . . . was directly calculated to produce conviction in the minds of those who heard him, that his whole soul was engaged in it."[58] He and Cowdery set out that day to collect funds to redeem their lands.

To their surprise, the spiritual experiences in the temple were not over.[59] The next Sunday, about a thousand people attended the morning service and returned in the afternoon for the sacrament. At the conclusion, Joseph and Cowdery went into one of the pulpits and had the veil dropped, cutting them off from view of the congregation. In seclusion, they experienced one of Joseph's most spectacular visions, later recorded by Warren Cowdery, Joseph's clerk and Oliver's brother.

> They saw the Lord standing upon the breast work of the pulpit before them, and under his feet was a paved work of pure gold, in color like amber: his eyes were as a flame of fire; the hair of his head was like the pure snow, his counte-

nance shone above the brightness of the sun, and his voice was as the sound of the rushing of great waters, even the Voice of Jehovah, saying, I am the first and the last, I am he who liveth, I am he who was slain. I am your Advocate with the Father. Behold your sins are forgiven you. You are clean before me, therefore, lift up your heads and rejoice, let the hearts of your brethren rejoice and let the hearts of all my people rejoice, who have with their might, built this house to my name. For behold I have accepted this house and my name shall be here; and I will manifest myself to my people, in mercy, in this House, yea I will appear unto my servants and speak unto them with mine own voice, if my people will keep my commandments and do not pollute this Holy House.[60]

What could this staggering experience have meant to Joseph and Cowdery? Unfortunately, Joseph's detailed Ohio journal ends with Warren Cowdery's entry. The long run of reports abruptly halts, not to be resumed for two years. We have no idea what Joseph and Cowdery said when they came from behind the veil, or how widely they shared the account. The vision was not included in editions of the *Doctrine and Covenants* published during Joseph's lifetime, and no manuscript copies exist save Warren Cowdery's and the one Willard Richards copied into Joseph's history for the Church newspaper in 1843.[61] Joseph never mentioned the event in his other writings. There is no evidence he told the Kirtland Saints.

Warren Cowdery reported additional visitors behind the veil that day. Moses appeared, and then Elias, followed by Elijah. Each personage presented "keys"—that is, the power and right to perform certain acts on God's behalf: Moses, to gather Israel; Elias, for the gospel of Abraham; and Elijah for turning the hearts of the fathers to the children and children to the fathers, in fulfillment of a prophecy in Malachi. No explanation of these keys was given. The gathering of Israel was familiar by this time, but the significance of the gospel of Abraham and uniting the hearts of fathers and children could only be surmised.[62]

The episode behind the veil is mysteriously suspended at the end of the diary without comment or explanation, as if Joseph was stilled by the event.[63] Joseph would have needed time to understand Elijah's part in the order of heaven. As for Abraham, Joseph had been translating his writings since the Egyptian scrolls were purchased the previous summer, and Abraham's gospel still was not clear. How did it differ from the gospel the Saints already had? In time, the name of Abraham would be invoked to explain marriage practices too radical to be announced.

Besides marking the completion of the temple, the April 3 vision signaled the coming of incommunicable revelations. The frequency of announced revelations slowed in the ensuing years. Doctrine came through sermons, offhand comments, and letters, reports on revelations rather than full revelations themselves. An air of mystery and reticence rises around the Prophet. He had conscientiously worked to install the order of heaven in Kirtland as rapidly as new light came to him, introducing washings and anointings and ceremonial order. After the temple dedication, he confidently informed the Saints that he had completed the organization of the Church and given them all the instruction they needed. Zion could now be built. But then just as he was setting to work on Zion, an enigmatic revelation intervened. The revelation behind the veil suggested that Joseph was moving ahead of his followers. He began to speak of revelations they could not bear.[64]

EIGHTEEN

REVERSES

APRIL 1836–JANUARY 1838

Bretheren we have waided through a scene of affliction and sorrow thus far for the will of God, that language is inadequate to describe pray ye therefore with more earnestness for our redemption.
JOSEPH SMITH TO JOHN CORRILL AND OTHERS, September 4, 1837

THE DEDICATION OF THE TEMPLE in 1836 was a high point. After its completion, Joseph Smith's life descended into a tangle of intrigue and conflict. To this point, the Church had suffered little internal contention. Joseph's most virulent critics had been newspaper editors and lapsed Mormons.[1] By the winter of 1837, however, factions in Kirtland, believing Joseph had fallen, were trying to depose him. Joseph was accused of false steps in the promotion of a Kirtland bank and of moral transgression in taking an additional wife—or worse. Some of his most trusted associates lost confidence in him, and for the first time, loyalty became a central issue. Who would stand by him, who would turn against him?

Unfortunately, Joseph's own words are rarely heard in this dark time. There are no more dictated journals, no writing by his hand. Clerks made his diary entries, sometimes only listing official acts. Not even the birth of Joseph's son Frederick is mentioned. The revelations decreased too. Between the dedication of the Kirtland temple in the spring of 1836 until the Prophet fled Kirtland in early 1838, only two brief revelations were recorded. From then until the end of his life, only twenty more were added to the canon. His speeches are known only from notes by listeners. On the large issues of the next eight years—plural marriage, the temple endowment, the plans for the Kingdom of God—we hear virtually nothing from Joseph himself. He moves behind a screen of other minds: those of clerks who wrote his diaries, hearers who took notes on his sermons, enemies who charged him with dire crimes, official letters written by others, sensational reports by newspaper editors, and later remembrances of loyal old comrades and embittered former friends.

The image of Joseph Smith shifts and goes out of focus. We know the facts of his life—a succession of battles and defeats, widening influence and doctrinal exposition, a reach for power and glory, and finally gunshots and death—but not his personality or attitudes. Was he the same hopeful Joseph Smith of the Kirtland years, the person who yearned to be the friend of God, or did he develop an insatiable appetite for position and eminence. Did he give way to his lusts? The answers depend on who speaks.

FANNY ALGER

There is evidence that Joseph was a polygamist by 1835. Was he also an adulterer? In an angry letter written in 1838, Oliver Cowdery referred to the "dirty, nasty, filthy affair" of Joseph Smith and Fanny Alger.[2] What did that mean? Had Joseph been involved in an illicit affair? Some of his critics tried to depict him as a libertine going back to the New York years. One of Emma's cousins by marriage, Levi Lewis, said Martin Harris spoke of Joseph's attempt to seduce Elizabeth Winters, a friend of Emma's in Harmony. But the reports are tenuous. Harris said nothing of the event in his many descriptions of Joseph, nor did Winters herself when interviewed much later.[3] Considering how eager the Palmyra neighbors were to besmirch Joseph's character, their minimal mention of moral lapses suggests libertinism was not part of his New York reputation. In Kirtland, the situation was more complicated.

Alger was fourteen when her family joined the Church in Mayfield, near Kirtland, in 1830. In 1836, after a time as a serving girl in the Smith household, she left Kirtland and soon married. Between those two dates, perhaps as early as 1831, she and Joseph were reportedly involved, but conflicting accounts make it difficult to establish the facts—much less to understand Joseph's thoughts. Was he a blackguard covering his lusts with religious pretensions, or a prophet doggedly adhering to instructions from heaven, or something in between?

Rumors of Mormon sexual license were circulating by 1835, when an "Article on Marriage" published in the *Doctrine and Covenants* said that Church members had been "reproached with the crime of fornication and polygamy." Coming from faithful Mormons, this evidence of marital irregularities cannot be ignored, but neither can it be taken at face value. From the Münster Anabaptists of the sixteenth century to the camp meetings of the nineteenth, critics expected sexual improprieties from religious enthusiasts. Marital experiments by contemporary radical sects increased the suspicions.[4] John Humphrey Noyes, founder of the Oneida community, concluded that "there is no more reason why sexual intercourse should be restricted by law, than why eating and drinking should be." With old barriers coming down, people were on the lookout for sexual aberrations. What, if anything, lay behind the accusations of the Mormons is uncertain. They were apparently on edge themselves; the seventies resolved to expel any of their members guilty of polygamy.[5]

No one intimated in 1835 that Joseph's actions caused the rumors. The sources written before 1839 indicate that most Church leaders knew nothing of a possible marriage. What they did know is suggested by the minutes of Oliver Cowdery's excommunication trial before the Far West High Council in April 1838, one of the few contemporaneous sources. Cowdery, long Joseph's friend and associate in visions, was a casualty of the bad times. In 1838, he was charged with "seeking to destroy the character of President Joseph Smith jr by falsly insinuating that he was guilty of adultry &c."[6] Fanny Alger's name was never mentioned, but doubtless she was the woman in question.

The Far West court did not accuse Joseph of being involved with Alger. Some councilors had heard the rumors, but concluded they were untrue. They were concerned only with Cowdery's insinuations. He was on trial for false accusations, not Joseph for adultery. David Patten, an apostle, "went to Oliver Cowdery to enquire of him if a certain story was true respecting J. Smith's committing adultery with a certain girl, when he turned on his heel and insinuated as though he was guilty." Thomas Marsh, another apostle, reported a similar experience. "Oliver Cowdery cocked up his eye very knowingly and hesitated to answer the question, saying he did not know as he was bound to answer the question yet conveyed the idea that it was true." George Harris testified that in conversation between Cowdery and Joseph the previous November, Cowdery "seemed to insinuate that Joseph Smith jr was guilty of adultery." Eventually the court concluded that Cowdery had made false accusations, and cut him off from the Church.[7]

Cowdery denied that he had lied about Joseph and Alger. Cowdery had heard the accusations against him when he wrote to Joseph in January 1838. "I learn from Kirtland, by the last letters, that you have publickly said, that when you were here I confessed to you that I had willfully lied about you." He demanded that Joseph retract the statement. In a letter to his brother Warren, Cowdery insisted he would never dishonor the family name by lying about anything, much less about the Smiths, whom he had always defended. In his conversations with Joseph, Cowdery asserted, "in every instance, I did not fail to affirm that what I had said was strictly true," meaning he believed Joseph did have an affair. His insinuations were not lies but the truth as he understood it.[8]

Cowdery and Joseph aired their differences at a meeting in November 1837 where Joseph did not deny his relationship with Alger, but contended that he had never confessed to adultery. Cowdery apparently had said otherwise, but backed down at the November meeting. When the question was put to Cowdery "if he [Joseph] had ever acknowledged to him that he was guilty of such a thing . . . he answered No."[9] That was all Joseph wanted: an admission that he had not termed the Alger affair adulterous. As Cowdery told his brother, "just before leaving, he [Joseph] wanted to drop every past thing, in which had been a difficulty or difference—he called witnesses to the fact, gave me his hand in their presence, and I might have supposed of an honest man, calculated to say nothing of former matters."[10]

These scraps of testimony recorded within a few years of the Alger business show how differently the various parties understood events. In the contemporaneous documents, only one person, Cowdery, believed that Joseph had had an affair with Fanny Alger. Others may have heard the rumors, but none joined Cowdery in making accusations.[11] David Patten, who made inquiries in Kirtland, concluded the rumors were untrue. No one proposed to put Joseph on trial for adultery. Only Cowdery, who was leaving the Church, asserted Joseph's involvement. On his part, Joseph never denied a relationship with Alger, but insisted it was not adulterous. He wanted it on record that he had never confessed to such a sin. Presumably, he felt innocent because he had married Alger.

After the Far West council excommunicated Cowdery, Alger disappears from the Mormon historical record for a quarter of a century. Her story was recorded as many as sixty years later by witnesses who had strong reason to take sides.[12] Surprisingly, they all agree that Joseph married Fanny Alger as a plural wife. Ann Eliza Webb Young, the notorious divorced wife of Brigham Young who toured the country lecturing against the Mormons, thought the relationship was scandalous but reported that Fanny's parents "considered it the highest honor to have their daughter adopted into the Prophet's family, and her mother has always claimed that [Fanny] was sealed to Joseph at that time." Ann Eliza's father, Chauncey Webb, who reportedly took Alger in when Emma learned of the marriage, said Joseph "was sealed there secretly to Fanny Alger," Mormon language for marriage.[13]

On the believers' side, Mosiah Hancock wrote in the 1890s about Joseph engaging Levi Hancock, Mosiah's father, to ask Alger's parents for permission to marry. Levi Hancock was Alger's uncle and an appropriate go-between. He talked with Alger's father, then her mother, and finally to Fanny herself, and all three consented. As in many subsequent plural marriages, Joseph did not steal away the prospective bride. He approached the parents first to ask for their daughter's hand. Hancock performed the ceremony, repeating words Joseph dictated to him. The whole process was formal and, in a peculiar way, old-fashioned.[14]

Most of the other stories about Joseph's plural marriage in Kirtland come from one individual without confirmation from a second source. Ann Eliza, for example, included a story of Fanny being ejected by a furious

Emma, one of the few scraps of information about her reaction. Ann Eliza could not have been an eyewitness because she was not yet born, but she might have heard the story from her parents, who were close to the Smiths. Are such accounts to be believed? One of the few tales that appears in more than one account was of Oliver Cowdery experimenting with plural wives himself, contrary to Joseph's counsel.[15] That pattern of followers marrying prematurely without authorization was repeated later when some of Joseph's followers used the doctrine of plural marriage as a license for marrying at will. Stories like these, all of them from intensely partisan witnesses, must be treated with caution.

On that principle, the date when plural marriage was begun will remain uncertain. Todd Compton, putting the evidence together in his massive history, concluded that Joseph began practicing plural marriage around 1833. The sources offer conflicting testimony on when the principle was revealed. When a plural marriage revelation was finally written down in 1843, it referred to a question about Old Testament polygamy: "You have enquired of my hand to know and understand wherein I the Lord justified my servants, Abraham, Isaac and Jacob; as also Moses, David and Solomon, my servants, as touching the principle and doctrine of their having many wives and concubines." Joseph frequently inquired about biblical practices while revising the scriptures, and it seems possible that he received the revelation on plural marriage in 1831 while working on the Old Testament.[16]

Because plural marriage was so sexually charged, the practice has provoked endless speculation about Joseph's motives. Was he a libertine in the guise of a prophet seducing women for his own pleasure? The question can never be answered definitively from historical sources, but the language he used to describe marriage is known. Joseph did not explain plural marriage as a love match or even a companionship. Only slight hints of romance found their way into his proposals. He understood plural marriage as a religious principle. Levi Hancock remembered the Prophet telling him in 1832: "Brother Levi, the Lord has revealed to me that it is his will that righteous men shall take Righteous women even a plurality of Wives that a Righteous race may be sent forth uppon the Earth preparatory to the ushering in of the Millenial Reign of our Redeemer."[17] As Joseph described the practice to Hancock, plural marriage had the millennial purpose of fashioning a righteous generation on the eve of the Second Coming.

The end of Joseph's relationship with Fanny Alger is as elusive as the beginning. After leaving Kirtland in September 1836, Alger, reportedly a comely, amiable person, had no trouble remarrying. Joseph asked her uncle Hancock to take her to Missouri, but she went with her parents instead. They stopped in Indiana for the season, and while there she married Solomon Custer, a non-Mormon listed in the censuses as grocer, baker, and merchant. When her parents moved on, Alger remained in Indiana with her husband. She bore nine children. After Joseph's death, Alger's brother asked her about her relationship with the Prophet. She replied: "That is all a matter of my—own. And I have nothing to Communicate."[18]

CLAY COUNTY

Joseph had believed that the endowment of power in the temple would open the gates to Jackson County. Either an army of Saints would sweep through, or their enemies' hearts would be softened. Two days after the temple dedication, Joseph and the other presidents "met in the most holy place in the Lords house and sought for a revelation from Him to teach us concerning our going to Zion."[19] Suspension of Joseph's journal in early April obscures what happened next, but by the summer of 1836, the Saints were further than ever from their goal.

On June 29, 1836, a public meeting in Liberty, Missouri, voted that the Saints must leave Clay County, which had been their home since they were driven from Jackson County in late 1833. Now "the clouds of civil war are rolling up their fearful masses," the drafting committee reported, "and hanging over our devoted country. Solemn, dark terrible." The report recalled the sympathy shown the penniless Saints when they first arrived. Now, when they were purchasing land and increasing their numbers, their alien character was becoming obvious: "They are Eastern men, whose manners, habits, customs and even dialect, are essentially different from our own." Worst of all, "they are non-slave holders, and opposed to slavery; which, in this peculiar period, when abolition has reared its deformed and haggard visage in our land, is well calculated to excite deep and abiding prejudices."[20]

Mormon opposition to slavery had come up earlier in a Jackson County manifesto claiming that Mormons planned to introduce free blacks into the county. The Church had tried to neutralize the charge in a letter to the editor in the April 1836 *Messenger and Advocate* that responded to an abolitionist lecture in Kirtland, which Church leaders feared would be interpreted as a sign of friendship for the abolitionist cause. Writing in Joseph Smith's name, the author denied that there was any local sympathy for the speaker. "All except a very few, attended to their own avocations and left the gentleman to hold forth his own arguments to nearly naked walls." The letter echoed the antiabolitionist feeling that was peaking in the United States in 1836. Andrew Jackson had proposed that "incendiary publications" be barred from the mails. Southern congressmen successfully sponsored legislation to block petitions for ending the slave trade in Washington, D.C. Abolitionists were being mobbed everywhere. Caught up in this wave of antiabolitionist enthusiasm, the letter repeated all the familiar biblical arguments in support of slavery and warned traveling elders against preaching to slaves without their masters' permission.[21]

The *Messenger and Advocate*'s feeble attempt to allay suspicion had no effect on the Clay County committee that recommended Mormon withdrawal. The committee admitted that the county had not "the least right, under the constitution and laws of the country, to expel them by force." But the committee feared an irrepressible conflict if the Mormons did not voluntarily leave. "The religious tenets of this people are so different from the present churches of the age, that they always have and always will, excite deep prejudices against them, in any populous country."[22] They would be happiest living alone in unsettled frontier regions. The Mormons were given time to sell any property over forty acres at a fair price and then they were to leave.

The Church leaders in Clay County and Kirtland responded in the spirit of the committee's proposals. They agreed on the terms suggested, and the departure was so amicable that the citizens in Clay raised funds to help the poorest Saints. In defense of the Church's reputation, a letter from Kirtland did reply to the Clay County charge of Mormon abolitionism by pointing to the antiabolitionist letter in the April *Messenger and Advocate*. On another count, the reason for the Saints' poverty was the persecution they had suffered.[23] Nothing was said about religious tenets "so different from the present churches of the age." Their silence acknowledged the truth of that charge.

FINANCES

When the Saints were driven from Jackson County three years earlier, Joseph had been stunned for months, scarcely knowing what to do. This time, after dispatching letters to the Clay County officials, the Kirtland leaders set off on a trip east. Joseph and Hyrum, Rigdon and Cowdery took passage from Fairport on Lake Erie the very day the letters were dated, their destinations New York City and Salem, Massachusetts. The purpose of the journey goes unstated, but in Salem, a revelation assured them, "I have much treasure in this city for you, for the benefit of Zion; and many people in this city whom I will gather out in due time for the benefit of Zion."[24] Uncertain of his next step, Joseph was casting about for financial resources.

The revelation put the best face on a misbegotten venture.[25] Long after the event, Ebenezer Robinson, a printer in Nauvoo, remembered that a convert named Burgess had persuaded Church leaders that a large sum of money was hidden in the cellar of a Salem house. Perhaps Joseph believed he could identify the site using his boyhood gifts as a treasure-seeker. Less than encouraging, the Salem revelation opened with the words "I the Lord your God am not displeased with your coming this journey, notwithstanding your follies," and tried to deflect the men to missionary work. "There are more treasures than one for you in this city." The "wealth pertaining to gold and silver" could be obtained "in due time," implying that meanwhile they should concentrate on people. For two weeks, the men taught from house to house, taking time out to visit the famous East India Marine Society museum like ordinary tourists. On August 20, Rigdon lectured on "Christianity" at the lyceum. All the while they looked for the treasure-house. On August 19, Joseph wrote Emma that "we have found the house since Bro. Burgess left us, very luckily and providentially, as we had one spell been most discouraged." They were plotting how to get possession. "The house is occupied, and it will require much care and patience to rent or buy it." Joseph said they were willing to wait months if necessary, but by September, the party was back in Kirtland with no treasure for their pains.[26]

The Kirtland leaders grasped at the slimmest hopes. The temple had left a debt of around $13,000, and in the summer of 1836, the Church faced the additional expense of establishing a new stake of Zion in Missouri. At the June trial of two brethren accused of insufficient generosity, Frederick Williams put it bluntly: "The church [is] poor, Zion [is] to be built and we have not means to do it unless the rich assist, & because the rich have not assisted, the heads of the church have to suffer and are now suffering under severe embarrassments and are much in debt."[27] In December 1836, elders in the branches were told to stop "sending their poor from among them, and moving them to this place, without the necessary means of subsistence," a policy Joseph must have lamented.[28]

Joseph opened a merchandise store, but the venture called for still more capital. The month after he returned from Salem, he borrowed $11,000 for land purchases and store inventory. John Corrill heard the store inventory eventually cost between $80,000 and $90,000. The borrowing went on through 1837 until Joseph had run up debts of over $100,000.[29]

While risky, the indebtedness was not extravagant. The lenders would not have extended credit were Joseph and the Church without prospects. Creditors doubtless viewed the loans as capital investments, not credit for personal consumption. The loans were secured by store goods or land, with many notes showing multiple signatures. The Kirtland leaders followed standard practices for merchants and land brokers developing the midwestern economy: they borrowed to build a business. To make the Mormon market especially attractive, the Church could almost guarantee an ingathering of Saints eager to buy land. Developers all over the country were borrowing for land under less favorable circumstances. Assured by the Church's prospects, lenders extended credit even as the debt rose.[30]

To raise more capital, Church leaders planned a bank. Like stores and

mills, banks were multiplying in the 1830s. Twenty banks had been chartered in Ohio since 1830. In November 1836, Church leaders dispatched
Cowdery to New York to purchase plates for printing currency, and Orson
Hyde was sent to the state capitol in Columbus to apply for a charter. On
November 2, the Kirtland Safety Society bank was organized and began
selling stock. As usual, Joseph thought big. Capital stock was set at $4 mil-
lion, though the roughly 200 stock purchasers put up only about $21,000 in
cash.[31] Heber C. Kimball subscribed for $50,000 in shares for only $15.
The rest of the issue was secured by land. In actuality, the Safety Society
was a partial "land bank," a device New Englanders had once resorted to in
their cash-poor, land-rich society. Land bank notes, secured by the farms of
participants, gave landowners liquidity to initiate commercial ventures
when capital was lacking.[32] Unfortunately, the hybrid Kirtland bank—
based partly on land and partly on specie—set up expectations for redeeming notes in hard money.

The disappointments began almost immediately. Cowdery brought
back the plates and printed notes, but Hyde failed to obtain the charter
from the Ohio legislature, which knew the pitfalls of underfunded banks.
Hard-money Democrats saw the weakness in the Kirtland operation immediately.[33] The Mormons adjusted by organizing themselves into an "anti-
banking" company and, spiting the legislature, stamped the word "anti"
before the word "banking," and began issuing notes.

The issue of about $100,000 made no claim that the bills were legal ten-
der; the notes were the promissory notes of a private company. In an earlier
day, they would have been called a "medium of trade," replacing barter as a
means of exchange, allowing farmers to buy and sell by paying cash, instead
of working out more complicated exchanges.[34] In a simpler and more iso-
lated society, where mutual trust was high, the scheme might have worked.
In Kirtland, the bank failed within a month. Business started on January 2,
1837. Three weeks later, the bank was floundering. Skeptical (and perhaps
mean-spirited) customers presented their notes for redemption, and the
bank's pitiful supply of liquid capital was exhausted within days. On January
23, payment stopped. From then on, the value of the notes plummeted,
falling to one-eighth of their face value by February. All the investors lost
their capital, Joseph as much as anyone. He had bought more stock than
eighty-five percent of the investors. As treasurer and secretary and signers
of the notes, Joseph and Rigdon begged the note holders to keep them,
promising that the economy would benefit. In June, faced with complete
collapse, both resigned. In August, Joseph publicly disavowed the Kirtland
notes in the Church newspaper.[35] The bank staggered on until November,
long since moribund.

Meanwhile, Joseph's enemies attacked. A local mill owner, Grandison

Newell, a longtime enemy of the Mormons, entered a suit against Joseph for issuing bills of credit illegally. The charterless Kirtland Safety Society fell under the ban of an 1816 Ohio law forbidding private companies to issue money. The case was heard in March 1837 and held over to October, when Joseph was fined $1,000, adding to his huge debt. Creditors everywhere were closing in on their debtors. The nationwide collapse of the speculative bubble in 1837 tightened credit throughout the country. The Mormons' creditors were as zealous as any.[36] Kirtland merchants refused to sell the Saints flour, driving up the price and forcing them to trade with neighboring towns. Sidney Rigdon told the Church in an April meeting that "the gentiles are striving to besiege the saints in Kirtland & would be glad to starve the saints to death."[37]

Everyone who accepted Safety Society notes at face value suffered from the collapse. Losses are estimated at $40,000, about the cost of the Kirtland temple. Mormons, who invested in the bank and trusted the notes, suffered most. Jonathan Crosby lacked the money to invest in the bank, but he took the bills in payment for his work. When flour rose to $10 a barrel, Crosby could not purchase provisions. "I was then compelled to stop work, and spent a day running about town trying to buy some food with Kirtland money, but could get nothing for it." Emma Smith gave him a ham and forty pounds of flour.[38]

The bank episode not only hurt the Saints financially, it tried their faith. The notes had their Prophet's signature on the face. He had encouraged investment; his enthusiasm persuaded subscription. Wilford Woodruff marveled at Joseph's vision of Kirtland:

> Joseph presented to us in some degree the plot of the city of Kirtland . . . as it was given him by vision. It was great marvelous & glorious. The city extended to the east, west, North, & South. Steam boats will come puffing into the city. Our goods will be conveyed upon railroads from Kirtland to many places & probably to Zion. Houses of worship would be reared unto the most high. Beautiful streets was to be made for the Saints to walk in. Kings of the earth would come to behold the glory thereof & many glorious things not now to be named would be bestowed upon the Saints.

Carried along by the booster spirit that infected virtually every western town in these decades, Joseph promised too much. Town promoters like William Ogden in Chicago or, later, William Larimer in Denver believed they could create something out of nothing and did. Overly optimistic, Joseph started construction on a new house. Other brethren went heavily into debt expecting to profit in the predicted boom. John Corrill remembered that some brethren "suffered pride to arise in their hearts, and became desirous

of fine houses, and fine clothes, and indulged too much in these things, sup-
posing for a few months that they were very rich."[39]

A year earlier, in 1836, they had seemed to be succeeding. A visitor to
Kirtland that fall was "astonished to see that a city had sprung up since I was
there last March. I should think there were between 100 and 200 houses
(perhaps more) [and] new buildings, most of them are small and plain, but
some of them are elegant." By April 1837, when the bank was floundering,
Joseph was still telling his people that "this place must be built up, and
would be built up, and that every brother that would take hold and help
secure and discharge those contracts that had been made, should be rich."[40]
His hopes were doomed. When the effects of the 1837 panic and the subsequent depression spread, any chance of Kirtland and its bank prospering
was destroyed. Far from flourishing as their prophet had foretold, the
Saints were caught in a downward spiral of personal losses and narrowing
opportunities.

Widespread apostasy resulted. The volatility in prices, the pressure to
collect debts, the implication of bad faith were too much for some of the
sturdiest believers. The stalwarts Parley and Orson Pratt faltered for a few
months. David Patten, a leading apostle, raised so many insulting questions
Joseph "slaped him in the face & kicked him out of the yard." Joseph's
counselor Frederick G. Williams was alienated and removed from office.
One of the Prophet's favorites, his clerk Warren Parrish, tried to depose
him. Heber C. Kimball claimed that by June 1837 not twenty men in Kirtland believed Joseph was a prophet.[41]

WILFORD WOODRUFF'S KIRTLAND

In later retellings, the turmoil of this bad time overshadows the ordinary
course of life in Kirtland in 1837. Brigham Young and Heber Kimball told
grim stories. Eliza Snow, who was living in Joseph's household, added a terrifying account of apostates with bowie knives in the temple. The tales were
recounted years later to emphasize the importance of loyalty in trying circumstances, but they had the effect of making 1837 appear like an unbroken
fall into apostasy and ruin. In the worst of these times, Joseph kept the support of hundreds and probably thousands of loyal followers. Apostasy was
rife, but the Church was not near collapse. As leaders defected, men of equal
ability rose to take their places. By 1837, Mormonism had developed such
momentum that the loss of a few high-placed men could not slow it down.
While Joseph was fending off critics in Kirtland, the Missouri Church leaders were building a Zion in Far West. Elsewhere, the traveling elders were
gathering converts faster than Joseph's opponents could make apostates.[42]

A more balanced picture comes from the diary of Wilford Woodruff, a
thirty-year-old convert who made nearly daily entries from January to May

1837, the period when opposition was taking shape. Woodruff began his diary—perhaps the best by a nineteenth-century Mormon—as he left on his first mission in January 1835. The son of a Connecticut miller, he had moved to New York in 1832 to farm with his brother. Perpetually dissatisfied with existing churches, he was looking for an authoritative version of Christianity. "I believed the Church of Christ was in the wilderness," he later wrote, "and that there had been a falling away from the pure and undefiled religion before God." When he heard a Mormon elder preach, Woodruff believed immediately and joined in 1833. A rock-solid, intense man, with glowing deep-set eyes, he volunteered for Zion's Camp, the proving ground for later Mormon leaders.[43]

After a mission to Kentucky and Tennessee, Woodruff returned to Kirtland in November 1836. Although not eminent enough to be called in for the endowment of power earlier that spring, Woodruff was well acquainted in town. Joseph greeted him on his arrival, one friendly face among many. Woodruff wrote: "I was truly edified to again strike hands with President Joseph Smith Jr. & many other beloved saints of God who are rolling on the mighty work of God & of Israel."[44]

Woodruff's circle of friends represented a substantial second-rank, self-motivated priesthood who were "rolling on the mighty work." A passionate enumerator, Woodruff summed up his labors for 1836 by noting he traveled 6,557 miles, held 153 meetings, started 1 congregation, baptized 27 persons, blessed 19 children, healed 4 persons of disease, and "had three mobs Come together against me But always as yet deliverd from their hands." Woodruff was one of scores, perhaps hundreds, of Mormon missionaries gathering converts across the United States. The *Messenger and Advocate* carried frequent reports from the field, and a new journal was envisioned just to publish their letters.[45] Many of these men scarcely knew Joseph Smith and honored him more for his office than for his personal influence on their lives. They preached, debated, baptized, withstood mobs, and healed the sick on their own.

In Kirtland, Woodruff attended school with fellow veterans of the missionary wars. "There is an enjoyment in meeting our brethren & companions in tribulation that the world Knows not," he wrote. On the first Sunday in Kirtland, Joseph spoke in the morning meeting, and in the afternoon, Woodruff and Abraham Smoot were asked to speak. For the rest of the winter, Joseph appears in the diary only intermittently in occasional group settings. He gave sermons and officiated at occasional marriages, but appeared more like an eminent neighbor than an overwhelming presence.[46]

Woodruff was more involved with the seventies, who met on Tuesday evenings through the winter. They assembled to ordain initiates and receive instruction. "We had an interesting meeting," Woodruff wrote after one gathering. "Much of the spirit of Prophecy was poured out upon those

Presidents while ordaining the third seventy." Woodruff wrote a diary page on his own ordination. In a blessing given by Zebedee Coltrin, Woodruff was promised he would heal the sick, cause the blind to see and the deaf to hear, and have power to "waft myself (as did Philip) from River to river from Sea to sea & from Continant to Continant for the Purpose of Preaching the gospel of Jesus Christ."[47]

During the day, Woodruff studied Latin and Greek at a school taught by "Professor Haws." On January 4, the school was examined and a four-week recess declared. With time on his hands, Woodruff visited the Kirtland Safety Society office on January 6 to see the first notes issued to Jacob Bump. Joseph told them he had received a revelation about the society in "an audable voice," not just by impressions of the Spirit. Joseph did not disclose the revelation but "remarked that if we would give heed to the Commandments the Lord had given this morning all would be well." Woodruff entered his own small prayer asking that the society would "become the greatest of all institutions on EARTH."[48]

From then on, Woodruff wrote news of the bank along with other events. At one Thursday prayer meeting, Woodruff heard "an account of the general gathering of Israel in the gift of tongues." The next Sunday at Bishop Newel Whitney's house, Woodruff "had a vary happy time in speaking Singing hearing & interpeting tongues & in prayer with the family." A week later, five elders of the Church laid their hands on Abraham Smoot and "immediately healed" him of his pain and fever. Into these happy accounts, Woodruff interjected the jarring note that on January 24 he feared "a mob from Panesville to visit us that night & demolish our Bank & take our property but they did not appeare."[49]

Messages coming from Church leaders suggest more internal tension than Woodruff himself felt. As early as December 1836, warnings were being delivered in Sunday meetings. "O what a meeting," Woodruff wrote. "On this day the God of Israel Sharply reproved this stake of Zion [Kirtland] through the Prophets & Apostles for all our sins & backsliding & also a timely warning that we may escape the Judgments of God that otherwise will fall on us." A month later, Brigham Young "warned us not to murmur against Moses [or] Joseph or the heads of the Church." Complaints spread as the bank collapsed. The next Sunday, Sidney Rigdon "exhorted the Church to union that they might be prepared to meet every trial & difficulty that awates them." Two days later, David Whitmer rebuked the seventies for their pride. "A scourge awates this stake of Zion even Kirtland if their is not great repentance." Everyone knew this, Whitmer said, "esspecially the heads of the Church."[50]

Joseph preached on Sunday, February 19, after having been away on business for a few days. While he was gone, "many were stir'd up in their hearts & some were against him as the Israelites were against Moses."

Woodruff thought Joseph silenced the critics. "When he arose in the power of God in their midst, as Moses did anciently, they were put to silence for the complainers saw that he stood in the power of a Prophet." Joseph spoke again the next Sunday with the same effect.[51] Though his friend Warren Parrish was to defect in a few months, Woodruff showed no uncertainty about the Church leadership.

Interspersed with the warning sermons were Woodruff's reports of a missionary pair who had baptized 267 persons in Canada over the last eight months, a "great" patriarchal blessing, a funeral, a Church court where a brother was chastized and restored to fellowship, and the healing of a boy from pleurisy. Woodruff, meanwhile, had returned to his Latin studies. On March 24, he wrote that "I left school in view of spending some time in studying History & preparing for the endowment." He reported events at one of the regular Thursday prayer meetings where the Saints spent the whole day in prayer and fasting. After scripture reading and brief remarks, the veils were lowered, dividing the room into four segments, two for women and two for men. "The time was taken up during the day in each appartment in singing, exortation, & prayer. Some had a tongue, others an interpetation, & all was in order." Woodruff, who had missed the temple dedication the previous spring, had his own Pentecost. "The gifts were poured out upon us. Some had the administering of angels & the image of GOD sat upon the countenances of the Saints." Finally, at four in the afternoon, the veils were lifted bringing participants in view of one another, when the "Saints fell upon their knees & all as one man, vocally poured forth rejoicing, supplication & Prayer before the God of Israel." To close, they made a contribution to the poor and then departed.[52]

The spiritual experiences occurred without noticeable direction from Joseph. He was not there when initiates were instructed in the rituals of washing and anointing. When the rituals were instituted the previous spring, Joseph had closely supervised them; a year later, the seventies performed the ordinances on their own. Woodruff was sent to President Williams to "have the perfumes & oil prepared against the day following." That night they performed their first washings. "After washing our bodies from head to foot in soap & watter we then washed ourselves in clear watter next in perfumed spirits. The spirit of God was with us & we had a spiritual time."[53] Once washed, the men became officiators. Woodruff said, "I washed & perfumed the bodies of a number of my Brethren & the interview Closed after expressing our feelings to each other." That evening they met in the upper part of the temple for the anointing with oil. Fifteen of the seventies were anointed and many received a blessing from President Coltrin. At ten the meeting closed, all without Joseph appearing. The second- and third-rank leaders managed on their own.[54]

Joseph was more in evidence on April 6, 1837, the Church's seven-year anniversary conference. In a preliminary meeting, he and Rigdon ordained new leaders of the Seventy and sealed a blessing upon the newly anointed. They all then shouted "HOSANNA, Hosanna, Hosanna, to GOD & the LAMB, Amen, & Amen, & Amen," Woodruff wrote, and "if ever a shout entered the Cabinet of heaven that did & was repeated by angels on high & caused the power of God to rest upon us." Afterward, the men joined the Saints in the lower court where the veils were once more dropped, and the Twelve assisted the seventies' presidents in washing feet, culminating the series of temple rituals. Heber Kimball pronounced Woodruff "clean from the Blood of this generation." Then the veils were rolled up.[55]

Woodruff did not feel the bank trouble threatened Joseph's authority. After hearing his address at the April 6 conference, he felt the Prophet was "Clothed with the power, spirit, & image of GOD." Woodruff concurred when the Prophet said the dissenters "have become Covenant Breakers for which they will feel the wrath of God."[56] Woodruff found evidence of Joseph's greatness in his sermons:

> Joseph is as a father to Ephraim & to all Israel in these last days. He mourns because of unbelief & the negligence manifest with many who have receieved the gospel in obeying the commands of God. He fears lest but few be left to receieve an inheritance. There is not a greater man than Joseph standing in this generation. . . . Nothing short of a God can comprehend his Soul.

Paradoxically, the trials of 1837, instead of tearing Joseph down, built him up.[57]

"The power, gifts, and graces of the gospel" continued to visit Woodruff, but by June the sky blackened. On May 28 he noted that "the same spirits of murmering, complaining, & of mutiny, that I spake of in Feb. 19th in this journal, hath not slept from that day to the present. They have been brewing in the family Circle in the secret Chamber & in the streets untill many & some in high places had risen up against Joseph." Warren Parrish arose in public meeting and "in the blackness of his face & corruption of his heart stretched out his puny arm and proclaimed against Joseph." Woodruff had stopped boarding with his old friend. "O, Warren Warren," Woodruff lamented, "when thou art converted strengthen thy brethren. O my God deliver me from such a crime."[58] On May 31, Woodruff left Kirtland on another mission.

APOSTASY

The bank failure, suspicions about Joseph's morals, and economic stress combined to bring on the apostasies of 1837.[59] When Joseph, battered by creditors, tried to collect payment for three city lots he had sold Parley Pratt in the inflationary delirium a few months earlier, Pratt exploded in rage and frustration: "If you are still determined to pursue this wicked course, until yourself and the church shall sink down to hell, I beseech you at least, to have mercy on me and my family." His brother Orson and Lyman Johnson brought charges against Joseph for lying, extortion, and "speaking disrespectfully, against his brethren behind their backs." It took months for the Pratts to recover their composure and return to the fold.[60]

In retaliation, charges were brought against the complainers. At a May 29 high council meeting, five brethren accused Parrish, Parley P. Pratt, David Whitmer, Frederick G. Williams, and Lyman Johnson—all high Church officers—of following a course that "has been injurious to the Church of God." For once the council system was unequal to the occasion. Whitmer and Williams denied the high council's jurisdiction because a revelation had said that presidents were to be tried by a bishop's court. Pratt objected to Rigdon and Joseph's sitting on the case since they had previously spoken against him; Cowdery admitted that he had too. Rigdon and Cowdery then withdrew from the council, both claiming Pratt was guilty. Williams said he could not preside because he had been accused. The council "then dispersed in confusion."[61]

In the middle of the disarray, Joseph was hauled off to court on another charge. Grandison Newell, who had gone after Joseph Smith for breaking the banking laws, brought a suit against Joseph on June 3, 1837, for plotting Newell's assassination. The angry Newell had sponsored Doctor Philastus Hurlbut's search for the Spaulding manuscript and had led a band of rowdies who pelted Parley Pratt with eggs while he preached in Mentor. The Mormons suspected Newell of getting up a mob to attack the bank. In the 1837 suit, Newell's star witness was an excommunicated Mormon named Solomon Denton, once a helper in the Smith household, who testified that Joseph had approached him to assassinate Newell. Orson Hyde testified for the prosecution that Joseph had said in January or February 1837 that Newell "should be put out of the way, or where the crows could not find him." When the shocked Hyde asked what he meant, Joseph assured him he had spoken "inadvertently [in] the heat of passion." Hyde told the court, "I have known him for some time and think him to be possessed of much kindness and humanity toward his fellow beings." With little evidence to support Newell's suspicion, the court acquitted Joseph, insinuating, according to Newell, that "my hatred, not my fear, induced the prosecution."[62]

Mary Fielding, a recent convert from Canada who witnessed the disaffection, wrote home in mid-June that "truely my heart has almost bled" for Joseph. Besides facing the dissidents, he was struck down by a nearly fatal illness. In early June, he was incapacitated while his critics reviled him in meetings. One Sunday, Parley Pratt preached that Joseph "had committed great sins." After Rigdon defended the Prophet, Pratt left in protest. Mary Fielding stayed to hear Cowdery attempt a reconciliation, but when Orson Pratt attacked Joseph, she walked out too. Parrish, who had climbed into Joseph's seat on the stand, spoke last, and the meeting broke up without the Lord's Supper. "Many tears ware that day shed by those who had come up here to worship God in his house," said Fielding. She walked home by way of Joseph's house "not knowing wether he live till next morn."

Fielding found Joseph able to walk, but illness and contention had worn him down. Fielding said that "he feels himself to be but a poor Creature and can do nothing but what God enables him to do." "When he was too weak to pray himself," he told his visitors, "the enemy strove with all his power to get his Spirit." "The strugle sometimes became so great that he had to call upon his wife or some Friend to pray that the good spirit might conquer." At the same time, Joseph was blessed "with such glorious visions as made him quite forget that his body was afflicted."[63]

By mid-June, Fielding could write that the Lord "begins to pour out his spirit upon us in mighty power and I truely feel encouraged to hope that we shall ere long have order & peace restored to the Church." Hyrum spoke in meeting on feeling humble as a little child, breaking into tears as he spoke. By early July, meetings were back to normal. "It was truely gratifying," Fielding wrote, to see Joseph Smith Sr., "the venerabl Patriarch with his two aged Brothers in the upper Stand and in the next, four of his Sons with president Rigdon in their midst."[64] She noticed how proud Lucy was of the Smith men, her eyes "are frequently baithed in tears when she looks at, or speaks of them." At the regular Thursday meeting, "many spake in tongues & others prophesied & interpreted." It was one of the best meetings the Kirtland Saints could remember. "Some of the Sisters while engaged in conversing in tongues their countenences beaming with joy, clasped each others hands & kissd in the most affectionate manner." "The Bretheren as well as the Sisters were all melted down and we wept and praised God together." Fielding thought angels entered the room.[65]

ZION

While he was fending off the apostates, Joseph looked beyond Kirtland to a broader field. The Twelve Apostles had been contemplating a European mission in keeping with their commission to carry the gospel to the world, and in June 1837, Joseph called Heber C. Kimball to lead a band of seven to England. On June 13, they set out to begin a work that over the next fifteen years would yield 51,000 converts.[66]

Three weeks later, 1,500 Saints in Far West broke ground for a new temple in Missouri. By the day's end, an excavation for a 110-by-80-foot foundation had been dug. William Phelps reported that the Missouri Saints were increasing daily, and "we shall soon have one of the most precious spots on the Globe." A few months later, in September, a conference in Kirtland discussed the need for more gathering places—as many as eleven new stakes— and more missionaries. During the conference, 109 elders accepted mission calls. A circular letter from the bishopric showed the enthusiasm for Zion was still high. "Whatever is glorious.—Whatever is desirable—Whatever pertains to salvation, either temporal or spiritual. Our hopes, our expectations, our glory and our reward, all depend on our building Zion according to the testimony of the prophets."[67]

To promote the work and probably to escape trouble, on July 26, 1837, Joseph left Kirtland with Hyrum, Rigdon, David Patten, and Thomas March, headed for Canada. He had gone north once before when Hurlbut was pursuing him. This time vexatious lawsuits in Painesville delayed him for a day, but by taking circuitous routes, he eluded his creditors and reached a port on Lake Erie.[68] His absence gave the dissenters free rein in Kirtland, shattering the calm of the past month. Eliza Snow, who was there, later said that the dissenters "claimed that the Temple belonged to them." Headed by Warren Parrish, the ringleader, and "armed with pistols and bowie-knives," they occupied the east pulpits one Sunday morning when Joseph Sr. was conducting. One usurper started heckling the speaker, and Father Smith told him to wait his turn. At this, Parrish, Apostle John Boynton, and others drew their pistols and knives. Boynton threatened to "blow out the brains of the first man who dared to lay hands on him." Amid the shrieks, women and children tried to jump out the window. Constables carried off the troublemakers, who, as a countermeasure, charged Joseph Sr. and eighteen others with assault, battery, and riot.[69]

The violent outburst seemed like a complete collapse. Snow herself said that "nearly, if not every quorum was more or less infected." And yet, after his return from Canada, Joseph held a conference where the Church leaders were presented for a sustaining vote, and Joseph put himself before the membership. He and the First Presidency were sustained unanimously, and three dissidents were excluded from the Twelve.[70] The next Sunday, the three spoke in meeting, confessed their sins, and were forgiven. They were restored to full fellowship and reappointed to their former positions.[71] Joseph did not fear them and was quick to forgive. The three brethren administered the sacrament to the congregation.

Joseph did not seem to worry about his position in the Church. At the September conference, he announced that Oliver Cowdery was in transgression, and soon after chastised John Whitmer and William Phelps in Missouri, with a warning to David Whitmer. Joseph was not concerned that criticism of these longtime leaders might weaken his own authority. To check on progress in Far West, he and Rigdon traveled west in October, where he aired the complaints against the Missouri leaders and his former counselor Frederick G. Williams, but they all were sustained in their positions save Williams.[72] On the same visit, Joseph confronted Cowdery about the accusation of adultery with Fanny Alger.

While he dealt with disaffection in Missouri in November, the Kirtland dissenters rallied again. Parrish, Boynton, and Luke Johnson, the off-and-on-again apostles, aided by Joseph Coe and others, undertook to take over the Church under the banner of "the old standard." The title implied the dissenters held to the original restored gospel while objecting to more recent developments.[73] They claimed that thirty of the most talented men in Kirtland had joined them, and support was solicited in Missouri from the Whitmers, Cowdery, Williams, and William McLellin.[74]

This time punishment was swift. In late December, twenty-eight men were cut off from the Church, bringing the total to more than forty that year. But excommunication did not silence the group. In mid-December, they were "very violent in their opposition to the President and all who uphold him." The "old standard" faction was determined to hold their meetings in the temple even "if it is by the shedding of blood." They claimed to be the legitimate Church, making Joseph the apostate.[75] They called themselves the Church of Christ, the Church's first name.

Joseph and Rigdon left Kirtland in the night on January 12, 1838.[76] The lawsuits were building up, and apostates were feared to be plotting more desperate measures. Joseph claimed that armed men—whether Mormons or irate creditors, he did not say—pursued them for two hundred miles from Kirtland. Joseph and Rigdon had resolved in November to move to Missouri, but their leave-taking in January was precipitous. Brigham Young had gone three weeks earlier, forced to leave, he later said, by enemies "who threatened to take my life because I would proclaim publicly and privately that I knew by the power of the Holy Ghost that President Joseph Smith was a Prophet of the most high God." Emma was pregnant when she followed Joseph in a wagon with the three children. Soon after they left, the Church printing office went up in flames, scorching the nearby temple.[77]

The turmoil in Joseph's mind in 1837 seems to have matched the disruptions in the Church. The despair he felt during his June illness may have been with him at other times. Reading between the lines of the sparse records, it appears that the letdown after the Kirtland endowment puzzled and depressed him. He had anticipated triumph and instead suffered defeat. Where was God during these setbacks? Only one revelation during the year was deemed worthy of inclusion in the later *Doctrine and Covenants*. Only one letter in Joseph's voice went into the record. His usual inspiration seemed closed, or at least he chose to keep silent about it. Except for the bold stroke of the English mission, he seems to have lost his way. The bank, his great hope for Kirtland, had crashed, injuring and alienating his friends. He knew only dark days. He wrote to John Corrill in Missouri in September that "we have waided through a scene of affliction and sorrow thus far for the will of God, that language is inadequate to describe." Though he blessed the God "who has delivered you many times from the hands of your Enimies," he had no counsel to offer, no revelation, no bright prospect. He sent them a copy of the Kirtland High Council minutes for September 3, that the Missouri Saints may know "how to proceed to set in order & regulate the affairs of the Church in Zion whenever they become disorganized."[78] He had nothing more to say.

NINETEEN

TRIALS

JANUARY–JULY 1838

We will never be the aggressors, we will infringe on the rights of no people; but shall stand for our own until death. We claim our own rights, and are willing that all others shall enjoy theirs.

No man shall be at liberty to come into our streets, to threaten us with mobs, for if he does, he shall attone for it before he leaves the place, neither shall he be at liberty, to villify and slander any of us, for suffer it we will not in this place.

SIDNEY RIGDON, Oration, July 4, 1838

EMMA WAS SIX MONTHS PREGNANT when she and Joseph left Kirtland with Sidney Rigdon in January 1838. They struggled west on bad roads in bitter cold with little money. At one point, Joseph was looking for work cutting cordwood when a local member supplied them with funds. In Paris, Illinois, the tavern keepers turned the Mormons away until Joseph threatened to burn down one of their houses if his family was refused. At the Mississippi, they crossed on broken ice. Finally in early March, 120 miles from Far West, the Smiths were met with money and teams. On March 13, two months and a day after leaving Kirtland, the brethren came out to escort them the last eight miles. "We were greeted on every hand by the saints who bid us welcom[e]" to the "land of their inheritance," Joseph wrote back to Kirtland. "Verily our hearts were full and we feel greatfull to Almighty God for his kindness unto us."[1]

In a year and a half, the Missouri Saints had erected a thriving city with 100 buildings, a public square, and a temple site. Far West followed Joseph's and Frederick G. Williams's plan for the City of Zion, with four main streets 132 feet wide and the rest 82½ feet. In the surrounding countryside, the Saints opened as many as 2,000 farms. One outsider said that it was "by magic that the wild prairies over a large tract were converted into cultivated fields." Already rising land prices were forcing newcomers into outlying areas, where they could enter a government land claim at $1.25 an acre. Most Mormon settlers dwelt in cabins or small shanties, and many could afford only 40 acres, but two or three years' wages paid for a small

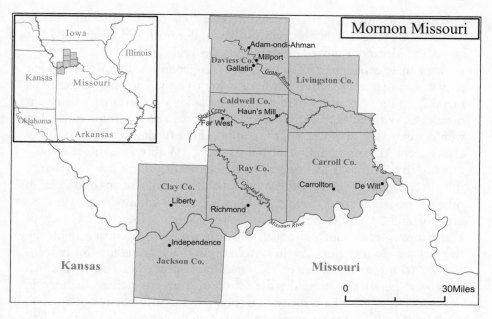

farm. The Caldwell County population would rise to around 5,000 in 1838, virtually all Mormons. Mormons elected the magistrates, county clerk, and military officers. William W. Phelps was postmaster and justice of the county court.[2] When Joseph arrived in 1838, a new City of Zion was on its way to completion. Within a year, it would all be lost.

A NEW ZION

The conception of Far West was Joseph's, but Phelps, Edward Partridge, John Corrill, Isaac Morley, John Whitmer, and a handful of others actually planted the city on the raw prairie. Joseph's vision of Zion now had a life of its own. When Far West grew too crowded, Joseph told them to expand the city to four square miles rather than one, and he authorized the leaders to look for additional lands outside the county's bounds, but local leaders made most decisions. When Edward Partridge wrote his brother in October 1837 that "our town or city is called Far West," the words "our town" were entirely justified.[3]

The Mormons had taken an interest in this tract in the spring of 1836, four months before the Clay County citizens formally asked them to leave. A few Mormon exiles from Jackson County had been among the first settlers in the largely uninhabited area. Most settlers preferred the timbered lands along the rivers to the open prairies, "peering one over another, as far as the eye can glance." The area the Mormons took up was about two-thirds prairie, tough grasslands with sod a foot thick, requiring special plows to break it up, though rich soil lay underneath.[4] Hoping to be left alone, the Mormons moved on to the less desirable lands.

After their experience in Jackson and Clay counties, the Mormons felt they must ask nearby settlers for permission to move in. They requested a meeting in Ray County, where the desired lands were located, to present their case. Without hesitation, the Ray citizens said no. Mormon migration would "retard the prosperity of the county, check further emigration of any class except Mormons, and disturb the peace."[5] With no assurance of protection, the Mormons had to pull back. Before they left Clay, they wrote the governor about their "fear lest the inhabitants will rise up to mob us, in other places, or in other Counties." They wanted to know whether the governor would "quell these mobs, and help us obtain a location." Governor Dunklin was less sympathetic than when they had appealed to him during the Jackson County riots. Again he told them to use the courts for redress, but, he admitted, "there are cases, sometimes, of individual outrage which may be so popular as to render the action of courts of justice nugatory, in endeavoring to afford a remedy." He suggested that the Saints themselves must be at fault for the citizens' enmity, but could not say why. As the Mormons said, "*not one* solitary *instance* of crime" had been lodged against them in either Jackson or Clay courts. The governor noted somewhat diffidently, "Your neighbors accuse your people, of holding illicit communications with the Indians, and of being opposed to slavery," for which he had no evidence. He was helpless to offer a solution. "All I can say to you is, that in this Republic, the *vox populi* is the *vox Dei*."[6]

With no protection from the government, the Saints depended on the goodwill of their neighbors, which Ray County refused to give. The impasse was broken when Alexander Doniphan of Clay County, a member of the state legislature and the Mormons' legal counsel, submitted a bill to create two counties out of northern Ray County: Caldwell County, just north of Ray, for the Mormons, and Daviess, immediately above Caldwell, which would be open to all. The framers of the legislation probably thought that Caldwell would hold the Saints. They would live there and nowhere else.[7] Mormons would control local government, and other citizens would leave them alone. Doniphan apologized for not getting the entire region for the Mormons, considering their rapidly expanding numbers, but opposition from the Jackson County representative and the governor—by this time Lilburn Boggs, a resident of Jackson County—prevented it. The bill, signed into law on December 19, 1836, cut Caldwell's size to roughly eighteen miles from north to south and twenty-four miles east to west. The compromise placated the citizens of Ray, who understood the Mormons would be restricted to the undesirable northern prairie lands and would not live among the Missourians in Ray. The Mormons meanwhile bought out all the non-Mormon settlers in Caldwell, including the bee men who hunted wild honey on the prairies. (An 1838 dispute about the state boundary in northern Missouri was called "The Honey War.") By late 1836, the Mormons, still wary of potential mobbings, began moving in.[8]

All this was history when Joseph reached Far West in the spring of 1838. The site gave him his first opportunity to construct a city from the ground up. He had scarcely been there a month when a revelation called the Saints in Caldwell "my Church in Zion," implying that Far West was to take the place of Independence. "Let the City Far West, be a holy and consecrated land unto me," the Lord said, "and it shall be called most holy for the ground upon which thou standest is holy." A temple was to be constructed, and the new Zion was to be "for a defence and for a reffuge from the storm and from wrath when it shall be poured out without mixture upon the whole earth." Then "other places should be appointed for stakes in the regions round about as they shall be manifested unto my Servant Joseph."[9]

In the late spring, Joseph began looking for more land. On May 18, he headed north with a large party "for the purpose of laying off stakes of Zion in Daviess County." On the open prairies, they saw deer, turkey, partridges, elk, and a wolf that Joseph set his dog after. When they reached the Grand River angling to the southeast, they thought about steamboats hauling in freight. Hiking through the timber along the river, they came to the place where Lyman Wight operated a ferry at the bottom of Tower Hill. Inspired by what he saw, Joseph invested the place with a history, partly from the *Book of Mormon*, partly from the Bible. He spotted "an old Nephitish Alter and Tower," and then received a revelation that said Spring Hill was named by the Lord "Adam-ondi-Ahman," because "it is the place where Adam shall come to visit his people, or the Ancient of days shall sit as spoken of by Daniel the Prophet." The name of the site, Adam-ondi-Ahman, meant "the place where Adam dwelt," presumably after his expulsion from the Garden.[10]

For two weeks, the party surveyed lands, intending to purchase everything between Adam-ondi-Ahman and Far West twenty-five miles to the south. After that they would obtain the land to the north. Joseph returned to Far West just before Emma bore a son (whom they named Alexander Hale Smith), but the rest of the party went on surveying and building houses until June 5. The Church did not have the resources to purchase the land outright, but they entered preemption rights with the government, which would permit them to buy the land for $1.25 an acre in November when it was to be opened for sale.[11]

The surveying went on outside Caldwell, beyond the limits of the informal agreement limiting the Mormons to one county. Since the terms were never specified, the Mormons may have thought that staying away from Ray County to the south was all that mattered.[12] With migrants pouring in, Joseph could scarcely keep his people out of open areas. He heard in early May that two hundred wagons would be arriving from Canada in three weeks. A few days later, a reconciled Parley Pratt, fresh from New York, brought word of Saints "flocking from all parts of the world to this land, to avoid the destructions which are coming." Kirtland Saints were planning to come too. More than five hundred left on July 6 and arrived on October 2. By that time, a Mormon living at Far West reported that "emigration to the stakes of Zion is verry great almost every day witnesseth from 1 to 30 teams with furniture & families Teniment room verry scirce in this place, many families have to live in their tents & waggons." Joseph encouraged the immigrants with a revelation promising to "make solitary places to bud and to blossom, and to bring forth in abundance." By May the habitable parts of Caldwell were mostly settled, and there were 150 houses in Far West. In June, Joseph organized a stake at Adam-ondi-Ahman in Daviess, and by October, 200 houses had been built there. One observer said the city had 500 people in it before Gallatin, the county seat of Daviess, had five houses.[13] The expansion beyond Caldwell would prove to be fatal.

DISSENT

Joseph soon learned that the disaffection in the Kirtland Church had spread to Caldwell County, beginning with the Missouri Presidency. Not long after Caldwell was settled, the Missouri Saints began to doubt the faithfulness of David Whitmer, William Phelps, John Whitmer, and Oliver Cowdery. John Corrill, a member of the Missouri bishopric with Edward Partridge, thought that a misunderstanding about land purchases aroused suspicion of Phelps and Whitmer, presidents of the Missouri Church. Some time in the winter of 1836–37, Church members came to doubt them "on account of their having entered the town plot and some other lands in their own names," suggesting they were speculating in Caldwell County lands. The land was soon deeded to the bishop, the Church officer responsible for land, but complaints accumulated.[14]

In January 1838, a group of apostles and high councilors appointed a committee to make inquiries. Soon after, "the excitement rose so high that they turned them out of their presidential office." At a February council meeting, George Morey, a high councilor, set "forth in a very energetic manner, the proceedings of the Presidency as being iniquitous." The four were accused of various infractions of the Word of Wisdom and of selling their lands in Jackson County, signaling a lack of faith in the Saints' return to their promised land. Cowdery admitted to drinking tea three times a day for his health, and the Whitmers contended tea and coffee were not covered by the revelation. As for their property, the four threatened to leave if they were forbidden to sell their Jackson lands. Phelps said he "would move out of the accursed place." Moreover, they "would not be controlled by an ecclesiastical power of revelation whatever in their temporal concerns."

Considering the answers unsatisfactory, the council removed the four from office.[15] By this time popular feelings were at fever pitch. "Had we not taken the above measures," Thomas Marsh wrote Joseph, "we think that nothing could have prevented a rebellion against the whole high council and bishop; so great was the disaffection against the presidents." Joseph approved the "Judicious High Council" that cut off Phelps and Whitmer, adding that "the saints at this time are in union & peace & love prevails throughout, in a word Heaven smiles upon the saints in Caldwell," as if the removal of dissenters had brought the harmony essential to Zion.[16]

The individual complaints against the Missouri Presidency blended with the larger issue of loyalty to Joseph Smith. The Prophet had warned the Missouri Saints the previous fall about the transgressions of the four men. The high council's investigations only confirmed his earlier suspicions. In a public meeting, Apostle David Patten "spake with much zeal against this Presidency, and in favor of Br. Joseph Smith jr." Somehow, opposition to the Missouri Presidency was interpreted as support of Joseph. A new phrase was added to entries in the minutes about the appointment of faithful brethren who were called men "in good standing & friends to Joseph Smith jr, the Prophet." Friendship to Joseph divided true Saints from false. That summer Patten wrote a long discourse for the *Elders Journal* on the scriptural foundation of Joseph's authority.[17]

Although Joseph's own position was never seriously threatened, after the repeated struggles with the Kirtland dissenters he had lost patience with the opposition. He did what he could to end controversy, but when reconciliation failed, he cut his brethren off to preserve "union & peace love." He would tolerate failings in his closest followers, but not disloyalty.

In April, Joseph attended the trial of his "bosom friend" Oliver Cowdery, whose relationship with the Church had been deteriorating for nearly a year. In September 1837, Joseph publicly announced that Cowdery was "in transgression," though he retained his positions as assistant counselor to Joseph and one of the presidents of the Church in Far West. After dropping him from the Far West Presidency in January, the high council tried him for his Church membership on April 12, 1838. One of the nine charges was falsely insinuating that Joseph had committed adultery. He was also accused of urging vexatious lawsuits against the Mormons, leaving his calling to make money, and counterfeiting. Perhaps the heart of the matter was stated in a charge of "virtually denying the faith by declaring that he would not be governed by any ecclesiastical authority nor Revelation whatever in his temporal affairs."[18]

Cowdery was charged with "selling his lands in Jackson County contrary to the Revelations," a sign he was withdrawing from the economic order of the Church. Joseph told the council that Cowdery had said he wanted "to get property and if he could not get it one way he would another." For a couple of years, Cowdery had been trying to develop a law practice and obtain political office. The Saints suspected him of drumming up business by urging their enemies to bring suits for debts. He was charged with leaving "the calling, in which God had appointed him, by Revelation, for the sake of filthy lucre, and turning to the practice of the Law."[19]

In response to the charge of selling land in Jackson County, Cowdery launched into a discourse about *"allodial"* tenure as contrasted to *"feudal"* tenure, strange language for a Church court. Allodial holdings allowed a person to dispose of land without the permission of an overlord. In America, he reminded the council, land was held allodially, unlike under the feudal regimes of Europe. He might have added that freehold tenure was widely considered to be the economic basis of a republican society. By limiting land sales, he implied, the Church had reverted to feudalism. He was unwilling, the letter went on, to subject himself to "any ecclesiastical authority or pretended revelation." He based his actions on "the three great principles of English liberty . . . 'the right of personal security; the right of personal liberty, and the right of private property. . . . This attempt to controll me in my temporal interest, I conceive to be a disposition to take from me a portion of my Constitutional privileges and inherent rights."[20] Cowdery was speaking as a citizen of a republic rather than as a member of the Church that he had once thought was the kingdom of God on earth.

Cowdery's letter is a reminder of the complex ideological environment of Mormons in the 1830s. Most of the time they spoke Kingdom of God language, using words like "faith," "righteousness," "Zion, "gathering," "priesthood," and "temple." At the same time, as American citizens, they knew the political language of rights and freedom. Most Church discourse was conducted using scriptural language, but they all knew republican speech as well. Cowdery showed how easily a disaffected member could slip out of millennial, scriptural discourse into political talk, using republicanism to discredit Church leaders. Democratic discourse transformed obedience, faith, and loyalty into fanaticism and blind submission. The injunction not to sell land in Jackson County became a feudal imposition, a trespass on American property rights. "My venerable ancestor was among that little band, who landed on the rocks of Plymouth in 1620," Oliver informed his judges, invoking an event as familiar as the stories in the Bible. Cowdery's Plymouth ancestor, he told the council, "brought those maxims, and a body of those laws" on which "now stands our great and happy Government." How could he yield to a *"petty"* ecclesiastical government? "I am wholly unwilling to exchange them for any thing less liberal, less benevolent, or less free."[21] The Church and kingdom Cowdery had once thrilled to had become a petty satrap.

Cowdery's letter sounded incongruous in the context of a Church trial, but it was only the opening round in a battle of republicanisms in 1838. Joseph thought republican too. Shortly after arriving in Far West, he dictated the "Motto of the Church of Christ of *Latterday Saints*." Instead of sounding like scripture, the motto's first line was "The Constitution of our country formed by the Fathers of Liberty." Since the expulsion from Jackson County, Joseph had viewed the Constitution as a bulwark, though no authorities enforced its principles for the Mormons. His motto proclaimed, "Wo, to tyrants, Mobs, Aristocracy, Anarchy and Toryism," republican words for the dark side, referring in one sweep to their enemies in Jackson, unsympathetic government officials, and the Kirtland dissenters. "Exalt the standard of Democracy! Down with that of Priestcraft, and let all the people say Amen!" he concluded the motto. The only scriptural note struck was a call for "Peace and good order in society Love to God and good will to man."[22]

DANITES

This republican language would be heard again in June 1838 after the "Danites," or "Daughters of Zion," were organized. In the impassioned accounts of Mormon crimes written in the aftermath of the Mormon war in 1838, the later conflict that resulted in expulsion of Mormons from Missouri, the Danites figured as an example of religious power run amok. The Danites were said to be a secret society, several hundred strong, organized in June 1838, to drive out dissenters, using violence if necessary.[23] "They ran into awful extremes," John Corrill later said, "for it seemed that they felt justified, and thought it was the will of God to use any measures whatever, whether lawful or unlawful, to accomplish" their end. The leader of the Danites, Sampson Avard, described them as a seditious government within the lawful government, supporting the charge of treason brought against Joseph after the Mormon war.[24]

In later court hearings, Joseph was held responsible for Danite excesses. Some historians depict the Danites as Joseph's private army, dispatched at his command to expunge enemies of the Church. In contrast, many Mormons, both then and now, blame Avard for the Danites. Avard, an ambitious adventurer, it was said, formed a band of ruffians who harassed dissenters at his command rather than Joseph's. Unfortunately, the secrecy of the organization and the obscurity of the records hinder efforts to distribute blame between the two. Was a vengeful Joseph the inspiration for the Danites, or was the band the work of the unscrupulous Avard?

The situation was further complicated by George Robinson, Sidney Rigdon's son-in-law and keeper of Joseph's journal, being a Danite supporter. Robinson may exaggerate the First Presidency's backing. He also depicts the Presidency, not Joseph, as the effective governing body of the Church. Smith recedes as a personality in Robinson's records, and the Presidency as a group, with Rigdon as First Counselor, appears to be in charge. In Robinson's record, Joseph goes along with Rigdon, rather than taking the lead, making it difficult to determine the degree of Joseph's involvement.[25]

Resentment against dissenters was already boiling when Avard arrived in June. Corrill said that "notwithstanding the dissenters had left the church, yet the old strife kept up." The Far West defectors—particularly Cowdery, the Whitmers, and Phelps—were accused of stealing and counterfeiting, and bringing "vexatious lawsuits" to collect debts and question land titles. Reed Peck, a Mormon drawn unwillingly into the Danite movement and who left the Church by the end of 1838, said a secret meeting held in mid-June was called by Dimick Huntington and Jared Carter—not Avard—to decide how to expel the dissenters. Peck said someone proposed "to kill these men that they would not be capable of injuring the church."[26]

Although none of the Presidency attended the Danite organizational meeting, Peck assumed Joseph and Rigdon knew about it. Perhaps by coincidence, on June 17, the Sunday following the meeting, Rigdon preached a vitriolic sermon based on the theme of salt losing its savor and being cast out and trodden underfoot. Peck, who recorded the most incendiary passages, remembered Rigdon saying that "they had a set of men among them that had dissented from the church and were doing all in their power to destroy the presidency laying plans to take their lives &c., accused them of counterfeiting lying cheating and numerous other crimes and called on the people to rise en masse and rid the county of such a nuisance." According to Peck, Rigdon hinted at lynching. Joseph, a dim figure at the meeting, gave only a short speech. Peck thought the Prophet sanctioned Rigdon's message but remembered Joseph adding, "I don't want the brethren to act unlawfully"—a constant theme that year. Corrill accused Joseph and Rigdon of backing violent measures, but, according to Corrill's own account, "they both denied it promptly."[27]

Soon after the sermon, eighty-three prominent members in Far West, many of them probably Danites by then, signed an ultimatum demanding the departure of the offenders. The letter summarized the mounting complaints against Cowdery, John and David Whitmer, and Phelps. "You have had the audacity," the letter concluded, "to threaten us that, if we offered to disturb you, you would get up a mob from Clay and Ray counties. For the insult, if for nothing else, and for your threatening to shoot us if we offered to molest [you], we will put you from the county of Caldwell, so help us God!" Fearing for their property and perhaps their lives, the dissenters fled. A gleeful George Robinson noted in the Prophet's journal that "these men took warning, and soon they were seen bounding over the prairie like the scape Goat to carry of [f] their own sins."[28]

When he formed the Danites, Avard was a relative newcomer. An immigrant physician from the Isle of Guernsey, he had preached for a time as a Campbellite minister in Pennsylvania before being baptized by Orson Pratt in 1835 and called to lead the local branch of the Church. Avard moved to Kirtland in 1836, and a year later, for reasons unknown, had his license as a high priest revoked. Joseph's attorney later described Avard as "a very eccentric genius, fluent, imaginative, sarcastic, and very quick in replying to questions." The Mormon historian B. H. Roberts thought that Avard had attempted to wrest control of the Canadian Church from the hands of John Taylor, for which he earned a severe rebuke from Joseph. Cowdery wrote his brothers that "Avard arrived sometime since. He appears very friendly, but I look upon him with so much contempt that he will probably get but little from me."[29]

Although the Far West Mormons ousted the dissenters without Avard's provocation, he gave shape to their outrage. He formed the Far West activists into a society bound by oaths, backing one another to the death. Avard played upon the members' loyalty to Joseph Smith, putting them under oath to be completely submissive to the Presidency.[30] The reasoning, as John Corrill explained, was that

> as the presidency stood next to God, or between God and the church, and was the oracle through which the word and will of God was communicated to the church, they esteemed it very essential to have their word, or the word of God through them, strictly adhered to. They therefore entered into a covenant, that the word of the presidency should be obeyed, and none should be suffered to raise his hand or voice against it.[31]

Peck later wrote that Avard insisted the people were bound to obey God's prophet in all things, "and whatever he requires you shall perform being ready to give up life and property for the advancement of the cause. When any thing is to be performed no member shall have the privilege of judging whether it would be right or wrong but shall engage in its accomplishment and trust God for the result."[32] Peck, Corrill, and a few others later said they objected to Avard's oaths, but could not extricate themselves. They kept quiet for fear they would be run out of town like other dissenters. Corrill blamed the society's extremes on Avard, who was "indefatigable in accomplishing their purposes, for he devoted his whole talents to it, and spared no pains; and, I thought, was as grand a villain as his wit and ability would admit of."[33]

Corrill suspected that Avard spoke for Joseph and Rigdon, but admitted "how much he was assisted by the presidency I know not." Peck, a Danite adjutant, said, "Dr. Avard, in speaking to the society, remarked, that it would be impossible for the presidency to explain the object of the society to every member, but that the presidency would explain their views or wishes to the head officers, and they to the members of the society." After a secret meeting, Corrill approached Rigdon, and "he told me I ought not to have any thing to do with it; that they would do as they pleased."[34] Yet later, the Presidency blessed the officers at a meeting. Corrill testified:

> There was at this meeting a ceremony of introducing the officers of the society to the presidency, who pronounced blessings on each of them, as introduced, exhorting to faithfulness in their calling, and they should have blessings. After this, President Smith got up and made general remarks, about, in substance, as follows: relating the oppressions the society had suffered, and they wanted to be prepared for further events; but said he wished to do nothing unlawful, and, if the people would let him alone, they would preach the gospel and live in peace.[35]

Peck observed that Dr. Avard "did not explain to the presidency what his teaching had been in the society." Corrill remembered strong talk. Joseph said that "if they came on us to molest us, we would establish our religion by the sword; and that he would become to this generation a second Mahomet." Although Avard may have concealed the Danite oaths, Joseph certainly favored evicting dissenters and resisting mobs.[36]

Corrill and Peck used republican language to combat the Danites. "It was clearly evident to me," Corrill wrote the next year, "that the leaders of this faction intended to set up a monarchical government, in which the presidency should tyranize and rule over all things." Those words made the authority of the Prophet, otherwise considered a blessing to the Saints, appear tyrannical. Once the language of the American Revolution snapped into place, the divine powers of the Prophet became oppressive, and the issue became one of freedom rather than truth. When Joseph attempted to reinstitute the consecration of properties at Far West, Peck charged that "no monarch on earth ever had supreme power over his subjects more than they over the inhabitants of caldwell county."[37]

On the Sunday after the apostates were driven from Far West, Sidney Rigdon attempted to explain the treatment of the dissenters. He preached on the republican basis of their expulsion, admitting that "certain characters in the place had been crying 'you have broken the law—you have acted contrary to the principles of republicanism.' " In actuality, Rigdon claimed, the reverse was true:

> When a country, or body of people have individuals among them with whom they do not wish to associate and a public expression is taken against their remaining among them and such individuals do not remove it is the principle of republicanism itself that gives that community a right to expel them forcibly and no law will prevent it.[38]

That was sound reasoning in a nation that had driven out Tories during the Revolution.[39] But it was also the reasoning the mob used to justify expulsion of the Mormons from Jackson County.

The clash between Mormonism and republicanism was brilliantly summed up in an exchange between John Corrill and Joseph Smith late in the summer. For some time, George Robinson noted, Corrill had been out of step "with the great wheal which is propelled by the arm of the great Jehovah."[40] To justify himself, Corrill insisted that "he will not yeald his Judgement, to any thing proposed by the Church, or any individuals of the Church, or even the voice of the great (I am,) given through the appointed organ, as revelation, but will always act upon his Judgment." Corrill posed the question: must an individual sacrifice his autonomy to the revealed will of God, or should he decide for himself in all things? In republican theory, the individual was supreme. In the Kingdom of God, was an individual required to sacrifice that autonomy?

According to Robinson, Corrill, who had accepted Joseph's revelations while serving in the Church, "says he will always say what he pleases, for he says he is a republican, and as such he will do, say, act, and believe, what he pleases." To which Robinson added: "Let the reader mark such republicanism as this, That a man should oppose his own Judgment to the Judgment of God, and at the same time profess to believe in the same God." The question could not have been stated more forcefully. How could a believer in God put his own will and judgment up against the will and judgment of God? On the other hand, how could an independent republican yield his judgment to another man, even one speaking for God? The exchange laid bare the source of Mormonism's conflict with democratic society. Mormons believed they were building Zion according to God's commands; to apostates and outsiders they looked like mindless zealots obeying a tyrant.[41]

In 1838, the practical form of this question involved submission to law. The Missourians believed that Mormons thought Joseph's revelations put them beyond the law. Since the word of God outranked the law of the land,

Mormons were suspected of breaking the law whenever the Prophet required it. Joseph had indeed grown impatient with what he called "vexatious lawsuits," and repeatedly said he would not submit to such harassment any longer. His April motto pronounced woe to "those who invent or seek out unrighteous and vexatious lawsuits under the pretext or color of law or office, either religious or political." Corrill remembered Joseph saying that he "had been before courts some twenty odd times; they had never found any thing against him, and that . . . he would submit to it no longer." His feelings differed little from those of thousands of rural Americans who felt justice was defeated in the courts through the lawyers' devilish management of mysterious rules that the defendants could scarcely comprehend. But to worried observers, these impatient eruptions sounded ominous. When Rigdon proclaimed that "he would not suffer people to come into their streets and abuse them, nor would they suffer vexatious law suits," it sounded like a scofflaw policy. A lawless spirit ran through the Danite schemes, Peck thought. "They consider themselves accountable only at the bar of God for their conduct, and consequently acknowledged no law superior to the 'word of the Lord through the prophet.' "[42] In later court hearings, Rigdon's declaration that "neither will we permit any man or set of men to institute vexatious law-suits against us, to cheat us out of our just rights; if they do, wo be unto them" was interpreted as a fixed policy to flout the law, rather than a frustrated outburst from people harried endlessly in the courts.[43]

Through the summer, the Mormons were perplexed about how far to trust the law and when to take the law into their own hands. Behind Mormon actions during the Mormon war was the memory of Jackson County in 1833. None of the Jackson citizens' complaints against the Mormons had been brought to court. Missouri citizens had not trusted the law but treated the Mormons like wartime enemies, expelling them without due process. The Church had turned to the governor for redress and been told that, unlike the citizens who drove them out, the Mormons must rely on the courts. Individual mobbers must be taken to court and required by due process of law to compensate the Mormons for their depredations. Non-Mormon citizens could circumvent the law; Mormons could not.

With the threat of mob attacks rising in the summer of 1838, the Mormons teetered on the boundary between law and war. They feared they would come under attack again, especially when the influx of Mormon immigrants made it impossible to restrict settlement to Caldwell County. The governor told them that neither the courts nor the state militia could give assistance to such a hated people. How should they react to an attack? Could they rely on the courts that had always failed them? Should they allow themselves to be forced out again as before? What should they do in the face of an aggressor who annoyed, harassed, and attacked?

They had lived in the South long enough to know that southern officials ignored the crimes of rioters. Judges and sheriffs closed their eyes to the crimes of the people. As one student of mobs has written, "the more mob violence accelerated in deadliness in the South, the less likely authorities were to interfere," or if they did, they took the side of the mob. The free black who killed a deputy sheriff in a scuffle in St. Louis in 1836 had been burned alive while two thousand people looked on. A city alderman declared he would shoot anyone who interfered, and no one did. Judge Luke Lawless discharged the perpetrators on the grounds that doing the popular will could never constitute a crime. In the South in 1835, seventy-nine riots took place in which sixty-three people died, seven or eight by prolonged torture. In only four of the seventy-nine cases was there even a hint of official interference or inquiry.[44]

The Saints lived in a world where rioters acted with impunity. Aware of the realities, Joseph decided that the Saints could not back down again. They could not allow themselves to be driven repeatedly from place to place. He endorsed the bellicose declaration of Sidney Rigdon at a celebration in Far West on July 4, 1838. The Saints made a grand occasion of the holiday, parading around Far West, raising a tall liberty pole, and conducting a ceremony at the temple site. Danite officers sat on the stand, alongside Caldwell County militia officers, a sign Joseph acknowledged the role of both in protecting the Saints.[45] Rigdon, the orator of the day, reminded the Saints of their sufferings in this supposed land of liberty. "Our cheeks have been given to the smiters, and our heads to those who have plucked off the hair. We have not only when smitten on one cheek turned the other, but we have done it again and again, until we are wearied of being smitten, and tired of being trampled on." Now the time had come, Rigdon declared: "From this day and this hour, we will suffer it no more." "That mob that comes on us to disturb us; it shall be between us and them a war of extermination. . . . We will never be the aggressors, we will infringe on the rights of no people; but shall stand for our own until death."[46]

The Mormon press printed Rigdon's talk, and Joseph urged the elders to get a copy, underscoring the passage saying the Saints would not "be mob[b]ed any more without taking vengeance." Although possibly published as a warning, the heated language inflamed the Missourians. Corrill reported that "there were one or two sentences to which considerable exception was taken by the people of other counties." Within the Church, the militant elements took heart, believing the Presidency was in their camp. John D. Lee, one of the Danite leaders, later said the Daviess County stake leaders organized the "Host of Israel" into camps of hundreds, fifties, and tens that summer.[47] Both sides were poised to react when the first event in the Mormon war occurred on August 6.

TWENTY

WAR

I have received by Amos Rees Esq. of Ray county and Wiley C. Williams Esq. one of my aids, information of the most appalling character, which entirely changes the face of things, and places the Mormons in the attitude of an open and avowed defiance of the laws, and of having made war upon the people of this State. Your orders are, therefore, to hasten your operations with all possible speed. The Mormons must be treated as enemies, and must be exterminated or driven from the State if necessary for the public peace.
LILBURN W. BOGGS TO GEN. JOHN B. CLARK, October 27, 1838

JOSEPH'S HAPPY PROSPECTS HAD faded quickly in Far West. Hope for the new land, its beauty, its expanse briefly invigorated him, and then the struggle with the dissenters, the Danites, and the growing animosity in upper Missouri darkened the picture. As if borne down by troubles during the summer of 1838, he mysteriously recedes in the records. Sidney Rigdon preached the sermons. George Robinson's minutes credited the Presidency with leading the Church. Judging from the records, Joseph was uncustomarily passive, leaving a power vacuum for Sidney Rigdon, Sampson Avard, and Lyman Wight to fill. Little direct evidence remains of Joseph's thoughts and feelings; little he did went on record.

When war between the Mormons and Missourians broke out in the fall of 1838, Joseph remained in the background, more buffeted by events than directing their course. He favored resistance to the mobs, but others took the lead. The militants appear to have called the shots. When action was required, they headed the troops. Near the end, when the Mormons' Missouri Zion was in tatters, Joseph emerged again as the central figure. By November 1838, an army of Missourians was camped before Far West ready to drive the Saints from the state. Joseph was the one to surrender, and became at once the target of the state's prosecution.

GALLATIN

Since politics usually underlay the conflicts between Mormons and their neighbors, it was fitting that an election ignited the clash in Missouri. As

Mormon numbers increased, the non-Mormons watched local government fall into the hands of people they saw as deluded fanatics. A powerless minority of Saints could be tolerated; a majority in control of elections could not. The Mormons constituted at least a third of the voters in Daviess County in 1838, and more were coming. The Missourians wanted the Mormons out before the county was engulfed.[1]

William Peniston, a local Whig politician and colonel of the county militia, instigated the fight. He had asked for Mormon support in his candidacy for the state legislature and was disappointed when the Saints threw their support to the Democratic candidate. On August 6, election day in Gallatin, the Daviess County seat, Peniston's "flaming speech," as John Corrill called it, incited the hundred or so old settlers at the polls to stop the Mormons from voting, even though no Mormon candidates were on the ballot. Responding to the call, the mostly southern locals tried to scare off the two or three dozen Mormon voters. One Missourian announced that Mormons should not vote "no more than the negroes." The Mormons refused to be intimidated, and when one of them was challenged as he approached the polls, a fight began. After a few blows, a Mormon gave the Danite signal of distress, and others joined the fray. The combatants banged each other up with clubs and rocks, and then the Mormons withdrew.[2]

Rumors flew. Word reached Far West of two or three murdered Mormons lying in the streets of Gallatin and the settlers threatening to take vengeance on the Daviess Saints. A small party of volunteers, with Joseph among them, hurried to Adam-ondi-Ahman, and more collected through the day. After learning that no Mormons had been killed, the group conferred about the next step. Corrill thought the Saints made a mistake at this point: "Instead of returning home again, as they ought to have done, they took a notion to make the citizens agree to live in peace, and not come out in mobs."[3]

The Mormons were most worried about Adam Black, a hostile justice of the peace.[4] Knowing the Gallatin fight would eventually get into the courts, the Mormons wanted his assurance of impartiality. On August 8, a party of about fifty mounted Mormons led by Sampson Avard called on Black and required him to sign an affidavit to deal even-handed justice. After objecting to the intimidation—he later called Avard "a mean man"—Black wrote a statement agreeing to support the constitutions of the state and of the United States, swearing he was "not attached to any mob nor will not attach him self to any such people. And so long as they [the Mormons] will not molest me, I will not molest them." That evening a few of the cooler heads in Daviess County called on the Mormons to calm their fears. The next day, the parties entered into a "covenant of peace . . . to preserve each others rights" and to allow offenders to be dealt with "according to law and Justice."[5] Everyone knew that if justice broke down, war would come next.

None of the accounts of the foray into Daviess County put Joseph at the forefront of events. The horsemen from Far West went under the command of militia officers and the Danite chief Avard, with Joseph in the pack. Joseph later said that Sampson Avard invited him to go along; he did not commission Avard to lead the party. Nor was Joseph among the number who first visited Adam Black. Joseph sat outside by a spring while the others talked. He was brought in only at the end at the judge's request. Black, however, held Joseph and Lyman Wight responsible when a few days later he brought a complaint to Austin King, the circuit judge in Richmond, Ray County, naming Smith and Wight as heading the group that intimidated him into signing the statement.[6] Joseph was thought to personify the Mormons' terrifying lawlessness. The officers who delivered the writ for his arrest on August 13 expected Joseph to resist; a man who spoke for God would naturally consider himself above the law. Joseph's refusal to be tried in Daviess, where a fair judgment was impossible, started a rumor that he refused to submit to all legal processes. The bellicose Wight's comment that "the law had never protected him, and he owed them no obedience" was thought to characterize all Mormons. The frightened Missourians could not believe that Joseph would submit once his safety was assured. An investigating committee from Chariton County, delegated to find out if intervention was justified, found that both Joseph and Wight were "willing to give themselves up to an officer, to administer law, but not willing to be taken by a mob who were threatening their lives daily."[7]

After the election fight on August 6, nothing could halt the growing animosity. People all over the region were ready to take up arms. Peniston and Black solicited support from seven adjoining counties, many of which sent investigating committees. As far away as Jackson County, a meeting of citizens declared that they "know the Mormons to be a set of fanatics and impostors and that they are a pest to the community at large." A committee from nearby Livingston County reported that men were collecting from eleven counties to take Wight and Smith. Robinson worried that "this looks a little to[o] much like mobocracy, it foretells some evil intentions, the whole uper Missouri is all in an uproar and confusion."[8]

Hoping for government protection, on September 2, the Mormons wrote to David Atchison, their Clay County friend and the elected commander of all troops in northeast Missouri. Before their request for protection arrived, Atchison had been called out by the adjutant general of the state militia to quiet affairs in Daviess County. Atchison reached Far West on September 3 and persuaded Joseph to submit to a trial in Daviess County. Atchison stationed a militia company on the border of Caldwell in case trouble arose. Under Atchison's protection, the Prophet and Wight appeared before Judge King on September 7 and were bound over on a $500 bond to appear at the next term of the Daviess circuit court on November 29.[9]

His task completed, Atchison withdrew his forces, but a few days later, on September 10, Judge King ordered him back. Not satisfied with the court's decision, marauders continued to harass outlying Mormon farmers, using a rumor that the Mormons were in league with the Indians to justify the attacks. The threats grew so ominous that Joseph ordered all Mormon families in Daviess into Adam-ondi-Ahman. Reed Peck felt that the Daviess citizens, backed by small parties from other counties, were determined to rid the county of Mormons. At the same time, the Daviess citizens, fearing reprisals, also abandoned their farms. When Atchison returned, the county appeared deserted.[10]

Alexander Doniphan, a brigade commander under Atchison, arrived first. He found the Daviess vigilante camp six miles south of Adam-ondi-Ahman, under the command of Dr. William W. Austin of Carroll County, who had interrupted anti-Mormon action in his own county to rally to the support of Daviess. Though they claimed to be acting in self-defense, Austin's company refused to disband at Doniphan's request, though Doniphan believed they would not attack while his force remained. In Adam-ondi-Ahman, Wight, who was preparing his forces for a siege, showed a similar reluctance, but eventually "professed entire willingness to disband and surrender up to me every one of the Mormons accused of crime." Atchison doubted the peace would hold. "From the state of feeling in the county of Daviess and the adjoining counties," he wrote the governor on September 20, "it is very much to be feared it will break out again, and if so, without the interposition of the Commander-in-Chief, the consequences will be awful."[11]

Calm prevailed for a moment. "Whatever may have been the disposition of the people called Mormons, before our arrival here," General Hiram Parks wrote the governor, "since we have made our appearance they have shown no disposition to resist the laws, or of hostile intentions." Atchison reported that "there is no cause of alarm on account of the Mormons; they are not to be feared; they are very much alarmed." But appearances could be deceiving. Atchison understood the Mormon resolve not to be driven out again: "If an attack is made upon the Mormons in Daviess county, for the purpose of driving them from that county, it is very much to be feared that the Mormons, to a man, will assist the Mormons of that county."[12]

Through September, the Missouri officials tried to deal with the conflict through the judicial system, hoping to prevent war. Judge King insisted on bringing accused criminals to hearings before regularly constituted courts.[13] Atchison and Doniphan aided King in finding the accused, and the Mormons, trusting the two friendly generals, eventually cooperated.

In late September, the action shifted south to Carroll County, where the Mormons had settled in De Witt near the Missouri River. The Mormon presence had been opposed from the time the Saints moved there in July. The Missourians had supposed Mormons would confine themselves to

Caldwell County and were dismayed to find them spilling over into Carroll. The question of Mormon immigration was put on the ballot at the August 6 election, and only eight votes in the entire county were cast in favor of letting Mormons move in.[14]

From then on, the Saints were bullied and threatened. In late August, vigilantes under William Austin gathered outside De Witt in a quasi-siege. Austin's company had moved north in September when news of the Daviess County struggle reached Carroll, and then returned late in the month after Atchison persuaded them to withdraw. Under Austin's leadership, the vigilantes once again deployed themselves outside De Witt, and on September 20 demanded that the Mormons leave. After talking to the vigilantes' leader, an investigating committee of Missourians from Chariton County wrote back that "to use the gentleman's language, they are waging a war of extermination, or to remove them from the said county." On October 1 Austin underscored his ultimatum by burning a house.[15]

On hearing the news, Joseph hurried to De Witt to confer with the Saints, and the Mormons sent an appeal to the governor. The emissary reported that the governor told them to fight their own battles.[16] Samuel Lucas, an old enemy of the Mormons, wrote the governor that a fight would obliterate the Mormons:

> It will create excitement in the whole upper Missouri, and those base and degraded beings will be exterminated from the face of the earth. If one of the citizens of Carroll should be killed, before five days I believe that there will be from four to five thousand volunteers in the field against the Mormons, and nothing but their blood will satisfy them.[17]

The Carroll citizens called upon other counties to send men to help expel "these detestable fanatics." Hoping to restore order, Judge King ordered General Hiram Parks to the scene with the intention of dispersing the mob, but Parks's forces were badly outnumbered and untrustworthy. If he took any action to defend the Mormons, Parks believed, his own troops would desert him, and anti-Mormon reinforcements would pour in from the surrounding counties. "Nothing seems so much in demand here (to hear the Carroll county men talk,) as Mormon scalps—as yet they are scarce."[18]

Seeing the hopelessness of the De Witt Saints' plight, Colonel George Hinkle, the Caldwell County militia officer in charge of the Mormon forces, realized he must surrender. Austin's men kept firing on the Saints, some were starving as a result of the siege, others were losing cattle and having their houses burnt. Hinkle negotiated with the vigilantes to buy out Mormon property and let the Saints depart. In mid-October, the De Witt Mormons limped northward with a report that the mob was headed for

Daviess. Atchison told the governor that Austin's company pulled a cannon with them, and "the same lawless game is to be played over, and the Mormons to be driven from that county and probably from Caldwell county."[19]

The expulsion from Carroll came as a shock. Joseph feared that the anticipated campaign to expel all Mormons was about to begin. In Daviess, houses were being burned and cattle driven away. Previously, the Mormons had agreed to buy out the anti-Mormon citizens in Daviess. The return of the vigilantes would stop the acquisitions and end the peace. General Parks, who had been on the scene in late September, believed that if the property exchange stopped, "the determination of the Daviess county men is to drive the Mormons with powder and lead."[20]

Three days after the De Witt Saints arrived, Joseph rallied his forces in Caldwell. The Mormons heard reports of mobs converging from all points of the compass.[21] At this point, rather than relying on Rigdon to speak for the Church, Joseph himself stepped forward. Corrill said Joseph repeated the policy he had voiced for months.

> They (the church) had been driven from place to place; their property destroyed; their rights as citizens taken from them; abuse upon abuse practised upon them from time to time; they had sought for redress through the medium of the law, but never could get it; the State of Missouri refused to protect them in their rights; the executive had been petitioned many times, but never would do any thing for them.

While they were at De Witt, the governor "refused to do any thing for them." Now the Mormons would take care of themselves.[22]

General Parks asked the Mormons why they had five hundred men under arms. He was told "they intended to defend that place; they had been driven from De Witt and other places, and here they were determined to stand and die, rather than be driven from that place." Albert Rockwood's diary for October 15 reported:

> A meeting was called this day to make arrangments for the defence of the Brethren in Davies Co. Oaur lives Honours & Fortunes are pledged to defend the constitution of the U.S.A. and our individual rights and our Holy Religion. the strong bands of union appear to be wreathed around the heart of evry man & woman, come life or come death come what will here we stand or here we die is the will of the Lord.[23]

Militant self-defense meant driving out mob members from Daviess and confiscating their property.[24] The Mormons, in short, were to wage war on their enemies, as the Missourians had waged war on them. As the legally organized militia in Caldwell, the Mormons had a right to mobilize in self-defense, but to carry operations into Daviess, they needed authorization from Circuit Judge Austin King, and they only had a call out from a Caldwell County judge. The Mormons later claimed that General Parks advised them to defend themselves, but that was probably a rationalization after the fact. To maintain legal coloration, they marched under the command of the appointed Caldwell County militia officers. Joseph removed Avard from his command.[25]

To enforce military order, the people in Far West were put under martial law. Those refusing to fight had to contribute supplies. Warren Foote, whose family had just arrived in Missouri, said Joseph "was very plain and pointed in his remarks, and expressed a determination to put down the mob or die in the attempt." Those who were thought to be aiding the enemy were forbidden to depart. John Corrill, who believed the campaign would fail and wanted to escape, could find no way. Thomas Marsh and Orson Hyde fled in the night.[26]

Mormon strategy went beyond protection of their own people to attacking suspected mobbers. Mormon militia were to confiscate the property of hostile Daviess citizens and force them to move, thus destroying the vigilantes' home base. Enemies only were to be attacked. The confiscated property was to be deposited in the bishop's storehouse for the use of Mormons who had suffered losses in earlier battles.

Corrill knew the campaign was doomed. Mormon depredations would bring down Missourians from surrounding counties to crush the Saints. Colonel Hinkle begged Joseph to halt his disastrous course, but he pressed on, perhaps thinking the God of Israel would come to their rescue. He talked of the stone in Daniel's prophecy rolling forth to crush all other kingdoms. The Bible offered countless passages to prove that God would give His people victory. General Atchison reported after the Mormon raids on Daviess that "it seems that the Mormons have become desperate, and act like mad-men."[27]

The Mormon forces from Far West marched to Adam-ondi-Ahman on Tuesday, October 16. An unseasonal storm on Wednesday dropped six inches of snow, and the army threw snowballs at one another. On Thursday, October 18, war parties were dispatched to Gallatin, Millport, and Splawn's Ridge. In Gallatin, the company under David Patten removed the goods from Stolling's store, and the building was burned. A tailor's shop received similar treatment. Elsewhere around fifty buildings were burned. Within four days, Joseph's uncle John Smith reported that "we have driven most of the enemy out of the Co."[28]

The Mormons claimed the action was entirely defensive and not as violent as rumored. They said the Missourians torched their own buildings and blamed the Mormons. "They had recourse to this stratagem," Hyrum

Smith later swore in an affidavit, "to set their houses on fire, and send runners into all the counties adjacent to declare to the people that the 'Mormons' had burnt up their houses and destroyed their fields."[29] The day after the raid on Millport, James Turnur, a Missourian, came upon a small group of horsemen looking at a burning building in the town.

> I went up to Millport in company with young Mr. Morin: directly after our arrival, I saw Joseph Smith, jr., Hiram Smith, Lyman Wight and two others, ride up. Mr. Cobb, the mail rider, and several of the Bleckleys, came up also. Cobb observed, "See what the damned Mormons have done!" speaking of the burning. Hiram Smith asked how he knew it was the Mormons? He said they had burnt Gallatin. Some of the Mormons replied, that Gallatin was burnt by the mob from Platte.[30]

Uncertainty about the identity of culprits continued into the trial of the Mormons accused of depredations. The prosecutors at the court hearing following the conflict could not produce a single eyewitness to Mormons burning houses.[31] But some Mormon burnings likely did occur. William W. Phelps overheard an agreement between Joseph and Wight to burn buildings, and Parley Pratt, one of the company leaders, acknowledged:

> It is said that some of our troops, exasperated to the highest degree, retalliated in some instances by plundering and burning houses, and bringing the spoil to feed the hungry and clothe the naked, whose provisions and clothing had been robbed from them; and upon the whole I am rather inclined to believe it was the case; for human nature cannot endure all things.[32]

The Church's representative at the U.S. Senate hearings a few years later admitted that "small parties on both sides were on the alert, and probably done some damages." Many witnessed Mormon forces raiding enemy supplies for the bishop's storehouse in Adam-ondi-Ahman, in retaliation for the previous destruction of Mormon property.[33]

The week after the Mormon raids, Daviess County was a battle zone. Mormon families were driven from their farms by retaliating citizens, and Lyman Wight and others continued to plunder non-Mormon houses. Wight, whom General Atchison had earlier characterized as "a bold, brave, skilfull, and, I may add, a desperate man," had been hungering for war since Zion's Camp. He is reputed to have said that the Mormons would soon be knocking at the gates of St. Louis, as if the armies of Israel were destined to conquer the whole country.[34] John D. Lee later said Daviess fell into chaos for a week: "The burning of houses, farms, and stacks of grain was generally indulged in by each party. Lawlessness prevailed, and pillage was the rule."[35]

In a subsequent encounter, a band of Mormons, hearing of the cannon

Carroll County vigilantes were hauling to Daviess, surprised them in their encampment. The field piece had been buried in a road, but a rooting hog uncovered a portion of the ordnance, and the Mormons dug it up. A few days later, on October 24, the Mormons learned of a group of armed men approaching in a threatening posture. They actually were a contingent of the Richmond County militia under Samuel Bogart, but they looked like a mob on the prowl. The misapprehension proved to be a serious mistake. David Patten was sent out to drive them back, and as they approached the Missourian encampment on Crooked River in Ray County, the two groups exchanged fire. Patten was mortally wounded, as were two other Mormons, and a Missourian died in the fight.[36] The skirmish at Crooked River led to the charge of treason against Joseph Smith and the Mormon leaders. Resisting a band of vigilantes was justifiable, but attacking a militia company was resistance to the state.

Joseph disappeared from view during the military action. He had emerged to encourage Mormon forces on their departure for Daviess, and he and Hyrum had accompanied the troops to Adam-ondi-Ahman, leaving Rigdon in Far West. But Joseph did not command troops or bear arms. A hostile witness at Joseph's hearing said that "it was not usual for any of the presidency, composed of President Smith and his counsellors, to take arms and go into the ranks."[37] Joseph was said to have gone with Patten's company to Gallatin on October 18, but in the reports he is assigned no role and his location during the raids is unknown.[38] The affidavits describing the Mormon attacks said nothing about him on the field of battle. The military bands were led by Patten, Wight, and Seymour Brunson. In Joseph's own account of events, he sympathized with his suffering followers. "My feelings were such as I cannot describe when I saw them flock into the village, almost entirely destitute of clothes, and only escaping with their lives."[39]

Albert Rockwood, a militant eyewitness, thought the Mormon action a success. He noted on October 23, a week after the Mormon troops left Far West for Daviess, that "the Mob have been dispersed by the Brethren nor have they had any assistance from the Malitia neither do we desire any."[40] He did not know that reports of the Mormon raids had already reached the governor. William Peniston, the Mormons' old Daviess enemy, was the first to write about the plundering and the burned houses. "These facts are made known to you, sir, hoping that your authority will be used to stop the course of this banditti of Canadian refugees, and restore us to our lost homes." From October 21 to October 24 more than a dozen affidavits and reports by military and civil officials poured in, many of them addressed to Boggs in Jefferson City.[41]

General Atchison warned the governor that the conflict was beyond the scope of the law. "The great difficulty in settling this matter," Atchison wrote on October 22, "seems to be in not being able to identify the offenders." Without specific culprits on either side, no prosecutions could take place. Yet the citizens demanded action:

I am convinced that nothing short of driving the Mormons from Daviess county will satisfy the parties opposed to them; and this I have not the power to do, as I conceive, legally. . . . I do not feel disposed to disgrace myself, or permit the troops under my command to disgrace the State and themselves by acting the part of a mob. If the Mormons are to be driven from their homes, let it be done without any color of law, and in open defiance thereof; let it be done by volunteers acting upon their own responsibilities.[42]

By this time, the governor was not listening to Atchison. Peniston had warned Boggs that people were accusing the general of "political juggling" in hopes of getting the Mormon vote. Atchison was relieved of his command, and Boggs took action contrary to his general's advice. On October 27, the governor wrote General John B. Clark, Atchison's replacement, that events of "the most appalling character" entirely changed the face of things. The Mormons were "in the attitude of an open and avowed defiance of the laws, and of having made war upon the people of this State." "Your orders are, therefore, to hasten your operations with all possible speed," Boggs declared. "The Mormons must be treated as enemies, and must be exterminated or driven from the State if necessary for the public peace—their outrages are beyond all description."[43]

When the Mormons were expelled from Jackson County in 1833, Boggs—the husband of Daniel Boone's granddaughter—had been lieutenant governor and a leading merchant in the county. Though not involved in the mobs himself, he had not defended the Mormons either. Elected governor in 1836, he promoted internal improvements and founded a state bank. In 1838, having observed firsthand the turmoil the Mormons caused, Boggs saw expulsion as a solution to an old problem as well as a response to the immediate emergency.[44] However he felt personally about the Mormons, Boggs could not resist the popular will. He was caught in the predicament that Alexis de Tocqueville perceived as the classic dilemma of democratic society: the majority ruled even when it trampled the rights of a minority.[45] No agency of government could stand against overwhelming popular opinion. As Tocqueville could have predicted, the Mormons had no redress, no matter how grievous the crimes against them.

Northern Missouri citizens were fixed on expulsion before the governor gave them legal support. On October 30, a party of Missourians, still unaware of Boggs's order to Clark, attacked a small settlement of Saints at Haun's Mill fifteen miles east of Far West. The commander later claimed they were fired upon, but the Mormons were totally unprepared. The attackers killed everyone who could not get away, including children, leaving seventeen dead. The conflict had gone beyond threats, whippings, plundering, and burning. Now children's blood had been shed. At a hearing before Judge King in Richmond, a military officer estimated that "the whole number of the Mormons killed through the whole difficulty, as far as I can ascertain, are about 40, and several wounded. There has been one citizen killed, and about 15 badly wounded."[46]

SURRENDER

The war rapidly concluded after the Haun's Mill massacre. On October 30, Joseph Smith found an army of Missouri militia men drawn up a mile and a half south of Far West, temporarily under the command of Samuel Lucas of Jackson County, the ranking officer until General Clark arrived. Joseph spoke bravely of taking a stand, but when he got news of the Haun's Mill attack, he foresaw the same fate for Far West and Adam-ondi-Ahman. John Corrill, Reed Peck, and George Hinkle from the Mormon side entered into negotiations with Alexander Doniphan acting for Lucas. Both Peck and Corrill claimed Joseph was eager to sue for peace. Corrill said he was told "to beg like a dog for peace, and afterwards [Joseph] said he would rather go to States-prison for twenty years, or would rather die himself than have the people exterminated."[47]

On October 31, Lucas presented terms to Hinkle and required him to bring Joseph and other key leaders into the Missourian camp. Failing that, Lucas threatened to reduce Far West to ashes. As legal support for the threat, he showed the Mormons the governor's order. Lucas gave them an hour to decide and prepared his 2,500 men for battle. Seeing the Missouri forces approaching, the Far West leaders hurriedly complied. Near sunset, Joseph and four others walked the six hundred yards between the Mormon lines and the advancing militia and put themselves into the hands of their enemies.[48]

Joseph thought he went to negotiate, as the head of the opposing forces, but Lucas wanted prisoners charged with crimes against the state. He had told Hinkle that Joseph would be taken captive if the peace terms were accepted; if they were turned down, he would be returned to Far West and the Mormons would take the consequences. Instead of negotiating, as he should have since the terms were not yet accepted, Lucas dealt with Joseph like a prisoner of war. A guard of fifty men escorted the Mormons through lines of jeering soldiers, who were delighted to have captured the infamous Prophet. As Joseph said, "Instead of being treated with that respect which is due from one citizen to another, we were taken as prisoners of war, and were treated with the utmost contempt." Parley Pratt said that "these all set up a constant yell, like so many bloodhounds let loose upon their prey." A Missourian later remembered the five Mormons "were about as badly scared set as I ever saw," save for Lyman Wight, who "stood like a lion . . . without a sign of fear about him." That night Joseph slept in the rain on the ground, surrounded by an armed guard. That was far from what he expected, and he ever after thought that Hinkle had betrayed him.[49]

Seeing no alternative, Joseph acceded to Lucas's terms. The Mormons were to give up their arms and leave the state. Those accused of crimes were to be surrendered and tried. Mormon property in Missouri was to be confiscated to reimburse the Daviess citizens whose houses had been burned. The Mormons were to give up everything except their lives. Hinkle thought the demands beyond reason and wanted to seek better. He argued they were being asked to give up "their most sacred rites as citizens of a republican state." Joseph, with little faith in republican rights, sent word to comply anyway.[50] With 2,500 Missouri militia men camped outside of Far West, he had no stomach for battle. The Mormons were to give up their Zion.

Lucas, the Saints' old Jackson County enemy, seeking drumhead justice, held a court-martial the night of Joseph's capture. Joseph was convicted of treason against the state with no opportunity to defend himself, and with the other prisoners he was sentenced to be executed the next morning. Lucas was halted in this illegal action (Joseph was not a militia member and thus was not subject to court-martial) only by the refusal of the Saints' friend Doniphan to carry out the execution order.[51] Doniphan would not even execute the four prisoners who were militia and subject to a military court.

On November 1, Far West surrendered. The soldiers searched the city for firearms, threatening and ridiculing the Saints. A few days later, a force dispatched to Adam-ondi-Ahman accepted the surrender of the Mormon leaders, who followed Joseph's instructions not to resist. The Mormon men came one by one to a table where they signed away their property to the state of Missouri while militia men stood by and struck anyone who protested. By this time the Mormons were willing to go. Marauders were attacking outlying farms, molesting women, whipping men, and killing animals.[52] Rockwood reported that "orders from the govenour are to exterminate the Mormons, the Brethren are hunted as wild game and shot down, severeal have been shot in site of the City, womin are ravished and houses rifled, one woman has been killed within less than 2 miles of this City, we are here as captives strictly guarded by the Malitia no person is allowed to go out of the City." The militia made no effort to protect the Mormons. Judge King told the Mormons to bring charges in court, returning now to law as the suitable recourse for offended parties and overlooking the gover-

nor's declaration of war.[53] Despite the coming winter, the Saints had no
desire to remain in Missouri.

CAPTIVES

Lucas brought Joseph and the other prisoners, Sidney Rigdon, Lyman
Wight, Parley Pratt, Amasa Lyman, Hyrum Smith, and George Robinson,
into Far West to let them pick up clothes and supplies for their imprisonment. Guards accompanied each prisoner to his house and stood by while
goodbyes were said. Emma and the children clung to Joseph and cried. A
guard pushed Joseph's son aside with a sword, saying, "God Damn you, get
away you little rascal or I will run you through."[54] Then the men were
loaded on a wagon and hurried off to Independence accompanied by three
hundred men commanded by Brigadier General Moses Wilson. Lucas
wanted the prisoners out of reach of the Mormon forces.

In Independence, the prisoners received good treatment. Joseph wrote
Emma on November 4, two days after their separation, saying that "we
have been protected by the Jackson County boys, in the most genteel
manner . . . instead of going to goal [jail] we have a good house provided
for us and the kindst treatment."[55] Any form of respect won his goodwill.
Warmed by his captors' kindness, Joseph did not condemn them, but he
was uncertain about his own fate. "What God may do for us I do not know
but I hope for the best always in all circumstances although I go unto
death." To Emma, he wrote, "I have great anxiety about you, and my lovely
children, my heart morns and bleeds for the brotheren, and sisters, and for
the slain of the people of God." He needed his family's support.

> Those little childrens are subjects of my meditation continually, tell them
> that Father is yet alive, God grant that he may see them again Oh Emma for
> God sake do not forsake me nor the truth but remember me, if I do not meet
> you again in this life may God grant that we may . . . meet in heaven, I cannot
> express my feelings, my heart is full, Farewell Oh my kind and affectionate
> Emma I am yours forever your Hu[s]band and true friend.[56]

The prisoners remained in Independence for only four days. When General John B. Clark took command from Lucas, he immediately returned the
prisoners to Richmond in Ray County, where the court of inquiry would be
held. Clark mistrusted Lucas's motives in carrying the Mormons to his
home county and wanted the prisoners in Richmond before the judge with
the right jurisdiction. On the morning of the inquiry, Joseph was still in a
hopeful mood. He wrote to Emma that the prisoners were chained together
in two-foot intervals: "Brother Robison is chained next to me he has a true

heart and a firm mind, Brother Whight, is next, Br. Rigdon, next, Hyram next, Parely next Amasa next, and thus we are bound together in chains as well as the cords of everlasting love, we are in good spirits and rejoice that we are counted worthy to be persecuted for christ sake." He was sure he would be acquitted and returned to his family. "The[re] is no possible dainger but what we shall be set at Liberty if Justice can be done." Mainly he wanted once more to convey his love for his wife and children: "Oh my affectionate Emma, I want you to remember that I am a true and faithful friend, to you and the chilldren, forever, my heart is intwined around you[r]s forever and ever, oh may God bless you all amen I am your husband and am in bands and tribulation."[57]

The inquiry before Judge Austin King of the Fifth Circuit Court in Richmond ran from November 12 to 28. The nearly fifty prisoners were accused of participating in the raids on Daviess County or the attack on Samuel Bogart and the Richmond County militia at Crooked River. For two weeks, the court heard testimony from over forty witnesses blaming Joseph for instigating the Mormon raids and setting up the Danites as a secret government. The majority of the state witnesses were or had been Mormons.[58] Joseph's old allies Thomas Marsh, Orson Hyde, and John Whitmer spoke against him, along with the negotiators he had trusted, George Hinkle, John Corrill, and Reed Peck. Sampson Avard said the Danite society was all Joseph's doing. Only seven Mormons testified or submitted affidavits on behalf of the defendants, most of them for Lyman Wight. Mormon witnesses were likely to be arrested themselves if they tried to testify. One Mormon, Ebenezer Robinson, who wrote after his disaffection from the Church, said that "the trial was a one-sided *exparte* affair, as our witnesses were treated so badly, and intimidated to such an extent it was considered useless to attempt to make an extended defense." Their attorneys advised the Mormons to hold back their witnesses until the actual trial. Producing them now would allow Bogart to drive them out of the state.[59]

The testimony put Joseph squarely at the center of a plot to erect an independent government that planned to wage war on the state of Missouri. Outside the courtroom, a hostile crowd muttered threats and intimidated the witnesses. At the end, the court found probable cause to charge Joseph and five others with "overt acts of treason." Another five, including Parley Pratt, were charged with murder because a Missourian was killed at Crooked River. The rest of the accused Mormons were dismissed. Outraged, the prisoners complained bitterly to one another, save for Joseph, who was silenced by a toothache and pain in his face.[60]

Because the Richmond jail was crowded, on December 1 the group charged with treason were sent chained and handcuffed to Liberty, the Clay county seat.[61] Two weeks later, Joseph wrote a long letter to the Church from Liberty jail. By then he was fuming. Brief criticism of Hinkle and Corrill in the November 12 letter expanded into pages of outrage. Joseph was angrier with the dissenters who turned on him at the trial than with the militia mob. He ransacked the scriptures for precedents. He cited Haman, who sought the life of Mordecai and the Jews. "Those who have sought by their unbelief and wickedness and by the principle of mobocracy to destroy us and the people of God . . . like Haman shall be hanged upon their own gallows." "These men like balaam being greedy for a reward sold us into the hands of those who loved them." "We classify them . . . with the company of Cora and Dathan and Abiram." In a more secular vein, he called them "ill bred and ignorant . . . so very ignorant that they cannot appear respectable in any decent and civilized society." In the end, Joseph delivered the traitors "unto the buffetings of satan untill the day of redemption that they may be dealt with according to their works."[62]

Joseph denied wrongdoing in Daviess County. He was innocent, he said, and only the testimony of traitors had prevented his acquittal. The mobbers had conspired to "plunder to starve and to exterminate and burn the houses of the mormons these are the characters that by their treasonable and overt acts have desolated and laid waste Daviess County." The one Missourian death, at the battle of Crooked River in Ray County, he said, resulted from the Mormons' defense against an enemy that sprang wolflike on the Mormons and then retreated into the brambles. The accusers, Joseph insisted, "represent us falsely; we say unto you that we have not committed treason, nor any other unlawful act in Daviess County." He showed no regret for mistaken policies or any sense that the Church had erred. He was outraged and innocent. The letter urged the brethren to "be not afraid of your adversaries contend earnestly against mobs, and the unlawful works of dissenters and of darkness."[63] Far from breaking his spirit, defeat and imprisonment made him bolder.

REPRISE

How responsible was Joseph for the debacle in Missouri? The December letter helps answer the question by shedding light on his attitudes toward the Saints' enemies in the preceding months when the spotty diaries reveal so little. The letter gives clear evidence of Joseph's willingness to do battle against the attacking Missourians and of his impatience with dissenters among the Saints. The letter leaves little doubt that he would have favored the expulsion of Cowdery, Phelps, and Whitmer in June when the leading brethren in Far West signed the ultimatum. One can also picture him arousing the Mormon militia to defend themselves against the invading mob in October. "Go tell the army to retreat in 5 minutes or we'll give them hell," he later recounted.[64] When he was insulted, betrayed, or attacked, anger poured from his heart.

On the other hand, the letter is a rhetorical flourish, not one advocating offensive action. The dissenters are left in the hands of God. No actual revenge or sabotage is advocated. When it came to violence, Joseph was a man of words. In 1834, he had mobilized an army to march on Jackson County, but stopped short of an attack. Four years later, he urged the defense of Daviess, but did not carry a gun in the Mormon raids. How aggressively he wanted his troops to act at Gallatin and Millport is unclear. He certainly wanted Mormon enemies removed, but would he have fought to remove them or burned their houses? He believed his people could rightfully confiscate property in compensation for their own losses to the Missourians but no more. He is not known to have ordered any greater violence.

As the December letter said, he believed the Missourians burned their own houses and blamed it on the Mormons. His military instincts were defensive. When it was time to attack, he pulled back.[65] As the militia approached Far West on October 30, he talked militantly, but recommended surrender. Any Mormon aggression beyond these limits probably occurred without his authorization.

Whether Joseph Smith was guilty of treason in 1838 remains moot.[66] He was no more guilty than the mobs that had driven the Mormons out of Jackson and De Witt. Joseph thought the Saints acted only in self-defense. Was there no legal justification for resisting attacks when the government refused to help? The editor of the *St. Louis Republican* offered a judgment on the Missouri conflict:

> It does not appear, from any thing which I have seen, having the semblance of truth, that the Mormons offered any resistance to the properly constituted authorities of the county, civil and military. They did desire to protect themselves, their families and their property, from the licentiousness of a mob; and they did, furthermore, retaliate upon some portion of that mob, for burning Mormon houses and Mormon property in one county, by doing a similar act of injustice in another. But Squire Black, and those who acted with him, in retailing the enormities of the Mormons to the governor, singularly enough, forgot to mention that *their* patriotic band had been before them in scattering their firebrands.[67]

Yet Joseph must take responsibility for the Mormon raids on their Daviess County enemies. His angry rhetoric stirred the blood of more militant men. After the Daviess raids, Rockwood wrote his father that "the Prophet has unsheathed his sword and in the name of Jesus declares that it shall not be sheathed again untill he can go unto any County or state in safety and in peace." Words like that licensed Lyman Wight's desperate plans. Joseph's approval of Rigdon's salt sermon with its strong threats against dissenters had justified the Danites' expulsion of the Whitmers, Cowdery, and Phelps. Later Joseph repudiated the Danites, speaking of "many false and pernicious things which were calculated to lead the saints far astray," wrongly "taught by Dr. Avard as coming from the Presidency." Had the Presidency known of these corruptions, Joseph insisted, "they would have spurned them and their authors from them as they would the gates of hell."[68] But by giving them places of honor at the July 4 celebration, he acknowledged their legitimacy.

Joseph had enough power to be a target for an ambitious character like Avard who recognized that loyalty to the Prophet was an asset. Joseph's hold on the Saints could be turned to advantage by making that loyalty the basis of a private militia under Avard's control. He won support by purporting to represent the Prophet and making submission to Joseph the heart of the Danite pledge. Considering that Avard was the chief witness for the prosecution at the Mormon hearing, he appears to have acted with consummate cynicism. After he was cut off from the Church the following March, he gave no signs of ever having sincerely believed.[69] He was astute enough to recognize Joseph's influence and to use it for his own ends.

We cannot tell how clearly Joseph understood that power had slipped from his hands in that year. In retrospect, it seems possible that Wight and other militants took the Prophet's call for self-defense to extremes Joseph would not have approved. With only partial backing from Joseph, Avard organized the Danite band in a form Joseph later denounced as a combination of "frauds and secret abominations."[70] He may not have understood his error in 1838, but later, in Nauvoo, he kept control of the key institutions. He served as mayor and took command of the Nauvoo legion. Under his direction, the legion restricted itself to parades, ceremonies, maneuvers, and speeches. No engagements ever occurred. No Lyman Wight was permitted to take the Saints into battle.

Whatever Joseph learned in 1838, the need for restraint was not the lesson all Mormons took from the Missouri conflicts. The war scarred the men who had battled with mobs and militia. Many left Missouri defeated and embittered. Alanson Ripley told Joseph that "when I reflect upon the cause of your afflictions it is like fire in my bones, and burns against your enemies to the bare hilt . . . those who were butchered at Haun's Mill crieth for vengeance . . . I from this day declare myself the Avenger of the blood of those innocent men, and the innocent cause of Zion."[71]

Ripley was ready to strike if attacked again. For half a century, the war poisoned Mormon memory.

TWENTY-ONE

IMPRISONMENT

Your humble servant Joseph Smith Jr prisoner for the Lord Jesus Christ's sake and for the saints taken and held by the power of mobocracy under the exterminating reign of his excelancy the Governor Lilburn W. Boggs. . . . Forasmuch as we know that the most of you are well acquainted with the rongs and the high toned injustice and cruelty that is practiced upon us whereas we have been taken prisoners charged falsly with every kind of evil and thrown into prison inclosed with strong walls surrounded with a strong guard who continually watch day and knight as indefatigable as the devil is in tempting and laying snayers for the people of God. Therefore dearly and beloved Brethren we are the more ready and willing to lay claim to your fellowship and love.

JOSEPH SMITH AND OTHERS TO THE CHURCH, March 20, 1839

EMMA VISITED JOSEPH IN LIBERTY JAIL three times before she left Far West in mid-February 1839. In early December, she had traveled the forty miles to Liberty with six-year-old Joseph III and Phebe Rigdon, Sidney's wife, and their son Wickliffe. The women found their husbands locked in the frigid, smelly cellar of a tiny jailhouse, suffering from bad food and poor ventilation. Within three weeks, Emma returned with the wives of two other prisoners. Joseph asked for quilts, which Emma lacked herself but got from a neighbor. In January, she again returned to Liberty with Mary Fielding Smith, Hyrum's wife, and Mary's sister Mercy. The visitors and prisoners sang and prayed through the night, and Joseph blessed Joseph III.[1]

Joseph dispatched counsel to his flock whenever he could. "Brethren fear not but be strong in the Lord and in the power of his might," the First Presidency wrote from Liberty in early January.

> Neither think strange concerning the firy trials with which we are tried as though some strange thing had happened unto us. Remember that all have ben pertakers of like afflictions. Therefore rejoice in our afflictions by which we are perfected and through which the captain of our salvation was perfected also.[2]

Joseph's system of government by councils proved its worth in his absence. All through December, the high council with Brigham Young presiding met to strengthen one another and fill vacancies. In January, Joseph told Young and Heber Kimball, the senior apostles after the death of David Patten and the defection of Thomas Marsh, the Twelve were to manage the Church, and with council support, Young supervised the Caldwell exodus. Joseph also instructed Young and Kimball not to leave the state themselves. He felt bound by a revelation requiring the Twelve to plant a cornerstone for the Far West temple on April 26, before departing for Britain.

He was less exacting about the gathering, as there was no place to go. English converts could stay in England for the time being, or migrate to the United States. "America will be a Zion to all that choose to come to it," he said, meaning that, for the moment, all the continent was secure against coming calamities. A few months later, he shrank the gathering to "places of refuge and safty that God shall open unto them betwean Kirtland and Far West." Meanwhile, the missionary work was to speed forward. "The convertion of the world need not stop, but under wise management can go on more rapidley than ever."[3]

Joseph worried about his upcoming trial. Although he spoke confidently of acquittal, his life was at stake. If convicted of treason, he would be executed, and the likelihood of exoneration was slight. On January 24, the Mormon prisoners petitioned the state legislature for a change of venue and a new trial judge. No county would be sympathetic, but a fair trial in upper Missouri was impossible. Judge King, who would likely preside, had already publicly pronounced the defendants guilty. Hoping for some relief, the prisoners requested that their case be heard on a plea of habeas corpus. The Clay County judge refused the pleas of all but the ailing Sidney Rigdon, who spoke for himself from a cot. Winning over the court with his eloquence, he was released on bail on January 25. He stole away at night ten days later, fearing the Missourians would kill him if he were caught.[4]

In March, Joseph again appealed for a writ of habeas corpus, this time to the Missouri Supreme Court. He complained that he had been held nearly five months, at times in chains, without justification. Joseph denied wrongdoing. The supposedly treasonous statements attributed to him were false; he "did not promulgate such ridiculous and absurd sentiments." Witnesses who heard his speeches would support his claims if allowed to testify. Furthermore, Joseph said, he "had nothing to do with burning in Daviess county; that the prisoner made public proclamation against such things; that the prisoner did oppose Dr. Avard and George M. Hinkle against the vile measures with the mob, but was threatened by them if he did not let them alone." The statement tacitly acknowledged the struggle for control in the Mormon camp. In the heat of battle, hawks like Avard and Wight had taken command and perpetrated "vile measures" against Joseph's wishes.[5]

None of the petitions brought results. By mid-March, Joseph had lost faith in his lawyers, who, he believed, had not petitioned vigorously enough. Fearing a fair trial was impossible and a lynching likely if they were acquitted, the prisoners attempted to escape, as though prisoners of war. They bored holes in the foot-thick oak walls until the auger handles gave out. A friend unwittingly dropped a hint that aroused suspicion, and they were discovered while working on the outer stone walls. From then on, every visitor was searched for escape tools and kept from talking alone with the prisoners.[6]

The six men—Joseph, Hyrum, Wight, Caleb Baldwin, Sidney Rigdon (until his release in late January), and the six-foot-six Alexander McRae—were confined in a room about fourteen by fourteen feet in a small rock building with walls four feet thick. The lower floor, where the prisoners were housed most of the time, had two small grated iron windows and a trapdoor to the floor above. The men slept on dirty straw on an earthen floor. McRae remembered food "so *filthy* that we could not eat it until we were driven to it by hunger." When they fell to vomiting after a meal, Hyrum suspected poison. After the attack, he said, "[W]e would lie some two or three days in a torpid, stupid state, not even caring or wishing for life." Joseph said only that the food was "scant, uniform, and coarse."[7]

Outside the windows, curiosity-seekers jeered them. Hyrum said that "we are often inspected by fools who act as though we were elaphants or dromadarys or Sea hogs or some monstrous whale or sea serpents." The guards were worse than the curious. The prison was a "hell," Hyrum wrote Edward Partridge, "surrounded with demons if not those who are damned . . . where we are compeled to hear nothing but blasphemos oaths and witness a scen of blasphemy and drunkenness and hypocracy and debaucheries of evry description." Earlier, at the Richmond jail, the guards, whom Parley Pratt described as a "noisy, foul-mouthed, vulgar, disgraceful rabble," had boasted in the prisoners' hearing of defiling Mormon women. They went on for hours with "obscene jests," "dreadful blasphemies," and "filthy language." Finally after midnight, his patience exhausted, Joseph rose and thundered at them to be silent—or either they or he would die that instant. According to Pratt, the rebuke quieted the guards. Writing years later, Pratt remembered the majesty of the Prophet standing in his chains in a dungeon.[8]

By late March, Joseph wrote Emma that "my nerve trembles from long confinement," making it impossible to write with a steady hand. He asked her not to "think I am babyish, for . . . I bare with fortitude all my oppression." And the same for the others: "Not one of us have flinched yet."[9]

PRISON LETTERS

With Joseph confined, the Saints moved east to Illinois and eastern Iowa. Generals Clark and Lucas had given them permission to stay in Caldwell County until spring if they planted no crops, but roaming vigilantes forced most of the Saints to depart in midwinter. Bishop Partridge thought each family should manage its own escape. Brigham Young decided the families should cooperate. Young's committee resolved to "stand by & assist each other to the utmost of our ability in Removeing from this state." By pooling their property, the Saints could help all the worthy poor "untill there shall not be one left in the County whoo have a desire to Remove." With no agreed-upon destination, the Saints ended up scattered along the Mississippi River from Keokuk, Iowa, to Quincy, Illinois. The largest group accumulated in Quincy, the largest town along that stretch of river. Emma was housed with Judge Cleveland just outside of Quincy; Brigham Young's family was nearby. Joseph followed the Saints in his mind as they struggled east to Illinois: "My heart bleeds continually when I contemplate the distress of the Church Oh that I could be with them I would not shrink at toil and hardship to render them comfort and consolation."[10]

A packet of messages from Quincy arrived on March 19, one from Emma and another from Joseph's brother Don Carlos, who wrote that all the Smiths had made it to Illinois. Bishop Partridge reported kind treatment by the Illinois people. The next day Joseph wrote a lengthy reply, unburdening his feelings in an effusion of instruction, reflection, and emotion. In a single day, he dictated a letter to fellow prisoner Alexander McRae that comes to sixteen printed pages. All five prisoners signed the letter, but Joseph's mind and heart were on the pages. The words came rapidly from his lips without calculated organization. No paragraphs break up the flow; sentences merge; frequent misplaced and misspelled words show the rush in which the dictation was scribbled down. Yet parts of the letter rose to a level that merited later canonization in the *Doctrine and Covenants*.[11]

Joseph's wrath spilled onto the first few pages. He could not forget the "blasphemy and drunkeness and hypocracy and debaucheries of evry description," nor the "cries of orphans and widdows." The "blood of inocent women and children" now stains the soil of Missouri: "But oh! the unrelenting hand the inhumanity and murderous disposition of this people it shocks all nature it beggers and defies all description. it is a tail of wo a lamentable tail yea a sorrifull tail too much to tell too much for contemplation too much to think of for a moment." He prayed God to avenge the sufferings of the powerless: "In the fury of thine hart with thy sword avenge us of our rongs remember thy suffering saints oh our God and thy servants will rejoyce in th[y] name for ever."[12] Then, after calling down the curses of heaven on his enemies, he spoke with equal passion of "how swe[e]t the voice of a friend." The "fearsness of a tiger" and the "vivasity of lightning" receded from his mind, he said, "untill finally all enmity malice and hatred and past diferances misunderstandings and mismanagements be slain victoms at the feet of hope."[13]

Despite mistreatment by the governor, courts, and militia, Joseph did not become cynical about government. The March 20 letter shows him moving toward greater political involvement. He saw more clearly than ever that constitutional rights were the Saints' best and perhaps only defense. The beauty of the United States Constitution was that it "garentees to al parties sects and demominations and clases of religeon equal and coher[ent and] indefeasible right": "Hence we say that the constitution of the unit[ed] States is a glorious standard it is founded [in] the wisdom of God it is a heavenly banner it is to all those who are privilaged with the sweats of its liberty like the cooling shades and refreshing watters of a greate rock in a thirsty and weary land." True, the Saints had been deprived of protection, but the "fruit is no les presious and delisious to our taist." He realized, as the historian John Wilson has noted, that citizens can only make constitutional principles work by entering the political arena.[14]

By the time he wrote, Joseph had conceived a strategy. For the Saints to claim their rights, the story of persecution had to be told. He urged the people to gather the facts and "present the whole concatination of diabolicalil rascality and nefarious and murderous impositions that have been practised upon this people that we may not only publish to all the world but present them to the heads of the government in all there dark and hellish hugh." The story would appeal to potential friends who might support the Mormons even if they were skeptical about Mormon beliefs. Joseph thought that the mobbers constituted only a fraction of the Missourians, probably basing his hopes on sympathetic newspaper accounts, and that the number of sympathizers had grown. "As nigh as we can learn the publick mind has been for a long time turning in our favor and the majority is now friendly."[15] Rallying the support of sympathetic non-Mormons might persuade the government to grant justice to the Saints.

Ironically, persecution moderated the Saints' relationship with the rest of the world. For conversion purposes, the errors in other religions could be emphasized, but for political purposes, goodwill was more important. Potential friends had to be treated respectfully. In the Liberty letter, Joseph urged the Saints to respect other religious beliefs. He had never advocated forceful imposition of Mormonism, but here he said Mormons must guard against becoming antagonistic or aggressive. They must "be awair of those prejudices which sometimes so strongly presented themselves and are so congenial to human nature against our neighbors friends and bretheren of the world who choose to differ with us in opinion and in matters of faith." These people, Joseph reminded the Saints, had every right to their own beliefs. "Our religeon is betwean us and our God their religeon is betwean them and their God." Of course, common faith bound the Saints firmly to one another, but our faith "gives scope to the mind which inables us to conduct ourselves with grater liberality to word all others that are not of our faith than what they exercise to wards one another." Toleration and respect "approximate nearer to the mind of God."[16]

While in prison, Joseph mulled over the problems of the past year. The Missourians were to blame, of course, but he now saw that the Church had erred, and he had made mistakes himself. The wrong men had gained the upper hand: "an aspiring spirit . . . has oftentimes urged men fo[r]wards to make foul speaches and influaance the church to reject milder councils and has eventually been the means of bringing much death and sorrow upon the church." He did not say which speeches he now considered "foul," but he saw that undue militance had brought "death and sorrow." The rejected "milder councils" were presumably his. He had mistakenly yielded to those who favored "vile measures." Thinking of the Danites, Joseph cautioned against "the organization of bands or companies by covenant or oaths by penalities or secrecies," which weakened "pure friendship."

Joseph resolved not to repeat his own errors. He pledged himself to "disapprobate every thing that is not in accordance with the fullness of the gospel of Jesus Christ and is not of a bold and frank and an upright nature." From now on, he promised, the leaders "will not hold their peace as in times past when they see iniquity begining to rear its head for fear of traitors or the concequinces that shall flow by reproving those who creap in unawairs." They would reprove without fear of offense. Henceforth, he would "be always ready to obey the truth without having mens persons in admiration."[17]

Apart from the leaders' mistakes, Joseph saw that the Church had been in error. The tone and spirit of their meetings had been unworthy. Beware, he warned, of "a fanciful and flowe[r]y and heated immagination," perhaps a reference to Sidney Rigdon. "The things of God Are of deep import and time and expeariance and carful and pondurous and solom though[ts] can only find them out." Joseph tried to define an emotional posture suitable for the pursuit of divine knowledge. What was the right walk for a man officiating in the priesthood? "Thy mind O Man, if thou wilt lead a soul unto salvation must streach as high as the utmost Heavens, and sear[c]h in to and contemplate the lowest conside[r]ations of the darkest abyss." The Saints had to rise to their revelations. "How much more dignifide and noble are the thoughts of God, than the vain immaginations of the human heart," which were too often ignoble and crude. "How vane and trifling, have ben our spirits, our Conferencs our Coun[c]ils," Joseph wrote, "to low to mean to vulgar to condecending, for the dignifide Characters of the Cald and Chosen of God."[18]

As a poor man from a poor family, Joseph was sensitive about inequality. He worried that some Saints tried to raise themselves above the rest while neglecting the poor. Remember those "in bondage and in heaviness and in deep aflection," he urged them. Those who "aspire after their own aggrandisement and seek their own oppulance while their brethren are groning in poverty" cannot benefit from the holy spirit. "We ought at all times to be verry carefull that such highmindedness never have place in our harts but condesend to men of low estate and with all long suffering bare the infermities of the weak." "The things of this world" and aspiring "to the honors of men" corrupted the priesthood.[19]

Repairing their mistakes, however, did not deal with the underlying question: why God had allowed the Missourians to abuse the Saints. If this was His work, where was He? The succession of failures, beginning with Jackson County and continuing through the Far West surrender, was too much for John Corrill, the steady, clear-headed Missouri leader. At the end of his 1839 account of early Mormonism, Corrill explained why he abandoned the movement:

> When I retrace our track, and view the doings of the church for six years past, I can see nothing that convinces me that God has been our leader; calculation after calculation has failed, and plan after plan has been overthrown, and our prophet seemed not to know the event till too late. If he said go up and prosper, still we did not prosper; but have labored and toiled, and waded through trials, difficulties, and temptations, of various kinds, in hope of deliverance. But no deliverance came.[20]

Everything Corrill said was true. The great work had met defeat after defeat. None of the Mormon settlements had lasted in Ohio or Missouri. Joseph's seven-year stay in Kirtland was the longest in any gathering place. At Far West, the Saints survived barely two years. The gathering led to one disaster after another, as local citizens turned against the expanding Mormon population. Joseph lost old friends and trusted supporters: Oliver Cowdery, David Whitmer, Frederick G. Williams, William W. Phelps, Orson Hyde, Martin Harris, and Thomas B. Marsh all left him in 1838, worn down by failures and perceived missteps.[21] Six of the seven—all but Whitmer—returned to the Church before they died, and Phelps and Hyde within a few months. But the events of 1838 brought these faithful souls to the breaking point.

In March 1839, as Joseph was about to be tried for his life, the demoralized Saints were strung between Far West and Illinois. If ever there was a moment to give up the cause, this was it. Joseph puzzled over the Saints' suffering in the cause of God. Why had they been defeated? He never questioned his own revelations, never doubted the validity of the commandments. He did not wonder if he had been mistaken in sending the Saints to Missouri or requiring them to gather.[22] He questioned God's disappearance. Where was He when the Saints needed Him? "O God where art thou and where is the pavilion that covereth thy hiding place how long shall thy hand be stayed?" Joseph asked the question over and over. He had assured the Saints early in his imprisonment that God was with them in their afflictions. Yet he asked again in the Liberty Jail letter: "How long shall they suffer these rongs and unlawfull oppressions before thine hart shall be softened towards them and thy bowels be moved with compassion?"[23]

One long passage near the end of the letter turned the raw Missouri experience into a theology of suffering. The passage interwove Joseph's ongoing feelings about his own past with the struggle in Missouri. The opening sentence, "the ends of the Earth shall inquire after thy name and fools shall have thee in derision," was the way he felt about his life from boyhood. He was both noted and derided. He and his family had felt the sting of social insult from their time in the Palmyra cabin, and now more than ever he was publicly scorned. But in the very next line was the answer: "The pure in heart and the wise and the noble and the virtuous shall seek council and authority and blesings constantly from under thy hand." He would be honored and respected in the society he was creating himself, a society composed of the virtuous and wise. Traitors and enemies tore at this fabric and tried to wrest this society from him, but only "for a small moment and thy voice shall be more terrible in the midst of thine enemies than the fierce lion."

Meanwhile he would pass through tribulation, be put in peril, accused falsely, torn from his family, cast into the pit, sentenced to death, and all nature conspire against him. And why? "If fearse winds become thine enemy if the heavens gether blackness and all the elements combine to hedge up the way and above all if the verry jaws of hell shall gape open her mouth wide after thee know thou my son that all these things shall give thee experiance and shall be for thy good." The abuse, the injustice, the horror—all were for experience. "The son of man hath descended below them all art thou greater than he?" Christ had gone through worse and so Joseph must submit too. The voice of God told him to "endure it well."[24]

"Experience" was an unusual word to answer the problem of evil. Nothing was said about purification, or the greater glory of God, or redemption. The word "experience" suggested life was a passage. The enduring human personality was being tested. Experience instructed. Life was not just a place to shed one's sins but a place to deepen comprehension by descending below them all. The Missouri tribulations were a training ground.[25]

And for what? Experience implied a future elevation or condition. An earlier revelation said the Saints "must needs be chastened, and tried, even as Abraham" when commanded to offer Isaac. "For all those who will not endure chastening, but deny me, cannot be sanctified."[26] Joseph did not use the term here, but the reasoning brought back into view the earlier word "fulness." In an earlier revelation, Joseph wrote humans grew from grace to grace like Christ. Here growth into a fulness comes from suffering. Those who would be like Christ must suffer like Christ.

RETURN

The day after dictating the letter to the Church, Joseph answered a letter from his "Affectionate Wife." Emma had written, her "hands stiffened with hard work" and "heart convulsed with intense anxiety," concluding, "I hope there is better days to come to us yet." In reply, Joseph promised that "if God will spare my life once more to have the privelege of takeing care of you I will ease your care and indeavour to cumfort your heart." He spoke of the children and of his dog, "old major." At this low point, he could promise little. "If the heveans linger it is nothing to me I must stear my bark safe which I intend to do." He closed "yours forever," adding a pitiful postcript: "Dear Emma do you think that my being cast into prison by the mob renders me less worthy of your friendsship?"[27]

By early April, the prisoners had learned that they would be transferred to Daviess County for the long-awaited trial and then to some southern county where a less prejudiced jury could be assembled for the final trial. Writing Emma, Joseph was unsure what to expect but knew "we cannot get into a worse hole then this is." He thought of her and the children continually. "I would gladly walk from here to you barefoot, and bareheaded, and half naked, to see you." "You should not let those little fellows, forgit me, tell them Father loves them with a perfect love." But after these assurances of devotion, he again struck an uncertain note:

> I find no fault with you, attall I know nothing but what you have done the best you could, if there is any thing it is known to yourself, you must be your own Judge. . . . if ether of us have done wrong it is wise in us to repent of it, and for God sake, do not be so foolish as to yield to the flattery of the Devel, falshoods, and vainty, in this hour of trouble, that our affections be drawn, away from the right objects.

Joseph gave no indication what was worrying him. He said only, "[M]y heart has often been exceding sorrowful when I have thaught of these thing[s]." Emma, he urged, should not be "self willed, neither harber a spirit of revevenge," but against whom or what he did not say. Please, he begged, "never give up an old tried friend, who has waded through all manner of toil, for your sake, and throw him away becau[se] fools may tell you he has some *faults*."[28] He spoke as if Emma harbored resentment against him. At this point, the manuscript page is torn away.

On April 6, Joseph and the other prisoners left Liberty Jail, under a fifteen-man guard, arriving in Gallatin two days later. On April 10, a grand jury met in the front rooms of Elisha Creekmore's house; it returned indictments for arson, riot, burglary, treason, and receiving stolen goods. Judge Thomas C. Burch agreed to a change of venue to Boone County, and the prisoners set off for Columbia in a two-horse wagon with Sheriff William Morgan of Daviess County and four guards. While traveling east through Chariton County, the prisoners escaped, perhaps with the guards' connivance. The prisoners had long suspected they were an embarrassment to the state because the vigilante action and Boggs's extermination order would cause a scandal if widely publicized. At the same time, the prisoners believed the mob still sought to lynch them, whatever the outcome of the trial. Considering themselves prisoners of war in a hostile country, they had attempted escapes before; this time they succeeded. Hyrum said Sheriff Morgan agreed to get drunk and look the other way.[29] With two horses they had recently purchased, the five men headed for Illinois, traveling the back roads under assumed names. On April 22, 1839, they arrived in Quincy. After nearly six months of separation, Joseph and Emma were reunited. One of the new apostles, Wilford Woodruff, noted in his journal that "Brother Joseph . . . greeted us with great Joy . . . was frank open & familiar as usual. Sister Emma was truly happy."[30]

In Joseph's absence, several leaders questioned the advisability of gathering the Saints after the disaster in Missouri. Gathering aroused antagonism. Shouldn't they settle in scattered smaller groups rather than in a single large city? The leaders' uncertainty about an overall strategy prevented them from contracting for land while Joseph was in prison.[31] With his return in late April, debate ceased. Joseph later said, "I cried Lord what will thou have me to do? & the answer was 'build up a city & call my saints to this place!' " Two days after his arrival, a council commissioned him to locate land in Iowa on the west bank of the Mississippi and urged the Saints to move to the town of Commerce on the Illinois side.[32] The Saints were to gather as before, with Commerce at the center.

For months, Mormon leaders had been negotiating for property. Besides Commerce, the most likely site was directly across the Mississippi in Lee County, Iowa, where Isaac Galland, a local editor, purported doctor, and land dealer, owned a large tract. Joseph was drawn to Galland's proposal of twenty thousand acres for $2 an acre with nothing down and the payments stretched over twenty years. To an impoverished people, those terms seemed heaven-sent. The land could be occupied without raising cash, and the debt paid off later as farms became productive. Galland presented himself as a friend to the Church. Besides offering favorable terms, he wrote to the governor and the attorney general of Iowa, asking that the Saints be treated fairly. Joseph wrote Galland a long letter from prison about Mormon beliefs, and in July, he was baptized. Whether this was to ingratiate himself with potential customers or out of sincere belief is unclear.[33]

Galland offered the Saints easy terms because his title to the Iowa land was clouded and was not settled until the United States Supreme Court intervened in 1850. Galland was selling part of the 119,000-acre Half-Breed Tract designated by Congress in 1824 for the abandoned children of Indian women and white trappers, traders, and soldiers. Under pressure from speculators, Congress permitted "half-breeds" to sell their property, resulting in many conflicting claims. The legislature of the Wisconsin Territory, where the tract was once located, appointed a commission to settle the title controversies, but Congress organized the Iowa Territory in 1838, and with the tract in the new jurisdiction, the commission was dissolved. Miffed by their dismissal, the old commission members sued for pay in the form of land titles from the tract, complicating the picture. When the Mormons signed the contract, so many claimants were vying for the land, Galland scarcely could be said to own it.

Joseph appointed a stake of Zion in Lee County, Iowa, naming it Zarahemla after the *Book of Mormon* city, but the settlement never flourished. Migrants avoided the dubious titles and were rebuffed by the previously settled Iowans.[34] The largest Mormon growth occurred across the river in Hancock County, Illinois. The Mormons were attracted to a two-mile-long peninsula jutting into the Mississippi River on an arc just north of the Des Moines rapids near Keokuk, Iowa. The site had long been considered a promising place for a commercial town because of its proximity to the rapids, a natural point for upriver trade. The town laid out there was named Commerce.

For steamboat navigation, the Mississippi was divided into three legs. The first leg, extending from New Orleans to St. Louis, allowed for large cargoes on big steamboats from the Louisiana gulf. The second segment, from St. Louis to the Des Moines rapids, was dominated by the river port Quincy, where pork and corn flowed for transport in smaller vessels to St. Louis and southern ports downstream. The third leg extended from the twelve-mile Des Moines rapids to the lead mines around Galena in northwest Illinois. Because navigation over the rapids was only possible at certain seasons, Commerce had the potential to become the leading port of this third leg, comparable to Quincy just downstream. Because bluffs came down to the river's edge on the Illinois side, the peninsula, the only land at water level for miles, was an attractive site for a port.[35]

Seeing the potential, visionaries founded the town of Commerce in 1824.

Two Connecticut speculators, Horace Hotchkiss and John Gillett, platted a second town, Commerce City, alongside the first. Joseph first bought land on the peninsula from Galland and a farmer named Hugh White. Through the summer Joseph also entered into contracts with Hotchkiss and Gillett for 500 additional acres, including all of Commerce City and most of Commerce.[36] Eventually the Church owned all but 125 acres of the peninsula. Hotchkiss and Gillett offered sound titles but at a high price. Even though land was not moving during the depression following the Panic of 1837, Hotchkiss drove a hard bargain. The total cost, including interest of eight percent, came to $114,500, to be paid over twenty years at a rate of $3,000 a year most years with balloon payments of $26,250 at the tenth year and $25,000 at the twentieth.

The burden of that debt weighed on Joseph through most of his Nauvoo years. He originally hoped to pay much of it through donations, enabling him to provide town lots for the poor at a minimal cost. When donations fell short, he was forced to repay the loan through land sales, which meant that the financial solvency of the Church depended on high immigration rates. To concentrate the population in Nauvoo, Joseph eventually closed down seven stakes he had planned elsewhere in Illinois and urged all the Saints to come to the stakes at Nauvoo and Zarahemla.[37]

The Nauvoo landscape did not captivate Joseph as Independence and Far West had done. Instead of rhapsodizing about the garden of nature on the banks of the Mississippi, his history said the place "was literally a wilderness," with only one stone house and three log houses. "The land was mostly covered with trees & bushes, & much of it so wet that it was with the utmost difficulty a foot man could get through & totaly impossible for teams." Water seeping out of the bluffs along the eastern edge of the marshy peninsula required the Saints to dig a drainage canal, and even then the land was too wet to permit cellars. The wet spots and the nearby river were a breeding ground for mosquitoes. "Commerce was so unhealthy," Joseph's history said, "very few could live there." The Saints suffered from a terrible plague of malaria in 1839, and the next two summers were even worse. Joseph did not invest any of this landscape with religious history as he had in Far West, where Adam was said to have dwelt. Nor did he call Nauvoo "Zion" as he had Far West. Even though he was giving up the campaign to recover Jackson County, Nauvoo was not an equivalent. It was called a stake of Zion, like Kirtland or Zarahemla, not Zion itself. The most enthusiasm he could muster when proposing a stake at Commerce was to say "he believed it to be a good location, and well adapted to the circumstances of the Saints."[38]

Yet here, in this compromise location, Joseph built his most successful city. As his history put it, "No more eligible place presenting itself I considered it wisdom to make an attempt to build up a city." He laid out a plat roughly on the pattern of the previous cities of Zion but without a central public square. At Water and Main, two broader streets that crossed near the lower end of the peninsula, Joseph eventually built a store, a hotel, and a mansion to mark the commercial and cultural center of the city. Within five years, the population would grow to 15,000 in Nauvoo and the immediate vicinity. When Joseph died in 1844, Nauvoo was as large as Chicago.[39]

For at least a month after his escape from Missouri, Joseph's energies were depleted from his long imprisonment. Hyrum spoke for all the prisoners when he wrote that "I feel my body broken down and my health very much impaired."[40] For ten days that month, Joseph traveled around the countryside just visiting the scattered Saints. In mid-July, malaria struck, and for weeks he ministered to ailing Mormons, anointing their heads with oil and laying on his hands to bless them. The disease struck Joseph too. On one memorable day, he forced himself to rise and set out to heal the suffering Saints. Wilford Woodruff noted:

> There was many Sick among the Saints on both sides of the river & Joseph went through the midst of them taking them by the hand & in a loud voice Commanding them in the name of Jesus Christ to arise from their beds & be made whole & they leaped from their beds made whole by the power of God. Elder Eligah Fordham was one among the number & he with the rest of the sick rose from his bed & followed Joseph from house to house & it was truly a time of rejoicing.

Joseph kept thinking the disease was dissipating but it dragged on until September. Woodruff took a course of Thomsonian medicine, a healing system based on the belief that the stomach determined one's health. The body could be healed by emptying and warming the stomach, so Woodruff "took 3 emetics & steamed 15 minutes" in order "to clens my System." Joseph later preached a sermon against the belief that only the wicked suffer from disease. "It is an unhallowed principle to say that such and such have transgressed because they have been preyed upon by disease or death for all flesh is subject to death."[41] He had seen too many good people suffer to believe otherwise.

Through the summer, Joseph and Emma and the four children occupied a log house in Commerce with one room on the ground floor and one room above. Joseph's parents lived in the summer kitchen, which was connected to the house by a shed roof. Even these limited quarters were filled with guests. During the malaria epidemic, sick families moved in with the Smiths, sleeping in bedrolls on the floor, forcing Joseph and Emma to move outside into a tent. The high council, sympathetic to Emma, voted in October that the Smiths be "exempt from receiving in future such crowds of visitors as have formerly thronged his house."[42]

THE TWELVE

A non-Mormon attorney who was acquainted with Joseph during the prison months said that "he possessed the most indomitable perseverance." The Twelve learned the truth of this observation when Joseph required them to leave for England as commanded in a revelation, even though the Mormon war left their families in a desperate plight. All of them lost property and were struggling to gain a foothold in Iowa or Illinois; Joseph needed their help more than ever. But the commandment had to be obeyed. Heber Kimball had spent nearly a year in Great Britain in 1837 and 1838, assisting in baptizing some 1,500 converts, and during the good times in Missouri, Joseph planned to send a larger contingent of apostles and missionaries.[43] Now, when a new city was getting started and strong leaders were needed more than ever, Joseph sent away his most trusted followers to fulfill a revelation.

The revelation had instructed the Twelve to leave from the town square at Far West on April 26, 1839, easy enough when the Saints controlled the place. After the expulsion, a visiting Mormon risked his life by entering the state. Joseph told the Twelve they must obey anyway, and they did. Leaving Illinois secretly on April 17, seven of the Twelve Apostles and about twenty Church members stole into the deserted Far West square before dawn on April 26 and conducted their business. The council excommunicated nearly three dozen dissenters who had testified against the Church leadership or abandoned the Saints. Two new apostles were ordained. Alpheus Cutler, the Far West temple's master builder, supervised the placement of a foundation stone, and each apostle prayed in order of his seniority in the quorum. Then everyone slipped away in the early morning light.[44]

For the next three months, Joseph instructed the men who would go to Britain. After a two-year hiatus, the flow of doctrine began again. Perhaps because of poor record keeping, it appeared that Joseph had stopped revealing doctrine after the Kirtland temple dedication in 1836. Nothing of note was added to the corpus of beliefs or to ceremonial practices in 1837 or 1838. But a letter from Liberty Jail noted that "I never have had opportunity to give them [the Church] the plan that God has revealed to me," as if he was storing up revelations.[45] When Joseph met with the Twelve in 1839, the newly appointed apostles John Taylor and Wilford Woodruff began taking notes.[46] Their records show a prophet whose mind still overflowed with information about heaven and God, though he seemed wary of telling all he was thinking. Church members had to be prepared first. He told the Twelve everything revealed to him would be revealed to them, "& even the least Saint may know all things as fast as he is able to— bear them."[47]

Joseph spoke to the Twelve about angels with an easy familiarity that must have thrilled his hearers. He told the apostles that "when an angel of God appears unto man face to face in personage & reaches out his hand unto the man & he takes hold of the angels hand & feels a substance the Same as one man would in shaking hands with another he may then know that it is an angel of God." An angel's hand could be felt because angels are resurrected. An angel of the devil, who never had a body, will extend his hand but when one grasps it nothing will be felt. Thus he may be detected.[48] The instructions implied that the Twelve would find this rule useful when angels appeared to them.

Joseph's theology was as independent and idiosyncratic as ever. A sermon in June set out to address the Christian doctrine of election, traditionally a problematic theological principle that raised the question of how to recon- cile God's election with the moral agency of human beings.[49] If God decreed who was to be saved, what part did human effort play? Joseph's sermon, instead of proposing an answer, finessed moral agency and discoursed instead on the Holy Ghost. In Joseph's version, election was about how the Holy Ghost changed one's composition. The problem for him was how Gentiles became Israelites. The Holy Ghost, which, he explained, had "no other effect than pure intelligence," affected Israelites and Gentiles differ- ently. The Holy Ghost "is more powerful in expanding the mind enlighten- ing the understanding & storeing the intellect with present knowledge of a man who is of the literal Seed of Abraham than one that is a gentile." Work- ing in non-Israelites, the Holy Ghost had first to "purge out the old blood & make him actually of the seed of Abraham" before the intelligence could flow.[50] Election in Joseph's mind involved adoption into Abraham's progeny and gaining the resulting blessings of intelligence. Nothing was said about divine decrees or the place of good works in salvation.

He did cite the scriptural phrases about making "your calling and elec- tion sure," and being "sealed with that holy Spirit of promise," along with John's reference to "another Comforter, that he may abide with you for ever." The Second Comforter, he explained, came to those who hungered and thirsted after righteousness and lived by every word of God. Receiving that Second Comforter made one's calling and election sure. When believ- ers had shown themselves "determined to serve him at all hazard," then they would receive the other Comforter, "no more or less than the *Lord Jesus Christ* himself. . . . When any man obtains this last Comforter he will have the personage of Jesus Christ to attend him or appear unto him from time to time." Joseph's long quest to prepare his people to see the face of

God appears here again in the form of Christ dwelling with the believer. "He will manifest the Father unto him & they will take up their abode with him, & the visions of the heavens will be opened unto him & the Lord will teach him face to face & he may have a perfect knowledge of the mysteries of the kingdom of God."[51]

That emphasis on intelligence—a perfect knowledge of the mysteries coupled with the promise that hungry souls would see Christ—was classic Joseph Smith. "The day must come when no man need say to his neighbor know ye the Lord for all shall know him . . . from the least to the greatest." He gave tips on how to receive revelation:

> A person may profit by noticing the first intimation of the Spirit of Revelation for instance when you feel pure Inteligence flowing unto you it may give you sudden strokes of ideas that by noticeting [*sic*] it you may find it. fulfilled the same day or soon . . . and thus by learning the Spirit of god. & understanding it you may grow into the principle of Revelation. until you become perfect in Christ Jesus.[52]

Joseph's doctrine of election, unconcerned about justifying the ways of God to man, described the flow of pure intelligence to the worthy, avoiding the theological conundrums of Calvinism.

The other distinctive topic that summer, Joseph's expanded view of administrative organization in heaven, had no connection to conventional Christian ideas. From the beginning of the Church, he had been fascinated with administrative structures, especially the ranks of the priesthood and the organization of councils. The great priesthood revelation of 1835 summoned up an organization that involved every priesthood holder in a baroque elaboration of quorums and councils. In his 1839 teachings to the Twelve, Joseph tied these councils and priesthood keys to patterns in the heavens. "The Priesthood is an everlasting principle & Existed with God from Eternity." He meant that the keys and councils of the earthly Church descended from the persons who governed in heaven. Adam, Joseph told the apostles, "obtained the first Presidency & held the Keys of it." Just as the Latter-day Church had a president, Adam was president of the earth. After Adam, who was also the archangel Michael, came Noah, later known as the angel Gabriel. At some time in the future, Michael-Adam, also known as the Ancient of Days, would hold a council as president of the human family, where he would report to Christ on the work done on earth. As president, Adam passed along keys to those who presided under him: Noah, Moses, Elias, Peter, James, and John. They in turn conveyed the keys to the modern Saints. Joseph had long taught that the order of the Latter-day Church emulated the order of the ancient church. Here he revealed the connection to heaven.[53] The little church in Commerce descended from the eternal order of the angels.

Future Church president John Taylor scribbled down these words as Joseph spoke to the Twelve. Later, Willard Richards, another apostle, copied them into his notebook. Intellectually and spiritually, these men lived in the world Joseph created. His teachings were fresh in their minds when the Twelve left in the late summer for New York City on their way to England. Brigham Young and Heber Kimball, sick with chills and fever, could scarcely crawl into their wagons and wave farewell to their wives and children. Neither blamed Joseph for imposing impossible tasks on them. They felt privileged to go.[54]

HISTORY

In his spare moments in June and July, Joseph wrote his history with his clerk, James Mulholland, an Irish immigrant who had kept a scanty journal for Joseph since the previous fall. Joseph had begun the history in April 1838, starting with his birth and continuing to the reception of the gold plates in 1827. He now picked up where he had left off, carrying the account down to September 1830. After Mulholland's death in late 1839, a new clerk took over, and the history continued; beginning in 1842 it was published serially in the Church newspaper *Times and Seasons*.[55]

Joseph had always been conscious of making history. After 1828, he was scrupulous about writing down the revelations and tried to preserve letters. When the Mormons were leaving Missouri, Mulholland passed many Church papers along to his sister-in-law Ann Scott, who carried them for days in large handmade cotton bags fastened with bands buttoned around her waist. Scott gave them to Emma, who carried them to Illinois. When she walked across the Mississippi ice in February with two children in her arms, the bags banged against her legs.[56]

These documents were available to Joseph as he began dictating again in 1839.[57] In some respects, he told a story he had told before. The 1838 text was written in the same register as Joseph's brief 1832 history, his first formal attempt to describe his early revelations down to 1828. Both accounts tell the story of a confused boy visited by the powers of heaven. But the 1838 and 1839 history was a new work, written in a different spirit. The 1832 account, written when Joseph was just twenty-six, tells of a lonely adolescent, occupied with spiritual agonies, trying to account for his fabulous experiences. The 1838 account has a more confident public tone. Joseph, still the perplexed youth, is also the prophet about to usher in the last dispensation.

The 1838 and 1839 history marks Joseph's emergence as the preeminent figure in the Mormon story. Previously he had been reticent about his personal experiences. Judging from tracts, newspaper articles, and accounts of sermons, missionaries rarely mentioned him. But his importance grew. His life fascinated Mormons and outsiders alike. He had to account for himself to one curious traveler after another. Intrigued newspaper editors published stories about him. In 1843 he was the subject of a biography. Joseph opened his 1838 history with a reference to "the many reports which have been put in circulation by evil disposed and designing persons." He was news. In the 1838 history, Joseph attempted to set the story straight and to promote the cause. Moroni had told him that his name should be known "for good and evil among all nations kindreds and tongues."[58] As prophesied, he had become a celebrity. Now he turned his story to the advantage of the Church.

It would be years, however, before Joseph's story would become part of the missionary message. When he sent the Twelve to England in the summer of 1839, Joseph said nothing of himself in their instructions (save for reminding them that if they suffered, he had suffered too). He was more concerned with developing the Twelve into an effective working unit. Joseph cautioned them to forgive one another and be merciful. Don't seek to "excell one above another but act for each others good & honorably make mention of each others name in our prayers."[59] He did not want the quorum to deteriorate under Brigham Young, as it had under Thomas Marsh. Joseph seemed to understand that the genius of the Church lay in the extension of his power to this quorum and to the hundreds of elders teaching in cities and towns all over the country. He wanted to extend his work through the world, not his own personage. By working through the Twelve, he multiplied himself, and they extended their reach through the Seventy and all the other elders trudging from village to village with the *Book of Mormon* in their packs.[60]

The mission of the Twelve was one of many difficult undertakings that year. The defeat in Missouri notwithstanding, Joseph was still determined to build a city. As he said in his long prison letter, "our harts do not shrink neither are our spirits altogether broken." Neither their losses nor guilt about the Daviess County raids weighed them down. When the Mormons thought of Missouri, they did not remember looting houses or burning stores. They believed that they had acted solely in their own defense. They were the victims. As evidence of their sincerity, they asked for a full investigation. Let the federal government conduct an inquiry and judge for itself. The Missourians had proposed an inquiry but then pulled back when the investigating committee realized that the evidence collected was "not of the character which should be desired for the basis of a fair and candid investigation." The Saints had no such hesitation. In prison, Joseph had asked the Missouri Mormons to write accounts of the abuses heaped upon them.[61] He was sure that an investigation would vindicate the Saints. By the fall of 1839, he was ready to lay the case before the president of the United States.

TWENTY-TWO

WASHINGTON

SEPTEMBER 1839–JUNE 1840

Smith, the prophet, remained in Washington a great part of the winter, and preached often in the city. I became well acquainted with him. He was a person rather larger than ordinary stature, well proportioned, and would weigh, I presume, about one hundred and eighty pounds. He was rather fleshy, but was in his appearance amiable and benevolent. He did not appear to possess any harshness or barbarity in his composition, nor did he appear to possess that great talent and boundless mind that would enable him to accomplish the wonders he performed.

JOHN REYNOLDS, *My Own Times*, 1855

JOSEPH STARTED FOR WASHINGTON, D.C., on October 29, 1839, riding in a two-horse carriage with Sidney Rigdon, "Judge" Elias Higbee, and Orrin Porter Rockwell. Higbee, ten years Joseph's senior, had been elected judge in Mormon Caldwell County. Though he lacked formal legal training, his common sense and personal composure suited him for negotiations with Congress and the president. Rockwell, an early convert to Mormonism and zealously loyal to Joseph, would come into his own later as a western scout, hunter, and gunman.[1] On the Washington trip, his job was probably to protect Joseph from vengeful Missourians.

Rigdon had considered a Washington visit before Joseph escaped from prison. He planned to ask state legislatures for resolutions in support of the Saints, and then request reparations for the Missouri losses from Congress. He may have been thinking of an old states' rights tradition that assumed the states could pass resolutions on national issues. By fall 1839, Joseph and Higbee had decided to accompany Rigdon, and, in the end, they bore the burden of the Washington mission. Rigdon suffered a recurrence of the malarial fevers from the summer epidemic, making travel impossible. The party rested at Springfield for five days but then pressed on without him. Unfortunately, the letters of introduction from Illinois leaders were written for Rigdon, and he had to append endorsements for Joseph and Higbee. The letter asked President Van Buren and the heads of departments to "place all confidence in them as gentlemen." Rigdon caught up with the party in Columbus, Ohio, but by that time they were far behind schedule, and Joseph and Higbee hurried on by stage, leaving Rigdon, Rockwell, and Robert Foster, a physician who had joined them to look after Rigdon, to follow later in the carriage.[2]

Passing through the mountains in the stage, Higbee and Joseph had an unnerving experience. While the driver took a glass of grog in a public house, something startled the horses and they bolted. A terrified woman, fearful the coach would roll over, tried to throw her baby out the window to save its life. Joseph stopped her and then opened the door and climbed along the outside to the driver's seat. Higbee jumped out hoping to stop the horses but only injured himself. After a three-mile run, Joseph finally brought the horses to a halt. The relieved passengers commended him for his courage, discovering at the journey's end that he was the Mormon prophet.[3]

PETITIONS

In Washington, Joseph and Higbee found cheap accommodations at the Gadsby Hotel on Third Street and Missouri Avenue. By 1839, Pennsylvania Avenue had been paved with macadam, but the city was still raw. Livestock were corralled on the Mall in front of the Capitol waiting their turn at the slaughterhouse. Sheep, pigs, and geese roamed the streets, as they did in most American cities. Charles Dickens, who visited the city in 1842, noted the spacious avenues that "only want houses, roads, and inhabitants."[4] Washington was still a city of unfulfilled pretensions.

On November 29, the day after their arrival, Joseph and Higbee knocked on the front door of the White House. They may have had an appointment—a possible reason for hurrying ahead—but in those days appointments were not necessary. The porter received guests and decided whom to admit. President Martin Van Buren, a Democrat from New York, customarily saw anyone with political influence, and he doubtless knew of the influx of Mormon voters into Illinois. John Reynolds, an Illinois congressman, likewise conscious of the Mormon vote, accompanied Joseph and Higbee upstairs to the parlor and made the introductions.[5]

At the White House, Joseph and Higbee "found a very large and splendid palace, surrounded with a splendid enclosure, decorated with all the fineries and elegancies of this world." Van Buren had redone everything during his occupancy, repainting, repapering, revarnishing, even gilding the chandeliers. Critics later charged Van Buren with extravagance, calling the White House "a Palace as splendid as that of the Caesars, and as richly adorned as the proudest Asiatic mansion."[6]

Joseph and Van Buren had plain origins in common, but Van Buren, the son of a farmer turned tavern keeper, had outgrown his past. During his long career in politics, he developed a taste for high living, mingling with New York society, and drinking fine wine. Small and dapper, he was well-dressed and courtly in manner. Though liked by almost everyone who knew him personally, he failed to win over Joseph.

Joseph asked Reynolds to introduce him as a "Latter Day Saint," which brought a smile to Van Buren's face. His demeanor changed when they got down to business. After looking over the letters of introduction, the president looked up with a half frown. "What can I do? I can do nothing for you! If I do anything, I shall come in contact with the whole state of Missouri." Van Buren's first reaction was political. He faced a difficult election in 1840. The Whigs would choose their candidate, William Henry Harrison, the next week, and Van Buren would be nominated by the Democratic Party in May.[7] Missouri was one of his strongholds, and he had to calculate the political damage from helping a small, unpopular sect.

Joseph and Higbee did not like Van Buren, not even the way he looked. In a letter home reporting their "eye witnesses of his Majesty," they derided his "ordinary" features, "frowning" brow, and "considerable," but "not well proportioned," body.[8] They were to see Van Buren two months later and hear his famous declaration about their cause being just and still he could do nothing for them, but already Joseph and Higbee knew they would never vote for such a frivolous man.

They turned next to the Illinois senators and congressmen, who were ready to assist an influential constituent. The delegation heard the two Mormons out in one of the Capitol's committee rooms. Senator Richard Young even lent them money, which Higbee repaid by crediting Young's account with a Quincy merchant. Impressed, Joseph and Higbee reported that "the gentlemen from Illinois are worthy men, and have treated us with the greatest kindness." Congress was less impressive. Overall they felt there was "little solidity and honorable deportment among those who are sent here to represent the people; but a great deal of pomposity and show."

> There is such an itching disposition to display their oratory on the most trivial occasions, and so much etiquette, bowing and scraping, twisting and turning, to make a display of their witticism, that it seems to us rather a display of folly and show, more than substance and gravity, such as becomes a great nation like ours.[9]

The Illinois congressmen helped Higbee and Joseph plan their presentation to Congress. The 678 petitioners requested compensation ranging from 63 cents to $505,000 for their losses in Missouri. One congressman took the well-worn position that the Mormons should seek redress in the Missouri courts. The others saw that would not work. Ultimately, Senator Young offered to present the Mormon petition to the Senate.[10]

IN PUBLIC

With their petition on its way, Joseph and Higbee had no further business until the hearing. Joseph left for Philadelphia by rail about December 21 and did not return to Washington until the end of January. Growing Mormon congregations in the middle states were eager to see the Prophet. In New York, Mormon preaching had filled the thousand-seat Columbian Hall three times a Sunday. Other branches were thriving in Pennsylvania and New Jersey. Joseph spent a few days in Monmouth, New Jersey, with a branch of ninety, and near the end of his Pennsylvania stay preached in Brandywine, just west of Philadelphia.[11]

Joseph spoke to sophisticated general audiences as well as to the Saints. In Philadelphia, he "electrified" an audience of three thousand with the story of his visions and the recovery of the *Book of Mormon*. He was learning to adapt to his listeners. President Van Buren had asked Joseph and Higbee what distinguished their faith from others. Joseph had answered that "we differed in mode of baptism, and the gift of the Holy Ghost by the laying on of hands." Higbee commented that "we considered that all other considerations were contained in the gift of the Holy Ghost," code for the revelations and spiritual gifts. Earlier, Joseph had presented his religion to Isaac Galland in the broadest, most liberal terms. "Mormonism is truth," he told Galland, who had pretensions to some education. "The first and fundamental principle of our holy religion is, that we believe that we have a right to embrace all, and every item of truth, without limitation or without being circumscribed or prohibited by the creeds or superstitious notions of men." Joseph meant new revelation, but the word "truth" emphasized the generosity and openness of his religion compared to orthodoxies fenced in by creeds. "We believe that we have a right to revelations, visions, and dreams from God, our heavenly Father; and light and intelligence, through the gift of the Holy Ghost, in the name of Jesus Christ, on all subjects pertaining to our spiritual welfare."[12] The wording conveyed the liberation that so many early converts experienced and that made them feel progressive and forward-looking, not retrograde.

In Washington on February 5, Joseph spoke to a group that included an educated New Yorker, Matthew Davis, an experienced journalist. Davis expected something different from the notorious "Joe Smith" than what he heard. In a letter to his wife, he reported "no levity—no fanaticism—no want of dignity in his deportment," traits a pretended prophet would surely show. The recently deposed New York prophet Matthias habitually wore a green frock coat and crimson sash. Of Joseph, Davis said, "in his garb there are no peculiarities; his dress being that of a plain, unpretending citizen." (Joseph purchased three new suits in Washington.) "He is not an educated man; but he is a plain, sensible, strong minded man. . . . He is, by profession, a farmer; but is evidently well read."[13]

In the Washington lecture, Joseph underscored beliefs held in common with other Christians. "We teach nothing but what the Bible teaches. We believe nothing, but what is to be found in this Book." He believed in the Fall, but repudiated predestination and original sin. Christ washed away the sins of infants so that all were born pure and undefiled. In this liberal period, Davis was not surprised to learn that the Prophet had abandoned Calvinist doctrines, but then Joseph went on to more unconventional principles. God is eternal, without beginning or end, and so is the soul of man, Joseph told them, a view that foreshadowed his radical doctrine of man becoming god. Punishment, on the other hand, since it commences in the next life, will eventually end.[14]

Davis was impressed. Nothing Joseph said in the two-hour address was calculated to "impair the morals of Society, or in any manner to degrade and brutalize the human species." Davis felt Joseph's precepts would "soften the asperities of man towards man," and lead to more rational relationships. He had changed his opinion of the Mormons, Davis told his wife. Joseph "displayed strongly a spirit of Charity and Forbearance." "There was no violence; no fury; no denunciation. His religion appears to be the religion of meekness, lowliness, and mild persuasion." Joseph insisted more than once that "all who would follow the precepts of the Bible, whether Mormon or not, would assuredly be saved."[15]

That Joseph claimed the Mormon Bible "was communicated to him, *direct from Heaven,*" did not diminish Davis's admiration. "If there was such a thing on Earth, as the Author of it," he recorded Joseph as saying, "then he (Smith) was the Author; but the idea that he wished to impress was, that he had penned it as dictated by God." Joseph told the audience he was no savior or worker of miracles. "All this was false. He made no such pretensions. He was but a man, he said—a plain untutored man; seeking what he should do to be saved." "Every thing he says," Davis noted, "is said in a manner to leave an impression that he is sincere."[16]

Another reporter from a Christian journal heard part of another address the night before to "an intelligent congregation, including several members of congress." Judging from the report, Joseph's lack of formal education did not make him diffident. The reporter wrongly guessed that he "has evidently a good English education," and considered him "an energetic, impassioned speaker." Because Joseph dwelt on the sufferings of the Mormons, the reporter thought he was dodging the subject of the *Book of Mormon*, but noted that nonetheless Joseph said "he was inspired to write the golden Bible."[17]

Others who met Joseph personally thought less of his intellectual powers than did his Washington audience. John Reynolds, the Illinois congressman who saw much of Joseph that winter, thought he lacked "that great talent and boundless mind that would enable him to accomplish the wonders he performed," but neither did he "appear to possess any harshness or barbarity in his composition."[18] Peter Burnett, counsel for Joseph Smith during his imprisonment and later governor of California, thought that "his appearance was not prepossessing, and his conversational powers were but ordinary. You could see at a glance that his education was very limited. He was an awkward but vehement speaker. In conversation he was slow, and used too many words to express his ideas, and would not generally go directly to a point." And still, like so many educated people who met Joseph, Burnett was impressed.

> With all these drawbacks, he was much more than an ordinary man. . . . His views were so strange and striking, and his manner was so earnest, and apparently so candid, that you could not but be interested. There was a kind, familiar look about him, that pleased you. He was very courteous in discussion, readily admitting what he did not intend to controvert, and would not oppose you abruptly, but had due deference to your feelings. He had the capacity for discussing a subject in different aspects, and for proposing many original views, even of ordinary matters.

His sincerity and candor, Burnett thought, gave Joseph influence even with his enemies. After Joseph was arrested in 1838, Burnett saw him among a crowd of hostile Missourians, "conversing freely with every one, and seeming to be perfectly at ease." "In the short space of five days," Burnett recalled, "he had managed so to mollify his enemies that he could go unprotected among them without the slightest danger." Among his own followers, he was dominant. He "deemed himself born to command, and he did command." By comparison, Sidney Rigdon, though a man of superior education and fine appearance, "did not possess the native intellect of Smith, and lacked his determined will."[19]

Joseph stayed in Washington only a week or two in February. He saw the president again and was told definitely that nothing could be done. Joseph attributed Van Buren's timidity to political ambition, which was likely true, but the president did not have the authority under the Constitution or federal law to intervene in local disturbances unless invited to do so by the governor or a federal court officer.[20] Van Buren's rebuff stung Joseph, and when an interview with John C. Calhoun, the powerful South Carolina senator, was no more satisfactory, the Prophet abandoned the capital. He wrote home his usual plaintive words of affection: "My dear Emma my heart is intwined arround you and those little ones."[21]

With the help of the Illinois delegation, Joseph and Higbee had pared down the petition to the Senate and House, reporting losses of two million dollars and appending a long litany of abuses beginning in Jackson County and going through Governor Boggs's extermination order. They pointed out the impossibility of obtaining justice among a hostile population. "For ourselves we see no redress, unless it be awarded by the Congress of the United States."[22]

The petition was referred to the Senate Judiciary Committee under the chairmanship of Senator Garret Wall of New Jersey. Since the state of Missouri was being accused of crimes against the Mormons, its delegation was invited to attend the committee's hearings. They had meanwhile written home for information and received the record of testimony at Judge Austin King's November 1838 hearings. Up to this point, the state had done nothing to justify the governor's extermination order, and the Mormon memorial argued that the failure to bring extradition proceedings against Joseph was a tacit admission of the state's culpability. With its reputation in jeopardy, Missouri rushed off supporting materials to its congressmen.[23]

The Missouri delegation grounded its case as much on religious doctrines as on alleged crimes. Senator Linn and Congressman Jameson "summoned all the energies of their mind," Higbee reported, to prove Joseph Smith led the people by revelation in political matters, causing the Mormons to vote in a bloc. The Missourians tried to "make us treasonable characters" by showing that "everything both civil and political among us is done by revelation." Higbee insisted that this was false. Everyone exercised "the right of judgment according to his better judgment," in accord with the "democratic principles . . . taught us from our infancy." If they voted together, it was for the party that defended their rights, not because the Prophet commanded them.[24]

The Missourians' stout defense put the Judiciary Committee in a dilemma. They could not rule in favor of the Mormons without a full-scale investigation of the war, something the Missourians did not want and Congress could not easily accomplish. Eventually the committee retreated from a decision on the merits of the case and instead ruled that redress could only be had in the Missouri courts. "It can never be presumed," the committee said, "that a State either wants the power, or lacks the disposition, to redress the wrongs of its own citizens." Higbee accurately called the decision a defeat. Seeking justice in the Missouri courts was futile. Higbee stayed in Washington until the Senate accepted the committee's report on March 23, then headed back to Nauvoo, closing a chapter on Mormonism and Missouri. Joseph and his people would never recover their property. Not until late in the twentieth century did the state of Missouri issue a formal apology for the order to expel the Mormons.[25]

THE PUBLIC DEBATE

Though stymied in Washington, Joseph did not slacken his appeals to public opinion. His associates continued to circulate four accounts of the Missouri persecutions published in 1839 and a fifth that appeared the following year. Parley Pratt republished his *Late Persecution* twice, and Sidney Rigdon's *An Appeal to the American People* had a second edition. The Mormons may have hoped that an informed electorate would throw out "unfeeling and unprincipled demagogues" like Senator Benton of Missouri and "others of the 'Golden humbug,' firm of Vanburen &, co." Higbee believed that more publicity might influence Congress to reverse its decision.[26] Joseph was encouraged by groups such as the Cincinnati citizens who heard their case and resolved that the story "ought to be spread before the American people and the world"—exactly the sentiment of his long letter from Liberty. The editor of the *Quincy Argus*, prefacing a collection of Mormon documents, said the events in Missouri "concern *every Freeman* of these States."[27]

The literature on the Mormon war in Missouri did have a long-term effect on Mormonism's public image. Mormons were depicted as a persecuted minority who had suffered unjustly for their religious beliefs. The Quincy editor, who disclaimed any belief in the Mormons' "creed, character or conduct," felt obligated to expose the "injustice they have received from the People, Authorities, Executive, and Legislature of Missouri."[28] Defenders like Atchison and Doniphan in Missouri took the Mormons' side. Later a land developer and would-be politician from Pennsylvania, Thomas Kane, would take up the Mormons as a personal crusade. These sympathizers had little to gain personally but felt the Mormons deserved better. The accounts of the persecutions turned the expulsion from Missouri into an asset in the battle for popular support.

The persecution literature told one Mormon story, but there were others. After 1837, the number of Mormon-related items in print mushroomed, some positive, most not. On the positive side, Parley Pratt published one of the most popular missionary tracts of all time in 1837, *A Voice of Warning and Instruction to All People, Containing a Declaration of the Faith and Doctrine of the Church of the Latter-Day Saints, Commonly Called Mormons*. It was countered the next year by four anti-Mormon pamphlets with titles like *Mormonism Exposed*. After that, the assaults kept coming year after year as Mormonism proved to be good press. Three of the 1838 anti-Mormon pamphlets were published in New York; the other in England.[29]

Mormonism had been noticed in the national press before, but never with such intensity. The earliest stories had passed off the *Book of Mormon* and Joseph's visions as entertaining diversions. Mormonism was a folly, not a threat. Serious criticism came primarily from people close to Mormonism. Ezra Booth, the author of nine acrimonious letters printed in the *Ohio Star* in 1831, was a disillusioned Mormon. Doctor Philastus Hurlbut, an excommunicated apostate, collected affidavits about the Smiths' money-digging in Palmyra. Eber D. Howe's 1834 *Mormonism Unvailed*, which included both Booth's and Hurlbut's writings, was the work of a newspaper editor in nearby Painesville, Ohio. The people most exercised about Mormons were disaffected former adherents and near neighbors. The Campbellite leader Alexander Campbell, who published a critique of the *Book of Mormon* in 1831, was a former colleague of Sidney Rigdon. He was moved to attack the book when he heard of conversions among his Kirtland followers.

In 1838, the menace of Mormonism began to concern a much wider circle. The first of the three anti-Mormon pamphlets to appear that year was the work of Origen Bacheler, a polemicist who had no direct contact with the body of Mormons. The pamphlet was the published version of a debate between Bacheler and Parley Pratt (with Pratt's side omitted). Pratt had come to New York in the summer of 1837 to purge himself of his ill feelings toward Joseph after the Kirtland bank debacle. He had faltered when Joseph tried to collect payment for a Kirtland city lot and was alienated from the Prophet for three months. In New York, he wrote *A Voice of Warning* and debated Bacheler. Bacheler gave credit to Pratt for his personal demeanor. "To be sure, you have a very demure countenance; you are quite moderate in your manner of speech; and you appear very cool and self-possessed," but, he added, are not many knaves "smooth as razors dipped in oil?" Pratt withdrew from debate after six meetings, but Bacheler unloaded his criticisms twice more and still was not finished with Mormonism. The back of the pamphlet advertised eight additional points he intended to argue in a subsequent work.[30]

Bacheler focused his criticism on the *Book of Mormon*. He gave example after example of errors in style, reasoning, and historical fact, much in the spirit of Thomas Paine's iconoclastic attack on the Bible in *The Age of Reason*, published in 1794. In fact, Bacheler patterned his treatment of Mormonism after Paine. Paine had brought evidence "to show the imposition and falsehood of Isaiah" and every other book in the Bible. His aim, he said, was "to show that the Bible is spurious, and thus, by taking away the foundation, to overthrow at once the whole structure of superstition raised thereon." Paine wrote: "Whenever we read the obscene stories, the voluptuous debaucheries, the cruel and torturous executions, the unrelenting vindictiveness, with which more than half the Bible is filled, it would be more consistent that we call it the word of a demon than the word of God." A Boston newspaper, appalled at Paine's audacity, had called him "a lying, drunken, brutal infidel."[31] Bacheler administered the same medicine to the *Book of Mormon*: slashing prose, scorn for the text, and complete confidence in rational analysis.

Bacheler arranged his evidence in categories like "Barbarisms," "Improbabilities," "Absurdities," and "Contradiction of Fact." He lumped together the colloquial New England language as "Jonathanisms," which he thought unworthy of God. Some phrases struck Bacheler as ridiculously funny: " 'ye *wear* stiff *necks* and high *heads*' . . . Wear necks and heads! A curious kind of stocks and hats, to be sure. Genuine Mormon *manufacture*." Bacheler denied the Mormon claim that the book harmonized with the Bible. Where in the Bible did Smith find the prophet Lehi, whose visions are given in the first chapter of the *Book of Mormon*? "Now ask the Jews if they ever had such a prophet; and they are quite as likely to know, as the juggling, money-digging, fortune-telling impostor, Smith."[32]

As Bacheler went on laying out one absurdity after another, his outrage at "the miscreants who are battening on the ignorance and credulity of those upon whom they can successfully play off this imposture" intensified. The *Book of Mormon* is "the most gross, the most ridiculous, the most imbecile, the most contemptible concern, that was ever attempted to be palmed off upon society as a revelation." Joseph Smith and his witnesses are "perhaps the most infamous liars and impostors that ever breathed." The deceit they practice on the unsuspecting believers is nearly criminal. "By their deception and lies, they swindle them out of their property, disturb social order and the public peace, excite a spirit of ferocity and murder, and lead multitudes astray on the subject in which, of all others, they have the deepest interest." Bacheler believed they must be dealt with: "They can be viewed in no other light than that of monstrous public nuisances, that ought forthwith to be abated."[33]

Publishing conventions for over a century had permitted feverish writing on public issues. Bacheler's rhetoric did not distinguish him from scores of other polemicists of his time. Still, the anger in his words raises the question of why Mormonism was so threatening. Why did Bacheler write so passionately against the productions of a "blockhead" like Joseph Smith? Why did he claim the Mormon conspirators were "the most vile, the most impudent, the most impious knot of charlatans and cheats with which any community was ever disgraced and cursed"?[34]

Bacheler had earlier attacked Universalism and later wrote against Episcopalianism. Like other rationalists of his day, he may have felt crushed between skepticism on the one hand and superstition on the other. On one side, Paine and the infidels were assaulting Christianity, and on the other, the uneducated masses were falling into the clutches of charlatans like "Joe Smith." In 1831 Bacheler published an exchange of letters with the atheist Robert Dale Owen on belief in God and the authenticity of the Bible. For ten weeks the two traded blows on God and then launched into a debate on the Bible. While skeptics were closing in from the rationalist side, Mormonism was spreading superstition on the other. Joseph Smith's success seemed to show that the popular masses would put their faith in any cock-eyed story. The foundation on which rational Christianity stood was proving to be uncomfortably narrow.[35]

In the introduction to a later edition of the letters, Bacheler put the issue as he saw it. "Religion is the all-important thing, or else it is a gross imposition on mankind. . . . If it is true, it ought to be maintained; if false, overthrown." Everything hung on religion's rationality. The thousands of Mormon conversions posed the question: Was faith in orthodox Christianity any different? Was it another religious imposture battening on human credulity just like Mormonism? The pretensions of Joseph Smith put all revealed religion to the test. Unless Mormonism could be distinguished from rational religion, all of Christianity was in danger. While protecting the innocent from the Mormon imposture, Bacheler was defending Christianity itself.[36]

The critics' writings largely controlled the reading public's image of the Prophet for the next century, with unfortunate results for biographers. The sharp caricature of "Joe Smith" as fraud and con man blotted out the actual person. He was a combination of knave and blockhead. No one had to explain what motives drove him. He was a fixed type, the confidence man, well known in the literature of antebellum America.[37] Americans knew all about these insidious scoundrels who undermined social order and ruined the lives of their unsuspecting victims. Joseph Smith became the worst of the type—a religious fraud who preyed upon the sacred yearnings of the human soul. James M'Chesney, the author of another of the anti-Mormon pamphlets in 1838, thought the Mormons were "miserable enemies of both God and man—engines of death and hell." Combat with them was "desperate, the battle is one of extermination."[38]

Joseph Smith as a person did not figure in this literature, but then neither did he in the writings of Mormons. Defenders of the faith like Orson and Parley Pratt contended with the critics, but said little either way about Joseph Smith. They spoke of revelation in the passive voice, as if it was received without anybody to receive it. For the first hundred pages, Parley Pratt's *Voice of Warning* did not mention the Church, much less Joseph

Smith. Pratt emphasized the gathering of Israel in the last days and the abstract need for revelation. Finally, on page 122, he announced that revelation had come without saying anything of the revelator. "Suddenly a voice is heard from the wilderness, a cry salutes the ears of mortals, a testimony is heard among them, piercing to the inmost recesses of their hearts." The *Book of Mormon* was "brought to light by the ministering of angels, and translated by Inspiration"—all in the passive voice. Pratt tells the story of finding the book and publishing it without mentioning Joseph Smith or even indicating that an actual person did the work. When people are mentioned as receiving revelation, they are a faceless group. "This manifestation was by the ministering of Angels, and by the voice of Jehovah, speaking from the heavens in plainness, unto men who are now living among you."[39] The revelations came down like rain on a company of nameless prophets.

Joseph first figured as a person in a tract by Pratt's brother Orson, published in Edinburgh in 1840, *An Interesting Account of Several Remarkable Visions, and of the Late Discovery of Ancient American Records.*[40] Orson recounted the First Vision story from Joseph Smith's 1838 history and reprinted long excerpts from Oliver Cowdery's 1834 letters to the *Messenger and Advocate* on Moroni and the plates, but added nothing from personal experience about the Prophet's character or teachings. The Joseph he presented was the persona the Prophet had created for himself in his history, the perplexed innocent searching for truth. And yet Orson Pratt's pamphlet was a breakthrough. Joseph Smith was at last given a name and a role in print as the searching youth to whom God and angels appeared.

Pratt's work had little impact on the treatment of Mormons in the national press. There the Mormons figured in two diametrically opposed stories. In one version, they were a misguided but mistreated religious minority who had unjustly suffered for their beliefs, a story resonating with the American story of persecuted Pilgrims fleeing to the New World. In the other version, Joseph was a stereotypical fanatic foisting his schemes on an ignorant public, a blaspheming scoundrel who made dupes of his followers. Orson Pratt's searching visionary and the reasonable and forceful leader admired by Matthew Davis and Peter Burnett were virtually unknown.

TWENTY-THREE

BEAUTIFUL PLACE

APRIL 1840–APRIL 1841

The name of our city (Nauvoo,) is of Hebrew origin, and signifies a beautiful situation, or place, carrying with it, also, the idea of rest; and is truly descriptive of this most delightful situation.

JOSEPH SMITH, SIDNEY RIGDON, AND HYRUM SMITH
TO THE SAINTS SCATTERED ABROAD, January 15, 1841

EIGHTEEN FORTY MAY HAVE BEEN the happiest year of Joseph Smith's life. Exultant after the annual conference in April 1840, he was free at last to construct a city. For nine years, circumstances had frustrated him. The 1833 expulsion had stopped activity in Jackson County; in Kirtland, Joseph's only civic achievement after seven years was the construction of the temple; at Far West, war blasted his hopes. In Nauvoo in 1840, the way at last seemed clear. Although Commerce's marshy ground was not ideal, land was available on long credit, and the Illinois citizens welcomed the Mormons. For a year, Joseph devoted himself almost entirely to city-building.

His happy mood shines through four official reports to the Church between August 1840 and April 1841. In September the First Presidency wrote:

The work of the Lord in these last days, is one of vast magnitude and almost beyond the comprehension of mortals: its glories are past description and its grandour insurpassable. . . . The purposes of our God are great, his love unfathomable, his wisdom infinite, and his power unlimited; therefore, the Saints have cause to rejoice and be glad, knowing that "this God is our God forever and ever and he will be our guide unto death."[1]

The feeling in April 1841 was the same. The First Presidency made known "with unfeigned pleasure . . . the steady and rapid increase of the church in this State, the United States, and in Europe. . . . Peace and prosperity attend us; and we have favor in the sight of God and virtuous men."[2]

How should we read the optimism of the reports? Joseph knew better than anyone the problems facing the Church. They lacked the resources for building a city; Joseph verged on bankruptcy much of the time. Enmity from Missouri was spilling over into Illinois and would soon break out in the press. Did he realize that the Church ran on his vision and grit, and that he had to manufacture progress by sheer will? If he lost his nerve, the Zion campaign would collapse.

Joseph generated positive energy even from defeat. His reaction to the report of the Senate Judiciary Committee is one example. The advice to take their grievances to the Missouri courts brought "deep sorrow, regret and disappointment to Church leaders," but the April 1840 conference dismissed the report, appealing "to the Courts of Heaven, believing, that the great Jehovah, who rules over the destiny of nations, and who notices the falling sparrows, will undoubtedly redress our wrongs." Instead of feeling like pitiful victims, the Saints turned their anger on the hardhearted officials. Joseph predicted ruin for a government that ignored a suffering people. If just causes found no favor, the nation would be brought to "the very verge of crumbling to peices and tumbling to the ground." The Latter-day Saints, the people the government had disregarded, would save it. At that day "when the constitution is upon the brink of ruin this people will be the Staff up[on] which the Nation shall lean and they shall bear the constitution away from the very verge of destruction."[3] Joseph, who loved and hated the United States, saw the collapsing country supported by his own people.

By mid-1840, the recent expulsion no longer looked like a total disaster. Joseph was turning the Missouri conflict into a usable past. During the war, "nothing but death presented itself, and destruction, inevitable," he wrote, yet the Saints escaped. They were "like the children of Israel who came out of the land of Egypt." With his remarkable facility for giving meaning to events, Joseph turned the Missouri expulsion into a modern exodus. "Two years ago, mobs were threatening, plundering, driving and murdering the saints. [N]ow we can enjoy peace, and can worship the God of heaven and earth without molestation." The Saints can thank God "who looked upon our distresses and delivered us from danger and death." The Missouri exodus was a deliverance.[4]

A revelation in January 1841 freed the Saints from Missouri like Israel sloughing off Egypt. For years, holding on to property in Jackson County was a sign of faithfulness. The 1841 revelation told them they could sell their lands and "build a house to my name, even in this place," meaning Nauvoo.[5] Though Jackson County remained the symbol of the perfect Mormon society, they could realize this ideal in another place. In July, Joseph designated all of North and South America as Zion. Cities could arise wherever the Saints lived. He proposed founding twelve stakes of Zion in Illinois and Iowa, and the number could be multiplied.[6]

Intermittent trouble did not dampen Joseph's spirits. In early July, ruffians from Tully, Missouri, kidnapped four Illinois Mormons accused of stealing and carried them across the Mississippi. The Missourians hung one by a noose until he nearly strangled, beat up others, and held them all in prison for three days, to "enforce the law." Two months later, in September, Missouri officials tried to capture Joseph. They recognized that unless the state attempted to recover the five Mormons who had escaped custody in April 1839, it implicitly admitted its error in charging them in the first place. Governor Thomas Reynolds, Boggs's successor in Missouri, instituted extradition proceedings. Illinois's Governor Carlin signed the writ, but the sheriff was unable to locate any of the five men, and no further proceedings were instituted for six months.[7]

Neither incident dismayed Joseph. He was more affected by the death of his father in September, mourned as the patriarch who laid on hands and blessed people.[8] Although the old man had failed by every measure of material success, Joseph Jr. never showed anything but love and respect for his father. Lucy reported that on his deathbed, Joseph Sr. promised Joseph Jr. he would live to finish his work. (Lucy's preliminary manuscript said, "Your children after you shall live to finish your work.")[9]

Three months before Joseph Sr.'s death, Emma bore another son, Don Carlos, adding a fourth boy to the family, along with the adopted Julia and two daughters of Edward Partridge, the Missouri bishop who died in 1840. Joseph built a kitchen wing on the back of the Smiths' log house in the spring, leaving the two main rooms for sleeping quarters. To be on the safe side, he constructed a secret room under hinged stairs leading to the cellar in case Missouri tried to recapture him.[10]

WORLD CITY

Returning from four months in the East, Joseph marveled at Nauvoo's progress. The marshy city no longer looked so bad: "There is now every prospect of our haveing a good society, a peaceable habitation and a desirable residence here." By summer he was talking like a booster once again.[11] Nauvoo, he wrote a prospective convert, "is probably the best & most beautiful site for a city on the River." "If we are suffered to remain there is every prospect of its becoming one of the largest cities on the river if not in the western world." Quincy and Alton, the two most advanced Illinois towns along the Mississippi, each contained about 2,300 people in 1840. Chicago was 4,470, and Springfield, the state capital, just 2,579. Joseph said Nauvoo had nearly 3,000 people, probably including the surrounding countryside, and more were on the way.[12]

The City of Zion was conceived as an international religious capital.[13] Joseph reminded the Saints at the October conference that Zion was to

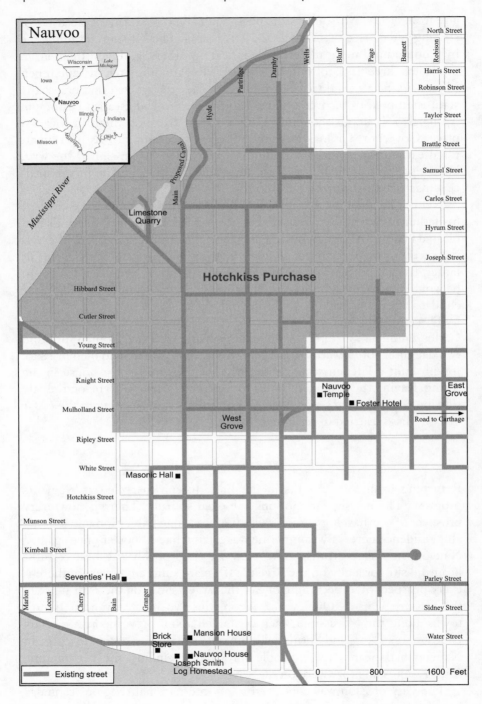

Nauvoo

Wisconsin
Lake Michigan
Iowa
Nauvoo
Illinois
Indiana
Missouri
Mississippi
Ohio R.

Mississippi River

Proposed Canal

Limestone Quarry

North Street
Harris Street
Robinson Street
Taylor Street
Brattle Street
Samuel Street
Carlos Street
Hyrum Street
Joseph Street

Wells
Bluff
Page
Barnett
Robison
Durphy
Partridge
Hyde
Main

Hotchkiss Purchase

Hibbard Street
Cutler Street
Young Street

Knight Street
Mulholland Street
Ripley Street
White Street
Hotchkiss Street
Munson Street
Kimball Street

West Grove

Nauvoo Temple
Foster Hotel

East Grove

Road to Carthage

Masonic Hall ■

Seventies' Hall ■

Parley Street

Marlon
Locust
Cherry
Bain
Granger

Sidney Street

Brick Store ■
■ Mansion House

Water Street

■ Nauvoo House
Joseph Smith
Log Homestead

0   800   1600 Feet

Existing street

"become the praise, the joy, and the glory of the whole earth." A sardonic report in the *Alton Telegraph* downriver a hundred and fifty miles commented that "they doubt not but that they shall be endued when necessary, with power from on high to proclaim to all the nations of the earth, in their own tongues, the wonderful works of God." Joseph told the Saints "we may soon expect to see flocking to this place, people from every land and from every nation." The missionaries would gather converts to Nauvoo as the center of a great world movement.[14]

The missionaries thought of themselves as shepherds of Israel, gathering in God's people from their long dispersion across the earth.[15] The chief meaning of "restoration" for this first generation of Mormons was the restoration of Israel. Wherever it was scattered, Israel was to return to its own land and regain the favor of God. The *Book of Mormon* message was directed to the Lamanites, the American branch of Israel, and another branch of Israel was lost in the north countries, presumably the ten lost tribes. Then there were the Jews, the most obvious branch of extant Israel. For two years, Joseph had contemplated contacting them. The revelations spoke of two cities, Jerusalem and Zion, developing on parallel tracks.[16] While he was gathering converts to his Zion, the Jews were to collect in Jerusalem. In 1840 the time seemed right to inquire into the Jews' progress.

Joseph chose Orson Hyde to undertake a fact-finding mission to Israel. Hyde, a store clerk converted in the first wave of Kirtland converts in 1831, was well suited for a difficult and sensitive mission. He was among the Twelve Apostles chosen in 1835. While on a mission in Canada in 1836, he published the Church's first missionary tract, a broadside entitled *A Prophetic Warning to all the Churches, of Every Sect and Denomination, and to Every Individual into Whose Hands It May Fall.*[17] Hyde had asked to accompany Heber C. Kimball on the first mission to Britain in 1837. During the Missouri wars, he had become disillusioned with Joseph Smith, but within six months he was restored to his positions. He had dealt with government officials, and was an eloquent speaker and experienced missionary.

Hyde said Joseph had set him apart to go to Jerusalem and be "a watchman unto the house of Israel" as early as 1833. Hyde later saw London, Amsterdam, Constantinople, and Jerusalem in a vision and was told "here are many of the children of Abraham whom I will gather to the land that I gave to their fathers; and here also, is the field of your labors." Reporting his vision at the April 1840 general conference, Hyde said he planned to visit the Jews in these cities and "gather up all the information he could, respecting their movements, expectations &c, and communicate the same to this Church, and to the nation at large." He went not to convert but to reconnoiter. Apostle John Page, who spoke with much force on "the gathering of the Jews" at the conference, was called to accompany Hyde.[18]

Joseph was enthralled with Israel's destiny. "Those engaged in seeking the outcasts of Israel," he wrote Hyde and Page, "cannot fail to enjoy the Spirit of the Lord, and have the choisests blessings of Heaven rest upon them in copious effusions." Joseph may have identified with Israel because they were "outcasts." The revelation on the consecration of properties in 1831 had said God would "consecrate of the riches of the Gentiles unto my people which are of the house of Israel," as if Israel had been deprived and now must have riches restored. Joseph knew Israel had sinned and been cast out, and yet they still were the Lord's favorites, the elect praised by the apostle Paul.[19] The idea of hidden greatness, yet to be vindicated, appealed to a man whose family had lived in obscurity while believing themselves chosen. Anyone who took Israel to heart, he assured Hyde and Page, would enjoy a vast expansion of his powers:

> Inasmuch as you are to be instrumental in this great work, he will endow you with power, wisdom, might, and intelligence; and every qualification necessary; while your minds will expand wider and wider, until you can circumscribe the earth, & the Heavens, reach forth into eternity; [and] contemplate the mighty acts of Jehovah, in all their variety & glory.

He was certain, he told them, that "inasmuch as you feel interested for the covenant people of the Lord, the God of their Father[s] shall bless you."[20]

Page dropped out before the mission began, but Hyde sailed for Liverpool on February 13, 1841. Upon arrival, he wrote a letter to Solomon Hirschel, chief rabbi of the Jews in London, urging him to lead the Jews to the Holy Land. Hyde proceeded to Rotterdam and Amsterdam and then across Europe. He taught English to a family in Regensburg for seven weeks while learning German and then headed to the Adriatic, where he took passage from Constantinople for Beirut.[21] On October 21, he arrived in Jerusalem.

Hyde was skeptical that Christian missionaries in Palestine could convert Jerusalem's 7,000 Jews.[22] On Sunday, October 24, he climbed to the Mount of Olives and wrote a prayer "to dedicate and consecrate this land . . . for the gathering together of Judah's scattered remnants." He prayed to "inspire the hearts of kings" to realize that God will "restore the kingdom unto Israel—raise up Jerusalem as its capital, and constitute her people a distinct nation and government" with a descendant of David on the throne. On the Mount of Olives, Hyde erected one pile of stones, and on Mount Zion another, to witness the dedication of the land for the return of the Jewish branch of scattered Israel.[23]

Hyde returned to the United States with no converts, no connections with influential Jews, nothing concrete, only the symbolism of the new

Israel greeting the old. Hyde asked Joseph where converted Jews were to gather; Nauvoo, Joseph enthusiastically replied.[24] He needed their acumen and capital in developing his city—a temporary respite since the Jews' true home was Jerusalem. In his own scheme of things, Joseph would have to recruit the Nauvoo population from other branches of Israel.

His hopes for Nauvoo rose with rapidly increasing migration. The first boatload of English Mormon immigrants left the Liverpool docks on June 6, 1840, the beginning of a later flood. By 1841, British membership was 5,814, with more eager to migrate than funds allowed. Brigham Young, leader of the 1839 contingent of missionaries, sent the Saints off by the shipload. In the first three years of organized migration, more than 2,800 Saints crossed the sea from Britain, some landing in New York, but most in New Orleans. Joseph liked to stroll to the Nauvoo docks to welcome boatloads of converts. The British Saints hoped he would come to England; instead, he offered "a pressing invitation to come and see me" in Nauvoo.[25]

Success in Britain dispelled any thought that Mormonism was an American religion. The *Book of Mormon* may have had a special appeal for Americans, but in England Brigham Young and Willard Richards found "the people of this land much more ready to receive the gospel than those of America." As in America, the missionaries attracted radical Protestants, many from the United Brethren, a Methodist offshoot searching for the New Testament gospel's promise of spiritual gifts. Within six months of the apostles' arrival, over a thousand, including scores of lay preachers, accepted the message of Wilford Woodruff and other missionaries in Herefordshire where the United Brethren were concentrated.[26] The typical English convert was a dissatisfied Christian seeking religion along the margins of conventional church life. And, as Brigham Young said in a report to Joseph, "almost without exception it is the poor that receive the gospel." Though poor men themselves, the apostles were appalled by the miserable living conditions they encountered. In the Midlands manufacturing towns, Young and Richards found workers who "labor 12 hours in a day for almost nothing rather than starve at once." Mormonism thrived among radical religionists who welcomed a reordering of their destitute world. Brigham wrote Joseph that "they do not seem to understand argument, simple testimony is enough for them."[27]

The British mission tested Joseph Smith's ecclesiastical organization. Could the Church thrive without his immediate direction? In Britain the quorum of the Twelve Apostles, the solid men who took over the Church after Joseph's death, proved it could. Brigham Young showed himself to be a master of organization in Britain: he saw to the publication of 5,000 copies of the *Book of Mormon* and 3,000 hymn books, began the monthly newspaper the *Latter-day Saints' Millennial Star,* oversaw immigration, and organized congregations of new members. The momentum continued into the 1850s. When all but two apostles left Great Britain, the Church kept growing under the direction of local authorities. As Joseph said, the Church was now organized and "the leaven can spread."[28]

Reports from Britain, added to missionary successes in North America, raised spirits in Nauvoo. In an effervescent epistle in October 1840, the Presidency saw Nauvoo standing in the center of a vast campaign to encircle the globe with missionaries.

> Wherever the faithful laborer has gone forth reaping, sowing the seed of truth, he has returned with joy, bringing his sheaves with him. . . .
>
> On the Islands of the sea, viz. great Britain, there continues to be a steady flow of souls into the church. . . .
>
> If the work roll[s] forth with the same rapidity it has heretofore done, we may soon expect to see flocking to this place, people from every land and from every nation, the polished European, the degraded Hottentot, and the shivering Laplander. Persons of all languages, and of every tongue, and of every color; who shall with us worship the Lord of Hosts in his holy temple.

Missionaries were sent to Australia and the East Indies. "I feel desirous," Joseph wrote the Twelve, "that every providential opening of that kind should be filled, and that you should, prior to your leaving England, send the Gospel into as many parts as you possibly can."[29]

THE CHARTER

By 1840, Joseph was pleased with the quality of the converts coming to the Church. He had been accustomed to receiving plain people with little education or experience in large affairs. But now "many wealthy and influential characters have embraced the gospel," the First Presidency reported somewhat optimistically, "so that not only will the poor rejoice in that they are exalted, but the rich in that they are made low." In Illinois, a number of leading men sympathized with the Saints. Isaac Galland had sold them land and eventually joined the Church. John C. Bennett, M.D., the quartermaster general of Illinois, had been baptized. Joseph seems to have been unaware of how Mormon numbers increased the interest of ambitious politicians and businessmen. He had trouble distinguishing true friends from self-serving schemers. In Bennett, who was later shown to be a villain, Joseph at first saw "a man of enterprize, extensive acquirements, and of independent mind," who was "calculated to be a great blessing to our community."[30]

Bennett rose meteorically in Nauvoo's civic affairs and fell just as fast. He first wrote Joseph Smith on July 25, 1840, expressing sympathy for the Saints' sufferings. Bennett believed that his state militia office would dazzle the simple Mormons and give him privileged status when he joined. He was partly right. By fall, he had Joseph's backing and was sent to lobby the Illinois legislature for a city charter. On February 1, 1841, Bennett was elected mayor of Nauvoo. An ambitious, restless, enterprising man, with dark, intense eyes, Bennett had flitted from one project to another before he attached himself to the Mormons at age thirty-six. Not content with a medical practice, for a time he was a Methodist itinerant. He dreamed of establishing a college and asked for support from the Methodists, the Disciples of Christ, and the Ohio legislature. He threw himself into projects and then abruptly withdrew when his schemes were rejected. He dropped Methodism when its adherents refused support for the college, and pulled out of the Disciples of Christ when they too were critical.[31]

Resolved to found a college, he established Christian College in New Albany, Indiana, without adequate funding or faculty. He believed that professional men should be credited for their experience, and peddled degrees in medicine, law, and theology to anyone who would pay. When doctors pronounced the procedure unethical, Bennett closed the institution and returned to Ohio. Impressed with his credentials and abilities, Willoughby University at Chagrin, Ohio, had him open a medical department. He was dismissed when reports of his diploma mill caught up with him.[32]

While in Ohio in 1832, Bennett met Joseph Smith, but Bennett showed no interest in joining the Mormons; he made friends instead with their critic Eber D. Howe. When Bennett later published an attack on the Mormons, he borrowed heavily from Howe's *Mormonism Unvailed.* After leaving Willoughby, Bennett wandered the Midwest, living in six localities in three states before settling in Illinois. In 1838 he got authorization from the state legislature for a militia unit, the Invincible Dragoons, with himself as brigadier general, and won election to the unpaid position of the state's quartermaster general. By this time, his wife had abandoned him because of his recurring extramarital affairs, and he was looking for a new cause. Bennett later said he never believed Joseph's doctrine but saw a grand opportunity in the Mormons.[33]

After Bennett's third letter, Joseph assured him that he could be of service in Nauvoo. Joseph kept his eyes open for talented people, especially educated men, who were scarce among converts. Joseph had asked Howard Coray to clerk for him at their first meeting, because he was told Coray was attending college. Bennett was a polished speaker and experienced lobbyist, and the Saints were seeking political influence. Joseph said Bennett was superior to Paul as an orator. At the October conference in 1840, Bennett gave a fawning address on the Saints' persecutions and prospects, whereupon the conference appointed him to a committee with Joseph Smith to seek a charter for Nauvoo.[34]

Bennett's connections with the state political parties paid off. The proposed charter passed both houses with scarcely a debate. Drafted by Joseph and Bennett, the charter maximized local self-rule, capitalizing on the legislature's inexperience in granting city charters. The first of the Illinois charters had been bestowed in 1837 on Chicago; only four more had been granted before Nauvoo applied, but this assembly would pass seven during its session in 1840–41. City charters differed on details such as term length for city officials—one year in some charters, two years in Nauvoo's—and residence qualifications for voting. Nauvoo voters needed only to meet the liberal state voting requirement of six months in the state (U.S. citizenship was not required because Democrats benefited from the immigrant vote) and sixty days in Nauvoo.[35]

No one complained about these variations. More contentious was the charter's authorization of the city council to pass any law not in conflict with the state and federal constitutions. Although this was later considered far too generous, the Chicago and Alton charters had similarly liberal provisions. Critics complained even more about the Nauvoo Municipal Court's authority to issue writs of habeas corpus, a power that enabled Joseph to elude his Missouri pursuers when they tried to extradite him. That authority was unusual, though Alton had been granted the same power in 1839. Overall, the Nauvoo charter invested the city officers with considerable authority—it was certainly among the most liberal to that point—to protect the Saints from legal incursions by their enemies. None of the provisions were unprecedented or "anti-republican," as Thomas Ford, governor of Illinois at the time of Joseph's death, later claimed.[36] The charter implemented the Jeffersonian principle of distributing power to the level of society closest to the people.

Governor Thomas Carlin signed the charter bill on December 16, 1840, and it went into effect on February 1, 1841. The charter's passage added to Joseph's ebullience. In January 1841, the First Presidency sent greetings to the Saints throughout the world and reported that the charter secured the "great blessings of civil liberty . . . all we ever claimed." Under the provisions "of our *magna charta*," the Church could concentrate on advancing the great work throughout the world. "Not only has it spread through the length and breadth of this vast continent; but on the continent of Europe, and on the Islands of the sea, it is spreading in a manner entirely unprecedented in the annals of time." To Joseph's knowledge, the gospel had never seen greater success in the history of the world. He urged everyone to come to Nauvoo, especially the rich who could build up manufactures and purchase farms, thus preparing for the gathering of the poor. He admitted that "the idea of a general gathering has been associated with most cruel and oppressing scenes," but he hoped those days were behind them. The gathering remained essential. "By a concentration of action, and a unity of effort, we can only accomplish the great work of the last days, which we could not do in our remote and scattered condition."[37]

Through the winter and spring of 1841, Joseph enthusiastically built the city. A revelation in mid-January gave detailed instructions for constructing a hotel called the Nauvoo House. "And let it be a delightful habitation for man, and a resting place for the weary traveller, that he may contemplate the glory of Zion, and the glory of this the corner stone thereof." Joseph foresaw a stream of guests coming to view Nauvoo, and suitable accommodations were needed. The same revelation directed Joseph to send a proclamation to "all the Kings of the world" and "the high minded Governors of the nation in which you live, and to all the nations of the earth scattered abroad." The powers of the earth were "to give heed to the light and glory of Zion." The doctrines of the revelations had always made the great work a global, world-shaking enterprise. Now success in making converts and founding a city led the Saints to think "the set time has come to favor her." Nauvoo's temple would "undoubtedly attract the attention of the great men of the earth." "Awake, O kings of the earth!" the revelation proclaimed. "Come ye, O! come ye with your gold and your silver, to the help of my people—to the house of the daughter of Zion."[38]

That winter, Joseph and Bennett put the city government together. In his inaugural address as mayor on February 3, 1841, Bennett called for the suppression of tippling houses, the organization of the University of the City of Nauvoo, the formation of the militia under the name of the Nauvoo Legion, and the construction of a wing dam in the Mississippi and a ship canal down the center of the peninsula to provide both navigation and water power. Not wasting a minute, Joseph that very day presented a bill organizing the university and appointing a board of trustees with Bennett as chancellor. Joseph also submitted a bill organizing the male citizens of the city and other volunteers from Hancock County into the Nauvoo Legion. By the end of the day, Joseph had been appointed chair of committees on the canal, the regulation of liquor, health, and a city code. Events proceeded speedily. On February 8, Joseph introduced a bill for surveying a canal and another on temperance. A week later the council passed an ordinance against vending whiskey in small quantities, effectively restricting the opening of saloons. The next week the city's elementary schools were put under the jurisdiction of the university's board of trustees, and the Nauvoo House Association and the Nauvoo Agricultural and Manufacturing Association were incorporated. On March 1, the council absorbed the old town of Commerce into Nauvoo and divided the city into four wards, appointing officers for each: constable, surveyor and engineer, market master, a weigher and sealer, and a collector.[39] Under Bennett and Joseph's leadership, Nauvoo became a functioning city in less than a month.

While the city rose before his eyes, Joseph could not escape debt, poverty, and ill health. The Nauvoo House and the university were never completed. The peninsula still suffered from fevers in the summer, and even the sick needed work. How was he to employ the thousands of minimally skilled working-class poor arriving from Liverpool? Many knew nothing of farming, the chief employment.[40] Joseph wanted to help, but huge debts prevented him from simply giving away land. What could poor converts do?

He decided not to institute the consecration of properties in Illinois. The system had had mixed success in Jackson County and Caldwell. Knowing the Saints would wonder about consecration—a command by revelation— he told an Iowa high council in early 1840 that "the Law of consecration could not be kept here, & that it was the will of the Lord that we should desist from trying to keep it." He assured them that he himself "assumed the whole responsibility of not keeping it untill proposed by himself." A year later, he told the Nauvoo Lyceum, "If we were eaquel in property at present, in six months we would be worse than Ever for there is too many Dishonest men amongst us."[41]

Spurred by Bennett, Joseph dreamed of industrial projects. The wing dam Bennett proposed was to project two miles up the Mississippi. A head of water would accumulate where the dam met the land, and the flow could be channeled down a canal running south along Main Street. Using the canal as a mill race, small manufacturers could harness the water's power. At the southern end of the canal, where Main Street met the Mississippi again, the water was to accumulate in a basin, generating more power. A stratum of solid limestone across the northern end defeated the proposed canal; the settlers lacked the means to cut a channel through the rock. But the city's economy called for grand schemes. Two years later, Joseph was still calculating how to construct a dam that would utilize the river's power.[42]

At the general conference in April 1841, the First Presidency issued another hopeful report. The troubles in Missouri were over, and the citizens of Illinois promised enjoyment of "all the blessings of civil and religious liberty, guaranteed by the constitution." Joseph did regret that construction on Nauvoo's public buildings was slow "in consequence of the impoverished condition of the saints." He called on his listeners to show their zeal, to contribute labor or "their gold and their silver, their brass, and their iron, with the pine tree and box tree, to beautify the same"—a biblical flourish. Once again, the report projected an air of assurance and forward-looking optimism.[43]

Like previous proclamations and announcements, the report aimed to show progress. Inadvertently, the promotional language also reflected a subtle doctrinal shift. Joseph called the people to gather as vigorously as ever, but in a new spirit. The initial call to Jackson County warned of calamities to come. Millennial storms were about to burst, and Zion was the place of refuge. The people were to flee the scene of future devastation into the safety of the holy city. Underlying the gathering was danger and fear as much as hope and promise.

In 1840 and 1841, the refuge principle was reduced to a minor theme. In January 1841, the Presidency reminded the Saints of prophetic warnings through the ages about gathering before the Lord returns to "take vengeance upon the ungodly." Many scriptures could be cited to support the point, the Presidency said, but "believing them to be familiar to the Saints we forbear." Instead they underscored the happy prospects of those who came to Zion:

> Let the brethren who love the prosperity of Zion, who are anxious that her stakes should be strengthened, and her cords lengthened, and who prefer her prosperity to their chief joy, come, and cast in their lots with us, and cheerfully engage in a work so glorious and sublime, and say with Nehemiah, "we his servants will arise and build."

From being heavily negative, the appeal of Zion had become almost entirely positive. The aphorism from Nehemiah struck the note of the new gathering: "arise and build." The Presidency urged people to come for a higher life, "for their prosperity and everlasting welfare, and for the carrying out the great and glorious purposes of our God."[44]

That new emphasis changed the look of things. The Presidency explained to the Saints that the new name of their city, Nauvoo, was Hebrew for "a beautiful situation, or place," and is "truly descriptive of this most delightful situation."[45] The congeniality of Illinois, the warm reception in England, and missionary success everywhere made the world appear happier. The positive outlook and zeal for the city began to work their influence on the Saints' apocalyptic outlook. They no longer wanted an immediate end to the wicked world. Joseph spoke of the Second Coming as further in the future. In a sermon urging people to "build up the cities of the Lord," he told them "Zion and Jerusalem must both be built up before the coming of Christ." That would take time. "More than 40 years will pass before this work will be accomplished and when these cities are built then shall the coming of the Son of Man be."[46]

The work would bless the whole world, not just the fortunate few. Joseph envisioned Nauvoo as an open city. Having lived with diversity of belief all his life, he had always opened his doors to visitors and shown tolerance for other beliefs. Now with a city of his own, he opened wide the gates. In Nauvoo, he told the Saints, "We claim no privilege but what we feel cheerfully disposed to share with our fellow citizens of every denomination." The city's ordinance on religious liberty listed the Mormons as only one of the denominations granted freedom to worship:

> Be it ordained by the City Council of the City of Nauvoo, That the Catholics, Presbyterians, Methodists, Baptists, Latter-Day Saints, Quakers, Episcopalians, Universalists, Unitarians, Mohammedans, and all other religious sects, and denominations, whatever, shall have free toleration, and equal privileges, in this city.

Everyone was welcome. "Far from being restricted to our own faith," he wrote in a public epistle, "let all those who desire to locate themselves in this place, or the vicinity, come, and we will hail them as citizens and friends."[47] As he had told the Twelve Apostles that fall, "A man filled with the love of God, is not content with blessing his family alone, but ranges through the whole world anxious to bless the whole human family."[48]

TWENTY-FOUR

TEMPORALITIES AND SPIRITUALITIES

1841

On Sunday I attended one of their meetings, in front of the Temple, now build-ing, and one of the largest buildings in the State.—There could not have been less than 2,500 people present, and as well appearing as any number that could be found in this or any State.—Mr. Smith preached in the morning, and one could have readily learned then the magic by which he has built up this Society, because as we say in Illinois—"they believe in him," and in his honesty.

CORRESPONDENT TO THE *JULIET COURIER*, June 1841

JOSEPH WOULD HAVE GLADLY LEFT the city's real estate business to others. After contracting with Isaac Galland and Horace Hotchkiss for large tracts on both sides of the Mississippi, he would have liked someone else to survey, set prices, negotiate with buyers, and enter the deeds—a time-consuming business even with the help of clerks. He wanted to give land to the poor, especially to widows and orphans. To finance these free gifts, he wanted others to pay generously. The high council priced Nauvoo lots from $200 to $800, leaving room for negotiation. All these judgments required patience and wisdom and exposed Joseph to criticism for gouging and unfair treatment.[1]

In June 1840, he asked the high council to appoint someone else to attend to "the temporalities of the Church." His brother Don Carlos resorted to writing him a letter because, he said, "I have no opportunity to converse with you—you are thronged with business." Joseph wanted to free himself for "the spiritualities"—translation and revelation—but his appeal went unheeded. The high council supplied another clerk, leaving Joseph responsible for the debts and the final disposition of land. He oversaw the business for another year, until the Twelve Apostles returned and took on much of the responsibility. In January 1841, he assumed the title of "trustee-in-trust" for the Church, as required by the Illinois statute on reli-gious societies.[2]

DOCTRINE

From the beginning, Joseph had been both revelator and organizer. He was chief visionary as well as chief executive. He confided to a friend, "I have to labor under a load that is intolerable to bear." Yet in 1840 and 1841, the peak time for organizing city government, Joseph continued to elaborate his cosmology. He revealed ideas on topics ranging from Creation and the nature of the body to priesthood and baptism for the dead. Revelations came like water from an inexhaustible spring. He wrote from the Missouri jail, "As well might man streach forth his puny arm to stop the Missouri River in its dicread cours or to turne it up stream as to hinder the Almighty from pooring down knoledge from heaven upon the heads of the Latter day saints."[3]

As new doctrine piled up, he did not abandon the simpler doctrines of the Church's early period. The *Times and Seasons* reported him "observing that many of the saints who had come from different States and Nations, had only a very superficial knowledge of these principles, not having heard them fully investigated." Joseph then taught faith, repentance, baptism, and the gift of the Holy Ghost by the laying on of hands.[4]

By 1841, the missionary gospel was settling into a well-defined formula. In a pamphlet written for the citizens of Salem, Massachusetts, Erastus Snow and Benjamin Winchester, two experienced missionaries, laid out their version of the fundamentals.

    1. Faith and repentance.
    2. Baptism by immersion.
    3. Laying on of hands for the Holy Ghost.
    4. Gifts of the Spirit as promised in the New Testament.
    5. Restoration of the New Testament church organization.
    6. Christian virtues like brotherly kindness and love.
    7. The authority of the priesthood restored by angels.
    8. The Second Coming at the beginning of the millennium.
    9. Gathering of Israel to the City of Zion.
   10. The added revelation of the Book of Mormon.

Snow and Winchester's was one of several summaries published from 1839 to 1841. Parley and Orson Pratt published their list in 1840, and Joseph would soon sum up Latter-day Saint belief for the Chicago newspaper editor John Wentworth in the formulation later adopted by the Church as the Articles of Faith.[5] Although Joseph himself presented new doctrines in public sermons in Nauvoo and touched on others during his preaching tour in Pennsylvania, New Jersey, and Washington, D.C., he wanted the fundamentals to come first.[6]

After the completion of the council system in 1835, the number of written revelations opening with lines like "verily thus saith the Lord" diminished. Instead of formal, dictated revelations, the later teachings were delivered in sermons, conversations, or letters. Many are known today only from notes taken down by William Clayton, a literate English convert, or William McIntire, a tailor who spelled haphazardly.[7] The doctrine of baptism for the dead was given in a sermon and enlarged in letters. The revelation on eternal marriage was written because Hyrum requested it. Almost everything else, among them many of the richest passages in Joseph Smith's thought, is delineated only in ragged, compacted listeners' notes.

These later teachings had the air of the 1835 priesthood revelation, which was spoken as if by a guide familiar with priesthood. In the 1841 sermons, Joseph spoke like a witness or an initiate in heavenly mysteries, rather than a prophet delivering revelations from the Lord's mouth. Occasionally, he mentioned "the visions that roll like an overflowing surge before my mind"; these apparently yielded the knowledge he dispensed in the sermons.[8]

One of Joseph's most famed statements was a casual aside to a Methodist preacher: "There is no such thing as immaterial matter. All spirit is matter but is more fine or pure and can only be discerned by purer eyes. We cant see it but when our bodies are purified we shall see that it is all matter." No one at the time made anything of the radical idea. Clayton remarked only that "the gentleman seemed pleased and said he should visit Nauvoo immediately." Clayton thought the Methodist's reaction was as noteworthy as the revision of Christian metaphysics.[9]

When he spoke the words, Joseph probably did not consider the long-standing philosophical argument about the nature of matter. Metaphysical materialism—the idea that there was no spirit, only matter—was the subject of extensive debate in the late eighteenth century. Materialists usually were atheists, but one who was not was the Unitarian Englishman Joseph Priestley, whose letters on materialism were published in 1778. Priestley denied the existence of spirit. The body, not some immaterial "mind," was the seat of perception and thought. Priestley admitted that if matter was all, the human personality vanished when the body died, since spirit provided continuity at death. But he accepted the doctrinal consequence, speculating that personality evaporated temporarily at death until the resurrection restored the body and its mental and spiritual faculties.[10]

The debate did not affect Joseph. He made no effort to meet objections or deal with complexities. His material spirits, made of what he called "refined" matter, persisted through death like immaterial spirits in traditional Christian thought. He probably was scarcely aware of the philosophical implications. Later Mormon thinkers dealt with the problems when they assembled Joseph's theology posthumously. In Nauvoo, people were intrigued by his aphorisms, and passed notes from hand to hand; Willard Richards copied John Taylor's notes of one of Joseph's sermons into a collection Richards called his "Pocket Companion." But the ideas were not incorporated into the missionary message, made the subject of sermons, or systematized. They were informally circulated and gradually assimilated into Mormon thinking; some were added to the *Doctrine and Covenants* in 1876.[11]

One of the exaltation revelations of 1832 and 1833 had touched lightly on the eternity of matter and intelligence: "Intelligence, or the light of truth was not created or made, neither indeed can be," and "the elements are eternal."[12] After 1840, these bits were elaborated and underscored. Statements in Nauvoo began to populate the universe with realities—intelligences and matter—as eternal as God. One senses in these teachings a concern about nothingness. In a famous analogy, Joseph took a ring from his finger. "Take a ring, it is without beginning or end; cut it for a beginning place, and at the same time you have an ending place." The comparison showed a concern for the certainty of human existence. Would intelligence—personality—be assured of continuance if it had originally been created? Something made could also be unmade. "If the soul of man had a beginning it will surely have an end." Joseph's metaphysics removed even the possibility of extinction. "More painful to me [are] the thoughts of an[ni]hil[a]tion than death," he once said.[13] He envisioned a world where not even God could extinguish a human personality. Intelligence has existed forever with God Himself, and, though banished and punished, could not be terminated.

Joseph's concern about nothingness can also be seen in his views of God. By 1841, he had moved from a traditional Christian belief in God as pure spirit to a belief in His corporeality. God had a body after which humans were modeled. The concept was foreshadowed in the *Book of Mormon*, where the brother of Jared saw first the Lord's finger and then the entire "body of my spirit," but the doctrine of a corporeal God was not fully articulated until later. In 1841, Joseph taught that "there is no other God in heaven but that God who has flesh and bones," stressing that anything "without body or parts is nothing." Here he echoed Thomas Jefferson's idea that to speak of God, angels, or soul as immaterial was "to talk of *nothings*."[14] A nonmaterial God was a vacuity, a God with no substance. The supernal was not to be found outside of material existence but within it.

In Joseph's view, making God corporeal did not reduce Him: Joseph had little sense of the flesh being base. In contrast to conventional theologies, Joseph saw embodiment as a glorious aspect of human existence. An early revelation had said that only when joined with "element" could a spirit attain a fulness of joy, and in 1841 Joseph taught that "the great principle of happiness consists in having a body." From Joseph's perspective, the melding of matter and spirit at birth was a major purpose for coming to earth. In a sense embodiment was the very purpose of earth life. "We came to this earth that we might have a body," Clayton quoted Joseph saying, "and present it pure before God in the Celestial Kingdom." God had a body and so should every person.[15]

Piece by piece, Joseph redefined the nature of God, giving Him a form and a body and locating Him in time and space. Taken as a whole, the bits and pieces of the Nauvoo metaphysical doctrines were gradually coalescing into a new story of Creation and the purpose of life. Joseph would pull the parts together in one grand narrative in the King Follett sermon of April 1844, but portions crept into the early sermons in Nauvoo. By emphasizing the eternity of matter and intelligence, Joseph modified the Creation story until it appeared that God had not created anything ex nihilo. He did not make the earth "out of Nothing; for it is contrary to a Rashanall mind & Reason. that a something could be Brought from a Nothing." In Joseph's view, God assembled the earth from preexisting material and then drew a cohort of spirits from the pool of eternal intelligences to place upon it. "The elements are eternal." "Spirits are eternal." God's work was to organize the matter that had always existed. Joseph once said "this earth was organized or formed out of other planets which were broke up and remodelled and made into the one on which we live." God built earths and heavens as an artisan makes cabinets or houses and gave them to His children to use.[16]

A decade before, the Book of Moses had spoken of God making many worlds through his only begotten son. Even then it was clear that Creation was not a single big bang, but a series of lesser creations. The reason for it all, as explained in 1830, was "to bring to pass the immortality and eternal life of man." By 1841, this idea included God making one earth after another where embodied spirits formed in His image might dwell. "God is Good & all his acts is for the benifit of infereir inteligences," Joseph said.[17] On these earths, the intelligences would enjoy the blessings of a body and progress toward eternal life. God was a Father-gardener making places for His children to grow.

The most striking of the Nauvoo doctrinal developments was the new emphasis on family. Binding families together, as if their existence too was in jeopardy if not sealed by God's power, underlay both baptism for the dead and plural marriage. Joseph first mentioned baptism for the dead in a funeral sermon on August 15, 1840, and within weeks, baptisms were being performed in the Mississippi River. Although unknown in contemporary

Christianity, the practice grew from Paul's comment in the Bible: "else what shall they do which are baptized for the dead, if the dead rise not at all?"[18] Joseph summed up the doctrine in an October letter to the Apostles in England:

> The Saints have the privelege of being baptized, for those of their relatives who are dead, who they believe would have embraced the gospel if they had been priveleged with hearing it, and who have received the gospel in the spirit, through the instrumentality of those who have been commissioned to preach to them while in prison.

In the April 1841 conference, Joseph and Rigdon discoursed on the doctrine, and it soon became the subject of poetry in the *Times and Seasons.* Over six thousand baptisms for the dead were performed in 1841, most for relatives and close friends, a few for notable figures like Thomas Jefferson and George and Martha Washington.[19]

The sermons on baptism for the dead emphasized the justice of bringing the saving ordinances to the millions who had died without an opportunity to receive their benefits. As Joseph said, "It presents the gospel of Christ in probably a more enlarged scale than some have imagined it." In an 1836 vision, Joseph had seen his eldest brother, Alvin, in the celestial kingdom even though he died in Joseph's youth. Joseph was told that all who would have believed had they lived would be rewarded as if they had accepted the Gospel in mortality. Alvin believed and needed only the necessary ordinances. Baptism for the dead made the scriptural insistence on being born of water before entering the Kingdom of Heaven reasonable. Otherwise either the command to baptize or the justice of God was compromised. Under the new doctrine, everyone would have a chance, if the Saints were diligent in performing the ordinance.[20]

Besides equity, however, baptism for the dead united the human family. Joseph himself underscored its value in turning the hearts of the children to their fathers. Something had to bond all the generations from the first to the last, going back through time, as the prophet Malachi had written, or the earth would be wasted. Locating names and baptizing vicariously created the welding link.

Nothing in his later life excited Joseph more than the idea of joining together the generations of humanity from start to finish. From the beginning, he had the idea of linking the present to the past by replicating the ancient order of things in the present. Baptism for the dead was another tie. In "the dispensation of the fulness of times," it was necessary that "a whole, and complete and perfect union, and welding together of dispensations and keys, and powers and glories should take place, and be reveald, from the days of Adam even to the present time."[21] As Joseph envisioned history, the prophets of the past were as concerned about current affairs as the modern Saints. "These men are in heaven, but their children are on Earth. . . . All these authoritative characters will come down & join hand in hand in bringing about this work." For their part, modern Saints must reach back to help the dead. "Their salvation is necessary and essential to our salvation." "They without us, cannot be made perfect . . . neither can we without our dead, be made perfect." Baptism was the means of helping past generations find salvation. This was what Malachi meant by the hearts of the children turning to their fathers and fathers to their children.[22]

Joseph's story of the earth and its people, more than any set of abstract qualities, conveyed his understanding of God. When the work was finished, the priesthood keys would be returned to Adam, who would turn over the earth and its inhabitants to Christ, who holds the "Keys of the Universe." The presentation of the earth to Christ, with its inhabitants bound together by priesthood ordinances, was the culmination of history. Then "this earth will be rolled back into the presence of God and crowned with Celestial Glory," completing the cycle. One more earth had fulfilled its mission. As the Lord said in Joseph's vision ten years earlier, "As one earth shall pass away, and the heavens thereof, even so shall another come, and there is no end to my works, neither to my words."[23]

TEMPLE

The narrative came together in the temple, the anchor of Joseph's cities. Baptisms for the dead, which at first were performed in the river, were meant for the temple. If the Saints failed to build the temple with dispatch, they were told, they would be rejected as a people.[24] Knowing a temple was expected, the Saints had selected a site on a bluff overlooking the city and begun work before a revelation in January 1841 confirmed their choice. In October 1840, a committee was formed to supervise construction. A quarry soon opened, and plans were made to cut and mill timber in Wisconsin and float the lumber down the Mississippi. From several designs, the plan of William Weeks was accepted, and the foundation was soon excavated.[25] By April 6, 1841, the site was ready for cornerstones, presenting Joseph the opportunity for another public ceremony.

This time Joseph added to the usual priesthood ceremonies the drills and splendor of civic life. Fourteen companies of the Nauvoo Legion mustered for review, and cannon boomed as Major General John C. Bennett and Lieutenant General Joseph Smith came in on horseback, resplendent in "rich and costly dresses" that "would have become a Bonaparte or a Washington." While the band played, the ladies of Nauvoo presented Joseph with a silk flag. Then the militia and the spectators removed to the temple ground, and the militia formed a hollow square around the foundation space. Officers, dignitaries, choir, and band occupied the center, the ladies stood just outside the foundation with the gentlemen behind them, and the infantry and cavalry ringed the whole.[26]

As always on such occasions, Sidney Rigdon delivered the address. Then the leaders moved to the cornerstones. In the southeast corner, Joseph blessed the stone on behalf of the First Presidency, praying the construction would "be accomplished speedily; that the Saints may have a place to worship God, and the Son of Man have where to lay his head." Following Joseph, the various quorums blessed the stones in the three other corners.[27]

The occasion doubtless lifted the spirits of many who remembered the Saints' miserable condition two years earlier. The absence of profanity and intoxication pleased Don Carlos Smith, the editor of the *Times and Seasons*. He liked the whole demeanor of the assemblage.

> Such an almost countless multitude of people, moving in harmony, in friendship, in dignity, told with a voice not easily misunderstood, that they were a people of intelligence and virtue, and order; in short, that they were *saints;* and that the God of love, purity, and light was their God, their exemplar, and director; and that they were blessed and happy.[28]

The comment revealed the Saints' pleasure in being a godly civic people. They dedicated the temple surrounded by a city militia under the legal umbrella of a city charter. At last they had become a civic society.

Through the fall of 1841, temple construction proceeded with dispatch. The Saints donated ten percent of their time to work on the building and ten percent of their produce to meet the costs. Joseph said construction work was as important as missionary labors. Women made stockings and mittens for the workers. Letters to Church members everywhere requested donations, and bonded agents were dispatched to collect them.[29] Eliza Snow contributed poetry on temple construction to the *Times and Seasons:*

> Come, and bring in your treasures—your wealth from abroad:
> Come, and build up the city and Temple of God:
> A stupendous foundation already is laid,
> And the work is progressing—withhold not your aid.[30]

By June 1841, a baptismal font was under way, a large "sea," as the font in Solomon's temple was called, sixteen by twelve by seven feet built from pine planks glued together. To support the basin, following the pattern in Solomon's temple, Elijah Fordham carved twelve oxen to be leafed with gold. On November 8, 1841, a temporary font was dedicated and baptisms began, with water flowing from a thirty-foot well in the east end of the basement. They had come a long way, but it would take another five years to complete the temple.[31]

The doctrinal outpouring of the winter of 1840–41 slowed during the fall, when Joseph's teachings turned back to administrative problems. Two revelations given in March and July 1841 dealt with the Zarahemla stake in Iowa, and Brigham Young, relieved of missionary responsibilities, was told to take care of his family. Sermons also came down a notch doctrinally. "Preached to a large congregation at the stand on the science & practice of Medicine," noted an entry in Joseph's history for September 5, 1841. On November 7, one listener noted, he "delivered unto us an Edifying address showing us what temperance faith virtue, charity & truth was."

Joseph did offer an observation on the "difference between an angel and a ministering spirit; the one a resurrected or translated body, with its spirit, ministering to embodied spirits—the other a disembodied spirit, visiting and ministering to disembodied spirits." Jesus, while still a spirit between death and the resurrection, taught the disembodied spirits in prison. After the resurrection, when embodied again, he appeared to His disciples on earth. But that provocative thought was not followed by anything more of the kind between June and December 1841, at least on the record. In December, Joseph acknowledged to the Twelve that people complained about not hearing more from God. "Some say Joseph is a fallen Prophet because he does not bring forth more of the word of the Lord." Joseph blamed it on the Saints' unbelief: they were not ready to receive more. But it was just as likely that pressing temporalities preoccupied him. Among Joseph's greatest sorrows, his brother Don Carlos, age twenty-six, and his namesake, Joseph's fourteen-month-old son Don Carlos, died of malaria within a little more than a week of each other, on August 7 and 15, 1841. The following February, Emma would lose another son in childbirth, the fifth of her children to die in infancy.[32]

LAW AND POLITICS

In the summer of 1841, the Missouri courts tried again to extradite Joseph on the old charges of treason, arson, and robbery coming out of the 1838 Mormon war. A writ in September 1840 had failed when the sheriff could not locate him. In June 1841, the writ was delivered again. On Saturday, June 5, the Adams County sheriff, Thomas King, along with a Missouri officer, arrested Joseph at the Heberlin Hotel in Bear Creek, twenty-eight miles south of Nauvoo. Sent to Quincy, Joseph was brought before Charles Warren, an equity court official who issued a writ of habeas corpus, permit-

ting Joseph to return home. By chance, Stephen Douglas, a member of the
Illinois State Supreme Court, was in Quincy and agreed to hear the case the
next Tuesday in Monmouth, forty miles northeast of Nauvoo.[33]

Douglas, a rising political star in Illinois Democratic politics, was in a
position to help or hurt the Mormons. He was just five feet tall and weighed
little more than a hundred pounds, but he had a huge head and chest and
was a furious debater. Born in 1813 in Vermont, Douglas later read law in
New York and then moved to Morgan County, Illinois. Drawn to politics,
Douglas joined the Democrats and attained notoriety for routing a Whig
who was attacking Andrew Jackson's veto of the National Bank. Delighted
with their new champion, the Democrats carried him around the town
square on their shoulders. Soon known as the "Little Giant," he was elected
to the state legislature, and in 1841 was appointed to the state supreme
court.

In the 1840 presidential election, the Mormons had voted for the Whig
William Henry Harrison, a vote against Martin Van Buren. By 1841 they
were drifting back toward their natural home in the Democratic Party, and
growing fast enough to hold the balance of power in the area of the Quincy
circuit, where Douglas was assigned. He was on a mission to recover them
for the Democrats when he visited in May 1841 and received the freedom
of the city for his help in obtaining their charter while secretary of state.
A month later, he was fortuitously in a position to hear the case of the
Prophet's extradition.[34]

The Missouri attorneys wanted Joseph, who was technically a fugitive
from justice, returned to Missouri for trial. Joseph's attorneys wanted to
block the action and at the same time have the Illinois court decide the
merits of the case. One attorney, Charles Warren, read a petition claiming
the Missouri indictment was a fraud, having been obtained under duress.
Another, O. H. Browning, delivered an impassioned two-hour account of
the Saints' suffering and ill treatment. By whatever means, Joseph felt he
had to avoid extradition. He was convinced that the Missourians would
never fairly judge his case—the killers of the Mormon settlers at Haun's
Mill had never been brought to justice. Once in Missouri, his life would be
in danger.[35] If Missouri cleared him, Governor Boggs would implicitly be
convicted of waging an unjust war against his own people.

Judge Douglas decided the case on a technicality. Rather than vindicating
the Saints, he declared the writ of extradition void. After the first attempt to
recover Joseph the previous September, the sheriff had returned the writ to
the governor, in effect invalidating it and a companion writ issued at the
same time. Joseph could not be arrested again on the same writ. The decision pleased Joseph. "Thus have I been once more deliverd from the fangs
of my cruel persecutors, for which I thank God, my heavenly Father."

Stephen Douglas could consider his political mission accomplished. The next December, Joseph would call Douglas "a *Master Spirit*, and *his friends are our friends.*"[36]

Joseph noted the hostility of the courthouse crowd and realized that popular opinion was turning against the Saints after two years of sympathy. At Monmouth, Joseph could not leave his room for meals. The people crowded in on the Prophet and his witnesses. Some Monmouth citizens offered to pay the prosecuting attorneys.[37] In this politicized age, the Mormons' growing electoral power and their vacillation between political parties made enemies. Joseph tried to proclaim his neutrality—"we care not a fig for *Whig* or *Democrat.*" What mattered to him was the politicians' position on Mormon issues. "We shall go for our *friends*, our TRIED FRIENDS, and the cause of *human liberty*, which is the cause of God."[38] But he could not escape politics. Lauding the Democrat Douglas as "a master spirit" provoked the first public opposition to the Mormons, not surprisingly, in a Whig newspaper.

THOMAS SHARP

Joseph's leading critic from the summer of 1841 to the end of his life was Thomas Sharp, editor of the *Warsaw Signal*, a weekly or sometimes semi-weekly newspaper published twenty-five miles downstream in Warsaw, a little port town of about five hundred inhabitants. Sharp, the son of a Methodist minister, came to Illinois in September 1840 after a law apprenticeship in Pennsylvania. He opened a law office in Warsaw and by November was the editor of the *Western World*, which six months later he renamed the *Warsaw Signal*.[39]

At first Sharp was a neutral observer. In a January 1841 issue, he reported the issuance of the Nauvoo charter without editorial comment. In April Joseph invited him to the cornerstone ceremony, gave him a place of honor on the stand, and invited him and other guests to the Smiths' house for a turkey dinner. In his editorial, Sharp said blandly of the ceremony, "On the whole, the exercises passed off with the utmost order, without accident or the slightest disturbance."[40]

Sharp broke with the Mormons in the *Signal*'s May 19, 1841, issue when he objected to Stephen Douglas's appointment of Bennett as master of chancery in Hancock County. The recently arrived Bennett, Sharp commented, "joins a sect and advocates a creed in which no one believes he has any faith." The line criticized Bennett more than the Mormons, but Sharp later observed that some recent Mormon immigrants were leaving Nauvoo dissatisfied with the city and the leadership, a report damaging to Joseph's recruiting efforts. Growing a little testy, Sharp warned that if Mormons "as a people, step beyond the proper sphere of a religious denomination, and become a political body, as many of our citizens are beginning to apprehend will be the case, then this press stands pledged to take a stand against them." His newspaper, he said, "is bound to oppose the concentration of political power in a religious body, or in the hands of a few individuals."[41]

Joseph immediately dispatched a letter terminating his subscription to Sharp's paper.

> SIR—You will discontinue my paper—its contents are calculated to pollute me, and to patronize the filthy sheet—that tissue of lies—that sink of iniquity—is disgraceful to any moral man. Yours, with utter contempt.
>
> JOSEPH SMITH.
>
> P.S. Please publish the above in your contemptible paper.
>
> J.S.

Sharp, just twenty-two, replied with the sarcasm and scorn he was to practice from then on. He published Joseph's letter as a "highly important revelation . . . forwarded us, from his holiness, the Prophet," and then published his own "revelation" showing how much Joseph still owed on his subscription.[42]

Joseph's letter triggered a vitriolic attack by Sharp on the Nauvoo Legion: "Every thing they say or do seems to breathe the spirit of military tactics. Their *prophet* appears, on all great occasions in his splendid regimental dress. . . . Truly *fighting* must, be a part of the creed of these Saints!"[43] Sharp disregarded the temple, the weekly sermons, the influx of hundreds of converts, and the city's economic prospects, and made the militia, an organization found in cities and counties all over the state, the true revelation of Mormonism's character. To Sharp's mind, the militia was a sign of the Saints' essential militarism. What he most feared in Mormonism, and what he found, was militant fanaticism.

Sharp was equally alarmed about Mormon candidates for county offices. When two Mormons ran for school board, Sharp warned that Mormonism, "the vilest system of knavery that has ever yet seen the light of heaven, is preparing for your necks a yoke, and for your consciences iron bondage." The prospect of two Mormons on the school board threatened disaster. Sharp warned his readers they were in danger of being ruled by

> a politico-military Church, . . . if you suffer yourself to be defeated in this contest, be assured, that you will surrender the county to be governed hereafter by *one* who has, under the garb of religion, defied the laws of man, and desecrated those of heaven—A man whom fortune and impudence *alone* has elevated from the dregs of the earth, yea! from the station of a "money dig-

ger," to the leader of a fanatical band, which now numbers thousands—A man whose history proves him to be a greater knave, a more consummate impostor and a more impious blasphemer than any whose acts *disgrace* the annals of villainy or hypocrasy.

The Prophet was a tyrant and his followers a "powerful band" of fanatic slaves, "able, from the peculiarity of their situation, and the corrupting power of party spirit, to sway the destinies of the whole county, and probably the state."[44]

"I ask you candidly, fellow citizens," Sharp wrote in July 1841, "if there is not need of an Anti-Mormon Party in this county?" He called for action, and support soon materialized. A convention that summer admitted the absence of verifiable Mormon offenses, but was "guided . . . by a desire to defend ourselves against a despotism, the extent and consequences of which we have no means of ascertaining." They assumed that a man claiming to hear from God "wishes to place his authority above that of the State." A prophet necessarily created a sovereignty in competition with the voice of the people.[45]

Sensing the rising tide of animosity, the *Times and Seasons* editors in Nauvoo printed imaginary religious dialogues to show how rational and open Mormons were, how willing to debate, how confident of their religion's clarity and truth. They knew they spoke into a whirlwind. Eighteen forty-one was a bad year for the Mormons; a flurry of anti-Mormon books and critical articles appeared in print. "The minds of thousands," they acknowledged, were primed to believe nearly any violent story about Mormons.[46] The *Times and Seasons* editors invited anyone to visit Nauvoo and see for themselves its industrious citizens, brick and frame houses, and rising hotel and temple:

> If they will wait over Sunday, they will then see the saints congregating together from a circuit of six or seven miles, some on horseback—in wagons and in carriages—There they will see native born Americans from every state of the Union, the enterprising Englishman, the hardy Scotchman, the warm hearted son of Erin, the Pennsylvania Dutchman, and the honest Canadian, all joining in harmonious praises to Heaven's holy King.

The Mormon editors hoped these sights would allay the fear of Mormon militarism. They would see that "the noise and confusion which is said to be in our midst—'the clash of arms and din of war,'" was only "prejudice against us."[47]

To counter the *Warsaw Signal*, the editors reprinted favorable articles from other papers. A reporter from the *Juliet Courier* was impressed with "the plain hospitality of the Prophet Smith, to all strangers visiting the town, aided as he is, in making the stranger comfortable by his excellent wife, a woman of superior ability." The reporter visited meetings, heard preaching, observed Mormons laboring, and then wondered why the fuss:

> It has been a matter of astonishment to me, after seeing the prophet, as he is called, Elder Rigdon and many other gentlemenly men, any one may see at Nauvoo, who will visit there, why it is that so many professing christianity, and so many professing to reverence the sacred principles of our constitution, which gives free religious toleration to all, have slandered, and persecuted this sect of Christians.

The author urged free discussion about the Mormons and hoped that "no such degrading brutish persecutions, will be got up in Illinois as was in Missouri." Bolstered by such reports, the *Times and Seasons* insisted all was well in Illinois. "Perfect harmony and good feeling prevails between us and our neighbors, with the exception of two or three individuals, whose names are not worthy of mention."[48]

LAND AND DEBT

Despite the paper's claim, Nauvoo's prosperity was tenuous at best. The site had no natural economic advantages, as its precipitous economic decline after the Mormons' departure was to prove. Land sales and construction were the city's chief industries, and the supply of land was inadequate for the burgeoning population. In Iowa the faulty titles to Isaac Galland's Half-Breed Tract were about to be exposed, and in Illinois, Joseph had trouble making payments for the Hotchkiss purchase.

The debt to the partners Horace Hotchkiss, John Gillett, and Smith Tuttle put terrible financial pressures on Joseph. Joseph's brother Don Carlos wrote that Joseph was "all the time (almost) in the *narrows*, straining the last link, as it were, to get out of *this & that Pinch*."[49] In August 1839, Joseph had signed two notes for $25,000 each plus fees, one due in ten years and the other in twenty. These constituted the principal payments which Joseph thought the Church would be able to pay when they came due. The more immediate pressure came from the interest payments of $3,000 that were due each year for twenty years beginning in August 1840.[50] To raise the money, Hotchkiss (the lead partner) had urged Joseph to mobilize the Saints' friends in Washington to support the Mormon petition for redress. If the petition were granted by Congress, reparations would supply the interest payments. If that failed, he told them, they must rely on the "honorable conduct of your own people; their pure morals—their correct habits—their indefatigable industry—their untiring perseverance—and their well directed enterprise."[51]

Joseph saw no way of meeting the payment schedule. As early as July 28, 1840, he wrote Hotchkiss to say poverty and sickness would prevent them from making the first payment on time. Apparently Hotchkiss was satisfied, for no more was heard from him on the subject in 1840. For the future, the Church devised a scheme for paying without raising the cash. Church agents would persuade Saints in the East to exchange their properties for bills that would be good for payment on Nauvoo lands. When they arrived in Nauvoo, they could purchase new lands with these bills. The titles of the eastern lands, meanwhile, would be signed over to Hotchkiss, in effect funding the Nauvoo land purchase.[52]

The success of the venture depended on the effectiveness of the Church agents in persuading eastern converts to cooperate. To represent the Church, Joseph commissioned his brothers Hyrum and William to accompany Isaac Galland east, but Hyrum fell ill soon after departure and returned to Nauvoo, leaving the enterprise with the other two. A few exchanges may have been completed, but in August 1841, Joseph heard from Hotchkiss that Galland had never made it to Connecticut with the exchanged titles. Instead Galland wrote Hotchkiss that he was leaving for the West without coming to Connecticut or reporting if any exchanges were made. "Permit me to ask," Hotchkiss wrote Joseph, "whether this is a proper return for the confidence we have bestowed and for the indulgence we have extended."[53]

Joseph shot back an angry letter. He believed that Hotchkiss had verbally agreed to delay the $3,000 interest payments for five years—perhaps the reason Hotchkiss had stopped pressing for the 1840 payment. In Joseph's view, they had agreed that eastern lands were to go toward both principal and interest, and Hotchkiss would not "coerce" payment while the Saints were getting established. Joseph thought he had renegotiated the terms of the loan, while Hotchkiss wanted interest now as stated in the original agreement.[54]

Joseph was partly a victim of the nineteenth-century rhetoric of financial obligations. Letters about debt often sounded like correspondence between old friends. Hotchkiss appeared to be solicitous, giving fatherly advice and inviting Joseph to stay at his house on visits. Joseph in turn inquired after Hotchkiss's health. He spoke of repaying the debt as his utmost desire, hindered only by the Saints' poverty. "Every exertion on our part shall be made to meet the demands against us, so that if we cannot accomplish all we wish to, it will be our misfortune and not our fault." They spoke of good faith, honor, and confidence, personal rather than financial qualities, as if this were a gentlemen's transaction. When informed that the fixed provisions actually prevailed, Joseph charged Hotchkiss with being hardhearted. What about our destitution after Missouri? he wondered, asking, "Have you no feelings of commiser[a]tion?" He complained that the part of the plat purchased was "a *deathly sickly* hole." Then he issued the final challenge: either take back the property, or let us try to make the best of it. "Coersive measures," he reminded Hotchkiss, "would kill us in the germ."[55]

Under the circumstances, Hotchkiss, like other land speculators of his day, could only wait and keep pressing. So long as there was a prospect for a return, speculators were best advised to let their purchasers labor on, especially if they were improving the land, as the Mormons were. The Saints had to pay off the loan to get clear title; failure meant losing the land and their improvements. Joseph understood the speculators' position and counted on Hotchkiss to tolerate delays.

Meanwhile, Joseph had turned over responsibility for managing the Nauvoo settlements to the Twelve Apostles. The Twelve had originally been in charge of Church affairs outside of the stakes, but Joseph announced at a special conference that they should now "stand in their place next to the first presidency" in "attend[ing] to the settling of emigrants." Thereafter, Brigham Young's hand can be seen in the Church's business affairs. He issued an epistle urging support of the plan for exchanging eastern lands for Nauvoo properties, and delivered an address on the necessity of obtaining proper title at the general Church conference in October. The leaders read a calming letter from one of Hotchkiss's partners, Smith Tuttle, showing that both sides had an interest in restoring amicable relations. Joseph replied with a conciliatory letter of his own. He said he intended to pay the interest a year in advance if possible using eastern land titles instead of cash. Unfortunately, he explained, he had no means now in his hands. The villain in the story was Galland, who had gone West with the money meant for Hotchkiss. So far Galland had not returned to Nauvoo.[56]

Joseph wanted friendship with the Hotchkiss partnership, whose "sincerity" he did not doubt. The Saints would bear their "misfortunes of life, and shoulder[ed] them up handsomely like men." At the end, Joseph revealed how much the culture of honor had formed his inner being. "We ask nothing . . . but what ought to be required between man and man . . . bearing our own part in every thing which duty calls us to do, as not inferior to any of the human race." The heart of the culture of honor was to do your part but tolerate no implication of inferiority. "We are the sons of Adam," he wrote. "We are the *free born sons* of *America;* and having been trampled upon and our rights taken from us, even our Constitutional rights . . . will afford a sufficient excuse, we hope, for any harsh remarks that may have been dropped by us, when we thought there was an assumption of superiority designed to gall our feelings." He could not bear to be treated like an inferior. "We are very sensitive as a people—we confess it."

Yet he was contrite too. "May God forbid that pride, ambition, a want of humanity or any degree of importance, unjustly should have any dominion in our bosoms." "We want to be pardoned for our sins, if any we have committed." In the end, he agreed to pay the interest he had previously contested.[57]

With the Hotchkiss connection restored, Joseph turned to Galland, who had still not appeared. Although presumably he owed the Church money, Galland could claim payment on the extensive Iowa and Illinois lands he had sold Joseph. The contesting debts led to an impasse. After an exchange of letters with Galland and a visit from Brigham Young, some unspecified accommodation was reached. Joseph revoked Galland's agency and power of attorney, and Galland withdrew from the Church. A month later, the Saints learned the Galland titles to Iowa lands were invalid, and settlers there would have to vacate. Joseph chose not to prosecute, and the Galland affair dropped from view.[58]

Joseph's financial dealings took a strange turn in the spring of 1842, when he was informed that he was eligible to declare bankruptcy under a new federal law passed in 1841 by the Whig government. Following the Panic of 1837, thousands of petitioners had appealed to Congress for bankruptcy relief. The Whigs had blamed Democratic policies for the depression, and believed that debt relief advertised the Democrats' blunders. The statute allowed debtors to petition for relief by listing their assets and liabilities. If the accounting was not successfully challenged and no fraud was proven, the debtors were legally discharged without the approval of their creditors. The law threw the balance too much in favor of the debtors and was repealed in March 1843, but during this window of liberality, thousands of debtors sought relief.[59]

The idea was to reach an agreement about distributing inadequate resources. Joseph engaged Calvin Warren, a Quincy attorney, to pursue the matter. Warren, who had hoped to attract Mormons to a small town he had laid out a mile south of Warsaw, entered his own bankruptcy proceedings at the same time. Over a dozen other Mormons, including Sidney Rigdon, also appeared before the commissioners.[60]

Joseph spent two days assembling a "list of Debtors & invoice of Property" and on Monday, April 18, 1842, testified to the lists before the county commissioners.[61] Most who filed applications were discharged from their debts, but complications inevitably arose in evaluating a bundle of properties as complex as Joseph's. Later, after John C. Bennett was expelled from the Church, he charged Joseph with fraudulently transferring personal property to himself as trustee-in-trust of the Church to escape personal liabilities. The charge, never confirmed, led the U.S. Attorney for Illinois, Justin Butterfield, to protest Joseph's invoice.[62] At Joseph's hearing in October 1842, Butterfield objected that Joseph had hidden property. Butterfield feared the federal government would lose payment for a steamboat bought by a Mormon businessman, Peter Haws, with a note that Joseph Smith and others countersigned. The steamboat was wrecked within a few weeks of Haws's purchase, and Butterfield thought Joseph was the only one of the four signatories with any prospect of compensating the government. To satisfy the federal attorney, the Nauvoo High Council proposed to give the government a bond secured by real estate. The negotiations bogged down, however, and were not completed until 1852, when the government was paid in full.[63]

With objections hanging over the proceedings, Joseph was never discharged from his debts under the federal bankruptcy law.[64] Until the charges of fraud were settled, he could not be. But the imminent possibility of being discharged altered his relations with his creditors, who thought they were about to lose their legal hold on him.[65] Joseph wrote Hotchkiss in May 1842 pleading his dire circumstances—the loss of property in Missouri and the pressure of unjust debts—as a reason for resorting to bankruptcy. He assured Hotchkiss that he was not insolvent: "There is property sufficient in the inventory to pay every debt and some to spare." Joseph wanted to pay all of his creditors and "have enough left, for one loaf more for each of our families."[66]

Reassurances notwithstanding, the Hotchkiss partners were dismayed. Joseph's bankruptcy raised the possibility of losing their investment. In addition to the prospect of no further payments, they were threatened by taxes. As holders of the titles, they were responsible for the levies on the land, and Mormon improvements were continually raising the assessed valuations. If the taxes weren't paid, all of their holdings might be sold at a sheriff's auction. To avert the difficulties, Hotchkiss offered long-term leases in return for reasonable rent, an arrangement that would tie up his capital but bring in revenue for taxes. In the absence of good records after 1843, the outcome is unknown. Possibly Hotchkiss lost everything.[67] He may have suffered the fate of many speculators who obtained land at low prices in the expectation of huge gains only to find the complexities of introducing settlers and collecting payment insurmountable. In the end, speculators often came to ruin.[68]

After 1842, Joseph Smith could not be brought down by his creditors. The bankruptcy proceedings stood in the way, and because of the defaults, his credit was good only among the Saints. The outsiders to whom he owed money ceased to harass him, but other vexations took their place. The Missourians would soon renew their extradition proceedings. Sharp and a small army of antagonists would intensify their campaigns of vilification and exposure. The temple and the Nauvoo House, two huge construction projects, remained to be completed.

One would think that the incessant drumming of opposition and business would have drowned out Joseph's revelations, but his was a strange kind of prophethood. No withdrawn mystic contemplating his visions in the isolation of a cave, he was a city-builder, a Church president, and now in Nauvoo a general and soon-to-be mayor. He stood at the center of every project and every controversy. And still, the revelations kept coming, each more daring than the last. The year 1842 brought another florescence.

TWENTY-FIVE

STORIES OF ETERNITY

SPRING 1842

A man is saved no faster than he gets knowledge for if he does not get knowledge he will be brought into Captivity by some evil power in the other world as evil spirits will have more knowledge & Consequently more power than many men who are on the earth. Hence it needs Revelation to assist us & give us knowledge of the things of God.

JOSEPH SMITH, April 10, 1842

BY THE MIDDLE OF 1842, the time of peace in Nauvoo was drawing to a close. By summer, Joseph was entangled in the conflicts that would end in his death two years later. And yet these tempestuous years saw momentous doctrinal and ecclesiastical innovations. A series of events compressed into a few months in the spring of 1842 seemed to signal a fresh vision of the Church's course. The organization of the Relief Society gave women an unprecedented role in church government. Soon after, Joseph embraced Freemasonry and introduced a new endowment ceremony for the temple. In March, his final translation, the Book of Abraham, which he had labored over since 1835, was published in the *Times and Seasons*. Perhaps most fateful, the number of Joseph's wives increased dramatically.

These developments added new depth to the Mormon worldview. Joseph almost always wound theology around his organizational changes. Everything he did, he often said, was patterned after the order of heaven; everything was situated against a ground of history and cosmology. In Nauvoo, his theology became increasingly dramaturgical, not only in the temple ritual, where a reenactment of the Creation and the Fall was the form of instruction, but in his comments about primordial events. Developments in Nauvoo were linked to dramatic occurrences at the foundation of the world, so that the elaboration of institutions in the spring of 1842 also added to the stories of eternity.

MARRIAGE

Of all the events, the resumption of plural marriage was the most disturbing. After marrying Fanny Alger sometime before 1836, Joseph, it appears, married no one else until he wed Louisa Beaman on April 5, 1841, in Nauvoo. (Historians debate the possibility of one other wife in the interim.) In the next two and a half years, Joseph married about thirty additional women, ten of them already married to other men.[1] Nothing confuses the picture of Joseph Smith's character more than these plural marriages. What lay behind this egregious transgression of conventional morality? What drove him to a practice that put his life and his work in jeopardy, not to mention his relationship with Emma? Was he a dominant male whose ego brooked no bounds? Joseph exercised such untrammeled authority in Nauvoo that it is possible to imagine him thinking no conquest beyond his reach. In theory, he could take what he wanted and browbeat his followers with threats of divine punishment.

This simple reading of Joseph's motives is implicit in descriptions of him as "a charismatic, handsome man." They suggest he was irresistible and made the most of it. Other Mormon men went along out of loyalty or in hopes of sharing the power. But missing from that picture is Joseph's sense of himself. In public and private, he spoke and acted as if guided by God. All the doctrines, plans, programs, and claims were, in his mind, the mandates of heaven. They came to him as requirements, with a kind of irresistible certainty. The revelations weighed him down with impossible tasks like translation, gathering, constructing a temple, or building a city. More than once he told the Church he had completed the work and had no more to accomplish, as if he hoped the revelations would subside.[2] Then a new commandment would force itself upon him, and the work would resume.

Joseph ordinarily followed the commandments punctiliously, as if disobedience put him at risk. In the case of plural marriage, he held off for two or three years before marrying Fanny Alger, and then after this one unsuccessful attempt, waited another five years. The delay showed an uncharacteristic reluctance, hard for one who feared God. In some of Joseph's revelations the Lord speaks as a friend, but in others with the voice of thunder. Writing to a woman whom he hoped would be his wife, he described the two sides of the image: "Our heavenly father is more liberal in his views, and boundless in his mercies and blessings, than we are ready to believe or receive, and at the same time is as terrible to workers of iniquity, more awful in the executions of his punishments, and more ready to detect every false way than we are apt to suppose him to be."[3] God was both kind and terrible. By delaying plural marriage, Joseph risked provoking God's wrath. Mary

Rollins Lightner, one of his plural wives, later said Joseph told her about the pressure he was under. "The angel came to me three times between the year of '34 and '42 and said I was to obey that principle or he would [s]lay me." Others told the story with an additional detail: the angel held a drawn sword.[4]

The possibility of an imaginary revelation, erupting from his own heart and subconscious mind, seems not to have occurred to Joseph. To him, the words came from heaven.[5] They required obedience even though the demand seemed contradictory or wrong. The possibility of deception did occur to him. Satanic counterfeits concerned Joseph; he talked to the Saints about the detection of fraudulent angels. But when Lightner asked if perhaps plural marriage was of the devil, Joseph said no. In his mind, the revelation came from God, and he had to obey or suffer. The written form of the revelation, recorded in 1843 (later canonized as *Doctrine and Covenants* 132) said bluntly, "I reveal unto you a New and an Everlasting Covenant and if ye abide not that Covenant, then are ye damned."[6]

Joseph never wrote his personal feelings about plural marriage. Save for the revelation given in the voice of God, everything on the subject comes from the people around him. But surely he realized that plural marriage would inflict terrible damage, that he ran the risk of wrecking his marriage and alienating his followers. How could the faithful Emma, to whom he pledged his love in every letter, accept additional wives? His followers would see the revelation as an unforgivable breach of the moral law and reject it altogether, or, even worse, use it as a license for free love. Either way, their reactions would jeopardize the Zion project. As for the world at large, plural marriage would confirm all their worst fears. Sexual excess was considered the all too common fruit of pretended revelation. Joseph's enemies would delight in one more evidence of a revelator's antinomian transgressions. He also risked prosecution under Illinois's antibigamy law.[7]

In approaching Joseph Bates Noble in the spring of 1841 about marrying his wife's sister, Louisa Beaman, Joseph asked Bates, a man he had known since Kirtland, to keep quiet. "In revealing this to you I have placed my life in your hands, therefore do not in an evil hour betray me to my enemies." Louisa Beaman was twenty-six when she married Joseph Smith.[8] Alone since her mother's death in September 1840, Beaman had moved in with Joseph and Mary Noble. To disguise the wedding, Joseph asked Noble to perform the ceremony in a grove near Main Street with Louisa in man's clothing.

Partly to maintain secrecy, Joseph could not have spent much time with Beaman or any of the women he married. He never gathered his wives into a household—as his Utah followers later did—or accompanied them to public events. Close relationships were further curtailed by business. Joseph had to look after Emma and the children, manage the Church, govern the city, and evade the extradition officers from Missouri. As the marriages increased, there were fewer and fewer opportunities for seeing each wife.

Even so, nothing indicates that sexual relations were left out of plural marriages; Noble testified many years later that Joseph spent the night with Louisa after the wedding. But there was no "mormon seraglio or Nauvoo harem," as his enemies charged. Not until many years later did anyone claim Joseph Smith's paternity, and evidence for the tiny handful of supposed children is tenuous. For the most part, the women went about their business as before. Only the slightest hints suggest that Joseph was in Louisa's company after their marriage, though he may have contributed to her support.[9]

The marital status of the plural wives further complicated the issue. Within fifteen months of marrying Louisa Beaman, Joseph had married eleven other women. Eight of the eleven were married to other men. All told, ten of Joseph's plural wives were married to other men. All of them went on living with their first husbands after marrying the Prophet. The reasons for choosing married women can only be surmised. Not all were married to non-Mormon men: six of the ten husbands were active Latter-day Saints.[10] In most cases, the husband knew of the plural marriage and approved. The practice seems inexplicable today. Why would a husband consent?

The only answer seems to be the explanation Joseph gave when he asked a woman for her consent: they and their families would benefit spiritually from a close tie to the Prophet. Joseph told a prospective wife that submitting to plural marriage would "ensure your eternal salvation & exaltation and that of your father's household. & all your kindred." A father who gave his daughter to the Prophet as a plural wife was assured that the marriage "shall be crowned upon your heads with honor and immortality and eternal life to all your house both old and young." The relationship would bear fruit in the afterlife. There is no certain evidence that Joseph had sexual relations with any of the wives who were married to other men.[11] They married because Joseph's kingdom grew with the size of his family, and those bonded to that family would be exalted with him.[12]

In October 1841, Joseph married Zina Huntington Jacobs, wife of Henry Jacobs. Zina was a pious young woman of twenty who had spoken in tongues and heard angels singing. Joseph and Emma had cared for Zina and her siblings for three months in 1839–40 after their mother died. When Joseph explained plural marriage to her the following year, her first response was to resist. Accepting Henry, who was courting her at the time, meant saying no to Joseph.[13] Zina changed her mind after her brother told her about the angel threatening Joseph's "position and his life." That image

plus her own inquiries convinced her. "I searched the scripture & buy humble prayer to my Heavenly Father I obtained a testimony for my self that
God had required that order to be established in this church." Even after
this assurance, she despaired of the consequences. "I mad[e] a greater sacri-
fise than to give my life for I never anticipated a gain to be looked uppon as
an honerable woman by those I dearly loved." On October 27, 1841, her
brother Dimick performed the marriage on the banks of the Mississippi.
Little more is known of Zina's relationship with Joseph. Her diary says
nothing about visits. In 1843 while Henry was away on a mission, she,
"being lonely," opened a school in her house. The records don't reveal how
much Henry knew about the marriage at first, but in 1846 he stood by in the
temple when Zina was sealed posthumously to Joseph Smith for eternity.[14]

The personal anguish caused by plural marriage did not stop Joseph
Smith from marrying more women. He married three in 1841, eleven in
1842, and seventeen in 1843. Historians debate these numbers, but the total
figure is most likely between twenty-eight and thirty-three. Larger numbers have been proposed based on the sealing records in the Nauvoo temple. Eight additional women were sealed to Joseph in the temple after his
death, possibly implying a marriage while he was still alive. Whatever the
exact number, the marriages are numerous enough to indicate an impersonal bond. Joseph did not marry women to form a warm, human companionship, but to create a network of related wives, children, and kinsmen that
would endure into the eternities. The revelation on marriage promised
Joseph an "hundred fold in this world, of fathers and mothers, brothers and
sisters, houses and lands, wives and children, and crowns of eternal lives in
the eternal worlds."[15] Like Abraham of old, Joseph yearned for familial
plentitude. He did not lust for women so much as he lusted for kin.

Romance played only a slight part. In making proposals, Joseph would
sometimes say God had given a woman to him, or they were meant for each
other, but there was no romantic talk of adoring love. He did not court his
prospective wives by first trying to win their affections. Often he asked a
relative—a father or an uncle—to propose the marriage. Sometimes one of
his current wives proposed for him. When he made the proposal himself, a
friend like Brigham Young was often present. The language was religious
and doctrinal, stressing that a new law has been revealed. She was to seek
spiritual confirmation. Once consent was given, a formal ceremony was
performed before witnesses, with Joseph dictating the words to the person
officiating.[16]

Joseph himself said nothing about sex in these marriages. Other marriage
experimenters in Joseph's times focused on sexual relations. The Shakers
repudiated marriage altogether, considering sex beastly and unworthy of a
millennial people. John Humphrey Noyes's Oneida community objected to

the possessiveness of the marriage relationship and thought free intercourse was as necessary to openness and love as communal property.[17] Joseph, so far as can be told, never discussed the sexual component of marriage, save for his concern about adultery.

We might expect that Joseph, the kind of dominant man who is thought to have strong libidinal urges, would betray his sexual drive in his talk and manner. Bred outside the rising genteel culture, he was not inhibited by Victorian prudery. But references to sexual pleasure are infrequent. Years later, William Law, Joseph's counselor in the First Presidency, said he was shocked once to hear Joseph say one of his wives "afforded him great *pleasure.*" That report is one of the few, and the fact that it shocked Law suggests such comments were infrequent.[18] As Fawn Brodie said, "There was too much of the Puritan" in Joseph for him to be a "careless libertine." Indeed, the practice of plural marriage went against the teachings of other revelations. In one of the Book of Mormon's most impassioned sermons, the prophet Jacob chastised the Nephite men for taking additional wives and concubines. "Ye have broken the hearts of your tender wives," Jacob preached. "For I, the Lord God, delighteth in chastity of women. And whoredoms is an abomination before me." The offenders would be visited with "a sore curse, even unto destruction." A revelation given in Kirtland in 1831 underscored the same prohibition: "Thou shalt not commit adultery; and he that committeth adultery and repenteth not, shall be cast out."[19]

With these prohibitions emblazoned in his own revelations, Joseph was torn by the command to take plural wives. What about the curses and destruction promised adulterers? What about the heart of his tender wife? In 1838 when Joseph was accused of a relationship with Fanny Alger, his only concern had been to insist that he had never confessed to adultery. The written revelation on marriage noted that "ye have asked concerning adultery," and defined precisely what constituted adultery.[20] The question obviously bothered him.

Joseph explained to Nancy Rigdon, Sidney Rigdon's daughter, who refused Joseph's proposal of marriage, how he justified the apparent breach of the moral code.[21] The path to happiness, he assured her, was "virtue, uprightness, faithfulness, holiness, and keeping all the commandments of God." Even in taking additional wives, he had to think of himself as virtuous. But the phrase about "keeping the commandments of God" suggested how plural marriage was justified. "God said thou shalt not kill,—at another time he said thou shalt utterly destroy." What was a believer to do with conflicting injunctions? Joseph reached a terrifying answer: "that which is wrong under one circumstance, may be and often is, right under another." This unnerving principle was the foundation of the government of God. "Whatever God requires is right, no matter what it is," he wrote Nancy,

"although we may not see the reason thereof till long after the events tran-
spire."[22]

The idea actually informed every revealed religion. A few years later the
Christian evangelist and antislavery advocate Charles Finney was to say with
respect to slavery that "no human legislation can make it right or lawful to
violate any command of God." To Finney the higher law—equality—
prevailed over human law, and justified attacks on slavery. The same sentiment coming from Joseph with plural marriage in mind froze the heart.[23]
He could not have chosen words better suited to strike terror into the
rational mind. He was saying that any moral rule, any commonsense limitation on any human constraint, could be overthrown by a revelation. The
assertion confirmed the fears of rational Christians for centuries about the
social chaos inherent in revealed religion.

Joseph quickly qualified what he had said. Although "every thing that
God gives us is lawful and right, and 'tis proper that we should enjoy his
gifts and blessings whenever and wherever he is disposed to bestow," casual
liaisons were not authorized. A gift taken was not a gift given. "Blessings
and enjoyments" taken arbitrarily "without law, without revelation, without
commandment, those blessings and enjoyments would prove cursings and
vexations in the end, and we should have to go down in sorrow and wailings
of everlasting regret."[24]

To Joseph's mind, revelation functioned like law. The revelations came
as "commandments," the name he gave to all the early revelations. They
required obedience. The marriage revelation laid down rules about adultery, binding partners to each other by covenant. If a woman "be not in the
new and everlasting covenant, and she be with another man, she has committed adultery." The same for men. "If her husband be with another
woman, and he was under a vow, he hath broken his vow, and hath committed adultery." The rules were as strict under plural marriage as under monogamy, except that revelation set the standard.[25]

The shock of plural marriage was further mitigated by precedents in the
Bible. The sermon against adultery in the *Book of Mormon* began with the
Old Testament. "David and Solomon truly had many wives and concubines," the prophet Jacob acknowledged, and they sinned in the practice.
The Old Testament sanctioned plural marriage, but not for selfishly "multiply[ing] wives to himself," as Solomon and David evidently did. But what
about the other biblical polygamists not mentioned in the *Book of Mormon*
who did multiply wives to themselves? Did Abraham sin in marrying Hagar?
Implicitly recognizing the contradiction, the *Book of Mormon* offered an
explanation. "For if I will, saith the Lord of Hosts, raise up seed unto me,"
Jacob wrote, "I will command my people: otherwise, they will hearken unto
these things." Monogamy was the usual practice, but in certain instances
God commanded polygamy.[26]

The disjuncture between the *Book of Mormon* prohibitions of polygamy and the Old Testament practice apparently caused Joseph to question. The plural marriage revelation, not written down until July 1843, opened with the observation that "you have enquired of my hand to know and understand wherein I the Lord justified my servants, Abraham, Isaac and Jacob; as also Moses, David and Solomon, my servants, as touching the principle and doctrine of their having many wives and concubines." In answer to the question, Joseph learned that plural marriage was a divine commandment. "God commanded Abraham," the revelation said, "and Sarah gave Hagar to Abraham to wife. And why did she do it? Because this was the Law." Abraham was the precedent. The scriptural justification for plural marriage was the admonition to "go ye, therefore, and do the works of Abraham."[27]

Joseph told the Twelve about plural marriage soon after their return in 1841, and they began marrying other women soon after. Before Joseph died, as many as twenty-nine other men had married at least one additional wife under his authorization.[28] The practice had to be generalized because the revelation tied marriage to the highest form of exaltation. Marriage was the basis for human exaltation, whether plural or not. Later in Mormon history, exaltation through marriage was separated from multiple wives. The plural marriage revelation still describes the modern Mormon view of marriage and family, although Latter-day Saints abandoned plural marriage more than a century ago.[29]

At the base was priesthood sealing, the practice of binding people together by priesthood authority. The revelation informed the Saints that no marriages, monogamous or plural, would last after death unless sealed by priesthood authority.

> All Covenants, Contracts, bonds, obligations, oaths, vows, performances, connections, associations, or expectations that are not made or entered into and sealed by the Holy Spirit of Promise, of him who is anointed, both as well for time and for all Eternity . . . are of no efficacy, virtue, or force in and after the resurrection.[30]

The powers of this world ended at death; only the power of God could ordain eternal marriages.

To those sealed by the priesthood, the promises were startling. When out of the world, the revelation said, sealed couples would pass by the angels and go on to godhood. Their state was quite different from those married by worldly authority. In the afterlife, the worldly wed became single again, and a permanent cap limited their progress. "Therefore they cannot be enlarged, but remain separately and singly" and are appointed "angels in heaven, which angels are ministering servants, to minister for those who are worthy of a far more, and an exceeding, and an eternal

weight of glory." The key word in the passage was "enlarged." Single people could not expand; married pairs could. And how? Through "a continuation of the seeds forever and ever." They kept bearing children. This
capacity to "enlarge" made them, in effect, gods:

> Then shall they be Gods, because they have no end; therefore shall they be
> from everlasting to everlasting, because they continue; then shall they be
> above all because all things are subject unto them. Then shall they be Gods,
> because they have all power, and the angels are subject unto them.[31]

The great, godly power was procreation, the continuation of seed. The
ultimate social order of heaven was familial.

Before the marriage revelation, women were in the shadows in Joseph's
theology, implied but rarely recognized. Now they moved to the center.
"The continuation of the seeds" involved bearing and nurturing children,
the work of parents. In 1843, Joseph said that "in order to obtain the highest degree of celestial glory, a man must enter into this order of the priesthood; and if he dont, he cant obtain it. He may enter into the other but that
is the end of his kingdom he cannot have an increase."[32] The marriage revelation was still addressed to men and spoke of their increase and their
power, but they could have none of these alone. To be exalted, men and
women must be bound together.

Joseph had never tried to demean women. Emma had gone to the Hill
Cumorah with him to obtain the plates and later helped record the translation. When he lost the 116 pages, he thought first of her disappointment.
The revelation to Emma in 1830 said her time was to be given "to writing,
and to learning much"—no marginal activities. But like so many Victorians,
Joseph thought of women in helping roles. Women nurtured children and
cared for the sick. Revelations were addressed to the "Elders of my church,"
rarely to women.[33] In church as in politics or the economy of the day,
women and children were subsumed under a male head.

The marriage revelation did not overturn the family order. If anything,
women were more entrenched than ever in the roles of mother and wife. But
procreation was lifted to the highest level of human and divine endeavor.
Mothering was precisely what made "gods." And with mothering highlighted, the greatest work was not accomplished in the priesthood councils
where women were absent, but at home, where women were present and
central.[34] The marriage revelation redressed the balance of the political and
the familial, shifting emphasis from the corporate to the personal. While
women gained by this shift, the revelation also relieved the loneliness and
burden of male autonomy. Men would not become gods alone. Through
the continuation of seed, husbands and wives passed by the angels and

became gods together—and only together. Women—in partnership, not as individuals—were at last represented in Joseph's theology.

The revelation's tone was more political than sentimental. There are no scenes of smiling children playing at their parents' feet, the standard trope of later Victorian heavens. Men and women who married by God's law would inherit "thrones, kingdoms, principalities, and powers, dominions, all heights & depths." This was the language of government, not sentimentalism. Echoing the words of the Revelation of St. John, the Lord told Joseph, "I . . . prepare a throne for you in the kingdom of my Father, with Abraham your father," presumably with a queen or queens beside him.[35] The marriage covenant prepared the Saints less for wedded bliss than for heavenly rule.

The marriage revelation culminated the emergence of family theology. More than any previous revelation, this one put family first. In the first decade of the Church, the city (not the parish) was the primary social organization, and the council was the characteristic governing body: the First Presidency, the stake high councils, the council of the Twelve Apostles. In the middle of the decade, priesthood was associated with lineage. Revelations described the descent of the priesthood from father to son; the office of patriarch was by right passed to a son; and the bishopric ideally went to descendants of Aaron. The Book of Abraham described Abraham's quest for priesthood descending through "the fathers."[36]

In Nauvoo, the family side of priesthood came forward. Bonding families became the center of Joseph's doctrine. Malachi's phrase about turning the hearts of the children to the fathers inspired the practice of baptisms for the dead, tying family to family together through history, thus creating a "welding link" going back in time. The earth would be wasted, Joseph read Malachi to say, if families were not bound together across the generations. Priesthood marriage welded contemporary husbands, wives, and children together for eternity, making the family the one institution sure to survive death. Family did not displace councils in earthly Church government, but family was identified as the fundamental governing body in the hereafter. After death, husbands and wives as kings and queens would rule over principalities and powers.[37]

Joseph's family doctrine did not grow out of a diagnosis of social ills, like *The Peace Maker, or the Doctrines of the Millennium* by Udney Hay Jacob, a book favoring plural marriage published in 1842 by the Mormon press in Nauvoo. Jacob, who was not a Mormon at the time, argued for easy divorce and polygamous marriage in order to reduce the sexual influence of women and restore male authority. Society, Jacob believed, was suffering from the decay of patriarchal dominance and would perish unless men were put back in charge. Women were lording it over their husbands, Jacob thought, because of men's sexual needs. Polygamy would liberate men and restore their rightful authority.[38] Joseph's plural marriage revelation also gave husbands the upper hand, but it said nothing about loss of control or family deterioration. The revelation was about bonding, not dominance; its concern was to preserve family into eternity.

THE RELIEF SOCIETY

In the same spring when Joseph was enlarging his circle of wives, he gave women a new role in Church organization. The formation of a women's society in Nauvoo in 1842 spurred his thinking. The society began with the benevolent impulse of twenty-three-year-old Sarah Granger Kimball, an eminent young matron. Her father, Oliver Granger, had been sheriff and colonel of the militia in Ontario County, the Smiths' home county in New York, before he joined the Mormons and moved to Kirtland in 1833. Sarah's non-Mormon husband, Hiram Kimball, was a merchant and land speculator. Sarah married him in 1840 and lived in the finest house in Nauvoo. Like others of her class, Sarah Kimball believed her social position carried a responsibility for helping the underprivileged, and in Nauvoo in 1842 the needs were evident on every street. For forty years, women's organizations around the country had pursued a host of worthy causes—aid to the poor, schools for indigent children, missionary work, and the distribution of Bibles. Thousands of benevolent societies had sprung up, especially in New England and in the path of Yankee westward settlement. To ambitious and improving women, forming a "Ladies' Society," as Sarah Kimball called it, was a natural extension of their nurturing office in the home. Kimball thought first of paying her seamstress to stitch shirts for the temple workmen, but then decided to organize a wider effort. At the first meeting on March 4, 1842, the group moved to organize formally.[39]

At the women's behest, Kimball went to Eliza R. Snow, well-known in Nauvoo for her literary experience, with a request for a constitution and bylaws. Joseph took an interest when Snow brought the documents to him for approval. He called them "the best he had ever seen," but said he had "something better for them than a written Constitution." He wanted to organize the women, he said, "under the priesthood after the pattern of the priesthood." Those words implied that he considered a women's organization part of the ancient order of things. When he met with the women on March 17, Joseph told the women they should put aside the usual model for benevolent societies. He told them to elect a president who would choose counselors to preside over the society, just as the First Presidency presided over the Church. Let additional officers "be appointed and set apart, as Deacons, Teachers, &C. are among us." The society's duties were to mesh with the priesthood's. They were to care for the poor as originally intended but also "to assist; by correcting the morals and strengthening the virtues of the community, and save the Elders the trouble of rebuking." The women were not ordained to the priesthood, and the name of the society—The Female Relief Society of Nauvoo—did not imply priesthood, but priesthood was the pattern. Two weeks later, in urging them to select worthy members, Joseph told the society to act "according to the ancient Priesthood." He wanted to "make of this Society a kingdom of priests."[40] For the first time, women had a place in the evolving Church organization.

In recent, more feminist times, the Relief Society's minutes have been scrutinized for signs that priesthood was being given to the sisters. The minutes have Joseph saying "I now turn the key to you in the name of God and this Society shall rejoice and knowledge and intelligence shall flow down from this time." Since the word "key" was associated with priesthood, the statement has a priesthood ring. Even then, the question of priesthood authority was raised. Some members objected to women "laying hands on the sick" as if they were priesthood holders. Joseph answered the critics by saying "all that believe whether male or female" had the promise of casting out devils and healing the sick. He replied that "there could be no more sin in any female laying hands on the sick than in wetting the face with water." Women did not need priesthood to minister. "It is no sin for any body to do it that has faith," Joseph said. Women administered by faith, not priesthood.[41]

More significant was Joseph's promise that "Females, if they are pure and innocent can come into the presence of God." In most salvationist churches, those words would have meant a return to heaven after death. For Mormons, the words referred to Joseph's long quest to bring his people into the presence of God while still on earth. The revelations associated the vision of God with the temple and the endowment of power. Until then, the endowment had been given solely to men, the only ones to receive washings and anointings in Kirtland. By including women among those who were to see God, Joseph brought them into the circle of the endowed who would be cleansed and purified in the temple. In the middle of his talk about women healing the sick, he interjected a seemingly unconnected remark about the temple: "the Church is not now organiz'd in its proper order, and cannot be until the Temple is completed." The remark implied women would understand their place in "the proper order" when they entered the temple.[42]

At the launching of the Relief Society, Emma Smith was made president. Joseph had not forgotten the 1831 revelation about her calling "to expound scriptures, and to exhort the church." He read the entire text at the society's organizational meeting and commented that "she was ordain'd at the time the Revelation was given, to expound the scriptures to all; and to teach the female part of the community." Emma probably had more influence over him than any living person. He worried about displeasing her and begged her forgiveness for unknown infractions. Her appointment to head the Relief Society, perhaps a small compensation for the sorrows she bore, was part of his envisioned family order. They would share the burdens of leadership together.[43]

In his comments to the society, Joseph tried to steady the boat he knew was rocking because of the plural-marriage rumors. On the one hand, he urged them to "purge out iniquity," his Puritanical conscience requiring him to insist on virtue in the Church. On the other hand, he asked them to show mercy; don't "think yourselves more righteous than others." Perhaps in an indirect plea to Emma he asked the sisters to treat their husbands "with mildness and affection." "When a man is borne down with trouble—when he is perplexed, if he can meet a smile, [not] an argument—if he can meet with mildness, it will calm down his soul and smoothe his feelings." In this turbulent spring filled with stress and suspicion, Joseph appealed to the new president of the Relief Society for understanding. "When the mind is going to despair it needs a solace."[44]

ENDOWMENT

The concept of the temple had steadily expanded since it was first mentioned in a revelation in late 1830. In Independence, the temple was understood as a place for the Lord to return—a place to lay His head when He came.[45] In Kirtland, Joseph added administrative offices, a meetinghouse and school, and, more significantly, performed the rituals of washing and anointing in the House of the Lord. In Nauvoo, the ceremonies were further elaborated to include baptism for the dead, endowments, and priesthood marriages.

The elaboration of function was not reflected in the architecture in Nauvoo. The floor plans for the new temple looked very much like Kirtland's. Two assembly rooms once again sat atop each other with pulpits at opposite ends for the leaders arrayed in their priesthood ranks, from the First Presidency and high priests down through teachers and deacons. The Nauvoo temple provided distinctive space for only one temple ordinance, baptisms for the dead, which were performed in a large basement font. Otherwise there were no rooms designed specifically for temple ceremonies. As in Kirtland, the third floor was divided into small, plain offices with none of them designated as ritual spaces.

The architectural carryover from Kirtland, however, did not mean that Joseph did not have more in mind for Nauvoo when the temple was begun.[46] Sermons and revelations alluded to something additional on the way. The idea of a place for recovering ancient knowledge was emphasized in January 1841: "Let this house be built unto my name, that I may reveal mine ordinances therein unto my people; for I design to reveal unto my church, things which have been kept hid from before the foundation of the world—things that pertain to the dispensation of the fullness of times."[47]

To the washings and anointings of Kirtland, the Nauvoo endowment added instruction based on the biblical story of the Creation, a recurring narrative in Joseph's revelations. Both the Book of Moses and the Book of Abraham contained a creation story; a third version framed the endowment ceremony. The endowment presented a reenactment of the Creation, the Fall, and the establishment of priesthood order among humans after the earth was formed. This was the primordium, the time when God imprinted the earth and fixed the pattern for human existence. The drama foreshadowed Joseph's mission to install the priesthood order among the Saints in his day, as the prophets had been trying to do from the beginning.

Portions of the temple ritual resembled Masonic rites that Joseph had observed when a Nauvoo lodge was organized in March 1842 and that he may have heard about from Hyrum, a Mason from New York days. The Nauvoo endowment was first bestowed just six weeks after Joseph's induction. The similarities were marked enough for Heber Kimball to quote Joseph saying that Freemasonry "was taken from preasthood but has become degen[e]rated. but menny things are perfect."[48] Joseph often requested revelation about things that caught his attention. His revision of the Bible had sparked questions that resulted in revelations such as the vision of three glories. Tensions in South Carolina brought on a revelation about coming civil war. He had a green thumb for growing ideas from tiny seeds. Masonic rites seem to have been one more provocation.

Freemasonry, emerging from a slump after the anti-Masonic frenzy of the early 1830s, began in Nauvoo with a few Mormon Masons who wanted to organize a lodge. Fewer than two hundred Masons were distributed among five lodges in Illinois in 1841, but in the next year, six new lodges were organized in the state besides the Mormon lodges.[49] James Adams, a Mormon convert and probate judge in Springfield, encouraged Mormon Masons to apply. In June 1841, they petitioned for sponsorship and received it from Abraham Jonas, a Jewish Mason and Grand Master of the Grand Lodge of Illinois. Jonas's belief in equality and brotherhood disposed him to befriend the Saints, and he was also seeking support in his run for the state legislature. Jonas formed the Mormons into a temporary lodge of Ancient York Masons with George Miller as "Worshipful Master" and Hyrum Smith as "Senior Warden." The new lodge quickly received membership applications from forty-one Mormons including Joseph, Sidney Rigdon, and five of the Twelve Apostles.

In March 1842, Jonas came to Nauvoo to install the new members.[50]

Joseph became an "Entered Apprentice" Mason on March 15, 1842. Jonas dubbed Joseph a Mason "on sight" to allow him to officiate as chaplain while being installed. The next day Joseph rose through degrees of "Fellow Craft" and "Master Mason." Impressed though he must have been, his journal entry for the installation expressed most pleasure in the celebration following the initiation. The Masonic procession began at Joseph's store near the river and marched to the grove at the base of the temple bluff, where three thousand people gathered. Joseph reported that "a Large number of people assembled on the occasion, the day was exceedingly fine, all things were done in order, and universal satisfaction manifested."[51]

If Joseph thought of Freemasonry as degenerate priesthood, he did nothing to suppress his rival. Once the Nauvoo lodge was organized, Mormons joined in large numbers. Eleven of the Twelve Apostles became Freemasons. By October 1842, the 253 members of the Nauvoo lodge outnumbered the 227 Masons in all the other Illinois lodges combined. The Mormons organized four additional lodges over the next year. In June, less than seven weeks after bestowing the endowment on the first group of brethren, Joseph celebrated "St. Johns day," in honor of John the Baptist, a Masonic favorite, by riding in procession to a public celebration attended by thousands. In April 1844, the Saints dedicated the Nauvoo Masonic Hall, the finest completed building in the city.[52]

Masonic instruction would have attracted Joseph. Masonic candidates sought light, a powerful word in Joseph's revelations. Biblical imagery was mixed generously with a conglomeration of symbols—grips, signs, tools, architecture, objects, scriptures, stories, actions, many of them references to the craft of masonry. After the ceremony initiating members into a higher degree, a lecture summarized the symbols and their importance for instilling virtue and brotherhood.[53] The outcome was a circle of committed brethren, loyal to each other to the death, forming a bulwark against a wicked world. After the Masonic installation and the first endowment ceremony, Heber Kimball wrote Parley Pratt that "Brother Joseph feels as well as I Ever see him. one reason is he has got a Small Company. that he feels safe in thare ha[n]ds." Kimball probably referred to the men who had been endowed, but the Masonic lodge was one more line of defense against a hostile world.[54]

Intrigued by the Masonic rites, Joseph turned the materials to his own use. The Masonic elements that appeared in the temple endowment were embedded in a distinctive context—the Creation instead of the Temple of Solomon, exaltation rather than fraternity, God and Christ, not the Worshipful Master. Temple covenants bound people to God rather than to each other. At the end, the participants entered symbolically into the presence of God.[55]

Endowment, Joseph's name for the temple ceremony, connected it to

promises made long before his encounter with Freemasonry. In early revelations, the word "endowment" referred to seeing God, a bequest of Pentecostal spiritual light. The use of the word "endowment" in Nauvoo implied
that the goal of coming into God's presence would be realized now through
ritual rather than a transcendent vision. This transition gave Mormonism's search for direct access to God an enduring form. David Hume, the
eighteenth-century empiricist and critic of "enthusiastic" religion, had
observed that outbursts of visions and revelations soon sputtered out. They
lacked form to keep them alive. They could not endure because they had
"no rites, no ceremonies, no holy observances, which may enter into the
common train of life, and preserve the sacred principles from oblivion." To
remain in force, "enthusiasm" had to be embodied in holy practice. Ann
Taves, a modern scholar of religion, has added that "direct inspiration survives only when it is supported by a sacred mythos embedded in sacred
practices."[56] The Mormon temple's sacred story stabilized and perpetuated
the original enthusiastic endowment.

The resemblances of the temple rites to Masonic ritual have led some
to imagine the endowment as an offshoot of the fraternal lodge movement.
Between 1840 and 1900, membership in lodges leapt from around 2,500 to
over 6,000,000. The lodges' success attested to the need for bonding
among American males. In the hard world of emergent capitalism, the
lodges set up an alternative universe of virtue and friendship encased in
imagery and ancient rites.[57] On the surface, the temple resembles the cloistered, brotherly world of the lodges. But the spiritual core of the Nauvoo
endowment was not male bonding. By 1843 women were sitting in the
ordinance rooms and passing through the rituals. Adam and Eve, a male-
female pair, were the representative figures rather than the Masonic hero
Hiram Abiff. The aim of the endowment was not male fraternity but the
exaltation of husbands and wives.[58]

The Nauvoo endowment is more akin to aspects of Kabbalah, the alternative Jewish tradition that flourished for centuries alongside rational Judaism. As one commentator explains, Kabbalah's central impulse was a
desire to encounter God: "The position of classical Judaism was that the
essence of God is unknowable: 'Thou canst not see My Face.' The Kabbalists sought not only to define and characterize the Godhead—through
a kind of spiritualized cosmogonic physics—but to experience it."[59] Joseph's
governing passion was to have his people experience God. To be sure,
Joseph was not seeking a mystic God known through some transcendent
fusion. Joseph's God existed in time and space in a bodily form. Nonetheless, the fundamental trajectory of the endowment coincided with the passions and expectations of mystics for centuries past and especially with the
Kabbalistic dream of conjunction with the divine.[60]

How Joseph Smith could have tied into this line of religious inquiry remains a mystery. Scholars have pointed to Kabbalistic books in the possession of Alexander Neibaur, a Jewish Mormon convert who knew Joseph in Nauvoo. But these came on the scene a decade after Joseph's revelations defined the endowment of power as an encounter with God. We can scarcely imagine him steeping himself in Kabbalistic literature in Manchester and Harmony. More reasonable is Harold Bloom's conclusion that Joseph's desire for God's presence came out of his own religious experience and genius.[61] He had an uncanny ability to recover long-lost traditions for use in modern times.

Joseph first bestowed the endowment on nine men on May 4, 1842, in the second-floor rooms of his brick store. Having arranged the room with scenery and props the day before, he spent the day, his journal said, giving "certain instructions concerning the priesthood."[62] Later, his clerk Willard Richards gave a more detailed description of Joseph's instructions

> in the principles and order of the priesthood, attending to washings anointing, endowments, and the communications of keys, pertaining to the Aronic Priesthood, and so on to the highest order of the Melchisedek Priesthood, setting forth the order pertaining to the Ancient of days, & all those plans & principles by which any one is enabled to secure the fulness of those blessings which has been prepared for the church of the first-born, and come up, and abide in the presence of Eloheim in the eternal worlds. In this council was instituted the Ancient order of things for the first time in these last days. And the communications I made to this council were of things spiritual, and to be received only by the spiritual minded: and there was nothing made know to these men but what will be made known to all the Saints, of the last days, so soon as they are prepared to receive, and a proper place is prepared to communicate them, even to the weakest of the Saints.[63]

Because the endowment was necessary for salvation, all were to enter into this order, even "the weakest of the Saints." In the winter of 1845–46, at the end of the Mormon stay in Nauvoo, carpenters labored on the temple long after they knew they would be forced out. In the final months, while they gathered supplies and built wagons for the winter trek across Iowa, 5,600 Saints passed through the temple. Brigham Young, the master organizer of the journey, spent his nights instructing the people in the endowment. Young believed that the presentation of the ordinances in the House of the Lord held the people together in that dispiriting time.[64]

ABRAHAM

The same month in which Joseph organized the Relief Society and entered Masonry, he published the Book of Abraham. Parts had been translated when the text was first purchased from the traveling exhibitor Michael Chandler in 1835, but in the press of business Joseph had trouble getting back to it. He had originally spoken of two texts, one about Abraham and the other about Joseph of Egypt. Nothing was ever seen of the Joseph text. The portions of Abraham that appeared in the *Times and Seasons* ran for two issues and then abruptly ended as if another installment was on the way.

The newspaper's introduction of Abraham was brief:

A TRANSLATION

Of some ancient Records that have fallen into our hands, from the Catecombs of Egypt, purporting to be the writings of Abraham, while he was in Egypt, called the BOOK OF ABRAHAM, written by his own hand, upon papyrus.[65]

Joseph had been similarly unforthcoming about the *Book of Mormon* when it was first published. Nothing is said about the process of translation, who did it, or by what means. In a gesture toward scripture, the printer divided the text into thirty-two verses.

The Book of Abraham had no immediate applicability to Church affairs. It contained no divine directives and was not even proposed as new scripture until 1876. The book sits suspended out of time, its importance suggested only by its top billing above the "History of Joseph Smith" in the newspaper. But Joseph hired Reuben Hedlock to engrave three pictures found on the scrolls, a job that took months. There is no question that Joseph valued this book, which shows him in his pure revelatory mode.

The book, generously enlarging the Bible story, follows Abraham's life from his youth in Ur of the Chaldees through his departure for Canaan and journey into Egypt.[66] After expanding these familiar accounts, Joseph's Abraham inserts a disquisition on astronomy.[67] Abraham receives instruction through a Urim and Thummim, a revelatory instrument like the one Joseph received with the plates of the *Book of Mormon*, and talks with the Lord "face to face" about the stars. The text says the astronomical information was revealed for Abraham's use in Egypt. Joseph interpreted one of the three facsimiles to be a picture of Abraham in Egypt "reasoning upon the principles of Astronomy, in the kings Court," while Pharaoh and his prince listen. The "explanation" of another facsimile gives the stars and planets Egyptian names. One is "called in Egyptian Enish-go-on-dosh." Stars are named "Kli-flos-is-es," "Hah-ko-kau-beam," and "Oliblish." The name for the "firmanent of the heavens," on the other hand, is given in Hebrew as "Raukeeyang."[68]

Joseph had offered astronomical speculations before, and all of these excursions conformed to a Copernican view of the stars and planets, not the older views of Ptolemy. The Ptolemaic system, with stars and planets circling the earth at the center of Creation, had appealed to early Christian theologians because it imagined God outside the heavens, creating and controlling a fixed system of stars and planets revolving around the earth, the scene of man's redemption. The Copernican system—with the sun, not the earth, at the center of the solar system circled by planets—shocked theologians. If the earth was not unique and central, Christ's redemptive role was open to question. As Emerson wrote, "the irresistible effect of Copernican astronomy has been to make the great scheme of salvation of man absolutely incredible." It took centuries for Christians to accommodate the new conceptions of the universe.[69]

After Copernicus, astronomers identified other planets revolving around the sun and postulated the existence of many other planets in distant solar systems. Many Copernican astronomers believed the universe was infinite, filled with innumerable star systems. The Book of Moses, Joseph's 1830 revelation, incorporated this astronomy by populating the heavens with numerous worlds, all made through Christ, all redeemed by Him. "Worlds without number have I created," the Lord tells Moses. Joseph's revelation drew out precisely what an expanding universe implied for the earth as one dot in a voluminous expanse of stars and planets. Joseph's Enoch spoke of "millions of earths like this."[70] By making God the creator of many earths, Joseph dealt with the theological problem of an infinite universe jeopardizing the role of a creator God. His theology recognized that an expanding universe meant endless expansion for God too.

Alexandre Koyré in his seminal study *From the Closed World to the Infinite Universe* posed another problem. "An infinite and eternal world . . . can hardly admit creation. It does not need it; it exists by virtue of this very infinity."[71] If the universe is endless in time and space, what need for God? Rather than struggle against the universe's infinity, Joseph's revelations accepted it. All matter was as eternal as God, he taught. Most Christian theologians could not relinquish the idea of a time prior to Creation when there was nothing (not even time) but God. God must be the creator of it all, or He was no God. In Joseph's revelations, God formed individual earths inside time and space rather than creating the universe as a whole from the outside. God did not have to create and control existence in order to be God. He could dwell within eternal time and space, making worlds and peopling them with spirits. He was the master of the universe rather than its originator.

The Abrahamic astronomy, unlike the astronomy of the Book of Moses, was a peculiar mixture of the Ptolemaic and the Copernican. In keeping with the new astronomy, Abraham speaks of central, powerful stars "governing" the planets as the sun governs the solar system: "And I saw the stars also that they were very great, and that one of them was nearest unto the throne of God; and there were many great ones, which were near unto it."[72] These great stars govern lesser planets and stars, like the sun governs the planets of the solar system, but in a different way. Abraham says nothing about orbits, solar systems, or gravity, the means of governance in scientific astronomy, but power still radiated from one to the other as the new astronomy prescribed.

More in the spirit of Ptolemy than Copernicus, Abraham's universe was ranked and ordered. For Abraham the key is being "nearest unto the throne of God," as if nearness brought power. Stars at this center held greater sway than more remote objects. A "set time" governed each star or planet. On "Kolob," the great star nearest to God's throne, one revolution equaled one thousand years in earth time, the equation given by Peter in the New Testament. Kolob's greatness and its slowness went together. By the same measure, the moon ruled the earth by night (because "it moveth in order more slow") and the sun ruled by day. Abraham's astronomy envisioned an ascending order of planetary rule based on slowness of time. Wherever there was one planet or star, "there shall be another planet whose reckoning of time shall be longer still; and thus there shall be the reckoning of the time of one planet above another, until thou come nigh unto Kolob, which Kolob, is after the reckoning of the Lord's time; which, Kolob, is set nigh unto the throne of God, to govern all those planets which belong to the same order of that upon which thou standest."[73] The series moved from the earth's "order" of planets upward through ever slowing planets, moons, suns, and stars to Kolob.

The destruction of Ptolemaic astronomy had wrecked the idea of ascent from the dank earth to the stars and then to God's heaven. The Copernican system replaced the old order with an infinite scattering of stars and planets of various sizes and orbits in no hierarchical arrangement, making the universe no longer a cosmos.[74] Abraham's astronomy with its multiple worlds partook of the new Copernican universe, while the tight ordering of planetary rule restored the spirit of the old Ptolemaic.

This fundamental cosmic order was mirrored in humans' relationship with God. Midway through the text, the Lord compares humans to the stars. The ranking of the planets and stars, the Lord said, carries over to the ranking of spirits: "The Lord said unto me, these two facts do exist, that there are two spirits, one being more intelligent than the other, there shall be another more intelligent than they; I am the Lord thy God, I am more intelligent than they all." Like the stars, the spirits rise in ascending order to God, echoing the traditional idea of the Great Chain of Being.[75] The verse suggests that the source of God's authority comes from his being the highest and greatest of the intelligences, "more intelligent than they all." Years earlier, Joseph had written that "the glory of God is intelligence, or, in other words, light and truth."[76] Now he showed a universe filled with individual intelligences ruled by a God who was "more intelligent than they all." God's power grew out of his glory and intelligence rather than his having created everything out of nothing.

This assembly of ranked stars and ranked intelligences added to Joseph's stories of eternity. The revelations extended God's history back into the primordium before the world was. Earlier, the *Book of Mormon* took priesthood back to "the foundation of the world." The ceremonial dramas in the endowment began with God planning the earth and sending emissaries to create it. The Book of Abraham returned to pre-earth history to describe the role of the pre-mortal spirits. Abraham envisioned God descending to an assemblage of intelligences to organize them:

> Now the Lord had shewn unto me, Abraham, the intelligences that were organized before the world was; and among all these were many of the noble and great ones, and God saw these souls that they were good, and he stood in the midst of them, and he said, these, I will make my rulers; for he stood among those that were spirits, and he saw that they were good; and he said unto me, Abraham, thou art one of them, thou wast chosen before thou wast born.

God, the most intelligent of the intelligences, and perhaps more intelligent than all of them combined, chose from the ranks of intelligences those he could trust to govern the earth. Christ, preeminent among them, was given responsibility for creation with the aid of others in the council: "And there stood one among them that was like unto God, and he said unto those, who were with him, we will go down, for there is space there, and we will take of these materials, and we will make an Earth whereon these may dwell." In the creation account that follows, the text speaks of "Gods" forming the earth. The earth was the work of multiple creators: "And then the Lord said, let us go down; and they went down at the beginning, and they organized and formed, (that is, the Gods,) the heavens and the earth."[77]

On the eve of the Creation, evil enters the picture, for at this moment Satan offers to take charge. A decade earlier, the Book of Moses had spoken of Satan's offer to redeem all mankind without exception and his asking for God's glory in return. God rejects Satan's proposal because he "sought to destroy the Agency of man" and take glory to himself. "Give me thine honor, which is my power." Abraham briefly alludes to this contest in which Satan is cast out: "And the Lord said, who shall I send? And one answered like unto the Son of Man, here am I, send me. And another answered and said, here am I, send me. And the Lord said, I will send the first." The first, of course, is Christ, and the second, Satan, whose rejection turns him into a rebel. "And the second was angry, and kept not his first estate, and, at that day, many followed after him."[78] Satan takes with him a great number of the intelligences. Like Milton's Lucifer, Abraham's Satan is a magnetic figure. He draws followers who become angels to the devil.

The prehistory of the earth, like all foundation stories, implied the purpose of the existence that followed. All the misled spirits lost "their first estate," as Abraham puts it. Those who remained and came to earth kept theirs, but here they would be tested again: "And they, who keep their first estate, shall be added upon; and they, who keep not their first estate, shall not have glory in the same kingdom, with those who keep their first estate; and they, who keep their second estate, shall have glory added upon their heads for ever and ever."[79] The first estate presumably came to the intelligences by following God up until the Creation; the second estate is acquired by remaining true through the trials of earth life. Those who keep both estates receive boundless glory.

From Joseph's three Creation stories and comments in his sermons emerges a patchy but coherent picture of the primordial history of humanity. At the center are God and the intelligences, the primal and uncreated stuff of individual persons. All intelligences are ranked. God's great virtue is the superiority of His intelligence. The intelligences ascend in order to God. (Arguably, they descend too.) God's great work is to lead those intelligences, who are embodied in His own image, to immortality and eternal life—to bestow on them the fulness of His own glory. To do this, He enlists "noble and great ones," the greatest being Christ, who becomes His Only Begotten Son. With the aid of these great ones, Christ creates the earth.

Earth life becomes a test. As Abraham's Christ puts it: "We will prove them herewith, to see if they will do all things whatsoever the Lord their God shall command them." If the intelligences obey and hearken to God's spirit as they did in the earth's prehistory, they will have glory added upon their heads forever and ever—virtually without limit, meaning an eternal increase of intelligence and glory. That expansion begins during life on earth. A year after publishing Abraham, Joseph observed: "Whatever principle of intelligence we obtain in this life will rise with us in the resurrection: and if a person gains more knowledge in this life through his diligence & obedience than another, he will have so much the advantage in the world to come." Intelligence, which here means more than knowledge and intellectual capacity, goes with light rather than darkness, good rather than evil. Clever as Satan is, "light and truth forsaketh that evil one." Intelligence seems closely related to comprehension, including the understanding of good and evil. Through obedience and following the light, intelligence goes on growing through eternity.[80]

No other nineteenth-century religious imagination filled time and space with stories like these. William Blake's mystical forays have a similar spirit but lack the single narrative core. Thomas Dick, a Scottish Presbyterian minister, shared Joseph's interest in the theological implications of an open universe with innumerable worlds, but Dick's *Philosophy of a Future State*, a book Sidney Rigdon owned, could only conceive of celestial spirits spending eternity observing the wonders of God's extensive creations.[81] He had no story of eternity to tell. Only Joseph Smith wrote a pre-earth history of God and then filled out humanity's future in the expanding universe.

Did Joseph realize he was departing from traditional Christian theology? The record of his revelations and sermons gives no sense of him arguing against received beliefs. He does not refer to other thinkers as foils for his views. He was only vaguely aware of overthrowing entrenched theological traditions in making matter and intelligence eternal or in depicting the Saints on their way to becoming gods. His storytelling was oracular rather than argumentative. He made pronouncements on the authority of his own inspiration, heedless of current opinion.

Yet stroke by stroke over the years, Joseph's revelations pictured a world of infinite possibilities, one compatible with the new astronomy of infinite space, and with America's expansive sweep towards the Pacific. Joseph's contemporary, the French political philosopher Alexis de Tocqueville, wrote that when "castes disappear and classes are brought together," as they were in America, "when men are jumbled together and habits, customs, and laws are changing . . . when old conceptions vanish and new ones take their place, then the human mind imagines the possibility of an ideal but always fugitive perfection." It is hard to think of a time in the world's history when a culture of boundlessness prevailed so widely as in America in the 1840s or was expressed with greater bravura than in the revelations of Joseph Smith.[82]

TWENTY-SIX

PERILS

As for the perils which I am called to pass through they seem but a small thing to me, as the envy and wrath of man have been my common lot all the days of my life.

JOSEPH SMITH TO ALL THE SAINTS, Sept. 1, 1842

EVEN THE UNITED STATES IN THE 1840s could not support Joseph Smith's lofty ambition. The luxuriance of his designs doomed him to controversy, opprobrium, and violence, as was already evident in 1842. In an August letter to the *New York Herald*, John C. Bennett, Joseph's Judas, called for war on the Mormons: "Nothing short of an excision of the cancer of Mormonism will effect a cure." Military power must "perform the operation at the edge of the sword, point of the bayonet, and mouth of the cannon." The *Boston Transcript* agreed that Mormonism was "a cancer upon our free institutions," and the sooner it was "CUT OFF the better."[1]

Joseph's sunny spring of 1842, with its flowering of doctrine, ritual, and institutions, turned cold in mid-May. The summer brought only strife and fear. At the center of the reversal was Bennett, Joseph's collaborator in founding Nauvoo. Bennett's success in obtaining a charter for the city in December 1840 was rewarded by election as first mayor in February 1841 and appointment as major general in the Nauvoo Legion, making him its effective commander. Bennett never aspired to spiritual leadership. He preached politics and urban improvements, not theology. He was not included in the select group to whom Joseph gave the endowment in 1842. Yet he was for a time the confidant of the Prophet. His sudden rise to power was another sign of the vacuum of experienced leadership. Joseph trusted converts with literary or administrative talent before their character was tested. Only after homegrown leaders like Brigham Young developed could Joseph reduce his dependence on these frail reeds. Bennett's political influence seemed a godsend when he first appeared; in the end he was a disaster. Thomas Ford, governor of Illinois in 1842, called Bennett "probably the greatest scamp in the western country."[2]

Joseph heard rumors of Bennett's shady character not many months after his arrival in Nauvoo in the late summer of 1840.[3] Bennett, it was said, had a respectable wife who had left him in the face of repeated infidelities. Joseph chose to disregard the accusations until a letter from Hyrum Smith in June 1841 confirmed the speculation. When confronted with the facts, Bennett broke into a paroxysm of remorse. He pled for forgiveness and begged not to be exposed, showing his desperation by swallowing poison.[4] Persuaded of Bennett's sincerity, Joseph agreed to overlook the past and leave him in his posts. In need of Bennett's political and oratorical skill, Joseph propped him up for over a year.

Joseph broke with Bennett in May 1842 after learning that he had been making overtures to various Nauvoo women, wed and unwed. Bennett told one woman after another that illicit sexual intercourse was acceptable if kept secret. Church leaders, Bennett claimed, were engaging in the same practice. It was a nightmare for Joseph to have his carefully regulated celestial marriages debased into a device for seducing the unsuspecting, and Bennett was not the only one who did it. Chauncey Higbee was brought before the high council in May 1842 for approaching three women with the same line. Higbee's victims testified that he had "taught the doctrine that it was right to have free intercourse with women if it was kept secret &c and also that Joseph Smith [au]therised him to practice these things."[5] The rationalizations were an unintended consequence of the plural marriage doctrine, now warped into a scheme for tricking women. Bennett never denied his Nauvoo adulteries, but he charged Joseph Smith with exactly the same wrongdoing.[6]

The growing ill will came out at the May 1842 review of the Nauvoo Legion. Joseph's journal at the time spoke happily of the occasion: "The day was very fine, & passed away very harmoniously, without drunkenness, noise or confusion." But several years later, Joseph's clerk Willard Richards described a plot against Joseph's life during a sham battle. Bennett asked Joseph to take a position at the rear of the cavalry without his usual guards. Albert Rockwood, the commander of Joseph's bodyguards, objected, and Joseph selected another spot with Rockwood by his side. The entry has Joseph commenting that "the gentle breathings of that spirit" whispered "there was 'mischief concealed in that sham battle.' "[7]

A few days later, on May 11, Joseph signed a certificate disfellowshiping Bennett, suspending his Church privileges, but not nullifying his membership. Joseph did not immediately deliver the certificate, waiting to see what direction Bennett would take. On May 17, Hyrum confronted Bennett with charges of seducing women. Confessing his sins, Bennett resigned as mayor but wept and begged forgiveness.[8] Still unwilling to cut Bennett off, Joseph exacted a statement swearing that the Prophet did not license illicit sexual relations. In an affidavit before Alderman Daniel Wells,

Bennett avowed that he "never was taught any thing in the least c[o]ntrary to the strictest principles of the Gospel, or of virtue, or of the laws of God, or man, under any occasion either directly or indirectly, in word or deed, by Joseph Smith." Thirteen witnesses attested that they heard Bennett's testimony. Two days later Joseph made Bennett testify again, before the city council this time, that "any one who has said that I have stated that General Joseph Smith has given me authority to hold illicit intercourse with women is a Liar in the face of God."[9]

The breach between Joseph and Bennett, however, could not be healed. At a high council trial on May 25, a victim accused Bennett of teaching her that illicit sexual relations were innocent, by claiming that Joseph was entering into such relationships. At this point, Joseph delivered the disfellowshiping notice. Again Bennett groveled. Hyrum, always suspicious of Bennett, advised no relenting, but Joseph hesitated, agreeing not to publish Bennett's misdeeds in the *Times and Seasons*. The next day Bennett confessed to the Nauvoo Masonic Lodge. He "cried like a child & begged that he might be spared." Joseph spoke on his behalf.[10]

Joseph went from the lodge meeting to the Female Relief Society, where he preached to the sisters about his efforts to bring iniquity to light. He was torn by Bennett's behavior. He wanted to recover the man in whom he had put so much trust. He told the sisters that it was

> melancholy and awful that so many are under the condemnation of the devil & going to perdition.
>
> With deep feeling [he] said that they are our fellows—we lov'd them once, shall we not encourage them to reformation? We have not [yet] forgiv'n them seventy times—perhaps we have not forgiven them once.[11]

He was still unsure how to deal with Bennett—to condemn and cast him out, or to forgive and attempt a reformation.

Joseph let Bennett down gently, stripping him of authority in the city and the Church, taking over as mayor without fanfare.[12] But in early June, news came of Bennett's earlier expulsion from an Ohio Masonic lodge, a fact not verified before, and Joseph learned of additional men who had adopted Bennett's rationalization of illicit sexual relations. In midmonth, Joseph published Bennett's disfellowshiping letter in the *Times and Seasons* and backed his expulsion from the Nauvoo Masonic Lodge. On June 18, Joseph spoke against Bennett's "iniquity & wickedness" in an open meeting.[13]

All along Bennett had pled not to be exposed, once claiming it would break his mother's heart. He could deal with the high council, the Masons, and Joseph and Hyrum, when they brought charges against him, but he could not bear the world to know his shame. On June 21, with his story now in the open, he left town, claiming Orrin Porter Rockwell was trying to kill him. He returned briefly a week later, but reconciliation was now impossible.[14]

During the first ten days of July, Bennett sat in Carthage, twenty miles from Nauvoo, writing furious letters. The *Sangamo Journal* editor, who had earlier refused to publish Bennett's favorable account of the Prophet, urged Bennett to write an exposé.[15] Bennett obliged with a long list of accusations published in seven letters from July to September, writings later expanded into a book. Bennett claimed that the Prophet had sent Danites to murder him, and that Joseph, not Bennett, was the seducer of women. The oath attesting to Joseph's moral purity was extracted, Bennett claimed, at gunpoint. He asserted that he knew all along Joseph was an adulterer but feared to say so. Joseph, among his lesser sins, was taking illegal advantage of the bankruptcy law and cheating on Masonic regulations for advancement through the ranks.[16]

Joseph realized that Bennett could arouse the countryside against the Mormons. The Missouri government had been attempting to extradite the Prophet for over a year on the old charges, and the Illinois countryside, thanks partly to Thomas Sharp's prodding, bristled with anti-Mormon sentiment. There were rumors of Bennett forming an anti-Mormon party. In the force of rising hostility, Joseph feared he might be kidnapped and carried to Missouri. He imagined the Missouri expulsion repeated in Illinois and the Mormons forced from their homes once more.[17]

In midsummer, Joseph wrote to Governor Carlin of Illinois to say that Bennett had been dismissed from his city offices and to ask for advice on how to react if attacked. "In case of any mob coming upon us, I wish to be informed by the Governor what will be the best course for us to pursue, and how he wishes us to act in regard to this matter." Joseph was asking about self-defense. Mormon self-defense had provoked the extermination order in Missouri. Would it bring the same reaction in Illinois? He signed the letter, "Joseph Smith, Lieutenant-General, Nauvoo Legion."[18]

Joseph thought he might reduce animosity if he could "correct the public mind." A common accusation in Missouri was that Joseph put his revelations above the law. To answer the charge, a meeting of Nauvoo citizens resolved that so far as they knew Joseph was "a good, moral, virtuous, peaceable and patriotic man, and a firm supporter of law, justice and equal rights; that he at all times upholds and keeps inviolate the constitution of this State and of the United States." The Female Relief Society drew up a petition, signed by nearly a thousand women, speaking of Joseph's "virtue integrity honesty." A newspaper, the *Nauvoo Wasp*, was founded to counter "the shafts of slander." The Nauvoo City Council assured Governor Carlin that to their knowledge Joseph Smith had "violated no Law, nor has he in any wise promoted sedition, or Rebellion."[19] The council did not know that

Joseph was then breaking the state's antibigamy law, putting the law of God above the law of man. Though he was law-abiding in most respects, plural marriage put Joseph at odds with moral and legal conventions of all kinds.

Throughout July, the Saints collected affidavits attesting to Bennett's misdoings. People who had known Bennett recounted his unforced confessions, repeating the affirmations that Joseph had never authorized adultery. Bennett, meanwhile, journeyed from city to city, lecturing against the Mormons. From St. Louis, he published a letter claiming Joseph's complicity in an assassination attempt on Lilburn Boggs. He persuaded Martha Brotherton, a former Mormon who had fled Nauvoo, to tell the story of Brigham Young's proposal of plural marriage. Enough editors credited Bennett's sensational disclosures for him to get frequent hearings. By late July he was in Louisville, publishing his exposures in the *Louisville Daily Journal*. Then it was on to Cleveland, Buffalo, and New York City.[20]

In New York, to his surprise, Bennett found Willard Richards. They met at the house of James Arlington Bennet, a non-Mormon sympathizer who lent moral support to the Saints. John C. Bennett wanted to turn James Arlington Bennet against the Prophet, but the latter thought the former mayor of Nauvoo was a character "of the very worst stamp." James A. Bennet had earlier written a letter to the *New York Herald* over the pseudonym "Cincinnatus" and hoped it would counteract some of the bad effects of Bennett's virulent writing.[21]

Richards was one of the missionaries that Joseph and the Twelve had dispatched to "deluge the States with a flood of truth." When they asked for volunteers, 380 men came forward. From then on, Bennett was likely to face objections from Mormon elders wherever he lectured.[22] His campaign was further handicapped by his previous notoriety as a prominent Mormon, Nauvoo mayor, and major general of the legion. Even Thomas Sharp, the zealous anti-Mormon editor of the *Warsaw Signal*, questioned Bennett's motives. Having lost his high position in Nauvoo, was Bennett seeking vengeance? His extravagant charges in *The History of the Saints; or an Exposé of Joe Smith and Mormonism*, a book based on his letters to the *Sangamo Journal* and published in Boston in October 1842, at the climax of his lecture tour, gave editors pause. The *New York Herald* could not "believe half the filthy things it contains." The *Boston Post* thought it a "heap of monstrosities." Thomas Ford, after looking into Bennett, concluded "he was everywhere accounted the same debauched, unprincipled and profligate character." Yet many editors thought Bennett presented the "true character" of the Mormons. They cautioned readers to discount Bennett's claims, but considered the book a needed antidote to a poisonous religious sect. "Cancer" was a word commonly used.[23]

In *History of the Saints*, Bennett explained that his conversion to Mormonism was a public-spirited desire to expose a plot. He considered Joseph's ambitions stupendous and terrifying. Smith was entertaining a "deep-laid scheme" to erect "a despotic military and religious empire, the head of which, as emperor and pope, was to be Joseph Smith, the Prophet of the Lord." The aim was control of the entire region between the Rockies and the Allegheny Mountains, starting with dominance of Missouri, Illinois, and Iowa. The rest of the states would be "licked up like salt." Bennett claimed he was trying to save the nation "from the most dreadful evils—civil war, despotism, and the establishment of a false and persecuting religion."[24]

As supposed religious fanatics, the Mormons followed a well-known plan. Mormon ambitions, Bennett claimed, could be foretold before they acted from knowledge "of the course of such fanatics afforded us by history." Fanatics always forced their beliefs on the rest of the world and exterminated anyone who resisted. For support Bennett referred to another anti-Mormon book published that summer, Jonathan Baldwin Turner's *Mormonism in All Ages*, which Bennett quoted at length.[25]

Turner, a Yale-educated professor at Illinois College in Jacksonville, was among a band of New Englanders who came to Illinois to raise the level of civilization in the West and prevent the spread of Catholicism. By 1842 he had come to believe that Mormonism might take over the region. The Mormons, Turner was convinced, were one more example of a phenomenon that repeated itself through the ages. It coupled the innate human desire to worship with people's perverse resistance to doctrinal orthodoxy. When a desire for power on the part of a few was added to these human traits, fanatical beliefs were bound to result. Fanaticism stretched back to antiquity. Mormonism, Turner thought, was one of the many hideous errors imposed by scheming charlatans on the credulous multitude throughout history. Mormonism's early success foreshadowed a time when it might unite with other delusions and dominate the nation. "Mormonism, if suffered to spread extensively, and unite with Atheism and Romanism, its natural allies, will soon have power to disturb, not single states only, but the entire Union."[26]

While Turner diagnosed the Mormon cancer sociologically, Bennett's contribution to anti-Mormon lore was his description of the Prophet's "Seraglio." The harem idea sparked Bennett's imagination, as it captivated sensationalist writers on Mormonism for the rest of the century. He imagined three orders of women dedicated to the pleasures of Mormon men: the "Cyprian Saints," the "Chambered Sisters of Charity," and in the highest degree, "Cloistered Saints," or "Consecratees of the Cloister." The levels measured degrees of honor and respect, beginning with prostitutes and rising to the *"secret, spiritual wives"* of eminent Church leaders. Bennett saw in Mormonism "licentious Oriental courts, where debauchery has been, for ages, systematized and sanctioned by law and religion on the most extensive scale." Like an Oriental despot, Joseph schemed to dominate the Gentiles and control the West.[27]

The *New York Herald*'s James Gordon Bennett dismissed *History of the Saints* as a work of vengeance by a disappointed man. John C. Bennett may indeed have entertained ambitions for an inland empire under Mormon domination like the one he attributed to Joseph Smith. His charges against Joseph seem to have come out of his own fantasies. Bennett admitted he was the leading spirit in the Nauvoo Legion. He may have thought of himself as the brains of the Mormon kingdom, the one capable of organizing a city and protecting it with an army, while Joseph recruited the soldiers. Earlier, Bennett had spoken to the Saints of "armies of chariots and horsemen, and strong cohorts of footmen, great and terrible, with spears and banners, and the implements of war, forming to the sound of the clarion," implying these were Mormon forces.[28] He had asserted that "the master spirits of the age must rise," obviously himself and probably Joseph.[29] Along with a military empire, he was well on his way to making Nauvoo his private harem.

Bennett's fabulous exaggerations do not diminish the book's significance in the history of Mormonism. *History of the Saints* performed a notable cultural work in antebellum America: it dehumanized Joseph Smith. Bennett stripped Joseph of any human qualities, meaning that no sympathy or understanding had to be extended to him. Joseph was a fanatic, not a person, a threat and a horror, not a human being with feelings and rights. There need be no compunctions about using force against him. At the close of the book, Bennett urged his readers to stop Joseph Smith:

> If this Mormon villain is suffered to carry out his plans, I warn the people of these United States, that less than twenty years will see them involved in a civil war of the most formidable character. They will have to encounter a numerous and ferocious enemy, excited to the utmost by fanaticism and by pretended revelations from God, and led on by reckless, ambitious, and, in some respects, able scoundrels, who will not pause in the execution of their projects, even though to accomplish them they should deluge this fair land with the blood of her sons, and exterminate the results of the toil and the civilization of more than two centuries.

Bennett appealed to his fellow citizens to overcome their apathy. "Quit the forum for the field, and, meeting the Mormons with their own arms, crush the reptile before it has grown powerful enough to sting them to the death." The editor of a Burlington, Iowa, newspaper, thirty miles from Nauvoo, concluded that if half of Bennett's charges were true, the Mormons were "more diabolical, more dangerous and more deserving of destruction than any that can be found in the darkest dungeon in the land."[30]

DISSENSION

Besides poisoning the public mind, Bennett's attack sowed dissension among the Mormons themselves. His letter in the July 15 issue of the *Sangamo Journal* accused Joseph of making advances to Sarah Pratt, wife of one of Joseph's longtime loyal associates, Orson Pratt. Bennett claimed that while Pratt was in England with the other apostles in 1841, Joseph had proposed marriage. In *History of the Saints*, Bennett claimed that Sarah replied, "I believe in no such revelations," and sent the Prophet away. In a later private conversation, according to Bennett, who had become her confidant, she gave an impassioned speech about fearing and trembling "for the weak and uneducated of my sex," in the clutches of "an unprincipled libertine, sensualist, and debauchee."[31]

Bennett's disclosure stunned Orson Pratt. Had the Prophet tried to seduce his wife? To make matters worse, a story circulated of Bennett's possible involvement with Sarah. Nauvoo residents swore they witnessed long nocturnal visits and glimpses of the two in compromising positions. The non-Mormon but friendly Nauvoo resident Jacob Backenstos signed an affidavit stating flatly that Bennett had "illicit intercourse with Mrs. Orson Pratt." In public meeting, Joseph spoke openly about Bennett's relations with Sister Pratt.[32]

Orson Pratt faced two equally repulsive stories. Either his wife had received a proposal of marriage from the man Pratt thought was the Lord's anointed (Bennett's story), or she had compromised her virtue with John C. Bennett (Joseph's story). No contemporary report of Sarah's own version remains (save Bennett's account), but forty years later, after Orson's death, and after she had left the Church, she told a story that substantially supported Bennett against Joseph.[33] If that was the story she gave at the time, Orson was forced to choose between his wife and the Prophet, dreadful alternatives.

On July 15, Orson Pratt left a note to his wife and disappeared. "My sorrows are greater than I can bear! Where I am henceforth it matters not," he wrote. For a day he could not be found. Fearing Pratt would take his own life, Joseph organized a search of the city. While the search went on, Joseph called meetings to explain Pratt's plight and to further expose Bennett's schemes. Pratt was finally discovered five miles down the river sitting dazed on a log. Two days after the disappearance, Brigham Young wrote to Pratt's brother Parley: "Br Orson Pratt is in trubble in consequence of his wife, his feelings are so rought up that he dos not know whether his wife is wrong, or whether Josephs testimony and others are wrong and due Ly and he decived for 12 years—or not; he is all but crazy about matters." Relating the incident later, Young said Pratt's "mind became so darkened by the influence and statements of his wife, that he came out in rebellion against Joseph, refusing to believe his testimony or obey his counsel. He said he would believe his wife in preference to the Prophet." Joseph told Pratt that "if he did believe his wife and follow her suggestions, he would go to hell."[34]

In this rebellious mood, Orson Pratt refused to vote for a resolution supporting Joseph Smith's character. At a public meeting on July 22, Pratt rose to explain his opposition. In reply, Joseph asked, "Have you personally a knowledge of any immoral act in me toward the female sex, or in any other way?" Since Pratt was relying on the testimony of his wife and Bennett, his answer had to be no. After laboring with Pratt for days, the apostles decided he would not yield. On August 20, 1842, he was excommunicated.[35]

Bennett hoped to enlist Pratt and other disaffected Mormons in bringing Joseph down. George Robinson, Sidney Rigdon's son-in-law and once Joseph's clerk, connived with Bennett to rally the opposition. Robinson wrote on August 8 that Orson and Sarah Pratt, Rigdon, and probably others would soon "come out" with public denunciations.[36] Rigdon, whose poor health had reduced his role in the Presidency, had been further alienated by Joseph's proposal of plural marriage to his daughter Nancy. Through the fall, Robinson informed Bennett on the state of this incipient alliance. Joseph declared in a special conference on August 29, "As to all that Orson Pratt, Sidney Rigdon, or George W. Robinson can do to prevent me, I can kick them off my heels, as many as you can name."[37]

In early January, Bennett wrote to Rigdon and Orson Pratt as "Dear Friends," detailing his plans to drag Joseph into Missouri to stand trial on the old charges of murder, burglary, and treason. In addition, "We shall try Smith on the Boggs case," Bennett confided as if he were a principal in the scheme. "The war goes bravely on," he reported cheerfully. And then more ominously: "Smith thinks he is now safe—the enemy is near, even at the door. He has awoke the wrong passenger." Bennett promised that when the officers came for Joseph, Bennett himself would be nearby.[38]

But back in Nauvoo, Orson Pratt began to mend. He published a statement in an October 1842 issue of the *Nauvoo Wasp* denying Bennett's claim that he and Sarah were leaving Nauvoo and planning to expose Mormonism. When Rigdon passed along Bennett's January letter, Pratt handed it to Joseph. Perhaps as a result of this visible sign of support, Pratt's case was reconsidered by the council of the Twelve. Joseph ruled on a technicality that Pratt had not been officially excommunicated back in August. Then the two men spoke directly about Sarah. "She lied about me," said Joseph. "I never made the offer which she said I did." He advised Orson to divorce Sarah and begin another family. Orson, still loyal to his wife, demurred. He was reinstated as an apostle, and that afternoon both he and Sarah were rebaptized in the Mississippi.[39] By the time Orson left Nauvoo in 1846, he had taken four additional wives.

IN HIDING

Joseph was on the run during the summer of 1842, trying to elude arrest for his suspected complicity in the attempt to assassinate Lilburn W. Boggs, the former governor of Missouri. About nine o'clock on the evening of May 6, 1842, while reading the newspaper in his Independence house, Boggs received a damaging but not fatal blast of buckshot to his head from a shot through the window. Suspicion was first directed to Boggs's rivals in a heated campaign for a state senate seat, but two weeks later, anti-Mormons in Illinois reported rumors that Joseph Smith was responsible. The *Quincy Whig* claimed Joseph had predicted Boggs's violent death a year before. Joseph denied the charge in a letter to the editor, but the rumors would not die. Governor Carlin told the Prophet his own followers had reported the supposed prophecy. In one of his letters to the *Sangamo Journal*, Bennett claimed Joseph had offered a five-hundred-dollar reward for Boggs's death. Still angry with the former governor for his treatment of the Saints, the *Wasp* commented that "who did the noble deed remains to be found out."[40]

Bennett named Orrin Porter Rockwell as the likely assassin. He reported that Joseph said months before that Rockwell had left Nauvoo to *"fulfill PROPHECY."* Rockwell, a rough and ready loyalist of Joseph's, had been employed as the Prophet's bodyguard on his trip to Washington in 1839. Joseph called Rockwell "an innocent and a noble boy," but he was later to acquire a reputation as a gunslinging lawman in Utah. Months before the shooting, Rockwell had moved to Independence, the home of his in-laws, while awaiting the birth of his fourth child. There he worked as a stableman under an assumed name. Immediately after the shooting, he left for Nauvoo, arriving on May 14. Bennett's charges made Rockwell and Joseph prime suspects, and in late July, Bennett traveled to Missouri to publicize his suspicions. On July 20, Boggs charged Rockwell with the crime and asked Illinois to deliver him to Jackson County for trial. All the evidence was circumstantial, but against the history of the Boggs's treatment of the Mormons, the accusation seemed plausible.[41] Not until Rockwell was arrested, tried, and acquitted a year later would his innocence be proven.

Joseph was certain the Missourians would kill him the moment they had him in custody. He saw extradition proceedings as a pretext for kidnapping. To protect the Prophet, Joseph's allies in Nauvoo erected all the legal protections possible, utilizing the Nauvoo municipal courts as the chief bastion. On July 5, the city council passed an ordinance empowering the city courts to examine all outside arrest warrants and issue writs of habeas corpus. A warrant for Joseph's extradition would fall under this law, which required the municipal court to review such cases.[42]

The city council appealed to Governor Carlin to disregard the "false statements & seditious designs of John Cook Bennett," but all pleas were in vain. By August 8, the extradition papers had passed from Governor Thomas Reynolds of Missouri through Carlin to the deputy sheriff of Adams County. With two assistants, the sheriff arrested Rockwell in Nauvoo and took Joseph Smith into custody as an accessory before the fact. Now was the moment for putting the Nauvoo habeas corpus machinery to the test. The city council, which functioned as the municipal court, issued a writ, which gave the sheriff pause. Unsure of his legal grounds, he went back to Carlin for instructions. By the time he returned two days later, the prisoners were gone. Rockwell left for Philadelphia, and Joseph went into hiding.[43]

For the next three months, Joseph spent nearly half his time concealed in friends' houses outside of Nauvoo. He headed first for his uncle John Smith's across the river in the Mormon settlement of Zarahemla. From there, he sent word to Emma to meet him at an island in the Mississippi between Nauvoo and Montrose, bringing Hyrum and five trusted friends. The party set off in a skiff at night and met Erastus Derby rowing Joseph in from the Iowa side. The eight men and Emma sat in their skiffs near the mouth of a slough and discussed a course of action. They had heard that the governor of Iowa had issued a warrant for Joseph and Rockwell, making Iowa no more safe than Illinois. With little solid information to go on, the group surmised that Boggs was trying to extradite Joseph illegally, working through a justice of the peace instead of Governor Reynolds, turning the whole procedure into a legal sham. Boggs and the Missourians, the Mormons were sure, would do anything to get Joseph back "wether by legal or illegal means." The group agreed that for the time being Joseph should go into hiding at Edward Sayers's, outside of Nauvoo. Having decided on a plan, the party split up, and Jonathan Dunham rowed Joseph upstream while Albert Rockwood traveled upriver on foot to mark the landing place with signal fires.[44]

In order to visit her husband, Emma had to leave town without revealing her destination. She walked to Elizabeth Durfee's, where William Clayton, Joseph's clerk, picked her up and drove out of town in a carriage with the top down to advertise her departure. Clayton drove downstream four miles in the opposite direction from the hiding place, before turning off toward the prairie. They circled back north, staying away from Nauvoo, until they were near the farm. For the last mile, Emma and Clayton went through the timber on foot. After spending the night together at Sayers's, Joseph and Emma "both felt in good spirits" the next morning, Clayton noted, "and were very chearful." They talked, and Joseph read to Emma from his history.[45]

Emma carried back a letter from Joseph to Wilson Law, newly elected major general of the Nauvoo Legion. Joseph was going into wartime mode. With memories of the Missouri expulsions in mind, he was convinced "a mob spirit for the purpose of carrying out mob violence" was rising once more. This time he was determined not to surrender. "I never would suffer myself to go into the hands of the Missourians alive," he told Law. "If I by any means should be taken, these are therefore to command you forthwith, without delay, regardless of life or death to rescue me out of their hands." Perhaps uneasy about ordering the use of force, Joseph underscored the illegality of his arrest within Nauvoo where the charter gave the Saints control of all legal proceedings, "nothing short of the supreme court of this State, having authority to dis-annul them." Wanting to preserve the peace if possible, he would go into hiding. "But if this policy cannot accomplish the desire; let our Charter, and our municipality; free trade and Sailors rights be our motto, and go a-head David Crockett like, and lay down our lives like men." He invoked George Washington, the Spirit of '76, Captain Moroni's title of liberty, and the eternal God. "Let us plead the justice of our cause; trusting in the arm of Jehovah the Eloheem who sits enthroned in the heavens: that peradventure he may give us the victory."[46]

The next day, rumors circulated that the sheriffs were returning to Nauvoo to search every house. The alarmed brethren decided they must talk to Joseph. Seven of them set off by different routes about 9 p.m. and converged on Sayers's farm. They sat huddled in the woods in the warm August night and discussed plans. Everything else failing, they would send Joseph to the Wisconsin pine country, where Mormon workers were cutting lumber for the temple. Joseph himself was undecided. He would go, he wrote Wilson Law, "if I knew that they would oppress me alone and let the rest of you dwell peacably and quietly." Departure would make sense "if by that means wee could prevent the profusion [of] Blood." Law advised Joseph to remain in Nauvoo under shield of the municipal courts. If he stayed in hiding until the gubernatorial elections, his enemies would not guess he was there. Without Joseph as a prize, Law surmised, "they will not attempt any violence on the city."[47]

Until he heard from Law, Joseph was serious about leaving Nauvoo. He told Emma he was "tired of the mean, low, and unhallowed vulgarity, of some portions of the society in which we live." Six months away with his family "would be a savor of life unto life." He gave Emma detailed instructions about how to pack saddlebags and a valise and put them in a buggy with a trunk containing his heavy clothes. William Clayton was to come

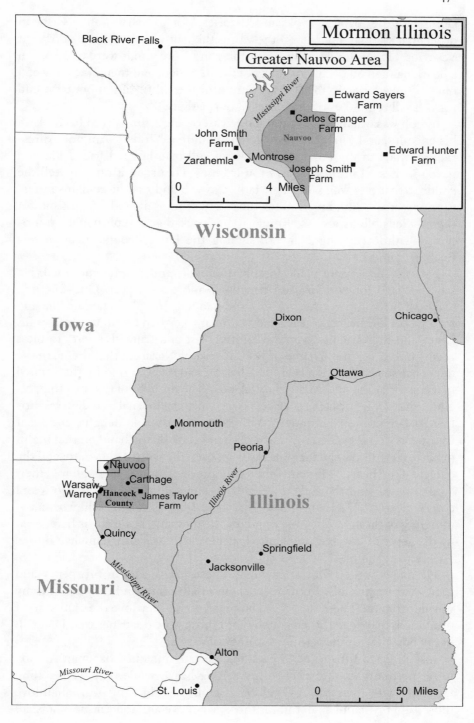

Mormon Illinois

Greater Nauvoo Area

Black River Falls

Mississippi River

Edward Sayers
Farm

Carlos Granger
Farm

Nauvoo

John Smith
Farm

Zarahemla

Montrose

Edward Hunter
Farm

Joseph Smith
Farm

0   4 Miles

Wisconsin

Iowa

Dixon

Chicago

Ottawa

Monmouth

Peoria

Nauvoo

Carthage

Warsaw
Warren

Hancock
County

James Taylor
Farm

Illinois River

Illinois

Quincy

Springfield

Jacksonville

Missouri

Mississippi River

Alton

Missouri River

St. Louis

0   50 Miles

along with the "papers, books and histories," for "we shall want a scribe in order that we may pour upon the world the truth like the Lava of Mount Vesuvius." Household furniture, clothes, and store goods were to be put in a boat, manned by twenty or thirty of the best men, and then "we will wend our way like larks up the Mississippi untill the to[we]ring mountains and rocks, shall remind us of the places of our nativity."[48]

Joseph was exhausted. He wanted to cast off everything, turn his back on his enemies, and retreat to his wife and children. "Tongue can not express the gratitude of my heart, for the warm and true-hearted friendship you have manifested in these things toward me." He urged Emma to "tell the children that it is well with their father, as yet; and that he remains in fervent prayer to Almighty God for the safety of himself, and for you and for them." Sensible as always, Emma wrote back that Joseph could be protected without leaving Nauvoo, signing the letter "yours affectionately forever, Emma."[49]

Fatigue and anxiety made Joseph vulnerable and a little emotional. He felt the need for comfort and friendship more than ever. One Tuesday, when all the company save for Clayton had left, Joseph dictated a blessing for Erastus Derby, his courier and boatman, and then began to speak of his "pure and holy friends, who are faithful, just and true." He felt "to bless them, and to say in the name of Jesus Christ of Nazareth that these are the ones that shall inherit eternal life." Joseph had been moved by the council in the skiffs at the mid-Mississippi island. As he thought of that meeting, his emotions, always near the surface, poured into the journal in the high sentimental language of his time: "With what unspeakable delight, and what transports of joy swelled my bosom, when I took by the hand on that night, my beloved Emma, she that was my wife, even the wife of my youth; and the choice of my heart." He remembered all they had passed through together: "the fatigues, and the toils, the sorrows, and sufferings, and the joys and consolations from time to time." Now here she was again. "Oh! what a comingling of thought filled my mind for the moment, again she is here, even in the seventh trouble, undaunted, firm and unwavering, unchangeable, affectionate Emma."[50]

He named other faithful friends. "These I have met in prosperity and they were my friends, I now meet them in adversity, and they are still my warmer friends. These love the God that I serve; they love the truths that I promulge; they love those virtuous, and those holy doctrines that I cherish in my bosom with the warmest feelings of my heart."

Joseph listed fifteen men by name, and one unnamed oarsman. "Many were my thoughts that swelled my aching heart, while they were toiling faithfully with their oars." Of all his friends, he said, "my heart shall love those; and my hands shall toil for those, who love and toil for me, and shall ever be found faithful to my friends."[51]

Joseph may have been a lonely man who needed people around him every moment. He told the Relief Society in Nauvoo how important consolation was to husbands after bearing the burdens of the day. During his exile he wrote of fighting off loneliness. "I have been kept from melancholy and dumps, by the kind-heartedness of brother [Erastus] Derby, and his interesting chit-chat . . . which has called my mind from the more strong contemplations of things, and subjects that would have preyed more earnestly upon my feelings."[52]

On August 18, Joseph wrote to Newel and Elizabeth Whitney asking them to come with their seventeen-year-old daughter Sarah Ann. Three weeks before, on July 27, Joseph had married Sarah Ann. The Whitneys had reacted to the marriage request with the usual horror, but had agreed to pray about it. They prayed unceasingly, until finally "we were seemingly wrapt in a heavenly vision, a halo of light encircled us, and we were convinced in our minds that God heard and approved our prayers." When Joseph invited the three to visit him in hiding, he told them his feelings were "so strong for you since what has pased lately between us." Then he spoke of his loneliness after just a few days without company. "If you three would come and see me in this my lonely retreat, it would afford me great relief, of mind, if those with whom I am alied, do love me, now is the time to afford me succour, in the days of exile."[53]

The Whitneys stole away from Nauvoo without Emma knowing. She was unaware of this marriage, and perhaps most of the others. Joseph would have preferred to take new wives with her consent, and may have asked for her cooperation. The later marriage revelation required men to consult with their wives, and allowed them to go ahead on their own only if their wives refused. In 1843 Joseph would approach Emma for consent, but her earlier opposition meant the 1842 marriages entangled Joseph in subterfuge and deception. Newel was to come ahead of the women and knock at Joseph's window, taking care to arrive when Emma was not there. The letter was to be burned upon receipt—though it survived to tell its tale. "Keep all locked up in your breasts, my life depends upon it," he warned them. The main reason for coming, he said, was to "git the fulness of my blessings sealed upon our heads," a reference perhaps to the sealing of Newel and Elizabeth in eternal marriage three days later. In closing, he appealed to them to consider "how lonesome I must be."[54]

Despite the concealment that lay between him and Emma, Joseph relied on her judgment and ability. Though he knew she would disapprove of his other wives, she was his chief contact with the city while he remained in hiding. When rumors went around that his whereabouts were known, she was the one who warned him to move from the Sayerses' to Carlos Granger's. When she was not with him, her letters conveyed information about business matters, showing her familiarity with real estate transactions.[55]

In August, Emma wrote two letters to Governor Carlin. She had met the governor in July when a delegation of Relief Society women conveyed a petition on behalf of the Saints. In hopes of ending the extradition proceedings, Emma pled with the governor on behalf of a people "who are not guilty of any offense against the laws of the Country; and also the life of my husband; who has not committed any crime whatever." When the governor professed himself bound by the law to deliver Joseph to Missouri, she wrote again asking him to "thoroughly acquaint yourself with the illegality of the prosecution instituted against Mr. Smith." This time she examined the Nauvoo charter and the ordinance granting authority to issue writs of habeas corpus. "Now, dear sir, where can be the justice in depriving us of these rights which are lawfully ours, as well as they are the lawful rights of the inhabitants of Quincy and Springfield?" Emma argued that Joseph could not be extradited to Missouri as a "fugitive" from justice; he had been in Illinois when Boggs was shot and could not be a fugitive from Missouri justice. She presented legal arguments and then appealed to the governor's common sense. "It only requires . . . a knowledge of the outrages committed by some of the inhabitants of that State upon the people called Mormons, and that pass'd unpunished by the administrators of the law; to know that there is not the least confidence to be placed in any of those men that were engaged in those disgraceful transactions."[56]

Emma's brisk letter evoked a sharp reply from Carlin. Laying aside the usual niceties due a lady correspondent, he launched an attack on her legal arguments. The charter authorized Nauvoo's municipal courts to issue writs in cases arising from city ordinances, he wrote Emma, not those originating in state or constitutional law. The claim to issue writs for all charges, Carlin erupted, "is most absurd & rediculous, and an attempt to exercise it, is a gross usurpation of power." Carlin dismissed the assertion that kidnappers from Jackson County lay in wait to abduct Joseph: "not one word of it is true." In his impatience, the governor neglected to deal with Emma's argument that the extradition was illegal because Joseph was not a fugitive from Missouri justice, having been in Illinois at the time of the Boggs shooting.[57]

After two weeks in hiding, Joseph was told to come home. Clayton noted that Joseph "received a few lines from sister Emma informing him that she would expect him home this evening believing that she could take care of him better at home than elsewhere." Joseph came as instructed. Emma may have sensed that Joseph was sinking into melancholy. The day before his return, his ruminations about friends had turned his mind to the past. "I have remembered the scenes of my child-hood. I have thought of my father who is dead, who died by disease which was brought upon him through suffering by the hands of ruthless mobs." Death lay heavy on his mind. He apparently was building a tomb for his family, and spoke of his father in elegaic language akin to the needlework depictions of tombs and weeping willows stitched by young ladies. "Sacred to me is his dust, and the spot where he is laid. Sacred to me is the tomb I have made to encircle o'er his head." He went over the names of other family members, living and dead. He wanted to bring them all together in death. "Let my father, Don Carlos, and Alvin, and children that I have buried be brought and laid in the tomb I have built. Let my mother, and my brethren, and my sisters be laid there also; and let it be called the Tomb of Joseph, a descendant of Jacob."[58]

STRATEGY

Once Joseph was back in Nauvoo, his spirits revived. He organized the corps of missionaries going out to counteract John Bennett's charges and saw to the publication of affidavits attesting to Bennett's corruption. When he showed up on the podium in the middle of a meeting in the grove, his sudden appearance "caused much animation and joy." Joseph felt that between the Nauvoo courts and his exile, he had outmaneuvered his enemies. "He had not fought them with the sword nor by carnal weapons; he had done it by stratagem or by outwitting them." He told the congregation, "We don't want or mean to fight with the sword of the flesh but we will fight with the broad sword of the spirit," perhaps a caution to men in the congregation who were all too ready to take up arms. Joseph made a show of strength—it was not in his nature to back down—but he veered from outright warfare. "I will fight them," he assured his hearers, "if they dont take off oppression from me. I will do as I have done this time, I will run into the woods. I will fight them in my own way."[59]

He could never settle the issue in his own mind—to run or to fight.[60] With his onetime advisor John C. Bennett out of the picture, Joseph needed a counselor wise in the ways of the world. In September, Joseph explained his dilemma in a letter to James Arlington Bennet, who besides being an author was a former military officer. James Arlington, fifty-four, had come on the Nauvoo scene through his *American System of Practical Book-keeping*, a well-known textbook adopted by the University of Nauvoo. Later the university bestowed an honorary degree on him.[61] Through this correspondence, an acquaintance with the Mormons began. Though he had encountered the Saints through John C. Bennett, the university's chancellor, James Arlington Bennet took Joseph's side. From then on, James Arlington remained a friend of the Prophet's, though little more. Bennet told Joseph frankly that "I have been long a Mormon in sympathy alone and probably can never be one in any other way, yet I feel that I am a friend of the people." He lightheartedly underwent baptism at Brigham Young's hands in 1842—Bennet called it "a glorious frolic in the clear blue ocean"—but refused to go west or become more involved.[62]

In his letter, Joseph spoke candidly to this man he had never met. "My bosom swells, with unutterable anguish," Joseph wrote in September 1842, "when I contemplate the scenes of horror that we have pass'd through in the State of Missouri and then look, and behold, and see the storm, and cloud, gathering ten times blacker—ready to burst upon the heads of this innocent people." What was he to do? "Shall we bow down and be slaves?" He wished the nation would come to the Saints' rescue and "wrench these shackles from the feet of our fellow citizens," but, failing that, should the Mormons defend themselves? On balance, he thought not. "The Legion, would all willingly die in the defence of their rights; but what would that accomplish?" Joseph had tried to calm the more militant Mormons. "I have kept down their indignation, and kept a quiet submission on all hands, and am determined to do so, at all hazards." He knew the attempt to drive away the mob in Daviess County had backfired; he did not want another extermination order. "Our enemies shall not have it to say, that we rebel against government, or commit treason; however much they may lift their hands in oppression, and tyranny." He was willing to submit to the government, he said, "although it leads us to the slaughter, and to beggary."[63]

Restraint seemed the best policy. And yet, with his instincts running in the opposite direction, he was not sure. "I wish you would write to me in answer to this and let me know your views." He was not concerned for himself. "I am ready to be offered up a sacrifice, in that way that can bring to pass, the greatest benifit, and good." But was that right? He needed advice. "I would to God that you could know all my feelings on this subject and the real facts in relation to this people." He suggested an investigating committee made up of wise outsiders to offer an impartial judgment to "an enlightened world" on whether the Mormons deserved "such high-handed treatment."[64]

Bennet had kept up with Mormon affairs through the newspapers and visitors like Willard Richards. Based on what he knew, he concurred in Joseph's conviction about Missouri justice: "how easy it would be to suborn witnesses against you who would seal your fate." On the other hand, "it will not do to oppose force to force, for your protection, as this in the present case would be treason against the State and would ultimately bring to ruin all those concerned." Avoiding the sheriff was the best Joseph could do for the moment. Yet after this cautious counsel, Bennet went off on a speculation worthy of John C. Bennett: "I most ardently wish that you had one hundred thousand *true* men at Nauvoo and that I had the command of them—*Times and things would soon alter.* I hope to see the day before I die that such an army will dictate times from Nauvoo to the enemies of the Mormon people." What was he thinking? Was Bennet imagining a Mormon kingdom in the midsection of the nation, defended by a huge army, with himself at the head? Was Bennet thinking along the same lines as Bennett? After all the persecution, Bennet told Joseph, "you will only be made a greater Prophet and a greater man a greater *Emperor.*" The open spaces of the West seemed to spark dreams of empire, and Joseph struck one observer after another as a likely leader of a great inland kingdom.[65]

While brooding over the Saints' predicament and reflecting on friendship and death, Joseph meditated on doctrine. In early September, he submitted two letters to the Saints about regulating baptism for the dead. In the first he grew philosophical: "The envy and the wrath of man have been my common lot all the days of my life and for what cause it seems mysterious, unless I was ordained from before the foundation of the world for some good end, or bad as you may choose to call it." He seemed resigned. "Deep water is what I am wont to swim in, it all has become a second nature to me."[66] He reflected on the doctrine and particularly the management of baptisms for the dead, instructing the Saints to appoint a recorder to witness the baptisms. As usual Joseph elevated this seemingly perfunctory procedure into something much larger. The witness was appointed "that in all your recordings it may be recorded in heaven . . . [that] whatsoever you bind on earth may be bound in heaven, and whatsoever you loose on earth may be loosed in heaven."

The letter is an example of Joseph's remarkable power to make religion. A clerical process, recording the baptisms, Joseph said, involved binding in heaven, the authority granted to Peter in the New Testament. Joseph said these very records would be opened when the dead, "small and great, stand before God." In other words, the baptismal records were the books to be reviewed on Judgment Day! In a move typical of Joseph, he made the transcendent literal and the mundane heavenly. The simple practice of noting the names of people being baptized for the dead became a heavenly act, a performance of sealing and judging. "Whatsoever you record on earth shall be recorded in heaven; and whatsoever you do not record on earth, shall not be recorded in heaven." He knew this would strike many as "a very bold doctrine," but then, in another typical move, he planted this present practice in history. "In all ages of the world, whenever the Lord has given a dispensation of the Priesthood to any man, by actual revelation, or any set of men; this power has always been given." The practice you are to follow now, he said, is practice of the people of God in all ages. History and heaven converged in the simple practice of recording names and actions at a baptism. In the space of a few paragraphs, the baptismal record became the book of life, recording became sealing, and the great powers promised to Peter were requisitioned for the Saints.[67]

Nowhere in his revelations does Joseph show more enthusiasm for his own work than in this letter. Whatever the miseries of the moment, he thrilled to think how the past had been welded to the present through the visions of the previous twenty years. Even after all the tension, fear, and melancholy of the summer, his unbounded enthusiasm for his revelations could not be suppressed.

> Now what do we hear in the gospel which we have received? A voice of glad-ness—a voice of mercy from heaven—a voice of truth out of the earth—glad tidings for the dead; a voice of gladness for the living and the dead; glad tid-ings of great joy! . . . What do we hear? Glad tiding from Cumorah! Moroni, an angel from heaven, declaring the fulfilment of the prophets—the book to be reveal'd! A voice of the Lord in the wilderness of Fayette, Seneca County, declaring the three witnesses to bear record of the Book. The voice of Michael on the banks of the Susquehanna, detecting the devil when he appeared as an angel of light. The voice of Peter, James & John, in the wilderness, between Harmony, Susquehanna County, and Colesville, Broom County, on the Sus-quehanna river, declaring themselves as possessing the keys of the kingdom, and of the dispensation of the fulness of times. And again, the voice of God in the chamber of old father Whitmer in Fayette, Seneca County, and at sundry times, and in divers places, through all the travels and tribulations, of this Church of Jesus Christ of Latter Day Saints. And the voice of Michael the archangel—the voice of Gabriel, and of Raphael, and of divers angels, from Michael or Adam, down to the present time; all declaring, each one their dis-pensation, their rights, their keys, their honors, their majesty & glory, and the power of their Priesthood; giving line upon line; precept upon precept; here a little and there a little: giving us consolation by holding forth that which is to come confirming our hope.[68]

No passage better captures Joseph Smith's restoration than this one, min-gling the names of "divers angels"—Michael, Gabriel, Raphael—with spe-cific, mundane places that one could locate on a map—Fayette, Seneca County, Colesville, Broome County, and the banks of the Susquehanna River. That mixing of the mystical with the plain was pure Joseph Smith. This very concreteness gave him his highest pleasure. After the doleful days in exile, the memory of angels delivering their keys to places where he had stood cheered his heart.

TRIALS

On September 3, Joseph went into hiding again. At noon on the first Satur-day in September, a well-armed deputy sheriff with two other men appeared at the Smiths' front door. Joseph was at the table eating dinner with his family when the threesome knocked. While John Boynton delayed the officers, Joseph slipped out the back and ran through a cornfield to the Whitneys'. The sheriff asked Emma for permission to search the house. She inquired if he had a warrant, which he did not, but she gave permission anyway. Two more men returned to search again after sundown. After dark, Joseph left the Whitneys' for Edward Hunter's.[69]

Joseph remained out of sight the next week, returning again when Emma said she wanted him back home. The next three months followed that pattern, times at home alternating with times away.[70] In late September, he was back. Emma fell ill with a fever, and Joseph sat with her day after day. The news that Governor Carlin had offered a $200 reward for Joseph's capture did not send him into hiding. After a week, Emma was so ill that she was baptized twice in the river, doing her "much good." Still she grew worse "and continues very sick indeed." After two weeks, she began to mend a little, allowing Joseph to go into hiding again.[71] This time he traveled through the night and part of the next day to the house of James Taylor. He returned home again on October 20 for a short visit with Emma and then returned to Taylor's. Finally on October 28, he returned for a longer stay, Emma being "some worse." She was up and down through the fall.[72]

In December 1842, this in-and-out life ended. The extradition proceedings were halted when Justin Butterfield, the United States district attorney for Illinois, passed along his opinion that the extradition of the Prophet was unconstitutional.[73] (Ironically, Butterfield was then prosecuting Joseph for payment on the steamboat that the federal government had sold to Peter Haws and that Joseph had co-signed for.) The constitutional provision for extradition, Butterfield told Sidney Rigdon, allowed a state to recover a "fugitive from justice," that is, a suspect who had fled the state, but Joseph was not in Missouri on May 6, when the crime occurred. If he had committed a crime, it occurred in Illinois, and Illinois officials, not the Missourians, would have to prosecute—a sophisticated version of Emma's position. Illinois's newly elected governor, Thomas Ford, accepted Butterfield's opinion, but was reluctant to reverse the action of his predecessor. Butterfield advised Joseph to take his case to the state supreme court, assuring him the justices were unanimously in his favor.[74] On December 27, Joseph, surrounded by fifteen supporters, left for the state capital in Springfield. At Joseph's request, Butterfield himself presented the petition, not to the Illinois Supreme Court, as it happened, but to the United States Circuit Court.[75] On January 5, Judge Nathaniel Pope handed down a favorable judgment. The Missouri writ for Joseph's extradition on charges of conspiring to kill Boggs was dead.

The case was argued at great length by Butterfield and then summarized and analyzed with equal intensity by Judge Pope. The judge delivered his opinion to a courtroom filled with spectators "of a very respectable class." Though doubtless curious about the fate of a man who called himself a prophet, the spectators were aware that the case had broader significance. In delivering an opinion on Joseph as a fugitive from justice, Pope linked the case to a far more controversial group of fugitives: runaway slaves. The abolitionist attack on slavery had been mounting for the past half dozen years, and in many northern states, the opposition focused on southern attempts to recover fugitive slaves. Just months before Joseph's hearing, the U.S. Supreme Court had ruled in *Prigg v. Commonwealth of Pennsylvania* that state governments should not pass laws interfering with the Fugitive Slave Act of 1793. That was federal business, and the states were not to interfere. Joseph was in the same position as a fugitive slave. Butterfield asked at one point if Joseph Smith had "the Rights of a negro," by which he meant whether federal law applied in this case, rather than the actions of the Missouri chief executive. Rather than give way to Missouri's wishes, Butterfield argued, Illinois must abide by the U.S. Constitution, which provided for extradition only for those who had fled justice. Judge Pope's ruling said "a criminal, fugitive from the one State to the other, could not be claimed as of right to be given up."[76] Joseph, like a fugitive slave, could not be recalled by state action.

During the time in Springfield, Willard Richards, the clerk for the trip, kept track of of public opinion. When Josiah Lamborn, the Illinois attorney general who was arguing that Joseph should be turned over to Missouri, observed that "Mr. Smith is a very good looking, jovial man," Richards put it down. As usual, Joseph won over the people he dealt with personally. "A peculiarly pleasant and conciliatory feeling prevailed through the company," Richards said of an informal gathering that included Lamborn and the marshal who had Joseph in custody. "The Marshall invited Joseph to a family dinner when he was freed." A New York reporter was impressed with the figure he cut. "The prophet is a large, portly, and fine looking man," he wrote, "six feet without shoes, looks about forty or forty-two, and weighs 220 pounds, eyes light blue, approaching to grey, light brown hair, peaked nose, large head." Strangely, the reporter judged Joseph had "little self esteem," but did see in him "more of the intellectual than the animal." Joseph was dressed in the costume he so often wears in posthumous portraits: "box coat, black, blue dress coat and pants, black silk velvet vest, white cravat, a large gold ring on the finger next to the little one of his left hand, a black cane, and wears a continual smile on his countenance."[77]

From the Mormons' point of view, the hearing was a success. Besides receiving a favorable verdict, "the utmost decorum and good feeling prevailed. Much prejudice was allayed." After the hearing, Judge Pope, obviously curious, invited Joseph into his room. Pope and Butterfield wanted to know if Joseph really believed himself to be a prophet. Joseph dodged the question by referring to a biblical passage about the testimony of Jesus being the spirit of prophecy. Every preacher should be a prophet. Butterfield asked about the price of lots in Nauvoo, and the other lawyers laughed, "saying he would be a Mormon in 6 weeks if he would go to Nauvoo."[78]

Joseph came away from Springfield happy: "I have met with less prejudice and better and more noble and liberal feelings on the part of the people generally than I expected." On the way home, Wilson Law composed a song that began

> And are you sure the news is true?
> And are you sure he's free?
> Then let us join with one accord,
> And have a Jubilee

The song was sung over and over, the company adding new verses as they went.

> We'll have a Jubilee, My friends
> We'll have a Jubilee
> With heart and voice we'll all rejoice
> In that our Prophet's free.

The jubilation went beyond their relief about Joseph. The Missouri extradition, combined with John C. Bennett's charges, had threatened the Church. The legal struggle could have ignited more persecution. After just three years in Illinois, the Saints foresaw another Missouri. But, for the moment, the fear was lifted. The law had come down on their side. "The whole party were very cheerful," Richards noted, and sang over and over:

> And now we're bound for home my friend
> A bond of brothers true
> To cheer the heart of those we love
> In beautiful Nauvoo.[79]

TWENTY-SEVEN

THICKETS

1843

It is my meditation all the day & more than my meat & drink to know how I shall make the saints of God to comprehend the visions that roll like an overflowing surge, before my mind.

JOSEPH SMITH, April 16, 1843

BACK IN NAUVOO AFTER THE Springfield hearing, Joseph continued in an exultant mood. The charges against him had been heard in the state capital and dismissed; the Missourian plots to recapture him had been defeated; and John Bennett had failed to gain allies in the Church. On Tuesday, January 17, Joseph declared a day of "humiliation fasting & prayer & thanksgiving" with meetings held in each city ward. The next day, he and Emma entertained over fifty invited guests at four long tables in his Nauvoo mansion. Joseph handed out cards printed with new verses of the Jubilee song celebrating his vindication in Springfield. While he and Emma served the guests, Joseph announced that this was their sixteenth wedding anniversary. There were "many jokes," and after dinner people told stories.[1]

The description of the dinner came from Willard Richards, Joseph's personal secretary from December 1842 to the end of his life in June 1844. Since Joseph wrote so little about himself, we must rely on images filtered through the eyes of the people who knew him, and Richards, who virtually shadowed Joseph for the last year and a half of his life, wrote more about him than anyone. Richards was a close observer of Joseph's idiosyncrasies, noting his manners, his originality, his bravado. Richards picked up on details like the announcement of the wedding anniversary and the fact that Emma and Joseph waited on the guests. He wrote down Joseph's colorful phrases like "the opinions of men, so far as I am concerned, are to me as the crackling of the thorns under the pot, or the whistling of the wind." He noted Joseph's broad humor, as when he "laid down on the writing table with back of the head on Law Books saying write and tell the world I acknowlidge myself a very great lawyer. I am going to study law and this is the way I study and fell asleep and went to snoring."[2]

A stout man with dark brows and piercing eyes, Richards came from rural Massachusetts. As a young man, he had lectured on electricity and other scientific subjects, until he decided to study the Thomsonian method of treating illness with herbs. He was practicing near Boston in 1836 when he read the *Book of Mormon* and was converted. Six months later Richards was on his way to Britain with the first party of Mormon missionaries. There he was ordained an apostle. After four years, he returned to the United States with his bride, Jennetta, a British convert. Sensing capacity, Joseph appointed Richards a recorder and historian of Church business. Though Richards suffered from a tremor that must have affected his hand-writing, in December 1842 he took on the responsibility of keeping Joseph's journal.[3]

Richards gives us the playful Joseph Smith. Richards tells us when Joseph "pulled up Bro[ther] Moses with one hand pulling sticks," or "throwed the bully of Ramus wrestling." Although the incidents went into Richards's record, one cannot tell if he was amused or shocked by the Prophet's behav-ior. "About 4 [Joseph] took a game of ball east of Main street." Another day, he went out with Frederick, his six-year-old son, "to slide on the ice." Richards has Joseph cutting down a tree, attending "Mr. Vicker's perfor-mance of wire dancing, Legerdemain Magic, &c.," drinking "a glass of wine with Sister Richards of her mother's make in England." One day in May, Joseph set off with a party of a hundred on the Church's new steamboat, the *Maid of Iowa*, for twelve hours of merriment. Now that the Smiths had a house large enough for company, they entertained. We hear of large crowds for Christmas and another wedding anniversary celebration the next year.[4]

Richards does not betray his own feelings about a Prophet who wrestled and went to magic shows, but some visitors were dismayed. Charlotte Haven, an observant young lady from New Hampshire who heard Joseph report on his Springfield adventures, was appalled. "His language and man-ner were the coarsest possible. His object seemed to be to amuse and excite laughter in his audience." Expecting more from a man who claimed to be a prophet, she thought nothing he said "impressed upon his people the great object of life." Joseph appeared raucous and impious. He uttered not a word "calculated to create devotional feelings."[5] Haven did not happen upon a heavy doctrinal sermon like the one Wilford Woodruff recorded a week later in three compact pages of notes.[6] She caught Joseph entertaining his audience with the broad humor of the frontier orator. Abraham Lincoln used the same kind of rough talk to hold the attention of the crowd in New Salem and Springfield.

Joseph seemed to be aware of the seeming incongruity. "Many think a prophet must be a great deal better than any body else," he told a congregation. But if he were that much better, Joseph said with characteristic hyperbole, "I would be raised up to the highest heaven, and who should I have to accompany me?" That half-humorous exaggeration kept Joseph on a level with his audience. He spoke their rough language and shared their rough work. When seventy men gathered one cold February day to saw wood for the Prophet, he went with them to cut and draw a five-foot log. Rather than watching from behind a curtained window, he entered into the "pleasentry, good humor, and feeling."[7]

Richards seemed a little uncomfortable when Joseph began to boast. At Springfield, Richards noted that Joseph was criticized for lacking meekness. In the aftermath of his triumph, he cut loose with extravagant comments about his mastery: "I am a Lawyer. I am [a] big lawyer and comprehend heaven, earth, and hell to bring forth knowledge which shall cover up all Lawyers and doctors." Theologically, it was true that prophetic knowledge outranked legal knowledge, but did Joseph believe he was a master lawyer? Richards elsewhere recorded Joseph saying that by his doctoring he had "never failed" to administer comfort to "thousands" of sick people.[8] Later in an otherwise sober appeal for Vermont support of the Mormon petitions to Congress, Joseph inserted an extravagant aside about how people of various tongues expressed dismay.

> Were I a Chaldean I would exclaim: Keed'nauh ta-meroon le-hoam elauhayuh dey-shemayauh. . . .
> An Egyptian: Su e-eh-m: (What other persons are those?) A Grecian: Diaboles bassileuei: (The Devil reigns.) A Frenchman: Messieurs sans Dieu, (Gentlemen without God:) A Turk. Ain shems: (The fountain of light). . . .

And so on through seventeen languages. Among his other skills, the passage implied, Joseph was fluent in many tongues.[9]

The bragging is so exaggerated and so comical, one wonders what lay behind it. The literary scholar Kenneth Lynn, in a meditation on frontier humor, asks what motivated classic frontier boasts like "I am a man; I am a horse; I am a team. I can whip any man in all Kentucky, by G-d." For the frontiersman, Lynn speculates, "tall talk that began in whimsicality and ended in blasphemy . . . was a way of beating the wilderness at its own game, of converting terror into *joie de vivre* and helplessness into an exhilarating sense of power." One can glimpse in Joseph's boasts not horror at the wilderness but a desperate realization of the Saints' lowly social station. They were outcasts, subject to unending ridicule and scorn. Joseph's boasts made fantastic claims to learning and position, as a lawyer, a doctor, a linguist, a politician, the positions in respectable society from which his family and the Church were excluded. Lynn says frontiersmen sometimes "staged a ludicrously savage exhibition" to purposely shock eastern visitors, gaining a "splendid revenge" on sophisticates and thus "making would-be laughers laughable." Joseph's extravagant claims punctured the pretensions of the learned who looked down their noses at his pitiful collection of followers. Lynn said of Davy Crockett, "every defeat, big or small, was an unforgivable insult."[10] In that spirit, Joseph summed up his feelings once by declaring, "I bear record this morning that all the combined powers of Earth and hell shall not over come this boy." He could not bear to be degraded, and he craved respect. Richards noted the times when Joseph received unexpected regard. In February 1843, "some 7 or 8 young men called to see me, part of them from the city of N[ew] York. They treated me with the greatest respect."[11]

Soon after his return from Springfield, Joseph reported a violent dream:

> I dreamed this morning that I was in the Lobby of the Representative House at Springfield when some of the members who did not like my being there began to mar and cut and pound my shins with pieces of Iron. I bore it as long as I could, then Jumped over the rail into the hall, caught a rod of Iron and went at them cursing and swearing at them in the most awful manner and drove them all out of the house. I went to the door and told them to send me a clerk and I would make some laws that would do good. There was quite a collection around the State house trying to raise an army to take me and there were many horses tied around the square. I thought they would not have the privilege of getting me so I took a rod of Iron and mowed my way through their ranks, looking after their best race horrse thinking they might catch me when the[y] could find me when I was awoke.[12]

Joseph dreamed he had to fight his way out of the hall at Springfield. If he felt this way about a triumph, how must he have felt when actually besieged? Was he under constant pressure to either fight or flee?

Joseph was happiest in the company of plain men: "I love that man better who swears a stream as long as my arm and [is attentive to] administering to the poor and dividing his substance, than the long smoothed faced hypocrites." Having plain folks around him was his kind of heaven. He once said, "That same sociality which exists amongst us here will exist among us there only it will be coupled with eternal glory which glory we do not now enjoy." Company comforted him. He would feel blessed, he said, "if I am to be afflicted in this world to have my lot cast where I can find brothers and friends all around me."[13]

But even among his friends he felt cut off. He wanted desperately "to express my feelings once to my friends, but I never expect to." Separation from family and friends worried him. "If I had no expectation of seeing my mother, brother[s], and Sisters and friends again my heart would burst in a moment and I should go down to my grave." He was concerned about Saints who died in "a strange land," away from the company of their friends. His theological passion to weld families together extended to being buried close to the people he loved. He told a Nauvoo congregation that if buried together "in the morn of the resurrection they may come forth in a body and come right up out of their graves and strike hands immediately in eternal glory." He feared being left alone.[14]

MYSTERIES

Joseph's comments about resurrection registered with Richards because he was attuned to doctrine. He considered it his job to gather the pearls that Joseph strewed and to deposit them in the diary. Ever since Joseph emerged from Liberty Jail, he had dispensed doctrinal knowledge through sermons, letters, and comments. Earlier the Saints had thought of Joseph knocking at heaven's door and learning from God through formal revelations.[15] By Nauvoo, he was considered an experienced heavenly traveler, who knew the ways of the ancient prophets, conversed with angels, and might at any moment pass along gems of truth.

William Clayton, another of Joseph's confidants, who served as a second diarist from 1842 to 1844, was even more alert to doctrine than Richards. One of the first British converts, Clayton had resigned his job as a textile mill accountant soon after his baptism in 1837, to work full-time as a missionary. He arrived in Nauvoo in November 1840 and was called as assistant temple recorder to Richards in January 1842. In September, Joseph asked Clayton to record revelations that came along in the course of his conversation. Until Joseph's death, Clayton was with the Prophet most days, paying particular heed to doctrinal statements.

Accounts by the sensitive and emotional Clayton were often more poetic than Richards's staccato, abbreviated notes. Richards recorded one famous epigram as "The earth in its sanctified and immortal state will be a Urim & Thummim for all things below it in the scale of creation, but not above it." Clayton elaborated the sentence to read "The earth when it is purified will be made like unto crystal and will be a Urim & Thummim whereby all things pertaining to an inferior kingdom on all kingdoms of a lower order will be manifest to those who dwell on it."[16]

Clayton had a great relish for mysteries. On the day when Joseph commented on the earth as a Urim and Thummim, Clayton was the one who posed the question "Is not the reckoning of gods time, angels time, prophets time & mans time according to the planet on which they reside?" Yes, answered Joseph, and then extended the answer:

But there is no angel ministers to this earth only what either does belong or has belonged to this earth and the angels do not reside on a planet like our earth but they dwell with God and the planet where he dwells is like crystal, and like a sea of glass before the throne. This is the great Urim & Thummim whereon all things are manifest both things past, present & future and are continually before the Lord. . . . Then the white stone mentioned in Rev[ela-tion] c 2 v 17 is the Urim & Thummim whereby all things pertaining to an higher order of kingdoms even all kingdoms will be made known and a white stone is given to each of those who come into this celestial kingdom, whereon is a new name written which no man knoweth save he that receiveth it. The new name is the key word.

Sayings like these, drawing on the imagery in the Revelation of St. John, fascinated the Saints. Joseph had said, "Could you gaze in[to] heaven 5 minutes you would know more than you would by read[ing] all that ever was written on the subject," and his descriptions proved the point. His words were noted, circulated, and eventually printed.[17]

The view of heaven as a crystalline sea of glass seemed like a departure from Joseph's earlier ideas. He stood in the tradition of heavenly speculators who saw heaven more as an extension of earth than as an ascetic existence devoted to contemplation of God. A sea of glass and fire, while glorious, sounded severe and inhospitable. Emanuel Swedenborg, the most imagina-tive of the eighteenth-century seers, pictured a heaven with houses and gar-dens, a view that later dominated nineteenth-century speculations. In that vein, Joseph had earlier said that the earth itself would be celestialized and celestial beings would possess it like inheritances in the City of Zion. Earth, it was implied, would be an Eden-like green rather than a sea of glass and fire. On the other hand, an earth that was a Urim and Thummim and a white stone that revealed higher kingdoms had its appeal. The Urim and Thummim coming with the plates had thrilled Joseph; it allowed him to "see any thing."[18] With his characteristic generosity, he wanted everyone to have a seerstone. What better heaven than access to boundless knowledge?

Joseph considered revelations like these to be of immense importance. In his last years more than ever, he stressed that "knowledge is power & the man who has the most knowledge has the greatest power." "The reason why God is greater than all others is He knows how to subject all things to himself." Knowledge was power over evil, power over matter. "God has more power than all other beings, because he has greater Knowledge, and hence he knows how to subject all other beings to him." Joseph said in a sermon in 1843 that "the principle of knowledge is the principle of Salva-tion." Knowledge was the way to ascend. One declaration that reached the *Doctrine and Covenants* was "Whatever principle of intelligence we obtain in this life will rise with us in the ressurection; and if a person gains more knowledge in this life through his diligence & obedience than another, he will have so much the advantage in the world to come." In the meantime, in a more human way, knowledge was also comfort: "I am glad I have the privilege of communicating to you some things which if grasped closely will be a help to you when the clouds are gathering and the storms are ready to burst upon you like peals of thunder. Lay hold of these things and let not your knees tremble, nor hearts faint."[19] Godly knowledge stabilized and reassured Joseph. It was his salvation, and he believed it would redeem the Saints.

During the spring of 1843, he and Willard Richards became absorbed in another kind of knowledge. On March 10 at 6:50 p.m., they observed a light in the form of a sword in the southwest sky for about two hours. Richards also described a "large circle seen around the moon" with four other circles of light, and drew diagrams with notes about their colors. Entry after entry for the next few days noted this strange phenomenon. According to Richards, Joseph said that "the above is a diagram of one of the signs of the times designed to represent 'A union of power and combination of Nations.' " The morning after the sword appeared, Joseph interpreted it to mean that "there will be a speedy and bloody war, and the broad sword seen last evening is the sure sign thereof."[20]

The two were sensitized to signs in the sky because of widespread speculation that the Second Coming would occur in 1843. Orson Pratt said at the April general conference that "the 2d advent of the Son of God is a subject which occupies the attention of the people of this day." The reason was the popular fascination with the widely publicized predictions of William Miller, an unlearned Baptist preacher from Massachusetts. Miller, who was converted from Deism in 1816, thought the Bible contained a complete outline of human history down to the end of the world, all written in code. The scholars were to crack the code by matching clues in the scripture to actual historical events. Miller began his calculations with a passage in Daniel 8:14 about 2,300 days passing before the sanctuary would be cleansed. Like many students of the Millennium, Miller assumed that in biblical code a day equaled a year, permitting him to measure the time to the end once he fixed on a beginning point. Miller selected the declaration of Artaxerxes I of Persia in 458 BCE permitting the exiled Jewish priest Ezra to rebuild the Temple in Jerusalem. With this date as the baseline, Miller calculated that the cleansing of the sanctuary, interpreted to mean the coming of Christ, would occur in 1843, 2,300 years later.[21] In 1836, he laid out the scheme in *Evidence from Scripture and History of the Second Coming of Christ about the Year 1843*.

Miller was one of many millenarians who predicted that the Second Coming would happen in the mid-1840s. He had presented his ideas for years with little effect when a Boston preacher, Joshua V. Himes, began promoting Miller's analysis in the periodical *Signs of the Times*, first published in March 1840. Miller was reluctant to specify an exact date, but finally concluded that it would be between March 1843 and March 1844. The identification of a specific time for the end of the world caused a sensation. Newspaper editors poked fun at Miller, a palsied, graying, self-taught farmer-preacher, but people packed the meetinghouses when he spoke. Even skeptics were watching and waiting.[22]

In the general excitement over Miller's predictions, Joseph's followers wanted his opinion on the Second Coming. Seeking light on the subject, he received a partial answer. On a Sunday morning in April, three weeks before one of the Millerite dates, he told the people what he had learned: "I earnestly desired to know concerning the coming of the Son of Man and prayed, when a voice Said to me, 'Joseph my son, if thou livest until thou art 85 years old thou shall see the face of the Son of Man. Therefore let this suffice and trouble me no more on this matter.' "[23] A few days later at a conference in the temple, he ventured an interpretation: "I took the liberty to conclude that if I did live till that time he would make his appearance but I do not say whether he will make his appearance or I shall go where he is." That put the Second Coming at least forty-eight years away and left time, Joseph observed, for prophesied events like the return of Judah and the healing of the Dead Sea. Besides that, the Saints had yet to build cities, establish stakes, and preach the gospel in every land.[24] Most rode out the year without being swept up in the millennial furor.

Not long after the Miller excitement, Joseph's prophetic powers were put to the test. In April, a dozen men in Kinderhook, Pike County, Illinois, said they had dug twelve feet into a mound on the property of a local merchant, Robert Wiley, and found six small bell-shaped brass plates with undecipherable writing on them. Within a few weeks, the plates were in Joseph's hands with a request for a translation. Wiley claimed he began the dig after dreaming about treasure in the mound three nights in succession. The more likely story is that Wiley, one W. Fugate, and a local blacksmith named Whitton counterfeited the plates by engraving the characters with acid. They cast this lure before the Mormon prophet in hopes of catching him in a feigned translation. A letter was sent to the *Times and Seasons* explaining the find, and the plates were taken to Nauvoo. An editorial in the *Quincy Whig*, a paper hostile to the Mormons, baited the Prophet by saying that "some pretend to say that Smith, the Mormon leader, has the ability to read them." In a classic temptation, the paper observed that if he could, "it would go to prove the authenticity of the Book of Mormon."[25]

John Taylor, editor of the *Times and Seasons*, classed the Kinderhook plates with the discoveries of Mayan ruins recently described in John Lloyd Stephens and Frederick Catherwood's immensely popular *Incidents of Travel in Central America.* Taylor, like all Mormons at the time, counted every building and artwork in ancient Mexico as evidence for the *Book of Mormon.* When the *Book of Mormon* first came out, Taylor pointed out, the inhabitants of the Americas were thought to have been "a rude, barbarous race, uncouth, unlettered, and without civilization." The *Book of Mormon* appeared like "a wild speculation." Now the picture was changing daily. The "various relics that have been found indicative of civilization, intelligence, and learning" give testimony to the authenticity of the book. The Kinderhook find, showing that ancient people wrote on plates, should "convince the skeptical that such things have been used and that even the obnoxious Book of Mormon may be true." Taylor had no doubt "but Mr. Smith will be able to translate them."[26]

Taylor said he had not ascertained Joseph's opinion, but the Prophet had his chance when "several gentlemen" showed him the plates. Richards said Joseph sent William Smith for a Hebrew Bible and lexicon, as if he was going to translate conventionally. Clayton, in a conflicting account, wrote that "Joseph has translated a portion and says they contain the history of the person with whom they were found and he was a descendant of Ham through the loins of Pharaoh king of Egypt, and that he received his kingdom from the ruler of heaven and earth." Joseph seemed to be stepping into the trap, but then he pulled back. Pressure from Taylor and the *Quincy Whig* did not push him any further. After the first meeting, no further mention was made of translation, and the Kinderhook plates dropped out of sight. Joseph may not have detected the fraud, but he did not swing into a full-fledged translation as he had with the Egyptian scrolls. The trap did not quite spring shut, which foiled the conspirators' original plan. Instead of exposing the plot immediately, as they had probably intended to do, they said nothing until 1879, when one of them signed an affidavit describing the fabrication. Church historians continued to insist on the authenticity of the Kinderhook plates until 1980 when an examination conducted by the Chicago Historical Society, possessor of one plate, proved it was a nineteenth-century creation.[27]

EMMA AND JOSEPH

Plural marriage was the most difficult trial of 1843. Nothing Joseph had done put the Church and his own reputation in greater jeopardy. The doctrine shocked his faithful followers, while Emma vacillated between acceptance and rejection. Yet Joseph would not and probably felt that he could not stop. He saw himself in the tradition of Abraham and Solomon, Old Testament patriarchs commanded by God to marry plurally. In the first six months of 1843, Joseph married twelve women, two of them already married to other men, one single and fifty-eight years old. Five of the women boarded in Joseph's household when he married them. Emma probably knew nothing of these marriages at first and then temporarily accepted them before regretting her action and demanding that all five leave.

Plural marriage was practiced secretly in 1843 and would be until well after Joseph's death. The doctrine was not publicly announced until 1852. In Joseph's journal, Willard Richards recorded Joseph's marriages in code. Some marriages he omitted, probably because he did not know that they had taken place. To safeguard his burdensome secret, Joseph publicly and repeatedly denied he was advocating polygamy. In his mind, he wasn't. He distinguished between authorized celestial marriage and the illegal practice of bigamy or the radical ideology of spiritual wives. By denying his involvement, Joseph was trying to wall off John C. Bennett's lascivious schemes for enticing women into illicit relations from the carefully regulated performance of priesthood marriages. To admit he was practicing polygamy would have authorized behavior he condemned. He taught his complicated religious version privately to trusted individuals and small groups, telling the Twelve Apostles about the doctrine in the summer of 1841 after their return from Great Britain, and others one by one.[28] The message was always the same: This is a revelation from God to your prophet. Seek your own inspiration, and you will know for yourself. If you deny it, you will lose your blessings.

The reaction was almost invariably negative. One young woman, Lucy Walker, was struck with horror on hearing the doctrine. She was fifteen when the Prophet invited her to live in his house. Her parents had joined the Mormons in 1832 in Vermont and later migrated to New York, to Missouri, and then on to Illinois, where Lucy's mother died of malarial fevers. Joseph told Lucy's father he would look after the children while John Walker went on a mission. Lucy's older brother Lorin, a worker on Joseph's farm, was fast becoming a favorite. The children were treated like sons and daughters. Lucy worked as Emma's maid while going to school.

In 1842, when Lucy was fifteen or sixteen, Joseph told her, "I have a message for you. I have been commanded of God to take another wife, and you are the woman." Lucy was astounded. "This announcement was indeed a thunderbolt to me." Do you believe me to be a Prophet of God? Joseph asked. "Most assuredly I do," she reported herself as saying in her later autobiography. "He fully Explained to me the principle of plural or celestial marriage. Said this principle was again to be restored for the benefit of the human family. That it would prove an everlasting blessing to my father's house. And form a chain that could never be broken, worlds without end." "What have you to say," Joseph asked her. "Nothing," she replied. Rather than exert more pressure, Joseph backed away. "If you will pray sincerely

for light and understanding in relation thereto, you Shall receive a testimony of the correctness of this principle." Lucy felt "tempted and tortured
beyond endureance untill life was not desireable." "Oh let this bitter cup
pass," she moaned.[29]

For months Joseph said nothing more. Then in the spring of 1843, he
spoke with Lucy's brother William, following the usual pattern of asking
for permission from a relative. William told Joseph that Lucy must decide
for herself. In April 1843, Joseph spoke again and this time he exerted pressure: "I will give you untill to-morrow to decide this matter. If you reject
this message the gate will be closed forever against you." Lucy hated that.

> This arroused every drop of scotch in my veins. . . . I felt at this moment that
> I was called to place myself upon the altar a liveing Sacrafice, perhaps to
> brook the world in disgrace and incur the displeasure and contempt of my
> youthful companions; all my dreams of happiness blown to the four winds,
> this was too much, the thought was unbearable.

Facing an ultimatum, Lucy bluntly refused, unless God Himself told her
otherwise, and "emphatically forbid him speaking again to me on this Subject." Joseph blithely replied, "God Almighty bless you," promised her a
manifestation, and left.

After a sleepless night in prayer, Lucy felt something in her room. "My
room became filled with a heavenly influence. To me it was in comparison
like the brilliant sunshine bursting through the darkest cloud. . . . My Soul
was filled with a calm sweet peace that I never knew. Supreme happiness
took possession of my whole being." Going down the stairs to "go out into
the morning air," she met Joseph, who took her by the hand, led her to a
chair, and "placed his hands upon my head, and blessed me with Every
blessing my heart could posibly desire." On May 1, 1843, William Clayton
married Joseph to Lucy. "It was not a love matter," she wrote later, "but
simply the giving up of myself as a sacrifice to establish that grand and glorious principle that God had revealed to the world." After Joseph's death,
Lucy bore nine children as the plural wife of Heber C. Kimball.[30]

Lucy's autobiography fits the standard pattern for the celestial marriage
narratives written in Utah a quarter of a century or more after Nauvoo.
The circumstances encouraged the plural wives of Joseph (now married to
other men) to be candid about their torment when the Prophet made his
proposal. The revulsion the women felt at first made the subsequent confirmation all the more compelling. Women were free to enlarge upon their
initial anguish, which must have been real, especially for the younger
women. (Ten of Joseph's wives were under twenty.) They had to give up
romance, cut themselves off from friends, perhaps suffer disgrace if they

became pregnant. Their dreams of happiness, as Lucy said, were "blown to the four winds." The point of the narratives was that spiritual confirmation alone persuaded them to comply.

Emma was more resistant. She probably knew of plural marriage but had no idea of the extent of her husband's practice. Aware of her opposition, Joseph could not bring himself to explain what he was doing. Caught between the plural marriage revelation and Emma's opposition, he moved ahead surreptitiously, making the recovery of his domestic life almost impossible.[31]

One story told in Utah in the 1880s had Emma pushing one of Mormondom's most honored women, Eliza Roxcy Snow, down the stairs upon discovering she was married to Joseph, but the evidence for the incident is shaky. Snow was a refined, intelligent woman who had been brought into the Smith household to teach their children. She joined the Mormons in 1835 along with her sister Leonora and moved to Kirtland, where she boarded with the Smiths and taught school. Slender and ramrod straight, Snow was the most intellectual of all the women converts. She wrote poetry and prepared a constitution for the Female Relief Society. Repelled at first by the practice of plural marriage, she concluded that she was "living in the Dispensation of the fulness of times, embracing all other Dispensations," and so "surely Plural Marriage must necessarily be included." Brigham Young performed the ceremony for Joseph and Eliza on June 29, 1842. She was thirty-eight, two years older than Joseph. She later spoke of him as "my beloved husband, the choice of my heart and the crown of my life."[32]

In August 1842, Emma invited Eliza to move back into the Smith household. In December, Eliza began teaching the Smith children and ran a school for them and others until March 1843. Eliza noted in her diary that on February 11, 1843, while still teaching, she moved out of the Smiths' house without saying why, though the reason could well be that on the same day, Joseph's mother, Lucy Mack Smith, moved in. Later gossip blamed Emma.[33] All the versions of the Eliza story, however, were attenuated. Most of them were tales told many decades after the fact and were second- or third-hand hearsay. Some had Emma pushing Eliza, others said she beat her. None hold up under scrutiny.[34] They have to be read skeptically because of the widespread dislike for Emma among the Utah Mormons. Brigham Young never forgave her for breaking with the Church and not coming west. She was considered a traitor to Mormonism because she remained behind and denied, in carefully worded statements that skirted the truth, that Joseph took additional wives. When her sons, then leaders of a rival branch of Mormonism, the Reorganized Church of Jesus Christ of Latter Day Saints, came to Utah on missions in the 1860s, they tried to trace and discredit every claim that Joseph had multiple wives. In response, the Utah church secured scores of affidavits from people who knew of the practice in Nauvoo.[35] Besides proving the existence of plural marriage, the affidavits attempted to refute the hypothesis that Joseph's relations with his plural wives were purely spiritual. Some members of the Reorganized Church accepted ceremonial marriages but thought Joseph never slept with his wives.[36] To rebut that view, the affidavits noted the occasions when Joseph occupied the same room with a wife, facts that might have been omitted had not the Utah Mormons been determined to prove that Joseph and his plural wives were married as completely as the later polygamists under Brigham Young.

While Joseph was alive, there were times when Emma countenanced plural marriage. In May 1843 she approved two wives, Eliza and Emily Partridge, daughters of Edward Partridge and helpers in the Smith household. The sisters were an awkward selection because Joseph had already married them two months earlier in March without Emma's knowledge. When Joseph proposed, Emily and Eliza, nineteen and twenty-three, went through the usual turmoil. At first they turned Joseph down, but by the time he told Emily that "the Lord had commanded him to enter into plural marriage and had given me to him," she was prepared. They married on March 4, 1843. "Well I was married there and then," she wrote many years later. "Joseph went home his way and I going my way alone. A strange way of getting married wasent it?" Eliza Partridge married him four days later. In May, they both went through the ceremony again with Emma present.[37] About the same time, Emma agreed to accept Maria and Sarah Lawrence, two other young women living in the Smiths' house.[38]

Emma's concurrence brought about a reconciliation, which led in turn to her and Joseph's priesthood marriage. Joseph probably would not have had the sealing performed while Emma opposed the plural-marriage revelation. But on a cold Sunday evening, May 28, 1843, in the upper room of Joseph's redbrick store, Joseph and Emma were "sealed" for eternity by the power of the priesthood.

Unfortunately, the reconciliation did not last. Emma had agreed to the plural marriages, but she immediately regretted it. "Before the day was over she turned around or repented of what she had done and kept Joseph up till very late in the night talking to him," Emily Partridge wrote in the 1880s, when revealing Emma's faults was thought to aid the Utah Church. "She kept close watch of us. If we were missing for a few minutes, and Joseph was not at home, the house was searched from top to bottom and from one end to the other, and if we were not found, the neighborhood was searched until we were found." One day Emma heard Joseph talking to Eliza Partridge in an upstairs room. Joseph closed the door and held it shut, while Emma called Eliza's name and tried to open the door. "She seemed much irritated," he reported to William Clayton.[39]

The situation deteriorated. In her 1884 reminiscence, Emily wrote of Emma:

> She sent for us one day to come to her room. Joseph was present, looking like a martyr. Emma said some very hard things—Joseph should give us up or blood should flow. She would rather her blood would run pure than be poluted in this manner. Such interviews were quite common, but the last time she called us to her room, I felt quite indignant, and was determined it should be the last, for it was becoming monotonous, and I am ashamed to say, I felt indignant towards Joseph for submitting to Emma.

Emma wanted the marriages to the Partridge girls ended. Emily said, "Joseph asked her [Emma] if we made her the promises she required, if she would cease to trouble us, and not persist in our marrying some one else. She made the promise. Joseph came to us and shook hands with us, and the understanding was that all was ended between us." Later he said to Emily privately, "You know my hands are tied. And he looked as if he would sink into the earth." Emma wanted the girls out of the house and the city. Emily said later that "my sister and I were cast off."[40]

Joseph was unsure how far the usually composed Emma would go in her anger. Near the end of June, he warned William Clayton that Emma "wanted to lay a snare for me." Joseph said that "he knew she was disposed to be revenged on him for some things she thought that if he would indulge himself she would too."[41] Clayton, trying to patch up relations with one of his own wives, was dumbfounded. Joseph warned him against getting involved. The staid and upright Emma, determined to regain her dignity, was looking for a way to punish her husband. Joseph was anxious and under pressure.

Emma had always performed her duties as wife of the Church president. She entertained housefuls of guests, appeared at reviews of the Nauvoo Legion, and took on multiple business duties, traveling to St. Louis in late April, for example, when Joseph dared not stir for fear of arrest. Emma believed in her husband's inspiration. She had been convinced ever since watching the *Book of Mormon* translation going on in her house in 1829. Late in life, she told a Mormon elder that the gold plates "lay in a box under our bed for months."

Knowing her basic faith, Hyrum thought Joseph should show Emma a written revelation on plural marriage. Hyrum had been reluctant to accept the principle himself until Brigham Young explained that it allowed him to be married to both Jerusha Barden, his deceased first wife, and to Mary Fielding, his current spouse. At the same time, he had the spiritual confirmation so many others reported.[42] On May 29, the day after Joseph was sealed to Emma, Hyrum was sealed to his two wives. In July, Hyrum argued that writing the revelation would win over Emma. To be sure of its accuracy, he asked Joseph to use the Urim and Thummim, but the Prophet said he knew it perfectly. On July 12, 1843, Joseph dictated to William Clayton for three hours in the upper office of his store.[43] Emma once said Hyrum's words were irresistible to her, but when he presented the revelation, she was adamant. He came away from Emma saying that he "had never received a more severe talking to in his life."[44]

The next day, Joseph and Emma talked for hours. Clayton was called into the room near the end to hear "an agreement they had mutually entered into. They both stated their feelings on many subjects & wept considerable." They were in impossible positions: Joseph caught between his revelation and his wife, Emma between a practice she detested and belief in her husband. The agreement represented some kind of compromise. Emma was beginning to think practically of the consequences of sharing her husband with other women. Two days later, Clayton made a deed to her for half of the steamboat *Maid of Iowa*, and sixty city lots.[45]

The assurance of financial security did not heal the breach. A month later, Joseph said that Emma had completely rejected plural marriage. She had given him the Partridge sisters but "he knew if he took them she would pitch on him & obtain a divorce & leave him." But Joseph told Clayton that he "should not relinquish any thing." He was unwilling to put away the women he had married. Even with his marriage at stake, he could not back down. Meanwhile, Emma kept watch for suspicious signs. She was "vexed & angry" when she found two letters from Eliza Snow in Joseph's pocket, and demanded to know if Clayton had delivered them. The next day, Emma learned from Flora Woodworth, another plural wife, that Joseph had given her a gold watch. Emma demanded its return. When Joseph learned of the incident, he reproved her, and on the return trip from the Woodworths, Emma "abused him much & also when he got home," Clayton reported. "He had to use harsh measures to put a stop to her abuse but finally succeeded."[46]

These events exhausted both Emma and Joseph. In the fall they stopped fighting. Joseph's mother, Lucy, fell ill, and Emma tended her until she became ill herself. They managed at the end of August to move into the new wing built on their house, enlarging it to seventeen or eighteen rooms, big enough to open a hotel. Joseph put up a sign outside advertising the "Nauvoo Mansion." A month later they held an open house and dinner for a hundred couples to mark the occasion. Other occupations and Emma's involvement in the elaboration of temple rituals may have combined to soften her on plural marriage for the moment. Three weeks later, Joseph told Clayton, Emma "was turned quite friendly & kind. She had been anointed."[47]

By "anointed" Joseph meant Emma had received an "endowment," the first woman to take part in the ceremony offered to nine men a year and a half before. The endowment was the heart of the temple rituals that had grown considerably since the Kirtland temple dedication. For a year after the bestowal of the expanded endowment in May 1842, no one else was endowed. During that year, the central importance of marriage, and of women, had emerged. When he renewed the ceremony on May 26, 1843, Joseph taught the participants about the "new and everlasting covenant," referring to marriage. By then he knew that men and women must marry by the power of the priesthood to reach the highest degree of celestial glory.[48]

The increased importance of marriage meant including women in the temple ceremonies. Emma was the natural choice to be endowed first. On or before September 28, she passed through the endowment ceremony.[49] From then on, she initiated other women into washings, anointings, and sealings. Heber Kimball noted in his journal that "January 1844 my wife Vilate and menny feemales was received in to the Holy Order, and was washed and inointed by Emma." By the time of Joseph's death in June 1844, sixty-five persons had been endowed.[50]

Those who had been endowed met almost weekly to induct others, hear instruction, and offer prayers. Called the "Quorum," the "Anointed Quorum," or the "Holy Order," this small group of endowed members held prayer circles, probably dressed in special temple clothing and partially reenacting the ceremonies.[51] A typical entry in Richards's record reads: "Prayer Meeting at Joseph's. Quorum present. . . . Hiram and his wife were blessed, ord[ained] and anointed. Prayer and singing." Sometimes the notes on the anointings themselves were coded. "Prayer Meeting in the evening at S E Room Jos[eph's] old house," one entry began. "R Cahoon and" [sequence in code] "wife anointed and Mother Smith." Although used intermittently, the coded words showed Richards's sense that the occasions were too sacred to be written for any eye to see.[52]

Joseph introduced a more advanced ordinance called the "second anointing," between September 28 and February 26. This ceremony, given to eighteen men and their wives, was Joseph's attempt to deal with the theological problem of assurance. How did a Christian, in the words of the first chapter of 2 Peter, "give diligence to make your calling and election sure"?[53] Calvinist theologians had argued over the question of certain knowledge for centuries. Was it possible to end doubt about one's standing with the Lord?[54] Preaching from 2 Peter 1 in May 1843, at the time he was reviving the endowment, Joseph had taught that the "more sure word of prophecy" meant "a mans knowing that he was sealed up unto eternal life by revelation and the spirit of prophecy through the power of the Holy priesthood." A few months later, the revelation on priesthood marriage had promised those who married eternally that they would surely enter into exaltation, even if they sinned, if once their bond was "sealed by the Holy Spirit of promise." Characteristically, Joseph embodied this process of certification in a ritual whose details were never described but that involved ordination as king and priest, words found in the Revelation of St. John: Christ "hath made us kings and priests unto God and his Father."[55]

The couples given the second anointing were noticeably quiet about the proceedings. Elizabeth Ann Whitney, one of the initiated, later said Joseph "had been strictly charged by the angel who committed these precious things into his keeping that he should only reveal them to such persons as were pure, full of integrity to the truth, and worthy to be entrusted with divine messages; that to spread them abroad would be like casting pearls before swine, and that the most profound secresy must be maintained."[56] Joseph was as tight-lipped as the rest.

Through the late fall and winter of 1843 and 1844, Joseph and Emma's relationship broke down only once. During Sunday dinner on November 5, Joseph became ill, rushed to the door, and vomited so violently that he dislocated his jaw. "Every symptom of poison," Richards noted in Joseph's diary. That night at the prayer meeting, Richards wrote in code that Joseph and Emma did not dress in the usual special clothing, a sign they were too much at odds to participate. The next day, Richards wrote that Joseph was "busy with domestic concerns." Years later, in the anti-Emma atmosphere of Utah, Brigham Young spoke of a meeting where Joseph accused his wife of slipping poison into his coffee. Brigham interpreted Emma's refusal to answer as an admission of guilt. Though there probably was an argument, the poisoning accusation was unfounded. Joseph was susceptible to vomiting anyway. He had even dislocated his jaw while vomiting once before; and five weeks after the 1843 dinner episode, he was sick again, vomiting more violently than ever. During this last bout, Joseph said gratefully, "My wife waited on me."[57]

Three days before the disrupted Sunday dinner, Joseph had taken another plural wife, fifty-six-year-old Fanny Murray, Brigham Young's widowed older sister.[58] According to Brigham's account thirty years later, Fanny insisted in conversation with Joseph and her brother that she would never marry again, though she knew this left her as a ministering spirit in heaven, the state of those not married by the priesthood. Joseph said she talked foolishly and offered to marry her right there, with Brigham performing the ceremony. Fanny changed her mind and agreed. At the end of December, she received her endowment and joined the anointed quorum.[59]

Fanny Murray was Joseph Smith's last plural wife. His marriages had dropped off sharply after July 1843. During his confrontation with Emma between July 12 and 16, Joseph may have agreed to add no more. He told

Clayton she would divorce him if he did. Whatever the arrangement, Joseph wed Melissa Lott on September 20, perhaps because he had proposed earlier in the summer.[60] Fanny Murray may have seemed like an innocent exception to him, but not to Emma.

In the winter, Emma fulfilled her role as president's wife to the utmost. On Christmas Day 1843, the Smiths entertained a large party at their house, spending the evening "in a most cheerful and friendly manner in Music, Dancing, &c." In the middle of the festivities a disheveled figure with long hair stumbled in, pretending to be a Missourian. Joseph scuffled with the man until he saw it was Orrin Porter Rockwell, now released from a Missouri prison where he had been held on suspicion of shooting Lilburn Boggs. Rockwell had been moved from jail to jail and was held for weeks before he was finally acquitted. After his release, he walked for twelve days to arrive in Nauvoo, as it happened, just in time for the party.[61]

The parties continued nonstop that winter. On New Year's Eve, a company of fifty musicians and singers serenaded the Smiths under their window with William Phelps's New Year hymn. On New Year's Day, another large party had supper at the Smiths' and "continued music and dancing till morning." On January 18, 1844, a "Cotillion Party" at the Nauvoo Mansion marked Joseph and Emma's wedding anniversary.[62]

Two weeks earlier, Joseph told Richards about Emma: "I was remarking to Bro[ther] Phelps what a kind, provident wife I had. That when I wanted a little bread and milk she would load the table with so many good things it would destroy my appetite." Emma entered the room at that moment, and Phelps said to her, "You must do as Bonaparte did have a little table, just large enough for yourself and your order thereon." Phelps pictured the two of them, Joseph and Emma, dining quietly together. Emma knew better. "Mr. Smith is a bigger man than Bonaparte," came her retort, perhaps wistfully. "He can never eat without his friends."[63]

TWENTY-EIGHT

CITY AND KINGDOM

1843–44

It is just as Joseph Smith said to a certain man who asked him, "How do you govern such a vast people as this?" "Oh," says Joseph, "it is very easy." "Why," says the man, "but we find it very difficult." "But," said Joseph, "it is very easy, for I teach them correct principles and they govern themselves."

JOHN TAYLOR, May 18, 1862

IN EARLY OCTOBER 1843, Emma and Joseph hosted a "luxurious feast for a pleasure party," celebrating the opening of a hotel in their newly expanded house. One hundred couples dined at "a well spread board." After the cloth was removed, the hotel's proprietor Robert D. Foster, chair of the event, proposed toasts. One was to "General Joseph Smith, whether we view him as a Prophet at the head of the church; a General at the head of the Legion; a Mayor at the head of the City Council; or as a Landlord at the head of his table." Another was to the Nauvoo Legion, "a faithful band of invincibles; ready at all times to defend their country," and a third to the Nauvoo Charter, a legislative decree "for the protection of the Saints." The longest toast was to Nauvoo itself:

> The great Emporium of the west, the centre of all centers, a city of three years growth—a population of eighteen thousand souls, congregated from the four quarters of the globe, embracing the intelligence of all nations, with industry, frugality, economy virtue; and brotherly love; unsurpassed in any age in the world—a suitable home for the saints.

At the end of the proceedings, Joseph offered his gratitude for "the pleasing prospects that surrounded him," and Foster thanked the guests on Emma's behalf.[1]

Ironically, the happy occasion presaged the coming conflicts. The institutions that Foster celebrated were the very ones the anti-Mormons most feared: the charter, the legion, and the Prophet's combination of religious and civil authority.[2] Even the growth of Nauvoo disturbed other Hancock

County residents who were fearful of Mormon domination at the polls. Foster's toast used the familiar language of boosterism. Hundreds of small western American towns aimed to build a "great Emporium." But only Nauvoo had a prophet as mayor, uniting religion and the state. Bringing God into the government created an alliance most Americans had rejected after the Revolution. The Nauvoo merger was all the more offensive because Joseph commanded a military force—the "invincibles" of Foster's toast—and possessed a city charter that gave the Mormons control over the municipal courts.

By 1843, it was clear that this combination would not be tolerated. Anti-Mormon committees throughout the county were calling for state intervention. Some were already talking of expulsion. But despite the growing opposition, Joseph would not back down. A religious society under religious government had been his goal for thirteen years. Instead of creating parishes, he built cities. Instead of leaving people to worship where they lived, he gathered them. He aimed for a new social order patterned after the "order of heaven." Mormon sufferings and his months in prison had not weakened his resolve. The final campaign of his last six months was to frame the constitution of a political Kingdom of God.

CAPITALISM

Joseph had the authority in Nauvoo to have instituted the egalitarian society prescribed in the early revelations on Zion. In Jackson County, families had given their property to the Church, receiving back a stewardship fitted to their needs and wants. Everyone was to receive an "inheritance," with surplus income after the first redistribution deposited in the bishop's storehouse for public use. The consecration of properties aimed to end poverty and establish equality. The early revelations stressed that "if ye are not equal in earthly things, ye cannot be equal in obtaining heavenly things," a criticism of the current economic order.[3] Once in control of Nauvoo, Joseph might have replaced the existing system.

He lived in a time of economic experimentation. As he was founding Nauvoo, a fellow Vermonter, Orestes Brownson, was blasting American capitalism. Two years older than Joseph Smith, the orphaned Brownson was living in Royalton, Vermont, the year Joseph was born in neighboring Sharon. About the same time the Smiths moved to New York, Brownson, age fourteen, migrated too. A passionately bookish person, he passed through phases of skepticism, Unitarianism, and Transcendentalism, eventually advocating social reforms to end inequality and exploitation.

In 1840, Brownson excoriated the capitalist economic order for the *Boston Quarterly Review*, a magazine he edited and largely wrote himself.

Offended by the vast discrepancy in wealth between owners and laborers, he condemned the "city nabobs, revelling in luxury" and the factory owners who employ workers "toiling as so many slaves." In 1844, disillusioned by democracy's failure to address economic injustices, Brownson became a Roman Catholic. He came to think that only an organization with authority and benevolent purpose could right the world's wrongs.[4]

Joseph shared Brownson's egalitarianism, but not his diagnosis. Unlike many social reformers, Joseph had no language of political economy. He did not see the economic system in itself as the source of injustice. A decade earlier, he had spoken of the selfishness of the rich, but never of capital, labor, or exploitation, or "nabobs revelling in luxury." Joseph did not base his reforms on a diagnosis of a diseased economic system; when property redistribution proved impractical, he adapted.

He was interested enough in schemes of economic reform to invite John Finch to lecture in Nauvoo while visiting the city. Finch was associated with Robert Owen, the Scottish industrialist-turned-socialist who had founded a utopian community at New Harmony, Indiana. Prevailed on to stay two extra days, September 13 and 14, 1843, Finch talked on "the present wretched condition of the working classes, and the causes of their misery" to an audience of nearly two thousand people. On the second day, discussion went on for five hours. Though Joseph listened to Finch, the Prophet said he "did not believe the doctrine." A few weeks later Joseph preached on "the folly of common stock," the idea of the communal sharing of property, much discussed in that decade.[5]

Joseph accepted the economy of private property and individual enterprise. Even under the consecration of properties, individual stewards operated independently in a market economy, though they were obligated to return their "surplus" to the bishop. More than once he tried his hand at business. In Nauvoo, Joseph opened a store with goods from St. Louis in a neat two-story brick building with faux-grained pillars and drawers. For a few days, he stood behind the counter waiting on customers. Later he purchased a half interest in the sixty-ton steamboat *Maid of Iowa* and obtained a monopoly on the ferry business from Nauvoo to Montrose, on the Iowa side of the Mississippi. The addition to his house permitted him to advertise the Nauvoo Mansion and take in paying guests. In a still grander entrance into the hostelry business, a revelation authorized the formation of a joint stock corporation to erect the spacious Nauvoo House.[6]

He also encouraged industrial enterprise in Nauvoo. In 1841, the legislature chartered the Nauvoo Agricultural and Mechanical Association to pool capital for industrial purposes. Under its auspices, work began on a pottery to employ English immigrants from the pottery districts. Joseph's friends started small manufacturing establishments, and Joseph would have liked more. In England, the Twelve Apostles called "for men of capital to go on first and make large purchases of land, and erect mills, machinery, manufactories, &c." Joseph wanted converts from English factories to produce the cloth, boots, and pottery Nauvoo needed. He urged Edward Hunter, a rich Pennsylvania convert, to persuade manufacturers of wool or cotton to "come on and establish their businesses." To facilitate manufacturing, Joseph proposed a canal down the middle of Main Street to create a mill race that could be tapped for water power.[7]

But capitalism never ruled Nauvoo as it did Chicago, a city that in 1844 was the same size as Nauvoo. The original name of the Nauvoo site, Commerce, was dropped after the Saints arrived. Rather than promising entrepreneurs great wealth, Joseph asked that "money be brought here to pay the poor for manufacturing." Profits were secondary to creating jobs. He invited "all ye rich men of the Latter Day Saints from abroad . . . to bring up some of their money and give to the Temple." He practiced capitalism without the spirit of capitalism. Summing up a day of waiting on customers in the store, he mused, "I love to wait upon the Saints, and be a servant to all, hoping that I may be exalted in the due time of the Lord."[8]

Joseph was not a successful entrepreneur. He sold goods on credit to every customer who walked in, whether or not they could pay, knowing that if he tried to collect, he risked being labeled a false prophet. Within two years, when competition from a second business district on the bluff pressured the store, it folded. The Nauvoo Mansion hotel lasted only five months before Joseph leased the house to Ebenezer Robinson and confined his own family of six plus two servants to three rooms. After two years of operation, the *Maid of Iowa* was in debt $1,700. The Wisconsin pinery business was in debt $3,000 after its first year. Construction on the Nauvoo House was finally abandoned. None of these projects enriched Joseph, who invested too much money in land for the shiploads of new migrants. When he died, his estate was insolvent.[9]

Nauvoo's architecture revealed the city's noncapitalist nature. Nauvoo had shops, hotels, and houses (mostly with one or two rooms down and one up) and then the extravagant temple. That huge structure, 128 feet long, 88 feet wide, and 165 feet tall, captured the spiritual essence of the city. Nauvoo was a religious capital, not a commercial center. Amazingly, the Nauvoo temple, valued at roughly three-quarters of a million dollars, was built without incurring much debt. Everyone contributed labor or money or both. The ten wards into which the city was divided organized teams to cut stone, manage cranes, and install beams and floors. Every able-bodied man in the city was asked to work one day in ten. Fortuitously, the rock ledge whose extension into the Mississippi River diverted the stream and first brought the Nauvoo peninsula into existence yielded the limestone for the walls, which were four to six feet thick. For internal framing, the Church sent 150 men to the Black River in Wisconsin, four hundred miles up the Mississippi, where they cut wood and sent down rafts of lumber annually. The full-time stonecutters and carpenters, all found among the Church membership, were paid with temple scrip that could be exchanged for meat, grain, and cheese that had been contributed as tithing to the temple storehouse. Mormon merchants accepted the scrip as payment on goods, though it required them to redeem the scrip for whatever the storehouse happened to hold.[10] Little money changed hands, and yet the temple kept rising.

Architect William Weeks, a convert from Massachusetts, drew Joseph's design. When Weeks objected to a set of small round windows, thinking half windows suited the building better, Joseph reminded him that the building had been seen in a vision. Josiah Quincy, the Boston Brahmin who toured the city with Joseph in May 1844, called the architecture "odd and striking." A New York paper said the design was "entirely original—unlike any thing in the world, or in the history of the world." Begun in October 1840, the building was ready for the performance of baptisms for the dead within a year. The Saints began meeting in the building on a temporary floor in October 1842.[11]

Joseph never saw the completed temple. He died with the walls just halfway up. But construction continued on even when the Saints knew they would be forced to leave. After the largest body departed in the winter and early spring of 1846, lingering members finished the interior and dedicated the temple in April.[12] Then that remnant fled too. To ensure that the Mormons would never return, an arsonist burned the building in 1848.

Before its destruction, the temple on the bluff was visible from far downriver. It was Nauvoo's equivalent of Chicago's Great Hall of the Board of Trade, erected three decades later. Each building represented its city's soul. A vast, elegantly ornamented space, the Board of Trade housed Chicago's central activity: trading commodities. The Great Hall, the essence of capitalism, shaped the activities of lumbermen, farmers, and cattlemen hundreds of miles away. They labored the year around to produce the commodities exchanged in the Great Hall. In Nauvoo, the temple was the magnet, attracting converts from all over North America and Great Britain who came to the temple for spiritual knowledge, the essence of the city's values.[13]

EXTRADITION

Joseph was two hundred miles north of Nauvoo in mid-June 1843 when he learned that Missouri was pursuing him again. He and Emma and the children were visiting her sister Elizabeth Wasson in Inlet Grove, near Dixon,

Illinois, when news arrived from Judge James Adams in Springfield that Governor Thomas Ford had agreed to turn Joseph over to Missouri. A Missouri sheriff and an Illinois constable were on their way to arrest Joseph and carry him across the Mississippi. Within hours, William Clayton and Stephen Markham were galloping north with the warning. Leaving around midnight, they rode night and day, stopping only briefly to rest their horses, and arrived at the Wassons' at 4 p.m. Wednesday, having covered 212 miles in sixty-six hours.[14]

The two law officers, Joseph Reynolds of Jackson County, Missouri, and Harmon Wilson of Carthage, Illinois, had hurried to Dixon, knowing that if Joseph heard they were coming he would slip away. They carried an extradition writ issued by Ford on behalf of the Missouri governor, requiring Joseph to answer the old charge of treason. Joseph had cleared himself of the attempted murder of Lilburn Boggs on the grounds he was not in Missouri when the attempt was made, but he had certainly been there during the Mormon war when he was accused of resisting the state militia. John C. Bennett and Boggs, both still furious, had persuaded Missouri's Governor Thomas Reynolds that the state's reputation depended on prosecuting Joseph, especially when the Mormons were publicizing their mistreatment. Thomas Ford reluctantly issued the writ.[15]

In Dixon, Reynolds and Wilson presented themselves as Mormon elders. On the way to the Wassons', they rode right by William Clayton and reached the house at two o'clock, while the family was eating. Joseph said the officers cocked pistols at his head and declared, "God damn you I will Shoot you." They bundled him into a wagon and with pistols in his sides headed to Dixon for fresh horses. Locked in a tavern, Joseph shouted through the window that he was being held prisoner. A lawyer who tried to get in had the door shut in his face, and Reynolds went back to "God damn you I will shoot you." Joseph said, "I turned to him opened my bosom & told him to shoot away."[16]

By this time, word of the struggle had spread through the town. A group of citizens, including the tavern owner, insisted that a local judge determine the legality of the proceedings. Meanwhile, Stephen Markham had entered complaints against the officers for threatening life and abusive treatment (because of the gun barrels in the Prophet's ribs), prompting Reynolds and Wilson to be taken into custody by local authorities. Both Joseph and his captors being under arrest, everyone slept that night under guard. The next day both parties obtained writs of habeas corpus from the local master in chancery, returnable before the judge of the Ninth Circuit in Ottawa, forty miles away. Finding him gone, the parties headed for Stephen Douglas's Fifth Circuit Court in Quincy.[17]

They set off on the two-hundred-mile journey south, Joseph in the cus-

tody of Reynolds and Wilson, and the two of them in the custody of Sheriff
Campbell of Lee County. Reynolds refused to let Joseph ride horseback,
fearful he would bolt. Joseph feared the river. He was sure the officers
wanted him aboard a steamboat that the Missouri kidnappers could raid.
He sent Clayton to dispatch rescuers, hoping to stay inland long enough for
help to arrive. When the message got to Nauvoo on Sunday, June 25,
Hyrum called a meeting at the Masonic Hall within thirty minutes. More
men showed up than the building would hold. Upwards of 300 volunteered
to ride, and 175 set out that night.[18]

One party went upstream in the *Maid of Iowa*, searching boats as they
went in case the arresting officers took the river route. Another party split
in two, sending some horsemen to Peoria and others to Monmouth. When
two Mormons finally intercepted the convoy, Joseph greeted his friends
"with tears [in] his eyes." Then he turned to his captors. "I am not going
[to] Missouri this time these [a]r[e] my boys."[19]

Reynolds tried to divert the party to the river. He was the fearful one
now, knowing people in Nauvoo would remember him from the Jackson
County persecutions. He and Wilson drew their pistols as the party headed
inland: "No by God we wont, we will never go by Nauvoo alive." But with
more Nauvoo men joining the party by the hour, the two were outnumbered. They were helpless when the decision was made to return the habeas
corpus writs to the Nauvoo municipal court rather than to Quincy, which
meant Joseph was as good as free. What had been a conveyance of prisoners became Joseph's triumphal return. Nauvoo sent out the brass band
and a parade of carriages full of leading citizens. Joseph's guard of over a
hundred horsemen, seeing the group approach, entwined wild prairie flowers around their bridles. When the two contingents met, Joseph greeted
Emma and Hyrum, mounted his favorite horse, Old Charley, and marched
slowly into town. Emma rode by his side, as the band played "Hail Columbia." Cheering citizens lined the streets while guns and cannons were fired.
Said one onlooker, "We shouted him welcome and shed tears of joy to see
him again delivered from his enemies." At the Nauvoo Mansion, fifty people sat down for dinner. Joseph put Reynolds and Wilson at the head of the
table.[20]

Later that afternoon Joseph addressed about seven thousand people at
the temple site. Uppermost in his thoughts was gratitude for the city's charter and its municipal courts. The right to issue a writ of habeas corpus had
saved his life. He was convinced that once taken across the river, he was
doomed. In Missouri he would never be tried in court but ambushed, kidnapped, and murdered before Reynolds ever got him to Daviess County.
Those dangers made the charter's power to erect a court and militia price-
less. Joseph said the Mormons had been "deprived of our rights & privi-

leges as Citizen[s] driven from town to town place to place State to State with the sacrifice of our homes & land & our blood been shed & many murdered." And it was true that the Missouri government had done little to protect Mormon rights. Generals Atchison and Doniphan were the only Missouri militia officers to defend them, and Atchison had been deprived of his command. Usually, state militias had turned on the Mormons rather than protecting them. No court had convicted or even tried a perpetrator for burning a Mormon house, whipping a Mormon man, or driving off Mormon cattle. As Governor Thomas Ford later wrote, democratic government is helpless to defend an unpopular group: "The people cannot be used to put down the people."[21] Joseph was grateful that Nauvoo's charter authorized a militia to ward off mobs and courts to prosecute persecutors— the only government protection the Mormons could count on.

Joseph's speech at the temple was characteristically ambivalent on how to react to the threats. Joseph knew how close he had come to being dragged off to his enemies' lair, and his reaction was to fight back. "The time has Come when forbearance is no longer a virtue," he declared. "If you are again taken unlawfully you are at liberty to give loose to Blood and Thunder." He would take no more. "Befor I will bear this unhallowed persecution any longer I will spill my Blood their is a time when bearing it longer is a sin I will not bear it longer I will spil the last drop of Blood I have." Then he appealed to the audience. "All that will not bear it longer say AH and, the Cry of AH rung throughout the Congregation," as one report said, like a "vast peal of thunder." Knowing he had support, Joseph told them, "I will lead you to battle & if you are not afraid to die & feel disposed to spill your Blood in your own defence you will not offend me."[22]

Yet Joseph also talked of caution and restraint, boasting of his kindness toward Reynolds and Wilson. "I have brought them to Nauvoo & treated them kindly I have had the privilege of rewarding them good for evil." He had not spilled their blood. After their attempts to run him to Missouri, he took them into his house and "set the best before them my house afforded & they were waited upon by my wife." Was that the model for treating one's enemies? He cautioned the crowd to "restrain your hand from violence, against these men." After saying he would lead the Saints into battle, he warned them "be not the aggressor bear untill they strike on the one cheek [then] offer the other." Joseph was advocating defensive war against an invading enemy. In his eyes, the Mormons were defending the same "privileges & freedom which our fathers fought bled & died for" in the Revolution.[23]

The next day, Reynolds and Wilson delivered up Joseph to the Nauvoo municipal court, and stormed off to Carthage, demanding that the governor dispatch the militia to arrest the Prophet. Fearing war, Ford refused.

Reynolds returned to Missouri empty-handed. Although it was not clear immediately, the campaign to extradite Joseph Smith had ended.[24]

POLITICS

The political fallout lasted longer. Joseph's escape from the arresting officers outraged Illinois citizens. Thomas Ford thought that the summer's events brought about Joseph's downfall: "From this time forth the whigs generally, and a party of the democrats, determined upon driving the Mormons out of the State; and everything connected with the Mormons became political."[25] No matter what the Mormons did, trouble followed. Their political vacillations added to the enmity. Switching from the Democrats to the Whigs and back again annoyed both parties. Through the 1830s, Mormon candidates for public office generally ran on the Democratic ticket, but President Martin Van Buren's refusal to help the Mormons after their expulsion from Missouri turned Joseph to the Whig candidate, William Henry Harrison, in 1840. Stephen Douglas briefly won the Mormons back to the Democrats in 1841 until a Democrat, Governor Thomas Carlin, served Joseph with extradition papers in the 1842 Boggs shooting, and a Whig judge cleared Joseph in Springfield.[26] That brought the Mormons back to the Whig camp. In June 1843, Cyrus Walker, Whig candidate for Congress and a leading defense lawyer in Illinois, agreed to defend Smith against Reynolds and Wilson after the Dixon arrest in return for the Mormon vote.[27] Both candidates, Walker and Joseph Hoge, the Democrat, supported the Mormon contention that the Nauvoo charter authorized the city's municipal court to issue writs of habeas corpus even on state charges— contrary to most expert legal opinion—but Joseph had already pledged his support to the Whig Walker.[28]

Everyone assumed the Whigs had sewn up the Mormon vote in the August 1843 elections. Then events in Springfield reversed the picture. When Reynolds ran to the Democrat Governor Thomas Ford after Joseph was released, Nauvoo feared Ford would return with a militia to recapture the Prophet. For a month that threat lingered over the city. Meanwhile the Whig Walker pled with Ford on the Mormons' behalf. Ford had no intention of invading the Mormon stronghold, but he was reluctant to deliver that happy news to Walker, who would surely claim the credit—and the Mormon vote for the Whigs. Instead, Ford said he needed to investigate and left for St. Louis on state business. When Nauvoo's emissary, Jacob Backenstos, arrived in Springfield a few days later, however, the governor's aide informed him that no militia would be sent. The aide also implied that votes for the Whigs in the August elections might reverse the decision. Backenstos returned to Nauvoo with the news that unless the Saints voted Democratic, the militia would be dispatched.[29]

Caught between Joseph's pledge and the threat of a militia invasion, the Mormons switched allegiances two days before the election. Joseph told the Saints he would vote for Walker, the Whig, as promised, but his brother Hyrum would vote for Hoge, the Democrat. "Bro Hiram tells me this morning that he has had a testimony that it will be better for this people to vote for hoge. & I never knew Hiram to say he ever had a revelation & it failed." In the final count, Hoge received about 3,000 Mormon votes and won by just 574 in the district. The Whigs were furious and, according to Ford, henceforth resolved to expel the Mormons.[30]

The Mormons had an awkward relationship with the political parties. Joseph claimed he wanted to remain outside the parties. "The Lord has not given me Revelation concerning politics," he said when explaining his vote for Walker. "I have not asked the Lord for it.—I am a third party [and] stand independent and alone." The problem was that Mormons felt none of the usual obligations that parties counted on. In his history of Illinois, Ford described the "little cliques of leaders in each county" and the "little big men in each neighborhood" who relied on the party for their own advancement.[31] Newspaper editors, merchants, and lawyers all benefited from such alliances and reliably stuck with their party. The parties consisted of networks of interwoven special interests.

No such ties bound the Mormons. Their single issue was protection from mobs, whether through preservation of the city charter or forestalling extradition proceedings. The usual party loyalties meant nothing. Mormons voted for the good of the Church, not for personal interest, so the huge Mormon vote, a majority in Hancock County, pivoted on this single factor. Mormons swung back and forth, tipping this way and that depending on extradition writs, militia threats, and attacks on the charter. The parties had no way of controlling or appealing to them except by promising favors like Walker's. Outsiders complained and asked Mormons to divide their vote, to join the network of personal interests and party connections that held both parties together. The practice of bloc voting, Ford said, "arrayed against them in deadly hostility all aspirants for office who were not sure of their support, all who have been unsuccessful in elections, and all who were too proud to court their influence."[32]

ALARMS

Ford said the Mormons' betrayal of the Whigs opened the spigots of the party press. From then on nothing was too extreme to be charged against the Mormons. "Every paper was loaded with account of the wickedness, corruptions, and enormities of Nauvoo." Two weeks after the August 1843 election, anti-Mormons collected in a convention at Carthage and appointed a nine-man committee to draft resolutions. "A certain class of people have obtruded themselves upon us," the committee reported, and have assumed "the sacred garb of Christianity" the better to "perpetrate the most lawless and diabolical deeds, that have ever, in any age of the world, disgraced the human species."

> We find them yielding implicit obedience to the ostensible head and founder of this sect, who is a pretended Prophet of the Lord, and under this Heaven-daring assumption, claiming to set aside, by his vile and blasphemous lies, all those moral & religious institutions which have been established by the Bible, & which have, in all ages been cherished by men, as the only means of maintaining those social blessings, which are so indispensably necessary for our happiness.
>
> We believe that such an individual, regardless as he must be, of his obligations to God, and at the same time entertaining the most absolute contempt for the laws of man, cannot fail to become a most dangerous character, especially when he shall have been able to place himself at the head of a numerous horde, either equally reckless and unprincipalled as himself, or else made his pliant tools by the most absurd credulity that has astonished the world since its foundation.

That was the anti-Mormon argument: a pretended prophet, at the head of a numerous horde of unprincipled or credulous believers, sets aside the moral law. As one anxious editor put it, "Revelation now has the balance of power" in the county. Terrified of this "latter-day would be Mahomet," the convention resolved to assert their rights, "peaceably, if we can, but forcibly if we must."[33]

As the pressure was turned up, nerves frayed in Nauvoo. Joseph, worried about a Missouri kidnapping attempt, turned on his own counselor, whom he suspected of selling out to his enemies. He had not entirely trusted Sidney Rigdon after John C. Bennett had solicited Rigdon's support to extradite Joseph for the Boggs shooting. At a public meeting in mid-August 1843, Joseph declared "there is a certain man in this city who has made a covenant to betray me." A steamboat captain had told Orson Hyde about a close associate of Joseph's who had plotted to destroy him when Governor Carlin issued the extradition writ in 1842. Joseph surmised that Rigdon was the guilty party. If the accusation proved true, Joseph exclaimed, "I most solemnly proclaim the withdrawal of my fellowship from this man." In his own defense, Rigdon obtained a letter from former governor Carlin denying their correspondence, but Joseph's suspicions were not allayed. He thought the letter evasive and brought up the charges again at a conference in October. He complained of Rigdon's diminished role in the Presidency and his failings as a postmaster. Rigdon defended himself on every count and pled with Joseph on the basis of "their former friendship, associations and sufferings and expressed his willingness to resign his place, though with sorrowful and indescribable feelings." Always the mediator, Hyrum gave a discourse on the need for the Saints to show mercy toward each other, and especially "towards their aged companion and fellow servant." On a motion seconded by Hyrum, the conference voted to retain Rigdon in the First Presidency. Frustrated, Joseph told the conference he still lacked confidence in Rigdon's "integrity and steadfastness."[34]

Joseph's anxiety showed itself in instance after instance through the fall. He paid a fine in August for striking Walter Bagby, the county tax collector. Joseph "became enraged" when he learned Bagby had been selling Mormon lots for late taxes. In September, he petitioned the state for more arms for the Nauvoo Legion and informed Governor Ford of the renewed anti-Mormon activity, which he feared would be linked to an invasion from Missouri. In early December, news came that two Mormons, a father and son, Daniel and Philander Avery, suspected of having stolen horses three years earlier in Missouri, had been kidnapped. Both were carried across the river and locked up. Joseph immediately informed Ford, appending a rumor that Missouri was coming after the Prophet too.[35]

The Avery kidnappings threw Nauvoo into a panic. Two days after hearing the news, Joseph ordered the Legion to stand ready to enforce city ordinances. The Nauvoo City Council passed an ordinance making it illegal to arrest Joseph Smith on the old Missouri charges on penalty of life imprisonment. On the same day, Joseph suggested the city petition Congress to make Nauvoo a territory with the right to call on federal troops in their own defense. Early the next week, the city council organized a police force of forty men.[36] The Mormons, sensing war, mobilized every resource.

Outsiders saw these measures as proof of Joseph Smith's megalomania. They could not understand his fear of attack. Even Ford did not understand. He told Joseph that only the judiciary, not the militia, could enforce laws. At the same time, he awkwardly attempted to reduce the excitement by mentioning that he had not yet read the voluminous accounts of Mormon suffering sent him the previous summer. And, he added, I "probably never will." Ford wanted peace but seemed callous to suffering. "Oh! Humanity where hast thou hidden thyself?" Joseph lamented.[37]

On December 18, the Nauvoo municipal court convicted John Elliot, a schoolmaster, of kidnapping Daniel Avery. Joseph then brought charges against Elliot for threatening Joseph's life. The Prophet was speaking at the second trial when news came that a mob was collecting in Warsaw to protect another alleged kidnapper, Colonel Levi Williams of Green Plains, whom the Mormons were trying to arrest. The news of a mob gave Joseph pause. He stopped in midtrial, withdrew his action, forgave Elliot, and invited him home for supper and a night's lodgings. Joseph immediately ordered Major Wilson Law to dispatch backup troops for the constable pursuing Williams, and to stand ready to defend the city against mob attack. The crisis passed when the Mormons backed down after learning that armed men stood ready to defend the colonel.[38]

Gradually life returned to normal. When Joseph heard an alarm gun fired in late December, he decided it was nothing serious. On Christmas Eve, a Mr. Richards, who collaborated in the Avery kidnapping, called on Joseph, and they made their peace. "He manifested some repentance and promised to use his influence to prevent Avery's conviction by the Missourians." In February, the ordinance forbidding the arrest of Joseph Smith was repealed at his suggestion.[39] The city had calmed.

TACTICS

Joseph returned to strategizing about the Mormon future. By the fall of 1843 he understood that Nauvoo was not a secure fortress. The militia could not stand up to the state, and the municipal courts were legally contested. The Saints needed broader support, and the Constitution of the United States seemed to hold the key—if interpreted properly. Joseph never lost hope that the federal government would come to the Saints' aid. He continued to believe that beyond the local enemies who encircled them there was widespread goodwill toward the Mormons, which, if mobilized and brought to bear on the federal government, would lead to the desired protection.

The oncoming presidential election offered an opening. The Mormon vote plus sympathy from around the country might catch the attention of national politicians. Church leaders were encouraged when Colonel John Frierson of Quincy, a Calhoun backer, offered to write Congressman Robert Barnwell Rhett of South Carolina seeking congressional support for the Mormons. On the same day that Frierson's proposal was discussed, the council decided to write five of the candidates for the presidency for their opinions on the Mormons: Whigs Lewis Cass, Richard M. Johnson, and Henry Clay; and Democrats Martin Van Buren and John C. Calhoun. (Ironically, the successful candidate in the 1844 election, James K. Polk, then a Democratic dark horse, was not on the list.) For the next month, the Twelve and Joseph moved ahead on three fronts: petitions to Congress, letters to the candidates, and appeals to various states for public support.[40]

Although appeals were sent to Massachusetts, Maine, New York, Tennessee, and Pennsylvania, the longest was *General Joseph Smith's Appeal to the Green Mountain Boys*, drafted by William Phelps (who had returned to the Church in 1840) with input from the Prophet.[41] The document measured the distance Joseph had come politically since organizing the Church in 1830. In the millenarian mood of the early years, the nation's destiny, its elections, even its history meant little in light of the Second Coming. The predicted calamities, preaching the gospel, and the gathering of Israel dwarfed talk about the Revolution, the Constitution, and the growth of the United States. That detachment had ended by the time of the appeal to the Vermonters. Joseph now depicted himself as a true-blue American.

> I was born in Sharon, Vermont, in 1805,—where the first quarter of my life, grew with the growth, and strengthened with the strength of that "first born" State of the "United Thirteen." From the old "French War" to the final consummation of American Independence, my fathers, heart to heart, and shoulder to shoulder, with the noble fathers of our liberty, fought and bled; and, with the most of that venerable band of patriots, they have gone to rest,—bequeathing a glorious country with all her inherent rights to millions of posterity.

Driven by political expediency, Joseph had made himself a son of America.

That identification was a prelude to a description of the ironies of his situation: Loyal though he was, Joseph and his followers had received no relief from religious persecution. Mormons were deprived of "the blessings and privileges of an American citizen." They did not enjoy "life and religion according to the most virtuous and enlightened, customs, rules, and etiquet of the nineteenth century." Joseph's rhetorical strategy paralleled that of Frederick Douglass in his 1852 address "What to the Slave Is the Fourth of July?" "I am not included within the pale of this glorious anniversary," Douglass reminded his listeners. In the Vermont appeal, Joseph made common cause with slaves, asking, "What must the manacled nations think of freemen's rights in the land of liberty?"[42] Neither slaves nor Mormons benefited from the nation's freedom.

Joseph invited his Green Mountain brethren to help him obtain justice from Missouri. He asked for no direct political help, no votes in Congress, no soldiers for the Nauvoo Legion, only for support in coming conflicts. The appeal concluded on an apocalyptic note. Let everyone in the nation, rich, learned, wise, noble, poor, needy, black, white, "cleave to the knowledge of God . . . and prepare to meet the judge of the quick and the dead, for the hour of his coming is nigh."[43]

As the appeal to Vermont was launched, Colonel Frierson helped draft a memorial to Congress asking for reparations, one more in a long series of petitions that had been submitted since the Missouri war. This large document, termed the "scroll petition," was carried to Washington by Orson Pratt, along with an appeal for territorial powers, and submitted to the Senate on April 5. Appended to it was a fifty-foot-long sheet containing the signatures of 3,419 people injured by the Missouri persecutions.[44]

These efforts brought no results. The appeals, memorials, and petitions fell on deaf ears, as did the letters to the presidential candidates. On November 4, 1843, Joseph addressed letters containing a single question, to all five candidates: *"What will be your rule of action, relative to us, as a people?"* The replies were uniformly unsatisfactory. Clay was completely noncommittal: "I can enter into no engagements, make no promises, give no pledges to any particular portion of the people." Calhoun delivered a small lesson in political theory: "the case does not come within the Jurisdiction of the Federal Government."[45]

Frustrated and disillusioned, Joseph replied to Calhoun on January 2, 1844. "If the General Government has no power, to re-instate expelled citizens to their rights, there is a monstrous hypocrite fed and fostered from the hard earnings of the people!" How could a government not protect its citizens against the flagrant violations the Mormons had suffered? Was it true that a government was powerless? "The States rights doctrine are what feed mobs," Joseph once said. "They are a dead carcass, a stink and they shall ascend up as a stink offering in the nose of the Almighty." Congress had the constitutional power to "protect the nation against foreign invasion and internal broil"; why not protect the nation's citizens when their rights were trampled on? He urged Calhoun to ponder "the sublime idea that Congress, with the president as Executor, is as Almighty in its sphere, as Jehovah is in his."[46]

Within two weeks of writing to Calhoun, Joseph was considering his own candidacy for the presidency. He lectured on the Constitution and the candidates in mid-January, and on January 29 the Twelve Apostles nominated him for the presidency of the United States.[47] The *Times and Seasons* explained that Joseph ran because no other candidates met the Church's needs:

> Under existing circumstances we have no other alternative, and if we can accomplish our object well, if not we shall have the satisfaction of knowing that we have acted conscientiously and have used our best judgment; and if we have to throw away our votes, we had better do so upon a worthy, rather than upon an unworthy individual, who might make use of the weapon we put in his hand to destroy us with.

Joseph himself saw the need to assert the Church's rights:

> I would not have suffered my name to have been used by my friends on any wise as president of the United States or Candidate for that office If I &

my friends could have had the privilege of enjoying our religious & civel rights. . . . I feel it to be my right & privilege to obtain what influence & power I can lawfully in the United States for the protection of injured innocence.

Although his candidacy may have been a gesture, Joseph immediately planned a campaign. He had the vast Mormon missionary force to stump for him, and he conceived of a series of conferences throughout the nation. "There is oretory enough in the Church," he told the Twelve, "to carry me into the Presidential chair the first slide." With a large field of candidates and no clear favorite, he may have thought he could gain votes through convert baptisms and steal the victory in a split vote.[48] In any event, a campaign would present the case for wrongs to the Mormons and spread the Church's message.

The candidacy pushed Joseph into the role of statesman, requiring him to take stands on issues outside the Mormon realm. To get up a platform, he put William Phelps to work on *General Smith's Views of the Powers and Policy of the Government of the United States.*[49] He took positions on the great issues of the day: the national bank, Andrew Jackson's bête noire; and the annexation of Texas as a slave state, which raised the question of slavery in the West. Both issues divided the parties internally. The Whigs had long favored the bank, but John Tyler, the nominally Whig president, had by twice vetoing bank bills relinquished control of the Whigs to the long-time party leader Henry Clay, who was pro-bank. The Democrats had opposed the national bank for fear of favoring the rich and powerful, but they began to waffle on the issue as time went by and party members did better in the market economy. The more entrepreneurial wing favored paper money credit provided by banks; the idealists, led by Van Buren, stuck by hard money.

On the vexed question of admitting Texas with its slaves, northern and southern Whigs divided. Clay, who took no clear stand, was eventually nominated by acclamation at the party's Baltimore convention in May. Among the Democrats, Calhoun strenuously favored a new state for slaveholders; Van Buren opposed it. Like Clay, Van Buren avoided the Texas question until passage of an annexation treaty smoked him out. Then he courageously opposed annexation, even though he knew that alienating the Democrats' southern wing would cost him the nomination. The party's eventual candidate was Tennessee's James K. Polk, an enthusiastic supporter of annexation.[50]

Joseph Smith's *Views* proved him to be an independent candidate. His platform cut across party lines. Like the Whigs, he favored the national bank—his statement that the economy needed "the fostering care of government," was standard Whig doctrine. But he would limit the national bank to issuing bills only to the amount of its capital stock, a hard-money practice contrary to the Whig position. As for the Democrats, he called Jackson's administration "the *acme* of American glory, liberty and prosperity," and the Democratic Van Buren's presidency its nadir. At a time when party loyalties were near their zenith, his platform cast parties aside: "We have had democratic presidents; whig presidents; a pseudo democratic whig president; and now it is time to have *a president of the United States.*"[51]

On the Texas question, Joseph, like the Democrats, was an expansionist, but in his own way. "Come Texas: come Mexico; come Canada; and come all the world—let us be brethren: let us be one great family; and let there be universal peace." He saw expansion as brotherhood. "If Texas petitions Congress to be adopted among the sons of liberty, give her the right hand of fellowship; and refuse no[t] the same friendly grip to Canada and Mexico." But he proposed to eliminate slavery in Texas once it was admitted, defeating the slaveholders' purpose. To further repel them, he was for ending slavery everywhere: "Break off the shackles from the poor black man, and hire them to labor like other human beings." Joseph blithely believed emancipation could be accomplished peacefully. He envisioned happy compliance, not war. "The southern people are hospitable and noble: they will help to rid so *free* a country of every vestige of slavery"—if they were compensated for their losses. He proposed to pay owners with revenues from the sale of public lands.[52]

Joseph's antislavery policy was not devised just for the campaign. When asked about slavery during his Springfield trial in December 1842, he had come out for manumission. Orson Hyde wanted to know "what would you advi[s]e a man to do who come in the [Church] having a hundred slaves?" "I have always advised such to bring their slaves into a free country," was Joseph's reply; "set them free, Educate them and give them their equal rights." A few days later, Hyde pressed the question again: "What is the situation of the Negro?" he wanted to know. Joseph had a ready answer:

They come into the world slaves, mentally and physically. Change their situation with the white and they would be like them. They have souls and are subjects of salvation. Go into Cincinati and find one educated [black man who] rid[e]s in his carriage. He has risen by the power of his mind to his exalted state of respectability. Slaves in Washington [are] more refined than the president.

Hyde was concerned that the blacks would try to rise above the whites. Of course they would, Joseph said. "If I raised you to be my equal and then attempt to oppress you would you not be indignant and try to rise above me?" At that point Joseph's sympathy for the blacks began to waver. "Had I any thing to do with the Negro," he said, voicing the view of many antislavery partisans, "I would confine them by strict Laws to their own Species [and] put them on a national Equalization." Probably by "confinement to their own species" he meant no intermarriage.[53]

Joseph Smith was proud of his *Views*. He read the pamphlet to visitors and printed 1,500 copies for distribution to politicians and newspaper editors. Idealistic but politically impractical, *Views* revealed him at his exuberant best. Slavery seemed as solvable as every other social problem. Joseph believed he could sweep away stubborn selfish interests in magnanimous gestures for the general good.

> I would, as the universal friend of man, open the prisons; open the eyes; open the ears and open the hearts of all people, to behold and enjoy freedom, unadulterated freedom: and God, who once cleansed the violence of the earth with a flood; whose Son laid down his life for the salvation of all his Father gave him out of the world; and who has promised that he will come and purify the world again with fire in the last days, should be supplicated by me for the good of the people.

He effectively expanded his Zion society to the entire nation. The confidence that his own people could become godly was extended to all citizens—even prisoners.[54] As prophet and priest, he would call down a heavenly blessing.

The *Times and Seasons* promoted Joseph's merits in article after article, and letters were dispatched explaining his position on Texas, banking, and prison reform. In April 1844, forty-seven conferences were scheduled in fourteen states, and 339 elders signed up to campaign. On May 17, the day that Democrats met in Baltimore to choose their candidates, a "convention of the state" was held in Joseph Smith's office. That night friends burned a barrel of tar in front of the mansion, lifted Joseph to their shoulders, and marched twice around the fire before escorting him home to the music of a band.[55]

THE KINGDOM

With one eye on Washington, Joseph also looked west. During the spring of 1844, while the presidential campaign gathered momentum, plans for a Mormon outpost in Texas, Oregon, or California took shape. Mormons had faced west ever since an 1830 revelation instructed them to look for the site of the New Jerusalem on the "borders of the Lamanites." Independence, the departure point for trading expeditions to Santa Fe and fur-trapping ventures up the Missouri, had been chosen as the site of Zion. The West had long served a role in the American imagination as a place for solving social problems. Labor reformers thought oppressed factory workers could find independence and dignity on farms of their own in the West. After Mark Twain's Huck Finn lost interest in life along the Mississippi, he lit out for the territories—as did Samuel Clemens himself. A half dozen years after Joseph considered migration west, California drew thousands of Americans in search of gold and improved fortunes. When the Mormons began to move into Illinois in the aftermath of the Missouri war, Stephen Douglas, always westward-thinking, suggested they move to Oregon. Joseph may have been considering California as early as 1842, when he realized Hancock County could never contain the stream of British immigrants flowing into Nauvoo.[56]

If the West was promise, it was also danger. When the new national government provided for western settlement in the Land Ordinance of 1785, Congress worried about the degraded forms of life springing up in the West. They provided land for schools in every township to prevent western settlers from regressing to savagery. Lyman Beecher urged Connecticut Congregationalists to send missionaries west to halt Roman Catholicism's encroachment into the vast "empty" western spaces.[57] The West was a stage for adventurers like Aaron Burr, whose filibustering expedition in the service of an inland empire caused his downfall. John C. Bennett played on long-standing fears when he informed the nation in 1842 that Joseph Smith planned to invade the West and establish a great inland empire dominated by a corrupt religion.

The prospect of a Mormon empire evoked horror and wonder. Before his apostasy, Bennett tantalized the Mormons with visions of their armies claiming great spaces, revealing his own feverish dreams. But the Mormons' friend James Arlington Bennet also hinted that he would join the Prophet on such a venture. The editor of the *New York Herald*, James Gordon Bennett, speculated in 1841 that "we should not be surprised if Joe Smith were made Governor of a new religious territory in the west, that may rival the Arabians one of these days," making reference to the Muslim empire. Bennett thought the Mormons would "one day, control the whole valley of the Mississippi, from the peaks of the Alleghanies to the pinnacles of the Rocky Mountains." Because of these preconceptions, every Mormon move west seemed like an imperial scheme. The apprehensions were part fantasy and part reality. Eventually, the Saints did build a vast inland empire, but one they conquered by industry rather than by arms.[58]

On February 20, 1844, three weeks after being nominated for the presidency, Joseph told the Twelve to send an exploring expedition to California and Oregon in search of locations "where we can remove after the Temple is completed and build a city in a day and have a government of our own in a healthy climate." He did not intend to abandon Nauvoo or the temple; Nauvoo would anchor the Mormon kingdom in the East while stakes were formed in the West. The next day the Twelve selected eight men for the assignment.[59]

All through the spring plans were made and information gathered. To survey the West, a party of twenty-five was to follow the Santa Fe Trail to New Mexico, press on to the Pacific, and then head north for Oregon, their mission to locate sites for large settlements.[60] In March, Lyman Wight and George Miller, writing from the Mormons' Wisconsin logging camp at Black River Falls, proposed a move to Texas. The Twelve sent a delegate to confer with Sam Houston, who assured them of a welcome in a region starved for inhabitants. To encompass these broad plans, Joseph revived his earlier conception of a greater Zion. "The whole of America is Zion," he told the Saints. "From henceforth the elders shall build churches where ever the people receive the gospel."[61]

In March 1844, the western explorations led to the addition of a political arm to the governing structure of the Church. Joseph may have been thinking of organizing a political kingdom for two years or even longer.[62] He had become convinced that sympathetic outsiders would cooperate with the Mormon priesthood, not only for the benefit of the Church but for the well-being of society as a whole. Westward explorations, which blended Mormon interests with the interests of other American migrants streaming toward Oregon, suggested the need for a body combining Church members and friendly outsiders. Between March 10 and March 13, 1844, Joseph formed the Council of Fifty, mostly drawn from the established Church elite but also including a handful of non-Mormons. The council was conceived as an initial step toward government for the Kingdom of God.[63]

The council's immediate task was to oversee the exploration of the West, its main work during the Nauvoo period.[64] It aimed, as William Clayton put it, "to seek out a location and a home where the saints can dwell in peace and health, and where they can erect the ensign & standard of liberty for the nations, and live by the laws of God without being oppressed and mobbed under a tyrannical government without protection from the laws."[65] Within two weeks of its organization, the council had devised a scheme for western settlement on a large scale. They wanted to establish a force, authorized by the United States Government, to guard American settlers moving west. In the name of Joseph Smith, the council asked Congress to authorize Smith to raise 100,000 "armed volunteers" to keep order, repel invasions by foreign powers, and protect settlers from Indians, robbers, and desperadoes. Not officially members of the United States Army, though acting in a military capacity, the volunteers were to save the cost of posting a standing army in the West. The council borrowed an idea from Benjamin Franklin, who

decades earlier had suggested settling the West with civilian militias marching to their new homes "under the conduct of the government to be established over them." More recently, Missouri senator Lewis F. Linn had
introduced a bill to militarize the overland route from Missouri to Oregon.
Apparently the council's deeper motive was to provide an authorized
defense force for the Saints in case of mob attack as they moved west. The
memorial asked that "no citizen of these United States shall obstruct, or
attempt to obstruct, or hinder, so *good*, so *great*, so *noble* an enterprize."[66]

Orson Hyde, who carried the memorial to Congress in April, soon ran
into problems. John Wentworth and James Semple, the Illinois congressmen who cooperated in submitting the memorial to Congress, warned
Hyde that a bill favoring one particular group in the West would face insurmountable obstacles. The Mormon presence, moreover, would endanger
the touchy relations with Britain over Oregon, where a treaty provided for
joint occupancy by the two nations.[67] Finally, President Tyler had already
proposed a line of forts along the Oregon Trail.[68]

Aware of these obstacles, Stephen Douglas advised the Mormons to set
out without authorization. He told Hyde that "in 5 years a noble State
might be formed, and then if they would not receive us into the Union, we
would have a government of our own." Governor Ford later recommended
California. No one understood that Mormons, fearing attacks from the
Missourians, felt a need for military protection.[69]

In the middle of the negotiations, Hyde received a reprimand from the
council. A provision in the memorial proposed to make Joseph Smith "a
member of the army of these United States" with authority to act in the
army's name. To overcome the objection that this was unconstitutional,
Hyde had removed the offending clause. Learning of his unilateral decision, the council reprimanded Hyde for compromising its dignity. Stung by
the criticism, Hyde wrote back a long apology that incidentally shed light
on the council's conception of itself:

> I am aware that our council stands on the summit of all earthly powers, and
> that he who presides over it is God's messenger to execute justice and judg-
> ment in the Earth, and that any seeming neglect to maintain his dignity and
> honor, and that also of the Council generally, touches a very tender place, and
> renders the delinquent justly entitled to the censure and warm reproof of
> your dignified and honorable body.

The words hint at the Council of Fifty's belief that it was more than a body
to coordinate the activities of the Church with the United States. The
council was, theologically speaking, "the summit of all earthly powers." In
the same spirit, Parley Pratt wrote in April that the Council of Fifty is "the

most exalted Council with which our earth is at present Dignified." Lyman Wight said to Joseph during the presidential campaign, "You are already president pro tem of the world."[70]

As the council's original records are not available to researchers, its exact nature is hard to determine, but the council may have considered itself the incipient organization for millennial rule, a shadow government awaiting the demise of worldly political authority and the beginning of Christ's earthly reign. In early April 1844, Joseph "prophecied the entire overthrow of this nation in a few years." Perhaps he believed that provision had to be made for impending chaos and, practical as always, took the first step. George Miller, a member of the council, said Joseph appointed some of the brethren as "princes in the Kingdom of God."[71] The phrase "Kingdom of God," usually understood to mean the Church or the regime of righteousness, was interpreted in 1844 to mean an actual government of the whole society. In a general conference address a month after the Council of Fifty's organization, Sidney Rigdon described the literal nature of the Kingdom: "When God sets up a system of salvation, he sets up a system of government; when I speak of a government I mean what I say; I mean a government that shall rule over temporal and spiritual affairs."[72] It would be typical of the literal-minded Joseph Smith to bring such a kingdom into being. While most millenarians waited for God to establish millennial rule, Joseph formed an actual government, just as he constructed an actual city rather than waiting for the New Jerusalem to descend from heaven. Taking his lead from Daniel's prophecy of a kingdom in the last days, Joseph told the Saints: "I calculate to be one of the Instruments of setting up the Kingdom of Daniel, by the word of the Lord, and I intend to lay a foundation that will revolutionize the whole world . . . it will not be by Sword or Gun that this Kingdom will roll on—the power of truth is such that—all nations will be under the necessity of obeying the Gospel." The mystical name for the Council of Fifty given by revelation was "the kingdom of God and his Law, with the keys and power thereof and judgments in the hands of his servants Ahman Christ."[73]

One historian has called Joseph's political involvement the "dreamlike . . . politics of utopia," which it may well be considered. But this was a century of dreamlike politics. Marx dreamed of government withering away. Dostoevsky envisioned a theocratic kingdom of God on earth. Inspired by dreams like these, revolutions tore up most of Europe in 1848. In the United States, the issue of God in government was still alive. Timothy Dwight, grandson of Jonathan Edwards and president of Yale College, had not long before lamented that the United States formed its Constitution "without any acknowledgement of GOD; without any recognition of his mercies to us, as a people, of his government, or even of his existence." How could the nation not be "*a smoke in the nostrils* of JEHOVAH." Orestes Brownson thought that church should be dissolved into state in order to infuse moral and religious values into everything. "Our views, if carried out," Brownson wrote, "would realize not a union, but the unity, the identity, of Church and State."[74] Different in detail, these schemes shared a dream of a God-backed, righteous government.

In forming a godly government, Joseph did not cite Dwight or the reformers, of whom likely he knew nothing, but relied on the Bible, the inspiration for the godly kingdoms. "It has been the design of Jehovah, from the commencement of the world, and is his purpose now," an 1842 editorial in the *Times and Seasons* argued, to "take the reins of government into his own hand." Under Moses, the motto of Israel was "The Lord is our lawgiver."

> This is the only thing that can bring about the "restitution of all things, spoken of by all the holy prophets since the world was". . . . Other attempts to promote universal peace and happiness in the human family have proved abortive; every effort has failed; every plan and design has fallen to the ground; it needs the wisdom of God, the intelligence of God, and the power of God to accomplish this.[75]

From a certain Christian perspective, government under God was logical and natural. To critics, of course, Joseph's plan for the Kingdom of God looked like a program for Mormon dominance. The council included only three outsiders, and Joseph was, as Hyde noted in his letter, "God's messenger to execute justice and judgment in the Earth." Did not that put all power in his hands? Joseph never understood this difficulty, thinking his authority and democracy entirely compatible. When a St. Louis reporter asked "by what principle I got so much power," Joseph answered "on the principle of truth and virtue which would last when I was dead." "I go emphatically, virtuously, and humanely for a THEODEMOCRACY," he wrote in the spring of 1844, "where God and the people hold the power to conduct the affairs of men in righteousness. And where liberty, free trade, and sailor's right, and the protection of life and property shall be maintained inviolate, for the benefit of ALL."[76]

He did not intend to force his religion on anyone. He thought of himself as the champion of free worship. Nauvoo's ordinance for religious freedom listed a dozen religions allowed to practice in the city. Josiah Quincy was surprised to hear Joseph invite a Methodist to preach from a Mormon pulpit. The socialist John Finch noted that "Joe Smith was in the practice of inviting strangers who visited Nauvoo, of every shade of politics and religion, to lecture to his people." Joseph could honestly say that "it is one of the first principles of my life and one that I have cultivated from my child-hood, having been taught it of my father, to allow every one the liberty of conscience." He made it an article of faith to allow people to "worship how, where, or what they may." He declared, "I am an advocate of unadulterated freedom."[77]

But Joseph's kingdom had no place for electoral politics. He saw in poli-tics "disappointed ambition, thirst for power, pride, corruption, party spirit, faction, patronage; perquisites, fame, tangling alliances; priest-craft and spiritual wickedness in *high places*."[78] He would never consider holding elec-tions for seats on the Council of Fifty, whose members were called by reve-lation. Worthiness meant more than popularity. Joseph would substitute *salus republicae suprema lex esto*, the good of the commonwealth is the high-est law, for *vox populi vox dei*, the voice of the people is the voice of God.[79] As he told the Nauvoo High Council: "It was the principles of democracy that the peoples voice should be heard when the voice was just, but when it was not just it was no longer democratic, but if the minority views are more just, then Aristarchy should be the governing principle. I.E. the wisest & best laws should be made." He was more devoted to rights and justice than to government by elections.[80] Rule by the wise seemed more sensible than government by the mistaken.

Instinctively, Joseph had returned to an older, more paternalistic politi-cal theory, exemplified in the "patriot king" ideal of government champi-oned by Henry St. John Bolingbroke, the eighteenth-century Tory, whose writings influenced American political philosophy down to Andrew Jack-son. The patriot king, a true father of his people, stood above party and ruled selflessly in their behalf. In an act shocking to democratic sensibilities, at the Council of Fifty meeting on April 11, 1844, "Prest J[oseph] was voted our P[rophet] P[riest] and K[ing] with loud Hosannas." The office of king came out of temple rituals where other Saints were anointed "kings and priests," according to the prescriptions in the Revelation of St. John, but here the title had overt political implications. Joseph was to be king in the Kingdom of God, or "King and Ruler over Israel." His election as king did not alter his behavior or give him additional power—he was still called "chairman" of the council—but it did indicate Joseph's frame of mind.[81]

Monarchy did not repel Joseph as it did other Americans. A righteous king was the best kind of ruler, the *Book of Mormon* had taught. Although it now seems like a far remove from American political reality, the idea of a benevolent ruler governing according to his best judgment rather than popular will was not foreign to political culture in the nineteenth century, when monarchs still governed most of Europe. "Nothing can so surely and so effectually restore the virtue and public spirit, essential to the preserva-tion of liberty, and national prosperity, as the reign of such a prince," Bolingbroke had written a century earlier, and that ideal of the virtuous ruler was perpetuated by the first five presidents of the United States.[82]

Joseph saw even more in kingship. By returning to the Bible for inspiration, he evoked an ancient idea that the king must rule as a priest as well. Joseph admired Melchizedek, a "king and priest to the most high God," who blessed the people in every way under "a perfect law of Theocracy holding keys of power and blessings stood as God to give laws to the people, administering endless lives to the sons and daughters of Adam." Joseph's aim was sacred kingship, a side of monarchy Britain had sloughed off by the eighteenth century.[83] He was for redemptive authority.

Judging by his practice, Joseph was drawn to constitutional, not absolute, monarchy. He was "voted" king, according to William Clayton, suggesting that the council elected its monarch. As a further limitation, Joseph ran the Church through councils, governing much like the traditional "king in council." Non-Mormon as well as Mormon members of the Council of Fifty had "a full and free opportunity of representing their views, interests and principles." A right to the ear of the king rather than outright voting power was the basis of their influence. Besides the restraint of conciliar government, an impeachment process provided for a trial of the president should he go astray.[84]

All these formed the rudiments of a constitution, but the emphasis was not on constitutional mechanisms for checking power. The Council of Fifty made an effort to write a constitution and then gave up. The virtuous men on the council constituted a "living constitution," as they were called; their character guarded against the misuse of power rather than relying on counterbalancing branches of government. It was a traditional idea. Timothy Dwight had said the ruler's "good-will to Mankind, accomplishes directly most of those desirable objects, at which the political Constitutions, and the Laws, of Society aim." Joseph had voiced this principle in his 1839 letter from Liberty Jail: "No power or influance can or ought to be maintained by virtue of the priesthood, only by persuasion, by long suffering, by gentleness and meakness and by love unfaigned." He had reverted to the Puritan, the biblical, and the patriot king ideal of the righteous ruler. Perhaps not coincidentally, Joseph set up the council at the very moment when United States presidents were giving up the idea of government by the virtuous in exchange for rule by party.[85] Joseph spoke for those who lamented the passing of an old ideal of righteous government.

To critics, the high sentiments gave little assurance that Joseph's authority would be held in check. They saw kingship not as the recovery of an ideal, but as an arrogant power grab. For Mormons, anointing Joseph a king held no terrors. William Clayton, clerk of the council, remembered that "the principles of eternal truths rolled forth to the hearers without reserve and the hearts of the servants of God [were] made to rejoice exceedingly." On April 18, 1844, Clayton recorded the fifty-two names of "those who have been called upon to form the grand K[ingdom] of G[od] by Revelation." He noted that "it seems like heaven began on earth and the power of god is with us."[86]

The Council of Fifty met nearly every week in the spring of 1844. Temporarily, it became the leading council in Church government. In the last days of Nauvoo, the members continued to meet, but in Utah, Brigham Young let the council lapse, reviving it only infrequently. In the 1880s, in an apocalyptic period when the Church was under pressure from the polygamy prosecutions and anticipating the Millennium, President John Taylor renewed the council's meetings.[87] Lacking a purpose in the twentieth century, the Council of Fifty became a historical artifact of Joseph's dream of organizing the Kingdom of God on earth.

TWENTY-NINE

CONFRONTATIONS

JANUARY–JUNE 1844

Joseph called upon the Citizens to defend the lives of their wives & children,
fathers and mothers, brothers & sisters from being murdered by the mob. He
urged them in strong terms not to shed innocent blood.—not to act in the least
on the offensive but invariably in the defensive and if we die—die like men of
God and secure a glorious resurrection. He concluded by invoking the Great
God to bless the people.

WILLIAM CLAYTON, Diary, June 18, 1844

JOSEPH'S POLITICAL BUSINESS ALONE was enough to keep him busy in the
hectic last six months of his life. He was mayor and chief magistrate of
the municipal court. In January he was nominated for the presidency of the
United States and began his campaign. In February, the search for a refuge
in the West began in earnest. In March he organized the political Kingdom
of God and began meeting weekly with the Council of Fifty. Besides mounting exploring expeditions, the council sent three delegates to Washington
to ask permission to send a volunteer military force into Texas, California,
and Oregon. The combination of grand operations and the pedestrian
duties of his civic offices seems more than one man could handle.

Adding to his worries, he had to deal with the fallout from plural marriage. Rogue missionaries teaching "spiritual wives" had to be disciplined.
A notice in the February 1, 1844, issue of the *Times and Seasons* announced:

> As we have lately been credibly informed, that an Elder of the Church of
> Jesus Christ, of Latter-day Saints, by the name of Hiram Brown, has been
> preaching Polygamy, and other false and corrupt doctrines, in the county of
> Lapeer, state of Michigan.
> This is to notify him and the Church in general, that he has been cut off
> from the church, for his iniquity.

Joseph and Hyrum taught against the doctrine from the pulpit. Joseph
insisted "the Church had not received any license from him to commit
adultery fornication or any such thing but to the contrary if any man Com-

mit adultery He Could not receive the Ce[le]stial kingdom of God."[1] The distinction between priesthood calls to take additional wives and unlicensed indulgence was clear to him if not always to others.

Through the spring, immigrants arrived by the boatload and had to be accommodated. Two hundred ten souls from Liverpool came on the *Maid of Iowa* in mid-April; a smaller company arrived the week before. Joseph had tried to greet each vessel personally, but in 1844 the press of other duties prevented his attendance at the wharf. He tried to find land for the newcomers where he could, but for the most part, they shifted for themselves, moving in with friends and family while getting settled.[2]

Sickness interrupted the flow of business with merciless regularity. When Willard Richards's wife fell ill, Joseph was called to her house. "Laid on hands. Directed some Raspberry tea and she was better." The pregnant Emma required more attention. He attended to her closely during a sick spell in mid-May. Still, he got away to the theater for performances of *Damon and Pythias* and *Idiot Witness*.[3]

His two ongoing building projects, the temple and the Nauvoo House, required constant attention. A single revelation in January 1841 had commanded construction of both buildings, and the two remained linked in Joseph's mind.[4] The 1841 revelation commanded the Church to make "a solemn proclamation" to "all the Kings of the world," the president, and the state governors. The temple, he was sure, would "undoubtedly attract the attention of the great men of the earth." He anticipated visits from eminent leaders—like Josiah Quincy and his friend Charles Francis Adams, who stopped in Nauvoo in May 1844. The city lacked a "place where men of wealth, character, and influence can go to repose themselfs and it is necessary we should have such a place." For three years, he pressed vigorously for construction on the Nauvoo House. In March 1844, finally recognizing that the double construction project exceeded the capacity of Nauvoo's economy, he suspended construction.[5]

Rational calculation could not justify two such vast projects as the temple and the Nauvoo House, any more than it made sense to practice plural marriage or gather to Zion. Joseph's revelations drove him beyond prudence. Once a doctrine or project came to him by revelation, he was indomitable. In 1844, he was more expansive than ever, despite the overload of business. He saw himself as a rough stone rolling down a hill. In the summer, he came to an abrupt halt.

DISSENT

Along with the rush of business, Joseph faced growing opposition within his own ranks. He was stunned by the defections of loyal followers. In the last six months of his life, both a counselor in the First Presidency and the commanding officer of the Nauvoo Legion turned against him. The surgeon general of the legion and two sons of his old friend and legal counsel Elias Higbee joined the group. By midspring 1844, a half dozen of his closest associates had publicly denounced him as a fallen prophet. In his anger and frustration, he berated them and cut them off.

William Law gained Joseph's confidence after he came to Nauvoo in 1839. An immigrant from Northern Ireland who had converted to Mormonism in Canada, Law was one of the few Saints to arrive with capital. He and his brother Wilson Law purchased land and constructed steampowered mills to produce flour and lumber. William Law, said to have "great suavity of manners and amiability of character," impressed Joseph. When Hyrum left the First Presidency to move into his father's position as patriarch, Law was made Joseph's counselor. Law admired Joseph. "I have carefully watched his movements since I have been here," he wrote a friend after a year, "and I assure you I have found him honest and honourable in all our transactions which have been very considerable I believe he is an honest upright man, and as to his follies let who ever is guiltless throw the first stone." Law was one of the nine trusted men given the endowment in May 1842, and he and his wife, Jane, were members of the Anointed Quorum that met regularly in prayer meetings in the fall of 1843.[6]

Law's disaffection began when Hyrum showed him the plural marriage revelation. Law had disputed John Bennett's charges of Nauvoo polygamy and temporarily allied with Hyrum and William Marks to deny the existence of the practice. After Hyrum accepted the revelation, he tried to persuade Law.[7] Although they considered plural marriage, William and Jane eventually decided Joseph had gone too far. On January 1, 1844, Law wrote in his diary that what he had learned "paralizes the nerves, chills the currents of the heart, and drives the brain almost to madness." Stories were later told of William pleading with Joseph, his hands around the Prophet's neck. Joseph had made the acceptance of plural marriage in principle a prerequisite to couples being sealed for eternity. William and Jane were torn, but by the end of 1843, they had made their decision against plural marriage. On January 8, 1844, Law learned he had been dropped from the First Presidency. Attempts at reconciliation failed, and he was excommunicated in April.[8]

Another dissenter, Robert Foster, a convert from England, had accompanied Joseph to Washington in 1839 as Sidney Rigdon's physician. In Nauvoo, Foster was appointed surgeon general in the Nauvoo Legion and justice of the peace in the municipal court. Like Law he invested in real estate near the temple, where he built the Mammoth Hotel. An early sign of trouble came when Joseph publicly taunted Foster for resisting Joseph's efforts to give first priority to land on the flat on Main Street near his house. The Church owned property there and Joseph wanted it developed first. "This is the way people swell like the ox or a toad," he said of Foster and the hill developers. When Joseph required new immigrants to buy from him, Foster and Law accused him of managing the real estate to his own advantage. His retort: "They are fools [and] ought to hide their heads in a hollow pumkin." Joseph also resented the diversion of lumber and resources to private house-building rather than to the construction of the temple and Nauvoo House. People like Foster, Joseph said, "build a great many little skeletons . . . but there is no flesh on them."[9]

Joseph and Foster still remained friendly. Foster gave the gracious toast at the Smiths' party in October 1843. More a civic figure than a religious leader, he was elected school commissioner in Hancock County in August 1843 with the Mormon vote and braved armed opposition from anti-Mormons when he tried to take office. Though Foster was firmly identified with the Mormons, he joined the dissidents in the winter of 1843–44. When a reform church was organized, Foster was selected one of its Twelve Apostles.[10]

Opposition to Joseph brought together men of diverse character. Chauncey Higbee, age twenty-three, son of Joseph's deceased legal adviser Elias Higbee, had been accused of seducing women during the time when John Bennett was operating in Nauvoo. His brother Francis Higbee felt threatened when Joseph proposed to a woman Higbee was courting. Joseph Jackson had been given a job as a real estate clerk when he arrived destitute in Nauvoo. After he was spurned in his suit for Lovina Smith, Hyrum's daughter, he became a borderline criminal. Robert Foster and William and Wilson Law were respectable men. The heart of their controversy with Joseph was plural marriage. Joseph had predicted his people would turn against him if he told them all he knew; in this instance, he was right.[11]

The dissenters troubled Joseph mainly because he feared plots to haul him away to certain death in Missouri. The previous December, Porter Rockwell had brought back reports of plans to ensnare Joseph. Rumors of traitors conspiring with his enemies made him wary. The dissenters, equally suspicious, feared harassment from the Nauvoo police, a force recently organized to protect the Prophet. William Marks, the president of the Nauvoo Stake High Council, who had rejected the plural marriage revelation, became excited when a bonfire was built near his house, fearing the police had been sworn to do away with him. During the city council's investigation of the occurrence in January 1844, even Hyrum was concerned that secret Danite bands were organizing as they had in Far West in 1838. People on both sides suspected plots and counterplots. The hearing in the council dissipated some of the tension; at the end Wilson Law declared, "I am Joseph's friend, he has no better friend in the world." But the reconciliation was temporary. The deep disagreement on principles went unresolved. Francis Higbee testified that "Mr Law, Mr Marks & probably one or two others could not subscribe to all things in the church."[12]

Francis Higbee thought Joseph had cast a slur on his character during the January city council hearing, and wrote a furious letter demanding vindication in ecclesiastical court. "Sir, you have struck a blow at evry thing which renders existence sweet," Higbee stormed. "You have sought to blast evry proud hope, and evry fond expectation, by throwing into free circulation reports, the truth of which, God is some day to Judge." In retribution, Joseph brought Higbee before the municipal court for slanderous and abusive language. There the Prophet's method of airing all grievances worked temporarily. At a city council meeting, Higbee acknowledged that he had said many hard things against Joseph and was forgiven. Joseph's journal says that "all difficulties between me and Francis M. Higby are eternally buried and I am to be his friend forever. To which F. M. Higby replied I will be his friend forever and his right hand man." Joseph ordered his criticisms of Higbee stricken from previous minutes.[13]

Trouble broke out again when Joseph spoke in public meeting against one of his critics. In a speech at the temple, he suggested by innuendo that Charles Foster, Robert Foster's brother, had written a critical letter to the *New York Tribune* about misappropriation of temple funds and the impossibility of completing the huge building. When Charles Foster asked from the audience if he was the man, Joseph indicated he was. Insulted, Foster retorted, "You shall hear from me." Joseph whipped back, "I fine you $10.00 for that threat and disturbing the meeting." Robert Foster rose to calm the situation and defend his brother. "No one has heard him threaten you," he insisted. But hundreds of voices in the audience cried, "I have." Joseph called for order and threatened to fine the doctor if he did not stop talking.[14]

By this time the dissidents were organizing. In mid-March, Joseph Jackson tried to recruit two Nauvoo citizens, Marenus G. Eaton and Abiathar Williams, with horror stories about "men tied hand and foot and run through the heart with a sword, and there heads taken off, and then buried." Eaton accompanied Jackson to the back room of the "Key Stone Store" on the hill, where Robert Foster and Chauncey Higbee added tales of many wives. They told Eaton that Joseph had tried to seduce Foster's wife with the spiritual wife doctrine. Foster caught them eating together and, after Joseph departed, demanded to know what was going on. When his wife said nothing, he threatened to shoot her, but she claimed innocence. Then he thrust a double-barreled pistol into her hand and demanded, "Defend yourself, for if you don't tell me, either you or I would shoot," whereupon she fainted. Finally, she told him what he had believed all along: Joseph "by preaching the spiritual wife system to her had endeavored to seduce her."[15]

When Joseph heard the story, he went to see Mrs. Foster with William Clayton and the German-speaking dentist, Alexander Neibaur. In the presence of the witnesses, Joseph asked Mrs. Foster if she "ever in her life knew him guilty of an immoral or indecent act." She answered no, and he asked if he used indecent language or preached the spiritual wife doctrine to her or proposed illicit conduct when he had dinner with her during Robert Foster's absence. Clayton said all the answers were no. The next day from the stand, Joseph told the congregation that a caucus planned to "destroy all the Smith family in a few weeks." He named Chauncey Higbee, Robert Foster, Joseph Jackson, and William and Wilson Law.[16]

Joseph made one more attempt at reconciliation with Robert Foster. In municipal court on April 13, he asked, "Have I ever misused you [in] any way?" Foster responded, "I do not feel at liberty to answer." "Did I ever wrong you in deal[ing] personally?" Still not at liberty. "Tell me where I have done wrong and I will ask your forgiveness. I want to prove to this company by your own testimony that I have treated you honorably." All Foster would say was "I shall testify no further at present." After the exchange, Joseph brought charges against Foster "for abusing my character privately, for throwing out slanderous insinuation against me, for conspiring against my peace and Safety, for conspiring against my life, for conspiring against the peace of my family."[17]

On April 18, four dissenters were excommunicated: Robert Foster, Wilson Law, William Law, and Jane Law. They were given no opportunity to defend themselves or bring witnesses. Contrary to standard protocol in Church courts, the defendants were not present.[18]

Cutting off the dissidents did not end the wrangling. A week after the excommunications, a city marshal arrested Augustus Spencer, another dissenter, for assaulting Spencer's brother Orson. Robert and Charles Foster and Chauncey Higbee came charging down the hill to complain. Charles Foster drew a pistol on Joseph in front of his office and had to be restrained. Foster and Higbee said that "they would be God damned if they would not shoot the Mayor." Robert Foster "swore by God they would see the Mayor &c. in hell before they would go." They all suspected Joseph of conniving at their destruction. Robert Foster told Joseph there was "Daniteism in Nauvoo."[19]

Suspicion ran high. The dissidents thought the secret police were after them, and Joseph believed the dissenters were plotting against his life. Charles Foster wanted to open the case before the public and publish the results in the *Warsaw Signal*. Joseph said he would agree if Foster would publish in a Nauvoo paper only and "not attempt to raise a mob." When Foster would not agree to be quiet, Joseph said he "had made the last overtures of peace" and "delivered him into the hand of God." The dissidents were relieved of their offices in the legion and proceedings were brought against them in the Nauvoo Masonic lodge. On April 21, 1844, the dissenters organized a reform church.[20]

ENEMIES

Mounting opposition outside of Nauvoo made dissension within the city doubly troubling. The *Warsaw Signal* would be delighted to print news of Mormon squabbling, and Joseph feared that advertising internal criticism would feed the anti-Mormon flames. Anti-Mormon committees organized prior to the elections of 1842 and 1843 came together again in January 1844 following an attempt by Nauvoo law enforcement officers to arrest Milton Cook, a non-Mormon, in Carthage on bastardy charges. Believing a non-Mormon would never receive justice in a Mormon court, a group of Carthaginians prevented the arrest. When the Nauvoo officers tried again, they faced a half dozen men with bayonets. In the ensuing melee, one Nauvoo man was injured. The Carthage anti-Mormon committee promised to defend citizens like Cook "at the point of the bayonet" if necessary.[21]

Not everyone was as virulent as the extremists on the committees. A number of newspaper editors, bellwethers of public opinion, tried to calm the hotheads. The *Alton Telegraph*, a Democratic paper published in the prosperous river port town 180 miles downstream from Nauvoo, was appalled at the kidnapping of the Averys in November 1843. "No matter how great the injury inflicted by those who have been kidnapped, upon their captors, the act is alike arbitrary, illegal and oppressive." The headline read "Unheard-of Outrage." Thomas Gregg, the editor of the *Warsaw Message*, assured his readers of his contempt for Joseph Smith but recommended moderation. "We feel sure that a majority even of his most firm supporters, would prefer peace and quietness, to rapine and violence."[22] The Quaker-reared Gregg proposed a public meeting in Carthage where grievances could be aired and a compromise effected. A correspondent from the fire-brands absolutely refused: "I say, No, Never!! Just as well might you call upon us to strike hands with Pirates, or to compromise with the Powers of Darkness." But the moderate Gregg persisted:

> We see no use in attempting to disguise the fact, that many in our midst contemplate a total extermination of that people; that the thousands of defenceless women and children, aged and infirm, who are congregated at Nauvoo, must be driven out—aye DRIVEN—SCATTERED—like the leaves before the Autumn blast! But what good citizen, let us ask—what lover of his country and his race, but contemplates such an event with horror?[23]

Through the spring of 1844, the *Quincy Whig* and the *Alton Telegraph* continued their cautious course, but the *Warsaw Message* fell into the hands of the anti-Mormon faction. On February 14, Thomas Sharp took over the editor's chair from Gregg and issued the paper under its old name of the

Warsaw Signal. The *Alton Telegraph* editorially urged the *Signal* to go easy on the Mormons and "allay, as far as possible, the excitement against that people." Sharp would have none of it.

> Now Mr. Telegraph, you know but little of the circumstances by which the people of this County are surrounded—you know nothing of the repeated insults and injuries received by our citizens from the Heads of the Mormon Church. . . . We say Mr. Telegraph, you can know nothing of these things, or you could not undertake to lecture us, for endeavoring to expose such a gang of outlaws, blacklegs and bloodsuckers.[24]

The moderates could not understand the extremists' fear and anger. According to the extremists, Mormons were not just a nuisance, they were a threat and an insult. Joseph's escape from arrest through habeas corpus writs in the Nauvoo municipal court and the prosecution of non-Mormons like Cook in Nauvoo courts became to the anti-Mormons examples of "galling oppression." Although Thomas Gregg thought Joseph was "steeped up to the very eyes in sin," Gregg was not personally insulted like Sharp, who felt invaded "by the repeated insults and injuries of this *Monster* in human shape."[25]

After breaking with Joseph, the more obstreperous dissenters—Charles Foster and the Higbees—joined forces with the anti-Mormons. A long letter from Foster detailing his complaints was printed in the *Signal,* and Chauncey Higbee became the Nauvoo precinct leader of the county anti-Mormon committee. William Law spoke on the usurpations in Nauvoo at a Carthage anti-Mormon meeting. At a similar meeting in Warsaw in June, Francis Higbee's name was "loudly called for." He recounted a Mormon history "characterised by the darkest and most diabolical deeds which has ever disgraced humanity"—exactly what the meeting wanted to hear.[26]

KING FOLLETT SERMON

With bombshells bursting around him, Joseph continued to meet weekly with the Council of Fifty to plan western explorations and keep the presidential campaign moving. Temple construction resumed as the spring weather allowed, and in the groves around the temple Joseph delivered theological addresses to his people. At the annual conference in April, he gave what the literary critic Harold Bloom has called "one of the truly remarkable sermons ever preached in America." Though never canonized as scripture, the King Follett sermon, known only through the overlapping notes of four diarists, has been called the culminating statement of Joseph Smith's theology.[27]

The April 7, 1844, morning session of the annual Church conference, held in a grove a quarter mile east of the temple, attracted the largest con-gregation ever assembled in Nauvoo. That afternoon, Joseph spoke for more than two hours, straining to speak over a high wind. The next day his voice was gone, and he could not speak at all.[28]

The occasion of the afternoon meeting was the accidental death of city constable King Follett, crushed when a tub of rocks fell on him in a well. Joseph was in a contemplative mood. He was thirty-eight and taking stock; perhaps he was a little melancholy, perhaps lonely. "You never knew my heart. No man knows my hist[ory]," he ruminated at the end. How could they know him, separated as he was by his visionary experiences. Sometime, somewhere, they would know one another. "When I am called at the trump & weighed in the balance you will know me then."[29]

Joseph said he would speak on the subject of death, but soon veered to the nature of God. His authority was being challenged; he was being called a false prophet, he admitted, but was "never in any nearer relationship to God than at the present time." He asked the congregation to consider this important subject. If he could explain the nature of God, "let every one sit in silence and never lift your voice against the servants of God again."[30]

He spoke confidently, as if he was giving the obvious meaning of the Bible, even in making the most startling assertions. To begin, he wanted to "refute the Idea that God was God from all eternity." "God that sits enthroned is a man like one of yourselves." The statement so astounded Thomas Bullock that he recorded the reverse: "He was God from the begin of all Eternity." But the other manuscripts concur in the opposite: Joseph wanted to say that God had a history. "We suppose that God was God from eternity. I will refute that Idea," Wilford Woodruff has Joseph declaring. "It is the first principle to know that we may converse with him and that he once was a man like us." The scriptural basis for the doctrine was Jesus's statement about doing nothing but what he saw the Father do. God "was once as one of us and was on a planet as Jesus was in the flesh." It was so obvious, Joseph asserted, "I defy all Hell and earth to refute it."[31]

The point of this radical doctrine was obvious: God was one of the free intelligences who had learned to become God. The other free intelligences were to take the same path. "You have got to learn how to make yourselves God, king and priest, by going from a small capacity to a great capacity to the resurrection of the dead to dwelling in everlasting burnings." Souls were meant to grow from smaller to greater. "You have got to learn how to be a god yourself in order to save yourself—to be priests & kings as all Gods has done—by going from a small degree to another—from exaltation to ex[altation]—till they are able to sit in glory as with those who sit en-throned." Christ was the model. What did Christ do? Joseph asked. Christ said: "I do the things that I saw the father do when worlds came into existence. I saw the father work out a kingdom with fear & trembling & I can do the same & when I get my K[ingdom] work[ed out] I will present [it] to the father & it will exalt his glory and Jesus steps into his tracks to inherit what God did before."[32]

The words evoked a hierarchy of gods, succeeding to higher stations of greater glory as kingdoms are presented to them and as rising souls below them ascend to godhood. As humankind's advocate and leader, Christ is the one through whom humans are saved; the kingdom prepared on earth is presented to Him, and He presents it to the Father, Elohim. In the light of this doctrine, the early statement from the 1830 revelations of Moses took on new depth. "This is my work and my glory to bring to pass the immortality & eternal life of man," God had said to Moses.[33] Now it could be seen that God's creation of humans contributed to His own glory as kingdoms of the rising gods were presented to him. As He glorified them, they glorified Him.

Critics are wrong when they say Joseph Smith created a heaven of multiple gods like the pagan pantheons of Zeus and Thor. The gods in Joseph Smith's heaven are not distinct, willful personalities pursuing their own purposes. The Christian trinity was Joseph's model; the gods are one as Christ and the Father are one, distinct personalities unified in purpose and will. A free intelligence had to become one with God in order to become as God. The gods had formed an eternal alliance, welding their wills into one. The idea of earth life was to join that alliance and participate in the glory and power of the gods. The way to become a god was to conform to the order of heaven and receive light and truth.[34] The unity and order Joseph strove to instill in the Church was a type of the higher unity among the gods in their heavens.

The King Follett discourse was the final and most complete presentation of Joseph Smith's dramaturgical theology. Joseph filled out the creation story he had been telling in various forms ever since Liberty Jail. The Creation came under the oversight of a "grand Council" of gods who "came together & concocked the plan of making the world & the inhabitants." These gods made the world not out of nothing, but from eternal matter, which they organized out of chaos. Intelligence existed eternally too. "God was a self exhisting being, man exhists upon the same principle." "God never had power to create the spirit of man, God himself could not create himself. Intelligence is Eternal & it is self exhisting."[35]

That made individual persons radically free. Their nature was not predetermined by their creator. They were what they were, not what God made them. Rather than God being the sovereign creator of all things from nothing, He was the most intelligent of the free intelligences. The universe is a school for these free, self-existing intelligences. God, finding "himself in

the midst of spirit and glory because he was greater[,] saw proper to institute laws whereby the rest could have a privilege to advance like himself."
God nurtures the intelligences, giving them laws to help them progress to
greater capacity. "God has power to institute laws to instruct the weaker
intelligences that thay may be exhalted with himself."[36] He is their teacher,
not their maker. Each one is free to choose. The intelligences have independent, self-existing wills, and each one must make the decision to ally
with God or not, to join the order of the gods or not.

This discourse envisioned a far different universe than the God-created
universe of traditional Christian theology. Instead of one overwhelming,
all-pervasive power governing the universe, making it essentially simple,
the universe was composed of a congeries of intelligences and self-existent
matter that God organized rather than made. He was bringing order out of
chaos rather than making something from nothing. Existence had an openness and freedom impossible under a theology of an omnipotent Creator-
God. Mormons later picked out a statement by William James as capturing
the spirit of Joseph's theology. James pictured God saying to other spirits:

> I am going to make a world not certain to be saved, a world the perfection of
> which shall be conditional merely, the condition being that each several agent
> does its own "level best." I offer you the chance of taking part in such a world.
> Its safety, you see, is unwarranted. It is a real adventure, with real danger, yet
> it may win through. It is a social scheme of co-operative work genuinely to be
> done. Will you join the procession? Will you trust yourself and trust the
> other agents enough to face the risk?[37]

Though emphasizing risks and dangers more than most Mormons would
like, James's statement approached Joseph's organizer-teacher God.

The discourse came in a spring when Joseph was running for president
and had organized the Kingdom of God in anticipation of the millennial
coming of Christ. Teaching about the gods seemed miles away from the hard
realities of politics and the plans for an earthly kingdom, but the two were
related. Joseph's ordination as king took on an entirely different meaning
when viewed against the King Follett sermon. Kingship in the nineteenth-
century context implied a royal line and aristocratic rule. The king was set
apart from the people as God is set apart from His creations. Both occupied
distinct and inaccessible realms and exercised powers peculiar to themselves. In having himself ordained king, Joseph appeared to set himself
above his people, reinstating the Great Chain of Being with fixed subordi-
nations and superordinations.

But the relationship took on a new meaning if people were invited to
become kings, priests, and gods themselves. They remained subjects, to be

sure, owing all deference and obedience to their sovereign, but they were subject to the monarch as princes and princesses are subject to their mothers and fathers. They subordinated themselves to the higher power in preparation for assuming that power themselves. The purpose of allegiance and obedience was not order and happiness but training. The subjects of the king were learning to become kings. King and subjects were separated by rank, not by class. All were members of the same order of beings as children are of the same order as their parents. Family became the ultimate and truest model of the heavenly order.

The King Follett doctrines can sound profoundly American. Every man a god and a king fulfilled democratic aspirations to a degree unknown in any other religion. Joseph's assertion that "all mind is susseptible of improvement" opened up the possibility of limitless growth. Mormons themselves have labeled the doctrine of eternal spirits "eternal progression," as if it meant rising ever higher in society, the essence of the American dream. It is the one teaching of Joseph Smith that Americans are most likely to admire.[38] True as these readings may be, they overlook the hierarchical elements in the King Follett doctrine. The sermon actually restores subordination and superordination in the spirit of the Great Chain of Being. God is superior to all other intelligences, and the Kingdom of God is made up of ranks of intelligent beings ruling under His authority. The rising free intelligences must submit to God, take upon them the name of Christ, conform to the order of heaven, and even obey priesthood authorities on the earth. Hierarchy, though certainly a benevolent one, is installed at the center of intelligent existence.

REFORM

In the stormy spring of 1844, the King Follett discourse rose like a castle in the weeds, a splendid, mysterious heterodoxy standing amid the bitterness in Nauvoo. The sermon thrilled many of the city's Mormons. Joseph Fielding, one of the Prophet's listeners, said, "Any one that could not see in him the Spirit of Inspiration of God must be dark, they might have known that he was not a fallen Prophet even if they thought he was fallen." People like Fielding loved accounts of the heavenly order. Not so the Laws, Fosters, and Higbees. William Law said the annual conference brought out "some of the most blasphemous doctrines . . . ever heard of," such as "other gods as far above our God as he is above us."[39]

At the first formal meeting of their reform church on April 28, the dissenters chose William Law to preside and selected two apostles.[40] The dissenters did not aim to overthrow Mormonism; in their view, Joseph was a fallen prophet, not a fraud. They held on to the *Book of Mormon* and the more conventional Christian doctrines of the early Church. What they hated was polygamy, the Kingdom of God, and the "tyranny" of Joseph Smith. They wanted to reform Mormonism from within by purging it of its excrescences. Law insisted he was only president of the new church, not a prophet, but otherwise their principles were meant to appeal to alienated Mormons who were offended by the rumors of spiritual wives and Joseph's merger of church and state. By canvassing the city, the dissenters by mid-May were attracting three hundred listeners to their meetings.[41]

To put teeth in their campaign, the seceders brought charges against Joseph in Carthage courts. On May 1, Francis Higbee charged Joseph in circuit court with speaking "false scandalous malicious and defamatory words" concerning Higbee's character. Three weeks later, William Law charged Joseph with living in adultery with a plural wife, Maria Lawrence. A Carthage grand jury issued indictments for perjury and polygamy on the witness of Joseph Jackson, Robert Foster, and William Law. Joseph could elude these court actions by the familiar device of taking them before the Nauvoo municipal court, but that could not stop the county sheriff. Twice during the month Joseph had to hide while officers waited around his house. These awkward disappearances displeased Emma, who was still suspicious of his whereabouts when out of sight. Joseph sent William Clayton to "find Emma's mind about him going home," and Clayton found her "crying with rage and fury because he had gone away." She was not well, and Joseph promptly hurried home.[42]

Joseph ultimately faced his accusers. At the Sunday meeting on May 26, before the entire congregation, he answered the specific charges about spiritual wives and malfeasance levied against him in the Nauvoo municipal court.[43] His main point as always was that he was not committing adultery, nor was he practicing "spiritual wifeism," another name for polygamy. To Joseph's enemies, the speech was blatant hypocrisy, but in his own mind, priesthood plural marriage was based on another principle than polygamy. He reassured the people about his state of mind. "The Lord has constituted me so curiously that I glory in persecution. . . . All hell, boil over! Ye burning mountains, roll down your lava! for I will come out on top at last." That was only one side of his feelings. At the end of the talk, he revealed his need for their love. "Don't forsake me. I want the friendship of the brethren." He would do all he could to be worthy of their loyalty. "As I grow older, my heart grows tenderer for you. I am at all times willing to give up everything that is wrong, for I wish this people to have a virtuous leader."[44]

About eight o'clock on the morning of Monday, May 27, Joseph, though not yet arrested, left for Carthage, to have the grand jury indictments investigated. For safety's sake, two dozen brethren joined him along the way. At noon, they arrived at A. Hamilton's Carthage Hotel, where Joseph Jackson,

Francis Higbee, and Chauncey Higbee were also lodging. To Joseph's surprise, Charles Foster joined his party, speaking more mildly than before. In the hotel, Foster took Joseph aside and told him that Joseph Jackson planned to kill him. Joseph later swore in court to the truth of Charles Foster's surprising behavior, adding that Foster had warned Joseph not to go out of doors or blood would be shed. "There were those who were determined I should not go out of the village alive." Apparently when Foster saw the cold-blooded Jackson loading his pistol, his animosity disappeared.[45] Joseph went ahead with the court proceedings, but one of the prosecution's material witnesses being absent, the case was deferred until the next term. Joseph's party watched Jackson closely as they left town, but he made no move. They arrived home about nine that evening.[46]

By the end of May, everyone involved seemed determined to drive through to the cataclysmic conclusion. The dissenters proceeded with their campaign to pull down Joseph Smith, even though they must have known that a revelation of his faults would provoke his enemies in surrounding towns. An exposé of evil doings in Nauvoo would fan the flames in Warsaw. The dissenters obtained a press in May, issued a prospectus, and on June 7, 1844, published a thousand copies of the one and only issue of the *Nauvoo Expositor*.[47]

The *Expositor* consisted of seven essays, some addressing potential Mormon converts, and others appealing more directly to the county's anti-Mormons. The "Preamble" was written to potential converts in a religious voice, likely William Law's, the reform church's leader and Joseph's former counselor in the First Presidency.[48] "It is with the greatest solicitude for the salvation of the Human Family," the first line began. The essayist, though turning against the Prophet, did not want to destroy the church. "Many of us have sought a reformation in the church," the editor wrote, but, failing that, had been driven to a desperate action. In the face of Joseph's moral crimes, he asked, "shall we lie supinely and suffer ourselves to be metamorphosed into beasts by the Syren tongue?" The writer assured his readers that the new church advocated the religion "originally taught by Joseph Smith." The reformers opposed only the recent doctrines. The paper aimed "to explode the vicious principles of Joseph Smith, and those who practice the same abominations and whoredoms"—meaning primarily polygamy. On top of that scandalous practice, the editor objected to the doctrine "that there are innumerable Gods as much above the God that presides over this universe, as he is above us."[49]

The more political voice in the *Expositor* wrote to gratify the county's anti-Mormons. The editors promised everything the anti-Mormons had been calling for, including "the rights of the old citizens of the county" to control elections. The people who had "borne the heat and burden of the day" as pioneers should "not have men imposed upon them, who are obnoxious, for good and sufficient reasons." The paper rallied the county to oppose Hyrum's candidacy for the state legislature in the August 1844 election on the grounds that he would be the pawn of Joseph Smith. In condemning the Prophet, Francis Higbee, the one editor to sign his essay, referred to the Prophet in one heading as "Joe Smith," a name never used in Nauvoo. The political editors favored repeal of the charter and limits on the power of municipal courts. The editors had no worries about an attack of Nauvoo. The Saints' mob anxieties were a bugaboo.[50] "The question is asked, will you bring a mob upon us?" The answer was that the use of armed men to enforce the law did not constitute a mob. "It will create no sympathy in that case to cry out, we are mobbed."[51]

Willard Richards wrote nothing about the Prophet's feelings at the appearance of the *Expositor.* William Clayton revealed little more. "Truly," he wrote, the paper "seems to be a source of falsehood and bitter misrepresentation." Both diarists recorded a visit from Robert Foster seeking reconciliation with Joseph. Perhaps feeling he had the upper hand now with the anti-Mormons in the county behind him, Foster wrote what Clayton called "a very saucy letter," refusing to deal with Joseph and his "unworthy, unprincipled, Clan." At the city council meeting the next day, Joseph argued the paper was "a nuisance, a greater nuisance than a dead carcass." The term "nuisance" came from a passage in Blackstone that he would use to justify suppression of the paper. The *Expositor* was a "nuisance" because it threatened to bring the countryside down on the Mormons. "It is not safe that such things should exist, on account of the mob spirit which they tend to produce."[52] Joseph would later quote Blackstone to Governor Thomas Ford to prove the city council acted legally.

The legal fine points were lost in the subsequent chaos. The city council met for six and a half hours on Monday, June 10, "investigating the Merits of the Nauvoo Expositor." They seemed to realize they were taking a huge risk when they finally passed an ordinance concerning libels, but they concluded that the action was necessary and legally justified.[53] Joseph, as mayor, ordered the city marshal, John P. Greene, to destroy the *Expositor* and the major general of the Nauvoo Legion to assist. "About 8 p.m. the Marshall returned and reported that he had removed the press, type, and printed papers, and fixtures into the street, and fired them." The posse, consisting of about a hundred men, gathered in front of Joseph's house after the work was done to hear a speech. "I would never submit to have another libellous publication . . . established in this city," he told them. "I cared not how many papers there were in the city if they would print the truth but would submit to no libe[l]s or slander."[54]

In the "considerable excitement" the day after, the dissenters stormed about saying "the Temple shall be thrown down Joseph['s] house burned & the printing office torn down," possibly thinking of an anti-Mormon invasion. Francis Higbee predicted "in 10 days there will not be a Mormon left in Nauvoo." Joseph's enemies were persuaded that he had crossed the line in closing the *Expositor*. Whether or not the law of libels or abatement of a nuisance justified the action, he had trespassed freedom of the press, which had become nearly a sacred right in the United States. Joseph was deaf to these ideas. He did not grasp the enormity of destroying a press, especially one that was attacking him. Fear of another mob drove his action.[55] In municipal court, Joseph spoke for more than an hour to a large assembly about his willingness to fight "if the mob compel me to it." In a proclamation issued on June 11, Joseph gave his reason for suppressing the *Expositor*. The paper was, he thought, an attempt to "excite the jealousy and prejudice of the people of the surrounding country, by libels, and slanderous articles upon the citizens and City Council, for the purpose of destroying the 'Charter' of said city, and for the purpose of raising suspicion, wrath, and indignation among a certain class of the less honorable portion of mankind, to commit acts of violence upon the innocent and unsuspecting."[56] Joseph failed to see that suppression of the paper was far more likely to arouse a mob than the libels. It was a fatal mistake.

The next day Francis Higbee entered a complaint before a Carthage justice of the peace, and two days after the event, Constable David Bettisworth was in Nauvoo to arrest the Prophet and his accomplices for riot in suppressing the press. The accused were released by the municipal court as usual, but the constable, who was "very wrathy," according to Clayton, was certain to return.[57]

Charles Foster immediately alerted the seceders' allies by reporting the press's destruction to the *Warsaw Signal*. Sharp was ready with suitable rhetoric.

> CITIZENS ARISE, ONE AND ALL!!!—Can you *stand* by, and suffer such INFERNAL DEVILS! to ROB men of their property and RIGHTS, without avenging them. We have no time for comment, every man will make his own. LET IT BE MADE with POWDER AND BALL!!![58]

To rid tender consciences of any compunction about taking up their guns, Sharp characterized Joseph and Hyrum as "Hellish Fiends." "Yes! Hyrum & Joe are as trult [*sic*] Devils, as though they had served an apprenticeship of half of eternity in the Infernal Pit." Anti-Mormon committees gathered immediately, setting off rumors that there were plans to expel the Mormons. At the Warsaw meeting, Sharp told the people that "if the safety of our lives and property cannot be ensured to us by legal means . . . the only recourse left us is to take up arms." The countywide meeting in Carthage on June 13 resolved to drive all the Saints in the outlying settlements into Nauvoo. At the same time, the Laws and Robert Foster fled the city.[59]

Three days after suppressing the *Expositor,* Joseph wrote to Isaac Morley about how to react to anti-Mormon demands that the Mormons in Lima, Illinois, give up their arms. The instructions were to give up their lives first. The same day news arrived of forty anti-Mormons drilling in Carthage and of an arms shipment landing in Warsaw.[60] In the morning, Joseph wrote to Governor Ford explaining the reasons for shutting down the *Expositor.*

In the middle of the afternoon, Joseph took a moment for "examining" Benjamin West's *Death on the Pale Horse,* on display in the "reading room" of his store.[61] A favorite work by the expatriate American painter, *Death* had been touring the country to attract paying customers. The title was taken from the Revelation of St. John where the pale horse follows three other horses carrying on their backs a conqueror, a rider who takes peace from the earth, and a third carrying a pair of balances.

> And I looked, and behold a pale horse: and his name that sat on him was Death, and Hell followed with him. And power was given unto them over the fourth part of the earth, to kill with sword, and with hunger, and with death, and with the beasts of the earth.[62]

West depicted this apocalyptic scene as a swirl of half-naked, contorted bodies about to be slain by armed riders on horseback. In the center, a dark, misty figure on a white horse is about to trample a man supporting a dead or dying woman with a child kneeling at her side. In the background storm clouds rile the sky. Perhaps for no other viewer of West's painting did art more accurately imitate life.

In his final two weeks, Joseph was cornered. Two forces bore down on him: law and order represented by Governor Thomas Ford, and the conspiracy to assassinate him led by Thomas Sharp. Ford, sensible and restrained, struggled to keep passions in Hancock County in check. He wanted Joseph to answer in court for destroying the *Expositor,* and the anti-Mormons to rely on the law for redress. Ford was convinced that one mistake would trigger a war.

The passionate Sharp had gone beyond law and order, thinking Joseph had eluded the law too many times. He had founded the *Warsaw Signal,* he said, for the purpose "of either correcting the unhallowed usurpation power of that band of villains, at Nauvoo, or their extermination from civilized society." All he waited for was an occasion to strike.

> It should be the firm determination of every one holding in veneration the institutions of his country, upon the first outrage against a citizen of this

county, to give those "Latter-day Devils," a scathing that will eclipse the "Missouri Persecutions," or in other words Missouri Justice.

The closing of the *Expositor* was a perfect excuse. The long campaign against Joseph and the Mormons made their "extermination from civilized society" the logical course of action. In an open letter to Joseph on June 5, Sharp had said that no one

> can picture a wretch so depraved, and loathsome as yourself. Yes Joe! we have that confidence in your saintship, that we do not believe that the concentrated extract of all the abominations of the Infernal Regions, can add one stain to the blackness of your character. Look in a mirror Joe and you will see the reflection of the most detestable wretch that the earth contains.

His followers were not that much better, "gathered as they are from all parts of the world, and bound together by religious fanaticism and rascality." Two weeks before the *Expositor* was destroyed, Sharp warned that "Joe Smith is not safe out of Nauvoo, and we would not be surprised to hear of his death by violent means in a short time."[63]

In advocating force, Sharp appealed to the primitive law of communal self-defense that had authorized mob actions from the Revolution to the killing of the abolitionist printer Elijah Lovejoy in Alton, Illinois, in 1837, ironically the same principle underlying the wrecking of the *Expositor*. The theory that a community had the right to enforce its will against impending danger had authorized vigilantism and lynchings in one community after another in every section of the nation. Relying on it to make his case, Sharp was sure of support when on June 12 he called for Joseph's assassination and the extermination of the Mormons.

Sometimes Joseph sensed his doom approaching and foretold his imminent death; then his native optimism would return and he predicted survival. The two people closest to him, Emma and Hyrum, believed he should submit to the law. They wanted him to go before the court and vindicate himself, as he had in the Boggs case. Joseph believed that Carthage meant death. For two weeks, he thrashed about seeking an alternative: using the legion to defend the city, going to Washington for aid, fleeing to the West—anything but submission to the mob collecting in Carthage.

On Sunday, June 16, on a rainy morning at the east grove, Joseph preached his last sermon. He took for his text the biblical verse that had governed his teachings for the past year: "And hath made us kings and priests unto God and his Father; to him be glory and dominion for ever and ever." He did not intend the sermon to be a concluding statement; it was an answer to the seceders. The *Expositor* had listed the plurality of gods among Joseph's doctrinal errors, and rather than smoothing away the doctrine's sharp edges to soothe his opponents, he was defiant. "The plurality of Gods is as prominent in the Bible as any doctrine—it is all over the face of the Bible," he proclaimed. He was thinking of Paul's statement, "there be gods many, and lords many . . . but to us there is but one God." Moreover, the Hebrew word *Elohim* "ought to be in the plural all the way thro—Gods— the heads of the Gods appointed one God for us." Likewise, the progression to godhood could be found everywhere in the scriptures. Christ's prayer in the garden for his followers to be one with the Father meant, in Joseph's reading, we shall be "as God—& he as the God of his Fa[the]r." As Christ becomes God the Father, we become one with Christ and rise up the ranks. This succession implied God had a father to whom He had ascended. "Paul says that which is Earthyly is in likeness of that which is Heavenly— hence if J[esus] has a Fa[the]r can we not believe that he had a Fa[the]r also?"

Joseph knew his leaps would terrify less intrepid souls. "I despise the idea of being scared to death," he said upon completing his proof of God the Father having a father. "When things that are great are passed over with[ou]t. even a thot I want to see all in all its bearings & hug it to my bosom." Then came a sentence that captured his spirit perfectly: "I never hear[d] of a man being d[amne]d for bel[ievin]g too much but they are d[amne]d for unbel[ief]." A few minutes later he stopped talking. The sky was pouring rain.[64]

Monday, June 17, began Joseph's final week in Nauvoo. Feeling the noose tightening, he turned Nauvoo into an armed camp. When news came on Tuesday that the mob "threaten[ed] extermination to the whole Church in Nauvoo," he assembled the legion and addressed them from the platform of a partially constructed building across from the Nauvoo Mansion. Standing in full military dress, he raised his sword to the sky and declared he would not give up without a fight. Clayton said that Joseph "urged them in strong terms not to shed innocent blood.—not to act in the least on the offensive but invariably on the defensive and if we die—die like men of God and secure a glorious resurrection." Then he put the city under martial law and marched the troops up Main Street. Through the week, armed Mormons moved in from the outlying settlements to prepare for battle. Reports of armed attack on Mormon farms arrived almost daily. Joseph deployed the troops throughout the city to prevent invasions by water or land.[65]

Joseph naively believed that benevolent higher officials would rescue him. That week he penned a letter to U.S. president John Tyler asking for aid while keeping Governor Ford informed of mob action in hopes he would intervene. Joseph had earlier explained to Ford the rationale for closing the *Expositor*, confident that he had acted legally. He never thought of himself as a lawbreaker. His reliance on the much-disputed municipal court, he said, came from his desire to observe legal procedures established under the Nauvoo Charter. He admitted he may have erred in judgment. "If it be so that we have erred in this thing. Let the Supreme Court correct the evil."[66]

Ford acknowledged that Joseph could have been deceived by self-serving politicians into believing the municipal court was authorized to hear all cases. Joseph's great error in the *Expositor* suppression, Ford said, was acting without allowing the proprietors to defend themselves. Joseph conceived of the suppression as an executive action of the city council; Ford thought it should have been a judicial proceeding with both sides heard. Joseph was quite willing to argue his position, but not before a Carthage court. "I have ever held myself in readiness to comply with your orders and answer for my proceedings before any legal tribunal in the state," but not where the witnesses would "put themselves into the power of an infuriated, blood thirsty mob."[67] In Missouri, witnesses sympathetic to the Mormons were subjected to intimidation. They would fare no better in Carthage.

Ford did not want a repeat of the expulsion that had brought so much condemnation on Missouri. "I was determined, if possible," he wrote afterwards, "that the forms of law should not be made the catspaw of a mob, to seduce these people to a quiet surrender, as the convenient victims of popular fury." On the other hand, outrage in Hancock County was fast getting out of control. Ford had to speak forcefully to the Mormons and above all bring Joseph Smith to justice or the populace would seize control. Ford dared not even call out the county militias, knowing they would turn into a mob and take vengeance on the Saints. A large armed force assembled from three counties had turned Carthage into an armed camp as bristling as Nauvoo.[68] These militants did not want a peaceful settlement. Even the Mormon sympathizers, the so-called "Jack Mormons," would suffer in the inevitable slaughter. Ford feared for his own safety. If Joseph Smith was mistreated in court or by a mob, would the Mormons take vengeance? Ford rather bravely thrust himself into the center of events in the futile belief he might negotiate a settlement.[69]

On Friday, June 21, Ford arrived in Carthage and sent for Mormon representatives to tell their side of the story. Fearing to venture into the camp of his sworn enemies, Joseph sent John Taylor to speak for him. On Saturday Ford conveyed his conclusions to the Prophet. The governor dismissed the widespread rumors about Mormons burning houses or stealing horses. Only one crime stood out to Ford: Joseph had broken the law in shutting down the press without a fair hearing and must come to Carthage to stand trial. "I now express to you my opinion that your conduct in the destruction of the press was a very gross outrage upon the laws and liberties of the people. It may have been full of libels, but this did not authorise you to destroy it." If Joseph did not submit to the law, there would be war. "If you by refusing to submit, shall make it necessary to call out the Militia I have great fears that your city will be destroyed and your people many of them exterminated." And yet the governor had no choice: "If no such submission is made as I have indicated I will be obliged to call out the Militia, and if a few thousands will not be sufficient many thousands will be."[70]

Joseph was hesitant. He wrote Ford on Saturday at noon, "We dare not come, though your Excell[enc]y promises protection. yet at the same time you have expressed fears that you could not control the mob.—in which case we are left to the mercy of the Merciless." But staying home was also dangerous. The militia would invade the city to capture the Prophet and bloodshed would follow. Faced with this dilemma, Joseph chose to flee. In the noon letter, he told Ford that "we shall leave the City forthwith—to lay the facts before the General government." Then in a rushed, broken sentence, he pleaded, "by every thing that is sacred we implore your exc[el]lency to come our helpless women & children to protected from Mob violence." Late Saturday night, he crossed the swollen Mississippi River. He and Hyrum and Willard Richards bailed the leaky boat with their boots while Porter Rockwell rowed. About daybreak Joseph wrote Emma from Montrose that he was on his way to Washington.[71]

Joseph remained on the Iowa side less than twelve hours. When Rockwell returned for horses he found frightened people in Nauvoo. They feared the posse would tear up the city in search of the Prophet. Vilate Kimball wrote Heber that "some were tryed almost to death to think Joseph should leve them in the hour of danger." Three Mormons crossed the river with a message from the governor saying he would hunt Joseph down if he hid, and guaranteeing him a safe trial if he submitted. Hyrum and Emma favored trusting to God and the courts. At 2 p.m. Joseph wrote Ford from the riverbank that he was coming in—if a protective posse could be provided. All he asked was that all be done "in due form of law."[72] By five o'clock on Sunday afternoon, June 23, Joseph was back in Nauvoo.

He left for Carthage on Monday morning, June 24, with the fourteen others charged with closing the *Expositor*. Four miles from his destination, he met Captain James Dunn of the McDonough County militia with sixty mounted men under orders from Ford to collect state-issued arms in Nauvoo. Joseph countersigned the order and then returned to Nauvoo with Dunn to aid in the collection. The return gave Joseph another chance to bid his family farewell. Clayton observed that Joseph "appeared to feel solemn and though[t]ful and from expressions made to several individuals he expects nothing but to be massacred." His choice was to "give himself up or the City be massacred by a lawless mob." After seeing Emma one last time, Joseph again departed for Carthage, arriving at Hamilton's Hotel around midnight.

All the next day, Tuesday, June 25, rumors circulated about plots to kill the Prophet and carry the violence to Nauvoo. To placate the armed militia in town, Ford practiced a little political theater, marching Joseph and Hyrum between lines of troops curious to see the object of their hatred. In the early afternoon, Joseph wrote Emma that the governor introduced Hyrum and himself "in a very appropriate manner as Gen. *Joseph Smith* & *General Hyrum Smith.*" Joseph appreciated the use of a military title rather than the usual "Joe." Optimistic for the moment, he told Emma, "I think the Gov. has & will succeed in enforcing the laws. I do hope the people of Nauvoo will continue placid pacific & prayerful."[73]

The court business of the day was to hear the charge of riot against Nauvoo's town officers. The defendants were released on bail of $500 each and bound over to the next term of the circuit court. Before the hearing, however, another charge, this one for treason, was brought against Joseph and Hyrum. Not the government, but dissenter Augustine Spencer accused them of calling out the legion to resist the state militia. The Mormons could see the dissenters were determined to keep Joseph and Hyrum in Carthage on one pretext or other. Ford considered the treason charge groundless since the city had had reason to fear a mob invasion, but he refused to intervene in a judicial proceeding. The justice of the peace, Robert Smith, committed Joseph and Hyrum to prison without a hearing, claiming he did so for their safety. John Taylor, the Mormon apostle, was furious. He told Ford if Joseph could be dragged to prison "at the instance of every infernal scoundrel whose oath could be bought for a dram of whiskey, his protection availed very little."[74]

Joseph's first action the next day, Wednesday, June 26, was to appeal to the governor for release from prison. He wanted to return to the safety of Nauvoo. Every time he was escorted through town, he was in danger. Joseph was searching for any venue where a fair and safe hearing was possible. At a meeting later in the morning, he assured Governor Ford of his willingness to appear in court, but not a court controlled by enemies.[75]

Ford told Joseph he planned to take a large body of armed militia to Nauvoo the next day to search the town for the counterfeiting equipment the Mormons were suspected of operating. The show of force would placate the angry citizens, Ford initially thought, and perhaps end the crisis. The next day he changed his mind when he learned that his own officers apparently proposed taking an armed band into Nauvoo, provoking a conflict, and then driving out the Mormons or slaughtering them. Later, in his *History of Illinois*, Ford tells of convincing his officers "that such wanton and unprovoked barbarity on their part would turn the sympathy of the people in the surrounding counties in favor of the Mormons." As Ford told the tale, a majority voted in favor of the invasion anyway.[76] Overruling them, he decided instead to go to Nauvoo with a small number of men to search for the counterfeiting gear.

A few Mormons believed that under pressure Ford agreed to sacrifice two lives to prevent the murder of more. Jonathan C. Wright, a Nauvoo city marshal, later testified that one of the officers urged Ford to placate the restive old citizens by allowing Joseph and Hyrum to be killed. According to Wright, Colonel Enoch Marsh of Alton told Ford: "You have now got the principle men here under your own control, they are all you want, what more do you want? When they are out of the way the thing is settled, and the people will be satisfied, and that is the easiest way you can dispose of it." Wright said Marsh told him that "Governor Ford concluded upon the whole that was the best policy, and I know it will be done."[77] The affidavit, sworn to in Utah in 1855, was far from proof that Ford was complicit in the assassination, but attests to the violent proposals then in the air.

At four o'clock on Wednesday afternoon, Joseph and Hyrum were brought before Robert Smith, the justice of the peace, to be examined on the treason charge. The hearing was postponed until noon the next day, and later to Saturday, while the defense collected witnesses from Nauvoo, and meanwhile Joseph and Hyrum returned to jail. A great deal of lore has grown up around Joseph's last night in prison where five friends kept him and his brother company. Hyrum read passages from the *Book of Mormon* about prophets in prison. Joseph preached to the guards. Willard Richards went on writing until his candle guttered out. Joseph lay on the floor between John Fullmer and Dan Jones and offered Fullmer his arm for a pillow. To Jones he whispered, "Are you afraid to die?"[78]

Early on Thursday morning, June 27, Joseph wrote Emma to tell her that Ford had decided to leave his troops in Carthage rather than indulge their wish to search Nauvoo. Still trusting the governor, Joseph instructed the people to "stay at home and attend to their own business and let there be no groups or gathering together unless by permission of the Gov." He assured Emma that "there is no danger of any 'exterminating order,' " though he was stoic about his own fate. "I am very much resigned to my lot knowing I am Justified and have done the best that could be done give my love to the children." His last known letter was addressed to a lawyer he wished to add to his counsel.[79] He believed his innocence could be proven in court.

Thomas Ford later tried to excuse himself for leaving the Carthage Greys, one of the militia units in town, to protect the prisoners while he left for Nauvoo. The Greys had been the most hostile of the armed men gathered in Carthage. Ford admitted that he "knew that this company were the enemies of the Smiths, yet I had confidence in their loyalty and integrity; because their captain was universally spoken of as a most respectable citizen and honorable man." Ford said he turned down "frequent appeals" to "make a clean and thorough work of the matter, by exterminating the Mormons, or expelling them from the State." When the Greys assured him they would not act without his permission, he believed them. As he told the story later, he did not think they would endanger the governor's life by killing the Prophet while he was in Nauvoo exposed to Mormon wrath.[80]

Ford heard rumors of assassination plots all the way to Nauvoo. Perhaps growing anxious, he postponed the search for the counterfeiting equipment and stayed only long enough to address the citizens.[81] Arriving about four, he went to the Mansion House, shaved, and climbed on the platform of the unfinished building across the street to address the citizens. He advised the Saints to lay aside their arms and warned them not to attack the dissenters' property. If they made a move, "thousands would assemble for the total destruction of their city." If he attempted to protect the Mormons with force, he warned, both he and they would be exterminated. When he asked the crowd if they would abide by the law, everyone raised their hands, but secretly "every breast was filled with indignation," Clayton noted in his journal. "The brethren generally have forebodings that the Governor is treacherous & full of prejudice against us."[82] They invited him to stay the night, but he left before sundown.

In Carthage, the friendly jailer had moved the prisoners into his own upstairs bedroom, a room without bars on the windows. Joseph spent Thursday, June 27, preparing for the treason trial scheduled for Saturday. He gave a long list of witnesses to Cyrus Wheelock, who earlier in the day had smuggled in a six-shooter in his overcoat. John Fullmer had previously given Joseph a single-shot pistol, which he passed along to Hyrum. In midafternoon, according to a familiar story, John Taylor sang "A Poor Way-faring Man of Grief"—whether all fourteen verses or not is not recorded—and then sang it again.[83] Hyrum read extracts from Josephus.

At four a new set of eight men replaced the afternoon guard while the main body of Carthage Greys camped a quarter of a mile away on the public square. Late in the afternoon, the jailer's boy told the prisoners the guards wanted wine; Willard Richards gave him a dollar. When the wine was returned, the prisoners, their spirits "dull and heavy," all partook. The guard turned to leave with the bottle. At the top of the stairs, someone called him two or three times, and he went down. The prisoners heard rustling and cries, then three or four shots. Looking through the curtain from the second-story bedroom window, Willard Richards saw a hundred armed men around the door. Men ran up the stairs and shots were fired through the open windows. The four men in the room sprang for their weapons—Joseph for the six-shooter, Hyrum for the single-shot, Richards and Taylor for canes. As they threw their weight against the door, musket balls from the landing punched through.[84]

Hyrum was the first to fall. A ball through the door struck him on the left side of the nose, throwing him to the floor. Three more balls entered his thigh, torso, and shin, killing him. John Taylor was hit in the thigh and fell against the windowsill, breaking his watch. Crawling toward the bed, he was struck again in the hip. Joseph pulled the trigger six times into the hall, dropped the pistol on the floor, and sprang to the window. With one leg over the sill, he raised his arms in the Masonic sign of distress.[85] A ball from the doorway struck his hip, and a shot from the outside entered his chest. Another hit under the heart and a fourth his collarbone. He fell outward crying, *"O Lord my God!"* Landing on his left side, he struggled to sit up against the curb of a well and died within seconds. Richards raised his head above the sill far enough to see that Joseph was dead and then turned to help John Taylor. Taylor's watch had stopped at sixteen minutes past five.[86]

EPILOGUE

You don't know me—you never will I don't blame you for not believing my
history had I not experienced it [I] could not believe it myself.

JOSEPH SMITH, Journal, April 7, 1844

WHEN THOMAS FORD GOT TO CARTHAGE about 10 p.m. on June 27, many
citizens were fleeing and more preparing to go. Ford himself soon hurried
away, traveling through the night to arrive at Quincy on June 29. The people of Warsaw had already evacuated women and children across the river.
All expected an assault from vengeful Mormons. The anti-Mormons hoped
the Mormons would attack, believing it would secure their downfall. The
Warsaw Signal reported that the legion would kill Ford in Nauvoo. "To have
the governor of the State assassinated by the Mormons," Ford explained in
his history of Illinois, "the public excitement would be greatly increased
against that people, and would result in their expulsion from the State at
least." When nothing happened, the *Signal* tried to justify the murders: "Is
it not better that the blood of two guilty wretches, whose crimes had long
awaited the vengeance of Heaven, has been shed and thus by cutting off the
fountain head to dry up the stream of corruption?" Unfazed by the enormity of the assassination, the anti-Mormons openly asked Governor Ford
for support in evicting the remaining Mormons. Weeks after the killing, the
governor's agents found "the temper of the people still greatly aroused
against the Mormons." Ford was almost speechless with anger. In an open
letter, he wrote: "I could not believe that so much stupidity and baseness, as
was necessary for such an enterprize as the murder of defenceless prisoners
in jail would be, could be mustered in Hancock county."[1]

In this atmosphere, the chances of convicting anyone were slight. The
assassination had been a group effort with no single perpetrator obviously
responsible. The mob at the jail on June 27 was composed of the militia
from Warsaw and Green Plains, where Sharp's influence was paramount,
and recruits from the other armed bands who had assembled in Carthage
before Joseph's death. Governor Ford had disbanded both the 1,400 troops

in Carthage and the 300 in Warsaw before proceeding to Nauvoo on June 27, but they reconstituted themselves as a posse comitatus, commissioned by the will of the community to rid the county of an offending nuisance. With the Carthage Greys 700 yards away on the town square, a hundred or more men, their faces blacked to hide their identities, sneaked into town in the late afternoon, hiding behind a rail fence and then suddenly rushing the jail. In the confusion of the attack, it would have been difficult even for those present to know which of the men killed the two Smiths.[2]

Willard Richards and John Taylor compiled a list of sixteen people they recognized in the mob. Sheriff Jacob Backenstos, a friendly non-Mormon, provided the names of sixty men, largely from Warsaw–Green Plains and Carthage, who "took an active part." Rather than charging everyone involved, Governor Ford recommended bringing charges against the vigilante leaders. Eventually the first five men on Backenstos's list stood trial in May 1845: Thomas Sharp, editor of the *Warsaw Signal*; Colonel Levi Williams of Green Plains; Jacob C. Davis, a Warsaw lawyer and state senator; Mark Aldrich, a Warsaw land agent; and William N. Grover, a Warsaw lawyer. At the trial, the defense argued that no single individual could be held responsible for the deaths of Joseph and Hyrum when the assassins were carrying out the will of the people. If the defendants were guilty, then so too were "every man, woman and child in the county guilty." After six days of testimony, the jury acquitted the defendants. O. H. Browning, the skillful attorney for the defense, had persuaded the judge, Richard M. Young, to dismiss the impaneled jury because of bias and to select special court agents, called elisors, to choose potential jurors from the onlookers. Since, to avoid confrontations, Mormons had decided not to attend the trial, none of them were in the pool. By this clever device, Mormons were excluded from the jury, though they were nearly a majority in the county.[3]

After his acquittal, Sharp continued to lead the opposition until the Mormons evacuated Nauvoo in the spring of 1846. Then he and the other anti-Mormon leaders receded back into the ordinary routines of small-town life. Sharp gave up the *Warsaw Signal* and became a justice of the peace. He served three terms as mayor of Warsaw, and a term as judge of Hancock County. No further causes aroused anything near the passion of his anti-Mormon campaign. The other defendants led similarly conventional lives. Two of the accused were elected to state and territorial legislatures. Two were postmasters. One was appointed U.S. district attorney.[4]

Anti-Mormon fury had erupted out of these otherwise unexceptional lives. Quite ordinary people were roused to levels of hatred and fear they never reached at any other time. "The unfortunate victims of this assassination, were generally and thoroughly hated throughout the country," Ford told the Mormons, thinking of the area around Hancock County. Among their nearest neighbors, Mormons were as generally detested as abolitionists in the antebellum South and, later, black freedmen during Reconstruction. One can only speculate on the reasons. It was not a hatred of the alien; the role of a prophet was well known to every believer in the Bible. It was more a fear of the familiar gone awry. Joseph was hated for twisting the common faith in biblical prophets into the visage of the arrogant fanatic, just as the abolitionists twisted the principle of equal rights into an attack on property in slaves.[5] Both turned something powerful and valued into something dangerous. Frustrated and infuriated, ordinary people trampled down law and democratic order to destroy their imagined enemies.

The Mormons scarcely knew how to react to the hatred and violence of the old citizens. After binding up John Taylor's wounds, Willard Richards wrote from the jail: "Joseph & Hyrum are dead. . . . The citizens here are afraid of the Mormons attacking them. I promised them NO!" At midnight he wrote again repeating his warning to Emma and Jonathan Dunham of the Nauvoo Legion: "I have pledged my word the Mormons will stay at home . . . and no violence will be on their part."[6]

The governor's aides helped wash Joseph's and Hyrum's bodies, and in the morning they were placed in oak boxes, loaded onto two wagons, and covered with brush to shade them from the sun. A mile from Nauvoo, the cortege was met by several thousand people who followed the wagons to the Nauvoo Mansion. Speakers mounted the platform on the unfinished buildings across the street where ten days earlier Joseph had rallied the legion and just the day before Governor Ford had addressed the Saints. Willard Richards spoke "with the earnestness of a hungry man begging for bread, to trust in the law for redress, and when that failed, to call upon God to avenge us of our wrongs."[7]

In the Mansion House, the bodies were washed again, and George Cannon took impressions for death masks. The bodies were dressed in white—shirt, pants, stockings, neckerchief, and shroud—and from early Saturday morning until late afternoon the Saints passed through the house. "Joseph looks very natural," Clayton commented, "except being pale through loss of blood." Hyrum, who had been hit in the nose by a musket ball, "does not look so natural." To foil any attempts to steal the bodies, the coffins were removed from the outer boxes, sand bags put in their places, and the boxes buried in the city graveyard. The actual coffins with the bodies inside were buried in the basement of the unfinished Nauvoo House. In the fall, the coffins were reburied in unmarked graves near the Smiths' original Nauvoo homestead on the banks of the Mississippi. The tomb near the temple where Joseph had hoped to be buried alongside his family did not receive him after all. In 1928, he was reinterred near the original graves with Hyrum on his left and Emma on his right.[8]

Tossed by a storm of conflicting feelings, Nauvoo was caught between an impulse to seek vengeance and a realistic fear of the consequences. "A few words," Clayton wrote on June 28, "would raise the City in arms & massacre the Cities of Carthage & Warsaw & lay them in ashes but it is wisdom to be quiet." The Saints were "still surrounded by a mob and threatened to be exterminated." When leaders spoke, the city was "exhorted to be peaceable and calm and use no threats." Most fell back into mournful resignation. "All seem to hang on the mercy of God and wait further events." The two agents sent by the governor to size up the situation in Nauvoo found "every thing quiet; the Mormons were disposed to obey the laws; neither to retaliate the deaths of the Smiths." Richards said the Saints "entered into covenants" with the governor "not to avenge the blood of the Martyrs."[9]

Emma, whose tortured relationship with Joseph had blighted her last years as his wife, struggled between her belief in him as a prophet and her love for him as a man. Her affection remained. Her son remembered her saying softly over his dead body, "Oh, Joseph, Joseph! My husband, my husband! Have they taken you from me at last!" When the bodies of Hyrum and Joseph were moved to the homestead site, she had a lock of her husband's hair snipped for a locket she wore all her life.[10]

Emma's alienation from the main body of the Church began almost immediately. Joseph left behind five children: the adopted Julia Murdock, age thirteen; Joseph III, eleven; Frederick Granger Williams, nearly eight; Alexander Hale, six; and the unborn David Hyrum. Emma thought immediately of her family's security. At issue was property. She wanted to preserve her assets from inclusion with the Church's, a nearly impossible distinction to maintain.[11] William Clayton felt she was grasping and unreasonable, and Brigham Young was suspicious. Uneasy in dealing with this powerful, willful woman, they left her out of their councils and even their socials. Her known opposition to plural marriage made her doubly troublesome. When most of the Saints moved west, she stayed behind. Knowing her life was in danger when anti-Mormon forces laid siege to the city, she moved temporarily to Fulton, Illinois, but returned to Nauvoo after six months and remained there the rest of her life. She lived to the end in the house she and Joseph had occupied and where his portrait hung on the wall. The property she held on to—the Nauvoo Mansion, the Nauvoo House, the homestead, and the farm—provided her a living but not an easy one. Responsibility for many of Joseph's debts reduced her resources drastically.[12]

In 1847, Emma married Major Lewis Bidamon, who had taken the Mormons' part during the battle for Nauvoo without becoming a believer. He was an enterprising man who made good use of Emma's property. At a low point after the Mormons left, he spent a fruitless year in the California goldfields. Bidamon had fathered an illegitimate child before marrying

Emma, his third wife, and at age sixty-two sired another. Emma generously brought up the youngest. Despite these lapses, the couple showed genuine affection for each other. Emma's children called Bidamon "Pa."[13]

With Joseph gone from her life, Emma withdrew from religion. She was reluctant to talk about Mormonism. Approached by representatives of one of the Mormon churches that sprang up after the exodus, she told them, "I have always avoided talking to my children about having anything to do in the church, for I have suffered so much I have dreaded to have them take any part in it." Her sons grew up believing the Bible and the *Book of Mormon* but with little knowledge of their father's teachings—and none about plural marriage. Eventually the reform Mormons who founded the Reorganized Church of Jesus Christ of Latter Day Saints, made up of Saints who had not gone west, persuaded Joseph III to take the leadership. Emma joined but never took a leading role. She fended off Joseph III's increasingly urgent questions about plural marriage, leaving the impression that her husband had never supported the principle but keeping the door open for the revelation she knew he had received. When asked about the *Book of Mormon* and Joseph's translation, she professed complete belief.[14] Like the 1844 reform group led by William Law, she believed in the early Joseph whose doctrines conformed to conventional Christianity. Until her death in 1879, the memory she chose to perpetuate for her children was of this milder Prophet rather than the religious revolutionary of the Nauvoo years.

Others tried to claim Joseph's memory to consolidate their power in the Church. Joseph had never explicitly named a successor, and events complicated the natural descent of authority. The two remaining Smith brothers were in line because of kinship. Clayton said confidently that Joseph had said "if he and Hyrum were taken away Samuel H. Smith would be his successor," but Samuel died on July 30 from bilious fever, leaving only William Smith.[15] Lucy Smith campaigned for William to become presiding patriarch, Hyrum's office at his death, and after receiving that ordination, he made a bid for the Church presidency, but his unstable character kept him from being a serious contender. William was excommunicated in 1845, for teaching plural marriage illegally and opposing the leadership of Brigham Young. For years he wandered erratically from one variant of Mormonism to another, finally settling in the Reorganized branch of Mormonism.[16]

James J. Strang, who was baptized only in February 1844, claimed that Joseph had written a letter commissioning him to lead the Church. Although the letter proved to be counterfeit, Strang leveraged his slight claim to authority by recording new revelations, using a seerstone, and saying an angel ordained him in direct imitation of Joseph. Strang practiced baptism for the dead, instituted an endowment ceremony, restored the order of Enoch, and prospered until he began polygamy. Charismatic and colorful,

Strang attracted two thousand followers, among them Martin Harris, and John C. Bennett, whose dreams of a religious empire persisted despite his opposition to Joseph. Strang imitated Joseph in death as in life. In 1856, he was assassinated by dissenters and non-Mormons.[17]

Sidney Rigdon's claim was undercut by his intermittent involvement at Nauvoo. Rigdon had dropped out of the First Presidency after imprisonment in Missouri in 1839, hampered by his own reticence and ill health. In 1842, after breaking with Joseph over the Prophet's proposal of plural marriage to Rigdon's daughter Nancy, he was suspected of sympathizing with John C. Bennett. A year later Joseph tried to remove Rigdon from the Presidency. In early 1844, however, after Law's defection, Rigdon to his great delight was restored to the inner councils of the Church. In June, to keep out of harm's way, he went to Pittsburgh. Upon hearing of Joseph's death, he speedily returned.[18]

In a public meeting in August, Rigdon reported a vision where the Lord had shown him "there must be a Guardian appointed to build the Church up to Joseph." Rigdon's main point was that

> this Church must be built up to Joseph, and that all the blessings we receive must come through him. I have been ordained a spokesman to Joseph, and I must come to Nauvoo and see that the Church is governed in a proper manner. Joseph sustains the same relationship to this Church as he has always done: no man can be the successor of Joseph. . . . The martyred prophet is still the head of this Church.

It was a remarkable argument. Rigdon was in effect denying Joseph's death. Joseph remained the head of the Church, and Rigdon was only "commanded to speak for him."[19]

In a sense, all the claimants drew Joseph's mantle around them. They were not successors but agents or replicas of the man who had dominated the Mormon movement for fourteen years. Brigham Young, president of the Twelve, presided at the meeting where Rigdon made his case. Young took another approach, proposing that the Twelve lead the Church. In later recountings, his supporters in the audience thought he looked like Joseph standing there. One couple wrote that Young "favours Br Joseph, both in person, & manner of speaking more than any person ever you saw, looks like another." Wilford Woodruff said, "It was evident to the Saints that the mantle of Joseph had fallen upon" Brigham Young. As the years went by, the resemblance stories accumulated. Scores of people remembered thinking Joseph stood before their eyes. When Young rose to speak, said George Morris, "I was sitting right Before Him holding down my Head—reflecting about what Rigdon had said—when I was startled by Earing Josephs Voice—

he had a way of Clearing his Throat before he began to speak—by a peculier Effort of His own—like Ah-hem—I raised my Head sudinly—and the first thing I saw was Joseph." These reminiscences were offered as faith-promoting stories, as if the Lord vouched for Young by showing him to be another Joseph. At the August meeting when the issue was posed, the congregation sustained Brigham Young and the Twelve as the new Presidency with little visible resistance. Rigdon, increasingly erratic thereafter, left for Pennsylvania, where the remnant churches he formed faded in and out of existence until he died in New York in 1876.[20]

Calling on Joseph's charisma was one approach to succeeding him; another was to rely on his organization. Who had the right to be president? Brigham Young instinctively made succession a priesthood issue. When he heard of Joseph's death, the first thing he wondered was "whether Joseph had taken the keys of the kingdom with him from the earth," meaning priesthood authority. Young was thinking not of Joseph, but of Joseph's system of priesthood keys and councils. Once he came to the conclusion that the keys had remained with the Church, and the Twelve possessed them, the right course was obvious: the Twelve should become the new First Presidency. When he spoke to the Saints in the August meeting in Nauvoo, he said he wanted to "speak of the organization of the Church."[21]

Appealing to the Church on these terms assumed that the members had incorporated the constitution of priesthood authority into their thinking. Young's case worked because Joseph had laid the foundation in the early years. He had organized the Church by councils and then invested this governance system with charisma. The priesthood who manned the councils had "keys," the powers to act for God. Young's success demonstrated that the Church now existed in the minds of thousands of Mormons. In 1846, over ten thousand of them would march across the plains under Young's direction.[22] Before they left, they labored on the temple down to the final hour in order to receive the endowment they were convinced would exalt them. They did these things within the framework of a religious culture that had come into being in the fourteen years since Joseph organized the Church of Christ in 1830 with a few dozen members.

OBITUARIES

In the months after Joseph Smith's assassination, newspaper editors wrote more about his death than his life. The brutality of popular anger fascinated them more than the visionary who had passed from their midst. They condemned the assassination—or justified it—and said nothing about Joseph's mark on history. No one asked what Joseph Smith had accomplished during his thirty-eight years on earth.[23]

Within the Church, someone, probably John Taylor, wrote a tribute.[24] One paragraph listed the accomplishments from the believers' point of view:

> Joseph Smith, the prophet and seer of the Lord, has done more, (save Jesus only,) for the salvation of men in this world, than any other man that ever lived in it. In the short space of twenty years, he has brought forth the Book of Mormon, which he translated by the gift and power of God, and has been the means of publishing it on two continents: has sent the fulness of the-everlasting gospel which it contained, to the four quarters of the earth; has brought forth the revelations and commandments which compose this book of Doctrine and Covenants, and many other wise documents and instructions for the benefit of the children of men: gathered many thousands of the Latter-Day Saints: founded a great city: and left a fame and name that cannot be slain.

The statement was remarkable for making Joseph almost purely a prophet. His personal virtues and defects, his family and friends, the affection of his people were left out—and not unjustly. His followers had thought of him first and foremost as a prophet ever since John Whitmer recorded his name in the history book as "Joseph the Seer." He had never been considered a model man, nor had he encouraged adulation. "I do not wish to be a great deal better than any body else," he told one congregation.[25] His ambition was invested in what he called "the work."

The newspaper editors, almost without exception, thought of him as a religious fanatic. In a July 1844 article, the *Quincy Whig*—one of the moderate Illinois presses—regretted Smith's murder but found good reason for it.

> The aim and object of him, who called himself their Prophet, was to collect about him a people, devoted to his will and obedient to all his commands. To this end he pretended to be inspired by God himself, to be favored with frequent revelations, and to announce to his followers, from time to time, the commands of the great Jehovah. . . . The Mormons thus associated and thus taught, have been the blind, fanatical, unreasoning followers of such an arch impostor.[26]

Nothing admirable or even interesting could make its way past this fixed view of the impostor and his followers. The character of the fanatic was like racial stereotypes in excluding human qualities. Outside observers saw only a man who pretended to be inspired of God and made himself master of thousands. No one saw him as a biblical prophet.

James Gordon Bennett, the energetic editor of the *New York Herald*, famous for his interest in the bizarre and sensational, came closer to understanding Joseph's historical role. Bennett had been the first New York City reporter to cover Mormonism. In 1831, when he toured upstate New York, all he could learn about Joseph Smith was that "he hung round the villages and strolled round the taverns without any end or aim—without any positive defect or as little merit in his character." A decade later, in 1842, after years of running Mormon stories in the *Herald*, Bennett published a report from a "Nauvoo correspondent." "The Mormons, under the guidance of their great prophet and seer, the famous Joe Smith," it was reported, "are organizing a religious empire in the far west that will astonish the world in these latter days." Bennett's correspondent sensed that Mormonism was more than a church. The article said that Joseph Smith was "without a parallel in the history of nations since the time of Mahomet. . . . Both combined religion, political, moral, and social institutions in one mass of legislation and empire."[27]

The *Herald*'s florid picture came close to describing Joseph's own ambitions for the Latter-day Saints, although he would have preferred "Zion" or "the Kingdom of God" as a name rather than "empire." Almost from the beginning, he wanted more than a church. He was not satisfied with conversions or building up a congregation. Six months after the organization of the Church, the revelations directed him to organize "Zion." The word implied a society, and in Joseph's revelations, Zion became a city.[28] The unit of organization was not the parish or the synod but the community. He worked all his life to organize communities, and in the end he succeeded. The judgment of history has been that Joseph's great achievement was the creation of the Mormon people.

Forming a "kingdom" was exactly what the critics feared. To them, the Church looked like an authoritarian regime with Joseph as the potentate. And yet this Zion was in its way democratic. The historian Nathan Hatch has observed that Joseph used his immense authority "to return power to illiterate men." His was a religion for and by the people. It was not *of* the people—electoral democracy was absent—but if democracy means participation in government, no church was more democratic. Joseph was a plain man himself, and he let plain men run the councils and preside over the congregations. They were ordained elders and high priests, and they did the preaching. In his theology, unexceptional people could aspire to the highest imaginable glory. In belated recognition of this populist side, Joseph Smith's Mormonism came to be understood in the twentieth century as an American religion.[29]

That Mormonism was profoundly if strangely democratic was to the Saints themselves, of course, secondary. Democracy was not mentioned in the hymn that William Phelps wrote for the dedication of the Kirtland temple:

> The Spirit of God like a fire is burning;
> The latter day glory begins to come forth;
> The visions and blessings of old are returning,
> The angels are coming to visit the earth.
> We call in our solemn assemblies, in spirit,
> To spread forth the kingdom of heaven abroad,
> That we through our faith may begin to inherit
> The visions, and blessings, and glories of God.[30]

For Phelps, and probably all the Saints in Kirtland, Joseph's work was not about democracy but about knowledge, power, visions, and blessings. The Saints believed that Joseph brought in the latter-day glory. They were happy to grant him the authority of a prophet if he would connect them with heaven, and that was the key to his success. The Saints' belief was the cement of the Zion society. Mormon communities were held together by their faith in the religious culture Joseph created—the theology, cosmology, and ritual order pointing toward exaltation.

The ideal of this social order was peace and righteousness, but every year of his fourteen years as head of the Church, he faced opposition from within and without. Instead of the unity and peace he desired, there was conflict and anxiety. The Church suffered one debilitating setback after another. Skepticism and ridicule escalated into physical attacks, expulsion, and finally murder. Contention could have broken the Church, and many members did fade away or stomp off in anger, but Joseph never wavered, and the Church survived.

Only a person of powerful conviction could have remained productive and hopeful through the discouragements. For years, the kingdom existed primarily in Joseph's mind. He was one of those unlettered men who could have built a railroad or governed a state. Josiah Quincy saw in him "that kingly faculty which directs, as by intrinsic right."[31] But where his powers came from is a mystery. His upbringing seems so inadequate to his ambitions. He was undoubtedly blessed with intelligence and will, and the Bible, his chief cultural resource, was a trove of possibilities, but how was he able to perceive what lay in its pages? Whence the new scripture, the global schemes for a kingdom, the stories of eternity? He lacked the learning to conceive of the world on such a scale.

His people marveled that he did so much when he was just one of them, and his accomplishments—translations, cities, missions, gatherings, priesthoods, temples, cosmologies, governments—are astonishing by any standard. Joseph Smith himself did not take credit for his achievements. All he could speak of were his "marvilous experience." Perhaps his signal trait was trust in his own inspiration. He knew he was no more than a rough stone cut from a Vermont hillside. He told one audience "he was but a man, . . . a plain, untutored man; seeking what he should do to be saved."[32] But his revelations enabled him, as one scholar has said of prophets, "to do unaccustomed things." It was his calling, as Joseph himself put it, to "lay a foundation that will revolutionize the whole world."[33]

NOTES

CITATION ABBREVIATIONS

APR   Joseph Smith Jr. *An American Prophet's Record: The Diaries and Journals of Joseph Smith.* Edited by Scott H. Faulring. Salt Lake City, Utah: Signature Books in association with Smith Research Associates, 1989.

BioS   Lucy Mack Smith. *Biographical Sketches of Joseph Smith the Prophet and His Progenitors for Many Generations.* Liverpool, Eng.: S. W. Richards, 1853.

BofC   Joseph Smith Jr., comp. *A Book of Commandments, For the Government of the Church of Christ, Organized According to the Law, on the 6th of April, 1830.* Zion, Mo.: W. W. Phelps, 1833.

BofM   Joseph Smith Jr., trans. *The Book of Mormon: An Account Written by the Hand of Mormon, Upon Plates Taken from the Plates of Nephi.* Palmyra, N.Y.: E. B. Grandin, 1830.

CA   Church Archives. The Church of Jesus Christ of Latter-day Saints. Salt Lake City, Utah.

D&C   Joseph Smith Jr., comp. *Doctrine and Covenants of the Church of Jesus Christ of Latter-day Saints: Containing Revelations Given to Joseph Smith, the Prophet, with Some Additions by His Successors in the Presidency of the Church.* Salt Lake City, Utah: The Church of Jesus Christ of Latter-day Saints, 1981.

D&C [1835]   Joseph Smith Jr. and others, comps. *Doctrine and Covenants of the Church of the Latter-day Saints: From the Revelations of God.* Kirtland, Ohio: F. G. Williams and Co., 1835.

D&C [1844]   Joseph Smith Jr., comp. *The Doctrine and Covenants of the Church of Jesus Christ of Latter-day Saints; Carefully Selected from the Revelations of God.* 2d ed. Nauvoo, Ill.: John Taylor, 1844.

E&MS   *Evening and Morning Star* [Independence, Missouri], 1831–33; [Kirtland, Ohio], 1833–34.

EMD   Dan Vogel, ed. *Early Mormon Documents,* 5 vols. Salt Lake City: Signature Books, 1996–2003.

FARMS   Foundation for Ancient Research and Mormon Studies.

FWR   Donald Q. Cannon and Lyndon W. Cook, eds. *Far West Record: Minutes of The Church of Jesus Christ of Latter-day Saints, 1830–1844.* Salt Lake City, Utah: Deseret Book, 1983.

HC   Joseph Smith Jr. *History of The Church of Jesus Christ of Latter-day Saints.* Edited by B. H. Roberts. 7 vols., 2d ed. rev. Salt Lake City, Utah: Deseret Book, 1971.

JS   Joseph Smith Jr.

JSC   Joseph Smith Jr. Collection, 1805–1844. Church Archives, The Church of Jesus Christ of Latter-day Saints, Salt Lake City, Utah.

JST   Joseph Smith Translation.

LDS   The Church of Jesus Christ of Latter-day Saints.

M&A   *Messenger and Advocate* [Kirtland, Ohio], 1834–36.

ManH   Manuscript History of the Church. Historian's Office. Church Archives. The Church of Jesus Christ of Latter-day Saints. Salt Lake City, Utah.

MoU   Eber D. Howe. *Mormonism Unvailed* [sic]: *Or, A Faithful Account of that Singular Imposition and Delusion.* Painesville, Ohio: By the author, 1834.

PJS   Joseph Smith Jr. *The Papers of Joseph Smith.* Edited by Dean C. Jessee. 2 vols. Salt Lake City, Utah: Deseret Book, 1989–92.

PreM   Lucy Mack Smith, Preliminary Manuscript [1844–45]. Church Archives. The Church of Jesus Christ of Latter-day Saints. Salt Lake City, Utah. In Lucy Mack Smith, *Lucy's Book: A Critical Edition of Lucy Mack Smith's Family Memoir,* ed. Lavina Fielding Anderson. Salt Lake City, Utah: Signature Books, 2001.

PWJS   Joseph Smith Jr. *The Personal Writings of Joseph Smith.* Edited by Dean C. Jessee. Rev. ed. Salt Lake City, Utah: Deseret Book, 2002.

RLDS   Reorganized Church of Jesus Christ of Latter Day Saints (now named Community of Christ).

T&S   *Times and Seasons* [Nauvoo, Ill.], 1839–46.

WJS   Joseph Smith Jr. *The Words of Joseph Smith: The Contemporary Accounts of the Nauvoo Discourses of the Prophet Joseph.* Edited by Andrew F. Ehat and Lyndon W. Cook. Provo, Utah: Religious Studies Center, Brigham Young University, 1980.

PREFACE

1   For review of the biographies, see Bushman, "Joseph Smith for the Twenty-first Century," 155–71; Bitton, *Images of the Prophet Joseph Smith,* 138–64. The volume of the scholarship can be measured in Allen, Walker, and Whittaker, *Studies in Mormon History.* For the DVDs, see *Selected Collections.*

2   Bate, *Samuel Johnson;* Bloom, *American Religion,* 126.

3   Steven Shields tallies almost two hundred distinct "church organizations of fellowships" tracing their lineage to Joseph Smith. Shields, "Latter Day Saint Churches," 49.

4   One early acquaintance who knew Joseph before 1821 (when he was fifteen or younger) did say he was a "very passable exhorter" in Methodist meetings. Turner, *History,* 214.

5   *BofC,* 58:1 (*D&C,* 56:1).

6   JS, Journal, May 21, 1843, in *APR,* 378–79.

7   *WJS,* 355 (April 7, 1844).

8   Damrosch, *Quaker Jesus,* 71; History [1832], in *PJS,* 1:3; *Pittsburgh Weekly Gazette,* Sept. 15, 1843, in *PJS,* 1:443.

9   Armstrong, *Muhammad,* 14.

PROLOGUE

1   Quincy, *Figures of the Past,* 378–79; JS, Journal, in *APR,* 480.

2   Ford, *History of Illinois,* 334.

3   Quincy, *Figures of the Past,* 380–81.

4   Quincy, *Figures of the Past,* 382. Cf. Adams, "Charles Francis Adams," 4–36.

5   Indenture, JS to Ebenezer Robinson, Jan. 23, 1844.

6   Quincy, *Figures of the Past,* 381–82, 277–78. The account was first published in a New York literary magazine and republished in Quincy's posthumous memoirs. New York *Independent,* Dec. 29, 1881, 4–5; Jan. 9, 1882, 2–4; Quincy, *Figures of the Past,* 376–400.

7   Quincy, *Figures of the Past,* 397–98.

8   Quincy, *Figures of the Past,* 394–95.

9   Quincy, *Figures of the Past,* 376.

10   Quincy, *Figures of the Past,* 394–95.

11 Emerson, "An Address," in *Works*, 1:84, 90, 92.

12 Phebe Peck to Anna Pratt, Aug. 10, 1832, in Johnson, " 'Give Up All and Follow Your Lord': Testimony and Exhortations in Early Mormon Women's Letters," 93.

13 William Clayton to Edward Martin, Nov. 29, 1840.

14 Quincy, *Figures of the Past*, 376–77, 400.

15 Quincy, *Figures of the Past*, 397.

16 JS, Journal, May 15, 1844, in *APR*, 479.

CHAPTER 1   THE JOSEPH SMITH FAMILY

1   *BioS*, 279.

2   PreM, 220.

3   Martha Jane Knowlton Coray, a Nauvoo schoolteacher, and her husband, Howard, a former clerk of Joseph Smith's, recorded Lucy Smith's narrative in a series of notebooks from which a preliminary manuscript was prepared. The Corays and Lucy Smith further revised the manuscript, and Orson Pratt published *Biographical Sketches* [*BioS*] in Liverpool in 1853 with Lucy Smith's permission. Brigham Young appointed a committee to correct inaccuracies and make other editorial changes. This version was published in 1902 as *History of the Prophet Joseph by His Mother Lucy Smith, as Revised by George A. Smith and Elias Smith*. A later edition based on the 1902 edition was published in 1945 as *History of Joseph Smith, by His Mother, Lucy Mack Smith*, by Preston Nibley. For a discussion of the history of the manuscript and the significance of the revisions in the 1902 edition, see the critical text L. M. Smith, *Lucy's Book*, 66–166.

4   *BioS*, 278, 281–82.

5   *BioS*, 56.

6   *BioS*, 15, 21, 23, 30, 33–36, 279, 281.

7   *BioS*, 8, 33.

8   Anderson, *New England Heritage*, 5–7, 202, n. 2; Mack, *Solomon Mack*, 4–5. Mack's autobiography, *Solomon Mack*, is conveniently reprinted with excellent notation in Anderson, *New England Heritage*, 44–73. Mack gave his birthday as Sept. 26, 1735. Mack, *Solomon Mack*, 3, 5. Lucy Mack Smith gave the same date. *BioS*, 15. The vital records of Lyme, Conn., show Sept. 15, 1732. For a discussion of the point, see Anderson, *New England Heritage*, 203, n. 8. For John Mack and the Lyme economy, see Main, "Early Lyme," 31, 36. Main calculates that John Mack doubled the value of the estate left by his father.

9   Mack, *Solomon Mack*, 5–11; Anderson, *New England Heritage*, 10–12. Solomon Mack and his brother Elijah were said to have built a gristmill in about 1776 near Gilsum's stone bridge. Hayward, *Town of Gilsum*, 207.

10 Mack, *Solomon Mack*, 10, 12–14; Hayward, *Town of Gilsum*, 34.

11 Mack, *Solomon Mack*, 14–17; Anderson, *New England Heritage*, 19. McCurdy was from a New Hampshire town that originally was part of Gilsum. Solomon Mack gives the name as Cordy, but probate records say McCurdy or McCordy. Anderson, *New England Heritage*, 214, n. 49. Solomon had been in debt to John McCurdy, one of the richest men in Connecticut, who died in 1786 with an estate valued at £37,118. Main, "Early Lyme," 42, 45.

12 Mack, *Solomon Mack*, 17, 20; Anderson, *New England Heritage*, 19, 21; PreM, 245.

13 PreM, 10; *BioS*, 36.

14 Mack, *Solomon Mack*, 11–12; *BioS*, 36.

15 *BioS*, 23–29. Anderson, *New England Heritage*, 80–88, collates the various accounts of the sickness of the two sisters.

16 *BioS*, 36–37.

17   Mack, *Solomon Mack*, 62, 63, 66; *BioS*, 19; PreM, 35; Anderson, *New England Heritage*, 232, n. 80.

18   PreM, 230–31; *BioS*, 25, 53, 21, 24–29.

19   PreM, 258; *BioS*, 37; Porter, *Study of the Origins*, 5; Anderson, *New England Heritage*, 21–22, 129.

20   Brooke, *Refiner's Fire*, 65–67, spins out the possible implications of this testimony.

21   The standard works on the Smith ancestry are M. Anderson, *Ancestry and Posterity*, and J. F. Smith, "Asahel Smith," 87–101. For Samuel Smith, see Anderson, *New England Heritage*, 115–17. The obituary appeared in *Salem* (Mass.) *Gazette*, Nov. 22, 1785. On the significance of the moderator's office, see Cook, *Leadership and Community*. On the town of Topsfield, see Cannon, "Topsfield, Massachusetts," 56–76.

22   Anderson, *New England Heritage*, 117–26. A year after his marriage, Asael was listed in the tax rolls with his father and brother and no property assigned to his name, suggesting he was still living at home. Anderson, *New England Heritage*, 248, n. 124.

23   Porter, *Study of the Origins*, 5; Anderson, *New England Heritage*, 127–28. On the Smith family migration, see Garrard, "Asael Smith Family," 14–31.

24   Anderson, *New England Heritage*, 129. Tunbridge was organized as a town on Mar. 21, 1786, and sent a representative to the legislature the following year. Child, *Orange County*, 473, 478.

25   The complete heading of the letter is "A few words of advice which I Leave to you my Dear wife and children whom I Expect ear Long to Leave." The holograph is in the Church Archives. The document was published by J. F. Smith in "Asahel Smith," 91–96. The best modern edition is in Anderson, *New England Heritage*, 160–65, esp. 160, 163, 162. Citations are to this edition.

26   Anderson, *New England Heritage*, 164, 190.

27   Anderson, *New England Heritage*, 142–48.

28   Anderson, *New England Heritage*, 147–52, 163, 276–80. Of the thirteen members of the Asael Smith family, seven accepted the Mormon faith, three died before they had an opportunity, and three rejected it. John Smith, who was baptized in 1832, was the first to join after Joseph Sr.

29   Allen and Eddy, *Unitarians and Universalists*, 388–407; Bressler, *Universalist Movement*, 12, 14–17. The Arminians had no patience with Murray. Wright, *Unitarianism in America*, 189–90.

30   Anderson, *New England Heritage*, 161–62.

31   Lucy Smith, *BioS*, 154–57; Anderson, *New England Heritage*, 133–36, 140–41. A daughter-in-law of Asael's said he renounced Universalism on his deathbed. Anderson, *New England Heritage*, 288, n. 218.

32   *BioS*, 140, 45. Evidence for a son prior to Alvin is found in Patriarchal Blessings, Book A, 1. Addressing the Smith family in 1834, Joseph Smith Sr. speaks of "three seats" vacated by death: "The Lord in his just providence has taken from me at an untimely birth a son. . . . My next son, Alvin . . . was taken. . . ." I am grateful to Richard Lloyd Anderson for this reference. The Smiths also lost Ephraim in 1810. Larry Porter found Lucy Smith's 1799 date for Alvin's birth in conflict with the 1798 date in the Tunbridge vital records. Porter, *Study of the Origins*, 12, n. 12. For price rises in the 1790s, see U.S. Department of Commerce, *Historical Statistics*, 202, 205.

33   *BioS*, 45; Child, *Orange County*, 343, 535; Crockett, *Vermont*, 2:502–3, 513, 521. The mercantile business frequently attracted ambitious men of small fortunes. Gross, *Minutemen*, 91–92.

34   *BioS*, 49, 51; Boorstin, *National Experience*, 7–8.

35   *BioS*, 49–51.

36   PreM, 286; *BioS*, 51. Larry Porter suggests the possibility that the farm was sold in the family. In June 1803, Asael Smith mortgaged two of his lots to Thomas Emerson of

Topsfield for $700, which may have provided him cash to make the purchase. Porter, *Study of the Origins*, 6–7, 12, n. 19.

37 Porter, *Study of the Origins*, 7–9. For the moves of a family of comparable economic circumstances, see the case of Ezekiel Brown, told in Gross, *Minutemen*, 89–94.

38 Porter, *Study of the Origins*, 6–7; BioS, 40, 51; Anderson, *New England Heritage*, 24–25; Bennett, "Solomon Mack," 36.

39 BioS, 56. Porter, *Study of the Origins*, 7, assembles evidence that the attending doctor was Joseph Adam Denison of Bethel, Vt., a community twelve miles northwest of Sharon.

40 BioS, 40–41, 56. Solomon Mack was having trouble holding on to the farm. There is evidence of a second mortgage in 1807, and he lost the farm to the previous owner in 1811. Solomon received $500 for the land, which had been priced at $800, an indication that he had not paid in full when it was deeded back. Anderson, *New England Heritage*, 25–26, 29.

41 Dan Vogel argues the opposite in "Joseph Smith's Family Dynamics," 51–74.

42 Hill, *Joseph Smith*, 35; PreM, 299–300; Chase, *Dartmouth College*, 1:634–35. Katharine was born July 28, 1812. BioS, 41.

43 BioS, 60.

44 Gallup, *Epidemic Diseases*, 69–70, 75; BioS, 59–61.

45 BioS, 63.

46 BioS, 62–66; PreM, 306; ManH A-1, in *PJS*, 1:268, n. 1. For a technical description of the infection and the operation, and for the history of Dr. Nathan Smith, see Wirthlin, "Boyhood Operation," 131–54, and "Nathan Smith," 319–37.

47 BioS, 65.

48 ManH A-1, in *PJS*, 1:268, n. 1; BioS, 62–63, 65, 69. On his lame leg, see Woodruff, *Journals*, 2:258 (July 14, 1843). William D. Morain, a surgeon himself, has written a psychoanalytic study of the effects of this traumatic event on Joseph. Morain argues it scarred him permanently and disrupted normal behavior through his life. *Sword of Laban*. Clinicians do trace personality disorders back to childhood traumas, but broader statistical investigations show that many children survive such events and function normally. Cohen and Cohen, "The Clinician's Illusion."

49 BioS, 63–64.

50 BioS, 64.

51 PreM, 307.

52 BioS, 61, 63.

53 BioS, 64–65.

54 BioS, 54–55, 70, 183–84.

55 BioS, 46.

56 BioS, 46.

57 Heyrman, *Southern Cross*; Hardman, *Charles Grandison Finney*; Boles, *Great Revival*; Cross, *Burned-Over District*; Rawlyk, *Canada Fire*.

58 BioS, 37, 47; cf. Matt. 7:7; John 14:1.

59 BioS, 21, 47–48; PreM, 276–78.

60 PreM, 291; BioS, 54.

61 BioS, 59–61; W. Smith, Interview (1893), in *EMD*, 1:512.

62 Mack, *Solomon Mack*, 18, 23, 25; BioS, 56, 60–61; BioS, 57–58; W. Smith, *Mormonism*, 5.

63 The evidence, which is exceedingly thin, is found in "Birthplace and Early Residence," 315–16. The Middletown, Vermont, town historian Barnes Frisbie later claimed that Joseph Sr. was involved with a family of money-diggers and radical religionists headed by Nathaniel Wood and with a money-digger named Winchell, but the connection has never been proven satisfactorily. Barnes Frisbie, Account (1867), in *EMD*, 1:599–600, 617–21. Joseph Sr.'s treasure-seeking activities in New York are the main reason for believing he was involved in treasure-seeking earlier.

64 Hall, *Worlds of Wonder,* 137–38, 162, 164.

65 PreM, 310–11.

66 Anderson, *New England Heritage,* 142–47. On the Smiths' move to New York, see Garrard, "Asael Smith Family," 14–31.

67 *BioS,* 66; Ludlum, *Early American Winters,* 190–94; Child, *Orange County,* 535; Stilwell, *Migration from Vermont,* 125–39, 151. The unseasonably cold weather across North America and northern Europe in 1816 is generally attributed to the volcanic explosion of Tamboro on the Indonesian island of Sumbawa in 1815, which blew at least 150 cubic kilometers of volcanic ash and pulverized rock into the atmosphere. Post, *Subsistence Crisis,* 1–5.

68 Many Vermonters on their way to New York took the St. Lawrence turnpike from Plattsburg to Carthage, opened in 1812 and 1813. Stilwell, *Migration from Vermont,* 139. Judging from the $150 debt that Lucy paid at the last minute, the Smith debts could easily have amounted to $200 or $300. PreM, 34.

69 *BioS,* 67; Stilwell, *Migration from Vermont,* 135; PreM, 312–13.

70 PreM, 312–14; *BioS,* 67–68; Joseph Smith, ManH A-1, in *PJS,* 1:268–69, n. 1.

71 *BioS,* 68–69. Lydia Mack was injured when the sleigh in which she was riding overturned. She died about 1818. ManH A-1, in *PJS,* 1:268–69, n. 1; Anderson, *New England Heritage,* 31–32.

72 The accounts of Joseph Jr. and Lucy differ slightly on details of the journey. Lucy says she paid Howard; Joseph says his father gave Howard the money. Joseph says the incident with the wagon took place in Utica; Lucy, who presumably had a more accurate sense of location than her ten-year-old son, said it occurred twenty miles west of Utica. PreM, 314–17; *BioS,* 69; ManH A-1, in *PJS,* 1:268–69, n. 1.

73 ManH A-1, in *PJS,* 1:268–69, n. 1.

74 ManH A-1, in *PJS,* 1:268–69, n. 1; *BioS,* 70; PreM, 317.

CHAPTER 2   THE FIRST VISIONS

1 For the settlement of the Massachusetts–New York boundary dispute, see Cochran, *New York,* and Billington, *Westward Expansion,* 251–59.

2 McNall, *Genesee Valley,* 70, 96–98; Spafford, *Gazeteer* (1824), 80; Spafford, *Gazeteer* (1813), 152; Backman, *First Vision,* 27–28.

3 Backman, *First Vision,* 32–33; Spafford, *Gazeteer* (1813), 7; Spafford, *Gazeteer* (1824), 80.

4 Spafford, *Gazeteer* (1824), 400–401; Backman, *First Vision,* 45; Shaw, *Erie Water West,* 130; Miller, *Economic Development,* 94.

5 McKelvey, *Rochester,* 71–72, 75–76, 100; McNall, *Genesee Valley,* 100; Cross, *Burned-Over District,* 70. In 1827 Rochester had eight newspapers. McKelvey, *Rochester,* 151; Shaw, *Erie Water West,* 240; Spafford, *Gazeteer* (1824), 484.

6 Backman, *First Vision,* 30.

7 *BioS,* 70; Tucker, *Origin,* 12. Wheat harvesters made $1.50 a day in the Genesee Valley. McNall, *Genesee Valley,* 112; Backman, *First Vision,* 44.

8 Marquardt and Walters, *Inventing Mormonism,* 4; Backman, *First Vision,* 41, 43; Porter, *Study of the Origins,* 139–40. The price is indeterminate because the terms of the purchase agreement are unknown, but the property was assessed for $700 in the 1821 property tax list. Marquardt and Walters, *Inventing Mormonism,* 7. The method of payment is unclear too. Lucy Smith speaks of three payments. PreM, 320–21. William Smith said payments of $100 were made annually. W. Smith, *Mormonism,* 12. The draft manuscript of Lucy Smith's *BioS* implies that the first payment was made before the Smiths began working the farm; the published version leaves the impression they raised the money while they worked the farm. PreM, 318–19; *BioS,* 70.

9 The uncertain time of the Manchester move makes the dating of other events, such as

the First Vision, complicated, since Joseph related subsequent happenings to the move. "Sometime in the second year after our removal to Manchester," he says, referring to the revivals that aroused his questions about a true church. ManH A-1, in *PJS*, 1:269. Porter, *Study of the Origins*, 16–17, presents evidence for the move to "Manchester" in 1818. Marquardt and Walters, *Inventing Mormonism*, 7, dates the move in 1822. Lucy indicates they moved to their farm in late 1822 or 1823, perhaps the time when they left the house on the Jennings property. PreM, 321.

10 Marquardt and Walters, *Inventing Mormonism*, 6, argues for a second log house on their own property. Lucy said the land agent instructed them to build a house on the property, which would be to the owner's advantage should the new purchasers default on the payments. PreM, 319. But the valuation of their Manchester property did not go up until 1823, when the frame house was being constructed; a new log house would have raised the value. They were also in the Palmyra road records for these years, suggesting they were technically still in the town bounds though working a farm in Manchester. *EMD*, 3:414, 425–26.

11 Tucker, *Origin*, 12. Joseph Sr. appears on the Palmyra road tax list for 1817–22, Alvin in 1820–22, and Hyrum in 1821. Palmyra road lists (1817–22), in *EMD*, 3:414.

12 Porter, *Study of the Origins*, 16–17. For descriptions of the house, see Tucker, *Origin*, 13; *BioS*, 71.

13 Ellis, *Landlords and Farmers*, 40, 73, 101–102; *BioS*, 70; W. Smith, Notes (ca. 1875), in *EMD*, 1:489. Orsamus Turner recalled only a small spot near the Smith house cleared of underbrush in 1819 or 1820. *History*, 212–13, n. See also Tucker, *Origin*, 13.

14 W. Smith, Notes (ca. 1875), in *EMD*, 1:489; Spafford, *Gazeteer* (1824), 400–401; Ellis, *Landlords and Farmers*, 75–76, 91, 101–102, 113; Tucker, *Origin*, 3. One Palmyra resident said the Smiths were coopers by trade. Benjamin Saunders, Interview (1884), in *EMD*, 2:137. Lucy later said they made 1,000 pounds of maple sugar a year. PreM, 322.

15 U.S. Department of Commerce, *Historical Statistics*, 209.

16 *BioS*, 70–71; Tucker, *Origin*, 14; Backman, *First Vision*, 44. PreM, 321, says Alvin returned home "with the necessary amount money for all except the last payment." It is unlikely that he could have earned the required amount in a single year. The more modest statement in the published version seems closer to the truth.

17 PreM, 321–22; *BioS*, 71; Bushman, *Refinement of America*, 238–79, 378–80, 384–85, 426–28.

18 *BofC*, 22:1 (*D&C*, 21:1).

19 *BioS*, 73, 84.

20 Turner, *History*, 213–14; Clark, *Gleanings*, 225; History [1832], in *PJS*, 1:7; Tucker, *Origin*, 17, says that as Joseph grew up, he "learned to read comprehensively," but Tucker mentioned only cheap fiction and the Bible. On the literary environment of Palmyra and Manchester, see Paul, "Manchester (New York) Library," 333–56. For an argument for Joseph's much wider reading, see Quinn, *Early Mormonism*, 181–93, 228.

21 The neighbors had an opportunity to record their impressions of young Joseph when Doctor Philastus Hurlbut, an ex-Mormon, collected affidavits in late 1833. E. D. Howe, editor of the *Painesville Telegraph*, published them in his exposé, *MoU*, 231–67.

22 *BioS*, 56–59, 70–74. For the *Book of Mormon* comparisons, see *BofM*, 18–21, 23–26 (1 Nephi 8 and 11), and *BioS*, 58–59; *BofM*, 122 (2 Nephi 33:10–15) and *BioS*, 281–82. For the relationship of Joseph Smith Sr.'s dreams and the dreams of Nephi and Lehi in the *Book of Mormon*, see Hougey, "*Lehi Tree-of-Life*," and Griggs, "Book of Mormon," 259–78.

23 *BioS*, 71, 58.

24 Backman, *First Vision*, 61–71, esp. 68, estimates the Presbyterian membership in Palmyra village at 65, and the Society of Friends at 30. The Macedon Baptists listed 146 members.

25 Cross, *Burned-Over District*, 3–13, 151–69, esp. 157; Kling, *Field of Divine Wonders;* Johnson, *Islands of Holiness.*

26 Backman, *First Vision*, 67; Hotchkin, *Western New York*, 378; *BioS*, 72.

27 Walters, "New Light," 227–44, stirred a debate on the timing of the revivals. For the argument that revivals in 1824 were the background for Joseph's first vision, see Marquardt and Walters, *Inventing Mormonism*, 15–41. The rebuttal is in Backman, *First Vision*, 53–111.

28 History [1832], in *PJS*, 1:5; ManH A-1, in *PJS*, 1:270.

29 Tucker, *Origin*, 18; Turner, *History*, 214; ManH A-1, in *PJS*, 1:270; Alexander Neibaur, Journal, May 24, 1844, in *PJS*, 1:461. William Smith said a "Mr. Lane," a Methodist preacher, stirred up a revival in the neighborhood. W. Smith, *Mormonism*, 6. On the Rev. George Lane, see Porter, "Reverend George Lane," 321–40.

30 ManH A-1, in *PJS*, 1:270; Backman and Allen, "Western Presbyterian Church," 482–84. On the contested question of when Lucy joined the Presbyterian church, see William Smith, Interview (1893), in *EMD*, 1:512; ManH A-1, 1:270; Porter, *Study of the Origins*, 18; *EMD*, 3:497–501. All the circumstantial evidence notwithstanding for an 1820 membership, the date of Lucy Smith's engagement to Presbyterianism remains a matter of debate. It is possible to argue plausibly that she did not join until later Palmyra revivals in 1824. Hill, "First Vision Controversy," 39–42; Marquardt and Walters, *Inventing Mormonism*, xxviii, 16–17.

31 Turner, *History*, 214; *M&A*, Feb. 1835, 78; History [1832], in *PJS*, 1:6.

32 ManH A-1, in *PJS*, 1:271; History [1832], in *PJS*, 1:3–4.

33 ManH A-1, in *PJS*, 1:271; James 1:5–7. William Smith later said Joseph had heard the Rev. George Lane use the James text in a sermon titled "What church shall I join?" William Smith, Interview (1893), in *EMD*, 1:513.

34 On praying vocally, see ManH A-1, in *PJS*, 1:272. The year of the First Vision is a matter of dispute. In his first written account, Joseph said he made his inquiry "in the 16th year of my age," which would be 1821. In 1838, he said it was the spring of 1820. History [1832]; ManH A-1, in *PJS* 1:6, 269. William Smith gives Joseph's age as "about seventeen," placing the vision in 1823. W. Smith, *Mormonism*, 7. In telling his story, Joseph himself usually said he was "about fourteen years old" or "about fourteen years of age," as if he was uncertain about the exact date. *PJS*, 1:429, 444, 448; Backman, *First Vision*, 158. See also Anderson, "Circumstantial Confirmation," 398–401.

35 *Pittsburgh Gazette*, Sept. 15, 1843, in *PJS*, 1:444. For a discussion of the First Vision in Mormon theology, see Allen, " 'First Vision' in Mormon Thought," 29–45, and "Emergence of a Fundamental," 43–61; Hill, "On the First Vision," 90–99; Howard, "Joseph Smith's First Vision," 23–29.

36 History [1832], in *PJS*, 1:3, 6–7; *BofC*, 24:6 (*D&C*, 20:5). For other visionaries in Joseph's period, see Bushman, "Visionary World," and Winiarski, "Souls Filled," 3–46.

37 History [1832], in *PJS*, 1:5–7.

38 Bushman, "Visionary World," 195–96; Allen, "Emergence of a Fundamental," 43–61; PreM, 343.

39 JS, Journal, Nov. 9, 1835, in *PJS*, 2:68–69; ManH A-1, in *PJS*, 1:272.

40 History [1832], in *PJS*, 1:7; Jessee, "Early Accounts," 283–87. The accounts are conveniently reproduced in Jessee, "First Vision," 1–33. On the import of the changes, see Lambert and Cracroft, "Literary Form," 31–42, and, from another perspective, Howard, "Analysis of Six Contemporary Accounts," 95–117. For a literary analysis of the 1838 account, see King, "Joseph Smith as Writer," 197–205.

41 History [1832], in *PJS*, 1:7; ManH A-1, in *PJS*, 1:273; Colossians 2:22.

42 ManH A-1, in *PJS*, 1:273, n. 1; *FWR*, 23 (Oct. 25, 1831). The failure to tell his mother about the vision led to her mixing up the sequence of events. In the draft of the *BioS* she connected Joseph's confusion about the churches with the visit of Moroni. William,

who probably got the story from his mother, made the same mistake. PreM, 335; W. Smith, *Mormonism*, 8–9; JS, Journal, Nov. 9, 1835, in *PJS*, 2:69.

43   ManH A-1, in *PJS*, 1:273. *Wayne Sentinel*, Oct. 22, 1823; Thompson, *Christian Guide*, 71; Crawford, "Nathan Cole," 96; Winiarski, "Heavenly Visions," 3–46; Kirchner, "Spiritual Dreams," 198–229.

44   Amatus, "While People Continue," 349; ManH A-1, in *PJS*, 1:273–74. The New England divines Joseph Bellamy and Samuel Hopkins both argued against personal revelations. Bellamy, *True Religion*, 92; Hopkins, *System of Doctrines*, 1:603–4. The announcement of a general apostasy among the churches would have been familiar to the Methodist preacher. That was the common message of the visions; see, for example, *Sense of the United Non-conforming Ministers*, 6. I am indebted to Michael Crawford for this reference. Asa Wild carried the same information away from his vision. *Wayne Sentinel*, Oct. 22, 1823. Cf. E. Smith, *Elias Smith*. Marvin Hill, "Role of Christian Primitivism," enlarges on the belief in apostasy among a number of lay Christians in the early nineteenth century. See also Hill, "Shaping of the Mormon Mind," 351–72.

45   ManH A-1, in *PJS*, 1:275.

46   ManH A-1, in *PJS*, 1:275; W. Smith, *Mormonism*, 9–10, 12; History [1832], in *PJS* 1:5; Anderson, "New York Reputation," 306. On school attendance: Ashurst-McGee, "Josiah Stowell Jr.," 113; Christopher M. Stafford, Statement (1885), and John Stafford, Statement (1881), in *EMD*, 2:194, 122.

47   PreM, 320–21, 349; BioS, 71, 86–87; JS, Journal, August 23, 1842, in *PJS*, 2:440–41; Marquardt and Walters, *Inventing Mormonism*, 6.

48   The article for land does not exist but a reference to it appears in an 1825 document concerning the property of their neighbor to the south. Nicholas Everston heirs to Squire Stoddard, Nov. 2, 1825, Ontario County Land Records, Deeds, 44:219–21. Don Enders provided this reference.

49   Patriarchal Blessings, Book A, 1–2; Barton Stafford, Affidavit (1833), and David Stafford, Affidavit (1833), in *MoU*, 249–51. Alcohol consumption in America was at its peak in the 1820s. Lender and Martin, *Drinking in America*, 46–47; Rorabaugh, *Alcoholic Republic*, 145, 175, 187. Smith family "cider" for purchases 1827–28 are listed in Lemuel Durfee, Account Books, May 31, Sept. 1, 1827; May 13, June 20, 1828, in *EMD*, 3:458–59.

50   Patriarchal Blessings, Book A, 1–3. For a hostile assessment of Joseph Sr., see Turner, *History*, 213. The Smiths were remembered as good workers but poor. Backman, *First Vision*, 119–20.

51   ManH A-1, in *PJS*, 1:273, 275. The only other evidence of persecution are a reminiscence by Thomas H. Taylor of Manchester about Joseph being ducked in a pond for teaching what he believed, and an inexplicable attempt on his life recorded by Lucy Smith. She said an unknown attacker took a shot at Joseph one day as he entered the yard. The times of both incidents are uncertain. Thomas H. Taylor, Interview (1881), in *EMD*, 2:118; BioS, 73.

52   *Wayne Sentinel*, Sept. 30, 1824; W. Smith, *Mormonism*, 13; Backman, *First Vision*, 119; BioS, 73.

53   BofC, 24:5 (D&C, 20:5); ManH A-1, in *PJS*, 1:276, n. 2; *Saints' Herald*, June 1, 1881, 163, 167. Martin Harris was brought before a high council in 1834 for saying Joseph drank while translating the Book of Mormon. Harris said the drinking happened before the translation began. Kirtland High Council, Minutes, Feb. 12, 1834. Josiah Stowell Jr., who knew Joseph Smith from about 1825 through 1827, said Joseph took a glass but never got drunk. Ashurst-McGee, "Josiah Stowell Jr.," 113. For references to Joseph's drinking, see *EMD*, 2:22, n. 4.

54   T&S, April 1, 1842, 749; History [1832], in *PJS*, 1:7; ManH A-1, in *PJS*, 1:275–76.

55   This memory may not be entirely trustworthy because Lucy thought Moroni was the

one to tell Joseph the churches were wrong. Her lack of knowledge of the First Vision confused her sense of the sequence of events. PreM, 335.

56 ManH A-1, in *PJS*, 1:276. The frame house remained unfinished in 1823, and unless some family members slept there to relieve congestion, Joseph received Moroni in the cabin. Porter, *Study of the Origins*, 25–26. In 1835 Oliver Cowdery commented that Joseph prayed when "slumber had spread her refreshing hand over others beside him." *M&A*, Feb. 1835, 79.

57 ManH A-1, in *PJS*, 1:276–78. Joseph said nothing about forgiveness of sins in his 1838 account, but Oliver Cowdery mentioned this personal message twice in his 1835 letters. *M&A*, Feb. 1835, 78–79; and July 1835, 155–56. In his 1838 account, Joseph said the angel called himself "Nephi," a puzzling mistake. For discussion of possible reasons why, see L. M. Smith, *Lucy's Book*, 336–37; *PJS*, 1:277; Quinn, *Early Mormonism*, 198–99.

58 ManH A-1, in *PJS*, 1:278–79.

59 ManH A-1, in *PJS*, 1:280–81; *BioS*, 81–82.

60 History [1832], in *PJS*, 1:8; *BioS*, 81–82; ManH A-1, in *PJS*, 1:281.

61 *M&A*, July 1835, 152–58; Oct. 1835, 196–97; ManH A-1, in *PJS*, 1:281 and n. 1. Lucy Smith mentioned four pillars of cement. PreM, 346.

62 ManH A-1, in *PJS*, 1:280; History [1832], in *PJS*, 1:8; *BioS*, 83, 85; PreM, 346–47; Knight, "Joseph Knight's Recollection," 31; *M&A*, Oct. 1835, 197–98. Joseph's money-digging associates told a story of a toad in the box that metamorphosed into a man and struck Joseph down. Willard Chase, Affidavit (1833), in *MoU*, 242, and Benjamin Saunders, Interview (1884), in *EMD*, 2:137.

63 W. Smith, *Mormonism*, 9–10; *BioS*, 84; PreM, 344. In the accounts of Lucy Smith and William Smith, Joseph went to the hill a day or more after Moroni's visit. On at least one intervening evening the family gathered around to hear him tell about the angel's visit. PreM, 341–44.

64 *BioS*, 87.

65 *Bios*, 88–91; ManH A-1, in *PJS*, 1:269, 282; JS, Journal, Dec. 18, 1835, in *PJS*, 2:118.

66 *BioS*, 90–91; Walters, "New Light."

67 PreM, 349, 359. Don Enders supplied this reading of the payment situation.

68 *BioS*, 91–93; ManH A-1, in *PJS*, 1:282. Joseph Lewis and Hiel Lewis, Statement (1879), in *EMD*, 4:304–305. Josiah Stowell may have had a cousin in Palmyra, Simpson Stowell. Porter, *Study of the Origins*, 48. On Joseph Knight, see Hartley, *Stand by my Servant Joseph.*

69 *Russell Stoddard v. Joseph Smith*, Feb. 18, 1825, Court of Common Pleas, Ontario Co., Court Record, Disposition of Court Cases. Don Enders, who provided this reference, has identified nine properties that Greenwood repossessed in 1824 and 1825.

70 *BioS*, 40, 91, 94–98; Porter, *Study of the Origins*, 36–37; McNall, *Genesee Valley*, 40, 43; W. Smith, *Mormonism*, 13–14. The Durfee deed of purchase is reproduced in *EMD*, 3:429–31. The years 1824 and 1825 were especially hard in New York and Pennsylvania. In some places land could be purchased for the cost of the improvements. Ellis, *Landlords and Farmers*, 125–26.

71 *BioS*, 98, 129; Porter, *Study of the Origins*, 36–37; W. Smith, *Mormonism*, 14. Lucy said Durfee took six months' labor of fifteen-year-old Samuel as one year's rent. PreM, 372. The arrangement was renewed after the first year. Lemuel Durfee, Account Book, Apr. 16, 1827, in *EMD*, 3:457–58. Hyrum married Jerusha Barden in Manchester. *BioS*, 40.

72 *BioS*, 40. Lucy Smith said Joseph Jr. wished to marry Emma Hale in Dec. 1825, which would have been less than one month after he met her. Lucy was putting the house in order to receive the bride when Stoddard ordered the family out. PreM, 362–64.

73 For the holdings of Stowell and Knight, see Porter, *Study of the Origins*, 48–49, 71–73.

74 Knight, Autobiographical Sketch, 1862, 1; *BioS*, 91–92; ManH A-1, in *PJS*, 1:282; Porter, *Study of the Origins*, 36, 48–49, 71. Lucy Smith said Stowell learned about the

mine from an old document that fell into his hands. *BioS*, 91; see also *M&A*, Oct. 1835, 196–201. An account in the *Amboy Journal*, Apr. 30, 1879, claimed that a woman named Odle told William Hale, a distant relative of Isaac's, about the treasure. *EMD*, 4:301. Martin Harris said Joseph and his father were part of a company to dig for treasure. *Tiffany's Monthly*, Aug. 1859, 164. Larry Porter has identified the signatories to the agreement, all of whom lived in the vicinity. Porter, *Study of the Origins*, 48–49. Emily C. Blackburn, the author of *The History of Susquehannah County*, published in 1873, gave directions to the place where the digging purportedly went on. See also Porter, *Origins*, 49, 65, n. 46.

75 *BioS*, 91–92. Quinn, *Early Mormonism*, 42–44, also describes a green stone which Joseph obtained later when he worked in Susquehanna County. W. D. Purple, who attended a court hearing in Bainbridge in 1826 where Joseph Smith was charged with disorderly conduct, told a story of him seeking his first stone under a tree near Lake Erie. William D. Purple, Reminiscence (1877), in *EMD*, 4:133–34.

76 *BioS*, 91–92. Willard Chase claimed that he found the stone. *MoU*, 240–41. B. H. Roberts says the stone was found in the well of Clark Chase, as does Pomeroy Tucker. Roberts, *Comprehensive History*, 1:129; Tucker, *Origin*, 19; cf. Widtsoe, *Joseph Smith*, 260–67. Martin Harris said the well was Mason Chase's. *Tiffany's Monthly*, Aug. 1859, 169.

77 Emma Smith Bidamon, to Emma Pilgrim, March 27, 1870, in *EMD*, 1:532. On JS stones, see Quinn, *Early Mormonism*, 42–44, 242–47; Ashurst-McGee, "Pathway to Prophethood," chapter 4.

78 *Tiffany's Monthly*, Aug. 1859, 164; Isaac Hale, Affidavit (1834), in *MoU*, 263; Tucker, *Origin*, 19–20; *EMD*, 4:252. The 1826 court record has Joseph say that "while at Palmyra he had frequently ascertained . . . where lost property was of various kinds; that he has occasionally been in the habit of looking through this stone to find lost property for 3 years." *EMD*, 4:250. In *Tiffany's Monthly*, Aug. 1859, 164, Martin Harris said that Joseph found a pin in a pile of shavings with the aid of the stone. The most comprehensive account of the seerstone is Van Wagoner and Walker, " 'Gift of Seeing,' " 48–68.

79 Brodie, *No Man Knows*, 18–21, 29–31. The affidavits were published in *MoU*, 232–67.

80 Willard Chase, Affidavit (1833), in *MoU*, 240–41; Tucker, *Origin*, 19; Abel Chase, Interview (1881), and John Stafford, Interview (1881), in *EMD*, 2:85, 106, 121; Caroline Rockwell Smith, Statement (1885), in *EMD*, 2:199; *BioS*, 102, 109. For another Palmyra seerstone, see *Wayne Sentinel*, Dec. 27, 1825.

81 William Stafford, Affidavit (1833), and Peter Ingersoll, Affidavit (1833), in *MoU*, 238–39, 232–33; Cornelius Stafford, Statement (1885), and Caroline Rockwell Smith, Statement (1885), in *EMD*, 2:196, 199.

82 On the Cowderys' connection with Nathaniel Woods, see Quinn, *Early Mormonism*, 35–36, and Morris, "Cowdery's Vermont Years," 106–29. On the lore, see *Rochester Gem*, May 15, 1830; *New York Folklore Quarterly*, 1:20; 2:174–81; 3:252–53; 13:215–17; Dorson, *Long Bow*, 115, 119, 179–180, 182; Frisbie, *History of Middletown*, 44–65. For further evidence of treasure-seeking and stone-looking, see *Lyons* (N.Y.) *Advertiser*, Aug. 29, 1827; *Palmyra Reflector*, Feb. 1, 1831; *Ontario* (N.Y.) *Depository*, Feb. 9, 1825; *Wayne Sentinel*, Oct. 29, 1823, Feb. 16, Mar. 2, Dec. 27, 1825; *Norwich* (N.Y.) *Journal*, July 2, 1828; Priest, *Wonders of Nature*, 562–63. See also Tanner and Tanner, *Money Digging*.

83 Barton, *Disappointment*, 41; Thomas, *Religion and Decline*, 231–37. See also Leventhal, *In the Shadow*; Butler, "Magic," 317–46, and *Sea of Faith*, 230–31; Watson, *Annals of Philadelphia*, 1:273–74. Besides seeking treasure, Goodwin Wharton joined forces with John Wildman, the former Leveller, to find the Urim and Thummim from the breastplate of the High Priest of the Temple. Thomas, *Religion and Decline*, 236–37.

84 William Stafford, Affidavit (1833), and Peter Ingersoll, Affidavit (1833), in *MoU*, 238, 232–33; Anderson, "New York Reputation," 296; Kirkham, *New Witness*, 2:363.

85 Quinn, *Early Mormonism*, 66–72, 82–86, 103–109, 315–16, and figs. 28a and b, 37–38,

43–44, 50–53, 58–59. The question of Moroni being a biblical angel or a guardian spirit of a treasure hoard is taken up in Quinn, *Early Mormonism*, 138–47; Thomas, "Form Criticism," 145–60; and Ashurst-McGee, "Moroni," 39–75.

86   PreM, 323; Peter Ingersoll, William Stafford, Willard Chase, and Henry Harris, Affidavits (1833); Abigail Harris, Statement (1833), all in *MoU*, 232–34, 238, 239, 242, 251–53; *Tiffany's Monthly*, Aug. 1859, 164. *Tiffany's Monthly* was a spiritualist journal that was willing to admit supernatural influence in Joseph Smith's revelations, but attributed them to "a band of spirits, of not very exalted character." In *Tiffany's* view Joseph Smith was a sincere but misled medium. The *Tiffany's* interview with Martin Harris has him say that the company of money-diggers consisted of Josiah Stowell, Mr. Beman, Samuel Lawrence, George Proper, Joseph Smith Jr., his father, and Hyrum Smith. Joseph Capron claimed "the family of Smiths held Joseph Jr. in high estimation on account of some supernatural power, which he was supposed to possess." *MoU*, 237–38, 259. The huge literature on Joseph Smith Jr., and treasure-seeking includes Taylor, "Treasure Seeking," 18–28; Walker, "American Treasure Hunting," 429–59; Hill, "Money-Digging Folklore," 473–88; Anderson, "Mature Joseph Smith," 489–560.

87   ManH A-1, in *PJS*, 1:280; *M&A*, Oct. 1835, 198–99; PreM, 340–41.

88   *Tiffany's Monthly*, Aug. 1859, 169. Dan Vogel makes a case for Joseph Jr.'s aggressive involvement in "Locations," 197–231. Ingersoll related a similar story of Joseph Sr. leading the search and Joseph Jr. not present. *MoU*, 232–33, 238–39.

89   Isaac Hale, Affidavit (1834), Alva Hale, Statement (1834), in *MoU*, 263, 268; *EMD*, 4:291. Isaac Hale said Joseph Jr. was "very saucy and insolent to his father." *MoU*, 263. In the *Elders' Journal* for 1838, published in Far West, the question was asked, "Was not Joseph Smith a money-digger?" "Yes, but it was never a very profitable job for him as he only got fourteen dollars a month for it." *HC*, 3:29. The reference is apparently to Joseph's work with Stowell in Harmony.

90   Oliver Cowdery said that while Joseph was in the Bainbridge area and before he received the plates, an "officious person complained of him as a disorderly person," but he was "honorably acquitted." *M&A*, Oct. 1835, 201. For the evidence for a trial or preliminary hearing, see Walters, "Court Trials," 123–55, and "From Occult to Cult," 121–31. For an analysis of the contradictions in the various court transcripts and of the questionable circumstances under which some of the supporting evidence was discovered, see Hill, "Joseph Smith and the 1826 Trial," 223–33. Cf. Brodie, *No Man Knows*, 20–31; and Tanner and Tanner, *Joseph Smith's 1826 Trial*.

91   Three accounts of the trial or hearing are known to exist: one by A. W. Benton, a physician living in South Bainbridge, who published a brief account in the *Evangelical Magazine and Gospel Advocate*, Apr. 9, 1831; a second by W. D. Purple, another physician present at the hearing, published in the *Chenango Union* (Norwich, N.Y.), May 3, 1877; and a third, presumably an actual record torn from the book of the presiding justice of the peace, Albert Neely, and published first in *Fraser's Magazine*, Feb. 1873, and subsequently in the article on Mormonism by the Episcopal bishop of Utah, Daniel S. Tuttle, in Tuttle, "Mormons." All three of the accounts are reprinted conveniently in *EMD*, 4:95–99, 129–37, 248–56. The quotation above is at *EMD*, 4:253. The court appearance has been the subject of a long debate summarized in Madsen, "1826 Trial," 91–108. Cf. Editorial Note, *EMD*, 4:239–48.

92   Bainbridge (N.Y.) Court Record (1826), in *EMD*, 4:249–50. Jonathan Thompson, a believer in Joseph's "professed skill," told the court that Joseph led them to the chest "but on account of an enchantment, the trunk kept settling away." Bainbridge (N.Y.) Court Record (1826), in *EMD*, 4:254.

93   William D. Purple, Reminiscences (1877), in *EMD*, 4:135; Roswell Nichols, Statement (1833), in *MoU*, 257. Dan Vogel finds evidence of treasure-seeking in the fall of 1826 and winter of 1827, but it is attenuated. Vogel, "Locations," 229–31. In a final

brush with treasure-seeking, Joseph may have sought a hidden cache of gold and silver in Salem in 1836. *Deseret News*, Dec. 25, 1852 (*D&C*, 111); Brodie, *No Man Knows*, 192–93. In Nauvoo an English convert gave a pair of seerstones used by Church members in England to George A. Smith. George Smith showed the stones to Joseph, "who pronounced them to be a Urim and Thummim as good as ever was upon the earth, but he said, 'They have been consecrated to devils.' " Mace, Autobiography, 48–49.

94 *EMD*, 4:249. Porter, *Study of the Origins*, 69, 73, summarizes the evidence of Joseph's school attendance in Chenango County and possibly Broome County. For his involvement in wool carding, see Austin, *Mormonism*, 32.

95 *T&S*, June 1, 1844, 549–52; Ashurst-McGee, "Josiah Stowell Jr.," 114; Knight, Autobiographical Sketch, 1.

96 Joseph Knight Jr.'s account gives Nov. 1827, rather than 1826, as the date of Joseph's arrival back in Colesville, but since Knight's date conflicts with the well-documented chain of events following Sept. 23, 1827, it seems best to assume that Knight was off by a year. Knight, Autobiographical Sketch, 1.

97 *BioS*, 93; ManH A-1, in *PJS*, 1:313–14. The best summary of the Hale family's history is Porter, *Study of the Origins*, 616–50. The Hales later publicly repudiated Joseph Smith. *Susquehannah Register*, May 1, 1834; Isaac Hale, Affidavit (1834), in *MoU*, 263.

98 Porter, *Study of the Origins*, 75; ManH A-1, in *PJS*, 1:282–83; Walters, "Occult to Cult," 123; Newell and Avery, *Mormon Enigma*, 1–2, 17–18. Emily Coburn said that Emma taught school before she married. Porter, *Study of the Origins*, 77; for further details on the circumstances of the marriage, see 73–78. Isaac Hale said Joseph carried Emma off, but Emma herself told the story differently. Isaac Hale, Affidavit (1834), in *MoU*, 263. The most authoritative study of Joseph Smith's appearance is Hatch, *Joseph Smith Portraits*. Hatch concludes that the best portrait was a full-length profile done in Nauvoo in 1842, probably by Sutcliffe Maudsley, a British convert. The background of the portrait is described in Anderson, "139-Year-Old Portraits," 62–64.

99 ManH A-1, in *PJS*, 1:282–83. Peter Ingersoll, Affidavit (1833), and Isaac Hale, Affidavit (1834), in *MoU*, 263–64. Peter Ingersoll transported the Smiths to Harmony and later claimed that in the conversation with Isaac Hale, Joseph acknowledged that "he could not see in a stone now, nor never could." *MoU*, 234. Isaac Hale's account is more to be trusted in view of the fact that Joseph never repudiated the powers of the stone on any other occasion.

100 Peter Ingersoll, Affidavit (1833), in *MoU*, 235.

101 Joseph Knight Sr., Joseph's employer and friend, reported on the Alvin requirement. Knight, "Joseph Knight's Recollection," 31. The evidence is summarized in Quinn, *Early Mormonism*, 158, 163–64. Quinn argues that the rumor of Alvin's body being exhumed was connected with the requirement of bringing him to the hill in 1824. Taking the corpse along seemed to be the only way to obey the command. Quinn, *Early Mormonism*, 160–61.

102 Quinn, *Early Mormonism*, 159.

103 Morain, *Sword of Laban*, argues that the leg operation permanently scarred Joseph's psyche, accounting for his bizarre religious experiences. For other psychoanalytic diagnoses, see Anderson, *Inside the Mind*; Vogel, "Joseph Smith's Family Dynamics," 51–74; and Groesbeck, "Dreams and Visions," 22–29.

104 *BioS*, 98–99.

CHAPTER 3   TRANSLATION

1 Brodie, *No Man Knows*, 37. For the sources, see *EMD*, 1:43–44; Vogel, *Making of a Prophet*, 98.

2 *EMD*, 2:483, 486; 3:178; Tucker, *Origin*, 31–32. For an example of speculative recon-

struction, see Persuitte, *Joseph Smith*, 54–63, 83. Vogel's language is "would have" and "could have." Vogel, *Making of a Prophet*, 98–99.

3   On Joseph Knight's involvement in early Mormonism, see Hartley, *Stand by My Servant*. Knight and Willard Chase both said Samuel Lawrence had gone to the Hill Cumorah at one time. Knight, "Joseph Knight's Recollection," 32–33; Willard Chase, Affidavit (1833), in *MoU*, 243. Knight recalled Joseph instructing his father to tell Lawrence that if he showed up at the hill, Joseph would "thrash the stumps with him." Knight, "Joseph Knight's Recollection," 33.

4   Quinn, *Early Mormonism*, 166–67, argues there were astrological reasons for going at that hour.

5   *BioS*, 100.

6   *BioS*, 100–101.

7   *BioS*, 101; PreM, 378–79; Knight, "Joseph Knight's Recollection," 33. A description attributed to Martin Harris added that the glasses were about two inches in diameter, perfectly round, and five-eighths of an inch thick at the center, thinning at the edges. *Tiffany's Monthly*, Aug. 1859, 164–65; *Latter-day Saints Millennial Star*, Jan. 30, 1882, 87; cf. W. Smith, *Mormonism*, 12.

8   *BioS*, 101–102, 104. Martin Harris said the plates were first hidden in a hollow oak tree top. *Tiffany's Monthly*, Aug. 1859, 166; cf. *MoU*, 246. Willard Chase said Joseph asked him to make a box. Willard Chase, Affidavit (1833), in *MoU*, 245.

9   *BioS*, 102–104; PreM, 381–84. Brigham Young went on to say, "When Joseph obtained the treasure, the priests, the deacons, and religionists of every grade, went hand in hand with the fortune-teller, and with every wicked person, to get it out of his hands, and, to accomplish this, a part of them came out and persecuted him." *Journal of Discourses*, 2:180–81 (Feb. 18, 1852).

10 *BioS*, 104–105; *Tiffany's Monthly*, Aug. 1859, 166; Lorenzo Saunders, Interview (1885), in *EMD*, 3:178. Willard Chase said Joseph told him the plates weighed between forty and sixty pounds. Willard Chase, Affidavit (1833), in *MoU*, 245–46.

11 *BioS*, 105–106; Knight, "Joseph Knight's Recollection," 33–34.

12 *BioS*, 106, 108; Knight, "Joseph Knight's Recollection," 33–34.

13 On Beaman, also spelled Beman, see Quinn, *Early Mormonism*, 39, 388, nn. 78–79.

14 *Tiffany's Monthly*, Aug. 1859, 167; Knight, "Joseph Knight's Recollection," 33–34; *Kansas City Daily Journal*, June 5, 1881, cited in Whitmer, *Interviews*, 60–61. Willard Chase later claimed he was promised "a share in the book" in return for making a box for the plates. Willard Chase, Affidavit (1833), in *MoU*, 245.

15 *BioS*, 108–109; *Tiffany's Monthly*, Aug. 1859, 167.

16 *Tiffany's Monthly*, Aug. 1859, 164, 166–68; Lucy Harris, Statement (1833) in *MoU*, 255; *BioS*, 110–11. For background on Martin Harris, see Walker, "Martin Harris," 29–43; and Gunnell, "Martin Harris."

17 *BioS*, 111–12; *Tiffany's Monthly*, Aug. 1859, 167. Martin Harris said his wife and daughter returned from the visit to the Smiths with a report of having hefted the plates in their box. *Tiffany's Monthly*, Aug. 1859, 168.

18 *Tiffany's Monthly*, Aug. 1859, 168–70.

19 *BioS*, 113; *Tiffany's Monthly*, Aug. 1859, 170. Joseph Knight said Emma wished to return to her family in Harmony because she was feeling unwell. Knight, "Joseph Knight's Recollection," 34.

20 Isaac Hale, Affidavit (1834), in *MoU*, 264; Knight, "Joseph Knight's Recollection," 34.

21 ManH A-1, in *PJS*, 1:278, 284; PreM, 393; Knight, "Joseph Knight's Recollection," 34.

22 History [1832], in *PJS*, 1:9; *BioS*, 113–14.

23 Knight, "Joseph Knight's Recollection," 34; PreM, 393; *BioS*, 113–14; ManH A-1, in *PJS*, 1:284–85. John Clark, who says Harris called on him before setting out for the east, reported that he went "in quest of some interpreter who should be able to decipher the mysterious characters of the golden Bible." *Gleanings*, 222, 232.

24 Kimball, "Anthon Transcript," 328–30, 334; ManH A-1, in *PJS*, 1:285–86.

25 Kimball, "Anthon Transcript," 336–37. The treatise Anthon referred to must have been Champollion's *Précis du système Hiéroglyphique des Anciens Égyptiens* (Paris, 1824), his only major work on Egyptian to that point.

26 The 1834 Anthon letter first appeared in *MoU*, 269–72, and the 1841 letter in Clark, *Gleanings*, 233–38. Both are reprinted in *EMD*, 4:377–86.

27 Clark, *Gleanings*, 233. Two versions of the Anthon Transcript were published in 1844. David Whitmer's grandson donated a copy to the RLDS Church in 1903. David Whitmer earlier claimed that Martin Harris gave him the original. Kimball, "Anthon Transcript," 346–49. See also Ashment, "Anthon Transcript," 29–31. On the authenticity of the characters, see Crowley, "Anthon Transcript," 14–15, 58–60, 76–80, 124–25, 150–51, 182–83, 542–43, 576, 583.

28 Sorenson, "Mesoamerican Record," 414–17.

29 ManH A-1, in *PJS*, 1:285. Crowley, "Anthon Transcript," 76, has identified transcript characters that somewhat resemble Chaldaic, Arabic, and Assyriac and could have led Anthon to his opinion. One difficulty with the Harris story is that the characters in the Anthon Transcript are still undecipherable. Either Anthon was bluffing or Harris was mixed up.

30 ManH A-1, in *PJS*, 1:285. Harris says he subsequently went to Mitchill, who confirmed Anthon's judgment; Anthon said Harris arrived with a note from Mitchill. ManH A-1, in *PJS*, 1:285–86; Clark, *Gleanings*, 233.

31 *Palmyra Freeman*, ca. Aug. 1829, in *EMD*, 2:222; *BioS*, 115; John Gilbert, Memorandum (1892), in *EMD*, 2:547. Kimball, "Anthon Transcript," 330, 343; Tucker, *Origin*, 42; Clark, *Gleanings*, 229–30. Charles Butler, the Geneva banker to whom Martin Harris applied for a loan to subsidize printing of the *Book of Mormon*, recalled Harris saying that the professor at Columbia thought the characters "very curious, but admitted that he could not decypher them." Bennett, "1831 Report," 362. W. W. Phelps, a printer in Canandaigua, knew about Anthon by late 1830. W. W. Phelps's letter of Jan. 15, 1831, addressed to E. D. Howe, appeared in *MoU*, 273–74.

32 Isaiah 29:11–12; History [1832], in *PJS*, 1:9; Knight, "Joseph Knight's Recollection," 35. In his Feb. 1835 letter on Joseph Smith in the *Messenger and Advocate*, Oliver Cowdery said the angel told Joseph that "the scriptures must be fulfilled before it is translated, which says that the words of a book, which were sealed, were presented to the learned; for thus has God determined to leave men without excuse." Orson Pratt said Joseph Smith had no knowledge of Isaiah 29 before Harris went to New York City. *Journal of Discourses*, 2:288 (Jan. 7, 1855). Before his death Martin Harris is reported to have said that he had no knowledge of the prophecy either. Metcalf, *Ten Years*, 71.

33 Knight, "Joseph Knight's Recollection," 34; *BioS*, 115–17.

34 ManH A-1, in *PJS*, 1:286; Clark, *Gleanings*, 230–31; Charles Anthon to E. D. Howe, Feb. 17, 1834, in *MoU*, 270.

35 PreM, 411; ManH A-1, in *PJS*, 1:286; History [1832], in *PJS*, 1:10; cf. *BofC*, 4:1 (*D&C*, 5:1).

36 *BioS*, 118; Porter, *Study of the Origins*, 55–56. On the baby's name, see Anderson, "139-Year-Old Portraits," 64.

37 *BioS*, 120–21.

38 *BioS*, 121–23. Some Palmyrans believed that Mrs. Harris burned the manuscript. Tucker, *Origin*, 45–46. Lucy Smith implied divine retribution when she reported that a dense fog covered Martin Harris's fields and blighted his wheat on the day he discovered the loss. *BioS*, 123–24.

39 PreM, 419; *BioS*, 1:121, 124.

40 History [1832], in *PJS*, 1:10; ManH A-1, in *PJS*, 1:287; *BioS*, 125; *BofC*, 2:1–4 (*D&C*, 3:1–3, 5–8).

41 *BofC*, 2:4 (*D&C*, 3:9–10).

42 ManH A-1, in *PJS*, 1:287, 319; *BofC*, 2:3 (*D&C*, 3:1, 4). See also Howard, *Restoration Scriptures*, 146.

43 *BofC*, 2:6 (*D&C*, 3:19).

44 For a reflection on the crucial transition of 1828–29, see Staker, "Seer Story," 235–74.

45 Joseph Lewis and Hiel Lewis, Statement (1879), in *EMD*, 305–306.

46 *BioS*, 125–26. Although the assertion clashes with other accounts, David Whitmer said Moroni did not return the Urim and Thummim in September. Instead Joseph used a seerstone for the remaining translation. *Kansas City Journal*, June 19, 1881, *Omaha Herald*, Oct. 17, 1886; Interview (1885), in Whitmer, *Interviews*, 72, 157, 200. Of the translation process, Emma said, "The first that my husband translated, was translated by the use of the Urim, and Thummim, and that was the part that Martin Harris lost, after that he used a small stone, not exactly black, but was rather a dark color." Emma Smith Bidamon to Emma Pilgrim, Mar. 27, 1870, in *EMD*, 1:532.

47 Knight, "Joseph Knight's Recollection," 35–36; ManH A-1, in *PJS*, 1:288; *BioS*, 124, 126–27.

48 Knight, "Joseph Knight's Recollection," 35–36; *BofC*, 3:1 (*D&C*, 4:1–2). Virtually all of the language of section *BofC* 3 (*D&C* 4) comes from the Bible: Isaiah 29:14 (verse 1); Mark 12:30; Luke 10:27 (verse 2); 1 Corinthians 1:8; John 4:35–36 (verse 4); 1 Corinthians 13:13 (verse 5); 2 Peter 1:5–7 (verse 6); Matthew 7:7–8, Luke 18:1, James 1:5 (verse 7).

49 Emma Smith, Notes to Interview (1879), in *EMD*, 1:538–39; *BioS*, 124. Emma gave the information in an interview Feb. 4–10, 1879, with her son, Joseph Smith III, published in *Saints' Herald*, Oct. 1, 1879, 289–90.

50 *M&A*, Oct. 1834, 14; *BioS*, 128–29.

51 Information on Oliver Cowdery may be found in Gunn, *Oliver Cowdery*; Anderson, "Second Witness," 15–16, 18, 20–22, 24. Oliver Cowdery was a third cousin of Lucy Smith.

52 *BioS*, 128–30.

53 *M&A*, Oct. 1834, 14; ManH A-1, in *PJS*, 1:288; *Saints' Herald*, Oct. 1, 1879, 289–90; Clark, *Gleanings*, 230. Tucker, *Origin*, 36, said a blanket hung between Oliver and Joseph. But Elizabeth Ann Whitmer Cowdery, who saw and heard translation "for hours" in Fayette, said Joseph "never had a curtain drawn between him and his scribe." Affidavit (1870), in *EMD*, 5:260.

54 The description of translation comes from Emma Smith, Oliver Cowdery, David Whitmer, Martin Harris, and William Smith. *Saints' Herald*, Oct. 1, 1879, 289–90; May 19, 1888, 310; Neal, *Oliver Cowdery's Defence*, 6; Whitmer, *All Believers*, 12, 30; Whitmer, *Interviews*, passim; Clark, *Gleanings*, 240; *Latter-day Saints Millennial Star*, Jan. 30, 1882, 78–79, 86–87; W. Smith, *Mormonism*, 11. Comprehensive accounts are Van Wagoner and Walker, " 'Gift of Seeing,' " 48–68; and Skousen, "Original Manuscript," 61–93. Richard Howard has pointed out that early newspaper accounts of the translation make no mention of the Urim and Thummim. The first was in the *Evening and Morning Star* (Independence, Mo.), Jan. 1833. Previously the instrument was called "interpreters." Howard, *Restoration Scriptures*, 152–53. The descriptions of translation are compiled in Welch, "Miraculous Translation," 118–213.

55 The most recent and ambitious effort to explain the *Book of Mormon* as a composition is Vogel, *Making of a Prophet*, 111–465. Some believing Mormons adopt versions of the composition theory, speculating that Joseph began with an ancient text but liberally injected interpositions of his own. Ostler, "Modern Expansion," 66–123.

56 Michael Quinn refers to the "myth" of Joseph's ignorance and points to the ample opportunities for extensive reading in the village bookstores and nearby libraries. Quinn, *Early Mormonism*, 179–93.

57 Skousen, "Original Manuscript," 61–93, esp. 71–75 and 79–82; Lancaster, "Method of Translation," 14–18, 22, 23; Knight, "Joseph Knight's Recollection," 35; History [1832], in *PJS*, 1:9. Royal Skousen's critical text is published as Skousen, *Original Manuscript*, and *Printer's Manuscript*.

58 *M&A*, Oct. 1834, 14. In a pamphlet purportedly published at Norton, Ohio, in 1839, after his alienation from Joseph Smith, Cowdery supposedly said, "I have sometimes had seasons of skepticism, in which I did seriously wonder whether the Prophet and I were men in our sober senses when he would be translating from plates through 'the Urim and Thummimn' and the plates not be in sight at all." Quoted in Neal, *Oliver Cowdery's Defence*, 6, 22. The pamphlet is called in question because the only source is a reprint by a fervent anti-Mormon, R. B. Neal, in 1906. No original is known to exist, and there is no evidence for a printing establishment in Norton, Ohio, in 1839. Anderson, "Second Witness," 17.

59 *BofC*, 5:6, 11 (*D&C*, 6:14, 22–23); ManH A-1, in *PJS*, 1:289.

60 Morris, "Vermont Years," 106–29; *BofC*, 7:3; 5:3, 5 (*D&C*, 8:6, 6:7, 10–13); cf. Exodus 7, Numbers 17, Hebrews 9:4. The phrase "gift of Aaron" comes from the 1835 ed. of the *Doctrine and Covenants*, section 34, verse 3.

61 *BofC*, 2:4; 5:11–13 (*D&C*, 3:11; 6:25–28); ManH A-1, in *PJS*, 1:289; *BofC*, 7:1–2 (*D&C*, 8:1–4); see also *BofC*, 4:2–10 (*D&C*, 5:4, 31).

62 *BofC*, 8:1–4 (*D&C*, 9:8, 11, 1, 2). Cowdery helped Joseph translate the Book of Abraham. *HC*, 2:236, 286; *M&A*, Dec. 1835, 234–37.

63 *BofC*, 9:3, 7, 9–10 (*D&C*, 10:14, 18, 31, 39–42). The order of translation has been established through analysis of the handwriting of the original manuscript. The bulk of the writing in the fragments of 1 Nephi that have been saved is in the hand of Oliver Cowdery, with a number of passages in a hand that most resembles John Whitmer's. Anything in these two hands must have been written after April 6, when Oliver arrived in Harmony. Oliver's is the first hand to appear, writing 1 Nephi 2:2–23. There is no evidence of Emma Smith's hand, as would be expected had Joseph begun with 1 Nephi after the loss of the first 116 pages. Joseph did not meet John Whitmer until after June 1, 1829, when Joseph and Oliver moved to Fayette from Harmony. Thus it is unlikely that Emma and Joseph began work on 1 Nephi in the winter of 1829 when they resumed translating. Work on 1 Nephi probably began in late May. It also appears that the Book of Mosiah in the current *Book of Mormon* is not complete. It begins abruptly without the introduction that Mormon affixed to all the other books he abridged. Possibly the first pages of Mosiah were among the 116 that were lost. The evidence implies Joseph and Oliver began work on Mosiah when they began translating together in April 1829, finished the book to the end, and then went back and translated 1 Nephi up through Mosiah. The handwriting analysis was accomplished by Dean Jessee and presented in "Mormon Manuscript," 259–78.

The order of translation in turn bears on the date of section 10, currently dated "summer 1828" in modern editions of the *Doctrine and Covenants*. The manuscript version of the *History of the Church* gives May 1829 for the date of section 10. The *Book of Commandments*, the first printed version of the *Doctrine and Covenants*, also dated the section May 1829. A later editor, however, changed the date to summer 1828, because the directions for translating 1 Nephi are in that section. The revelation would have lost its point by May 1829, if Joseph had begun the translation of 1 Nephi long before. On the other hand, if Joseph had not translated 1 Nephi by May because he had started with Mosiah when he resumed work after the loss of the 116 pages, section 10 was relevant in May.

In conjunction with the dating change of section 10, the text of the manuscript was also altered. Insertions and interpositions in the manuscript in another hand changed the words so as to fit section 10 into the chronology where the later editor believed it rightfully belonged. With the information provided by Dean Jessee's analysis, confidence is restored in the original manuscript and dating. The emendations in the Manuscript History of the Church are in vol. A-1, 11. For further information on writing the history, see Jessee, "Joseph Smith's History," 439–73; Marquardt, *Joseph Smith Revelations*, 41.

64   Knight, "Joseph Knight's Recollection," 36; ManH A-1, in *PJS*, 1:292–93.

65   *M&A*, Oct. 1834, 14–15; ManH A-1, in *PJS*, 1:289. The relevant passages in the Book of Mormon are *BofM*, 349, 452, 510, 512 (Alma 45:18; 3 Nephi 1:3; 28:7, 38).

66   *M&A*, Oct. 1834, 14–15; ManH A-1, in *PJS*, 1:289–90; *T&S*, Aug. 1, 1842, 865–66 (*D&C*, 13). Quinn, *Origins of Power*, 15–16, says the division into greater and lesser priesthoods was a retroactive addition. Lucy Smith said that "one morning they sat down to their work, as usual, and the first thing which presented itself through the Urim and Thummim, was a commandment for Joseph and Cowdery to repair to the water, and attend to the ordinance of Baptism." *BioS*, 131.

67   The reference to John the Baptist in the current section 27 of the *Doctrine and Covenants* was added in 1835. Woodford, "Historical Development," 1:393–98; Marquardt, *Joseph Smith Revelations*, 72–73. According to the *Painesville Telegraph*, Nov. 16, 1830, Cowdery was claiming authority from angels much earlier.

68   History [1832], in *PJS*, 1:3; *BofC*, 24:6–11 (*D&C*, 20:5–10); David Whitmer interview with Zenas H. Gurley (1885) and William E. McLellin to Joseph Smith III (1872), in *EMD*, 5:136–37, 329; *M&A*, Oct. 1834, 15. The significance of the John the Baptist visit is analyzed in Prince, *Power from on High*, 5–9, and Cannon and *BYU Studies* staff, "Priesthood Restoration Documents," 162–207.

69   ManH A-1, in *PJS*, 1:291.

70   ManH A-1, in *PJS*, 1:291.

71   Porter, *Study of the Origins*, 61, 91–95; ManH A-1, in *PJS*, 1:293–94; *BioS*, 137.

72   *Deseret Evening News*, Mar. 25, 1884; Porter, *Study of the Origins*, 95; Jessee, "Mormon Manuscript," 273, 276–77; ManH A-1, in *PJS*, 1:293; Whitmer, *All Believers*, 30; David Whitmer, Interview (1882), in Whitmer, *Interviews*, 86.

73   ManH A-1, in *PJS*, 1:294.

74   *BofC*, 4:3 (*D&C*, 5:7).

75   *BofC*, 4:2, 4, 8 (*D&C*, 5:2, 10, 11, 13, 24); *BofM*, 548, 86, 110 (Ether 5:2–4, 2 Nephi 11:3, 27:12); ManH A-1, in *PJS*, 1:295–96; *M&A*, Sept. 1835, 178 (*D&C*, 17).

76   *BioS*, 138; *Kansas City Journal*, June 5, 1881, in Whitmer, *Interviews*, 62. Lucy Smith remembered Martin accompanying her and Joseph Sr. on the trip to the Whitmers'. *BioS*, 138.

77   David Whitmer gave an account of the vision in *Kansas City Journal*, June 5, 1881, and *Saints' Herald*, Mar. 1, 1882, in Whitmer, *Interviews*, 63–64, 86–87. Joseph Smith's account is in ManH A-1, in *PJS*, 1:296–97.

78   Miller, Diary, Oct. 21, 1848.

79   Harris, quoted in ManH A-1, in *PJS*, 1:296–98.

80   *BioS*, 139.

81   Joseph makes no mention of a visit to Palmyra between the experiences of the three and the eight witnesses. He places the visit later. ManH A-1, in *PJS*, 1:297–98, 300.

82   ManH A-1, in *PJS*, 1:298; Testimony of Eight Witnesses, *BofM*, unnumbered page. For further information on this group, see Anderson, "Five Who Handled."

83   *HC*, 1:56 n; Vogel, "Witnesses' Testimony," 79–122; Vogel, *Making of a Prophet*, 466–69. For the later lives of the three men, see Anderson, *Investigating the Book of Mormon Witnesses*.

84   David Whitmer said the translation was completed around July 1, 1829. *Kansas City Journal*, June 5, 1881, in Whitmer, *Interviews*, 62. Lucy Smith placed completion prior to the vision of the three witnesses, which would have been near the middle of June. *BioS*, 138; cf. Whitmer, *All Believers*, 30.

85 ManH A-1, in *PJS*, 1:299–300; *T&S*, Oct. 1, 1842, 936 (*D&C*, 128:21). David Whitmer claimed that he and at least five others were ordained elders by August 1829: Joseph Smith, Oliver Cowdery, Peter Whitmer, Samuel H. Smith, and Hyrum Smith. *All Believers*, 32.

86 ManH A-1, in *PJS*, 1:298–300; Porter, *Study of the Origins*, 30; Tucker, *Origin*, 51–53. The copyright is published in *EMD*, 3:462–63. Lucy Smith said that a gang of Palmyra toughs planned to stop Joseph from signing the agreement, but he walked unharmed between them as they lined the fence along his route. *BioS*, 141–43.

87 Tucker, *Origin*, 50, 52–55; Porter, *Study of the Origins*, 30. Tucker said Joseph Smith applied unsuccessfully to George Crane, a Quaker living in Macedon, for funding. Lucy Smith understood that Martin Harris contracted for half the costs and Joseph and Hyrum for the other half. *BioS*, 142. The Harris mortgage, dated August 25, 1829, is published in *EMD*, 3:475–77.

88 *BioS*, 142–43; Tucker, *Origin*, 53; Gregg, *Prophet of Palmyra*, 39–43; John H. Gilbert to James T. Cobb, Feb. 10, 1879, quoted in Porter, *Origins*, 30, 32; Oliver Cowdery to JS, Dec. 28 and Nov. 6, 1829, JSC.

89 JS to Oliver Cowdery, Oct. 22, 1829, in *PWJS*, 251–52. Lucy Smith implies that Joseph returned to Harmony immediately after contracting with Grandin, which would have been in late June or July, but in addition to Joseph's own word in the above letter, Pomeroy Tucker and Stephen Harding say they saw him in the printing office after work on the Book of Mormon began. *BioS*, 142; Tucker, *Origin*, 56; Gregg, *Prophet of Palmyra*, 38–39.

90 The present chapter 1 of 1 Nephi and the first three verses of chapter 2. Rich, "Dogberry Papers," 316–17. Lucy Smith identifies Dogberry as Abner Cole. *BioS*, 148.

91 *BioS*, 149; Oliver Cowdery to JS, Dec. 28, 1829, JSC.

92 *BioS*, 149–50; Rich, "Dogberry Papers," 317–18. Dogberry's subsequent paper, the *Liberal Advocate*, is described in Barnes, "Obediah Dogberry," 1–24.

93 Rich, "Dogberry Papers," 316; *BioS*, 143–47; Backman, *First Vision*, 182–83; Backman and Allen, "Western Presbyterian Church," 482–84.

94 Oliver Cowdery to JS, Nov. 6, 1829, JSC; *BioS*, 150–51; Joseph Smith Sr. and Martin Harris agreement, Jan. 16, 1830, in *EMD*, 3:485. On the Toronto trip, see Whitmer, *All Believers*, 30–31; *BioS*, 151.

95 Grandin announced in the *Wayne Sentinel*, Mar. 19, 1830, that the Book of Mormon would be ready in the coming week. For publication details, see Crawley, *Descriptive Bibliography*, 29–32.

96 Knight, "Joseph Knight's Recollection," 36–37; *BofC*, 16:27, 37–38 (*D&C*, 19:26, 35). On poor sales, see *BioS*, 152; Tucker, *Origin*, 60.

97 Diedrich Willers to Reverend Brethren (1831), in *EMD*, 5:271. Francis Kirkham has compiled a great many of the news articles on Mormonism in *New Witness*, 2:28–50. The articles noted by Kirkham (plus one additional essay in the *Painesville Telegraph*) appeared in the following order: *Wayne Sentinel*, June 26, 1829; *Rochester Advertiser*, Aug. 3, 1829; *Palmyra Reflector*, Sept. 2, 1829; *Rochester Gem*, Sept. 5, 1829; *Palmyra Reflector*, Sept. 16, 1829; *Painesville Telegraph*, Sept. 22, 1829; *Palmyra Reflector*, Oct. 7, Dec. 9, 1829, Jan. 2, 13, 22, Feb. 27, 1830; *Wayne Sentinel*, Mar. 26, 1830; *Rochester Republican*, Mar. 30, 1830; *Rochester Daily Advertiser*, Apr. 2, 1830; *Palmyra Reflector*, Apr. 19, May 1, 1830; *Horn of the Green Mountains* (Manchester, Vt.), May 4, 1830; *Rochester Gem*, May 15, 1830.

98 *Rochester Daily Advertiser*, Apr. 2, 1830, and *Horn of the Green Mountains*, May 4, 1830, reprinted in Kirkham, *New Witness*, 2:30, 31.

99 Kirkham, *New Witness*, 2:31–32, 40–41, 47–48. For the religious language, see Taves, *Experiencing Religion*, 18, 131–33, 142–43.

100 *BofM*, v, vi.
101 *BofM*, vi.

CHAPTER 4   A NEW BIBLE

1 Twain quoted in Cracroft, "Mark Twain," 137; De Voto, "Mormonism," 5; Bloom, *American Religion*, 86; Brodie, *No Man Knows*, 69; Rees, "American Renaissance," 83. For literary investigations of the *Book of Mormon*, see, for example, King, "Joseph Smith as Writer," 192–205; King, "Account of My Conversion," 26–28; King, "Language Themes in Jacob 5," 140–73; Arnold, *Sweet Is the Word*; Card, "Artifact or Artifice," 13–45; Thomas, *Digging in Cumorah*; Rust, *Feasting on the Word*; Brown, *Jerusalem to Zarahemla*.
2 John H. Gilbert, Memorandum (1892), in *EMD*, 2:543. "The book is chiefly garbled from the Old and New Testaments," a Palmyra correspondent wrote to an Ohio paper. *Painesville Telegraph*, March 22, 1831. See also *Rochester Gem*, Sept. 5, 1829.
3 *MoU*, 11; Buell, *New England Literary Culture*, 183.
4 Welch, Seely, and Seely, *Glimpses of Lehi's Jerusalem*.
5 *BofM*, 7, 9, 39, 42, 49, 59–60 (1 Nephi 1:18–19; 2:2–6, 16, 20; 16:14; 17:1, 4, 8; 18:23; 2 Nephi 1:4–5).
6 *BofM*, 72, 474, 547–48, 574 (2 Nephi 5:10, 16; 3 Nephi 9:19; Mormon 8:1; Moroni 1:1–4); Bushman, "Lamanite View," 2:52–72; ManH A-1, in *PJS*, 1:277–78.
7 *BofM*, 445–46, 471–72, 476–85, 490, 496–502, 506 (Helaman 14:3–5, 20; 3 Nephi 8:23; 11:7, 12–14, 21–22; 12:1; 17:21; 18:5–6, 20–21; 26:14); Matthew 3:17; 17:5. On the debate over the sermon, see Larson, "Sermon on the Mount," 23–45, and Welch, *Sermon at the Temple*.
8 *BofM*, 519–20, 531–32 (Mormon 2:1; 1:15; 2:2; 8:1–5).
9 *BofM*, 521, 523–24 (Mormon 2:13–14; 3:3, 9–12, 14–15).
10 *BofM*, 239, 173, 151 (Alma 7, Mosiah 9; Words of Mormon 3).
11 On the structure of the Book of Mormon, see Brewster, "Theory of Evolutionary Development," 109–40; and Brown, "Lehi's Personal Record," 19–42. On Mormon as editor, see Hardy, "Mormon as Editor," 15–28.
12 Hoskisson, "Names in the Book of Mormon," 580–81; and the special issue on names in *Journal of Book of Mormon Studies* 9, no. 1 (2000).
13 *BofM*, 251–52 (Alma 11:4–19); Welch, "Weighing and Measuring," 36–45; Smith, "Weights and Measures"; Ricks and Hamblin, *Warfare in the Book of Mormon*; and Hamblin, "Importance of Warfare," 523–43.
14 *BofM*, 305 (Alma 30:16–17).
15 *T&S*, Feb. 1, 1841, 305–306; Welch, "Miraculous Translation," 102, estimates there were sixty-three translating days.
16 *Wayne Sentinel*, June 26, 1829; *Painesville Telegraph*, Sept. 22, 1829 (from *Palmyra Freeman*, ca. Aug. 1829).
17 *Palmyra Reflector*, Jan. 6, 18, 1831.
18 Campbell, *Delusions*, 11, 13, 15.
19 Campbell, *Delusions*, 6; *Western Banner*, May 28, 1839.
20 *MoU*, 278–87, esp. 279 and 283.
21 Spaulding, *Manuscript Found*; Bush, "Spalding Theory," 40–69; *MoU*, 278, 100, 289–90.
22 Tucker, *Origin*, 27, 45; Bush, "Spalding Theory," 49–50.
23 Bush, "Spalding Theory," 53–55.
24 Brodie, *No Man Knows*, 69.
25 Vogel and Metcalfe, *American Apocrypha*, ix.
26 Vogel and Metcalfe, *American Apocrypha*, ix; Hutchinson, "Word of God," 1–2; G.

Smith, "B. H. Roberts," 94–111; Vogel, *Mormon Scripture*, vii–ix. Robert Price, a non-Mormon, makes the same plea in "Prophecy and Palimpsest," 67–82.

27 Vogel and Metcalfe, *American Apocrypha*, viii, ix; Vogel, "Anti-Masonry," 275–320, and " 'Anti-Masonick Bible,' " 17–30; Vogel, "Anti-Universalist Rhetoric," 21–54; Wright, "Isaiah in the Book of Mormon," 157–234; Murphy, "Lamanite Genesis," 47–77; Ashment, "Ancient Egyptian," 374. For attempts to mediate and moderate this conflict, see Rees, "American Renaissance," 104–109; and Thomas, *Digging in Cumorah*, 1–32.

28 Bloom, *Omens of Millennium*, 51.

29 Givens, *American Scripture*, 180–84; Rees, "American Renaissance," 87–88; Midgley, "Critics and Their Theories," 101–39, esp. 126–28.

30 FARMS is now one component of the Institute for the Study and Preservation of Ancient Religious Texts (ISPART).

31 Salmon, "Parallelomania," 129–56. For a non-Mormon assessment of the apologetic scholarship, see Mosser and Owen, "Mormon Apologetic Scholarship," 203; and for a critical analysis by a Mormon, see Judkins, "Book of Mormon Apologetics." Representative apologetics can be found in Nibley, *Lehi in the Desert*, and *Approach to the Book of Mormon*. See also Brown, *Jerusalem to Zarahemla*; Welch, *Sermon at the Temple*; and Parry, Peterson, and Welch, *Echoes and Evidences of the Book of Mormon*.

32 Welch, "Chiasmus in the Book of Mormon," 69–84; Welch, *Chiasmus in Antiquity*. On the ignorance of chiasmus in Joseph Smith's time, see Welch, "Chiasmus in 1829," 47–80, responding to Quinn, *Early Mormonism*, 500–501, which claims chiasmus was available to Joseph Smith by 1825.

33 Nibley, *Approach to the Book of Mormon*, 296–310; Tvedtnes, "Feast of the Tabernacles," 2:197–237; Ricks, "Kingship, Coronation, and Covenant," 233–75; Nibley, *Since Cumorah*, 149–50; Hamblin, "Reformed Egyptian"; Hess, "Botanical Comparisons," 87–102; Ricks and Welch, *Allegory of the Olive Tree*; Aston and Aston, *Footsteps of Lehi*; Aston, "Arabian Bountiful," 4–21; Brown, "Ancient Yemen," 66–68; and Aston, "Altars from Nahom," 56–61.

34 The rejoinder to the Asian DNA argument is given in *Journal of Book of Mormon Studies* 12, no. 1 (2003). The leading figure in assembling evidence from Meso-America is John L. Sorenson. In addition to his work on geography cited below, see his *Nephite Culture and Society* and "Mesoamerican Record," 391–521.

35 The current state of Mormon scholarship is summarized in Givens, *American Scripture*, 117–57; and the 900-page Largey, *Book of Mormon Reference*. Collections of current work can be found in Reynolds, *Authorship* and *Authorship Revisited*. The balance of evidence for both ancient and modern authorship has led one scholar to argue the *Book of Mormon* is a pseudepigraphic text, that is, an ancient writing with modern interpolations by Joseph Smith. Ostler, "Modern Expansion," 66–123. A similar view is expressed by a non-Mormon, Krister Stendahl, in "Third Nephi," 139–54.

36 The major study is Sorenson, *Ancient American Setting*. His effort to persuade Mormons of the limited view is "Changing Understanding," 26–37, 12–23. Critical of Sorenson's claims is Wunderli, "Critique of a Limited Geography," 161–97. On the disruptive effect of the new theory on Mormon views of Indians, see Metcalfe, "Reinventing Lamanite Identity," 20–25.

37 On the opposition of Michael Coe, a Yale archeologist, and others, see Givens, *American Scripture*, 146–49. For a respectful treatment, see T. Smith, "Biblical Culture," 3–21.

38 From the *New-Yorker*; reprinted in *T&S*, Feb. 1, 1841, 305–306.

39 Gordon, "Foreword," xi–xiii. See also a description of the multiple landings controversy in Stengel, "Diffusionists Have Landed," 35–39, 42–46. For a bibliography of other work on transatlantic contacts, see Sorenson, *Pre-Columbian Contact*.

40 Among other non-Mormon scholars to offer supportive opinions are Charlesworth, "Messianism," 99–137, and Stendahl, "Third Nephi," 139–54.

41 Mosser and Owen, "Mormon Scholarship," 185, 189. For bibliography, see Parry, Miller, and Thorne, *Publications on the Book of Mormon*.

42 *BioS*, 152; JS to N. C. Saxton, Jan. 4, 1833, in *PWJS*, 297; *Palmyra Reflector*, July 7, 1830. In the Oct. 30, 1830, issue of the *Brattleboro Messenger*, the editor suggested that the *Book of Mormon* could have been "designed to explain the ancient fortifications and other things seen in the west." Cited in Vogel, *Indian Origins*, 30.

43 Taylor, *William Cooper's Town*, 39; *Wayne Sentinel*, Apr. 24, 1829. An 1855 census recorded 4,619 Iroquois on seven New York reservations. Hauptman, *Iroquois Dispossession*, 216.

44 Dan Vogel inventories the Indian sites in the larger Smith neighborhood, in *Indian Origins*, 26–27. Vogel, the most thorough investigator of the Indian background of the *Book of Mormon*, reports that local sources on Indians "do not prove but merely suggest Joseph's exposure to the subject." Vogel, *Indian Origins*, 9. References mention the Smiths' search for treasure as associated with Indians, but the natives were not noted for accumulating riches. Vogel, *Indian Origins*, 17–18.

45 Sanders, *Indian Wars*, 111–12, 119; *Palmyra Herald*, Feb. 19, 1823.

46 Givens, *American Scripture*, 94. On Noah, see *Wayne Sentinel*, Sept. 27, Oct. 4, 11, 1825. Other newspaper references include *Palmyra Register*, Jan. 21, 1818; May 26, 1819 (which refers to a civilized race being exterminated by the present Indians); *Palmyra Herald*, Oct. 30, 1822; Feb. 19, 1823; *Wayne Sentinel*, Aug. 16, 1825; Aug. 17, Oct. 5, Nov. 9, 1827.

47 John Smith, Lecture 13, Natural Philosophy Lectures, Dartmouth College, January 6, 1779. Smith thought the Indians were most likely descended from Phoenicians driven off course during a voyage from their homes in Carthage in northern Africa and from Scythians and probably others.

48 Popkin, "Jewish Indian Theory," 63–82; Sanders, *Indian Wars*, 119.

49 E. Smith, *View of the Hebrews*; Morris, "Cowdery's Vermont Years," 106–29. The most insistent argument for the influence of *View of the Hebrews* on the Book of Mormon is Persuitte, *Joseph Smith and the Origins*.

50 Givens, *American Scripture*, 96–98; *T&S*, June 1, 1842, 813–14.

51 Spaulding, *Manuscript Found*, 15, 23, 46–47.

52 For Mormon speculations, see Vogel, *Indian Origins*, 30. On Latin American antiquities in this period, see Vogel, *Indian Origins*, 21–52. The story of the explorations of John Lloyd Stephens and Frederick Catherwood is told in Webster, *Ancient Maya*, 21–28. The publication of the book was noted in Nauvoo: "Messrs. Stephens and Catherwood have succeeded in collecting in the interior of America a large amount of relics of the Nephites, or the ancient inhabitants of America treated of in the Book of Mormon, which relics have recently been landed in New York." *HC*, 5:44.

53 Givens, *American Scripture*, 126–30. The most successful attempts at geographical reconstruction are Sorenson, *Ancient American Setting* and *Mormon's Map*. For a recent speculation that the Malay Peninsula better conforms to the *Book of Mormon* descriptions, see Olsen, "Malay Site," 30–34.

54 *Palmyra Reflector*, July 7, 1830; Spaulding, *Manuscript Found*, 9, 15, 28.

55 The most complete mound reference is *BofM*, 267 (Alma 16:11).

56 *BofM*, 342–43 (Alma 43:20, 37); Fluharty, "Book Ahead of Its Time," 4. *View of the Hebrews* and the *Book of Mormon* converged more in purpose than in content. They joined at two key points: Indians were Israel and would be restored in the last days along with the rest of Israel, and American Christians were to do the work. "Thou nation of the last days, shadowing with thy wings of liberty and peace," Ethan Smith has Isaiah address the United States, "pity, instruct, and save my ancient people and brethren; especially that outcast branch of them, who were the natives of your soil." *View of the Hebrews*, 247.

57 *BofM*, 731, 228 (2 Nephi 5:21, 24; Alma 3: 5–8, 11); Norman, "Lingering Racism," 119–36. On Hamitic racism, see Evans, "Strange Odyssey," 15–43; Braude, "Sons of Noah," 103–42.

58 See, for example, Clinton, *Discourse Delivered*.

59 *BofM*, 289–90, 422, 441–49, 456 (Alma 23:5–13, 18; 26:33; Helaman 6:1, 4; 13–15; 3 Nephi 2:14–16). The Lamanites were also more rigorous in expelling the Gadianton bands. *BofM*, 425 (Helaman 6:37–38).

60 *BofM*, 29, 30, 125–26, 496, 501 (1 Nephi 13:12–20, 30; Jacob 2:12; 3 Nephi 20:14, 21:22).

61 *BofM*, 32–33 (1 Nephi 14:1–2, 6–7).

62 Walker, *David Walker's Appeal*, 68, 89, 91; Hickman, "New World Baroque," 147.

63 Barlow, *Mormons and the Bible*, 27. Many of these are duplicates. The phrase "and it came to pass" occurs 168 times. The common phrase analysis is reported in Jenkins, "Common Phrases," 28.

64 *BofM*, 103, 32 (2 Nephi 25:5; 1 Nephi 13:40). The quoted or excerpted chapters are Isaiah 2–14 and 48–54, plus a discourse on Isaiah 29 that reproduces virtually the entire chapter. The Isaiah passages are found in *BofM*, 52–56, 75–78, 86–102, 107–112, 185–86, 501–502 (1 Nephi 20–21; 2 Nephi 7–8; 12–24, 26–27; Mosiah 14; and 3 Nephi 22). On Mormon scriptures and the Bible, see Jackson, "Sacred Literature," 163–91; and Barlow, *Mormons and the Bible*.

65 *BofM*, 30 (1 Nephi 13:26, 28); *T&S*, March 1, 1842, 709. On the Book of Mormon meeting the need for an authoritative scripture, see Gutjahr, *American Bible*, 155.

66 Harold Bloom comments that "Mormonism is a wonderfully strong misprision, or creative misreading, of the early history of the Jews. So strong was this act of reading that it broke through all the orthodoxies." Bloom, *American Religion*, 84. All visionaries implicitly or explicitly bring canonical texts into question. Damrosch, *Quaker Jesus*, 269.

67 *BofM*, 115 (2 Nephi 29:4).

68 *BofM*, 116, 303 (2 Nephi 29:12; Alma 29:8).

69 *BofM*, 115–16 (2 Nephi 29:3, 10–11, 13).

70 *BofM*, 114 (2 Nephi 28:29–30). See also *BofM*, 130 (Jacob 4:8). Joseph's future role is made explicit in *BofM*, 67 (2 Nephi 3:5–18).

71 For the American desire to have a Christ story, see Forsberg, "Popular Literature," 69–86.

72 *BofM*, 29 (1 Nephi 13:12–13, 17, 20).

73 *BofM*, 216–20 (Mosiah 28:10; 29:11–13, 25, 37–41).

74 *BofM*, 220, 231–32, 366, 407–408, 410, 415, 452, 466 (Mosiah 29:39, 42; Alma 4:15–18, 50:37–40; Helaman 1:1–13, 2:1, 3:37; 3 Nephi 1:1–2, 6:19).

75 *BofM*, 30, 32, 108, 112–13, 165, 534–39, 586–87 (1 Nephi 13:26, 14:12; 2 Nephi 26:20, 28:4–6, 12–14; Mosiah 4:26; Mormon 8:28–41, 9:7–26; Moroni 10:7, 9, 24). For other Christians, the word "restoration" meant the restoration of the New Testament church. For early Mormons, restoration first meant restoring Israel. This gave Mormonism a strong Old Testament cast from the beginning. For the effect of Old and New Testament forms of restoration on Mormon theology and dissent, see Shipps, *Sojourner*, 246, 292–96.

76 Timothy Powell has investigated the idea of conflicting strains existing within the same cultural space. Powell, *Ruthless Democracy*.

77 Hatch, *American Christianity*, 116; *BofM*, 108 (2 Nephi 26:20). For a similar view in American poetry, see Forsberg, "Popular Literature," 83.

78 *BofM*, 81, 165, 237, 416, 535 (2 Nephi 9:30; Mosiah 4:26; Alma 5:55; Helaman 4:12; Mormon 8:39).

79 *BofM*, 58, 108, 113, 507–508, 516, 534 (1 Nephi 22:23; 2 Nephi 26:20; 28:12–13; 3 Nephi 27:11; 4 Nephi 1:26, 29–30; Mormon 8:28). The *Book of Mormon* critique

echoed John Wesley's complaints about religious formalists a hundred years earlier. See Taves, *Experiencing Religion*, 16.

80 Arac, "Narrative Forms," 736. The protest against the dominant culture may be the most American of the Book of Mormon's traits. See Forsberg, "Popular Literature," 83, 94–95.

81 Richardson, *Emerson*, 4–5, 14, 44, 69. On the necessity of preparation before producing major literary works, see Rees, "American Renaissance," 91–93.

82 *Saints' Herald*, 26 (Oct. 1, 1879): 290. Attempts at an explanation can be found in Shipps, "Prophet Puzzle," 3–20; Vogel, " 'Prophet Puzzle' Revisited," 49–68; Foster, "Religious Genius," 183–208; Sandberg, "Knowing Brother Joseph," 319–46; Dunn, "Automaticity," 17–46.

83 Vogel, *Making of a Prophet*, 111–465; R. D. Anderson, *Inside the Mind*, 9–12, 43–54, 65–68, 125–214; Groesbeck, "Symbolic History," 34–45, esp. 43.

84 *BofM*, 142 (Jacob 7:26); *BofC*, 48:14 (*D&C*, 45:13).

85 *BofM*, 70–71 (2 Nephi 4:33–34); JS to Emma Smith, June 6, 1832, in *PWJS*, 264.

86 David Persuitte argues that the Book of Mormon's religion was a cynical effort to appeal to popular faith. Persuitte, *Joseph Smith and the Origins*, 89–90.

87 *BofM*, 412–26 (Helaman 3–6), is one example.

88 Pratt, *Autobiography*, 38; Thayer quoted in Porter, *Origins*, 35.

89 *BofM*, 587–88 (Moroni 10:32–33).

90 The argument was made in Shipps, *Mormonism*.

91 Woodruff, *Journals*, 2:139 (Nov. 28, 1841); Barney, "Documentary Hypothesis," 57–99.

CHAPTER 5   THE CHURCH OF CHRIST

1 Knight, "Joseph Knight's Recollection," 36–37; ManH A-1, 1:302. Quinn, *Early Mormonism*, 176, argues that April 6 was chosen for its astrological importance.

2 ManH A-1, in *PJS*, 1:302; *T&S*, Mar. 1, 1842, 708; Edward Stevenson, Diary, Dec. 22–23, 1877, in Whitmer, *Interviews*, 11. Larry Porter provides evidence for the Fayette organization in "Organizational Origins," 149–64. The case for a Manchester organization is made in Marquardt and Walters, *Inventing Mormonism*, 154–72. For an assessment that acknowledges the evidence for Manchester but concludes that the location of the organization is not material, see Peterson, Review of *Inventing Mormonism*, 216–27, which includes a helpful table comparing the accounts. David Whitmer's claim for Fayette is found in Whitmer, *All Believers*, 33. The *Book of Commandments* (1833) identifies six revelations (chapters 17 to 22 [*D&C*, 23, 21]) as being given on Apr. 6, 1830, in Manchester.

3 ManH A-1, in *PJS*, 1:302–303. Joseph Smith's draft history says that "we met to gether, (being six in number) besides a number who were believing." History [1838 draft], in *PJS*, 1:241. The names of the organizers are known from a statement submitted by Joseph Knight Jr., Aug. 11, 1862, at Salt Lake City. For a full discussion, see Porter, *Study of the Origins*, 109, n. 69, and Anderson, "Six Who Organized," 44–45. Joseph Knight said that Joseph Smith received the revelation recorded in *BofC*, 22 (*D&C*, 21), on the day of organization. Knight, "Joseph Knight's Recollection," 37.

4 *T&S*, Mar. 1, 1842, 708–709, hints at the possibility of preaching. Lucy Smith said Joseph preached to them in Manchester several times. PreM, 477. But Joseph's draft history in 1838 said the first public sermon was delivered by Oliver Cowdery at the Whitmer house on Apr. 11, 1830. History [1838 draft], in *PJS*, 1:244.

5 *BioS*, 57, 72; William Smith, Interview (1893), in *EMD*, 1:512–13.

6 Knight, "Joseph Knight's Recollection," 37; ManH A-1, in *PJS*, 1:303; *BioS*, 151; PreM, 477. Lucy Smith said the baptism occurred in the morning, but Joseph Knight and Joseph Smith Jr. place it after the organizational meeting.

7   *BofC*, 3:1, 5:1, 10:1, 11:1, 12:1 (*D&C*, 4:1, 6:1, 11:1, 12:1, 14:1).

8   *BofC*, 9:14, 16, 14:3 (*D&C*, 10:53, 61–62, 16:6); *BofC*, 12:4, 13:3, 15:45 (*D&C*, 14:8, 15:6, 18:41); *BofC*, 4:5 (*D&C*, 5:14).

9   *BofC*, 24:31–37, 40, 49 (*D&C*, 20:38–46, 48, 57, 70). On elders, priests, and teachers, see *BofM*, 228, 574–75 (Alma 6:1; Moroni 2:2, 3:1, 4:1). On the high priest, see *BofM*, 220, 232 (Mosiah 29:42; Alma 4:18). On the twelve disciples, see *BofM*, 479, 493–94, 507, 515, 574 (3 Nephi 12:1, 19:4–6, 27:1–3; 4 Nephi 1:14; Moroni 2).

10 *BofC*, 24:35, 37, 40, 43–44 (*D&C*, 20:45, 49, 56, 62, 64); Whitmer, *All Believers*, 32; *BofM*, 212, 223 (Mosiah 27:5; Alma 1:26).

11 *BofC*, 15:30, 42 (*D&C*, 18:28, 37). For an argument that twelve apostles were appointed as early as 1830, see Prince, *Power from On High*, 56–58. According to Michael Quinn, the word "apostle" referred to charisma before 1835. Quinn, *Origins of Power*, 10–14.

12 *BofC*, 22:1, 4–5 (*D&C*, 21:1, 4–5). Even in the disillusionment of his later years, David Whitmer remembered that "we had all confidence in Brother Joseph, thinking that as God had given him so great a gift as to translate the Book of Mormon, that everything he would do must be right." *All Believers*, 34.

13 JS to N. C. Saxton, Jan. 4, 1833, in *PWJS*, 296.

14 *BofC*, 24:7, 6–11 (*D&C*, 20:6, 5–10). The "Articles and Covenants" is based on the 1829 "Articles of the Church of Christ" prepared by Oliver Cowdery and printed in Faulring, "Section 20," 57–91. On the development of this revelation, see Faulring, "Organizing the Church," 60–69.

15 *BofC*, 24:50, 21 (*D&C*, 20:71, 32).

16 ManH A-1, in *PJS*, 1:304; History [1838 draft], in *PJS*, 1:244; Porter, *Origins*, 101–102; *HC*, 1:117, n.; *Deseret News*, Mar. 24, 1858; *BofC*, 34:2–3 (*D&C*, 31:2); Chamberlin, "Short Sketch," 4–5; Porter, "Missing Pamphlet," 113–40; Porter, "Early Missionary," 316–17. On Marsh, see Anderson, "Thomas B. Marsh," 129, 135.

17 Vogel, *Religious Seekers*; Bushman, "Visionary World," 183–204. For a combination of radical Protestant and Masonic influences on early converts, see Brooke, *Refiner's Fire*, 144–45, 187, 238–39, 306–10. For Brigham Young as a seeker, see Esplin, "New York Roots," 20–53.

18 *BioS*, 151–53, 166–67.

19 Hartley, *Stand by My Servant*, 98. For a discussion of the early converts, see Porter, *Origins*, 32–35, 78–83, 100–105.

20 Porter, *Origins*, 33–34; Lucy Mack Smith to Solomon Mack, Jan. 6, 1831, in Johnson, "Mormon Women's Letters," 85–89.

21 Anderson, *New England Heritage*, 148–49; quoted in *BioS*, 156. John Smith later wrote, "We had always been accustomed to being treated with much harshness by our brother." *BioS*, 155.

22 Knight, "Joseph Knight's Recollection," 37; History [1838 draft], in *PJS*, 1:248. For the timing of the move of Joseph Smith Sr. and Lucy Smith, see Porter, *Origins*, 37–38.

23 ManH A-1, in *PJS*, 1:305.

24 ManH A-1, in *PJS*, 1:306–307. For a modern evaluation of the miraculous healing, see Hartley, *Stand by My Servant*, 62–70.

25 *FWR*, 1–2 (June 9, 1830); Journal History, June 9, 1830; Cannon, "Licensing," 97. Joseph's 1838 history says the conference assembled on June 1. History [1838 draft], in *PJS*, 1:249.

26 *FWR*, 1–2 (June 9, 1830); ManH A-1, in *PJS*, 1:307–309.

27 History [1838 draft], in *PJS*, 1:250.

28 History [1838 draft], in *PJS*, 1:251; Porter, *Study of the Origins*, 79–80; Knight, Autobiographical Sketch, 2.

29 Knight, "Joseph Knight's Recollection," 38; History [1838 draft], in *PJS*, 1:252–53; Walters, "Court Trials," 124.

30 History [1838 draft], in *PJS*, 1:252; *T&S*, June 1, 1844, 549–52; A. W. Benton, Reminiscence (1831), in *EMD*, 4:97; Hill, *Joseph Smith*, 113. On confusion about the date of the trial, see Walters, "Court Trials," 124–25; Knight, "Joseph Knight's Recollection," 38; ManH A-1, in *PJS*, 1:312.

31 Walters, "Court Trials," 125; *T&S*, June 1, 1844, 549–50.

32 ManH A-1, in *PJS*, 1:314–15.

33 ManH A-1, in *PJS*, 1:317; Knight, Autobiographical Sketch, 2; *T&S*, June 1, 1844, 551–52.

34 History [1838 draft], in *PJS*, 2:258; Knight, Autobiographical Sketch, 2.

35 ManH A-1, in *PJS*, 1:318. *D&C* [1835], 50:3 (*D&C*, 27:12); *Journal of Discourses*, 23:183 (May 6, 1882); Addison Everett to Oliver B. Huntington, Feb. 17, 1881, in Oliver Boardman Huntington, Journal, Jan. 31, 1881.

The exact time of the visit of Peter, James, and John has always been a puzzle in Mormon history. Neither Joseph nor any of the other early chroniclers mentioned the event in their histories. It is usually assumed that the visitation must have occurred after the appearance of John the Baptist on May 15, 1829, and before the organization of the Church on Apr. 6, 1830. Larry C. Porter has placed the visit of Peter, James, and John in late May 1829. Porter, "Aaronic and Melchizedek Priesthoods," 30–47. Porter relies on a second letter of Addison Everett, written to Joseph F. Smith, Jan. 16, 1882, a year after the first letter cited in the text. The second letter says that Joseph and Oliver went to Colesville while translating the *Book of Mormon* and received the Melchizedek Priesthood while returning to Harmony, fixing the event in 1829. The letter is problematic, however, not only because it contradicts the first, in which no mention is made of translating, but because it seems to mix up events in 1829 and 1830. It says that Joseph moved from Harmony to Fayette in August 1829 when he actually moved in June. It was in 1830 that he moved in August. There are, moreover, no mentions in other records of a visit to Colesville in May 1829, or of persecution there, or of a trial involving Mr. Reed, conditions Everett associates with the visit. On the other hand, the visit to Colesville, the trial, and the assistance of Mr. Reed are all well-attested occurrences in the summer of 1830. Joseph inserted the first reference to Peter, James, and John in a revelation dated Aug. 1830. That is why in the text above the visit of Peter, James, and John is assigned to the summer of 1830. But the difficulties with both of the proposed dates—summer 1829 or summer 1830—means that we will not know for certain until more information is uncovered. See also B. H. Roberts's note in *HC*, 1:40–41 n.; Anderson, "Reuben Miller," 277–78, 282–85. For the various accounts of priesthood restoration, see Anderson, "Second Witness," 15–20; Cannon and *BYU Studies* staff, "Priesthood Restoration Documents," 162–207, reprinted in Welch, *Opening the Heavens*, 215–63.

36 The twins, who died at birth, were possibly premature. Newell and Avery, *Mormon Enigma*, 39.

37 *BofC*, 26:3, 6–7, 11 (*D&C*, 25:4, 7–8, 11).

38 *BofC*, 26:10, 25:14, 7–8, 5, 28 (*D&C*, 25:10, 24:9, 5, 3, 18); Indenture, Joseph Smith and Isaac Hale, Aug. 25, 1830, JSC. On the loan and payment to Isaac Hale, see *EMD*, 4:427–35. Porter, *Origins*, 62, presents evidence from the federal census that a boy between ten and fifteen was living with Joseph and Emma that summer and attending school.

39 Porter, *Study of the Origins*, 63; History [1838 draft], in *PJS*, 1:261–62. The Hale and Lewis statements about Joseph Smith are found in *MoU*, 262–67.

40 History [1838 draft], in *PJS*, 1:259–60.

41 History [1838 draft], in *PJS*, 1:260; ManH A-1, in *PJS*, 1:320.

42 Knight, "Journal," 64–65; History [1838 draft], in *PJS*, 1:263; Whitmer, *All Believers*, 31–36, 42, 49, 53, 55–56, 58.

43 ManH A-1, in *PJS*; 1:323; History [1838 draft], in *PJS*, 1:263; *BofC*, 30:12–13; *FWR*, 3 (Sept. 26, 1830); Knight, "Journal," 64–65; Journal History, Sept. 26, 1830.

44 *BofC*, 22:1; 30:2–3, 5–6 (*D&C*, 21:1, 28:2–3, 5–7).

45 Knight, "Journal," 64–65; *BofC*, 30:11 (*D&C*, 28:11); ManH A-1, in *PJS*, 1:323.

46 At the same time, David Whitmer remembered, Joseph handed the seerstone to Oliver Cowdery, saying "that he was through with it, and he did not use the stone any more." *All Believers*, 32.

47 Brodhead, "John Brown," 535.

48 *BofC*, 2:6 (*D&C*, 3:18).

49 *Ravenna* (Ohio) *Star*, Dec. 8, 1831; *BofC*, 30: 8–9 (*D&C*, 28:9); Revelation 21:2; *BofM*, 566, 501 (Ether 13:4; 3 Nephi 21:23).

50 *BofC*, 29:8–9, 17–24 (*D&C*, 29:7–8, 14–21). For the New Jerusalem in the broader context of Mormon millenarianism, see Underwood, *Millenarian World*, 30–41.

51 Porter, *Study of the Origins*, 37–38, 118; *BioS*, 159, 171; Hill, *Joseph Smith*, 118–19.

52 *BioS*, 170; ManH A-1, in *PJS*, 1:348.

53 Rigdon, "Life and Testimony," 18–25; Chase, "Sidney Rigdon."

54 ManH A-1, in *PJS*, 1:339–44; Hill, *Joseph Smith*, 120–22.

55 Whitmer, *All Believers*, 35; *BofC*, 37:5–6, 18–22, 24–25 (*D&C*, 35:4, 17–20, 23).

56 Porter, *Study of the Origins*, 116–17; Knight, "Joseph Knight's Recollection," 38.

57 *BofC*, 39:1, 4 (*D&C*, 37:1, 3); Porter, *Study of the Origins*, 117–18. The *Painesville Telegraph* reported the arrival of Whitmer in the week prior to the paper's issue of Jan. 18, 1831.

58 ManH A-1, in *PJS*, 1:346; *BofC*, 40:22, 27–29, 18 (*D&C*, 38:28, 31–33, 22); Porter, *Study of the Origins*, 106, 119. Lucy wrote her brother Solomon Mack on Jan. 6, 1831, that God "has now mad[e] a new and everlasting covenant and all that will hear his voice and enter he says they shall be gathered together into a land of promise and he himself will come and reign on earth with them a thousand years." Johnson, "Mormon Women's Letters," 87.

59 *BofC*, 40:30, 33, 15 (*D&C*, 38:37, 18, 35, 39). John Whitmer said some of the Saints doubted the revelation to move to Ohio, thinking that Joseph "invented it himself to deceive the people that in the end he might get gain." Porter, *Study of the Origins*, 124.

60 *BofC*, 40:35 (*D&C*, 38:40); Knight, Autobiographical Sketch, 2; Porter, *Study of the Origins*, 116–17; Knight, "Joseph Knight's Recollection," 38. Lucy Smith says Ezra Thayer and Newel Knight also accompanied the first group, but Newel Knight led the Colesville Mormons to Ohio later in the spring. *BioS*, 171. Joseph speaks loosely of traveling to Ohio with Sidney Rigdon and Edward Partridge, but the two groups arrived a few days apart, Sidney on February 1, 1831, and Joseph a few days later. ManH A-1, in *PJS*, 1:346; Porter, *Study of the Origins*, 117; *BofC*, 37:23 (*D&C*, 35:22).

61 *BioS*, 172–83; Porter, *Study of the Origins*, 123, 125–27; Porter and Shipps, "Colesville, New York," 201–11.

62 Porter, *Study of the Origins*, 127–28.

CHAPTER 6 JOSEPH, MOSES, AND ENOCH

1 *Woman's Exponent*, Sept. 1, 1878, 51.

2 Bennett, "Report," 355.

3 *MoU*, 248–49, 261–62.

4 ManH A-1, in *PJS*, 1:273–74; Isaac Hale, Affidavit (1834), in *MoU*, 263–65.

5 History [1832], in *PJS*, 1:3.

6 *T&S*, Feb. 15, 1843, 108.

7 The closest parallel I have found are the second-generation Shaker visionaries after Ann Lee who recorded revelations and read them like scripture. Philemon Stewart's *A Holy, Sacred and Divine Roll and Book*, published by the United Society of Believers in

1843, came in two parts with more than 400 pages. The book directed the Shakers to distribute it to the rulers of the world and lay it beside the Bible in their pulpits. Yet, *A Holy, Sacred and Divine Roll and Book* was discredited after a couple of years. The Shakers' Millennial Laws, though in part informed by the visionaries' revelations, were more a handbook of instructions than scripture. Stein, *Shaker Experience*, 177–98.

8   Ann Lee's belief in continuing revelations prevented her from writing them down. She and her successor Lucy Wright did not want the believers fixed on certain rules or doctrines when new revelations were always coming to displace the old. Stein, *Shaker Experience*, 95.

9   *BofC*, 1:1 (*D&C*, 1:1).

10   *BofC*, 2:2 (*D&C*, 3:3–4).

11   The voice is reminiscent of the distinction Søren Kierkegaard made in his essay on the difference between an apostle and a genius. "An apostle has no other evidence than his own statement, and at most his willingness to suffer everything joyfully for the sake of that statement." Kierkegaard, "Difference," 105.

12   Whitmer, *Book of John Whitmer*, 55.

13   *BofC*, 50:1 (*D&C*, 47:1).

14   William Phelps to Sally Phelps, ca. Jan. 1836, in Van Orden, "Kirtland Letters," 578.

15   JS to Hyrum Smith, Mar. 3, 1831, in *PWJS*, 257.

16   Pratt, *Autobiography*, 65–66.

17   Hancock, Diary, 45.

18   JS to William W. Phelps, July 31, 1832, in *PWJS*, 273.

19   When he was about to return to Kirtland from New York, Sidney Rigdon sent copies of Joseph's revelations ahead of him. Van Wagoner, *Sidney Rigdon*, 76.

20   *BofC*, 22:1 (*D&C*, 21:1); Bushman, "Visionary World," 183–204.

21   Finney, *Memoirs*, 9–20; E. Smith, *Elias Smith*, 134–75.

22   Irwin, *American Hieroglyphics*, 4–6, 8; Wilson, *American Egyptology*, 17–19; "Zodiac of Denderah," 242; "Egyptian Antiquities," 361–89; Everett, "Hieroglyphics," 95–127, "Egyptian History," 27–53, and "Hieroglyphic System," 339–51.

23   Knight, "Joseph Knight's Recollection," 33. How Joseph found his stones—brown and white—is explained in Ashurst-McGee, "Pathway to Prophethood," 198–283.

24   There is evidence that the translation stone was given him after he lost the Urim and Thummim when the 116 pages disappeared. Van Wagoner and Walker, " 'The Gift of Seeing,' " 54. Much later William Hine said that Joseph Smith translated American hieroglyphs while treasure-scrying. The 1826 court record has a witness who said Joseph pretended to read from a book using his white stone. Bainbridge (N.Y.) Court Record, March 20, 1886, in *EMD*, 4:253. For a longer analysis of Joseph Smith's identity as translator, see Bushman, "Joseph Smith as Translator," 69–85.

25   For the skeptical view see Anderson, *Inside the Mind*, and Morain, *Sword of Laban*.

26   *BofM*, 172–73 (Mosiah 8:13, 16). Bushman, "Joseph Smith as Translator," 69–85.

27   JS, *New Translation*, 591 (Moses 1:1); *BofM*, 5 (1 Nephi 1:1); *T&S*, March 1, 1842, 704 (Abraham 1:1).

28   For the story of the revision, see Matthews, *Joseph Smith's Translation*. For the manuscripts, see JS, *New Translation*. A second temple was meant for "the work of the printing of the translation of my scriptures." *D&C* [1835], 83:3 (*D&C*, 94:10).

29   Thomas Campbell, quoted in Barlow, *Mormons and the Bible*, 7–8.

30   Packer, "Transcendentalists," 2:366; Brown, *Biblical Criticism*, 10–26. For a discussion of the complex impact on literature, see Buell, *New England Literary Culture*, 166–68.

31   Campbell, *Sacred Writings*; Webster, *Holy Bible*.

32   Church, "Thomas Jefferson's Bible," 145–61.

33   JS, Journal, Oct. 15, 1843, in *APR*, 420; Barlow, *Mormons and the Bible*, 54. A 1936 book about American translations of the Bible said Joseph Smith's work contained "the most

astonishing claims ever made in connection with the Bible, and the most peculiar alterations of any Bible in English ever published." Simms, *Bible in America*, 235.

34 History [1838 draft], in *PJS*, 1:250–59.

35 *T&S*, Jan. 16, 1843, 71.

36 JS, *New Translation*, 591 (Moses 1:1–2). The parenthetical references are to the 1981 edition of *The Pearl of Great Price*.

37 JS, *New Translation*, 591, 593–94 (Moses 1:4, 6, 33, 24).

38 Genesis 3:15; Edwards, *Work of Redemption*, in *Works*, 2:7, 17–18, 28–29. On typology, see Miner, *Uses of Typology*; Bercovitch, *Puritan Origins*, 35–40, 46–48, 59–73; Brumm, *Religious Typology*; Lowance, *Language of Canaan*.

39 *E&MS*, Jan. 1833, [73] (Moses 6:51); Charles, "Mormon Christianizing," 35–39.

40 JS, *New Translation*, 591–92 (Moses 1:6, 8, 10).

41 JS, *New Translation*, 592–93 (Moses 1:12–15, 18–22). Paragraphing added.

42 JS, *New Translation*, 593–94 (Moses 1:25, 27–28). Paragraphing added.

43 JS, *New Translation*, 594 (Moses 1:30–31). Paragraphing added.

44 JS, *New Translation*, 594 (Moses 1:33, 36–38). Paragraphing added.

45 *BofM*, 66–67 (2 Nephi 3:1–11, 15–17).

46 Bloom, *American Religion*, 99, 101.

47 A translation and commentary are in Metzger, "Fourth Book of Ezra," 1:517–59. I am grateful to Anthony Grafton of Princeton University for this reference. 4 Ezra (or 2 Esdras) was included in the Apocrypha of the Church of England and other Protestant churches. Stone, "Esdras," 2:612.

48 Hugh Nibley is the great Mormon expositor of the apocryphal connections. See his *Enoch the Prophet*.

49 JS, *New Translation*, 3–25; Matthews, *Joseph Smith's Translation*, 26–27, 64–65.

50 The page count was derived by comparing the LDS edition of the Bible, published in 1979, with *The Pearl of Great Price*, published in 1981. By mid-January, the revelations to Moses were circulating among the Mormons in Kirtland. *Painesville Telegraph*, Jan. 18, 1831.

51 Genesis 5:21–24; Luke 3:37; Hebrews 11:5; Jude 1:14; VanderKam, *Enoch*, preface, 175, 183, 185. Jed Woodworth put me in touch with the literature on Enoch and provided an assessment of Richard Laurence's translation in his "Enoch in Early American History."

52 Michael Quinn claims there is a link to Laurence's 1821 translation of Enoch and cites a reference to Enoch in a book advertised in a Palmyra newspaper. He does not find the actual Book of Enoch in Palmyra or vicinity, only this reference in a scholarly commentary. Quinn, *Early Mormonism*, 190–92.

53 Laurence, *Book of Enoch*, chaps. 7, 9–10, 12, 25–26. Laurence thought there was even evidence of three distinct persons in Enoch's Godhead. Laurence, *Book of Enoch*, xlviii–lvi.

54 As Hugh Nibley has shown, the Slavonic version of Enoch's story, found later in the century, has more in common with Joseph's Enoch. Nibley, *Enoch the Prophet*, 138–281. Latter-day Saint attention to the various Enoch stories has prompted one specialist to note that "among twentieth-century Christians, only the Ethiopian Church and the Church of Jesus Christ of Latter-day Saints consider the Enochic writings to be authoritative." Nickelsburg, *I Enoch*, 82.

55 JS, *New Translation*, 610 (Moses 6:27–28).

56 Woodford, "Historical Development," 2:993–94; Whittaker, "Substituted Names," 103–12.

57 JS, *New Translation*, 610 (Moses 6:31).

58 ManH A-1, in *PJS*, 1:274.

59 JS, *New Translation*, 611 (Moses 6:35–36, 38–39).

60   *E&MS*, Aug. 1832, [18] (Moses 7:2–4, 24–26).

61   *E&MS*, Aug. 1832, [18] (Moses 7:28–30).

62   *E&MS*, Aug. 1832, [18] (Moses 7:33, 34, 36, 37).

63   *E&MS*, Aug. 1832, [18] (Moses 7:41).

64   *BofM*, 530, 583–85 (Mormon 6:17, 19; Moroni 9).

65   *E&MS*, Aug. 1832, [18] (Moses 7:58).

66   For the case that "restorationist" denominations did yearn for a return to a favored era, see Hughes and Allen, *Protestant Primitivism*.

67   Quoted in ManH A-1, in *PJS*, 1:276, n. 2; *BofC*, 16:18; 48:14 (*D&C*, 19:18; 45:12).

68   On Joseph Smith's theodicy, see Paulsen, "Problem of Evil," and Paulsen and Ostler, "Sin, Suffering, and Soul-Making."

69   Joseph seems also to have identified personally with Enoch. When outside pressures led to the adoption of borrowed names for Church leaders, Joseph took the name of Enoch in the revelations. Whittaker, "Substituted Names," 103–12.

70   *E&MS*, Aug. 1832, [18–19] (Moses 7:18, 62–64).

71   Bloom, *American Religion*, 100; Shipps, *Mormonism*, 51–56. For the blending of the present with the *Book of Mormon* past, see Bushman, "Early Mormon History," 3–18. The seventeenth-century New England Puritans blended present and historical past with similar facility. Bozeman, *Primitivist Dimension*.

72   JS, *New Translation*, 851; Matthews, *Joseph Smith's Translation*, 37, 40–49, 207.

73   *BofC*, 48:54–55 (*D&C*, 45:60–61); Matthews, *Joseph Smith's Translation*, 73.

74   Matthews, *Joseph Smith's Translation*, 40.

75   Jackson and Jasinski, "Inspired Translation," 35–64. As Robert Matthews notes in his study of the Joseph Smith translation, "a passage that had been revised and recorded once was later further revised and recorded. Some passages were revised even a third time." *Joseph Smith's Translation*, 61.

76   JS, Journal, Jan. 29, 1836, in *PJS*, 2:162; Pratt quoted in Matthews, "Joseph Smith—Translator," 84.

77   *WJS*, 355 (Apr. 7, 1844).

CHAPTER 7   THE KIRTLAND VISIONARIES

1   Milton Backman gives a useful summary of Kirtland's demography and economy in *Heavens Resound*, 33–37, 139.

2   Foote, Autobiography, 8–9. For a survey of the Kirtland topography and economy, see Layton, "Kirtland," 423–38. On the economy of the region at the time, see Hurt, *Ohio Frontier*, 20; Lewis, "Economic Landscape," 116–75; and Stewart, *Northeastern Ohio*, 1:179–284.

3   Knepper, *Ohio and Its People*, 144–49.

4   Rose, *Cleveland*, 113, 169.

5   For Painesville, see Stewart, *Northeastern Ohio*, 1:295–98.

6   *MofU*; Howe, *Autobiography*.

7   Newell and Avery, *Mormon Enigma*, 37–38; Rollins, Reminiscences, 3.

8   *BofC*, 43:9 (*D&C*, 41:7).

9   Cox, " 'Father Isaac Morley,' " [1]. For a map showing the Morley farm's location, see Backman, *Heavens Resound*, 78.

10 The best edition of Whitmer's history is Whitmer, *Book of John Whitmer*.

11 ManH A-1, in *PJS*, 1:352; Matthews, *Joseph Smith's Translation*, 31–32; *FWR*, v, vii, xi, xii.

12 Marini, *Radical Sects*, 63, 66, 73–74, 76, 80; Hatch, *American Christianity*, 40. The visionary impulse remained strong among the Shakers after Ann Lee's death. Stein, *Shaker Experience*, 166–67.

13 Wigger, *Taking Heaven*, 53, 54, 107, 110. John Brooke finds traces of hermetic doctrine in the visionary culture but only by exaggerating the evidence and making many speculative leaps. Brooke, *Refiner's Fire*, 30–58. There is more evidence of magical practice mingling with Christian belief. See Obelkevich, *South Lindsey*, 259–312, and Quinn, *Early Mormonism*.

14 *MoU*, 261–62; *Woman's Exponent*, Sept. 1, 1878, 51; Crosby, "Biographical Sketch," [3].

15 Tullidge, *Women of Mormondom*, 44–45. John Brooke presents tentative figures to show that early converts came from families that "had long stood outside the mainstream of New England orthodoxy." Brooke, *Refiner's Fire*, 65, 306–309. For a statistical analysis of Mormon cultural origins, see Grandstaff and Backman, "Kirtland Mormons," 47–66.

16 Wigger, *Taking Heaven*, 124, 181–89. Later this supernaturalist impulse was channeled into spiritualism. Cross, *Burned-Over District*, 341–52. Cross's concept of "ultraism" comes close to Wigger's "supernaturalism."

17 Backman, *Heavens Resound*, 38–39.

18 *Woman's Exponent*, Sept. 1, 1878, 51.

19 Van Wagoner, *Sidney Rigdon*, 44–45; Backman, *Heavens Resound*, 13–14.

20 *MoU*, 113–14, 118. When Joseph met Walter Scott in Cincinnati in June 1831, their basic disagreement was over New Testament gifts. ManH A-1, in *PJS*, 1:356.

21 Quoted in Van Wagoner, *Sidney Rigdon*, 44, 62; Backman, *Heavens Resound*, 15–16. Campbell ascribed Rigdon's conversion to "a peculiar mental and corporeal malady to which he has been subject for some years. Fits of melancholy succeeded by fits of enthusiasm accompanied by some kind of nervous spasms and swoonings." *Millennial Harbinger*, Feb. 7, 1831, 100.

22 Acts 2:43–45; 4:32. Thomas Campbell, Alexander's father, attacked the communal organization in a letter to Sidney Rigdon, Feb. 4, 1831. *MoU*, 121. For a comparison of the early Mormon and Disciples movements, see Hughes, "Mormons and Churches of Christ," 348–63.

23 Morley, "Isaac Morley"; Whitmer, *Book of John Whitmer*, 27. Levi Hancock, visiting the "Family," felt sorry for the load taken on by Morley, "one of the most honest patient men I ever saw." "The company he maintained looked large enough to bring on a famine." Hancock, Diary, 42.

24 Quoted in Anderson, "Preaching in Ohio," 488.

25 Shaker visionaries also received visits from "native spirits" and translated native songs and messages. Stein, *Shaker Experience*, 176.

26 Corrill, *Brief History*, 8–10, 17.

27 *MoU*, 104–105; Hancock, Diary, 41. Some of the most extravagant visions are recounted in Backman, "Non-Mormon View," 309–10.

28 Corrill, *Brief History*, 16.

29 *MoU*, 116; ManH A-1, in *PJS*, 1:347; Hancock, Diary, 39–40, 46–47; Corrill, *Brief History*, 14; Mark 16:15, 18.

30 Whitmer, *Book of John Whitmer*, 37; *MoU*, 216; ManH A-1, in *PJS*, 1:349; *BofC*, 45:2–3 (*D&C*, 43:2–3).

31 The Shakers, who did not curtail their visionaries as decisively, suffered the consequences. The visionaries' contradictory and sometimes extreme revelations opened up rifts in the organization and eventually resulted in a burnout of the visionary impulse. Stein, *Shaker Experience*, 183–87.

32 Corrill, *Brief History*, 17; Pratt, *Autobiography*, 65; JS to Hyrum Smith, Mar. 3, 1831, in *PWJS*, 257.

33 Corrill, *Brief History*, 17–18; *BofC*, 53:1–4, 17–21 (*D&C*, 50:1–4, 17–22); John 16:13; *D&C* [1835], 7:36; 82:5 (*D&C*, 88:118; 93:29–30); JS and others to Edward Partridge and the Church, Mar. 20, 1839, in *PWJS*, 440; Clayton, Journal, Apr. 2, 1843 (*D&C*, 121:33, 42; 130:18–19); *BofC*, 44:46 (*D&C*, 42:61). Lucy Smith, who arrived in Kirt-

land in time to observe the contortions of the possessed, said Joseph emphasized that "when a man speaks by the Spirit of God, he speaks from the abundance of his heart—his mind is filled with intelligence." *BioS*, 171–72.

34   *BofC*, 53:25, 27 (*D&C*, 50:29, 31). Joseph later said tongues were provided to teach the gospel to people in foreign lands. Kirtland High Council, Minutes, Sept. 8, 1834. George A. Smith was still preaching against the visionaries in Nauvoo in 1842. *T&S*, Apr. 1, 1842, 745–47.

35   *BofC*, 29:9; 41:12; 40:18, 28; 43:4 (*D&C*, 29:8; 39:13; 38:22, 32; 41:3).

36   *BofC*, 44:5 (*D&C*, 42:4); Corrill, *Brief History*, 17. Levi Hancock was ordained an elder the morning after his baptism in 1830. Almost immediately, he started preaching "from place to place where the folks were well acquainted with me." Hancock, Diary, 34.

37   *BofC*, 44:13 (*D&C*, 42:12); *MoU*, 115.

38   Wigger, "Early American Methodism," 180.

39   Hatch analyzes the Mormon democratic impulses in his *American Christianity*, 113–22.

40   *BofC*, 44:12 (*D&C*, 42:11).

41   *BofC*, 41:4 (*D&C*, 39:6). Cf. *BofC*, 44:8 (*D&C*, 42:7).

42   Whitmer, *Book of John Whitmer*, 42, 47. For a description of missionary work out of Kirtland, see Bitton, "Missionary Activity," 497–516.

43   Van Wagoner, *Sidney Rigdon*, 93–94. Parley Pratt's abbreviated version is in Pratt, *Autobiography*, 65. Oliver Cowdery had been well received by Kitchel in the fall of 1830. Anderson, *Book of Mormon Witnesses*, 55.

44   Whitmer, *Book of John Whitmer*, 56–57. Six hundred is Milton Backman's population estimate in *Heavens Resound*, 51. Parley Pratt exuberantly claimed over a thousand members in Ohio and several hundred in New York. *Autobiography*, 64.

45   Marquardt, *Joseph Smith Revelations*, 108, 111; *BofC*, 44:26–29 (*D&C*, 42:30–35).

46   *BofC*, 52:19–20 (*D&C*, 49:20). For a recent study of communal societies as a group, see Pitzer, *America's Communal Utopias*, which contains a thorough bibliography and listing of communities. The classic work is Bestor, *Backwoods Utopias*. For the numbers of utopian communities, see Clark, *Communitarian Moment*, 12.

47   Richard Van Wagoner, following Fawn Brodie, credits Sidney Rigdon's interest in Robert Owen's ideas with inspiring the consecration of properties. Besides the lack of evidence for Rigdon's interest, Owenite plans bore little resemblance to the Mormon program. Van Wagoner, *Sidney Rigdon*, 49–50, 54, 85–86; Brodie, *No Man Knows*, 105.

48   The revelation makes no reference to the New Testament practice of common property, the inspiration for Isaac Morley's Kirtland "Family." No telltale New Testament phrases like "all things in common" appear in the revelation. Instead the revelation invoked Enoch's City of Zion where "they were of one heart and of one mind, and dwelt in righteousness; and there was no poor among them." *E&MS*, Aug. 1832, [18] (Moses 7:18). Later the system was referred to as "the Order of Enoch."

49   *D&C* [1835], 13:8, 11 (*D&C*, 42:30, 38); *BofC*, 40:30 (*D&C*, 38:35). See also Matthew 25:40.

50   *BofC*, 58:19, 21 (*D&C*, 56:16–17); *BofM*, 81–82, 165, 231, 237, 416, 535 (2 Nephi 9:30, 42; Mosiah 4:26; Alma 4:12; 5:55; Helaman 4:12; Mormon 8:37–39).

51   Newell and Avery, *Mormon Enigma*, 38–39; *Woman's Exponent*, Sept. 1, 1878, 51; Rollins, Reminiscences, 3; Murdock, Diary, 2; Morton, "Julia Murdock Smith," 37–39.

52   The living arrangements of the Smiths in the spring of 1831 are not clearly explained in the existing sources. For two attempts, see Morley, "Isaac Morley," 17–19, and Newell and Avery, *Mormon Enigma*, 39.

53   William McLellin admired the "peace, order, harmony" of Mormon meetings in Missouri in August 1831 compared to the "shouting, screaming, jumping" in other churches. McLellin, *Journals*, 34 (Aug. 21, 1831).

54   *BofC*, 40:28; 45:16; 46:2 (*D&C*, 38:32; 43:16; 44:2).

55 Hancock, Diary, 48; *MoU*, 188–89. Participants differ on the date, but June 3 seems to be the best guess. Levi Hancock gave June 4 as the date. Diary, 47. Parley Pratt said June 6. *Autobiography*, 72. John Whitmer, the Church historian, recorded June 3. *Book of John Whitmer*, 69; *FWR*, 6–7 (June 3, 1831). John Smith agreed with Whitmer. J. Smith, Diary, 3–4.

56 Hancock, Diary, 48–49. Ezra Booth, an elder who shortly apostatized, reported a failed attempt at healing at the conference. *MoU*, 190–91. Hancock, a solid reporter, said nothing about it.

57 Whitmer, *Book of John Whitmer*, 85. John Corrill, who was at the meeting, said "some doubting took place among the elders, and considerable conversation was held on the subject. The elders not fairly understanding the nature of the endowments, it took some time to reconcile all their feelings." *Brief History*, 18.

58 ManH A-1, in *PJS*, 1:353; Hancock, Diary, 49; Whitmer, *Book of John Whitmer*, 71. John Corrill was not thrown by what he saw at the meeting. "The same visionary and marvellous spirits, spoken of before, got hold of some of the elders; it threw one from his seat to the floor; it bound another, so that for some time he could not use his limbs nor speak; and some other curious effects were experienced, but, by a mighty exertion, in the name of the Lord, it was exposed and shown to be from an evil source." Corrill, *Brief History*, 18.

59 "High priest" appears in Old and New Testaments (Leviticus 21:10 and Hebrews 3:1, for example), and was the chief administrative officer in lodges of Royal Arch Masons. Mackey, *Lexicon of Freemasonry*, 195–96.

60 The account of John the Baptist and the Aaronic Priesthood (*D&C*, 13) did not appear in the *Doctrine and Covenants* until 1876, though John's bestowal of priesthood was mentioned in the 1835 edition. *D&C* [1835], 50:2 (*D&C*, 27:7–8). John's prayer, differently worded, was included in Oliver Cowdery's 1834 account of John's appearance. *M&A* 1 (Oct. 1834): 16. It was published in the current form in *T&S* in 1842. Cook, *Revelations*, 23. The history of section 27 is detailed in Woodford, "Historical Development," 1:393–98. The truncated version of section 27 appears as section 28 in the 1833 *Book of Commandments*. For the background, see Quinn, *Origins of Power*, 1–38; Prince, *Power from On High*, 1–10.

61 A Universalist magazine made Satan the founder of priesthood: "The father of priesthood commenced his work, when coiled around the tree of knowledge." *Gospel Advocate*, Mar. 21, 1829, 105. Miriam Murdock has explored this theme in "Patterns of the Priesthood."

62 David Whitmer blamed the introduction of the priesthood on Sidney Rigdon. *Omaha Herald*, Oct. 17, 1886, in Whitmer, *Interviews*, 202–203.

63 Holland, "Priest, Pastor, and Power," 9–10; Cannon, "Licensing," 96–105. One early form of discipline in the Church was to be "silenced from holding the office of Elders" without excommunication, implying that offices could be given and taken away. *FWR*, 11–12 (Sept. 1, 6, 1831).

64 Genesis 14:18–20; Hebrews 5:6; 7:1–3; *FWR*, 7 (June 3, 1831); Whitmer, *Book of John Whitmer*, 69.

65 ManH A-1, in *PJS* 1:353. The passage appeared in the *T&S*, Feb. 1, 1844, publication of Joseph's history, but then was crossed out by Willard Richards in the manuscript and new wording supplied: "I conferred the high priesthood for the first time, upon several of the Elders." When the change was made cannot be determined, nor whether Joseph Smith authorized it.

66 Whitmer, *Book of John Whitmer*, 70–71. Oliver Cowdery likewise was ordained to the high priesthood after returning from Missouri. *FWR*, 10 (Aug. 28, 1831).

67 *HC*, 1:176, n.

68 For the bestowal of the Melchizedek Priesthood in 1831, see Hill, *Quest for Refuge*, 25; Corrill, *Brief History*, 18.

69 Pratt, *Autobiography*, 72. Quinn, *Origins of Power*, 26, interprets a later statement by Brigham Young to mean Peter, James, and John did not restore the Melchizedek Priesthood until 1831 and in Kirtland. Young's statement is ambiguous. *Journal of Discourses*, 9:89–90 (May 7, 1861).

70 Joseph's 1838 history had already given an account of praying for the Melchizedek Priesthood in June 1829, when he and Oliver Cowdery were instructed to ordain one another elders. ManH A-1, in *PJS*, 1:299–300. This entry in Joseph's history vests the office of elder with the Melchizedek Priesthood in 1829, making the first bestowal of that same priesthood on the elders in 1831 redundant. A Campbellite in Kirtland in the fall of 1830 heard the Mormon missionaries say that "no legal administrator" was on the earth to administer baptism "until God had called them to the office." Quoted in Backman, "Non-Mormon View," 308. For an effort to work out the gradually unfolding of priesthood, see Prince, *Power from On High*. Prince accepts the reality of the revelations but believes Joseph Smith did not have the vocabulary to understand the experiences at first.

71 For a discussion of ordination to the ministry in seventeenth-century New England, see Davies, *American Puritans*, 215–25.

72 *D&C* [1835], 4:3 (*D&C*, 84:20–21).

73 Brodie, *No Man Knows*, 111; Kimball, "Melchizedek," 17–28. Melchizedek also had overtones of the king-priest who combined religion and state power, a theme Joseph would return to toward the end of his life. Kenny, *Elias Smith*, 184.

74 *BofM*, 259–60 (Alma 13:6, 18); JS, *New Translation*, 641 (JST Genesis 14:27–29). Alma said "an exceedingly great many" were ordained high priests and entered the rest of the Lord. Alma 13:12.

75 JS, *New Translation*, 641 (JST Genesis 14:26–33).

CHAPTER 8   ZION

1 Whitmer, *Book of John Whitmer*, 69, 81; *BofC*, 54 (*D&C*, 52); Oliver Cowdery to JS, April 8, 1831, JSC. For Cowdery's mission, see Walker, "Native American," 5–9; Romig, "Lamanite Mission," 24–33.

2 *BofC*, 30:8–9 (*D&C*, 28:9). The phrase "on the borders by the Lamanites" may be an anachronism. The version published in the *Ohio Star* in Dec. 1831 had the words "among the Lamanites." Marquardt, *Joseph Smith Revelations*, 85.

3 ManH A-1, in *PJS*, 1:354, strikeout omitted. *BofC*, 44:9, 47, 51 (*D&C*, 42:9, 62, 67); cf. *BofC*, 44:29; 54:44 (*D&C*, 42:35; 52:43).

4 ManH A-1, in *PJS*, 1:356–57.

5 Romig, *Early Jackson County*, iv–v.

6 ManH A-1, in *PJS*, 1:357. See also Anderson, "Jackson County," 270–93.

7 *MoU*, 194, 202; *BofC*, 59:19 (*D&C*, 58:15); Romig, "Lamanite Mission," 30–32; Partridge, "Edward Partridge," 64.

8 *D&C* [1835], 27:1–5 (*D&C*, 57:2–13); Romig, *Early Jackson County*, iv. On the courthouse, see Parkin, "Courthouse Mentioned," 451–57. For maps, see Parkin, "Independence, Missouri," 41.

9 Porter, "Colesville Branch," 281–311; Whitmer, *Book of John Whitmer*, 86–87.

10 ManH A-1, in *PJS*, 1:359. Joseph borrowed much of his language from an 1834 description of Missouri by William W. Phelps. Anderson, "Missouri 'Documentary History,'" 491–92, 496–98, 500–501. *BofC*, 60:25, 28 (*D&C*, 59:16, 18).

11 *BofC*, 59:4–5, 8 (*D&C*, 58:3, 4, 7).

12 *BofC*, 59:56–59 (*D&C*, 58:44–56).

13 Ezra Booth said some in the party accused Joseph and Rigdon of "excessive cowardice." *MoU*, 204–205.

14 ManH A-1, in *PJS*, 1:362; *BofC*, 62:3, 7, 25 (*D&C*, 61:3, 6, 23); Cahoon, Diary, Aug. 9, 1831.

15 Chidester and Linenthal, *American Sacred Space*, 5–19.

16 The temple lot, like contested sacred space in Jerusalem, has been the source of endless conflict over the years. See, for example, Romig, "Temple Lot Suit," 3–15; and Campbell, "Images of the New Jerusalem."

17 Revelation 3:12, 21:2; *BofM*, 566 (Ether 13:4); Marini, *Radical Sects*, 50, 55; Bozeman, *Primitivist Dimension*, 203, 209, 218–19, 230–31; Forman, *Brazilian Peasantry*, 227–29; Hatch, *American Christianity* 32; Raboteau, *Slave Religion*, 270; Vogel, *Religious Seekers*, 190–93; Bloch, *Visionary Republic*, 114, 141, 182–83.

18 Fogarty, *American Communal*, xxiv.

19 *BofC*, 48:14 (*D&C*, 45:12–13); Moorhead, "Mainstream Protestantism," 73–81; Augustine quote in Brown, *Augustine*, 315. Some millennialists believed the change would come through steady improvement in human civilization effected by reforms, technology, and evangelization. Others thought only a cataclysmic end to the old order could make room for a righteous society. At one time, historians thought these two points of view divided "postmillennialists" from "premillennialists." The postmillennialists, who expected Christ to come after the millennium, had confidence in the capacity of human civilization—especially American civilization—to improve by ordinary historical processes. Those who believed Christ would come before the millennium—premillennialists—relied solely on God's power to destroy evil and reconstruct a holy order. The earth had to be cleansed before a new beginning could be made. On closer examination, this division breaks down; the extreme poles on the millennial spectrum are closer than once believed. Many postmillennialists, it turns out, also anticipated calamities that would shake the old order, and many premillennialists, on the other hand, exerted themselves to ready the world for Christ. Stein, "Apocalypticism Outside," 109.

20 *BofC*, 48:59, 63–64 (*D&C*, 45:66, 69).

21 Ravitzky, "Contemporary Judaism," 215; Numbers and Butler, *Millerism*; Greenberg, *Nat Turner*.

22 *BofC*, 64:30–32 (*D&C*, 63:29–31). For a broad exposition of Mormon millenarian ideas, see Underwood, *Millenarian World*, and Stein, "Signs of the Times," 59–65. For a continuation of the analysis to the end of the nineteenth century, see Erickson, *Millennial Deliverance*.

23 *BofC*, 45:25–26 (*D&C*, 43:22). Cf. *BofC*, 29:9–26 (*D&C*, 29:8–23). The authoritative study of the Shaker movement is Stein, *Shaker Experience*.

24 JS, Journal, Nov. 13, 1833, in *PJS*, 2:11; Stein, *Shaker Experience*, 29, 70–71, 75, 80.

25 Matthew 24; Revelation 8–9; *BofC*, 29:11, 22; 45:18, 24–26 (*D&C*, 29:9,19, 43:18, 21–22).

26 Doan, *Miller Heresy*, 72; Oates, *Approaching Fury*, 28; *BofM*, 115–16 (2 Nephi 29), among many others; *E&MS*, Aug. 1832 [18] (Moses 7:61). The moderate evangelist Charles Finney preached that "to create all things new in the moral order of things," Christ had "to reform or destroy, all governments that dont obey God." Quoted in Noll, *America's God*, 380. For a different read on the year, see Masur, *Year of Eclipse*.

27 *D&C* [1835], 24 (*D&C*, 65).

28 ManH A-1, in *PJS*, 1:362; *BofC*, 64:7, 38–40 (*D&C*, 63:6, 36–37).

29 Richey, *Early American Methodism*, 45; *BofC*, 45:29; 48:67 (*D&C*, 43:24; 45:71). *D&C* [1835], 27:1 (*D&C*, 57:4), spoke of the division between Jew and Gentile at the frontier of American settlement, with the Indians on one side and the American Gentiles on the other.

30 *D&C* [1835], 82:2; 97:10; (*D&C*, 101:77, 80); *BofC*, 40:17–18 (*D&C*, 38:21–22). The neglect of the United States came to an end after the persecution of the Mormons in

Missouri when Joseph Smith had to appeal to principles of American justice to gain redress; the Constitution particularly was acknowledged favorably. *D&C* [1835], 85:2 (*D&C*, 98:5–7).

31 Van Wagoner, *Sidney Rigdon*, 102. On the new centering of Zion, see Olsen, *Cosmic Symbolism*, 26–29.

32 *FWR*, 12 (Sept. 12, 1831). The Booth letters were republished in the *Painesville Telegraph* and again in *MoU*, 175–221. They are analyzed in Parkin, "Mormons in Ohio," 101–20.

33 Quoted in Hayden, *History of the Disciples*, 250; *Latter-day Saints' Millennial Star*, Dec. 31, 1864, 834.

34 Whitmer, *Book of John Whitmer*, 57–58, 70–71, 87; *MoU*, 180–81, 189–90, 183–210; ManH A-1, in *PJS*, 1:363–64.

35 *MoU*, 179–80. Booth thought other aspects of the Mormon gospel attracted converts: "repentance and baptism for the remission of sins, and the laying on of hands for the reception of the Holy Ghost." The Mormons preceded baptism with the words "having authority given me of Jesus Christ," he said. Many had been ordained to the high priesthood in the order of Melchizedek, and "profess to be endowed with the same power as the ancient apostles were." *MoU*, 180.

36 *MoU*, 191, 177, 181.

37 *MoU*, 193, 202–206; *BofC*, 65:9 (*D&C*, 64:7); Hayden, *History of the Disciples*, 252; *HC*, 1:261, n.

38 The attendees are listed in *FWR*, 6–7 (June 3, 1831). For a list of later apostates, see Backman, *Heavens Resound*, 327–28. The one-fifth figure is derived from the biographical appendix in *FWR*, 245–98. Of the approximately 320 Mormons on the list, 65 apostatized.

39 Other apostates were cut off for their sins, and in some cases, transgression and doubt may have overlapped. Three 1831 revelations condemned adultery, as if it were a particular problem. *BofC*, 47:1–8, 21–24; 64:16, 18 (*D&C*, 42:74–83; 63:14, 16); *D&C* [1835], 74:5 (*D&C*, 66:10). Ezra Booth hinted that both Ziba Peterson and Oliver Cowdery were involved in transgression in Missouri. *MoU*, 208.

40 On the Johnsons, see Perkins, "John Johnson Family," 54–59.

41 Newell and Avery, *Mormon Enigma*, 40–41; Whitmer, *Book of John Whitmer*, 101; Van Wagoner, *Sidney Rigdon*, 5–6, 8–10, 29, 100, 102–103, 109, 171, 220–21.

42 Juster, *Anglo-American Prophecy*, 58; Towle, *Vicissitudes Illustrated*, 137, 142. For Towle's place among the women evangelists, see Brekus, *Female Preaching*, 208, 213, 227.

43 Quoted in Towle, *Vicissitudes Illustrated*, 144–45.

44 *FWR*, 27 and n. 2 (Nov. 1, 1831). The process of compiling the revelations began in July 1830. After receiving *BofC* 25, 26, and 27 (*D&C*, 24, 25, and 26) Joseph Smith began to arrange and copy the revelations. Garrett, "Coming Forth," 90. On the publishing history, see Crawley, *Descriptive Bibliography*, 37–42.

45 *BofC*, 24 (*D&C*, 20).

46 Walker, *Creeds and Platforms*; ManH A-1, in *PJS*, 1:273; JS, Journal, Jan. 1, 1843, in *APR*, 264.

47 The Shakers believed their Millennial Laws were partially a product of revelation. Stein, *Shaker Experience*, 183, 198. But they did not rely on day-to-day administrative revelations like the Mormons.

48 Hall, *Cultures of Print*, 143–45.

49 *FWR*, 26–28, 31–32 (Nov. 1–2 and 12–13, 1831). On the resulting *Book of Commandments*, see Crawley, *Descriptive Bibliography*, 37–42.

50 *D&C* [1835], 90:2 (*D&C*, 71:9).

51 ManH A-1, in *PJS*, 1:367; *D&C* [1835], 25:2 (*D&C*, 67:5).

52 *D&C* [1835], 25:2 (*D&C*, 67:6–7); ManH A-1, in *PJS*, 1:367.

53 McLellin has been maligned for making the attempt, but there is no evidence he brought up the question in the first place or was a doubter. McLellin's role in the incident has been analyzed in Grandstaff, "McLellin and the Book of Commandments," 23–48. As one evidence of McLellin's good standing after the incident, a revelation a week earlier assigned him to go into the eastern countries with Samuel Smith, preaching and healing. *D&C* [1835], 74:3–5 (*D&C*, 66:7–9), cf. *D&C* [1835], 22:1 (*D&C*, 68:7–8). McLellin, who saw many revelations received, later marveled at their effectiveness:

> The scribe seats himself at a desk or table, with pen, ink, and paper. The subject of inquiry being understood, the Prophet and Revelator inquires of God. He spiritually sees, hears, and feels, and then speaks as he is moved upon by the Holy Ghost, the "thus saith the Lord," sentence after sentence, and waits for his amanuenses to write and then read aloud each sentence. Thus they proceed until the revelator says Amen, at the close of what is then communicated. I have known both those men mentioned above, to seat themselves, and without premeditation to thus deliver in broken sentences, some of the most sublime pieces of composition which I ever perused in any book. Quoted in Grandstaff, "McLellin and the Book of Commandments," 40.

54 *FWR*, 29 (Nov. 8, 1831).
55 *BofC*, 1:5 (*D&C*, 1:24). On the theological import of revising the revelations, see Best, "Changes in the Revelations," 87–112. The changes are analyzed in Woodford, "Historical Development," and Marquardt, *Joseph Smith Revelations*.
56 *BofC*, 30:2 (*D&C*, 28:2).
57 *BofC*, 1:4 (*D&C*, 1:20); *D&C* [1835], 22:1 (*D&C* 68:2–4).
58 *FWR*, 21 (Oct. 25, 1831); Hancock, Diary, 34; *D&C* [1835], 25:1, 3 (*D&C*, 67:3, 10).
59 The early English Friends and the later Shakers licensed everyone to speak the word of God in a roughly parallel way. These inspired speeches were written and distributed and were believed to be equal to scripture, though they never became scripture like the Bible. Hall, *Cultures of Print*, 143–45.
60 *D&C* [1835], 86:4 (*D&C*, 82:14); Isaiah 54:2; *D&C* [1835], 86:4 (*D&C*, 82:13). The word "stake" in *Doctrine and Covenants* 68:25 was an 1835 addition, but "stake" appeared in the *Book of Mormon* and in the revelations beginning in 1832. Woodford, "Historical Development," 2:864–65; *BofM*, 501, 587 (3 Nephi 22:2; Moroni 10:31); Marquardt, *Joseph Smith Revelations*, 208.
61 *D&C* [1835], 83:1 (*D&C*, 94:1).

CHAPTER 9 THE BURDEN OF ZION

1 Whitmer, *Book of John Whitmer*, 102; *D&C* [1835], 90 (*D&C*, 71). Ambrose Palmer, a recent convert, said the letters gave Mormonism "such a coloring, or appearance of falsehood, that the public feeling was, that 'Mormonism' was overthrown." Quoted in Van Wagoner, *Sidney Rigdon*, 110. See also Rowley, "Ezra Booth Letters," 133–37.
2 Van Wagoner, *Sidney Rigdon*, 111; ManH A-1, in *PJS*, 1:370.
3 ManH A-1, in *PJS*, 1:364; *MoU*, 205, 202.
4 *D&C* [1835], 90:2 (*D&C*, 71:7). Milton Backman estimates 600 members by the spring of 1831. *Heavens Resound*, 51. William W. Phelps counted 810 members in Missouri in November 1832. *E&MS*, Nov. 1832, [45].
5 Joseph himself gives the best account of the attack in ManH A-1, in *PJS*, 1:374–78. The story has been given numerous retellings. Two of the best are Newell and Avery, *Mormon Enigma*, 41–44, and Van Wagoner, *Sidney Rigdon*, 114–18.

6   A newspaper account said twenty-five or thirty men were involved. *Geauga Gazette*, Apr. 17, 1832. Luke Johnson estimated between forty and fifty. *Latter-day Saints' Millennial Star*, Dec. 31, 1864, 834.

7   ManH A-1, in *PJS*, 1:375, 377–78.

8   Van Wagoner, *Sidney Rigdon*, 115; *MoU*, 178, 195.

9   Ryder, quoted in Hayden, *History of the Disciples*, 221.

10   *Latter-day Saints' Millennial Star*, Dec. 31, 1864, 834.

11   Brodie, *No Man Knows*, 119; Van Wagoner, *Sidney Rigdon*, 120, n. 28; ManH A-1, in *PJS*, 1:374.

12   Quoted in ManH A-1, in *PJS*, 1:376. Cf. *Latter-day Saints' Millennial Star*, Dec. 31, 1864, 834–35.

13   *Latter-day Saints' Millennial Star*, Dec. 31, 1864, 835; ManH A-1, in *PJS*, 1:373–74, 378.

14   ManH A-1, in *PJS*, 1:378. Van Wagoner looks at the medical implications in *Sidney Rigdon*, 117–18.

15   ManH A-1, in *PJS*, 1:378; Hill, *Joseph Smith*, 146; Newell and Avery, *Mormon Enigma*, 43–44; PreM, 565.

16   ManH A-1, in *PJS*, 1:378–80. Sidney Rigdon's version of the trip is reprinted in Cook, *Revelations*, 316.

17   In the printed version, Frederick G. Williams replaced Gause in the revelation. *D&C* [1835], 79:1 (*D&C*, 81:1). Woodford, "Historical Development," 2:1017, 1023.

18   Woodford, "Jesse Gause," 362–64; Quinn, "Jesse Gause," 487–93; Cook, *Revelations*, 171–72; *PJS*, 2:547.

19   ManH A-1, in *PJS*, 1:379–80.

20   Van Wagoner, *Sidney Rigdon*, 71, 123; *BofC*, 43:11 (*D&C*, 41:9). For more on Partridge, see Wixom, *Edward Partridge*, and Partridge, "Edward Partridge," 50–73.

21   *BofC*, 59:18–19 (*D&C*, 58:14–15); E. Young, Reminiscence, 6, 8.

22   *FWR*, 40–42 (Mar. 10, 1832); ManH A-1, in *PJS*, 1:380.

23   ManH A-1, in *PJS*, 1:380.

24   *D&C* [1835], 75:2 (*D&C*, 78:3, 9–10).

25   *D&C* [1835], 86:4 (*D&C*, 82:11–12); Arrington, "Mormon Communitarianism," 356, n. 2. On the United Firm, see Cook, *Law of Consecration*, 57–70.

26   *D&C* [1835], 75:1 (*D&C*, 78:4–7).

27   *D&C* [1835], 86:4 (*D&C*, 82:17–19). In joining the society by covenant (renewed each year), Shakers accepted the principle of joint interest whereby all members had "an Equal right and privilege, according to their Calling and needs, in things both Spiritual and temporal." Full membership went only to adults who gave their substance to the church for the "mutual good" and for such "Charitable uses" as the officers saw fit. Stein, *Shaker Experience*, 45–46.

28   Clark, *Communitarian Moment*, 2.

29   On Brigham Young's experiments with consecrated properties and the subject as a whole, see Arrington, Fox, and May, *City of God*. For modern Mormon idealism, Lucas and Woodworth, *Working Toward Zion*.

30   *FWR*, 50 (May 29, 1832). On the brick house, see Romig and Siebert, "Printing Operation," 54–55.

31   *FWR*, 46 (Apr. 30, 1832); ManH A-1, *PJS*, 1:381; Crawley, *Descriptive Bibliography*, 32.

32   *E&MS*, June 1832, [6]; Hatch, *American Christianity*, 126–27, 142, 144, 145.

33   *BofC*, 57:5 (*D&C*, 55:4); Van Orden, "Conversion of William W. Phelps," 207–12.

34   ManH A-1, in *PJS*, 1:384; *E&MS*, June 1832, [6]. For an example of closeness, see JS to William W. Phelps, Nov. 27, 1832, *PWJS*, 285–87.

35   ManH A-1, in *PJS*, 1:383.

36   *BofM*, 70 (2 Nephi 4:17); History, [1832], in *PJS*, 1:5–6.

37   JS to Emma Smith, June 6, 1832, in *PWJS*, 264–65; JS to William W. Phelps, July 31, 1832, in *PWJS*, 272.

38 JS to Emma Smith, June 6, 1832, in *PWJS*, 239.

39 ManH A-1, in *PJS*, 1:383–84.

40 *BioS*, 196–97; Newell and Avery, *Mormon Enigma*, 44–45.

41 PreM, 561–62; Cahoon, Diary, July 5, 1832.

42 Van Wagoner, *Sidney Rigdon*, 126–27. The evidence for the event occurring in July—not April, the date Lucy Smith gives—is found in Arrington, *Charles C. Rich*, 332, n. 15. That Rigdon was back in the good standing by July 31, 1832, is shown by a comment in Joseph Smith's letter to William W. Phelps on that date. *PWJS*, 272–73. Hyrum wrote that "28th [Jul.] 1832 Brother Sidney was ordaind to the high priesthood the second time." H. Smith, Diary, July 28, 1832.

43 JS to William W. Phelps, July 31, 1832, in *PWJS*, 270–71. Cahoon, Diary, Apr. 1832.

44 JS to William W. Phelps, July 31, 1832, in *PWJS*, 269–73; *BofC*, 1:4 (*D&C*, 1:19).

45 JS to William W. Phelps, July 31, 1832, in *PWJS*, 272–75.

46 *D&C* [1835], 4:16, 22 (*D&C*, 84:96, 114); ManH A-1, in *PWJS*, 277–78.

47 Burroughs and Wallace, *Gotham*, 419–22, 446–49, 455–60, 475–76, 575–80.

48 JS to Emma Smith, Oct. 13, 1832, in *PWJS*, 278.

49 JS to Emma Smith, Oct. 13, 1832, in *PWJS*, 278–79.

50 JS to Emma Smith, Oct. 13, 1832, in *PWJS*, 279–80; Newell and Avery, *Mormon Enigma*, 46. The Smith family had a tradition going back to Grandfather Asael Smith of naming the third son after the father. Joseph Smith Jr., was a third son, and so was Joseph III. Lucy Mack Smith's third daughter was named Lucy. Mark Ashurst-McGee drew my attention to this peculiar fact.

51 For Brigham Young's conversion, see Arrington, *Brigham Young*, 19–34; and Esplin, "New York Roots," 20–53.

52 Quoted in Arrington, *Brigham Young*, 26.

53 Quoted in Arrington, *Brigham Young*, 28–29.

54 Arrington, *Brigham Young*, 31–33; England, *Brother Brigham*, 62–89; Matthew 10:9–10.

55 In a sample of fifty-three life histories that mentioned conversion, only eleven described their first meeting with Joseph Smith. Of these eleven, four registered an impression, two favorable, and two neutral or negative. Bushman, "Conversion of 'Feeble Souls.' "

56 Crosby, "Biographical Sketch," [9]; Arrington, *Brigham Young*, 37.

57 Young, *Manuscript History*, 4–5.

58 After Joseph's death, and after Brigham Young had led a large body of Mormons to Utah, a note was added to Joseph's history that attributed to Joseph a more favorable judgment of Brigham: "Brother Joseph Young is a great man, but Brigham is a greater, and the time will come when he will preside over the whole Church." Quoted in *PJS*, 1:386, n. 2.

59 JS to William W. Phelps, July 31, 1832, in *PWJS*, 274. For the Nullification Crisis, see Freehling, *Nullification Controversy*, and Ellis, *Nullification Crisis*.

60 ManH A-1, in *PJS*, 244; *E&MS*, Jan. 1833, [62].

61 ManH A-1, in *PJS*, 244–45 (*D&C*, 87:1–6); *BofM*, 497, 500, 528 (3 Nephi 20:16; 21:12; Mormon 5:24).

62 It was first published in 1851 in Great Britain in a miscellany of revelations called *The Pearl of Great Price*. Alluding to the revelation, Joseph Smith told a newspaper editor in January 1833 that "not many years shall pass away before the United States shall present such a scene of *blood shed* as has not a parallel in the history of our nation." JS to N. C. Saxton, Jan. 4, 1833, in *PWJS*, 298.

63 "A Mormon Prophecy," *Philadelphia Sunday Mercury*, May 5, 1861, reproduced in Woodford, "Historical Development," 2:1110. The publication history is found on pages 1115–17.

64 JS to William W. Phelps, July 31, 1832, in *PWJS*, 285–86. This portion of the letter was included among Joseph Smith's revelations in the 1876 edition of the *Doctrine and Covenants*. Woodford, "Historical Development," 2:1080.

65 On interpretation of one "mighty and strong," see Woodford, "Historical Development," 2:1083.

66 JS to William W. Phelps, July 31, 1832, in *PWJS*, 287.

CHAPTER 10 EXALTATION

1 Joseph and Rigdon were preaching against Booth until January 10, 1832, when a revelation commanded them to return to translation. ManH A-1, in *PJS*, 1:370; *D&C* [1835], 29:2 (*D&C*, 73:3–4). On the "economy of God," see Woodford, "Historical Development," 2:935.

2 *D&C* [1835] 91, 4, 7, 82 (*D&C*, 76, 84, 88, 93).

3 The summary stated that "by the transgression of these holy laws, man became sensual and devilish, and became fallen man. Wherefore, the Almighty God gave his only begotten Son." *BofC*, 24:14–15 (*D&C*, 20:20–21).

4 Ostler, "Mormon Concept of Grace," 57–84, esp. 70–71.

5 Grant Underwood, an editor of *The Papers of Joseph Smith*, hypothesizes that possibly Joseph first revised John 5:29, then received the revelation, then revised the passage further. Personal communication with the author.

6 ManH A-1, in *PJS*, 1:37–72; *D&C* [1835], 91:3 (*D&C*, 76:15–17).

7 The strains in Calvinist theology and in attitudes toward authority are analyzed in Wright, *Unitarianism in America*; Foster, *New England Theology*; and Fliegelman, *Prodigals and Pilgrims*.

8 *D&C* [1835], 91:3 (*D&C*, 76:11, 20, 22–24).

9 Philo Dibble said about twelve men were in the room when the vision was given. Joseph and Rigdon seemed to be looking out a window and describing what they saw. "Recollections of the Prophet," 303–304. For a question about the authenticity of Dibble's story, see Van Wagoner, *Sidney Rigdon*, 119, n. 17.

10 Woodford, "Historical Development," 2:935; *D&C* [1835], 91:3–4 (*D&C*, 76:31–33).

11 Unlike "celestial" and "terrestrial," words in common usage, "telestial" was not a known word. It has the ring of *telos*, meaning "end" or "uttermost," a Greek word that appears in the New Testament in 1 Corinthians 15:24, a few verses before a passage on bodies celestial and terrestrial in verse 40. Speaking of the order of resurrection beginning with the righteous, Paul writes, "then cometh the end [*telos*] when he [Christ] shall have delivered up the kingdom to God, even the Father; when he shall have put down all rule and all authority and power." Jed Woodworth pointed out this connection.

12 *D&C* [1835], 91:8, 7 (*D&C*, 76:104–106, 81, 89).

13 *D&C* [1835], 91:6, 5 (*D&C*, 76:75–76, 54, 51–53, 58–59). See also Psalms 82:6, and John 1:12 and 10:34.

14 1 Corinthians 15:40–42.

15 McDannell and Lang, *Heaven*, 199–200. The three heavens in "The Vision" echo Paul's reference to a man caught up into the "third heaven" in 2 Corinthians 12:2.

16 Although there is no evidence Joseph read the books on heaven, by 1839 he knew about Swedenborg's ideas. Hunter, *Edward Hunter*, 51. On the Swedenborg connection, see Meyers, "Swedenborgian and Mormon Eschatology," 58–64, and Quinn, *Early Mormonism*, 174, 217–18, 520, n. 319.

17 Clayton, Journal, May 16, 1843 (*D&C*, 131:1); *D&C* [1835], 91:7, 4 (*D&C*, 76:106, 85, 37, 44).

18 *D&C* [1835], 91:7 (*D&C*, 76:89). Grant Underwood has argued that Mormons disregarded the doctrine of the three degrees of glory in the 1830s and 1840s, sticking with the standard heaven and hell. "Persistent Protestantism," 93–97.

19 *D&C* [1835], 7:5, 7, 10 (*D&C*, 88:22, 33, 40). The same sentiment is voiced in Alma's

expostulation in the *Book of Mormon:* "he that knoweth good and evil, to him it is given according to his desires; whether he desireth good or evil, life or death, joy or remorse of conscience." *BofM*, 303 (Alma 29:5).

20 Miller, *Universalist Church.* The doctrine of hell was equally repulsive to the Unitarians. Channing, *Works*, 3:221. Universal salvation met resistance too. Saum, *Pre–Civil War America*, 44–47.

21 *BofM*, 221–23, 263, 265–67, 283, 337–40 (Alma 1:4, 16; 14:18; 15:15; 16:11; 21:4; 42). Cf. *BofM*, 337, 63–64 (Alma 41:10–13; 2 Nephi 2:10–13). For an elaboration of the anti-Universalism in the *Book of Mormon*, see Vogel, "Anti-Universalist Rhetoric," 21–52. A rejoinder is Tanner, "Anti-Universalist Rhetoric?" 418–33.

22 *BofC*, 16:7, 11–12 (*D&C*, 19:6, 10, 12).

23 Materials on the rocky reception of "The Vision" are assembled in Woodford, "Historical Development," 2:929–33, and Quinn, *Early Mormonism*, 216.

24 Murdock, Diary, 27–29; ManH B-1, 792; *E&MS*, July 1832, [10–11]. Probably Phelps was responsible for putting "The Vision" into poetic verse in 1843. Hicks, "Poetic Paraphrase," 63–84.

25 McDannell and Lang, *Heaven*, 199–203.

26 Emerson, *Departed Saints*, 11.

27 *D&C* [1835], 91:5 (*D&C*, 76:56); Revelation 1:6; 5:10; 20:6. Cf. 2 Peter 1:3.

28 Hoge, *Heavenly Rest*, 17–25; Nott, *Future Habitation of Believers*, 5–7; McDannell and Lang, *Heaven*, 199.

29 *D&C* [1835], 91:7, 5 (*D&C*, 76:95, 93, 58–59). Cf. 1 Corinthians 13:12; John 1:17; Revelation 1:6; Psalms 82:6; John 10:34; Romans 8:16–17.

30 ManH A-1, in *PJS*, 1:372.

31 *D&C* [1835], 91:5 (*D&C*, 76:57); Revelation 1:6; Emerson, *Departed Saints*, 11.

32 Kirtland Revelation Book, 84–86, Revelations Collection, later incorporated into *D&C*, 107:64–68; Pratt, *Journals*, 11 (Jan. 25, 1832); Cahoon, Diary, Jan. 1832; ManH A-1, in *PJS*, 1:371.

33 Hebrews 7:12; *D&C* [1835], 4:2–4 (*D&C*, 84:14, 19, 26–27).

34 *D&C* [1835], 4:2 (*D&C*, 84:6–17).

35 *D&C* [1835], 4:2, 6; 3:18–27 (*D&C*, 84:16–17, 32–34; 107:41–52). The revelation included John the Baptist in the lineage of priests, linking Joseph Smith and Oliver Cowdery to the ancient order. *D&C* [1835], 4:4 (*D&C*, 84:27–28).

36 *D&C* [1835], 4:3 (*D&C*, 84:20, 22).

37 Exodus 33:11; *D&C* [1835], 4:4 (*D&C*, 84:23–24). Exodus 33:20 has God say, "Thou canst not see my face; for there shall no man see me, and live." Joseph revised this passage to read, "Thou canst not see my face at this time," for no "sinful man" shall see God's face and live. JS, *New Translation*, 701 (Exodus 33:20).

38 Exodus 19:10–11; 20:19; *D&C* [1835], 4:4 (*D&C*, 84:24–26).

39 JS, *New Translation*, 641 (Genesis 14:31). John Corrill said some elders were disappointed that the endowment amounted only to a bestowal of the priesthood. Corrill, *Brief History*, 18.

40 *D&C* [1835], 25:3; 4:6 (*D&C*, 67:10; 84:31, 32, 38).

41 Redle, "Beatific Vision," 2:186–91; and Bastian, "Light of Glory," 8:755.

42 *D&C* [1835] 4:22 (*D&C*, 84:114); Whitmer, *Book of John Whitmer*, 102–103. Mormon scriptures added two earlier instances of a whole people entering God's presence: the city of Salem in Melchizedek's time, and Enoch's Zion. JS, *New Translation* (Moses 7:18–21); *E&MS*, Aug. 1832, [18].

43 John 13:5, 14; Exodus 28, 29.

44 Bloom, *American Religion*, 32.

45 *BofM*, 259 (Alma 13:8); *D&C* [1835], 3:1 (*D&C*, 107:3).

46 Kirtland High Council, Minutes, Dec. 27–28, 1832; JS to William W. Phelps, Jan. 11,

1833, in *PWJS*, 292. Verses 1–126 of the current revelation were delivered at this time. Verses 127–137 were received Jan. 3, 1833. Woodford, "Historical Development," 2:1128.

47   For Swedenborg in America, see Block, *Swedenborgianism*.

48   John 1:1–9; *D&C* [1835], 7:2 (*D&C*, 88:6–10). Paragraphing added.

49   *D&C* [1835], 7:18 (*D&C*, 88:67).

50   John Brooke argues for the resemblance of Joseph's teachings to the hermetic impulse toward divinization—becoming God. But Brooke could not find the actual connections to Joseph Smith. Brooke, *Refiner's Fire*, 204–207. The closest hermetic-linked influence was Freemasonry, which had given up on divinization in favor of moral instruction. Masons defined their order as "a beautiful system of morality, veiled in allegory, and illustrated by symbols." Mackey, *Lexicon of Freemasonry*, 169. Hermetic philosophy, moreover, did not foresee facing God, but merging with Him. French, *John Dee*, 115–16.

51   Jonsson, *Emanuel Swedenborg*, 92–118; Emerson, *Nature*, in *Collected Works*, 1–37.

52   *D&C* [1835], 82:2 (*D&C*, 93:17).

53   *D&C* [1835], 82:2–3 (*D&C*, 93:12, 17–20); Matt. 28:18. These ideas about light reach back to Neoplatonic notions developed by Pseudo-Dionysius and Francesco Patrizi da Cherso. Schützinger, "Light," 8:750.

54   Quoted in Peters, *Christian Perfection*, 115–16, 112, 118.

55   *D&C* [1835], 82:4, 6 (*D&C*, 93:26, 28, 36).

56   *D&C* [1835], 82:4 (*D&C*, 93:24).

57   *D&C* [1835], 82:5 (*D&C*, 93:29–34). Paragraphing added.

58   *D&C* [1835], 82:4 (*D&C*, 93:23); Lindquist, "Pre-existent Intelligences," 119–31. On the history of this doctrine in Mormon thought, see Ostler, "Idea of Pre-existence," 59–78.

59   *D&C* [1835], 82:6 (*D&C*, 93:28, 39).

60   *D&C* [1835], 4:6 (*D&C*, 84:38).

61   *D&C* [1835], 82:6 (*D&C*, 93:37); *T&S*, Mar. 15, 1842, 720 (Abraham 3:22).

62   *D&C* [1835], 82:8 (*D&C*, 93:47).

63   *D&C* [1835], 7:21–22; 84:5 (*D&C*, 88:77–81; 90:15). The phrase "school of the prophets" was a later addition to the revelation. Marquardt, *Joseph Smith Revelations*, 229–30.

64   *D&C* [1835], 7:20, 19, 38, 37, 36 (*D&C*, 88:74, 69, 124, 121, 118).

65   *D&C* [1835], 7:37 (*D&C*, 88:122).

66   *D&C* [1835], 7:38–43 (*D&C*, 88:125–35).

67   *D&C* [1835], 7:36 (*D&C*, 88:119, 118); *M&A*, Mar. 1836, 277 (*D&C*, 109:7–8).

68   *D&C* [1835], 4:6, 7:18 (*D&C*, 84:33, 88:67).

69   *Omaha Herald*, Oct. 17, 1886, in Whitmer, *Interviews*, 204; Trollope, *Domestic Manners*, 24, 83.

70   *D&C* [1835], 80:1–3 (*D&C*, 89:10–11, 9, 18). Hyrum Smith defined "hot drinks" to mean tea and coffee. *T&S*, June 1, 1842, 800. For a period discussion, see Alcott, *Tea and Coffee*.

71   For the background of the "Word of Wisdom," see Ford, "Word of Wisdom," 129–54; Bush, "Word of Wisdom," 47–65; Peterson, "Word of Wisdom." The published collection of Graham's lectures was titled *Lectures on the Science of Human Life*. Another attack on tea and coffee appeared in Alcott, *Tea and Coffee*. On the climate of dietary reform, see Nissenbaum, *Sylvester Graham*.

72   Isaiah 40:31; *D&C* [1835], 80:3 (*D&C*, 89:1920); *Journal of Discourses*, 12:157–58 (Feb. 8, 1868).

73   On the history of the "Word of Wisdom," see Alexander, "Principle to Requirement," 78–88, and Peterson and Walker, "Word of Wisdom Legacy," 29–64.

74   French, *John Dee*, 77, 116.

75 *D&C*, [1835] 7:3, 6; 82:5 (*D&C*, 88:15, 28; 93:33–34); *BofC*, 48:18 (*D&C*, 45:17); Clayton, Journal, Feb. 9, Apr. 2, 1843 (*D&C*, 129:1, 130:22).

76 Entries from Kirtland High Council, Minutes, kept by Frederick G. Williams, were the basis for Joseph Smith's later history. It recorded Church business at the frequent "conferences" during February and March but said nothing about the school's activities. Reminiscences of the school were recorded in the minutes of a much later School of the Prophets convened in the 1870s and 1880s in Utah. See School of the Prophets, Minutes, Nov. 12, 1870, June 3, 1871; Oct. 3, 11, 1883.

77 Sorensen, "Schools of the Prophets," 3:1269; PreM, 567; Backman, *Heavens Resound*, 265; Coltrin, Diary, Jan. 24, 1833; *D&C* [1835], 84:5, 3–4 (*D&C*, 90:15, 7–11).

78 Kirtland High Council, Minutes, Jan. 23, 1833. Writing long after the fact, Lucy Smith got the date wrong. PreM, 566–67.

79 The washing of feet had been planned for some time. A letter to the Missouri church on January 14, 1833, mentioned the command of the Lord to purify themselves and wash hands and feet. Twelve High Priests to the Bishop, Council, and Inhabitants of Zion, Jan. 14, 1833, JSC. Coltrin, Diary, Jan. 24, 23, 1833, places these events on January 24. On the background of the practice, see Grow, "Washing of Feet."

80 Kirtland High Council, Minutes, Jan. 23, 1833; Twelve High Priests to the Bishop, Council, and Inhabitants of Zion, Jan. 14, 1833, JSC; ManH A-1, 564. William W. Phelps, July 31, 1832, in *PWJS*, 287.

CHAPTER 11   CITIES OF ZION

1 *D&C* [1835], 95:2 (*D&C*, 95:10); *FWR*, 78 (July 31, 1834).

2 Joseph Smith, Sidney Rigdon, and F. G. Williams, Kirtland, to William W. Phelps and others in Independence, June 25, 1833, JSC. For a discussion of the Mormon population in Kirtland, see Backman, *Heavens Resound*, 139.

3 In April 1833, Albert Brown was appointed to raise money for continuing to rent a house where meetings had been held the past winter. Kirtland High Council, Minutes, April 30, 1833. The next fall they rented the schoolhouse on Kirtland flats for one congregation and held a second meeting in Uncle John Smith's house. JS to Vienna Jacques, Sept. 4, 1831, in *PWJS*, 319; Backman, *Heavens Resound*, 275–76.

4 Hancock, Diary, 76. Lucy Smith, attuned to class distinctions in material culture, said that the "majority" of Kirtland leaders wanted a temple built of logs. PreM, 581.

5 *BofC*, 38:6 (*D&C*, 36:8); *D&C* [1835], 7:36, 39 (*D&C*, 88:119, 128–29); JS to William W. Phelps, Jan. 11, 1833, in *PWJS*, 293.

6 Nathaniel Wood, whose short-lived religious adventure in Vermont around 1800 is said to have involved Oliver Cowdery's father, also received a command to build a temple. Quinn, *Early Mormonism*, 35. Taylor Petrey argues that the more radical sects in this period used the Old Testament as a basis for their practices. Petrey, " 'Old Testament Hermeneutic.' " For the use of the word "temple" in the construction of a Congregational meetinghouse in Quincy, Massachusetts, see Lunt, *Two Discourses*, 125–29.

7 Hamilton, *Mormon Architecture*, 38, 40; Shipps, *Mormonism*, 51–56; Andrew, *Early Temples*, 142; Cranford, "Mormon and Masonic Temples," 13–14. A Gothic-styled Masonic temple was built in New York City in 1826.

8 *BofM*, 72 (2 Nephi 5:16); *Chardon Spectator and Geauga Gazette*, Aug. 17, 1833; 1 Kings 6.

9 Jan Shipps discusses the tensions in Mormonism's blend of Old and New Testament religion. *Mormonism*, 46–65.

10 *BofC*, 38:6 (*D&C*, 36:8); *D&C* [1835], 27:1, 4:2 (*D&C*, 57:3; 84:4).

11 *D&C* [1835], 7:36, 39; 83:1–2 (*D&C*, 88:119, 127–28; 94:3, 7); Andrew, *Early Temples*, 46; Robison, *First Mormon Temple*, 55.

12 2 Chronicles 5:13–14; *D&C* [1835], 4:2, 83:2, 95:2 (*D&C*, 84:5, 94:8, 95:8). See also JS to William W. Phelps, Jan. 11, 1833, in *PWJS*, 293.

13 Backman, *Heavens Resound*, 144–45; Robison, *First Mormon Temple*, 33; Johnson, *Life's Review*, 9; Kirtland High Council, Minutes, Mar. 23, 1833.

14 *D&C* [1835], 83:2–3 (*D&C*, 94:4, 10–11); Hyrum Smith, Reynolds Cahoon, and Jared Carter to the Church of Christ in _____, June 1, 1833, JSC. The committee was appointed at a conference of high priests on May 4. Kirtland High Council, Minutes, May 4, 1833.

15 Cook, *Revelations*, 322; *D&C* [1835], 95:3 (*D&C*, 95:13–14). On the temple revelation, see Backman, *Heavens Resound*, 149; Robison, *First Mormon Temple*, 8, 24, n. 3; and *Painesville Telegraph*, May 20, 1836. On the Gothic windows, see Andrew, *Early Temples*, 43–46; and Robison, *First Mormon Temple*, 78. For the Gothic revival in America as a whole, see Howe and Warren, *Gothic Revival Style*.

16 *D&C* [1835], 95:3 (*D&C*, 95:16–17); Andrew, *Early Temples*, 46–50. On the veils, room divisions, pulpits, and courts, see Robison, *First Mormon Temple*, 19–20, 59–68, 85–95.

17 ManH A-1, 302; *PWJS*, 647; Robison, *First Mormon Temple*, 28; *HC*, 1:400. A verbal description of the Missouri temple interior appears in "Plat of the City of Zion, June [24], 1833," reprinted in Hamilton, *Mormon Architecture*, 34–36. The Missouri Saints were told to build two other temples in addition to the one described, one for the presidency and one for printing. JS, Sidney Rigdon, and Frederick G. Williams to Beloved Brethren, Aug. 6, 1833, JSC. For an analysis of the Missouri temple, see Robison, *First Mormon Temple*, 9–16, and Andrew, *Early Temples*, 32–35.

18 Backman, *Heavens Resound*, 139.

19 Joseph wrote, "I have always felt as though a letter written to any one in authority in Zion, would be the property of all, & it mattered but little to whom it was directed." JS to Edward Partridge, May 2, 1833, JSC. Phelps later claimed he was "leader of spiritual affairs" as printer to the Church. Phelps, "Short History," 2–3.

20 Orson Hyde and Hyrum Smith, to the Bishop, Council, and the Inhabitants of Zion, Jan. 14, 1833, JSC; Kirtland High Council, Loose Minutes, Jan. 13, 1833, JSC; JS to William W. Phelps, Jan. 11, 1833, in *PWJS*, 292.

21 Orson Hyde and Hyrum Smith to the Bishop, Council, and the Inhabitants of Zion, Jan. 14, 1833, JSC; ManH A-1, 282; JS to Brethren in Zion, Apr. 21, 1833, JSC; *FWR*, 60–61 (Feb. 26, 1833); *D&C* [1835], 84:8 (*D&C*, 90:34).

22 Joseph Smith is put in the context of other utopians in Tyler, *Freedom's Ferment*, 86–107. For an analysis of the differences between Joseph's two plans, see Hamilton, *Mormon Architecture*, 18–19, and Romig and Siebert, "Development of Zion," 286–304. For American town plans, see Reps, *City Planning*.

23 For the history of the city plans, see Hamilton, *Mormon Architecture*, 15–18, 34.

24 On the larger amended plan, two instead of three squares stood at the center. Plat for the City of Zion, June [24], 1833. One of the twenty-four, temple number 5, was designated as the temple shown in the design sent to Zion. Romig and Siebert, "Concept of Temples," 105–106. W. Ray Luce, seizing upon the explanatory note calling temples "Houses of worship, schools, etc.," argues that the large number of temples was necessary to seat the City of Zion for Sunday services. If each temple housed 500, a population of 12,000 could be housed. Luce, "Mormon Architecture," 36.

25 Plat of the City of Zion, June [24], 1833; Kirtland High Council, Minutes, June 24, 1833.

26 Wills, *John Wayne's America*, 304, 349, n. 9.

27 Steven L. Olsen has explicated the religious meaning of the city in "City of Zion," 203–11, and at greater length in "Cosmic Symbolism."

28 For example, William Mulder claimed that the plan was an "idealized New England village" in his "Mormonism's 'Gathering,'" 253.

29 Thompson and Welpton, *Population Trends*, 26; Jackson, "Mormon Village," 223–40;

Francaviglia, *Mormon Landscape*, 80–82; Sellers, "Mormon Community Planning," 24–30; Romig and Siebert, "Concept of Temples," 102. The classic work on Mormon city planning is Nelson, *Mormon Village*. A recent synthesis is Hamilton, *Mormon Architecture*.

30 Plat for the City of Zion, June [24], 1833. In 1838, Joseph told the Saints that they must live in cities "according to the order of God." JS, Journal, Aug. 6, 1838 in *PJS*, 2:266.

31 Hartley, "Nauvoo Stake," 57–80.

32 Hamilton, *Mormon Architecture*, 18–22. These themes are developed more fully in Bushman, *Making Space*, and Meinig, "Mormon Corridor."

33 See Flanders, *Nauvoo*, 115–43.

34 Pratt, *Autobiography*, 100; *D&C* [1835], 81:1–4 (*D&C*, 97:3–5, 7, 9, 11, 14, 16, 18–19, 26).

35 For the early signs of antagonism, see Jennings, "Zion Is Fled," 124–25, and "Mormon Press," 63–64.

36 "Petition to Governor Daniel Dunklin, [Sept. 28, 1833]," in *E&MS*, Dec. 1833, 114; E. Young, Reminiscence, 11–12; Pratt, *Autobiography*, 103; Corrill, *Brief History*, 19. Isaac McCoy, a Baptist missionary, foresaw the problem of political dominance too. Hill, *Quest for Refuge*, 210–11, n. 82. The difference between the Mormon "yankee" and the Missouri "frontiersman" is emphasized in Jennings, "Social Conflict," 99–119. See also Bushman, "Mormon Persecutions," 11–20.

37 *BofC*, 54:43 (*D&C*, 52:42); *E&MS*, July 1833, 110; Gregg, *Commerce of the Prairies*, 218. Max Parkin estimates that Edward Partridge held title to 2,260 acres of Mormon lands in Jackson County, with another 155 held by individual Church members. "Clay County," 301–303. Partridge himself said he held title to 2,136 acres. Johnson, *Redress Petitions*, 513.

38 *E&MS*, July 1833, 109; Jan. 1834, 122. For Phelps's disavowal, see Crawley, *Descriptive Bibliography*, 37. For an analysis of Missouri opposition to free black people, see Jennings, "Mormon Press," 65–68.

39 Whitmer, *Book of John Whitmer*, 103–105; *E&MS*, Dec. 1833, 114. The manifesto is reproduced in full in John Whitmer to Oliver Cowdery and JS, July 29, 1833, JSC, and Jennings, "Zion Is Fled," 135–37.

40 The title "The Manifesto of the Mob" was given the document by the compilers of Joseph Smith's history. *HC*, 1:374. On the tradition of crowd action, see Brown, *American Violence*; Feldberg, *Turbulent Era*; Grimsted, "Rioting," 361–97; Grimsted, *American Mobbing*; Mason, "Anti-Mormon Conflict."

41 "Petition to Governor Daniel Dunklin, [Sept. 28, 1833]," in *E&MS*, Dec. 1833, 114; John Whitmer to Oliver Cowdery and JS, July 29, 1833, JSC. For the quasi-legality of mob action, see Nelson, "Anti-Mormon Mob Violence," 353–88.

42 "Petition to Governor Daniel Dunklin, [Sept. 28, 1833]," in *E&MS*, Dec. 1833. On the background to this incident, see Jennings, "Mormon Press," 57–76. Destruction is recounted in Romig and Siebert, "Printing Operation," 51–66.

43 *Jeffersonian Republican*, Aug. 17, 1833; *Western Monitor*, Aug. 2, 1833, in ManH A-1, 330–37; *MoU*, 142. The account from the *Missouri Intelligencer*, Aug. 10, 1833, is reproduced in Mulder and Mortensen, *Among the Mormons*, 77–80.

44 Edward Partridge and others, Memorial to the Legislature of Missouri, Dec. 10, 1838; Edward Partridge, Affidavit, May 15, 1839; and Orrin Porter Rockwell, Affidavit, Feb. 3, 1840, in Johnson, *Redress Petitions*, 15–16, 512–18, 528.

45 For an account by a Mormon eyewitness, see Whitmer, *Book of John Whitmer*, 106. The resolutions circulated widely. See, for example, *U.S. Telegraph*, Aug. 21, 1833; *New-York American*, Aug. 27, 1833; *Erie Gazette*, Sept. 5, 1833.

46 *Missouri Intelligencer*, Aug. 10, 1833; *Jeffersonian Republican*, Aug. 17, 1833; John Whitmer to Oliver Cowdery and JS, July 29, 1833, JSC. On Mormon involvement with slaves, see *E&MS*, Jan. 1834, 122, and Jennings, "Mormon Press," 73–76.

47 *Jeffersonian Republican*, Aug. 17, 1833; *Missouri Intelligencer*, Aug. 10, 1833. The same

agreement is reproduced in *MoU*, 142–43. For the Mormon account of the day's events, see "Petition to Governor Daniel Dunklin, [Sept. 28, 1833]," in *E&MS*, Dec. 1833, 114.

48   *E&MS*, Dec. 1833, 115; JS, Sidney Rigdon, and Frederick G. Williams to Beloved Brethren, Aug. 6, 1833, JSC; *D&C* [1835], 85:3 (*D&C*, 98:14, 16).

49   Oliver Cowdery to William W. Phelps and others, Aug. 10, 1833, in *PWJS*, 305–306. On the meeting of the council, see Frederick G. Williams to Dear Brethren, Oct. 10, 1833, JSC.

50   William Phelps, John Whitmer, Edward Partridge, Isaac Morley, John Corrill, and Sidney Gilbert. Partridge, Morley, and Corrill were bishops.

51   JS to William W. Phelps and others, Aug. 18, 1833, in *PWJS*, 308–309.

52   JS to William W. Phelps and others, Aug. 18, 1833, in *PWJS*, 307–10.

53   JS to William W. Phelps and others, Aug. 18, 1833, in *PWJS*, 310–12; Oliver Cowdery to William W. Phelps et al., Aug. 10, 1833, in *PWJS*, 305; Frederick G. Williams to Dear Brethren, Oct. 10, 1833, JSC.

54   Whitmer, *Book of John Whitmer*, 89; *BofC*, 40:18 (*D&C*, 38:22). Early Methodists disregarded the nation too. Richey, *Early American Methodism*, 33–46.

55   *D&C* [1835], 85:2 (*D&C*, 98:5–6); JS to William W. Phelps and others, Aug. 18, 1833, in *PWJS*, 310.

56   ManH A-1, 328–29. A similar observation was made years ago in Moore, *Religious Outsiders*, 34–35.

57   *Missouri Intelligencer*, Nov. 16, 1833; *Jeffersonian Republican*, Nov. 30, 1833; *New-York American*, Dec. 3, 1833; *Boston Recorder*, Dec. 14, 1833. Even the obstreperous Ohio newspaper editor E. D. Howe was convinced that the proceedings "on the part of the people of Jackson county, were in total disregard of all law, and must be condemned by all." *MoU*, 144.

58   For examples of washing his feet after rejections, see Pratt, *Journals*, 34, 36 (Feb. 27; Mar. 21, 1834); Woodruff, *Journals*, 1:70, 100–101 (May 22; Oct. 12, 1836); McLellin, *Journals*, 61, 174 (Nov. 18, 1831; May 7, 1835).

59   Colonel John Sconce of Ray County, Missouri, was one of the first of these sympathizers. He befriended the Mormons in June 1834 after Joseph led a band of men to Missouri in hopes of restoring the Saints to their lands. According to Heber C. Kimball, Joseph gave Sconce "a relation of the sufferings of our people in Jackson county, and also of all our persecutions generally, and what we had suffered by our enemies for our religion." Sconce reacted exactly as hoped. He and his friends "offered him [Joseph] their hands, and said they would use their influence to allay the excitement which every where prevailed against us." Conversion to Mormonism never came up in the conversation. It was enough that the visitors "wept because they saw we were a poor afflicted people." *T&S*, Feb. 15, 1845, 804.

60   *E&MS*, Aug. 1834, 183–84.

61   Kirtland High Council, Minutes, Sept. 11, 1833. The shift in emphasis led to momentary confusion about Zion's location. A few Saints concluded that Zion consisted of the broad swath from Ohio to Missouri, a view that would have diffused the gathering and made it no more than a westward movement. ManH A-1, 360.

62   Kirtland High Council, Minutes, Sept. 28, 1833.

63   JS to Vienna Jacques, Sept. 4, 1833, in *PWJS*, 318–19.

64   "Petition to Governor Daniel Dunklin, [Sept. 28, 1833]," in *E&MS*, Dec. 1833, 114–15; Daniel Dunklin to Edward Partridge and others, Oct. 19, 1833, Phelps Collections. The lawyers asked for the exorbitant sum of $250 each, they said, because "by this engagement we must expect to lose the greatest part of it, which will be to all of us a considerable loss." Quoted in Launius, *Alexander William Doniphan*, 15. See also Anderson, "Atchison's Letters," 6.

65 According to John Corrill, the hostilities recommenced as soon as the Missourians found "that we were about to appeal to the law for redress." Corrill, *Brief History*, 19.

66 *E&MS*, Jan. 1834, 125; Corrill, *Brief History*, 20; Jennings, "Zion Is Fled," 144–52. Orson Hyde reported two men beaten with stones and clubs. *E&MS*, Dec. 1833, 118. There were reports of other whippings and many threats. *E&MS*, Dec. 1833, 119; Jan. 1834, 124. A dispute developed about whether the Mormons had received maltreatment. The citizens may have considered attacks on property within the bounds of propriety for a vigilante action, while bodily injuries were not. *E&MS*, Dec. 1833, 119.

67 Isaac McCoy, quoted in Jennings, "Isaac McCoy," 71. See also the document signed by Jackson County leaders on November 8, 1833, expressing a belief in the Mormons' "late attempt to massacre our people." They thought Edward Partridge should be charged with "forming a conspiracy to murder and rob the other inhabitants of the county." Jennings, "Isaac McCoy," 75–76.

68 Jennings, "Isaac McCoy," 70; *FWR*, 213; *E&MS*, Jan. 1834, 125; Jennings, "Expulsion of the Mormons," 47–48. The grisly story told in the ManH A-1, 366–76, is based on John Corrill to Oliver Cowdery, Dec. 1833, in *E&MS*, Jan. 1834, 124–26. For a modern version sympathetic to the Mormons, see Jennings, "Expulsion of the Mormons," 41–63. For descriptions of the Mormon losses in Jackson County, see Johnson, *Mormon Redress Petitions*, xxix, and passim. On the reception in Clay County, see Parkin, "Clay County," 8–51. By the end of the year, the Saints had spread to the neighboring counties of Ray, Lafayette, and Van Buren.

69 ManH A-1, 366–76, esp. 373. Boggs's son later denied that his father took part in the Jackson County expulsion. Boggs, "Lilburn W. Boggs," 107.

70 *D&C* [1835], 94:4 (*D&C*, 100:13); Frederick G. Williams to Dear Brethren, Oct. 10, 1833, JSC; JS to Edward Partridge, Dec. 5, 1833, JSC; *BofC*, 59:4–6 (*D&C*, 58:3–4); *D&C* [1835], 94:4 (*D&C*, 100:13); JS to Edward Partridge and others, Dec. 10, 1833, in *PWJS*, 329.

71 JS to Edward Partridge and others, Dec. 10, 1833, in *PWJS*, 329–31.

72 Quoted in Ames, Autobiography, [10].

73 *D&C* [1835], 97:1–4, 9–10 (*D&C*, 101:2–6, 17, 67, 70–73). The revelation called for "wise men" to make the purchases. Phelps, "Short History," 4.

CHAPTER 12   THE CHARACTER OF A PROPHET

1 Joel Hills Johnson actually said Joseph called himself a "great, green lubberly fellow," and Johnson concurred. Andrus and Andrus, *They Knew the Prophet*, 29.

2 Shurtliff, "Biographical Sketch," 19; Mary Isabella Hales Horne, quoted in Hales, *Windows*, 31; Charlotte Havens to Sister Isa, Jan. 22, 1843, in Mulder and Mortensen, *Among the Mormons*, 118; Burnett, *Old California Pioneer*, 40–41. For the firsthand observations of Joseph Smith, see Hill, "Joseph Smith the Man," 175–86.

3 Quinn, *Early Mormonism*, 122; JS, Journal, Jan. 11, 1834, in *PJS*, 2:20; Kirtland High Council, Minutes, June 21, 23, 1833. Hurlbut had cut short his Church mission in Pennsylvania to court a woman in Jefferson, Ohio. On this and Hurlbut generally, see Adams, "Doctor Philastus Hurlbut," 76–93.

4 Winchester, *Spaulding Story*, 9. The Hurlbut story is summarized in Van Wagoner, *Sidney Rigdon*, 134–36. Joseph recalled Hurlbut saying "that if he ever became convinced that the book of Mormon was false, he would be the cause of my destruction, &c." JS, Journal, Jan. 11, 1834, in *PJS*, 2:20.

5 Adams, "Doctor Philastus Hurlbut," 82–83; Van Wagoner, *Sidney Rigdon*, 135. Other inquiries about the Smiths in the same years got a response different from Hurlbut's.

Mormons who passed through Palmyra often inquired about Joseph's reputation and heard nothing damaging. One visitor in 1835 "went about from house to house to inquire [into] the character of Joseph Smith . . . previous to his receiving the book of the plates of Mormon. The answer was that his character was as good as young men in general." Hale, Diary, 1–2.

6 Presidency of the High Priesthood to the Brethren Scattered from Zion [ca. 1834], JSC; JS to William W. Phelps and others, Aug. 18, 1833, in *PWJS*, 311.

7 Quinn, *Origins of Power*, 84; G. Smith, "History," 11; JS, Journal, Jan. 11; April 1, 1834, in *PJS*, 2:19, 28–29.

8 Hurlbut had been humiliated by the revelation of an affair between his wife and one of his Campbellite backers. Van Wagoner, *Sidney Rigdon*, 136. The hostile affidavits and reports appear in *MoU*, 232–69, and again with annotation in *EMD*, 2:13–72. For assessment, see Anderson, "New York Reputation," 283–314; and Anderson, *New York Reputation Reexamined*.

9 Presidency of the High Priesthood to the Scattered Brethren from Zion, [ca. 1834], JSC; *MoU*, 258, 262. Hurlbut probably authored the Palmyra and Manchester group statements and then asked for signatures. *EMD*, 2:18, 48; Anderson, *New York Reputation Reexamined*, 30–31; Backman, *Heavens Resound*, 202. Hurlbut looked for people with the story he wanted to hear. Benjamin Saunders said Hurlbut "came to me but he could not get out of me what he wanted; so [he] went [to] others." Benjamin Saunders, Interview (1884), in *EMD*, 2:139.

10 Whitmer, *Book of John Whitmer*, 55–56; History [1832], in *PJS*, 1:1; Jessee, "Joseph Smith's History," 439–73.

11 *BioS*, 84; History [1832], in *PJS*, 1:3, 5–6.

12 History [1832], in *PJS*, 1:6–8.

13 History [1832], in *PJS*, 1:10, 3.

14 JS, Journal, Nov. 27–28; Dec. 4, 1832, in *PJS*, 2:2, 5.

15 JS, Journal, Jan. 31; March 1, 3, 1834, in *PJS*, 2:21–22.

16 JS, Journal, Jan. 11, 16, 1834, in *PJS*, 2:18–19.

17 Kirtland High Council, Minutes, Feb. 24, 1834.

18 *BofM*, 290–93, 367–69, 523–24 (Alma 24, 51:13–21; Mormon 3:7–16).

19 *BofC*, 64:30–32 (*D&C*, 63:29–31); *D&C* [1835], 85:7 (*D&C*, 98:47–48). For a helpful discussion of the issue, see Walker, "Dilemmas of War," 43–56. On Mormon pacifism, see Mason, "Mormon Peacebuilding," 12–45.

20 Quinn, *Origins of Power*, 80–86; Quinn, "Culture of Violence," 166–67.

21 Kirtland High Council, Minutes, Feb. 24, 1834.

22 *D&C* [1844], 101:3, 5 (*D&C*, 103:15–16, 20, 24–25); Hill, *Quest for Refuge*, 45.

23 Crawley and Anderson, "Zion's Camp," 406–20; Daniel Dunklin to Gentlemen, Feb. 4, 1834; Edward Partridge and 113 others to Andrew Jackson, Apr. 10, 1834; Lewis Cass to A. S. Gilbert and others, May 2, 1834; A. S. Gilbert and others to Daniel Dunklin, Apr. 24, 1834, all in Phelps Collection.

24 Kirtland High Council, Minutes, Mar. 17, 1834; JS, Journal, Feb. 26; Mar. 28, 1834, in *PJS*, 2:21, 27; *D&C* [1844], 101:6 (*D&C*, 103:32–33); JS, Frederick G. Williams, and Oliver Cowdery to Orson Hyde, Apr. 7, 1834, JSC.

25 JS, Journal, Apr. 19, 1834, in *PJS*, 2:31–32.

26 A later account said the number had grown to 130 before they left New Portage. ManH A-1, 478. Milton Backman's compilation lists 207 men, 11 women, and 11 children. Backman, *Zion's Camp*, 93–95. Cf. *T&S*, Jan. 1, 1846; Bradley, *Zion's Camp*, 263–80. On the Hyrum Smith party, see Launius, *Zion's Camp*, 45, 93–103.

27 *Painesville Telegraph*, May 9, 1834. Wilford Woodruff carried a rifle, dirk, sword, and pistol. He gave the sword to Joseph upon request. Alexander, "Woodruff and Zion's Camp," 137. For the tendency to see harsh repression in the motives of priests, see Whittier, *Supernaturalism of New England*, 42–43.

28 Van Orden, "Expeditions from Kirtland," 28. On the women and children, see Radke, "Zion's Camp," 147–65.

29 For Heber C. Kimball's firsthand account, see *T&S*, Jan. 15, 1845, 771–73; Feb. 1, 1845, 787–90; Feb. 15, 1845, 803–805; Mar. 15, 1845, 838–40.

30 *T&S*, Jan. 15, 1845, 772; A. S. Gilbert and William W. Phelps to Daniel Dunklin, May 7, 1834, Phelps Collection.

31 Mancill, "Hyrum Smith's Division," 167–88; G. Smith, Memoirs, 2, 21, 30; Wight, quoted in Romig and Siebert, "Legions of Zion," 26–27; *T&S*, Feb. 1, 1845, 789; G. Smith Statement, Oct. 10, 1864, Zion's Camp Festival Papers. Levi Hancock heard Joseph teaching restraint during the Zion's Camp expedition. Hancock, Diary, 80.

32 On the whole episode, see Crawley and Anderson, "Zion's Camp," 406–20.

33 George A. Smith said, "I could not write at the time and consequently kept no journal," but wrote from memory later. G. Smith, Memoirs, 42–43.

34 G. Smith, Memoirs, 9, 14–15, 26, 33.

35 G. Smith, Memoirs, 9, 14, 17–19, 21, 37–38. G. Smith Statement, Oct. 10, 1864, Zion's Camp Festival Papers.

36 *D&C* [1844], 101:3 (*D&C*, 103:20); *T&S*, Jan. 15, 1845, 772; Hancock, Diary, 81. Reuben McBride said Joseph told them he had seen angels. McBride, Reminiscence, 3.

37 G. Smith, Memoirs, 14; JS to Emma Smith, June 4, 1834, in *PWJS*, 345. Heber C. Kimball said the overcounting occurred many times. *T&S*, Jan. 15, 1845, 773.

38 G. Smith, Memoirs, 16.

39 G. Smith, Memoirs, 18.

40 JS to Emma Smith, June 4, 1834, in *PWJS*, 345.

41 ManH A-1, 483. Willard Richards, working as Church historian, compiled this section of his history, presumably under Joseph's direction, in 1842–43. In his manuscript version, the words "hill Cumorah" and "Nephites" are crossed out, but whether at Joseph's insistence is unknown. On this and a table of the major sources, see Godfrey, "Zelph Story," 43, 47, 50–53. On Zelph and Book of Mormon geography, see Cannon, "Zelph Revisited," 97–111. Kenneth Godfrey has identified seven accounts of the Zelph story in Zion's Camp diaries. "Significance of Zelph," 70–79.

42 Hancock, Diary, 79.

43 G. Smith, Memoirs, 38, 19.

44 G. Smith, Memoirs, 20.

45 JS to Emma Smith, June 4, 1834, in *PWJS*, 344–46.

46 G. Smith, Memoirs, 29; *T&S*, Feb. 1, 1845, 788–89. Levi Hancock's version was slightly less gory. "Joseph said, if you do not get rid of that feeling you will have your flesh eaten off from you and you cannot help it." Hancock, Diary, 80.

47 G. Smith, Memoirs, 34–35. The horn was used to call the men to prayer morning and evening. *T&S*, Jan. 15, 1845, 771.

48 Daniel Dunklin to Colonel J. Thornton, June 6, 1834, in *E&MS*, July 1834, 175; Jennings, "Army of Israel," 120. The most balanced account of Mormon–Jackson County negotiations is in Jennings, "Army of Israel," 107–35. On Jackson County fears, see 117–18.

49 ManH A-1, 491; *History of Jackson County*, 261; *E&MS*, July 1834, 175; quotes from Launius, *Alexander William Doniphan*, 22, and ManH A-1, 493.

50 John Corrill and A. S. Gilbert to Alexander Doniphan and David Atchison, June 14, 1834, Phelps Collection; William W. Phelps and others to Samuel C. Owens and others, [July 23, 1833], Phelps Collection.

51 Jennings, "Army of Israel," 124–25.

52 ManH A-1, 495. "Brother Joseph said it was the angel of the Lord who sank the boat." Pratt, *Autobiography*, 125.

53 ManH A-1, 496; *History of Jackson County*, 262–63; *HC*, 2:99–100.

54 Pratt, *Autobiography*, 123–24; JS and others to John Lincoln and others, June 21, 1834,

in *E&MS*, July 1834, 176; cf. *T&S*, Feb. 15, 1845, 804; *HC*, 2:121–22; Samuel Owens to Amos Reese, June 26, 1834, Phelps Collection. Joseph reported the outcome of the meeting to Governor Dunklin on June 26. A. S. Gilbert, William W. Phelps, and John Corrill to Daniel Dunklin, June 26, 1834, Phelps Collection.

55 *E&MS*, July 1834, 176; G. Smith, Memoirs, 38; *D&C* [1844], 102 (*D&C*, 105).

56 G. Smith, Memoirs, 38; Whitmer, *Book of John Whitmer*, 133; *D&C* [1844], 102:2–3, 5, 8–9 (*D&C*, 105:2–6, 8–9, 13–14, 16–17, 28–31). Joseph acknowledged that even faithful members wanted to engage the Jackson County citizenry. Kirtland High Council, Minutes, Feb. 14, 1835. See also McBride, Reminiscence, 2–3.

57 *D&C* [1844], 102:3, 2, 10, 11 (*D&C*, 105:10–11, 5, 33, 24–27, 38–39); ManH A-1, 503–504; *FWR*, 68–69, (June 23, 1834).

58 G. Smith, Memoirs, 38; ManH A-1, 509; *T&S*, Mar. 15, 1845, 840.

59 G. Smith, Memoirs, 41, 43; Jennings, "Army of Israel," 132–33; *T&S*, Mar. 15, 1845, 839.

60 *T&S*, Feb. 1, 1846, 1107; Whitney, *Life of Heber C. Kimball*, 60.

61 ManH A-1, 506, 505; *T&S*, Mar. 15, 1845, 839; G. Smith, Memoirs, 42.

62 JS to John Thornton, Alexander Doniphan, and David Atchison, June 25, 1834, in *T&S*, Feb. 1, 1846, 1106; G. Smith, Memoirs, 40, 50; Jennings, "Army of Israel," 134; *T&S*, Mar. 15, 1845, 840; ManH A-1, 525. The ledger of monies collected and dispersed for Zion's Camp is reproduced in Talbot, "Zion's Camp," 132–36.

63 G. Smith, Memoirs, 55, 51, 53–54, 57–58; ManH A-1, 526–29.

64 Brodie, *No Man Knows*, 159; *D&C* [1844], 102:7 (*D&C*, 105:23–24); *FWR*, 76, 78 (July 12, 31, 1834). P. A. M. Taylor calls Zion's Camp a "total failure" in his *Expectations Westward*, 16.

65 Launius, *Zion's Camp*, 167; Van Orden, "Zion's Camp," 206. For participants' reflections on the meaning of the march, see Zion's Camp Festival Papers. On the training for future leaders, see Alexander, "Woodruff and Zion's Camp," 130–46.

66 JS to Lyman Wight and others, Aug. 16, 1834, JSC. For an evaluation of Zion's Camp, see Esplin, "Emergence of Brigham Young," 119–24.

67 Kirtland High Council, Minutes, Aug. 11, 23, 28–29, 1834; *E&MS*, Aug. 1834, 182.

68 Kirtland High Council, Minutes, Aug. 28, 1834.

69 Kirtland High Council, Minutes, Aug. 29, 1834.

70 Kirtland High Council, Minutes, Aug. 29, 1834.

71 Kirtland High Council, Minutes, Aug. 11, 1834.

72 Kirtland High Council, Minutes, Aug. 29, 1834. Sylvester's statement is in *M&A*, Oct. 1834, 11.

73 JS to Lyman Wight and others, Aug. 16, 1834, JSC.

74 Kirtland High Council, Minutes, Aug. 23, 1834.

75 Hill, *Quest for Refuge*, 53; Quinn, *Origins of Power*, 85.

76 JS to Emma Smith, May 19, 1834; June 4, 1834, in *PWJS*, 341, 345–46.

CHAPTER 13 PRIESTHOOD AND CHURCH GOVERNMENT

1 JS to Lyman Wight and others, Aug. 16, 1834, JSC.

2 For examples, see *FWR*, 11–33 (Aug. 24; Sept. 1, 6, 12, 29; Oct. 1, 10–11, 21, 25–26; Nov. 1–2, 8–9, 11–13, 29, 1831).

3 *FWR*, 12, 15, 17–18 (Sept. 6; Oct. 10–11, 21, 1831).

4 Kirtland High Council, Minutes, Dec. 27–28, 1832. The revelation was *D&C* [1835], 7 (*D&C*, 88).

5 *FWR*, 33–38 (Nov. 29–30; Dec. 1, 6–7, 1831).

6 *FWR*, 71 (July 12, 1834). In November 1835 Joseph admitted his hasty judgment. "I

supposed I had established this church on a permanent foundation when I went to the Missouri and indeed I did so, for if I had been taken away it would have been enough, but I yet live, and therefore God requires more at my hands." JS, Journal, Nov. 12, 1835, in *PJS*, 2:76.

7   *D&C* [1835], 84:5 (*D&C*, 90:16).

8   Kirtland High Council, Minutes, Feb. 17, 12, 1834.

9   Kirtland High Council, Minutes, Mar. 28, 1835.

10 On the evolution of church government, see Prince, *Power from On High*; Quinn, *Origins of Power*; Esplin, "Emergence of Brigham Young."

11 *BofC*, 24:43 (*D&C*, 20:61–63); Faulring, "Organizing the Church," 60–69. On the duties of deacons, teachers, and priests during Joseph Smith's lifetime, see Hartley, "Aaronic Priesthood Offices," 85–89.

12 *BofC*, 24:6–7 (*D&C*, 20:5–8), with *D&C* [1835], 2:2 (*D&C*, 20:5–8).

13 *BofC*, 44:26–29 (*D&C*, 42:30–34). The office of bishop became attached to individual stakes in 1839. Beecher, "Office of Bishop," 104.

14 The number twelve for members of a council had been observed for nearly a year. Kirtland High Council, Minutes, June 21, 23, 1833. Right up to the eve of formally organizing the high council, priesthood holders of various ranks participated in councils. JS and Orson Hyde to J. G. Fosdick, Feb. 3, 1834, Cowdery Letter Book, 23–24.

15 Kirtland High Council, Minutes, Feb. 17, 1834.

16 *FWR*, 70–71 (July 3, 1834). For a discussion of the "nebulous" boundaries between these two high councils, see Howard, *Church Through the Years*, 1:256–58.

17 Bushman, *Making Space*, and chapter 11 supra.

18 Corrill, *Brief History*, 25.

19 *BofC*, 15:27–42 (*D&C*, 18:26–39).

20 Kirtland High Council, Minutes, Feb. 14–15, 1835.

21 Exodus 24:1, 11; Numbers 11:16; Luke 10:1, 17; Kirtland High Council, Minutes, Feb. 12, 21, 28, 1835; *D&C* [1835], 3:11 (*D&C*, 107:25); Young, *Organization of the Seventies*, 1–2. On the Seventy, see Baumgarten, "Function of the Seventies." On the Seventy as "apostles," see Quinn, *Origins of Power*, 68–69.

22 Kirtland High Council, Minutes, Feb. 27, May 2, 1835.

23 Quinn, "Sacral Power Structure," 12 (fig. 1). Within a year, by revelation and by practice, the Twelve's authority began to extend into the stakes. Prince, *Power from On High*, 61. On the Twelve Apostles, see Esplin, "Quorum of the Twelve," 54–84.

24 *D&C* [1835], 3:11 (*D&C*, 107:23).

25 Kirtland High Council, Minutes, Feb. 17, 1834; *D&C* [1835], 5:4–5 (*D&C*, 102:6, 8).

26 *HC*, 2:31.

27 Kirtland High Council, Minutes, Jan. 18; Feb. 14, 28, 1835. These themes are developed in Bushman, "Theology of Councils," 433–45.

28 *D&C* [1835], 5:10 (*D&C*, 102:23); *FWR*, 71–72 (July 7, 1834); JS to Brother Carter, Apr. 13, 1833, JSC.

29 Kirtland High Council, Minutes, Feb. 27, 1835.

30 JS to Brother Carter, Apr. 13, 1833, JSC; *BofC*, 59:33 (*D&C*, 58:26).

31 Woodford, "Historical Development," 3:1399, 1403. Michael Marquardt tentatively dates the revelation April 28–30, 1835. Marquardt, *Joseph Smith Revelations*, 267, n. 6.

32 *D&C* [1835], 3:14–15, 11 (*D&C*, 107:36, 37, 23).

33 *D&C* [1835], 4:3; 3:9 (*D&C*, 84:20, 19; 107:19).

34 JS to Brother Carter, Apr. 13, 1833, JSC; *D&C* [1835], 3:3 (*D&C*, 107:8).

35 *D&C* [1835], 3:31 (*D&C*, 107:65).

36 The references to the First Presidency in *Doctrine and Covenants* 68:16–21 do not appear in the version of that revelation printed in the *Evening and Morning Star* in October 1832. They do appear in the 1835 edition of the *Doctrine and Covenants*, pre-

sumably added to bring the revelation up-to-date. Woodford, "Historical Development," 2:855–56.

37 The priesthood quorums mentioned in the November 1831 revelation did not come into being for a number of years either. The first one known to be organized were the teachers in December 1834. "Teacher's Quorum Minutebook, Dec., 1834–Dec., 1845," cited in Prince, *Power from On High*, 51. A reference in Samuel Smith's diary suggests the possibility of quorums being organized in January 1832: "Presidents were chosen by the difrent grades of oficers to Preside over them according to the Holy order of God." Samuel Smith, Diary, Jan. 25, 1832, Lee Library; cited in Quinn, *Origins*, 40.

38 *D&C* [1835], 84:5; 3:3 (*D&C*, 90:13–16; 107:8).

39 *D&C* [1835], 5:13; 3:38–41 (*D&C*, 102:32; 107:85–89); *OED*, 2d ed., s.v. "quorum."

40 Stein, *Shaker Experience*, 43–45, 133–34.

41 *D&C* [1835], 3:2 (*D&C*, 107:5). For a comparison of the names of the temples in Zion and names on the Kirtland temple altars, see Quinn, *Origins of Power*, 50.

42 Vogel and Dunn, "Glossalalia," 11, 13–15, 18. Johnson, "Mormon Women's Letters," 77–107. On the predominance of patriarchy in the Hebrew Bible, see Fuchs, *Sexual Politics*. On women's role in early Mormonism, see Bradley, "Women's Engagement," 57–70; Newell and Avery, "Religious Life," 151–62.

43 *D&C* [1835], 3:8 (*D&C*, 107:16).

44 *D&C* [1835], 3:8–9, 32; 22:2 (*D&C*, 107:17–18, 70; 68:10–12); Marquardt, *Joseph Smith Revelations*, 171.

45 *D&C* [1835], 3:17–18 (*D&C*, 107:39–40); Ephesians 4:11. For efforts to understand the terminology, see Quinn, *Origins of Power*, 49. On the office of patriarch, see Bates and Smith, *Lost Legacy*.

46 Kirtland High Council, Minutes, Jan. 23, 1833.

47 JS, Journal, Nov. 19; Dec. 18, 1833, in *PJS*, 2:12–13, 15–17. On the relationship of family and Mormon priesthood, see Quinn, "Prosopographical Study," 125–76.

48 The dispute is over whether it was December 1833 or December 1834. The earlier date, until recently the most generally accepted, is based on an entry in December 18, 1833, by Oliver Cowdery in Joseph Smith Sr.'s patriarchal blessing book. Joseph Smith did not record the event in his history and mentioned it only in retrospect years later. ManH C-1, 20–21. Michael Quinn, the chief critic of the Dec. 18, 1833, date, points out that Joseph Sr. did not give blessings to his children until Dec. 9, 1834, a puzzling year-long lapse before exercising his office if he had been ordained a year earlier. Quinn, *Origins of Power*, 47. The traditional chronology is laid out by Bates and Smith, *Lost Legacy*, 34–37.

49 Patriarchal Blessings, Book A, 9.

50 Patriarchal Blessings, Book A, 1–2.

51 Patriarchal Blessings, Book A, 3; Woodruff, *Journals*, 1:109 (Nov. 27, 1836).

52 *T&S*, Mar. 1, 1842, 704 (Abraham 1:3); Bates and Smith, *Lost Legacy*, 34.

53 "Every father, after he has received his patriarchal blessing, is a Patriarch to his own family; and has the right to confer patriarchal blessings upon his family." *T&S*, June 1, 1845, 921.

54 *D&C* [1835], 2:16 (*D&C*, 20:65). Marquardt, *Joseph Smith Revelations*, 67.

55 *D&C* [1835], 3:11 (*D&C*, 107:22). Licenses for priesthood offices were granted "by the authority of this church." For examples, see Kirtland Elders' Certificates, 1836–38.

56 *D&C* [1835], 3:1 (*D&C*, 107:1–4).

57 *D&C* [1835], 4:2; 3:18–27, 3 (*D&C*, 84:6–17; 107:40–52, 8). For a textual analysis of the Melchizedek passages in the *Book of Mormon*, see Wright, "Transformation of Hebrews," 165–229. A rejoinder is Skousen, "Critical Methodology," 121–44.

58 Bushman, *King and People*, 176–210. The classic description of power in the eighteenth century is Bailyn, *Ideological Origins*.

59 *D&C* [1835], 3:37 (*D&C*, 107:82–84).

60 Corrill, *Brief History*, 24–25.

61 In one instance, Joseph had to bow to popular will when a conference insisted on sustaining Sidney Rigdon as a counselor in the First Presidency in 1843, contrary to Joseph's wishes. Van Wagoner, *Sidney Rigdon*, 323–24.

62 *D&C* [1835], 3:9; 4:3 (*D&C*, 107:18; 84:20).

63 *D&C* [1835], 3:11 (*D&C*, 107:30).

64 JS and others to the Church at Quincy, Mar. 20, 1839, in *PWJS*, 440–41 (*D&C*, 121:39, 41–42, 36).

65 JS to the Church at Quincy, Mar. 20, 1839, in *PWJS*, 440–41 (*D&C*, 121:39, 41–42, 36).

66 John Jay to George Washington, June 27, 1786, in Morison, *Sources*, 214–15.

67 *D&C* [1835], 3:9–11; 4:6 (*D&C*, 107:27, 18, 20; 84:35–38); Ketcham, *Presidents Above Party*.

68 JS to the Church at Quincy, Mar. 20, 1839, in *PWJS*, 441 (*D&C*, 121:41, 46).

69 Quoted in *Latter-day Saints' Millennial Star*, Nov. 15, 1851, 339.

70 JS to Lyman Wight and others, Aug. 16, 1834, JSC.

71 Hume, *Essays*, 42.

CHAPTER 14   VISITORS

1 JS, Journal, Sept. 22, 23, 1835, in *PJS*, 2:39, 105.

2 JS, Journal, Sept. 23, 1835, in *PJS*, 2:39, 41.

3 The entire article appears in Bennett, "Report," 356–63.

4 Thomas Shaw to the Saints of the Most High, Apr. 21, 1835, in *M&A*, May 1836, 316; Whitmer, *Book of John Whitmer*, 165.

5 The comparisons are elaborated upon in Lively, "Minority Millenarian Groups," 81–85.

6 Flegg, *Gathered Under Apostles*, 75, 47; Sandeen, *Roots of Fundamentalism*, 14–16. On Irving, see Oliphant, *Life of Edward Irving*, and Dallimore, *Charismatic Movement*. Carlyle's long tribute is in Carlyle, *Reminiscences*, 55–267.

7 Flegg, *Gathered Under Apostles*, 39; Dallimore, *Charismatic Movement*, 77; Sandeen, *Roots of Fundamentalism*, 3–41.

8 ManH A-1, in *PJS*, 1:279; Shaw, *Catholic Apostolic Church*, 25, 34–36, 51. On Irving's trial and condemnation, see Strachan, *Pentecostal Theology*, 151–201.

9 Shaw, *Catholic Apostolic Church*, 49–53, 78–79; Flegg, *Gathered Under Apostles*, 68–69.

10 Whitmer, *Book of John Whitmer*, 167; Kirtland High Council, Minutes, June 14–15, 1835; *Painesville Telegraph*, Feb. 26, 1836. In February 1836, two gentlemen from Scotland called on Joseph to inquire about the work of the Lord. JS, Journal, Feb. 28, 1836, in *PJS*, 2:180–81.

11 Sandeen, *Roots of Fundamentalism*, 3–58; Berlin, "Joseph S. C. F. Frey."

12 Garrison and DeGroot, *Disciples of Christ*, 207–18; Ahlstrom, *Religious History*, 445–52; Kenny, *Elias Smith*, 105–107, 139–49, 189–90.

13 *T&S*, Apr. 1842, 746. Mormon missionaries later had success among Irvingites in Canada. Underwood, *Millenarian World*, 136–37.

14 John 10:16; Ezekiel 37:15–20; Isaiah 29:4–14. Cf. *BofM*, 486, 67, 109–12 (3 Nephi 15:21–24; 2 Nephi 3:12; 2 Nephi 27).

15 Quincy, *Figures of the Past*, 383.

16 JS, Journal, Nov. 9, 1835, in *PJS*, 2:68.

17 JS, Journal, Nov. 10, 1835, in *PJS*, 2:74.

18 Johnson and Wilentz, *Kingdom of Matthias*, 3, 6, 172–73.

19 Matthias's story is brilliantly told in Johnson and Wilentz, *Kingdom of Matthias*, 49–164.

20 Thomas, *Mary Baker Eddy's Path*, 148–50, 172–300.

21 Quoted in Finney, *Memoirs*, 10.

22 Gerona, "Early American Quaker Dreams," and chapter 7 supra.

23 Turner, *Origins of Unbelief*, 141–67.

24 Kirtland High Council, Minutes, Apr. 21, 1834; Givens, *Viper on the Hearth*, 82–93; JS, Journal, Nov. 6, 1835, in *PJS*, 2:66; *BofM*, 111, 113, 130, 532, 536–37 (1 Nephi 27:23, 28:6; Jacob 4:8; Mormon 8:6, 9:11, 20); *BofC*, 10:11 (*D&C*, 11:25). The philosopher Richard Rorty, representing a modern mentality, has said that over the past three centuries we have learned that "the world does not speak. Only we do." Quoted in Delbanco, *Death of Satan*, 220.

25 *BofM*, 115–16 (2 Nephi 29:3–4, 9); *BofC*, 24:9–10 (*D&C*, 20:11); JS, Journal, Jan. 21, 1836, in *PJS*, 2:155.

CHAPTER 15   TEXTS

1   Porter, "William Earl McLellin," 295–324; McLellin, *Journals*, 174 (May 6, 1835).

2   McLellin, *Journals*, 174–75, 179, 182–83 (May 7, 24; June 7, 1835).

3   McLellin, *Journals*, 176–78, 180 (May 11, 14, 17–18, 1835); Porter, "William Earl McLellin," 296–97. Steven Harper, who studied the diaries of over fifty Mormon missionaries from the 1830s, concludes that "all the missionaries wrote of emphasizing the Book of Mormon" in their preaching. Harper, "Mormon Proselyting," 20, 26, n. 85.

4   JS to William W. Phelps, Jan. 14, 1833, in *PWJS*, 293.

5   *M&A*, Oct. 1834, 2.

6   Best, "Changes in the Revelations," 891; JS, Journal, Apr. 19, 1834, in *PJS*, 2:31. JS to Dear Brethren, June 15, 1835, JSC.

7   *D&C* [1835], preface; Kirtland High Council, Minutes, Sept. 24, 1834. For a description of the book's editing, see Marquardt, *Joseph Smith Revelations*, 3–19, and Howard, *Restoration Scriptures*, 149–66.

8   Underwood, "First Reference Guide," 120.

9   Campbell, *Christian System*, 11; Wood, "Evangelical America," 379; Higham, *Boundlessness to Consolidation*.

10 Lectures on Faith, in *D&C* [1835], 9, 36, 10, 26, 35, 41, 42, 55. The first five lectures sound nothing like Joseph Smith. Lectures 6 and 7 could possibly be his. For reproduction and commentary, see Dahl and Tate, *Lectures on Faith*. Noel Reynolds tentatively attributes them to Sidney Rigdon in "Authorship Debate," 355–82.

11 Kirtland High Council, Minutes, Aug. 17, 1835; *HC*, 2:245. The events leading up to the publication are detailed in Woodford, "Historical Development," 1:37–41, and Garrett, "Coming Forth," 89–103.

12 *FWR*, 111 (Apr. 24, 1837); Kirtland High Council, Minutes, Aug. 19, 1834; *D&C* [1835], preface; Whitmer, *All Believers*, 51. The objections of David Whitmer and others to the *Doctrine and Covenants* are summarized in Van Wagoner, *Sidney Rigdon*, 162–63.

13 Rough Draft Notes, ManH, Jan. 1, 1843. The theme of Joseph's creedlessness is developed in Hickman, "Romantic Theology."

14 *WJS*, 256 (Oct. 15, 1843); Best, "Changes in the Revelations," 92–101, 107–11; Woodford, "Revelations," 26–33. Chronological compilation returned in the 1876 edition of the *Doctrine and Covenants*. Crawley, *Descriptive Bibliography*, 278; Woodford, "Historical Development," 1:76–81, 95; 3:1835.

15   *WJS*, 184 (Apr. 8, 1843). On the centrifugal forces, see Arrington, "Centrifugal Tendencies," 165–77.

16   ManH B-1, 595; William W. Phelps to Sally Phelps, July 19–20, 1835, in Van Orden, "Kirtland Letters," 554–55. The exhibition notice in the March 27, 1835, issue of the *Painesville Telegraph* is reprinted in Larson, "Joseph Smith and Egyptology," 162–63.

17   Peterson, "Tombs of Egypt," 137–53; Peterson, "Antonio Lebolo," 15–20; Peterson, *Book of Abraham*, 53–63, 86–102; *M&A*, Dec. 1835, 233–37. Hugh Nibley believes Lebolo obtained mummies from an English traveler, Sir Frederick Henniker, not from his own excavations. Nibley, *Joseph Smith Papyri*, 3–4.

18   Albert Brown to James Brown, Nov. 1, 1835, in Brown, "Book of Abraham," 402–403. For a description of the mummies, see *M&A*, Dec. 1835, 233–35; Kimball, "Mormon Mummies," 84; Peterson, "Mormon Mummies," 128. Joseph Coe and Simeon Andrews each contributed $800; Joseph Smith raised the additional third through contributions. Joseph Coe to JS, Jan. 1, 1844, JSC.

19   JS, Journal, Oct. 1, 7; Nov. 17, 19, 24–26; Dec. 16, 1835, in *PJS*, 2:45, 50, 85, 87–88, 90, 106; Nibley, "Kirtland Egyptian Papers," 354–56; William W. Phelps to Sally Phelps, Sept. 11, 1835, in Van Orden, "Kirtland Letters," 563; Clark, *Story*, 145, 166–69; Gee, *Joseph Smith Papyri*, 4. Oliver Cowdery speculated in December 1835 that the translation would fill volumes. *M&A*, Dec. 1835, 236.

20   Whitmer, *Book of John Whitmer*, 167.

21   *M&A*, Dec. 1835, 236; JS, Journal, Oct. 3, 19, 24, 29; Nov. 17, 30; Dec. 7, 10, 12, 14, 16, 23, 1835; Jan. 12, 30; Feb. 3, 11, 17, 1836, in *PJS*, 2:46, 53, 56, 85, 92, 97, 101–104, 106, 120, 132, 167, 169, 173, 176; Quincy, *Figures of the Past*, 386–87; Peterson, *Book of Abraham*, 125–27, 191–202.

22   Genesis 11:27–32.

23   *T&S*, Mar. 1, 1842, 704–706 (Abraham 1:2); Mar. 15, 1842, 719 (Abraham 1:20; 2:1, 18, 20). On the names, see Gee and Ricks, "Case Study," 63–98.

24   *T&S*, Mar. 1, 1842, 704 (Abraham 1:1–3).

25   *T&S*, Mar. 1, 1842, 704–705 (Abraham 1:8–12, 15–17, 20).

26   *T&S*, Mar. 1, 1842, 705 (Abraham 1:21–27).

27   *E&MS*, Aug. 1832, [18] (Moses 7:8); *T&S*, Mar. 1, 1842, 705 (Abraham 1:21, 26).

28   Peterson, *Ham and Japheth*; Davis, *Slavery and Human Progress*; Jordan, *White over Black*; Genesis 9:25–27; Braude, "Sons of Noah," 103–42; Evans, "Strange Odyssey," 15–43.

29   *T&S*, Mar. 1, 1842, 705 (Abraham 1:26); Dain, *American Race Theory*, 105–108. The *Book of Mormon* mentions a "curse" resulting in a "skin of blackness," but the curse could be removed through righteous living. See Mauss, *All Abraham's Children*, 116–18. For an association of Ham with kingship, see Braude, "The Sons of Noah," 117, 131.

30   Ronald K. Esplin has identified circumstantial evidence and later accounts that implicate Joseph Smith in denial of the priesthood to blacks. "Priesthood Denial," 394–402.

31   Bush, "Mormonism's Negro Doctrine," 14, 16–17; JS, Journal, Jan. 14, 1836, in *PJS*, 2:137; *T&S*, Oct. 1840, 188. In 1836, Abel received a patriarchal blessing from Joseph Smith Sr. declaring him "ordained an Elder and annointed to secure thee against the power of the destroyer." Quoted in Bringhurst, "Elijah Abel," 24.

32   Quoted in JS, Journal, Jan. 2, 1843, in *APR*, 269. Joseph said on this occasion that he would "confine them by strict Laws to their own Species." In Nauvoo, Joseph fined black men who attempted to marry white women. Launius, *Invisible Saints*, 59–60.

33   *T&S*, May 15, 1844, 528; Acts 17:26.

34   *T&S*, Mar. 1, 1842, 705 (Abraham 1:28); *D&C* [1835], 4:2–3; 3:19–27 (*D&C*, 84:6–17, 107:42–52).

35   For a comparison with the tales about the Orient, see Collings, "Oriental Tale." For American foundation narratives, see Arac, "Narrative Forms," 605–777.

36 JS, Journal, Nov. 14, 1835, in *PJS*, 2:79.

37 The exact period of translation attempts is not known for sure, except that it occurred before 1837. Manuscripts in the hand of Warren Parrish, who apostatized in 1837, run into Abraham 2. William W. Phelps's comment to his wife in September 1835, about the translating being ended for the time being, suggests fall 1835. Joseph's journal notes days devoted to translation. Nibley, "Kirtland Egyptian Papers," 351, 355–56; William W. Phelps to Sally Phelps, Sept. 11, 1835, in Van Orden, "Kirtland Letters," 563; JS, Journal, Oct. 1; Nov. 19, 24, 1835, in *PJS*, 2:45, 87–88.

38 JS, Journal, Oct. 1, 1835, in *PJS*, 2:45; *BofC*, 8:3 (*D&C*, 9:8). Hugh Nibley worked out this explanation for the strange accumulation of documents inscribed with Egyptian characters and various attempted translations in the handwriting of the men around Joseph Smith in 1835–37. Nibley, "Kirtland Egyptian Papers," 350–99.

39 "Grammar & A[l]phabet of the Egyptian Language," Kirtland Egyptian Manuscripts.

40 For the story of the recovery, see Todd, *Book of Abraham*, 333–66. For color reproduction and discussion of the fragments, see Gee, *Joseph Smith Papyri*.

41 Heward and Tanner, "Abraham Identified," 93–95; Howard, "Book of Abraham," 91; Parker, "Joseph Smith Papyri," 86–88; Wilson, "Summary Report," 67–85; Ashment, "Reappraisal," 33–48; Nibley, "Response," 49–51; Ritner, "Breathing Permit," 161–80; Nibley, " 'Book of Breathings' " 153–87; Baer, "Breathing Permit," 109–34; Ashment, "Reducing Dissonance," 221–35; Thompson, "Egyptology," 143–60; Ashment, "Joseph Smith's Identification," 121–26; Ritner, "Thirty-four Years Later," 97–119.

42 Nibley has argued that the pictures in Egyptian texts do not necessarily correspond to the content nearby. The Book of Abraham facsimiles therefore do not positively prove the extant text corresponds to the translated text. Nibley, *Joseph Smith Papyri*, 2–3.

43 Parrish quote in Gee, "Eyewitness, Hearsay, and Physical Evidence," 203; Nibley, *Joseph Smith Papyri*, 47–51. For a meditation on Joseph Smith's translation, see Sandberg, "The Book of Abraham," 319–46.

44 Tvedtnes, Hauglid, and Gee, *Life of Abraham*, 49, 135–53.

45 Judkins, "Alchemical Imagination." The dictionary is Alexander, *Pocket Dictionary*, s.v. "Abram." For a detailed comparison of the Book of Abraham and the ancient stories of Abraham, see Tvedtnes, Hauglid, and Gee, *Life of Abraham*; Nibley, *Abraham in Egypt*; and Cook, "Tales of the Prophets," 127–46.

46 JS, Journal, Nov. 15, 1843, in *APR*, 427.

47 Seixas had taught Hebrew to Theodore Parker, the eminent Boston Unitarian preacher. Grodzins, *American Heretic*, 510, n. 26.

48 JS, Journal, Feb. 15, 17, 19, 1836, in *PJS*, 2:175–77; Seixas certificate for JS, Mar. 30, 1836, JSC. The story of the Hebrew school is given in Zucker, "Student of Hebrew," 41–55.

49 *BofC*, 7:4 (*D&C*, 8:11); JS, *New Translation*, 608 (Moses 6:5); 6:5; *T&S*, Mar. 1, 1842, 705 (Abraham 1:28, 31); *BofM*, 116 (2 Nephi 29:13).

50 *T&S*, Mar. 1, 1842, 709–10.

CHAPTER 16   STRIFE

1 Warren Parrish was called to be "the Lords Scribe, for the Lords Seer." JS, Journal, Nov. 14, 1835, in *PJS*, 2:79. For a description of this journal, see *PJS*, 2:38; on Parrish, see Jessee, "Joseph Smith's History," 446–49.

2 The honor culture prevailed among gentlemen in both the North and the South, though spoken with a different dialect. Freeman, *National Politics*, xvi, 168–70.

3 The classic analysis of the honor culture is Wyatt-Brown, *Southern Honor*. Wyatt-

Brown argues that the "ethical code" that remained strong in the antebellum South faded in the North, marked for example by the end of punishment by public shaming. The culture of honor was not obliterated, however. The "hill people" who lived on the outskirts of towns or in the deep backcountry were considered by residents of the center villages as almost a race apart—proud, stiff, crude, and hypersensitive. Bushman, *Refinement of America*, 379–80. For honor among the poor, see Gorn, *Manly Art*, 143; and Spierenburg, *Men and Violence*, 10. On Andrew Jackson, see Wyatt-Brown, "Andrew Jackson's Honor," 1–36. The culture of honor is widely distributed through time and space. Stewart, *Honor*.

4 Joseph's associates spoke the language of insult and honor with equal fluency. For a ripe example, see Warren Parrish's exchange with the Hebrew teacher Daniel Peixotto. JS, Journal, Jan. 18, 1836, in *PJS*, 2:149–52.

5 Kirtland High Council, Minutes, Sept. 19, 1835.

6 Benjamin F. Johnson to George S. Gibbs, Apr.–Oct. 1903, in LeBaron, *Benjamin Franklin Johnson*, 221. Luke Johnson said Joseph once kicked a Baptist minister into the street in Kirtland after he called Joseph "a hypocrite, a liar, and impostor and a false prophet." Joseph said, "I whipped him till he begged." *Latter-day Saints' Millennial Star*, Jan. 7, 1865, 7; JS, Journal, Jan. 1, 1843, in *APR*, 267. For more on Joseph's rebukes, see Bushman, "Character of Joseph Smith," 26–28.

7 Kirtland High Council, Minutes, Sept. 16, 1835.

8 Kirtland High Council, Minutes, Sept. 16, 1835.

9 *M&A*, Apr. 1837, 487; Kirtland High Council, Minutes, Sept. 16, 1835.

10 Kirtland High Council, Minutes, Aug. 4, 1835, JSC.

11 Quoted in Esplin, "Emergence of Brigham Young," 168.

12 Kirtland High Council, Minutes, Sept. 26, 1835; JS, Journal, Sept. 26, 1835, in *PJS*, 2:43.

13 Kirtland High Council, Loose Minutes, Aug. 4, 1835, JSC; JS, Journal, Nov. 3, 1835, in *PJS*, 2:63–64.

14 JS, Journal, Nov. 5, 12, 1835, in *PJS*, 65–66, 2:75; Kimball, Journal and Record, 30.

15 JS, Journal, Jan. 16, 1836, in *PJS*, 2:143–47.

16 JS, Journal, Jan. 16, 1836, in *PJS*, 2:147–48. To conclude the controversy, the writer of a letter against the Twelve, Warren Cowdery, apologized publicly. *M&A*, Feb. 1836, 263. The fall's controversies are described in detail in Esplin, "Emergence of Brigham Young," 166–87.

17 JS, Journal, Nov. 8, 1835, in *PJS*, 2:67–68.

18 JS, Journal, Jan. 6, 1836, in *PJS*, 2:129.

19 JS, Journal, Oct. 26, 1835, in *PJS*, 2:54; Bushman, "Farmers in Court," 388–413. For the legal exemptions, see *PJS*, 2:54–55, n. 1.

20 For William Smith, see Bates, "Problematic Patriarch," 11–23.

21 A year earlier, Heber Kimball had reduced Joseph to tears by telling a tale of his daughter escaping a threatened punishment by praying to God her mother's heart would relent. Journal History, Dec. 22, 1834.

22 Kirtland High Council, Minutes, Oct. 29, 1835; Wyatt-Brown, *Honor and Violence*, 36–37; JS, Journal, Oct. 29, 1835, in *PJS*, 2:59.

23 JS, Journal, Oct. 30–31, 1835, in *PJS*, 2:60–61.

24 JS, Journal, Nov. 3, 1835; Dec. 15, 17, 1835, in *PJS*, 2:64, 105–11.

25 JS, Journal, Nov. 18; Dec. 12, 16–18, 1835, in *PJS*, 2:86, 102, 106–107, 110, 115.

26 JS, Journal, Dec. 18, 1835, in *PJS*, 2:116; Kirtland High Council, Minutes, Dec. 28, 1835.

27 JS, Journal, Dec. 18–19, 1835, in *PJS*, 2:116–19.

28 JS, Journal, Jan. 1, 1836, in *PJS*, 2:125.

29 JS, Journal, Jan. 1, 1836, in *PJS*, 2:126. For William Smith's confession, see Kirtland High Council, Minutes, Jan. 2, 1835.

30   JS, Journal, Nov. 16, Dec. 18, 1835, in *PJS*, 2:80–84, 113; JS to the Church at Quincy, Mar. 20, 1839, in *PWJS*, 441.

31   JS, Journal, Jan. 17, 1836, in *PJS*, 2:149. Joseph was not alone in his desire for surcease. "To live and live beloved," John Winthrop wrote, "is the soul's paradise." Quoted in Delbanco, *American Dream*, 36.

32   JS, Journal, Dec. 10, 1835, in *PJS*, 2:99–100. On Joseph's benevolence, see Bushman, "Character of Joseph Smith," 31–33.

33   Kirtland High Council, Minutes, May 2, 1835.

34   *M&A*, Nov. 1835, 209; Sept. 1835, 179–82.

35   JS, Journal, Oct. 5, 29; Nov. 27, 1835, in *PJS*, 2:47, 58, 90.

36   JS, Journal, Sept. 24, 1835, in *PJS*, 2:42; Whitmer, *Book of John Whitmer*, 173.

37   JS to Hezekiah Peck and others, Aug. 31, 1835, in *PWJS*, 365–66; JS, Journal, Sept. 24, 1835, in *PJS*, 2:42; *HC*, 2:329.

38   Kirtland High Council, Loose Minutes, Aug. 4, 1835, JSC. The linkage had been evident for a year and a half. Oliver emphasized the interconnection in a letter to John Boynton in May 1834: "We want you to understand that the Lord has not promised to endow his servants from on high only on the condition that they build him a house; and if the house is not built the Elders will not be endowed with power, and if they are not they can never go to the nations with the everlasting gospel." Oliver Cowdery to John F. Boynton, May 6, 1834, Cowdery Letter Book.

39   George Hinkle to R. Ruben Middleton, Oct. 22, 1835, in Journal History, Oct. 22, 1835.

40   William Phelps to Sally Phelps, Sept. 16, 1835; Dec. 18, 1835, in Van Orden, "Kirtland Letters," 565, 569.

CHAPTER 17   THE ORDER OF HEAVEN

1   JS, Journal, Jan. 13, 1836, in *PJS*, 2:136; Matthew 17:4.

2   JS, Journal, Jan. 7, 9, 1836, in *PJS*, 2:130–31.

3   JS, Journal, Jan. 7, 1836, in *PJS*, 2:130; *D&C* [1835], 3:1 (*D&C*, 107:3).

4   *BioS*, 204; JS, Journal, Oct. 17, Nov. 8, Dec. 29, 1835, in *PJS*, 2:52, 68, 123; Newell and Avery, *Mormon Enigma*, 56.

5   JS, Journal, Oct. 30, Dec. 24, 1835, in *PJS*, 2:59–60, 120; *Journal of Discourses*, 1:215 (Oct. 9, 1852); Anderson, *Joseph Smith's Kirtland*, 48. On a paid ministry in the early years, see Quinn, *Extensions of Power*, 204–205.

6   JS, Journal, Dec. 9, 1835, in *PJS*, 2:97–98; Crosby, "Biographical Sketch," 75.

7   Backman, *Heavens Resound*, 138; Robison, *First Mormon Temple*, 78; JS, Journal, Nov. 12, 1835, in *PJS*, 2:75; Arrington, *Brigham Young*, 51. Tradition credits Mormon women with contributing glassware for the finish coat of stucco. Millett's son said people were sent to gather old crockery and glass from surrounding towns. Robison, *First Mormon Temple*, 79.

8   Crosby, "Biographical Sketch," 76–77; Robison, *First Mormon Temple*, 47; *M&A*, Oct. 1835, 207; JS, Journal, Jan. 11; Nov. 29, 1834; Sept. 23; Oct. 6; Nov. 27, 29; Dec. 4, 1835, in *PJS*, 2:19, 34–35, 41, 48–49, 91, 94–95. By 1836–37, Joseph and his co-signers' debt probably amounted to around $100,000. Hill, Rooker, and Wimmer, *Kirtland Economy*, 24–29.

9   Kimball, Journal and Record, 33; Robison, *First Mormon Temple*, 99. George A. Smith thought the cost was not less than $100,000. *Journal of Discourses*, 2:214 (Mar. 18, 1855). John Corrill said that "the cost was nearly $40,000." Corrill, *Brief History*, 21. The same figure was given by Truman Coe, an outside observer. Coe, "Description," 351.

10   The school began on November 2, the first Monday in November 1835. The move occurred on January 18, 1836. JS, Journal, Nov. 1–2, 1835; Jan. 18, 1836, in *PJS*,

2:62–63, 149; *D&C* [1835], 7:36–46; 92:3 (*D&C*, 88:119, 118–141; 95:17); Johnson, *Life's Review*, 15.

11 Backman, *Heavens Resound*, 276; Robison, *First Mormon Temple*; JS, Journal, Jan. 4, 1836, in *PJS*, 2:128–29. On the singing school, see Hicks, *Mormonism and Music*, 39–40.

12 *BofC*, 40:28 (*D&C*, 38:32); *D&C* [1835], 4:3–4; 95:2 (*D&C*, 84:20–25; 95:8). Cf. *BofC*, 45:16 (*D&C*, 43:16); Oliver Cowdery to J. G. Fosdick, Feb. 4, 1834, Cowdery Letter Book.

13 Kirtland High Council, Minutes, Feb. 15, 1835; *M&A*, Feb. 1835, 69; JS, Journal, Oct. 5, 1843; Dec. 15, 1835; Jan. 13, 11, 24, 1836, in *PJS*, 2:47–48, 106, 132, 161. Cf. *Journal of Discourses*, 19:16, 18–19 (May 20, 1877); Post, *Treatise*, 9.

14 JS, Journal, Nov. 12, 1835, in *PJS*, 2:76–77. The term "solemn assembly" came from Joel 1:14: "Sanctify ye a fast, call a solemn assembly, gather the elders and all the inhabitants of the land into the house of the Lord your God, and cry unto the Lord." The words were then repeated in Joseph's revelations. *D&C* [1835], 7:19; 95:1; *M&A*, Mar. 1836, 277–78 (*D&C*, 88:70; 95:7; 109:6, 10).

15 Backman, *Heavens Resound*, 149; *HC*, 1:400; *Journal of Discourses*, 1:133–35 (Apr. 6, 1853). The nearest models available to Joseph were Masonic cornerstone ceremonies, occasions featuring an array of emblematic objects. Bullock, *Freemasonry*, 137.

16 *D&C* [1835], 3:11–15 (*D&C*, 107:21–37).

17 Kirtland High Council, Minutes, Aug. 17, 1835; Jan. 13, 1836; *HC*, 2:244–46; JS, Journal, Jan. 13, 1836, in *PJS*, 2:132–36; William W. Phelps to Sally Phelps, Jan. 1836, in Van Orden, "Kirtland Letters," 576. Joseph apparently intended to require this cumbersome procedure for all Church appointments; in mid-February, a resolution required the unanimous voice of "the several bodies that constitute this quorum who are appointed to do church business in the name of said church." JS, Journal, Jan. 15; Feb. 12; March 3, 17, 1836, in *PJS*, 2:139–40, 174–75, 182–85, 189; Partridge, Diary, Jan. 15, 1836.

18 *Journal of Discourses*, 2:215 (Mar. 18, 1855); Newell and Avery, "Religious Life of Women," 151–62.

19 JS, Journal, Jan. 20, 1836, in *PJS*, 2:153–54. Historians have disputed the authority of Joseph Smith to perform a wedding without a license, but Ohio law recognized marriages performed according to the regulations of a religious society. For a discussion of the laws and the debate, see Bradshaw, "Marriages in Ohio," 23–69.

20 Kirtland High Council, Minutes, Jan. 12, 15, 1836; JS, Journal, Jan. 14–15, 1836, in *PJS*, 2:136–40.

21 Exodus 25:22; 1 Kings 8:1–8. For the urge to create sacred space in churches, see Buggeln, *Connecticut's Churches*, 136–42, 154–56.

22 These confessions came the day after Joseph's meeting with the Twelve when their differences had been aired. See Esplin, "Emergence of Brigham Young," 183–86.

23 JS, Journal, Jan. 17, 1836, in *PJS*, 2:149; William W. Phelps to Sally Phelps, Jan. 1836, in Van Orden, "Kirtland Letters," 576. Cf. Cowdery, " 'Sketch Book,' " 416 (Jan. 17, 1836).

24 Kirtland High Council, Minutes, Jan. 22–23, 1833; John 13:4–11. Baptists practiced feet-washing; Sidney Rigdon had been involved in the ceremony while he was a Baptist preacher. Van Wagoner, *Sidney Rigdon*, 173.

25 JS, Journal, Jan. 21, 1836, in *PJS*, 2:155–56. Joseph implied that they washed their entire bodies, and John Corrill reported the same. Corrill, *Brief History*, 23. Orson Pratt later said the washings included hands, faces, and feet. *Journal of Discourses*, 19:16 (May 20, 1877).

26 JS, Journal, Jan. 21, 1836, in *PJS*, 2:156; Cowdery, " 'Sketch Book,' " 416, 418–19 (Jan. 16, 21, 1836); Partridge, Diary, Jan. 21, 1836.

27   Roman Catholics had practiced washing of feet from an early time. Maundy Thursday was appointed for washing of feet. Ahaus, "Orders," 11:282–83; Thurston, "Washing," 15:557. On the Shaker feasts, see Stein, *Shaker Experience*, 176–77.

28   Exodus 30:22–30, 40:12–15; Cowdery, " 'Sketch Book,' " 419 (Jan. 21, 1836). Cf. Snow, Dec. 15, 1836, Journal and Letterbook.

29   JS, Journal, Jan. 21, 1836, in *PJS*, 2:157–58. Cf. Cowdery, "Sketch Book," 419 (Jan. 21, 1836).

30   Partridge, Diary, Jan. 21, 1836; JS, Journal, Jan. 21, 1836, in *PJS*, 2:159.

31   JS, Journal, Jan. 22, 1836, in *PJS*, 2:159; Partridge, Diary, Jan. 22, 1836. Joseph may not have seen that some were disappointed when they failed to experience the manifestations. William McLellin claimed to see nothing of spiritual importance. Porter, "William Earl McLellin," 320. Thomas Marsh, the head of the Twelve Apostles, later appointed a time when the Twelve were to demand a visit of an angel by sheer force of will—without success. Cowdery, " 'Sketch Book,' " 420 (Jan. 23, 1836); Woodruff, *Journals*, 5:297 (Feb. 23, 1859).

32   For a more elaborate summary of the procedures, see Cook, *Revelations of the Prophet*, 216–17. Other more modest accounts of the ordinances can be found in Whitmer, *Book of John Whitmer*, 173–75; Kirtland Elders' Quorum, *Record*, 3–12, 26, 28, 30 (Jan. 1, 4, 8, 11, 19; Feb. 2, 9, 16, 17, 18, 19; Mar. 1836); Lyman Wight to Wilford Woodruff, Aug. 24, 1857; Cowdery, " 'Sketch Book,' " 420–22 (Jan. 25; Feb. 6, 1836).

33   JS, Journal, Jan. 27, 1836, in *PJS*, 2:160. Edward Partridge said the tongues lasted for ten or fifteen minutes. Partridge, Diary, Jan. 22, 1836.

34   JS, Journal, Jan. 28, 1836, in *PJS*, 2:163–64; Kirtland Elders' Quorum, *Record*, 4 (Jan. 28, 1836); Corrill, *Brief History*, 23.

35   The priests, teachers, and deacons were anointed in late January. Partridge, Diary, Jan. 26, 1836.

36   JS, Journal, Jan. 30, 1836, in *PJS*, 2:167.

37   Cowdery, " 'Sketch Book,' " 416 (Jan. 17, 1836); *M&A*, Jan. 1836, 256.

38   William W. Phelps to Sally Phelps, Jan. 1836, in Van Orden, "Kirtland Letters," 574. The accounts of the anointings frequently mention purification or sanctification. Cowdery, " 'Sketch Book,' " 420 (Jan. 24, 1836); Kirtland Elders' Quorum, *Record*, 31 (Jan. 25, 1836).

39   Later the elders straightened themselves out and were blessed spiritually. Kirtland Elders' Quorum, *Record*, 6 (Feb. 6, 1836). Cowdery reported that "many saw visions, many prophesied, and many spoke in tongues." Cowdery, " 'Sketch Book,' " 422 (Feb. 6, 1836). JS, Journal, Feb. 6, 1836, in *PJS*, 2:169–71; Kirtland Elders' Quorum, *Record*, 6 (Feb. 6, 1836).

40   JS, Journal, Feb. 7, 1836, in *PJS*, 2:170.

41   JS, Journal, Mar. 2, 4, 9, 14, 16, 24, 1836, in *PJS*, 2:182, 185, 187, 189, 191; *HC*, 2:413, 416, 417, 427; Hicks, *Mormonism and Music*, 18–23; Crawley, *Descriptive Bibliography*, 59.

42   JS, Journal, Mar. 27, 1836, in *PJS*, 2:192–93.

43   *PJS*, 2:193, n. 1; JS, Journal, Mar. 27, 1836, in *PJS*, 2:191; Post, Journal, Mar. 27, 1836; Woodford, "Historical Development," 3:1441. Children attended too. Madsen, *Joseph Smith*, 72.

44   JS, Journal, Mar. 27, 23, 1836, in *PJS*, 2:194–95. Joseph's journal does not mention the sustaining of the high priests, possibly an oversight.

45   In the *Messenger and Advocate* account of the dedication, the substance of Sidney Rigdon's talk was given at some length. *M&A*, Mar. 1836, 275–77, 281.

46   Woodford, "Historical Development," 3:1440; Cowdery, " 'Sketch Book,' " 426 (Mar. 19, 1836), mentions Sidney Rigdon, Hyrum Smith, Warren Parrish, and Oliver and Warren Cowdery.

47   *M&A*, Mar. 1836, 278–80 (*D&C*, 109:12, 35–36, 25–26, 39, 47, 76).

48 JS, Journal, Mar. 27, 1836, in *PJS*, 2:203; Taves, *Experiencing Religion*, 111–14; Partridge, Diary, Mar. 27, 1836; *M&A*, Mar. 1836, 281; Post, Journal, March 27, 28, 1836; Cowdery, " 'Sketch Book,' " 426 (Mar. 27, 1836). Cf. *Journal of Discourses*, 11:10 (Nov. 15, 1864); Acts 2:2–3.

49 JS, Journal, Mar. 29, 1836, in *PJS*, 2:203.

50 JS, Journal, Mar. 29, 1836, in *PJS*, 2:204–205; Partridge, Diary, Mar. 29, 1836.

51 Post, Journal, Mar. 30, 1836; Corrill, *Brief History*, 23.

52 JS, Journal, Mar. 30, 1836, in *PJS*, 2:207.

53 David Whitmer said much later, in 1886, that the endowment "was a grand fizzle," a "trumped-up yarn." *Omaha Herald*, Oct. 17, 1886, in Whitmer, *Interviews*, 204–205. Their views are counterbalanced by many more who reported the events in their diaries and reminiscences. Buerger, *Mormon Temple Worship*, 20–34; Harper, "Temple Experience," 327–71; Bradley and Woodward, *4 Zinas*, 61–62; Tullidge, *Women of Mormondom*, 94–95; Madsen, *Joseph Smith*, 76–79. Lucy Smith called the experiences "the endowment." PreM, 594. The meaning for later Mormons was summed up by Orson Pratt in 1875. *Journal of Discourses*, 18:132 (Oct. 9, 1875).

54 *The Return*, June 1889, 90–91; JS, Journal, Mar. 30, 1836, in *PJS*, 2:206–207.

55 A Congregationalist minister, Thomas Upham, wrote in 1845 that "the love of manifestations, of that which is visible and tangible," was "one of the evils of the present age." Upham, *Life of Faith*, 153.

56 Emerson, "Divinity School Address," in *Works*, 347. In 1836, a sensational year for Transcendentalist publications, Emerson published *Nature;* George Ripley published *Discourses on the Philosophy of Religion;* Orestes Brownson published *New Views of Christianity, Society, and Church;* Bronson Alcott published *Conversations with Children on the Gospels.*

57 Stein, *Shaker Experience*, 167–81; Numbers, *Ellen G. White*, 14–21. Finney explored his perfectionist ideas in *Lectures to Professing Christians* (1837). See also Hirrel, *New School Calvinism.*

58 JS, Journal, Mar. 30, Apr. 2, 1836, in *PJS*, 2:206, 208. On the Thursday after the March 27 dedication, a second dedication was conducted for the overflow. JS, Journal, Mar. 31, 1836, in *PJS*, 2:207–208.

59 Other spiritual meetings succeeded the great revelation of April 3. Kimball, Journal and Record, 36; Woodruff, *Journals*, 5:120 (Nov. 8, 1857).

60 JS, Journal, Apr. 3, 1836, in *PJS*, 2:209–210.

61 Woodford, "Historical Development," 3:1460–61.

62 Malachi 4:5–6. On traditions of Elijah, see Ricks, "Jewish Passover," 483–86. On the opacity of Elijah's keys in 1836, see Prince, *Power from On High*, 35–36.

63 Moses, Elias, and Elijah are not named in the brief summary of angelic visitors (*T&S*, Oct. 1, 1842, 936; *D&C*, 128:20–21), nor did the revelation appear in the *Doctrine and Covenants* in Joseph's lifetime. Joseph said nothing about the visit of Elijah, even when teaching about Elijah's mission. *WJS*, 43 (Oct. 5, 1840), 318 (Jan. 21, 1844), 327–36 (Mar. 10, 1844).

64 George A. Smith said later of the temple dedication: "If the Lord had on that occasion revealed one single sentiment more, or went one step further to reveal more fully the law of redemption, I believe He would have upset the whole of us." *Journal of Discourses*, 2:215 (Mar. 18, 1855).

CHAPTER 18 REVERSES

1 For the apostate critics, see Parkin, "Mormons in Ohio," 89–133.

2 Oliver Cowdery to Warren A. Cowdery, Jan. 21, 1838, Cowdery Letter Book.

3   *Susquehannah Register, and Northern Pennsylvanian*, May 1, 1834, in *EMD*, 4:296–97.

4   *D&C* [1835], 101:4; Foster, *Communal Experiments*. For the next couple of years, the question of polygamy was thrown up to the Mormons and repeatedly denied. It was "daily and hourly asked by all classes of people," the *Elders' Journal* complained. "Do the Mormons believe in having more wives than one?" *Elders' Journal*, Nov. 1837, 28; July 1838, 43; *M&A*, May 1837, 511.

5   Quoted in Foster, *Religion and Sexuality*, 81; *M&A*, May 1837, 511.

6   *FWR*, 163 (Apr. 12, 1838).

7   *FWR*, 167, 169 (Apr. 12, 1838).

8   Oliver Cowdery to JS, Jan. 21, 1838, quoted in Oliver Cowdery to Warren A. Cowdery, Jan. 21, 1838, Cowdery Letter Book.

9   *FWR*, 120, 167–68 (Nov. 6, 1837; Apr. 12, 1838). Cf. *Elders' Journal*, July 1838, 45. David Patten testified that Cowdery once claimed that "Joseph told him, he [Joseph] had confessed to Emma." *FWR*, 167 (Apr. 12, 1838).

10   Oliver Cowdery to Warren A. Cowdery, Jan. 21, 1838, Cowdery Letter Book.

11   In an 1842 affidavit, Fanny Brewer, who left the Church during the troubles of 1837 and 1838, referred to "much excitement against the Prophet" in those years. There were rumors of "an unlawful intercourse between himself and a young orphan girl residing in his family and under his protection." Quoted in Brotherton, *Mormonism*, 10.

12   In 1872, William E. McLellin told Joseph Smith III that he repeated the rumors about Joseph being discovered with Fanny Alger in a barn to Emma Smith, and she corroborated the stories. William E. McLellin to Joseph Smith III, July 1872. *Saints' Herald*, Oct. 1, 1879, 289. Todd Compton, the most thorough student of Joseph Smith's plural wives, discounts McLellin's story because it contradicts the accounts of Chauncey Webb and Emma Smith's later statements on polygamy. Compton, *In Sacred Loneliness*, 35. When McLellin joined the Mormons, a revelation warned: "Commit not adultery, a temptation with which thou hast been troubled." *D&C* [1835], 74:5 (*D&C*, 66:10).

13   Young, *Wife No. 19*, 66–67; the elder Webb quoted in Wyl, *Joseph Smith*, 57.

14   Hancock, Autobiography, 61–64. For the reliability of the Hancock account, see Compton, "Mormonism's First Plural Wife?," 183–88.

15   Young, *Wife No. 19*, 66–67; Walker, *Diary*, 1:349 (July 26, 1872); Benjamin F. Johnson to George S. Gibbs, Apr.–Oct. 1903, in LeBaron, *Benjamin Franklin Johnson*, 225. On Ann Eliza Young's birth date, see Compton, *In Sacred Loneliness*, 645.

16   Compton, *In Sacred Loneliness*, 4, 33; Revelation, July 12, 1843, Revelations Collection (*D&C*, 132:1); Bachman, "Plural Marriage," 67, 71–72. According to Mosiah Hancock, his father learned about plural marriage from the Prophet in 1832. Hancock, Autobiography, 61. Brigham Young is quoted as saying that Joseph and Cowdery had the doctrine revealed to them while translating the Book of Mormon—locating it in 1829. Walker, *Diary*, 1:349 (July 26, 1872). Joseph Bates Noble put it during the time when the Bible was being revised, between 1831 and 1833. Bachman, "Plural Marriage," 61. Lyman Johnson, who knew Joseph well while the Smiths stayed at his parents' house in Hiram, Ohio, in 1831 and 1832, told Orson Pratt that "Joseph had made known to him as early as 1831 that plural marriage was a correct principle." *Latter-day Saints' Millennial Star*, Dec. 16, 1878, 788. William Phelps wrote to Brigham Young in 1861 that in 1831 Joseph had advocated marriage to Native American women as second wives on the same basis. Bachman, "Plural Marriage," 68–70. In 1905, Mary Elizabeth Rollins Lightner said that Joseph had told her in 1842 that God had commanded him in 1834 to take her as a plural wife. "He said *I* was the first woman God commanded him." Lightner to Emmeline B. Wells, Summer 1905, Lightner Collection. The evidence for an early revelation on plural marriage is summarized in Compton, *In Sacred Loneliness*, 26–27.

17   Quoted in Hancock, Autobiography, 61. Joseph did tell Levi Hancock, "I love Fanny." Hancock, Autobiography, 63.

18 Compton, *In Sacred Loneliness*, 39–41.

19 JS, Journal, Mar. 29, 1836, in *PJS*, 2:203–204.

20 *M&A*, Aug. 1836, 353–54.

21 Filler, *Crusade Against Slavery*, 71–81, 97–100; Stauffer, *Radical Abolitionists*, 100; *M&A*, Apr. 1836, 289–91.

22 *M&A*, Aug. 1836, 354–55. John Corrill's cool analysis was that Clay County objected to the Mormons "either because they hated our religion, or were afraid we would become a majority, or for some other cause, I know not what (for the Mormons had committed no crime)." Corrill, *Brief History*, 26.

23 *M&A*, Aug. 1836, 359–61; Sidney Rigdon and others to John Thornton and others, July 25, 1836, in *M&A*, Aug. 1836, 355–59.

24 ManH B-1, 748; Parkin, "Clay County," 260; Sidney Rigdon and others to John Thornton, July 25, 1836, in *M&A*, Aug. 1836, 359; *Deseret News*, Dec. 25, 1852 (*D&C*, 111:2).

25 For an account that puts the Salem trip in the context of Joseph's quests for treasure, see Quinn, *Early Mormonism*, 261–64.

26 *The Return*, July 1889, 105–106; Godfrey, "More Treasures than One," 196–99; *Deseret News*, Dec. 25, 1852 (*D&C*, 111:2, 4, 10); Proper, "Joseph Smith and Salem," 93–94; ManH B-1, 749; Guest Register Book, Aug. 9, 1836, East India Marine Society; JS to Emma Smith, Aug. 19, 1836, in *PWJS*, 390.

27 *M&A*, Apr. 1827, 488; Heber C. Kimball, Journal and Record, 33; Kirtland High Council, Minutes, June 16, 1836. John Corrill thought the debt was more like fifteen to twenty thousand dollars. Corrill, *Brief History*, 26.

28 Backman, *Heavens Resound*, 139; *M&A*, Jan. 1837, 443.

29 Corrill, *Brief History*, 26–27. Debt figures have been compiled from court records where Joseph was sued for nonpayment. The exact total from these sources comes to $102,307.81. Hill, Rooker, and Wimmer, *Kirtland Economy*, 27–35.

30 The argument for the debt's rationality is made in Hill, Rooker, and Wimmer, *Kirtland Economy*.

31 Backman, *Heavens Resound*, 314; *M&A*, Sept. 1836, 375; ManH B-1, 750; Van Wagoner, *Sidney Rigdon*, 182. Four million dollars was the capitalization of the anti-banking company organized on January 2, 1837. *M&A*, Jan. 1837, 441. The largest bank in the state had only $2 million capitalization. Adams, "Kirtland Bank," 477.

32 S. Kimball, *Heber C. Kimball*, 40. On land banks in Connecticut, see Bushman, *Puritan to Yankee*, 124–34.

33 Adams, "Kirtland Bank," 467–82. Marvin Hill suggests that Whigs in the Ohio legislature were rejecting bank proposals from Democrats. Hill, *Quest for Refuge*, 56. The Mormons attributed the refusal to religious prejudice. *Journal of Discourses*, 13:106–107 (Oct. 9, 1868).

34 *M&A*, Jan. 1837, 441; Fielding, "Mormon Economy," 351; Backman, *Heavens Resound*, 317.

35 *Painesville Telegraph*, Jan. 19, 1837; Backman, *Heavens Resound*, 317; Van Wagoner, *Sidney Rigdon*, 185; Hill, Rooker, and Wimmer, *Kirtland Economy*, 76–80; Sampson and Wimmer, "Kirtland Safety Society," 428; *M&A*, Aug. 1837, 560. The Mormons applied to the Ohio legislature for a second charter on February 10, 1837, also without success. Adams, "Kirtland Bank," 477–79.

36 Van Wagoner, *Sidney Rigdon*, 186.

37 Backman, *Heavens*, 322; ManH B-1, 761; *Journal of Discourses*, 13:106 (Oct. 8–9, 1868); Crosby, Autobiography, in Godfrey, Godfrey, and Derr, *Women's Voices*, 55; Woodruff, *Journals*, 1:138 (Apr. 9, 1837). A table of suits is in Hill, Rooker, and Wimmer, *Kirtland Economy*, 30–33. See also Firmage and Mangrum, *Zion in the Courts*, 56–58.

38 Backman, *Heavens Resound*, 320; Crosby, "Biographical Sketch," 76–77.

39   Crosby, "Biographical Sketch," 76–77; *M&A*, Apr. 1837, 488; Woodruff, *Journals*, 1:134 (Apr. 6, 1837); Hill, *Quest for Refuge*, 55; Boorstin, *National Experience*, 115–23, 161–68; Heber C. Kimball, Journal and Record, 40; Corrill, *Brief History*, 27.

40   *Lisbon* (Ohio) *Aurora*, Jan. 19, 1837; Woodruff, *Journals*, 1:108 (Nov. 25, 1836); Kimball, Journal and Record, 39–40; *M&A*, Apr. 1837, 488.

41   Woodruff, *Journals*, 5:63 (June 25, 1857); Williams, "Frederick Granger Williams," 256–57. The best account of dissent in Kirtland is Esplin, "Emergence of Brigham Young," 281–307. See also Hill, "Cultural Crises," 286–97; PreM, 596–97; *Journal of Discourses*, 4:108; 11:11 (Nov. 15, 1864).

42   *Journal of Discourses*, 11:11 (Nov. 15, 1864). Milton Backman notes that none of the bank's largest shareholders and only eight percent of all shareholders left the Church. Backman, "Kirtland Temple," 221.

43   Jessee, "Kirtland Diary," 365–69; Woodruff, *Journals*, 1:5–6 [ca. Dec. 1833]. On Woodruff, see Alexander, *Wilford Woodruff*.

44   Woodruff, *Journals*, 1:107 (Nov. 25, 1836).

45   Woodruff, *Journals*, 1:113–14 (Dec. 31, 1836); *M&A*, Jan. 1837, 440–41.

46   Woodruff, *Journals*, 1:107, 109–11 (Nov. 25, 27; Dec. 1, 18, 1836).

47   Woodruff, *Journals*, 1:112–13, 118–19 (Dec. 20, 27, 1836; Jan. 3, 1837).

48   Woodruff, *Journals*, 1:111–12, 119–20 (Dec. 5, 19–20, 1836; Jan. 4, 6, 1837).

49   Woodruff, *Journals*, 1:120–21, 123 (Jan. 5, 8, 16, 24, 1837).

50   Woodruff, *Journals*, 1:111, 121–22 (Dec. 11, 1836; Jan. 10, 15, 17, 1837).

51   Woodruff, *Journals*, 1:125 (Feb. 19, 26, 1837).

52   Woodruff, *Journals*, 1:122–27 (Jan. 22–23, 28; Mar. 4, 23–24, 1837).

53   Woodruff, *Journals*, 1:128–29 Mar. 23; Apr. 3, 1837).

54   Woodruff, *Journals*, 1:129 (Apr. 14, 1837).

55   Woodruff, *Journals*, 1:132–33 (Apr. 6, 1837). For another account of the April 6 meetings, see *M&A*, Apr. 1837, and First Council of the Seventy, Minutes, Apr. 6, 1837.

56   Woodruff, *Journals*, 1:134, 138 (Apr. 6, 19, 1837).

57   Woodruff, *Journals*, 1:138–39 (Apr. 9, 1837).

58   Woodruff, *Journals*, 1:146–48 (Apr. 20; May 28, 1837). Parrish later said that Joseph and Rigdon "lie by revelation, swindle by revelation, cheat and defraud by revelation, run away by revelation, and if they do not men[d] their ways, I fear they will at last be damned by revelation." *Painesville Republican*, Feb. 15, 1838.

59   For a general analysis using sociological terminology, see Jorgensen, "Mormon Fissiparousness," 15–39.

60   Parley P. Pratt to JS, May 22, 1837, in *Zion's Watchman*, Mar. 24, 1838; Complaint, Lyman E. Johnson and Orson Pratt, May 29, 1837, Whitney Collection.

61   Kirtland High Council, Minutes, May 29, 1837.

62   Firmage and Mangrum, *Zion in the Courts*, 55–56; Pratt, *Autobiography*, 138–39; *Painesville Telegraph*, June 9, 30, 1837. On Newell, see Parkin, "Mormon Political Involvement," 498–501, and Adams, "Newell's Obsession," 159–88. On Denton's service to Joseph, see JS, Journal, Nov. 22, 1838, in *PJS*, 2:15.

63   Mary Fielding to Mercy Fielding, [June 15, 1837], Mary Fielding Smith Collection.

64   Mary Fielding to Mercy Fielding Thompson, July 8, 1837, Mary Fielding Smith Collection.

65   Mary Fielding to Mercy Fielding Thompson, July 8, 1837, Mary Fielding Smith Collection.

66   Jensen and Thorp, *Victorian Britain*, xi; Esplin, "Thomas B. Marsh," 179; *D&C* [1844], 104:11, 9 (*D&C*, 112:27–28, 24).

67   William W. Phelps to Dear Brother, July 7, 1837, in *M&A*, July 1837, 529; Kirtland High Council, Minutes, Sept. 17, 1837; Mary Fielding to Mercy Fielding Thompson and Robert Thompson, Oct. 7, 1837, Mary Fielding Smith Collection; Esplin, "Emer-

gence of Brigham Young," 300. Newel K. Whitney, Reynolds Cahoon, and Vinson Knight to the Saints Scattered Abroad, Sept. 18, 1837, in *M&A*, Sept. 1838, 563.

68 ManH B-1, 767; Esplin, "Emergence of Brigham Young," 292–93. A mob attacked the Canada party on their return and put them in jail. With the connivance of the Mormon housekeeper, Joseph and Rigdon escaped together. Mary Fielding to Mercy Thompson, [Sept. 1837], Mary Fielding Smith Collection.

69 Snow, *Lorenzo Snow*, 20–21; *The State of Ohio vs. Joseph Smith Sen. and Others*, Aug. 14, 1837, Cowdery Court Docket. The Church leaders were acquitted. The August date for the Parrish skirmish is fixed by a reference in a letter from Mary Fielding to Mercy Thompson, [Sept.] 1837, which speaks of "a terrible stir with Wm. Parish." This chronology was first worked out in Esplin, "Emergence of Brigham Young," 293–98.

70 Snow, *Lorenzo Snow*, 20; Kirtland High Council, Minutes, Sept. 3, 1837. Brigham Young later said he packed the front seats with sympathetic members just to be sure. Esplin, "Emergence of Brigham Young," 296.

71 Kirtland High Council, Minutes, Sept. 3, 1837; JS, Journal, Mar. 13, 1838, in *PJS*, 2:218.

72 JS, Journal, Mar. 13, 1838, in *PJS*, 2:219–20; Romig, "David Whitmer," 34–36. Joseph wanted to keep Williams in the First Presidency but the congregation refused. Hyrum Smith was sustained in his place. *FWR*, 122 (Nov. 7, 1837).

73 The "old standard" group's choice of the first name of the Church, "the Church of Christ," may have influenced the expansion of the Church's name to the "Church of Jesus Christ of Latter Day Saints" in April 1838. *Elders' Journal*, July 1838, 37; Aug. 1838, 52 (*D&C*, 115:3–4). George A. Smith later said the dissenters wanted to strip away all but the bare fundamentals. "Their plan was to take the doctrines of the Church, such as repentance, baptism for the remission of sins, throw aside the Book of Mormon, the Prophet and priesthood, and go and unite the whole Christian world under these doctrines." *Journal of Discourses*, 11:11 (Nov. 15, 1864). For attempts to discipline them, see Kirtland High Council, Minutes, Oct. 22, Nov. 1, 1837.

74 *Journal of Discourses*, 11:11 (Nov. 15, 1864); Crosby, Autobiography, in Godfrey, Godfrey, and Derr, *Women's Voices*, 56. In addition to the Parrish faction, a Colin Brewster had claimed a visit of Moroni and the power to translate from the Book of Mormon. Vogel, "James Colin Brewster," 120–39. Lucy Smith said a young seer, Adaline Bernard, told the dissenters Joseph was in transgression. PreM, 599–603.

75 Esplin, "Emergence of Brigham Young," 305; Hepzibah Richards to Willard Richards, Jan. 18, 1838, in Godfrey, Godfrey, and Derr, *Women's Voices*, 71.

76 On the pressure from creditors, see Van Wagoner, *Sidney Rigdon*, 203; *Latter-day Saints' Millennial Star*, Jan. 7, 1865, 5. A revelation on Jan. 12, 1838, commanded the Presidency to leave. JS, Journal, July 8, 1838, in *PJS*, 2:255.

77 Young, "History of Brigham Young," 13; Hepzibah Richards to Willard Richards, Jan. 19, 1838, in Godfrey, Godfrey, and Derr, *Women's Voices*, 71.

78 Corrill, *Brief History*, 26; *D&C* [1844], 104 (*D&C*, 112); JS to John Corrill and others, Sept. 4, 1837, in *PWJS*, 391–92.

CHAPTER 19 TRIALS

1 ManH B-1, 780, 784; JS, Journal, Dec. 19, 1842, in *APR*, 259–60; Newell and Avery, *Mormon Enigma*, 69–70; JS, Journal, Mar. 29, 1838, in *PJS*, 2:221.

2 Peck, Historical Sketch, 12. The story of Mormon development of Caldwell County is told in Gentry, *Northern Missouri*, 29–39.

3 Quoted in Gentry, *Northern Missouri*, 30.

4 *M&A*, July 1836, 341; Faragher, *Sugar Creek*, 63.

5 Quoted in Gentry, *Northern Missouri*, 21.
6 William W. Phelps and others to Daniel Dunklin, July 7, 1836; Daniel Dunklin to William W. Phelps and others, July 18, 1836; both in Phelps Collection.
7 *Missouri Argus*, Sept. 27, 1838, Feb. 15, 1839; *History of Caldwell*, 103–105, 117; Launius, *Alexander William Doniphan*, 39–40; LeSueur, *Mormon War*, 25–26.
8 *History of Van Buren County, Iowa*, 407–10; Gentry, *Northern Missouri*, 19–24.
9 JS, Journal, Apr. 26, 1838, in *PJS*, 2:232; *Elders' Journal*, Aug. 1838 (*D&C*, 115:3, 6, 7, 18).
10 JS, Journal, May 18–19, 1838, in *PJS*, 2:243–44 (*D&C*, 116). The name "Adam-ondi-Ahman" first appears in a March 1832 revelation. *D&C* [1835], 75:3 (*D&C*, 78:15). For the larger meaning of the site to Latter-day Saints, see Gentry, "Adam-ondi-Ahman," 553–76; Matthews, "Adam-ondi-Ahman," 27–35. Brigham Young later said Joseph announced that "Jackson County was the garden of Eden." Journal History, Mar. 15, 1857.
11 JS, Journal, May 20–June 5, 1838, in *PJS*, 2:245–48; Gentry, "Land Question," 47–50.
12 When they did start buying land to the north, no one complained until trouble broke out; Doniphan himself raised no objections. Newspapers brought up the informal agreement only in August 1838, long after Mormon settlement began and only when other conflicts were starting up. LeSueur, *Mormon War*, 25; *Western Star*, Sept. 14, 1838, cited in *Missouri Argus*, Sept. 27, 1838. For a discussion of the issue, see Launius, *Alexander William Doniphan*, 38–40; Anderson, "Atchison's Letters," 15; Baugh, *Call to Arms*, 14.
13 JS, Journal, May 5, 7, 1838, in *PJS*, 238–39; *HC*, 3:87–148; Rockwood, "Journal," 21 (Oct. 14, 1838); *Deseret News*, Apr. 2, 1853 (*D&C*, 117:8); *Elders' Journal*, July 1838, 33; John Smith, Journal, June 28, 1838; Hill, *Quest for Refuge*, 74.
14 *E&MS*, Aug. 1832, [18] (Moses 7:18); Corrill, *Brief History*, 27–28; *Elders' Journal*, July 1838, 37, 46. Oliver Cowdery to Warren A. and Lyman Cowdery, Feb. 4, 1838, Cowdery Letter Book; Marsh, "History," 6.
15 Corrill, *Brief History*, 27–28; *FWR*, 135–38 (Jan. 20, 26; Feb. 5, 1838).
16 Thomas B. Marsh to JS, Feb. 15, 1838, in *Elders' Journal*, July 1838, 45; JS, Journal, March 29, 1838, in *PJS*, 2:222.
17 JS, Journal, Mar. 13, 1838, in *PJS*, 219–20; *FWR*, 138, 142–43 (Feb. 5, 24, 1838); Oliver Cowdery to Warren A. and Lyman Cowdery, Feb. 24; Mar. 10, 1838; Cowdery Letter Book.
18 JS, Journal, Mar. 13, 1838, in *PJS*, 2:219–20; *FWR*, 135–36, 162–69 (Jan. 26; Apr. 12, 1838). For Cowdery's view of the dispute, see Oliver Cowdery to Brigham Young and others, Dec. 25, 1843, Young Office Files.
19 *FWR*, 163 (Apr. 12, 1838). On seeking political patronage, see Oliver Cowdery to John A. Bryan, Oct. 15, 1835; Oliver Cowdery to William Kenmore, Oct. 15, 1835; Oliver Cowdery to R. M. Johnson, Oct. 30, 1835; James M. Carrel to R. M. Williams, Oct. 29, 1835, all in Cowdery Letter Book. Cowdery was elected justice of the peace in Kirtland.
20 *FWR*, 164–65 (Apr. 12, 1838); Oliver Cowdery to Warren A. and Lyman Cowdery, Feb. 4, 1838, Cowdery Letter Book.
21 *FWR*, 165 (Apr. 12, 1838).
22 JS, Journal, Mar. 13, 1838, in *PJS*, 2:213–14. Joseph labeled the Parrish faction in Kirtland "the Aristocrats or Anarchys." JS, Journal, Mar. 29, 1838, in *PJS*, 2:221.
23 On the number of Danites, see LeSueur, "Danites Reconsidered," 39; Hartley, *John Lowe Butler*, 42, 48; John N. Sapp, Affidavit, Sept. 4, 1838, in *Document*, 17; Quinn, *Origins of Power*, 479–90.
24 Corrill, *Brief History*, 31; Sampson Avard, Testimony (Nov. 1838), in *Document*, 97–102.
25 JS, Journal, July 27, 1838, in *PJS*, 2:262; Hill, *Quest for Refuge*, 75, 77. On the Danites, see Gentry, "Danite Band," 421–50, and LeSueur, "Danites Reconsidered," 1–15. For a review of the historiography, see LeSueur, "Mormon Experience," 98–104. LeSueur concludes that "while the degree of the prophet's involvement is unclear, there can be

no doubt that he knew and approved of the group's activities." "Danites Reconsidered," 48–49. On the Danites in anti-Mormon fiction, see Cornwall and Arrington, "Mormon Danites," 147–65.

26 Corrill, *Brief History*, 29; Peck, Historical Sketch, 23; Sampson Avard and others to Oliver Cowdery and others, June 1838, in *Document*, 103–106, and conveniently reproduced in Gentry, *Northern Missouri*, 58–60.

27 Corrill, *Brief History*, 25–26, 29–30, 32; Peck, Historical Sketch, 24–25; Whitmer, *Book of John Whitmer*, 184–85.

28 Gentry, *Northern Missouri*, 60; Quinn, *Origins of Power*, 94; JS, Journal, July 4, 1838, in *PJS*, 2:249. Peck claimed the dissenters were told "preparations were being made to hang them up." Peck, Historical Sketch, 26. John Whitmer said "they had threatened to kill us." Whitmer, *Book of John Whitmer*, 184.

29 Burnett, *Old California Pioneer*, 38; Roberts, *John Taylor*, 42–43; Gentry, "Danite Band," 426.

30 Corrill, *Brief History*, 30; Sampson Avard Testimony (Nov. 1838), in *Document*, 97–98; *The Return*, Sept. 1889, 131–32.

31 Corrill, *Brief History*, 30.

32 Peck, Historical Sketch, 38–39, 41.

33 Corrill, *Brief History*, 30–32, 36–37; Peck, Historical Sketch, 56–57.

34 Corrill, *Brief History*, 31; Reed Peck, Testimony (Nov. 1838), in *Document*, 117; John Corrill, Testimony (Nov. 1838), in *Document*, 110.

35 John Corrill, Testimony (Nov. 1838), in *Document*, 111; Sampson Avard, Testimony (Nov. 1838), in *Document*, 97. See also Peck, Historical Sketch, 46. Luman Shurtliff, a believing Mormon, recalled the time when Joseph and Hyrum gave him countersigns, which may or may not have been Danite. Shurtliff, Autobiography, 122.

36 Reed Peck, Testimony (Nov. 1838) in *Document*, 117; John Corrill, Testimony (Nov. 1838), in *Document*, 111; Thomas B. Marsh, Affidavit, Oct. 24, 1838, in *Document*, 58.

37 Corrill, *Brief History*, 32; Peck, Historical Sketch, 35–36.

38 Quoted in Peck, "Historical Sketch," 32–33.

39 Avard, Testimony (Nov. 1838), in *Document*, 97.

40 JS, Journal, Aug. 31, 1838, in *PJS*, 2:279.

41 JS, Journal, Aug. 31, 1838, in *PJS*, 2:279. For a similar analysis, see Hill, "Mormon Reaction," 24–33, and Winn, *Exiles*, 117–28.

42 Rigdon, *Oration*, 12; Peck, Historical Sketch, 42–43. Immediately after the attack on Gallatin, Thomas Marsh testified that "the prophet inculcates the notion, and it is believed by every true Mormon, that Smith's prophecies are superior to the law of the land." Thomas B. Mar[s]h, Affidavit, Oct. 24, 1838, in *Document*, 58. Cf. John Whitmer, Testimony (Nov. 1838); in *Document*, 138–39.

43 Quoted in John Corrill, Testimony (Nov. 1838), in *Document*, 111; Hill, *Quest for Refuge*, 75.

44 Grimsted, *American Mobbing*, 13–15, 103–104.

45 Swartzell, *Mormonism Exposed*, 16; *Elders' Journal*, Aug. 1838, 60; JS, Journal, July 4, 27, 1838. The Caldwell County militia was organized in August 1837. Lyman Wight, Affidavit, July 1, 1843, in *T&S*, July 15, 1843, 265.

46 Rigdon, *Oration*, 12.

47 Lee, *Mormonism Unveiled*, 57; Corrill, *Brief History*, 31–32; Van Wagoner, *Sidney Rigdon*, 221; *Elders' Journal*, Aug. 1838, 54; Sidney Rigdon to Sterling Price, Sept. 8, 1838.

CHAPTER 20   WAR

1 LeSueur, *Mormon War*, 59. On electoral conflict in Kirtland, see Hill, *Quest for Refuge*, 66.

2 Sidney Rigdon to Sterling Price, Sept. 8, 1838, CA; JS, Journal, May 10, 1838, in *PJS*,

2:240; Corrill, *Brief History*, 33. For the politics, see Hill, *Quest for Refuge*, 82–84. "Negroes" quote in LeSueur, *Mormon War*, 61. Accounts of the election scuffle are given in Gentry, *Northern Missouri*, 91–94; Durham, "Election Day Battle," 36–61; and LeSueur, *Mormon War*, 59–64. For the Danite role, see Hartley, *John Lowe Butler*, 389–91.

3   LeSueur, *Mormon War*, 64; Sidney Rigdon to Sterling Price, Sept. 8, 1838, CA; Greene, *Expulsion*, 19; Rigdon, *Appeal*, 22–23; JS, Journal, Aug. 7, 1838, in *PJS*, 2:268; Corrill, *Brief History*, 34.

4   Joseph was told that Adam Black had headed a mob assembled at Millport in Daviess County. Rough Draft Notes, ManH, Sept. 5, 1838; JS, Affidavit, Sept. 5, 1838, in Rigdon, *Appeal*, 21–22.

5   JS, Journal, Aug. 8, 9, 1838, in *PJS*, 2:270–71; Rigdon, *Appeal*, 20; Sidney Rigdon to Sterling Price, Sept. 8, 1838, CA; David R. Atchison to JS, Sept. 1, 1838, JSC. Rigdon said Black treated the Mormon delegation "insultingly, and would give no satisfaction, afterwards giving a statement." Sidney Rigdon to Sterling Price, Sept. 8, 1838, CA.

6   JS, Affidavit, Sept. 5, 1838, in Rigdon, *Appeal*, 21–22; Greene, *Expulsion*, 25; Adam Black, Affidavit, Sept. 18, 1838, in *Document*, 161. Rigdon said that "if there were any one person who might be said to command more than another, it was Dr. Avard. He was the person who called for the people to go, and he was the one who took the direction of the concern." Sidney Rigdon to Sterling Price, Sept. 8, 1838, CA.

7   *Missouri Republican*, Sept. 8, 1838; Corrill, *Brief History*, 34; Sidney Rigdon to Sterling Price, Sept. 8, 1838, CA; Chariton Committee to the citizens of Chariton, Sept. 10, 1838, in *Niles National Register*, Oct. 13, 1838, 103. Wight said he was willing to be tried by Austin King or a "jury of 12 men"—so long as none "should belong to any mob." Sidney Rigdon to Sterling Price, Sept. 8, 1838, CA.

8   JS, Journal, Sept. 2, 1838, in *PJS*, 2:281–82; *Missouri Argus*, Sept. 6, 13, 1838; Anderson, "Boggs' 'Order,' " 37; Corrill, *Brief History*, 34; JS, Journal, Sept. 2, 1838, in *PJS*, 2:282. For action in various counties, see LeSueur, *Mormon War*, 70; Baugh, *Call to Arms*, 50–51.

9   JS, Journal, Sept. 2, 1838, in *PJS*, 281–82. On Atchison, see Parrish, *David Rice Atchison*. The course of events was recorded by Robinson day by day in Joseph Smith's Scriptory Book. JS, Journal, Aug. 11–Sept. 7, 1838, in *PJS*, 2:271–85. A broader account that alters details of Robinson's record is Baugh, *Call to Arms*, 51–53.

10 Baugh, *Call to Arms*, 53–56; JS, Journal, Sept. 2, 1838, in *PJS*, 281–82. Another rumor had the Mormons in league with abolitionists. Sidney Rigdon to Sterling Price, Sept. 8, 1838, CA.

11 Alexander Doniphan to David R. Atchison, Sept. 15, 1838, in *Document*, 25; David R. Atchison to Lilburn W. Boggs, Sept. 20, 1838, in *Document*, 27. On Doniphan, see Launius, *Alexander William Doniphan*.

12 Hiram G. Parks to Lilburn W. Boggs, Sept. 25, 1838, in *Document*, 32; David R. Atchison to Lilburn W. Boggs, Sept. 20, 27, 1838, in *Document*, 27, 34.

13 Austin A. King to David R. Atchison, Sept. 10, 1838, in *Document*, 28; Parrish, *David Rice Atchison*, 24–25; Launius, *Alexander William Doniphan*, 51–53.

14 Baugh, *Call to Arms*, 66–68.

15 Committee of Chariton County, Report, Oct. 5, 1838, in *Document*, 36; Rockwood, "Journal," 21 (Oct. 14, 1838).

16 JS, Journal Extract, Nov. 1839, in *PWJS*, 472–73; De Witt Mormons to Lilburn W. Boggs, Sept. 22, 1838, in *Document*, 29; Greene, *Expulsion*, 26. Boggs denied he told the Mormons to fight.

17 Samuel Lucas to Lilburn W. Boggs, Oct. 4, 1838, in *Document*, 34–35.

18 Carroll County to Howard County citizens, Oct. 7, 1838, in *Document*, 40; Hiram G. Parks to David R. Atchison, Oct. 7, 1838, in *Document*, 37. The De Witt story is narrated in LeSueur, *Mormon War*, 88, 101–11, and Baugh, *Call to Arms*, 66–76.

19 David R. Atchison to Lilburn W. Boggs, Oct. 9, 16, 1838, in *Document*, 38–39; JS, Journal Extract, Nov. 1839, in *PWJS*, 473. Samuel Bogart, probably unaware of the agreement to sell out to the Mormons, thought the vigilantes were going north to protect the Daviess citizens. Samuel Bogart to Lilburn W. Boggs, Oct. 13, 1838, in *Document*, 41.

20 JS, Journal Extract, Nov. 1839, in *PWJS*, 475; Hiram G. Parks to Lilburn W. Boggs, Sept. 25, 1838, in *Document*, 32–33. Albert Rockwood, writing regular reports at the time, said: "Verry great fear rests on the Missourians in Davis county they are now selling their property verry low to the Brethren. in many cases they sell their real Estate with their houses and crops on the ground for less than the crop is worth Davis County is now considered in the possession of the Brethren." Rockwood, "Journal," 18 (Oct. 6, 1838).

21 Hyrum Smith, Affidavit, July 1, 1843, in *T&S*, July 1, 1843, 246–48.

22 Corrill, *Brief History*, 36–37. For Sampson Avard's version, see Avard, Testimony (Nov. 1838), in *Document*, 99.

23 Hiram G. Parks to David R. Atchison, Oct. 21, 1838, in *Document*, 47; Rockwood, "Journal," 22 (Oct. 15, 1838).

24 Hiram G. Parks to David R. Atchison, Oct. 21, 1838, in *Document*, 47; Rockwood, "Journal," 22 (Oct. 15, 1838); John Corrill, Testimony (Nov. 1838), in *Document*, 112.

25 ManH B-1, 837; Baugh, *Call to Arms*, 89; Sampson Avard, Testimony (Nov. 1838), in *Document*, 99. Later Mormons believed the march into Daviess was "agreeably to the order of Gen. Doniphen." Rough Draft Notes, ManH, Oct. 5, 1838. In an attempt at observing the legal proprieties, they asked a Caldwell County judge, probably a Mormon, to authorize them. Baugh, *Call to Arms*, 14, 84. At testimony in Nauvoo Municipal Court in 1842, both Hyrum Smith and Lyman Wight testified that Generals Doniphan and Atchison authorized Wight to disperse the gathering mob in Daviess in October 1838. *T&S*, July 1, 1843, 248–49; July 15, 1843, 265–66.

26 John Corrill, Testimony (Nov. 1838), in *Document*, 112; Foote, Autobiography, 24; Corrill, *Brief History*, 37, 39; Thomas B. Marsh, Affidavit, Oct. 24, 1838, in *Document*, 57. For Hyde's confession, see Hyde, "History," 16. Marsh, who like Hyde returned to the Church, recounted in 1857: "I got a beam in my eye & thought I could discover a beam in Joseph's eye tho it was nothing but a mote." Marsh, "History," 2.

27 George M. Hinkle, Testimony (Nov. 1838), in *Document*, 128; Sampson Avard, Testimony (Nov. 1838), in *Document*, 99–100; David R. Atchison to Lilburn W. Boggs, Oct. 22, 1838, in *Document*, 46. On Mormon belief about Daniel's prophecy of a kingdom and the accompanying militarism, see Whittaker, "Book of Daniel," 155–201.

28 John Cleminson, Testimony (Nov. 1838), in *Document*, 114, 115; Patrick Lynch, Testimony (Nov. 1838), in *Document*, 145; John Smith, Journal, Oct. 22, 1838. For attempts at discriminating between friends and enemies, see Thomas J. Martin, Affidavit, Oct. 22, 1838; Charles Bleckley, Testimony (Nov. 1838), James Cobb, Testimony (Nov. 1838), Jesse Kelly, Testimony (Nov. 1838); all in *Document*, 46, 136–37. On Mormon burnings, see Hill, *Quest for Refuge*, 91.

29 JS, Journal Extract, Nov. 1839, in *PWJS*, 475; Hyrum Smith, Affidavit, July 1, 1843, in Johnson, *Mormon Redress Petitions*, 623–24.

30 James B. Turnur, Testimony (Nov. 1838), in *Document*, 139.

31 Philip Covington, Affidavit, Sept. 22, 1838; William P. Peniston to Lilburn W. Boggs, Oct. 21, 1838; Samuel Venable, Affidavit, Oct. 22, 1838; Jonathan J. Dryden, Affidavit, Oct. 22, 1838; James Stone, Affidavit, Oct. 22, 1838; Thomas J. Martin, Affidavit, Oct. 22, 1838; Thomas C. Burch to Lilburn W. Boggs, Oct. 23, 1838; C. R. Morehead, William Thornton, and Jacob Gudgel, Report, Oct. 24, 1838; John Corrill, Testimony (Nov. 1838); Jeremiah Myers, Testimony (Nov. 1838); Andrew J. Job, Testimony (Nov. 1838); George W. Worthington, Testimony (Nov. 1838); Joseph H. McGee, Testimony (Nov. 1838); Ezra Williams, Testimony (Nov. 1838); Timothy Lewis, Testimony

(Nov. 1838); Patrick Lynch, Testimony (Nov. 1838), all in *Document*, 43–46, 50, 52, 57, 100, 112, 132, 140, 141, 144, 145. See also Reed Peck, Testimony (Nov. 1838), in *Document*, 123, 118. Porter Yale, who had been taken captive by the Mormons, heard an order to burn the store at Gallatin, but did not see it done. Porter Yale, Testimony (Nov. 1838), in *Document*, 142–43. John Cleminson, a disaffected Mormon who was in Adam-ondi-Ahman as the forces were coming back from Daviess, testified at the hearing that "it was said by some that the Mormons were burning their own houses, and by others, that the mob were burning them; and so much was said about it, that I did not know when I got the truth." John Cleminson, Testimony (Nov. 1838), in *Document*, 115. Brigham Young saw Missourians vacating their land and setting fire to their houses. "History," 18. Fifty years after the fact, Joseph McGee, who was on the scene, wrote an account of Mormon burnings, but in his statement before the court he did not claim to be an eyewitness. *North Missourian*, Feb. 28, 1888; McGee, *Grand River*, [12]; Joseph H. McGee, Testimony (Nov. 1838), in *Document*, 141.

32 William Phelps, Affidavit, *Document*, 123; Pratt, *Late Persecutions*, 32–33.

33 Elias Higbee to JS, Feb. 22, 1840, JSC. Phineas Richards wrote in January 1839 that the elders "went at it and drove the mob by the hundreds, hunted them from every valley, from every secret place. They fled like wind . . . leaving their cannon and many other valuable things behind which were taken as spoil." Quoted in Hill, *Quest for Refuge*, 91. An account of events sent to the governor by the Mormons on Dec. 10, 1838, admitted that "instances have been of late, where individuals have trespassed upon the rights of others, and thereby broken the laws of the land." Memorial to Missouri Legislature, Dec. 10, 1838, JSC. Cf. *The Return*, March 1890, 235; Huntington, Autobiography, 32, and note 32 above.

34 David R. Atchison, Affidavit, Sept. 20, 1838, in *Document*, 28; Sampson Avard, Testimony (Nov. 1838), in *Document*, 99.

35 David R. Atchison, Affidavit, Sept. 20, 1838, in *Document*, 28; Sampson Avard, Testimony (Nov. 1838), in *Document*, 99; Lee, *Mormonism Unveiled*, 70; George Hinkle, Testimony (Nov. 1838), in *Document*, 129; LeSueur, *Mormon War*, 133, 147–50, 155–57.

36 Rockwood, "Journal," 24 (Oct. 25, 1838). On the question of who fired first, John Lockhart, a member of the Missourian company, testified in court that he heard a percussion cap burst without the gun firing and ordered the guard with him to shoot back. John Lockhart, Testimony (Nov. 1838), in *Document*, 142. See also Baugh, "Bogart's 1839 Letter," 54.

37 John Cleminson, Testimony (Nov. 1838), in *Document*, 116. Peter Burnett said, "Smith was not in any of the combats, so far as I remember." Burnett, *California Pioneer*, 39. Lyman Wight and Hyrum Smith later testified that Joseph was exempt because of the boyhood operation on his leg. Lyman Wight, Affidavit, July 1, 1843, in *T&S*, July 15, 1843, 265; Hyrum Smith, Affidavit, July 1, 1843, in *T&S*, July 1, 1843, 246.

38 Not that Joseph was not known to be in charge. Albert Rockwood noted that "Brother Joseph Smith Jr & Lyman White were at the head of the armey of Isreal that went up to the relief of the Brethren in Davies County." Rockwood, "Journal," 19 (Oct. 6, 1838). George Hinkle said that neither Joseph nor Hyrum "seemed to have any command as officers in the field, but seemed to give general directions." George M. Hinkle, Testimony (Nov. 1838), in *Document*, 126.

39 JS, Journal Extract, Nov. 1839, in *PWJS*, 474.

40 Rockwood thought the Danites led the raids rather than the militia. Rockwood, "Journal," 23 (Oct. 22–23, 1838).

41 William Peniston to Lilburn W. Boggs, Oct. 21, 1838, in *Document*, 44; and generally, *Document*, 43–60.

42 David R. Atchison to Lilburn W. Boggs, Oct. 22, 1838, in *Document*, 46–47.

43 William Peniston to Lilburn W. Boggs, Oct. 21, 1838, in *Document*, 44; Lilburn W.

Boggs to John B. Clark, Oct. 27, 1838, in *Document*, 61. On the order, see Baugh, "Lilburn W. Boggs," 111–32, and Hartley, "Extermination Order," 1–30.

44 Gordon, "Political Career," 111–22; McLaws, "Attempted Assassination," 50–62; Baugh, "Lilburn W. Boggs," 111–32.

45 Three years earlier, in the first volume of *Democracy in America*, 252, Tocqueville had diagnosed the helplessness of a hated minority:

> When a man or a party suffers an injustice in the United States, to whom can he turn? To public opinion? That is what forms the majority. To the legislative body? It represents the majority and obeys it blindly. To the executive power? It is appointed by the majority and serves as its passive instrument. To the police? They are nothing but the majority under arms. A jury? The jury is the majority vested with the right to pronounce judgment; even the judges in certain states are elected by the majority. So, however iniquitous or unreasonable the measure which hurts you, you must submit.

46 Baugh, *Call to Arms*, 127, 118–23; Daniel Ashby to John B. Clark, Nov. 28, 1838; John B. Clark to Lilburn W. Boggs, Nov. 29, 1838; in *Document*, 82–83, 92, 93. Rockwood put the number of Mormon dead at 30. Rockwood, "Journal," 28 (Nov. 11, 1838). On December 9, Parley Pratt wrote between 30 and 100. Parley P. Pratt to Dear Sister, Dec. 9, 1838, in Rockwood, "Journal," 32. For a detailed account of Haun's Mill, see Blair, "Haun's Mill Massacre," 62–67, and Baugh, "Joseph Young's Affidavit," 188–202.

47 George M. Hinkle, Testimony (Nov. 1838), in *Document*, 127–28; Corrill, *Brief History*, 40–41; LeSueur, *Mormon War*, 125–28, 158–60, 168.

48 LeSueur, *Mormon War*, 170–73; Baugh, *Call to Arms*, 149. Eliza Snow estimated the militia numbers at 9,500. Snow, "Letter," 546. John Corrill said 3,000. Corrill, *Brief History*, 42.

49 Pratt, *Autobiography*, 204; Baugh, *Call to Arms*, 141; JS, Journal Extract, Nov. 1839, in *PWJS*, 476. Albert Rockwood thought the Church leaders had gone to the militia camp as hostages, not as prisoners. Rockwood, "Journal," 25–26 (Oct. 31, 1838). Hinkle denied wrongdoing. "When the facts were laid before Joseph, did he not say, 'I will go'?" George M. Hinkle to William W. Phelps, Aug. 14, 1844, in Hinkle, "Biographical Sketch," 451. Brigham Young, like Joseph, spoke of Hinkle's "treachery." Young, "History," 19.

50 Samuel D. Lucas to Lilburn W. Boggs, Nov. 2, 1838, in *Document*, 73; LeSueur, *Mormon War*, 169; Baugh, *Call to Arms*, 141.

51 Launius, *Alexander Doniphan*, 64–65. Doniphan wrote Lucas, "It is cold-blooded murder. I will not obey your order." *History of Caldwell*, 137. Lucas denied holding the court-martial in Samuel D. Lucas to Lilburn W. Boggs, Nov. 11, 1838, in *Document*, 64.

52 Huntington, Autobiography, 18; Baugh, *Call to Arms*, 151; Young, "History," 18. A Missourian critical of the government's action objected that hostile citizens "are now constantly strolling up and down Caldwell county, in small companies armed, insulting the women in any and every way, and plundering the poor devils of all the means of subsistence (scanty as it was) left them, and driving off their horses, cattle, hogs, &c., and rifling their houses and farms of every thing therein, taking beds, bedding, wardrobe and all such things as they see they want, leaving the poor Mormons in a starving and naked condition." M. Arthur to Representatives from Clay County, Nov. 29, 1838, in *Document*, 94. For a description of the harassment, see LeSueur, *Mormon War*, 180–81.

53 Rockwood, "Journal," 27 (Nov. 3, 1838); General Wilson to John B. Clark, Nov. 12, 1838, in *Document*, 78; Austin A. King to Lilburn W. Boggs, Dec. 23, 1838, in *Document*, 95.

54   Baugh, *Call to Arms*, 152; JS, Journal Extract, Nov. 1839, in *PWJS*, 476–77; JS, Journal, Dec. 30, 1842, in *APR*, 261.

55   JS to Emma Smith, Nov. 4, 1838, in *PWJS*, 399–401; Lyman Wight, Journal, Nov. 3–5, 1838, quoted in *History of the Reorganized Church*, 295–96. Joseph may have been putting a good face on his situation. In a later account he said that in Jackson County they "had to sleep on the floor with nothing but a mantle for our covering, and a stick of wood for our pillow." JS, Journal Extract, Nov. 1839, in *PWJS*, 477.

56   JS to Emma Smith, Nov. 4, 1838, in *PWJS*, 400.

57   JS to Emma Smith, Nov. 12, 1838, in *PWJS*, 405–406.

58   Half of the Mormon witnesses testified under pressure and were not dissenters. LeSueur, *Mormon War*, 201–202. LeSueur counts twenty non-Mormon and twenty-one Mormon witnesses. Hill numbers the witnesses at forty-two. *Quest for Refuge*, 234, n. 244.

59   Pratt, *Autobiography*, 230–33; *The Return*, Mar. 1890, 235–36; LeSueur, "High Treason," 3–30.

60   LeSueur, *Mormon War*, 198–99; *T&S*, Sept. 1840, 163; Hyrum Smith, Affidavit, July 1, 1843, in *T&S*, July 1, 1843, 253–54; Madsen, "Missouri Court," 92–136.

61   Hyrum Smith, Affidavit, July 1, 1843, in *T&S*, July 1, 1843, 254.

62   JS to the Church in Caldwell County, Dec. 16, 1838, in *PWJS*, 415–17, 421–22.

63   LeSueur, *Mormon War*, 198–99; *T&S*, Sept. 1840, 163; Hyrum Smith, Affidavit, July 1, 1843, in *T&S*, July 1, 1843, 253–54.

64   Quoted in JS, Journal, Dec. 30, 1842, in *APR*, 262.

65   Lyman Wight had to pressure Joseph on the eve of the Daviess raids to go beyond the strict limits of the law, and only reluctantly did he agree. William W. Phelps, Testimony (Nov. 1838), in *Document*, 123; Hill, *Quest for Refuge*, 97.

66   LeSueur argues that the charges were valid and the Mormon defense unjustified. LeSueur, *Mormon War*, 205–18, esp. 217.

67   Printed in *Arkansas Gazette*, Dec. 5, 1838.

68   Rockwood, "Journal," 25 (Nov. 3, 1838); JS to the Church of Caldwell County, Dec. 16, 1838, in *PWJS*, 420.

69   John B. Clark to Lilburn W. Boggs, Nov. 29, 1838, in *Document*, 90.

70   JS to the Church of Caldwell County, Dec. 16, 1838, in *PWJS*, 420.

71   Alanson Ripley to JS and others, Apr. 10, 1839, JSC.

CHAPTER 21   IMPRISONMENT

1   Newell and Avery, *Mormon Enigma*, 77–78. Lyman Wight later claimed the Prophet ordained his son to succeed him on this occasion. Launius, *Joseph Smith III*, 10. No other prisoners remembered such a charge.

2   JS, Sidney Rigdon, and Hyrum Smith to Heber C. Kimball and Brigham Young, Jan. 16, 1839, *PWJS*, 424.

3   *FWR*, 221–25 (Dec. 13, 19, 26, 1838); First Council of the Seventy, Minutes, Dec. 28, 1838; Jan. 5, 1839; JS, Sidney Rigdon, and Hyrum Smith to Heber C. Kimball and Brigham Young, Jan. 16, 1839, in *PWJS*, 424; Hartley, "Winter Exodus," 6–40; JS and others to Edward Partridge and the Church, Mar. 20, 1839, in *PWJS*, 442.

4   Joseph Smith and others to James M. Hughes, Jan. 24, 1839, JSC; Van Wagoner, *Sidney Rigdon*, 254–55. Hyrum Smith said the judge himself warned Rigdon of his danger. Hyrum Smith, Affidavit, July 1, 1843, in *T&S*, July 1, 1843, 254.

5   Pratt, *Autobiography*, 232–33; Joseph Smith and others to George Tompkins, Mar. 15, 1839, JSC.

6   JS and others to Edward Partridge and the Church, Mar. 20, 1839, in *PWJS*, 432; Hyrum Smith to Mary F. Smith, Mar. 16, 1839, Mary Fielding Smith Collection.

7   Jenson, *Autobiography*, 163; Jessee, "Prison Experience," 25; Arrington, "Liberty Jail," 21; *Deseret News*, Nov. 2, 1854; Hyrum Smith, Affidavit, July 1, 1843, in *T&S*, July 1, 1843, 254; JS to Isaac Galland, Mar. 22, 1839, in *PWJS*, 456. Wight said the jailer gave them dregs of coffee and tea from his own table, and sometimes after drinking it the prisoners were blind for two or three days. Jessee, "Prison Experience," 27–28.

8   H. Smith Diary, Mar. 18 and Apr. 3, 1839; JS and others to Edward Partridge and the Church, Mar. 20, 1839, in *PWJS*, 431; Pratt, *Autobiography*, 228–29.

9   JS to Emma Smith, Mar. 21 and Apr. 4, 1839, in *PWJS*, 449, 464.

10 *T&S*, Sept. 1840, 165; Rough Draft Notes, ManH, Jan. 16, 1839; Far West Committee, Minutes, Jan. 29, 1839; JS to Presendia Huntington Buell, Mar. 15, 1839, *PWJS*, 427. On the Mormons in Quincy, see Black and Bennett, *City of Refuge*.

11 Emma Smith to JS, Mar. 7, 1839, JSC; *HC*, 2:272–74; JS and others to Edward Partridge and the Church, Mar. 20, 1839, in *PWJS*, 431. Joseph's letter is published with canonized portions offset in Jessee and Welch, "Joseph Smith's Letter," 125–45. Earlier scholars believed parts of the letter were written on March 25. Sperry, *Doctrine and Covenants*, 635. On American prison letters, see Philip, *Prison Communications*.

12 JS and others to Edward Partridge and the Church, Mar. 20, 1839, in *PWJS*, 443, 432.

13 JS and others to Edward Partridge and the Church, Mar. 20, 1839, in *PWJS*, 430, 434. In another letter, he wrote to a Church sister not to think of revenge on their enemies. God "must do his own work or it must fall to the ground we must not take it in our hands to avenge our wrongs." JS to Presendia Huntington Buell, Mar. 15, 1839, in *PWJS*, 428.

14 JS and others to Edward Partridge and the Church, Mar. 20, 1839, in *PWJS*, 445; Wilson, "Early Mormon Movement," 76.

15 For examples of sympathetic stories, see *Arkansas Gazette*, Dec. 5, 1838; *New-Yorker*, Sept. 21, 1839, 11; *Peoria Register*, May 18, 1839; *Daily National Intelligencer*, May 31 and Sept. 21, 1839; *Pennsylvanian for the Country*, Jan. 24, 1839; *Northampton Courier*, May 15, 1839; *Western Reserve Chronicle*, Mar. 5, June 18, and Oct. 1, 1839.

16 JS and others to Edward Partridge and the Church, Mar. 20, 1839, in *PWJS*, 432, 444–45.

17 JS and others to Edward Partridge and the Church, Mar. 20, 1839, in *PWJS*, 430–31, 435–36, 444.

18 JS and others to Edward Partridge and the Church, Mar. 20, 1839, in *PWJS*, 436.

19 JS and others to Edward Partridge and the Church, Mar. 20, 1839, in *PWJS*, 440 (*D&C*, 121:35).

20 Corrill, *Brief History*, 48.

21 Sidney Rigdon is reputed to have said he did not care to serve a God who let them be "hauled around as we had been." Van Wagoner, *Sidney Rigdon*, 261.

22 JS and others to Edward Partridge and the Church, Mar. 20, 1839, in *PWJS*, 442.

23 JS and others to Edward Partridge and the Church, Mar. 20, 1839, in *PWJS*, 431 (*D&C*, 121:1). For a similar line of questioning, see Plea to Lord, Jan. 1839, in ManH.

24 JS and others to Edward Partridge and the Church, Mar. 20, 1839, in *PWJS*, 441–42 (*D&C*, 122:1–9). "It seems to me that man was meant to have sorrow & grief in all his Days if he will be saved in the world to come." Hyrum Smith to Mary F. Smith, March 23, 1839, Mary Fielding Smith Collection.

25 On Joseph Smith and the problem of evil, see Paulsen and Ostler, "Problem of Evil," 237–84.

26 *D&C* [1835], 97:2 (*D&C*, 101:4–5).

27 Emma Smith to JS, Mar. 7, 1839, JSC; JS to Emma Smith, Mar. 21, 1839, in *PWJS*, 448–49.

28 JS to Emma Smith, Apr. 4, 1839, in *PWJS*, 463–65.

29 Burnett, *California Pioneer*, 38–39, 41; Jessee, "Prison Experience," 33; *HC*, 3:310; Hyrum Smith, Affidavit, July 1, 1843, in *T&S*, July 1, 1843, 255–56. Joseph Smith III

remembered the sheriff later coming to collect $800, suggesting a bribe. *Saints' Herald*, Nov. 13, 1934, 1454.

30 JS, Journal, Apr. 16, 22, 1839, in *PJS*, 2:318; Baugh, "Gallatin Hearing," 31–65; Woodruff, *Journals*, 329–30 (May 3, 1839); Young, "History," 23.

31 Albert Rockwood noted that "it is thought by some we shall not gather again in large bodies." Albert P. Rockwood to Dear Beloved Father, Jan. 30, 1839, in Rockwood, "Journal," 34. For a statement of the reservations, see Far West Committee, Minutes, Feb. 1839, and Esplin, "Emergence of Brigham Young," 373. On March 5, Partridge wrote the prisoners about the decision not to buy. Edward Partridge to JS and others, Mar. 5, 1839, JSC.

32 *WJS*, 192 (Apr. 13, 1843); Quincy Council, Minutes, Apr. 24, 1839, JSC; JS, Journal, Apr. 24, 1839, in *PJS*, 2:318.

33 Van Wagoner, *Sidney Rigdon*, 264; Cook, "Isaac Galland," 267; Ford, *History of Illinois*, 406; *HC*, 3:317–18; JS to Isaac Galland, Mar. 22, 1839, in *PWJS*, 454–61; JS, Journal, July 3, 1839, in *PJS*, 2:325. Galland did promote the *Book of Mormon* on his journeys and argued with fellow passengers about religion. Isaac Galland to Joseph Smith and others, July 24, 1839, JSC; Cook, "Isaac Galland," 282.

34 The story of Galland and the Iowa land purchases is told in Flanders, *Nauvoo*, 27–38, and Leonard, *Nauvoo*, 41–58. For maps, see Kimball, "Nauvoo West," 133–34; and Leonard, *Nauvoo*, 50, 56.

35 Meyer, *Heartland Quilt*, 85–90; Mahoney, "Urban History," 318–39; Rowley, "River Town," 255–72.

36 Flanders, *Nauvoo*, 40; Alanson Ripley, Statement; Leonard, *Nauvoo*, 57. At first Joseph spoke of Nauvoo as a city alongside the other two cities. Eventually the whole peninsula was called Nauvoo. JS to Isaac Galland, Sept. 11, 1839, JSC.

37 General Conference of the Church, Minutes, Oct. 6, 1839, JSC; JS to the Church, May 27, 1839, JSC; Flanders, *Nauvoo*, 41–49.

38 Rough Draft Notes, ManH, June 11, 1839; Garrett, "Disease and Sickness," 169–82; Flanders, *Nauvoo*, 53–54; *D&C*, 115:6–7; 117:8–9, 14; General Conference of the Church, Minutes, Oct. 5, 1839, JSC.

39 Rough Draft Notes, ManH, June 11, 1839; Enders, "Nauvoo Streets," 409–15. Without adding in the surrounding countryside, Susan Easton Black estimates Nauvoo's population at 12,000 by 1844. Black, "Population of Nauvoo," 93.

40 *HC*, 3:374; JS, Journal, June 1839, in *PJS*, 2:321–24.

41 Woodruff, *Journals*, 1:347–48 (July 22, 29, 1839); *WJS*, 15 (Sept. 29, 1839). For firsthand descriptions, see Esplin, "Sickness and Faith," 425–34.

42 PreM, 702; Newell and Avery, *Mormon Enigma*, 83–84; Nauvoo High Council, Minutes, Oct. 20, 1839.

43 Kimball, *Diaries*, 25, n. 40.

44 *D&C*, 118:4–5; Arrington, *Brigham Young*, 73; Esplin, "Emergence of Brigham Young," 38–83; Porter, "Missouri Storm," 121–65.

45 JS to Presendia Huntington Buell, Mar. 15, 1839, in *PWJS*, 427.

46 JS to Presendia Huntington Buell, Mar. 15, 1839, in *PWJS*, 427; *WJS*, 3–8 (June 27; July 2, 7, 1839).

47 JS to Presendia Huntington Buell, Mar. 15, 1839, in *PWJS*, 427; *WJS*, 3–8 (June 27; July 2, 7, 1839).

48 *WJS*, 6 (June 27, 1839).

49 On the Calvinist doctrine of election in Joseph's time, see Foster, *New England Theology*, 112, 305, 502–503.

50 *WJS*, 4 (June 27, 1839).

51 2 Peter 1:10; Ephesians 1:13; John 14:16, 21; *WJS*, 5 (June 27, 1839).

52 *WJS*, 4, 5–6 (June 27, 1839).

53 *WJS*, 8–9 (ca. July–Aug. 1839). In his prison letter of March 20, Joseph spoke of "the councyl of the eternal God of all other Gods." JS and others to Edward Partridge and the Church, Mar. 20, 1839, in *PWJS*, 437.

54 *WJS*, 17, n. 1; 22, n. 1; Allen, Esplin, and Whittaker, *Men with a Mission*, 70–73.

55 *PJS*, 2:301–302, 574; Jessee, "Joseph Smith's History," 439–73, esp. 464.

56 Newell and Avery, *Mormon Enigma*, 79. This slightly mythic tale, whether precisely true or not, attests to the importance of records in Mormon culture.

57 JS, Journal, June 11, 1839, in *PJS*, 2:321.

58 Caswall, *Prophet of the Nineteenth Century*; ManH A-1, in *PJS*, 1:267. On Caswall, see Foster, "Henry Caswall," 144–59.

59 *WJS*, 7 (July 2, 1839); JS, Journal, July 2, 1839, in *PJS*, 2:325.

60 *WJS*, 7–8 (July 2, 1839).

61 JS and others to Edward Partridge and the Church, Mar. 20, 1839, in *PWJS*, 432; Missouri Senate, Proceedings, Dec. 18, 1838, in *Document*, 2; Emma Smith to JS, March 7, 1839, JSC.

CHAPTER 22   WASHINGTON

1 Rough Draft Notes, ManH, Oct. 29, 1839; Black, *Doctrine and Covenants*, 134–35; Schindler, *Orrin Porter Rockwell*.

2 Sidney Rigdon to Joseph Smith and others, Apr. 10, 1839, JSC; J. M. Smith, "Kentucky Resolutions," 221–45; General Conference of the Church, Minutes, Oct. 5, 1839, JSC; JS to Emma Smith, Nov. 9, 1839, in *PWJS*, 485; Sidney Rigdon to Martin Van Buren, Nov. 9, 1839, Van Buren Papers; James Adams to Martin Van Buren, Nov. 7, 1839, Van Buren Papers; Rough Draft Notes, ManH, Nov. 8, 19, 1839. For a detailed account of the journey, see Van Wagoner, *Sidney Rigdon*, 268–69.

3 JS and Elias Higbee to Hyrum Smith and others, Dec. 5, 1839, JSC; Rough Draft Notes, ManH, Nov. 27, 1839.

4 JS and Elias Higbee to Hyrum Smith and others, Dec. 5, 1839, JSC; Van Wagoner, *Sidney Rigdon*, 269; Lewis, *District of Columbia*, 16; Young, *Washington Community*, 20; Remini, *Henry Clay*, 378.

5 Reynolds, *My Own Times*, 575. Joseph mentioned Reynolds's presence at a conference at Montrose the following spring. *Peoria Register and North-Western Gazetteer*, Apr. 17, 1840.

6 JS and Elias Higbee to Hyrum Smith and others, Dec. 5, 1839, JSC; Seale, *President's House*, 2:214, 222.

7 Reynolds, *My Own Times*, 575; JS and Elias Higbee to Hyrum Smith and others, Dec. 5, 1839, JSC. In 1840, Van Buren won Missouri 56.4% to 43.6%. Chambers, "Election of 1840," 1:656–58, 661, 666, 690.

8 JS and Elias Higbee to Hyrum Smith and others, Dec. 5, 1839, JSC.

9 JS and Elias Higbee to Hyrum Smith and others, Dec. 5, 1839, JSC; Hyrum Smith to JS and Elias Higbee, Jan. 2, 1840, JSC.

10 JS and Elias Higbee to Seymour Brunson and others, Dec. 7, 1839, JSC. The sum of all the amounts mentioned in the petitions came to $2,275,789. Johnson, *Mormon Redress Petitions*, xxv, xxviii.

11 Rough Draft Notes, ManH, Dec. 21, 30, 1839; Jan. 25, 27, 1840; Orson Pratt to Sarah Pratt, Jan. 6, 1840, in *T&S*, Feb. 1840, 61; JS to Emma Smith, Jan. 20, 1840, in *PWJS*, 489–90.

12 Benjamin Winchester to Dear Brother, Feb. 10, 1840, in *T&S*, May 1840, 104; Philadelphia, Pennsylvania Branch, Minutes, Jan. 13, 1840; Pratt, *Autobiography*, 330;

JS and Elias Higbee to Hyrum Smith, Dec. 5, 1839, JSC; JS to Isaac Galland, March 22, 1839, in *PWJS*, 458–59.

13 Nauvoo High Council, Minutes, Sept. 5, 1840; Matthew L. Davis to Mary Davis, Feb. 6, 1840.

14 Matthew L. Davis to Mary Davis, Feb. 6, 1840.

15 Matthew L. Davis to Mary Davis, Feb. 6, 1840. A reporter who heard Joseph speak in 1837 called his discourse "mild and persuasive." *New-Yorker*, July 8, 1837, 251.

16 Matthew L. Davis to Mary Davis, Feb. 6, 1840.

17 *WJS*, 34–35 (Mar. 6, 1840).

18 Reynolds, *My Own Times*, 575.

19 Burnett, *Old California Pioneer*, 41.

20 Commentators have overemphasized the relevance of states' rights doctrine in tying Van Buren's hands. The Saints were not asking the federal government to intervene in Missouri; the request was for compensation for losses. In this case, states' rights was a background issue. Gordon, *Mormon Question*, 1–9; Firmage and Mangrum, *Zion in the Courts*, 81.

21 Rough Draft Notes, ManH, Feb. 6, 1840; JS to Emma Smith, Jan. 20, 1840, in *PWJS*, 490.

22 Joseph Smith, Sidney Rigdon, and Elias Higbee to the U.S. Senate and House, Jan. 27, 1840, JSC.

23 Elias Higbee to JS, Feb. 20, 1840, JSC. For information on congressmen, see *Biographical Directory*, 1182, 1294, 1871.

24 Elias Higbee to JS, Feb. 21, 1840; Elias Higbee to JS, Feb. 22, 1840, JSC.

25 U.S. Congress, Senate Committee on the Judiciary, *Mormons;* Elias Higbee to JS, Feb. 22, 26, 1840, JSC; Elias Higbee to JS, Mar. 24, 1840, JSC; Reynolds, *My Own Times*, 575–76. For the response in Nauvoo, see General Conference of the Church, Resolutions, Apr. 6, 1840, JSC. For the modern apology, see *New York Times*, June 25, 1976.

26 Bishop, *Brief History;* Greene, *Expulsion;* Taylor, *Short Account;* Pratt, *Late Persecution;* Rigdon, *Appeal;* Crawley, *Descriptive Bibliography*, 90, 100, 102–103, 124; Elias Smith to Elias Higbee, Mar. 7, 24, 1840, JSC; Elias Smith to JS, Mar. 24, 1840, JSC.

27 Greene, *Expulsion*, 42, iii.

28 Greene, *Expulsion*, iii.

29 Flake and Draper, *Mormon Bibliography*, 2:763; Sunderland, *Mormonism Exposed*, first in *Zion's Watchman*, Jan. 13, 20, 27; Feb. 3, 10, 17, 24; Mar. 3, 1838; Bacheler, *Mormonism Exposed;* M'Chesney, *Antidote to Mormonism;* Livesey, *Exposure of Mormonism*. For the early anti-Mormon press in Britain, see Foster, *Anti-Mormon Pamphleteering*.

30 Bacheler, *Mormonism Exposed*, 6–9.

31 Paine, *Age of Reason*, 141, 140, 60; Philip Foner introduction in Paine, *Age of Reason*, 40.

32 Bacheler, *Mormonism Exposed*, 11, 12, 14, 17, 20, 26.

33 Bacheler, *Mormonism Exposed*, 5, 36, 48.

34 Bacheler, *Mormonism Exposed*, 5–6, 36.

35 *Trial of the Commonwealth;* Bacheler, *Episcopacy;* Turner, *Origins of Unbelief*, 141–67; Hall, "Victorian Connection," 561–74.

36 *Discussion of the Existence*, 3; Givens, *Viper on the Hearth;* Bushman, *Joseph Smith and Skepticism*. Christian rationalists sometimes had difficulty in finding footing between skepticism and mindless credulity. E. D. Howe, an earlier rationalist critic of Mormonism, went on to doubt Christianity too. Howe, *Autobiography*, 54.

37 *Salem* (Mass.) *Register*, Oct. 19, 1843; *New-Yorker*, July 8, 1837, 250–51.

38 Halttunen, *Confidence Men*, 1–12; Davis, "Counter-Subversion," 205–24; Kirkham, *New Witness*, 2:162.

39 Pratt, *Voice of Warning*, 122, 125, 128–29, 140.

40 Pratt, *Remarkable Visions*.

CHAPTER 23   BEAUTIFUL PLACE

1   First Presidency to the Saints, Sept. 1840, in *T&S*, Oct. 1840, 178.

2   First Presidency, Report [Apr. 1841], in *T&S*, Apr. 15, 1841, 384.

3   General Conference of the Church, Resolutions, Apr. 6, 1840, JSC; Coray, "1840 Discourse," 392. Brigham Young may have had this talk in mind when he told the Church much later that Joseph said the Constitution "will hang upon a single thread," and this people will save it. *Journal of Discourses*, 7:15 (July 4, 1854). See also Cannon, *United States Constitution*, 6, 12–13.

4   First Presidency to the Saints, Sept. 1840, in *T&S*, Oct. 1840, 178; First Presidency, Report, [Oct. 1840,] in *T&S*, Oct. 1840, 187. For Joseph's larger project of representing Mormons as modern Israel, see Shipps, *New Religious Tradition*, 51–64; and Moench, "New Israel," 42–56.

5   *T&S*, June 1841, 427 (*D&C*, 124:51, 55).

6   Coray, "1840 Discourse," 392.

7   *T&S*, July 1840, 141–42; Sept. 1840, 169–70; *Weekly North American*, Aug. 7, 1840; Hill, *Quest for Refuge*, 106; Leonard, *Nauvoo*, 276–97.

8   PreM, 714–25; *T&S*, Sept. 1840, 170–73; Oct. 1840, 190–91; JS to Robert Foster, Mar. 11, 1840, in *PWJS*, 499.

9   *BioS*, 267; PreM, 717. Lucy was dictating after Joseph's death when the question of succession was in the air. The manuscript version supported putting a Smith into office.

10 Newell and Avery, *Mormon Enigma*, 89–90.

11 JS to Robert Foster, Mar. 11, 1840, in *PWJS*, 500; Abbott, *Boosters and Businessmen*, 115; Cronon, *Nature's Metropolis*, 31–46.

12 JS to John C. Bennett, Aug. 8, 1840, JSC; *Sixth Census*, 377, 387, 391. For a population comparison, see Gaustad and Barlow, *Historical Atlas*, 296–97.

13 *D&C* [1835], 100:2 (*D&C*, 133:7–9).

14 First Presidency, Report, [Oct. 1840,] in *T&S*, Oct. 1840, 187–88; *Alton Telegraph*, Nov. 14, 1840; *D&C* [1835], 100:2 (*D&C*, 133:8–13).

15 For a discussion of this dual impulse, see Green, "Jews in LDS Thought," 137–64, and "Gathering and Election," 195–228.

16 Isaiah 11:11, 51:11; *BofM*, 68, 131–39, 502 (2 Nephi 3:24, Jacob 5, 3 Nephi 22:10); *T&S*, Aug. 1, 1844, 595 (*D&C*, 77:9); JS, Journal, Apr. 3, 1836, in *PJS*, 2:210 (110:11); *D&C* [1835], 100:2 (*D&C*, 133:12–13).

17 Although thought to be Jewish because of Joseph's statement that in going to Jerusalem he returned to the land of his fathers, Hyde himself said he had no Jewish ancestors and none have been discovered. Hyde, *Orson Hyde*, 489–91. For a description of the tract and the circumstances of publication, see Crawley, *Descriptive Bibliography*, 63–64.

18 Orson Hyde to JS, June 15, 1841, in *T&S*, Oct. 1, 1841, 552–53; General Conference of the Church, Minutes, Apr. 6, 1840, JSC.

19 Draper and Draper, "Gathering of the Jews," 139–50; [JS] to Dear Brethren, May 14, 1840, JSC; *BofC*, 44:32 (*D&C*, 42:39); *WJS*, 73–74 (May 16, 1841).

20 [JS] to Dear Brethren, May 14, 1840, JSC.

21 Quist, "John E. Page," 55; *T&S*, Oct. 1, 1841, 552–54; Orson Hyde to JS, July 17, 1841, in *T&S*, Oct. 15, 1841, 570; Epperson, *Mormons and Jews*, 152–55; Hyde, *Voice from Jerusalem*, 34. The best account of Hyde's journey is Hyde, *Orson Hyde*, 124–43.

22 Hyde, *Voice from Jerusalem*, 7.

23 Hyde, *Voice from Jerusalem*, 7–10, 16, 30, 32.

24 Hyde, *Voice from Jerusalem*, 22; JS to the Twelve, Dec. 15, 1840, in *PWJS*, 521. Hyde's

mission became national news. *Salem Register,* May 5, 1842; *Weekly North American,* May 1, 1840.

25 Esplin, "Emergence of Brigham Young," 431, 449, 471–72, 476; Arrington, *Brigham Young,* 94; Taylor, *Expectations Westward,* 43, 116; *HC,* 4:232. Between 1837 and 1846, the Mormons baptized 17,849 converts in Great Britain and 4,700 emigrated to the U.S. Harrison, "Early Victorian Britain," 14. On the immigration routes, see Gaustad and Barlow, *Historical Atlas,* 298.

26 Underwood, "Religious Milieu," 31–48, esp. 47; Esplin, "Emergence of Brigham Young," 452; Taylor, *Expectations Westward,* 37; Thorp, " 'Field Is White,' " 323–44.

27 Brigham Young to JS, May 7, 1840, JSC; Allen, Esplin, and Whittaker, *Men with a Mission,* 392; Harrison, "Victorian Britain," 1–15.

28 Esplin, "Emergence of Brigham Young," 392, 480; Allen, Esplin, and Whittaker, *Men with a Mission;* Crawley, *Descriptive Bibliography,* 108–13, 121–24, 148–51; JS to the Twelve, Dec. 15, 1840, JSC.

29 First Presidency, Report, [Oct. 1840,] in *T&S,* Oct. 1840, 187–88; JS to the Twelve, [Oct. 1840,] JSC.

30 *Weekly North American,* Mar. 21, 1840; First Presidency to the Saints Scattered Abroad, Jan. 15, 1841, in *T&S,* Jan. 15, 1841, 275.

31 John C. Bennett to JS and Sidney Rigdon, July 25, 27, 1840, JSC; A. Smith, *John Cook Bennett,* 3–12. Acquaintances said of Bennett that he believed himself "the smartest man in the nation; and if he cannot at once be placed at the head of the heap, he soon seeks a situation." George Miller to Dear Sir, Mar. 2, 1841, in *T&S,* July 1, 1842, 842.

32 A. Smith, *John Cook Bennett,* 17–33.

33 The complexities of Bennett's life are detailed in A. Smith, *John Cook Bennett.* His denial of belief in Mormon doctrine is stated in Bennett, *History of the Saints,* 5. See also A. Smith, "Bennett's Nauvoo," 111–18.

34 Coray, Journal, 3; Coray, "Recollections," 344; *WJS,* 59 (Jan. 5, 1841); General Conference of the Church, Minutes, Oct. 3, 1840, in *T&S,* Oct. 1840, 186–87.

35 John C. Bennett to the *Times and Seasons,* Dec. 16, 1840, in *T&S,* Jan. 1, 1841, 266–67; A. Smith, *John Cook Bennett,* 58–59; Leonard, *Nauvoo,* 101; Flanders, *Nauvoo,* 96; Kimball, "Wall to Defend," 491–97; Bennett and Cope, "Chartering the City," 17–40, esp. 22 and 34.

36 Kimball, "Nauvoo Charter," 39–47; Bennett and Cope, "Chartering the City," 26; Ford, *History of Illinois,* 265.

37 *T&S,* Jan. 15, 1841, 281–85; First Presidency to the Saints Scattered Abroad, Jan. 15, 1841, in *T&S,* Jan. 15, 1841, 273–74, 276.

38 *T&S,* June 1, 1841, 427, 424–25 (*D&C,* 124:60, 3, 6, 11); JS to the Elders in England, [Jan. 1841,] in *T&S,* Jan. 1, 1841, 260.

39 *T&S,* Feb. 2, 15, 22; Mar. 1, 15; Apr. 1, 1841, 316–22, 336–38, 355–56, 37–71; Nauvoo City Council, Minutes, Feb. 3, 8, 15, 22, Mar. 1, 1841.

40 Leonard, *Nauvoo,* 184–87. "You will discover that the greater part of the English brethren, have always worked under masters; and they have not so much notion of planning and shifting for themselves, particularly in a strange country, as the Americans." Orson Hyde to JS, June 15, 1841, in *T&S,* Oct. 1, 1841, 554.

41 Iowa High Council, Record, Mar. 6, 1840; *WJS,* 68 (Mar. 30, 1841).

42 Enders, "Dam for Nauvoo," 246–54; Flanders, *Nauvoo,* 151–53.

43 First Presidency, Report [Apr. 1841,] in *T&S,* Apr. 15, 1841, 385–86.

44 First Presidency to the Saints Scattered Abroad, Jan. 15, 1841, in *T&S,* Jan. 15, 1841, 276.

45 First Presidency to the Saints Scattered Abroad, Jan. 15, 1841, in *T&S,* Jan. 15, 1841, 273–74. On the origins of the name, see Leonard, *Nauvoo,* 58–59.

46 Coray, "1840 Discourse," 393. The belief in the Millennium remained strong despite the delay of the date. *T&S*, May 15, 1841, 411.

47 *T&S*, Mar. 1, 1841, 336–37; First Presidency to the Saints Scattered Abroad, Jan. 15, 1841, in *T&S*, Jan. 15, 1841, 277. In a more informal vein, Emma told her brother David Hale, "I feel quite anxious that all of my Fathers family should come and cettle in this country as I think it is far better than any other place east of here, I should also like to have you all investigate our doctrines and all become good Mormons, as we are generaly called, but there is no compulsion as to the subject of our religion, you can live here if you are not Mormons." Lorenzo D. Wasson and others to David Hale, Feb. 1841, CA.

48 JS to the Twelve, Oct. 1840, JSC.

CHAPTER 24 TEMPORALITIES AND SPIRITUALITIES

1 JS, Journal, Apr. 13, 1843, in *APR*, 363; Nauvoo High Council, Minutes, Oct. 20, 1839. Joseph's effort to find land for John Bernhisel illustrates the complexity of the land agent's work. JS to John M. Bernhisel, Apr. 13, 1841, JSC. Brigham Young and the Twelve acknowledged the complaints in 1841. "Let us not for a moment lend an ear to evil and designing men, who would subvert the truth, and blacken the character of the servant of the Most High God, by publishing abroad that the prophet is enriching himself on the spoils of the brethren." Brigham Young and others to the Brethren Scattered Abroad, Oct. 12, 1841, in *T&S*, Oct. 15, 1841, 569.

2 Don Carlos Smith to JS, June 3, 1841, JSC; Nauvoo High Council, Minutes, June 20; July 3, 1840; *WJS*, 75 (Aug. 16, 1841); Leonard, *Nauvoo*, 166, 175, 177; JS to Hancock County Recorder, Feb. 2, 1841, JSC. Joseph vetoed the first attempt of the high council to relieve him of his business responsibilities. What dissatisfied him is not clear. Nauvoo High Council, Minutes, June 27, 1840.

3 JS to Oliver Granger, May 4, 1841, JSC; JS and others to Edward Partridge and the Church, Mar. 20, 1839, in *PWJS*, 437 (*D&C*, 121:33).

4 *WJS*, 72 (May 16, 1841).

5 Snow and Winchester, *Citizens of Salem*; Whittaker, "Benjamin Winchester," 49; Crawley, *Descriptive Bibliography*, 104–106, 127–29; Whittaker, " 'Articles of Faith,' " 63–92.

6 *WJS*, 33 (Feb. 5, 1840). At the October 1841 conference Brigham Young "addressed the Elders at some length, on the importance of teaching abroad the first principles of the gospel, leaving the mysteries of the kingdom to be taught among the saints." *T&S*, Oct. 15, 1841, 578.

7 Allen, *William Clayton*; for McIntire, see *WJS*, 84–85, n. 14.

8 JS, Journal, Apr. 16, 1843, in *APR*, 366.

9 Clayton, Journal, May 17, 1843 (*D&C*, 131:7–8). Brooke, in *Refiner's Fire*, 3–5, and passim, makes much of the idea.

10 One of Priestley's reasons for denying the existence of spirit was that it led to the notion of "*the pre-existence of souls*," one of the corruptions of Christianity underlying belief in Christ's divinity. His ultimate aim was to overturn the atonement, which he thought was a slur on God's character. Price and Priestley, *Materialism and Philosophical Necessity*, xiv–xviii.

11 *WJS*, 17, n. 1; Cook, *Revelations*, 286–93.

12 *D&C* [1835], 82:5 (*D&C*, 93:29, 33).

13 *WJS*, 60 (Jan. 5, 1841); Palmer, Reminiscences, 304–306; JS, Journal, Apr. 16, 1843, in *APR*, 367.

14 *BofM*, 544 (Ether 3:15–16); *WJS*, 60 (Jan. 5, 1841). Jefferson quote from Gaustad,

Thomas Jefferson, 144. David Paulsen argues that Joseph Smith understood the embodiment of God and Christ by 1830. Paulsen, "Divine Embodiment," 19–21. On the evolving understanding of God, see Alexander, "Mormon Doctrine," 53–66.

15 *D&C* [1835], 82:5 (*D&C*, 93:33); *WJS*, 60 (Jan. 5, 1841). Later Joseph taught the eternal importance of procreation. Revelation, July 12, 1843, Revelations Collection (*D&C*, 132:19–20). Another revelation explained that celestial persons received a "natural body" in the resurrection. *D&C* [1835], 6:6 (*D&C*, 88:28).

16 *WJS*, 60–61 (Jan. 5, 1841). For other teachings on eternal matter and spirit, see *WJS*, 9 (July–Aug. 1839); *D&C* [1835], 82:5 (*D&C*, 93:29–35). For the ideas of fellow Vermonter Ethan Allen on eternal matter and intelligence, see Allen, *Oracle of Man*, 57–71, esp. 69.

17 *WJS*, 68 (Mar. 18, 1841).

18 *T&S*, June 1, 1841, 426 (*D&C*, 124:29); JS to the Church, Sept. 6, 1842, in *T&S*, Oct. 1, 1842, 935 (*D&C*, 128:18); *WJS*, 49, n. 1; Bishop, "Baptism for the Dead," 87; 1 Corinthians 15:29. John Brooke has found baptism for the dead among the German pietist mystics at Ephrata in the 1740s. *Refiner's Fire*, 243. For the practice in postbiblical times, see Trumbower, *Posthumous Salvation*.

19 JS to the Twelve, [Oct. 1840,] JSC; General Conference, Minutes, Apr. 8, 1841, in *T&S*, Apr. 15, 1841, 387–88; *T&S*, Oct. 1, 1841, 565; Bishop, "Baptism for the Dead," 88–90; Black and Black, *Annotated Record*.

20 JS to the Twelve, [Oct. 1840,] JSC; JS, Journal, Jan. 21, 1836, in *PJS*, 2:157; General Conference, Minutes, Oct. 3, 1841, in *T&S*, Oct. 1, 1841, 578. For a discussion of the Saints' interest in salvation for the dead before 1840, see Prince, *Power from On High*, 142–45.

21 JS, Journal, Sept. 11, 1842, in *PJS*, 2:473 (*D&C*, 128:18). In a message to the Church, Brigham Young and the Twelve said that "this dispensation comprehends all the great works of all former dispensations." Brigham Young and others to the Brethren Scattered Abroad, Oct. 12, 1841, in *T&S*, Oct. 15, 1841, 569.

22 *WJS*, 9–10 (Aug. 8, 1839); JS, Journal, Sept. 11, 1842, in *PJS*, 2:472–73 (*D&C*, 128:15, 17–18); Malachi 4:6. The implications of "welding" are explicated in Hickman, "New World Baroque."

23 *WJS*, 9–10, 60 (Aug. 8, 1839, Jan. 5, 1841); JS, *New Translation*, 594 (Moses 1:38).

24 *T&S*, June 1, 1841, 426 (*D&C*, 124:29–35). In the temple, Joseph declared in January 1841, "all the functions of the priesthood" could be exercised. First Presidency to the Saints Scattered Abroad, Jan. 15, 1841, in *T&S*, Jan. 15, 1841, 274.

25 Huntington, Autobiography, 32–33; Journal History, Apr. 6, 1841; *T&S*, June 1, 1841, 426 (*D&C*, 128:43); General Conference, Minutes, Oct. 4, 1840, in *T&S*, Oct. 1840, 186; *T&S*, Sept. 15, 1841, 543; Arrington, "William Weeks," 337–59. On Wisconsin lumbering, see Flanders, *Nauvoo*, 183–85, and Rowley, "Wisconsin Pineries," 119–48.

26 *T&S*, Apr. 15, 1841, 375–76, 381.

27 Van Wagoner, *Sidney Rigdon*, 283; *T&S*, Apr. 15, 1841, 377; Clayton, *Journals*, 85–86 (Apr. 6, 1841).

28 *T&S*, Apr. 15, 1841, 377.

29 *WJS*, 70 (Apr. 9, 1841); Brigham Young and others to the Brethren Scattered Abroad, Oct. 12, 1841, in *T&S*, Oct. 15, 1841, 567. For examples of bonded agents, see H. W. Miller, Bond, Apr. 10, 1841; William Smith, Bond, Apr. 13, 1841; Leonard Soby, Bond, Apr. 15, 1841; Ira Miles, Certificate, Oct. 11, 1842, all in Whitney Collection.

30 *T&S*, Aug. 2, 1841, 494.

31 *T&S*, July 1, 1841, 455; *Salem Register*, Aug. 9, 1841. November 8 was a private ceremony; the formal opening was November 21. Young, *Manuscript History*, 112 (Nov. 21, 1841); Colvin, *Nauvoo Temple*, 184–87; Woodruff, *Journals*, 2:138 (Nov. 21, 1841).

32 *Deseret News*, Jan 25; Apr. 18, 1855 (*D&C*, 125, 126); Rough Draft Notes, ManH,

Sept. 5, 1841; *WJS*, 80, 77 (Nov. 7, 1841; Oct. 2, 1841); 1 Peter 3:17–18, 4:6; Woodruff, *Journals*, 2:142–43 (Dec. 19, 1841); *HC*, 4:393–98, 402; Newell and Avery, *Mormon Enigma*, 102–3.

33   *T&S*, June 15, 1841, 447; Firmage and Mangrum, *Zion in the Courts*, 94.

34   JS to Editors of the *Times and Seasons*, May 6, 1841, in *T&S*, May 15, 1841, 414; Johannsen, *Stephen A. Douglas*, 105; Capers, *Stephen A. Douglas*, 5–12.

35   *T&S*, June 15, 1841, 447–49.

36   Firmage and Mangrum, *Zion in the Courts*, 94; *History of Adams County*, 106; Rough Draft Notes, ManH, June 10, 1841; JS to Friends in Illinois, Dec. 20, 1841, in *T&S*, Jan. 1, 1842, 651. For an analysis of Douglas's courtship of the Mormons, see Flanders, *Nauvoo*, 225, and Van Orden, "Stephen A. Douglas," 359–78.

37   ManH C-1, 1205–6.

38   JS to Friends in Illinois, Dec. 20, 1841, in *T&S*, Jan. 1, 1842, 651.

39   Sharp's early life and his first reactions to the Mormons are outlined in Hamilton, "Sharp's Turning Point," 16–22. For further information on Sharp, see Gregg, *Hancock County*, 748–57; Launius, "Sharp's Unfinished History," 27–45; Hampshire, "Thomas Sharp," 82–100.

40   Quoted in Marshall, "Thomas Sharp's Turning Point," 19. Sharp's observations were reprinted in the *New-Yorker*, Apr. 24, 1841, 92.

41   Quoted in Marshall, "Thomas Sharp's Turning Point," 20; Gregg, *Hancock County*, 749.

42   JS to Thomas Sharp, May 26, 1841, and Sharp's undated reply in *Warsaw Signal*, June 2, 1841.

43   *Warsaw Signal*, July 21, 1841.

44   *Warsaw Signal*, July 21, 28, 1841.

45   *Warsaw Signal*, July 28, 1841; Hallwas, "Mormon Nauvoo," 167; *T&S*, Oct. 1, 1841, 562–63; Hallwas and Launius, *Cultures in Conflict*, 78–82.

46   *T&S*, July 1, 15, 456–57; Aug. 2, 1841, 480, 495. For examples of the image of Mormon militants, see *Manufacturers and Farmers Journal*, Aug. 9, 29, 1841; May 4, 1843; *New-York Tribune*, May 17, 1843; Parsons, *Mormon Fanaticism*, 81–83. Sharp's inflammatory articles circulated in the East. *Fitchburg* (Mass.) *Sentinel*, Jan. 6, 1842; *Connecticut Courant*, Aug. 14, 1841; *New-York Tribune*, Dec. 7, 1841; Gregg, *Hancock County*, 750.

47   *T&S*, Aug. 2, 1841, 496–97.

48   *T&S*, Aug. 2, 496–97; Sept. 15, 1841, 543.

49   Don Carlos Smith to JS, June 3, 1841, JSC.

50   Flanders, *Nauvoo*, 42, 129; Leonard, *Nauvoo*, 58. Two additional notes of $1,250 were due in five and ten years, and $2,000 was due to Hugh White for his share of the Hotchkiss partnership. Flanders's analysis of the debt obligations is based on his research in the deed book.

51   Horace R. Hotchkiss to Sidney Rigdon and JS, Mar. 17, 1840, JSC; Horace R. Hotchkiss to JS, Apr. 1, 1840, JSC.

52   JS to Horace R. Hotchkiss, July 28, 1840, JSC; Smith Tuttle to JS, Sept. 1841, JSC; Flanders, *Nauvoo*, 130. Joseph outlined the plan in a letter to Hotchkiss on August 25, 1841, in JSC.

53   William Smith to JS, Aug. 5, 1841, JSC; Smith Tuttle to JS, Sept. 1841, JSC; Horace R. Hotchkiss to Joseph Smith, July 24, 1841, JSC.

54   JS to Horace R. Hotchkiss, Aug. 25, 1841, JSC.

55   Horace R. Hotchkiss to Sidney Rigdon and JS, Mar. 17, 1840, JSC; Horace R. Hotchkiss to JS, Apr. 1, 1840, JSC; JS to Horace R. Hotchkiss, July 28 and Aug. 25, 1841, JSC.

56   Conference, Minutes, Aug. 16, 1841, in *T&S*, Sept. 1, 1841, 521; Arrington, *Brigham Young*, 98–100; Brigham Young and others to the Brethren Scattered Abroad, Oct. 12, 1841, in *T&S*, Oct. 15, 1841, 568; JS to Smith Tuttle, Oct. 9, 1841, JSC.

57 JS to Smith Tuttle, Oct. 9, 1841, JSC.

58 Hill, *Joseph Smith*, 291; Flanders, *Nauvoo*, 132–34.

59 Balleisen, *Bankruptcy*, 12–13, 104–107, 123.

60 Oaks and Hill, *Carthage Conspiracy*, 53–54; *Nauvoo Wasp*, May 7, 1842; Flanders, *Nauvoo*, 169. Oaks and Bentley count twenty-six Mormons who applied for bankruptcy under the law. "Steamboat *Nauvoo*," 751.

61 JS, Journal, Apr. 15–16, 18, 1842, in *PJS*, 2:377. Joseph's list of debts totaled $73,066.38. Oaks and Bentley, "Steamboat *Nauvoo*," 753. An eastern newspaper reported Joseph's debts at $100,000. *Portland Maine Transcript*, June 18, 1842, 79.

62 Bennett, *History of the Saints*, 96–98. The transfer deed had actually been made out on October 5, 1841, during the conference when Joseph, with the help of Brigham Young, was straightening out his financial affairs. Flanders, *Nauvoo*, 170. For an argument against the validity of Bennett's charges, see Oaks and Bentley, "Steamboat *Nauvoo*," 759–62.

63 Oaks and Bentley, "Steamboat *Nauvoo*," 735–82; Cannon, "Bankruptcy Proceedings," 425–33.

64 This is the judgment of Flanders, *Nauvoo*, 319. Justin Butterfield twice recommended that Joseph be discharged, but the U.S. Treasury solicitor demurred. Oaks and Bentley, in "Steamboat *Nauvoo*," 762–65. Joseph was still trying to pay Butterfield for the steamboat in 1844. William Clayton to Justin Butterfield, Jan. 18, 1844, Fleming Collection.

65 Joseph asked Butterfield about the state of his obligation to Hotchkiss once bankruptcy was declared. Butterfield told him that if the debts were discharged the obligation to pay was dissolved, but the possessors of the Hotchkiss lots, lacking a title, could not sell the property. The property rights reverted to the original owner. JS, Journal, Jan. 5, 1843, in *APR*, 285.

66 JS to Horace R. Hotchkiss, May 13, 1842, JSC; JS to Horace Hotchkiss, Nov. 26, 1842, Whitney Collection.

67 Flanders, *Nauvoo*, 171–75. In March 1843, the Hancock County recorder, unable to find a deed or power of attorney authorizing Hotchkiss's purchase of the lands in 1836, questioned the legality of the purchase. The recorder recommended that Joseph "make n[o] payment to said Hotchkiss & Gillett until such search of Record be made." Hancock County Recorder to Sir, Mar. 8, 1843, Whitney Collection.

68 This was the fate of the famous William Cooper, as eloquently described in Taylor, *William Cooper's Town*.

CHAPTER 25   STORIES OF ETERNITY

1 I follow the count of Compton, *In Sacred Loneliness*, save for Lucinda Pendleton Morgan Harris, whose marriage to Joseph Smith in 1838 is contested by Anderson and Faulring, "Plural Wives," 75, 109–11. Cf. Compton, "Trajectory of Plurality," 1–38. Other marriage experiments are analyzed in Foster, *Religion and Sexuality*.

2 Quote from G. Smith, "Nauvoo Roots," 10. The acceptance of plural marriage as a test of loyalty is developed in Daynes, *Marriage System*, 17–35; and Ehat, "Temple Ordinances," 46–75.

3 JS to Nancy Rigdon, [1842] in *PWJS*, 539. Joseph's first recorded revelation in 1828 had been a ferocious rebuke, and other reprimands followed through the years. *BofC*, 2:5 (*D&C*, 3:15) specifically warned him not to allow "the counsel of thy director to be trampled upon."

4 Quote from Compton, *In Sacred Loneliness*, 212. On the angel with a sword, see Joseph B. Noble, Affidavit, June 26, 1869, Affidavits. Benjamin F. Johnson to George S.

Gibbs, Apr.–Oct. 1903, in LeBaron, *Benjamin F. Johnson*, 227; Snow, *Lorenzo Snow*, 69–70.

5   Stephen, "Autonomous Imagination," 41–67.

6   *WJS*, 6, 12, 20, n. 21 (June 27; ca. July–Aug. 1839); Compton, *In Sacred Loneliness*, 212; *T&S*, Apr. 1, 1842, 745; JS, Journal, May 1, 1842, in *PJS*, 2:379; JS, Journal, Feb. 9, 1843, in *APR*, 300; Revelation, July 12, 1843, Revelations Collection (*D&C*, 132:4).

7   G. D. Smith, "Nauvoo Roots," 2, n. 4. In a forthcoming paper, M. Scott Bradshaw argues the difficulty of proving bigamous relations in Joseph's case.

8   Joseph B. Noble, Affidavit, June 26, 1869, Affidavits.

9   Compton, *In Sacred Loneliness*, 12–15, 59–60; Newell and Avery, *Mormon Enigma*, 136; Francis Higbee to Mr. Gregg, May 1844, quoted in G. D. Smith, "Nauvoo Roots," 7. On Joseph's paternity, see Compton, *In Sacred Loneliness*, 12, and Leonard, *Nauvoo*, 345. On the ambiguities of the evidence, see Daynes, *Marriage System*, 29–30, and Anderson and Faulring, "Plural Wives," 82–83.

10 Compton, "Trajectory of Plurality," 2, and *In Sacred Loneliness*, 15–16. Marriage to two of these nine has been questioned: Elizabeth Davis Durfee and Sarah Kingsley Cleveland. Anderson and Faulring, "Plural Wives," 75. The number rises to eleven married women if the debated marriage to Lucinda Pendleton (Harris) is included. The data on the wives was compiled by David Allred and Benjamin Pykles from the information in Compton, *In Sacred Loneliness*. See also Van Wagoner, "Mormon Polyandry," 69–83.

11 Whitney, Autobiography, [2]; Revelation, July 27, 1842, Revelations Collection; Bradley and Woodward, "Nauvoo Marriages," 96. Compton believes sexual relations were likely part of all these marriages. Compton, *In Sacred Loneliness*, 14–15.

12 For a rationale for marriages to married women, see Cooper, *Mormon Covenant Organization*, 142–47; Miles, "Economics of Salvation," 34–45; and Young, *Essential*, xxv. Six of the eight married women in 1841 and 1842 are known to have been sealed to Joseph in the temple after his death. Compton, *In Sacred Loneliness*, 4–5. The belief in salvation through connection to Joseph Smith and other leading figures led eventually to sealing of nonrelatives to these men. Irving, "Law of Adoption," 291–314.

13 Bradley and Woodward, "Nauvoo Marriages," 90–93. "Nearly everyone who has commented on their first introduction to polygamy wrote that they at first looked at it with revulsion and shock, and fought the idea for a time." Compton, *In Sacred Loneliness*, 238.

14 Bradley and Woodward, "Nauvoo Marriages," 90–93, 96, 99–100; Young, Autobiography, [1]; Young, "Diary," 291–92 (June 5–26, 1844); Compton, *In Sacred Loneliness*, 71; Bradley and Woodward, *4 Zinas*, 132.

15 Compton, *In Sacred Loneliness*, 4–6, 10, 8; Leonard, *Nauvoo*, 345; Anderson and Faulring, "Plural Wives," 75–77; Revelation, July 12, 1843, Revelations Collection (*D&C*, 132:55). See also Brodie, *No Man Knows*, 461–65.

16 Compton, *In Sacred Loneliness*, 212 and passim. When Joseph's close associates recalled their plural marriages in Nauvoo, they recounted a ceremony with an officiator and witnesses present. Adeline B. A. Benson, Affidavit, Sept. 5, 1869; Pamelia A. Benson, Affidavit, Sept. 6, 1869; Orson Hyde, Affidavit, Sept. 15, 1869; Eliza Partridge, Affidavit, July 1, 1869; Mary Ann Pratt, Affidavit, Sept. 3, 1869; Patty Sessions, Statement, June 1867; Catharine Phillips Smith, Affidavit, Jan. 28, 1903; all in Affidavits. Martha McBride Kimball, who married Joseph Smith in August 1842, testified the ceremony was performed "in said Church according to the laws of the same regulating marriage." Martha McBride Kimball, Affidavit, July 8, 1869, Affidavits.

17 Foster, *Religion and Sexuality*, 16; Goodliffe, "Economics and Marriage," 71–79; Clark, "Women and the Body," 145–53.

18 Cook, *William Law*, 99. One made much of a supposed comment of Joseph's that "whenever I see a pretty woman, I have to pray for grace." Wyl, *Joseph Smith*, 55.

19 Brodie, *No Man Knows*, 297; *BofM*, 127 (Jacob 2:35, 28, 33); *BofM*, 44:23 (*D&C*, 42:24). Perhaps knowledge of the marriage revelation had moved some of the brethren to unauthorized experiments, for the records kept returning to the theme. *BofC*, 64:18 (*D&C*, 63:16); *D&C* [1835], 74:5 (*D&C*, 66:10).

20 Almera W. Johnson Barton, Affidavit, Aug. 1, 1833, in Affidavits; *Elders' Journal*, July 1838, 45; *FWR*, 167–68 (Apr. 12, 1838); Revelation, July 12, 1843, Revelations Collection (*D&C*, 132:44). The rules are reminiscent of the Deuteronomic code on adultery. Deuteronomy 22:13–30.

21 On Joseph's proposal to Nancy Rigdon, see Van Wagoner, *Sidney Rigdon*, 294–302. In a letter to the *Nauvoo Wasp*, Sept. 3, 1842, Sidney Rigdon said Nancy denied the letter was in Joseph's hand and furthermore said that Joseph denied writing it, but the letter has been accepted by Dean Jessee, editor of Joseph Smith's personal writings, as authentic. *PWJS*, 537.

22 JS to Nancy Rigdon, [1842,] in *PWJS*, 538–39.

23 Quoted in Hardman, *Charles Grandison Finney*, 369–70.

24 JS to Nancy Rigdon, [1842,] in *PWJS*, 539.

25 Revelation, July 12, 1843, Revelations Collection (*D&C*, 132:42–43). On the regulation of plural marriage in Utah, see Daynes, *Marriage System*, 194–96. A year after Joseph's death, Parley Pratt caught the spirit of strict regulation in an admonition to couples seeking to be sealed: "There is not a more unlawful, and unjustifiable principle in exist[e]nce, and one more calculated to injure and destroy the church than the principle of seeking to enjoy those blessings in the wrong place and time, that is to say, without complying with the requisitions of heaven." "Proclamation," in *The Prophet* (New York), May 24, 1845.

26 *BofM*, 127 (Jacob 2:24, 30). Deuteronomy 17:17 and 21:15–17 acknowledge plural marriage but not to excess. I thank Jack Welch for these references.

27 Revelation, July 12, 1843, Revelations Collection (*D&C*, 132:1, 34, 32). Early Mormons cited Milton justifying plural marriage on the basis of the biblical predents. Milton, *Christian Doctrine*, in *Complete Poems*, 994; Tanner, "Mormon of Milton," 203.

28 G. D. Smith, "Nauvoo Roots," 33. Danel Bachman counts just nineteen. Bachman, "Plural Marriage," 189.

29 Revelation, July 12, 1843, Revelations Collection (*D&C*, 132:29).

30 Revelation, July 12, 1843, Revelations Collection (*D&C*, 132:7).

31 Revelation, July 12, 1843, Revelations Collection (*D&C*, 132:16–17, 19–20).

32 Clayton, *Journals*, 102 (May 16, 1843) (*D&C*, 131:2–3).

33 *BofC*, 26:7, 38:4, 43:3, 45:1, 53:1, 59:1, 62:1, 63:1, 64:1 (*D&C*, 25:8, 36:7, 41:2, 43:1, 50:1, 58:1, 61:1, 62:1, 64:1). Even the "law" given in February 1831 was addressed to the "elders of my church," though it obviously had wider application. *BofC*, 44:1 (*D&C*, 42:1). The two exceptions were revelations to Emma Smith and Vienna Jacques. *BofC*, 26 (*D&C*, 25); *D&C* [1835], 84:7 (*D&C*, 90:28–31).

34 The combination of the civic and the domestic was typical of women's involvement in the public sphere in Joseph's time. Boylan, *Women's Activism*, 6–7. Women were also involved in baptisms for the dead. Bishop, "Baptism for the Dead," 87–88.

35 Revelation 3:21; Revelation, July 12, 1843, Revelations Collection (*D&C*, 132:19, 49). For domestic heavens in the period just following Joseph Smith, see McDannell and Lang, *Heaven*, 264–75. For a discussion of the walled-off family, see Fliegelman, *Patriarchal Authority*, 264–66.

36 *T&S*, Mar. 1, 1842, 704 (Abraham 1:2).

37 *WJS*, 8–9 (ca. July–Aug. 1839).

38 Foster, "Defense of Polygamy," 21–24; Foster, *Religion and Sexuality*, 175–77.

39 *PJS*, 2:548, 562; Leonard, *Nauvoo*, 52–53; Derr, Cannon, and Beecher, *Women of Covenant*, 26–27; Melder, *Women's Rights*, 62–76; Boylan, *Women's Activism*; *Woman's Exponent*, Sept. 1, 1883, 51.

40 Derr, Cannon, and Beecher, *Women of Covenant*, 26–27; *Woman's Exponent*, Sept. 1, 1883, 51; Female Relief Society, Minutes, Mar. 17, 30, 1842.

41 *WJS*, 118, 115–16 (Apr. 28, 1842). For varying discussions of women and the priesthood in Joseph's time, see Prince, *Power from On High*, 201–09; Quinn, "Priesthood Since 1843," 365–409; Howard, "Priesthood for Women," 18–30; Holzapfel and Holzapfel, *Women of Nauvoo*, 119–26.

42 *WJS*, 117, 115 (Apr. 28, 1842).

43 *BofC*, 26:6 (*D&C*, 25:7); *WJS*, 105 (Mar. 17, 1842); JS, Journal, Mar. 17, 1842, in *PJS*, 2:371. The minute taker, Eliza R. Snow, called Emma Smith the "Presidentess" and after Joseph's death referred to Brigham Young's wife Mary Ann with the same title, as though the wife of the Church president implied leadership. *WJS*, 104 (Mar. 17, 1842); Derr, "Lion and the Lioness," 64. By Joseph's death in 1844, over 1,300 names were on the rolls of the Relief Society. Ward, "Female Relief Society," 86–203.

44 Bergera, "Plural Marriage," 59–90; Female Relief Society, Minutes, Mar. 30, 1842; *WJS*, 118 (Apr. 28, 1842).

45 *BofC*, 38:6; 44:29 (*D&C*, 36:8; 42:36); *D&C* [1835], 100:1 (*D&C* 133:2).

46 Brown, "Temple Work," 360–74. For an argument that the architectural similarities meant Joseph did not construct the endowment ceremonies until after the building was planned, see Prince, *Power from On High*, 132–33.

47 *T&S*, June 1, 1841, 426 (*D&C*, 124:40–41).

48 Brooke, *Refiner's Fire*, 249–53; Heber C. Kimball to Parley P. Pratt, June 17, 1842, Pratt Correspondence. On Masonry and the endowment, see Fielding, "Journal," 147. Benjamin Johnson said Joseph told him, "Freemasonry, as at present, was the apostate endowments, as sectarian religion was the apostate religion." Johnson, *Life's Review*, 85. For the literature on Mormonism and Masonry, see Homer, "Freemasonry," 2–113. See also Prince, *Power from On High*, 134–48.

49 Homer, "Freemasonry," 9–10, 27; Leonard, *Nauvoo*, 318; Godfrey, "Masons," 83.

50 Morcombe, "Masonry and Mormonism," 448; Jonas quote from Leonard, *Nauvoo*, 315; Lyon, "Free Masonry at Nauvoo," 76; Nauvoo Masonic Lodge, *Minutes*, 20–23 (Mar. 15–16, 1842).

51 JS, Journal, Mar. 15, 1842, in *PJS*, 2:370; Woodruff, *Journals*, 2:158–59 (Mar. 15, 1842).

52 Homer, "Freemasonry," 30–31; JS, Journal, June 24, 1843, in *APR*, 388; Leonard, *Nauvoo*, 391; Allen, "Masonic Hall," 39–49.

53 Morgan, *Illustrations of Masonry*, gives a taste of Masonic rituals.

54 Heber C. Kimball to Parley P. Pratt, June 17, 1842, Pratt Correspondence; Bullock, *Freemasonry*.

55 Michael Quinn emphasizes the temple endowment's ascent into heaven as a distinguishing feature. *Early Mormonism*, 184–90.

56 Hume, *Essays*, 76–78; Taves, *Experiencing Religion*, 46.

57 Homer, "Freemasonry," 27; Stevens, *Fraternities*, xvi; Carnes, *Secret Ritual*; Clawson, *Constructing Brotherhood*.

58 In the higher orders of Masonry, the search for the celestial received greater emphasis than in the first degrees Joseph passed through. Homer, "Freemasonry," 16–17, 106–107. For a reading that emphasizes the common effort to overcome competitiveness, see Epperson, "Virtue of Friendship," 88–91.

59 Ozick, "Gershom Scholem," 145.

60 Owens, "Kabbalah," 173–78; Quinn, "Prayer Circles," 79–105; Nibley, "Prayer Circle," 41–78. For discussions of Kabbalah, see Scholem, *Kabbalah*, and Idel, *Absorbing Perfections*.

61 Owens, "Kabbalah"; Brooke, *Refiner's Fire*, 252; Bloom, *American Religion*, 99, 105.

62 JS, Journal, May 4, 1842, in *PJS*, 2:380. On the props and scenery, see *Deseret Semi-Weekly News*, Feb. 15, 1884, 2.

63   Rough Draft Notes, ManH, May 4, 1842; Ehat, "4 May, 1842," 48–62; Prince, *Power from On High*, 137, n. 87.

64   Allen, *William Clayton*, 176–80.

65   *T&S*, Mar. 1, 1842, 704.

66   See chapter 15, above.

67   Joseph had been discoursing on astronomy for a number of years. *WJS*, 45, n. 1; JS, Journal, Oct. 1 and Dec. 16, 1835; May 6, 1838, in *PJS*, 2:45, 106, 239.

68   *T&S*, Mar. 15, 719–21 and May 16, 1842, 783–84 (Abraham, 3:1, 11, facsimile 3, facsimile 2). On names in Abraham, see Gee and Ricks, "Historicity," 63–98.

69   Emerson quote in Richardson, *Emerson*, 5. The idea of multiple earths had been assimilated into orthodox Christian thought in Chalmers, *Christian Revelation*, 26–29, 34–35, 40, and others, but it was to remain controversial through the nineteenth century. Crowe, *Extraterrestrial Life*, 241–46.

70   JS, *New Translation*, 594 (Moses 1:33); *E&MS*, Aug. 1832, [18] (Moses 7:30). On Joseph Smith and multiple worlds see Paul, *Mormon Cosmology*, 75–98.

71   Koyré, *Infinite Universe*, 275.

72   *T&S*, Mar. 15, 1842, 719 (Abraham 3:2).

73   2 Peter 3:8; *T&S*, Mar. 15, 1842, 719 (Abraham 3:3–6, 8–9).

74   Derek Jensen describes the efforts of eighteenth-century astronomers to restore hierarchy within a Copernican universe. Jensen, "Cosmologies."

75   Genesis 22:17; Revelation, July 12, 1843, Revelations Collection (*D&C*, 132:30); *T&S*, Mar. 15, 1842, 720 (Abraham 3:19). The Ptolemaic system had its ascending intelligences too. Intelligences were the motor force that turned the spheres and moved the stars and planets, and they rose from low to high depending on the rank of their spheres. Ptolemy, like Abraham, envisioned a hierarchical order, both physical and intellectual, embedded in nature.
       Joseph's writings on intelligences and stars have a medieval spirit. As Christian philosophers absorbed conceptions of "motor intelligences," they debated the question of how these intelligences were created. Hellenic and Arabic opinion tended to make them subcreations rather than the creations of God. Higher intelligences beget lesser intelligences farther down the line. Christians insisted that all were creations of God. Though scarcely aware of the controversy, Joseph took a stand in this debate by declaring none of the intelligences were created. Bemrose, *Angelic Intelligences*, 23–31.

76   *D&C* [1835], 86 (*D&C*, 93:36).

77   *BofM*, 258 (Alma 13:3); *T&S*, Mar. 15, 1842, 720 (Abraham 3:22–24). For ancient stories of creation by councils, see Peterson, "Divine Nature," 471–594. Comparisons of the Moses and Abraham creation accounts are found in Norman, "Adam's Navel," 81–97; Hutchinson, "Creation Narratives," 11–74.

78   Revelation 12:7–9; JS, *New Translation*, 599–600 (Moses 4:1–4); *T&S*, Mar. 15, 1842, 720 (Abraham 3:27–28).

79   *T&S*, Mar. 15, 1842, 720 (Abraham 3:26).

80   Clayton, Journal, Apr. 2, 1843 (*D&C*, 130:18–19); *D&C* [1835], 82:6 (*D&C*, 93:36–37); JS, Journal, Dec. 28, 1842, in *APR*, 259.

81   Brodie, *No Man Knows*, 171–72. Joseph may have also owned the book. In January 1844, he donated Dick's "Philosophy" to the Nauvoo Library and Literary Institute, but whether it was Dick's *Philosophy of Religion* or his *Philosophy of a Future State* is unknown. Godfrey, "Nauvoo Library," 388. Dick believed in gradations of intelligence in the world and in the universe. He also conceived of "THE THRONE OF GOD" at the center of the universe, around which all other bodies circulated. "This grand central body may be considered as the *Capital* of the universe." Dick, *Philosophy of a Future State*, in *Works*, 87, 91–92, 95, 102–103. On Dick, see Astore, *Thomas Dick*.

82   Tocqueville, *Democracy in America*, 453. "Boundlessness" is John Higham's term in his essay *Boundlessness to Consolidation*.

CHAPTER 26   PERILS

1   John C. Bennett to James Gordon Bennett, Aug. 27, 1842, in *New York Herald*, Aug. 30, 1842; *Boston Daily Evening Transcript*, Sept. 8, 1842.

2   Ford, *History of Illinois*, 263. A. Smith, *John Cook Bennett*, offers a clear, balanced, well-researched narrative of Bennett's Nauvoo career and his break with Joseph Smith. For a partisan assessment, see Skinner, "John C. Bennett," 249–65.

3   JS to the Church, June 23, 1842, in *T&S*, July 1, 1842, 839.

4   George Miller to Dear Sir, Mar. 2, 1841, in *T&S*, July 1, 1842, 842; JS to the Church, June 23, 1842, in *T&S*, July 1, 1842, 839–40; JS to Thomas Carlin, June 24, 1842, in JSC.

5   JS to Thomas Carlin, June 24, 1842, JSC; JS to the Church, June 23, 1842, in *T&S*, July 1, 1842, 840; Nauvoo High Council, Minutes, May 20, 1842. See also JS, Journal, May 24, 1842, in *PJS*, 2:387; Bergera, "Plural Marriage," 67–71. Chauncey Higbee's brother Francis may have been involved in the same scandal. JS, Journal, June 29, 1842, in *PJS*, 2:395.

6   A. Smith, *John Cook Bennett*, 89. The others charged with seducing women in this period or marrying illegally are analyzed in Bergera, "Plural Marriage," 74–90. Most made no claim to be authorized by Joseph Smith.

7   JS, Journal, May 7, 1842, in *PJS*, 2:381; Rough Draft Notes, ManH, May 7, 1842; Jessee, "Joseph Smith's History," 441.

8   Once John Taylor (not the apostle), acting in his priesthood office of teacher, shadowed Bennett and reported his suspicious movements. John Taylor, Testimony, 1:397–98, in U.S. Court of Appeals. Hyrum, who at this point was unaware of Joseph's plural marriage doctrine, wanted to prosecute Bennett immediately. Bennett begged to meet with Joseph, whom he thought had a softer heart. Hyrum Smith, Affidavit, July 23, 1842, in *T&S*, Aug. 1, 1842, 870–71; Ehat, "Temple Ordinances," 56–59. Bennett claimed Joseph allowed him to withdraw from the Church "if he desires to do so." *Sangamo Journal*, July 8, 1842.

9   John C. Bennett, Affidavit, May 17, 1842, in *T&S*, July 1, 1842, 841; *Nauvoo Wasp*, June 25, 1842; JS, Journal, May 29, 1842, in *PJS*, 2:385; Nauvoo City Council, Minutes, May 19, 1842. Bennett resigned as mayor amid rumors that he had built a brothel in the city. The previous week, the city council had passed an ordinance against brothels. Nauvoo City Council, Minutes, May 14, 19, 1842; *Nauvoo Wasp*, May 21, 1842. On the brothel, see John Taylor, Testimony, 1:403–404, in U.S. Court of Appeals.

10 Nauvoo High Council, Minutes, May 25, 1842; *Nauvoo Wasp*, May 21, 1842; *T&S*, June 15, 1842, 830; Hyrum Smith, Affidavit, July 23, 1842, in *T&S*, Aug. 1, 1842, 870–71; JS, Journal, May 26, 1842, in *PJS*, 2:387–88; Rough Draft Notes, ManH, May 25–26, 1842.

11 Female Relief Society, Minutes, May 26, 1842.

12 Bennett had to be removed from the Church, from the mayorship, from the Masonic lodge, and from the Nauvoo Legion. JS, Journal, May 26, 1842, in *PJS*, 2:387; Nauvoo City Council, Minutes, May 19, 1842; Nauvoo Lodge, Minutes, June 2; July 7–8, 1842; Nauvoo Legion, Record, Aug. 3, 1842. Bennett sent a letter in support of Joseph's character to the *Sangamo Journal* in Springfield, a letter the editor refused to publish, but the gesture did not quiet growing suspicions. *Nauvoo Wasp*, June 18, 1842; A. Smith, *John Cook Bennett*, 90–91.

13 Nauvoo High Council, Minutes, May 20, 24–25, 27–28, 1842; JS, Journal, May 26, June 4, 1842, in *PJS*, 2:387, 389; A. Jonas to George Miller, May 4, 1842, Freemasonry Letters; Bergera, "Plural Marriage," 66–72; *T&S*, June 15, 1842, 830, 842; Nauvoo Lodge, Minutes, July 7–8, 1842; Woodruff, *Journals*, 2:179 (June 18, 1842).

14 Rough Draft Notes, ManH, May 25, 1842; A. Smith, *John Cook Bennett*, 91–93.

15 A. Smith, *John Cook Bennett*, 98.

16 *Sangamo Journal*, July 8, 15 (two letters), 22; Aug. 19 (two letters); Sept. 21, 1842; John
C. Bennett to Mr. Edwards, June 27, 1842, in *Burlington* (Iowa), *Hawk Eye*, June 30,
1842; Bennett, *History of the Saints*, 287–88; A. Smith, *John Cook Bennett*, 101–102.

17 *T&S*, July 1, 1842, 840; *Nauvoo Wasp*, June 25, 1842; JS to Thomas Carlin, June 30,
1842, JSC.

18 JS to Thomas Carlin, June 24, 1842, *JSC*.

19 Rough Draft Notes, ManH, July 22, 1842; Jolley, "Nauvoo Newspaper," 487–96; *T&S*,
Aug. 1, 1842, 869; Female Relief Society, Petition [July 1842,] 6; *T&S*, Aug. 1, 1842,
869; Nauvoo City Council and Citizens to Thomas Carlin, July 22, 1842, in Nauvoo
City Council, Minutes, July 22, 1842.

20 *T&S*, Aug. 1, 1842, 869–75; *Affidavits and Certificates*; Crawley, *Descriptive Bibliography*,
202–204; A. Smith, *John Cook Bennett*, 105–109; Martha H. Brotherton to John C.
Bennett, July 13, 1842, in Bennett, *History of the Saints*, 236–40.

21 Richards, Journal, Aug. 4, 7, 1842; A. Smith, *John Cook Bennett*, 109; Bennett to JS,
Aug. 16, 1842, in *PJS*, 2:460. The letter, dated May 8, 1842, appeared in the May 16,
1842, issue of the *New York Herald*.

22 JS, Journal, Aug. 26, 29, 1842, in *PJS*, 2:443–44, 447; A. Smith, *John Cook Bennett*,
117–18, 120–21. Bennett lectured against Mormonism on the same platform as Origen
Bacheler, an old enemy of the Saints. *New York Herald*, Aug. 31, 1842.

23 *Warsaw Signal*, Aug. 6, 1842; A. Smith, *John Cook Bennett*, 124; *Missouri Reporter*, in
T&S, Aug. 1, 1842, 877; *New York Herald*, Oct. 21, 1842; A. Smith, "Introduction,"
xxxii–xxxiii; Ford, *History of Illinois*, 263; Bennett, *History of the Saints*, xxxii; *Boston Daily
Evening Transcript*, Sept. 8, 1842. The *St. Louis Gazette* and *Missouri Reporter* remained
suspicious of Bennett. Kimball, "St. Louis," 497.

24 Bennett, *History of the Saints*, 5–6, 293, 8.

25 For an analysis of Bennett's use of other histories, see Crawley, *Descriptive Bibliography*,
202–203. For a history of the idea of fanaticism, see Colas, *Civil Society and Fanaticism*.

26 Doyle, *Jacksonville, Illinois*, 21–33, 127; Billington, *Protestant Crusade*; Turner, *Mormonism in All Ages*, 65–66, 70, 72, 8. On Turner, see Carriel, *Jonathan Baldwin Turner*.
For the similarities to anti-Catholic writings, see Davis, "Counter-Subversion,205–24.

27 Givens, *Viper on the Hearth*, 130–37; Bennett, *History of the Saints*, 130–37, 220–24,
218–20, 278.

28 *New York Herald*, July 22; Oct. 21, 1842; *T&S*, Feb. 1, 1842, 681; Aug. 1, 1842, 876.

29 John C. Bennett to JS, March 8, 1842, in *T&S*, Mar. 15, 1842, 724.

30 Bennett, *History of the Saints*, 306–307; *Burlington Hawk Eye*, Nov. 10, 1842, quoted in
A. Smith, "Introduction," xxxii.

31 Bennett, *History of the Saints*, 228–29.

32 Bennett, *History of the Saints*, 231–32; J. B. Backenstos, Affidavit, July 28, 1842, in *Affidavits and Certificates*; JS, Journal, July 15, 1842, in *PJS*, 2:399. The date of the public
discussion differs in the accounts. Joseph's journal dates it as July 15; the *Sangamo Journal*, July 14. England, *Orson Pratt*, 79.

33 Van Wagoner, "Sarah M. Pratt," 72, 96–97.

34 Orson Pratt, Statement, July 14, 1842; JS, Journal, July 15, 1842, in *PJS*, 2:399; *Warsaw Signal*, July 16, 1842; England, *Orson Pratt*, 79; Brigham Young to Parley P. Pratt,
July 17, 1842, CA; Young, *Manuscript History*, 120–21 (Aug. 8, 1842).

35 *T&S*, Aug. 1, 1842, 869; Woodruff, *Journals*, 2:187 (Aug. 20, 1842).

36 Robinson thought Rigdon would break with Joseph over the marriage proposal to Rigdon's daughter Nancy. George W. Robinson, Nauvoo, to John C. Bennett, Aug. 8,
1842, in *History of the Saints*, 247.

37 George W. Robinson to John C. Bennett, Sept. 16, 1842, in *History of the Saints*,
248–49; *WJS*, 129 (Aug. 29, 1842). Robinson, bitter over being "roughly handled" by
the Saints, announced his withdrawal from the Church in July. George W. Robinson to
Bartlett and Sullivan, July 12, 1842, in *Quincy Whig*, July 23, 1842.

38 John C. Bennett to Sidney Rigdon and Orson Pratt, Jan. 10, 1843, copied in JS to Justin Butterfield, Jan. 16, 1843, Whitney Collection.

39 Orson Pratt to Mr. Editor, Sept. 26, 1842, in *Nauvoo Wasp*, Oct. 1, 1842; Quorum of the Twelve, Minutes, Jan. 20, 1843; Quinn, "Rebaptism at Nauvoo," 28; Woodruff, *Journals*, 2:213 (Jan. 19, 1843).

40 McLaws, "Attempted Assassination," 50–62; *Quincy Whig*, May 21, 1842; Thomas Carlin to JS, June 30, 1842, in *PJS*, 2:423; *Nauvoo Wasp*, May 28, 1842; *Sangamo Journal*, July 22, 1842; A. Smith, *John Cook Bennett*, 103–104. George Hinkle, a former Mormon, also claimed that Joseph prophesied Boggs's violent death. George Hinkle to JS, June 12, 1842, JSC. Joseph denied the charge. JS to Mr. Bartlett, May 22, 1842, in *Nauvoo Wasp*, May 28, 1842.

41 JS, Journal, Aug. 23, Dec. 9, 1842, in *PJS*, 2:439, 499–500; Schindler, *Orrin Porter Rockwell*, 67–82; Leonard, *Nauvoo*, 279; Thomas Reynolds, Extradition Request, July 22, 1842, in *PJS*, 2:503–504.

42 Nauvoo City Council, Minutes, July 5; Aug. 8, 1842; *Nauvoo Wasp*, July 16, 1842.

43 Nauvoo City Council and Citizens to Thomas Carlin, July 22, 1842, in Nauvoo City Council, Minutes, July 22, 1842; JS, Journal, Aug. 8, 10, 1842, in *PJS*, 402–403; Snow, Journal, Aug. 9, 1842, in Snow, *Writings*, 53; Jennings, "Anti-Mormon Letters," 275–92; *Nauvoo Wasp*, Aug. 13, 1842; Gayler, "Extradite Joseph," 28–29; Schindler, *Orrin Porter Rockwell*, 79.

44 JS, Journal, Aug. 11, 1842, in *PJS*, 2:403–405.

45 JS, Journal, Aug. 13–14, 1842, in *PJS*, 2:406–7.

46 JS to Wilson Law, August [14?], 1842, in *PJS*, 2:408–10.

47 JS, Journal, Aug. 15, 1842, in *PJS*, 2:411, 413–14; JS to Wilson Law, Aug. 16, 1842, in PJS, 2:425–26; Wilson Law to JS, Aug. 16, 1842; Wilson Law to JS, Aug. 17, 1842, both in *PJS*, 2:426–29.

48 JS to Emma Smith, Aug. 16, 1842, in *PWJS*, 555–56.

49 JS to Emma Smith, Aug. 16, 1842; Emma Smith to JS, [Aug. 1842,] both in *PJS*, 2:429–33.

50 JS, Journal, Aug. 16, 1842, in *PJS*, 2:415–16.

51 JS, Journal, Aug. 16, 1842, in *PJS*, 2:416–17. In the longing for absent friends, Joseph's sentiments are reminiscent of a poem by Abraham Lincoln, published unattributed in the *Quincy Whig*, May 5, 1847: "Where many were, how few remain / Of old, familiar things."

52 JS to Emma Smith, Aug. 16, 1842, in *PJS*, 2:429.

53 *Woman's Exponent*, Dec. 15, 1878, 105; JS to the Whitneys, Aug. 18, 1842, in *PWJS*, 566–67.

54 Revelation, July 12, 1843, Revelations Collection (*D&C*, 132:64–65); Compton, *In Sacred Loneliness*, 350; JS to Sarah Ann Whitney, Mar. 23, 1843; JS to the Whitneys, Aug. 18, 1842, in *PWJS*, 566–67.

55 JS, Journal, Aug. 17, 1842, in *PJS*, 2:418; Emma Smith to JS, May 16, 1842, in *PJS*, 2:433. For more on Emma's business capacity, see Newell and Avery, *Mormon Enigma*, 130.

56 Snow, Journal, July 29, 1842, in Snow, *Writings*, 52; Thomas Carlin to Emma Smith, Aug. 24, 1842, in *PJS*, 2:450–52; Emma Smith to Thomas Carlin, Aug. 16, 27, 1842, in *PJS*, 2:434, 453–54.

57 Thomas Carlin to Emma Smith, Sept. 7, 1842, in *PJS*, 2:476–78.

58 JS, Journal, Aug. 23, 1842, in *PJS*, 2:438–43.

59 JS, Journal, Aug. 26, 27, 29, 1842, in *PJS*, 2:443–47.

60 JS, Journal, Aug. 29, 1842, in *PJS*, 2:445–47.

61 In the early editions of his bookkeeping text, Bennet spelled his name with two "t's"; by 1842 he was using one. In 1846 he published a book on the art of swimming. A. Smith, *John Cook Bennett*, 67–68.

62   James Arlington Bennet to JS, Sept. 1, 1842, in *PJS*, 2:480; James Arlington Bennet to JS, Oct. 24, 1843, in *T&S*, Nov. 1, 1843, 371; Cook, "James Arlington Bennet," 247–49.

63   JS to James Arlington Bennet, Sept. 8, 1842, in *PWJS*, 576–78.

64   JS to James Arlington Bennet, Sept. 8, 1842, in *PWJS*, 578–79.

65   James Arlington Bennet to JS, Sept. 1, 1842, in *PJS*, 2:480–81. Turner, *Mormonism in All Ages*, grew out of the same fantasy, one also evoked by Beecher, *Plea for the West*. See the analysis of these schemes in Pykles, "Anti-Mormon Rhetoric."

66   JS to All the Saints, Sept. 1, 1842, in *PWJS*, 571 (*D&C*, 127:2).

67   JS to the Church, Sept. 6, 1842, in *PJS*, 2:469–71 (*D&C*, 128:1–13); Matthew 16:16–19.

68   JS to the Church, Sept. 6, 1842, in *PJS*, 2:473–74 (*D&C*, 128:20–21).

69   JS, Journal, Sept. 3, 1842, in *PJS*, 2:448–50; Snow, Journal, Sept. 4, 1842, in Snow, *Writings*, 55.

70   JS, Journal, Sept. 9–11, Oct. 2, 10, 21; Nov. 16, 1842, in *PJS*, 2:468, 485, 487–88, 493. Thomas Sharp thought Joseph was hiding in Nauvoo, but it was rumored that he had escaped to Canada. *Warsaw Signal*, Sept. 3, 1842; *Niles National Register*, Oct. 1, 1842.

71   *Sangamo Journal*, Sept. 30, 1842. News had arrived of more sheriffs on their way to make an arrest. Snow, Journal, Oct. 9, 1842, in Snow, *Writings*, 57.

72   JS, Journal, Sept. 29–Oct. 5, 7, 20, Nov. 1, Dec. 1, 1842, in *PJS*, 2:484–88, 490, 495; Quinn, "Rebaptism at Nauvoo," 229–31.

73   Justin Butterfield to Sidney Rigdon, Oct. 20, 1842, in *T&S*, Dec. 15, 1842, 33–36. Judge Stephen Douglas also assured Joseph the writ should be revoked. JS, Journal, Dec. 9, 1842, in *PJS*, 2:499; Clayton, Journal, Dec. 14, 1842.

74   Thomas Ford to JS, Dec. 17, 1842, in *PJS*, 2:504–505; JS, Journal, Dec. 9, 1842, in *PJS*, 2:500–2; Justin Butterfield to JS, Dec. 17, 1842, in *PJS*, 2:505–506. Ford recommended the same course and agreed to abide by the decision. Clayton, Journal, Dec. 14, 1842.

75   Richards, Journal, Dec. 27, 1842; JS, Journal, Dec. 27, 1842, in *APR*, 258–59.

76   JS, Journal, Jan. 5, 1843, in *APR*, 279; *T&S*, Jan. 16, 1843, 65–67; Arnold, *Illinois-Bar*, 135.

77   JS, Journal, Jan. 2, 1843, in *APR*, 269; *New York Herald*, Jan. 18, 1843.

78   JS, Journal, Jan. 4–6, 1843, in *APR*, 278, 284–86; Revelation 19:12.

79   JS, Journal, Jan. 5, 7, 1843, in *APR*, 285, 287–90; Clayton, Journal, Jan. 7, 1843. Willard Richards said he helped Law compose the verses. Rough Draft Notes, ManH, Jan. 7, 1843; *Nauvoo Wasp*, Jan. 14, 1843.

CHAPTER 27   THICKETS

1   *WJS*, 155 (Jan. 17, 1843); JS, Journal, Jan. 18, 1843, in *APR*, 292–93; Young, Diary, 27; Rough Draft Notes, ManH, Jan. 18, 1843.

2   JS, Journal, May 21; Mar. 18, 1843, in *APR*, 379, 335.

3   Brief sketches of Richards's life can be found in Black, *Doctrine and Covenants*, 241–43; and Jenson, *Biographical Encyclopedia*, 1:53–56.

4   JS, Journal, Mar. 11, 13, 18; Feb. 8, 20; May 3, 6, 9; Oct. 3; Dec. 25, 1843; Jan. 18, 23, 1844, in *APR*, 332–33, 335, 300, 306, 375–76, 417, 435, 441–42. On Joseph and sports, see Baugh, "Athletic Nature," 137–50.

5   Charlotte Haven to Sister Isa, Jan. 22, 1843, in Mulder and Mortensen, *Among the Mormons*, 118–19.

6   Woodruff, *Journals*, 2:153 (Jan. 22, 1843).

7   JS, Journal, May 21 and Feb. 20, 1843, in *APR*, 378, 306–307.

8   JS, Journal, Jan. 2; Feb. 25, 1843, in *APR*, 270, 313. On Joseph's doctoring, see JS, Journal, Apr. 29, 1843, in *APR*, 369.

9   William W. Phelps drafted the appeal. JS, Journal, Nov. 21; Dec. 4, 1843, in *APR*, 428; JS, *Green Mountain Boys*, 4. Joseph was genuinely fascinated by languages. In 1842–43 he studied German. JS, Journal, Feb. 3, 5; Mar. 1, 1843, in *APR*, 298–99; Young, Diary, 27; Gellinek, *Young Schleiermacher*, 40, 56–57. What he knew of languages, he brought into his sermons, prefacing a commentary on the meaning of "paradise," for example, by saying, "I will turn linguist." JS, Journal, June 11, 1843, in *APR*, 384.

10 Lynn, *Southwestern Humor*, 27–29, 34. Josiah Quincy was surprised to hear Joseph use "forcible vulgarisms" like "I have proved that point as straight as a loon's leg." Quincy, *Figures of the Past*, 385.

11 JS, Journal, Apr. 6, Aug. 27, and Feb. 12, 1843, in *APR*, 348, 409, 303. When a Methodist minister used the term "Joe Smith" in a sermon, Joseph retorted, "It would have been more respectful to have said Lieutenant-General Joseph Smith." Quincy, *Figures of the Past*, 393.

12 JS, Journal, Jan. 20, 1843, in *APR*, 293–94.

13 JS, Journal, May 21; Apr. 2, 16, 1843, in *APR*, 378, 339, 365 (*D&C*, 130:2).

14 JS, Journal, Apr. 16, 1843, in *APR*, 367, 365; Woodruff *Journals*, 2:226–27 (Apr. 16, 1843); *WJS*, 194. For the central place of friendship in Joseph Smith's thinking, see Epperson, "Virtue of Friendship," 77–105.

15 Joseph could also combine the formal with the offhand. See JS, Journal, May 19, 1842, in *PJS*, 2:384.

16 JS, Journal, Apr. 2, 1843, in *APR*, 339; Clayton, Journal, Apr. 2, 1843. On Clayton, see Allen, *William Clayton*; and Clayton, *Journals*, xi–lxxiii.

17 Clayton, Journal, Apr. 2, 1843; Revelation 4:6, 15:2; JS, Journal, Oct. 9, 1843, in *APR*, 418; Woodford, "Historical Development," 3:1701–24.

18 *D&C* [1835], 6:4 (*D&C*, 88:16–18); *D&C* [1844], 101:2 (*D&C*, 103:7); JS, Journal, Apr. 2, 1843, in *APR*, 339 (*D&C*, 130:2); Knight, "Joseph Knight's Recollection," 33. On speculations on heaven, McDannell and Lang, *Heaven*, 183–84, 191–227; Schulz, *Paradise Preserved*.

19 *WJS*, 202 (May 17, 1843), 189–90 (Apr. 8, 1843), 183 (Apr. 8, 1843), 207 (May 2, 1843); Woodruff, *Journals*, 2:229 (May 14, 1843); Clayton, Journal, Apr. 2, 1843 (*D&C*, 130:18–19); JS, Journal, Apr. 16, 1843, in *APR*, 366.

20 JS, Journal, Mar. 10–11, 13–14, 20, 23 1843, in *APR*, 334–36; cf. Woodruff, *Journals*, 2:219, 221–22 (March 10, 20–25; April 2, 1843). On astrology and early Mormonism, see Quinn, *Early Mormonism*, 277–82; and Whittaker, "Almanacs," 89–113.

21 JS, Journal, Apr. 7, 1843, in *APR*, 352; Boyer, "Fundamentalist Apocalyptic," 3:145–46; Stein, "Apocalypticism," 3:115–16.

22 Knight, *Millennial Fever*, 17, 126, 47, 72–92, 131; Doan, *Miller Heresy*, 32–38, 46–52.

23 JS, Journal, Apr. 2, 1843, in *APR*, 340 (*D&C*, 130:14–15); Anderson, "Millenarian Time Table," 55–66.

24 JS, Journal, Apr. 6, 1843, in *APR*, 349. The Mormons looked for the Second Coming in 1890 and 1891. Erickson, *Millennial Deliverance*.

25 *Quincy Whig*, May 3, 1843.

26 Webster, *Ancient Maya*, 21–28; *HC*, 5:372–79.

27 JS, Journal, May 7, 1843, in *APR*, 376; Clayton, Journal, May 1, 1843. Clayton's date of May 1 conflicts with Richards's date of May 7. B. H. Roberts was still defending the plates' authenticity when he edited *The History of the Church*. See *HC*, 5:378–79. On the history of the plates, see Kimball, "Kinderhook Plates," 66–74; Ashurst-McGee, "Kinderhook Plates."

28 Ehat, "Temple Ordinances," 65–75.

29 Kimball, Autobiographical Sketch, 10–11; Kimball, Affidavit, Dec. 17, 1902, Affidavits.

30 Kimball, Autobiographical Sketch, 11–12; Kimball, Testimony, 3–4; Lucy Walker

Smith Kimball, Affidavit, Dec. 17, 1902, Affidavits; *Woman's Exponent*, Jan. 1911, 43. Lucy's story is told in Compton, *In Sacred Loneliness*, 458–65.

31 Scholars estimate that Emma probably knew about no more than a dozen women whom Joseph had married. Newell and Avery say eleven at most. *Mormon Enigma*, 151. It is possible he told her about them all in July 1843, when they seem to have reached an agreement that he would stop the practice.

32 Compton, *In Sacred Loneliness*, 308–13, esp. 312–13.

33 Snow, Journal, Aug. 14, 18; Dec. 12, 1842; Feb. 11; Mar. 17, 1843, in Snow, *Writings*, 54, 64, 66; JS, Journal, Feb. 11, 1843, in *APR*, 303. One story has it that just before Eliza's departure, Emma learned the truth about her relation to Joseph and drove her out with a broom, ending Eliza's pregnancy. Published in 1886 by an anti-Mormon author, Wilhelm Ritter von Wymetal, who had lived in Utah for four or five months, the story was based on gossip. Wymetal gave no source for the account of Eliza other than to say it was common knowledge. A correspondent for the *Berliner Tageblatt*, Wymetal published *Joseph Smith, the Prophet, His Family and His Friends* at the peak of the antipolygamy campaign when vilification of the Mormons was credible. On Wymetal, whose pen name was "W. Wyl," see *EMD*, 2:528, n. 1.

34 A former servant in the Smith household told Mary Ann Barzee Boice some time after 1884 that "Emma went up stairs pulled Eliza R. Snow down stairs by the hair of her head." After writing the story, Boice added the notation "this I give as a rumer only." Quoted in Newell and Avery, *Mormon Enigma*, 134. A Snow family tradition, attributed to LeRoi Snow, a nephew of Eliza's born when she was seventy-two, held that Emma knocked Eliza down the stairs. LeRoi Snow's notes, compiled for a biography of Eliza, said Charles C. Rich witnessed Emma pushing a pregnant Eliza down the steps after seeing Joseph kiss her goodbye, but the information came from a letter of 1844. None of the accounts hold up under scrutiny. Beecher, Newell, and Avery, "Emma and Eliza," 87–95.

35 Brigham Young told the Smith sons their mother was a "wicked woman." Quoted in Newell and Avery, *Mormon Enigma*, 281, 199–209. One hundred thirty-three depositions are listed in Bachman, "Plural Marriage," 346–54. Many of them are reprinted in Jenson, "Plural Marriage," 219–34; and J. F. Smith, *Plural Marriage*, 81–105.

36 Jason Briggs, a principal in forming the Reorganized Church, believed Joseph's plural marriages were spiritual only. J. F. Smith, *Plural Marriage*, 63–64.

37 Young, Diary, 124; Eliza Partridge, Affidavit, July 1, 1869, Affidavits; Young, "Incidents," 186. Emily Partridge gave the date as May 11, 1843, with the ceremony performed by Judge James Adams. Since Adams was not in Nauvoo on that date, scholars have concluded the actual date was May 23. Newell and Avery, *Mormon Enigma*, 333, n. 54.

38 Lucy Walker Kimball, Affidavit, Dec. 17, 1902, Affidavits; *Woman's Exponent*, Jan. 1911, 43; Lucy Walker Kimball, Testimony, 2:461, in U.S. Court of Appeals.

39 Young, Diary, 2; Clayton, Journal, May 23, 1843.

40 Young, Diary, 2; Compton, *In Sacred Loneliness*, 410–11; Young, "Incidents," 186.

41 Clayton, Journal, June 23, 1843. A few weeks earlier Joseph had asked Clayton "if I had used any familiarity with E[mma]. I told him by no means & explained to his satisfaction." Clayton, Journal, May 29, 1843.

42 Newell and Avery, *Mormon Enigma*, 139; Madsen, Statement; Brigham Young, Discourse, Oct. 8, 1866, Historian's Office Speeches. Before that, Hyrum might have tried to smoke out members rumored to be taking plural wives. Clayton noted in his journal on May 23, 1843, "Conversed with H C. K[imball]. concerning a plot that is being laid to entrap the brethren of the secret priesthood by bro. H. and others." Presumably "H" is Hyrum. As late as May 14, 1843, Hyrum spoke against polygamy from the pul-

pit. Richards, *Diary*, May 14, 1843. On Hyrum's conversion to plural marriage, see Ehat, "Temple Ordinances," 56–59.

43 JS, Journal, May 29; July 12, 1843, in *APR*, 381, 396; Clayton, Journal, July 12, 1843; William Clayton, Affidavit, Nov. 11, 1871, Affidavits. The story of Hyrum and Emma appears in William Clayton, Affidavit, Feb. 16, 1874, Affidavits, and published in Jenson, "Plural Marriage," 225–26. Details are added in Clayton's 1871 letter to Madison Scott printed in J. F. Smith, *Plural Marriage*, 92–93.

44 Newell and Avery, *Mormon Enigma*, 161; William Clayton, Affidavit, Feb. 16, 1874, Affidavits. Upon Hyrum's return, Joseph said quietly, according to Clayton, "I told you, you did not know Emma as well as I did."

45 JS, Journal, July 13, 1843, in *APR*, 396; Clayton, Journal, July 13, 15, 1843.

46 Clayton, Journal, Aug. 16, 21, 23, 1843. Joseph paid more attention to Flora than to his other plural wives. Clayton's journal records visits to her on May 2, June 1, and August 26, 28, and 29. The last three visits may have been to compensate for Emma's hard treatment.

47 JS, Journal, Oct. 3, 1843, in *APR*, 417; Clayton, Journal, Oct. 19, 1843. Joseph's body-guard, Allen J. Stout, later testified that he overheard Emma tell Joseph that Satan inspired her opposition to plural marriage. Jenson, "Plural Marriage," 230–31. For other evidence to her softening, all of it late, see Newell and Avery, *Mormon Enigma*, 160–61.

48 JS, Journal, May 26, 1843, in *APR*, 381; Young, *Manuscript History*, 129 (May 26, 1843); Madsen, "Mormon Women," 86; Compton, " 'Kingdom of Priests,' " 55–57; Clayton, *Journals*, 110 (Apr. 2, 1843) (*D&C*, 131:1–4); Bergera, "Eternal Sealings," 41–66.

49 Richards's notes for September 28 mention only that Joseph was "anointed and ordn to the highest and holiest order of the priesthood (and companion.)" These words most likely refer to the "second anointing" with Emma. Did she receive her endowment on the same occasion or earlier? The record is unclear but the consensus among historians is that she had received her endowment at least by this date. Madsen, "Mormon Women," 85; Prince, *Power from On High*, 189; Quinn, "Prayer Circles," 86; Ehat, "Temple Ordinances," 94, 107.

50 Kimball, Journal, Jan. 1844. See also Ehat, "Temple Ordinances," 119; Quinn, *Origins of Power*, 496–98; Ehat, "Temple Ordinances," 119, 107. Devry Anderson counts twenty-nine women and thirty-seven men. Anderson, "Anointed Quorum," 152.

51 Ehat, "Temple Ordinances," 101, lists eighteen different names linked to the quorum.

52 JS, Journal, Oct. 8; Nov. 12, 1843, in *APR*, 418, 426. For other coded entries of quorum meetings, see JS, Journal, Oct. 22, 27; Nov. 15, 22, 1843, in *APR*, 423–24, 427–28. For other uncoded entries, see JS, Journal, Sept. 28; Oct. 1, 8; Dec. 2, 9–10, 17, 23, 30–31, 1843; Jan. 7, 25–27; Feb. 4, 10, 18, 26; Mar. 3, 1844, in *APR*, 416, 418, 429, 431–32, 435, 437–38, 442–43, 445–46, 449–50. The code was Taylor shorthand. Ehat, "Temple Ordinances," 62. For the chronology of the prayer circles and the anointed quorum, see Quinn, *Origins of Power*, 491–502. As the number of endowed persons increased after the temple was available, the anointed quorum stopped meeting. Quinn, "Prayer Circles," 94–95.

53 Quinn, *Origins of Power*, 115; 2 Peter 1:10. Buerger, *Mysteries of Godliness*, 63, counts twenty men receiving the second anointing and sixteen of their wives. Anderson, "Anointed Quorum," 152, 154, counts nineteen men and seventeen women.

54 Bell, *Calvin and Scottish Theology*; Jinkins, *Theology of Atonement*.

55 2 Peter 1:19; Clayton, *Journals*, 103 (May 17, 1843); Revelation, July 12, 1843, Revelations Collection (*D&C*, 132:19, 26); Revelation 1:6. Joseph participated in this ordinance on Sept. 28, 1843. JS, Journal, Sept. 28, 1843, in *APR*, 416; Clayton, *Journals*, 122 (Oct. 19, 1843); Woodruff, "Historian's Private Journal," 1858, 24.

56 *Woman's Exponent*, Dec. 15, 1878, 105. Whitney was speaking about plural marriages as

well as temple ordinances. For an attempt to piece together the lean records, see Buerger, "Second Anointing," 10–44.

57 JS, Journal, Nov. 5–6; Dec. 15, 1843, in *APR*, 426, 432; Brigham Young, Discourse, Oct. 7, 1866, Historian's Office Speeches.

58 Compton, *In Sacred Loneliness*, 609–17.

59 *Journal of Discourses*, 16:166–67 (Aug. 31, 1873); Compton, *In Sacred Loneliness*, 617.

60 Compton, *In Sacred Loneliness*, 6, 597–98.

61 JS, Journal, Dec. 25, 1843, in *APR*, 435–36; Schindler, *Orrin Porter Rockwell*, 99–101.

62 JS, Journal, Dec. 31, 1843; Jan. 1, 18, 1844, in *APR*, 437, 441. Another cotillion was held the following week. JS, Journal, Jan. 23, 1844, in *APR*, 442.

63 JS, Journal, Jan. 4, 1844, in *APR*, 437–38.

CHAPTER 28   CITY AND KINGDOM

1 *Nauvoo Neighbor*, Oct. 4, 1843; JS, Journal, Oct. 3, 1843, in *APR*, 417.

2 On the unusual powers of the Nauvoo Legion, see Gardner, "Nauvoo Legion," 181–97.

3 *D&C* [1835], 75:1 (*D&C*, 78:6). Cf. *D&C* [1835], 23:1–2; 26:3; 86:4 (*D&C*, 51:3, 9; 70:14; 82:17–18).

4 *Boston Quarterly Review*, July 1840, 368, in Hollinger and Capper, *American Intellectual Tradition*, 297. For a time, Brownson's brother Oran associated with the Mormons. Schlesinger, *Orestes A. Brownson*, 186–87.

5 JS, Journal, Sept. 13–14, 24, 1843, in *APR*, 413, 415; *New Moral World*, Oct. 5, 1844. My thanks to James Lucas for this last reference.

6 Flanders, *Nauvoo*, 162, 161, 175–77, 154; Leonard, *Nauvoo*, 145; Enders, "*Maid of Iowa*," 321–35; *T&S*, June 1, 1841, 427 (*D&C*, 124:56–72).

7 Flanders, *Nauvoo*, 146–52, 154; Twelve Apostles to the Church in England, Scotland, Ireland, Wales, and the Isle of Man, Apr. 15, 1841, in *Latter-day Saints' Millennial Star*, Apr. 1841, 309–12; JS to Edward Hunter, Dec. 21, 1841, JSC; Hunter, *Edward Hunter*, 69–70; Leonard, *Nauvoo*, 491–94; *Nauvoo Neighbor*, May 17, 1843. The city also proposed a dam in the Mississippi for generating water power and creating a harbor. Nauvoo City Council, Minutes, Dec. 8, 1843; *Nauvoo Neighbor*, Dec. 9, 1843, Extra.

8 JS, Journal, Oct. 15, 1843, in *APR*, 421–22; JS to Edward Hunter, Jan. 5, 1842, JSC.

9 Leonard, *Nauvoo*, 144–47; Flanders, *Nauvoo*, 160–64, 161; Launius and McKiernan, *Red Brick Store*, 16; JS to Ebenezer Robinson, Jan. 23, 1844; Clayton, Journal, Apr. 15, 1844; Rowley, "Wisconsin Pineries," 127; JS, Journal, Mar. 4, 1844, in *APR*, 451.

10 Flanders, *Nauvoo*, 157, 207–208, 156, 158, 183–84; Nauvoo High Council, Minutes, Aug. 20, 1842; Hartley, "Nauvoo Stake," 58–62; Rowley, "Wisconsin Pineries," 119–48; Leonard, *Nauvoo*, 248–51; Lyman Wight and others to Joseph Smith and others, Feb. 15, 1844, JSC.

11 ManH E-1, 1875–76; Hamilton, *Mormon Architecture*, 40–41; Quincy, *Figures from the Past*, 389; Leonard, *Nauvoo*, 250; *New York Weekly Argus*, quoted in Ostler, "Nauvoo Saints," 30; JS, Journal, Oct. 23, 30, 1842, in *PJS*, 2:488, 490. On Weeks, see Arrington, "William Weeks," 337–59.

12 Leonard, *Nauvoo*, 250–51, 261.

13 Cronon, *Nature's Metropolis*, 34–43, 52–54; Bushman, *Making Space*, 18–25.

14 Clayton, Journal, June 18, 20–21, 1843; Rough Draft Notes, ManH, June 18, 21, 1843; Richards, Journal, June 17, 1843. The two carried $450 in their saddlebags to hire lawyers. The entire story is told in Hill, *Joseph Smith*, 324–26.

15 *Quincy Whig*, June 28, 1843; *Illinois State Register*, July 3, 1843; A. Smith, *Saintly Scoundrel*, 136–37; Ford, *History of Illinois*, 315.

16 Clayton, Journal, June 23, 1843; Rough Draft Notes, ManH, June 23, 1843; Conover, Statement; Woodruff, *Journals*, 2:252 (June 30, 1843); *Nauvoo Neighbor*, July 5, 1843.

17 *Nauvoo Neighbor*, July 5, 1843; Rough Draft Notes, ManH, June 23–24, 1843; Clayton, Journal, June 23, 1843.

18 Rough Draft Notes, ManH, June 27, 25, 1843; Conover, Statement; Woodruff, *Journals*, 2:252, 245–46 (June 30, 25, 1843); JS, Journal, June 25, 1843, in *APR*, 388.

19 Burbank, Autobiography, 43–44; Conover, Statement.

20 Rough Draft Notes, ManH, June 27–28, 18, 30, 1843; Conover, Statement; Clayton, Journal, June 30, 1843; JS, Journal, June 30, 1843, in *APR*, 389–99; Needham, "Letter," 41 (July 7, 1843); Fielding, "Journal," 144.

21 *WJS*, 220 (June 30, 1843); Ford, *History of Illinois*, 249.

22 *WJS*, 217–18, 223 (June 30, 1843).

23 *WJS*, 217–19 (June 30, 1843).

24 Nauvoo Municipal Court, Docket, June 30; July 1, 1843; JS to Nauvoo Municipal Court, June 30, 1843, JSC; Writ, Nauvoo Municipal Court, June 30, 1843, JSC; JS, Journal, June 30; July 2, 1843, in *APR*, 389, 392; *Nauvoo Neighbor*, July 12, 1843; Thomas Ford to Joseph H. Reynolds, July 6, 1843, in *HC*, 5:492; Ford, *History of Illinois*, 316–17, 320.

25 Ford, *History of Illinois*, 319.

26 Ford, *History of Illinois*, 314.

27 Hill, *Quest for Refuge*, 129; Ford said the Mormons had been leaning toward Walker from the beginning of the year. Ford, *History of Illinois*, 314.

28 Ford, *History of Illinois*, 319, 314–16; Hill, *Quest for Refuge*, 129; Oaks, "Habeas Corpus," 243–88.

29 Ford, *History of Illinois*, 317–19. Backenstos returned to Nauvoo on August 1. JS, Journal, Aug. 1, 1843, in *APR*, 401. On Backenstos, see Whitman and Varner, "Jacob B. Backenstos," 150–78, esp. 155. Marvin Hill argues that the Mormons decided to switch to the Democrats before they heard from Backenstos. *Quest for Refuge*, 132.

30 *WJS*, 237 (Aug. 6, 1843); Clayton, Journal, Aug. 6, 1843; *Illinois State Register*, Sept. 1, 1843; Ford, *History of Illinois*, 319; JS, Journal, Aug. 7, 1843, in *APR*, 403.

31 *WJS*, 236 (Aug. 6, 1843); Ford, *History of Illinois*, 273–74.

32 Ford, *History of Illinois*, 329–30.

33 Ford, *History of Illinois*, 319; *Warsaw Message*, Sept. 6, 13, 1843.

34 JS, Journal, Mar. 27; Aug. 27, 13, 1843, in *APR*, 337, 406, 408, 410–11; Van Wagoner, *Sidney Rigdon*, 314–15, 322–24; Clayton, Journal, Aug. 13, 1843; *T&S*, Sept. 15, 1843, 330; Laub, "Journal," 159.

35 Clayton, Journal, Aug. 1, 1843; *Warsaw Message*, Aug. 13, 1843; Jan. 3, 1844; JS, Journal, Sept. 19; Dec. 5–6, 1843, in *APR*, 415, 430; JS to Thomas Ford, Sept. 20; Dec. 6, 1843, JSC; *Nauvoo Neighbor*, Dec. 20, 1843; *T&S*, Nov. 1, 1843, 375–76.

36 *Nauvoo Neighbor*, Dec. 13, 1843; Nauvoo City Council, Minutes, Dec. 8, 16, 12, 1843; JS, Journal, Dec. 8, 13, 1843, in *APR*, 431. On the petition for territorial powers, see JS, Journal, Dec. 21, 1843; Feb. 12, 1844, in *APR*, 434, 446; Nauvoo City Council, Minutes, Dec. 8, 16, 1843; JS and others to United States Congress, Dec. 21, 1843, JSC.

37 Thomas Ford to JS, Dec. 12, 1843, JSC; ManH E-1, 1804.

38 *HC*, 6:109; Aaron Johnson to JS, Dec. 18, 1843, JSC; *Warsaw Message*, Jan. 3, 1844; JS, Journal, Dec. 18–19, 1843, in *APR*, 432–34; Woodruff, *Journals*, 2:332 (Dec. 18, 1843); *Nauvoo Neighbor*, Dec. 20, 1843; Clayton, Journal, Dec. 19, 1843.

39 JS, Journal, Dec. 21, 24, 1843; Feb. 12, 1844, in *APR*, 434–35, 446; *Nauvoo Neighbor*, Feb. 14, 1844.

40 Joseph L. Heywood to JS, Oct. 23, 1843, JSC; JS, Journal, Nov. 2, 1843, in *APR*, 425; Clayton, Journal, Nov. 2, 1843.

41 For the Massachusetts appeal, see JS, Journal, Feb. 2, 1844, in *APR*, 444, and Joseph

Young and Phinehas Richards to Inhabitants of Massachusetts, Feb. 1, 1844, in *Nauvoo Neighbor*, Feb. 7, 1844; for the Maine appeal, see Benjamin Andrews to Fellow-Citizens, [n.d.,] in *T&S*, Jan. 15, 1844, 403–406; for Pennsylvania, see Sidney Rigdon to Pennsylvania Congress, [n.d.,] in *T&S*, Feb. 1, 1844, 418–23; for Tennessee, see A. Young to State of Tennessee, [n.d.,] in *Nauvoo Neighbor*, Feb. 28, 1844; for New York, see JS, Journal, Dec. 4, 1843, in *APR*, 430.

42 JS, *Green Mountain Boys*, 3; "What to the Slave Is the Fourth of July," Hollinger and Capper, *American Intellectual Tradition*, 501.

43 JS, *Green Mountain Boys*, 7. An anonymous author, in the Green Mountain Boys' reply in a letter to Thomas Sharp, called Joseph Smith an "infamous wreck." Hampshire, "Thomas Sharp," 88.

44 Johnson, *Mormon Redress Petitions*, 563–614; Crawley, *Descriptive Bibliography*, 232, 269–70.

45 JS, Journal, Nov. 4, 1843, in *APR*, 425; JS to John C. Calhoun, Nov. 4, 1843, in Calhoun, *Papers*, 531; *Nauvoo Neighbor*, Jan. 10, May 29, 1844; Henry Clay to JS, Nov. 15, 1843, Smith, in Clay, *Papers*, 891; John F. Cowan to JS, Jan. 23, 1844, JSC; John C. Calhoun to JS, Dec. 2, 1843, in Calhoun, *Papers*, 583.

46 *WJS*, 259 (Nov. 29, 1843); JS to John C. Calhoun, Jan. 2, 1844, in Calhoun, *Papers*, 664, 666; Durham, *Joseph Smith*, 136–37.

47 JS, Journal, Jan. 19, 29, 1844, in *APR*, 441, 443. Joseph offered the vice presidential nomination first to James Arlington Bennet, then to Solomon Copeland of Tennessee, and finally to Sidney Rigdon. JS, Journal, Mar. 4, 8, 20; May 6, 1844, in *APR*, 451, 457, 460, 477.

48 *T&S*, Feb. 15, 1844, 441; *WJS*, 320 (Feb. 8, 1844); JS, Journal, Jan. 19, 1844, in *APR*, 443. Two questions underlie the large literature on Joseph Smith's candidacy: Did he think he could win? And did he plan to make over the United States government into the Kingdom of God? For a sample of the debate see Leonard, *Nauvoo*, 334–40; Hill, *Quest for Refuge*, 137–40; Winn, *Exiles*, 195–207; Hansen, *Quest for Empire*, 75–78; Wood, "Presidential Campaign," 167–93. George Miller, an advocate of moving to Texas, wrote in his 1855 autobiography that "if we succeeded in making a majority of the voters converts to our faith, and elected Joseph president, in such an event the dominion of the kingdom would be forever established in the United States; and if not successful, we could fall back on Texas, and be a kingdom notwithstanding." George Miller to Dear Brother, June 28, 1855, in Miller, "De Tal Palo Tal Astilla," 132.

49 JS, Journal, Jan. 29, 1844, in *APR*, 444; Crawley, *Descriptive Bibliography*, 244–47. *Views* was published in the *T&S*, May 15, 1844, 528–33. One of the manuscript versions omits the words "General Smith's" from the title. JS, "Views," Feb. 7, 1844, JSC. John Bernhisel may have helped with the composition. Poll, "Presidency, 1844," 19.

50 For a summary of the issues and the coalitions, see Sellers, "Election of 1844," 1:747–73.

51 JS, *Views*, 5–8.

52 JS, *Views*, 7–8.

53 JS, Journal, Dec. 30, 1843; Jan. 2, 1844, in *APR*, 260, 269.

54 JS, Journal, Feb. 18–19, 24–25, 27, 1844, in *APR*, 446, 448, 449; Flanders, *Nauvoo*, 156; JS, *Views*, 8; Durham, *Joseph Smith*, 167. For more in this vein, see JS to *Times and Seasons*, Apr. 15, 1844, in *T&S*, Apr. 15, 1844, 508–10.

55 *T&S*, Apr. 15, 1844, 501–502, 504–11; JS, Journal, May 17, 1844, in *APR*, 479–80. In "Electioneers," 147–80, Margaret C. Robertson argues the missionaries did more proselytizing than campaigning.

56 On the Mormon turn to the West, see Esplin, "Promised Refuge," 85–111; and Christian, "Mormon Foreknowledge," 403–15.

57 Beecher, *Plea for the West*.

58 *New York Weekly Herald*, July 3, 1841, and Jan. 15, 1842; Pykles, "Anti-Mormon Rhetoric."

59 JS, Journal, Feb. 20–21, 1844, in *APR*, 447; Woodruff, *Journals*, 2:21 (Feb. 21, 1844); Willard Richards to Orson Hyde, May 25, 1844, Richards Papers; *WJS*, 363–64 (Apr. 8, 1844).

60 Leonard, *Nauvoo*, 325.

61 Quinn, *Origins of Power*, 132–33; Van Wagenen, *Texas Republic*, 38–42; JS, Journal, Apr. 8, 1844, in *APR*, 468; Parley P. Pratt to JS, Apr. 19, 1844, JSC.

62 This surmise is based on the revelation of the Council of Fifty's name in April 1842 and an editorial on the government of God in *T&S*, July 15, 1842, 855–58. Council of Fifty minutes in 1880 said that "it was organized by the Lord. April 7th 1842." Quinn, "Council of Fifty," 164. But in 1845, William Clayton spoke of "the organization of the kingdom of God on the 11th of March last." Clayton, Journal, Jan. 1, 1845.

63 JS, Journal, Mar. 10–13, 1844, in *APR*, 459; Quinn, "Council of Fifty," 164–66; Ehat, "Kingdom of God," 265, 267.

64 The council also sent embassies to England and Russia for reasons hard to identify now, but possibly associated with settling the claims of these nations to Oregon. Quinn, *Origins of Power*, 132–33.

65 Clayton, Journal, Mar. 1, 1845.

66 Morris, *Encyclopedia of American History*, 188; JS, Journal, Mar. 25, 31, 1844, in *APR*, 461–62; JS to United States Congress, March 26, 1844, JSC; Bitton, "Lyman Wight," 5–26; Watt, "Wilford Woodruff and Lyman Wight," 110; Franklin, *Papers*, 457, 460; Billington, *Westward Expansion*, 524; Van Wagenen, *Texas Republic*, 26–27.

67 JS, Journal, Apr. 4, 1844, in *APR*, 463; Orson Hyde to JS, Apr. 25, 26, 1844, JSC.

68 Orson Hyde to JS and others, June 11, 1844, JSC.

69 Orson Hyde to JS, Apr. 26, 1844, JSC; Clayton, *Journals*, 163 (Apr. 15, 1845); Orson Hyde to JS and others, June 11, 1844, JSC.

70 Orson Hyde to JS, Apr. 5 and June 9, 1844, JSC; Parley P. Pratt to JS, Apr. 19, 1844, JSC; Lyman Wight and Heber C. Kimball to JS, June 19, 1844, JSC. See also note 48.

71 Quinn, "Council of Fifty," 163; Ehat, "Kingdom of God," 257, 265–66; Clayton, Journal, Apr. 13, 1844; George Miller to Dear Brother, June 27, 1855, in Miller, "De Tal Palo Tal Astilla," 131.

72 *T&S*, May 1, 1844, 524.

73 *WJS*, 367 (May 12, 1844); Clayton, Journal, Jan. 1, 1845.

74 Flanders, "Politics in Utopia," 156; Frank, *Dostoevsky*; Silverman, *Timothy Dwight*, 138–39; Brownson, "Laboring Classes," in Hollinger and Capper, *American Intellectual Tradition*, 305.

75 *T&S*, July 15, 1842, 856–57; Acts 3:19–21. The essay was signed "ED" when Joseph Smith was the paper's editor. He may not have written the editorial but would have approved it.

76 Harris, "Dwight's Civic Participation," 449–68; Ehat, "Kingdom of God," 257; Orson Hyde to JS and others, June 9, 1844, JSC; JS, Journal, Apr. 25, 1844, in *APR*, 473; JS to *Times and Seasons*, Apr. 15, 1844, in *T&S*, Apr. 15, 1844, 508–10.

77 Quincy, *Figures of the Past*, 393; *New Moral World*, Oct. 5, 1844; JS, Journal, Oct. 15, 1843, in *APR*, 420; *T&S*, Mar. 1, 1842, 710, in *PJS*, 1:437; JS to *Times and Seasons*, Apr. 15, 1844, in *T&S*, Apr. 15, 1844, 508–10.

78 JS, *Views*, 6. For a general disgust with politics, see Altschuler and Blumin, *Rude Republic*.

79 Clayton, Journal, Apr. 18, 1844. In a letter responding to a critic, Joseph said the people should be "honored as noble in their patriotism; and almighty in their majesty: *vox populi; vox Dei!*" JS to *Times and Seasons*, Apr. 15, 1844, in *T&S*, Apr. 15, 1844, 508–10. But he did not mean they should elect every officer of government. He once said, "We

are republican & wish to have the people rule but rule in righteousness." *WJS*, 323 (Mar. 7, 1844).

80   Nauvoo City Council, Minutes, Mar. 9, 1844. Timothy Dwight argued that "our holy religion makes good men." Dwight approvingly quoted New Jersey's Governor Paterson: *"where private virtue cannot be found, it is vain to look for public."* Quoted in Harris, "Dwight's Civic Participation," 454.

81   Ketcham, *First American Presidency*, 29–30, 51–68; Clayton, Journal, Apr. 11, 1844; Jan. 1, 1845; Revelation, June 27, 1882, in Collier, *Unpublished Revelations*, 133. See also Quinn, *Origins of Power*, 124.

82   *BofM*, 218 (Mosiah 29:13); Bolingbroke, *Idea of a Patriot King* (1738), Letter 2, 26. On the persistence of the patriot king ideal in America down to Joseph's time, see Ketcham, *Presidents Above Party*, 73, 89, 94–95, 100–101, 115, 125, 130–33. The *Book of Mormon* was ambivalent about kings: good kings were a blessing, bad kings a curse. *BofM*, 548–50, 217–21 (Ether 6; Mosiah 29).

83   JS, Journal, Aug. 27, 1843, in *APR*, 409.

84   Revelation, June 27, 1882, in Collier, *Unpublished Revelations*, 135; *D&C* [1835], 3:34, 37 (*D&C*, 107:76, 82). Robert Kraynak argues that constitutional monarchy and Christianity—at least Roman Catholic Christianity—are a better fit than Christianity and democracy. *Christian Faith and Modern Democracy*, 233–40.

85   JS, Journal, Mar. 10, 1844, in *APR*, 458; Ehat, "Kingdom of God," 259; Collier, *Unpublished Revelations*, 95; Harris, "Dwight's Civic Participation," 456; JS and others to the Church, Mar. 20, 1839, in *PWJS*, 441 (*D&C*, 121:41); Ketcham, *Presidents Above Party*, 142–44.

86   Clayton, Journal, Jan. 1 and Apr. 18, 1844.

87   JS, Journal, Mar. 10–14, 19–20, 26; Apr. 4, 11, 14, 25; May 3, 6, 13, 24, 1844, in *APR*, 458–61, 463, 470–71, 473, 476–78, 483; Clayton, Journal, Mar. 14, 26, 1844; Hansen, *Quest for Empire*, 173–79; Quinn, "Council of Fifty," 176.

CHAPTER 29   CONFRONTATIONS

1   *T&S*, Feb. 1, 1844, 423; Lucinda Sagers to First Presidency and Twelve, Apr. 10, 1844, JSC; JS, Journal, Apr. 8, 1844, in *APR*, 468; Woodruff, *Journals*, 2:328 (Nov. 25, 1843).

2   JS, Journal, Apr. 13, 1844; Apr. 12, 1843, in *APR*, 471, 360; Allen, *William Clayton*, 50, 63–64.

3   JS, Journal, May 31, 19–24, 9, 1844, in *APR*, 486, 480–83, 477; Carmack, "Nauvoo Theater," 96.

4   JS, Journal, Feb. 21 and Apr. 6, 1843, in *APR*, 310, 342.

5   *T&S*, June 1, 1841, 424 (*D&C*, 124:2–3); Joseph Smith to the Twelve, [Oct. 1840,] JSC; JS, Journal, Apr. 6, May 15, Feb. 21, 1843; in *APR*, 343, 479, 309; Woodworth, "1844 Visit," 84. On promotion of the Nauvoo House, see JS, Journal, Apr. 19, 23, 1843, in *APR*, 370, 373; Clayton, *Journals*, 98 (Apr. 6, 1843); Woodruff, *Journals*, 2:218 (Mar. 21, 1843). On the decision to halt construction, see JS, Journal, Mar. 4, 1844, in *APR*, 451.

6   Cook, *William Law*, 1–4, 8–10; *T&S*, Feb. 1, 1841, 310; William Law to Bro. Russell, Nov. 29, 1840, in Cook, "Letters," 217–18; Ehat, "Temple Ordinances," 107.

7   William Law, Affidavit, May 4, 1844, in *Warsaw Signal*, June 12, 1844; *Nauvoo Expositor*, June 7, 1844.

8   William Law, Affidavit, May 4, 1844, in *Warsaw Signal*, June 12, 1844; *Nauvoo Expositor*, June 7, 1844; Law, Diary, Jan. 1, 1844, in Cook, *William Law*, 37, 46; Glaser, "William Law," 163–75; Clayton, Journal, June 12, 1844. Alexander Neibaur heard that Jane Law asked Joseph to marry her if she could not be married to William, and

that William could not be sealed to Jane because he was an adulterer. Neibaur, Journal, May 24, 1844. Cf. *Nauvoo Neighbor*, Extra, June 17, 1844. For the stories of Joseph approaching Jane Law, see Jackson, *Adventures*, 19–21; Ford, *History of Illinois*, 322.

9 JS, Journal, Apr. 22; Dec. 18; Feb. 21, 13, 1843; Jan. 21, 1844, in *APR*, 272, 433, 308–309, 304, 442; William Clayton to Emigrants, Dec. 16, 1843, in *Nauvoo Neighbor*, Feb. 14, 1844.

10 JS, Journal, Mar. 3, Aug. 12, 1843; Apr. 28, 1844, in *APR*, 324, 403, 475; *Nauvoo Neighbor*, Oct. 4, 1843.

11 Nauvoo High Council, Minutes, May 20, 24–25, 1842; June 8, 1844; *T&S*, May 15, 1842, 538–39; Francis Higbee to *Signal*, [May 1844,] in *Warsaw Signal*, May 29, 1844; PreM, 736–37; Thomas Grover, Affidavit, July 6, 1869; David Fullmer, Affidavit, June 15, 1869, both in *Affidavits*; *Latter-day Saints' Millennial Star*, Sept. 1, 1851, 258.

12 JS, Journal, Jan. 3–4, 1844; Dec. 19, 1843, in *APR*, 437, 436; Nauvoo City Council, Minutes, Dec. 29, 12, 1843; Jan. 3, 5, 1844.

13 Francis M. Higbee to JS, Jan. 10, 1844, JSC; Rough Draft Notes, ManH, Jan. 16, 1844; JS, Journal, Jan. 16, 1844, in *APR*, 440–41; Nauvoo Municipal Court, Docket, Jan. 5, 1844; Nauvoo City Council, Minutes, Jan. 16, 1844; *T&S*, May 15, 1844, 538.

14 JS, Journal, Mar. 7, 1844, in *APR*, 454; Woodruff, *Journals*, 2:355 (Mar. 7, 1844); Fielding, "Journal," 146. Foster's letter, dated Jan. 10, 1844, and addressed to the *New York Tribune*, was reprinted in the *Quincy Whig*, Feb. 21, 1844.

15 Abiathar Williams, Affidavit, Mar. 27, 1844; M. G. Eaton, Affidavit, Mar. 27, 1844, both in *T&S*, May 15, 1844, 541–42; Clayton, Journal, Mar. 23, 27, 1844.

16 Clayton, Journal, Mar. 23, 27, 1844; *WJS*, 337–38 (Mar. 24, 1844); Fielding, "Journal," 146.

17 JS, Journal, Apr. 13, 1844, in *APR*, 470–71.

18 Richards, Journal, Apr. 18, 1844; JS, Journal, Apr. 18, 1844, in *APR*, 471–72. For the protocol, see Nauvoo High Council, Minutes, July 11, 1840; Law, Diary, Apr. 19, 1844, in Cook, *William Law*, 50–51.

19 *Nauvoo Neighbor*, May 1, 1844; JS, Journal, Apr. 26–27, 1844, in *APR*, 473–74; Charles A. Foster to Editor, Apr. 29, 1844, in *Warsaw Signal*, May 8, 1844. For the rest of the story see *Nauvoo Neighbor*, May 1, 1844. Joseph Jackson told a co-conspirator that Joseph had tried to hire him to kill William Law. Chauncey L. Higbee, Affidavit, Apr. 21, 1844, in *Warsaw Signal*, May 8, 1844.

20 JS, Journal, Apr. 27, 29–30, 18, 1844, in *APR*, 474–76; Nauvoo Legion, Court Martial Minutes, May 9, 1844, Legion Records; Nauvoo Masonic Lodge, Minutes, May 2, 7, 1844; Law, Diary, June 1, 1844, in Cook, *William Law*, 54.

21 *Warsaw Message*, Jan. 10, 17, 1844; *Nauvoo Neighbor*, Jan. 10, 1844. The *Message* denied that anyone was injured.

22 *Alton Telegraph*, Dec. 30, 1843; reprinted in *Warsaw Message*, Jan. 10, 1844.

23 *Warsaw Message*, Jan. 17, 1844; Hallwas, *Thomas Gregg*, 47; Hill, *Quest for Refuge*, 134.

24 *Alton Telegraph*, Feb. 3 and Mar. 25, 1844; *Quincy Whig*, Feb. 28, 1844; *Warsaw Signal*, Apr. 25, 1844.

25 *Warsaw Message*, Jan. 10, 17; Feb. 7, 1844; Charles A. Foster to Editor, Apr. 12, 1844, in *Warsaw Signal*, Apr. 25, 1844. In mid-February 1844, moderates in Warsaw passed resolutions disavowing the "sentiments, policy, and intention" of the anti-Mormons. *Nauvoo Neighbor*, Feb. 21, 1844.

26 Charles A. Foster to Editor, Apr. 12, 1844, in *Warsaw Signal*, Apr. 25, 1844; Law, Diary, June 10, 1844, in Cook, *William Law*, 55; *Warsaw Signal*, June 14, 1844.

27 Bloom, *American Religion*, 95. For discussions of the texts, see JS, *King Follett Discourse*; Cannon, "King Follett Discourse," 179–92; Hale, "Textual History," 4–12; Larson, "Amalgamated Text," 193–208. For the appearance of King Follett doctrines in earlier teachings, see Hale, "King Follett," 209–25.

28 JS, Journal, Apr. 7, 1844, in *APR*, 464; *WJS*, 343, 348, 355, 362 (Apr. 7, 1844).

29 *WJS*, 340, 351, 355, 362 (Apr. 7, 1844); History [1832], in *PJS*, 1:3.

30 *WJS*, 340 (Apr. 6, 1844); JS, Journal, Apr. 7, 1844, in *APR*, 465.

31 *WJS*, 355, 341, 357, 350, 344, 345 (Apr. 7, 1844).

32 *WJS*, 344–45, 357–58, 345 (Apr. 7, 1844).

33 JS, *New Translation*, 594 (Moses 1:39).

34 *WJS*, 378–83 (June 16, 1844); John 17:3; Hale, "Doctrine of Deity," 23–27; *D&C* [1835], 82:4–6 (*D&C*, 93:27–28, 31–32, 39). For a summary of the scholarly literature showing the plurality of gods in the ancient Hebrew religion, see Barney, "Genesis 1:1," 107–24, and Owens, "Kabbalah," 178–84.

35 *WJS*, 345–46 (Apr. 7, 1844). On the overall doctrine, see Hale, "King Follett," 209–25; Ostler, "Idea of Pre-Existence," 59–78.

36 *WJS*, 360, 346 (Apr. 7, 1844).

37 James, *Pragmatism*, 121; Paulsen, "God of Abraham," 114–46.

38 *WJS*, 346 (Apr. 7, 1844); Brodie, *No Man Knows*, 300, 402.

39 Fielding, "Journal," 146, 148; Law, Diary, Apr. 15, 1844, in Cook, *William Law*, 49.

40 JS, Journal, Apr. 28, 1844, in *APR*, 475.

41 *Warsaw Signal*, May 8, 15, 1844; *Nauvoo Neighbor*, May 1, 1844; William Law to Editors, Aug. 1844, in Hallwas and Launius, *Mormon War*, 164.

42 *Francis M. Higbee v. Joseph Smith*, May 1, 1844; Nauvoo Municipal Court, Docket, May 6, 8, 1844; *T&S*, May 15, 1844, 536–42; Clayton, Journal, May 23, 1844; *The People v. Joseph Smith*, May 23, 1844; Cook, *William Law*, 30; JS, Journal, May 20, 21, 25, 1844, in *APR*, 480–81, 483; Clayton, Journal, May 21, 1844.

43 Joseph blamed his troubles on a "paper against adulterers and adulteresses" brought out by the Relief Society, presumably an essay titled the "Voice of Innocence," published in the *Nauvoo Neighbor*, Mar. 20, 1844. The brief essay by Phelps on behalf of the women defended the reputation of Nauvoo's widows and Hyrum Smith during the trial of Orsimus F. Bostwick for slandering Hyrum by accusing him of evil relations with Nauvoo women. Why Joseph faulted the essay is not clear. JS, Journal, Feb. 26, 1844, in *APR*, 447–48, 492; *WJS*, 376.

44 JS, Journal, May 25, 1844, in *APR*, 483; Hallwas and Launius, *Mormon War*, 138–39; *WJS*, 373, 376–77 (May 26, 1844). One Nauvoo leader, stake president William Marks, said that three weeks before his death Joseph repented of plural marriage and planned to give it up, but this runs contrary to everything else Joseph said in this period. Howard, "Mormon Polygamy," 146.

45 JS, Affidavit, June 21, 1844, JSC; JS, Journal, May 27, 1844, in *APR*, 484; John P. Greene, Affidavit, June 21, 1844, JSC.

46 *Warsaw Signal*, May 29, 1844; JS, Journal, May 27, 1844, in *APR*, 484–85; Clayton, Journal, May 27, 1844.

47 Prospectus, *Nauvoo Expositor*, May 10, 1844; *Nauvoo Expositor*, June 7, 1844; Law, Diary, June 1, 7, 1844, in Cook, *William Law*, 55; *Warsaw Signal*, May 15, 1844.

48 Law, Diary, Jan. 8, 1844, in Cook, *William Law*, 47. Law was stung by his Church trial; it was held in what he thought was the wrong court and using illegal methods. Law, Diary, Apr. 19, 1844, in Cook, *William Law*, 51–52.

49 *Nauvoo Expositor*, June 7, 1844.

50 *Nauvoo Expositor*, June 7, 1844. The call for repeal of the charter is in the section titled "Citizens of Hancock County." The political reformers spoke out in the sections of the *Expositor* headed "Introductory," "Joe Smith—The Presidency," "Miscellany," "Citizens of Hancock County," "The Mormons," "Extract from General Smith's Views," and the *Prospectus*. The cautionary sentence was "let us not follow their desperado measures, and thereby dishonor ourselves in revenging our own wrongs."

51 *Nauvoo Expositor*, June 7, 1844.

52 JS, Journal, June 7, 8, 1844, in *APR*, 488; Clayton, Journal, June 7, 1844; Robert D. Foster to JS, June 7, 1844, JSC, and published in *Warsaw Signal*, June 12, 1844; *Nauvoo Neighbor*, June 19, 1844; Nauvoo City Council, Minutes, June 8, 1844; Oaks, "Suppression," 862–903, esp. 889; *HC*, 6:438, 432. For attempted reconciliations with William Law, see Law, Diary, Mar. 29, Apr. 15, and May 13, 1844, in Cook, *William Law*, 48, 50, 52.

53 JS, Journal, June 10, 1844, in *APR*, 489; Nauvoo City Council, Minutes, June 8, 10, 1844. To justify the decision, the city council published the full transcript of the deliberations—twice. *Nauvoo Neighbor*, June 17, Extra; June 19, 1844.

54 Rough Draft Notes, ManH, June 10, 1844; Law, Diary, June 10, 1844, in Cook, *William Law*, 56; Nauvoo City Council, Minutes, June 10, 1844; JS, Journal, June 10, 1844, in *APR*, 489.

55 Clayton, Journal, June 12, 1844; JS, Journal, June 11, 1844, in *APR*, 490. John Hallwas argues Joseph could not tolerate individualism and pluralism. Hallwas, "Non-Mormon Perspective," 62.

56 JS, Proclamation, June 11, 1844, in *PWJS*, 603; *Nauvoo Neighbor*, June 12, 1844. "Bro. Joseph called a meeting at his own house and told the people or us that God showed him in an open vision in daylight that if he did not destroy that press, Printing press, it would cause the Blood of the Saints to flow in the Streets." Laub, "Journal," 160.

57 JS, Journal, June 12, 1844, in *APR*, 490; Clayton, Journal, June 12, 1844; JS to Nauvoo Municipal Court, Record, June 12, 1844, JSC.

58 *Warsaw Signal*, June 12, 1844.

59 *Warsaw Signal*, June 13–14, 19, 1844; JS, Journal, June 13, 1844, in *APR*, 491; Clayton, Journal, June 15, 1844; Isaac Morley to JS, June 16, 1844, JSC; Law, "Wilson Law," 244–46; Law, Diary, June 12, 1844, in Cook, *William Law*, 56.

60 JS to Isaac Morley, June 16, 1844, in *PWJS*, 609; Clayton, Journal, June 15, 1844; JS, Journal, June 15, 1844, in *APR*, 491.

61 JS, Journal, June 15, 1844, in *APR*, 491–92; *Nauvoo Neighbor*, June 12, 1844. West, an American-born painter who had thrived in England as a portraitist and history painter, had completed the first version of the picture in 1796 during England's war with Revolutionary France. A second version, painted in 1817, with a Christ figure in the scene was the one touring the United States. The painting was on display at the American Academy of Fine Arts in New York from April 9 to July 9 in 1836. Voorsanger and Howat, *Art and the Empire City*, 76. In September 1845, the *Rochester Democrat* reported that the painting was on display there after touring the South and West. Darrell Babidge located this reference.

62 Revelation 6:2–8.

63 *Warsaw Signal*, June 5, May 29, 1844.

64 Revelation 1:6; 1 Corinthians 8:5–6; Barney, "Joseph Smith's Emendation," 103–35; 1 Corinthians 8:4–6, 15:46–48; John 5:19; 10:33–34; 17:9–11; 1 John 5:7–8; Exodus 3:16; Romans 8:15–17; *WJS*, 378–83 (June 16, 1844).

65 Clayton, Diary, June 18, 1844; Laub, "Journal," 160; JS to Nauvoo City Marshall, June 18, 1844, JSC; JS, Journal, June 18–20, 1844, in *APR*, 494–95; *HC*, 6:505–14, 516–18, 528–32; JS to Jonathan Dunham, June 22, 1844, JSC.

66 JS to John Tyler, June 20, 1844, JSC; JS to Thomas Ford, June 16, 14, 1844, in *PWJS*, 607–608, 604–605; JS to Thomas Ford, June 22, 1844, JSC.

67 Thomas Ford to JS and City Council, June 22, 1844, JSC; Thomas Ford to JS and others, Nauvoo, June 21, 1844, JSC; JS to Thomas Ford, June 22, 1844, noon, in *PWJS*, 613.

68 Ford, *History of Illinois*, 332; Thomas Ford to JS and City Council, June 22, 1844, JSC. Sharp reported that militia men in Missouri and Iowa had also committed to march against the Mormons. *Warsaw Signal*, June 19, 1844. Ford refused a request of Carthage

citizens to assist in executing the court process against Joseph. Clayton, *Journal*, June 18, 1844; Ford, *History of Illinois*, 324.

69 Ford, *History of Illinois*, 330, 333–34; "Enoch March," in *HC*, 5:587.

70 Thomas Ford to JS and others, June 21, 1844, JSC; Ford, *History of Illinois*, 331; Thomas Ford to JS and City Council, June 22, 1844, JSC.

71 Taylor, Statement, 21–23; JS to Thomas Ford, 22 June 1844, noon, JSC; ManH F-1, 147; JS to Emma Smith, June 23, 1844, in *PWJS*, 616; *HC*, 6:545–47. On the Mississippi floods, see Ford, *History of Illinois*, 334–35. Later additions by Church clerks speak of Joseph heading for the Rocky Mountains. Correspondence at the time referred only to Washington. John C. Calhoun Jr., who happened into Nauvoo at this critical moment, may have advised an appeal to Washington. Taylor, Statement, 25; Cannon, "Joseph Smith," 777.

72 Vilate Kimball to Heber C. Kimball, June 9, 1844, with addendum June 24, 1844, in Kimball, "Martyrdom Letters," 235; Clayton, *Journal*, June 23, 1844; JS and Hyrum Smith to Thomas Ford, June 23, 1844, in *PWJS*, 617–18; Leonard, *Nauvoo*, 375–76. Well after the event, a complicated scenario of Joseph's hours in Montrose was devised by Church historians. *HC*, 6:548–50.

73 Thomas Ford to JS and others, June 24, 1844, JSC; Richards, *Journal*, June 24, 1844; JS to Jonathan Dunham, June 24, 1844, JSC; Clayton, *Journal*, June 24, 1844; Cyrus Wheelock to George A. Smith, Dec. 29, 1854; Dan Jones to Thomas Bullock, Jan. 20, 1855, in Jones, "Martyrdom," 97–98; JS to Emma Smith, June 25, 1844, in *PWJS*, 620.

74 Richards, *Journal*, June 25, 1844; Cyrus Wheelock to George A. Smith, Dec. 29, 1854; *T&S*, July 1, 1844, 562; Ford, *History of Illinois*, 337–38; Taylor, Statement, 31–32; ManH F-1, 159–61.

75 JS, *Journal*, May 27, 1844, in *APR*, 484; JS to Thomas Ford, June 26, 1844, in *PWJS*, 624–25. Richards, *Journal*, June 26, 1844, says JS asked his attorneys to change the venue to Quincy. Joseph assured Ford of his willingness to appear in court so long as he was safe.

76 Ford, *History of Illinois*, 340–41; Richards, *Journal*, June 26, 1844; Clayton, *Journal*, June 26, 1844.

77 Ford, *History of Illinois*, 342. Jonathan C. Wright, Affidavit, Jan. 13, 1855, in *HC*, 6:587–88. An earlier account by Wright has Ford questioning March about the best policy but giving no approval either way. Jonathan Wright to Willard Richards, Apr. 1, 1848.

78 John S. Fullmer to George A. Smith, Nov. 27, 1854, Leonard, *Nauvoo*, 385–86. Dan Jones to Thomas Bullock, Jan. 20, 1855, in Jones "Martyrdom," 101; ManH F-1, 173.

79 JS to Emma Smith, June 27, 1844, in *PWJS*, 629–30; JS to O. H. Browning, June 27, 1844, in *PWJS*, 634–35.

80 Ford, *History of Illinois*, 343, 345–46; Huntress, "Thomas Ford," 41–52.

81 Ford, *History of Illinois*, 346–47.

82 Ford, *History of Illinois*, 347; Clayton, *Journal*, June 27, 1844.

83 John S. Fullmer to George A. Smith, Nov. 27, 1854; and Cyrus Wheelock to George A. Smith, Dec. 29, 1854; Hicks, "Carthage Jail," 389–400.

84 Richards, *Journal*, June 27, 1844. The Carthage coroner, Thomas Barnes, claimed the guards fired blanks. Kimball, "Thomas L. Barnes," 143.

85 Leonard, *Nauvoo*, 396–97, 725 n. 46; Kimball, "Thomas L. Barnes," 143.

86 *T&S*, July 15, Aug. 1, 1844, 586, 599; *Warsaw Signal*, June 29, 1844; Taylor, Statement, 47–54; Oaks and Hill, *Carthage Conspiracy*, 21; Clayton, *Journal*, June 28, 1844. Clayton said the attackers set Joseph up against the well. *Journal*, June 28, 1844. The accounts of the assassination differ in details. Glen Leonard has correlated them in *Nauvoo*, 396–97.

EPILOGUE

1 Ford, *History of Illinois*, 348–51; *Warsaw Signal*, June 27, 29, 1844, Extra; Thomas Ford to M. R. Deming, June 30, 1844, Richards Papers; *Quincy Whig*, July 10, 1844. Ford's account may have been influenced by the report of the scheme to provoke the Mormons in Daniels, *Account of the Murder*, 8.

2 *Warsaw Signal*, June 19, 1844, Extra. The most detailed account of the assassination is Leonard, *Nauvoo*, 392–98.

3 Journal History, June 29, 1844; Roberts, *Comprehensive History*, 2:307; Clayton, Journal, July 6, 1844; Leonard, *Nauvoo*, 415; Oaks and Hill, *Carthage Conspiracy*, 90–112, 163–71, 184–85, 213–14; Hallwas and Launius, *Mormon War*, 259–62.

4 Hallwas and Launius, *Mormon War*, 30; Oaks and Hill, *Carthage Conspiracy*, 217–19. Mormon folklore has created stories of the murderers' gruesome ends. Poulsen, "Persecutors of Joseph Smith," 63–70.

5 Thomas Ford to William W. Phelps, July 22, 1844, Richards Papers; *Quincy Whig*, July 24, 1844.

6 Willard Richards and John Taylor to Nauvoo, June 27, 1844, Richards Papers; Willard Richards, John Taylor, and Samuel H. Smith to Emma Smith and Jonathan Dunham, June 27, 1844, in *T&S*, July 1844, 561.

7 Richards, Journal, June 28, 1844; *Nauvoo Neighbor*, July 3, 1844; Leonard, *Nauvoo*, 399–400; Mace, Autobiography, 110. On the Mormon reaction, see Bitton, *Martyrdom Remembered*, 3–36.

8 Bitton, *George Q. Cannon*, 46; Clayton, Journal, June 28, 1844; Leonard, *Nauvoo*, 400–404; Bernauer, "Final Burial," 17–33.

9 Clayton, Journal, June 28, 1844; *Quincy Whig*, July 10, 1844; Willard Richards to Brigham Young, June 30, 1844, Richards Papers. When Robert Foster returned to conclude his business in Nauvoo, the city council had to assign him a bodyguard to protect him from Porter Rockwell, M. G. Eaton, and Theodore Turley, who were "raging and threaten his life." Clayton, Journal, July 7, 1844.

10 Launius, *Joseph Smith III*, 21; Newell and Avery, *Mormon Enigma*, 213.

11 Emma pressed immediately for the appointment of a trustee-in-trust whom she approved, presumably William Marks, whom she thought of as an ally. But Marks had opposed plural marriage and was unacceptable to others. Clayton, Journal, July 12–15, 1844. Newel K. Whitney and George Miller were appointed trustees for the Church on August 9. Clayton, Journal, Aug. 9, 1844.

12 Clayton, Journal, Aug. 15, 18, 1844; Launius, *Joseph Smith III*, 35–45; Newell and Avery, *Mormon Enigma*, 210–12, 238–49, 252, 259.

13 Newell and Avery, *Mormon Enigma*, 246–49; Avery and Newell, "Lewis C. Bidamon," 375–88.

14 Briggs, "Visit to Nauvoo," 453; Newell and Avery, *Mormon Enigma*, 272, 296, 298, 302; Launius, *Joseph Smith III*, 96–118, 201–206; Avery, *Mission to Madness*, 46–48; Newell, "Polygamy Question," 11–12; Derr, "Eliza R. Snow," 117, n. 10.

15 Clayton, Journal, July 12, 1844. The succession question has been debated in the scholarly literature. Quinn, "Succession Crises," 187–233; Ehat, "Temple Ordinances," 188–247; Esplin, "Succession of Continuity," 301–41; Blair, "Moderate Mormonism," 207–30. Brigham Young acknowledged Samuel's right to the presidency. Woodruff, *Journals*, 2:436 (Aug. 8, 1844). But Young also admitted that Joseph had predicted that upon his unborn son David "will rest the responsibility that now rests upon me." Quoted in Avery, *Mission to Madness*, 45.

16 Quinn, *Origins of Power*, 153, 647, 213–25, 653–54; Bates, "William Smith," 11–23.

17 Van Noord, *James Jesse Strang*, 6, 33–35, 49–50, 60–65, 76–78, 81–83; Quinn, *Origins of Power*, 209–12.

18 Quinn, *Origins of Power*, 161–64; Van Wagoner, *Sidney Rigdon*, 335–36.

19 Clayton, Journal, Aug. 4, 1844; ManH F-1, 295–96; Richards, Journal, Aug. 7, 1844. Wilford Woodruff called Rigdon's reasoning "a kind of second class vision." Woodruff, *Journals*, 2:434 (Aug. 7, 1844).

20 Van Wagoner, *Sidney Rigdon*, 339–41, 354–55, 367–450. The question of the authenticity of the transformation has generated a literature of its own. See Jorgensen and others, "Mantle of the Prophet," 125–204; Harper, "Mantle of Joseph," 35–71; Van Wagoner, "Transfiguration of Brigham Young," 1–24.

21 Young, *Manuscript History*, 171 (July 16, 1844); Arrington, *Brigham Young*, 111; ManH F-1, 297; General Church Minutes, Aug. 8, 1844. The constitutional issue Brigham had to settle was the preeminence of the council of the Twelve over the high council of Mormonism's central city, Nauvoo. The revelation on priesthood, *D&C* [1835], 3 (*D&C*, 107), was slightly ambiguous on the point. Michael Quinn discusses the complexities in *Origins of Power*, 173–75. Later, members of the Twelve reported receiving the keys from Joseph in March 1844. Madsen, *Joseph Smith the Prophet*, 101, 169–70, n. 25; Esplin, "Joseph Smith's Mission," 308–309. Andrew Ehat has argued for the Twelve as legitimate successors on the basis of priesthood ordinances. Ehat, "Temple Ordinances," 194.

22 Bennett, *Mormon Exodus*, 40. Probably a majority of Mormons went west with Brigham Young, but not much more. May, "Demographic Portrait," 37–69, esp. 150.

23 Bitton, *Martyrdom Remembered*, 41–59; Ellsworth, "American Press Reactions," 71–82.

24 The tribute was completed soon enough to be included in the 1844 edition of the *Doctrine and Covenants*. Woodford, "Historical Development," 3:1794.

25 *D&C* [1844], 111:3 (*D&C*, 135:3); Whitmer, *Book of John Whitmer*, 55; *WJS*, 204, 206 (May 21, 1843).

26 *Quincy Whig*, July 4, 1844.

27 Bennett, "Report," 357–58; *New York Weekly Herald*, Jan. 15, 1842.

28 *BofC*, 44 (*D&C*, 42).

29 Hatch, *American Christianity*, 11, 3–16; Remini, *Joseph Smith*, 181; Brodie, *No Man Knows*, 403–4; Bloom, *American Religion*, 96–111.

30 *M&A*, Mar. 1836, 280.

31 *WJS*, 34 (Feb. 5, 1840); Quincy, *Figures from the Past*, 381.

32 *WJS*, 34 (Feb. 5, 1840).

33 History [1832], in *PJS*, 1:3; Brodhead, "John Brown," 529–31, 534–35; *WJS*, 367 (May 12, 1844).

SOURCES CITED

Abbott, Carl. *Boosters and Businessmen: Popular Economic Thought and Urban Growth in the Antebellum Middle West.* Westport, Conn.: Greenwood Press, 1981.

Abzug, Robert H. *Cosmos Crumbling: American Reform and Religious Imagination.* New York: Oxford University Press, 1994.

Adair, Douglass. *Fame and the Founding Fathers: Essays by Douglass Adair.* Edited by Trevor Colbourn. New York: W. W. Norton, 1974.

Adams, Charles Francis. "Charles Francis Adams Visits the Mormons in 1844." Edited by Henry Adams. *Proceedings of the Massachusetts Historical Society* 68 (1944–47): 4–36. Offprint.

Adams, Dale W. "Chartering the Kirtland Bank." *BYU Studies* 23, no. 4 (1983): 467–82.

———. "Doctor Philastus Hurlbut: Originator of Derogatory Statements About Joseph Smith, Jr." *John Whitmer Historical Association Journal* 20 (2000): 76–93.

———. "Grandison Newell's Obsession." *Journal of Mormon History* 30, no. 1 (2004): 159–88.

Affidavits and Certificates Disproving the Statements and Affidavits Contained in John C. Bennett's Letters. Aug. 31, 1842. Nauvoo, Ill., 1842.

Affidavits on Celestial Marriage, 1869–1915. Church Archives. The Church of Jesus Christ of Latter-day Saints. Salt Lake City, Utah.

Ahaus, Hubert. "Orders." In *The Catholic Encyclopedia*, edited by Charles G. Herbermann and others, 15 vols., 11:279–83. New York: Robert Appleton, 1907–12.

Ahlstrom, Sidney E. *A Religious History of the American People.* New Haven, Conn.: Yale University Press, 1972.

Alcott, Bronson. *Conversations with Children on the Gospels.* Boston: J. Munroe, 1836.

Alcott, William Andrus. *Tea and Coffee: Their Physical, Intellectual and Moral Effects on the Human System,* 5th ed. New York: Fowler and Wells, 1836.

Alexander, Archibald. *A Pocket Dictionary of the Holy Bible.* Philadelphia: American Sunday School Union, 1830.

Alexander, Thomas G. "The Reconstruction of Mormon Doctrine." In *Line upon Line: Essays on Mormon Doctrine,* edited by Gary James Bergera, 53–66. Salt Lake City, Utah: Signature Books, 1989.

———. *Things in Heaven and Earth: The Life and Times of Wilford Woodruff, a Mormon Prophet.* Salt Lake City, Utah: Signature Books, 1991.

———. "Wilford Woodruff and Zion's Camp: Baptism by Fire and the Spiritual Confirmation of a Future Prophet." *BYU Studies* 39, no. 1 (2000): 130–46.

———. "The Word of Wisdom: From Principle to Requirement." *Dialogue: A Journal of Mormon Thought* 14, no. 3 (1981): 78–88.

Allen, Ethan. *Reason the Only Oracle of Man.* Bennington, Vt.: Haswell and Russell, 1784.

Allen, James B. "Emergence of a Fundamental: The Expanding Role of Joseph Smith's First Vision in Mormon Religious Thought." *Journal of Mormon History* 7 (1980): 43–61.

———. "Nauvoo's Masonic Hall." *John Whitmer Historical Association Journal* 10 (1990): 39–49.

———. *No Toil nor Labor Fear: The Story of William Clayton*. Provo, Utah: Brigham Young University Press, 2002.

———. "The Significance of Joseph Smith's 'First Vision' in Mormon Thought." *Dialogue: A Journal of Mormon Thought* 1, no. 1 (1966): 29–45.

Allen, James B., Ronald K. Esplin, and David J. Whittaker. *Men with a Mission: The Quorum of the Twelve Apostles in the British Isles, 1837–1841*. Salt Lake City, Utah: Deseret Book, 1992.

Allen, Joseph Henry, and Richard Eddy. *A History of the Unitarians and Universalists in the United States*. New York: Scribner, 1903.

Altschuler, Glen C., and Stuart M. Blumin. *Rude Republic: Americans and Their Politics in the Nineteenth Century*. Princeton, N.J.: Princeton University Press, 2000.

Amatus. "While People Continue in the Body, They Are to Expect No Account from the Invisible World, but What Is Contained in the Bible." *Connecticut Evangelical Magazine* 5 (1805): 346–50.

Ames, Ira. Autobiography and Journal, 1858. Church Archives. The Church of Jesus Christ of Latter-day Saints. Salt Lake City, Utah.

Anderson, A. Gary. "Thomas B. Marsh: The Preparation and Conversion of an Emerging Apostle." In *Regional Studies in Latter-day Saint Church History: New York*, edited by Larry C. Porter, Milton V. Backman, Jr., and Susan Easton Black, 129–48. Provo, Utah: Department of Church History and Doctrine, Brigham Young University, 1992.

Anderson, Devery S. "The Anointed Quorum in Nauvoo, 1842–45." *Journal of Mormon History* 29, no. 2 (2003): 137–57.

Anderson, Karl Ricks. *Joseph Smith's Kirtland: Eyewitness Accounts*. Salt Lake City, Utah: Deseret Book, 1989.

Anderson, Lavina Fielding. "139-Year-Old Portraits of Joseph and Emma Smith." *Ensign* 11 (March 1981): 62–64.

Anderson, Mary Audentia Smith. *Ancestry and Posterity of Joseph Smith and Emma Hale*. Independence, Mo.: Herald Publishing House, 1929.

Anderson, Richard Lloyd. "Atchison's Letters and the Causes of Mormon Expulsion from Missouri." *BYU Studies* 26, no. 3 (1986): 3–47.

———. "Circumstantial Confirmation of the First Vision Through Reminiscences." *BYU Studies* 9, no. 3 (1969): 373–404.

———. "Clarifications of Boggs's 'Order' and Joseph Smith's Constitutionalism." In *Regional Studies in Latter-day Saint Church History: Missouri*, edited by Arnold K. Garr and Clark V. Johnson, 27–83. Provo, Utah: Department of Church History and Doctrine, Brigham Young University, 1994.

———. "Five Who Handled the Plates." *Improvement Era* 72 (July 1969): 38–40, 42, 44–47.

———. "The Impact of the First Preaching in Ohio." *BYU Studies* 11, no. 4 (1971): 474–96.

———. *Investigating the Book of Mormon Witnesses*. Salt Lake City, Utah: Deseret Book, 1981.

———. "Jackson County in Early Mormon Descriptions." *Missouri Historical Review* 65, no. 3 (1971): 270–93.

———. "Joseph Smith and the Millenarian Time Table." *BYU Studies* 3, nos. 3–4 (1961): 55–66.

———. *Joseph Smith's New England Heritage: Influences of Grandfathers Solomon Mack and Asael Smith*, 2d ed., rev. Salt Lake City, Utah: Deseret Book; Provo, Utah: BYU Press, 2003.

———. "Joseph Smith's New York Reputation Reappraised." *BYU Studies* 10, no. 3 (1970): 283–314.

———. "The Mature Joseph Smith and Treasure Searching." *BYU Studies* 24, no. 4 (1984): 489–560.

———. "New Data for Revising the Missouri 'Documentary History.' " *BYU Studies* 14, no. 4 (1974): 488–501.

———. "Reuben Miller, Recorder of Oliver Cowdery's Reaffirmations." *BYU Studies* 8, no. 3 (1968): 277–93.

———. "The Second Witness of Priesthood Restoration." *Improvement Era* 71 (Sept. 1968): 15–16, 18, 20–22, 24.

———. "Who Were the Six Who Organized the Church on 6 April 1830?" *Ensign* 10 (June 1980): 44–45.

Anderson, Richard Lloyd, and Scott H. Faulring. "The Prophet Joseph Smith and His Plural Wives." *FARMS Review of Books* 10, no. 2 (1998): 67–104.

Anderson, Robert D. *Inside the Mind of Joseph Smith: Psychobiography and the Book of Mormon.* Salt Lake City, Utah: Signature Books, 1999.

Anderson, Roger I. *Joseph Smith's New York Reputation Reexamined.* Salt Lake City, Utah: Signature Books, 1990.

Andrew, Laurel B. *The Early Temples of the Mormons: The Architecture of the Millennial Kingdom in the American West.* Albany: State University of New York Press, 1978.

Andrus, Hyrum L. and Helen Mae Andrus, comps. *They Knew the Prophet.* Salt Lake City, Utah: Bookcraft, 1974.

Arac, Jonathan. "Narrative Forms." In *The Cambridge History of American Literature. Volume 2, 1820–1865,* edited by Sacvan Bercovitch and Cyrus Patell, 605–777. Cambridge: Cambridge University Press, 1995.

Armstrong, Karen. *Muhammad: A Biography of the Prophet.* San Francisco: HarperSanFrancisco, 1992.

Arnold, Isaac N. *Reminiscences of the Illinois-Bar Forty Years Ago.* Chicago: Fergus, 1881.

Arnold, Marilyn. *Sweet Is the Word: Reflections on the Book of Mormon—Its Narrative, Teachings, and People.* American Fork, Utah: Covenant Communications, 1996.

Arrington, J. Earl. "William Weeks, Architect of the Nauvoo Temple." *BYU Studies* 19, no. 3 (1979): 337–59.

Arrington, Leonard J. *Brigham Young: American Moses.* New York: Alfred A. Knopf, 1985.

———. "Centrifugal Tendencies in Mormon History." In *To the Glory of God: Mormon Essays on Great Issues,* edited by Truman G. Madsen and Charles D. Tater Jr., 165–77. Salt Lake City, Utah: Deseret Book, 1972.

———. *Charles C. Rich: Mormon General and Western Frontiersman.* Provo, Utah: Brigham Young University Press, 1974.

———. "Church Leaders in Liberty Jail." *BYU Studies* 13, no. 1 (1972): 20–26.

———. "Early Mormon Communitarianism." *Western Humanities Review* 7 (Autumn 1953): 341–69.

Arrington, Leonard J., Feramorz Y. Fox, and Dean L. May. *Building the City of God: Community and Cooperation Among the Mormons.* Salt Lake City, Utah: Deseret Book, 1976.

Ashment, Edward H. "The Book of Mormon and the Anthon Transcript: An Interim Report." *Sunstone* 5, no. 3 (1980): 29–31.

———. "The Facsimiles of the Book of Abraham: A Reappraisal." *Sunstone* 4, no. 5–6 (1979): 33–48.

———. "Joseph Smith's Identification of 'Abraham' in Papyrus JS 1, the 'Breathing Permit of Hôr.' " *Dialogue: A Journal of Mormon Thought* 33, no. 4 (2000): 121–26.

———. " 'A Record in the Language of My Father': Evidence of Ancient Egyptian and Hebrew in the Book of Mormon." In *New Approaches to the Book of Mormon: Explorations in Critical Methodology,* edited by Brent Lee Metcalfe, 329–93. Salt Lake City, Utah: Signature Books, 1993.

———. "Reducing Dissonance: The Book of Abraham as a Case Study." *The Word of God: Essays on Mormon Scripture.* Edited by Dan Vogel, 221–35. Salt Lake City, Utah: Signature Books, 1990.

Ashurst-McGee, Mark. "Joseph Smith, the Kinderhook Plates, and the Question of Revelation." Unpublished paper read at the annual meeting of the Mormon History Association, 1996.

———. "Joseph Smith and the Restoration of the House of Israel." Unpublished paper. Archive of Restoration Culture. Joseph Fielding Smith Institute for Latter-day Saint History. Brigham Young University.

———. "The Josiah Stowell Jr.–John S. Fullmer Correspondence." *BYU Studies* 38, no. 3 (1999): 108–17.

———. "Moroni: Angel or Treasure-Guardian?" *Mormon Historical Studies* 2, no. 2 (2001): 39–75.

———. "A Pathway to Prophethood: Joseph Smith Junior as Rodsman, Village Seer, and Judeo-Christian Prophet." Master's thesis, Utah State University, 2000.

Aston, Warren P. "The Arabian Bountiful Discovered? Evidence for Nephi's Bountiful." *Journal of Book of Mormon Studies* 7, no. 1 (1998): 4–21.

———. "Newly Found Altars from Nahom." *Journal of Book of Mormon Studies* 10, no. 2 (2001): 56–61.

Aston, Warren P., and Michaela Knoth Aston. *In the Footsteps of Lehi: New Evidence for Lehi's Journey Across Arabia to Bountiful.* Salt Lake City, Utah: Deseret Book, 1994.

Astore, William J. *Observing God: Thomas Dick, Evangelicalism, and Popular Science in Victorian Britain and America.* Burlington, Vt.: Ashgate, 2001.

Atchison, David R. Letter to Joseph Smith, Sept. 1, 1838. Church Archives. The Church of Jesus Christ of Latter-day Saints. Salt Lake City, Utah.

Austin, Emily M. *Mormonism: Or, Life among the Mormons.* Madison, Wisc.: M. J. Cantwell, 1882.

Avery, Valeen Tippetts. *From Mission to Madness: Last Son of the Mormon Prophet.* Urbana: University of Illinois Press, 1998.

Avery, Valeen Tippetts, and Linda King Newell. "Lewis C. Bidamon, Stepchild of Mormonism." *BYU Studies* 19, no. 3 (1979): 375–88.

Bacheler, Origen. *Episcopacy.* Pawtucket, R.I.: R. W. Potter, 1845.

———. *Mormonism Exposed: Internally and Externally.* New York: n.p., 1838.

Bachman, Danel W. "A Study of the Mormon Practice of Plural Marriage Before the Death of Joseph Smith." Master's thesis, Purdue University, 1975.

Backman, Milton V. "Establish a House of Prayer, a House of God: The Kirtland Temple." In *The Prophet Joseph: Essays on the Life and Mission of Joseph Smith,* edited by Larry C. Porter and Susan Easton Black, 208–25. Salt Lake City, Utah: Deseret Book, 1988.

———. *The Heavens Resound: A History of the Latter-day Saints in Ohio, 1830–1838.* Salt Lake City, Utah: Deseret Book, 1983.

———. *Joseph Smith's First Vision: The First Vision in Its Historical Context.* Salt Lake City, Utah: Bookcraft, 1971.

———. "A Non-Mormon View of the Birth of Mormonism in Ohio." *BYU Studies* 12, no. 3 (1972): 306–11.

———, comp. *A Profile of Latter-day Saints of Kirtland, Ohio, and Members of Zion's Camp, 1830–1839: Vital Statistics and Sources.* Provo, Utah: Department of Church History and Doctrine, Brigham Young University, 1982.

Backman, Milton V., and James B. Allen. "Membership of Certain of Joseph Smith's Family in the Western Presbyterian Church of Palmyra. *BYU Studies* 10, no. 4 (1970): 482–84.

Baer, Klaus. "The Breathing Permit of Hôr: A Translation of the Apparent Source of the Book of Abraham." *Dialogue: A Journal of Mormon Thought* 3, no. 3 (1968): 109–34.

Bailyn, Bernard. *The Ideological Origins of the American Revolution.* Cambridge: Belknap Press of Harvard University Press, 1967.

Balleisen, Edward J. *Navigating Failure: Bankruptcy and Commercial Society in Antebellum America.* Chapel Hill: University of North Carolina Press, 2001.

Barlow, Philip L. *Mormons and the Bible: The Place of the Latter-day Saints in American Religion.* New York: Oxford University Press, 1991.

Barnes, Joseph W. "Obediah Dogberry: Rochester Freethinker." *Rochester History* 36, no. 3 (1974): 1–24.

Barney, Kevin L. "Examining Six Key Concepts in Joseph Smith's Understanding of Genesis 1:1." *BYU Studies* 39, no. 3 (2000): 107–24.

———. "Joseph Smith's Emendation of Hebrew Genesis 1:1." *Dialogue: Journal of Mormon Thought* 30, no. 4 (1997): 103–35.

———. "Reflections on the Documentary Hypothesis." *Dialogue: A Journal of Mormon Thought* 33, no. 1 (2000): 57–99.

Barton, Andrew. *Disappointment: Or, the Force of Credulity.* Edited by David Mays. Gainesville: University Presses of Florida, 1976.

Bastian, R. J. "Light of Glory." In *New Catholic Encyclopedia*, 15 vols., 8:755. New York: McGraw-Hill, 1967.

Bate, W. Jackson. *Samuel Johnson.* New York: Harcourt Brace Jovanovich, 1977.

Bates, Irene M. "William Smith, 1811–93: Problematic Patriarch." *Dialogue: A Journal of Mormon Thought* 16, no. 2 (1983): 11–23.

Bates, Irene M., and E. Gary Smith. *Lost Legacy: The Mormon Office of Presiding Patriarch.* Urbana: University of Illinois Press, 1996.

Baugh, Alexander L. *A Call to Arms: The 1838 Mormon Defense of Northern Missouri.* Ph.D. diss., Brigham Young University, 1996; reprint, Provo, Utah: Joseph Fielding Institute for LDS History and BYU Studies, 2000.

———. " 'For This Ordinance Belongeth to My House': The Practice of Baptism for the Dead Outside the Nauvoo Temple." *Mormon Historical Studies* 3, no. 1 (2002): 47–58.

———. "Joseph Smith's Athletic Nature." In *Joseph Smith: The Prophet, the Man*, edited by Susan Easton Black and Charles D. Tate, 137–50. Provo, Utah: Religious Studies Center, Brigham Young University, 1991.

———. "Joseph Young's Affidavit of the Massacre at Haun's Mill." *BYU Studies* 38, no. 1 (1999): 188–202.

———. "Missouri Governor Lilburn W. Boggs and the Mormons." *John Whitmer Historical Association Journal* 18 (1998): 111–32.

———. "Samuel Bogart's 1839 Letter About the Mormons to the Quincy Postmaster." *Nauvoo Journal* 7, no. 2 (1995): 52–56.

———. " 'We Took Our Change of Venue for the State of Illinois': The Gallatin Hearing and the Escape of Joseph Smith and the Mormon Prisoners from Missouri, April 1839." In *A City of Refuge: Quincy, Illinois*, edited by Susan Easton Black and Richard E. Bennett, 31–65. Salt Lake City, Utah: Millennial Press, 2000.

Baumgarten, James N. "The Role and Function of the Seventies in LDS Church History." Master's thesis, Brigham Young University, 1960.

Beecher, Catharine E. *Treatise on Domestic Economy: For the Use of Young Ladies at Home, and at School.* Boston: T. H. Webb, 1842.

Beecher, Dale. "The Office of Bishop." *Dialogue: A Journal of Mormon Thought* 15, no. 4 (1982): 103–15.

Beecher, Lyman. *A Plea for the West.* Cincinnati: Truman and Smith; New York: Leavitt, Lord, 1835.

Beecher, Maureen Ursenbach, Linda King Newell, and Valeen Tippetts Avery. "Emma and Eliza and the Stairs." *BYU Studies* 22, no. 1 (1982): 87–96.

Bell, M. Charles. *Calvin and Scottish Theology: The Doctrine of Assurance.* Edinburgh: Handsel, 1985.

Bellamy, Joseph. *True Religion Delineated: Or, Experimental Religion, as Distinguished from Formality on the One Hand, and Enthusiasm on the Other, Set in a Scriptural and Rational Light.* Boston: S. Kneeland, 1750.

Bemrose, Stephen. *Dante's Angelic Intelligences: Their Importance in the Cosmos and in Pre-Christian Religion.* Rome: Edizioni di Storia e Letteratura, 1983.

Bennet, James Arlington. *The American System of Practical Book-keeping, Adapted to the Com-*

merce of the United States, in Its Domestic and Foreign Relations . . . 19th ed. New York: Collins, Keese, 1839.

Bennett, Archibald F. "Solomon Mack and His Family." *Improvement Era* 58, 59 (Sept. 1955–May 1956): 8-part series, intermittent.

Bennett, James Gordon. "James Gordon Bennett's 1831 Report on 'The Mormonites.'" Edited by Leonard J. Arrington. *BYU Studies* 10, no. 3 (1970): 353–64.

Bennett, John Cook. *The History of the Saints; Or, An Exposé of Joe Smith and Mormonism.* Boston: Leland & Whiting, 1842.

Bennett, Richard E. *We'll Find the Place: The Mormon Exodus, 1846–1848.* Salt Lake City, Utah: Deseret Book, 1997.

Bennett, Richard E., and Rachel Cope. " 'A City on a Hill'—Chartering the city of Nauvoo." In *John Whitmer Historical Association Journal,* Nauvoo Conference Special Edition (2002), 17–40.

Bercovitch, Sacvan. *The Puritan Origins of the American Self.* New Haven, Conn.: Yale University Press, 1975.

Bergera, Gary James. "The Earliest Eternal Sealings for Civilly Married Couples Living and Dead." *Dialogue: A Journal of Mormon Thought* 35, no. 3 (2002): 41–66.

———. " 'Illicit Intercourse,' Plural Marriage, and the Nauvoo Stake High Council, 1830–1844." *John Whitmer Historical Association Journal* 23 (2003): 59–90.

Berlin, George L. "Joseph S. C. F. Frey, the Jews, and Early Nineteenth-Century Millenarianism." *Journal of the Early Republic* 1, no. 1 (1981): 27–49.

Bernauer, Barbara Hands. "Still 'Side by Side'—The Final Burial of Joseph and Hyrum Smith." *John Whitmer Historical Association Journal* 11 (1991): 17–33.

Best, Karl F. "Changes in the Revelations, 1833 to 1835." *Dialogue: A Journal of Mormon Thought* 25, no. 1 (1992): 87–112.

Bestor, Arthur E. *Backwoods Utopias: The Sectarian Origins and the Owenite Phase of Communitarian Socialism in America, 1663–1829,* 2d ed., enlarged. Philadelphia: University of Pennsylvania Press, 1970.

Billington, Ray Allen. *The Protestant Crusade, 1800–1860: A Study of the Origins of American Nativism.* New York: Rinehart, 1952.

———. *Westward Expansion: A History of the American Frontier,* 2d ed. New York: Macmillan, 1960.

Biographical Directory of the American Congress, 1774–1971. Washington, D.C.: Government Printing Office, 1971.

"Birthplace and Early Residence of Joseph Smith, Jr." *Historical Magazine* 2d ser., 8 (Nov. 1870): 315–16.

Bishop, Francis G. *A Brief History of the Church of Jesus Christ of Latter day Saints, from Their Rise Until the Present Time; Containing an Account of, and Showing the Cause of Their Sufferings in the State of Missouri, in the Years 1833–38.* Salem, N.C.: Blum and Son, 1839.

Bishop, M. Guy. "What Has Become of Our Fathers? Baptism for the Dead at Nauvoo." *Dialogue: A Journal of Mormon Thought* 23, no. 2 (1990): 85–97.

Bitton, Davis. *George Q. Cannon: A Biography.* Salt Lake City, Utah: Deseret Book, 1999.

———. *Images of the Prophet Joseph Smith.* Salt Lake City, Utah: Aspen Books, 1996.

———. "Kirtland as a Center of Missionary Activity, 1830–1838." *BYU Studies* 11, no. 4 (1971): 497–516.

———. *The Martyrdom Remembered: Reactions to the Assassination of the Prophet Joseph Smith.* Salt Lake City: Aspen Books, 1994.

———. "Mormon in Texas: The Ill-Fated Lyman Wight Colony, 1844–1858." *Arizona and the West* 11, no. 1 (1969): 5–26.

Black, Susan Easton. "How Large Was the Population of Nauvoo?" *BYU Studies* 35, no. 2 (1995): 91–94.

———. "Isaac Galland: Both Sides of the River." *Nauvoo Journal* 8, no. 2 (1996): 3–9.

————. "John Farnham Boynton." *Nauvoo Journal* 8, no. 1 (1996): 3–6.

————. *Who's Who in the Doctrine and Covenants.* Salt Lake City, Utah: Bookcraft, 1997.

Black, Susan Easton, and Richard E. Bennett, eds. *A City of Refuge: Quincy, Illinois.* Salt Lake City, Utah: Millennial Press, 2000.

Black, Susan Easton, and Harvey Bischoff Black, comps. *Annotated Record of Baptisms for the Dead, 1840–1845: Nauvoo, Hancock County, Illinois.* 7 vols. Provo, Utah: Center for Family History and Genealogy, Brigham Young University, 2002.

Blair, Alma R. "The Haun's Mill Massacre." *BYU Studies* 13, no. 1 (1972): 62–67.

————. "Reorganized Church of Jesus Christ of Latter Day Saints: Moderate Mormonism." In *The Restoration Movement: Essays in Mormon History,* edited by F. Mark McKiernan, Alma R. Blair, and Paul M. Edwards, 207–30. Lawrence, Kans.: Coronado Press, 1973.

Bloch, Ruth H. *Visionary Republic: Millennial Themes in American Thought, 1756–1800.* Cambridge: Cambridge University Press, 1985.

Block, Marguerite Beck. *The New Church in the New World: A Study of Swedenborgianism in America.* New York: Henry Holt, 1932.

Bloom, Harold. *American Religion: The Emergence of the Post-Christian Nation.* New York: Simon & Schuster, 1992.

————. *Omens of Millennium: The Gnosis of Angels, Dreams, and Resurrection.* New York: Riverhead Books, 1996.

Boggs, William M. "A Short Biographical Sketch of Lilburn W. Boggs, by His Son." *Missouri Historical Review* 4, no. 2 (1910): 106–10.

Boles, John B. *The Great Revival, 1707–1805: The Origins of the Southern Evangelical Mind.* Lexington: University Press of Kentucky, 1972.

Bolingbroke, Henry St. John, Viscount. *Letters on the Spirit of Patriotism: On the Idea of a Patriot King: and on the State of Parties, at the Accession of King George the First.* Philadelphia: Franklin and Hall, 1749.

Boorstin, Daniel J. *The Americans: The National Experience.* New York: Random House, 1965.

Boyer, Paul. "The Growth of Fundamentalist Apocalyptic in the United States." In *The Encyclopedia of Apocalypticism,* edited by Bernard McGinn, John J. Collins, and Stephen J. Stein, 3 vols., 3:140–78. New York: Continuum, 1998.

Boylan, Anne M. *The Origins of Women's Activism: New York and Boston, 1797–1840.* Chapel Hill: University of North Carolina Press, 2002.

Bozeman, Theodore Dwight. *To Live Ancient Lives: The Primitivist Dimension in Puritanism.* Chapel Hill: University of North Carolina Press, 1988.

Bradley, James L. *Zion's Camp, 1834: Prelude to the Civil War.* Salt Lake City, Utah: Publishers Press, 1990.

Bradley, Martha Sonntag. " 'Seizing Sacred Space': Women's Engagement in Early Mormonism." *Dialogue: A Journal of Mormon Thought* 27, no. 2 (1994): 57–70.

Bradley, Martha Sonntag, and Mary Brown Firmage Woodward. *4 Zinas: A Story of Mothers and Daughters on the Mormon Frontier.* Salt Lake City, Utah: Signature Books, 2000.

————. "Plurality, Patriarchy, and Priestess: Zina D. H. Young's Nauvoo Marriages." *Journal of Mormon History* 20, no. 1 (1994): 84–118.

Bradshaw, M. Scott. "Joseph Smith's Performance of Marriages in Ohio." *BYU Studies* 39, no. 4 (2000): 23–69.

Braude, Benjamin. "The Sons of Noah and the Construction of Ethnic and Geographical Identities in the Medieval and Early Modern Periods." *William and Mary Quarterly,* 3d ser., 54, no. 1 (1997): 103–42.

Brekus, Catherine A. *Strangers and Pilgrims: Female Preaching in America, 1740–1845.* Chapel Hill: University of North Carolina Press, 1998.

Bressler, Ann Lee. *The Universalist Movement in America, 1770–1880.* New York: Oxford University Press, 2001.

Brewer, Priscilla J. "The Shakers of Mother Ann Lee." In *America's Communal Utopias*, edited by Donald E. Pitzer, 37–56. Chapel Hill: University of North Carolina Press, 1997.

Brewster, Quinn. "The Structure of the Book of Mormon: A Theory of Evolutionary Development." *Dialogue: A Journal of Mormon Thought* 29, no. 2 (1996): 109–40.

Briggs, Edmund C. "A Visit to Nauvoo in 1856." *Journal of History* 9 (Oct. 1916): 446–62.

Bringhurst, Newell G. "Elijah Abel and the Changing Status of Blacks Within Mormonism." *Dialogue: A Journal of Mormon Thought* 12, no. 2 (1979): 22–36.

Brodhead, Richard H. "Prophets, Publics, and Publication: The Case of John Brown." *Proceedings of the American Antiquarian Society* 111, pt. 2 (2001): 529–51.

Brodie, Fawn M. *No Man Knows My History: The Life of Joseph Smith the Mormon Prophet*. New York: Alfred A. Knopf, 1945.

Brooke, John L. *The Refiner's Fire: The Making of Mormon Cosmology, 1644–1844*. New York: Cambridge University Press, 1994.

Brotherton, Edward. *Mormonism: Its Rise and Progress, and the Prophet Joseph Smith*. Manchester, Eng.: J. and S. Smith, [1842].

Brown, Albert. "A Letter Regarding the Acquisition of the Book of Abraham." Edited by Christopher C. Lund. *BYU Studies* 20, no. 4 (1980): 402–403.

Brown, Jerry Wayne. *The Rise of Biblical Criticism in America, 1810–1870: The New England Scholars*. Middletown, Conn.: Wesleyan University Press, 1969.

Brown, Lisle G. "The Sacred Departments for Temple Work in Nauvoo: The Assembly Room and the Council Chambers." *BYU Studies* 19, no. 3 (1979): 360–74.

Brown, Peter. *Augustine of Hippo: A Biography*. Berkeley: University of California Press, 1969.

Brown, Richard Maxwell. *Strain of Violence: Historical Studies of American Violence and Vigilantism*. New York: Oxford University Press, 1975.

Brown, S. Kent. *From Jerusalem to Zarahemla: Literary and Historical Studies of the Book of Mormon*. Provo, Utah: Religious Studies Center, Brigham Young University, 1998.

———. "Lehi's Personal Record: Quest for a Missing Source." *BYU Studies* 24, no. 1 (1984): 19–42.

———. " 'The Place That Was Called Nahom': New Light from Ancient Yemen." *Journal of Book of Mormon Studies* 8, no. 1 (1999): 66–68.

Brownson, Orestes. *New Views of Christianity, Society, and the Church*. Boston: J. Munroe, 1836.

Brumm, Ursula. *American Thought and Religious Typology*, trans. John Hoogland. New Brunswick, N.J.: Rutgers University Press, 1970.

Buell, Lawrence. *New England Literary Culture: From Revolution Through Renaissance*. Cambridge: Cambridge University Press, 1986.

Buerger, David John. " 'The Fulness of the Priesthood': The Second Anointing in Latter-day Saint Theology and Practice." *Dialogue: A Journal of Mormon Thought* 16, no. 1 (1983): 10–44.

———. *The Mysteries of Godliness: A History of Mormon Temple Worship*. San Francisco: Smith Research Associates, 1994.

Buggeln, Gretchen Townsend. *Temples of Grace: The Material Transformation of Connecticut's Churches, 1790–1840*. Hanover, N.H.: University Press of New England, 2003.

Bullock, Stephen C. *Revolutionary Brotherhood: Freemasonry and the Transformation of the American Social Order, 1730–1840*. Chapel Hill: University of North Carolina Press, 1996.

Burbank, Daniel. Autobiography, 1863. Church Archives. The Church of Jesus Christ of Latter-day Saints. Salt Lake City, Utah.

Burnett, Peter H. *An Old California Pioneer*. 1880; reprint, Oakland, Calif.: Biobooks, 1946.

Burroughs, Edwin G., and Mike Wallace. *Gotham: A History of New York City to 1898*. New York: Oxford University Press, 1999.

Bush, Lester E. *Health and Medicine Among the Latter-day Saints: Science, Sense, and Scripture*. New York: Crossroad Publishing, 1993.

———. "Mormonism's Negro Doctrine: An Historical Overview." *Dialogue: A Journal of Mormon Thought* 8, no. 1 (1973): 11–68.

————. "The Spalding Theory Then and Now." *Dialogue: A Journal of Mormon Thought* 10, no. 4 (1977): 40–69.

————. "The Word of Wisdom in Early Nineteenth-Century Perspective." *Dialogue: A Journal of Mormon Thought* 14, no. 3 (1981): 46–65.

Bushman, Richard Lyman. "The Book of Mormon in Early Mormon History." In *New Views of Mormon History: A Collection of Essays in Honor of Leonard J. Arrington*, edited by Davis Bitton and Maureen Ursenbach Beecher, 3–18. Salt Lake City, Utah: University of Utah Press, 1987.

————. "The Character of Joseph Smith." *BYU Studies* 42, no. 2 (2003): 23–34.

————. "Early Mormonism and the Conversion of 'Feeble Souls.' " Unpublished paper.

————. "Farmers in Court: Orange County, North Carolina, 1750–1776." In *The Many Legalities of Early America*, edited by Christopher L. Tomlins and Bruce H. Mann, 388–413. Chapel Hill: University of North Carolina Press, 2001.

————. *From Puritan to Yankee: Character and the Social Order in Connecticut, 1690–1765.* Cambridge: Harvard University Press, 1967.

————. *Joseph Smith and Skepticism.* Provo, Utah: Brigham Young University Press, 1974.

————. "Joseph Smith as Translator." In *The Prophet Puzzle: Interpretive Essays on Joseph Smith*, edited by Bryan Waterman, 69–85. Salt Lake City, Utah: Signature Books, 1999.

————. "A Joseph Smith for the Twenty-First Century." In *Believing History: Latter-day Saint Essays*, edited by Reid L. Neilson and Jed Woodworth. New York: Columbia University Press, 2004.

————. *King and People in Provincial Massachusetts.* Chapel Hill: University of North Carolina Press, 1985.

————. "The Lamanite View of Book of Mormon History." In *By Study and Also by Faith: Essays in Honor of Hugh W. Nibley . . .* , edited by John M. Lundquist and Stephen D. Ricks, 2 vols., 2:52–72. Salt Lake City, Utah: Deseret Book; Provo, Utah: FARMS, 1990.

————. *Making Space for the Mormons.* Logan: Utah State University Press, 1997.

————. "Mormon Persecutions in Missouri, 1833." *BYU Studies* 3, no. 1 (1960): 11–20.

————. *The Refinement of America: Persons, Houses, Cities.* New York: Alfred A. Knopf, 1992.

————. "The Theology of Councils." In *Revelation, Reason, and Faith: Essays in Honor of Truman G. Madsen*, edited by Donald W. Parry, Daniel C. Peterson, and Stephen D. Ricks, 433–45. Provo, Utah: FARMS, Brigham Young University, 2002.

————. "The Visionary World of Joseph Smith." *BYU Studies* 37, no. 1 (1997–98): 183–204.

Butler, Jon. *Awash in a Sea of Faith: Christianizing the American People.* Cambridge: Harvard University Press, 1990.

————. "Magic, Astrology, and the Early American Religious Heritage, 1600–1700." *American Historical Review* 84, no. 2 (1979): 317–46.

Butterfield, Abel. Letter to John Lufkin, July 24, 1837. Jacob K. Butterfield Letters. Utah State Historical Society, Salt Lake City.

Cahoon, Reynolds. Diaries, 1831–1832. Church Archives. The Church of Jesus Christ of Latter-day Saints. Salt Lake City, Utah.

Calhoun, John C. *The Papers of John C. Calhoun: Volume 17, 1843–1844.* Edited by Clyde N. Wilson. Columbia: University of South Carolina Press, 1986.

Campbell, Alexander. *The Christian System, in Reference to the Union of Christians, and a Restoration of Primitive Christianity, as Plead in the Current Reformation.* Pittsburgh: Forrester and Campbell, 1839.

————. *Delusions: An Analysis of the Book of Mormon; With an Examination of Its Internal and External Evidences, and Refutation of Its Pretences to Divine Authority.* Boston: Benjamin H. Greene, 1832.

————, comp. *The Sacred Writings of the Apostles and Evangelists of Jesus Christ, Commonly Styled the New Testament.* Trans. from the original Greek by George Campbell, James Macknight, and Philip Doddridge. Buffaloe, Va.: A. Campbell, 1826.

Campbell, Courtney S. "Images of the New Jerusalem: Latter Day Saint Faction Interpretations of Independence, Missouri, 1830–1992." Ph.D. diss., 2 vols., University of Kansas, 1993.

Cannon, Brian Q. "John C. Calhoun, Jr., Meets the Prophet Joseph Smith Shortly Before the Departure for Carthage." *BYU Studies* 33, no. 4 (1993): 772–80.

Cannon, Brian Q., and *BYU Studies* staff. "Priesthood Restoration Documents." *BYU Studies* 35, no. 4 (1995–96): 162–207.

Cannon, Donald Q. "The King Follett Discourse: Joseph Smith's Greatest Sermon in Historical Perspective." *BYU Studies* 18, no. 2 (1978): 179–82.

———. "Licensing in the Early Church." *BYU Studies* 22, no. 1 (1982): 96–105.

———. "Topsfield, Massachusetts: Ancestral Home of the Prophet Joseph Smith." *BYU Studies* 14, no. 1 (1973): 56–76.

———. "Zelph Revisited." In *Regional Studies in Latter-day Saint Church History: Illinois*, edited by H. Dean Garrett, 97–111. Provo, Utah: Department of Church History and Doctrine, Brigham Young University, 1995.

———, ed. *Latter-day Prophets and the United States Constitution.* Provo, Utah: Religious Studies Center, Brigham Young University, 1991.

Cannon, Donald Q., and Lyndon W. Cook, eds. *Far West Record: Minutes of the Church of Jesus Christ of Latter-day Saints, 1830–1844.* Salt Lake City, Utah: Deseret Book, 1983.

Cannon, M. Hamlin, ed. "Documents: Bankruptcy Proceedings Against Joseph Smith in Illinois." *Pacific Historical Review* 14, no. 4 (1945): 425–33.

Capers, Gerald M. *Stephen A. Douglas: Defender of the Union.* Boston: Little, Brown, 1959.

Card, Orson Scott. "The Book of Mormon—Artifact or Artifice?" In *A Storyteller in Zion: Essays and Speeches by Orson Scott Card*, 13–45. Salt Lake City, Utah: Bookcraft, 1993.

Carlyle, Thomas. *Reminiscences.* Edited by James Anthony Froude. New York: Charles Scribner's Sons, 1881.

Carmack, Noel A. "A Note on Nauvoo Theater." *BYU Studies* 34, no. 1 (1994): 94–100.

Carnes, Mark C. *Secret Ritual and Manhood in Victorian America.* New Haven, Conn.: Yale University Press, 1989.

Carriel, Mary. *The Life of Jonathan Baldwin Turner.* Urbana: University of Illinois Press, 1961.

Caswall, Henry. *The Prophet of the Nineteenth Century; Or, the Rise, Progress, and Present State of the Mormons, or Latter-day Saints.* London: J. G. F. and J. Rivington, 1843.

Chalmers, Thomas. *A Series of Discourses on the Christian Revelation, Viewed in Connection with the Modern Astronomy.* Glasgow: For John Smith and others, 1817.

Chamberlin, Solomon. "A Short Sketch of the Life of Solomon Chamberlain," ca. 1858. Church Archives. The Church of Jesus Christ of Latter-day Saints. Salt Lake City, Utah.

Chambers, William Nisbet. "Election of 1840." In *History of American Presidential Elections, 1789–1868*, edited by Arthur M. Schlesinger, 4 vols., 1:643–744. New York: Chelsea Publishers in association with McGraw-Hill, 1971.

Champollion, Jean-François. *Précis du système Hiéroglyphique des Anciens Égyptiens, ou Recherches.* Paris: Imprimerie Royale, 1824.

Channing, William E. *The Works of William E. Channing*, 6 vols. 4th ed. Boston: James Munroe, 1845.

Charles, Melodie Moench. "The Mormon Christianizing of the Old Testament." *Sunstone* 5, no. 6 (1980): 35–39.

Charlesworth, James H. "Messianism in the Pseudepigrapha and the Book of Mormon." In *Reflections on Mormonism: Judaeo-Christian Parallels*, edited by Truman Madsen, 99–137. Provo, Utah: Religious Studies Center, Brigham Young University, 1978.

Chase, Daryl. "Sidney Rigdon—Early Mormon." Master's thesis, University of Chicago, 1931.

Chase, Frederick. *A History of Dartmouth College and the Town of Hanover, New Hampshire.* Edited by John P. Lord. 2 vols. Cambridge, Mass.: John Wilson and Son, 1891.

Chidester, David, and Edward T. Linenthal, eds. *American Sacred Space.* Bloomington: Indiana University Press, 1995.

Child, Hamilton. *Gazeteer of Orange County, Vt., 1762–1888.* Syracuse, N.Y.: Syracuse Journal, 1888.

Christian, Lewis Clark. "Mormon Foreknowledge of the West." *BYU Studies* 21, no. 4 (1981): 403–15.

Church, F. Forrester. "Thomas Jefferson's Bible." In *The Bible and Bibles in America,* edited by Ernest Frerichs, 145–61. Atlanta: Scholars Press, 1988.

Clark, Allison. "Women and the Body in Early Nineteenth-Century Shakerism and Mormonism." In *Archive of Restoration Culture: Summer Fellows' Papers, 1997–1999, 145–54.* Provo, Utah: Joseph Fielding Smith Institute for Latter-day Saint History, Brigham Young University, 2000.

Clark, Christopher. *The Communitarian Moment: The Radical Challenge of the Northampton Association.* Ithaca, N.Y.: Cornell University Press, 1995.

Clark, James R. *The Story of the Pearl of Great Price.* Salt Lake City, Utah: Bookcraft, 1955.

Clark, John A. *Gleanings by the Way.* Philadelphia: W. J. & J. K. Simon; New York: R. Carter, 1842.

Clawson, Mary Ann. *Constructing Brotherhood: Class, Gender, and Fraternalism.* Princeton, N.J.: Princeton University Press, 1989.

Clay, Henry. *The Papers of Henry Clay: Volume 9: The Whig Leader, January 1, 1837–December 31, 1843.* Edited by Robert Seager. Lexington: University Press of Kentucky, 1988.

Clayton, William. *An Intimate Chronicle: The Journals of William Clayton.* Edited by George D. Smith. Salt Lake City, Utah: Signature Books in association with Smith Research Associates, 1991.

———. Diary. 1844. Church Archives. The Church of Jesus Christ of Latter-day Saints. Salt Lake City, Utah.

———. Journals, 1842–1846. Church Archives. The Church of Jesus Christ of Latter-day Saints. Salt Lake City, Utah.

———. Letter to Edward Martin. Nov. 29, 1840. Church Archives. The Church of Jesus Christ of Latter-day Saints. Salt Lake City, Utah.

Clinton, DeWitt. *Discourse Delivered before the New-York Historical Society, at Their Anniversary Meeting, 6th December, 1811.* New York: James Eastburn, 1812.

Cochran, Thomas C. *New York in the Confederation: An Economic Study.* Philadelphia: University of Pennsylvania Press, 1932.

Coe, Truman. "Truman Coe's 1836 Description of Mormonism." Edited by Milton V. Backman. *BYU Studies* 17, no. 3 (1977): 347–55.

Cohen, P., and J. Cohen. "The Clinician's Illusion." *Archives of General Psychiatry* 41, no. 12 (1984): 1178–82.

Colas, Dominique. *Civil Society and Fanaticism: Conjoined Histories.* Trans. by Amy Jacob. Stanford, Calif.: Stanford University Press, 1997.

Collier, Fred C., comp. *Unpublished Revelations of the Prophets and Presidents of the Church of Jesus Christ of Latter Day Saints: Volume 1.* 2d ed. Salt Lake City, Utah: Collier's Publishing, 1981.

Collings, Rosalyn M. " 'Wanderers in a Strange Land': The Oriental Tale and the Book of Mormon." Unpublished paper. Archive of Restoration Culture. Joseph Fielding Smith Institute for Latter-day Saint History, Brigham Young University.

Coltrin, Zebedee. Diaries, 1832–1834. Church Archives. The Church of Jesus Christ of Latter-day Saints, Salt Lake City, Utah.

Colvin, Don F. *Nauvoo Temple: A Story of Faith.* American Fork, Utah: Covenant Communications, 2002.

Compton, Todd. "Fanny Alger Smith Custer: Mormonism's First Plural Wife?" *Journal of Mormon History* 22, no. 1 (1996): 174–207.

———. " 'Kingdom of Priests': Priesthood, Temple, and Women in the Old Testament and in the Restoration." *Dialogue: A Journal of Mormon Thought* 36, no. 3 (2003): 41–59.

————. *In Sacred Loneliness: The Plural Wives of Joseph Smith*. Salt Lake City, Utah: Signature Books, 1997.

————. "A Trajectory of Plurality: An Overview of Joseph Smith's Thirty-three Plural Wives." *Dialogue: A Journal of Mormon Thought* 29, no. 2 (1996): 1–38.

Conover, Peter. Statement, 1854. Historian's Office. Church Archives. The Church of Jesus Christ of Latter-day Saints, Salt Lake City, Utah.

Cook, Bradley J. "The *Book of Abraham* and the Islamic Qiṣaṣ-al-Anbiyā (Tales of the Prophets) Extant Literature." *Dialogue: A Journal of Mormon Thought* 33, no. 4 (2000): 127–46.

Cook, Edward M. *The Fathers of the Towns: Leadership and Community Structure in Eighteenth-Century New England*. Baltimore: Johns Hopkins University Press, 1976.

Cook, Lyndon W. " 'Brother Joseph Is Truly a Wonderful Man, He Is All We Could Wish a Prophet to Be': Pre-1844 Letters of William Law." *BYU Studies* 20, no. 2 (1980): 207–18.

————. "Isaac Galland—Mormon Benefactor." *BYU Studies* 19, no. 3 (1979): 261–84.

————. "James Arlington Bennet and the Mormons." *BYU Studies* 19, no. 2 (1979): 247–49.

————. *Joseph Smith and the Law of Consecration*. Orem, Utah: Grandin Book, 1985.

————. *The Revelations of the Prophet Joseph Smith: A Historical and Biographical Commentary of the Doctrine and Covenants*. Salt Lake City, Utah: Deseret Book, 1985.

————. *William Law: Biographical Essay, Nauvoo Diary, Correspondence, Interview*. Orem, Utah: Grandin Book, 1994.

Cooper, Rex Eugene. *Promises Made to the Fathers: Mormon Covenant Organization*. Salt Lake City: University of Utah Press, 1990.

Coray, Howard. "Howard Coray's Recollections of Joseph Smith." Edited by Dean C. Jessee. *BYU Studies* 17, no. 3 (1977): 341–47.

————. Journal. L. Tom Perry Special Collections. Harold B. Lee Library. Brigham Young University.

Coray, Martha Jane Knowlton. "Joseph Smith's July 19, 1840 Discourse." Edited by Dean C. Jessee. *BYU Studies* 19, no. 3 (1979): 390–94.

Cornwall, Rebecca Foster, and Leonard J. Arrington. "Perpetuation of a Myth: Mormon Danites in Five Western Novels, 1840–90." *BYU Studies* 23, no. 2 (1983): 142–65.

Corrill, John. *A Brief History of the Church of Christ of Latter Day Saints*. St. Louis, Mo.: Printed for the Author, 1839.

Cox, Cordelia Morley. "A Sketch of the Life of My Father Isaac Morley Senior One of the Pioneers to Salt Lake Valley in 1848." L. Tom Perry Special Collections. Harold B. Lee Library. Brigham Young University.

Cowdery, Oliver. Letter Book, Docket, and Correspondence, 1833–1894. Huntington Library. San Marino, Calif.

————. "Oliver Cowdery's Kirtland, Ohio, 'Sketch Book.' " Edited by Leonard J. Arrington. *BYU Studies* 12, no. 4 (1972): 410–26.

Cracroft, Richard H. "The Gentle Blasphemer: Mark Twain, Holy Scripture, and the Book of Mormon." *BYU Studies* 11, no. 2 (1971): 119–40.

Cranford, Sara. " 'Holiness to the Lord': Mormon and Masonic Temples, 1830–1846." Unpublished paper. Archive of Restoration Culture. Joseph Fielding Smith Institute for Latter-day Saint History. Brigham Young University.

Crawford, Michael J. "The Spiritual Travels of Nathan Cole." *William and Mary Quarterly*, 3d ser., 33 (1976): 89–126.

Crawley, Peter. *A Descriptive Bibliography of the Mormon Church: Volume 1, 1830–1847*. Provo, Utah: Religious Studies Center, Brigham Young University, 1997.

————. "Two Rare Missouri Documents." *BYU Studies* 14, no. 4 (1974): 502–27.

Crawley, Peter, and Richard Lloyd Anderson. "The Political and Social Realities of Zion's Camp." *BYU Studies* 14, no. 4 (1974): 406–20.

Crockett, Walter Hill. *Vermont: The Green Mountain State*, 5 vols. New York: Century History, 1921–23.

Cronon, William. *Nature's Metropolis: Chicago and the Great West*. New York: W. W. Norton, 1991.

Crosby, Jonathan. "A Biographical Sketch of the Life of Jonathan Crosby Written by Himself." Utah State Historical Society. Salt Lake City.

Cross, Whitney R. *The Burned-Over District: The Social and Intellectual History of Enthusiastic Religion in Western New York, 1800–1850*. Ithaca, N.Y.: Cornell University Press, 1950.

Crowe, Michael J. *The Extraterrestrial Life Debate, 1750–1900: The Idea of Plurality of Worlds from Kant to Lowell*. Cambridge: Cambridge University Press, 1986.

Crowley, Ariel L. "The Anthon Transcript: An Evidence for the Truth of the Prophet's Account of the Origin of the Book of Mormon." *Improvement Era* 45, 47 (January–March 1942, September 1944): 4-part series.

Dahl, Larry E., and Charles D. Tate, eds. *The Lectures on Faith in Historical Perspective*. Provo, Utah: Religious Studies Center, Brigham Young University, 1990.

Dain, Bruce. *A Hideous Monster of the Mind: American Race Theory in the Early Republic*. Cambridge: Harvard University Press, 2002.

Dallimore, Arnold. *Forerunner of the Charismatic Movement: The Life of Edward Irving*. Chicago: Moody Press, 1983.

Damrosch, Leo. *The Sorrows of the Quaker Jesus: James Nayler and the Puritan Crackdown on the Free Spirit*. Cambridge: Harvard University Press, 1996.

Daniels, William M. *A Correct Account of the Murder of Generals Joseph and Hyrum Smith: At Carthage, on the 27th Day of June, 1844*. Nauvoo, Ill.: John Taylor, 1845.

Davies, Horton. *The Worship of the American Puritans, 1629–1730*. New York: Peter Lang, 1990.

Davis, David Brion. *Slavery and Human Progress*. New York: Oxford University Press, 1984.

———. "Some Themes of Counter-Subversion. An Analysis of Anti-Masonic, Anti-Catholic, and Anti-Mormon Literature." *Mississippi Valley Historical Review* 47, no. 2 (1960): 205–24.

Davis, Matthew L. Letter to Mary Davis. Feb. 5, 1840. Church Archives. The Church of Jesus Christ of Latter-day Saints. Salt Lake City.

Daynes, Kathryn M. *More Wives than One: Transformation of the Mormon Marriage System, 1840–1910*. Urbana: University of Illinois Press, 2001.

De Pillis, Mario S. "The Quest for Religious Authority and the Rise of Mormonism." *Dialogue: A Journal of Mormon Thought* 1, no. 1 (1966): 68–88.

De Voto, Bernard. "The Centennial of Mormonism." *American Mercury* 19 (1930): 1–13.

Delbanco, Andrew. *The Death of Satan: How Americans Have Lost the Sense of Evil*. New York: Farrar, Straus and Giroux, 1995.

———. *The Real American Dream: A Meditation on Hope*. Cambridge: Harvard University Press, 1999.

Derr, Jill Mulvay. "The Lion and the Lioness: Brigham Young and Eliza R. Snow." *BYU Studies* 40, no. 2 (2001): 54–101.

———. "The Significance of 'O My Father' in the Personal Journey of Eliza R. Snow." *BYU Studies* 36, no. 1 (1996–97): 84–126.

Derr, Jill Mulvay, Janath Russell Cannon, and Maureen Ursenbach Beecher. *Women of Covenant: The Story of the Relief Society*. Salt Lake City, Utah: Deseret Book, 1992.

Dick, Thomas. *The Philosophy of a Future State*. In *The Works of Thomas Dick, L.L.D*. Hartford, Conn.: Sumner and Goodman, 1843.

Discussion on the Existence of God and the Authenticity of the Bible, between Origen Bacheler and Robert Dale Owen. London: J. Watson, 1853.

Divett, Robert T. "His Chastening Rod: Cholera Epidemics and the Mormons." *Dialogue: A Journal of Mormon Thought* 12, no. 3 (1979): 6–15.

Doan, Ruth Alden. *The Miller Heresy, Millennialism, and American Culture*. Philadelphia: Temple University Press, 1987.

Document Containing the Correspondence, Orders, &C. In Relation to the Disturbances with the Mormons; and the Evidence Given before the Hon. Austin A. King, Judge of the Fifth Judicial

Circuit of the State of Missouri, at the Court-House in Richmond, in a Criminal Court of Inquiry, Begun November 12, 1838, on the Trial of Joseph Smith, Jr., and Others, for High Treason and Other Crimes against the State. Fayette, Mo.: Boon's Lick Democrat, 1841.

Dorson, Richard M. *Jonathan Draws the Long Bow.* Cambridge: Harvard University Press, 1946.

Doyle, Don Harrison. *The Social Order of a Frontier Community: Jacksonville, Illinois, 1825–70.* Urbana: University of Illinois Press, 1978.

Draper, Richard D., and Jessica E. Draper. "The Gathering of the Jews as Understood in the Nauvoo Period." In *Regional Studies in Latter-day Saint Church History: Illinois,* edited by H. Dean Garrett, 139–50. Provo, Utah: Department of Church History and Doctrine, Brigham Young University, 1995.

Dunn, Scott C. "Automaticity and the Dictation of the Book of Mormon." In *American Apocrypha: Essays on the Book of Mormon,* edited by Dan Vogel and Brent Lee Metcalfe, 17–46. Salt Lake City, Utah: Signature Books, 2002.

Durham, G. Homer. *Joseph Smith, Prophet-Statesman.* Salt Lake City, Utah: Bookcraft, 1944.

Durham, Reed C. "The Election Day Battle at Gallatin." *BYU Studies* 13, no. 1 (1972): 36–61.

Edwards, Jonathan. *A History of the Work of Redemption.* In *The Works of President Edwards.* 8 vols. Worcester, Mass.: Isaiah Thomas, 1808–9.

Eggleston, Edward. *The Hoosier Schoolmaster: A Story of Backwoods Life in Indiana.* New York: Grosset and Dunlap, 1913.

"Egyptian Antiquities." *North American Review* 29 (Oct. 1829): 361–89.

Ehat, Andrew F. " 'It Seems Like Heaven Began on Earth': Joseph Smith and the Constitution of the Kingdom of God." *BYU Studies* 20, no. 3 (1980): 253–79.

———. "Joseph Smith's Introduction of Temple Ordinances and the 1844 Mormon Succession Question." Master's thesis, Brigham Young University, 1982.

———. " 'Who Shall Ascend into the Hill of the Lord?': Sesquicentennial Reflections of a Sacred Day, 4 May 1842." In *Temples of the Ancient World: Ritual and Symbolism,* edited by Donald W. Parry, 48–62. Salt Lake City, Utah: Deseret Book; Provo, Utah, FARMS, 1994.

Eliade, Mircea. *The Sacred and the Profane: The Nature of Religion.* New York: Harcourt, Brace Jovanovich, 1959.

Ellis, David Maldwyn. *Landlords and Farmers in the Hudson-Mohawk Region, 1790–1850.* Ithaca, N.Y.: Cornell University Press, 1946.

Ellis, Richard E. *The Union at Risk: Jacksonian Democracy, States' Rights, and the Nullification Crisis.* New York: Oxford University Press, 1987.

Ellsworth, Paul D. "Mobocracy and the Rule of Law: American Press Reaction to the Murder of Joseph Smith." *BYU Studies* 20, no. 1 (1979): 71–82.

Emerson, Brown. *Departed Saints with Christ; A Sermon, Preached at Essex, Dec. 15, 1818, at the Interment of Mrs. Hannah Crowell, Late Consort of Rev. Robert Crowell.* Salem, Mass.: John D. Cushing, 1819.

Emerson, Ralph Waldo. *The Collected Works of Ralph Waldo Emerson,* volume 1. Edited by Robert E. Spiller and Alfred R. Ferguson. Cambridge: Belknap Press of Harvard University Press, 1971.

Enders, Donald L. "A Dam for Nauvoo: An Attempt to Industrialize the City." *BYU Studies* 18, no. 2 (1978): 246–54.

———. "Platting the City Beautiful: A Historical and Archeological Glimpse of Nauvoo Streets." *BYU Studies* 19, no. 3 (1979): 408–15.

———. "The Steamboat *Maid of Iowa:* Mormon Mistress of the Mississippi." *BYU Studies* 19, no. 3 (1979): 321–35.

England, Breck. *The Life and Thought of Orson Pratt.* Salt Lake City: University of Utah Press, 1985.

England, Eugene. *Brother Brigham.* Salt Lake City, Utah: Bookcraft, 1980.

Epperson, Steven. " 'The Grand, Fundamental Principle': Joseph Smith and the Virtue of Friendship." *Journal of Mormon History* 23, no. 2 (1997): 77–105.

————. *Mormons and Jews: Early Mormon Theologies of Israel.* Salt Lake City, Utah: Signature Books, 1992.

Erickson, Dan. *"As a Thief in the Night": The Mormon Quest for Millennial Deliverance.* Salt Lake City, Utah: Signature Books, 1998.

Esplin, Ronald K. "Brigham Young and Priesthood Denial to the Blacks: An Alternate View." *BYU Studies* 19, no. 3 (1979): 394–402.

————. "Brigham Young and the Transformation of the 'First' Quorum of the Twelve." In *Lion of the Lord: Essays on the Life and Service of Brigham Young,* edited by Susan Easton Black and Larry C. Porter, 54–84. Salt Lake City, Utah: Deseret Book, 1995.

————. "Conversion and Transformation: Brigham Young's New York Roots and the Search for Bible Religion." In *Lion of the Lord: Essays on the Life and Service of Brigham Young,* edited by Susan Easton Black and Larry C. Porter, 20–53. Salt Lake City, Utah: Deseret Book, 1995.

————. "The Emergence of Brigham Young and the Twelve to Mormon Leadership, 1830–1841." Ph.D. diss., Brigham Young University, 1981.

————. "Joseph, Brigham and the Twelve: A Succession of Continuity." *BYU Studies* 21, no. 3 (1981): 301–41.

————. "Joseph Smith's Mission and Timetable: 'God Will Protect Me Until My Work Is Done." In *The Prophet Joseph Smith: Essays on the Life and Mission of Joseph Smith,* edited by Larry C. Porter and Susan Easton Black, 280–319. Salt Lake City, Utah: Deseret Book, 1988.

————. " 'A Place Prepared': Joseph, Brigham, and the Quest for Promised Refuge in the West." *Journal of Mormon History* 9 (1982): 85–111.

————. "Sickness and Faith, Nauvoo Letters." *BYU Studies* 15, no. 4 (1975): 425–34.

————. "Thomas B. Marsh as President of the First Quorum of the Twelve, 1835–1838." In *Hearken O Ye People: Discourses on the Doctrine and Covenants,* 167–90. Sandy, Utah: Randall Book, 1984.

Evans, William McKee. "From the Land of Canaan to the Land of Guinea: The Strange Odyssey of the 'Sons of Ham.' " *American Historical Review* 85, no. 1 (1980): 15–43.

Everett, Edward. "Hieroglyphics." *North American Review* 32 (1831): 95–127.

————. "Egyptian History." *American Quarterly Review* 4 (1828): 27–53.

————. "Hieroglyphic System." *American Quarterly Review* 9 (1831): 339–51.

Faragher, John Mack. *Sugar Creek: Life on the Illinois Prairie.* New Haven, Conn.: Yale University Press, 1986.

Far West Committee. Minutes, 1839. Church Archives. The Church of Jesus Christ of Latter-day Saints. Salt Lake City, Utah.

Faulring, Scott H. "The Book of Mormon: A Blueprint for Organizing the Church." *Journal of Book of Mormon Studies* 7, no. 1 (1998): 60–69.

————. "An Examination of the 1829 'Articles of the Church and Christ' in Relation to Section 20 of the Doctrine and Covenants." *BYU Studies* 43, no. 4 (2004): 57–91.

Feldberg, Michael. *The Turbulent Era: Riot and Disorder in Jacksonian America.* New York: Oxford University Press, 1980.

Female Relief Society of Nauvoo. Minutes, 1842–1844. Church Archives. The Church of Jesus Christ of Latter-day Saints. Salt Lake City, Utah.

————. Petition, ca. July 1842. Church Archives. The Church of Jesus Christ of Latter-day Saints. Salt Lake City, Utah.

Fielding, Joseph. " 'They Might Have Known That He Was Not a Fallen Prophet'—The Nauvoo Journal of Joseph Fielding." Edited by Andrew F. Ehat. *BYU Studies* 19, no. 2 (1979): 133–66.

Fielding, Robert Kent. "The Growth of the Mormon Church in Kirtland, Ohio." Ph.D. diss., Indiana University, 1957.

————. "The Mormon Economy in Kirtland, Ohio." *Utah Historical Quarterly* 27 (Oct. 1959): 331–56.

Filler, Louis. *Crusade Against Slavery: Friends, Foes, and Reforms, 1820–1860*. Algonac, Mich.: Reference Publications, 1986.

Finney, Charles G. *Lectures to Professing Christians*. New York: J. S. Taylor, 1837.

———. *Memoirs of Rev. Charles G. Finney, Written by Himself.* New York: A. S. Barnes, 1876.

Firmage, Edwin Brown, and Richard Collin Mangrum. *Zion in the Courts: A Legal History of the Church of Jesus Christ of Latter-day Saints, 1830–1900*. Urbana: University of Illinois Press, 1988.

First Council of the Seventy. Minutes, 1835–1839. Church Archives. The Church of Jesus Christ of Latter-day Saints. Salt Lake City, Utah.

Flake, Chad J., and Larry W. Draper, eds. *A Mormon Bibliography, 1830–1930: Books, Pamphlets, Periodicals, and Broadsides Relating to the First Century of Mormonism*. 2 vols. 2d ed., rev. and enlarged, Provo, Utah: Religious Studies Center, Brigham Young University, 2004.

Flanders, Robert Bruce. "The Kingdom of God in Illinois: Politics in Utopia." In *Kingdom on the Mississippi Revisited: Nauvoo in Mormon History*, edited by Roger D. Launius and John E. Hallwas, 147–59. Urbana: University of Illinois Press, 1996.

———. *Nauvoo: Kingdom on the Mississippi*. Urbana: University of Illinois Press, 1965.

———. "To Transform History: Early Mormon Culture and the Concept of Time and Space." *Church History* 40 (1971): 108–17.

Flegg, Columba Graham. *Gathered Under Apostles: A Study of the Catholic Apostolic Church*. New York: Clarendon Press, 1992.

Fleming, Helen Vilate Bourne. Collection, 1836–1963. Church Archives. The Church of Jesus Christ of Latter-day Saints. Salt Lake City, Utah.

Fliegelman, Jay. *Prodigals and Pilgrims: The American Revolution Against Patriarchal Authority, 1750–1800*. Cambridge: Cambridge University Press, 1982.

Fluharty, Spencer. "A Book Ahead of Its Time: Concepts of Lamanite Culture and the White Man's Indian." Unpublished paper. Archive of Restoration Culture. Joseph Fielding Smith Institute for Latter-day Saint History. Brigham Young University.

Fogarty, Robert S., ed. *Dictionary of American Communal and Utopian History*. Westport, Conn.: Greenwood Press, 1980.

Foote, Warren. Autobiography, 1817–1901. L. Tom Perry Special Collections. Harold B. Lee Library. Brigham Young University.

Ford, Clyde. "The Origin of the Word of Wisdom." *Journal of Mormon History* 24, no. 2 (1998), 129–54.

Ford, Thomas. *A History of Illinois, From Its Commencement as a State in 1818 to 1847*. New York: Ivison and Phinney, 1854.

Forman, Shepard. *The Brazilian Peasantry*. New York: Columbia University Press, 1975.

Forsberg, Clyde R. "Retelling the Greatest Story Ever Told: Popular Literature as Scripture in Antebellum America." *Dialogue: A Journal of Mormon Thought* 29, no. 4 (1996): 69–86.

Foster, Craig L. "Henry Caswall: Anti-Mormon Extraordinaire." *BYU Studies* 35, no. 4 (1995–96): 144–59.

———. *Penny Tracts and Polemics: A Critical Analysis of Anti-Mormon Pamphleteering in Great Britain, 1837–1860*. Salt Lake City, Utah: Greg L. Kofford, 2002.

Foster, Frank Hugh. *A Genetic History of the New England Theology*. New York: Russell and Russell, 1963.

Foster, Lawrence. "A Little-Known Defense of Polygamy from the Mormon Press in 1842." *Dialogue: A Journal of Mormon Thought* 9, no. 4 (1974): 21–34.

———. "The Psychology of Religious Genius: Joseph Smith and the Origin of New Religious Movements." In *The Prophet Puzzle: Interpretive Essays on Joseph Smith*, edited by Bryan Waterman, 183–208. Salt Lake City, Utah: Signature Books, 1999.

———. *Religion and Sexuality: The Shakers, the Mormons, and the Oneida Community*. Urbana: University of Illinois Press, 1984.

———. *Women, Family, and Utopia: Communal Experiments of the Shakers, the Oneida Community, and the Mormons*. Syracuse, N.Y.: Syracuse University Press, 1991.

Francaviglia, Richard V. *The Mormon Landscape: Existence, Creation, and Perception of a Unique Image in the American West*. New York: AMS Press, 1978.

Francis M. Higbee v. Joseph Smith. May 1, 1844. Hancock County Courthouse, Carthage, Ill.

Frank, Joseph. *Dostoevsky: The Mantle of the Prophet, 1871–1881*. Princeton, N.J.: Princeton University Press, 2002.

Franklin, Benjamin. *The Papers of Benjamin Franklin. Volume 5, July 1, 1753, Through March 31, 1755*. Edited by Leonard W. Labaree. New Haven, Conn.: Yale University Press, 1962.

Freehling, William W. *Prelude to Civil War: The Nullification Controversy in South Carolina, 1816–1836*. New York: Harper and Row, 1965.

Freeman, Joanne B. *Affairs of Honor: National Politics in the New Republic*. New Haven, Conn.: Yale University Press, 2001.

Freemasonry Letters. Nauvoo, 1842. Church Archives. The Church of Jesus Christ of Latter-day Saints. Salt Lake City, Utah.

French, Peter J. *John Dee: The World of an Elizabethan Magus*. London: Routledge and Kegan Paul, 1972.

Frisbie, Barnes. *The History of Middletown, Vermont, in Three Discourses*. Rutland, Vt.: Tuttle and Co., 1867.

Froom, Le Roy Edwin. *The Prophetic Faith of Our Fathers: The Historical Development of Prophetic Interpretation*. 4 vols. Washington, D.C.: Review and Herald, 1946–1954.

Fuchs, Esther. *Sexual Politics in the Biblical Narrative: Reading the Hebrew Bible as a Woman*. Sheffield, Eng.: Sheffield Academic Press, 2000.

Fullmer, John S. Letter to George A. Smith, Nov. 27, 1854. Historian's Office. The Church of Jesus Christ of Latter-day Saints. Salt Lake City.

Gallup, Joseph A. *Sketches of Epidemic Diseases in the State of Vermont; From Its First Settlement to 1815*. Boston: T. B. Wait and Sons, 1815.

Gardner, Hamilton. "The Nauvoo Legion, 1840–1845 — A Unique Military Organization." *Journal of the Illinois Historical Society* 64, no. 2 (1961): 181–97.

Garrard, LaMar E. "The Asael Smith Family Moves from Vermont to New York, 1806 to 1820." In *Regional Studies in Latter-day Saint Church History: New York*, edited by Larry C. Porter, Milton V. Backman, and Susan Easton Black, 14–31. Provo, Utah: Department of Church History and Doctrine, Brigham Young University, 1992.

Garrett, H. Dean. "The Coming Forth of the Doctrine and Covenants." In *Regional Studies in Latter-day Saint Church History: Ohio*, edited by Milton V. Backman, 89–103. Provo, Utah: Department of Church History and Doctrine, Brigham Young University, 1990.

———. "Disease and Sickness in Nauvoo." In *Regional Studies in Latter-day Saint Church History: Illinois*, edited by H. Dean Garrett, 169–82. Provo, Utah: Department of Church History and Doctrine, Brigham Young University, 1995.

Garrison, Winfred Ernest, and Alfred T. DeGroot. *The Disciples of Christ: A History*. St. Louis: Christian Board of Publication, 1948.

Gaustad, Edwin Scott. *Sworn on the Altar of God: A Religious Biography of Thomas Jefferson*. Grand Rapids, Mich.: W. B. Eerdmans, 1996.

Gaustad, Edwin Scott, and Philip L. Barlow. *New Historical Atlas of Religion in America*. New York: Oxford University Press, 2001.

Gayler, George R. "Attempts by the State of Missouri to Extradite Joseph Smith, 1841–1843." *Missouri Historical Review* 58, no. 1 (1963): 21–36.

Gee, John. "Eyewitness, Hearsay, and Physical Evidence of the Joseph Smith Papyri." In *The Disciple as Witness: Essays on Latter-day Saint History and Doctrine in Honor of Richard Lloyd Anderson*, edited by Stephen D. Ricks, Donald W. Parry, and Andrew H. Hedges, 175–217. Provo: FARMS, Brigham Young University, 2000.

———. *A Guide to the Joseph Smith Papyri*. Provo, Utah: FARMS, Brigham Young University, 2000.

Gee, John, and Stephen D. Ricks. "Historical Plausibility: The Historicity of the Book of Abraham as a Case Study." In *Historicity and the Latter-day Saint Scriptures*, edited by Paul

Y. Hoskisson, 63–98. Provo, Utah: Religious Studies Center, Brigham Young University, 2001.

Gee, Lysander. Letter to Alexander McRae. April 2, 1879. Church Archives. The Church of Jesus Christ of Latter-day Saints. Salt Lake City, Utah.

Gellinek, Christian. *Young Schleiermacher and the Transatlantic Connection: A Mosaic of Early Mormonism.* Münster: Agenda, 2004.

General Church Minutes, 1839–1877. Historian's Office. Church Archives. The Church of Jesus Christ of Latter-day Saints. Salt Lake City, Utah.

Gentry, Leland H. "Adam-ondi-Ahman: A Brief Historical Survey." *BYU Studies* 13, no. 4 (1973): 553–76.

———. "The Danite Band of 1838." *BYU Studies* 14, no. 4 (1974): 421–50.

———. *A History of the Latter-day Saints in Northern Missouri from 1836 to 1839.* Ph.D. diss., Brigham Young University, 1965; reprint, Joseph Fielding Smith Institute for LDS History and BYU Studies, 2000.

———. "The Land Question at Adam-ondi-Ahman." *BYU Studies* 26, no. 2 (1986): 45–56.

Gerona, Carla. "Stairways to Heaven: A Cultural History of Early American Quaker Dreams." Ph.D. diss., Johns Hopkins University, 1998.

Givens, Terryl L. *By the Hand of Mormon: The American Scripture That Launched a New World Religion.* New York: Oxford University Press, 2002.

———. *The Viper on the Hearth: Mormons, Myths, and the Construction of Heresy.* New York: Oxford University Press, 1997.

Glaser, John Fredrick. "The Disaffection of William Law." *Restoration Studies* 3 (1986): 163–75.

Godfrey, Kenneth W. "Joseph Smith and the Masons." *Journal of the Illinois State Historical Society* 64, no. 1 (1971): 79–90.

———. "More Treasures than One: Section 111." In *Hearken O Ye People: Discourses on the Doctrine and Covenants,* 191–204. Sandy, Utah: Randall Book, 1984.

———. "A Note on the Nauvoo Library and Literary Institute." *BYU Studies* 14, no. 3 (1974): 386–89.

———. "What Is the Significance of Zelph in the Study of Book of Mormon Geography?" *Journal of Book of Mormon Studies* 8, no. 2 (1999): 70–79.

———. "The Zelph Story." *BYU Studies* 29, no. 2 (1989): 31–56.

Godfrey, Kenneth W., Audrey M. Godfrey, and Jill Mulvay Derr, eds. *Women's Voices: An Untold History of the Latter-day Saints.* Salt Lake City, Utah: Deseret Book, 1982.

Goodliffe, Elizabeth. "Joseph Smith and John Humphrey Noyes: Two Millennialists' Views on Economics and Marriage." In *Archive of Restoration Culture: Summer Fellows' Papers, 1997–1999,* 71–80. Provo, Utah: Joseph Fielding Smith Institute for Latter-day Saint History, Brigham Young University, 2000.

Gordon, Cyrus H. "Foreword." In *Unexpected Faces in Ancient America, 1500 B.C.–A.D. 1500: The Historical Testimony of Pre-Columbian Artists,* by Alexander von Wuthenau. New York: Crown, 1975.

Gordon, Joseph F. "The Political Career of Lilburn W. Boggs." *Missouri Historical Review* 52, no. 2 (1958): 111–22.

Gordon, Sarah Barringer. *The Mormon Question: Polygamy and Constitutional Conflict in Nineteenth-Century America.* Chapel Hill: University of North Carolina Press, 2002.

Gorn, Elliott J. *The Manly Art: Bare-Knuckle Prize Fighting in America.* Ithaca, N.Y.: Cornell University Press, 1986.

Graham, Sylvester. *Lectures on the Science of Human Life.* Boston: Marsh, Capen, Lyon and Webb, 1839.

Grandstaff, Mark R. "Having More Learning than Sense: William E. McLellin and the Book of Commandments Revisited." *Dialogue: A Journal of Mormon Thought* 26, no. 4 (1993): 23–48.

Grandstaff, Mark R., and Milton V. Backman. "The Social Origins of the Kirtland Mormons." *BYU Studies* 30, no. 2 (1990): 47–66.

Green, Arnold H. "Gathering and Election: Israelite Descent and Universalism in Mormon Discourse." *Journal of Mormon History* 25, no. 1 (1999): 195–228.

———. "Jews in LDS Thought." *BYU Studies* 34, no. 4 (1994–95): 137–64.

Greene, John P. *Facts Relative to the Expulsion of the Mormons or Latter Day Saints, from the State of Missouri, under the "Exterminating Order."* Cincinnati: R. P. Brooks, 1839.

Greenberg, Kenneth S., ed. *The Confessions of Nat Turner and Related Documents.* Boston: Bedford Books of St. Martin's Press, 1996.

Gregg, Josiah. *Commerce of the Prairies.* Edited by Max L. Moorhead. Norman: University of Oklahoma Press, 1954.

Gregg, Thomas. *History of Hancock County, Illinois. Together with an Outline History of the State, and a Digest of State Laws.* Chicago: Charles C. Chapman, 1880.

———. *The Prophet of Palmyra.* New York: J. B. Alden, 1890.

Griggs, C. Wilfred. "The Book of Mormon as an Ancient Book." *BYU Studies* 22, no. 3 (1982): 259–78.

Grimsted, David. *American Mobbing, 1828–1861: Toward Civil War.* New York: Oxford University Press, 1998.

———. "Rioting in Its Jacksonian Setting." *American Historical Review* 77, no. 2 (1972): 361–97.

Grodzins, Dean. *American Heretic: Theodore Parker and Transcendentalism.* Chapel Hill: University of North Carolina Press, 2002.

Groesbeck, C. Jess. "The Book of Mormon as a Symbolic History: A New Perspective on Its Place in History and Religion." *Sunstone*, no. 131 (March 2004): 35–45.

———. "The Smiths and Their Dreams and Visions." *Sunstone* 12, no. 2 (1988): 22–29.

Gross, Robert A. *The Minutemen and Their World.* New York: Hill and Wang, 1976.

Grow, Matthew. " 'Clean from the Blood of This Generation': The Washing of Feet and the Latter-day Saints." Unpublished paper. Archive of Restoration Culture. Joseph Fielding Smith Institute for Latter-day Saint History. Brigham Young University.

Guest Register Book. East India Marine Society (now Peabody Essex Museum). Salem, Mass.

Gunn, Stanley R. *Oliver Cowdery: Second Elder and Scribe.* Salt Lake City, Utah: Bookcraft, 1962.

Gunnell, Wayne Cutler. "Martin Harris—Witness and Benefactor to the Book of Mormon." Master's thesis, Brigham Young University, 1955.

Gutjahr, Paul C. *An American Bible: A History of the Good Book in the United States, 1777–1880.* Stanford, Calif.: Stanford University Press, 1999.

Hale, Aroet Lucious. Diary. L. Tom Perry Special Collections. Harold B. Lee Library. Brigham Young University.

Hale, Van. "Defining the Mormon Doctrine of Deity: What Can Theological Terminology Tell Us About Our Own Beliefs?" *Sunstone* 10, no. 1 (1985): 23–27.

———. "The Doctrinal Impact of the King Follett Discourse." *BYU Studies* 18, no. 2 (1978): 209–25.

———. "The King Follett Discourse: Textual History and Criticism." *Sunstone* 8, no. 5 (1983): 4–12.

———. "The Origin of the Human Spirit in Early Mormon Thought." In *Line upon Line: Essays on Mormon Doctrine,* edited by Gary James Bergera, 115–26. Salt Lake City, Utah: Signature Books, 1989.

Hales, Kenneth Glyn, comp. *Windows: A Mormon Family.* Tucson, Ariz.: Skyline Printing, 1985.

Hall, David D. *Cultures of Print: Essays in the History of the Book.* Amherst: University of Massachusetts Press, 1996.

———. "The Victorian Connection." *American Quarterly* 27, no. 5 (1975): 561–74.

———. *Worlds of Wonder, Days of Judgment: Popular Religious Belief in Early New England.* Cambridge: Harvard University Press, 1989.

Hallwas, John E. "Mormon Nauvoo from a Non-Mormon Perspective." *Journal of Mormon History* 16 (1990): 53–69.

———. *Thomas Gregg: Early Illinois Journalist and Author.* Macomb, Ill.: Western Illinois University, 1983.

Hallwas, John E., and Roger D. Launius, eds. *Cultures in Conflict: A Documentary History of the Mormon War in Illinois.* Logan: Utah State University Press, 1995.

Halttunen, Karen. *Confidence Men and Painted Women: A Study of Middle-Class Culture in America, 1830–1870.* New Haven, Conn.: Yale University Press, 1982.

Hamblin, William J. "The Importance of Warfare in the Book of Mormon." In *Book of Mormon Authorship Revisited: The Evidence for Ancient Origins*, edited by Noel B. Reynolds, 523–43. Provo: FARMS, 1997.

———. "Reformed Egyptian." Criticism Papers, FARMS, 1995. L. Tom Perry Special Collections, Harold B. Lee Library, Brigham Young University.

Hamilton, C. Mark. *Nineteenth-Century Mormon Architecture and City Planning.* New York: Oxford University Press, 1995.

Hamilton, Marshall. "Thomas Sharp's Turning Point: Birth of an Anti-Mormon." *Sunstone* 13, no. 5 (1989): 16–22.

Hamilton, Thomas. *Men and Manners in America.* 2 vols. Edinburgh: W. Blackwood, 1833.

Hampshire, Annette B. "Thomas Sharp and Anti-Mormon Sentiment in Illinois, 1842–1845." *Journal of the Illinois State Historical Society* 72, no. 2 (1979): 82–100.

Hancock, Levi. Diary. L. Tom Perry Special Collections. Harold B. Lee Library. Brigham Young University.

Hancock, Mosiah. Autobiography. Church Archives. The Church of Jesus Christ of Latter-day Saints. Salt Lake City, Utah.

Hansen, Klaus J. *Quest for Empire: The Political Kingdom of God and the Council of Fifty in Mormon History.* East Lansing: Michigan State University Press, 1967.

Hardman, Keith J. *Charles Grandison Finney, 1792–1875: Revivalist and Reformer.* Syracuse, N.Y.: Syracuse University Press, 1987.

Hardy, Grant R. "Mormon as Editor." In *Rediscovering the Book of Mormon*, edited by John L. Sorensen and Melvin J. Thorne, 15–28. Salt Lake City, Utah: Deseret Book; Provo, Utah: FARMS, 1991.

Harper, Reid L. "The Mantle of Joseph: Creation of a Mormon Miracle." *Journal of Mormon History* 22, no. 2 (1996): 35–71.

Harper, Steven C. "Missionaries in the American Religious Marketplace: Mormon Proselytizing in the 1830s." *Journal of Mormon History* 24, no. 2 (1998): 1–29.

———. " 'A Pentecost and Endowment Indeed': Six Eyewitness Accounts of the Kirtland Temple Experience." In *Opening the Heavens: Accounts of Divine Manifestations, 1820–1844*, edited by John W. Welch with Erick B. Carlson, 327–71. Provo, Utah: Brigham Young University Press; Salt Lake City, Utah: Deseret Book, 2005.

———. "Pentecost Continued: A Contemporaneous Account of the Kirtland Temple Dedication." *BYU Studies* 42, no. 2 (2003): 4–22.

Harris, Marc L. "Revelation and the American Republic: Timothy Dwight's Civic Participation." *Journal of the History of Ideas* 54, no. 3 (1993): 449–68.

Harris, William. *Mormonism Portrayed; Its Errors and Absurdities Exposed, and the Spirit and Danger of Its Authors Made Manifest.* Warsaw, Ill.: Sharp and Gamble, 1841.

Harrison, John F. C. "The Popular History of Early Victorian Britain: A Mormon Contribution." In *Mormons in Early Victorian Britain*, edited by Richard L. Jensen and Malcolm R. Thorp, 1–15. Salt Lake City: University of Utah Press, 1989.

Hartley, William G. " 'Almost Too Intolerable a Burthen': The Winter Exodus from Missouri, 1838–39." *Journal of Mormon History* 18, no. 2 (1992): 6–40.

———. "From Men to Boys: LDS Aaronic Priesthood Offices, 1829–1996." *Journal of Mormon History* 22, no. 1 (1996): 80–136.

———. "Missouri's 1838 Extermination Order and the Mormons' Forced Removal to Illinois." In *A City of Refuge: Quincy, Illinois*, edited by Susan Easton Black and Richard E. Bennett, 1–30. Salt Lake City, Utah: Millennial Press, 2000.

———. *My Best for the Kingdom: History and Autobiography of John Lowe Butler, A Mormon Frontiersman*. Salt Lake City, Utah: Aspen Books, 1993.

———. "Nauvoo Stake, Priesthood Quorums, and the Church's First Wards." *BYU Studies* 32, no. 1–2 (1992): 57–80.

———. *Stand by My Servant Joseph: The Story of the Joseph Knight Family and the Restoration*. Provo, Utah: Joseph Fielding Smith Institute for LDS History; Salt Lake City, Utah: Deseret Book, 2003.

Hatch, Ephraim. *Joseph Smith Portraits: A Search for the Prophet's Likeness*. Provo, Utah: Religious Studies Center, Brigham Young University, 1998.

———. "What Did Joseph Smith Look Like?" *Ensign* 11 (March 1981): 65–73.

Hatch, Nathan O. *The Democratization of American Christianity*. New Haven, Conn.: Yale University Press, 1989.

Hauptman, Laurence M. *Conspiracy of Interests: Iroquois Dispossession and the Rise of New York State*. Syracuse, N.Y.: Syracuse University Press, 1999.

Hayden, A. S. *Early History of the Disciples in the Western Reserve, Ohio*. Cincinnati: Chase and Hall, 1875.

Hayward, Oliver S., and Constance E. Putnam. *Improve, Perfect, and Perpetuate: Dr. Nathan Smith and Early American Medical Education*. Hanover, N.H.: University Press of New England, 1998.

Hayward, Silvanus. *History of the Town of Gilsum, New Hampshire from 1752 to 1879*. Manchester, N.H.: John B. Clarke, 1881.

Heimert, Alan. *Religion and the American Mind: From the Great Awakening to the Revolution*. Cambridge: Harvard University Press, 1966.

Hess, Wilford M. "Botanical Comparisons in the Allegory of the Olive Tree." In *The Book of Mormon: Jacob Through Words of Mormon: To Learn with Joy*, edited by Monte S. Nyman and Charles D. Tate, 87–102. Provo, Utah: Religious Studies Center, Brigham Young University, 1990.

Heward, Grant S., and Jerald Tanner. "The Source of the Book of Abraham Identified." *Dialogue: A Journal of Mormon Thought* 3, no. 2 (1968): 92–98.

Heyrman, Christian Leigh. *Southern Cross: The Beginnings of the Bible Belt*. New York: Alfred A. Knopf, 1997.

Hickman, Jared Winston. " 'No Creed to Circumscribe My Mind': Joseph Smith, Ralph Waldo Emerson, and Romantic Theology." Unpublished paper. Archive of Restoration Culture. Joseph Fielding Smith Institute for Latter-day Saint History. Brigham Young University.

———. " 'The Whole of America Is Zion': Joseph Smith, the New World Baroque, and Comparative American Literary Studies." Honors thesis, Bowdoin College, 2001.

Hicks, Michael. "Joseph Smith, W. W. Phelps, and the Poetic Paraphrase of 'The Vision.' " *Journal of Mormon History* 20, no. 2 (1994): 63–84.

———. *Mormonism and Music: A History*. Urbana: University of Illinois Press, 1989.

———. " 'Strains Which Will Not Soon Be Allowed Die . . .': 'The Stranger' and Carthage Jail." *BYU Studies* 23, no. 4 (1983): 389–400.

Higham, John. *From Boundlessness to Consolidation: The Transformation of American Culture, 1848–1860*. Ann Arbor, Mich.: William L. Clements Library, 1969.

Hill, Donna. *Joseph Smith, the First Mormon*. Garden City, N.Y.: Doubleday, 1977.

Hill, Marvin S. "Counter-Revolution: The Mormon Reaction to the Coming of American Democracy." *Sunstone* 13, no. 3 (1989): 24–33.

————. "Cultural Crises in the Mormon Kingdom: A Reconsideration of the Causes of Kirtland Dissent." *Church History* 49, no. 3 (1980): 286–97.

————. "The First Vision Controversy: A Critique and Reconciliation." *Dialogue: A Journal of Mormon Thought* 15, no. 2 (1982): 31–46.

————. "Joseph Smith and the 1826 Trial: New Evidence and New Difficulties." *BYU Studies* 12, no. 2 (1972): 223–33.

————. "Joseph Smith the Man: Some Reflections on a Subject of Controversy." *BYU Studies* 21, no. 2 (1981): 175–86.

————. "Money-Digging Folklore and the Beginnings of Mormonism: An Interpretive Suggestion." *BYU Studies* 24, no. 4 (1984): 473–88.

————. "On the First Vision and Its Import in the Shaping of Early Mormonism." *Dialogue: A Journal of Mormon Thought* 12, no. 1 (1979): 90–99.

————. "Quest for Refuge: An Hypothesis as to the Social Origins and Nature of the Mormon Political Kingdom." *Journal of Mormon History* 2 (1975): 3–20.

————. *Quest for Refuge: The Mormon Flight from American Pluralism.* Salt Lake City, Utah: Signature Books, 1989.

————. "The Role of Christian Primitivism in the Origin and Development of the Mormon Kingdom, 1830–1844." Ph.D. diss., University of Chicago, 1968.

————. "The Shaping of the Mormon Mind in New England and New York." *BYU Studies* 9, no. 3 (1969): 351–72.

Hill, Marvin S., C. Keith Rooker, and Larry T. Wimmer. *The Kirtland Economy Revisited: A Market Critique of Sectarian Economics.* Provo, Utah: Brigham Young University Press, 1977.

Hinkle, S. J. "A Biographical Sketch of G. M. Hinkle," *Journal of History* 13 (1920): 444–53.

Hirrel, Leo P. *Children of Wrath: New School Calvinism and Antebellum Reform.* Lexington: University Press of Kentucky, 1998.

Historian's Office. Reports of Speeches, ca. 1845–1885. Church Archives. The Church of Jesus Christ of Latter-day Saints. Salt Lake City, Utah.

History of Adams County, Illinois, Containing a History of the County—Its Cities, Towns, etc. Chicago: Murry, Williamson, and Phelps, 1879.

History of Caldwell and Livingston Counties, Missouri: Written and Compiled from the Most Authentic Official and Private Sources, including a History of Their Townships, Towns and Villages, Together with a Condensed History of Missouri. St. Louis: National Historical Co., 1886.

The History of Jackson County, Missouri: Containing a History of the County, Its Cities, Towns, etc. Kansas City, Mo.: Union Historical Co., 1881.

The History of the Reorganized Church of Jesus Christ of Latter Day Saints. Volume 2, 1836–1844. Independence, Mo.: Herald House, 1896.

History of Van Buren County, Iowa. Chicago: Western Historical Company, 1878.

Hofstadter, Richard. *The Paranoid Style in American Politics, and Other Essays.* New York: Alfred A. Knopf, 1965.

Hoge, John Blair. *The Heavenly Rest; A Sermon, Delivered at Martinsburgh, July Twenty-first, 1819, on Occasion of the Death of Mrs. Ann Boyd.* Martinsburgh, Va.: J. Alburtis, 1819.

Holbrook, Joseph. Reminiscences, ca. 1860–1871. Church Archives. The Church of Jesus Christ of Latter-day Saints. Salt Lake City, Utah.

Holland, David. "Priest, Pastor, and Power: Joseph Smith and the Question of Priesthood." In *Archive of Restoration Culture: Summer Fellows' Papers, 1997–1999*, 9–16. Provo, Utah: Joseph Fielding Smith Institute for Latter-day Saint History, Brigham Young University, 2000.

Hollinger, David A., and Charles Capper, eds., *The American Intellectual Tradition: A Sourcebook.* 2 vols. 4th ed. New York: Oxford University Press, 2001.

Holzapfel, Richard Neitzel, and Jeni Broberg Holzapfel. *Women of Nauvoo.* Salt Lake City, Utah: Bookcraft, 1992.

Homer, Michael W. " 'Similarity of Priesthood in Masonry': The Relationship Between Freemasonry and Mormonism." *Dialogue: A Journal of Mormon Thought* 27, no. 3 (1994): 2–113.

Hopkins, Samuel. *The System of Doctrines, Contained in Divine Revelation, Explained and Defended.* 2 vols. Boston: Isaiah Thomas and Ebenezer T. Andrews, 1793.

Hoskisson, Paul Y. "Names in the Book of Mormon." In *Book of Mormon Reference Companion*, edited by Dennis L. Largey, 580–81. Salt Lake City, Utah: Deseret Book, 2003.

Hotchkin, James H. *A History of the Purchase and Settlement of Western New York, and of the Rise, Progress, and Present State of the Presbyterian Church in That Section.* New York: M. W. Dodd, 1848.

Hougey, Hal. *The Truth About the "Lehi Tree-of-Life" Stone.* Concord, Calif.: Pacific Publishing, 1963.

Howard, Richard P. "An Analysis of Six Contemporary Accounts Touching Joseph Smith's First Vision." *Restoration Studies* 1 (1980): 95–117.

———. "The Changing RLDS Response to Mormon Polygamy: A Preliminary Analysis." *Restoration Studies* 3 (1986): 145–62.

———. *The Church Through the Years.* 2 vols. Independence, Mo.: Herald Publishing House, 1992–93.

———. "Joseph Smith's First Vision: The RLDS Tradition." *Journal of Mormon History* 7 (1980): 23–29.

———. *Restoration Scriptures: A Study of Their Textual Development*, 2d ed., rev. Independence, Mo.: Herald Publishing House, 1995.

———. "A Tentative Approach to the Book of Abraham." *Dialogue: A Journal of Mormon Thought* 3, no. 2 (1968): 88–92.

———. "What Sort of Priesthood for Women at Nauvoo?" *John Whitmer Historical Association Journal* 13 (1993): 18–30.

Howe, Eber D. *Autobiography and Recollections of a Pioneer Printer.* Painesville, Ohio: Telegraph Steam Printing House, 1878.

———. *History of Mormonism: Or, A Faithful Account of that Singular Imposition and Delusion.* Painesville, Ohio: By the Author, 1840.

Howe, Katherine S., and David B. Warren. *The Gothic Revival Style in America, 1830–1870.* Houston: Museum of Fine Arts, 1976.

Hughes, Nimrod. *A Solemn Warning to All the Dwellers upon Earth, Given Forth in Obedience to the Express Command of the Lord God . . .* Trenton, N.J.: n.p., 1811.

Hughes, Richard T. "Two Restoration Traditions: Mormons and Churches of Christ in the Nineteenth Century." In *The Stone-Campbell Movement: An International Religious Tradition*, edited by Michael W. Casey and Douglas A. Foster, 348–63. Knoxville: University of Tennessee Press, 2002.

Hughes, Richard T., and C. Leonard Allen. *Illusions of Innocence: Protestant Primitivism in America, 1630–1875.* Chicago: University of Chicago Press, 1988.

Hullinger, Robert. *Joseph Smith's Answer to Skepticism.* Salt Lake City, Utah: Signature Books, 1992.

Hume, David. *Essays: Moral, Political, Literary.* Edited by Eugene F. Miller. Rev. ed. Indianapolis, Ind.: Liberty Classics, 1985.

Hunter, William E. *Edward Hunter: Faithful Steward.* Salt Lake City, Utah: Publisher's Press, 1970.

Huntington, Oliver Boardman. Autobiography. L. Tom Perry Special Collections. Harold B. Lee Library. Brigham Young University.

———. Diaries, 1843–1922. L. Tom Perry Special Collections. Harold B. Lee Library. Brigham Young University.

Huntington, William. Diaries and Autobiography, 1784–1846. L. Tom Perry Special Collections. Harold B. Lee Library. Brigham Young University.

Huntress, Keith. "Governor Thomas Ford and the Murderers of Joseph Smith." *Dialogue: A Journal of Mormon Thought* 4, no. 2 (1969): 41–52.

Hurt, R. Douglas. *The Ohio Frontier: Crucible of the Old Northwest, 1720–1830*. Bloomington: Indiana University Press, 1996.

Hutchinson, Anthony A. "A Mormon Midrash? LDS Creation Narratives Reconsidered." *Dialogue: A Journal of Mormon Thought* 21, no. 4 (1998): 11–74.

———. "The Word of God Is Enough: The Book of Mormon as Nineteenth-Century Scripture." In *New Approaches to the Book of Mormon*, edited by Brent Lee Metcalfe, 1–19. Salt Lake City, Utah: Signature Books, 1993.

Hyde, Myrtle Stevens. *Orson Hyde: The Olive Branch of Israel*. Salt Lake City, Utah: Agreka Books, 2000.

Hyde, Orson. "History of Orson Hyde." Histories of the Twelve, ca. 1830–1880. Historian's Office. Church Archives. The Church of Jesus Christ of Latter-day Saints, Salt Lake City.

———. *A Voice from Jerusalem, or a Sketch of the Travels and Ministry of Elder Orson Hyde*. Boston: Albert Morgan, 1842.

Idel, Moshe. *Absorbing Perfections: Kabbalah and Interpretation*. New Haven, Conn.: Yale University Press, 2002.

"An Interesting Testimony." *Improvement Era* 6 (May 1903): 507–10.

Iowa High Council. Record, 1839–1841. Church Archives. The Church of Jesus Christ of Latter-day Saints. Salt Lake City, Utah.

Irving, Gordon. "The Law of Adoption: One Phase of the Development of the Mormon Concept of Salvation, 1830–1890." *BYU Studies* 14, no. 3 (1974): 291–314.

Irwin, John T. *American Hieroglyphics: The Symbol of the Egyptian Hieroglyphics in the American Renaissance*. New Haven, Conn.: Yale University Press, 1980.

Jackson, Joseph H. *A Narrative of the Adventures and Experiences of Joseph H. Jackson, in Nauvoo, Disclosing the Depths of Mormon Villainy*. Warsaw, Ill.: n.p., 1844.

Jackson, Kent P. "The Sacred Literature of the Latter-day Saints." In *The Bible and Bibles in America*, edited by Ernest S. Frerichs, 163–91. Atlanta: Scholars Press, 1988.

Jackson, Kent P., and Peter M. Jasinski. "The Process of Inspired Translation: Two Passages Translated Twice in the Joseph Smith Translation of the Bible." *BYU Studies* 42, no. 2 (2003): 35–64.

Jackson, Richard H. "The Mormon Village: Genesis and Antecedents of the City of Zion Plan." *BYU Studies* 17, no. 2 (1977): 223–40.

James, William. *Pragmatism*. 1907; Cambridge: Harvard University Press, 1975.

Jenkins, Kenneth D. "Common Phrases Between the King James Version and the Book of Mormon." 3 vols., Provo, Utah: FARMS.

Jennings, Warren A. "The Army of Israel Marches into Missouri." *Missouri Historical Review* 62, no. 2 (1968): 107–35.

———. "The City in the Garden: Social Conflict in Jackson County, Missouri." *The Restoration Movement: Essays in Mormon History*, edited by F. Mark McKiernan, Alma R. Blair, and Paul M. Edwards, 99–119. Lawrence, Kans.: Coronado, 1973.

———. "The Expulsion of the Mormons from Jackson County, Missouri." *Missouri Historical Review* 64, no. 1 (1969): 41–63.

———. "Factors in the Destruction of the Mormon Press in Missouri, 1833." *Utah Historical Quarterly* 35, no. 1 (1967): 57–76.

———. "Isaac McCoy and the Mormons." *Missouri Historical Review* 61, no. 1 (1966): 62–82.

———. "Two Iowa Postmasters View Nauvoo: Anti-Mormon Letters to the Governor of Missouri." *BYU Studies* 11, no. 3 (1971): 275–92.

———. "Zion Is Fled: The Expulsion of the Mormons from Jackson County, Missouri." Ph.D. diss., University of Florida, 1962.

Jensen, Derek. " 'One of Them Was Nearest unto the Throne of God': Nineteenth-Century Cosmologies and the Book of Abraham." Unpublished paper. Archive of Restoration

Culture. Joseph Fielding Smith Institute for Latter-day Saint History. Brigham Young University.

Jensen, Richard L., and Malcolm R. Thorp, eds. *Mormons in Early Victorian Britain*. Salt Lake City: University of Utah Press, 1989.

Jenson, Andrew. *Autobiography of Andrew Jenson*. Salt Lake City, Utah: Deseret News, 1938.

———. *Latter-day Saint Biographical Encyclopedia*. 4 vols. Salt Lake City, Utah: Andrew Jenson Historical Company, 1901–36.

———. "Plural Marriage." *Historical Record* 6 (May 1887): 219–34.

Jessee, Dean C. "The Earliest Documented Accounts of Joseph Smith's First Vision." In *Opening the Heavens: Accounts of Divine Manifestations, 1820–1844*, edited by John W. Welch with Erick B. Carlson, 1–33. Provo, Utah: Brigham Young University Press; Salt Lake City, Utah: Deseret Book, 2005.

———. "The Early Accounts of Joseph Smith's First Vision." *BYU Studies* 9, no. 3 (1969): 275–94.

———. "The Original Book of Mormon Manuscript." *BYU Studies* 10, no. 3 (1970): 259–78.

———. " 'Walls, Grates, and Screeking Iron Doors': The Prison Experience of Mormon Leaders in Missouri, 1838–1839." In *New Views of Mormon History: A Collection of Essays in Honor of Leonard J. Arrington*, edited by Davis Bitton and Maureen Ursenbach Beecher, 19–42. Salt Lake City: University of Utah Press, 1987.

———. "The Writing of Joseph Smith's History." *BYU Studies* 11, no. 4 (1971): 439–73.

Jessee, Dean C., and John W. Welch. "Revelations in Context: Joseph Smith's Letter from Liberty Jail, March 20, 1839." *BYU Studies* 39, no. 3 (2000): 125–45.

Jinkins, Michael. *A Comparative Study in the Theology of Atonement in Jonathan Edwards and John McLeod Campbell: Atonement and the Character of God*. San Francisco: Mellen Research University Press, 1993.

Johannsen, Robert W. *Stephen A. Douglas*. New York: Oxford University Press, 1973.

Johnson, Benjamin F. *My Life's Review: Autobiography of Benjamin Franklin Johnson*. Provo, Utah: Grandin Book, 1997.

Johnson, Charles A. *The Frontier Camp Meeting: Religion's Harvest Time*. Dallas: Southern Methodist University Press, 1955.

Johnson, Clark V., ed. *Mormon Redress Petitions: Documents of the 1833–1838 Missouri Conflict*. Provo, Utah: Religious Studies Center, Brigham Young University, 1992.

Johnson, Curtis D. *Islands of Holiness: Rural Religion in Upstate New York, 1790–1860*. Ithaca, N.Y.: Cornell University Press, 1989.

Johnson, Janiece. " 'Give Up All and Follow Your Lord': Testimony and Exhortations in Early Mormon Women's Letters, 1831–1839." *BYU Studies* 41, no. 1 (2002): 77–107.

Johnson, Paul E., and Sean Wilentz. *The Kingdom of Matthias*. New York: Oxford University Press, 1994.

Jolley, Jerry C. "The Sting of the *Wasp*: Early Nauvoo Newspaper—April 1842 to April 1843." *BYU Studies* 22, no. 4 (1982): 487–96.

Jones, Dan. "The Martyrdom of Joseph Smith and His Brother Hyrum." Translated by Ronald D. Dennis. *BYU Studies* 24, no. 1 (1984): 78–109.

Jonsson, Inge. *Emanuel Swedenborg*. Translated by Catherine Djurklou. New York: Twayne, 1971.

Jordan, Winthrop D. *White over Black: American Attitudes Toward the Negro, 1550–1812*. Baltimore: Penguin Books, 1968.

Jorgensen, Danny L. "Dissent and Schism in the Early Church: Explaining Mormon Fissiparousness." *Dialogue: A Journal of Mormon Thought* 28, no. 3 (1995): 15–39.

Jorgensen, Lynne Watkins, and *BYU Studies* Staff. "The Mantle of the Prophet Joseph Passes to Brother Brigham: A Collective Spiritual Witness." *BYU Studies* 36, no. 4 (1996–97): 125–204.

Journal History of the Church of Jesus Christ of Latter-day Saints. Church History Library. The Church of Jesus Christ of Latter-day Saints. Salt Lake City, Utah.

Journal of Discourses, 26 vols. Liverpool, Eng.: F. D. Richards, 1855–86.

Judkins, Benjamin N. "Recent Trends in Book of Mormon Apologetics: A Critical Assessment of Methodological Diversity and Academic Viability." Unpublished paper. Archive of Restoration Culture. Joseph Fielding Smith Institute. Brigham Young University.

———. " 'Then Shall They Be Gods': Abraham, Egypt and the Alchemical Imagination." Unpublished paper. Archive of Restoration Culture. Joseph Fielding Smith Institute for Latter-day Saint History. Brigham Young University.

Juster, Susan. *Doomsayers: Anglo-American Prophecy in the Age of Revolution*. Philadelphia: University of Pennsylvania Press, 2003.

Kenny, Michael G. *The Perfect Law of Liberty: Elias Smith and the Providential History of America*. Washington, D.C.: Smithsonian Institution Press, 1994.

Kerber, Linda K. *Women of the Republic: Intellect and Ideology in Revolutionary America*. Chapel Hill: University of North Carolina Press, 1980.

Ketcham, Ralph. *Presidents Above Party: The First American Presidency, 1789–1829*. Chapel Hill: University of North Carolina Press, 1984.

Kierkegaard, Søren. "The Difference Between a Genius and an Apostle." In *Without Authority*, edited and translated by Howard V. Hong and Edna H. Hong, 91–108. Princeton, N.J.: Princeton University Press, 1997.

Kimball, Heber C. Journal and Record, 1837–1845. Church Archives. The Church of Jesus Christ of Latter-day Saints. Salt Lake City, Utah.

———. *On the Potter's Wheel: The Diaries of Heber C. Kimball*. Edited by Stanley B. Kimball. Salt Lake City, Utah: Signature Books, in association with Smith Research Associates, 1987.

———. Papers, 1837–1866. Church Archives. The Church of Jesus Christ of Latter-day Saints. Salt Lake City, Utah.

Kimball, James L. "The Nauvoo Charter: A Reinterpretation." In *Kingdom on the Mississippi Reconsidered: Nauvoo in Mormon History*, edited by Roger D. Launius and John E. Hallwas, 39–47. Urbana: University of Illinois Press, 1996.

———. "A Wall to Defend Zion: The Nauvoo Charter." *BYU Studies* 15, no. 4 (1975): 491–97.

Kimball, Lucy Walker. Autobiographical Sketch. Church Archives. The Church of Jesus Christ of Latter-day Saints. Salt Lake City, Utah.

———. Testimony. Church Archives. The Church of Jesus Christ of Latter-day Saints. Salt Lake City, Utah.

Kimball, Richard Ian. " 'A Dark and Dubious Field': Melchizedek in the World of Joseph Smith." *Archive of Restoration Culture: Summer Fellows' Papers, 1997–1999*, 17–28. Provo, Utah: Joseph Fielding Smith Institute for Latter-day Saint History, Brigham Young University, 2000.

Kimball, Stanley B. "The Anthon Transcript: People, Primary Sources, and Problems." *BYU Studies* 10, no. 3 (1970): 325–52.

———. *Heber C. Kimball: Mormon Patriarch and Pioneer*. Urbana: University of Illinois Press, 1981.

———. "Kinderhook Plates Brought to Joseph Smith Appear to Be a Nineteenth-Century Hoax." *Ensign* 11 (August 1981): 66–74.

———. "Nauvoo West: The Mormons of the Iowa Shore." *BYU Studies* 18, no. 2 (1978): 132–42.

———. "New Light on Old Egyptiana: Mormon Mummies, 1848–71." *Dialogue: A Journal of Mormon Thought* 16, no. 4 (1983): 72–90.

———. "The Saints and St. Louis, 1831–1857: An Oasis of Tolerance and Security." *BYU Studies* 13, no. 4 (1973): 489–519.

———. "Thomas L. Barnes: Coroner of Carthage." *BYU Studies* 11, no. 2 (1971): 141–47.

Kimball, Vilate. "Life in Nauvoo, June 1844: Vilate Kimball's Martyrdom Letters." Edited by Ronald K. Esplin. *BYU Studies* 19, no. 2 (1979): 231–40.

King, Arthur Henry. "An Account of My Conversion." In *The Abundance of the Heart*. Salt Lake City, Utah: Bookcraft, 1986.

———. "Joseph Smith as Writer." In *The Abundance of the Heart*. Salt Lake City, Utah: Bookcraft, 1986.

———. "Language Themes in Jacob 5: 'The Vineyard of the Lord of Hosts Is the House of Israel' (Isaiah 5:7)." In *Allegory of the Olive Tree: The Olive, the Bible, and Jacob 5*, edited by Stephen D. Ricks and John W. Welch, 140–73. Salt Lake City, Utah: Deseret Book; Provo, Utah: FARMS, 1994.

Kirchner, Ann. " 'Tending to Edify, Astonish, and Instruct': Published Narratives of Spiritual Dreams and Visions in the Early Republic." *Early American Studies* 1 (2003): 198–229.

Kirkham, Francis W. *A New Witness of Christ in America*. 2 vols. Salt Lake City: Utah Printing, 1951.

Kirtland Egyptian Manuscripts, ca. 1835–1842. Church Archives. The Church of Jesus Christ of Latter-day Saints. Salt Lake City, Utah.

Kirtland Elders' Certificates, 1836–1838. Church Archives. The Church of Jesus Christ of Latter-day Saints. Salt Lake City, Utah.

Kirtland Elders' Quorum. *The Kirtland Elders' Quorum Record, 1836–1841*. Edited by Lyndon W. Cook and Milton V. Backman. Provo, Utah: Grandin Books, 1985.

Kirtland High Council. Minutes, 1832–1837. Church Archives. The Church of Jesus Christ of Latter-day Saints. Salt Lake City, Utah.

Kling, David W. *A Field of Divine Wonders: The New Divinity and Village Revivals in Northwestern Connecticut, 1792–1822*. University Park: Pennsylvania State University Press, 1993.

Knepper, George W. *Ohio and Its People*. 3rd ed. Kent, Ohio: Kent State University Press, 2003.

Knight, George R. *Millennial Fever and the End of the World: A Study of Millerite Adventism*. Boise, Idaho: Pacific Press, 1993.

Knight, Joseph Jr. Autobiographical Sketch, 1862. Church Archives. The Church of Jesus Christ of Latter-day Saints. Salt Lake City, Utah.

Knight, Joseph Sr. "Joseph Knight's Recollection of Early Mormon History." Edited by Dean C. Jessee. *BYU Studies* 17, no. 1 (1976): 29–39.

Knight, Newel. "Newel Knight Journal." In *Scraps of Biography. Tenth Book of the Faith-Promoting Series*, 46–104. Salt Lake City, Utah: Juvenile Instructor Office, 1883.

Koyré, Alexandre. *From the Closed World to the Infinite Universe*. Baltimore: Johns Hopkins University Press, 1957.

Kraynak, Robert P. *Christian Faith and Modern Democracy: God and Politics in the Fallen World*. Notre Dame, Ind.: University of Notre Dame Press, 2001.

Lambert, Neal E., and Richard H. Cracroft. "Literary Form and Historical Understanding: Joseph Smith's First Vision." *Journal of Mormon History* 7 (1980): 31–42.

Lancaster, James E. " 'By the Gift and Power of God': The Method of Translation of the Book of Mormon." *Saints' Herald* 109 (November 15, 1962): 14–18, 22, 23.

Largey, Dennis L., ed. *Book of Mormon Reference Companion*. Salt Lake City, Utah: Deseret Book, 2003.

Larson, John. "Joseph Smith and Egyptology: An Early Episode in the History of American Speculation About Ancient Egypt, 1835–1844." In *For His Ka: Essays Offered in Memory of Klaus Baer*, edited by David Silverman, 159–78. Chicago: Oriental Institute of the University of Chicago, 1994.

Larson, Stan. "The King Follett Discourse: A Newly Amalgamated Text." *BYU Studies* 18, no. 2 (1978): 193–208.

———. "The Sermon on the Mount: What Its Textual Transformation Discloses Concerning the Historicity of the Book of Mormon." *Trinity Journal* 7, no. 1 (1986): 23–45.

Laub, George. "George Laub's Nauvoo Journal." Edited by Eugene England. *BYU Studies* 18, no. 2 (1978): 151–78.

Launius, Roger D. "Alexander William Doniphan and the 1838 Mormon War in Missouri." *John Whitmer Historical Association Journal* 18 (1998): 63–110.

———. *Alexander William Doniphan: Portrait of a Missouri Moderate*. Columbia: University of Missouri Press, 1997.

———. "Anti-Mormonism in Illinois: Thomas C. Sharp's Unfinished History of the Mormon War." *Journal of Mormon History* 15 (1989): 27–45.

———. *Invisible Saints: A History of Black Americans in the Reorganized Church*. Independence, Mo.: Herald Publishing House, 1988.

———. *Joseph Smith III: Pragmatic Prophet*. Urbana: University of Illinois Press, 1988.

———. "A Question of Honor? A. W. Doniphan and the Mormon Expulsion from Jackson County." *Nauvoo Journal* 10, no. 2 (1998): 3–17.

———. *Zion's Camp: Expedition to Missouri, 1834*. Independence, Mo.: Herald Publishing House, 1984.

Launius, Roger D., and F. Mark McKiernan. *Joseph Smith, Jr.'s Red Brick Store*. Macomb: Western Illinois University, 1985.

Laurence, Richard, trans. *The Book of Enoch the Prophet: An Apocryphal Production, Supposed for Ages to Have Been Lost; But Discovered at the Close of the Last Century in Abyssinia*. 3rd ed., rev. Oxford: S. Collingwood, 1838.

Law, Wilson. "Wilson Law: A Sidelight on the Expositor Incident." Edited by Steven G. Barnett. *BYU Studies* 19, no. 2 (1979): 244–46.

Layton, Robert L. "Kirtland: A Perspective on Time and Place." *BYU Studies* 11, no. 4 (1971): 423–38.

LeBaron, E. Dale. *Benjamin Franklin Johnson: Friend to the Prophets*. Provo, Utah: Benjamin F. Johnson Family Organization, 1997.

Lee, John D. *Mormonism Unveiled; Or the Life and Confessions of the Late Mormon Bishop, John D. Lee*. St. Louis: Bryan, Brand, 1877.

Lender, Mark Edward, and James Kirby Martin. *Drinking in America: A History*. Rev. ed. New York: Free Press; London: Collier Macmillan, 1987.

Leonard, Glen M. *Nauvoo: A Place of Peace, a People of Promise*. Salt Lake City, Utah: Deseret Book; Provo, Utah: Brigham Young University Press, 2002.

LeSueur, Stephen C. "Danites Reconsidered: Were They Vigilantes or Just the Mormons' Version of the Elks Club?" *John Whitmer Historical Association Journal* 14 (1994): 1–15.

———. *The 1838 Mormon War in Missouri*. Columbia: University of Missouri Press, 1987.

———. " 'High Treason and Murder': The Examination of Mormon Prisoners at Richmond, Missouri, in November 1838." *BYU Studies* 26, no. 2 (1986): 3–30.

———. "The Mormon Experience in Missouri, 1830–39." In *Excavating Mormon Pasts: The New Historiography of the Last Half Century*, edited by Newell G. Bringhurst and Lavina Fielding Anderson, 87–112. Salt Lake City, Utah: Greg Kofford Books, 2004.

Leventhal, Herbert. *In the Shadow of the Enlightenment: Occultism and Renaissance Science in Eighteenth-Century America*. New York: New York University Press, 1976.

Levy, Leonard W. *The Emergence of a Free Press*. New York: Oxford University Press, 1985.

Lewis, David L. *District of Columbia: A Bicentennial History*. New York: W. W. Norton, 1976.

Lewis, Richard T. "The Development of the Economic Landscape." In *A Geography of Ohio*, edited by Leonard Peacefull, 110–26. Kent, Ohio: Kent State University Press, 1996.

Lightner, Mary Elizabeth Rollins. Collection, 1865–1957. Church Archives. The Church of Jesus Christ of Latter-day Saints. Salt Lake City, Utah.

———. Papers, 1865–1914. L. Tom Perry Special Collections. Harold B. Lee Library. Brigham Young University.

Lindquist, Danille Christensen. " 'Old Devils' or 'Joint-Heirs': Pre-existent Intelligences in Christian Theodicy and Mormon Doctrine." *Archive of Restoration Culture: Summer*

Fellows' Papers, 1997–1999, 119–31. Provo, Utah: Joseph Fielding Smith Institute for Latter-day Saint History, Brigham Young University, 2000.

Lively, Robert L. "The Catholic Apostolic Church and the Church of Jesus Christ of Latter-day Saints: A Comparative Study of Two Minority Millenarian Groups in Nineteenth-Century England." Ph.D. diss., Mansfield College, Oxford, 1977.

Livesey, Richard. *An Exposure of Mormonism, Being a Statement of Facts Relating to the Self-Styled "Latter-day Saints," and the Origin of the Book of Mormon.* Preston, Eng.: J. Livesey, 1838.

Lowance, Mason I. *The Language of Canaan: Metaphor and Symbol in New England from the Puritans to the Transcendentalists.* Cambridge: Harvard University Press, 1980.

Lucas, James W., and Warner P. Woodworth. *Working Toward Zion: Principles of the United Order for the Modern World.* Salt Lake City, Utah: Aspen Books, 1996.

Luce, W. Ray. "Building the Kingdom of God: Mormon Architecture Before 1847." *BYU Studies* 30, no. 2 (1990): 33–45.

Ludlum, David M. *Early American Winters, 1604–1820.* Boston: American Meteorological Society, 1966.

———. *Social Ferment in Vermont, 1791–1850.* New York: Columbia University Press, 1939.

Lundquist, John M., and Stephen D. Ricks, eds. *By Study and Also by Faith: Essays in Honor of Hugh W. Nibley . . .* 2 vols. Salt Lake City, Utah: Deseret Book; Provo, Utah: FARMS, 1990.

Lunt, William P. *Two Discourses, Delivered September 29, 1839, on Occasion of the Two Hundredth Anniversary of the Gathering of the First Congregational Church, Quincy.* Boston: James Munroe, 1840.

Lynn, Kenneth S. *Mark Twain and Southwestern Humor.* Boston: Little, Brown, 1959.

Lyon, T. Edgar. "Free Masonry at Nauvoo." *Dialogue: A Journal of Mormon Thought* 6, no. 1 (1971): 76–78.

M'Chesney, James. *An Antidote to Mormonism: A Warning to the Church and Nation; The Purity of Christian Principles Defended; And Truth Disentangled from Error and Delusion.* New York: By the Author, 1838.

Mace, Wandle. Autobiography, ca. 1890. Church Archives. The Church of Jesus Christ of Latter-day Saints. Salt Lake City, Utah.

Mack, Solomon. *A Narraitve* [sic] *of the Life of Solomon Mack.* Windsor, Vt.: n.p., [1811].

Mackey, Albert G. *A Lexicon of Freemasonry.* 2nd ed., enl. Charleston: Walker & James, 1852.

Madsen, Carol Cornwall. "Mormon Women and the Temple: Toward a New Understanding." In *Sisters in Spirit: Mormon Women in Historical and Cultural Perspective*, edited by Maureen Ursenbach Beecher and Lavina Fielding Anderson, 80–110. Urbana: University of Illinois Press, 1987.

Madsen, Gordon A. "Joseph Smith and the Missouri Court of Inquiry: Austin A. King's Quest for Hostages." *BYU Studies* 43, no. 4 (2004): 92–136.

———. "Joseph Smith's 1826 Trial: The Legal Setting." *BYU Studies* 30, no. 2 (1990): 91–108.

Madsen, Nels. Statement, 1931. Church Archives. The Church of Jesus Christ of Latter-day Saints. Salt Lake City, Utah.

Madsen, Truman G. *Joseph Smith the Prophet.* Salt Lake City, Utah: Bookcraft, 1989.

Mahoney, Timothy R. "Urban History in a Regional Context: River Towns on the Upper Mississippi, 1840–1860." *Journal of American History* 72, no. 2 (1985): 318–39.

Main, Jackson Turner. "The Economic and Social Structure of Early Lyme." In *A Lyme Miscellany*, edited by George J. Willauer, 29–47. Middletown, Conn.: Wesleyan University Press, 1977.

Manscill, Craig K. " 'Journal of the Branch of the Church of Christ in Pontiac, . . . 1834': Hyrum Smith's Division of Zion's Camp." *BYU Studies* 39, no. 1 (2000): 169–88.

Marini, Stephen A. *Radical Sects of Revolutionary New England.* Cambridge: Harvard University Press, 1982.

Marquardt, H. Michael. "Early Texts of Joseph Smith's Revelations, 1828–1833." *Restoration* 1 (July 1982): 8–11.

———. *The Joseph Smith Revelations: Texts and Commentary*. Salt Lake City, Utah: Signature Books, 1999.

———. "Martin Harris: The Kirtland Years, 1831–1870." *Dialogue: A Journal of Mormon Thought* 35, no. 3 (2002): 1–40.

Marquardt, H. Michael, and Wesley P. Walters. *Inventing Mormonism: Tradition and the Historical Record*. San Francisco: Smith Research Associates, 1994.

Marsden, George M. *The Evangelical Mind and the New School Presbyterian Experience: A Case Study of Thought and Theology in Nineteenth-Century America*. New Haven, Conn.: Yale University Press, 1970.

Marsh, Thomas B. "History of Thomas B. Marsh." Histories of the Twelve, ca. 1830–1880. Historian's Office. Church Archives. The Church of Jesus Christ of Latter-day Saints. Salt Lake City, Utah.

May, Dean L. "A Demographic Portrait of the Mormons, 1830–1980." In *After 150 Years: The Latter-day Saints in Sesquicentennial Perspective*, edited by Thomas G. Alexander and Jessie L. Embry, 37–69. Provo, Utah: Charles Redd Center for Western Studies, Brigham Young University, 1983.

Mason, Patrick Q. "The Possibilities of Mormon Peacebuilding." *Dialogue: A Journal of Mormon Thought* 37, no. 1 (2004): 12–45.

———. "Traditions of Violence: Early Mormon and Anti-Mormon Conflict in Its American Setting." Unpublished paper. Archive of Restoration Culture. Joseph Fielding Smith Institute for Latter-day Saint History. Brigham Young University.

Masur, Louis P. *1831, Year of Eclipse*. New York: Hill and Wang, 2001.

Matheny, Deanne G. "Does the Shoe Fit? A Critique of the Limited Tehuantepec Geography." In *New Approaches to the Book of Mormon: Explorations in Critical Methodology*, edited by Brent Lee Metcalfe, 269–328. Salt Lake City, Utah: Signature Books, 1993.

Matthews, Robert J. "Adam-ondi-Ahman." *BYU Studies* 13, no. 1 (1972): 27–35.

———. "Joseph Smith—Translator." In *Joseph Smith: The Prophet, the Man*, edited by Susan Easton Black and Charles Tate, 77–87. Provo, Utah: Religious Studies Center, Brigham Young University, 1993.

———. *"A Plainer Translation": Joseph Smith's Translation of the Bible—A History and Commentary*. Provo, Utah: Brigham Young University Press, 1985.

Mauss, Armand L. *All Abraham's Children: Changing Mormon Conceptions of Race and Lineage*. Urbana: University of Illinois Press, 2003.

———. "In Search of Ephraim: Traditional Mormon Conception of Lineage and Race." *Journal of Mormon History* 25, no. 1 (1999): 131–73.

McBride, Reuben. Reminiscence. Church Archives. The Church of Jesus Christ of Latter-day Saints. Salt Lake City, Utah.

McDannell, Colleen, and Bernhard Lang. *Heaven: A History*. New Haven, Conn.: Yale University Press, 1988.

McGee, Joseph H. *Story of the Grand River Country, Memoirs of Maj. Joseph H. McGee, 1821–1905*. Gallatin, Mo.: North Missourian Press, 1909.

McKelvey, Blake. *Rochester: The Water-Power City, 1812–1854*. Cambridge: Harvard University Press, 1945.

McLaws, Monte B. "The Attempted Assassination of Missouri's Ex-Governor, Lilburn W. Boggs." *Missouri Historical Review* 60, no. 1 (1965): 50–62.

McLellin, William E. *The Journals of William E. McLellin, 1831–1836*. Edited by Jan Shipps and John W. Welch. Provo, Utah: BYU Studies, Brigham Young University; Urbana: University of Illinois Press, 1994.

McLoughlin, William G. *Modern Revivalism: Charles Grandison Finney to Billy Graham*. New York: Ronald Press, 1959.

McNall, Neil Adams. *An Agricultural History of the Genesee Valley, 1790–1860.* Philadelphia: University of Pennsylvania Press, 1952.

Meinig, Donald W. "The Mormon Culture Region: Strategies and Patterns in the Geography of the American West, 1847–1964." *Annals of the Association of American Geographers* 55 (June 1965): 191–220.

Melder, Keith E. *Beginnings of Sisterhood: The American Woman's Rights Movement, 1800–1850.* New York: Schocken Books, 1977.

Metcalf, Anthony. *Ten Years Before the Mast.* Milad, Idaho: By the Author, 1888.

Metcalfe, Brent Lee. "Reinventing Lamanite Identity." *Sunstone*, no. 131 (March 2004): 20–25.

———, ed. *New Approaches to the Book of Mormon: Explorations in Critical Methodology.* Salt Lake City, Utah: Signature Books, 1993.

Metzger, B. M. "The Fourth Book of Ezra." In *The Old Testament Pseudepigrapha*, edited by James H. Charlesworth, 2 vols., 1:517–59. Garden City, N.Y.: Doubleday, 1983.

Meyer, Douglas K. *Making the Heartland Quilt: A Geographical History of Settlement and Migration in Early-Nineteenth-Century Illinois.* Carbondale: Southern Illinois University Press, 2000.

Meyers, Mary Ann. "Death in Swedenborgian and Mormon Eschatology." *Dialogue: A Journal of Mormon Thought* 14, no. 1 (1981): 58–64.

Midgley, Louis C. "Who Really Wrote the Book of Mormon? The Critics and Their Theories." In *Book of Mormon Authorship Revisited: The Evidence for Ancient Origins*, edited by Noel B. Reynolds, 101–39. Provo, Utah: FARMS, 1997.

Miles, Carrie A. "Polygamy and the Economics of Salvation." *Sunstone* 21, no. 3 (1998): 34–45.

Miller, George. "De Tal Palo Tal Astilla." Edited by H. W. Mills. *Publications of the Historical Society of Southern California Annual* 10 (1917): 86–172.

Miller, Nathan. *The Enterprise of a Free People: Aspects of Economic Development in New York State During the Canal Period, 1792–1838.* Ithaca, N.Y.: Cornell University Press, 1962.

Miller, Reuben. Diaries, 1848–1849. Church Archives. The Church of Jesus Christ of Latter-day Saints. Salt Lake City, Utah.

Miller, Russell E. *The Larger Hope: The First Century of the Universalist Church in America, 1770–1870.* Boston: Unitarian Universalist Association, 1979.

Milton, John. *The Christian Doctrine.* In *John Milton: Complete Poems and Major Prose*, edited by Merritt Y. Hughes. New York: Odyssey Press, 1957.

Miner, Earl, ed. *Literary Uses of Typology: From the Late Middle Ages to the Present.* Princeton, N.J.: Princeton University Press, 1977.

Mitchell, James, ed. *The Life and Times of Levi Scott, D.D., One of Three Bishops of the Methodist Episcopal Church.* New York: Phillips and Hunt, 1885.

Moench, Melodie. "Nineteenth-Century Mormons: The New Israel." *Dialogue: A Journal of Mormon Thought* 12, no. 1 (1979): 42–56.

Moore, R. Laurence. *Religious Outsiders and the Making of Americans.* New York: Oxford University Press, 1986.

Moorhead, James H. "Apocalypticism in Mainstream Protestantism, 1800 to the Present." In *The Encyclopedia of Apocalypticism*, edited by Bernard McGinn, John J. Collins, and Stephen J. Stein, 3 vols., 3:72–107. New York: Continuum, 1998.

Morain, William D. *The Sword of Laban: Joseph Smith, Jr., and the Dissociated Mind.* Washington, D.C.: American Psychiatric Press, 1998.

Morcombe, Joseph E. "Masonry and Mormonism: A Record of Events in Illinois and Iowa Transpiring Between the Years 1840 and 1846." *New Age* 2 (May–June 1905): 2-part series.

Morgan, William. *Illustrations of Masonry, By One of the Fraternity Who has Devoted Thirty Years to the Subject.* Chicago: Ezra A. Cook, 1827.

Morison, Samuel Eliot. *Sources and Documents Illustrating the American Revolution, 1764–1788.* 2nd ed. London: Oxford University Press, 1929.

Morley, Richard Henrie. "The Life and Contributions of Isaac Morley." Master's thesis, Brigham Young University, 1965.

Morris, Larry E. "Oliver Cowdery's Vermont Years and the Origins of Mormonism." *BYU Studies* 39, no. 1 (2000): 106–29.

Morris, Richard B., ed. *Encyclopedia of American History.* New York: Harper and Brothers, 1953.

Morton, Sunny McClellan. "The Forgotten Daughter: Julia Murdock Smith." *Mormon Historical Studies* 3, no. 1 (2002): 35–60.

Mosser, Carl, and Paul Owen. "Mormon Apologetic Scholarship and Evangelical Neglect: Losing the Battle and Not Knowing It?" *Trinity Journal* 19, no. 2 (1998): 179–205.

Mulder, William. "Mormonism's 'Gathering': An American Doctrine with a Difference." *Church History* 23, no. 3 (1954): 248–64.

Mulder, William, and A. Russell Mortensen, eds. *Among the Mormons: Historic Accounts by Contemporary Observers.* New York: Alfred A. Knopf, 1958.

Murdock, John. Diaries, 1832–1859. Church Archives. The Church of Jesus Christ of Latter-day Saints. Salt Lake City, Utah.

Murdock, Miriam. " 'Stepping Stones' of Understanding: Patterns of the Priesthood in Universalism, Freemasonry, and Mormonism." *Archive of Restoration Culture: Summer Fellows' Papers, 1997–1999,* 51–57. Provo, Utah: Joseph Fielding Smith Institute for Latter-day Saint History, Brigham Young University, 2000.

Murphy, Thomas W. "Lamanite Genesis, Genealogy, and Genetics." In *American Apocrypha: Essays on the Book of Mormon,* edited by Dan Vogel and Brent Lee Metcalfe, 47–77. Salt Lake City, Utah: Signature Books, 2002.

Nauvoo City Council. Minutes, 1841–1845. Church Archives. The Church of Jesus Christ of Latter-day Saints. Salt Lake City, Utah.

Nauvoo High Council. Minutes, 1839–1845. Church Archives. The Church of Jesus Christ of Latter-day Saints. Salt Lake City, Utah.

Nauvoo Legion. Records, 1841–1844. Church Archives. The Church of Jesus Christ of Latter-day Saints. Salt Lake City, Utah.

Nauvoo Masonic Lodge. Minutes, 1841–1846. Church Archives. The Church of Jesus Christ of Latter-day Saints. Salt Lake City, Utah.

———. *The Official Minutes of the Nauvoo Lodge. U.D.* Edited by Mervin B. Hogan. Des Moines, Iowa: Research Lodge No. 2, [1971].

Nauvoo Municipal Court. Docket, 1841–1874. Church Archives. The Church of Jesus Christ of Latter-day Saints. Salt Lake City, Utah.

Neal, R. B. *Oliver Cowdery's Defence and Renunciation.* Ashland, Ky.: Ashland Independent, 1906.

Needham, John. "John Needham's Nauvoo Letter: 1843." Edited by Maurine Carr Ward. *Nauvoo Journal* 8, no. 1 (1996): 38–42.

Neibaur, Alexander. Journal, 1841–1862. Church Archives. The Church of Jesus Christ of Latter-day Saints. Salt Lake City, Utah.

Nelson, Lowry. *The Mormon Village: A Pattern and Technique of Land Settlement.* Salt Lake City: University of Utah Press, 1952.

Nelson, Marie H. "Anti-Mormon Mob Violence and Rhetoric of Law and Order in Early Mormon History." *Legal Studies Forum* 21 (1997): 353–88.

Newell, Linda King. "Emma Hale Smith and the Polygamy Question." *John Whitmer Historical Association Journal* 4 (1984): 3–15.

Newell, Linda King, and Valeen Tippetts Avery. *Mormon Enigma: Emma Hale Smith, Prophet's Wife, "Elect Lady," Polygamy's Foe—1804–1879.* Garden City, N.Y.: Doubleday, 1984.

———. "Sweet Counsel and Seas of Tribulation: The Religious Life of Women in Kirtland." *BYU Studies* 20, no. 2 (1980): 151–62.

Nibley, Hugh. *Abraham in Egypt*. Edited by Garry P. Gillum. 2d ed. Salt Lake City, Utah: Deseret Book; Provo, Utah: FARMS, 2000.

———. *An Approach to the Book of Mormon*. Salt Lake City, Utah: Council of the Twelve Apostles of the Church of Jesus Christ of Latter-day Saints, 1957.

———. "The Early Christian Prayer Circle." *BYU Studies* 19, no. 1 (1978): 41–78.

———. *Enoch the Prophet*. Edited by Stephen D. Ricks. Salt Lake City, Utah: Deseret Book; Provo, Utah: FARMS, 1986.

———. "The Facsimiles of the Book of Abraham: A Response." *Sunstone* 4, no. 5–6 (1979): 49–51.

———. *Lehi in the Desert and The World of the Jaredites*. Salt Lake City, Utah: Bookcraft, 1952.

———. "The Meaning of the Kirtland Egyptian Papers." *BYU Studies* 11, no. 4 (1971): 350–99.

———. *The Message of the Joseph Smith Papyri: An Egyptian Endowment*. Salt Lake City, Utah: Deseret Book, 1975.

———. *The Myth Makers*. Salt Lake City, Utah: Bookcraft, 1961.

———. *Since Cumorah*. 2d ed. Salt Lake City, Utah: Deseret Book, 1988.

———. "What Is 'The Book of Breathings'?" *BYU Studies* 11, no. 1 (1971): 153–87.

Nickelsburg, George W. E. *I Enoch 1: A Commentary on the Book of 1 Enoch, Chapters 1–36; 81–108*. Edited by Klaus Baltzer. Minneapolis: Fortress, 2001.

Nissenbaum, Stephen. *Sex, Diet, and Debility in Jacksonian America: Sylvester Graham and Health Reform*. Westport, Conn.: Greenwood Press, 1980.

Noll, Mark A. *America's God: From Jonathan Edwards to Abraham Lincoln*. New York: Oxford University Press, 2002.

Norman, Keith E. "Adam's Navel." *Dialogue: A Journal of Mormon Thought* 21, no. 2 (1988): 81–97.

———. "The Mark of the Curse: Lingering Racism in Mormon Doctrine." *Dialogue: A Journal of Mormon Thought* 32, no. 1 (1999): 119–36.

Norton, Andrews. *The Evidences of the Genuineness of the Gospels*. 3 vols. Boston: John B. Russell, 1837–44.

Nott, Samuel. *The Future Habitation of Believers, Superior to Their Present, and the Importance of Being Ready for the Day of Judgment*. Hartford, Conn.: For Roger McCall, 1812.

Numbers, Ronald L. *Prophetess of Health: A Study of Ellen G. White*. New York: Harper and Row, 1976.

Numbers, Ronald L., and Jonathan M. Butler, eds. *The Diappointed: Millerism and Millenarianism in the Nineteenth Century*. Bloomington: Indiana University Press, 1987.

Nuttall, L. John. Papers, 1857–1904. L. Tom Perry Special Collections. Harold B. Lee Library. Brigham Young University.

O'Dea, Thomas. *The Mormons*. Chicago: University of Chicago, 1957.

O'Driscoll, Jeffrey S. *Hyrum Smith: A Life of Integrity*. Salt Lake City, Utah: Deseret Book, 2003.

Oaks, Dallin H. "Habeas Corpus in the States, 1776–1865." *University of Chicago Law Review* 32, no. 2 (1965): 243–88.

———. "The Suppression of the Nauvoo Expositor." *Utah Law Review* 9, no. 4 (1965): 862–903.

Oaks, Dallin H., and Joseph I. Bentley. "Joseph Smith and Legal Process: In the Wake of the Steamboat *Nauvoo*." *Brigham Young University Law Review* 3 (1976): 735–82.

Oaks, Dallin H., and Marvin S. Hill. *Carthage Conspiracy: The Trial of the Accused Assassins of Joseph Smith*. Urbana: University of Illinois Press, 1975.

Oates, Stephen B. *The Approaching Fury: Voices of the Storm, 1820–1861*. New York: HarperCollins, 1997.

Obelkevich, James. *Religion and Rural Society: South Lindsey, 1825–1875*. Oxford, Eng.: Clarendon Press, 1976.

Oliphant, Margaret. *The Life of Edward Irving, Minister of the National Scotch Church, London.* 3d ed., rev. London: Hurst and Blackett, 1864.

Olsen, Ralph A. "A Malay Site for Book of Mormon Events." *Sunstone,* no. 131 (March 2004): 30–34.

Olsen, Steven L. "Joseph Smith's Concept of the City of Zion." In *Joseph Smith: The Prophet, the Man,* edited by Susan Easton Black and Charles D. Tate, Jr., 203–12. Provo, Utah: Religious Studies Center, Brigham Young University, 1993.

———. *The Mormon Ideology of Place: Cosmic Symbolism of the City of Zion, 1830–1846.* Ph.D. diss., University of Chicago, 1985; reprint, Provo, Utah: Joseph Fielding Smith Institute for LDS History and BYU Studies, 2002.

Ostler, Blake T. "The Book of Mormon as a Modern Expansion of an Ancient Source." *Dialogue: A Journal of Mormon Thought* 20, no. 1 (1987): 66–123.

———. "The Development of the Mormon Concept of Grace." *Dialogue: A Journal of Mormon Thought* 24, no. 1 (1991): 57–84.

———. "The Idea of Pre-Existence in the Development of Mormon Thought." *Dialogue: A Journal of Mormon Thought* 15, no. 1 (1982): 59–78.

Ostler, Craig J. "Nauvoo Saints in the Newspapers of the 1840s." *Nauvoo Journal* 8, no. 1 (1996): 30–33.

Otto, Rudolph. *The Idea of the Holy: An Inquiry into the Non-rational Factor in the Idea of the Divine and Its Relation to the Rational.* New York: Oxford University Press, 1958.

Owens, Lance S. "Joseph Smith and Kabbalah: The Occult Connection." *Dialogue: A Journal of Mormon Thought* 27, no. 3 (1994): 117–94.

Ozick, Cynthia. "The Heretic: The Mythic Passions of Gershom Scholem." *The New Yorker,* Sept. 2, 2002, 143–48.

Packer, Barbara L. "The Transcendentalists." In *The Cambridge History of American Literature. Volume 2, 1820–1865,* edited by Sacvan Bercovitch and Cyrus Patell, 329–604. Cambridge: Cambridge University Press, 1995.

Paine, Thomas. *The Age of Reason.* n.p.: Carol Publishing Group, 1997.

———. *The Complete Religious and Theological Works of Thomas Paine, Volume 1.* New York: Freethought Press Association, 1954.

Palmer, James. Reminiscences, ca. 1884–1898. Church Archives. The Church of Jesus Christ of Latter-day Saints. Salt Lake City, Utah.

Parker, Richard A. "The Joseph Smith Papyri: A Preliminary Report." *Dialogue: A Journal of Mormon Thought* 3, no. 2 (1968): 86–88.

Parkin, Max H. "The Courthouse Mentioned in the Revelation on Zion." *BYU Studies* 14, no. 4 (1974): 451–57.

———. "A History of the Latter-day Saints in Clay County, Missouri, from 1833 to 1837." Ph.D. diss., Brigham Young University, 1976.

———. "Independence, Missouri." In *Historical Atlas of Mormonism,* edited by S. Kent Brown, Donald Q. Cannon, and Richard H. Jackson, 40–41. New York: Simon and Schuster, 1994.

———. "Mormon Political Involvement in Ohio." *BYU Studies* 9, no. 4 (1969): 484–502.

———. "The Nature and Causes of External and Internal Conflict of the Mormons in Ohio Between 1830 and 1838." Master's thesis, Brigham Young University, 1966.

Parrish, William E. *David Rice Atchison of Missouri: Border Politician.* Columbia: University of Missouri Press, 1961.

Parry, Donald W., Jeanette W. Miller, and Sandra A. Thorne, eds. *A Guide to Publications on the Book of Mormon: A Selected Annotated Bibliography.* Provo, Utah: FARMS, 1996.

Parry, Donald W., Daniel C. Peterson, and John W. Welch, eds. *Echoes and Evidences of the Book of Mormon.* Provo, Utah: FARMS, Brigham Young University, 2002.

Parsons, Tyler. *Mormonism Fanaticism Exposed.* Boston: [s.n.], 1842.

Partridge, Edward. Diary, 1835–1836. Church Archives. The Church of Jesus Christ of Latter-day Saints. Salt Lake City, Utah.

Partridge, M. Scott. "Edward Partridge in Painesville, Ohio." *BYU Studies* 42, no. 1 (2003): 59–73.

Patriarchal Blessings. Books A, B. Church Archives. The Church of Jesus Christ of Latter-day Saints. Salt Lake City, Utah.

Paul, Erich Robert. "Joseph Smith and the Manchester (New York) Library." *BYU Studies* 22, no. 3 (1982): 333–56.

———. *Science, Religion, and Mormon Cosmology.* Urbana: University of Illinois Press, 1992.

Paulsen, David L. "The Doctrine of Divine Embodiment: Restoration, Judeo-Christian, and Philosophical Perspectives." *BYU Studies* 34, no. 4 (1995–96): 6–94.

———. "The God of Abraham, Isaac, and (William) James." *Journal of Speculative Philosophy* 13, no. 2 (1999): 114–46.

———. "Joseph Smith and the Problem of Evil." *BYU Studies* 39, no. 1 (2000): 53–65.

Paulsen, David L., and Blake T. Ostler. "Sin, Suffering, and Soul-Making: Joseph Smith on the Problem of Evil." In *Revelation, Reason, and Faith: Essays in Honor of Truman G. Madsen,* edited by Donald W. Parry, Daniel C. Peterson, and Stephen D. Ricks, 237–84. Provo, Utah: FARMS, Brigham Young University, 2002.

The Pearl of Great Price: Being a Choice Selection from the Revelations, Translations, and Narrations of Joseph Smith, First Prophet, Seer, and Revelator to the Church of Jesus Christ of Latter Day Saints. Liverpool, Eng.: F. D. Richards, 1851.

Pease, Theodore Calvin. *The Frontier State, 1818–1848.* Springfield: Illinois Centennial Commission, 1918.

Peck, Reed. Historical Sketch, 1839. L. Tom Perry Special Collections. Harold B. Lee Library. Brigham Young University.

The People v. Joseph Smith. May 23, 1844. Hancock County Courthouse. Carthage, Illinois.

Perkins, Keith. "A House Divided: The John Johnson Family." *Ensign* 9 (Feb. 1979): 54–59.

Persuitte, David. *Joseph Smith and the Origins of the Book of Mormon.* Jefferson, N.C.: McFarland, 1985.

Peters, John Leland. *Christian Perfection and American Methodism.* New York: Abingdon Press, 1956.

Peterson, Daniel C. " 'Ye Are Gods': Psalms 82 and John 10 as Witnesses to the Divine Nature of Humankind." In *The Disciple as Scholar: Essays on Scriptures and the Ancient World in Honor of Richard Lloyd Anderson,* edited by Stephen D. Ricks, Donald W. Parry, and Andrew W. Hedges, 471–594. Provo, Utah: FARMS, Brigham Young University, 2000.

Peterson, H. Donl. "Antonio Lebolo: Excavator of the Book of Abraham." *BYU Studies* 31, no. 3 (1991): 5–29.

———. "The Mormon Mummies and Papyri in Ohio." In *Regional Studies in Latter-day Saint Church History: Ohio,* edited by Milton V. Backman, 123–38. Provo, Utah: Department of Church History and Doctrine, Brigham Young University, 1990.

———. "Sacred Writings from the Tombs of Egypt." In *The Pearl of Great Price: Revelations from God,* edited by H. Donl Peterson and Charles D. Tate, 137–53. Provo, Utah: Religious Studies Center, Brigham Young University, 1989.

———. *The Story of the Book of Abraham: Mummies, Manuscripts, and Mormonism.* Salt Lake City, Utah: Deseret Book, 1995.

Peterson, Paul H. "An Historical Analysis of the Word of Wisdom." Master's thesis, Brigham Young University, 1972.

———. Review of *Inventing Mormonism: Tradition and the Historical Record,* by H. Michael Marquardt and Wesley P. Walters. In *BYU Studies* 35, no. 4 (1995–96): 209–27.

Peterson, Paul H., and Ronald W. Walker. "Brigham Young's Word of Wisdom Legacy." *BYU Studies* 42, no. 3–4 (2003): 29–64.

Peterson, Thomas Virgil. *Ham and Japheth: The Mythic World of Whites in the Antebellum South.* Metuchen, N.J.: Scarecrow Press and American Theological Library Association, 1975.

Petrey, Taylor. " 'Temple of the Modern World: An Old Testament Hermeneutic and the Latter-day Saints' or 'Christian Temple Builders: Judaizers of the Modern World.' " Unpublished paper. Archive of Restoration Culture. Joseph Fielding Smith Institute for Latter-day Saint History. Brigham Young University.

Phelps, William W. Collection of Missouri Documents, 1833–1837. Church Archives. The Church of Jesus Christ of Latter-day Saints. Salt Lake City, Utah.

———. "A Short History of W. W. Phelps' Stay in Missouri, 1864." Church Archives. The Church of Jesus Christ of Latter-day Saints. Salt Lake City, Utah.

Philadelphia, Pennsylvania Branch. Minutes and Records, 1840–1854. Library-Archives. The Community of Christ. Independence, Missouri.

Philip, Cynthia Owen, ed. *Imprisoned in America: Prison Communications, 1776 to Attica*. New York: Harper and Row, 1973.

Pitzer, Donald E., ed. *America's Communal Utopias*. Chapel Hill: University of North Carolina Press, 1997.

Plat of the City of Zion, June [24], 1833. Church Archives. The Church of Jesus Christ of Latter-day Saints. Salt Lake City, Utah.

Plato. *The Dialogues of Plato*. Trans. by B. Jowett. 2 vols. New York: Random House, 1937.

Poll, Richard D. "Joseph Smith and the Presidency, 1844." *Dialogue: A Journal of Mormon Thought* 3, no. 3 (1968): 17–21.

Popkin, Richard H. "The Rise and Fall of the Jewish Indian Theory." In *Menasseh Ben Israel and His World*, edited by Yosef Kaplan, Henry Mechoulan, and Richard H. Popkin, 63–82. Leiden: E. J. Brill, 1989.

Porter, Larry C. "Beginnings of the Restoration: Canada, an 'Effectual Door' to the British Isles." In *Truth Will Prevail: The Rise of the Church of Jesus Christ of Latter-day Saints in the British Isles, 1837–1987*, edited by V. Ben Bloxham, James R. Moss, and Larry C. Porter, 3–43. West Midlands, Eng.: The Church of Jesus Christ of Latter-day Saints, 1987.

———. "Brigham Young and the Twelve in Quincy: A Return to the Eye of the Missouri Storm, 26 April 1839." In *A City of Refuge: Quincy, Illinois*, edited by Susan Easton Black and Richard E. Bennett, 121–65. Salt Lake City, Utah: Millennial Press, 2000.

———. "The Colesville Branch and the Coming Forth of the Book of Mormon." *BYU Studies* 10, no. 3 (1970): 365–85.

———. "The Colesville Branch in Kaw Township, Jackson County, Missouri, 1831–1833." In *Religious Studies in Latter-day Saint Church History: Missouri*, edited by Arnold K. Garr and Clark V. Johnson, 281–311. Provo, Utah: Department of Church History and Doctrine, Brigham Young University, 1994.

———. "The Odyssey of William Earl McLellin: Man of Diversity, 1806–83." In *The Journals of William E. McLellin, 1831–1836*, edited by Jan Shipps and John W. Welch, 290–378. Provo, Utah: BYU Studies, Brigham Young University; Urbana: University of Illinois Press, 1994.

———. "Organizational Origins of the Church of Jesus Christ, 6 April 1830." In *Regional Studies in Latter-day Saint Church History: New York*, edited by Larry C. Porter, Milton V. Backman, and Susan Easton Black, 149–64. Provo, Utah: Department of Church History and Doctrine, Brigham Young University, 1992.

———. "The Restoration of the Aaronic and Melchizedek Priesthoods." *Ensign* 26 (Dec. 1996): 30–47.

———. "Reverend George Lane—Good 'Gifts,' Much 'Grace,' and Marked 'Usefulness.' " *BYU Studies* 9, no. 3 (1969): 321–40.

———. "Solomon Chamberlain—Early Missionary." *BYU Studies* 12, no. 3 (1972): 314–18.

———. "Solomon Chamberlain's Missing Pamphlet: Dreams, Visions, and Angelic Ministrants." *BYU Studies* 37, no. 2 (1997–98): 113–140.

———. *A Study of the Origins of the Church of Jesus Christ of Latter-day Saints in the States of New York and Pennsylvania, 1816–1831*. Ph.D. diss., Brigham Young University, 1971;

reprint, Provo, Utah: Joseph Fielding Smith Institute for LDS History and BYU Studies, 2000.

Porter, Larry C., and Jan Shipps, eds. "The Colesville, New York, 'Exodus' Seen from Two Documentary Perspectives." *New York History* 62 (1981): 201–11.

Porter, Larry C., Milton V. Backman, and Susan Easton Black, eds. *Regional Studies in Latter-day Saint Church History: New York.* Provo, Utah: Department of Church History and Doctrine, Brigham Young University, 1992.

Post, John D. *The Last Great Subsistence Crisis in the Western World.* Baltimore: Johns Hopkins University Press, 1977.

Post, Stephen. Journal. Stephen Post Papers, 1835–1921. Church Archives. The Church of Jesus Christ of Latter-day Saints. Salt Lake City, Utah.

Post, Stephen. *A Treatise on the Melchisedek Priesthood, and the Callings of God.* Council Bluffs, Iowa: Nonpareil Printing Co., 1872.

Poulsen, Richard C. "Fate and the Persecutors of Joseph Smith: Transmutations of an American Myth." *Dialogue: A Journal of Mormon Thought* 11, no. 4 (1978): 63–70.

Powell, Timothy B. *Ruthless Democracy: A Multicultural Interpretation of the American Renaissance.* Princeton, N.J.: Princeton University Press, 2000.

Pratt, Orson. *A[n] Interesting Account of Several Remarkable Visions, and of the Late Discovery of Ancient American Records.* Edinburgh, Scot.: Ballantyne and Hughes, 1840.

———. *The Orson Pratt Journals.* Edited by Eldon J. Watson. Salt Lake City, Utah: Eldon Jay Watson, 1975.

———. Statement, July 14, 1842. Church Archives. The Church of Jesus Christ of Latter-day Saints. Salt Lake City, Utah.

Pratt, Parley P. *The Autobiography of Parley Parker Pratt.* Edited by Parley P. Pratt Jr. New York: Russell Brothers, 1874.

———. Correspondence, 1842–1855. Church Archives. The Church of Jesus Christ of Latter-day Saints. Salt Lake City, Utah.

———. *History of the Late Persecution Inflicted by the State of Missouri upon the Mormons.* Detroit: Dawson and Bates, 1839.

———. *A Voice of Warning and Instruction to All People: Containing a Declaration of the Faith and Doctrine of the Church of the Latter Day Saints, Commonly called the Mormons.* New York: W. Sandford, 1837.

Pred, Allan L. *Spatial Dynamics of U.S. Urban-Industrial Growth, 1800–1914: Interpretive and Theoretical Essays.* Cambridge: MIT Press, 1966.

Price, Richard, and Joseph Priestley. *A Free Discussion of the Doctrines of Materialism and Philosophical Necessity.* London: J. Johnson and T. Cadell, 1778.

Price, Robert M. "Prophecy and Palimpsest." *Dialogue: A Journal of Mormon Thought* 35, no. 3 (2002): 67–82.

Priest, Josiah. *The Wonders of Nature and Providence, Displayed.* Albany, N.Y.: Josiah Priest, 1825.

Prince, Gregory A. *Power from On High: The Development of Mormon Priesthood.* Salt Lake City, Utah: Signature Books, 1995.

Proper, David R. "Joseph Smith and Salem." *Essex Institute Historical Collections* 100 (April 1964): 88–97.

Pykles, Benjamin C. " 'Look Well to the West!': Anti-Mormon Rhetoric and Nineteenth-Century Views of the American West." Unpublished paper. Archive of Restoration Culture. Joseph Fielding Smith Institute for Latter-day Saint History. Brigham Young University.

Quincy, Josiah. *Figures of the Past: From the Leaves of Old Journals.* Boston: Roberts Brothers, 1883.

Quinn, D. Michael. "The Council of Fifty and Its Members, 1844 to 1945." *BYU Studies* 20, no. 2 (1980): 163–97.

———. *Early Mormonism and the Magic World View.* 2d ed., rev. Salt Lake City, Utah: Signature Books, 1998.

———. "From Sacred Grove to Sacral Power Structure." *Dialogue: A Journal of Mormon Thought* 17, no. 2 (1984): 9–34.

———. "Jesse Gause: Joseph Smith's Little-Known Counselor." *BYU Studies* 23, no. 4 (1983): 487–93.

———. "Latter-day Saint Prayer Circles." *BYU Studies* 19, no. 1 (1978): 79–105.

———. *The Mormon Hierarchy: Extensions of Power.* Salt Lake City, Utah: Signature Books in association with Smith Research Associates, 1997.

———. *The Mormon Hierarchy: Origins of Power.* Salt Lake City, Utah: Signature Books in association with Smith Research Associates, 1994.

———. "The Mormon Succession Crises of 1844." *BYU Studies* 16, no. 2 (1976): 187–233.

———. "Mormon Women Have Had the Priesthood Since 1843." In *Women and Authority: Re-emerging Mormon Feminism,* edited by Maxine Hanks, 365–409. Salt Lake City, Utah: Signature Books, 1992.

———. "National Culture, Personality, and Theocracy in the Early Mormon Culture of Violence." In *John Whitmer Historical Association Journal,* Nauvoo Conference Special Edition (2002), 159–86.

———. "Organizational Development and Social Origins of the Mormon Hierarchy, 1832–1932: A Prosopographical Study." Master's thesis, University of Utah, 1973.

———. "The Practice of Rebaptism at Nauvoo." *BYU Studies* 18, no. 2 (1978): 226–32.

———. *Same-Sex Dynamics Among Nineteenth-Century Americans: A Mormon Example.* Urbana: University of Illinois Press, 1996.

Quist, John. "John E. Page: An Apostle of Uncertainty." *Journal of Mormon History* 12 (1985): 53–68.

Quorum of the Twelve Apostles. Minutes, 1841–1846. Church Archives. The Church of Jesus Christ of Latter-day Saints. Salt Lake City, Utah.

Raboteau, Albert J. *Slave Religion: The "Invisible Institution" in the Antebellum South.* New York: Oxford University Press, 1978.

Radke, Andrea G. "We Also Marched: The Women and Children of Zion's Camp, 1834." *BYU Studies* 39, no. 1 (2000): 147–65.

Ravitzky, Aviezer. "The Messianism of Success in Contemporary Judaism." In *The Encyclopedia of Apocalypticism,* edited by Bernard McGinn, John J. Collins, and Stephen J. Stein, 3 vols., 3:204–29. New York: Continuum, 1998.

Rawlyk, George A. *The Canada Fire: Radical Evangelicalism in British North America, 1775–1812.* Kingston, Ont.: McGill–Queen's University Press, 1994.

"Recollections of the Prophet Joseph Smith." *Juvenile Instructor* 27 (May 15, 1892): 302–304.

Redle, M. J. "Beatific Vision." In *New Catholic Encyclopedia,* 15 vols., 2:186–93. New York: McGraw-Hill, 1967.

Rees, Robert A. "Joseph Smith, the Book of Mormon, and the American Renaissance." *Dialogue: A Journal of Mormon Thought* 35, no. 3 (2002): 83–112.

Remini, Robert V. *Henry Clay: Statesman for the Union.* New York: W. W. Norton, 1991.

———. *Joseph Smith.* New York: Viking, 2002.

Reps, John W. *The Making of Urban America: A History of City Planning in the United States.* Princeton, N.J.: Princeton University Press, 1965.

Revelations Collection, ca. 1831–1876. Church Archives. The Church of Jesus Christ of Latter-day Saints. Salt Lake City, Utah.

Reynolds, David S. *Faith in Fiction: The Emergence of Religious Literature in America.* Cambridge: Harvard University Press, 1981.

Reynolds, John. *My Own Times, Embracing Also, the History of My Life.* Belleville, Ill.: Perryman and Davison, 1855.

Reynolds, Noel B. "The Authorship Debate Concerning *Lectures on Faith:* Exhumation and

Reburial." In *The Disciple as Witness: Essays on Latter-day Saint History and Doctrine in Honor of Richard Lloyd Anderson*, edited by Stephen D. Ricks, Donald W. Parry, and Andrew H. Hedges, 355–82. Provo, Utah: FARMS, Brigham Young University, 2000.

———. *Book of Mormon Authorship*. Provo, Utah: Religious Studies Center, Brigham Young University, 1982.

———. *Book of Mormon Authorship Revisited: The Evidence for Ancient Origins*. Provo, Utah: FARMS, 1997.

Rhodes, Michael Dennis. "A Translation and Commentary of the Joseph Smith Hypocephalus." *BYU Studies* 17, no. 3 (1977): 259–74.

Rich, Russell R. "The Dogberry Papers and the Book of Mormon." *BYU Studies* 10, no. 3 (1970): 315–20.

Richards, Levi. Diaries, 1840–1843. Church Archives. The Church of Jesus Christ of Latter-day Saints. Salt Lake City, Utah.

Richards, Willard. Journals, 1836–1853. Church Archives. The Church of Jesus Christ of Latter-day Saints. Salt Lake City, Utah.

———. Papers, 1821–1854. Church Archives. The Church of Jesus Christ of Latter-day Saints. Salt Lake City, Utah.

Richardson, Ralph D. *Emerson: The Mind on Fire—A Biography*. Berkeley: University of California Press, 1995.

Richey, Russell E. *Early American Methodism*. Bloomington: Indiana University Press, 1991.

Ricks, Stephen D. "The Appearance of Elijah and Moses in the Kirtland Temple and the Jewish Passover." *BYU Studies* 23, no. 4 (1983): 483–86.

———. "Kingship, Coronation, and Covenant in Mosiah 1–6." In *King Benjamin's Speech: "That Ye May Learn Wisdom,"* edited by John W. Welch and Stephen D. Ricks, 233–75. Provo, Utah: FARMS, 1998.

Ricks, Stephen D., and John W. Welch, eds. *The Allegory of the Olive Tree: The Olive, the Bible, and Jacob 5*. Provo: FARMS, 1994.

Ricks, Stephen D., and William J. Hamblin, eds. *Warfare in the Book of Mormon*. Salt Lake City, Utah: Deseret Book; Provo, Utah: FARMS, 1990.

Rigdon, John W. " 'I Never Knew a Time When I Did Not Know Joseph Smith': A Son's Record of the Life and Testimony of Sidney Rigdon." Edited by Karl Keller. *Dialogue: A Journal of Mormon Thought* 1, no. 4 (1966): 15–42.

Rigdon, Sidney. *An Appeal to the American People: Being an Account of the Persecution of the Church of Latter Day Saints*. 2d ed., rev. Cincinnati: Shepard and Stearns, 1840.

———. Letter to Sterling Price, September 8, 1838. Church Archives. The Church of Jesus Christ of Latter-day Saints. Salt Lake City, Utah.

———. *Oration Delivered by Mr. S. Rigdon, on the 4th of July, 1838, at Far West, Caldwell County, Missouri*. Far West, Mo.: Journal Office, 1838.

Ripley, Alanson. Statement, ca. 1845. Historian's Office. Church Archives. The Church of Jesus Christ of Latter-day Saints. Salt Lake City, Utah.

Ripley, George. *Discourses on the Philosophy of Religion, Addressed to Doubters who Wish to Believe*. Boston: J. Munroe, 1836.

Ritner, Robert K. "The Breathing Permit of Hôr Among the Joseph Smith Papyri." *Journal of Near Eastern Studies* 62, no. 3 (2003): 161–80.

———. "The 'Breathing Permit of Hôr' Thirty-four Years Later." *Dialogue: A Journal of Mormon Thought* 33, no. 4 (2000): 97–119.

Roberts, Brigham H. *A Comprehensive History of the Church of Jesus Christ of Latter-day Saints*. 6 vols. Salt Lake City, Utah: Deseret News, 1930.

———. *The Life of John Taylor, Third President of the Church of Jesus Christ of Latter-day Saints*. Salt Lake City, Utah: George Q. Cannon and Sons, 1892.

Robertson, Margaret C. "The Campaign and the Kingdom: The Activities of the Electioneers in Joseph Smith's Presidential Campaign." *BYU Studies* 39, no. 3 (2000): 147–80.

Robinson, Joseph Lee. Autobiography and Journals, 1883–1892. Church Archives. The Church of Jesus Christ of Latter-day Saints. Salt Lake City, Utah.

Robison, Elwin C. *The First Mormon Temple: Design, Construction, and Historic Context of the Kirtland Temple*. Provo, Utah: Brigham Young University Press, 1997.

Rockwood, Albert Perry. "The Last Months of Mormonism in Missouri: The Albert Perry Rockwood Journal." Edited by Dean C. Jessee and David J. Whittaker. *BYU Studies* 28, no. 1 (1988): 5–41.

Rollins, James Henry. Reminiscences, 1896. Church Archives. The Church of Jesus Christ of Latter-day Saints. Salt Lake City, Utah.

Romig, Ronald E. "David Whitmer: Faithful Dissenter, Witness Apart." In *Differing Visions: Dissenters in Mormon History*, edited by Roger D. Launius and Linda Thatcher, 23–44. Urbana: University of Illinois Press, 1994.

———. *Early Jackson County, Missouri: The "Mormon" Settlement on the Big Blue River.* Independence, Mo.: Missouri Mormon Frontier Foundation, 1996.

———. "The Lamanite Mission." *John Whitmer Historical Association Journal* 14 (1994): 24–33.

———. "The Temple Lot Suit After 100 Years." *John Whitmer Historical Association Journal* 12 (1992): 3–15.

Romig, Ronald E., and John H. Siebert. "Contours of the Kingdom: An RLDS Perspective on the Legions of Zion." *Restoration Studies* 5 (1993): 25–40.

———. "First Impressions: The Independence, Missouri, Printing Operation, 1832–33." *John Whitmer Historical Association Journal* 10 (1990): 51–66.

———. "The Genesis of Zion and Kirtland and the Concept of Temples." *Restoration Studies* 4 (1988): 99–123.

———. "Jackson County, 1831–1833: A Look at the Development of Zion." *Restoration Studies* 3 (1986): 286–304.

Rorabaugh, W. J. *The Alcoholic Republic: An American Tradition.* New York: Oxford University Press, 1979.

Rose, William Ganson. *Cleveland: The Making of a City.* 2nd ed. Kent, Ohio: Kent State University Press in cooperation with Western Reserve Historical Society, 1990.

Rosenberg, Charles E. *The Cholera Years: The United States in 1832, 1849, and 1866.* Chicago: University of Chicago Press, 1962.

Ross, Dorothy. "Historical Consciousness in Nineteenth-Century America." *American Historical Review* 89, no. 4 (1984): 909–28.

Rough Draft Notes, ca. 1842–54. Manuscript History of the Church. Historian's Office. Church Archives. The Church of Jesus Christ of Latter-day Saints. Salt Lake City, Utah.

Rowe, David L. "The Millerites: A Shadow Portrait." In *The Disappointed: Millerism and Millenarianism in the Nineteenth Century*, edited by Ronald L. Numbers and Jonathan M. Butler, 1–16. Bloomington: Indiana University Press, 1987.

Rowley, Dennis. "The Ezra Booth Letters." *Dialogue: A Journal of Mormon Thought* 16, no. 3 (1983): 133–37.

———. "The Mormon Experience in the Wisconsin Pineries, 1841–1845." *BYU Studies* 32, no. 1–2 (1992): 119–48.

———. "Nauvoo: A River Town." *BYU Studies* 18, no. 2 (1978): 255–72.

Rugh, Susan Sessions. *Our Common Country: Family Farming, Culture, and Community in the Nineteenth-Century Midwest.* Bloomington: Indiana University Press, 2001.

Rust, Richard Dilworth. *Feasting on the Word: The Literary Testimony of the Book of Mormon.* Salt Lake City, Utah: Deseret Book; Provo, Utah: FARMS, 1997.

Salmon, Douglas F. "Parallelomania and the Study of Latter-day Saint Scripture: Confirmation, Coincidence, or the Collective Unconscious?" *Dialogue: A Journal of Mormon Thought* 33, no. 2 (2000): 129–56.

Sampson, D. Paul, and Larry T. Wimmer. "The Kirtland Safety Society: The Stock Ledger Book and the Bank Failure." *BYU Studies* 12, no. 4 (1972): 427–36.

Sandberg, Karl. "Knowing Brother Joseph Again: The Book of Abraham and Joseph Smith as Translator." In *The Prophet Puzzle: Interpretive Essays on Joseph Smith*, edited by Bryan Waterman, 319–46. Salt Lake City, Utah: Signature Books, 1999.

Sandeen, Ernest R. *The Roots of Fundamentalism: British and American Millenarianism, 1800–1930*. Chicago: University of Chicago Press, 1970.

Sanders, Daniel Clarke. *A History of the Indian Wars with the First Settlers of the United States to the Commencement of the Late War; Together with an Appendix, Not before Added to this History, Containing Interesting Accounts of the Battles Fought by Gen. Andrew Jackson*. Rochester, N.Y.: Edwin Scrantom, 1828.

Saum, Lewis O. *The Popular Mood of Pre–Civil War America*. Westport, Conn.: Greenwood Press, 1980.

Schaff, Philip. *The Creeds of Christendom*. 6th ed., rev. and enl. Grand Rapids, Mich.: Baker Book House, 1966.

Schindler, Harold. *Orrin Porter Rockwell: Man of God, Son of Thunder*. 2d ed., rev. Salt Lake City: University of Utah Press, 1983.

Schlesinger, Arthur M. *Orestes A. Brownson: A Pilgrim's Progress*. Boston: Little, Brown, 1939.

Schmidt, Leigh Eric. *Holy Fairs: Scottish Communions and American Revivals in the Early Modern Period*. Princeton, N.J.: Princeton University Press, 1989.

Scholem, Gershom. *Kabbalah*. New York: New American Library, 1974.

School of the Prophets. Salt Lake City Meetings. Minutes, 1867–1872, 1883. Church Archives. The Church of Jesus Christ of Latter-day Saints. Salt Lake City, Utah.

Schulz, Max F. *Paradise Preserved: Recreations of Eden in Eighteenth- and Nineteenth-Century England*. Cambridge: Cambridge University Press, 1985.

Schützinger, C. E. "Light." *New Catholic Encyclopedia*. 15 vols., 8:747–50. New York: McGraw-Hill, 1967.

Seale, William. *The President's House: A History*. 2 vols. Washington, D.C.: White House Historical Association, with the cooperation of the National Geographic Society, 1986.

Selected Collections of the Archives of the Church of Jesus Christ of Latter-day Saints. 2 vols. Provo, Utah: Brigham Young University Press, 2002.

Sellers, Charles. "Election of 1844." In *History of American Presidential Elections, 1789–1968*, edited by Arthur M. Schlesinger, 4 vols., 1:747–861. New York: Chelsea Publishers, in association with McGraw-Hill, 1971.

Sellers, Charles L. "Early Mormon Community Planning." *Journal of the American Institute of Planners* 28, no. 1 (1962): 24–30.

The Sense of the United Non-conforming Ministers. London, 1693.

Shaw, P. E. *The Catholic Apostolic Church, Sometimes Called Irvingite: A Historical Study*. Morningside Heights, N.Y.: King's Crown Press, 1946.

Shaw, Ronald E. *Erie Water West: A History of the Erie Canal, 1792–1854*. Lexington: University of Kentucky Press, 1966.

Shields, Steven L. "The Latter Day Saint Churches." In *America's Alternative Religions*, edited by Timothy Miller, 47–59. Albany: State University of New York Press, 1995.

Shipps, Jan. "A Little Known Account of the Murders of Joseph and Hyrum Smith." *BYU Studies* 14, no. 3 (1974): 389–92.

———. *Mormonism: The Story of a New Religious Tradition*. Urbana: University of Illinois Press, 1985.

———. "The Prophet Puzzle: Suggestions Leading Toward a More Comprehensive Interpretation of Joseph Smith." *Journal of Mormon History* 1 (1974): 3–20.

———. *Sojourner in the Promised Land: Forty Years Among the Mormons*. Urbana: University of Illinois Press, 2000.

Shurtliff, Luman Andros. Autobiography. Church Archives. The Church of Jesus Christ of Latter-day Saints. Salt Lake City, Utah.

———. "Biographical Sketch of the Life of Luman Andros Shurtliff." L. Tom Perry Special Collections. Harold B. Lee Library. Brigham Young University.

Silverman, Kenneth. *Timothy Dwight*. New York: Twayne, 1969.

Simms, P. Marion. *The Bible in America: Versions That Have Played Their Part in the Making of the Republic*. New York: Wilson-Erickson, 1936.

Sixth Census or Enumeration of the Inhabitants of the United States, as Corrected at the Department of State, in 1840. Washington, D.C.: Blair and Rives, 1841.

Skinner, Andrew C. "Joseph C. Bennett: For Prophet or Profit?" In *Regional Studies in Latter-day Saint Church History: Illinois*, edited by H. Dean Garrett, 249–65. Provo, Utah: Department of Church History and Doctrine, Brigham Young University, 1995.

Skousen, Royal. "Critical Methodology and the Text of the Book of Mormon." *Review of Books on the Book of Mormon* 6, no. 1 (1994): 121–44.

———. "Translating the Book of Mormon: Evidence from the Original Manuscript." In *Book of Mormon Authorship Revisited: The Evidence for Ancient Origins*, edited by Noel B. Reynolds, 61–93. Provo, Utah: FARMS, 1997.

———, ed. *The Original Manuscript of the Book of Mormon: Typographical Facsimile of the Extant Text*. Provo: FARMS, Brigham Young University, 2001.

———. *The Printer's Manuscript of the Book of Mormon: Typographical Facsimile of the Entire Text in Two Parts*. Provo, Utah: FARMS, Brigham Young University, 2001.

Smith, Andrew F. "John Cook Bennett's Nauvoo." In *John Whitmer Historical Association Journal*, Nauvoo Conference Special Edition (2002), 111–18.

———. "Introduction." In *The History of the Saints; Or, An Exposé of Joe Smith and Mormonism*, by John Cook Bennett, vii–xliii. 3rd ed. Urbana: University of Illinois Press, 2000.

———. *The Saintly Scoundrel: The Life and Times of Dr. John Cook Bennett*. Urbana: University of Illinois Press, 1997.

Smith, Elias. *The Life, Conversion, Preaching, Travels, and Sufferings of Elias Smith*. Portsmouth, N.H.: Beck and Foster, 1816.

Smith, Ethan. *View of the Hebrews: Or the Tribes of Israel in America*. 2d ed., enl. Poultney, Vt.: Smith and Shute, 1825.

Smith, George Albert. "History of George Albert Smith by Himself." George A. Smith Papers. Church Archives. The Church of Jesus Christ of Latter-day Saints. Salt Lake City, Utah.

———. Memoirs, 1817–1847. George A. Smith Papers. Church Archives. The Church of Jesus Christ of Latter-day Saints. Salt Lake City, Utah.

Smith, George D. " 'Is There Any Way to Escape These Difficulties?': The Book of Mormon Studies of B. H. Roberts." *Dialogue: A Journal of Mormon Thought* 17, no. 2 (1984): 94–111.

———. "Nauvoo Roots of Mormon Polygamy, 1841–46: A Preliminary Demographic Report." *Dialogue: A Journal of Mormon Thought* 27, no. 1 (1994), 1–72.

Smith, Hyrum. Diary and Accounts, 1831–1844. Church Archives. The Church of Jesus Christ of Latter-day Saints. Salt Lake City, Utah.

———. Diary, 1839–1840. Church Archives. The Church of Jesus Christ of Latter-day Saints. Salt Lake City, Utah.

Smith, James Morton. "The Grass Roots Origins of the Kentucky Resolutions." *William and Mary Quarterly*, 3rd ser., 27, no. 3 (1970): 221–45.

Smith, John. Diary, 1831–32. Church Archives, The Church of Jesus Christ of Latter-day Saints. Salt Lake City, Utah.

———. Journal, 1833–1841. Church Archives. The Church of Jesus Christ of Latter-day Saints. Salt Lake City, Utah.

———. Natural Philosophy Lectures. Dartmouth College. Dartmouth College Library. Hanover, New Hampshire.

Smith, Joseph Jr. Blessing to Sarah Ann Whitney. March 3, 1843. Church Archives. The Church of Jesus Christ of Latter-day Saints. Salt Lake City, Utah.

———. *General Joseph Smith's Appeal to the Green Mountain Boys*. Nauvoo: Taylor and Woodruff, 1843.

————. *General Smith's Views of the Power and Policy of the Government of the United States.* Nauvoo: John Taylor, 1844.

————. Indenture to Ebenezer Robinson. Jan. 23, 1844. Frederick M. Smith Library. Graceland University. Lamoni, Iowa.

————. *The Prophet Joseph Smith's King Follett Discourse: A Six-Column Comparison of Original Notes and Amalgamations with Introduction and Commentary,* edited by Donald Q. Cannon and Larry E. Dahl. Provo, Utah: BYU Printing Service, 1983.

————, trans. *Joseph Smith's New Translation of the Bible: Original Manuscripts.* Edited by Scott H. Faulring, Kent P. Jackson, and Robert J. Matthews. Provo, Utah: Religious Studies Center, Brigham Young University, 2004.

Smith, Joseph Fielding. "Asahel Smith of Topsfield, with Some Account of the Smith Family." *Topsfield Historical Society Historical Collections* 8 (1902): 87–101.

————. *Blood Atonement and the Origin of Plural Marriage: A Discussion.* Salt Lake City, Utah: Deseret News, 1905.

Smith, Lucy Mack. *Lucy's Book: A Critical Edition of Luck Mack Smith's Family Memoir.* Edited by Lavina Fielding Anderson. Salt Lake City, Utah: Signature Books, 2001.

Smith, Mary Fielding. Collection, ca. 1832–1848. Church Archives. The Church of Jesus Christ of Latter-day Saints. Salt Lake City, Utah.

Smith, Robert F. "Weights and Measures in the Time of Mosiah II." Provo, Utah: FARMS, 1983.

Smith, Samuel. Diary, 1831–1833. Church Archives. The Church of Jesus Christ of Latter-day Saints. Salt Lake City, Utah.

Smith, Timothy L. "The Book of Mormon in a Biblical Culture." *Journal of Mormon History* 7 (1980): 3–21.

Smith, William. *William Smith on Mormonism: A True Account of the Origin of the Book of Mormon.* Lamoni, Iowa: Herald Stream Book and Job Office, 1883.

Snow, Eliza R. *Biography and Family Record of Lorenzo Snow.* Salt Lake City, Utah: Deseret News Company, 1884.

————. "Eliza R. Snow Letter from Missouri." *BYU Studies* 13, no. 4 (1973): 544–52.

————. *The Personal Writings of Eliza Roxcy Snow.* Edited by Maureen Ursenbach Beecher. Logan: Utah State University Press, 2000.

Snow, Erastus, and Benjamin Winchester. *An Address to the Citizens of Salem and Vicinity.* [Salem, Mass.:] Observer Press, [1841].

Snow, Lorenzo. Journal and Letterbook, 1836–1845. Church Archives. The Church of Jesus Christ of Latter-day Saints. Salt Lake City, Utah.

Sorenson, John L. *An Ancient American Setting for the Book of Mormon.* Salt Lake City, Utah: Deseret Book; Provo, Utah: FARMS, 1985.

————. "The Book of Mormon as a Mesoamerican Record." In *Book of Mormon Authorship Revisited: The Evidence for Ancient Origins,* edited by Noel B. Reynolds, 391–521. Provo, Utah: FARMS, 1997.

————. "Digging into the Book of Mormon: Our Changing Understanding of Ancient America and Its Scripture." *Ensign* 14 (September 1984): 26–37; 14 (October 1984): 12–13.

————. *Mormon's Map.* Provo, Utah: FARMS, 2002.

————. *Nephite Culture and Society: Collected Papers.* Salt Lake City, Utah: New Sage Books, 1997.

————. *Pre-Columbian Contact with the Americas Across the Oceans: An Annotated Bibliography.* 2 vols. Provo, Utah: Research Press, 1990.

Sorensen, Steven R. "Schools of the Prophets." In *Encyclopedia of Mormonism,* edited by Daniel H. Ludlow, 5 vols., 3:1269–70. New York: Macmillan, 1992.

Spafford, Horatio Gates. *A Gazeteer of the State of New-York.* Albany, N.Y.: H. C. Southwick, 1813.

————. *A Gazeteer of the State of New-York.* Albany, N.Y.: B. D. Packard, 1824.

Spaulding, Solomon. *Manuscript Found: The Complete Original "Spaulding Manuscript."* Edited by Kent P. Jackson. Provo, Utah: Religious Studies Center, Brigham Young University, 1996.

Sperry, Sidney B. *Doctrine and Covenants Compendium*. Salt Lake City, Utah: Bookcraft, 1960.

Spierenburg, Pieter, ed. *Men and Violence: Gender, Honor, and Rituals in Modern Europe and America*. Columbus: Ohio State University Press, 1998.

Staker, Susan. "Secret Things, Hidden Things: The Seer Story in the Imaginative Economy of Joseph Smith." In *American Apocrypha: Essays on the Book of Mormon*, edited by Dan Vogel and Brent Lee Metcalfe, 235–74. Salt Lake City, Utah: Signature Books, 2002.

Stauffer, John. *The Black Hearts of Men: Radical Abolitionists and the Transformation of Race*. Cambridge: Harvard University Press, 2002.

Stearns, Norris. *The Religious Experience of Norris Stearns, Written by Divine Command, Shewing the Marvellous Dealings of God to His Soul, and the Miraculous Manner in Which He Was Delivered from the Jaws of Death and Hell; and His Soul Set at Liberty,—Likewise His Appointment to the Ministry; and Commision from on High, to Preach the Gospel to Every Creature*. Greenfield, Mass.: By the author, 1815.

Stein, Stephen J. "Apocalypticism Outside the Mainstream in the United States." In *The Encyclopedia of Apocalypticism*, edited by Bernard McGinn, John J. Collins, and Stephen J. Stein, 3 vols., 3:108–39. New York: Continuum, 1993.

———. *The Shaker Experience in America: A History of the United Society of Believers*. New Haven, Conn.: Yale University Press, 1992.

———. "Signs of the Times: The Theological Foundations of Early Mormon Apocalyptic." *Sunstone* 8, nos. 1–2 (1983): 59–65.

Steiner, George. *Real Presences*. Chicago: University of Chicago Press, 1989.

Stendahl, Krister. "The Sermon on the Mount and Third Nephi." In *Reflections on Mormonism: Judaeo-Christian Parallels*, edited by Truman G. Madsen, 139–54. Provo, Utah: Religious Studies Center, Brigham Young University, 1978.

Stengel, Marc K. "The Diffusionists Have Landed." *Atlantic Monthly* 285 (January 2000): 35–39, 42–44, 46–48.

Stephen, Michele. "Self, the Sacred Other, and Autonomous Imagination." In *Religious Imagination in New Guinea*, edited by Gilbert Herdt and Michele Stephen. New Brunswick, N.J.: Rutgers University Press, 1989.

Stevens, Albert C. *The Cyclopoedia of Fraternities*. 2d ed., rev. New York: E. B. Treat, 1907.

Stevenson, Edward. *Reminiscences of Joseph, the Prophet, and the Coming Forth of the Book of Mormon*. Salt Lake City: By the author, 1893.

Stewart, Frank Henderson. *Honor*. Chicago: University of Chicago Press, 1994.

Stewart, John Struthers. *History of Northeastern Ohio*. 3 vols. Indianapolis, Ind.: Historical Publishing Company, 1935.

Stewart, Philemon. *A Holy, Sacred and Divine Roll and Book*. Canterbury, N.H.: Printed in the United Society, 1843.

Stilwell, Lewis D. *Migration from Vermont*. Montpelier, Vt.: Vermont Historical Society, 1948.

Stone, Michael E. "Esdras, Second Book of." In *Anchor Bible Dictionary*, edited by David Noel Freedman, 6 vols., 2:609–14. New York: Doubleday, 1992.

Stone, William L. *Matthias and His Impostures: Or, the Progress of Fanaticism*. 3d ed. New York: Harper & Brothers, 1835.

Stout, Hosea. *On the Mormon Frontier: The Diary of Hosea Stout, 1844–1861*. Edited by Juanita Brooks. 2 vols. Salt Lake City: University of Utah Press and Utah State Historical Society, 1964.

Strachan, C. Gordon. *The Pentecostal Theology of Edward Irving*. London: Darton, Longman & Todd, 1973.

Sunderland, La Roy. *Mormonism Exposed and Refuted*. New York: Piercy and Reed, 1838.

Swartzell, William. *Mormonism Exposed: Being a Journal of a Residence in Missouri from the 28th day of May to the 20th of August, 1838*. Pekin, Ohio: By the author, 1840.

Talbot, Wilburn D. "Zion's Camp." Master's thesis, Brigham Young University, 1973.

Tanner, Jerald, and Sandra Tanner. *Joseph Smith's 1826 Trial*. Salt Lake City, Utah: Modern Microfilm, 1971.

———. *Joseph Smith and Money Digging*. Salt Lake City, Utah: Modern Microfilm, 1970.

Tanner, John S. "Making a Mormon of Milton." *BYU Studies* 24, no. 2 (1984): 191–206.

Tanner, Martin S. "Is There Anti-Universalist Rhetoric in the Book of Mormon." *Review of Books on the Book of Mormon* 6, no. 1 (1994): 418–33.

Taves, Ann. *Fits, Trances, and Visions: Experiencing Religion and Explaining Experience from Wesley to James*. Princeton, N.J.: Princeton University Press, 1999.

Taylor, Alan. "Rediscovering the Context of Joseph Smith's Treasure Seeking." *Dialogue: A Journal of Mormon Thought* 19, no. 4 (1986): 18–28.

———. *William Cooper's Town: Power and Persuasion on the Frontier of the Early American Republic*. New York: Alfred A. Knopf, 1995.

Taylor, John. "The John Taylor Nauvoo Journal, January 1845–September 1845." Edited by Dean C. Jessee. *BYU Studies* 23, no. 3 (1983): 1–105.

———. *A Short Account of the Murders, Roberies, Burnings, Thefts, and Other Outrages Committed by the Mob and Militia of the State of Missouri, upon the Latter Day Saints*. Springfield, Ill.: 1839.

———. Statement, 1855. Historian's Office. Church Archives. The Church of Jesus Christ of Latter-day Saints. Salt Lake City, Utah.

Taylor, Philip A. M. *Expectations Westward: The Mormons and the Emigration of Their British Converts in the Nineteenth Century*. Ithaca, N.Y.: Cornell University Press, 1966.

Thomas, Keith. *Religion and the Decline of Magic: Studies in Popular Beliefs in Sixteenth and Seventeenth Century England*. New York: Oxford University Press, 1971.

Thomas, Mark D. *Digging in Cumorah: Reclaiming Book of Mormon Narratives*. Salt Lake City, Utah: Signature Books, 2000.

———. "Form Criticism of Joseph Smith's 1823 Vision of the Angel Moroni." *Dialogue: A Journal of Mormon Thought* 35, no. 3 (2002): 145–60.

Thomas, Robert David. *"With Bleeding Footsteps": Mary Baker Eddy's Path to Religious Leadership*. New York: Alfred A. Knopf, 1994.

Thompson, John Samuel. *The Christian Guide to a Right Understanding of the Sacred Scriptures, Designed as a Select Commentary on the Four Evangelists*. Utica, N.Y.: A. G. Danby, 1826.

Thompson, Stephen E. "Egyptology and the Book of Abraham." *Dialogue: A Journal of Mormon Thought* 28, no. 1 (1995): 143–60.

Thompson, Warren S., and P. K. Whelpton. *Population Trends in the United States*. New York: McGraw-Hill, 1933.

Thorp, Malcolm R. "Early Mormon Confrontations with Sectarianism, 1837–40." In *Mormons in Early Victorian Britain*, edited by Richard L. Jensen and Malcolm R. Thorp, 49–69. Salt Lake City: University of Utah Press, 1989.

———. " 'The Field Is White Already to Harvest.' " In *Men with a Mission, 1837–1841: The Quorum of the Twelve Apostles in the British Isles*, edited by James B. Allen, Ronald K. Esplin, and David J. Whittaker, 323–44. Salt Lake City, Utah: Deseret Book, 1992.

Thurston, Herbert. "Washing of Feet and Hands." In *The Catholic Encyclopedia*, edited by Charles G. Herbermann and others, 15 vols., 15:557–58. New York: Robert Appleton, 1907–12.

Tindal, Matthew. *Christianity as Old as the Creation: Or, the Gospel, a Republication of the Religion of Nature*. Newburgh, N.Y.: David Denniston, 1798.

Tocqueville, Alexis de. *Democracy in America*. Edited by J. P. Mayer, and translated by George Lawrence. Garden City, N.Y.: Doubleday, 1966.

Todd, Jay M. *The Saga of the Book of Abraham*. Salt Lake City, Utah: Deseret Book, 1969.

Towle, Nancy F. *Vicissitudes Illustrated, in the Experience of Nancy Towle, in Europe and America.* Charleston, S.C.: James L. Burges, 1832.

Trial of the Commonwealth, versus Origen Bacheler, for a Libel on the Character of George B. Beals, Deceased, at the Municipal Court, Boston, March Term, A. D. 1829. Boston: John H. Belcher, 1829.

Trollope, Frances. *Domestic Manners of the Americans,* 2 vols., 2d. ed. London: Whittaker, Treacher, 1832.

Trumbower, Jeffrey A. *Rescue for the Dead: The Posthumous Salvation of Non-Christians in Early Christianity.* New York: Oxford University Press, 2001.

Tucker, Pomeroy. *Origin, Rise, and Progress of Mormonism.* New York: D. Appleton, 1867.

Tullidge, Edward W. *The Women of Mormondom.* New York: Tullidge and Crandall, 1877.

Turner, James. *Without God, Without Creed: The Origins of Unbelief in America.* Baltimore: Johns Hopkins University Press, 1985.

Turner, Jonathan Baldwin. *Mormonism in All Ages: Or, the Rise, Progress, and Causes of Mormonism.* New York: Platt and Peters; London: Willey and Putnam, 1842.

Turner, Orsamus. *History of the Pioneer Settlement of Phelps and Gorham's Purchase, and Morris' Reserve.* Rochester, N.Y.: William Alling, 1851.

Tuttle, Daniel S. "Mormons." In *A Religious Encyclopaedia: Or, Dictionary of Biblical, Historical, Doctrinal, and Practical Theology,* edited by Philip Schaff, 3 vols., 2:1575–81. New York: Funk and Wagnalls, 1882–83.

Tuveson, Ernest Lee. *Redeemer Nation: The Ideal of America's Millennialism.* Chicago: University of Chicago Press, 1968.

Tvedtnes, John A. "King Benjamin and the Feast of Tabernacles." In *By Study and Also By Faith: Essays in Honor of Hugh W. Nibley . . . ,* edited by John M. Lundquist and Stephen D. Ricks, 2 vols., 197–237. Salt Lake City, Utah: Deseret Book; Provo, Utah: FARMS, 1990.

Tvedtnes, John A., Brian M. Hauglid, and John Gee, comps. and eds. *Traditions About the Life of Abraham.* Provo, Utah: FARMS, 2001.

Tyler, Alice Felt. *Freedom's Ferment: Phases of American Social History from the Colonial Period to the Outbreak of the Civil War.* New York: Harper and Row, 1962.

Underwood, Grant. *The Millenarian World of Early Mormonism.* Urbana: University of Illinois Press, 1993.

———. "More Than an Index: The First Reference Guide to the Doctrine and Covenants as a Window into Early Mormonism." *BYU Studies* 41, no. 2 (2002): 116–47.

———. "The Religious Milieu of English Mormonism." In *Mormons in Early Victorian Britain,* edited by Richard L. Jensen and Malcolm R. Thorp, 31–48. Salt Lake City: University of Utah Press, 1989.

———. " 'Saved or Damned': Tracing a Persistent Protestantism in Early Mormon Thought." *BYU Studies* 25, no. 3 (1985): 85–103.

Updike, John. "Big Dead White Male: Ralph Waldo Emerson Turns Two Hundred." *The New Yorker* 79 (Aug. 4, 2003), 77–81.

Upham, Thomas C. *The Life of Faith.* Boston: Waite, Pierce, 1845.

U.S. Congress. Senate. Committee on the Judiciary. *In the Senate of the United States, March 4, 1840 . . . The Committee on the Judiciary, to Whom was Referred the Memorial of a Delegation of the Latter Day Saints, Commonly Called Mormons.* Washington, D.C.: Blair and Rives, 1840.

U.S. Department of Commerce. *Historical Statistics of the United States: Colonial Times to 1970.* Washington, D.C.: U.S. Bureau of the Census, 1975.

U.S. Eighth Circuit Court of Appeals. Testimony [1892]. 2 vols. Church Archives. The Church of Jesus Christ of Latter-day Saints. Salt Lake City, Utah.

Van Buren, Martin. Papers, 1787–1910. Library of Congress, Washington, D.C.

Van Noord, Roger. *King of Beaver Island: The Life and Assassination of James Jesse Strang.* Urbana: University of Illinois Press, 1988.

Van Orden, Bruce A. " 'By That Book I Learned the Right Way of God': The Conversion of William W. Phelps." In *Regional Studies in Latter-day Saint Church History: New York*, edited by Larry C. Porter, Milton V. Backman, and Susan Easton Black, 203–13. Provo, Utah: Department of Church History and Doctrine, Brigham Young University, 1992.

———. "Expeditions from Kirtland." In *Historical Atlas of Mormonism*, edited by S. Kent Brown, Donald Q. Cannon, and Richard H. Jackson, 28–29. New York: Simon and Schuster, 1994.

———. "Stephen A. Douglas and the Mormons." In *Regional Studies in Latter-day Saint Church History: Illinois*, edited by H. Dean Garrett, 359–79. Provo, Utah: Department of Church History and Doctrine, Brigham Young University, 1995.

———. "Writing to Zion: The William W. Phelps Kirtland Letters (1835–1836)." *BYU Studies* 33, no. 3 (1993): 542–93.

———. "Zion's Camp: A Refiner's Fire." In *The Prophet Joseph: Essays on the Life and Mission of Joseph Smith*, edited by Larry C. Porter and Susan Easton Black, 192–207. Salt Lake City, Utah: Deseret Book, 1988.

Van Wagenen, Michael. *The Texas Republic and the Mormon Kingdom of God*. College Station: Texas A&M University Press, 2002.

Van Wagoner, Richard S. "The Making of a Mormon Myth: The 1844 Transfiguration of Brigham Young." *Dialogue: A Journal of Mormon Thought* 28, no. 4 (1995): 1–24.

———. "Mormon Polyandry in Nauvoo." *Dialogue: A Journal of Mormon Thought* 18, no. 3 (1985): 67–83.

———. "Sarah M. Pratt: The Shaping of an Apostate." *Dialogue: A Journal of Mormon Thought* 19, no. 2 (1986): 69–99.

———. *Sidney Rigdon: A Portrait of Religious Excess*. Salt Lake City, Utah: Signature Books, 1994.

Van Wagoner, Richard S., and Steven Walker. "Joseph Smith: 'The Gift of Seeing.'" *Dialogue: A Journal of Mormon Thought* 15, no. 2 (1982): 48–68.

VanderKam, James C. *Enoch: A Man for All Generations*. Columbia: University of South Carolina Press, 1995.

Vogel, Dan. "Anti-Universalist Rhetoric in the Book of Mormon." In *New Approaches to the Book of Mormon: Explorations in Critical Methodology*, edited by Brent Lee Metcalfe, 21–52. Salt Lake City, Utah: Signature Books, 1993.

———. "Echoes of Anti-Masonry: A Rejoinder to Critics of the Anti-Masonic Thesis." In *American Apocrypha: Essays on the Book of Mormon*, edited by Dan Vogel and Brent Lee Metcalfe, 275–320. Salt Lake City, Utah: Signature Books, 2002.

———. *Indian Origins and the Book of Mormon: Religious Solutions from Columbus to Joseph Smith*. Salt Lake City, Utah: Signature Books, 1986.

———. "James Colin Brewster: The Boy Prophet Who Challenged Mormon Authority." In *Differing Visions: Dissenters in Mormon History*, edited by Roger D. Launius and Linda Thatcher, 120–34. Urbana: University of Illinois Press, 1994.

———. *Joseph Smith: The Making of a Prophet*. Salt Lake City, Utah: Signature Books, 2004.

———. "Joseph Smith's Family Dynamics." *John Whitmer Historical Association Journal* 22 (2002): 51–74.

———. "The Locations of Joseph Smith's Early Treasure Quests." *Dialogue: A Journal of Mormon Thought* 27, no. 3 (1994): 197–231.

———. "Mormonism's 'Anti-Masonick Bible.'" *John Whitmer Historical Association Journal* 9 (1989): 17–30.

———. "'The Prophet Puzzle' Revisited." In *The Prophet Puzzle: Interpretive Essays on Joseph Smith*, edited by Bryan Waterman, 49–68. Salt Lake City, Utah: Signature Books, 1999.

———. *Religious Seekers and the Advent of Mormonism*. Salt Lake City, Utah: Signature Books, 1988.

———. "The Validity of the Witnesses' Testimonies." In *American Apocrypha: Essays on the*

Book of Mormon, edited by Dan Vogel and Brent Lee Metcalfe, 79–122. Salt Lake City, Utah: Signature Books, 2002.

———, ed. *The Word of God: Essays on Mormon Scripture*. Salt Lake City, Utah: Signature Books, 1990.

Vogel, Dan, and Scott C. Dunn. " 'The Tongue of Angels': Glossolalia Among Mormonism's Founders." *Journal of Mormon History* 19, no. 2 (1993): 1–34.

Vogel, Dan, and Brent Lee Metcalfe, eds. *American Apocrypha: Essays on the Book of Mormon*. Salt Lake City, Utah: Signature Books, 2002.

Voorsanger, Catherine Hoover, and John K. Howat, eds. *Art and the Empire City: New York, 1825–1861*. New York: Metropolitan Museum of Art; New Haven, Conn.: Yale University Press, 2000.

Walker, Charles L. *The Diary of Charles Lowell Walker*. Edited by A. Karl Larson and Katharine Miles Larson. 2 vols. Logan: Utah State University Press, 1980.

Walker, David. *David Walker's Appeal, in Four Articles: Together with a Preamble, to the Coloured Citizens of the World, but in Particular, and Very Expressly, to Those of the United States of America: Third and Last Edition, Revised and Published by David Walker, 1830*. Baltimore: Black Classics Press, 1993.

Walker, Ronald W. "Martin Harris: Mormonism's Early Convert." *Dialogue: A Journal of Mormon Thought* 19, no. 4 (1986): 29–43.

———. "The Persisting Idea of American Treasure Hunting." *BYU Studies* 24, no. 4 (1984): 429–59.

———. "Seeking the 'Remnant': The Native American During the Joseph Smith Period." *Journal of Mormon History* 19, no. 1 (1993): 1–33.

———. "Sheaves, Bucklers, and the State: Mormon Leaders Respond to the Dilemmas of War." *Sunstone* 7, no. 4 (1982): 43–56.

Walker, Williston. *The Creeds and Platforms of Congregationalism*. New York: Charles Scribner's Sons, 1893.

Walters, Wesley P. "From Occult to Cult with Joseph Smith, Jr." *Journal of Pastoral Practice* 1, no. 2 (1977): 121–31.

———. "Joseph Smith's Bainbridge, N.Y., Court Trials." *Westminster Theological Journal* 36, no. 2 (1974): 123–55.

———. "New Light on Mormon Origins from Palmyra (N.Y.) Revival." *Bulletin of the Evangelical Theological Society* 10, no. 4 (1967): 227–44.

Ward, Maurine Carr. " 'This Institution Is a Good One': The Female Relief Society of Nauvoo, 17 March 1842 to 16 March 1844." *Mormon Historical Studies* 3, no. 2 (2002): 86–203.

Wasson, Lorenzo D. Letter to David Hale, Feb. 1841. Church Archives. The Church of Jesus Christ of Latter-day Saints. Salt Lake City, Utah.

Watson, John F. *Annals of Philadelphia: Being a Collection of Memoirs, Anecdotes, and Incidents of the City and Its Inhabitants, from the Days of the Pilgrim Founders*. 3 vols. Philadelphia: Elijah Thomas, 1857.

Watt, Ronald G. "A Dialogue Between Wilford Woodruff and Lyman Wight." *BYU Studies* 17, no. 1 (1977): 108–13.

Webster, David. *The Fall of the Ancient Maya: Solving the Mystery of the Maya Collapse*. New York: Thames and Hudson, 2002.

Webster, Noah. *The Holy Bible, Containing the Old and New Testaments, In the Common Version, with Amendments of the Language*. New Haven, Conn.: Durrie and Peck, 1833.

Welch, John W. "Chiasmus in the Book of Mormon." *BYU Studies* 10, no. 1 (1969): 69–84.

———. "How Much Was Known About Chiasmus in 1829 When the Book of Mormon Was Translated?" *FARMS Review* 15, no. 1 (2003): 47–80.

———. "The Miraculous Translation of the Book of Mormon." In *Opening the Heavens: Accounts of Divine Manifestations, 1820–1844*. Edited by John W. Welch with Erick B. Carlson, 77–213. Provo, Utah: Brigham Young University Press; Salt Lake City, Utah: Deseret Book, 2005.

————. *The Sermon at the Temple and Sermon on the Mount: A Latter-day Saint Approach.* Salt Lake City, Utah: Deseret Book; Provo, Utah: FARMS, 1990.

————. "Weighing and Measuring in the Worlds of the Book of Mormon." *Journal of Book of Mormon Studies* 8, no. 2 (1999): 36–45.

————, ed. *Chiasmus in Antiquity: Structures, Analyses, Exegesis.* Hildesheim, Germany: Gerstenberg Verlag, 1981; reprint, Provo, Utah: Research Press, 1999.

————. *Opening the Heavens: Accounts of Divine Manifestations, 1820–1844.* Provo, Utah: Brigham Young University Press; Salt Lake City, Utah: Deseret Book, 2005.

Welch, John W., David Ralph Seely, and JoAnn H. Seely, eds. *Glimpses of Lehi's Jerusalem.* Provo, Utah: FARMS, Brigham Young University, 2004.

Wheelock, Cyrus. Letter to George A. Smith. Dec. 29, 1854. Historian's Office. Church Archives. The Church of Jesus Christ of Latter-day Saints. Salt Lake City, Utah.

Whitman, Omer W., and James L. Varner. "Sheriff Jacob B. Backenstos: 'Defender of the Saints.' " *Journal of Mormon History* 29, no. 2 (2003): 150–78.

Whitmer, David. *An Address to All Believers in Christ.* Richmond, Mo.: n.p., 1887.

————. *David Whitmer Interviews: A Restoration Witness.* Edited by Lyndon W. Cook. Orem, Utah: Grandin Book, 1991.

Whitmer, John. *From Historian to Dissident: The Book of John Whitmer.* Edited by Bruce N. Westergren. Salt Lake City, Utah: Signature Books, 1995.

Whitney, Helen Mar Kimball. Autobiography, 1881. Church Archives. The Church of Jesus Christ of Latter-day Saints. Salt Lake City, Utah.

Whitney, Newel Kimball. Collection, 1825–1906. L. Tom Perry Special Collections. Harold B. Lee Library. Brigham Young University.

Whitney, Orson F. *Life of Heber C. Kimball, an Apostle: The Father and Founder of the British Mission.* Salt Lake City, Utah: Kimball Family, 1888.

Whittaker, David J. "Almanacs in the New England Heritage of Mormonism." *BYU Studies* 29, no. 4 (1989): 89–113.

————. "The 'Articles of Faith' in Early Mormon Literature and Thought." In *New Views of Mormon History: A Collection of Essays in Honor of Leonard Arrington,* edited by Davis Bitton and Maureen Ursenbach Beecher, 63–92. Salt Lake City: University of Utah Press, 1987.

————. "The Book of Daniel in Early Mormon Thought." In *By Study and Also by Faith: Essays in Honor of Hugh W. Nibley . . .* edited by John M. Lundquist and Stephen D. Ricks, 2 vols. Salt Lake City, Utah: Deseret Book; Provo, Utah: FARMS, 1990, 1:155–201.

————. "East of Nauvoo: Benjamin Winchester and the Early Mormon Church." *Journal of Mormon History* 21, no. 2 (1995): 30–83.

————. "Substituted Names in the Published Revelations of Joseph Smith." *BYU Studies* 23, no. 1 (1983): 103–12.

Whittier, John Greenleaf. *Supernaturalism of New England.* Edited by Edward Wagenknecht. Norman: University of Oklahoma Press, 1969.

Widtsoe, John A. *Joseph Smith: Seeker After Truth, Prophet of God.* Salt Lake City, Utah: Deseret News, 1951.

Wigger, John H. "Taking Heaven by Storm: Enthusiasm and Early American Methodism, 1770–1820." *Journal of the Early Republic* 14, no. 2 (1994): 167–94.

————. *Taking Heaven by Storm: Methodism and the Rise of Popular Christianity in America.* New York: Oxford University Press, 1998.

Wight, Lyman. Letter to Wilford Woodruff, August 24, 1857. Historian's Office Papers. Church Archives. The Church of Jesus Christ of Latter-day Saints. Salt Lake City, Utah.

Williams, Frederick G. "Frederick Granger Williams of the First Presidency of the Church." *BYU Studies* 12, no. 3 (1972): 243–61.

Wills, Garry. *John Wayne's America: The Politics of Celebrity.* New York: Simon and Schuster, 1997.

Wilson, John A. *Signs and Wonders upon Pharaoh: A History of American Egyptology.* Chicago: University of Chicago Press, 1964.

———. "A Summary Report." *Dialogue: A Journal of Mormon Thought* 3, no. 3 (1968): 67–85.

Wilson, John F. "Some Comparative Perspectives on the Early Mormon Movement and the Church-State Question, 1830–1845." *Journal of Mormon History* 8 (1981): 63–77.

Winchester, Benjamin. *The Origin of the Spaulding Story, Concerning the Manuscript Found.* Philadelphia: Brown, Bicking, and Guilpert, 1840.

Winiarski, Douglas L. "Souls Filled with Ravishing Transport: Heavenly Visions and the Radical Awakening in New England." *William and Mary Quarterly,* 3d ser., 61 (Jan. 2004): 3–46.

Winn, Kenneth H. *Exiles in a Land of Liberty: Mormons in America, 1830–1846.* Chapel Hill: University of North Carolina Press, 1989.

———. " 'Such Republicanism as This': John Corrill's Rejection of Prophetic Rule." In *Differing Visions: Dissenters in Mormon History,* edited by Roger D. Launius and Linda Thatcher, 45–69. Urbana: University of Illinois Press, 1994.

Wirthlin, LeRoy S. "Joseph Smith's Boyhood Operation: An 1813 Surgical Success." *BYU Studies* 21, no. 2 (1981): 131–54.

———. "Nathan Smith (1762–1828): Surgical Consultant to Joseph Smith." *BYU Studies* 17, no. 3 (1977): 319–37.

Wixom, Hartt. *Edward Partridge: The First Bishop of the Church of Jesus Christ of Latter-day Saints.* Springville, Utah: Cedar Fort, 1998.

Wood, Gordon S. "Evangelical America and Early Mormonism." *New York History* 61, no. 4 (1980): 359–86.

Wood, Timothy L. "The Prophet and the Presidency: Mormonism and Politics in Joseph Smith's 1844 Presidential Campaign." *Journal of the Illinois State Historical Society* 93, no. 2 (2000): 167–93.

Woodford, Robert J. "The Historical Development of the Doctrine and Covenants." 3 vols. Ph.D. diss., Brigham Young University, 1974.

———. "How the Revelations in the Doctrine and Covenants Were Received and Compiled." *Ensign* 15 (Jan. 1985): 26–33.

———. "Jesse Gause, Counselor to the Prophet." *BYU Studies* 15, no. 3 (1975): 362–64.

Woodruff, Wilford. *Wilford Woodruff's Journals, 1833–1898.* 9 vols. Edited by Scott G. Kenney. Midvale, Utah: Signature Books, 1983–85.

———. "Historian's Private Journal," 1858–1878. Church Archives. The Church of Jesus Christ of Latter-day Saints. Salt Lake City, Utah.

———. "The Kirtland Diary of Wilford Woodruff." Edited by Dean C. Jessee. *BYU Studies* 12, no. 4 (1972): 365–99.

———. *Leaves from My Journal.* Salt Lake City, Utah: Juvenile Instructor Office, 1881.

Woodworth, Jed. "Extra-Biblical Enoch Texts in Early American Culture." *Archive of Restoration Culture: Summer Fellows' Papers, 1997–1999,* 185–93. Provo, Utah: Joseph Fielding Smith Institute for Latter-day Saint History, 2000.

———. "Josiah Quincy's 1844 Visit with Joseph Smith." *BYU Studies* 39, no. 4 (2000): 71–87.

Wright, Conrad. *The Beginnings of Unitarianism in America.* Boston: Starr King Press, distributed by Beacon Press, 1955.

Wright, David P. "Isaiah in Book of Mormon: Or Joseph Smith in Isaiah." In *American Apocrypha: Essays on Joseph Smith,* edited by Dan Vogel and Brent Lee Metcalfe, 157–234. Salt Lake City, Utah: Signature Books, 2002.

———. " 'In Plain Terms That We May Understand': Joseph Smith's Transformation of Hebrews in Alma 12–13." In *New Approaches to the Book of Mormon: Explorations in Critical Methodology,* edited by Brent Lee Metcalfe, 165–229. Salt Lake City, Utah: Signature Books, 1993.

Wright, Jonathan. Letter to Willard Richards, April 1, 1848. Historian's Office. Church Archives. The Church of Jesus Christ of Latter-day Saints. Salt Lake City, Utah.

Wunderli, Earl M. "Critique of a Limited Geography for Book of Mormon Events." *Dialogue: A Journal of Mormon Thought* 35, no. 3 (2002): 161–97.

Wyatt-Brown, Bertram. "Andrew Jackson's Honor." *Journal of the Early Republic* 17, no. 1 (1997): 1–36.

———. *Honor and Violence in the Old South*. New York: Oxford University Press, 1986.

———. *Southern Honor: Ethics and Behavior in the Old South*. New York: Oxford University Press, 1982.

Wyl, Wilhelm. *Joseph Smith, the Prophet, His Family and His Friends: A Study Based on Facts and Documents*. Salt Lake City, Utah: Tribune Printing and Publishing, 1886.

Young, Ann Eliza. *Wife No. 19: or The Story of a Life in Bondage: Being a Complete Exposé of Mormonism, and Revealing the Sorrows, Sacrifices and Sufferings of Women in Polygamy*. Hartford, Conn.: Dustin, Gilman, 1876.

Young, Brigham. *The Essential Brigham Young*. Foreword by Eugene E. Campbell. Salt Lake City, Utah: Signature Books, 1992.

———. "History of Brigham Young." Histories of the Twelve, ca. 1850–1880. Church Archives. The Church of Jesus Christ of Latter-day Saints. Salt Lake City, Utah.

———. Letter to Parley P. Pratt, July 17, 1842. Church Archives. The Church of Jesus Christ of Latter-day Saints. Salt Lake City, Utah.

———. *Manuscript History of Brigham Young, 1801–1844*. Compiled by Eldon Jay Watson. Salt Lake City, Utah: Smith Secretarial Service, 1968.

———. Office Files, 1832–1878. Church Archives. The Church of Jesus Christ of Latter-day Saints. Salt Lake City, Utah.

Young, Emily Partridge. Diary and Reminiscences, 1874–1899. Church Archives. The Church of Jesus Christ of Latter-day Saints. Salt Lake City, Utah.

———. "Incidents of the Early Life of a Mormon Girl." Church Archives. The Church of Jesus Christ of Latter-day Saints. Salt Lake City, Utah.

———. Reminiscence, 1884. L. Tom Perry Special Collections. Harold B. Lee Library. Brigham Young University.

Young, James Sterling. *The Washington Community, 1800–1828*. New York: Columbia University Press, 1966.

Young, Joseph. *History of the Organization of the Seventies*. Salt Lake City, Utah: Deseret News, 1878.

Young, Zina Diantha. " 'All Things Move in Order in the City': The Nauvoo Diary of Zina Diantha Huntington Jacobs." Edited by Maureen Ursenbach Beecher. *BYU Studies* 19, no. 3 (1979): 285–320.

———. Autobiography. Zina Card Brown Family Collection, 1806–1972. Church Archives. The Church of Jesus Christ of Latter-day Saints. Salt Lake City, Utah.

Zion's Camp Festival Papers, 1864–67. Church Archives, The Church of Jesus Christ of Latter-day Saints. Salt Lake City, Utah.

"The Zodiac of Denderah." *North American Review* 17 (1823): 233–42.

Zucker, Louis C. "Joseph Smith as a Student of Hebrew." *Dialogue: A Journal of Mormon Thought* 3, no. 2 (1968): 41–55.

ILLUSTRATION CREDITS

INDEX

A NOTE ABOUT THE AUTHOR

Richard Lyman Bushman, Gouverneur Morris Professor of History, Emeritus, at Columbia University, grew up in Portland, Oregon, and earned his undergraduate and graduate degrees from Harvard University. He has also taught at Brigham Young University, Boston University, and the University of Delaware. His *From Puritan to Yankee: Character and Social Order in Connecticut, 1690–1765* won the Bancroft Prize in 1967. His other books include *Joseph Smith and the Beginnings of Mormonism* (1984), winner of the Evans Biography Award; *King and People in Provincial Massachusetts* (1985); and *The Refinement of America: Persons, Houses, Cities* (1992). A practicing Mormon, he lives in New York City with his wife, Claudia.

A NOTE ON THE TYPE

This book was set in Janson, a typeface long thought to have been made by the Dutchman Anton Janson, who was a practicing typefounder in Leipzig during the years 1668–1687. However, it has been conclusively demonstrated that these types are actually the work of Nicholas Kis (1650–1702), a Hungarian, who most probably learned his trade from the master Dutch typefounder Dirk Voskens. The type is an excellent example of the influential and sturdy Dutch types that prevailed in England up to the time William Caslon (1692–1766) developed his own incomparable designs from them.

Composed by North Market Street Graphics, Lancaster, Pennsylvania

Printed and bound by R. R. Donnelley & Sons, Harrisonburg, Virginia

Designed by M. Kristen Bearse